FEDERAL ESTATE AND GIFT TAXATION

EIGHTH EDITION

RICHARD B. STEPHENS
Late Professor Emeritus
University of Florida

GUY B. MAXFIELD
Professor of Law
New York University

STEPHEN A. LIND
Albert R. Abramson Distinguished
Professor of Law
Hastings College of the Law

DENNIS A. CALFEE
Professor of Law
University of Florida

ROBERT B. SMITH
Of Counsel, Sutherland, Asbill & Brennan
Atlanta, Georgia

2012 CUMULATIVE SUPPLEMENT
TO ABRIDGED STUDENT EDITION

WG&L

This publication is designed to provide accurate and authoritative information in regard to the subject matter covered. It is sold with the understanding that neither the author(s) nor the publisher is engaged in rendering legal, account-ing, or other professional service. If legal advice or other expert assistance is required, the services of a competent professional should be sought.

In response to IRS Circular 230 requirements, Thomson Reuters advises that any discussions of federal tax issues in its publications and products, or in third-party publications and products on its platforms, are not intended to be used and may not in fact be used to avoid any penalties under the Internal Revenue Code, or to promote, market, or recommend any transaction or sub-ject addressed therein.

PRINTED IN THE UNITED STATES OF AMERICA

THOMSON REUTERS

How to Use
This Supplement

This cumulative supplement brings the eighth edition of Stephens, Maxfield, Lind, Calfee, and Smith's *Federal Estate and Gift Taxation*, Abridged Student Edition, up to date. Each entry in the supplement is keyed to the main volume by chapter, paragraph (¶), and, where appropriate, specific page number. An italicized instruction line following the keyed-in reference to the main volume tells you exactly how the new material affects the original text and/or footnotes in the Student Edition. When using the Student Edition, the reader may determine quickly if there have been new developments by referring to the corresponding chapter, paragraph, and page in the supplement.

The Table of Contents lists sections that have been updated. To further aid readers in locating material in the supplement, the top of each page carries a reference to the paragraph number of the Student Edition to which it relates. The supplement also contains a Cumulative Index and Cumulative Tables of Internal Revenue Code Sections, Regulation, Rulings, and Cases covering material in both the Student Edition and this supplement.

The publisher has included all material from the supplement to the professional edition. Therefore, this supplement contains references to some paragraphs that are not included in the student edition.

Summary of Contents

PART II   THE ESTATE TAX

2   Imposition of Estate Tax
3   Credits Against Estate Tax
4   The Gross Estate
5   The Taxable Estate
6   Estates of Nonresident Noncitizens
7   Tax Conventions
8   Miscellaneous Estate Tax Provisions

PART III   THE GIFT TAX

9   Gift Tax: Determination of Liability
10   Gift Tax: Transfers Subject to Tax
11   Gift Tax Deductions

PART IV   GENERATION-SKIPPING TRANSFERS

12   Imposition of the Generation-Skipping Transfer Tax
13   Generation-Skipping Transfers
14   Taxable Amount
15   The Generation-Skipping Transfer Exemption
16   Applicable Rate and Inclusion Ratio
17   Other Definitions and Special Rules
18   Administrative and Miscellaneous Matters

PART V   SPECIAL VALUATION RULES

19   Special Valuation Rules

CUMULATIVE TABLE OF IRC SECTIONS
CUMULATIVE TABLE OF TREASURY REGULATIONS
CUMULATIVE TABLE OF REVENUE RULINGS, REVENUE PROCEDURES, AND OTHER
         IRS RELEASES
CUMULATIVE TABLE OF CASES
CUMULATIVE INDEX

Table of Contents

PART II THE ESTATE TAX

2 Imposition of Estate Tax

¶ 2.01 Section 2001. Imposition and Rate of Tax [Revised] S2-1
    [1] Computation of the Tentative Tax S2-2
        [a] Taxable Estate S2-3
        [b] Adjusted Taxable Gifts S2-3
            [i] Gifts made through August 5, 1997. . . . S2-4
            [ii] Gifts made after August 5, 1997. . . . . . S2-4
        [c] Tax Rates S2-7
    [2] Reductions in the Tentative Tax S2-9
    [3] Tax Planning S2-13
¶ 2.02 Section 2002. Liability for Payment S2-14
    [1] Estate Tax Return S2-14
    [3] Extension of Time for Payment S2-16
        [a] Section 6159 . . . . S2-16
        [b] Section 6161 . . . . S2-17
            [i] Short extensions. S2-17
            [ii] "Reasonable cause" extensions. S2-17
        [c] Section 6166 . . . . S2-17
            [ii] Qualification for extension. S2-17
            [iii] Period of extension. S2-19
            [v] Interest. S2-21
            [vi] The "gotcha." S2-21
            [vii] Declaratory judgments with respect to
                Section 6166. . . . . S2-22

3 Credits Against Estate Tax

¶ 3.02 Section 2010. Unified Credit Against the Estate Tax
    [Revised] S3-2
    [1] The Amount of the Credit S3-3
        [a] Basic Exclusion Amount S3-4
        [b] The Deceased Spousal Unused Exclusion
            Amount S3-4
            [i] The Amount of Unused Exclusion. S3-5
            [ii] The Election. S3-8
    [2] The Relationship to the Section 2505 Credit S3-9
    [3] Estate Tax Return Filing Requirements S3-10
¶ 3.03 Section 2011. Credit for State Death Taxes S3-12
    [1] Introduction S3-12
¶ 3.05 Section 2013. Credit for Tax on Prior Transfers S3-12
    [2] Computation of Credit in General S3-12
    [3] Adjustments S3-13

			[b]	Value of Property Transferred	S3-13
		[4]	Limitations on Credit	S3-13
			[a]	Tax Caused in Decedent's Estate	S3-13
¶ 3.06		Section 2014. Credit for Foreign Death Taxes	S3-14
		[3]	The Federal Estate Tax Formula	S3-14
			[b]	Value of the Property	S3-14

4   The Gross Estate

¶ 4.02		Section 2031. Definition of "Gross Estate"	S4-4
	[1]	Introduction	S4-4
	[2]	Fair Market Value	S4-4
		[a]	Introduction	S4-4
		[b]	General Valuation Methods	S4-5
			[i]	Income approach.	S4-5
			[ii]	Market approach.	S4-5
			[iii]	Asset-based (cost) approach.	S4-6
			[iv]	Combinations.	S4-6
		[c]	Valuation Determined by Agreements	S4-6
	[3]	Basic Valuation Approaches to Property Interests . . .	S4-6
		[a]	Tangible Personal Property	S4-6
		[b]	Real Property	S4-7
		[e]	Bonds	S4-8
		[f]	Closely Held Corporations	S4-8
	[4]	Adjustments for Premiums and Discounts	S4-9
		[a]	Introduction	S4-9
		[b]	Premium for Control	S4-9
			[ii]	Absence of attribution.	S4-9
			[iv]	Swing vote premium.	S4-10
		[c]	Discount for Minority Interest	S4-10
			[i]	Rationale.	S4-10
			[iii]	Amounts and cases.	S4-10
		[d]	Discount for Lack of Marketability	S4-11
			[ii]	Amounts and cases.	S4-11
		[e]	Other Significant Discounts	S4-11
			[i]	Fractional interest discount.	S4-11
			[iii]	Capital gains discount.	S4-12
			[iv]	Securities law discount.	S4-12
			[v]	Environmental hazards discount.	S4-13
			[vi]	Key person discount.	S4-13
			[vii]	Litigation discount.	S4-13
		[g]	Nonbusiness Assets Held in FLPS and FLLCs	S4-13
	[5]	Temporal Property Interests	S4-15
	[6]	Statutes Related to Valuation	S4-17
		[a]	Understatement Penalty and Reasonable Cause: Sections 6662 and 6664	S4-17
		[b]	Understatement of Taxpayer Liability by Return Preparer: Section 6694 [Revised]	S4-19
		[c]	Section 7491	S4-21
	[7]	Exclusion of the Value of Land Subject to a Qualified Conservation Easement	S4-22
		[a]	Introduction	S4-22
		[b]	Land Subject to a Qualified Conservation Easement	S4-22

		[ii] Qualified conservation easement.......	S4-22
¶ 4.03	Section 2032. Alternate Valuation Date		S4-22
	[1]	Introduction	S4-22
	[2]	Identification of Gross Estate..................	S4-24
	[3]	Exceptions to Usual Alternate Date	S4-24
		[a] Property Disposed of	S4-24
		[c] Changes Not Due to Market Conditions [New]	S4-25
¶ 4.04	Section 2032A. Valuation of Certain Farm, Etc., Real		
	Property		S4-25
	[1]	Introduction	S4-25
	[3]	Estate Qualification	S4-26
		[c] The 25 Percent Test	S4-26
		[ii] Material participation.	S4-26
		[iii] Active management.	S4-26
	[4]	Real Property Qualification	S4-26
	[5]	Valuation Methods	S4-27
		[a] Formula Farm Valuation	S4-27
	[6]	Election and Agreement	S4-27
	[7]	Recapture	S4-28
		[b] Recapture Events	S4-28
		[i] Dispositions.....................	S4-28
		[ii] Cessation of qualified use.	S4-28
¶ 4.05	Section 2033. Property in Which the Decedent Had an		
	Interest		S4-29
	[2]	Beneficial Interest	S4-29
		[a] State Law	S4-29
		[b] State Decrees	S4-30
	[3]	Routine Inclusions	S4-30
	[4]	Income Items	S4-31
	[5]	Partial Interests in Property	S4-31
		[b] Successive Interests in Property	S4-31
	[7]	Business Interests	S4-31
		[c] Limited Liability Companies	S4-31
¶ 4.07	Section 2035. Adjustments for Gifts Made Within Three		
	Years of Decedent's Death		S4-32
	[2]	The Section 2035(a) Rule (the First Prong)........	S4-32
		[b] Exceptions to Section 2035(a) Inclusion	S4-32
		[i] Section 2035(d): bona fide sales.	S4-32
	[3]	The Section 2035(b) Rule (the Second Prong)	S4-32
		[a] The Gift Tax Gross-Up Rule	S4-32
		[b] Gifts Made Within Three Years of Death	S4-33
	[4]	Pre-1982 Section 2035 and Its Background	S4-33
¶ 4.08	Section 2036. Transfers With Retained Life Estate		S4-33
	[1]	Excluded Transfers	S4-33
		[a] Sales for Full Consideration	S4-33
	[4]	Beneficial Interests in the Decedent	S4-34
		[b] Right to Income	S4-34
		[c] Enjoyment "Retained"	S4-34
	[5]	Control Over Others' Interests	S4-41
		[a] Right to Designate Retained Indirectly	S4-41
		[c] Right to Designate Who Benefits	S4-42
	[6]	Indirect Interests or Controls	S4-42
		[a] Settlor Trustee	S4-42

	[c]	Rent Paid by Transferor	S4-43
	[7]	Transfer by the Decedent	S4-43
	[a]	Indirect Transfers	S4-44
	[d]	Reciprocal Trusts	S4-44
	[8]	Amount to Be Included	S4-44
¶ 4.10		Section 2038. Revocable Transfers	S4-46
	[4]	Power in the Decedent	S4-46
	[a]	Power to Revoke	S4-46
	[b]	Power to Alter or Amend	S4-46
	[c]	Administrative Powers	S4-47
	[g]	Power in "Whatever Capacity"	S4-47
	[6]	Power Exercisable Only With Another	S4-47
¶ 4.11		Section 2039. Annuities	S4-48
	[3]	Qualifications	S4-48
	[a]	Contract or Agreement	S4-48
	[4]	Amount to Be Included	S4-48
	[a]	Valuation	S4-48
	[5]	Private Annuities	S4-49
	[6]	Exempt Annuities	S4-50
¶ 4.12		Section 2040. Joint Interests	S4-50
	[9]	Termination Prior to Death	S4-50
¶ 4.13		Section 2041. Powers of Appointment	S4-50
	[2]	Powers Within Section 2041	S4-50
	[b]	Powers That Overlap Interests	S4-51
	[3]	Definition of "General Power"	S4-51
	[4]	Exceptions to General Definition	S4-52
	[a]	Power Limited by a Standard	S4-52
	[c]	Post-1942 Powers With Another Person	S4-53
	[ii]	Power held with an adverse party.	S4-53
	[iii]	Power held with an equally interested party.	S4-54
	[6]	Treatment of Pre-1942 Powers	S4-55
	[d]	Partial Release of Pre-1942 Powers	S4-55
	[7]	Treatment of Post-1942 Powers	S4-55
	[a]	Possession	S4-55
	[f]	The Five-or-Five Rule	S4-56
	[8]	Nongeneral Powers	S4-56
	[b]	Nongeneral Powers That Are Treated As General Powers	S4-56
¶ 4.14		Section 2042. Proceeds of Life Insurance	S4-57
	[4]	Amounts Receivable by Other Beneficiaries	S4-57
	[a]	Incidents of Ownership	S4-57
	[e]	"Incidents" in Context	S4-57
	[5]	Incidents Incidentally Held	S4-58
	[b]	Partnership's Insurance on Partner	S4-58
	[6]	Assignment of Group Term Insurance	S4-58
	[8]	Policy Purchased With Community Property Funds	S4-61
	[9]	Relation of Section 2042 to Other Sections Defining "Gross Estate"	S4-62
	[b]	Near-Death Transfers	S4-62
¶ 4.15		Section 2043. Transfers for Insufficient Consideration	S4-62
	[1]	Marital Rights: The Negative Rule	S4-62
	[b]	The Negative Rule in a Divorce Situation	S4-62

| | | [i] | Claims. . . . . | S4-62 |
| ¶ 4.16 | Section 2044. Certain Property for Which a Marital Deduction Was Previously Allowed . . . . | | | S4-63 |

5   The Taxable Estate

¶ 5.03	Section 2053. Expenses, Indebtedness, And Taxes [Revised]				S5-4
	[1]	Introduction			S5-4
		[a]	The State Law Allowance Requirement		S5-6
		[b]	The Amount and Payment Requirements		S5-7
			[i]	Establishment of the liability.	S5-8
			[ii]	Bona fide liability.	S5-9
			[iii]	Payment.	S5-10
			[iv]	Timing of Post-death events.	S5-10
	[2]	Funeral Expenses			S5-12
		[a]	In General		S5-12
		[b]	The "Allowable" Test		S5-12
	[3]	Administration Expenses			S5-14
		[a]	Executor Commissions and Attorney Fees . . .		S5-16
		[b]	Commissions Paid to a Trustee		S5-19
		[c]	Miscellaneous Administration Expenses		S5-20
			[i]	Interest expenses.	S5-21
			[ii]	Selling expenses.	S5-23
			[iii]	Other deductible administration expenses.	S5-24
	[4]	Claims Against the Estate			S5-25
		[a]	Personal Obligations of Decedent		S5-26
			[i]	The consideration requirement.	S5-27
			[ii]	Community property issues.	S5-30
			[iii]	Section 2044 claims.	S5-30
		[b]	Existing at the Time of Death		S5-31
			[i]	Taxes as claims.	S5-31
			[ii]	Section 2053(d): Limited deductibility of certain foreign death taxes.	S5-33
		[c]	Contingency of a Claim		S5-34
			[i]	Introduction.	S5-34
			[ii]	Types of contingencies.	S5-37
			[iii]	Actual payment.	S5-38
	[5]	Mortgages			S5-40
	[6]	Special Rules and Limitations Related to Section 2053 Deductions.			S5-42
		[a]	The Section 642(g) Election		S5-42
		[b]	The Section 213(c)(2) Election		S5-45
		[c]	Special Rules for Property Not Subject to Claims		S5-46
			[i]	Introduction.	S5-46
			[ii]	Property not subject to claims.	S5-47
			[iii]	Section 2053(b): Expenses of administering property not subject to claims.	S5-48
			[iv]	Section 2053(c)(2): Limitation based on the value of property subject to claims.	S5-50

¶ 5.05   Section 2055. Transfers for Public, Charitable, and Religious Uses S5-51

     [1]   Qualified Recipients S5-51

         [a]   In General S5-51

         [b]   Section 2055(a) Organizations S5-52

         [c]   Tainted Organizations S5-52

     [2]   Transfers to Charity S5-53

         [a]   Outright Transfers S5-53

         [b]   Indirect Transfers S5-53

         [c]   Disclaimers S5-54

         [e]   Lifetime Transfers S5-54

     [3]   The Amount of the Deduction S5-54

         [a]   In General S5-54

         [b]   Expenses of an Estate Affecting the Deduction   S5-55

             [i]   Death taxes.   S5-55

     [4]   Split Interests: Mixed Private and Charitable Bequests   S5-56

         [a]   Background S5-56

         [b]   Present Law S5-56

     [5]   Qualified Remainder Interests S5-56

         [a]   The Charitable Remainder Annuity Trust S5-57

             [i]   Annuity trust requirements. S5-57

             [ii]   The amount of the deduction. S5-58

         [b]   The Charitable Remainder Unitrust S5-59

             [i]   Unitrust requirements. S5-59

             [ii]   The amount of the deduction. S5-60

         [c]   The Pooled Income Fund S5-61

             [ii]   The amount of the deduction. S5-61

     [6]   Charitable Lead Trusts S5-61

         [a]   Requirements S5-61

             [ii]   Similarities in requirements. S5-62

         [b]   The Amount of the Deduction S5-62

     [7]   Exceptions to the Split-Interest Rules S5-63

         [a]   Remainders in Residences and Farms S5-63

         [b]   An Undivided Portion of the Property S5-63

         [e]   Charitable Gift Annuity S5-64

     [8]   Curative Amendments Permitted S5-65

         [b]   Reformable and Qualified Interests S5-65

         [c]   Qualified Reformation S5-65

         [d]   Additional Rules Related to Reformations S5-66

¶ 5.06   Section 2056. Testamentary Transfers to Surviving Spouse   S5-66

     [3]   Interests Passing to a Surviving Spouse S5-66

         [a]   By Will or Inheritance S5-67

         [h]   Disclaimers S5-68

     [5]   Valuation of Interests Passing S5-68

         [a]   Taxes on Surviving Spouse's Interest S5-68

         [b]   Encumbrances on Surviving Spouse's Interest   S5-69

             [ii]   Administrative expenses. S5-69

     [7]   The Terminable Interest Rule S5-69

         [b]   Identifying Terminable Interests S5-69

         [d]   The Executor-Purchaser Provision S5-69

     [8]   Terminable Interests That Do Qualify S5-70

         [b]   Life Interests With Powers S5-70

		[i]	The surviving spouse must be entitled for life to all of the income from the entire interest or a specific portion of the entire interest, or to a specific portion of all the income from the entire interest.	S5-70
		[iii]	The surviving spouse must have the power to appoint the entire interest or the specific portion to either surviving spouse or spouse's estate.	S5-71
	[d]	Election With Respect to Life Estate for Surviving Spouse	S5-71
		[i]	The passing requirement.	S5-71
		[ii]	The qualifying income interest requirement.	S5-72
		[iii]	The election.	S5-74
	[e]	Special Rules for Charitable Remainder Trusts	S5-76
¶ 5.07	Section 2056A. Qualified Domestic Trusts	S5-77
	[2]	The Passing Requirement	S5-77
	[b]	The Surviving Spouse's Transfer to a QDOT	S5-77
	[c]	An Annuity or Other Arrangement Treated as Passing to a QDOT	S5-77
	[3]	Requirements of a QDOT	S5-78
	[c]	Regulatory Requirements to Ensure Collection of Deferred Tax	S5-78
		[iii]	Rules applicable to both classifications of QDOTs.	S5-78
	[d]	A QDOT Election	S5-78
	[4]	Taxation of QDOT Property	S5-79
	[a]	Events Triggering the Tax	S5-79
		[i]	Corpus distributions.	S5-79
		[ii]	The surviving spouse's death.	S5-79
	[c]	Liability for and Payment of the Tax	S5-80
	[5]	Exceptions If Surviving Spouse Becomes a U.S. Citizen	S5-80
¶ 5.08	Section 2057. Family-Owned-Business Deduction	S5-81
	[2]	Definition of "Qualified Family-Owned Business Interest"	S5-81
	[a]	In General	S5-81
	[c]	Additional Requirements With Respect to Entities	S5-81
		[ii]	Ownership requirements.	S5-81
	[3]	Estate Qualifications	S5-82
	[b]	Election and Agreement	S5-82
		[i]	The election.	S5-82
		[ii]	The agreement.	S5-82
		[iii]	Grace period.	S5-82
	[c]	The 50 Percent Test	S5-83
		[i]	In general.	S5-83
		[iii]	Adjusted value of qualified family-owned business interests.	S5-83
	[5]	The Recapture Rule	S5-83
	[b]	Recapture Events	S5-83

          [ii]   Dispositions. S5-83
     [c]   Measuring the Recapture Tax S5-84
          [iii] Applicable percentage. S5-84

6   Estates of Nonresident Noncitizens

¶ 6.01   Section 2101. Tax Imposed S6-2
         [1]   Introduction S6-2
         [2]   Computation of the Tax S6-2
         [3]   Citizen or Noncitizen; Resident or Nonresident S6-2
                [b]   Residence S6-2
         [4]   Return Requirements S6-3
¶ 6.02   Section 2102. Credits Against Tax S6-3
         [1]   Credit for State Death Taxes S6-3
         [4]   Unified Credit S6-4
¶ 6.03   Section 2103. Definition of "Gross Estate" S6-4
         [2]   Limitation on General Principles S6-4
                [a]   Real Property and Tangible Personal Property   S6-4
¶ 6.04   Section 2104. Property Within the United States S6-4
         [1]   Corporate Stock S6-4
         [2]   Property Subject to Lifetime Transfer S6-5
¶ 6.05   Section 2105. Property Without the United States S6-6
         [2]   Bank and Similar Deposits S6-6
                [a]   Deposits in Domestic Institutions S6-6
                       [i]   Qualifying deposits. S6-6
         [3]   Debt Obligations Treated as Outside the United
                States S6-6
                [b]   Portfolio Debt Obligations S6-6
         [5]   Stock in Regulated Investment Companies [New] . . .   S6-6
¶ 6.06   Section 2106. Taxable Estate S6-7
         [1]   Expenses, Claims, and Losses S6-7
         [2]   Charitable Bequests S6-7
¶ 6.07   Expatriation to Avoid Tax [Revised] S6-8
         [1]   Section 2801 . . . .   S6-9
                [a]   Requirements S6-9
                [b]   The Tax Imposed S6-10
                [c]   Credit S6-11
         [2]   Section 2107 . . . .   S6-11
                [a]   Requirements S6-13
                [b]   Special Situs Rule S6-14
                [c]   Credit S6-15

7   Tax Conventions

¶ 7.01   Introduction S7-1
         [1]   Purpose of Treaties S7-1
         [3]   The Basic Patterns of the Treaties S7-2
                [b]   Modern Treaties S7-2
         [4]   Comparison of the Treaties S7-2
¶ 7.02   Early Treaties S7-2
         [3]   Deductions, Unified Credit, and Taxation Based on
                Situs S7-2

¶ 7.03   Modern Treaties S7-3
           [1]   The Organization for Economic Cooperation and
                  Development Convention and U.S. Model
                  Conventions S7-3
                  [c]   Deductions, Exemptions, and Credits S7-3
           [3]   The Canadian Convention S7-3
           [5]   The German Convention S7-4
           [6]   The Netherlands Convention S7-5
           [7]   The Swedish Convention S7-5
           [8]   The United Kingdom and French Conventions S7-5
¶ 7.04   Procedural Provisions S7-6
           [1]   Competent Authority Assistance S7-6

8   Miscellaneous Estate Tax Provisions

¶ 8.01   Section 2201. Combat Zone–Related Deaths of Members of
           the Armed Forces and Deaths of Victims of Certain
           Terrorist Attacks S8-2
           [1]   Qualified Decedents S8-2
                  [b]   Specified Terrorist Victims S8-2
                  [c]   Astronauts [New] S8-3
           [2]   Effects of the Relief Provision S8-3
                  [a]   Rate Relief S8-3
                  [b]   Unified Credit Computation S8-3
¶ 8.02   Section 2203. Definition of "Executor" S8-4
¶ 8.03   Section 2204. Discharge of Executor From Personal
           Liability S8-4
           [1]   Debts Due the United States S8-4
           [2]   Procedure to Gain Release From Personal Liability   S8-4
¶ 8.04   Section 2205. Reimbursement Out of Estate S8-5
           [2]   State Statutes S8-5
¶ 8.07   Section 2207A. Right of Recovery in the Case of Certain
           Marital Deduction Property S8-6
           [1]   Introduction S8-6
           [2]   Estate Tax Recovery S8-6
           [4]   Whose Liability? S8-7
           [5]   The Possibility of Indirect Gifts S8-8
¶ 8.08   Section 2207B. Right of Recovery Where Decedent
           Retained Interest S8-8
           [2]   Estate Tax Recovery S8-8
¶ 8.09   Sections 2208 and 2209. Citizenship and Residence of
           Certain Residents of Possessions S8-8
¶ 8.10   Section 2210. Estate Tax for the Year 2010 [Revised] S8-9
           [1]   Introduction S8-9
           [2]   The Election S8-10
           [3]   Income Tax Consequences S8-11
                  [a]   Introduction S8-11
                  [b]   Adjustments to the Carry-Over Basis S8-14
                         [i]   Increase in basis regardless of the
                                recipient. S8-15
                         [ii]   Increase in basis for surviving spouses.   S8-15
                         [iii] Ownership. S8-16

		[iv]	Ineligible property.	S8-18
		[v]	Allocation of the basis adjustments. . . .	S8-19
	[c]	Special Rules for Treatment of Gain		S8-20
		[i]	Character.	S8-20
		[ii]	Pecuniary bequests.	S8-20
		[iii]	Liability in excess of basis.	S8-20
		[iv]	Sale of residence.	S8-21
		[v]	Certain foreign transfers.	S8-21
	[d]	Reporting Requirements		S8-21
		[i]	Lifetime gifts.	S8-22
		[ii]	Transfers at death.	S8-22
		[iii]	Penalties for failure to file required information.	S8-23

¶ 8.11		The "Sunset" Provision [New]	S8-24
[1]		The Estate Tax	S8-25
[2]		The Gift Tax	S8-25
[3]		The Generation-Skipping Transfer Tax	S8-26

PART III THE GIFT TAX

9 Gift Tax: Determination of Liability

¶ 9.02		Section 2501. Imposition of Tax	S9-2
[1]		Imposition of the Gift Tax on Nonresident Noncitizens [Revised]	S9-2
	[a]	General Rules for Nonresident Noncitizens . . .	S9-2
	[b]	Gift Taxation of Some Expatriates	S9-3
		[i]	Section 2801.	S9-4
		[ii]	Section 2501(a)(3).	S9-6
[2]		Transfers to Political Organizations	S9-10
¶ 9.03		Section 2502. Rate of Tax [Revised]	S9-10
[1]		Periodic Accounting for Gifts	S9-11
[2]		Rates.	S9-11
[3]		Method of Computation	S9-13
[4]		Liability for the Gift Tax	S9-15
¶ 9.04		Section 2503. Taxable Gifts	S9-15
[1]		The Annual Exclusion	S9-15
	[b]	Identification of Donees	S9-16
		[ii]	Gifts to other entities.	S9-16
		[iii]	Gift by an entity.	S9-16
		[iv]	Gifts to charitable organizations.	S9-16
		[v]	Straw person.	S9-16
[3]		Definition of "Future Interests"	S9-17
	[a]	Separate Interests Tested	S9-17
	[b]	Non-Income-Producing Property	S9-17
	[e]	Right to Enjoyment Suffices	S9-18
	[f]	*Crummey* Powers	S9-19
	[g]	Qualified Tuition Programs and Education Savings Accounts	S9-19
[5]		Special Statutory Rule for Minor Donees	S9-20
	[a]	First Requirement	S9-20

        [b]   Second Requirement S9-21
     [6]   Medical Expenses and Tuition S9-21
     [9]   Gift Tax Returns S9-21
     [10] Limitations on Assessment S9-22
         [a]   Commencement of Limitations Period S9-22
     [11] Donee and Fiduciary Liability S9-23

¶ 9.05   Section 2504. Taxable Gifts for Preceding Calendar Periods   S9-23
     [2]   Valuation for Prior Years S9-23
         [a]   Gifts Made Through August 5, 1997 . . . .   S9-23

¶ 9.06   Section 2505. Unified Credit Against the Gift Tax [Revised]   S9-23
     [1]   Amount of the Credit S9-25
     [2]   Relation to the Section 2010 Credit S9-28

10   Gift Tax: Transfers Subject to Tax

¶ 10.01 Section 2511. Transfers in General S10-2
     [2]   Indirect Gifts S10-2
         [b]   Transfers to Entities S10-3
            [ii]   Partnerships or limited liability
                  companies. S10-3
         [c]   Gifts by Entities S10-4
         [d]   Nature of the Transfer S10-4
         [h]   Gift by an Incompetent S10-4
     [3]   Property Interests Covered S10-4
         [c]   Uncertain Interests S10-5
         [e]   Savings and Formula Clauses S10-5
         [g]   Insurance and Annuities S10-7
     [5]   Revocable Transfers S10-11
         [d]   Transfers of Community Property S10-12
     [6]   Power to Change Beneficiaries S10-12
     [8]   Donor's Power Exercisable Only With Third Persons   S10-13
     [10] Relationship of the Gift Tax to the Income Tax and
         the Estate Tax S10-13
         [e]   Powers Held by the Transferor S10-13
     [11] Nonresident Noncitizens [Revised] S10-15

¶ 10.02 Section 2512. Valuation of Gifts S10-15
     [1]   Time of Valuation S10-15
         [a]   Valuation on Completion S10-16
     [2]   Methods of Valuation S10-16
         [b]   Special Approaches to Valuation S10-16
            [ii]   Insurance policies. S10-16
            [iii] Temporal property interests. S10-16
         [c]   Premiums and Discounts for Interests in
            Property S10-17
            [ii]   Minority interest discount. S10-17
            [iii] Discount for lack of marketability. S10-18
            [iv] Other discounts. S10-19
            [v]   Discount resulting from a gift on
                 formation. S10-20
         [d]   Statutes Applicable to Gift Tax Valuation S10-20
            [iii] Section 7477. . . . .   S10-20
     [3]   Consideration for a Transfer S10-21
     [4]   Transfers in the Ordinary Course of Business S10-22

	[5]	Family Obligations	S10-22
		[d] Elective Share Marital Rights	S10-22
	[6]	Other Receipts of Money's Worth	S10-22
		[c] Reciprocal Trusts	S10-23
		[d] Donee's Payment of Gift Tax	S10-23
¶ 10.03	Section 2513. Gifts by Husband or Wife to Third Party		S10-23
	[1]	Introduction	S10-23
	[3]	Signifying Consent	S10-24
		[a] Manner	S10-24
¶ 10.04	Section 2514. Powers of Appointment		S10-24
	[4]	Treatment of Post-1942 Powers	S10-24
		[a] In General	S10-24
		[c] Lapse of Power	S10-24
¶ 10.05	Section 2515. Treatment of Generation-Skipping Transfer Tax		S10-25
¶ 10.06	Section 2516. Certain Property Settlements		S10-25
	[2]	Statutory Requirements	S10-25
		[a] Type of Transfer	S10-25
	[3]	Comparative Estate Tax Treatment	S10-26
¶ 10.07	Section 2518. Disclaimers		S10-26
	[2]	Definition of "Qualified Disclaimer"	S10-26
		[b] Disclaimer Must Be Timely	S10-27
		[c] Disclaimer May Not Follow an Acceptance	S10-29
		[d] Persons to Whom the Interest Must Pass	S10-29
		[i] Disclaimer by a surviving spouse......	S10-31
		[ii] Disclaimers ineffective under local law.	S10-31
	[3]	Effective Date	S10-32
¶ 10.08	Section 2519. Disposition of Certain Life Estates		S10-32
	[1]	The General Rule	S10-32
		[a] Disposition of a Portion of the Transferee Spouse's Qualifying Income Interest	S10-32
		[b] Section 2519 Transfer	S10-33
	[2]	Meaning of "Disposition"	S10-34
	[3]	Gift Tax Liability	S10-34

11   Gift Tax Deductions

¶ 11.02	Section 2522. Charitable and Similar Gifts		S11-1
	[1]	Charitable Transfers in General	S11-1
		[a] Qualified Recipients	S11-1
		[b] The Amount of the Deduction	S11-2
		[c] Timing of the Deduction	S11-3
	[2]	Mixed Private and Charitable Gifts	S11-3
		[a] Introduction	S11-3
		[b] Qualified Remainder Interests	S11-3
		[i] The charitable remainder annuity trust.	S11-3
		[c] Temporary Interests Gifted to Charity: Charitable Lead Trusts	S11-4
		[d] Exceptions to the Split-Gift Rules	S11-5
		[e] Curative Amendments Permitted	S11-5
¶ 11.03	Section 2523. Gifts to Spouse		S11-6
	[2]	Basic Requirements	S11-6

[4]   Exceptions to the Terminable Interest Rule S11-6
        [c]   Qualified Terminable Interest Property S11-6
                [i]   Other QTIP consequences. S11-7
        [d]   Special Rule for Charitable Remainder Trusts   S11-8
[5]   Noncitizen Donee Spouses S11-8

PART IV   GENERATION-SKIPPING TRANSFERS

12   Imposition of the Generation-Skipping Transfer Tax

¶ 12.03   Section 2603. Liability for Tax S12-1
          [1]   General Rules S12-1

13   Generation-Skipping Transfers

¶ 13.01   Section 2611. "Generation-Skipping Transfer" Defined S13-1
          [2]   Transfers Excluded by Section 2611(b) S13-1
                  [a]   Transfers for Educational and Medical
                          Expenses S13-1
¶ 13.02   Section 2612. Taxable Terminations, Taxable Distributions,
          and Direct Skips S13-2
          [4]   Direct Skips S13-2
                  [b]   General Rule S13-2
                          [i]   First requirement: transfer subject to
                                  estate or gift tax. S13-2
                          [ii]   Second requirement: transfer of an
                                  interest to a skip person. S13-2

14   Taxable Amount

¶ 14.02   Section 2621. Taxable Amount in Case of Taxable
          Distributions S14-1
          [2]   Valuation of Property Received by the Transferee . . .   S14-1
          [3]   Reductions S14-1
¶ 14.05   Section 2624. Valuation S14-2
          [3]   Reduction for Consideration S14-2

15   The Generation-Skipping Transfer Exemption

¶ 15.02   Section 2631. The GST Exemption [Revised] S15-2
          [1]   Individual Allocation S15-3
          [2]   Use of the Exemption S15-6
          [3]   The Transferor Requirement S15-8
          [4]   Duration of the Exemption S15-9
¶ 15.03   Section 2632. Special Rules for Allocation of the GST
          Exemption S15-12
          [2]   Actual Allocation to Inter Vivos Transfers S15-12
                  [b]   Manner of Allocation S15-12
          [3]   Deemed Allocation to Inter Vivos Direct Skips S15-13
                  [a]   The Deemed Allocation S15-13
                  [b]   Delayed Direct Skips S15-13

        [c]   Opting Out of the Deemed Allocation S15-13

    [4]   Deemed Allocation to Inter Vivos Indirect Skips S15-14

        [d]   The Amount Deemed Allocated S15-14

        [e]   Elections S15-15

            [i]   Preventing automatic allocation. S15-15

            [ii]   Elective GST trusts. S15-16

    [5]   Retroactive Allocations S15-17

        [b]   Consequences of a Retroactive Allocation S15-17

            [ii]   Inclusion ratio valuation. S15-17

    [6]   Allocations Made at or After Death S15-17

        [c]   Inter Vivos Trusts Not Included in the Gross

                Estate S15-17

    [7]   Allocation of Residual Exemption S15-18

        [a]   In General S15-18

        [b]   Allocation Between Categories S15-18

            [ii]   Trusts with generation-skipping transfer

                 potential. S15-18

        [c]   Apportionment Within Categories S15-18

            [i]   Direct skips and trusts with

                generation-skipping transfer potential. S15-18

16   Applicable Rate and Inclusion Ratio

¶ 16.01   Section 2641. The Applicable Rate [Revised] S16-2

¶ 16.02   Section 2642. The Inclusion Ratio S16-5

    [3]   Calculation of the Inclusion Ratio for Taxable

          Terminations and Taxable Distributions S16-5

        [b]   Applicable Fraction S16-5

            [ii]   The denominator. S16-5

    [4]   Valuation Rules S16-5

        [c]   Allocation to Other Inter Vivos Transfers S16-5

    [5]   Redetermination of the Applicable Fraction S16-5

        [a]   In General S16-5

        [b]   Additional Exemption Allocations and

              Transfers to a Trust S16-6

            [iii] Additional transfers and exemption

                allocations. S16-6

        [c]   Consolidation of Separate Trusts S16-6

        [e]   Trust Severance [Revised] S16-7

        [f]   Recapture Tax Imposed Under Section 2032A   S16-11

            [ii]   Section 2032A property valued at fair

                market value in the denominator of the

                applicable fraction. S16-11

    [6]   Special Rules for Charitable Lead Annuity Trusts . . . S16-11

    [7]   Deferral of the Effect of Generation-Skipping

          Transfer Exemption Allocation and Direct and

          Indirect Skips on Certain Inter Vivos Transfers S16-12

        [a]   Introduction S16-12

        [b]   General Rules of Deferral S16-12

            [i]   Inclusion in the transferor's gross estate. S16-12

        [c]   Termination of the Estate Tax Inclusion

              Period S16-13

            [i]   Potential inclusion in the transferor's

                gross estate. S16-13

　　　　　　[9]　Statutory Relief Provisions S16-13
　　　　　　　　[a]　Election Relief S16-13
　　　　　　　　[b]　Substantial Compliance S16-17

17   Other Definitions and Special Rules

¶ 17.01   Section 2651. Generation Assignment................ S17-2
　　　　　　[2]　Classes of Beneficiaries S17-2
　　　　　　　　[a]　Related Beneficiaries S17-2
　　　　　　　　　　[ii]　Predeceased parent rule............ S17-2
　　　　　　　　　　[iii]　Overlapping related beneficiaries. S17-3
¶ 17.02   Section 2652. Other Definitions S17-4
　　　　　　[1]　Transferor S17-4
　　　　　　　　[a]　Introduction [Revised] S17-4
　　　　　　　　[b]　General Rules S17-5
　　　　　　　　[c]　Special Rules...................... S17-5
　　　　　　　　　　[i]　Qualified terminable interest property. S17-5
　　　　　　　　　　[ii]　Gift-splitting by married couples. S17-7
　　　　　　[2]　Trusts and Trustees S17-7
　　　　　　[3]　Interest S17-7
　　　　　　　　[b]　Present Right to or Permissible Noncharitable
　　　　　　　　　　Current Recipient of Income or Corpus S17-7
¶ 17.04   Section 2654. Special Rules S17-8
　　　　　　[2]　Single Trust Treated as or Divided Into Multiple
　　　　　　　　Trusts S17-8
　　　　　　　　[a]　Single Trust Treated as Multiple Trusts S17-8
　　　　　　　　[b]　Division of a Single Trust Into Multiple
　　　　　　　　　　Trusts S17-8
　　　　　　[3]　Disclaimers S17-9

18   Administrative and Miscellaneous Matters

¶ 18.01   Section 2661. Administration...................... S18-2
　　　　　　[2]　Deferral of Payment S18-2
　　　　　　　　[a]　Transfers at Death S18-2
¶ 18.02   Section 2662. Return Requirements S18-2
　　　　　　[2]　Returns Required S18-2
　　　　　　　　[a]　Taxable Distributions and Taxable
　　　　　　　　　　Terminations S18-2
　　　　　　　　[b]　Direct Skips...................... S18-3
　　　　　　[4]　When to File S18-3
　　　　　　　　[b]　Extensions of Time to File S18-3
　　　　　　[5]　Where to File S18-3
　　　　　　[6]　Information Returns S18-3
¶ 18.03   Section 2663. Regulations S18-4
　　　　　　[1]　Recapture Tax Under Section 2032A S18-4
　　　　　　　　[b]　Other Testamentary Transfers S18-4
　　　　　　[2]　Nonresident Noncitizen Transferor S18-4
　　　　　　　　[b]　Transfer of Property Situated in the United
　　　　　　　　　　States S18-4
　　　　　　　　[c]　Trusts Partially Subject to Chapter 13 ...... S18-4
¶ 18.04   The Generation-Skipping Transfer Tax in 2010, 2013 and
　　　　　　Thereafter [Revised] S18-5

[1]	The Generation-Skipping Transfer Tax in the Year 2010	S18-5
[2]	The Generation-Skipping Transfer Tax in the Year 2013 and Thereafter	S18-6

¶ 18.05 | Effective Dates | S18-6 |
[2]	Transitional Rules	S18-6
	[b] Trusts Irrevocable on September 25, 1985	S18-6
	[ii] Additions to corpus.	S18-6
	[iii] Consequences when tainted corpus is added.	S18-8
	[d] Mental Disability	S18-9
	[e] Permissible Modifications to Exempt Trusts	S18-9
	[i] Trustee's discretionary powers.	S18-9
	[ii] Settlement.	S18-10
	[iii] Judicial construction.	S18-11
	[iv] Other changes.	S18-12

PART V   SPECIAL VALUATION RULES

19   Special Valuation Rules

¶ 19.02 | Section 2701. Special Valuation Rules | S19-2 |
[3]	Exceptions	S19-2
	[b] Interests of the Same Class and Interests Proportionate to the Class	S19-2
[4]	Section 2701 Valuation Rules	S19-2
	[c] Distribution Rights	S19-2
	[i] Qualified payment rights.	S19-2
[5]	Special Rules Under Section 2701	S19-3
	[a] Section 2701(d)	S19-3
	[ii] Qualified payment elections.	S19-3
	[d] Open Statute of Limitations	S19-3

¶ 19.03 | Section 2702: Special Valuation Rules for Transfers of Interests in Trusts | S19-4 |
[1]	Introduction	S19-4
[2]	The General Rule	S19-4
	[a] The Requirements of Section 2702	S19-4
	[ii] Family members.	S19-4
	[iv] A retained interest.	S19-5
[3]	Exceptions	S19-5
	[a] Incomplete Gifts	S19-5
	[b] Qualified Interests	S19-5
	[i] Qualified income interests.	S19-5
	[d] Personal Residence Trusts	S19-7
	[i] Requirements applicable to both types of personal residence trusts.	S19-8
	[iii] A qualified personal residence trust.	S19-8
	[iv] The two personal residence trusts limitation.	S19-10
[4]	Special Rules Under Section 2702	S19-10
	[a] The Joint Purchase Rule	S19-10

		[d]	The Open Statute of Limitations	S19-11
		[e]	The Relationship of Section 2702 to Other Taxes	S19-11
			[i] The estate tax.	S19-11
		[f]	Effective Dates	S19-12
¶ 19.04			Section 2703. Certain Rights and Restrictions Disregarded	S19-12
	[2]		The General Rule of Section 2703	S19-12
	[3]		The Section 2703(b) Statutory Exception	S19-13
		[a]	Bona Fide Business Arrangement	S19-13
		[b]	Not a Device to Transfer Property to Members of Decedent's Family for Less Than Full and Adequate Consideration	S19-14
			[i] Not a family device.	S19-14
			[ii] Full and adequate consideration.	S19-14
		[c]	Similar Arrangement Test	S19-14
	[4]		Deemed Satisfaction	S19-15
	[6]		Establishing Valuation When a Right or Restriction Is Excepted From Section 2703	S19-15
		[a]	Estate Tax Valuation	S19-15
			[i] Restrictions on lifetime dispositions. . . .	S19-15
			[ii] Obligation of the estate to sell.	S19-16
	[7]		Effective Dates and Substantial Modification	S19-16

CUMULATIVE TABLE OF IRC SECTIONS T-1

CUMULATIVE TABLE OF TREASURY REGULATIONS T-57

CUMULATIVE TABLE OF REVENUE RULINGS, REVENUE PROCEDURES,
        AND OTHER IRS RELEASES T-87

CUMULATIVE TABLE OF CASES T-109

CUMULATIVE INDEX I-1

PART **II**

The Estate Tax

CHAPTER 2

Imposition of Estate Tax

¶ 2.01   Section 2001. Imposition and Rate of Tax [Revised] S2-1
     [1]   Computation of the Tentative Tax S2-2
         [a]   Taxable Estate S2-3
         [b]   Adjusted Taxable Gifts S2-3
             [i]   Gifts made through August 5, 1997. . . .   S2-4
             [ii]   Gifts made after August 5, 1997. . . . . .   S2-4
         [c]   Tax Rates S2-7
     [2]   Reductions in the Tentative Tax S2-9
     [3]   Tax Planning S2-13
¶ 2.02   Section 2002. Liability for Payment S2-14
     [1]   Estate Tax Return S2-14
     [3]   Extension of Time for Payment S2-16
         [a]   Section 6159 . . . .   S2-16
         [b]   Section 6161 . . . .   S2-17
             [i]   Short extensions. S2-17
             [ii]   "Reasonable cause" extensions. S2-17
         [c]   Section 6166 . . . .   S2-17
             [ii]   Qualification for extension. S2-17
             [iii]   Period of extension. S2-19
             [v]   Interest. S2-21
             [vi]   The "gotcha." S2-21
             [vii]   Declaratory judgments with respect to
                  Section 6166.   S2-22

¶ 2.01 SECTION 2001. IMPOSITION AND RATE OF TAX [REVISED]

Replace existing ¶ 2.01 with the following revised ¶ 2.01.

The federal estate tax is imposed by Section 2001(a) of the Internal Revenue Code (the Code) on the transfer of the taxable estate of every decedent who is either a citizen or a resident of the United States.[1] "Taxable estate" is a term of art defined in Section 2051.[2] The term "transfer" has less statutory significance than might at first be supposed;[3] the statutory plan presumes the requisite transfer of a property interest if its value is required to be included in the gross estate of a decedent.[4]

The method of computing the tax is provided by Section 2001(b) and the rates to be used are presented in a multipurpose rate table provided in Section 2001(c).[5] Prior to 1977, computation of the estate tax involved only the application of rates in a graduated rate table to the taxable estate. However, with the enactment of Section 2001(b) in the Tax Reform Act of 1976, Congress took steps toward integration of the gift and estate taxes. The estate tax computation involves essentially figuring a tentative tax on all gratuitous transfers made inter vivos after 1976 or at death. This is a combination of the aggregate value of the taxable estate[6] *and* adjusted taxable gifts,[7] terms discussed here.[8] The tentative tax is then reduced by subtracting an amount related to tax payable on lifetime gifts after 1976.[9] The computation does not tax any gratuitous transfers twice; the taxable estate is still the only amount being taxed. However, the amount of tax imposed on the taxable estate is dependent upon the decedent's post-1976 gratuitous transfers.

[1] Computation of the Tentative Tax

The first step in computing a decedent's estate tax liability is to compute a tentative tax[10] on the aggregate amount of the decedent's "taxable estate"[11] and

---

[1] The questions of citizenship and residence are discussed ¶ 6.01[3] in connection with the tax imposed on estates of nonresidents who are not citizens. IRC §§ 2101–2108. See also IRC §§ 2208, 2209. Cf. ¶ 9.02[1], ¶ 18.03[2].

[2] See ¶ 5.02.

[3] However, it is of constitutional significance that the estate tax is imposed on wealth *transfers*, not on wealth itself. An indirect tax such as a tax on the transmission of wealth is constitutional as long as it is imposed uniformly throughout the United States. In contrast, a direct tax on wealth must be apportioned among the states in accordance with their respective populations. See Tribe, American Constitutional Law, 841 (3d ed. 2000).

[4] IRC §§ 2031–2046, discussed in Chapter 4.

[5] The Section 2001(c) rate schedule is multipurpose, because it is used in computing the estate tax, the gift tax, and the tax on generation-skipping transfers. See infra ¶ 2.01[c].

[6] IRC § 2001(b)(1)(A). See IRC § 2051, infra ¶ 2.01[1][a].

[7] IRC § 2001(b)(1)(B). See infra ¶ 2.01[1][b].

[8] IRC § 2001(b)(1).

[9] IRC § 2001(b)(2).

[10] IRC § 2001(b)(1).

[11] IRC § 2001(b)(1)(A). See IRC § 2051, infra ¶ 2.01[1][a].

"adjusted taxable gifts."[12] The tax is determined by applying the Section 2001(c) rates to that aggregated amount.[13]

[a] Taxable Estate

The term "taxable estate" is discussed in detail in Chapters 4 and 5. It constitutes the decedent's gross estate which is made up of property owned by the decedent at death[14] and property that, although not owned by decedent at death, was the subject of some lifetime ownership, benefit or control resulting from a testamentary-like transfer by the decedent.[15] Property included in a decedent's gross estate is valued under either the method provided by Section 2031 or Section 2032A at the date of the decedent's death under Section 2031 or on the alternate valuation date under Section 2032.[16] The gross estate is then reduced by allowable deductions to determine the taxable estate.[17]

[b] Adjusted Taxable Gifts

The term "adjusted taxable gifts," defined in Section 2001(b), is the total amount of taxable gifts (within the meaning of Section 2503)[18] made by the decedent after December 31, 1976, other than gifts that are taken into account in determining the gross estate.[19] The exclusion of gifts included in the decedent's gross estate from adjusted taxable gifts prevents the value of the same gift from being included twice in the estate tax computation.[20]

The amount of adjusted taxable gifts is the fair market value of the property gifted at the time the gift tax transfer was completed. However, this does not necessarily mean that the decedent's lifetime determination of the amount

---

[12] IRC § 2001(b)(1)(B). See infra ¶ 2.01[1][b].

[13] See infra ¶ 2.01[1][c]. But sec IRC § 2201, ¶ 8.01.

[14] IRC § 2033. See ¶ 4.05; but see ¶ 4.02[7].

[15] See ¶¶ 4.07-4.16.

[16] See ¶¶ 4.02, 4.03, 4.04.

[17] See Chapter 5.

[18] Taxable gifts are gifts after gift-splitting under Section 2513, exclusions under Sections 2503(b) and 2503(e), and deductions allowed by Sections 2522 and 2523 as limited by Section 2524. See Chapters 9–11.

[19] See Chapter 4.

[20] See HR Conf. Rep. No. 1380, 94th Cong., 2d Sess. 3, 13 (1976), reprinted in 1976-3 CB (Vol. 3) 735, 747. See also Rev. Rul. 84-25, 1984-1 CB 191, which appropriately holds that a legally binding note issued by the decedent during life and subject to the gift tax (see ¶ 10.01[3][h] note 124), but unpaid at death, is not included in adjusted taxable gifts, because the assets to satisfy the note are included in the gross estate.

Similarly, the amount of adjusted taxable gifts is reduced by the amount of gifts made by the decedent's spouse that are included in the decedent spouse's gross estate under Section 2035 where a Section 2513 election applied to the transfer. IRC § 2001(e). Congress should have applied the Section 2001(e)(2) rule to inclusions of property in the estate of the decedent's spouse under Sections 2036–2038, as well as Section 2035, especially in view of the limited scope of Section 2035(a). See ¶ 4.07[2][b].

of the property gifted controls its amount in the estate tax computation. The rules governing the amount of adjusted taxable gifts depend upon the date that gift was made.

[i] Gifts made through August 5, 1997. The fair market value of property transferred by gift prior to August 6, 1997,[21] may be redetermined in the determination of the amount of adjusted taxable gifts at the time of filing the estate tax return, notwithstanding the expiration of the statute of limitations on the assessment of gift tax on such transfers.[22] In addition, legal issues involving the interpretation of gift tax law (such as deductions and qualification for the annual exclusion) may also be raised even though the gift tax statute of limitations has run.[23]

[ii] Gifts made after August 5, 1997. The amount of adjusted taxable gifts made after August 5, 1997,[24] is not subject to a redetemination adjustment in the estate tax computation if: (1) the gift was adequately disclosed;[25] (2) the transferred property's value is finally determined for gift tax purposes;[26] and (3) the statute of limitations with respect to the gift has expired.[27] Even though the statute refers merely to valuation, the nonadjustment rule applies to adjustments involving all issues relating to the *amount* of the gift, including valuation issues and legal issues involving the interpretation of the gift tax law.[28] If

---

[21] Prior to August 6, 1997, there was no statute that required the value of a gift as determined for gift tax purposes be used in valuing adjusted taxable gifts in a decedent's estate tax computation. Cf. IRC § 2504(c).

[22] Reg. §§ 20.2001-1(a), 25.2504-2(c) Ex. 3; Evanson v. United States, 30 F3d 960 (8th Cir. 1994); Levin v. Comm'r, 986 F2d 91 (4th Cir. 1993), cert. denied, Levin v. C.I.R., (1993, S CT) 510 US 816, 126 L Ed 2d 36; Estate of Smith v. Comm'r, 94 TC 872 (1990). Contra Boatmen's First Nat'l Bank of Kans. City v. United States, 705 F. Supp. 1407 (WD Mo. 1988). See Morris, "Troubling Transfer Tax Tie-Ins," 1991 Utah L. Rev. 749; Schlenger, Madden & Hayes, "IRS Can Revalue Gifts for Estate Tax Purposes," 21 Est. Plan. 366 (1994).

[23] Reg. § 20.2001-1(a).

[24] The Taxpayer Relief Act of 1997, Pub. L. No. 105-34, § 506(a), 111 Stat. 788, 855 (1997), reprinted in 1997-4 CB (Vol. 1) 1, 386. The regulations provide that these rules apply only if the estate tax return is filed after the date the regulations became final, December 3, 1999. Reg. § 20.2001-1(f).

[25] IRC § 2001(f)(2) (flush language); Reg. § 20.2001-1(c)(1). See IRC § 6501(c)(9).

[26] IRC § 2001(f)(2).

[27] IRC § 2001(f)(2)(A). See Reg. § 20.2001-1(b).
  The rule applies to Section 2701(d) transfers as well. IRC § 2001(f)(1)(B). See ¶ 19.02[5][a].

[28] IRC § 2001(f); Reg. § 20.2001-1(b). See Reg. § 301.6501(c)-1(f)(7) Ex. 2. This is a liberalization of the U.S. Treasury's policy prior to the adoption of final regulations. See TD 8845, Supplementary Information, Finalty with Respect to Adequately Disclosed Gifts, 64 Fed. Reg. 67,767, 67,768 (1999), reprinted in 1999-2 CB 683, 685. The proposed regulations had applied the nonadjustment rules only to issues of valuation. See Prop. Reg. §§ 20.2001-1(b), 20.2001-1(d), 20.2001-1(f) Ex. 2. Notice of Proposed Rulemaking and

these requirements are not all satisfied, then the amount of the adjusted taxable gifts may be redetermined in computing the decedent's estate tax.[29]

Adequate Disclosure. The rules of adequate disclosure apply for purposes of both the estate tax computation and the limitations period for the gift tax.[30] Adequate disclosure may be made either on the gift tax return reporting the transfer or on a statement attached to the gift tax return.[31] Adequate disclosure[32] essentially requires a description of the nature of the gift and the basis for determining the value of the reported gift.[33] The regulations provide a safe harbor to satisfy the description and basis of valuation adequate disclosure requirements that must include: (1) a description of the transferred property and any consideration received by the transferor;[34] (2) a listing of the identity of, and relationship between, the transferor and each transferee;[35] (3) if the property is transferred in trust, the trust's identification number and either a brief description of the terms of the trust *or* a copy of the trust instrument;[36] (4) *either* a detailed description of the method used in determining the fair market value of the property, including any relevant financial data (such as balance sheets), and a description of any discounts claimed in valuing the property;[37] *or*

Notice of Public Hearing, 63 Fed. Reg. 70,701, 70,704. (1998), reprinted in 1999-1 CB 813, 816. Seemingly, this change led the Treasury to use the term "amount" of adjusted taxable gifts in the final regulations rather than the term "value," which had been used in the proposed regulations.

[29] For example, even though the "adequate disclosure" regulations have been satisfied sufficiently to commence the running of the statute of limitations, the reported amount is not binding for purposes of computing adjusted taxable gifts unless the "final determination" requirement is also met.

[30] IRC §§ 2001(f), 6501(c)(9). See ¶ 9.05[2][b].

The adequate disclosure regulations also provide adequate disclosure rules with respect to nongift completed transfers and transactions (Reg. § 301.6501(c)-1(f)(4), see Reg. § 301.6501(c)(1)(f)(7) Ex. 6), incomplete transfers (Reg. § 301.6501(c)-1(f)(5)), and split gifts (Reg. § 301.6501(c)-1(f)(6)). See ¶ 9.04[7][a] text accompanying notes 252-259.

[31] IRC §§ 2001(f)(2) (flush language), 6501(c)(9).

[32] See Reg. §§ 301.6501(c)-1(f)(2), 301.6501(c)-1(f)(3). The adequate disclosure safe-harbor rules apply to gifts made after December 31, 1996, but only if the gift tax return for the gift is filed after the date that the regulations became final, December 3, 1999. Reg. § 301.6501(c)-1(f)(8). See supra note 24; ¶ 9.04[7][a] note 242.

[33] Reg. §§ 301.6501(c)-1(f)(2), 301.6501(c)-1(f)(3).

[34] Reg. § 301.6501(c)-1(f)(2)(i).

[35] Reg. § 301.6501(c)-1(f)(2)(ii).

[36] Reg. § 301.6501(c)-1(f)(2)(iii).

[37] Reg. § 301.6501(c)-1(f)(2)(iv).

If the transfer is of an *actively traded entity* on an established exchange, it will be considered adequately disclosed if the description includes the CUSIP number of the security and the mean between the highest and lowest quoted selling prices on the applicable valuation date. Reg. §§ 301.6501(c)-1(f)(2)(iv), 301.6501(c)-1(f)(7) Ex. 1.

If the transfer is of a *nonactively traded entity*, there is a more detailed requirement. If the valuation is based on the net value of the assets, a statement must be provided as to the valuation of 100 percent of the entity (without discounts), the pro rata portion subject

in the alternative, an adequate appraisal of the property[38] by a qualified appraiser;[39] *and* (5) a statement describing any position taken that is contrary to any proposed, temporary, or final Treasury regulations or revenue rulings published at the time of the transfer.[40]

Final Determination. The nonadjustment rules for adjusted taxable gifts in the computation of the estate tax also require a final determination of the prior amount of the adjusted taxable gifts.[41] A final determination occurs if: (1) the amount of the taxable gift as shown by the taxpayer on a gift tax return (or on a statement attached to the return) is not contested by the Internal Revenue Service (the Service) before the period for assessing gift tax on the transfer expires;[42] (2) the Service establishes an amount that is not contested by the tax-

---

to the transfer, and the fair market value reported on the return. Reg. §§ 301.6501(c)-1(f)(2)(iv), \ 301.6501(c)-1(f)(7) Ex. 3. The final step takes into consideration any discounting of the value of the property transferred. Id. See ¶ 4.02[4]. If 100 percent of the value of the entity is not disclosed, the taxpayer bears the burden of demonstrating that the fair market value is properly determined by a method other than a method based on the net fair market value of the assets held by the entity. Reg. § 301.6501(c)-1(f)(2)(iv).

Furthermore, if the nonactively traded entity that is transferred owns an interest in another nonactively traded entity or entities, the same analysis must be employed for each such entity, if such information is relevant and material in determining the value of the transferred interest. Reg. §§ 301.6501(c)-1(f)(2)(iv), 301.6501(c)-1(f)(7) Ex. 4. If the appraisal alternative is employed (see infra text accompanying notes 38 and 39), this requirement will be a part of the appraisal. Reg. § 301.6501(c)-1(f)(7) Ex. 5.

[38] The appraisal must provide all of the following information in order to meet the safe-harbor requirements: (1) the appraiser's background and credentials that qualify the appraiser to perform the appraisal; (2) the dates of the transfer and the appraisal, and the purpose of the appraisal; (3) a description of the property; (4) a description of the appraisal process; (5) a description of the assumptions, hypothetical conditions, and any limiting conditions and restrictions on the transferred property that affect the valuation reported; (6) the information considered in determining the appraised value, including all financial data used in determining the value of an ownership interest of a business so that another person can replicate the process and arrive at the appraised value; (7) the appraisal procedures used and the reasoning that supports them; (8) the valuation method used, the rationale for its use, and the procedure used in arriving at the fair market value; and (9) the specific basis for the valuation, such as specific comparable sales or transactions, sales of similar interests, asset-based approaches, merger-acquisition transactions, etc. Reg. §§ 301.6501(c)-1(f)(3)(ii), 301.6501(c)-1(f)(7) Ex. 5.

[39] Reg. §§ 301.6501(c)-1(f)(2)(iv), 301.6501(c)-1(f)(3).

The appraiser must not be the donor or the donee of the property, must not be related to the transferor (as defined in Section 2032A(e)(2), see ¶ 4.04[3][b][vii]), must not be employed by any of such persons, and must be qualified to appraise the type of property transferred. Reg. § 301.6501(c)-1(f)(3)(i).

[40] Reg. § 301.6501(c)-1(f)(2)(v).

[41] Section 2001(f) was amended in 1998 legislation to add a definition of the term "final determination." Internal Revenue Service Restructuring and Reform Act of 1998, Pub. L. No. 105-206, § 6007(e)(2)(B), 112 Stat. 685, 810 (1998), reprinted in 1998-3 CB 145, 270.

[42] IRC § 2001(f)(2)(A).

payer within the limitations period;[43] (3) the courts establish the amount in a final determination that is no longer subject to appeal;[44] *or* (4) the amount is established through a settlement agreement between the taxpayer and the Service.[45]

[c] Tax Rates

Once the total of the taxable estate and adjusted taxable gifts has been computed a tax is computed using the multipurpose rate table[46] which appears in Section 2001(c).[47] Over the years since the 1976 unification of the estate and gift taxes, the table has undergone a variety of changes, with the current rate schedule being the most favorable to taxpayers. In 1977, the top rate was 70 percent, which by 1984 was reduced to 55 percent for the years 1984-2001.[48] Both rates also were subject to a 5 percent surtax on transfers in excess of $10 million.[49] The top marginal rate was 50 percent for the year

---

[43] IRC § 2001(f)(2)(B).

[44] IRC § 2001(f)(2)(C). See Reg. § 20.2001-1(d).

[45] IRC § 2001(f)(2)(C). A settlement agreement includes a Section 7121 closing agreement, a Section 7122 compromise, or a settlement of a valuation issue binding on both parties. Reg. § 20.2001-1(d).

[46] The table also imposes the tax rates for the gift tax. IRC § 2502(a)(1). See ¶ 9.03[2]. The maximum tax rate imposed by the table is also used in computing the rate of tax on generation-skipping transfers. IRC § 2641. See ¶ 16.01.

The table does not apply in limited estate tax circumstances. IRC § 2201. See ¶ 8.01.

[47] The maximum rate for years 2010 to 2012 is 35 percent. IRC § 2001(c). The basic table as provided in Section 2001(c) was modified in prior years according to the rules of now-repealed Section 2001(c)(2). Under those modifications, the maximum rate under Section 2001(c) was as follows:

Calendar Years	Maximum Rate
1977–1981	70 percent
1982	65 percent
1983	60 percent
1984–2001	55 percent
2002	50 percent
2003	49 percent
2004	48 percent
2005	47 percent
2006	46 percent
2007–2009	45 percent
2010–2012	35 percent

The maximum rate for years after 2012 is discussed infra note 52.

[48] See supra note 47.

[49] For years beginning in 1998, the surtax wiped out only the graduated rates but not the unified credit, and, as a result, it was capped at $17,184,000. A flat 55 percent tax on $3 million (where the 55 percent rate kicked in under Section 2001(c)(1) as it applied in years from 1998 through 2001) was $1,650,000 which is $359,200 in excess of the $1,290,800 amount of tax in the tables. Since 5 percent of $7,184,000 equals $359,200,

2002 and the 5 percent surtax does not apply to estates of decedents dying after 2001.[50] The top marginal rate was gradually reduced from 50 percent to 45 percent in years 2003 to 2007.[51] In 2010 it was reduced to its current 35 percent rate level.[52]

However, the rates can properly be analyzed only by examining them in conjunction with the Section 2010 credit.[53] As a result of both the applicable credit amount,[54] which offsets tax attributable to the lower rates, and the ceiling on maximum rates, the estate tax is imposed at a flat 35 percent rate for years 2010 through 2012.[55]

---

and the surtax applied only to taxable amounts over $10 million, the 5 percent surtax terminated at $17,184,000 ($10 million plus $7,184,000). See the Taxpayer Relief Act of 1997, Pub. L. No. 105-34, § 501(a)(1)(D), 111 Stat. 788, 845 (1997), reprinted in 1997-4 CB (Vol. 1) 1, 59.

The surtax did not affect the maximum federal estate tax rate for purposes of computing the generation-skipping transfer tax. Conf. Rep. No. 495, 100th Cong., 1st Sess. 993–994 (1987), reprinted in 1987-3 CB 193, 273–274. See ¶ 16.01 text accompanying note 12.

[50] The Section 2001(c)(2) 5 percent surtax was repealed by the Economic Growth and Tax Relief Reconciliation Act of 2001 for years after 2001. Pub. L. No. 107-16, § 511(b), 115 Stat. 38, 70 (2001), reprinted in 2001-3 CB 9, 42. But see infra note 52.

[51] See supra note 47.

[52] IRC § 2001(c). Under the "sunset" provision effective on January 1, 2013, the top rate of 55 percent is restored as is the 5 percent surtax on transfers in excess of $10 million that eliminates the graduated tax rates. Economic Growth and Tax Relief Reconciliation Act of 2001, Pub. L. No. 107-16, § 901(a)(2), 115 Stat. 38, 150 (2001), reprinted in 2001-3 CB 9, 122, as amended by the Tax Relief Act of 2010, Pub. L. No. 111-312, §§ 101(a)(1), 304, 124 Stat. 3296, 3298, 3304 (2010). The "sunset" provision is discussed more fully at ¶ 8.11.

[53] The credit also determines estate tax filing requirements. See IRC § 6018, discussed at Supplement ¶ 3.02[3].

[54] See IRC § 2010(b), discussed Supplement ¶ 3.02. If a recomputation of the gift tax payable is required by Section 2001(b)(2), the gift tax history of the decedent's spouse (not of the decedent) is applied to the spouse's portion of the split gifts included in the decedent's gross estate. IRC § 2001(d). See infra ¶ 2.01[2] text accompanying note 77.

[55] In prior years, as a result of the Section 2010 credit, the effective marginal rates of estate tax were:

Year	Rates
1984–2001	37 to 55 percent
2002	41 to 50 percent
2003	41 to 49 percent
2004	45 to 48 percent
2005	45 to 47 percent
2006	46 percent
2007–2009	45 percent
2010–2012	35 percent

The Section 2001(c) table actually shows minimum rates of 18 percent, gradually rising to 35 percent, identified here as the lowest current effective estate and gift tax rates. Thirty

[2] Reductions in the Tentative Tax

The tentative tax on the sum of the taxable estate and adjusted taxable gifts is then reduced by the amount of gift taxes that would have been payable on gifts made after 1976.[56] Since gifts made after 1976 are pulled into the estate tax computation,[57] a reduction is properly provided for gift taxes on those gifts. Those gifts are not taxed again, but they do affect the amount of tax imposed on the taxable estate.

Over the years there have been reductions in the rates imposed on gratuitous transfers[58] and changes in the amount of the gift tax credit.[59] Since the taxable estate is taxed at the rates imposed at the date of the decedent's death,[60] the computation of the amount of taxes payable on gifts made after 1976 also must reflect the transfer tax rates at the decedent's death.[61] Thus in computing the Section 2001(b)(2) reduction, both the gift tax rates[62] and the gift tax credit amounts[63] must reflect the tax rates in effect on the date of the decedent's death.

The Code specifically requires a reduction for the amount of gift taxes that would have been payable on the post-1976 gifts had the rate schedule *in effect at death* applied at the time of the gifts.[64] This recomputation is required to prevent changes in the rate schedule from retroactively affecting the amount

---

five percent is the lowest current effective rate because all estate and gift taxes imposed at the lower rates are eliminated by the unified credit. As indicated in the table above, when the unified credit increased (see IRC § 2010(c)), the lowest effective rate also increased. The lower part of the table was needed when enacted to compute the tax previously imposed on generation-skipping transfers. The original tax on generation-skipping transfers was retroactively repealed in 1986. See ¶ 18.05.

[56] IRC § 2001(b)(2). Even though the reduction for gift taxes payable is not so labeled, it is essentially a credit because it is a direct reduction of tax liability, and not merely a reduction of the tax base.

As the Section 2001(b)(2) reduction relates only to post-1976 gifts, pre-1977 gifts that become a part of the decedent's taxable estate identified in Section 2001(b)(1)(A) are still permitted to qualify for the Section 2012 credit for the gift tax paid. The Section 2012 credit will eventually fade away as it is inapplicable to post-1976 gifts. See IRC §§ 2012(a), 2012(e); ¶ 3.04.

While Section 2001(b)(2) applies only to post-1976 gifts, the rate of tax paid on such gifts is affected by pre-1977 gifts (see ¶ 9.03[3]) that must be taken into account in making the Section 2001(b)(2) reduction. TAM 9642001 (Nov. 30, 1994).

[57] Post-1976 gifts are part of the amount identified in Section 2001(b)(1)(A) if they are brought within the gross estate. If such gifts are not brought within the gross estate, they appear in Section 2001(b)(1)(B).

[58] See Supplement ¶ 9.03[2].

[59] See Supplement ¶ 9.06.

[60] IRC § 2001(b)(1).

[61] IRC §§ 2001(b)(2), 2001(g).

[62] IRC §§ 2001(b)(2), 2001(g)(1).

[63] IRC §§ 2001(b)(2), 2001(g)(2).

[64] IRC § 2001(g)(1).

of tax effectively paid on prior gifts.[65] In instances in which taxpayers have not made any pre-1977 taxable gifts and their adjusted taxable gifts do not exceed $500,000, the tentative tax will be reduced by the gift taxes that were payable on gifts made after 1976 without recomputation based on rates effective at death, because the tax rate schedules on those gifts and estates are identical.[66]

The Code also specifically requires a recomputation of the gift tax credit for years after 1976. The amount of the credit allowed in determining the gift taxes payable is determined using the gift tax applicable exclusion amount that was available at the time the gift[67] was made, but with an applicable credit amount determined using the tax rates in effect at the time of the decedent's death.[68]

The rate and credit computations of Section 2001(b)(2) can become complicated. However, a simple example illustrates how they work. If a donor, having made no prior inter vivos gifts, made a taxable gift of $2 million in the year 2009 and died in 2011, the donor would have paid a $435,000 gift tax in 2009.[69] When the donor dies in 2011, since both the rates and the effective credit rates are reduced,[70] the donor's Section 2001(b)(2) reduction is only

---

[65] HR Conf. Rep. No. 201, 97th Cong., 1st Sess. 38, 156 (1981), reprinted in 1981-2 CB 352, 376. In the case of a rate reduction, this would result in a reduction of taxes.

[66] See IRC § 2001(c).

[67] Priv. Ltr. Rul. 9250004 (Aug. 24, 1992).

[68] IRC §§ 2001(b)(2), 2001(g)(2).
Since the applicable exclusion amount in years 1977 through 1986 was less than $500,000, no adjustment is necessary for those years. Additionally no adjustment is necessary for 2011 and 2012. For years 1987-2010 the adjustment to the maximum amount of credit is as follows:

Years	Applicable Exclusion Amount	Original Credit Amount	Adjusted Credit Amount
1987–1997	$ 600,000	$192,800	$190,800
1998	$ 625,000	$202,050	$199,550
1999	$ 650,000	$211,300	$208,300
2000–2001	$ 675,000	$220,550	$217,050
2002–2010	$ 1 million	$345,800	$330,800

[69] The tax was computed as follows:

§ 2502(a)(1) tax on $2 million, all gifts, including the current year	$780,800
§ 2502(a)(2) less tax on gifts in prior periods	-0
Tax on current year's gifts	$780,800
§ 2505 Credit reduction	-345,800
Tax liability in 2009	$435,000

Thus, there was a tax on the second $1 million taxed in part at 41, 43, and 45 percent rates.

[70] See supra text accompanying notes 59–68.

$350,000.[71] The amount of reduction is appropriate because it allows a Section 2001(b)(2) reduction in the taxes payable on the $1 million of gifts that were taxed, but at the currect 35 percent tax rate on such gifts.[72]

Even if there is no change in the rate schedule, if there is a difference between taxes *actually paid* and taxes *payable*, the reduction is based on the latter. Thus, subject to the rules of Section 2001(f),[73] an error in prior computation of the gift tax may be disregarded and the reduction is based on the amount of tax that should have been paid.[74] In addition, if the Section 2505 unified credit under the gift tax, although allowable, was not actually used, the amount of gift tax payable is reduced by the amount of credit that was allowable using the tax rates at the decedent's death; again, it is tax *payable* not tax *paid* that determines the amount to be subtracted.[75]

The reduction of an amount for gift tax payable may include not only an amount for gift tax payable by the decedent but also, in limited situations, an amount for gift tax payable by the decedent's spouse. If Section 2513 gift-splitting[76] was elected on a lifetime transfer actually made by the decedent and the value of the property transferred was subsequently pulled into the decedent's taxable estate, then an amount for gift tax payable by the decedent's

---

[71] The amount is computed as follows:

§ 2502(a)(1) tax at 2001 rates on $2 million the sum of all gifts including gifts made in the current year	$680,800
§ 2502(a)(2) tax at 2001 rates on all gifts in prior years	- 0
§ 2502(a) tax	$680,800
§ 2505 credit reduction using current rates (see supra note 68)	-330,800
	$350,000

[72] Another example may be helpful. If donor made the $2 million gift in 1995, the donor would have paid gift taxes of $588,000, $780,800 (using 1995 rates) less a credit of $192,800 (see supra note 68). However, the donor's Section 2001(b)(2) reduction would be only $490,000, $680,800 (using current rates) less a credit of $190,800 (see supra note 68).

[73] See supra ¶ 2.01[1][b][ii].

[74] For open years there may be an assertion of a deficiency or a right to a refund if the gift tax liability was improperly determined at the time of the gift. See ¶ 9.04[7].

[75] See ¶ 9.06. This result is harsh and was probably not intended by Congress. See McCord, 1976 Estate and Gift Tax Reform—Analysis, Explanation and Commentary 23 (West 1977). The taxpayer is not given an opportunity to postpone use of the Section 2505 unified gift tax credit. If it is not used as allowed in post-1976 gifts, it cannot be used against subsequent gifts. Rev. Rul. 79-398, 1979-2 CB 338. The credit allowable in a year is the maximum credit reduced by the credit "allowable" in prior calendar periods. IRC § 2505(a)(2). See Supplement ¶ 9.06[1]. Under prior law, the somewhat related Section 2521 $30,000 lifetime exemption was not required to be used at the earliest possible time. Reg. § 25.2521-1(a). See Stephens, Maxfield & Lind, Federal Estate and Gift Taxation, ¶ 10-2 (Warren, Gorham & Lamont, 3d ed. 1974).

[76] See ¶ 10.03.

spouse is also used to reduce the tentative tax.[77] The reduction is proper; as the value of all of the property is being pulled into the decedent's gross estate, the estate ought to be allowed a reduction in the estate tax computation for gift taxes on the value of the entire property. However, in codifying this rule, Congress expressly approved a complementary rule that in some circumstances is disadvantageous to the decedent's spouse: any Section 2505 credit used ineffectively (as it now turns out) by a spouse on the "split" lifetime transfer of the decedent is not restored for further use by the spouse in case of subsequent lifetime transfers.[78]

As indicated earlier, in addition to a reduction for an amount for gift tax payable, the tentative tax is further reduced by tax credits,[79] the most important of which is the unified credit provided by Section 2010.[80] Other credits,[81] which are discussed in Chapter 3, also reduce the net amount of estate tax payable.[82]

---

[77] IRC § 2001(d). This rule parallels pre-1977 law, which allowed a credit for gift tax under Section 2012 for payment by a donor's spouse of gift tax on split gifts if the gift was also taxed in the donor's estate. Under Section 2001(e), when the consenting spouse dies, the Section 2001(b)(2) reduction of an amount for the gift tax payable is reduced by the amount of the tax treated under Section 2001(d) as payable by the donor spouse if Section 2035 required inclusion of the gift in the donor spouse's estate. See supra ¶ 2.01[1][b] note 20. This adjustment, however, should not be greater than the Section 2001(d) amount that actually qualified as a Section 2001(b)(2) reduction in the donor spouse's estate. In this situation, the total amount of adjusted taxable gifts of the consenting spouse does not include the split portion of the donor decedent's gift included in the donor decedent's estate under Section 2035. See ¶ 2.01[1][b]. If the consenting spouse dies before the donor decedent and the gift is included in donor decedent's gross estate under Section 2035, the consenting spouse's federal estate tax return will likely have to be amended. See Rev. Rul. 81-85, 1981-1 CB 452. If the donor spouse dies within three years and if the consenting spouse pays tax on one half of the gift and lives beyond the reach of Section 2035, it is possible to have payment of the federal estate tax with dollars that are never included in the gross estate.

[78] Cf. Norair v. Comm'r, 65 TC 942 (1976), aff'd, 556 F2d 574 (4th Cir. 1977); Ingalls v. Comm'r, 336 F2d 874 (4th Cir. 1964); English v. United States, 284 F. Supp. 256 (ND Fla. 1968). The legislative history of Section 2001(d) expresses congressional approval of these results. HR Conf. Rep. No. 1380, 94th Cong., 2d Sess. 3, 13 (1976), reprinted in 1976-3 CB (Vol. 3) 735, 747.

[79] See Chapter 3.

[80] That credit replaced the Section 2052 $60,000 exemption, which operated as a deduction under pre-1977 law. Cf. ¶ 3.02[1]. The current credit is generally the tax imposed on a basic exclusion amount of $5 million, adjusted for inflation after 2011. See Supplement ¶ 3.02.

[81] See IRC §§ 2012–2016.

[82] Although Section 2001(b)(2) largely eliminates the use of the Section 2012 credit for gift taxes, that credit is still applicable with respect to pre-1977 gifts that find their way into the estate tax computation as part of the taxable estate, not as adjusted taxable gifts. See supra note 56.

[3] Tax Planning

Lifetime gifts made after 1976 are automatically pulled into the estate tax structure in computing the rate of tax on the taxable estate and are subject to the same multipurpose rate table. An initial reaction might be that inter vivos gifts made after 1976 will not result in any overall tax savings. Although the government, not the taxpayer, has use of any gift tax dollars paid during the donor's lifetime, there are offsetting factors. While lifetime gifts play a part in the computation of the estate tax, appreciation of the transferred property between the date the gift is made and the date of the donor's death is not included as a taxable amount. This is because adjusted taxable gifts are included in the transfer tax base at their value when the gift is complete.[83] Second, income generated by the gift property between the time of the gift and the time of death is not included in a decedent's gross estate. In addition, assuming a post-gift survival period of more than three years,[84] the amount of any gift tax payable is not included in the transfer tax base. Therefore, federal gift taxes paid on lifetime transfers reduce the tax base in a way that the federal estate taxes do not. Finally, there are still tax savings available by use of the annual exclusion under Section 2503(b),[85] which may be doubled by the provision that permits married taxpayers to split gifts,[85] and by use of the exclusion under Section 2503(e) for qualified transfers for tuition and medical expenses.[86] Congress has consciously retained these tax advantages for lifetime gifts.

Planning for estates is, of course, much more difficult because of the uncertainty after 2012.[87] With respect to other planning, the gift tax exclusions of Sections 2503(b) and 2503(e) and, in all likelihood,[88] the use of the Section

---

[83] Cf. ¶ 2.01[1][b][ii].

[84] IRC § 2035(b). See ¶ 4.07[3].

[85] Section 2503(b) is discussed ¶ 9.04[1].

[85] IRC § 2513. See ¶ 10.03.

[86] Section 2503(e) is discussed ¶ 9.04[2].

[87] A "sunset" provision restores the year 2001 estate tax in the year 2013. Economic Growth and Tax Relief Reconciliation Act of 2001, Pub. L. No. 107-16, § 901(a)(2), 115 Stat. 38, 150 (2001), reprinted in 2001-3 CB 9, 122, as amended by the Tax Relief Act of 2010, Pub. L. No. 111-312, §§ 101(a)(1), 304, 124 Stat. 3296, 3298, 3304 (2010). The "sunset" provision is discussed more fully at Supplement ¶ 8.11.

[88] The $5 million applicable exclusion amount of Section 2505 is safe in years 2011 and 2012. Seemingly it will be extended. However, if the estate tax applicable exclusion amount is reduced after that date (either by legislation or under the sunsetting provision (see supra note 88), without legislative assistance tax liability could arise at death as a result of the prior transfer. Assume that in 2013 the applicable exclusion amount is reduced to $3.5 million, the maximum tax rate is 35 percent, that Decedent, never having made any prior gifts, made a $5 million taxable gift in 2011, and died with a $2 million taxable estate. Under Section 2001, Decedent would have a $2,435,800 tax liability reduced by a Section 2010 credit of $1,205,800 or estate tax liability of $1,225,000. Decedent would be paying a 35 percent tax on the $2 million taxable estate or $700,000 but, in addition, a 35 percent tax on the $1.5 million applicable exclusion amount reduction of $525,000 or total tax of $1,225,000. The situation would be even more dramatic if the sunset provision ap-

2505 $5 million applicable exclusion amount remain the only safe bets with respect to inter vivos estate planning.[89]

---

plied and reduced the applicable exclusion amount to $1 million and raised the maximum rate to 55 percent. See Supplement ¶¶ 2.01[1][c] note 52, Supplement 3.02[1] note 11.

[89] See ¶¶ 9.04, 9.06.

¶ 2.02 SECTION 2002. LIABILITY FOR PAYMENT

[1] Estate Tax Return

Page 2-16:

Add to note 7.

The Service has released the revised Form 706, United States Estate (and Generation-Skipping Transfer) Tax Return (revised July 2011) for use by estates of decedents dying in calendar year 2010. The instructions discuss, among other things, that executors of estates of decedents dying in 2010 may elect modified carryover basis treatment for property passing from the decedent by filing Form 8939, Allocation of Increase in Basis for Property Acquired From a Decedent, instead of filing Form 706; executors electing modified carryover basis treatment should not use the Form 706 Schedule R or R-1 to allocate GST exemption but rather Schedule R or R-1 in Form 8939. The applicable exclusion amount for estates of decedents dying in calendar year 2010 is $5 million, the maximum estate tax rate is 35 percent and the applicable rate for generation-skipping transfers is zero. Inflation-adjusted changes for decedents dying in 2010 include the following: (a) the maximum reduction allowed as a result of special use valuation remains at $1 million and (b) the amount used in computing the 2 percent portion of estate tax payable in installments under Section 6166 has increased to $1,340,000. The return due date for decedents dying before December 17, 2010, is September 19, 2011. Form 706-NA, United States Estate (and Generation-Skipping Transfer) Tax Return (revised July 2011), for nonresident noncitizens dying in calendar year 2010 was also released. The Service has also released the revised Form 706, United States Estate (and Generation-Skipping Transfer) Tax Return (revised August 2011) for use by estates of decedents dying in calendar year 2011. The instructions note that the maximum estate and generation-skipping transfer tax rate is 35 percent and that the estate and gift tax credits are reunified and now receive a combined exclusion amount of $5 million. Importantly, the instructions provide that the unused exclusion amount of a predeceased spouse dying after December 31, 2010, may be added to the decedent's exclusion amount, if the predeceased spouse's executor elected portability on a timely filed Form 706. Estates electing to allow a surviving spouse to use a decedent's unused exclusion amount must file Form 706, even if no tax is due. Estates not electing to allow a surviving spouse to use a decedent's unused exclusion amount must either attach a statement to Form 706 indicating that the estate is not making the election under Section 2010(c)(5), or write "No Election Under Section 2010(c)(5)" across the top of the first page of Form 706. The following inflation-adjusted changes for decedents dying in 2011 apply: (a) the maximum reduction allowed as a result of special use valuation increases to $1,020,000 and (b) the amount used in computing the 2 percent portion of estate tax payable in installments under Section 6166 has increased to $1,360,000.

Add to note 8.

Revised Form 4768 and related instructions have been released by the Service (revised July 2008). The Service revised Form 4768 to add Part V – Notice to Applicant, which will be used to notify an executor whether the request for an extension has been accepted, denied or requires additional information. The Service's Small Business/Self-Employed Division posted a document that provides interim guidance for processing requests for an extension. The memorandum addresses the processing of Form 4768 and lists the criteria for transfer of extension requests to advisory, including such items as certain minimum balances, a third request for an extension, and requests for an extension of time to pay annual installments deferred under Section 6166. The guidance expires December 4, 2009. SBSE-05-1208-062.

Page 2-17:

Add to note 9.

The Service has released instructions for Form 4768 (revised January 2007) to be used with Form 4768, Application for Extension of Time to File a Return and/or Pay U.S. Estate (and Generation-Skipping Transfer) Taxes (revised January 2006). Estates of decedents who died in 2010 and request an extension on Form 4768 will have until March 2012, to file their estate tax returns and pay any estate tax due. Notice 2011-76, 2011-40 IRB __. Most 2010 decedents that timely file Form 4768 will have until March 19, 2012, to file the estate tax return and, for those decedents dying after December 16, 2010, the due date is fifteen months after the date of death.

Add to first paragraph of note 10.

Revised Form 4768 and related instructions have been released by the Service (revised July 2008). The Service revised Form 4768 to add Part V — Notice to Applicant, which will be used to notify an executor whether the request for an extension has been accepted, denied or requires additional information.

Replace the last paragraph of note 10 with the following.

The Commissioner's denial of an extension of time to file the estate tax return may be reviewed by the Court to determine whether such denial was arbitrary and an abuse of its discretion. Estate of Gardner v. Comm'r, 82 TC 989 (1984); see also Estate of Proske v. United States, 105 AFTR 2d 2010-2613 (DNJ 2010).

Add to note 11.

Estate of Baccei, No. 08-16965 (9th Cir. 2011), *aff'g* 102 AFTR 2d 2008-5801 (ND Cal. 2008) (late payment penalties assessed against estate where estate's accountant filed Form 4768, but failed to complete Part III of Form 4768, "Extension of Time to Pay —Section 6161" and doctrine of substantial compliance was inapplicable, notwithstanding letter accompanying the form requesting an extension of time to pay the tax, because the statutory requirements for requesting an extension of time to pay the tax were not met).

Page 2-18:

Add to note 14 following citation to Estate of Hinz v. Comm'r.

Estate of Landers v. Comm'r, TC Memo. 2006-230 (2006) (return preparer's hip fracture was not a reasonable cause for the late filing of the return and late payment of the tax and filing of the return was a nondelegable duty of the estate administrator). Estate of Zlotow-ski, TC Memo. 2007-203 (2007) (delay due to correspondence from the administrators under a second will in Germany which warned U.S. executors to stop interfering with estate was not a reasonable cause to file a late return). Welch v. United States, No. 03-5044 (DNJ 2006). Estate of Fuertes, 2009-2 USTC ¶ 60,581 (ND Tex. 2009) (attorney's mistaken assumption that there was an automatic six-month extension to file did not provide reasonable cause for estate's failure to timely file its estate tax return and pay the estate tax due and executrix's reliance on the attorney to file the return was a delegation of her unambiguous duty to timely file the return and not reliance on legal advice). Estate of Cederloff v. US, 2010-2 USTC ¶ 60,604 (D. Md. 2010) (difficulties in determining the value of the estate were not a sufficient justification for the late filing of the return nor was executor's claim of reliance upon the advice of a professional since the executor, who was an experienced attorney, was the professional upon whose advice he relied).

Add to note 16.

In Estate of Lee v. Comm'r, TC Memo. 2009-84 (2009), the Tax Court held that the executor filed the estate tax return late because he had reasonably relied on his attorney's advice that the estate had received a second six month extension of time to file. Although that advice was erroneous, the Court found that executor had nonetheless acted diligently in fulfilling his obligation to timely file the estate tax return and that his reliance on his attorney's advice was reasonable and in good faith. In Estate of Charania, 603 F3d 67 (1st Cir. 2010), the estate was not subject to late-filing penalties where the Service had previously abated a separate late filing penalty against the estate for reasonable cause. The Court found no plausible reason for treating the initial late filing penalty in a different manner than the penalty subsequently issued by the Service noting that "[a]ny other result would be arbitrary, capricious, and in derogation of the government's duty to turn square corners in dealing with taxpayers."

[3] Extension of Time for Payment

[a] Section 6159

Page 2-20:

Add to note 28 following the initial citation.

See Reg. § 301.6159-1.

Add to note 31.

See Reg. § 301.6159-1(e)(1).

Page 2-21:

Add to note 34 following the initial citation.

See Reg. § 301.6159-1(e)(2).

Add to note 35 following the initial citation.

See Reg. § 301.6159-1(e)(3).

[b] Section 6161

[i] Short extensions.

Page 2-21:

Add to note 38.

Estate of Baccei, No. 3:07-cv-05329 (ND Cal. 2008), late payment penalties were assessed against an estate where estate's accountant filed Form 4768, but failed to complete Part III of Form 4768, "Extension of Time to Pay — Section 6161". The doctrine of substantial compliance was inapplicable, notwithstanding a letter accompanying the form requesting an extension of time to pay the tax, because the statutory requirements for requesting an extension of time to pay the tax were not met.

Page 2-22:

Add to note 39.

But see CCA 200836027 (May 12, 2008) (interest accruing on an extension to pay estate tax granted under Section 6161 due to the estate's lack of liquid assets is, however, non-deductible personal interest under IRC § 163(h)(2) and cannot be deducted on estate's income tax return).

[ii] "Reasonable cause" extensions.

Page 2-22:

Add to note 41.

CCA 200628042 (June 15, 2006) (no reasonable cause exception exists for denial of Section 6166 election if election made on untimely filed estate tax return and no reasonable cause exception for avoiding late payment penalties as a result of late installment payment where estate did not request a Section 6161 extension of time to pay the installment).

[c] Section 6166

[ii] Qualification for extension.

Page 2-24:

Add to note 55.

CCA 200848004 (Aug. 26, 2008) (statement attached to request for extension of time to file return stating that it was expected that estate would be eligible to make a Section 6166 election was not a valid election for two reasons: (1) Section 6166 election must be attached to a timely filed estate tax return, not a request for an extension of time to file a return; and (2) statement did not purport to make a Section 6166 election, but only stated that it was anticipated that the estate would be eligible for such an election).

Add to end of first paragraph of note 57.

CCA 200628042 (June 15, 2006) (no reasonable cause exception exists for denial of election if election made on untimely filed estate tax return); Priv. Ltr. Rul. 200721006 (Feb. 14, 2007) (estate denied an extension of time to file election because the election under Section 6166 is prescribed by statute and is not a regulatory election to which Regulations Section 301.9100-3 would be applicable); Priv. Ltr. Rul. 201015003 (Oct. 26, 2009). CCA 200848004 (Aug. 26, 2008)(statement attached to request for extension of time to file return stating that it was expected that estate would be eligible to make a Section 6166 election was not a valid election for two reasons: (1) Section 6166 election must be attached to a timely filed estate tax return, not a request for an extension of time to file a return; and (2) statement did not purport to make a Section 6166 election, but only stated that it was anticipated that the estate would be eligible for such an election).

Page 2-26:

Add the following to the end of the first sentence of note 71.

and Priv. Ltr. Rul. 200529006 (Apr. 11, 2005) (involving the Section 6166(b)(1)(C) entity attribution rule).

Page 2-28:

Add to note 82.

Compare Priv. Ltr. Rul. 200339043 (June 25, 2003) (decedent's interests in two S corporations who together employ ten full-time employees and provide extensive repair and maintenance services to properties owned by corporations qualified as active business interests for purposes of Section 6166); Priv. Ltr. Rul. 200521014 (Feb. 17, 2005) (decedent's level of activity, including activities performed by her pre-deceased husband, her son and other agents and employees, indicated that the properties were part of a Section 6166 closely held business because the activities went beyond merely managing investment assets); Priv. Ltr. Rul. 200518011 (Jan. 14, 2005) (decedent's interest in two automobile dealership corporations, of which he was the director, president and treasurer and was actively involved in day-to-day operations including supervision of employees and decision-making, and related real property is treated as an interest in a single Section 6166 closely held business); Priv. Ltr. Rul. 200340012 (July 1, 2003) (due to decedent's high level of active involvement, decedent's interest in residential rental business qualified as an active business interest for purposes of Section 6166); and Priv. Ltr. Rul. 200842012 (July 18, 2008) (decedent's interest in corporation that owned, developed, managed, and leased property through corporation employees who engaged in activities that encompassed all aspects of the business including negotiating leases, managing tenant requests and concerns, and maintenance of the various properties meets requirements that corporation be involved in a closely held active trade or business) with CCA 200339047 (Aug. 25, 2003) (decedent's interest in corporation whose activities were limited to collecting rents on properties owned by corporation did not qualify for purposes of Section 6166) and CCA 200928037 (May 20, 2009) (debt owed to decedent's company by decedent's son's company for use of decedent's company's services and equipment is passive asset for Section 6166 purposes since it is not an asset needed for the conduct of decedent's company's active business). See Priv. Ltr. Rul. 200518047 (Jan. 27, 2005) where the Service qualified several, but not all, of decedent's real estate interests as closely held businesses under Section 6166 and Priv. Ltr. Rul. 200845023 (Aug. 6, 2008) (value of two parcels of real property out of three held by a decedent's wholly-owned limited liability company qualifies under Section 6166).

Add new paragraph to note 82.

In Revenue Ruling 2006-34, the Service provided a taxpayer-friendly update to the guidance it gave in Revenue Rulings 75-365, 75-366, and 75-367. In doing so, it provided some safe harbors and a non-exclusive list of factors likely to be relevant in determining whether a decedent's activities with respect to certain real estate holdings were sufficiently active to support a finding that the holdings constitute a closely held business interest for purposes of Section 6166. Revenue Ruling 2006-34 revokes Revenue Ruling 75-365 in its entirety as well as the portion of Revenue Ruling 75-367 relating to the eight rental homes. In its new ruling, the Service analyzed five situations in which decedent performed certain activities with respect to the real estate holdings prior to death:

1. Decedent owned a ten-store strip mall and personally handled the day-to-day operation, management and maintenance of the strip mall and performed most repairs. Any repairs decedent was unable to perform was performed by a third-party independent contractor selected and hired by the decedent.

2. Decedent owned a small office park consisting of several buildings and multiple tenants in each building. Decedent hired a property management company, in which decedent had no ownership interest, to lease, manage and maintain the office park and decedent relied exclusively on the property management company to provide all necessary services. Each month the property management company provided decedent with a monthly accounting statement and check for the net rental income.

3. Same as 2 except decedent owned 20 percent of the stock of the property management company.

4. Decedent owned the one percent general partner interest and a 20 percent limited partnership interest in a limited partnership, which owned three strip malls that constituted 85 percent of the value of the limited partnership. The partnership agreement required decedent, as general partner, to provide the limited partnership with all services necessary to operate the limited partnership's business for which decedent, since 1992, had received an annual salary. Decedent, either personally or with the assistance of employees or agents, performed substantial management functions at the strip malls.

5. Decedent owned 100 percent of the stock in an automobile dealership. Decedent made all decisions regarding the dealership and supervised all its employees. In addition to the stock, decedent owned real property that decedent leased to the dealership, which featured a showroom, offices, repair and inventory storage areas.

The Service stated that it will consider the following nonexclusive factors in determining whether the decedent's interest was an active trade or business: (1) The amount of time devoted to the trade or business; (2) whether an office was maintained during regular business hours; (3) involvement in finding new tenants and negotiating leases; (4) provision of landscaping or related services; (5) involvement in repairs and maintenance; (6) handling tenant repair requests and complaints. In evaluating these factors, the Service indicated that it would look to the involvement of the decedent, as well as that of the employees and agents of the decedent and any management company. In Situation 2, the Service determined that decedent was not carrying on an active trade or business. In the other four situations, however, the Service concluded that the decedent had been carrying on an active trade or business, because the services to the tenants were provided by the decedent or by the employees and agents of entities, in which decedent had a 20-percent-or-greater ownership interest.

[iii] Period of extension.

Page 2-32:

Add to note 115.

In United States v. Askegard et al., 2003-2 USTC ¶ 60,468 (DC Minn. 2003), defendant's motion for summary judgment in the government's suit to collect unpaid taxes on an estate that had elected to defer payment under Section 6166 was not barred by the statute of limitations since there was no showing by the estate that Section 6166(g)(1)(A) applied to commence the limitations period. See also United States v. Kulhanek, 2010-2 USTC ¶ 60,610 (WD Pa. 2010) (Service's claim for unpaid estate tax timely where estate had previously elected, under IRC § 6166, to pay estate tax in installments and, pursuant to IRC § 6503, that election caused the statute of limitations period for assertion of the claim to be suspended).

Add to note 116.

The Section 6324A lien is in lieu of the special estate tax lien imposed pursuant to Section 6324(a)(1). IRC § 6324A(d)(4); Reg. §§ 20.6324A-1(a), 301.6324A-1(e). Note, however, that in Chief Counsel Advice 200645027 (July 31, 2006), the Service's Office of Chief Counsel advised that the recording of a Section 6324A lien on estate property would divest a Section 6324(a)(1) special estate tax lien only with respect to the property identified in the Section 6324A lien agreement and not the remainder of the estate property still subject to the Section 6324(a)(1) lien.

Although the Service has the discretion to require a bond for estates that elect to defer payment of estate tax under Section 6166, the Tax Court in Estate of Roski, 128 TC 10 (2007), held that the Service does not have the authority to impose an absolute bond or special lien requirement in every case. The Court examined Sections 6166(k)(1) and 6166(k)(2) which incorporates the Service's discretionary authority under Section 6165 that the Service "may" require a bond. Allowing the Service to impose a bright-line bond requirement would add a requirement to the statute that Congress had not intended. In response to the decision in the *Roski* case, the Service announced that it will determine on a case-by-case basis whether security will be required when a qualifying estate makes a Section 6166 election by establishing criteria to identify the estates that run the risk of defaulting on their installment payments. Notice 2007-90. Accordingly, the Service has issued interim guidance for establishing installment payments and requesting bonds for Section 6324A special estate tax liens. SB/SE-05-0609-010. Among other items, this memorandum sets up the procedures to follow when determining whether to require a bond or special estate tax lien which includes an initial request made to the estate by the Advisory Estate Tax Group to voluntarily provide a bond or special estate tax lien. If the estate declines, the Advisory Estate Tax Group will make its determination based on a list of nonexclusive factors and other pertinent information and, after a preliminary determination is made, the estate will be notified and given the right to appeal.

The Office of Chief Counsel issued advice on the Service's acceptance of various forms of property interests as collateral for a Section 6324A lien—stock in a closely held corporation in Chief Counsel Advice 200747019 (October 11, 2007) and interest in a limited liability company in Chief Counsel Advice 200803016 (October 11, 2007). As the Chief Counsel advised therein, the Service may only accept such assets as collateral if the three requirements set forth in Section 6324A(b) are met: (1) the asset must be expected to survive the deferral period; (2) the asset must be identified in the written agreement described in Section 6324A(b)(1)(B); and (3) the value of the asset as of the agreement must be sufficient to pay the deferred tax plus the required interest. The Chief Counsel explained that if the three requirements are met, the Section 6324A lien arises and the Service must accept the collateral. See also FAA 20070801F (Chief Counsel's office discusses the practice of the Service entering into a security agreement to secure its interest in property offered as collateral supplementary to the Section 6324A lien agreement).

Importantly, the expiration of the statute of limitations for assessment does not bar the Service from obtaining security or additional security for unpaid assessments. If security is not provided, a Section 6166 election may be denied or terminated at any time. CCA 200627023 (May 19, 2006).

The Office of the Chief Counsel has also issued advice regarding the maximum value of collateral that the Service may require to secure a Section 6324A lien. CCA 200909044 (Dec. 2, 2008). The maximum value of required property under Section 6324A(b)(2) always includes the sum of the "deferred amount" plus the amount of interest that would be payable over the first four years of the deferral period. As to computation of the required interest amount, a flat 2 percent rate is permissible if it results in an amount that is less than or equal to the amount computed under the two-part interest rate structure under Section 6601(j). On April 1, 2009, the Small Business/Self-Employed Division of the Service posted a memorandum to its website providing interim guidance for processing of estate tax liens. SB/SE 05-0308-022. The Office of Chief Counsel, in a memorandum designated as Program Manager's Technical Advice (PMTA), has also explained various issues involving bonds and liens as security for estates that elect Section 6166 deferral of estate taxes including whether the amount of bonds or liens required to secure the estate tax attributable to a closely held business can include accrued interest or can be compromised; how and by whom the valuation of lien property can be determined; and whether pledged or mortgaged property can be used for Section 6324A special estate tax lien. PMTA 2009-046.

[v] Interest.

Page 2-33:

Add to note 126.

The "2 percent portion" for the year 2003 is indexed for inflation to $1.12 million from $1.1 million in 2002. Rev. Proc. 2002-70, 2002-46 IRB 845. The "2 percent portion" is $1,140,000 for the calendar year 2004. Rev. Proc. 2003-85, 2003-49 IRB 1104. The "2 percent portion" is $1,170,000 for the calendar year 2005. Rev. Proc. 2004-71, 2004-50 IRB __. The "2 percent portion" is $1,250,000 for the calendar year 2007. Rev. Proc. 2006-53. The "2 percent portion" is $1,280,000 for the calendar year 2008. Rev. Proc. 2007-66, 2007-__ IRB __. The "2 percent portion" is $1,330,000 for the calendar year 2009. Rev. Proc. 2008-66, IRB 2008-45. The "2 percent portion" is $1,340,000 for the calendar year 2010. Rev. Proc. 2009-50. The "2 percent portion" is $1,360,000 for the calendar year 2011. Rev. Proc. 2010-40.

Add to note 128.

In Private Letter Ruling 200529006 (Apr. 11, 2005), the Service ruled that the interest rate on the deferred estate tax payments is determined by dividing the estate tax due into two portions, and that the interest rate on the 45 percent portion is subject to change as the federal short-term rate changes.

[vi] The "gotcha."

Page 2-35:

Add to note 137.

CCA 200628042 (June 15, 2006) (no reasonable cause exception for avoiding late payment penalties as a result of late installment payment where estate did not request a Section 6161 extension of time to pay the installment).

Page 2-36:

Add to note 142.

Priv. Ltr. Rul. 200613020 (Dec. 14, 2005) (withdrawal by decedent's daughter of part or all of a partnership held by decedent's trust, as authorized by trust agreement, will not cause Section 6166(a) extension of time for payment of decedent's estate tax to cease to apply).

Page 2-37:

Add to note 150.

But see TAM 200648028 (Aug. 4, 2006) (estate's remittance, designated as payment of estate and GST taxes, would be applied as designated unless original designation rescinded. Section 6403 is inapplicable where a remittance is made before the Section 6166 election is made).

[vii] Declaratory judgments with respect to Section 6166.

Page 2-38:

Add to note 156.

In Rev. Proc. 2005-33, 2005-1 CB 1231, the Service provides guidance on exhausting administrative remedies before seeking declaratory judgment from the tax court pursuant to Section 7479 with respect to a Section 6166 election. In accordance with Revenue Procedure 2005-33, the Office of Chief Counsel has issued email advice that if the Service denies or terminates a Section 6166 election and if the other statutory requirements have been met, the estate has the right to petition the Tax Court for declaratory judgment relief pursuant to Section 7479. CCA 200915037 (Nov. 25, 2008). The Office of Chief Counsel further advised in the email that once IRS Appeals has reached a decision with respect to the election, a Letter 3750 should be sent detailing the rationale for the determination and alerting the estate's representatives of the right to petition for declaratory relief.

CHAPTER **3**

Credits Against Estate Tax

¶ 3.02	Section 2010. Unified Credit Against the Estate Tax	
	[Revised]	S3-2
	[1] The Amount of the Credit	S3-3
	[a] Basic Exclusion Amount	S3-4
	[b] The Deceased Spousal Unused Exclusion	
	Amount	S3-4
	[i] The Amount of Unused Exclusion.	S3-5
	[ii] The Election.	S3-8
	[2] The Relationship to the Section 2505 Credit	S3-9
	[3] Estate Tax Return Filing Requirements	S3-10
¶ 3.03	Section 2011. Credit for State Death Taxes	S3-12
	[1] Introduction	S3-12
¶ 3.05	Section 2013. Credit for Tax on Prior Transfers	S3-12
	[2] Computation of Credit in General	S3-12
	[3] Adjustments	S3-13
	[b] Value of Property Transferred	S3-13
	[4] Limitations on Credit	S3-13
	[a] Tax Caused in Decedent's Estate	S3-13
¶ 3.06	Section 2014. Credit for Foreign Death Taxes	S3-14
	[3] The Federal Estate Tax Formula	S3-14
	[b] Value of the Property	S3-14

¶ 3.02 SECTION 2010. UNIFIED CREDIT AGAINST THE ESTATE TAX [REVISED]

Replace existing ¶ 3.02 with the following revised ¶ 3.02.

Estates of decedents dying after 1976[1] are allowed a Section 2010 credit, which reduces and, in the case of most decedents, eliminates any estate tax liability.[2] As a result of the Section 2010 credit, if the decedent has no "adjusted taxable gifts"[3] and the decedent's "taxable estate"[4] does not exceed the "applicable exclusion amount"[5] available in the year of the decedent's death, the estate will incur no estate tax liability.[6] If the amount of the credit available under Section 2010 exceeds tax liability, no refund is allowed.[7]

---

[1] Prior to 1977, all estates were allowed a $60,000 specific exemption, which operated as a deduction in computing the taxable estate. IRC § 2052, repealed with respect to estates of decedents dying after 1976 by the Tax Reform Act of 1976, Pub. L. No. 94-455, § 2001(a)(4), 90 Stat. 1520, 1848 (1976), reprinted in 1976-3 CB (Vol. 1) 1, 324. In the Tax Reform Act of 1976, Congress eliminated the exemption, replacing it with a credit.

This is only one of several areas in which Congress has replaced deductions with credits. In such situations, congressional policy views credits as more equitable than deductions, because they reduce tax liability equally for taxpayers in all brackets, while deductions confer greater tax savings on taxpayers in higher brackets. See HR Rep. No. 1380, 94th Cong., 2d Sess. 15 (1976), reprinted in 1976-3 CB (Vol. 3) 735, 749. See also Surrey, "Tax Incentives as a Device for Implementing Governmental Policy: A Comparison with Direct Government Expenditures," 83 Harv. L. Rev. 705 (1970).

In other situations, credits have been replaced by deductions. See IRC §§ 2011, 2058; ¶¶ 3.03, 5.09. In such circumstances, congressional policy is reversed, although there may be additional motives, such as to raise additional federal revenue, for the policy reversal.

Since a flat rate tax is imposed on taxable transfers after the applicable exemption amount is taken into consideration, if Congress retains the current law beyond 2012 it would simplify the statutory process by returning to an exemption of the decedent's applicable exclusion amount for taxable testamentary transfers rather than pursuing the complicated credit mechanism. The credit mechanism was appropriate when transfers were taxed at graduated rates.

[2] For example, in 2007 the estate tax was levied on about 0.7 percent of decedents. The Congressional Budget Office, Economic and Budget Issue Brief: Federal Estate and Gift Taxes (Dec. 2009). It is estimated that a $5 million applicable exclusion amount will result in the estate tax being levied on about .14 percent of decedents in 2011, or 14 out of every 10,000 decedents. Gravelle, Estate Tax Options, CRS Report R41203 at 13 (Dec. 23, 2010).

[3] IRC § 2001(b) flush language, discussed at Supplement ¶ 2.01[1][b].

[4] IRC § 2051, discussed at Supplement ¶ 2.01[1][a].

[5] IRC §§ 2010(c)(2)- 2010(c)(4). See infra ¶ 3.02[1].

[6] For example, in 2011, the tax under Section 2001(c) on the first $5 million of taxable estate, assuming no post-1976 taxable gifts, is $1,730,800, exactly the amount of tax offset by the Section 2010 credit for decedents dying in 2011.

[7] Section 2010(d) limits the amount of the credit to the amount of estate tax imposed under Section 2001.

[1] The Amount of the Credit

Since its enactment for the year 1977,[8] the credit has been substantially increased over the years.[9] The amount is subject to a possible adjustment for inflation for the year 2012,[10] but, the amount is currently scheduled to be reduced in the year 2013.[11]

The Section 2010 credit is statutorily expressed as an "applicable exclusion amount," which is converted to an "applicable credit amount."[12] The applicable exclusion amount[13] is the sum of the basic exclusion amount[14] and, in the case of a surviving spouse, the deceased spousal unused exclusion amount.[15] The applicable credit amount is determined by applying the Section

---

[8] See supra note 1.

[9] See infra note 12.

[10] See infra text accompanying note 20.

[11] Under the "sunset" provision effective January 1, 2013, the $1 million applicable exclusion amount for the year 2006 will apply to the estates of decedents dying after the year 2012. Economic Growth and Tax Relief Reconciliation Act of 2001, Pub. L. No. 107-16, § 901(a)(2), 115 Stat. 38, 150 (2001), reprinted in 2001-3 CB 9, 122, as amended by the Tax Relief Act of 2010, Pub. L. No. 111-312, §§ 101(a)(1), 304, 124 Stat. 3296, 3298, 3304 (2010). The "sunset" provision is discussed more fully at Supplement ¶ 8.11.

[12] The amount of the credit from the years 1977 to 2011 is as follows:

Year of Death	Credit Amount	Exclusion Amount
1977	$ 30,000	$120,667
1978	34,000	134,000
1979	38,000	147,333
1980	42,500	161,563
1981	47,000	175,625
1982	62,800	225,000
1983	79,300	275,000
1984	96,300	325,000
1985	121,800	400,000
1986	155,800	500,000
1987–1997	192,800	600,000
1998	202,050	625,000
1999	211,300	650,000
2000 and 2001	220,550	675,000
2002 and 2003	345,800	1 million
2004 and 2005	555,800	1.5 million
2006–2008	780,800	2 million
2009	1,455,800	3.5 million
2010	1,730,800	5 million
2011	1,730,800	5 million*

---

* This amount is the Section 2010(c)(3) basic exclusion amount, which may be increased by the Section 2010(c)(4) deceased spousal unused exclusion amount.

[13] IRC § 2010(c)(2)-(4).

[14] IRC §§ 2010(c)(2)(A), 2010(c)(3). See infra ¶ 3.02[1][a].

[15] IRC §§ 2010(c)(2)(B), 2010(c)(4). See infra ¶ 3.02[1][b].

2001(c) rates in the year of the decedent's death to the applicable exclusion amount.

[a] Basic Exclusion Amount

For the years 2010 and 2011, the basic exclusion amount[16] is $5 million.[17] The $5 million basic exclusion amount generally[18] converts to an applicable credit amount of $1,730,800.[19] The $5 million basic exclusion amount is indexed for inflation for the year 2012.[20]

[b] The Deceased Spousal Unused Exclusion Amount

Historically, the applicable exclusion amount was personal to an individual and not assignable to others, although the marital deduction provisions[21] permitted spouses to engage in estate planning techniques that effectively allowed a predeceasing spouse to use the surviving spouse's unused applicable exclusion amount.[22] To avoid such complicated techniques and to add simplic-

---

[16] See supra note 12.

[17] IRC § 2010(c)(3)(A).

[18] The applicable credit amount is sometimes subject to a very minor reduction in amount. If a decedent made inter vivos gifts between September 8, 1976, and January 1, 1977, and used all or any portion of the now-repealed Section 2521 $30,000 specific lifetime exemption to reduce such gifts, Section 2010(b) requires a reduction in the amount of the Section 2010 credit by 20 percent of the amount of exemption so used. This results in a maximum Section 2010 credit reduction of $6,000 if the full $30,000 exemption was used during such period. Between the adoption of the Tax Reform Act of 1976 and December 31, 1976, there were substantial tax incentives for taxpayers with large estates to make inter vivos gifts at lower tax rates. Although Congress condoned a full use of the $30,000 exemption against gifts made before September 9, 1976, with no reduction in the Section 2010 credit, a credit reduction in the amount indicated was considered a proper cost for last-minute use of the exemption. A potential donor's prior gift history was an obvious factor in the decision whether to elect to use the Section 2521 exemption during that period. See Priv. Ltr. Rul. 7937010 (May 31, 1979) (a Section 2010(b) credit reduction was not restored even though the gift was subsequently included in decedent's estate under Section 2035).

The constitutionality of Section 2010(b) was upheld in United States v. Hemme, 476 US 558 (1986).

[19] The credit amount reflects the current maximum 35 percent tax rate. See Supplement ¶ 2.01[1][c].

[20] IRC § 2010(c)(3)(B). The amount of the inflationary adjustment is determined by multiplying the cost-of-living adjustment determined under a modified version of Section 1(f)(3) for the calendar year by $5 million. IRC § 2010(c)(3)(B). The section 1(f)(3) cost-of-living adjustment for 2012 is modified by taking into consideration the amount of inflation between 2010 and 2011. IRC § 2010(c)(3)(B)(ii). Inflationary adjustments to the basic exclusion amount will be made only in multiples of $10,000, rounded to the next lowest multiple of $10,000. IRC § 2010(c)(3) flush language.

[21] See ¶ 5.06.

[22] See, for example, ¶ 11.03[4][c][i] where a donor spouse makes an inter vivos gift with a QTIP election to a donee spouse who has minimal assets and who is going to pre-

ity to estate planning in the predeceasing spouse's estate by allowing spouses to transport their unused exclusion amounts,[23] Section 2010 now permits a predeceasing spouse to transport that spouse's unused exclusion amount to the surviving spouse.[24]

Under the portability provision the predeceased spouse's unused exclusion amount may be transported to the surviving spouse[25] and added to the surviving spouse's basic exclusion amount[26] to determine the surviving spouse's applicable exclusion amount.[27] The surviving spouse may then use the combined amounts under either the gift tax[28] or the estate tax but not the generation-skipping transfer tax.[29] The portability provision applies only to predeceasing spouses dying after December 31, 2010,[30] and may currently be used by the surviving spouse only through December 31, 2012.[31]

[i] The Amount of Unused Exclusion. The statute provides that the predeceasing spouse's unused exclusion amount is the lesser of the "basic" exclu-

---

decease the donor spouse with a life estate in the donee spouse and a secondary life estate in the donor spouse. This requires the predeceasing spouse to include the trust in that spouse's gross estate under Section 2044 and to use an otherwise unused amount of Section 2010 credit. See Priv. Ltr. Rul. 200406004 (Oct. 31, 2003). See Gans, Blattmachr & Zeydel, "Supercharged Credit Shelter Trust," 21 Prob. & Prop. 52 (July/Aug. 2007).

[23] Transporting the unused exclusion amount avoids the need to use a by pass trust in the predeceasing spouse's estate. See ¶ 5.06[6]. However, one continuing advantage of use of a bypass trust in moderate-sized estates is to avoid inclusion of the appreciation of the property between the time of the predeceasing spouse's death and the surviving spouse's death. See A.S. Gassman & C.J. Denicolo, "The Role of Credit Shelter Trusts Under the New Estate Tax Law," 38 Estate Planning, No. 6, 10 (June 2011). See also infra note 31. However, transporting the unused exemption amount, rather than using the bypass trust, could result in the appreciation of the property between the time of the predeceasing spouse's death and the surviving spouse's death receiving an increase in basis under Section 1014(a)(1).

[24] IRC §§ 2010(c)(2)(B), 2010(c)(4), 2010(c)(5).

[25] IRC §§ 2010(c)(4), 2010(c)(5).

[26] IRC § 2010(c)(3).

[27] IRC § 2010(c)(2).

[28] IRC §§ 2505(a)(1) (referring to the applicable credit amount), 2010(c)(1), 2010(c)(2). See Supplement ¶ 9.06[1] text accompanying notes 18–21.

[29] See IRC § 2631(c) referring only to the "basic" exclusion amount. See also IRC § 2010(c)(3), Supplement ¶ 15.02 text accompanying note 2. As a result, a decedent wanting to use their generation-skipping transfer tax exemption (see ¶ 15.02), should either use a bypass trust (see ¶ 5.06[6]), or use a QTIP trust and make a reverse QTIP election under Section 2652(a)(3) (see ¶ 17.02[1][c][i]).

Portability is also disallowed under the estate tax return filing requirement. See IRC § 6081(a)(1) also referring to the "basic" exclusion amount.

[30] IRC § 2010(c)(4).

[31] The provision is currently scheduled to sunset on January 1, 2013. Economic Growth and Tax Relief Reconciliation Act of 2001, Pub. L. No, 107-16 § 901(a)(2), 115 Stat. 38, 150 (2001), reprinted in 2001-3 CB 9, 122, as amended by the Tax Relief Act of

sion amount at the survivor's death,[32] or the predeceasing spouse's basic exclusion amount reduced by the predeceasing spouse's taxable estate and adjusted taxable gifts.[33] Thus the predeceasing spouse's unused exclusion amount may never exceed the "basic" exclusion amount, $5 million in 2011 and $5 million adjusted for inflation in 2012.[34] If a predeceasing spouse had a basic exclusion amount of $5 million, no adjusted taxable gifts, and a taxable estate of $2 million, and a Section 2010(c)(5)(A) election was made,[35] the transported amount to the surviving spouse would be $3 million.[36]

2010, Pub. L. No. 111-312, §§ 101(a)(1), 304, 124 Stat. 3296, 3298, 3304 (2010). The "sunset" provision is discussed more fully at Supplement ¶ 8.11.

However, the Obama administration has proposed the retension of a portability provision. Dept. of Treasury, "General Explanation of the Administration Fiscal Year 2012 Revenue Proposals," 124 (Feb. 14, 2011).

If sunsetting occurs, an issue arises. If a surviving spouse received an unused exclusion amount from a predeceasing spouse during 2011 and 2012 and Section 2010(c)(4) and (5) are sunsetted in 2013, if the surviving spouse dies after 2012, does the transported amount disappear or remain with the surviving spouse? Seemingly regulations enacted pursuant to Section 2010(c)(6) will resolve this and numerous other issues. Until this issue is resolved, it would seem preferable for a predeceasing spouse to use a bypass trust rather than making a marital deduction transfer to a surviving spouse, except in combined estates under $1 million. See also supra notes 11 and 23.

A similar issue arises if the transporting provision is retained but the basic exclusion amount is reduced after 2012, assume to $3.5 million. The Obama administration has proposed a $3.5 million basic exclusion amount. Dept. of Treasury, "General Explanation of the Administration's Fiscal Year 2012 Revenue Proposals," 141 (Feb. 14, 2011). If a surviving spouse has received a $5 million deceased spousal unused exclusion from a predeceasing spouse who died in 2011 or 2012 and if the surviving spouse dies after 2012, under Section 2010(c)(2) the surviving spouse's total applicable exclusion amount would be $7 million, $3.5 million under Section 2010(c)(3)(A) and $3.5 million under Section 2010(c)(4)(A).

[32] IRC § 2010(c)(4)(A). If the portability provision is retained (see supra note 31), in 2013 this basic exclusion amount may be reduced to $3.5 million (see supra note 31) or sunsetted to $1 million (see supra note 11).

[33] IRC § 2010(c)(4)(B). Section 2010(c)(4)(B)(ii) refers to an "amount . . . determined under Section 2001(b)(1)" which incorporates the taxable estate and adjusted taxable gifts. See Supplement ¶ 2.01[1].

[34] IRC § 2010(c)(4). See IRC § 2010(c)(3) and supra note 20. Although the basic amount is adjusted for inflation in 2012, once transported to a surviving spouse, it is not adjusted for inflation. If a predeceasing spouse dies in 2011, there is no inflation adjustment to the unused exclusion amount; whereas if the predeceasing spouse dies in 2012 an inflation adjustment may be made to the basic exclusion amount, but only for inflation prior to its being transported. IRC §§ 2010(c)(3), 2010(c)(4).

[35] See infra ¶ 3.02[1][b][ii].

[36] IRC § 2010(c)(4). See Staff of Joint Comm. on Tax'n, Technical Explanation of the Revenue Provisions Contained in the "Tax Relief...Act of 2010" Scheduled for Consideration by the United States Senate (JCX-55-10) at 52 Example 1 (Dec. 10, 2010).

The same result would be reached if predeceasing spouse had $2 million of adjusted taxable gifts and a zero taxable estate, resulting from the entire estate being transferred to the surviving spouse in a manner qualifying for a Section 2056 marital deduction. See ¶ 5.06.

A surviving spouse may use only their most recent ("last") deceased spouse's unused exclusion amount.[37] Thus, if the surviving spouse in the example[38] above remarried and that spouse also predeceased (predeceased spouse number two), the surviving spouse may only use the unused exclusion amount from predeceasing spouse number two.[39] If predeceased spouse number two had no unused exclusion amount or if predeceased spouse number two had an unused exclusion amount but the executor made no Section 2010(c)(5)(A) election,[40] there would be no unused exclusion amount to be transported to surviving spouse even if predeceased spouse number one had an unused exclusion amount and predeceasing spouse number one's executor made a Section 2010(c)(5)(A) election.[41]

A surviving spouse who remarries cannot transport an unused exclusion amount at death from a predeceasing spouse to a new spouse.[42] But, in addition under the current statute the surviving spouse cannot use the predeceasing spouse's unused exclusion amount in an inter vivos or testamentary transfer[43] without reducing the surviving spouse's unused basic exclusion amount that may be transported to a surviving spouse.[44] This result is not in keeping with the policy underlying the transporting rule[45] and is inconsistent with an exam-

---

[37] See IRC § 2010(c)(4)(B)(i) using the term "last" deceased spouse.

[38] See supra text accompanying notes 35 and 36.

[39] IRC § 2010(c)(4)(B)(i). Staff of Joint Comm. on Tax'n, Technical Explanation of the Revenue Provisions Contained in the "Tax Relief…Act of 2010" Scheduled for Consideration by the United States Senate (JCX-55-10) at 52 Example 2 (Dec. 10, 2010).

[40] See infra ¶ 3.02[1][b][ii].

[41] Thus, even if Surviving Spouse used Spouse Number One's unused exclusion amount inter vivos prior to marrying Spouse Number Two, Surviving Spouse would lose Spouse Number One's unused exclusion amount at Surviving Spouse's death. For example, assume Spouse Number One leaves their entire estate of $5 million to Surviving Spouse, who also has $10 million in assets, an election is made under Section 2010(c)(5)(A), and Spouse Number One's unused basic exclusion amount is transported to Surviving Spouse. Surviving Spouse now has $15 million in assets and a $10 million applicable exclusion amount ($5 million basic exclusion amount and $5 million unused spousal exclusion amount). Surviving Spouse makes a gift of $10 million in assets to Child. Surviving Spouse remarries Spouse Number Two who then dies with a taxable estate of $5 million. Surviving Spouse subsequently dies with a taxable estate of $5 million and adjusted taxable gifts of $10 million. Surviving Spouse's estate tax is computed on $15 million offset by an applicable credit amount determined using a $5 million applicable exclusion amount.

[42] IRC § 2010(c)(4)(A).

[43] The transfer would be one in which does not qualify for a marital deduction. IRC §§ 2056, 2523.

[44] IRC § 2010(c)(4).

[45] See Blattmachr, Gans & Zaritsky, "Estate Planning After the 2010 Tax Relief Act's Big Changes, But Still No Certainty," 114 J. Tax'n 68, 80 and note 67 (Feb. 2011).

ple in the legislative history.[46] A technical amendment should be made[47] to Section 2010(c)(4)(B)(i) to change deceased spouse's "basic exclusion amount" to deceased spouse's "applicable exclusion amount," so that the statute would read the predeceasing spouse's unused exclusion amount is the lesser of the "basic" exclusion amount at the survivor's death, or the predeceasing spouse's "applicable exclusion amount" reduced by the predeceasing spouse's taxable estate and adjusted taxable gifts.[48]

[ii] The Election. Portability of the unused exclusion amount is permitted only if the executor[49] of the predeceasing spouse's estate elects on a timely filed (including extensions) estate tax return of the predeceasing spouse to transport the unused exclusion amount.[50] The election, once made, is irrevocable.[51] The executor of the predeceasing spouse must file an estate tax return for the predeceasing spouse, even though that spouse might not otherwise be required to file such a return.[52] Seemingly the return is required in order to compute the unused exclusion amount. In making the election, the executor of the predeceasing spouse must agree to allow the Service to examine the estate and gift tax returns of the predeceasing spouse (notwithstanding any statute of limitations)[53] for purposes of determining the predeceasing spouse's unused exclusion amount available to the surviving spouse.[54]

---

[46] See Staff of Joint Comm. On Tax'n, Technical Explanation of the Revenue Provisions Contained in the "Tax Relief . . . Act of 2010" Scheduled for Consideration by the United States Senate (JCX-55-10) at page 53 Example 3 (Dec. 10, 2010).

[47] See Staff of Joint Comm. On Tax'n, "General Explanation of Tax Legislation Enacted in the 111th Congress" page 555 footnote 1582A (2011) supporting the need for such a technical correction.

[48] For example assume Deceased Spouse's entire estate of $5 million passes to Surviving Spouse who also has $5 million in assets. The Deceased Spouse's unused basic exclusion amount is transported to Surviving Spouse. Surviving Spouse now has $10 million in assets and a $10 million applicable exclusion amount ($5 million basic and $5 million unused spousal exclusion amount). Surviving Spouse gives $5 million in assets to the couple's child. Surviving Spouse remarries and leaves $5 million to New Spouse resulting in a zero taxable estate. Under the current statute Surviving Spouse would be able to transfer zero unused applicable exclusion amount to New Spouse. Under the technical amendment, Surviving Spouse would have a $5 million unused applicable exclusion amount to be transported to New Spouse. See also supra note 46.

[49] See ¶ 8.02.

[50] IRC § 2010(c)(5)(A).

[51] IRC § 2010(c)(5)(A).

[52] IRC § 2010(c)(5)(A). See infra ¶ 3.02[3]. The Service has issued guidance reminding estates of married individuals dying after 2010 that executors must file an estate tax return in order to pass along unused exclusion amount to the surviving spouse. Notice 2011-82, 2011-42 IRB __.

[53] IRC § 6501.

[54] IRC § 2010(c)(5)(B).

The Secretary has authority to prescribe regulations necessary or appropriate to carry out the portability rule.[55]

[2] The Relationship to the Section 2505 Credit

The Section 2010 credit generally effectively exempts from the federal transmission taxes otherwise taxable transfers not exceeding the applicable exclusion amount[56] for the year of the decedent's death. The estate tax credit is referred to as *unified* because it is also used to offset the federal transmission tax imposed on lifetime gifts.[57] However, the amount of the Section 2010 estate tax credit and the Section 2505 gift tax credit are not always equal in amount.[58]

Although the credit is spoken of as "unified," use of the Section 2505 gift tax credit does not reduce the amount of the Section 2010 estate tax credit. This appears to allow a decedent who made lifetime gifts the advantage of the use of two credits, but it does not.[59] Under the system, the unified credit is effectively used only once. This is statutorily so because, before credits, the amount of the estate tax is the tentative tax on the sum of the taxable estate plus adjusted taxable gifts, reduced by gift taxes that would have been payable on the gifts made by the decedent after 1976 at rates in effect at the time of

---

[55] IRC § 2010(c)(6).

[56] See supra text accompanying note 15.

[57] IRC § 2505, discussed ¶ 9.06.

The credit generally is also unified with the generation-skipping transfer tax exemption. IRC § 2631(c). See ¶ 15.02. Thus, an individual has a $5 million (adjusted for inflation in 2012) generation-skipping transfer tax exemption; however, there is no portability of a predeceasing spouse's unused exclusion amount under the generation-skipping transfer tax. See IRC § 2631(c) limiting the generation-skipping transfer tax exemption to the "basic" exclusion amount. See also IRC § 2010(c)(3)(A) and supra the text accompanying note 30.

[58] First, there is no inter vivos portability of the exclusion amount between spouses, even though a transported unused exclusion amount from a predeceased spouse may be used in an inter vivos transfer by a donor surviving spouse. See Supplement ¶ 9.06 note 33.

Second, while the credit amount under Section 2505 and the basic credit amount under the estate tax have generally been equal since 1977, for the years 2004 through 2010, the gift tax applicable exclusion amount was capped at $1 million. IRC § 2505(a)(1). Thus, the Section 2505 credit amount was $345,800. See Supplement ¶ 9.06[1].

Even though the Section 2010 credit and the Section 2505 credit were not equal in amount for the years 2004 through 2010, the credits were still "unified" because a single use of the credits is effectively allowed. See infra text accompanying notes 59–61.

In addition, there was a difference in the amount of the two credits in the first half of 1977, when only $6,000 of the unified credit could be used against liability for gift tax, as compared with the $30,000 available estate tax credit. See Tax Reform Act of 1976, Pub. L. No. 94-455, §§ 2001(a)(2), 2002(b)(2), 90 Stat. 1520, 1848, 1849 (1976), reprinted in 1976-3 (Vol. 1) 1, 324, 325.

[59] Cf. supra note 58.

the decedent's death. Use of the gift tax credit reduces taxes payable on the gifts and correspondingly reduces the reduction in estate tax liability permitted for gift taxes that would have been payable.[60] As a practical matter, there is no dual use of the credits, and use of the Section 2505 credit effectively reduces the amount of the Section 2010 credit. For example, if Decedent, who had previously not made any gifts, had made taxable gifts of $1 million in 2009 (and used the Section 2505 credit and paid no gift tax) and Decedent died in 2011 with a $5 million taxable estate, Decedent would incur $350,000 of estate taxes.[61]

Use of the gift tax credit is mandatory.[62] Failure to use the gift tax credit, if available, may result in no credit effectively being allowed. Furthermore, if more than the necessary gift tax is paid, estate tax liability will still be reduced only by gift taxes "payable" at rates in effect at the decedent's death, and, overall, an overpayment of gift taxes could effectively wipe out the estate tax credit.[63]

[3] Estate Tax Return Filing Requirements

The Section 2010 credit not only directly affects tax liability, but also indirectly affects the requirement for an estate to file an estate tax return. Section 6018(a)(1) provides the rules for filing estate tax returns. The filing requirements are based on the amount of the gross estate.[64] The amount of gross estate for which no return is required to be filed is closely equivalent to the

---

[60] Because the lifetime use of the credit merely neutralizes gifts that otherwise would have generated a gift tax, which in turn would have reduced the estate tax under Section 2001(b)(2), the credit has not been used in an estate tax sense when applied to lifetime gifts. In the end, the unified credit causes a single reduction for gift tax and estate tax purposes that does not exceed the estate tax unified credit.

[61] The computation is as follows:

IRC § 2001(b)(1) tax on $6 million	= $ 2,080,800
IRC § 2001(b)(2) reduction for gift tax payable	= − 0
IRC § 2010 credit	= −1,730,800
Estate tax due:	$ 350,000

[62] See Staff of Joint Comm. on Tax'n, 94th Cong., 2d Sess., General Explanation of the Tax Reform Act of 1976, at 531 (1976), reprinted in 1976-3 CB (Vol. 2) 1, 543 and Rev. Rul. 79-160, 1979-1 CB 313, illustrating the use of the Section 2505 credit.

[63] See Supplement ¶ 2.01[2]. For example if in 2011 Decedent made a taxable gift of $5 million, had not used Decedent's Section 2505 credit, and had paid $1,730,800 of gift taxes on the 2011 gift, at Decedent's death, Decedent's gift tax *payable* on the 2011 gift would still have been zero (after the Section 2505 credit available in the year the gift is applied). If Decedent died in 2012 with a $5 million taxable estate (and there was no post-2010 inflation), $1,730,800 of estate taxes would be due in 2012, resulting in a total of $3,461,600 of transfer taxes, effectively eliminating the unified credit.

[64] See Chapter 4.

basic exclusion amount.[65] If the decedent's gross estate exceeds the basic exclusion amount for the year of the decedent's death set forth in Section 2010(c)(3), a return must be filed.[66]

Returns are sometimes required for smaller gross estates. The critical gross estate figures for years after 1976 must be reduced by adjusted taxable gifts.[67] The reason for this reduction is that adjusted taxable gifts may operate to increase the tax amount. For example, if in 2011 a decedent had a taxable estate of $5 million and had made no adjusted taxable gifts, the decedent's estate tax would be $1,730,800, which would be offset by the unified credit. However, if the decedent had made adjusted taxable gifts, the tax on the $5 million taxable estate would be greater than the amount of the unified credit. Appropriately, a return must then be filed.

Returns are also required to be filed for a predeceasing spouse's gross estate which is below $5 million if the predeceasing spouse's executor elects to transport an unused exclusion amount to a surviving spouse.[68] In addition, but

---

[65] See supra ¶ 3.02[1][a] and infra text accompanying notes 67–69.

[66] Subject to the three reductions discussed infra text accompanying notes 67–69, the Section 6018(a) filing requirements for recent years are as follows:

Year of Death	A return must be filed if the gross estate exceeds
1977	$ 120,000
1978	134,000
1979	147,000
1980	161,000
1981	175,000
1982	225,000
1983	275,000
1984	325,000
1985	400,000
1986	500,000
1987 through 1997	600,000
1998	625,000
1999	650,000
2000 and 2001	675,000
2002 and 2003	1,000,000
2004 and 2005	1,500,000
2006 through 2008	2,000,000
2009	3,500,000
2010 and 2011	5,000,000
2012	5,000,000 (adjusted for inflation)

Under the sunset provision effective January 1, 2013, the $1 million applicable exclusion amount for the year 2006 will apply to the estates of decedents dying after the year 2012. Economic Growth and Tax Relief Reconciliation Act of 2001, Pub. L. No. 107-16, § 901(a)(2), 115 Stat. 38, 150 (2001), reprinted in 2001-3 CB 9, 122, as amended by the Tax Relief Act of 2010, Pub. L. No. 111-312, §§ 101(a)(1), 304, 124 Stat. 3296, 3298, 3304 (2010). The sunset provision is discussed more fully at Supplement ¶ 8.11.

[67] IRC § 6018(a)(3)(A). See supra note 66.

[68] IRC § 2010(c)(5)(A). See supra ¶ 3.02[1][b][ii].

less significantly, the critical gross estate figures must be reduced by the amount of the decedent's exempted lifetime transfers of property made between September 8, 1976, and January 1, 1977.[69]

Even though an estate tax return is not required to be filed, it may be wise to file one. The statute of limitations on assessment, the period specified in Section 6501 within which the government may assess tax in addition to that reported, does not commence until a return is filed. Filing a return with sufficient information starts the time clock.[70] An ancillary benefit of filing a return is that it provides a permanent source of information that may be used for determination of the income tax basis of assets acquired from the decedent.[71]

---

[69] IRC § 6018(a)(3)(B). This is required because of the reduction in the amount of credit required in these circumstances. See supra note 18. This reduction of the critical gross estate figures cannot exceed $30,000, the amount of the prior specific lifetime exemption. See IRC § 2521 (prior to repeal in the Tax Reform Act of 1976, Pub. L. No. 94-455, § 2001(b)(3), 90 Stat. 1520, 1849 (1976), reprinted in 1976-3 CB (Vol. 3) 1, 325).

[70] Estate of Lohman v. Comm'r, TC Memo. 1972-27 (1972) ("tentative return" put the Service on notice for statute of limitations purposes in an estate tax case).

[71] See IRC § 1014.

¶ 3.03 SECTION 2011. CREDIT FOR STATE DEATH TAXES

[1] Introduction

Page 3-12:

Add to note 16.

Cf. Estate of Hemphill v. Washington, 153 Wash. 2d 544, 105 P3d 391 (Wash. 2005), in which the Washington Supreme Court held that the state's pick-up tax regime referencing pre-EGTRRA Code is nonetheless based on current federal law and any state estate tax not fully absorbed by current federal credit is invalid independent tax.

¶ 3.05 SECTION 2013. CREDIT FOR TAX ON PRIOR TRANSFERS

[2] Computation of Credit in General

Page 3-32:

Add to note 22.

In Estate of Le Caer v. Comm'r, 135 TC No. 14 (2010), decedent's estate claimed the full amounts of both federal and state estate taxes paid by her predeceased husband's estate as an IRC § 2013 credit on her estate tax return. The Tax Court explained that there are no available exceptions to the application of the Section 2013(b) and Section (c) limitations which reduce the amount of the allowable credit and that Section 2013(a) specifically references federal estate taxes and there is no Section 2013 credit for state estate taxes paid.

Page 3-33:

Add new note 22.1 at the end of the runover sentence.

[22.1] In performing this calculation, the transferor's taxable estate is not reduced by the IRC § 2010 credit amount. See Estate of Le Caer v. Comm'r, 135 TC No. 14 (2010).

[3] Adjustments

[b] Value of Property Transferred

Page 3-34:

Add to note 29.

As required by Section 7520(c)(3), the Service issued proposed, temporary and final regulations on May 7, 2009, revising Table S and Table U(1), the tables used to value annuities, interests for life or a term of years, and reversionary and remainder interests in property, to reflect the mortality experience from the 2000 census (Life Table 2000CM). Transition rules allow taxpayers to use tables based on either Life Table 90CM or Life Table 2000CM to value gift, charitable and estate transfers made on or after May 1, 2009, and before July 1, 2009, and they must use the appropriate interest rate for the month in which the valuation date falls, regardless of which table is chosen. TD 9448; REG-107845-08. Reg. §§ 1.170A-12T, 1.642(c)-6T, 1.664-4T, 20.2031-7T, 20.2032A-1T, 20.2056A-4T, 25.2512-5T, 25.2522(c)-3, 1.7520-1T, 20.7520-1T, and 25.7520-1T. Publications 1457 and 1458 (Rev. May 2009), both of which include examples for using the mortality component tables, have been released. On August 10, 2011, the Service issued final regulations that removed the temporary regulations issued in TD 9448 and adopted as final the proposed regulations issued in REG-107845-08. The only substantive change was the deletion of an example in the Section 2032 regulations which the Service anticipates including in a different regulation project under that Code section. TD 9540; Reg. §§ 1.170A-12, 1.642(c)-6, 1.664-4, 20.2031-7, 20.2032-1, 20.2056A-4, 25.2512-5, 25.2522(c)-3, 1.7520-1, 20.7520-1, 25.7520-1.

Page 3-37:

Add to note 46 just before the cite to "TAM 8512004".

See ILM 200218003 (Jan. 7, 2002);

[4] Limitations on Credit

[a] Tax Caused in Decedent's Estate

Page 3-39:

Add new note 52.1 at the end of the first paragraph on page 39.

   [52.1] Miglio v. United States, 2011-2 USTC ¶ 60,622 (ND Ill. 2011) (decedent's estate not entitled to an estate tax credit for prior estate taxes paid by sisters' estates since decedent's estate owed no estate tax).

¶ 3.06 SECTION 2014. CREDIT FOR FOREIGN DEATH TAXES

[3] The Federal Estate Tax Formula

[b] Value of the Property

Page 3-47:

Add to note 22.

Priv. Ltr. Rul. 200627016 (Mar. 15, 2006) (Service explains the adjustment to the calculation of the foreign death tax credit for foreign property that qualifies for the marital deduction).

CHAPTER 4

The Gross Estate

¶ 4.02   Section 2031. Definition of "Gross Estate" S4-4
     [1]   Introduction S4-4
     [2]   Fair Market Value S4-4
         [a]   Introduction S4-4
         [b]   General Valuation Methods S4-5
             [i]   Income approach. S4-5
             [ii]   Market approach. S4-5
             [iii]   Asset-based (cost) approach. S4-6
             [iv]   Combinations.   S4-6
         [c]   Valuation Determined by Agreements S4-6
     [3]   Basic Valuation Approaches to Property Interests . . .   S4-6
         [a]   Tangible Personal Property S4-6
         [b]   Real Property S4-7
         [e]   Bonds S4-8
         [f]   Closely Held Corporations S4-8
     [4]   Adjustments for Premiums and Discounts S4-9
         [a]   Introduction S4-9
         [b]   Premium for Control S4-9
             [ii]   Absence of attribution. S4-9
             [iv]   Swing vote premium. S4-10
         [c]   Discount for Minority Interest S4-10
             [i]   Rationale. S4-10
             [iii]   Amounts and cases. S4-10
         [d]   Discount for Lack of Marketability S4-11
             [ii]   Amounts and cases. S4-11
         [e]   Other Significant Discounts S4-11
             [i]   Fractional interest discount. S4-11
             [iii]   Capital gains discount. S4-12
             [iv]   Securities law discount. S4-12
             [v]   Environmental hazards discount. S4-13
             [vi]   Key person discount. S4-13
             [vii]   Litigation discount. S4-13
         [g]   Nonbusiness Assets Held in FLPS and FLLCs   S4-13
     [5]   Temporal Property Interests S4-15

[6]   Statutes Related to Valuation S4-17
        [a]   Understatement Penalty and Reasonable Cause:
                Sections 6662 and 6664 . . . .   S4-17
        [b]   Understatement of Taxpayer Liability by
                Return Preparer: Section 6694 [Revised] S4-19
        [c]   Section 7491 . . . .   S4-21
[7]   Exclusion of the Value of Land Subject to a
        Qualified Conservation Easement S4-22
        [a]   Introduction S4-22
        [b]   Land Subject to a Qualified Conservation
                Easement S4-22
                [ii]   Qualified conservation easement. S4-22

¶ 4.03   Section 2032. Alternate Valuation Date S4-22
        [1]   Introduction S4-22
        [2]   Identification of Gross Estate S4-24
        [3]   Exceptions to Usual Alternate Date S4-24
                [a]   Property Disposed of S4-24
                [c]   Changes Not Due to Market Conditions [New]   S4-25

¶ 4.04   Section 2032A. Valuation of Certain Farm, Etc., Real
        Property S4-25
        [1]   Introduction S4-25
        [3]   Estate Qualification S4-26
                [c]   The 25 Percent Test S4-26
                        [ii]   Material participation. S4-26
                        [iii]   Active management. S4-26
        [4]   Real Property Qualification S4-26
        [5]   Valuation Methods S4-27
                [a]   Formula Farm Valuation S4-27
        [6]   Election and Agreement S4-27
        [7]   Recapture S4-28
                [b]   Recapture Events S4-28
                        [i]   Dispositions. S4-28
                        [ii]   Cessation of qualified use. S4-28

¶ 4.05   Section 2033. Property in Which the Decedent Had an
        Interest S4-29
        [2]   Beneficial Interest S4-29
                [a]   State Law S4-29
                [b]   State Decrees S4-30
        [3]   Routine Inclusions S4-30
        [4]   Income Items S4-31
        [5]   Partial Interests in Property S4-31
                [b]   Successive Interests in Property S4-31
        [7]   Business Interests S4-31
                [c]   Limited Liability Companies S4-31

¶ 4.07   Section 2035. Adjustments for Gifts Made Within Three
        Years of Decedent's Death S4-32
        [2]   The Section 2035(a) Rule (the First Prong) S4-32
                [b]   Exceptions to Section 2035(a) Inclusion S4-32
                        [i]   Section 2035(d): bona fide sales. S4-32
        [3]   The Section 2035(b) Rule (the Second Prong) S4-32
                [a]   The Gift Tax Gross-Up Rule S4-32
                [b]   Gifts Made Within Three Years of Death S4-33
        [4]   Pre-1982 Section 2035 and Its Background S4-33

¶ 4.08 Section 2036. Transfers With Retained Life Estate S4-33
   [1] Excluded Transfers S4-33
    [a] Sales for Full Consideration S4-33
   [4] Beneficial Interests in the Decedent S4-34
    [b] Right to Income S4-34
    [c] Enjoyment "Retained" S4-34
   [5] Control Over Others' Interests S4-41
    [a] Right to Designate Retained Indirectly S4-41
    [c] Right to Designate Who Benefits S4-42
   [6] Indirect Interests or Controls S4-42
    [a] Settlor Trustee S4-42
    [c] Rent Paid by Transferor S4-43
   [7] Transfer by the Decedent S4-43
    [a] Indirect Transfers S4-44
    [d] Reciprocal Trusts S4-44
   [8] Amount to Be Included S4-44
¶ 4.10 Section 2038. Revocable Transfers S4-46
   [4] Power in the Decedent S4-46
    [a] Power to Revoke S4-46
    [b] Power to Alter or Amend S4-46
    [c] Administrative Powers S4-47
    [g] Power in "Whatever Capacity" S4-47
   [6] Power Exercisable Only With Another S4-47
¶ 4.11 Section 2039. Annuities S4-48
   [3] Qualifications S4-48
    [a] Contract or Agreement S4-48
   [4] Amount to Be Included S4-48
    [a] Valuation S4-48
   [5] Private Annuities S4-49
   [6] Exempt Annuities S4-50
¶ 4.12 Section 2040. Joint Interests S4-50
   [9] Termination Prior to Death S4-50
¶ 4.13 Section 2041. Powers of Appointment S4-50
   [2] Powers Within Section 2041 . . . . S4-50
    [b] Powers That Overlap Interests S4-51
   [3] Definition of "General Power" S4-51
   [4] Exceptions to General Definition S4-52
    [a] Power Limited by a Standard S4-52
    [c] Post-1942 Powers With Another Person S4-53
     [ii] Power held with an adverse party. S4-53
     [iii] Power held with an equally interested
      party. S4-54
   [6] Treatment of Pre-1942 Powers S4-55
    [d] Partial Release of Pre-1942 Powers S4-55
   [7] Treatment of Post-1942 Powers S4-55
    [a] Possession S4-55
    [f] The Five-or-Five Rule S4-56
   [8] Nongeneral Powers S4-56
    [b] Nongeneral Powers That Are Treated As
     General Powers S4-56
¶ 4.14 Section 2042. Proceeds of Life Insurance S4-57
   [4] Amounts Receivable by Other Beneficiaries S4-57
    [a] Incidents of Ownership S4-57

		[e]	"Incidents" in Context	S4-57
	[5]	Incidents Incidentally Held		S4-58
		[b]	Partnership's Insurance on Partner	S4-58
	[6]	Assignment of Group Term Insurance		S4-58
	[8]	Policy Purchased With Community Property Funds		S4-61
	[9]	Relation of Section 2042 to Other Sections Defining		
		"Gross Estate"		S4-62
		[b]	Near-Death Transfers	S4-62
¶ 4.15		Section 2043. Transfers for Insufficient Consideration		S4-62
	[1]	Marital Rights: The Negative Rule		S4-62
		[b]	The Negative Rule in a Divorce Situation	S4-62
		[i]	Claims.	S4-62
¶ 4.16		Section 2044. Certain Property for Which a Marital		
		Deduction Was Previously Allowed		S4-63

¶ 4.02 SECTION 2031. DEFINITION OF "GROSS ESTATE"

Page 4-9:

Add to note 4.

The Service has revised the general procedures relating to the issuance of written guidance, including letter rulings and determination letters. See Rev. Proc. 2011-1. In addition, see Rev. Proc. 2011-2 for updated general procedures relating to the issuance of technical advice to a director or an appeals area director by the various offices of the Associate Chief Counsel. The Service has also released a revised list of issues on which it will not generally issue letter rulings or determination letters due to the inherently factual nature of the problems involved. Rev. Proc. 2011-3.

[1] Introduction

Page 4-10:

Add to note 6.

The Service has released a revised list of issues on which it will not generally issue letter rulings or determination letters due to the inherently factual nature of the problems involved. Rev. Proc. 2011-3.

[2] Fair Market Value

[a] Introduction

Page 4-10:

Add to note 8.

The Service has released a revised list of issues on which it will not generally issue letter rulings or determination letters due to the inherently factual nature of the problems involved. Rev. Proc. 2011-3.

Page 4-12:

Add to note 22 after citation to "Dunn".

, rev'd on another issue, 301 F3d 339 (5th Cir. 2002)

Page 4-14:

Add to note 28 just before the citation to "Freeman".

Estate of Leichter v. Comm'r, TC Memo. 2003-66 (2003) (the settlement of a probate court dispute between family members determining a value for the property approximately five months after the decedent's death was probative in determining that the value reported on the estate tax return was correct); Estate of Noble v. Comm'r, TC Memo. 2005-2 (2005) (the actual price paid for closely held stock in a sale that occurred approximately one year after decedent's death controlled the fair market value of decedent's interest in the stock for estate tax purposes).

Add to note 31.

But see AOD 2005-01, in which the Chief Counsel's Office has recommended that the Service not acquiesce to the *Mitchell* court's opinion involving the shifting of the burden of proof to the Service to prove the correctness of its valuation of stock.

Add to note 34 after citation to "Strangi".

, rev'd sub nom. (on another issue) Gulig v. Comm'r, 293 F3d 279 (5th Cir. 2002)

[b] General Valuation Methods

Page 4-16:

Add to note 38.

Estate of Deputy v. Comm'r, TC Memo. 2003-176 (2003) (taxpayer's expert discarded the income valuation approach which the court held governed the value of a long established, financially successful operating company).

[i] Income approach.

Page 4-16:

Add to note 40.

In Estate of Gallagher v. Comm'r, TC Memo. 2011-148 (2011), the Tax Court rejected the Service's use of the guideline company method, a market-based valuation approach, in valuing a closely held publishing company since the four companies used as comparables differed in size, products and revenue growth. The Tax Court instead relied on the discounted cash flow method, an income-based valuation approach, which was considered by the experts for both the estate and the Service, although the experts differed as to various adjustments and other factors in applying it.

[ii] Market approach.

Page 4-16:

Add to note 41.

In Estate of Gallagher v. Comm'r, TC Memo. 2011-148 (2011), the Tax Court rejected the Service's use of the guideline company method, a market-based valuation approach, in valuing a closely held publishing company since the four companies used as comparables differed in size, products and revenue growth. The Tax Court instead relied on the discounted cash flow method, an income-based valuation approach, which was considered by the experts for both the estate and the Service, although the experts differed as to various adjustments and other factors in applying it.

[iii] Asset-based (cost) approach.

Page 4-17:

Add to note 44.

Estate of Kelley v. Comm'r, TC Memo. 2005-235 (2005) (decedent's interests in FLP and LLC, which held only cash and certificates of deposit, valued using the net asset value approach).

Add to note 45 after citation to "Dunn".

, rev'd, 301 F3d 339 (5th Cir. 2002)

[iv] Combinations.

Add to note 47 just before first semi-colon.

, rev'd, 301 F3d 339 (5th Cir. 2002) (directing the Tax Court on remand to assign a weight of 85 percent to the earnings approach and 15 percent to the asset approach)

Page 4-17:

Add to end of note 47.

Anderson v. United States, 2006-1 USTC ¶ 60,516 (WD La. 2005) (value in decedent's estate of minority interests in LLCs that held mineral interests was determined using a combination of the net asset and market approaches with the net asset approach weighted two to one over the market approach).

[c] Valuation Determined by Agreements

Page 4-18:

Add to note 48 after citation to "True".

, aff'd, 390 F3d 1210 (10th Cir. 2004).

[3] Basic Valuation Approaches to Property Interests

[a] Tangible Personal Property

Page 4-20:

Add to note 59.

In Estate of Murphy, 2009-2 USTC ¶ 60,583 (WD Ark. 2009), the court found the appraisals of four works of art by the estate's experts and by the Art Advisory Panel more credible than the Service's expert who based his valuation on art sales too remote to be relevant. In a January 27, 2011, memorandum, SBSE-04-0111-008, the Service directed its examiners that referrals to the Service's Art Appraisal Services are mandatory when audits involve pieces of art valued on the return at $50,000 or more (more than doubling the previous threshold of $20,000). See also Estate of Mitchell v. Comm'r, TC Memo 2011-94 (2011) (estate's valuation of paintings by two Western artists, Frederic Remington and Charles M. Russell, more credible due to expert's more thorough research, expertise in American Western art, detailed description of comparable sales and more understandable report).

[b] Real Property

Page 4-20:

Add to note 61.

Estate of Kolczynski v. Comm'r, TC Memo. 2005-218 (2005) (highest and best use was a mixed use of recreation and timber farming).

Page 4-21:

Add to note 70.

Estate of Dunia v. Comm'r, TC Memo. 2004-123 (2004) (one particular comparable sale of a similarly-sized tract of land, with various adjustments, was the most relevant factor in establishing valuation; a sale of a portion of the property three years after the valuation was given limited weight). Estate of Langer v. Comm'r, TC Memo. 2006-232 (2006) (two parcels of undeveloped commercial property valued using the comparable sales method with the court arriving at the value of one parcel that was approximately mid-range between the values derived by the parties' experts and, for the other parcel, adopting the value posited by the Service's expert because of flaws in the estate's expert's appraisal).

Page 4-22:

Add to note 73.

Estate of Mitchell v. Comm'r, TC Memo 2011-94 (2011) (court values property leased to unrelated third party using an income capitalization method, as advocated by the estate's expert, rather than lease buy-out method used by the Service's expert).

Add to note 79.

Levy v. United States, 2010-2 USTC ¶ 60,608 (5th Cir. 2010) , cert. denied, 2011 WL 1481312 (2011) (appellate court affirmed trial court's admission of evidence concerning negotiations over the eventual sale of the property and the listing and final sale price).

Page 4-23:

Add to note 84.

In a January 4, 2011, memorandum, SBSE-04-0111-002, the Service set out the circumstances under which transfer tax cases should be referred to Engineering, including those involving corporate or valuation issues and in cases with real property assets having a return value of more than $500,000.

[e] Bonds

Page 4-26:

Add new note 100.1 to end of ¶ 4.02[3][e].

   100.1 In Technical Advice Memorandum 200303010 (Sept. 19, 2002), the Service rejected an argument that because a willing buyer would consider the built-in income tax liability associated with a Series E bond in determining the price of the bond the value of the bond should be reduced. The Service noted there is only one buyer of such bonds, the Treasury, and it purchases the bonds at the redemption price.

[f] Closely Held Corporations

Page 4-26:

Add to note 102.

In Blount Estate v. Comm'r, 428 F3d 1338 (11th Cir. 2005), the court held that insurance proceeds paid to a company upon a shareholder's death are not included in calculating the company's fair market value due to the company's contractual obligation to buy the decedent's shares. The court noted that Regulations Section 20.2031-2(f)(2) provides that, in valuing corporate stock, non-operating assets, including life insurance policies payable to the company, should be considered but only to the extent "that such non-operating assets have not been taken into account in the determination of net worth." The court found that this limiting language precluded the inclusion of the insurance proceeds because of the company's obligation to purchase the decedent's shares. See also A. Baer Revocable Trust v. United States, 2010-1 USTC ¶ 60,590 (D. Neb. 2010) (bequests that were contingent upon sale of stock in a private equity company for a profit during surviving spouse's life were held to have no value where company's joint venture with foreign country fell through after there was a change in leadership of the country making the stock essentially worthless).

In the runover sentence in the first paragraph, replace Revenue Ruling 55-60 *in the text with* Revenue Ruling 59-60.

Page 4-27:

Add to note 106.

In Estate of Giustina v. Comm'r, TC Memo 2011-141 (2011), the court valued decedent's interest in limited partnership that held an operating lumber company. The court began by using a weighted combination of valuation methods to value the partnership. The cash flow method represented the future cash flow of the partnership if it continues to operate and the asset method reflects the distribution each partner would receive if the partnership had liquidated its assets on the date of decedent's death. To then determine the partnership's value, the court weighted the likelihood that the partnership would continue to operate or liquidate.

Add to note 108 following citation to Northern Trust Co.*;*

Barnes v. Comm'r, TCMemo. 1998-413 (1998) (capitalization of dividend yield used to value gifts of stock in closely held corporation, since dividends are the primary way in which a prospective shareholder of such stock would obtain a return on his or her investment).

Page 4-28:

Add to note 110.

Estate of Noble v. Comm'r, TC Memo. 2005-2 (2005) (the actual price paid for closely held stock in a sale that occurred approximately one year after decedent's death controlled the fair market value of decedent's interest in the stock for estate tax purposes). Huber v. Comm'r, TC Memo. 2006-96 (2006) (value of donors' gifts of closely held stock established by arm's-length transactions of same stock which had utilized values established annually by appraiser, an independent accounting firm).

Add to note 113.

In Thompson Estate v. Comm'r, TC Memo. 2004-174 (2004), vacated to correct a calculation error, 100 AFTR2d 2007-5792 (2d Cir. 2007), cert. denied, No. 07-1061 (2008), the court criticized and ultimately rejected the valuation opinions of the parties' experts as to the valuation of closely held stock in a decedent's estate that differed by more than $30 million. The court explained that it may give different weight to the factors relied on by the parties and that it may make a valuation based on its own analysis of the evidence.

[4] Adjustments for Premiums and Discounts

[a] Introduction

Page 4-32:

Add to note 146.

See also Rev. Rul. 2008-35, 2008-29 IRB 116, where the Service ruled that an interest in a restricted management account (RMA) will be valued for transfer tax purposes without any reduction or discount for the restrictions imposed by the RMA agreement.

Compare with CCA 200941016 (Aug. 26, 2008) where the IRS Chief Counsel ruled that the account owner of an RMA was limited to a discount for potential damages for breach of contract for transfer tax purposes.

[b] Premium for Control

[ii] Absence of attribution.

Page 4-34:

Add to note 155.

TAM 200648028 (Aug. 4, 2006). See also Estate of Adler v. Comm'r, TC Memo 2011-28 (2011) (decedent's estate denied fractional interest discount on the value of a ranch included in decedent's estate that decedent had, during life, gratuitously transferred undivided one-fifth interests to his five children but had retained full use, control, income and possession of during his lifetime).

[iv] Swing vote premium.

Page 4-37:

Add to note 169 after citation to "True".

, aff'd, 390 F3d 1210 (10th Cir. 2004).

Page 4-38:

Add to note 170 after citation to "True".

, aff'd, 390 F3d 1210 (10th Cir. 2004).

[c] Discount for Minority Interest

[i] Rationale.

Page 4-38:

Add to note 172.

The Tax Court in Estate of Deputy v. Comm'r, TC Memo. 2003-176 (2003), rightly rejected an assertion by the government expert that no discount should apply to a noncontrolling interest on the theory that the company was to be valued on the income basis and all the shares (minority or majority) would be entitled to the same income rights; a theory that ignores the distinction between the company's income and the minority shareholder's access to it. In Estate of Gallagher v. Comm'r, TC Memo. 2011-148 (2011), the Tax Court reasoned that the minority interest discount applied to estate's interest in a closely held publishing company could be determined using the control premium due to their inverse relationship.

[iii] Amounts and cases.

Page 4-38:

Add to note 176.

Anderson v. United States, 2006-1 USTC ¶ 60,516 (WD La. 2005) (where valuation, in decedent's estate, of minority interests in LLCs was determined using a combination of the net asset approach and market approaches, see ¶ 4.02[2][b][iv], a 10 percent minority interest discount was proper for the net asset approach).

Estate of Litchfield, TC Memo. 2009-21 (2009) (siding with the estate's expert who used a weighted average of discounts for estate's interest in one closely-held corporation to take into account the corporation's unequal mix of farmland and marketable securities and a deeper discount due to estate's smaller interest in another closely-held corporation).

[d] Discount for Lack of Marketability

[ii] Amounts and cases.

Page 4-40:

Add to note 186.

Anderson v. United States, 2006-1 USTC ¶ 60,516 (WD La. 2005) (where valuation, in decedent's estate, of minority interests in LLCs was determined using a combination of the net asset approach and market approaches, see ¶ 4.02[2][b][iv], a 40 percent lack of marketability discount was appropriate for both the market and net asset approaches).

Estate of Litchfield, TC Memo. 2009-21 (2009) (reducing estate's expert's discount for estate's interests in two closely-held corporations given the lack of control discounts applied by the court, the estate's expert's use of outdated data in calculating the discounts and the lower discount applied by the estate's expert in an earlier gift tax valuation of one of the corporations). Estate of Gallagher v. Comm'r, TC Memo. 2011-148 (2011) (Tax Court applied the Service's discount of 31 percent for lack of marketability because there was only a one percent difference between the appraisal by the Service's expert and that of the estate's expert and the Court determined the Service's calculation to be reasonable).

Page 4-42:

Add to note 196.

But see Estate of Foster, TC Memo 2011-95 (2011) (no lack of marketability discount for marital trust assets that were frozen by co-trustee due to lawsuit since a willing buyer of the trust assets would not have insisted on a discount since the lawsuit would not have affected the buyer's rights).

[e] Other Significant Discounts

[i] Fractional interest discount.

Page 4-42:

Add to note 197.

But see Stone v. United States, 2007-1 USTC ¶ 60,540 (ND Cal. 2007), where a California district court held that an estate's undivided 50 percent interest in an art collection consisting of nineteen paintings was not entitled to a fractional interest discount. The court stated that a hypothetical seller of an undivided interest in an art collection would not sell a fractional interest in such a collection at a discount but would seek to sell the whole collection and split the proceeds. The court ruled, however, that the estate was entitled to a cost-to-partition discount and, following the parties' failure to reach agreement on an appropriate cost-to-partition discount, the matter came before the court again. In Stone v. United States, 100 AFTR2d 2007-5512 (ND Cal. 2007), aff'd, 103 AFTR2d 2009-1379 (9th Cir. 2009), the court held that the estate was entitled to a 5 percent discount which included a 2 percent discount for sales fees, a 1.8 percent discount for the cost to partition the collection, and a 1.2 percent discount for the uncertainties involved in waiting for the resolution of the partition action.

[iii] Capital gains discount.

Page 4-46:

Add to note 218 after citation to "Dunn".

, rev'd, 301 F3d 339 (5th Cir. 2002) (finding as a matter of law, with respect to a C corporation, that in making an asset-based valuation the value is to be discounted by the entire amount of capital gains tax that would be incurred if the corporation were liquidated)

Add to the end of note 218.

But see Estate of Jelke v. Comm'r, 507 F3d 1317 (11th Cir. 2007) vacating TC Memo. 2005-131 (2005), cert. denied, No. 07-1582 (2008), (approving of the Fifth Circuit's approach in *Dunn* and holding that decedent's interest in closely held investment holding company should be valued based on corporate net asset value calculated with a 100 percent reduction for built-in capital gains tax liability).

   Estate of Litchfield, TC Memo. 2009-21 (2009) (siding with the estate's expert and citing both *Dunn* and *Jelke*). Estate of Jensen v. Comm'r, TC Memo 2010-182 (2010) (although the Tax Court applied a present-value approach to determine a range of values for the estate's discount for built-in capital gains, instead of the dollar for dollar reduction adopted by the Fifth and Eleventh Circuits, it nonetheless accepted the estate's 100 percent discount for the built-in capital gains as falling within that range).

Add to note 219.

But see Estate of Dunn v. Comm'r, 301 F3d 339 (5th Cir. 2002) (holding as a matter of law that a liquidation is assumed with respect to an asset-based valuation and that, with respect to a C corporation, the asset value is to be discounted by the entire amount of capital gains tax that would be incurred if the corporation were liquidated).

   See, however, Estate of Smith v. United States, 300 F. Supp. 2d 474 (SD Tex. 2004), aff'd, 391 F3d 621 (5th Cir. 2004), in which the court refused to allow a discount for the income tax liability incurred by retirement account beneficiaries upon distribution. The court distinguished Eisenberg v. Commissioner, 155 F3d 50 (2d Cir. 1998), and concluded that under the hypothetical willing buyer-willing seller valuation structure property is to be valued at the price the hypothetical willing buyer would pay. Since the hypothetical willing buyer of the accounts would not be saddled with the income tax liability, no discount is appropriate. The court noted that Congress had chosen to address the issue of double taxation of retirement accounts through Section 691(c). Accord Estate of Kahn v. Comm'r, 125 TC No. 11 (2005); TAM 200247001 (Nov. 22, 2002). Cf. TAM 200444021 (June 21, 2004), discussed in ¶ 5.03[3][c] note 63 and ¶ 5.03[5][a] note 103.

[iv] Securities law discount.

Page 4-46:

Add to note 220.

   In Estate of Gimbel, TC Memo. 2006-270 (2006), decedent's estate included restricted stock representing 13 percent of the total outstanding shares of a publicly traded company. In valuing the stock, the court ruled that the company would repurchase 20 percent of the estate's shares and applied a 13.9 percent repurchase discount. The remaining shares would be valued using the "dribble-out" method because of the federal securities law restrictions and applied a 14.4 percent discount. Accordingly, the court applied a lack of liquidity and marketability discount to the estate's shares, as a whole, of 14.2 percent.

An interesting income tax case examined the challenges in applying an appropriate discount for the valuation of restricted shares held by the former owners of what later became Hotel.com during the frenzied internet stock environment of the late 1990's. Litman et al. v. US, 78 Fed. Cl. 90 (2007). In its analysis, the court found most persuasive the taxpayers' valuation expert who best emphasized the primary factors that should be taken into account, including risk in terms of volatility, in determining appropriate discounts.

[v] Environmental hazards discount.

Delete the word "not" in the first sentence of ¶ 4.02[4][e][v].

Add to note 222.

See TAM 200648028 (Aug. 4, 2006) (in the valuation of shares of a closely held corporation with a potential environmental clean-up liability, the Service advised that valuation would depend on the various facts on the valuation date including: (1) The extent to which the clean-up problem was known; (2) whether it was foreseeable that the corporation would have to pay the costs; and (3) whether the corporation would be entitled to any state or federal funding incentives to allay the cost).

[vi] Key person discount.

Page 4-47:

Add to note 224.

As noted in Okerlund v. United States, 90 AFTR2d 2002-6124 (Fed. Cl. 2002) (addressing the valuation of *Schwan's Sales Enters., Inc.*), even where a company has a key management figure, if his death has neither occurred nor is anticipated at the time of the transfer, the key person discount will be quite limited or inapplicable.

[vii] Litigation discount.

Add to note 225.

Estate of Foster, TC Memo. 2011-95 (2011) (estate not entitled to valuation discount relating to lawsuit concerning marital trust assets since a willing buyer of the trust assets would not have insisted on a discount since the lawsuit would not have affected the buyer's rights).

[g] Nonbusiness Assets Held in FLPS and FLLCs

Page 4-49:

Add to note 235.

The Service has issued Appeals Settlement Guidelines: Family Limited Partnerships and Family Limited Liability Corporations, effective October 20, 2006, which address, among other things, whether the fair market value of transfers of FLP or FLLC interests is properly discounted from the pro rata value of the underlying assets. The settlement guidelines provide the positions of both the government and the taxpayer and includes a discussion of the applicable case law with respect to each issue the Service addresses. The full text of the settlement guidelines is available on the Service's website.

Page 4-50:

Add to note 237 after citation to "Strangi".

, rev'd sub nom. (on another issue) Gulig v. Comm'r, 293 F3d 279 (5th Cir. 2002)

Add to first paragraph of note 238 after citation to "Strangi".

, rev'd sub nom. (on another issue) Gulig v. Comm'r, 293 F3d 279 (5th Cir. 2002)

Add to end of first paragraph of note 238.

The Service successfully attacked the restrictions on transferability of a buy-sell provision found in a limited partnership agreement in Holman v. Comm'r, Doc. No. 08-3774 (8th Cir. 2010). Restrictive sale agreements are disregarded in valuing gifts of limited partnership units unless the taxpayer can establish that the restriction satisfies the three-part exception under Section 2703(b). The Eighth Circuit held that the provision failed the first part of the exception in that the donors' stated purposes for creating the limited partnership, i.e., estate planning, tax reduction, wealth transference, protection against dissipation and wealth management education, were not bona fide business purposes.

Add to third paragraph of note 238 after citation to "Strangi".

, rev'd sub nom. (on another issue) Gulig v. Comm'r, 293 F3d 279 (5th Cir. 2002)

Page 4-51:

In note 241, add at end of the second sentence.

and Strangi v. Comm'r, 417 F3d 468 (5th Cir. 2005) aff'g TC Memo. 2003-145 (2003) (applying Section 2036(a)(1) on the basis of an implied agreement that the decedent was to receive the income and was to have the retained benefit of the property, and also applying Section 2036(a)(2) on the basis that the decedent and other family members (in their capacity as shareholders of a one percent corporate general partner) together could determine who would possess the property).

In note 241, delete the third sentence.

Add to end of note 241.

See also Estate of Disbrow v. Comm'r, TC Memo. 2006-34 (2006), where the tax court applied Section 2036(a)(1) in holding that the fair market value of decedent's residence, which she had transferred to a family partnership seven years prior to her death, was includible in her gross estate. The court noted that, although there were annual lease agreements between the decedent and the partnership, the rental amounts stated therein were significantly below the residence's fair rental value. In addition, notwithstanding the lease agreements, the court stated that there was an implied understanding between the decedent and the partnership that she would continue possession and enjoyment of the residence following its transfer and that the lease agreements were a subterfuge to hide the testamentary nature of the transfer. The court looked to the following indices that such an implied agreement existed: (1) the partnership was not a business operated for profit but was merely a device to remove the residence from the decedent's estate; (2) neither the decedent nor the partnership treated the decedent as a tenant; (3) decedent was almost 72 and in ill health when she transferred the residence to the partnership; (4) one of the partners admitted that the members of the partnership wanted the decedent to reside in the home as long as she could; and (5) decedent transferred the residence to the partnership on advice of counsel in order to minimize estate tax.

[5] Temporal Property Interests

Page 4-51:

Add to the end of the first paragraph of note 244.

As required by Section 7520(c)(3), the Service issued proposed, temporary and final regulations on May 7, 2009, revising Table S and Table U(1), the tables used to value annuities, interests for life or a term of years, and reversionary and remainder interests in property, to reflect the mortality experience from the 2000 census (Life Table 2000CM). Transition rules allow taxpayers to use tables based on either Life Table 90CM or Life Table 2000CM to value gift, charitable and estate transfers made on or after May 1, 2009, but before July 1, 2009, but they must use the appropriate interest rate for the month in which the valuation date falls, regardless of which table is chosen. TD 9448; REG-107845-08. Reg. §§ 1.170A-12T, 1.642(c)-6T, 1.664-4T, 20.2031-7T, 20.2032A-1T, 20.2056A-4T, 25.2512-5T , 25.2522(c)-3, 1.7520-1T, 20.7520-1T, and Reg. § 25.7520-1T. Publications 1457 and 1458 (rev. May 2009), both of which include examples for using the mortality component tables, have been released. On August 10, 2011, the Service issued final regulations that removed the temporary regulations issued in TD 9448 and adopted as final the proposed regulations issued in REG-107845-08. The only substantive change was the deletion of an example in the Section 2032 regulations which the Service anticipates including in a different regulation project under that Code section. TD 9540; Reg. §§ 1.170A-12, 1.642(c)-6, 1.664-4, 20.2031-7, 20.2032-1, 20.2056A-4, 25.2512-5, 25.2522(c)-3, 1.7520-1, 20.7520-1, 25.7520-1.

Page 4-52:

Add to note 244.

In Estate of Gribauskas v. Comm'r, 342 F3d 85 (2d Cir. 2003), the Second Circuit reversed the tax court and concluded that a departure from the tables is allowed in valuing lottery winnings where the tables produce a substantially unrealistic and unreasonable approach. Accord Estate of Shackleford v. United States, 262 F3d 1068 (9th Cir. 2001) (reducing the values under the tables for lottery winnings to reflect a lack of marketability due to restrictions on transferability). Balancing the Second and Ninth Circuit's rulings, however, are the rulings of the Fifth and Sixth Circuits. In Estate of Cook v. Comm'r, 349 F3d 850 (5th Cir. 2003), the Fifth Circuit affirmed the holding of the Tax Court and treated the lottery prize as a private annuity and concluded that the valuation tables produced a result that was not so unreasonable or unrealistic as to justify resort to an alternative valuation method. Siding with the Fifth Circuit, the Sixth Circuit reversed the Tax Court in Negron v. US, 07-4460 (6th Cir. 2009), and held that the annuity tables apply in valuing the remaining lottery payments notwithstanding the fact that the tables produced a value higher than the lump sum the estates actually received from the State of Ohio. Accord Estate of Donovan v. United States, 95 AFTR2d 2005-2131 (D. Mass. 2005), where the court noted that under the Second and Ninth Circuit holdings, nonmarketability should be factored into the valuation of such interests, but under the Fifth Circuit holding such a reduction would not be appropriate; and Davis v. United States, Doc. No. 1:04-CV-00273 (DNH 2007), where the district court concluded that any discount applicable to the nonmarketability of the lottery payments was not enough to render the amount determined by reference to the annuity tables "unrealistic and unreasonable." The *Davis* court distinguished *Shackleford* and *Gribauskas* on the basis that the value of the lottery payments in those cases was at least 25 percent less than the value determined by reference to the annuity tables.

　　　In Estate of Davenport, TC Memo. 2006-215 (2006), the Tax Court held that two annuities payable under a settlement contract are included in decedent's gross estate under Section 2033 and stated that it need not reach the question of whether the annuities would likewise be includable under Section 2039. Valuation of the annuities is determined by using the Section 7520 tables. In Anthony v. United States, No. 07-30089 (5th Cir. 2008), a case involving actual nontransferable private annuities established for the decedent pursuant to a structured settlement agreement after the decedent had sustained injuries in an automobile accident, the Fifth Circuit adopted the rationale of its *Cook* decision by valuing the estate's right to receive payments from the annuities for estate tax purposes by using the Section 7520 annuity tables. It held that the annuities were not a "restricted beneficial interest" thereby governed by Regulations Section 20.7520-3(b), which precludes the use of the annuity tables, and that the nontransferability of the annuities did not make use of the annuity tables "unrealistic or unreasonable."

Add to note 247.

Notice 2009-18 provides supplements to the actuarial tables prescribed under IRC § 7520 by providing factors for interest rates below 2.2 percent. As required by Section 7520(c)(3), the Service issued proposed, temporary and final regulations on May 7, 2009, revising Table S and Table U(1), the tables used to value annuities, interests for life or a term of years, and reversionary and remainder interests in property, to reflect the mortality experience from the 2000 census (Life Table 2000CM). Transition rules allow taxpayers to use tables based on either Life Table 90CM or Life Table 2000CM to value gift, charitable and estate transfers made on or after May 1, 2009, but before July 1, 2009, but they must use the appropriate interest rate for the month in which the valuation date falls, regardless of which table is chosen. TD 9448; REG-107845-08. Reg. §§ 1.170A-12T, 1.642(c)-6T, 1.664-4T, 20.2031-7T, 20.2032A-1T, 20.2056A-4T, 25.2512-5T, 25.2522(c)-3, 1.7520-1T, 20.7520-1T, and Reg § 25.7520-1T. Publications 1457 and 1458 (rev. May 2009), both of which include examples for using the mortality component tables, have been released. On August 10, 2011, the Service issued final regulations that removed the temporary regulations issued in TD 9448 and adopted as final the proposed regulations issued in REG-107845-08. The only substantive change was the deletion of an example in the Section 2032 regulations which the Service anticipates including in a different regulation project under that Code section. TD 9540; Reg. §§ 1.170A-12, 1.642(c)-6, 1.664-4 , 20.2031-7, 20.2032-1, 20.2056A-4, 25.2512-5, 25.2522(c)-3, 1.7520-1, 20.7520-1, 25.7520-1.

Page 4-53:

Add to note 250 after citation to "Gribauskas".

, rev'd, 342 F3d 85 (2d Cir 2003).

In note 251, replace Prop. Reg. § 1.643(b)-1 *with* Reg. § 1.643(b)-1.

Replace citation to McLendon v. Comm'r *in note 253 with the following.*

Estate of McLendon v. Comm'r, TC Memo. 1993-459 (1993), rev'd on other grounds, 135 F3d 1017 (5th Cir. 1998);

[6] Statutes Related to Valuation

[a] Understatement Penalty and Reasonable Cause: Sections 6662 and 6664

Page 4-54:

Replace the first two full paragraphs of ¶ 4.02[6][a] with the following.

Apart from the proper computation of tax, valuation is also important from a more practical perspective. If an asset is undervalued on the federal estate tax return, an underpayment of estate tax will necessarily result. If the underpayment of estate tax is attributable to a "substantial estate or gift tax valuation understatement,"[256] the estate will owe, in addition to the underpayment amount, a penalty equal to 20 percent of the underpayment amount.[257] The penalty does not apply at all unless the underpayment attributable to a substantial estate or gift tax valuation understatement for the estate tax return or the gift tax return for the year exceeds $5,000.[258] A substantial understatement occurs any time the value of property included in the gross estate (or the value of property transferred by gift for federal gift tax purposes) is 65 percent or less of the finally determined value.[259] Thus, if the personal representative states the value of an asset at $130,000, but the actual value of the asset is determined to be $200,000 or more, the substantial understatement penalty applies.

If the value of property included in the gross estate (or reported on the federal gift tax return) is 40 percent or less of the value finally determined, the

---

[256] IRC § 6662(b)(5).

[257] IRC § 6662(a). If there is no tax due, for example because of the unlimited marital deductions or charitable deduction, no penalty is imposed because there is no underpayment. See also the Appeals Settlement Guidelines: Family Limited Partnerships and Family Limited Liability Corporations, issued by the Service and effective October 20, 2006, which address, among other things, accuracy-related penalties with respect to FLPs and FLLCs. The settlement guidelines provide the positions of both the government and the taxpayer and includes a discussion of the applicable case law with respect to each issue the Service addresses. The full text of the settlement guidelines is available on the Service's website. In addition to the penalty imposed on the estate, penalties may also be imposed on the tax return preparer and/or on the appraiser in connection with an understatement of taxpayer liability. See infra ¶ 4.02[6][b].

[258] IRC § 6662(g)(2).

[259] IRC § 6662(g)(1). For returns filed prior to August 17, 2006, the percentage was 50 percent or less of the finally determined value. See Pension Protection Act of 2006, Pub. L. No. 109-280, § 1219(e)(1),__ Stat. __, __ (2006), reprinted in 2006-__ CB __, __.

penalty amount increases to 40 percent of the underpayment amount.[260] In the above example, the more drastic penalty would apply if the actual value of the asset is determined to be $325,000 or more.

---

[260] IRC §§ 6662(h)(1), 6662(h)(2)(C). For returns filed prior to Aug 17, 2006, the percentage was 25 percent or less of the finally determined value. See Pension Protection Act of 2006, Pub. L. No. 109-280, § 1219(e)(1), __ Stat. __, __ (2006), reprinted in 2006-__ CB __, __.

Page 4-55:

Add to note 261.

In Estate of Rector, TC Memo. 2007-367 (2007), the estate was held liable for the Section 6662(a) accuracy-related penalty due to its negligent failure to report $595,000 of prior gifts on decedent's estate tax return. Decedent's son, a co-executor of the estate, had extensive financial expertise and was a recipient of one-half of the unreported gifts and produced no evidence of reasonable cause or good faith for the omission. In Estate of Giustina v. Comm'r, TC Memo. 2011-141 (2011), however, the court found that the estate, in determining valuation of a partnership interest, had obtained legal counsel and a credible appraisal that capitalized cash flows, capitalized distributions and compared market values of other companies. The appraisal met the Section 6664(c)(1) reasonable cause for underpayment standard such that the Section 6662 penalty was not applicable.

Add to note 263.

In Thompson Estate v. Comm'r, 100 AFTR2d 2007-5792 (2d Cir. 2007), cert. denied, No. 07-1061 (2008), vacating and remanding TC Memo. 2004-174 (2004), the estate relied on an Alaska attorney and accountant to establish the value of the decedent's interest in a New York–based corporation, both with little experience in appraising similar companies. The court held that, although the tax court noted this inexperience, it failed to make a determination as to whether the estate's reliance on the appraisers was reasonable and in good faith and remanded the case back to the tax court for such a determination. On remand, in an unreported decision and order, the Tax Court concluded that the estate's reliance on its appraisers was reasonable and in good faith. Subsequently, in No. 09-3601-ag (2d Cir. 2010), the Second Circuit affirmed the Tax Court's judgment and held that, although the appraisers were inexperienced in valuing large corporations, they were sufficiently qualified for the estate's reliance on them to be reasonable. The Court also noted that the Tax Court did not find there was a conflict of interest where one of the appraisers also acted as an executor.

Add to note 264.

In Estate of Lee v. Comm'r, TC Memo. 2009-84 (2009), in a case involving an understatement of tax due to the denial of the marital deduction (see infra ¶ 5.06 note 17 for the basis of the denial), the Tax Court applied the test in Regulations Section 1.6664-4(c)(1) and held that the estate was not liable for the accuracy-related penalty. The Court found that the executor had (1) performed adequate due diligence of his attorney's qualifications before hiring her; (2) reasonably concluded that the attorney was a competent estate tax attorney; (3) supplied his attorney with all required documents and information to prepare the return; (4) reviewed the return in detail prior to filing it; and (5) questioned his attorney on the legitimacy of the deductions taken. Estate of Robinson, TC Memo 2010-168 (2010) (estate not liable for the accuracy-related penalty where the Court found that the personal representative reasonably and in good faith relied on a disbarred enrolled agent who prepared the estate tax return and provided the personal representative with erroneous advice).

Add new ¶ 4.02[6][b] to text and make existing ¶ 4.02[6][b] and ¶ 4.02[6][c] into ¶ 4.02[6][c] and ¶ 4.02[6][d], respectively.

[b] Understatement of Taxpayer Liability by Return Preparer: Section 6694 [Revised]

Section 6694 imposes penalties on tax return preparers. The provision potentially applies where there is an understatement of valuation but it applies more broadly where there is any understatement of liability.[264.1] The provision was substantially amended in both 2007[264.2] and 2008[264.3] As originally enacted, Section 6694 was applicable only to income tax return preparers, but the 2007 legislation broadened the scope of the provision so that it now applies to all "tax return preparers"[264.4] which includes preparers of estate, gift, and generation-skipping transfer tax returns.[264.5]

[264.1] There is no penalty if there is no understatement of liability with respect to which the penalty is assessed. IRC § 6694(d). See Reg. § 1.6694-1(d). In a memorandum issued by the Service's Small Business/Self-Employed Division, examination agents should be scouting for the possibility of tax preparer penalties in the preparation of every estate or gift tax return examination they undertake. The memorandum stressed, however, that estate and gift tax examinations are to be settled "separate and distinct" from any tax preparer penalty case and examiners must not discuss any possible preparer conduct penalties in the presence of the taxpayer. SBSE-04-0509-009. The Service subsequently reissued this memorandum to clarify its content which is to provide guidance about the procedures for the assertion of the Sections 6694 and 6695 penalties until the revised Internal Revenue Manual § 4.25.1 is published. SBSE-04-1010-044. The reissued memorandum makes clear that the statute of limitations on assessment under Sections 6694(a) and 6695 expires three years from the date the related return or claim for refund was filed.

[264.2] Small Business and Work Opportunity Tax Act of 2007, Pub. L. No. 110-28, § 8246, 121 Stat. 190 (2007), reprinted in 2007-__ CB __, __. The amended provision is discussed in Lipton, "What Hath Congress Wrought? Amended Section 6694 Will Cause a Problem for Everyone," J. Tax'n 68 (Aug. 2007).

[264.3] Tax Extenders and Alternative Minimum Tax Relief Act of 2008, Div. C of Pub. L. No. 110-343, § 506, 122 Stat. 3765 (2008), reprinted in 2008-__ CB __, __ (the "2008 Act").

[264.4] IRC § 7701(a)(36). A tax return preparer generally is any person who prepares for compensation any tax return or claim for refund. Reg. § 301.7701-15. See August, Grimes & Maxfield, "Final Regs. On Tax Return Preparer Penalties: Impact on Estate Planners," 36 Est. Plan., No. 5 at 3 (2009).

[264.5] IRC §§ 6694(a)(1), 6694(b)(1). See Reg. § 1.6694-1(b). The Service has identified tax returns and refund claims to which the penalties may apply. Rev. Proc. 2009-11, 2009-13 IRB __. The expanded rule applies to returns after May 25, 2007. Notice 2007-54, 2007-27 IRB 12. See also IR 2008-4, 2008-1 CB __ (National Taxpayer Advocate comment on Section 6694); Notice 2008-11, 2008-3 IRB 279 (clarifies guidance and transitional relief provided in Notice 2007-54); Notice 2008-13, 2008-3 IRB 282 (interim guidance on pre-2008 return preparations); and Notice 2009-5, 2009-3 IRB __ (modifies and clarifies Notice 2008-13 and provides interim guidance regarding the application of IRC § 6694(a) as revised by the 2008 Act).

In general, a tax return preparer is subject to a penalty if any part of an understatement of liability is due to an unreasonable position[264.6] and the return preparer knew (or reasonably should have known) of the position.[264.7] If a position is not disclosed, it is unreasonable unless there is or was "substantial authority" for the position.[264.8] If the position was adequately disclosed,[264.9] it is unreasonable unless there is a reasonable basis for the position.[264.10] The penalty for the unreasonable position violation is the greater of $1,000 or 50 percent of the preparer's income from the preparation of the return.[264.11] However, no penalty is imposed if there is reasonable cause for the understatement and the tax preparer acted in good faith.[264.12]

[264.6] IRC §§ 6694(a)(1)(A), 6694(a)(2).

[264.7] IRC § 6694(a)(1)(B). See Section 6694(a)(2)(C) for a separate rule applicable to tax shelters and Section 6662A reportable transactions.

[264.8] IRC § 6694(a)(2)(A). Notice 2009-5, 2009-3 IRB __, adopts the current regulatory rules of Regulation Section 1.6662-4(d) in defining substantial authority. In deciding if there is substantial authority for the tax treatment of an item, the weight of the authorities supporting the position must be substantial in relation to the weight of authorities on the other side. Reg. § 1.6662-4(d)(3)(i). In doing this balancing, factors such as identity of facts and persuasiveness of reasoning are considered. Reg. § 1.6662-4(d)(3)(ii). Authority that may be considered in determining whether there is substantial authority for a position include the Code, the regulations (including proposed and temporary regulations), revenue rulings (public and private) and procedures, court cases, legislative history, and other pronouncements by the Internal Revenue Service. Notably, conclusions reached in treatises, legal periodicals, and legal opinions are not considered authority. Reg. § 1.6662-4(d)(3)(iii). The jurisdiction of court cases in relation to the taxpayer's residence generally is disregarded except that there is substantial authority for the tax treatment of an item if the treatment is supported by controlling authority of a United States Court of Appeals to which the taxpayer has a right of appeal. Reg. § 1.6662-4(d)(3)(iv)(B). Substantial authority for the tax treatment of an item in a return exists if there was such authority at the time the return was filed or on the last day of the taxable year to which the return relates. Reg. § 1.6662-4(d)(3)(iv)(C).

[264.9] IRC § 6662(d)(2)(B)(ii)(I). See Reg. § 1.6694-2(d)(3).

[264.10] IRC § 6694(a)(2)(B). Reasonable basis has the same meaning as in Regulations Section 1.6662-3(b)(3). Reg. § 1.6694-2(d)(2). The regulations describe "reasonable basis" as "a relatively high standard of tax reporting, that is, significantly higher than not frivolous or patently improper." Reg. § 1.6662-3(b)(3). To satisfy the reasonable basis standard, the position has to be more than "merely arguable" or a "colorable claim." Reg. § 1.6662-3(b)(3). In determining whether the tax return preparer has a reasonable basis for a position, the preparer may rely in good faith without verification upon information furnished by the taxpayer and advice furnished by another advisor, another tax return preparer or other party, as provided in Reg. §§ 1.6694-1(e) and 1.6694-2(e)(5). Reg. § 1.6694-2(d)(2).

[264.11] IRC § 6694(a)(1). The regulations provide detailed rules for determining a preparer's income from the preparation of the return or the claim for refund. Reg. § 1.6694-1(f). See also note 264.1 supra.

[264.12] IRC § 6694(a)(3). The regulations provide a number of factors that the Service will consider in determining if the preparer acted with reasonable cause and in good faith, including the nature, frequency and materiality of the error or errors, the tax return

If any part of the understatement is due to preparer conduct that is a willful attempt to understate liability or a reckless or intentional disregard of rules or regulations,[264.13] a potentially stiffer penalty of the greater of $5,000 or 50 percent of the preparer's income from preparation of the return or claim is imposed.[264.14] The amount of this penalty is reduced by the amount of any penalty paid under the rule for understatements due to an unreasonable position.[264.15]

In addition to the penalties on tax return preparers, Section 6695A, added by the Pension Protection Act of 2006,[264.16] possibly may impose a penalty on the appraiser who prepares an appraisal that results in a substantial or gross valuation misstatement if the appraiser knew or reasonably should have known that the appraisal would be used in connection with a return or refund claim.[264.17]

---

preparer's normal office practice, reliance on the advice of others and reliance on generally accepted administrative or industry practice. Reg. § 1.6694-2(e).

[264.13] IRC § 6694(b)(2). See Reg. §§ 1.6694-3(b), 1.6694-3(c), 1.6694-3(d).

[264.14] IRC § 6694(b)(1). See Reg. § 1.6694-1(f).

[264.15] IRC § 6694(b)(3).

[264.16] Pub. L. No. 109-280, § 1219(b)(1), __ Stat. __, __ (2006), reprinted in 2006-__ CB __, __.

[264.17] An appraiser might be subject to penalties under IRC § 6694 as a nonsigning tax return preparer if the appraisal is a substantial portion of the return or claim for refund and the applicable standards of care under IRC § 6694 are not met. Summary of Contents and Explanation of Provisions, TD 9436 (Dec. 22, 2008). The Service's Small Business/Self-Employed Division provided guidance in a memorandum, dated August 18, 2009, which states that the new penalty provision lets the Service assert a penalty against any person who prepared an appraisal of the value of property and who knew, or reasonably should have known, the appraisal would be used in connection with a return or claim for refund where the appraisal results in a substantial valuation understatement. SBSE-04-0809-015. The memorandum provides that the penalty does not apply if the appraiser can establish that it was "more likely than not" that the appraisal was correct. Id. See Bogdanski, "For Appraisers, New Tax Qualification Rules and Special Penalty," 34 Est. Plan. 16 (June 2007).

[c] Section 7491

Page 4-55:

Add to note 265.

See, e.g., Kohler v. Comm'r, TC Memo. 2006-152 (2006). See W. Chiang, "Shifting the Burden of Proof to the IRS in Tax Court," 84 Prac. Tax Strategies 340 (Dec. 2009). Estate of Van v. Comm'r, TC Memo 2011-22 (2011).

Add to note 265, 266 and 267.

In Thompson Estate v. Comm'r, 100 AFTR2d 2007-5792 (2d Cir. 2007), cert. denied, No. 07-1061 (2008), the court explained that the reallocation of burden does not require the court to adopt an erroneous value offered by the taxpayer if the court rejects the Service's value; the burden of disproving the taxpayer's valuation can be satisfied by evidence in the record impeaching, undermining, or indicating error in the taxpayer's valuation.

[7] Exclusion of the Value of Land Subject to a Qualified Conservation Easement

[a] Introduction

Page 4-56:

Add to note 273.

; Deason, "Section 2031(c): Post-Mortem Estate Planning," 11 Back Forty—Newsl. of Land Conservation L. 1 (Winter 2006).

[b] Land Subject to a Qualified Conservation Easement

[ii] Qualified conservation easement.

Page 4-59:

Add to note 294.

See Turner v. Comm'r, 126 TC No. 16 (2006) (income tax case where court held that no contribution of a qualified conservation easement was made on land situated near George Washington's home in Mount Vernon because attempted grant did not satisfy the "conservation purposes" required by the statute).

¶ 4.03 SECTION 2032. ALTERNATE VALUATION DATE

[1] Introduction

Page 4-76:

Replace the runover sentence ending with note 2 with the following.

The election is made by proper notation on the estate tax return and generally cannot be withdrawn once made.²

---

² IRC § 2032(d)(1). The election may be made on the last estate tax return filed by the executor on or before the due date (including extensions of time to file actually granted) or, if a timely return is not filed, the first return filed after the due date, provided it is filed no later than one year after the due date (including extensions actually granted). Generally, the election is irrevocable. Id. An election may be revoked, however, on a subsequent return on or before the due date of the return (including extensions actually granted). Reg. § 20.2032-1(b)(1).

If, based on the return as filed, the estate would not qualify for the use of Section 2032, a protective election may be made to use Section 2032 if it is subsequently determined such a reduction will occur. Reg. § 20.2032-1(b)(2). See also Priv. Ltr. Rul. 201118013 (Jan. 20, 2011) (estate granted extension of time for making protective election where estate relied in good faith on tax professional who failed to make, or advise estate to make, such election). A protective election may not be revoked other than on a return filed before the due date of the return including extensions actually granted. Absent such a revocation, if the estate subsequently qualifies for the use of Section 2032, the protective election becomes effective and may not be revoked. Prior to this blanket rule a protective election was limited and conditioned upon a variety of factors. See, e.g., Estate of Mapes v. Comm'r, 99 TC 511, 527 (1992) (conditional upon failure to qualify for Section 2032A); TAM 9846002 (July 13, 1998) (conditional upon testamentary trust not qualifying for a marital deduction or surviving spouse's exercise of elective share rights); Priv. Ltr. Rul. 199942015 (July 22, 1999) (conditional upon date of death blockage discount).

Add to note 3.

; Priv. Ltr. Rul. 200438014 (May 25, 2004); Priv. Ltr. Rul. 200740009 (May 10, 2007) (following the timely filing of the estate's return, accountant recomputed the gross estate using the alternate valuation date and then filed a supplemental return making the election). But see Estate of Loree, 2008 WL 305550 (DNJ 2008) (estate denied a refund of estate tax because its amended estate tax return, electing to use the Section 2032 alternate valuation date, was not timely filed).

The Service issued final regulations amending Regulations Section 20.2032-1(b), which provide that a request under Regulations Sections 301.9100-1 and 301.9100-3 for an extension of time to make the alternate valuation election will not be granted unless the estate tax return is filed no later than one year after the due date of the return, including extensions. Reg. § 20.2032-1(b)(3). In the preamble to the final regulations, the Service notes that taxpayers may still receive an extension of time to make the election, even after the expiration of the one-year period imposed by Section 2032(d), so long as the estate tax return is filed no later than one year after the due date of the return, including extensions. Priv. Ltr. Rul. 200930028 (Apr. 9, 2009) (extension of time granted where accountant retained to prepare estate tax return did not consider alternate valuation date); Priv. Ltr. Rul. 200949022 (Aug. 17, 2009); Priv. Ltr. Rul. 201001014 (Sept. 23, 2009), Priv. Ltr. Rul. 201016006 (Oct. 27, 2009), Priv. Ltr. Rul. 201019002 (Dec. 15, 2009); Priv. Ltr. Rul. 201103003 (Sept. 15, 2010). In Private Letter Ruling 201033023 (May 19, 2010) the Service initially refused an extension of time to make an alternate valuation election where the election was not filed within one year of the due date of the return. However, in Private Letter Ruling 201109014 (Oct. 27, 2010), the Service reversed the prior refusal of an extension it made in Private Letter Ruling 201033023 and granted the estate an extension of time to make the election, Priv. Ltr. Rul. 201122009 (Feb. 24, 2011).

Page 4-77:

Replace the first clause of the sentence ending with note 9 with the following.

Back in the good (bad?) old days when individual income tax rates were as high as 70 percent or 50 percent rather than 35 percent on ordinary income (and the generally 15 percent rate on net capital gain),

Page 4-78:

Replace the clause of the sentence beginning just after reference to note 11 and ending with reference to note 12 with the following.

and the individual income tax rates at a maximum of 35 percent (or generally 15 percent on net capital gains)

Add to note 15.

The Service issued final regulations clarifying that in determining whether there has been a decrease in the sum of the estate and GST tax liability, as reduced by allowable credits, the calcluation is made with reference to the estate and GST tax payable by reason of the decedent's death—not taxes that will be paid on future taxable distributions and taxable terminations.

[2] Identification of Gross Estate

Page 4-78:

Add to note 16.

But see Kohler v. Comm'r, TC Memo. 2006-152 (2006), nonacq. 2008-9 IRB (AOD 2008-1).

Page 4-79:

Add to note 20.

See also TAM 200343002 (June 11, 2003). See ¶ 4.03[2][c], treating post death earnings of a corporation which were distributed as a dividend within the six-month period as excluded property, but retained earnings not distributed during the period as included property.

[3] Exceptions to Usual Alternate Date

[a] Property Disposed of

Page 4-84:

Add to note 40.

See also Kohler v. Comm'r, TC Memo. 2006-152 (2006) (citing Regulations Section 20.2032-1(c)(1), the Tax Court noted that stock exchanged for stock of the same corporation in a tax-free reorganization is not treated as distributed, sold, or otherwise disposed of under Section 2032(a)). The Service has stated, however, that it disagrees with the tax court on the valuation of estate's stock and will not follow its decision. Kohler v. Comm'r, TC Memo. 2006-152 (2006), nonacq. 2008-9 IRB. In Action on Decision 2008-01 (2008), the Service explained that it disagrees with the Tax Court's decision that, under Section 2032, the transfer restrictions and purchase option imposed on the stock pursuant to a post-death tax-free reorganization should be taken into account in valuing the stock in the estate. In response to the Tax Court's decision in Kohler, the Treasury has issued proposed regulations targeting such maneuvering. See ¶ 4.03[2].

Page 4-86:

[c] Changes Not Due to Market Conditions [New]

Taxpayers have occasionally been successful in triggering post-death events which have resulted in a decline in the value of estate assets that are not due to market conditions.[54.1] To preclude such maneuvering, the Treasury has taken the position that post-death changes in value due to "market conditions"[54.2] are taken into account under Section 2032, but that changes due to other post-death events will be ignored.[54.3] Where changes in value reflect both market conditions and post-death events, the property is valued at the decedent's date of death, with adjustments for any changes due to market conditions.[54.4] Post-death events not due to market conditions include, but are not limited to, a reorganization of an entity in which an estate holds an interest,[54.5] a distribution of cash or other property to the estate from such entity[54.6] or one or more distributions by the estate of a fractional interest in such entity.[54.7]

[54.1] See, e.g., Kohler v. Comm'r, TC Memo. 2006-152 (2006), nonacq. 2008-9 IRB (AOD 2008-1) (post-death reorganization of company with transfer restrictions and purchase option imposed on stock resulted in discounts on value of stock). But cf. Prop. Reg. § 20.2032-1(f)(3)(ii) Exs. 1, 3, 4, and 5.

[54.2] Market conditions are defined as events outside of the control of the decedent (or the decedent's executor or trustee) or other person whose property is being valued that affect the fair market value of property being valued. Prop. Reg. § 20.2032-1(f)(1).

[54.3] Prop. Reg. § 20.2032-1(f)(1).

[54.4] Prop. Reg. § 20.2032-1(f)(3)(i). See Prop. Reg. § 20.2032-1(f)(3)(ii) Exs. 2, 4, and 5.

[54.5] Prop. Reg. § 20.2032-1(f)(3)(i). See Prop. Reg. § 20.2032-1(f)(3)(ii) Exs. 1 and 3.

[54.6] Prop. Reg. § 20.2032-1(f)(3)(i).

[54.7] Prop. Reg. § 20.2032-1(f)(3)(i). See Prop. Reg. § 20.2032-1(f)(3)(ii) Exs. 4 and 5.

¶ 4.04 SECTION 2032A. VALUATION OF CERTAIN FARM, ETC., REAL PROPERTY

[1] Introduction

Page 4-90:

Add to note 11.

The ceiling on special-use valuation as adjusted for inflation was $800,000 in 2001, Rev. Proc. 2001-13, 2001-3 IRB 337; $820,000 in 2002, Rev. Proc. 2001-59, 2001-52 IRB 623; and is $840,000 in 2003, Rev. Proc. 2002-70, 2002-46 IRB 845. The ceiling on special-use valuation is $850,000 for the estate of a decedent dying in 2004. Rev. Proc. 2003-85, 2003-49 IRB 1104. The ceiling on special-use valuation is $870,000 for the estate of a decedent dying in 2005. Rev. Proc. 2004-71, 2004-50 IRB ___. The ceiling on special-use valuation is $900,000 for the estate of a decedent dying in 2006. Rev. Proc. 2005-70. The ceiling on special-use valuation is $940,000 for the estate of a decedent dying in 2007. Rev. Proc. 2006-53. The ceiling on special use valuation is $960,000 for the estate of a decedent dying in 2008. Rev. Proc. 2007-66, 2007-__ IRB __. The ceiling on special use valuation is $1,000,000 for the estate of a decedent dying in 2009. Rev. Proc. 2008-66, IRB 2008-45.

  If the estate of a decedent who dies in 2010 elects to use IRC § 2032A special use valuation, the aggregate decrease in the property's value may not exceed $1,000,000. Rev. Proc. 2009-50. If the estate of a decedent who dies in 2011 elects to use IRC § 2032A special use valuation, the aggregate decrease in the property's value may not exceed $1,020,000. Rev. Proc. 2010-40.

[3] Estate Qualification

[c] The 25 Percent Test

[ii] Material participation.

Page 4-106:

Add to the end of the first paragraph of note 127.

But cf. TAM 200911009 (Nov. 24, 2009) (for purposes of determining whether a retired taxpayer materially participated in a farming activity under Section 469, the Service looks to whether Section 2032A(b)(4) or Section 2032A(b)(5) would cause the taxpayer to satisfy the Section 2032A(b)(1)(C)(ii) requirements for the real property used in the activity if the taxpayer had died during the year).

[iii] Active management.

Page 4-109:

Add to note 144.

In TAM 200911009 (Nov. 24, 2009), a ruling as to whether a retired taxpayer was deemed to materially participate in a farming activity for purposes of Section 469, the Service looked to whether Sections 2032A(b)(4) or 2032A(b)(5) would cause the taxpayer to satisfy the Section 2032A(b)(1)(C)(ii) requirements for the real property used in the activity if the taxpayer had died during the year. The Service noted that if deceased spouse materially participated in activity for five of eight years before deceased spouse's retirement and taxpayer was retired from activity at deceased spouse's death, taxpayer will satisfy the Section 2032A(b)(1)(C)(ii) material participation requirements.

[4] Real Property Qualification

Page 4-111:

Add to note 165.

In TAM 200911009 (Nov. 24, 2009), a ruling as to whether a retired taxpayer was deemed to materially participate in a farming activity for purposes of Section 469, the Service looked to whether Sections 2032A(b)(4) or 2032(A)(b)(5) would cause the taxpayer to satisfy the Section 2032A(b)(1)(C)(ii) requirements for the real property used in the activity if the taxpayer had died during the year. The Service noted that if deceased spouse materially participated in activity for five of eight years before deceased spouse's retirement and taxpayer was retired from activity at deceased spouse's death, taxpayer will satisfy the Section 2032A(b)(1)(C)(ii) material participation requirements.

[5] Valuation Methods

Page 4-112:

Add to note 171.

Priv. Ltr. Rul. 200448006 (July 19, 2004) following *Hoover.*

[a] Formula Farm Valuation

Page 4-113:

Add to note 176.

The 2003 rates are set forth in Revenue Ruling 2003-53, 2003-22 IRB 969, and range from a low of 7.19 percent (Texas district) to a high of 9.18 percent (Columbia district). The average annual effective interest rates for the five Farm Credit System Bank Chartered Territories for 2004 are set forth in Revenue Ruling 2004-63, 2004-27 IRB 6. The average annual effective rates on new loans under the Farm Credit System for 2005 are set forth in Revenue Ruling 2005-41.

The average annual effective interest rates on new Farm Credit System Bank loans to be used in computing the special-use value of farm real property under Section 3032A for the year 2007 are set forth in Revenue Ruling 2006-32. The average annual effective interest rates on new Farm Credit System Bank loans to be used in computing the special use value of farm real property under Section 2032A for the year 2007 are set forth in Revenue Ruling 2007-45. The average annual effective interest rates on new Farm Credit System Bank loans to be used in computing the special use value of farm real property under Section 2032A for the year 2008 are set forth in Revenue Ruling 2008-44, 2008-32 IRB 292.

The average annual effective interest rates on new Farm Credit System Bank loans to be used in computing the special use value of farm real property under Section 2032A for the year 2009 are set forth in Rev. Rul. 2009-21, 2009-30 IRB 162. The average annual effective interest rates on new Farm Credit System Bank loans to be used in computing the special use value of farm real property under Section 2032A for years 2010 and 2011 are set forth in Revenue Ruling 2011-17.

[6] Election and Agreement

Page 4-119:

Add to note 215.

Priv. Ltr. Rul. 201015003 (Oct. 26, 2009) (late election valid on first filed estate tax return). See Priv. Ltr. Rul. 200438036 (May 10, 2004) (estate granted extension of time to make a late special use valuation on a supplemental estate tax return for farmland that estate's attorney and accountant belatedly realized were subject to inclusion in decedent's estate); Priv. Ltr. Rul. 200513014 (Nov. 16, 2004) (tax professional failed to advise personal representative to make an election or protective election to specially value decedent's farmland); Priv. Ltr. Rul. 200523015 (Mar. 7, 2005) (estate granted an extension to file a supplemental estate tax return and perfect the Section 2032A protective election made by the accountant to specially value decedent's farmland—accountant failed to notify the executor or estate's attorney that the election had to be perfected within sixty days of the issuance of the estate tax closing letter); Priv. Ltr. Rul. 200528019 (Mar. 14, 2005) (executor unaware of availability of Section 2032A election); Priv. Ltr. Rul. 200804014 (Sept.12, 2007) (estate granted an extension of time to perfect a protective election to specially value decedent's interest in certain farm and timberlands—accountant neglected to inform the executors that the protective election had to be perfected within sixty days of receiving a closing letter from the Service).

[7] Recapture

Page 4-125:

Add to note 254 preceding the last sentence.

The Service has released the revised version of Form 706-A, United States Additional Estate Tax Return (revised January 2007). The instructions to Form 706-A note that a qualified heir may apply for an automatic six-month extension of time to file Form 706-A by filing Form 4768, Application for Extension of Time to File a Return and/or Pay U.S. Estate (and Generation-Skipping Transfer) Taxes (revised July 2008). See supra ¶ 2.02[1], note 10. The Service has released revised Form 706-A, United States Additional Estate Tax Return (revised December 2008) and instructions.

[b] Recapture Events

[i] Dispositions.

Page 4-129:

Add to note 272.

See also Priv. Ltr. Rul. 200840018 (May 13, 2008) (proposed sale of qualified conservation easement on Section 2032A property would not qualify for IRC § 2032A(c)(8) exception).

Add to note 273.

Cf. Priv. Ltr. Rul. 200608012 (Nov. 3, 2005) (conveyance of groundwater rights under qualified real property, which were not part of the property specially valued under Section 2032A, and related grant of easement on the qualified real property did not constitute a disposition of the qualified use, except as to the portion of the property specifically used for removing groundwater).

Page 4-130:

Add to note 277.

Priv. Ltr. Ruls. 201129016, 018-020 (Apr. 6, 2011) (transfer of beneficiaries' farmland interest to four limited liability companies (LLCs) for a proportionate interest in the LLCs was not a disposition).

[ii] Cessation of qualified use.

Page 4-131:

Add to note 284.

Cf. Priv. Ltr. Rul. 200608012 (Nov. 3, 2005) (lease of groundwater rights under qualified real property, which were not part of the property specially valued under Section 2032A, and related grant of easement on the qualified real property did not constitute a cessation of the qualified use, except as to the portion of the property specifically used for removing groundwater).

Add to note 285.

Priv. Ltr. Ruls. 201129016, 018-020 (Apr. 6, 2011) (lease of farm to partnership where partnership had the option of either paying a fixed sum or a percentage of the crop yield was not a cessation of qualified use since the rental payment was substantially dependent upon the farm's production).

¶ 4.05 SECTION 2033. PROPERTY IN WHICH THE DECEDENT HAD AN INTEREST

[2] Beneficial Interest

Page 4-146:

Add to note 2.

As the Tax Court stated in Estate of Fortunato v. Comm'r, TC Memo. 2010-105 (2010), the existence of a beneficial interest is determined by the facts and circumstances and an individual may be deemed to own stock in a corporation where he or she has a beneficial interest, even if no stock certificates were issued to that person. In *Fortunato*, however, although decedent had a leadership role in his brothers' company and full access to the company's coffers for personal expenses, the Court nevertheless held that decedent did not own a property interest in the company at the time of his death. The Court pointed out that the decedent never desired or intended to be a shareholder because of his criminal past and long history of creditor problems and that he had no need to accumulate wealth since he had no spouse and was estranged from his children. Decedent also had none of the financial burdens associated with equity ownership having never made any contributions or loans to the company. Moreover, there was no evidence that decedent's brothers, who owned the company, ever wanted him to become a stockholder even though they relied on his business acumen in running the company's affairs.

Add to note 3.

But see Estate of Hester, 2007 WL 703170 (WD Va. 2007), aff'd, 2008-2 USTC ¶ 60,568 (4th Cir. 2008) (per curiam), where trustee improperly transferred assets of his predeceased wife's trust to his own account and commingled them with his assets; at his death, the misappropriated assets were includible in his estate.

[a] State Law

Page 4-147:

Add to note 6 after citation to "Estate of Frazier".

, rev'd on another issue, 87 AFTR2d (RIA) 2001-2216 (9th Cir. 2001)

Add to end of note 6.

Cameron v. United States, 94 AFTR2d 2004-6489 (WD Pa. 2004) (interest in trust not included in decedent's estate under state law); M. Schneider v. United States, 94 AFTR2d 2004-7104 (ED La. 2004) (same). Estate of Gore v. Comm'r, TC Memo. 2007-169 (2007) (value of assets included in decedent's estate under Section 2033—attempted assignment of assets to FLP did not result in a completed transfer under state law since decedent did not relinquish all incidents of ownership over the assets).

[b] State Decrees

Page 4-149:

Add to note 13 after citation to Rev. Rul. 73-142.

See Priv. Ltr. Rul. 200543037 (July 12, 2005) (state court order regarding payment of estate taxes given effect because the state court had jurisdiction over the parties and the subject matter, the time for appeal had passed, and the order was issued before the time of the event giving rise to federal estate taxes).

Page 4-150:

Add to note 17.

The Service may give "proper regard" to judicial action that is consistent with applicable state law that would be applied by the highest court of that state. See Priv. Ltr. Rul. 200615025 (Dec. 19, 2005) (judicial reformation of irrevocable trust due to scrivener's error will not result in adverse estate or gift tax consequences) and Priv. Ltr. Rul. 200730015 (Apr. 5, 2007) (same).

[3] Routine Inclusions

Page 4-151:

Add to note 25.

Of course, with tangible personal property, there may be the question of whether a decedent actually owned such property. In Estate of Trompeter v. Comm'r, 97 AFTR2d 2006-1447 (9th Cir. 2006) (unpublished per curiam opinion), the court reversed the Tax Court and held that the decedent did not own thirty-one unaccounted-for gold coins due to the lack of evidence supporting the finding that the coins were in the decedent's possession.

Page 4-153:

Add at the end of note 32.

, rev'd, 320 F3d 595 (6th Cir. 2003) (holding the taxpayer had adequately explained the reasons for the changes in payment dates and other factual matters that had caused the Tax Court to conclude there was no real expectation of repayment, and remanding the case to consider whether the value of the self-cancelling installment note was less than the value of the purchased property).

[4] Income Items

Page 4-154:

In note 40 replace ¶ 4.11[6] *with* ¶ 4.11[5].

Add to note 40.

In Estate of Davenport, TC Memo. 2006-215 (2006), the tax court held that two annuities payable under a settlement contract are included in decedent's gross estate under Section 2033 and stated that it need not reach the question of whether the annuities would likewise be includible under Section 2039.

[5] Partial Interests in Property

[b] Successive Interests in Property

Page 4-159:

Add to note 57.

A will even possess a taxable interest in the property of *B* if *A* is merely given a testamentary general power of appointment over a portion of *B*'s property in *B*'s revocable trust and *A* predeceases *B*. See Private Letter Ruling 200604028 (Sept. 30, 2005), in which husband and wife each intend to amend their respective revocable living trusts and, under the proposed reformation of wife's trust, if husband predeceases her, husband will have a testamentary general power of appointment over the assets in the trust equal to his unused applicable exclusion amount. The Service ruled that, if the husband predeceased the wife, the value of wife's trust assets over which husband possessed a general power of appointment would be includible in his gross estate under Section 2041.

[7] Business Interests

[c] Limited Liability Companies

Page 4-167:

Add to note 88.

In a gift tax case involving a single-member LLC organized under New York law, where donor had not elected to treat the LLC as a corporation under the "check-the-box" regulations, transfers of LLC interests to trusts were to be valued as transfers of interests in the

LLC, subject to valuation discounts for lack of marketability and control, and not as transfers of proportionate shares of the LLC's underlying assets. Pierre v. Comm'r, 133 TC No. 2 (2009). See John A. Bogdanski, "Much Ado About (A Tax) Nothing: *Pierre v. Commissioner*," 36 Est. Plan. 38 (Dec. 2009).

¶ 4.07 SECTION 2035. ADJUSTMENTS FOR GIFTS MADE WITHIN THREE YEARS OF DECEDENT'S DEATH

[2] The Section 2035(a) Rule (the First Prong)

[b] Exceptions to Section 2035(a) Inclusion

[i] Section 2035(d): bona fide sales.

Page 4-180:

Add new note 40.1 to the penultimate sentence of the first paragraph of ¶ 4.07[2][b][i].

[40.1] In TAM 200432015 (Mar. 10, 2004), decedent and spouse formed an LLC to which decedent transferred a life insurance policy. The policy's cash surrender value was initially credited wholly to decedent's capital account, although one half of the value was subsequently credited to the wife's capital account. At the time of the transfer, decedent also changed the beneficiary on the policy from spouse to the LLC. Decedent died approximately eleven months after the transfer. The Service advised that the entire amount of the policy was includible in decedent's gross estate under Section 2035(a). The Service concluded that the Section 2035(d) exception did not apply, since decedent's transfer of the policy to the LLC did not constitute a bona fide sale for adequate and full consideration in money or money's worth. Moreover, the Service ruled that decedent's estate was not entitled to a marital deduction for the policy proceeds because the LLC was the beneficiary of the policy.

[3] The Section 2035(b) Rule (the Second Prong)

[a] The Gift Tax Gross-Up Rule

Page 4-187:

Add to note 76.

But see CCA 201020009 (Apr. 16, 2010) where the Chief Counsel's Office advised that the payment of gift tax by a nonresident/noncitizen made within three years of death under Section 2035(b) is not a transfer within the meaning of Sections 2035-2038 and is, therefore, not property that is deemed situated within the United States at the time of payment under Section 2104(b). See ¶ 6.04[2].

Add to note 78.

In Estate of O'Neal v. United States, 92 AFTR2d 2003-6648 (ND Ala. 2003), the court held that the amount paid by decedent from his separate funds for portion of decedent's spouse's gift tax liability on gifts the spouses had elected to split must be added to decedent's estate.

Page 4-188:

Add the following to the beginning of note 81.

Step-transaction analysis can, of course, cause a payment by the surviving spouse to be treated as payment by the decedent. For example, Brown v. United States, 329 F3d 664 (9th Cir. 2003), held that a husband's transfer of $1,415,732 to his wife, which she used the next day to pay gift taxes for which they had joint and several liability, was to be treated as a payment of gift tax by the husband, who died within three years of the gift.

Page 4-189:

Add at end of note 83.

and is supported by *dicta* in Estate of Armstrong v. Comm'r, 119 TC No. 13 (2002) (a case in which there was no evidence the gift payment was ever made by the donor's children who had agreed to make it). The *Armstrong* court also rejected an argument that the children's agreement to pay the tax constituted consideration that offset the amount includible under Section 2035(b).

[b] Gifts Made Within Three Years of Death

Add to note 85.

A gift completed on Date One of Year One is outside the three-year period if the decedent died on Date One of Year Four. TAM 200432016 (Mar. 10, 2004).

[4] Pre-1982 Section 2035 and Its Background

Page 4-190:

Add to note 98.

The Tax Court rejected constitutional arguments against the application of Section 2035(b) based on equal protection and due process in Estate of Armstrong v. Comm'r, 119 TC No. 13 (2002).

¶ 4.08 SECTION 2036. TRANSFERS WITH RETAINED LIFE ESTATE

[1] Excluded Transfers

[a] Sales for Full Consideration

Page 4-192:

Add to note 5.

As required by Section 7520(c)(3), the Service issued proposed, temporary and final regulations on May 7, 2009, revising Table S and Table U(1), the tables used to value annuities, interests for life or a term of years, and reversionary and remainder interests in property, to reflect the mortality experience from the 2000 census (Life Table 2000CM). Transition rules allow taxpayers to use tables based on either Life Table 90CM or Life Table 2000CM to value gift, charitable and estate transfers made on or after May 1, 2009, but before July 1, 2009, but they must use the appropriate interest rate for the month in which the valuation date falls, regardless of which table is chosen. TD 9448; REG-107845-08. Reg. §§ 1.170A-12T, 1.642(c)-6T, 1.664-4T, 20.2031-7T, 20.2032A-1T, 20.2056A-4T, 25.2512-5T, 25.2522(c)-3, 1.7520-1T, 20.7520-1T, and Reg. § 25.7520-1T . Publications 1457 and 1458 (rev. May 2009), both of which include examples for using the mortality component tables, have been released. On August 10, 2011, the Service issued final regulations that removed the temporary regulations issued in TD 9448 and adopted as final the proposed regulations issued in REG-107845-08. The only substantive change was the deletion of an example in the Section 2032 regulations which the Service anticipates including in a different regulation project under that Code section. TD 9540; Reg. §§ 1.170A-12, 1.642(c)-6 , 1.664-4, 20.2031-7, 20.2032-1, 20.2056A-4, 25.2512-5, 25.2522(c)-3, 1.7520-1, 20.7520-1, 25.7520-1.

[4] Beneficial Interests in the Decedent

[b] Right to Income

Page 4-198:

Add to note 28.

Rev. Rul. 2004-64, 2004-27 IRB 7 (the *full value* of the corpus of an otherwise defective grantor trust was includible in the grantor's gross estate even though the trust had an independent trustee where the trust or governing law requires the trust to reimburse the grantor for income taxes payable by the grantor on the trust's income. If there were not such requirement or the independent trustee had discretionary powers under the governing instrument or governing law, there would be no Section 2036(a)(1) inclusion. If the grantor was the trustee with such discretion, Section 2036(a)(1) would apply). See also text in supplement ¶ 10.01[10][e] following note 233.3.

[c] Enjoyment "Retained"

Page 4-201:

Add to note 42.

In Estate of Stewart, 2010-2 USTC ¶ 60,596 (2d Cir. 2010), the Second Circuit held that only a portion of the value of real property decedent had previously gifted to her son was includible in her gross estate as a result of an implied agreement that she would retain the economic benefits of the commercial portion of the property. The Court found there was no indication of an implied agreement that decedent would retain a substantial economic benefit from the portion of the real property that her son used as his residence. See P.N. Jones and H.N. Mitchell, "A Divided Second Circuit Fractionalizes Section 2036 in Estate of Stewart," 113 J. Tax'n 220 (Oct. 2010) and John A. Bogdanski, "Upstairs, Downstairs: Retained Interests and Estate of Stewart," 2011 Tax Notes 36-37 (Jan. 18, 2011).

Add to note 45.

Estate of Tehan v. Comm'r, TC Memo. 2005-128 (2005). Estate of Van v. Comm'r, TC Memo 2011-22 (2011) (decedent's residence included in her gross estate even though she bought it with funds provided to her by her daughter and son-in-law and notwithstanding her gratuitous transfer of the residence to her daughter and grandchildren just prior to her death). But see Estate of Riese v. Comm'r, TC Memo 2011-60 (2011) where decedent had neither executed a rental agreement nor paid rent for the six month period between termination of the qualified personal residence trust (QPRT) which held the residence and decedent's death (see, generally, ¶ 19.03[3][d]). The Tax Court, however, held that the residence was not includible in decedent's gross estate where there was evidence of decedent's intent to pay rent following termination of the QPRT.

Page 4-202:

Add to note 46.

In Estate of Stewart, 2010-2 USTC ¶ 60,596 (2d Cir. 2010), decedent and her son occupied two floors of a five-story Manhattan brownstone owned by decedent. Prior to her death, decedent transferred a 49-percent interest in the brownstone to her son but continued to collect all the rent from the commercial tenant. The Second Circuit held that only a portion of the value of the property was includible in decedent's gross estate as a result of an implied agreement that she would retain the economic benefits of the commercial portion of the property. The Court found there was no indication of an implied agreement that decedent would retain a substantial economic benefit from the portion of the real property that her son used as his residence. See P.N. Jones and H.N. Mitchell, "A Divided Second Circuit Fractionalizes Section 2036 in Estate of Stewart," 113 J. Tax'n 220 (Oct. 2010) and John A. Bogdanski, "Upstairs, Downstairs: Retained Interests and Estate of Stewart," 2011 Tax Notes 36-37 (Jan. 18, 2011).

Add to note 49 before the last sentence.

This implied agreement doctrine has been recently approved by several circuit courts who have, in some cases, disregarded family limited partnerships and related entities created by or for a decedent and included the assets contributed by the decedent to such entity in the decedent's estate. Most recently, the much anticipated Strangi v. Comm'r, 96 AFTR2d 2005-5230 (5th Cir. 2005), aff'g TC Memo. 2003-145, was decided with a set of facts that, in many ways, exemplifies the type of case the Service has found the most success in litigating. Albert Strangi, the decedent, died in 1994, but in 1993, Strangi's son-in-law, an attorney, had taken over management of Strangi's daily affairs under a power of attorney while Strangi was being treated for cancer and other health problems. About two months prior to Strangi's death, the son-in-law formed a family limited partnership (FLP) and transferred almost $10 million of Strangi's assets thereto in exchange for limited partnership interests. Strangi retained minimal liquid assets outside the FLP and, before Strangi's death, the FLP made distributions of cash to Strangi for his needs and expenses. Strangi also continued to live in the residence transferred to the FLP and, after Strangi's death, the FLP made various distributions to Strangi's estate for funeral expenses, estate administration expenses, Strangi's personal debts, specific bequests, and decedent's federal and state estate taxes. Strangi's estate tax return reported the value of the FLP interest owned by the decedent before his death and the Service issued a notice of deficiency claiming that the value of the assets Strangi had transferred to the FLP were includible in his estate. The estate appealed and the Tax Court sided with the Service. The estate appealed and the Fifth Circuit has now affirmed the Tax Court's decision, concluding that the decedent and the other shareholders of the FLP had an implied agreement that the decedent would retain the enjoyment of his property after transfer to the FLP. The court noted that the decedent's retained benefits in the assets he had transferred, including the cash distributions, the continued use of the residence, and the post-death payments, plus decedent's lack of liquid assets after the transfers were made provided strong evidence that there was an understanding that partnership assets would be used to meet the decedent's needs. The Court also held that decedent's transfers to the FLP did not satisfy the Section 2036(a) exception for bona fide sales for adequate and full consideration since the transfer did not serve a substantial business or other non-tax purpose.

The Fifth Circuit's decision in *Strangi* arrived after both the First and Third Circuit had come to the same conclusion in cases with similar facts. In Estate of Abraham v. Comm'r, 408 F3d 26 (1st Cir. 2005), aff'g TC Memo. 2004-39, cert. denied, 547 US 1178; (2006). Three partnerhips were established on behalf of the decedent, who had advanced Alzheimer's disease, by her Massachusetts guardian along with decedent's children. Under the court decree authorizing the creation of the partnerships, partnership income was to be applied first to the care of the decedent. T he First Circuit affirmed the Tax Court's ruling that decedent retained the right to the income from the partnership interests and that there was at least an implied agreement among the decedent and other partners that decedent would continue to be entitled to the partnership's income if she needed it. In Estate of Turner v. Comm'r, 382 F3d 367 (3d Cir. 2004), aff'g TC Memo. 2002-246, the decedent had transferred nearly all of his wealth into partnerships established for him within approximately two years of his death at age 97. There was evidence that at the time of the transfer an implied agreement or understanding existed among the partners that the decedent would retain the enjoyment and economic benefit of the transferred property. The court rejected the estate's argument that the transfer constituted a bona fide sale for adequate and full consideration regarding the formation of the partnerships as nothing more than a mere "recycling of value" and noting the failure of the partnerships to engage in any sort of "legitimate business operations." Accord Estate of Korby, No. 06-1201 (8th Cir. 2006), aff'g TC Memo. 2005-102 (2005); Estate of Bigelow v. Comm'r, 100 AFTR 2d 2007-6016 (9th Cir. 2007), aff'g TC Memo. 2005-65 (2005); Estate of Harper v. Comm'r, TC Memo. 2002-121 (2002). The steady drumbeat of tax court cases that find an implied agreement among the decedent and the other partners of an FLP that the decedent would retain enjoyment of property transferred to the FLP within the meaning of Section 2036(a)(1) continues. In Estate of Rosen v. Comm'r, TC Memo. 2006-115 (2006), the court noted that the FLP was not a business operated for profit, decedent's relationship to the transferred assets did not change after the transfer and that the transfer was made on the advice of counsel to minimize transfer taxes. In addition, the court held that decedent's transfer was not a bona fide sale for full and adequate consideration. Among other things, the court noted the absence of a valid, functioning business operation and that the legitimate non-tax reasons proffered by the estate for establishing the FLP were theoretical justification rather than the actual motivation for the FLP's formation, which was to avoid gift and estate tax. In Estate of Erickson v. Comm'r, TC Memo. 2007-107 (2007), decedent's daughter, acting under a power of attorney for her mother, formed an FLP along with herself and a credit shelter trust created by decedent's predeceased husband over which decedent's daughter was co-trustee. The daughter's sister and husband also contributed assets to the FLP in exchange for LP and GP interests. In finding an implied agreement among the partners that decedent would retain possession and enjoyment of the assets she had transferred to the FLP, the tax court cited (1) the significant delay between the FLP's formation and funding; (2) the distribution of funds to meet the estate's tax liabilities which the court found tantamount to making funds available to decedent or her estate as needed; (3) the FLP's limited practical effect during decedent's life; (4) significant gifts made by decedent's daughter, as decedent's agent, two days before decedent's death; and (5) decedent had been diagnosed with Alzheimer's disease at age 86, two years before the FLP's creation, and had recently moved to a supervised living facility due to deteriorating health. The court rejected the estate's argument that the bona fide sales exception was applicable to the transaction because the FLP was not formed for a "legitimate and significant nontax reason." The court cited the facts and circumstances surrounding the FLP's formation which included the many passive assets held in the FLP that were managed by the same advisors both before and after the transfers and the unilateral formation of the FLP with decedent's daughter on all sides of the transaction. See also Estate of Gore v. Comm'r, TC Memo. 2007-169 (2007) (value of assets included in decedent's estate under Section 2033 due to incomplete assignment to FLP and, in the alternative, even if transfer was complete, inclusion under Section 2036(a) because decedent retained the right of possession or enjoyment of the assets pursuant to an implied agreement that she would have continued access to the assets) and Estate of Rector, TC Memo. 2007-367 (2007) (court finding an implied agreement between the decedent and her sons that she would continue to utilize the assets transferred to the FLP for her benefit citing, among other things, the FLP agreement which gave her the ability to control the transferred assets through her status as general partner and majority owner of the FLP and the transfer of practically all of the decedent's liquid assets to the FLP; the court also held that the assets were not transferred to the FLP in a bona fide sale for adequate and full consideration because the creation of the FLP did not change the underlying assets or the potential for profit). In Estate of Hurford, TC Memo. 2008-278 (2008), the decedent transferred assets she owned as well as assets held by trusts established by her predeceased spouse to three FLPs she had established. Prior to funding the FLPs, decedent purported to sell the FLP interests held by her and the trusts to two of her children through a private annuity agreement. The Tax Court held that an implied agreement existed that the decedent would continue to enjoy the property transferred for the FLP interests and that the private annuity agreement was a sham transaction noting, among other things, that the two children who were parties to the agreement intended to follow their mother's wishes and provide for the third child. Accordingly, these transfers were not bona fide sales for adequate and full consideration and decedent's gross estate includes the assets transferred to FLP which were subsequently exchanged for the private annuity. In Estate of Jorgensen, TC Memo. 2009-66 (2009), aff'd in an unpublished per curiam memorandum opinion, No. 09-73250 (9th Cir. 2011) the court ruled that assets decedent transferred to two family limited partnerships she and her predeceased husband (and his estate) had established and funded with cash and marketable securities were included in decedent's estate under Section 2036(a)(1). The court held that the transfers were not bona fide sales because decedent did not have a legitimate and significant non-tax reason for the transfers. The court found the non-arm's length nature of the transfers and the FLP's largely untraded marketable securities were of special significance. The court also held that there was an implied agreement that the decedent would retain the economic benefit from the property citing decedent's failure to retain sufficient assets after the transfers to satisfy her desire to make gifts to family members and to pay taxes and, after her death, that FLP assets were used to pay the estate's transfer tax obligations and administrative expenses. The estate was entitled, however, to equitable recoupment of the 2003 income taxes paid by the decedent's descendants for sales of certain FLP assets. In Estate of Malkin v. Comm'r, TC Memo. 2009-212 (2009), stock was included in decedent's estate that he had previously transferred to two family limited partnerships. The court found an implied agreement that decedent would retain the present economic benefit from the stock since the other limited partners failed to object to decedent's use of the transferred stock to secure personal loans. The court also noted that the stock transfers achieved nothing more than testamentary and tax benefits and, accordingly, that the transfers were not bona fide sales for full and adequate consideration. In Estate of Turner v. Comm'r, TC Memo. 2011-209 (2011), shares of stock, certificates of deposit and cash decedent had previously transferred to a family limited partnership (FLP) were included in his estate. The Tax Court held that the transfer of assets to the FLP was not a bona fide sale for adequate and full consideration since the nontax reasons for the transfer were not legitimate and significant. The Court noted that the assets held by the FLP at the time of decedent's death were not significantly different from those transferred to the FLP and management of the assets was the same before and after the transfer so FLP was not created for the purpose of consolidating or centralizing the management of assets. In addition, unlike the situation in *Estate of Stone v. Comm'r*, disputes among decedent's children were not threatening a family business or the assets transferred so FLP was not created to address family discord. The Court also held that there was an express and implied agreement that decedent would retain the right to possess and enjoy the transferred property noting, for example, that FLP agreement expressly gave decedent the right to terminate or dissolve the partnership at any time, decedent made personal gifts from FLP funds and made loans to and payments on behalf of FLP out of his personal funds for which he received no documentation recognizing such transactions, decedent and his spouse received $2,000 per month management fee although there was no evidence as to the nature and scope of decedent's duties that would make such a fee reasonable. According to the Court, decedent treated FLP as more of an investment account and its purpose was to be an estate planning vehicle through which the family could incur significant estate tax savings.

These implied agreement cases should be viewed alongside the tax court's rulings in Estate of Stone v. Comm'r, TC Memo. 2003-309 (2003); Estate of Bongard v. Comm'r, 124 TC No. 8 (2005); Estate of Mirowski v. Comm'r, TC Memo. 2008-74 (2008) and the Fifth Circuit's recent reversal of the tax court in Kimbell v. United States, 244 F. Supp. 2d 700 (ND Tex. 2003), rev'd, 371 F3d 257 (5th Cir. 2004). In *Stone*, the tax court found that the transfers decedent made to five partnerships were motivated primarily by investment and business concerns relating to the management of decedent's assets. The partnerships had economic substance as for-profit joint enterprises and, as a result, the transfers did not amount to a mere "circuitous recycling of value" and fell within the exception to Section 2036 as bona fide sales for full and adequate consideration in money or money's worth. Similarly, the decedent in *Bongard* created an LLC as a holding company to own stock in an operating business that was owned by decedent and an irrevocable trust decedent had previously created. Soon after forming the LLC, the decedent and the trust contributed a portion of their LLC interests to an FLP created by the decedent. The tax court concluded that the formation of the LLC was the result of an arm's-length agreement and covered by the bona fide sale exception. Business advisors had recommended formation of the LLC in order to raise capital for the operating business which the court viewed as a legitimate and significant non-tax business motivation. On the other hand, the tax court determined that the transfer of the LLC units to the FLP was not a bona fide sale for adequate and full consideration because the only benefit decedent received from the transfer to the FLP was in the form of transfer tax savings. The decedent in *Estate of Mirowski* transferred to a newly formed LLC substantial cash and securities as well as her deceased husband's patents and her 51 percent interest in the patents' license agreements. Shortly thereafter, decedent made a gift of a 16 percent interest in the LLC to each of her three daughters. Three days later, decedent's foot ulcer took an unexpected turn for the worse causing her death the following day. The tax court, in holding that none of the assets owned by the LLC was includable in decedent's estate, cited *Bongard* in concluding that decedent's primary purpose in creating the LLC was based on significant nontax reasons including (1) joint management of the family's assets by her daughters and eventually her grandchildren; (2) maintenance of the bulk of the family's assets in a single pool to maximize investment opportunities; and (3) providing for each of her daughters, and eventually her grandchildren, on an equal basis. The court also held that the LLC's operating agreement was not an express agreement that decedent would retain possession or enjoyment of the transferred assets since decedent, as general manager and majority member, lacked the authority to determine the timing and amount of LLC distributions. Importantly, after decedent's transfers to the LLC, she retained a sufficient amount of personal assets to continue her current standard of living. Accordingly, the court further held that there was no implied agreement that the decedent would retain the right to enjoyment of the transferred assets. In *Kimbell*, the Fifth Circuit held that the decedent's transfer of assets to an FLP fell within the bona fide sale for full and adequate consideration exception to Section 2036. In its ruling, the court noted the tax court's decision in *Stone* which held that the bona fide sale exception to Section 2036(a)(1) was met in a case that involved an operating business. The court then distinguished cases in which the tax court had ruled that formation of the partnership was a mere recycling of value by pointing out that none of those cases involved an operating business. In Estate of Shurtz v. Comm'r, TC Memo. 2010-21 (2010), decedent created an FLP over five years before her death in order to consolidate the interests held by multiple family members in a timberland company in Mississippi. In finding that the transfer of the decedent's assets to the FLP was a bona fide sale, the Tax Court, citing its holding in Bongard, noted the legitimate nontax reasons for creating the FLP, i.e., facilitating the active management of the transferred assets and protecting those assets from potential litigants. The court also held that decedent's interest in the FLP, received in exchange for her interest in the timberland company, represented adequate and full consideration because the participants in the FLP received interests proportionate to the value each contributed and the respective contributed assets were properly credited to the transferors' capital accounts. Accordingly, the fair market value of the decedent's interest in the FLP was includible in her estate rather than the value of the transferred assets.

At this juncture, a good question might be whether the transfer of assets by a decedent to an FLP that did not include nearly all of the decedent's wealth and which left decedent with substantial assets to live on outside of the partnership would pass muster with the court if the assets transferred to the FLP consisted of marketable securities and did not include an operating business. In Estate of Schutt, TC Memo. 2005-126 (2005), for example, decedent was the surviving spouse of a wealthy member of the DuPont family and, in 1998 and while in poor health, he participated in forming two Delaware Business Trusts (DBTs) taxable as partnerships. These DBTs were funded exclusively with two publicly traded stocks, DuPont and Exxon, almost half of which were transferred to the DBTs by the decedent. The other participants were various trusts established by his spouse and father-in-law over which decedent had the power to prevent diversification. The decedent's alleged motivation for creating the DBTs was to prevent future sales of these stocks by family members and these various trusts. There was substantial evidence that decedent had long believed that his "buy-and-hold" investment strategy was in the best interests of the family. The tax court discussed, among other things, the *Turner* and *Bongard* decisions and noted the estate's position was that the DBTs were formed in furtherance and protection of decedent's family's wealth by providing for centralized management of the family's holdings in DuPont and Exxon stock during his lifetime and, to the extent possible, after his death. The court concluded that there was considerable evidence that decedent genuinely desired that the family's holdings in these stocks would not be diversified which, to the court, constituted a significant and legitimate non-tax purpose for formation of the DBTs. Although the decision in *Schutt* might be viewed as instructive, the court repeatedly makes reference in the opinion to the "unique" facts of the case and it likely has little precedential value. Better facts make Estate of Miller, TC Memo. 2009-119 (2009), a much more interesting case. In *Miller*, decedent created an FLP two years after her husband's death with the stated purpose of continuing her husband's investment strategies (he was a stock charter) and, in 2002, she funded the FLP with approximately 77 percent of her assets. Their son, who was familiar with her husband's strategies, was named as the general partner and the court notes that he then spent forty hours per week actively trading and managing the FLP's assets whereas, before the transfer, the securities had remained idle. The Tax Court, citing *Mirowski* and *Schutt*, found that decedent's 2002 contribution came within the scope of the bona fide sale exception to Section 2036 because management of the securities in accordance with decedent's husband's investment strategies was a legitimate non-tax reason. Importantly, after the contribution, decedent was left with sufficient assets to cover her living expenses and estate tax liability. Not so, however, with contributions decedent made in 2003 after she had broken her hip and three weeks before she died. After the 2003 contributions, the court held that decedent continued to retain possession and enjoyment of the transferred assets since she no longer retained enough wealth to pay her estate tax liability. Accordingly, decedent's 2003 contributions were includible in her estate at their undiscounted fair market value. In Keller v. United States, 2009-2 USTC ¶ 60,579 (SD Tex. 2009), decedent formed an FLP and intended to fund it with $250 million in bonds located in two trusts created at her predeceased husband's death. Although all appropriate documents had been filed with the state, decedent died prior to the FLP's funding. The Tax Court noted, however, that under applicable (Texas) law "ownership of property intended to be a partnership asset is not determined by legal title, but rather by the intention of the parties," quoting Church v. United States, 2000-1 USTC ¶ 60,369 (WD Tex. 2000), aff'd without an opinion, 268 F3d 1063 (5th Cir. 2001), and held that the bonds were FLP property at decedent's death. In addition, the court found that the transfer of bonds to the FLP was a bona fide sale for full and adequate consideration under Sections 2036 and 2038. The decedent's motive, according to the court, was not the avoidance of tax, but the protection of family assets from depletion through divorce which was considered a legitimate business purpose. Legal formalities for the FLP had been met, including the FLP's capital accounts, and decedent did not retain possession or enjoyment of the FLP assets because she kept over $100 million in assets outside of the FLP. In Estate of Murphy, 2009-2 USTC ¶ 60,583 (WD Ark. 2009), the decedent created an FLP and an LLC (which served as general partner of the FLP) with the active support of two of his four children and funded the FLP and LLC with shares in three publicly traded corporations. Decedent's contributions totaled 41 percent of his net worth and he retained approximately $130 million in assets outside of the FLP. The court held that the assets in the FLP and LLC were not includible in decedent's gross estate because decedent's contribution fell within the bona fide sale exception of Section 2036. The court noted decedent's purpose for creating the FLP was to pool certain family assets, protect the assets from dissipation and allow for central management which were legitimate nontax reasons. In addition, the court observed that decedent retained sufficient assets outside of the FLP, he did not mingle these assets with FLP assets and the FLP assets were actively managed through decedent's son's position on the board of directors of the three corporations. Finally, the court noted that the contributions were credited to the capital accounts and each partner was entitled to his or her share, upon termination, as determined by the capital accounts. Accordingly, only the discounted value of decedent's interest in the FLP and LLC was includible in his gross estate. In Estate of Black, 133 TC No. 15 (2009), the decedent created an FLP, along with his son and trusts for his grandchildren, when decedent was still in good health and eight years prior to his death. The FLP was funded with stock in an insurance company that went public several years after decedent formed the FLP. Decedent had originally acquired the stock during his tenure at the company and the parties to the FLP received proportionate partnership interests in exchange for the transferred shares. In creating the FLP, decedent wanted to implement his buy and hold philosophy for the family's stockholdings and intended to prevent his grandchildren from selling the shares he had transferred to them in trust and to protect his son's shares from potential claims incident to divorce. After the FLP's formation, decedent retained approximately $4 million in assets outside of his FLP interests. The Tax Court held that the creation of the FLP was the result of an arm's length transaction and that the decedent received an interest in the FLP that was for adequate and full consideration. The court explained that decedent had a legitimate and significant nontax reason for forming the FLP and that the sale of the shares to the FLP was for adequate and full consideration because the partners received FLP interests proportionate to the value of the assets contributed. The court also noted that the respective contributed assets were properly credited to the transferor's capital accounts.

The Service has issued Appeals Settlement Guidelines: Family Limited Partnerships and Family Limited Liability Corporations, effective October 20, 2006, which address, among other things, estate inclusion of assets held in the entity pursuant to IRC Sections 2036 or 2038. The settlement guidelines provide the positions of both the government and the taxpayer and includes a discussion of the applicable case law with respect to each issue the Service addresses. The full text of the settlement guidelines is available on the Service's website.

Page 4-203:

Add a new paragraph following the last sentence of ¶ 4.08[4][c].

Another issue is whether a decedent has retained the right to income from property under Section 2036(a) if the decedent had the power to remove the property from the trust, even in a nonfiduciary capacity, but is required to transfer property of equivalent value to the trust. The Service has ruled that such a power is not a retained right to the income from the property under Section 2036.[53.1]

[53.1] Rev. Rul. 2008-22, 2008-16 IRB 796. See infra ¶ 4.08[6][a] n. 76. Cf. IRC § 675(4)(C) which treats such a power as a power triggering the grantor trust provisions under the income tax. Under the facts of the revenue ruling, the grantor must certify that the properties are of an equivalent value, and under local law the trustee of the trust must have a fiduciary obligation to ensure that the properties are of equivalent value. The revenue ruling thus provides an effective method to create a "defective" grantor trust. Priv. Ltr. Rul. 200944002 (July 15, 2009) (grantor's transfer into irrevocable trust deemed complete for gift tax purposes despite retention by grantor of power to substitute trust assets and retained substitution power will not result in inclusion of transferred assets in grantor's estate). See discussion of "defective" grantor trusts at ¶ 10.01[10][e] text accompanying note 233.3.

[5] Control Over Others' Interests

[a] Right to Designate Retained Indirectly

Page 4-204:

Add to note 56.

In Private Letter Rulings 2003500090 and 200350010 (Aug. 25, 2003), the Service evaluated a proposed gift by an irrevocable trust established by donor to a charitable foundation in which donor is sole director. The Service concluded that the proposed gift will not cause the corpus of the trust or the amount distributed to the foundation to be included in donor's estate under Section 2036 if the gift is conditioned on the foundation's agreement to segregate the gift and any income earned thereby from the foundation's other assets and to amend the foundation's bylaws to provide that neither the donor nor any related or subordinate party to donor shall vote on decisions concerning whether and when to distribute such segregated amounts. Priv. Ltr. Rul. 200523003 (Mar. 8, 2005) (where grantor of trusts is shareholder of corporate trustee, the firewall provisions in the corporate bylaws and trustee provisions precluded the grantor from having the required dominion and control for inclusion in grantor's gross estate under Section 2036). See also Priv. Ltr. Rul. 200548035 (Aug. 2, 2005) (trustee provisions in various family trusts which restricted grantors from directly participating in discretionary distribution decisions in combination with a "firewall" provision in the bylaws of a family-owned trust company prevented inclusion of the trusts in the gross estates of the trusts' grantors on the appointment of the family-owned trust company as trustee of the family trusts) and Private Letter Ruling 200531004 (Apr. 21, 2005) (because of firewalls and limitations, trust grantor's status as shareholder of corporation will not cause trust to be included in grantor's estate upon corporation's appointment as trustee and its exercise of discretionary distribution powers).

In Notice 2008-63, 2008-31 IRB, the Service proposed a revenue ruling that would allow families to use private trust companies as trustees of family trusts without adverse gift, estate or generation-skipping transfer tax consequences for either the grantor(s) of the trust or trust beneficiaries in carefully defined situations.

[c] Right to Designate Who Benefits

Page 4-206:

Add to note 64.

In Strangi v. Comm'r, TC Memo. 2003-145, aff'd, 96 AFTR2d 2005-5230 (5th Cir. 2005), the Tax Court held on remand (in the alternative to a Section 2036(a)(1) holding) that the ability of a 99 percent limited partner, who also owned 47 percent of the corporate general partner, to combine with two of four other shareholders of the corporate general partner and cause the partnership's dissolution and liquidation was the ability to determine who had possession and benefit of the property. However, in a footnote in the Fifth Circuit's opinion, the court declined to rule in the Section 2036(a)(2) issue because it had already determined that the transferred property was properly includible in the decedent's estate under Section 2036(a)(1). But see Kimbell v. United States, 371 F3d 257 (5th Cir. 2004), discussed infra note 69. The remand of the *Strangi* case is discussed in Gans & Blattmachr, "*Strangi*: A Critical Analysis and Planning Suggestions," 100 Tax Notes 1153 (Sept. 1, 2003). In Estate of Turner v. Comm'r, TC Memo. 2011-209 (2011), shares of stock, certificates of deposit and cash decedent had previously transferred to a family limited partnership (FLP) were included in his estate pursuant to Section 2036(a)(2) due to decedent's retained right, by both express and implied agreement, to designate which person or persons could possess or enjoy the property, or the income therefrom.

Page 4-207:

Add to note 69.

The District Court's ruling in the *Kimbell* case, which was reversed by the Fifth Circuit, 244 F. Supp. 2d 700 (ND Tex. 2003), rev'd, 371 F3d 257 (5th Cir. 2004), discussed supra note 49, relied on the *Alexander* case to conclude that Section 2036(a)(2) applied where a decedent holding a 99 percent limited partnership interest could remove and replace a general partner and thereby alter the time of payment of the income.

[6] Indirect Interests or Controls

[a] Settlor Trustee

Page 4-208:

Add to end of first paragraph of note 76.

See also Priv. Ltr. Rul. 200603040 (Oct. 24, 2005) and Priv. Ltr. Rul. 200606006 (Oct. 24, 2005) (citing Estate of Jordahl v. Comm'r, 65 TC 92 (1975), acq. 1977-1 CB 1, the Service ruled that grantor's retention of the power to substitute nontrust property for trust property may only be exercised in a fiduciary capacity and will not cause grantor trust's assets to be included in grantor's gross estate under Section 2036). In Revenue Ruling 2008-22, 2008-16 IRB 796, the Service cited *Estate of Jordahl v. Comm'r* and ruled that a grantor's retained power, exercisable in a nonfiduciary capacity, to acquire trust property by substituting property of equivalent value will not, by itself, cause inclusion in the grantor's estate under Section 2036, as long as the trustee has a fiduciary duty (under the trust instrument or local law) to ensure that the grantor complies with the terms of the power. In exercising this fiduciary duty, the trustee must ensure that the properties the grantor acquires and substitutes are, in fact, of equivalent value and that the grantor must not be able to exercise the power in a manner that can shift benefits among trust beneficiaries. Priv. Ltr. Rul. 200842007 (June 24, 2008) (grantor's substitution of stock he personally owns for assets of equal value held in grantor trust he created, and under which he holds a power of substitution, will not cause trust property to be included in grantor's estate).

Priv. Ltr. Rul. 200944002 (July 15, 2009) (grantor's transfer into irrevocable trust deemed complete for gift tax purposes despite retention by grantor of power to substitute trust assets and retained substitution power will not result in inclusion of transferred assets in grantor's estate).

[c] Rent Paid by Transferor

Page 4-211:

Add to note 86.

See also Estate of Disbrow v. Comm'r, TC Memo. 2006-34 (2006), where the tax court applied Section 2036(a)(1) in holding that the fair market value of decedent's residence, which she had transferred to a family partnership seven years prior to her death, was includible in her gross estate. The court noted that, although there were annual lease agreements between the decedent and the partnership, the rental amounts stated therein were significantly below the residence's fair rental value. In addition, notwithstanding the lease agreements, the court stated that there was an implied understanding between the decedent and the partnership that she would continue possession and enjoyment of the residence following its transfer and that the lease agreements were a subterfuge to hide the testamentary nature of the transfer. The court looked to the following indices that such an implied agreement existed: (1) the partnership was not a business operated for profit, but was merely a device to remove the residence from the decedent's estate; (2) neither the decedent nor the partnership treated the decedent as a tenant; (3) decedent was almost 72 and in ill health when she transferred the residence to the partnership; and (4) one of the partners admitted that the members of the partnership wanted the decedent to reside in the home as long as she could; (5) decedent transferred the residence to the partnership on advice of counsel in order to minimize estate tax.

[7] Transfer by the Decedent

Page 4-216:

Add to note 114.

See Priv. Ltr. Rul. 201116006 (Dec. 27, 2010), in which a former spouse's transfer of cash to an irrevocable trust, made in settlement of the divorcing parties' property and marital rights, with decedent receiving all trust income for life and holding a limited power of appointment to appoint the trust remainder to her surviving issue, constituted a transfer for full and adequate consideration under Section 2516. A taxable gift does occur upon the transfer of the trust remainder to decedent's surviving issue, upon decedent's failure to exercise power of appointment, with former spouse as the transferor. As a result, the value of the trust remainder is not included in decedent's gross estate under Section 2036 because the former spouse transferred the cash to the trust in satisfaction of his spousal support obligation.

[a] Indirect Transfers

Page 4-217:

Add to note 121.

A similar analysis was applied to include the assets of a supplemental needs trust in the estate of the deceased lifetime beneficiary where the trust was created under a court order to hold a settlement payment arising from a tort claim. Priv. Ltr. Rul. 200240018 (June 24, 2002).

[d] Reciprocal Trusts

Page 4-226:

Add to note 163.

Priv. Ltr. Rul. 200426008 (Mar. 10, 2004) (trusts were different in several respects and were not interrelated).

[8] Amount to Be Included

Page 4-227:

Add to note 167.

In Estate of Stewart, 2010-2 USTC ¶ 60,596 (2d Cir. 2010), the Second Circuit held that only a portion of the value of real property decedent had previously gifted to her son was includible in her gross estate as a result of an implied agreement that she would retain the economic benefits of the commercial portion of the property. The Court found there was no indication of an implied agreement that decedent would retain a substantial economic benefit from the portion of the real property that her son used as his residence and directed the Tax Court, on remand, to follow the approach set out in Revenue Ruling 79-109, 1979-1 CB 297, to determine the apportionment of the son's interest. See P.N. Jones and H.N. Mitchell, "A Divided Second Circuit Fractionalizes Section 2036 in Estate of Stewart," 113 J. Tax'n 220 (Oct. 2010) and John A. Bogdanski, "Upstairs, Downstairs: Retained Interests and Estate of Stewart," 2011 Tax Notes 36-37 (Jan. 18, 2011).

Delete the last two paragraphs of note 168.

Add the following new paragraph to the text following note 168.

The amount of inclusion is more difficult to compute where the decedent has retained an annuity interest,[168.1] a unitrust interest,[168.2] a pooled income fund[168.3] or retains the use of an asset for a term of years[168.4] and predeceases the term of years. The Service has historically maintained that Section 2036(a)(1) applies in such situations.[168.5] The Service has finalized regulations to determine the amount of Section 2036 inclusion in such circumstances.[168.6] The amount of inclusion is the portion of the trust corpus valued at the date of the decedent's death (or alternate valuation date) necessary to yield the annual payment (or use) using the appropriate Section 7520 interest rate in effect at the decedent's death (or alternate valuation date).[168.7] The regulations provide illustrations of the rules[168.8] and also provide that Section 2039, although potentially applicable, will not be applied in such circumstances.[168.9] Subsequent to the issue of these final regulations, the Service issued new proposed regulations which address the method for determining the amount of inclusion where

---

[168.1] See ¶¶ 5.05[5][a], 19.03[3][b][i].

[168.2] See ¶¶ 5.05[5][b], 19.03[3][b][i].

[168.3] See ¶ 5.05[5][c].

[168.4] See ¶ 19.03[3][d]. See also Reg. § 20.2036-1(c)(1)(ii) Ex. 2.

[168.5] Rev. Rul. 76-273, 1976-2 CB 268 (involving a CRUT) and Rev. Rul. 82-105, 1982-1 CB 133 (involving a CRAT); Priv. Ltr. Rul. 9412036 (Dec. 23, 1993) (GRUT); FSA 200036012 (May 25, 2000) (GRAT). See ¶ 19.03[3][b], note 120. Cf. ¶ 5.06[8][d], note 344. The rulings are now obsolete. It might be questioned whether there is a retention of "the income" generated by the corpus in such circumstances. See Estate of Becklenberg v. Comm'r, 273 F2d 297 (7th Cir. 1959); Estate of Bergan v. Comm'r, 1 TC 543 (1943), acq. 1943 CB 2. Because the transferred property generates the annuity or unitrust amount and a flat dollar amount is treated as income in establishing the value of the remainder, the Treasury's position seems proper.

[168.6] Regs. §§ 20.2036-1(c), 20.2039-1(e). The regulations are effective on or after July 14, 2008. Regs. §§ 20.2036-1(c)(3), 20.2039-1(f). For an article discussing final regulations, see Katzenstein, "Regs Clarify Estate Tax Inclusion of Trust Property, but Issues Remain" 36 Est. Plan., No. 6 at 3 (2009). See Blattmachr, Gans & Zeydel, "Final Regulations on Estate Tax Inclusion for GRATs and Similar Arrangements Leave Open Issues," 109 J. Tax'n 217 (2008); Herpe & Hunter, "Proposed Regulations Clarify Includibility of Grantor Retained Annuity Trust in Grantor's Gross Estate," 33 ACTEC J. 131 (2007).

[168.7] Reg. § 20.2036-1(c)(2)(i).

[168.8] See Reg. § 20.2036-1(c)(1)(ii) Ex. 2 (involving a personal residence retained for a term of years); Reg. § 20.2036-1(c)(2)(iii), Ex. 1 (involving a CRAT for a term of years or for life); Ex. 2 (involving a GRAT); Ex. 3 (involving a CRUT for a term of years or for life); Ex. 4 (involving a GRIT); Ex. 5 (involving a pooled income fund); Ex. 6 (involving a QPRT).

[168.9] Regs. §§ 20.2039-1(a), 20.2039-1(e).

the deceased grantor retains an interest that increases annually,[168.10] and they clarify the amount of inclusion if the decedent retained a right to receive the annual payment after the death of the current recipient.[168.11]

[168.10] Prop. Reg. § 20.2036-1(c)(2)(ii). The amount of inclusion is the sum of (1) the amount necessary to generate the payment due to the decedent at death and (2) the amount necessary to generate sufficient income to pay the increase for each succeeding year. See Prop. Reg. § 20.2036-1(c)(2)(iii), Ex. 7 (involving a graduated GRAT).

[168.11] Prop. Reg. § 20.2036-1(b)(1)(ii). See Prop. Reg. § 20.2036-1(c)(1)(ii), Ex. 1. The proposed regulations are generally applicable to the estates of decedents dying on or after the date the regulations are published as final.

The sentence beginning with Moreover, if, *starts a new paragraph.*

¶ 4.10 SECTION 2038. REVOCABLE TRANSFERS

[4] Power in the Decedent

[a] Power to Revoke

Page 4-254:

Add to text following the last sentence on page 4-254.

But a power to recover the trust property is not a power to revoke if the grantor, even in a nonfiduciary capacity, is required to transfer substitute property of an equivalent value to the trust.[23.1]

[23.1] Rev. Rul. 2008-22, 2008-16 IRB 796. See infra ¶ 4.10[4][c] n. 40.

[b] Power to Alter or Amend

Page 4-256:

Add to note 30.

In Private Letter Rulings 2003500090 and 200350010 (Aug. 25, 2003), the Service evaluated a proposed gift by an irrevocable trust established by donor to a charitable foundation in which donor is sole director. The Service concluded that the proposed gift will not cause the corpus of the trust or the amount distributed to the foundation to be included in donor's estate under Section 2038 if the gift is conditioned on the foundation's agreement to segregate the gift and any income earned thereby from the foundation's other assets and to amend the foundation's bylaws to provide that neither the donor nor any related or subordinate party to donor shall vote on decisions concerning whether and when to distribute such segregated amounts. Priv. Ltr. Rul. 200523003 (Mar. 8, 2005) (where grantor of trusts is shareholder of corporate trustee, the firewall provisions in the corporate bylaws and trustee provisions precluded the grantor from having the required dominion and control for inclusion in grantor's gross estate under Section 2038). See also Priv. Ltr. Rul. 200548035 (Aug. 2, 2005) (trustee provisions in various family trusts which restricted grantors from directly participating in discretionary distribution decisions in combination with a "firewall" provision in the bylaws of a family-owned trust company prevented inclusion of the trusts in the gross estates of the trusts' grantors on the appointment of the family-owned trust company as trustee of the family trusts).

In Notice 2008-63, 2008-31 IRB, the Service proposed a revenue ruling that would allow families to use private trust companies as trustees of family trusts without adverse gift, estate or generation-skipping transfer tax consequences for either the grantor(s) of the trust or trust beneficiaries in carefully defined situations.

[c] Administrative Powers

Page 4-258:

Add to note 40.

See also Priv. Ltr. Rul. 20603040 (Oct. 24, 2005) and Priv. Ltr. Rul. 200606006 (Oct. 24, 2005) (citing Estate of Jordahl v. Comm'r, 65 TC 92 (1975), acq. 1977-1 CB 1, the Service ruled that grantor's retention of the power to substitute nontrust property for trust property may only be exercised in a fiduciary capacity and will not cause grantor trust's assets to be included in grantor's gross estate under Section 2038). In Revenue Ruling 2008-22, 2008-16 IRB 796, the Service cited *Estate of Jordahl v. Comm'r* and ruled that a grantor's retained power, exercisable in a nonfiduciary capacity, to acquire trust property by substituting property of equivalent value will not, by itself, cause inclusion in the grantor's estate under Section 2038, as long as the trustee has a fiduciary duty (under the trust instrument or local law) to ensure that the grantor complies with the terms of the power. In exercising this fiduciary duty, the trustee must ensure that the properties the grantor acquires and substitutes are, in fact, of equivalent value and that the grantor must not be able to exercise the power in a manner that can shift benefits among trust beneficiaries. Priv. Ltr. Rul. 200842007 (June 24, 2008) (grantor's substitution of stock he personally owns for assets of equal value held in grantor trust he created, and under which he holds a power of substitution, will not cause trust property to be included in grantor's estate).

Priv. Ltr. Rul. 200944002 (July 15, 2008) (grantor's transfer into irrevocable trust deemed complete for gift tax purposes despite retention by grantor of power to substitute trust assets and retained substitution power will not result in inclusion of transferred assets in grantor's estate).

[g] Power in "Whatever Capacity"

Page 4-261:

Add to note 56.

See Priv. Ltr. Rul. 200531004 (Apr. 21, 2005) (no unqualified power of removal).

[6] Power Exercisable Only With Another

Page 4-265:

Add to note 70.

Private Letter Ruling 200247037 (Aug. 19, 2002) applied this rule where a division of a trust would have been ineffective without the consent of all parties holding an interest in a trust. In Private Letter Ruling 200919008 (Jan. 12, 2009), court-ordered modifications to administrative provisions of a series of irrevocable trusts, petitioned by the grantor, did not result in the inclusion of trust assets in the grantor's gross estate since they were made pursuant to state statute and with the consent of all beneficiaries.

¶ 4.11 SECTION 2039. ANNUITIES

Page 4-278:

Delete See FSA 200036012 (May 25, 2000) *in note 3.*

Add to note 3.

However, under Regulations Section 20.2039-1(e), Section 2039 will not be applicable if a decedent created a trust and retained the right to use property or an annuity, unitrust or other income interest in the trust (other than a trust constituting an employee benefit) where Section 2036 applies. See text in ¶ 4.08[8] accompanying notes 168.1–168.9. The regulations are effective on or after July 14, 2008. Reg. § 20.2039-1(f).

[3] Qualifications

[a] Contract or Agreement

Page 4-281:

Delete the last two sentences of note 14.

[4] Amount to Be Included

[a] Valuation

Page 4-285:

Add after the second sentence of the first paragraph of note 40.

As required by Section 7520(c)(3), the Service issued proposed, temporary and final regulations on May 7, 2009, revising Table S and Table U(1), the tables used to value annuities, interests for life or a term of years, and reversionary and remainder interests in property, to reflect the mortality experience from the 2000 census (Life Table 2000CM). Transition rules allow taxpayers to use tables based on either Life Table 90CM or Life Table 2000CM to value gift, charitable and estate transfers made on or after May 1, 2009, but before July 1, 2009, but they must use the appropriate interest rate for the month in which the valuation date falls, regardless of which table is chosen. TD 9448; REG-107845-08. Reg. §§ 1.170A-12T, 1.642(c)-6T, 1.664-4T, 20.2031-7T, 20.2032A-1T, 20.2056A-4T, 25.2512-5T, 25.2522(c)-3, 1.7520-1T, 20.7520-1T, and Reg. § 25.7520-1T. Publications 1457 and 1458 (rev. May 2009), both of which include examples for using the mortality component tables, have been released.

In note 40, the second paragraph, replace the last sentence with the following.

In Estate of Gribauskas v. Comm'r, 342 F3d 85 (2d Cir. 2003), the Second Circuit reversed the tax court and concluded that a departure from the tables is allowed in valuing lottery winnings where the tables produce a substantially unrealistic and unreasonable approach. Accord Estate of Shackleford v. United States, 262 F3d 1068 (9th Cir. 2001) (reducing the values under the tables for lottery winnings to reflect a lack of marketability due to restrictions on transferability). Balancing the Second and Ninth Circuit's rulings, however, are the rulings of the Fifth and Sixth Circuits. In Estate of Cook v. Comm'r, 349 F3d 850 (5th Cir. 2003), the Fifth Circuit affirmed the holding of the Tax Court and treated the lottery prize as a private annuity and concluded that the valuation tables produced a result that was not so unreasonable or unrealistic as to justify resort to an alternative valuation method. Siding with the Fifth Circuit, the Sixth Circuit reversed the Tax Court in Negron v. US, Dkt. No. 07-4460 (6th Cir. 2009), and held that the annuity tables apply in valuing the remaining lottery payments notwithstanding the fact that the tables produced a value higher than the lump sum the estates actually received from the State of Ohio. Accord Estate of Donovan v. United States, 95 AFTR2d 2005-2131 (D. Mass. 2005), where the court noted that under the Second and Ninth Circuit holdings, nonmarketability should be factored into the valuation of such interests, but under the Fifth Circuit holding such a reduction would not be appropriate; and Davis v. United States, No. 1:04-CV-00273 (DNH 2007), where the district court concluded that any discount applicable to the nonmarketability of the lottery payments was not enough to render the amount determined by reference to the annuity tables "unrealistic and unreasonable." The *Davis* court distinguished *Shackleford* and *Gribauskas* on the basis that the value of the lottery payments in those cases was at least 25 percent less than the value determined by reference to the annuity tables.

In Estate of Davenport, TC Memo. 2006-215 (2006), the Tax Court held that two annuities payable under a settlement contract are included in decedent's gross estate under Section 2033 and stated that it need not reach the question of whether the annuities would likewise be includable under Section 2039. Valuation of the annuities is determined by using the Section 7520 tables. In Anthony v. United States, No. 07-30089 (5th Cir. 2008), a case involving actual nontransferable private annuities established for the decedent pursuant to a structured settlement agreement after the decedent had sustained injuries in an automobile accident, the Fifth Circuit adopted the rationale of its *Cook* decision by valuing the estate's right to receive payments from the annuities for estate tax purposes by using the Section 7520 annuity tables. It held that the annuities were not a "restricted beneficial interest" thereby governed by Regulations Section 20.7520-3(b), which precludes the use of the annuity tables, and that the nontransferability of the annuities did not make use of the annuity tables "unrealistic or unreasonable."

[5] Private Annuities

Page 4-289:

Add new paragraph to note 54.

The Service has issued proposed regulations under Sections 72 and 1001 that would eliminate the income tax advantages of transferring appreciated property in exchange for a private annuity by causing the transferor's gain to be recognized in the year the transaction is effected rather than as payments are received. Prop. Reg. §§ 1.72-6(e), 1.1001-1(j). The proposed regulations would apply for transactions entered into after October 18, 2006, with certain transactions effected before April 19, 2007, subject to the current rules. In addition, the Service proposes to declare Revenue Ruling 69-74 obsolete effective contemporaneously with the effective date of these regulations. REG-141901-05.

[6] Exempt Annuities

Page 4-290:

Add to note 60.

In Sherrill v. United States, 97 AFTR2d 2006-735 (ND Ind. 2006), the proceeds of a decedent's individual retirement account, holding funds rolled over from a lump-sum distribution from an employer pension plan when the decedent retired in 1981, did not qualify for exclusion under the transition rules of the Tax Reform Act of 1984 or the transition rules of the Tax Reform Act of 1986. Accordingly, these proceeds were includible in decedent's estate under Section 2039(a).

¶ 4.12 SECTION 2040. JOINT INTERESTS

[9] Termination Prior to Death

Page 4-308:

Add to note 73.

In Estate of Goldberg, TC Memo. 2010-26 (2010), decedent had earlier transferred real property to him and his spouse and, after the death of his predeceased spouse, decedent (in his capacity as executor of his wife's estate) attempted to transfer the spouse's interest in the properties to a trust. When decedent died, only decedent's portion of the properties was included in his gross estate. The Tax Court held, however, that a transfer of property to a married couple is presumed to be a tenancy of the entirety in accordance with applicable state law. Since a tenancy by the entirety is not a divisible interest, decedent's estate included the entire value of the real property.

¶ 4.13 SECTION 2041. POWERS OF APPOINTMENT

[2] Powers Within Section 2041

Page 4-314:

Add to note 6.

Private Letter Ruling 200229013 (Apr. 9, 2002) ruled that the beneficiaries of a trust who also became the sole shareholders of a corporation which controlled the trust company that was to serve as trustee of the trust did not have a general power of appointment. The beneficiaries renounced their right to participate in any decisions regarding discretionary distributions to beneficiaries and under the bylaws of the controlled trust company one to three directors, who would be independent vis-a-vis the beneficiaries and the trust grantor, were always to serve as the members of the distribution committee.

In Private Letter Ruling 200734010 (Apr. 19, 2007), the board of directors of a corporation with the power to appoint successor trustees for a trust voted to appoint as successor trustee a bank or trust company designated by the trust beneficiaries. The bank or trust company must be qualified to accept trusts, not related to or subordinate to any trust beneficiary, engaged in the trust business for at least ten years and have assets under management of at least $1 billion. Although the trust beneficiaries had the power to remove and appoint successor trustees, such power was restricted and was similar to that described in Revenue Ruling 95-58. Accordingly, the Service ruled that the board's resolution did not cause the beneficiaries to have a general power of appointment.

In Notice 2008-63, 2008-31 IRB, the Service proposed a revenue ruling that would allow families to use private trust companies as trustees of family trusts without adverse gift, estate or generation-skipping transfer tax consequences for either the grantor(s) of the trust or trust beneficiaries in carefully defined situations.

[b] Powers That Overlap Interests

Page 4-316:

Add to note 14.

TAM 200532049 (Mar. 23, 2005) (ruling that predeceased spouse's interest in residence which decedent and spouse had earlier conveyed to their daughter with a reservation of a life estate in the property for their "own lives" caused inclusion in decedent's estate under IRC § 2041(a)(2)).

[3] Definition of "General Power"

Page 4-318:

Add to note 19.

TAM 200907025 (Oct. 28, 2008) (although decedent could receive from trust only income in the trustee's discretion during decedent's life and trust continued after decedent's death, trust did not restrict decedent's testamentary appointment power and decedent's exercise of that power in a pre-1942 trust caused the entire value of the trust to be includible in decedent's estate).

Add to note 20.

Priv. Ltr. Rul. 200548035 (Aug. 2, 2005) (trustee provisions in various family trusts which restricted beneficiaries of the trusts from directly participating in discretionary distribution decisions in combination with a "firewall" provision in the bylaws of a family-owned trust company precluded the beneficiaries from having the power to affect the beneficial enjoyment of the trust property within the meaning of Section 2041).

Priv. Ltr. Rul. 200748008 (July 25, 2007) (under the terms of the trust established by parents, trust beneficiaries do not have a general power of appointment over trust assets due to their potential role as trust protector or as trust's investment advisor).

In Notice 2008-63, 2008-31 IRB, the Service proposed a revenue ruling that would allow families to use private trust companies as trustees of family trusts without adverse gift, estate or generation-skipping transfer tax consequences for either the grantor(s) of the trust or trust beneficiaries in carefully defined situations.

Priv. Ltr. Rul. 200832015 (Mar. 26, 2008) (testamentary power of appointment exercisable in favor of donee's spouse or descendants or the descendants of the grantor, donee's grandmother, is not a general power — since power is testamentary, donee cannot exercise power in favor of donee or donee's creditors and donee's estate and the creditors of donee's estate are not within the class of permissible appointees).

Add to note 22.

To similar effect is Private Letter Ruling 200210038 (Dec. 5, 2001). Private Letter Ruling 200311020 (Dec. 9, 2002) ruled that a surviving spouse would not have a general power of appointment over a trust created under her deceased spouse's estate plan where the trust was to be reformed to correct a scrivener's error. See also Priv. Ltr. Rul. 200450033 (Aug. 17, 2004) (state court order reforming trust to correct scrivener's error such that a testamentary power of appointment held by surviving spouse was not a general power of appointment is consistent with state law, as it would be applied by the highest court of the state) and Priv. Ltr. Rul. 201002013 (Sept. 30, 2009) (judicial modification of trust document to correct a scrivener's error which had mistakenly granted the spouse a testamentary general power of appointment over the predeceased spouse's bypass trust will not cause the assets of the bypass trust to be included in surviving spouse's gross estate). Priv. Ltr. Ruls. 201006005, 201006023 (Oct. 27, 2009) (judicial modification of son's general power of appointment over trust as a limited power of appointment is consistent with trust grantor's intent and applicable state law and trust corpus will not be includible in son's gross estate under IRC § 2041). Priv. Ltr. Rul. 201020001 (Dec. 31, 2009) (as a result of judicial reformation of trust to correct scrivener's error, trustor's son and daughter-in-law do not possess a general power of appointment over trust principal). Priv. Ltr. Rul. 201132017 (May 10, 2011) (judicial modification of trust to correct scrivener's error that provided for the payment of surviving spouse's debts, expenses and death tax from the bypass trust instead of the survivor's trust, the intent of the settlors when the original trust was drafted, was consistent with applicable law as it would be applied by the highest court in the state and, consequently, the amendment did not provide the surviving spouse with a general power of appointment over the assets in the bypass trust).

[4] Exceptions to General Definition

[a] Power Limited by a Standard

Page 4-319:

In note 25, after IRC § 2041(b)(1)(A) *add the following.*

The limitation on the exercise of a power of appointment only in accordance with the standard may be imposed by state law. Rev. Proc. 94-44, 1994-2 CB 683; Priv. Ltr. Rul. 200530020 (Apr. 6, 2005) (enactment of state statute converting beneficiary/trustee's general power of appointment over trust income to a limited power results in no inclusion of trust income in estate).

Page 4-320:

Add to note 32.

Cf. Priv. Ltr. Rul. 200847015 (July 20, 2008), where trust document gave trustee-decedent the power to expend funds for a trust beneficiary's "comfort, and happiness." The Service ruled that decedent did not possess a general power of appointment over property held in trust since such power could only be exercisable pursuant to a spendthrift clause in the document which, not having been triggered during decedent's life, was not a power in existence at decedent's death.

Add to note 35 following citation to Morgan v. Comm'r.

In Private Letter Ruling 200637021 (June 2, 2006), the Service ruled that the resignation of an original cotrustee of a trust and the beneficiary's appointment as sole trustee will not cause beneficiary to have a general power of appointment over trust that provides the trustee with the discretion to make principal distributions to beneficiary for her care, maintenance and support. Although original cotrustee and beneficiary live in one state and trust was executed in another state, the Service found that the applicable laws of both states provide that the invasion power of the trustee-beneficiary was limited by an ascertainable standard within the meaning of Sections 2041 and 2514.

Add to end of first paragraph of note 37.

Estate of Chancellor v. Comm'r, TC Memo. 2011-172 (2011) (Miss. law) (power as co-trustee to invade trust corpus limited to "the necessary maintenance, education, health care, sustenance, welfare or other appropriate expenditures needed by [decedent] and the other beneficiaries of this trust taking into consideration the standard of living to which they are accustomed"). See also Priv. Ltr. Rul. 201039003 (June 25, 2010) (the Service ruled that "other life emergency" in a trustee's invasion power for "reasonable care, maintenance, or education, or on account of any illness, infirmity, or other life emergency" was related to the categories that clearly qualified as an ascertainable standard).

[c] Post-1942 Powers With Another Person

[ii] Power held with an adverse party.

Page 4-322:

Add to note 41.

Priv. Ltr. Rul. 200612002 (Nov. 23, 2005) (members of a power of appointment committee named in a trust instrument do not have a general power of appointment over trust property where the trust provides that income and principal of the trust would be distributed pursuant to the unanimous direction of the members of the committee or by agreement of the donor and one member of that committee to appoint the property to one or more members of a class which includes the donor, donor's descendants, committee members, a named beneficiary, and a named private foundation); Priv. Ltr. Rul. 200637025 (June 5, 2006) (members of a distribution committee named in a trust instrument do not have a general power of appointment over trust property where the trust provides that income and principal of the trust would be distributed pursuant to the agreement of the members of the distribution committee or by the donor and one member of that committee to appoint the property to one or more members of an identified class of recipients, including the donor, the donor's spouse, the donor's parents and their descendants and a charitable organization); Priv. Ltr. Rul. 200647001 (Aug. 7, 2006) (same); Priv. Ltr. Rul.

200715005 (Jan. 3, 2007) (upon the death of a distribution committee member, that member's power would devolve to the surviving member and the donor's son jointly); Priv. Ltr. Rul. 200729025 (Apr. 10, 2007) (upon the death of a committee member, that member's power will devolve to the surviving committee members and the grantor jointly). The Service has announced that it is reconsidering the gift tax consequences in a series of private letter rulings issued under Sections 2511 and 2514, which involved trusts that use distribution committees comprised of trust beneficiaries who direct distributions of trust income and principal. The Office of Chief Counsel has discovered that its rulings on the application of Section 2514 may not be consistent with Revenue Ruling 76-503, 1976-2 CB 275 and Revenue Ruling 77-158, 1977-1 CB 285, which provide that such committee members would be treated as possessing general powers of appointment because the committee members are replaced if they resign or die. IR-2007-127 (July 9, 2007); Priv. Ltr. Rul. 200715005 (Jan. 3, 2007) (upon the death of a distribution committee member, that member's power would devolve to the surviving member and the donor's son jointly); Priv. Ltr. Rul. 2007290025 (Apr. 10, 2007) (upon the death of a committee member, that member's power will devolve to the surviving committee members and the grantor jointly). The Service has announced that it is reconsidering the gift tax consequences in a series of private letter rulings issued under Sections 2511 and 2514, which involved trusts that use distribution committees comprised of trust beneficiaries who direct distributions of trust income and principal. The Office of Chief Counsel has discovered that its rulings on the application of Section 2514 may not be consistent with Revenue Ruling 76-503, 1976-2 CB 275 and Revenue Ruling 77-158, 1977-1 CB 285, which provide that such committee members would be treated as possessing general powers of apointment because the committee members are replaced if they resign or die. IR-2007-127 (July 9, 2007); Priv. Ltr. Rul. 200731019 (May 1, 2007) (upon the death of a committee member, that member's power will devolve to the surviving committee member and the grantor jointly (and a new committee member will be appointed)).

[iii] Power held with an equally interested party.

Page 4-324:

Add to note 50.

Priv. Ltr. Rul. 200612002 (Nov. 23, 2005) (members of a power of appointment committee named in a trust instrument do not have a general power of appointment over trust property where the trust provides that income and principal of the trust would be distributed pursuant to the unanimous direction of the members of the committee or by agreement of the donor and one member of that committee to appoint the property to one or more members of a class which includes the donor, donor's descendants, committee members, a named beneficiary, and a named private foundation); Priv. Ltr. Rul. 200637025 (June 5, 2006) (members of a distribution committee named in a trust instrument do not have a general power of appointment over trust property where the trust provides that income and principal of the trust would be distributed pursuant to the agreement of the members of the distribution committee or by the donor and one member of that committee to appoint the property to one or more members of an identified class of recipients, including the donor, the donor's spouse, the donor's parents and their descendants and a charitable organization). Priv. Ltr. Rul. 200647001 (Aug. 7, 2006) (same); Priv. Ltr. Rul. 200715005 (Jan. 3, 2007) (upon the death of a distribution committee member, that member's power would devolve to the surviving member and the donor's son jointly); Priv. Ltr. Rul. 200729025 (Apr. 10, 2007) (upon the death of a committee member, that member's power will devolve to the surviving committee members and the grantor jointly). The Service has announced that it is reconsidering the gift tax consequences in a series of private letter rulings issued under Sections 2511 and 2514, which involved trusts that use distribution committees comprised of trust beneficiaries who direct distributions of trust income and principal. The Office of Chief Counsel has discovered that its rulings on the application of Section 2514 may not be consistent with Revenue Ruling 76-503, 1976-2 CB 275 and Revenue Ruling 77-158, 1977-1 CB 285, which provide that such committee members would be treated as possessing general powers of appointment because the committee members are replaced if they resign or die. IR-2007-127 (July 9, 2007); Priv. Ltr. Rul. 200715005 (Jan. 3, 2007) (upon the death of a distribution committee member, that member's power would devolve to the surviving member and the donor's son jointly); Priv. Ltr. Rul. 200729025 (Apr. 10, 2007) (upon the death of a committee member, that member's power will devolve to the surviving committee members and the grantor jointly). The Service has announced that it is reconsidering the gift tax consequences in a series of private letter rulings issued under Sections 2511 and 2514, which involved trusts that use distribution committees comprised of trust beneficiaries who direct distributions of trust income and principal. The Office of Chief Counsel has discovered that its rulings on the application of Section 2514 may not be consistent with Revenue Ruling 76-503, 1976-2 CB 275 and Revenue Ruling 77-158, 1977-1 CB 285, which provide that such committee members would be treated as possessing general powers of appointment because the committee members are replaced if they resign or die. IR-2007-127 (July 9, 2007). Priv. Ltr. Rul. 200731019 (May 1, 2007) (upon the death of a committee member, that member's power will devolve to the surviving committee member and the grantor jointly (and a new committee member will be appointed)).

[6] Treatment of Pre-1942 Powers

[d] Partial Release of Pre-1942 Powers

Page 4-330:

Add to end of first paragraph of note 76.

See Priv. Ltr. Rul. 200812022 (Nov. 7, 2007) (beneficiary's partial release of a pre-1942 general power of appointment made during beneficiary's minority under state law but at an age expressly allowed in the trust and made prior to November 1, 1951, was valid and resulted in beneficiary no longer holding a general power of appointment over the trust's assets).

[7] Treatment of Post-1942 Powers

[a] Possession

Page 4-331:

Add new paragraph to note 78.

In Technical Advice Memorandum 200407018 (July 8, 2003), the duty of consistency required property to be included in surviving spouse's estate where predeceasing spouse was allowed a marital deduction with respect to property. Cf. Estate of Posner v. Comm'r, TC Memo. 2004-112 (2004) (decedent did not possess a Section 2041 power of appointment over marital trust property and, accordingly, the property was not includible in decedent's estate even though decedent's predeceased spouse's estate claimed a Section 2056(b)(5) marital deduction. The court rejected the Service's argument that the duty of consistency required inclusion. In order for the duty of consistency to apply, three elements must be present: (1) a representation by the taxpayer; (2) reliance by the Service;

(3) an attempt by the taxpayer to change the representation after the statute of limitations on assessment has run. The court held that the duty does not apply to a mutual mistake by the taxpayer and the Service involving a pure question of law).

Page 4-332:

Add to note 83.

In TAM 200847015 (July 30, 2008), the Service ruled that a decedent did not possess a general power of appointment over property held in trust and created by her pre-deceased husband even though, as trustee, the trust gave her the power to expend funds on behalf of a beneficiary, including herself, not in accordance with an ascertainable standard. Since such power could only be exercisable pursuant to a spendthrift clause in the document and, since such power had not been triggered during decedent's life, it was not a power in existence at decedent's death.

Page 4-333:

Add to note 87.

In Private Letter Ruling 200403094 (Sept. 24, 2003), husband created a revocable trust, funded with his separate property, in which wife is given a testamentary general power of appointment over the assets of the trust equal to her unused applicable exclusion amount. The Service ruled that if wife predeceases husband, the value of the trust assets over which wife possesses a general power of appointment will be included in her gross estate.

Similarly, in Private Letter Ruling 200604028 (Sept. 30, 2005), husband and wife each intend to amend their respective revocable living trusts. Under the proposed reformation of wife's trust, if husband predeceases her, husband will have a testamentary general power of appointment over the assets in the trust equal to his unused applicable exclusion amount. Husband plans to sign a new will appointing this property to his trust. The Service ruled that if husband predeceases wife, the assets in wife's trust subject to husband's general power of appointment will be included in husband's estate and, if husband exercises power, wife will make a Section 2501 completed gift to husband that qualifies for the Section 2523 marital deduction.

[f] The Five-or-Five Rule

Page 4-337:

Add to note 109 following citation to Priv. Ltr. Rul. 199933020.

Private Letter Ruling 201038004 (June 15, 2010) (if beneficiary dies during period when she holds a noncumulative right to withdraw trust income, the current year's trust income is includible in trust beneficiary's estate in addition to accumulated trust income due to the lapse of beneficiary's previous years' withdrawal rights to the extent such income exceeded the greater of $5,000 or five percent of the trust corpus).

[8] Nongeneral Powers

[b] Nongeneral Powers That Are Treated As General Powers

Page 4-341:

Add to note 122.

Private Letter Ruling 201029011 (Apr. 12, 2010) (decedent's exercise of her nongeneral power of appointment to create a power of appointment in each of her children to appoint property at the child's death among decedent's descendants living at the time of decedent's death did not postpone or suspend vesting of the trust assets beyond the perpetuities period and, therefore, did not result in inclusion of the trust assets in decedent's estate).

¶ 4.14 SECTION 2042. PROCEEDS OF LIFE INSURANCE

[4] Amounts Receivable by Other Beneficiaries

[a] Incidents of Ownership

Page 4-351:

Add to note 37.

Estate of Coaxum v. Comm'r, TC Memo 2011-135 (2011) (value of insurance policies includible in decedent's gross estate because decedent retained the right to change the beneficiaries on the policy until his death).

Add to note 40.

Priv. Ltr. Rul. 200822003 (Jan. 28, 2008) (trustee of irrevocable trust established by husband holds all incidents of ownership in second-to-die policies on the lives of married couple pursuant to split-dollar life insurance agreement designating the trust as the policies' owner and a collateral assignment executed by the trustee assigning the policies to the couple but retaining all rights of ownership in the policies except the rights of the couple or the survivor's estate to receive the amount due on termination of the agreement); Priv. Ltr. Rul. 200825011 (Feb. 5, 2008); Priv. Ltr. Rul. 200910002 (Sept. 30, 2008).

[e] "Incidents" in Context

Page 4-357:

Add to note 69.

and Priv. Ltr. Rul. 200314009 (Dec. 17, 2002) (settlor did not have incidents of ownership over a policy transferred to a trust where the trust was reformed to correct a scrivener's error so as to prevent the settlor from being able to appoint herself or any related or subordinate party within the meaning of Section 672 as successor trustee).

Add to note 73.

See also Priv. Ltr. Rul. 200404013 (Oct. 14, 2003) (proceeds payable to decedent's trust, the owner of the policy, not includible in spouse's estate under Section 2042(2) even though spouse is a trustee) and Priv. Ltr. Rul. 200518005 (Jan. 13, 2005) (proceeds of policies owned by trusts established by someone other than the taxpayer will not be included in income beneficiary/insured's estate after taxpayer renounces her co-trustee rights and later resigns as co-trustee and so long as the premiums are not paid from trust income) and Priv. Ltr. Rul. 200617008 (Dec. 13, 2005) (proceeds of life insurance policy on wife to be purchased by trust established by her predeceased husband after her resignation as trustee will not be includible in her gross estate since wife will never possess, or have the power to exercise, any incidents of ownership in the policy).

[5] Incidents Incidentally Held

[b] Partnership's Insurance on Partner

Page 4-360:

Add to note 93 prior to last sentence.

See also Priv. Ltr. Rul. 200747002 (June 21, 2007) (taxpayers do not retain incidents of ownership in policies purchased pursuant to the terms of a company buy-sell agreement which were later transferred to a limited liability company taxpayers created to hold the policies with management of the LLC vested in a bank rather than taxpayers). Priv. Ltr. Rul. 200947006 (July 20, 2009) (proceeds of policies to be paid to partnership at taxpayer's death will not be included in taxpayer's gross estate following proposed transactions by which two family trusts will take ownership of partnership, which will then own and be the designated beneficiary of the policies). Priv. Ltr. Rul. 200948001 (July 20, 2009) (same); Priv. Ltr. Rul. 200949004 (July 20, 2009).

[6] Assignment of Group Term Insurance

Page 4-362:

Add to end of ¶ 4.14[6].

The Treasury has issued final regulations dealing with split dollar life insurance arrangements.[103.1] Generally, a split dollar life insurance arrangement involves an ownership arrangement of a life insurance policy[103.2] where there is a splitting of the interests in the life insurance policy through either a sharing of the costs or of the benefits of the policy or both. The original form of split dollar life insurance arrangements involved an employer-employee joint ownership of an ordinary life policy where the employer owned the "equity" or cash surrender value interest in the policy and the employee owned the "term"

[103.1] Reg. §§ 1.61-22, 1.83-3(e), 1.83-6(a)(5), 1.301-1(q), 1.7872-15. The regulations apply to any split dollar arrangement entered into after September 17, 2003. Reg. §§ 1.61-22(j)(1)(i), 1.7872-15(n)(1).

[103.2] Term insurance generally is not a type of insurance which is held as split dollar life insurance. See Rev. Rul. 64-328, 1964-2 CB 11 (now obsolete, see Rev. Rul. 2003-105, 2003-2 CB ___). See also Reg. § 1.61-22(b)(1)(iii) which does not preclude term insurance from regulatory treatment, but does provide that a Section 79 group term life insurance policy is generally not a split dollar life insurance arrangement.

or insurance interest in the policy[103.3] or a "reverse" split dollar life insurance arrangement where the above interests were reversed with the employee owning the equity interest and the employer owning the term interest.[103.4] Split dollar life insurance arrangements now also to include arrangements between a corporation and a shareholder[103.5] and between private parties.[103.6] Today, generally a split dollar life insurance policy involves any arrangement between an owner and nonowner of a life insurance contract under which either party to the arrangement pays all or part of the premiums and at least one of the parties paying premiums is entitled to recover all or a portion of the premiums where such recovery is to be made from, or secured by, the proceeds of the contract.[103.7]

Most of the complicated tax consequences considered in the current finalized regulations with respect to split dollar life insurance arrangements involve the income tax consequences of such arrangements.[103.8] The regulations defer to general estate tax principles the determination of the *estate tax* consequences of split dollar life insurance arrangements.[103.9] Thus, the rules of Section 2042 apply[103.10] and authority found in rulings and cases decided prior to the promulgation of the regulations are used to determine the extent to which the proceeds of split dollar arrangements are currently included within an insured

---

[103.3] Rev. Rul. 64-328, 1964-2 CB 11 (now obsolete, see Rev. Rul. 2003-105, 2003-2 CB __). Such an arrangement permits the employer to provide a fringe benefit to an employee, but also allows the employer to recoup its investment at the insured's death or earlier termination of the arrangement. An employee benefits by acquiring insurance protection at a low cost and by having a leveraged value of the policy if there is a transfer of the employee's interest in the policy. Id. The premium paying arrangement could fall into several different classifications including a split with the employer paying all the premiums, a classical split with the employer paying premiums in an amount equal to the increase in the cash surrender value of the policy, or a level split premium amount between the employer and employee.

[103.4] See Priv. Ltr. Rul. 9026041 (Mar. 30, 1990). Cf. Priv. Ltr. Rul. 9636033 (Mar. 12, 1996) (private reverse split dollar arrangement). Since the employer owns the initial "term" insurance protection, this type of policy is appropriate to provide an employer "key person" type of insurance protection and also provide the employee the cash value of the insurance policy. The benefits vary depending upon how the proceeds are split.

[103.5] See Rev. Rul. 79-50, 1979-1 CB 138 (now obsolete, see Rev. Rul. 2003-105, 2003-2 CB __).

[103.6] See Reg. §§ 1.61-22(b)(1), 1.61-22(b)(2). See Amoia, Simmons & Slane, "Private Split Dollar—What's New about an Old Opportunity," NAEPC Journal of Estate & Tax Planning, (June, 2009).

[103.7] Reg. § 1.61-22(b)(1).

[103.8] Reg. §§ 1.61-22, 1.83-3(e), 1.83-6(a)(5), 1.301-1(q), 1.7872-15. The regulations also provide gift tax consequences of such arrangements. See ¶ 10.01[3][g].

[103.9] See Supplementary Information, 68 Fed. Reg. 54,336, 54,343 (adopted Sept. 17, 2003).

[103.10] If a third-party owner of some portion of the policy predeceased the insured, that portion of the value of the policy would be included in the third-party's gross estate under Section 2033. See ¶ 4.05[6].

decedent's gross estate. For example, to the extent that proceeds of a split dollar life insurance arrangement are paid directly or indirectly to the insured decedent's executor,[103.11] those proceeds should be included within the decedent's gross estate under Section 2042(1) with a deduction allowed under Section 2053(a)(4) for the value of any other person's right to recover a portion of those proceeds.[103.12] Similarly, if the insured decedent directly or indirectly held any incidents of ownership over the policy on the insured decedent's life, the proceeds should be included in the insured's gross estate under Section 2042(2)[103.13] again with a Section 2053(a)(4)[103.14] deduction for the value of any other person's right to recover a portion of the proceeds of such policy from the beneficiary of the proceeds.[103.15] Although this is the appropriate statutory result, some courts have simply included the proceeds net of the value of such other persons' rights in the proceeds in the insured's gross estate under Section 2042(1) or Section 2042(2).[103.16] A transfer of incidents of ownership by the insured decedent of a split dollar arrangement within three years of death will cause the proceeds of the policy to be included in the insured decedent's gross estate under Section 2035(a), again reduced by the value of any other person's right to such proceeds as the result of a Section 2053(a)(4) deduction.[103.17]

As in the case of non-split dollar life insurance arrangements,[103.18] incidents of ownership may be indirectly held by an insured if the insured owns a controlling interest in a corporation and the corporation owns incidents of ownership in the policy.[103.19] In such circumstances, if the corporation's share of the proceeds is not paid to the corporation[103.20] or is not paid in a manner that otherwise increases the value of the insured's stock of the corporation,[103.21] the insured decedent is deemed to indirectly hold the corporation's incidents of ownership in the policy and the proceeds are then included in the insured decedent's gross estate under Section 2042(2) as if the insured decedent had held

---

[103.11] See ¶ 4.14[3].

[103.12] Cf. IRC § 2053(c)(1)(A).

[103.13] See ¶ 4.14[4].

[103.14] Cf. IRC § 2053(c)(1)(A).

[103.15] Priv. Ltr. Rul. 9026041 (Mar. 30, 1990).

[103.16] Cf. Estate of Tomerlin v. Comm'r, TC Memo. 1986-147; Rev. Rul. 76-113, 1976-2 CB 376 (not split dollar life insurance). Technically, this result is statutorily inappropriate; but, it generally makes no difference to the decedent's estate tax consequences. A similar discrepancy in treatment but not in consequences occurs with respect to recourse and nonrecourse mortgages under Section 2053(a)(4) discussed at ¶ 5.03[b] text accompanying notes 148–152.

[103.17] See ¶ 4.14[9][b].

[103.18] See ¶ 4.14[5].

[103.19] Reg. § 20.2042-1(c)(6).

[103.20] See Reg. § 20.2031-2(f); Estate of Huntsman v Comm'r, 66 TC 861 (1976), acq. 1977-2 CB 1.

[103.21] See Reg. § 20.2031-2(f).

the incidents of ownership directly.[103.22] If some of the proceeds are paid to the corporation or paid in a manner that increases the value of the corporate stock, only the remaining proceeds would be included in the decedent's gross estate under Section 2042(2).[103.23] In applying these rules, if the corporation has only a right of reimbursement for its economic interest in the policy, the right of reimbursement is not itself a Section 2042(2) incident of ownership held by the corporation in the policy.[103.24] If the ownership arrangement is held in part by a partnership or a limited liability company rather than a corporation, similar results occur.[103.25]

[103.22] Estate of Levy v. Comm'r, 70 TC 873 (1978); Dimen v. Comm'r, 72 TC 198 (1979), aff'd, 633 F2d 203 (2d Cir. 1980). In these cases involving split dollar arrangements, the insured decedent did not directly own incidents of ownership, but the corporation which the decedent controlled held incidents of ownership over the policy, part of which proceeds were paid to the corporation (no Section 2042(2)) and part of which were paid to a third party (Section 2042(2) inclusion). See also Rev. Rul. 82-145, 1982-2 CB 213 (corporate incident of ownership attributed to controlling shareholder except to extent proceeds paid to corporation).

[103.23] Reg. § 20.2042-1(c)(6). For example, if an insured decedent directly held no incidents of ownership but controlled a corporation which held incidents of ownership, and the proceeds were paid in a manner that did not increase the value of the corporate stock, the proceeds would be included in the insured decedent's gross estate under Section 2042(2) as a result of Regulations Section 20.2042-1(c)(6). If, in that situation, the corporation had a valid claim against the beneficiary to some portion of the proceeds, the proceeds included in the insured decedent's gross estate under Section 2042(2) would be reduced by the amount of the corporation's claim to the proceeds deductible under Section 2053(a)(4). The value of the corporation's claim would be reflected in the insured's gross estate by the value of any stock that the insured owned in the corporation. IRC § 2033. If the insured decedent was a shareholder of the corporation, but did not control the corporation, there would be no Section 2042(2) inclusion of any proceeds in the insured decedent's gross estate.

[103.24] Rev. Rul. 76-274, 1976-2 CB 278, modified by Rev. Rul. 82-145, 1982-2 CB 213; Priv. Ltr. Rul. 9651030 (Sept. 20, 1996); Priv. Ltr. Rul. 9808024 (Nov. 20, 1997). Thus, if the insured and the insured's controlled corporation held no incidents of ownership in the policy, but the corporation had a right to recover a portion of the split dollar proceeds from the beneficiary, the right of reimbursement would not be any incident of ownership and there would be no Section 2042 inclusion in the insured's gross estate; however, the value of the insured's stock included under Section 2033 would be increased as a result of the corporation's right of recovery.

[103.25] Cf. Priv. Ltr. Rul. 9639053 (June 20, 1996). Priv. Ltr. Rul. 200925003 (Dec. 16, 2008) (if trust grantor/insured disposes of his general partnership interest in partnership which entered into split-dollar agreement with trust, trust grantor/insured would not hold any incidents of ownership in the policy). See ¶ 4.14[5][b].

[8] Policy Purchased With Community Property Funds

Page 4-366:

Add to note 125.

The Service has acquiesced in the result in Burris, 2003-17 IRB 1, and has issued Revenue Ruling 2003-40, 2003-17 IRB 1, ruling that where a Louisiana decedent (D) acquired a life insurance policy on D's life, designated D as owner and D's spouse as beneficiary, and D never transferred ownership of the policy, one half of the proceeds are includible in D's gross estate.

[9] Relation of Section 2042 to Other Sections Defining "Gross Estate"

[b] Near-Death Transfers

Page 4-368:

Add to note 136.

Cf. Priv. Ltr. Rul. 200617008 (Dec. 13, 2005) (proceeds of life insurance policy on wife to be purchased by trust established by her predeceased husband after her resignation as trustee will not be includible in her gross estate under Section 2035(a) if wife dies within three years of her resignation since wife will never possess, or have the power to exercise, any incidents of ownership in the policy).

Page 4-369:

Add to note 137.

Cf. Priv. Ltr. Rul. 200947006 (July 20, 2009) (proceeds of policies to be paid to partnership at taxpayer's death will not be included in taxpayer's gross estate under Section 2035 following proposed transactions by which two family trusts will take ownership of partnership, which will then own and be the designated beneficiary of the policies since, before and after the proposed transactions, taxpayer will not possess any incidents of ownership). Priv. Ltr. Rul. 200948001 (July 20, 2009) (same); Priv. Ltr. Rul. 200949004 (July 20, 2009).

¶ 4.15 SECTION 2043. TRANSFERS FOR INSUFFICIENT CONSIDERATION

[1] Marital Rights: The Negative Rule

[b] The Negative Rule in a Divorce Situation

[i] Claims.

Page 4-380:

Add to beginning of note 48.

Priv. Ltr. Rul. 200709014 (Nov. 16, 2006) (Section 2516 applies to the testamentary transfer of stock to ex-wife following death of ex-husband pursuant to separation agreement and, accordingly, if ex-husband is survived by ex-wife, the transfer would be treated as made for adequate and full consideration in money or money's worth for purposes of Section 2053(c)(1)).

¶ 4.16 SECTION 2044. CERTAIN PROPERTY FOR WHICH A MARITAL DEDUCTION WAS PREVIOUSLY ALLOWED

Page 4-387:

Add to note 10.

Citing Revenue Procedure 2001-38, the Service in Private Letter Ruling 200407016 (Oct. 24, 2003) treated a QTIP election made for a surviving spouse's life estate as null and void because the election was unnecessary to eliminate deceased spouse's estate tax liability; Priv. Ltr. Rul. 200603004 (Sept. 30, 2005) (estate's QTIP election for credit shelter trust is null and void because election was not necessary to reduce estate tax liability to zero).

Add to note 11 just before reference to Estate of Soberdash.

see also TAM 200407018 (July 8, 2003) (painting for which a marital deduction was erroneously claimed by the decedent's spouse's estate is includible in decedent's gross estate pursuant to the doctrine of duty of consistency). Cf. Estate of Buder, 436 F3d 936 (8th Cir. 2006) (doctrine of equitable recoupment was applied to reduce an estate's refund for taxes paid on a residuary trust that was improperly treated as a QTIP trust in the predeceased husband's estate).

Add to note 12.

This is the case even if no income distributions were ever made from the marital trust. In Estate of Miller, TC Memo. 2009-119 (2009), decedent's predeceased spouse's estate made a QTIP election with respect to a marital trust and claimed a marital deduction. Decedent's estate argued, however, that the marital trust should not be included in decedent's gross estate because she never needed nor withdrew the marital trust income. The court correctly pointed out that the inclusion of a marital trust in a surviving spouse's estate is not contingent on whether surviving spouse needed or even used the income but rather on whether she retained a qualifying income interest for life.

Page 4-388:

Add to note 19.

Cf. Estate of Black, 133 TC No. 15 (2009), where surviving spouse died within five months of her husband and prior to the funding of the marital trust, which was never funded because the marital trust was to terminate at surviving spouse's death. In order to calculate surviving spouse's gross estate, the deemed funding date of the pecuniary bequest made to the marital trust for Section 2044 purposes was the surviving spouse's date of death because that was the last possible date that the funding could occur.

CHAPTER **5**

The Taxable Estate

¶ 5.03	Section 2053. Expenses, Indebtedness, And Taxes [Revised]	S5-4
[1]	Introduction	S5-4
	[a] The State Law Allowance Requirement	S5-6
	[b] The Amount and Payment Requirements	S5-7
	[i] Establishment of the liability.	S5-8
	[ii] Bona fide liability.	S5-9
	[iii] Payment.	S5-10
	[iv] Timing of Post-death events.	S5-10
[2]	Funeral Expenses	S5-12
	[a] In General	S5-12
	[b] The "Allowable" Test	S5-12
[3]	Administration Expenses	S5-14
	[a] Executor Commissions and Attorney Fees	S5-16
	[b] Commissions Paid to a Trustee	S5-19
	[c] Miscellaneous Administration Expenses	S5-20
	[i] Interest expenses.	S5-21
	[ii] Selling expenses.	S5-23
	[iii] Other deductible administration	
	expenses.	S5-24
[4]	Claims Against the Estate	S5-25
	[a] Personal Obligations of Decedent	S5-26
	[i] The consideration requirement.	S5-27
	[ii] Community property issues.	S5-30
	[iii] Section 2044 claims.	S5-30
	[b] Existing at the Time of Death	S5-31
	[i] Taxes as claims.	S5-31
	[ii] Section 2053(d): Limited deductibility of	
	certain foreign death taxes.	S5-33
	[c] Contingency of a Claim	S5-34
	[i] Introduction.	S5-34
	[ii] Types of contingencies.	S5-37
	[iii] Actual payment.	S5-38
[5]	Mortgages	S5-40

[6]   Special Rules and Limitations Related to Section
2053 Deductions. S5-42
      [a]   The Section 642(g) Election S5-42
      [b]   The Section 213(c)(2) Election S5-45
      [c]   Special Rules for Property Not Subject to
            Claims. S5-46
            [i]   Introduction. S5-46
            [ii]   Property not subject to claims. S5-47
            [iii]   Section 2053(b): Expenses of
                 administering property not subject to
                 claims. S5-48
            [iv]   Section 2053(c)(2): Limitation based on
                 the value of property subject to claims.   S5-50

¶ 5.05   Section 2055. Transfers for Public, Charitable, and
Religious Uses S5-51
    [1]   Qualified Recipients S5-51
      [a]   In General S5-51
      [b]   Section 2055(a) Organizations S5-52
      [c]   Tainted Organizations S5-52
    [2]   Transfers to Charity S5-53
      [a]   Outright Transfers S5-53
      [b]   Indirect Transfers S5-53
      [c]   Disclaimers S5-54
      [e]   Lifetime Transfers S5-54
    [3]   The Amount of the Deduction S5-54
      [a]   In General S5-54
      [b]   Expenses of an Estate Affecting the Deduction   S5-55
            [i]   Death taxes.   S5-55
    [4]   Split Interests: Mixed Private and Charitable
Bequests S5-56
      [a]   Background S5-56
      [b]   Present Law S5-56
    [5]   Qualified Remainder Interests S5-56
      [a]   The Charitable Remainder Annuity Trust S5-57
            [i]   Annuity trust requirements. S5-57
            [ii]   The amount of the deduction. S5-58
      [b]   The Charitable Remainder Unitrust S5-59
            [i]   Unitrust requirements. S5-59
            [ii]   The amount of the deduction. S5-60
      [c]   The Pooled Income Fund S5-61
            [ii]   The amount of the deduction. S5-61
    [6]   Charitable Lead Trusts S5-61
      [a]   Requirements S5-61
            [ii]   Similarities in requirements. S5-62
      [b]   The Amount of the Deduction S5-62
    [7]   Exceptions to the Split-Interest Rules S5-63
      [a]   Remainders in Residences and Farms S5-63
      [b]   An Undivided Portion of the Property S5-63
      [e]   Charitable Gift Annuity S5-64
    [8]   Curative Amendments Permitted S5-65
      [b]   Reformable and Qualified Interests S5-65
      [c]   Qualified Reformation S5-65
      [d]   Additional Rules Related to Reformations S5-66

¶ 5.06   Section 2056. Testamentary Transfers to Surviving Spouse   S5-66
    [3]   Interests Passing to a Surviving Spouse S5-66
          [a]   By Will or Inheritance S5-67
          [h]   Disclaimers S5-68
    [5]   Valuation of Interests Passing S5-68
          [a]   Taxes on Surviving Spouse's Interest S5-68
          [b]   Encumbrances on Surviving Spouse's Interest   S5-69
              [ii]   Administrative expenses. S5-69
    [7]   The Terminable Interest Rule S5-69
          [b]   Identifying Terminable Interests S5-69
          [d]   The Executor-Purchaser Provision S5-69
    [8]   Terminable Interests That Do Qualify S5-70
          [b]   Life Interests With Powers S5-70
              [i]   The surviving spouse must be entitled
                    for life to all of the income from the
                    entire interest or a specific portion of
                    the entire interest, or to a specific
                    portion of all the income from the entire
                    interest. S5-70
              [iii]   The surviving spouse must have the
                    power to appoint the entire interest or
                    the specific portion to either surviving
                    spouse or spouse's estate. S5-71
          [d]   Election With Respect to Life Estate for
              Surviving Spouse S5-71
              [i]   The passing requirement. S5-71
              [ii]   The qualifying income interest
                    requirement.   S5-72
              [iii]   The election.   S5-74
          [e]   Special Rules for Charitable Remainder Trusts   S5-76
¶ 5.07   Section 2056A. Qualified Domestic Trusts S5-77
    [2]   The Passing Requirement S5-77
          [b]   The Surviving Spouse's Transfer to a QDOT   S5-77
          [c]   An Annuity or Other Arrangement Treated as
              Passing to a QDOT S5-77
    [3]   Requirements of a QDOT S5-78
          [c]   Regulatory Requirements to Ensure Collection
              of Deferred Tax S5-78
              [iii]   Rules applicable to both classifications
                    of QDOTs. S5-78
          [d]   A QDOT Election S5-78
    [4]   Taxation of QDOT Property S5-79
          [a]   Events Triggering the Tax S5-79
              [i]   Corpus distributions. S5-79
              [ii]   The surviving spouse's death. S5-79
          [c]   Liability for and Payment of the Tax S5-80
    [5]   Exceptions If Surviving Spouse Becomes a U.S.
          Citizen S5-80
¶ 5.08   Section 2057. Family-Owned-Business Deduction S5-81
    [2]   Definition of "Qualified Family-Owned Business
          Interest" S5-81
          [a]   In General S5-81

		[c]	Additional Requirements With Respect to Entities	S5-81
			[ii] Ownership requirements.	S5-81
	[3]		Estate Qualifications	S5-82
		[b]	Election and Agreement	S5-82
			[i] The election.	S5-82
			[ii] The agreement.	S5-82
			[iii] Grace period.	S5-82
		[c]	The 50 Percent Test	S5-83
			[i] In general.	S5-83
			[iii] Adjusted value of qualified family-owned business interests.	S5-83
	[5]		The Recapture Rule	S5-83
		[b]	Recapture Events	S5-83
			[ii] Dispositions.	S5-83
		[c]	Measuring the Recapture Tax	S5-84
			[iii] Applicable percentage.	S5-84

Page 5-7:

Replace existing ¶ 5.03 with revised ¶ 5.03.

¶ 5.03 SECTION 2053. EXPENSES, INDEBTEDNESS, AND TAXES [REVISED]

[1] Introduction

Section 2053 contains most of the estate tax rules designed to assure an application of the tax rates to a realistic taxable estate, determined by subtracting from the gross estate certain of the decedent's obligations existing at death and other reasonable charges involved in winding up the decedent's affairs and passing the property on to beneficiaries.[1] The value of property owned by a decedent at death, or treated as if owned by a decedent under the various sections defining the gross estate,[2] is obviously not a fair measure of the decedent's wealth or of what a decedent can actually pass on to survivors. A decedent's estate will be diminished by unavoidable funeral and related costs. The collection and distribution of a decedent's property will necessitate administrative expenditures. Creditors, including various tax collectors, may have substantial claims against a decedent that will have to be discharged out of the assets of a decedent's estate. Some of the decedent's property may be mortgaged and, even if the decedent had no personal liability for the mortgage debt, the value of the property is reduced by the charges against it. Subject to detailed rules, Section 2053 takes all these matters into account in allowing deductions toward the determination of the taxable estate to assure that the estate

---

[1] Items described in Section 2053 sometimes also reduce the amount of generation-skipping transfers. See IRC § 2622(b), discussed at ¶ 14.03[3], at note 15.

[2] See generally Chapter 4 (¶¶ 4.01–4.18 inclusive).

tax is imposed only on "what actually passes in value from the dead to the living."[3]

The four categories of deductions mentioned above areauthorized by Section 2053(a).[4] All are subject to important limitations[5] that are sometimes subject to a minor exception.[6] The four allowances will serve as the basic outline of the ensuing discussion along with the limitations,[7] which often apply to several or even all of the deduction provisions.

On the other hand this seems to be the place for a brief introduction to the proper approach to Section 2053(a), an excellent small segment of legislation woefully buffeted about and otherwise abused by judge and scholar alike. It is a great place to pause and consider for a moment the interpretation of federal statutes.

The meaning of the terms of the four categories of potentially deductible items listed in Section 2053(a), "funeral expenses," "administration expenses," "claims against the estate," and "mortgages," are answered primarily by resort to federal law. We have known this at least since 1938.[8] The meaning of a term in a federal statute raises a question of federal law not governed by local characterization.[9] If Ohio passes a statute authorizing an executor to purchase a round-the-world trip for a bereaved widow and designates it a funeral expense, the Ohio executor may be authorized to expend the money, but the trip is not a Section 2053(a)(1) funeral expense merely because of its local characterization as a funeral expense, as it is clearly not within the *congressional* meaning of that term. So in each of the four categories of Section 2053(a), an initial question is the meaning of the terms, a question of *federal law.*[10]

---

[3] Estate of Cafaro v. Comm'r, TC Memo. 1989-348 (1989) (addressing Section 2053(a)(3) claims against the estate).

[4] First, funeral expenses, Section 2053(a)(1); second, expenses of administering the probate estate, Section 2053(a)(2); third, claims against the estate, Section 2053(a)(3); and fourth, mortgages and other indebtedness on estate property for which the decedent is personally liable, Section 2053(a)(4).

[5] In addition to the requirements specified in Section 2053(a), see Sections 2053(b) and 2053(c)(2) discussed infra ¶ 5.03[6][c].

[6] See IRC § 2053(d), allowing a deduction for certain foreign death taxes, despite the general proscription of Section 2053(c)(1)(B), discussed infra ¶ 5.03[4][b][ii].

[7] See Reg. § 20.2053-1.

[8] Lyeth v. Hoey, 305 US 188, 193 (1938).

[9] Lyeth v. Hoey, 305 US 188, 194 (1938). See also United States v. White, 853 F2d 107, 113 (2d Cir. 1988), cert. denied, 493 US 5 (1989), rev'g and remanding 650 F. Supp. 904 (WDNY 1987) (reinforcing the notion of a "federal standard" for deductible administration expenses) and infra ¶ 5.03[3] text accompanying notes 78–80.

[10] Even here an element of local law enters in. The term "expense" connotes a paid obligation. The obligation to pay can arise only by way of local law. Consequently, the discussion here is about state-recognized obligations to make payments that are, for example, within the federal concept of funeral expenses. Cf. Reg. § 20.2053-6(f) (using local law to determine estate's portion of joint income tax liability).

The next question is whether the item to be deducted falls within the federal law meaning given the statutory term. This is a matter for a federal court's decision. A federal court deciding a tax case decides whether an item falls within the ambit of a term of a federal statute; and it does so even if this may involve in some part a determination of how local law applies, notwithstanding that a state court, other than the highest state court, has already decided the local issue.[11]

[a] The State Law Allowance Requirement

Beyond these basics, there looms in Section 2053 a question of state law expressly raised. All the listed items in Section 2053(a) pass final muster as estate tax deductions only if they are "allowable" under applicable local law. There is no federal law that purports to say whether they are allowable, in the obvious sense of this requirement. The question is whether state law permits the amount to be paid by the executor out of estate assets. This is a classic example of express reference to local law for a principle to be applied in the implementation of a federal statute. If Nevada expressly authorizes executors to purchase solid silver caskets and the cost of a casket is a funeral expense (as Congress has used the term), the cost of a solid silver casket becomes a funeral expense (federal question) allowable by local law (state question) that a federal judge cannot properly hold nondeductible because of some feeling of parsimony that the judge may harbor. Obviously, Congress is not required to allow estate tax deductions for the cost of solid silver caskets. Congress might instead allow a deduction for "reasonable funeral expenses."[12] Local law would not then play the same role. But in Section 2053(a) the selected litmus paper is the local rule of law on allowability.

Who decides whether local law actually allows the solid silver casket? Generally the federal judge deciding the tax case makes this determination. The Supreme Court in the *Bosch case* has directed courts deciding federal tax controversies to give proper regard to a local adjudication of significant rights and obligations; at the same time, it holds that such adjudications are not binding in the federal tax case unless they are decisions by a state's highest court.[13] The *Bosch* opinion itself confuses local law versus local decision issues,[14] but at least the opinion makes it clear that a decision below the level of state's highest court regarding state law allowance is not binding on the federal judge. Thus, the Commissioner may successfully challenge the deductibility of fu-

---

[11] Comm'r v. Estate of Bosch, 387 US 456 (1967). See infra text accompanying notes 13–16.

[12] Cf. IRC § 162(a)(1), regarding a "reasonable allowance" for salaries.

[13] Comm'r v. Estate of Bosch, 387 US 456 (1967). The doctrine is analyzed in the discussion of Section 2033 at ¶ 4.05[2][b].

[14] The *Bosch* opinion misapplies the *Erie* doctrine which concerns the controlling effect of local law, not local adjudications. See discussion of Section 2033, at ¶ 4.05[2][b], note 14.

neral expenses actually allowed in a state probate court proceeding and paid by the estate;[15] but, unless the contention is that the charges are not funeral expenses as Congress has used that term, the attack should address the question of whether the expenses are allowable under principles of local law. If the judge in a tax case decides that a probate judge erred in holding the purchase of a solid silver casket allowable under local law, the judge may disallow a deduction on the basis of a contrary interpretation of the local law, giving only "proper regard" to the local decision.[16]

To carry this a step beyond where it may need to be carried, suppose the local law authorizes the purchase of a casket "fitting to the decedent's economic situation in life." Local law is much more likely to raise this equivocal kind of issue than the black or white (silver or bronze?) issue suggested above. Judge Local approves the silver casket. Judge Federal, passing on the Commissioner's disallowance of the deduction, may reject Judge Local's interpretation of local law, reverse the decision, and hold the expenditure for the silver casket not "allowable" under the law governing administration of the estate (i.e., under local law).

These basic postulates are assumed in the discussion that follows, but, even if they are sound, the authors do not assert they are uniformly followed.

[b] The Amount and Payment Requirements

Another issue that permeates all of the subparts of Section 2053 is the time that the amount of the deduction is established. Unlike some Code sections which call for the determination of the amount of an item at the date of the decedent's death,[17] Section 2053 does not specifically provide the time for the determination of the amount of the deduction.[18] The amount of some of the Section 2053 deductible items, such as funeral and administrative expenses, are unknown at the date of the decedent's death and their amount can be determined only after the decedent's death;[19] while the amount of other items such as claims and mortgages generally can be determined at the time of the dece-

---

[15] See Reg. § 20.2053-1(b)(1). Cf. First Nat'l Bank of Ft. Worth v. US, 301 F. Supp. 667 (ND Tex. 1969) (disallowing attorney's fees allowed by a state probate court).

[16] Comm'r v. Estate of Bosch, 387 US 456, 465 (1967).

[17] See, e.g., IRC § 2031. Cf. IRC §§ 2032, 2032A.

[18] See, however, Ithaca Trust v. Comm'r, 279 US 151 (1929), where although Section 2055 does not provide for the time of the determination of the deductible amount, the value of a remainder interest which was deductible was to be made as of the date of the decedent's death unaffected by the death of the life beneficiary shortly after the decedent's death. See also FSA 200217022 (Jan. 17, 2002) (discussing Ithaca Trust v. Comm'r, 279 US 151 (1929) and Jacobs v. Comm'r, 34 F2d 233 (8th Cir. 1929), cert. denied, Jacobs v. Lucas, 280 US 603 (1929), where the Eighth Circuit stated in its interpretation of *Ithaca Trust* that the Supreme Court has not and never will say that claims against an estate "must be determined solely by the facts and conditions existing on the date of the decedent's death.").

[19] See infra ¶ 5.03[2][b]; ¶ 5.03[3] text accompanying notes 77–85.

dent's death.[20] However, especially with respect to claims which are contingent, there has been significant controversy as to when the amount of the claim is determined and whether post-death events may be taken into consideration in the determination.[21] It has also been unclear whether a deductible amount under any subpart of Section 2053 must be paid prior to allowance of a deduction.[22] In an effort to settle controversies between the Circuit Courts of Appeal,[23] avoid litigation, and provide uniform rules,[24] the Treasury has issued regulations[25] to eliminate the controversies.[26]

Under the regulations, events occurring after a decedent's death are considered when determining the amount deductible under Section 2053,[27] and a Section 2053 deduction is generally limited to an amount actually paid in satisfaction of deductible claim or expense.[28] Thus, generally, no deduction is allowed under any subpart of Section 2053 until both the amount of the item is established and until actual payment of the item occurs.[29]

The regulatory rules apply primarily to the deductibility of contingent claims[30] and have a less significant effect on the rules for deductibility of the other Section 2053 items.[31]

[i] **Establishment of the liability.** In order for a claim or expense to be deductible under Section 2053, the amount of the liability must be established and not merely contingent, vague, or estimated. The liability may be established in a variety of methods.[32] The amount of the liability may be established

---

[20] See infra ¶ 5.03[4] text accompanying note 145; infra ¶ 5.03[5] text accompanying note 252.

[21] See infra ¶ 5.03[4][c].

[22] Compare Section 2053(a) with Section 2053(b).

[23] See infra ¶ 5.03[4][c] text accompanying notes 209 and 210.

[24] See TD 9468 (Oct. 16, 2009); see also Guidance Under Section 2053 Regarding Post-Death Events, Supplementary Information (Apr. 23, 2007).

[25] Reg. § 20.2053. These regulations are effective as of October 20, 2009. Reg. §§ 20.2053-1(f), 20.2053-3(e), 20.2053-4(f), 20.2053-6(h), 20.2053-9(f), 20.2053-10(e). For a discussion on the final regulations, see Blattmachr, Gans and Zeydel, "Final Regs. on Deducting Expenses and Claims Under Section 2053," 37 Est. Plan. No. 5, 3 (May 2010) (Part 1) and 37 Est. Plan. No. 6, 15 (June 2010) (Part 2).

[26] Some might argue that the resolution should be determined by the Supreme Court or by Congress, but there seems to be little doubt that the regulations are reasonable and will not be set aside by the courts. See US v. Correll, 389 US 299 (1967); Chevron USA v. Natural Resources Defense Council, Inc., 467 US 837 (1984).

[27] Reg. § 20.2053-1(d)(2). See Reg. § 20.2053-4(a)(2).

[28] Reg. § 20.2053-1(b)(1).

[29] Reg. §§ 20.2053-1(b)(1), 20.2053-1(b)(3).

[30] See infra ¶ 5.03[4][c].

[31] See infra ¶ 5.03[2][b] text accompanying note 63, ¶ 5.03[3] text accompanying note 85, ¶ 5.03[5] text accompanying note 254.

[32] Reg. § 20.2053-1(b)(3). Deductibility in such situations is still dependent upon the other Section 2053 requirements: allowance by the statute, allowance by state law and

by a court with appropriate jurisdiction passing upon the facts upon which deductibility depends and rendering a final decision on the amount of the liability.[33] If an amount is allowed by local law and no court decree is required for payment, then local law will establish the liability.[34] The liability may also be established by a consent decree.[35] The consent must be a bona fide recognition of the validity of the issue and be accepted by the court as satisfactory evidence on the merits.[36] A settlement may also establish the amount of a liability if it resolves a bona fide issue in a genuine contest, is the product of arms-length negotiations by parties having adverse interests with respect to the claim or expense, and it is consistent with local law.[37] If the cost of defending the claim or contesting the expense, the delay associated with litigating such claim or expense, or another significant factor will impose a higher burden on the estate relative to the amount of the settlement, the settlement will be considered bona fide.[38]

[ii] **Bona fide liability.** The liability to pay a claim or expense must be bona fide in nature and not a transfer that is essentially donative in character.[39] Close scrutiny is employed if the claim or expense involves a related party.[40] The decedent's personal representative must establish the bona fide nature of the claim or expense.[41] If the obligation is to a decedent family member,[42] a re-

---

payment. Id. Additional rules may also be imposed under other regulations provisions. Reg. § 20.2053-1(b)(3)(v).

[33] Reg. § 20.2053-1(b)(3)(i). It must appear that the court actually passed on the merits of the liability, although it is presumed in an active and genuine contest. Id. See Reg. § 20.2053-1(b)(4) Ex. 1.

[34] Reg. § 20.2053-1(b)(3)(ii). See Reg. § 20.2053-1(b)(4) Ex. 2.

[35] Reg. § 20.2053-1(b)(3)(iii).

[36] Reg. § 20.2053-1(b)(3)(iii). Consent given by parties having adverse interests to the allowance of the amount is presumed to provide validity. Id. The consent decree will not be allowed to the extent not consistent with local law. Reg. § 20.2053-1(b)(4) Ex. 1.

[37] Reg. § 20.2053-1(b)(3)(iv). No deduction is allowed for an unenforceable claim or to the extent that a settlement exceeds an applicable limit under local law. Id.

[38] Reg. § 20.2053-1(b)(3)(iv).

[39] Reg. § 20.2053-1(b)(2)(i). A claim that would otherwise be allowed as a charitable deduction under Section 2055 need not meet this requirement.

[40] Reg. § 20.2053-1(b)(2)(ii). Such close scrutiny is commonly prevalent under the tax law. See, e.g., ¶¶ 4.08[1][a][i], 10.02[4], 19.04[3][a]. Cf. ¶ 19.03[2][a][ii].

[41] Evidence of such may include evidence that the claim arises in circumstances that would support a claim by unrelated persons and non-beneficiaries. See Estate of Hicks, TC Memo. 2007-182 (2007) (intra-family loan by parent to decedent funded by proceeds of a tort settlement was bona fide).

[42] Family members include one's spouse, the grandparents, parents, siblings, and lineal descendants of the decedent and the decedent's spouse, as well as the spouse and lineal descendants of any such grandparent, parent, and sibling including any adopted individuals, but not the spouses of lineal descendants. Reg. § 20.2053-1(b)(2)(iii)(A).

lated entity,[43] or a beneficiary of a decedent's estate or revocable trust,[44] a variety of factors are examined to determine if the claim or expense is bona fide.[45]

　　[iii] Payment. Generally, in addition to establishing the liability, an actual payment must be made to allow the deductibility of a claim or expense.[46] However, a significant exception applies to this rule and payment requirement is waived where the personal representative establishes the amount to be paid with reasonable certainty[47] and that the amount will be paid.[48] A deduction for a payment is not allowed to the extent that the claim or expense is or could be compensated for by insurance or otherwise could be reimbursed.[49]

　　[iv] Timing of Post-death events. As seen above, post-death events are taken into consideration in both determining the existence of a liability and the payment of the liability. If a deduction is allowed and the liability does not exist or actual payment is not made, the Commissioner must act within the statute of limitations to deny a deduction.[50] If the amount of the liability is not

---

　　[43] A related entity is an entity in which the decedent, either directly or indirectly, held a beneficial interest either at any time in the three-year period preceding death or at death. It does not include a publicly-traded entity or a closely held entity in which the decedent and the decedent's family members (see supra note 42) collectively own less than 30 percent of the beneficial ownership interests (whether voting or non-voting). Reg. § 20.2053-1(b)(2)(iii)(B).

　　[44] Reg. § 20.2053-1(b)(2)(iii)(C).

　　[45] Reg. § 20.2053-1(b)(2)(ii). Factors that are indicative (but not necessarily determinative) of the claim or expense may include, but are not limited to (1) the transaction occurs in the ordinary course of business, is negotiated at arm's length, and is free from donative intent; (2) the nature of the claim or expense is not related to an expectation or claim of inheritance; (3) there is an agreement between the parties which is substantiated with contemporaneous evidence; (4) performance is pursuant to an agreement which can be substantiated; (5) all amounts paid are reported by each party for Federal income and employment tax purposes. Id.

　　[46] Reg. § 20.2053-1(b)(1).

　　[47] No deduction is allowed for a vague or uncertain estimate or where a claim or expense is contested or contingent. Reg. § 20.2053-1(b)(4)(i).

　　[48] Reg. § 20.2053-1(d)(4)(i). Additional exceptions apply for payment of claims. See infra ¶ 5.04[3][c][iii]. In Marshall Naify Revocable Trust, 106 AFTR2d ¶ 2010-5280 (ND Cal. 2010), the court held that the amount an estate could deduct for pre-death state income taxes the estate was contesting was limited to the amount for which the claim was settled after the decedent's death. Since the value of the claim was not ascertainable with reasonable certainty at the time of the decedent's death, it was permissible for the court to consider post-death events in determining the amount of the deduction.

　　[49] Reg. § 20.2053-1(d)(3). An executor may certify on Form 706 that no reimbursement is available for a claim or expense if the executor neither knows or reasonably should have known of the availability of any such reimbursement. Id. Even if a reimbursement is possible, no reduction will occur for the reimbursement if the executor explains that the efforts in pursuit of reimbursement outweigh the benefits of the efforts. Id.

　　[50] Reg. § 20.2053-1(d)(2)(i). See IRC § 6501. There is no duty on the part of the personal representative to report after the period of limitation has expired. TD 9468 (Oct. 16,

established at the time of examination of the return by the Commissioner or it is not clear at that time that the amount will be paid and the deduction is disallowed in whole or in part, the personal representative of the decedent can file a refund claim if the amount is subsequently established or the liability is paid within the statue of limitations.[51]

If the liability is not established or paid by the time of the expiration of the statute of limitations for the decedent's estate tax return, the personal representative may file a protective claim for refund before the expiration of the statute of limitations.[52] The protective claim for refund must identify each liability or claim and must describe the reasons and contingencies delaying the determination of liability or the payment of the claim.[53] If a timely filed protective claim for refund becomes ready for consideration after the assessment period is expired, the Service will refrain from reexamining each item on the estate tax return and limit its examination to the deduction under Section 2053 that is related to the protective claim.[54] If a protective claim for refund is filed with respect to a claim or expense that would have been deductible under Section 2053 and is payable out of an amount that qualifies for a marital or charitable deduction, the marital or charitable deduction is not reduced until the claim or expense is actually paid.[55]

2009), Summary of Comments and Explanation of Revisions, Item 4. But see Reg. § 20.2053-3(b)(3), last sentence.

[51] Reg. §§ 20.2053-1(d)(2)(ii), 20.2053-1(d)(4)(ii). See IRC § 6511.

[52] Reg. §§ 20.2053-1(d)(5)(i), 20.2053-1(d)(7) Ex. 2. See Reg. § 20.2053-1(b)(4)(ii); IRC § 6511. In Revenue Procedure 2011-48, the Service provided guidance related to the filing and subsequent resolution of a protective claim for refund of estate tax. In particular, § 4 of the revenue procedure provides procedures for filing a Section 2053 protective claim.

[53] See Reg. § 20.2053-1(d)(5)(i).

[54] Notice 2009-84, 2009-44 IRB __. Cf. Lewis v. Reynolds, 204 US 218 (1932) (permitting the Service to examine any item on return). Form 706 may be revised to incorporate the protective claim for refund so that a separate form need not be filed. TD 9468 (Oct. 16, 2009). In Revenue Procedure 2011-48, the Service provided guidance related to the filing and subsequent resolution of a protective claim for refund of estate tax. In particular, § 5 of the revenue procedure lists procedures for notifying the Service that a protective claim is ripe for consideration. The Service cautions, however, that a taxpayer who chooses not to follow or fails to comply with the procedures set forth in Revenue Procedure 2011-48 for a Section 2053 protective claim is subject to all of the generally applicable provisions concerning claims for refund as well as to the specific Section 2053 provisions relating to such claims, and will not have the benefit of the limited review described in Notice 2009-84, 2009-44 IRB 592, and Revenue Procedure 2011-48.

[55] Reg. §§ 20.2053-1(b)(5)(ii), 20.2053-1(b)(7) Ex. 3. In addition, such action does not render the charitable deduction contingent and nondeductible. Id.

[2] Funeral Expenses

[a] In General

Funeral expenses deductible under Section 2053(a)(1) are not limited to the bare cost of the funeral ceremony. Reasonably interpreting the federal statutory term, the regulations have consistently recognized as funeral expenses reasonable expenditures for "a tombstone, monument, or mausoleum, or for a burial lot, either for the decedent or his family."[56] It is equally clear that costs for embalming, cremation, casket, hearse, limousines, and other amounts paid to the undertaker and for floral and other decorations are included. The cost of transporting the body to the place of burial is a funeral expense and so is the cost of transportation of the person accompanying the body.[57] Expenditures for the future care of the burial lot or mausoleum may qualify as a deduction,[58] but expenditures for the care of a lot in which the decedent is not buried[59] and expenditures made by a testamentary trust after settlement of the estate are not deductible as funeral expenses.[60]

[b] The "Allowable" Test

Conceivably, the statute could be read to permit the deduction of the amount of funeral expenses that local law would allow without regard to the amount actually expended.[61] However, this is not the law. The terms "expenses" and "allowable," both of which appear in Section 2053(a), impose limiting concepts. The regulations properly assert as a ceiling on the deduction of

---

[56] Reg. § 20.2053-2.

[57] Reg. § 20.2053-2. But see Estate of Berkman v. Comm'r, TC Memo. 1979-46 (1979) (cost of person's other family members not also deductible); Estate of Calcagno v. Comm'r, TC Memo. 1989-677 (1989) (establishing a scholarship fund for priests is not a funeral expense); Estate of Tuck, TC Memo. 1988-560 (1988) (disallowing deduction for bequest for the perpetual care of decedent's family cemetery located several miles away from where decedent buried); Estate of Davenport v. Comm'r, TC Memo. 2006-215 (2006) (expenses of funeral luncheon following the burial not deductible under the circumstances).

[58] Reg. § 20.2053-2. See Comm'r v. Estate of Cardeza, 173 F2d 19 (3d Cir. 1949) (allowing a deduction for a testamentary trust established to maintain a mausoleum).

[59] Rev. Rul. 57-530, 1957-2 CB 621; Estate of Gillespie v. Comm'r, 8 TC 838 (1947) (bequest for perpetual care of a family burial lot in which decedent is not interred is not deductible even though amounts allowed by local law).

[60] Carter v. US, 1 USTC ¶ 238 (ED Mo. 1927). (Cost of mausoleum incurred by trustee after discharge of executor and with no allowance by Probate Court nondeductible.)

[61] The term "allowable" sometimes carries such a connotation, e.g., Virginian Hotel Corp. v. Helvering, 319 US 523 (1943), and indeed that may be its meaning as it affects the deduction of claims against the estate. See, however, Reg. § 20.2053-1(b)(1).

expenses the amount "actually expended."[62] There is no "expense" within the scope of this provision unless there is an actual payment.[63] The actual expense must then pass the three further tests discussed in the Introduction to this section: (1) the funeral expense must be a funeral expense within the meaning of the federal statute; (2) it must be allowable under local law in that it is of the kind that governing law permits to be charged against estate assets;[64] and (3) the amount must not exceed that which local law permits.[65]

The term "allowable" obviously raises more than a mere question whether an expense can be paid; the question is whether it can be paid out of the decedent's estate, i.e., "out of property subject to claims."[66] This has presented problems in community property states. If funeral expenses are chargeable half and half against the decedent's and the surviving spouse's community property, only one half of the expenses are deductible—only the half allowable as properly payable out of the decedent's estate.[67] Predictably, state community property laws have been amended to effect more satisfactory estate tax results.[68]

A somewhat similar problem may arise in a common law state in which the surviving spouse's duty of support imposes on the surviving spouse primary liability for a deceased spouse's funeral expense.[69] If there is no provision in the decedent's will specifying payment out of the decedent's estate, the

---

[62] Reg. § 20.2053-2.

[63] Reg. § 20.2053-1(d)(1). Nevertheless, funeral expenses accrued but not paid when the return is filed, a likely occurrence with the nine-month filing period, generally may be deducted on the return. Reg. § 20.2053-1(d)(4). Cf. Reg. § 20.2053-1(d)(7) Ex. 1.

[64] Compare Ingleheart v. Comm'r, 77 F2d 704 (5th Cir. 1935) (perpetual care of cemetery lot not chargeable against the estate under Florida law) with Comm'r v. Estate of Cardeza, 173 F2d 19 (3d Cir. 1949) (perpetual care of mausoleum an allowable expense under Pennsylvania law).

[65] Reg. § 20.2053-1(b)(1). Quantitative limitations respected by local law are most likely to arise out of testamentary insistence on a modest burial.

[66] Reg. § 20.2053-1(a)(1). See infra ¶ 5.03[6][c]. Cf. Blackburn v. United States, 1960-2 USTC ¶ 11,964 (SD Ind. 1960) (no deduction for funeral expenses where a will contained no direction for payment, and absent such direction, funeral expenses were not payable out of the decedent's estate).

[67] Estate of Lang v. Comm'r, 97 F2d 867 (9th Cir. 1938) (Washington law); United States v. Collins, 399 F2d 90 (5th Cir. 1968) (pre-1967 Texas law); Estate of Pinkerton v. Comm'r, TC Memo. 1974-71 (1974) (pre-1970 California law); Rev. Rul. 70-156, 1970-1 CB 190 (pre-1970 California law). Cf. Estate of Orcutt v. Comm'r, TC Memo. 1977-178 (1977) (similar result as to pre-1975 California administration expenses).

[68] See Rev. Rul. 69-193, 1969-1 CB 222; Rev. Rul. 71-168, 1971-1 CB 271, reflecting the predictable changes in Texas and California law, respectively, and, for the future, reversing the results indicated in United States v. Collins, 399 F2d 90 (5th Cir. 1968), Estate of Pinkerton v. Comm'r, TC Memo. 1974-71 (1974), and Revenue Ruling 70-156, 1970-1 CB 190. See also Nev. Rev. Stat. § 150.230(4) (2001) (Nevada law amended to reach this result); Estate of Lee v. Comm'r, 11 TC 141 (1948) (funeral expenses fully deductible under Idaho law).

[69] See Bradley v. Comm'r, TCM ¶ 43,382 (1943).

estate is allowed no deduction, since the expenses are simply those of the surviving spouse and, not being properly chargeable against the decedent's estate, are not allowable under local law.[70]

Veterans Administration payments to cover burial and funeral expenses, excluded from the gross estate, constitute a reimbursement that reduces the amount otherwise deductible.[71] On the other hand, a lump-sum death payment under the Social Security Act, excluded from the gross estate, is not required to be applied to funeral or burial expenses and should not reduce the funeral expenses deduction under Section 2053(a)(1).[72]

A final hurdle for the deductibility of funeral expenses is imposed by Section 2053(c)(2), which, with an exception, limits the aggregate Section 2053(a) deductions to the value of estate assets subject to claims. This restriction, along with other restrictions, is discussed later in this section[73] after a consideration of other deductions that are more likely to invoke the limitation.

[3] Administration Expenses

Section 2053(a)(2) authorizes the deduction of administration expenses. The expenses that fall into this category are those "actually and necessarily...incurred...in the collection of assets, payment of debts, and distribution

---

[70] Rev. Rul. 76-369, 1976-2 CB 281 (analyzing controlling local law in several states). However, if the estate is secondarily liable and the surviving spouse is insolvent, a deduction should be allowed if the estate pays the expenses and the payment is properly approved by the local court. Id. If in a case of intestacy the estate is at least secondarily liable under local law and pays the funeral expenses with proper judicial sanction, again the deduction should be allowed, if the surviving spouse's insolvency saddles the estate with the obligation. Id.

[71] Rev. Rul. 66-234, 1966-2 CB, 436, 437. The Veteran's Administration burial allowance at the time of the Revenue Ruling was only available for claims by the undertaker. Under 38 CRF §§ 3.1601(1)(iii) and 3.1601(2)(iv), the executor of the estate may execute a claim for the V.A. burial and plot allowance.

[72] Benefits paid to a spouse or a person equitably entitled to the payments are not included in the gross estate. Rev. Rul. 55-87, 1955-2 CB 112. Under a prior version of the Social Security Act (old 42 USC § 402(I)), a lump-sum death payment made to someone other than the surviving spouse was required to be made to the funeral home or to the person who paid the funeral bill and was limited to the amount actually paid. The total amount of the funeral expenses were required to be reduced for payments made to someone other than the surviving spouse to determine the allowable deduction under Section 2053(a)(1). No reduction was required if the benefits were paid to the surviving spouse because the Act did not require that the payment be related to or used to defray funeral expenses. Rev. Rul. 66-234, 1966-2 CB 436. The Social Security Act was amended in 1981 to no longer require the lump-sum death payment to be paid directly to the funeral home or to the person who paid the funeral bill. Omnibus Budget Reconciliation Act of 1981, Pub. L. No. 97-35, § 2202(a)(1), 95 Stat. 831–838, 841 (1981). Given the 1981 amendments to the Social Security Act after Revenue Ruling 66-234, a lump-sum death payment should no longer be required to reduce funeral or burial expenses in the determination of the Section 2053(a)(1) deduction.

[73] See infra ¶¶ 5.03[6][c][iv], 5.03[6][c][i]-[iii].

of property to the persons entitled to it."[74] The regulations specifically recognize as administration expenses executor commissions and attorneys' fees,[75] as well as such miscellaneous expenses as court costs, surrogates' fees, accountants' fees, appraisers' fees, and clerical costs.[76]

As in the case of funeral expenses, the concern here is only with expenses "actually incurred." The "allowable" concept, equally applicable here, is again a matter of limitation, not authorization.[77] The regulations properly take the position that mere allowance of a deduction under state law is insufficient to permit a Section 2053(a)(2) deduction, unless the expense is an actual and necessary administration expense within the meaning of federal law.[78] The Seventh Circuit has improperly refused to follow that regulation and treats deductibility as governed by state law alone.[79] The better rule as adopted by a majority of the circuits, requires not only allowance by state law but also that the expenses be administration expenses within the meaning of that term in the federal statute.[80] As previously discussed, the question whether an administra-

---

[74] Reg. § 20.2053-3(a).

Administration expenses incurred with respect to property not subject to claims are sometimes permitted by Section 2053(b). See infra ¶ 5.03[6][c][iii].

Section 642(g) preludes deductibility of Section 2053(a)(2) administration expenses under the income tax unless the estate waives the right to a Section 2053(a)(2) estate tax deduction. See infra ¶ 5.03[6][a].

[75] Reg. §§ 20.2053-3(b), 20.2053-3(c). See infra ¶ 5.03[3][a]. See also infra ¶ 5.03[3][b] discussing deductibility of trustee fees.

[76] Reg. § 20.2053-3(d). See infra ¶ 5.03[3][c].

[77] See supra ¶ 5.03[2][b].

[78] Reg. § 20.2053-3(a). See supra ¶ 5.03[1] text accompanying notes 8–10.

[79] Jenner v. Comm'r, 577 F2d 1100 (7th Cir. 1978). Some authors agree. See Tow, "Estate of Love and § 2053(a)(2): Why State Law Should Control the Determination of Deductible Administrative Expenses," 12 Va. Tax Rev. 283, 334 (1992). Considering the same issue, see also Nantell & Rogers, "Deductibility of Administration Expenses Is Not Always Black and White," 16 Hamline L. Rev. 105, 145 (1992); Caron, "The Estate Tax Deduction for Administrative Expenses: Reformulating Complementary Rules for Federal and State Laws Under IRC § 2053(a)(2)," 67 Cornell L. Rev. 981, 1010 (1982).

[80] Estate of Smith v. Comm'r, 57 TC 650 (1972), aff'd without determining the validity of the regulations, 510 F2d 479 (2d Cir. 1975), cert. denied, 423 US 827 (1975); United States v. White, 853 F2d 107 (2d Cir. 1988), cert. denied, 493 US 5 (1989); Estate of Love v. Comm'r, 923 F2d 335 (4th Cir. 1991); Pitner v. United States, 388 F2d 651 (5th Cir. 1967); Estate of Millikin v. Comm'r, 125 F3d 339 (6th Cir. 1997) overruling Estate of Park v. Comm'r, 475 F2d 673 (6th Cir. 1973); Hibernia Bank v. United States, 581 F2d 741 (9th Cir. 1978); Marcus v. DeWitt, 704 F2d 1227 (11th Cir 1983). See also Estate of Posen v. Comm'r, 75 TC 355 (1980); Estate of Reilly v. Comm'r, 76 TC 369 (1981); Payne v. United States, 1975-1 USTC ¶ 13,059 (MD Fla. 1975); Hefner v. United States, 880 F. Supp. 770 (WD Okla. 1993).

The Tax Court opinion in *Smith* clearly rejects its improper earlier view rather casually expressed in Estate of Sternberger v. Comm'r, 18 TC 836 (1952), acq. 1953-1 CB 6, nonacq. 1953-1 CB 7, aff'd per curiam, 207 F2d 600 (2d Cir. 1953), rev'd on another issue, 348 US 187 (1955).

tion expense is allowable raises a local law issue,[81] a question as to the effect of a local decree,[82] a requirement that the amount of the expenses be determined,[83] and generally, that an actual payment be made.[84] As with funeral expenses, estimates are frequently permitted and a deduction allowed even though payment is not actually made.[85]

[a] Executor Commissions and Attorney Fees

Executor commissions and attorney fees are obvious examples of deductible administrative expenses.[86] An executor who is a lawyer may be paid deductible fees (subject to income tax) in both capacities, if the lawyer performs legal services.[87] Of course, not every payment made by an estate to an executor or administrator or to an attorney will qualify as an expense of administration. The reason for the payment, the reasonableness of the payment, and the capacity in which the payee receives the payment will all be relevant in determining whether the expenditure is deductible.[88] Thus, for example, a bequest to the executor, not paid as a commission, does not entitle the estate to a de-

---

See TAM 8826003 (Mar. 14, 1988) (providing a simple illustration of the issue where the Service refused to allow the costs of pet care as an administration expense, notwithstanding that the expenses had been approved by the local probate court, because it is the Service's position that Section 2053 applies only to those expenses necessary to preserve the property of the estate).

[81] See supra ¶ 5.03[1][a] text accompanying notes 13–16; Malone v. United States, 493 F. Supp. 527 (SD Tex. 1980) (attorney fees limited by state law); Estate of Grant v. Comm'r, TC Memo. 1999-396 (1999) (executor's fees limited by state law); Estate of Rabe v. Comm'r, TC Memo. 1975-26 (1975) (extraordinary executor fees disallowed in absence of state court approval); Estate of Dowlin v. Comm'r, TC Memo. 1994-183 (1994) (residence expense and extraordinary executor's fees not deductible in absence of proof of state court approval).

[82] E.g., First Nat'l Bank of Ft. Worth v. United States, 301 F. Supp. 667 (ND Tex. 1969) (unreasonable attorney fees not deductible even though allowed by probate court); Estate of Agnew v. Comm'r, TC Memo. 1975-173 (1975) (Tax Court independent determination from state court as to whether fees were necessary); Succession of Helis v. United States, 52 Fed. Cl. 745 (2002) (excessive executor fees awarded by local court presumptive evidence of reasonableness).

[83] See supra ¶ 5.03[1][b][i]. The foreign exchange rate in effect on the date of payment is used in determining the value of foreign administration expenses under Section 2053(a)(2). Rev. Rul. 80-260, 1980-2 CB 277.

[84] See supra ¶ 5.03[1][b][iii].

[85] See supra ¶ 5.03[2][b] text accompanying note 63. See also supra ¶ 5.03[1][b], infra text accompanying note 97.

[86] Reg. §§ 20.2053-3(b), 20.2053-3(c).

[87] Rev. Rul. 69-551, 1969-2 CB 177. Such fees are included in the lawyer's gross income under Section 61. See, for example, Fla. Stat. § 733.617(6).

[88] E.g., Estate of Agnew v. Comm'r, TC Memo. 1975-173 (1975) (Tax Court made determination of reasonableness of fees independent of state court); Estate of Craft v. Comm'r, 68 TC 249 (1977), aff'd per curiam, 608 F2d 240 (5th Cir. 1979) (excess fees reasonable and deductible). See also cases cited supra note 69 and infra note 83.

duction.[89] However, even if the estate loses an estate tax deduction in the case of a specific bequest that takes the place of commissions, the executor benefits by being permitted to exclude the amount received from gross income for income tax purposes.[90] Obviously, this inverse relationship between income and estate taxes has resulted in tax planning that broadly considers both the consequences to the estate and the executor of an estate where the executor is a friend or relative. Even if the decedent has provided in a will for both a bequest to the executor and payment of commissions, an executor who is willing to forgo the latter fees may be able to avoid both income and gift taxation on the fees if a timely waiver is executed.[91]

No deduction is allowed for attorney fees if the attorney is performing services primarily for the benefit of individual legatees or beneficiaries rather than for the estate.[92] In many cases, payment of such personal expenses by the estate will not be proper under state law, and thus the "allowable under local law" requirement of Section 2053(a) will not be fulfilled.[93] Even if this is not the case, the disallowance of such expenses may be proper on the ground that if they are not primarily or directly related to the administration of the decedent's estate, they are not "administration expenses" as that term is used in Section 2053(a).[94] In some cases it is unclear whether the expense was incurred for the benefit of a beneficiary or for the estate. One court has drawn

---

[89] Reg. 20.2053-3(b)(4).

[90] The value of property acquired by bequest is excluded from gross income under Section 102(a). United States v. Merriam, 263 US 179 (1923) (bequest made in "lieu of compensation" not taxable to executor), criticized in Bank of New York v. Helvering, 132 F2d 773 (2d Cir. 1943), and in Wolder v. Comm'r, 493 F2d 608 (2d Cir. 1974) (bequests were included in gross income as compensation for services).

[91] See Rev. Rul. 66-167, 1966-1 CB 20 (executor's waiver of fees avoided inclusion of the fees in gross income and transfer of the fees subject to the gift tax where, as a result of the waiver, the fees passed to a third party). Relative tax rates under the two taxes are a key to making decisions here, and one may want to waive only a portion of one's fees.

[92] Reg. §§ 20.2053-3(a), 20.2053-3(c)(3); Jacobs v. United States, 248 F. Supp. 695 (D. Tex. 1965); Estate of Hecksher v. Comm'r, 63 TC 485 (1975); Estate of Bartberger v. Comm'r, TC Memo. 1988-21 (1988); Estate of Baird v. Comm'r, TC Memo. 1997-55 (1997) (all involving fees not deductible because not for the benefit of the estate). But see Dulles v. Johnson, 155 F. Supp. 275, 282 (SDNY 1957); rev'd on other issues, 273 F2d 362 (2d Cir. 1959), cert. denied, 364 US 834 (1960); Peirce v. United States, 80-1 USTC ¶ 13,338 (WD Pa. 1980); Estate of Reilly v. Comm'r, 76 TC 369 (1980); Rev. Rul. 74-509, 1974-2 CB 302; TAM 200532049 (Mar. 23, 2005) (all allowing deductions that were beneficial to the estate).

[93] Estate of Baldwin v. Comm'r, 59 TC 654 (1973); Estate of McCoy v. Comm'r, TC Memo. 1961-40 (1961); J. Kessler, Admr., DC Cal., 2007-1 USTC ¶ 60,554.

[94] Cf. Reg. §§ 20.2053-3(a), 20.2053-3(b)(5), 20.2053-3(c)(3). Compare Estate of O'Neal v. United States, 258 F3d 1265 (11th Cir. 2001) (disallowing deduction for attorney's fees because of lack of substantiation that fees were incurred for work of the estate) with Whitt v. Comm'r, TC Memo. 1983-262 (1983), aff'd, 751 F2d 1548 (11th Cir. 1985) (allowing deduction for attorney's fees incurred to defend estate and executor against criminal charges). Estate of Goldberg, TC Memo. 2010-26 (2010) (estate did not provide

the line between expenses incurred in an internecine conflict among beneficiaries over their respective shares (not deductible) and those incurred in a dispute between the true beneficiaries as a group and other spurious contenders
(deductible).[95]

The term "expense" clearly connotes outgo; it is therefore appropriate for
the Treasury to condition a deduction for administration expenses on ultimate
payment.[96] However, it is quite common for executor and attorney fees to be
paid long after the filing of the estate tax return. It is therefore equally reasonable for the Treasury to permit the return to be prepared and filed on the basis
of estimates, with suitable provision for adjustment in the case of disallowance
on audit or in the case of nonpayment.[97]

---

any evidence related to the amount of the attorney fees, whether the fees were necessarily
incurred in the administration of the estate, or whether the fees were actually paid).

[95] Pitner v. United States, 388 F2d 651 (5th Cir. 1967). The opinion is noteworthy
also for its analysis of the meaning of "allowable" and its recognition that there can be
administration expenses when there is no "administration" because it is foreclosed by state
law (Texas) for lack of necessity. Id. at 655. Another case that fits within this distinction
is Porter v. Comm'r, 49 TC 207 (1967) (allowing a deduction for expenses incurred by
two children successfully asserting against their surviving parent their deceased parent's
interest in property held as community property under New Mexico law at the time of the
parents' divorce).

[96] Reg. §§ 20.2053-1(b)(1), 20.2053-3(b)(1), 20.2053-3(c)(1). See, e.g., Estate of
O'Neal v. United States, 258 F3d 1265 (11th Cir. 2001) (disallowing deduction where no
substantiation of legal fees).

The fees must also be reasonable. Reg. § 20.2053-1(c)(1). Pitner v. United States,
388 F2d 651 (5th Cir. 1967) (deduction must be reasonable under the circumstances); Estate of Mariano v. Comm'r, TC Memo. 1996-58 (1996), rev'd on other issue, 142 F3d
651 (3rd Cir. 1998) (some fees excessive); Estate of Prell v. Comm'r, 48 TC 67 (1967)
(factors to consider in determining reasonableness). Cf. Reg. § 20.2053-8(d) Ex. 1. Estate
of Goldberg, TC Memo. 2010-26 (2010) (estate did not provide any evidence related to
the amount of the attorney fees, whether the fees were necessarily incurred in the administration of the estate, or whether the fees were actually paid).

[97] Reg. §§ 20.2053-1(d)(4), 20.2053-1(d)(7) Ex.1, 20.2053-3(b)(1), 20.2053-3(c)(1).
Estimated executor's commissions are allowed if (1) the Commissioner is reasonably satisfied the commission will be paid; (2) the amount is allowable under state law; and (3)
the amount is in accordance with accepted practice in the jurisdiction for estates of similar
size and character. Reg. § 20.2053-3(b)(1). If these conditions are not met, a protective
claim for refund may be filed (see Reg. §§ 20.2053-3(b)(2), 20.2053-1(d)(5)) and the
amount may be adjusted (Reg. § 20.2053-3(c)(3)). If a deduction is allowed before payment and payment is waived or otherwise left unpaid, before the running of the statute of
limitations, the executor has a duty to notify the Commissioner and pay the resulting tax
with interest. Reg. § 20.2053-3(b)(3). There is no duty on the part of the personal representative to report after the period of limitation has expired. TD 9468 (Oct. 16, 2009),
Summary of Comments and Explanation of Revisions, Item 4. But see Reg.
§ 20.2053-3(b)(3), (last sentence), implying that the obligation exists after the running of
the statute of limitations. But see supra ¶ 5.03[1][b][iv] n. 50.

Estimated attorney's fees are deductible if the Commissioner is reasonably satisfied
that the amount will be paid and that the amount is reasonable taking into account the size
and character of the estate and the local law and practice. Reg. § 20.2053-3(c)(1). Cf.
Reg. § 20.2053-3(d)(3).

In this respect, attorney fees sometimes present a special problem, as they may depend on services performed in connection with an audit or even litigation of tax liability after the estate tax return is filed. In deficiency or refund litigation, it is prudent, and permitted by the regulations,[98] to assert early a right to refund based on anticipated attorney fees even though the amount cannot be established at the time. Similarly, attorney's fees may be incurred in defending the estate against other claims and their expenses, even if the estate is not ultimately victorious, if incurred in good faith are also deductible in the same manner.[99] If nothing is done in this respect until the litigation has run its course, a refund based on the attorney fees will likely be barred by the statute of limitations,[100] although last-minute thoughts that result in the amendment of a petition or complaint before judgment may get the attorney fees recognized, if a claim for refund on other grounds has been timely asserted.[101] In addition, this problem can be resolved by the filing of a protective claim for refund which must be filed prior to the running of the statute of limitations.[102]

[b] Commissions Paid to a Trustee

Commissions paid to a trustee generally do not qualify as administration expenses.[103] For example, fees paid to a trustee for services to be performed in the management of a testamentary trust after its creation are "not in settlement of a dead man's affairs, but for the benefit of the beneficiaries of the trust."[104] In fact, amounts paid to an executor for services, nominally for the settlement of the estate but actually in the capacity of trustee for beneficiaries, have been properly disallowed as deductions.[105] On the other hand, if a trustee performs

---

[98] Reg. § 20.2053-3(c)(2).

[99] Reg. § 20.2053-3(d)(3). Such expenses include costs related to arbitration, mediation, and associated with reaching a negotiated settlement. Id. Expenses incurred merely for the purpose of unreasonably extending the time for payment are not deductible. Id. Beat v. U.S., 2011-1 USTC ¶ 60,617 (Bankr. D. Kan. 2011) (court approved expenditure of attorney fees in executor's failed attempt to claim a marital deduction, based on a purported common law marriage with decedent, following jury trial which found that executor had reasonable cause and acted in good faith in claiming such deduction).

[100] United States v. Wells Fargo Bank, 393 F2d 272 (9th Cir. 1963); Estate of Swietlik v. United States, 779 F2d 1306 (7th Cir. 1985). See also Moir v. United States, 149 F2d 455 (1st Cir. 1945) (barring attorney's fees attempted to be deducted after final determination of estate tax liability by Tax Court). Cf. Rev. Rul. 78-323, 1978-2 CB 240 (allowing deduction for 60 days after Tax Court decision only to the extent the allowance of the deduction is reflected in final Tax Court decision).

[101] Bankers Trust Co. v. United States, 438 F2d 1046 (2d Cir. 1970).

[102] Reg. § 20.2053-3(c)(1). See Reg. § 20.2053-1(d)(4), supra ¶ 5.03[1][b][iv].

[103] Reg. § 20.2053-3(b)(5).

[104] Estate of Sharpe v. Comm'r, 148 F2d 179, 181 (3d Cir. 1945).

[105] Estate of Carson v. Comm'r, TC Memo. 1976-73 (1976) (disallowing expenses of selling property for the benefit of beneficiary); Estate of Eagan v. Comm'r, 18 BTA 875 (1930), acq. IX-2 CB 17 (disallowing executor's commissions for period executor deemed to be acting as trustee where will directed executor to retain and manage assets for benefi-

services concerning property included within the probate estate, services that would normally be undertaken by the executor, fees for such services may be proper administration expenses.[106] An example would be amounts paid to a trustee in connection with the setting up (not management) of a testamentary trust. When assets of an inter vivos trust are included in a decedent's gross estate, the trustee's commissions for termination of the trust are either excludible from the gross estate or deductible as a Section 2053 expense.[107]

[c] Miscellaneous Administration Expenses

In addition to the administration expenses listed above, there are numerous other types of deductible administration expenses. Again, to be deductible, such expenses must be allowable by state law,[108] they must be established as actually and necessarily incurred in the administration of the decedent's estate

---

ciary); Estate of Peckham v. Comm'r, 19 BTA 1020 (1930) (disallowing administration expenses incurred in preserving and maintaining estate beyond ordinary administration period where will directed six year administration and executors deemed to be acting as trustees).

[106] Reg. § 20.2053-3(b)(5). Cf IRC § 2053(b), involving trustees' fees on nonprobate assets, discussed at ¶ 5.03[6][c][iii].

[107] Haggart's Estate v. Comm'r, 182 F2d 514 (3d Cir. 1950); Estate of De Foucaucourt v. Comm'r, 62 TC 485 (1974). Cf. Reg. § 20.2053-8(d) Exs. 1, 2, and 4; infra ¶ 5.03[6][c][iii].

[108] See supra ¶ 5.03[1][a] text accompanying notes 13–16.

in the collection of assets, payment of debts and distribution of property, and, generally, they must be paid.[109]

[i] Interest expenses. If, for a purpose beneficial[110] to the estate, the decedent's executor permits post-death interest[111] to accrue on either the decedent's debts incurred before or the estate's debts incurred after the decedent's death, the interest generally[112] is an administration expense deductible if allowable under the state law.[113]

---

[109] Reg. § 20.2053-3(a). See Jenner v Comm'r, 577 F2d 1100 (7th Cir. 1978) (improperly concluding that deductibility of administration expenses was solely a matter of state law). But see supra ¶ 5.03[3] text accompanying notes 78–80. In Estate of Riese v. Comm'r, TC Memo 2011-60 (2011), the estate of decedent who failed to pay rent on residence following termination of qualified personal residence trust (QPRT) (see, generally, ¶ 19.03[3][d]) was entitled to Section 2053(a)(3) deduction for unpaid accrued rent during post-QPRT period because it was a debt owed by the decedent at the time of her death. See supra ¶ 5.03[4]. The estate was not, however, allowed a Section 2053(a)(2) administrative expense deduction for rent owed after decedent's death since, as the court noted, the estate "did not require a roof over its head" nor was the estate allowed an administrative expense deduction for investment management fees paid to decedent's son-in-law because no evidence was presented of what services were provided to the estate or that such fees were reasonable and necessarily incurred.

[110] Regulation Section 20.2053-3(a) provides that such expenses must be "necessarily...incurred" expenses. See Estate of Wheless v. Comm'r, 72 TC 470 (1979) (allowing interest deductions where executors were unable to liquidate pre-death debts without selling assets at sacrifice prices); Ballance v. United States, 347 F2d 419 (7th Cir. 1965) (permitting deduction of post-death interest on pre-death debt incurred to avoid sale of assets at sacrifice prices); Turner v. United States, 306 F. Supp. 2d 668 (ND Tex. 2004) (statutory interest incurred by estate while awaiting determination of charitable status of a beneficiary was deductible); Estate of Street v. Comm'r, TC Memo. 1994-568 (1994) (disallowing deduction because estate did not meet burden to show there was a liquidity problem necessitating a loan to pay taxes); Hibernia Bank v. United States, 581 F2d 741 (9th Cir. 1978) (interest on residential loan was not deductible administration expense because loan proceeds not needed to administer estate); Rev. Rul. 77-461, 1977-2 CB 324 (interest on installment obligation incurred during decedent's life was not an administration expense because it was not a necessary expense in winding up of estate). Cf. Welch v. Helvering, 290 US 111, 113 (1933) (defining "necessary" under Section 162(a) of the income tax as "appropriate and helpful").

[111] See Reg. § 20.2053-4(e)(2). Interest accrued before death for which the decedent was personally liable is deductible either as a claim against the estate under Section 2053(a)(3) or as a part of a secured indebtedness under Section 2053(a)(4). Reg. § 20.2053-4(e)(1), Reg. § 20.2053-7. See infra ¶¶ 5.03[4], 5.03[5].

[112] But see infra text accompanying notes 124–126.

[113] Reg. §§ 20.2053-3(a), 20.2053-3(d)(1). If interest is deducted as a Section 2053 administration expense, the Service takes the position that post-death interest accruing on deferred federal estate tax payable from a testamentary transfer is an expense that may reduce the value of the transfer for purposes of Section 2013 (see ¶ 3.05[3][b] text accompanying notes 47, 48, 49, 50), and does reduce the value of the transfer for the purposes of Sections 2055 (see ¶ 5.05[3][b][ii] text accompanying note 117) and 2056 (see ¶ 5.06[5][b][ii] text accompanying note 119). See also Reg. §§ 20.2013-4(b)(3)(i),

As with all deductible administrative expenses, any post-death interest must be determinable with reasonable accuracy and eventually be paid in order to be currently deductible.[114] Thus, if the interest obligation is subject to fluctuating rates[115] or there is a possibility of an acceleration of the loan,[116] the interest is deductible only as payment is made.[117]

Most of the cases considering the deductibility of interest as an administration expense involve interest accruing on a decedent's obligation to pay various types of taxes. Interest paid on a loan whose proceeds are used to pay the federal estate tax qualifies as an administration expense,[118] as does interest

---

20.2055-3(b)(3), 20.2055-3(b)(6), 20.2056(b)-4(d)(2), 20.2056(b)-4(d)(3), 20.2056(b)-4(d)(5) Ex. 4.

[114] Reg. § 20.2053-1(d)(4)(i). See supra ¶ 5.03[1] text accompanying notes 17–19. Cf. Succession of Helis v. United States, 56 Fed. Cl. 544 (2003) (denying deduction for Section 6166 interest (prior to Section 2053(c)(1)(D)) which might ultimately be refunded).

[115] Bailly v. Comm'r, 81 TC 949 (1983); Estate of Bliss v. Comm'r, TC Memo. 1985-529 (1985); Hoover v. Comm'r, TC Memo. 1985-183 (1985); Estate of Harrison v. Comm'r, TC Memo. 1987-8 (1987).

[116] Rev. Rul. 84-75, 1984-1 CB 193; Snyder v. United States, 582 F. Supp. 196 (D. Md. 1984). Compare Estate of Graegin v. Comm'r, TC Memo. 1988-477 (1988); Priv. Ltr. Rul. 9952039 (Sept. 30, 1999); Priv. Ltr. Rul. 9903038 (Oct. 2, 1998) (all involving full amount of interest currently deductible because no possibility of acceleration of payment).

[117] Reg. § 20.2053-1(d)(4)(ii). A protective claim may be filed. Reg. § 20.2053-1(d)(5). See ¶ 5.03[1][b][iv]. See also Rev. Rul. 80-250, 1980-2 CB 278.

[118] However, again the estate must prove that the interest was "actually and necessarily incurred." Reg. § 20.2053-3(a). Estate of Todd v. Comm'r, 57 TC 288 (1971), acq. 1973-2 CB 4; Hipp v. United States, 1972-1 USTC ¶ 12824 (DSC 1971); Estate of McKee v. Comm'r, TC Memo. 1996-362 (1996); Estate of Sturgis v. Comm'r, TC Memo. 1987-415 (1987); Estate of Gilman v. Comm'r, TC Memo. 2004-238 (2004); Estate of Webster v Comm'r, 65 TC 968 (1976), acq. in part, nonacq. in part, 1977-2 CB2, 3 (post-death interest on loans to purchase flower bonds was deductible); Estate of Buchholtz v. Comm'r, 70 TC 814 (1978) (same); Estate of Graegin v. Comm'r, TC Memo. 1988-477 (1988) (holding interest deductible even though loan was made by decedent's closely-held corporation). Estate of Murphy, 2009-2 USTC ¶ 60,583 (WD Ark. 2009) (interest deductible on loans from FLP to pay the estate tax liability because of decline in value of decedent's retained assets and appreciation of the assets held in the FLP that was formed by decedent). Estate of Keller, 2010-2 USTC ¶ 60,605 (SD Tex. 2010) (interest deductible on loan from FLP to pay the estate tax where court held that the loan had economic substance and was necessary to preserve the estate's liquidity). But see Estate of Lasarzig v. Comm'r, TC Memo. 1999-307 (1999) (interest on a loan to pay estate tax on QTIP trust whose assets were distributed and estate was no longer being administered was not necessarily incurred); Rupert v. United States, 358 F. Supp. 421 (MD Pa. 2004) (motion for summary judgment denied because estate did not satisfy burden to show interest expense was necessary); TAM 200513028 (Sept. 15, 2004) (loan not necessarily incurred where estate had sufficient liquid assets); Estate of Black, 133 TC No. 15 (2009) (loan unnecessary because the only difference between the loan and some other transaction to obtain the needed funds was that the loan interest gave rise to an estate tax deduction and that the estate's main beneficiary and the lending FLP's majority partner was decedent's son who was, in effect, paying interest to himself); Estate of Stick v. Comm'r, TC Memo

paid on a decedent's federal estate tax deficiency to the extent allowable by local law.[119] Similarly, post-death interest payments allowable by local law on the decedent's state or federal income tax deficiency,[120] state or federal gift tax deficiency,[121] state death tax deficiency,[122] or foreign death tax deficiency[123] are also deductible administration expenses.

There are some limitations on the above holdings. For decedent's dying after 1997, interest payments on estate taxes deferred under Section 6166 do not qualify for a Section 2053 deduction.[124] Interest that is refunded or reimbursed to the estate is not an expense and is therefore not deductible.[125] And interest related to the Section 2032A(c) recapture tax is not deductible because it is a tax on the qualified heir, not on the decedent.[126]

[ii] Selling expenses. If assets must be sold to realize cash to pay the decedent's debts, expenses, or taxes, to preserve the decedent's estate, or to discharge cash legacies, then related brokerage charges and other selling expenses

---

2010-192 (2010) (estate offered no proof that borrowing funds to pay its tax liabilities was necessary and estate had sufficient liquid assets to satisfy federal and state estate tax liabilities and funeral expenses).

[119] Rev. Rul. 79-252, 1979-2 CB 333. This includes Section 6161 interest on a failure to timely pay estate taxes. Estate of Bahr v. Comm'r, 68 TC 74 (1977), acq. 1978-1 CB 1; Rev. Rul. 81-154, 1981-1 CB 470 (same, but holding that a Section 6651 penalty for late filing of a return is not a deductible administration expense necessarily incurred by the estate). But see CCA 200836027 (May 12, 2008) (interest accruing on an extension to pay estate tax that was granted under Section 6161 due to the estate's lack of liquid assets is, however, nondeductible personal interest under IRC § 163(h)(2) and cannot be deducted on estate's income tax return).

[120] Rev. Rul. 69-402, 1969-2 CB 176; Maehling v. United States, 1967-2 USTC ¶ 12,486 (SD Ind. 1967).

[121] Estate of Webster v. Comm'r, 65 TC 968 (1976), acq. in part, nonacq. in part, 1977-2 CB 2, 3.

[122] Rev. Rul. 81-256, 1981-2 CB 183.

[123] Rev. Rul. 83-24, 1983-1 CB 229.

[124] IRC § 2053(c)(1)(D). The rationale for this appropriate deduction disallowance, as well as other aspects of the subsection, are discussed at ¶ 2.02[3][c][v].

For decedents dying prior to 1998, such interest was generally deductible. See Rev. Rul. 78-125, 1978-1 CB 292; Rev. Rul. 81-287, 1981-2 CB 183; Rev. Proc. 81-27, 1981-2 CB 548; Estate of Shapiro v. Comm'r, 111 F3d 1010 (2d Cir. 1997), cert. denied, 522 US 1045 (1998). But see Succession of Helis v. United States, 56 Fed. Cl. 544 (2003). However, for decedents dying before 1998, interest paid on estate taxes deferred under Section 6166 was not deductible under Section 2053 if there was an election to have Section 6601(j) as amended apply to installments due after the effective date of the election. Taxpayer Relief Act of 1997, Pub. L. No. 105-34, § 503(d)(2), 111 Stat. 788, 853, reprinted in 1997-4 CB 1457, 1539.

[125] Estate of O'Daniel v. United States, 6 F3d 321 (5th Cir. 1993). Cf. Axtell v. United States, 860 F. Supp. 795 (D. Wyo. 1994) (disallowing deduction for interest claimed after Section 6511 statute of limitations had run, even though interest would have been deductible had a Section 6166 election been made).

[126] Rev. Rul. 90-8, 1990-1 CB 173.

are deductible administration expenses if allowed by state law.[127] For example, underwriting fees incurred in marketing a large block of stock are deductible.[128] The cases require one of the above purposes for the sale[129] and, to the extent that the sale proceeds are used for other purposes,[130] exceed the appropriate purposes,[131] or are speculative,[132] that portion of the selling expenses is nondeductible.

[iii] Other deductible administration expenses. It is not possible here to suggest all the other types of deductible administration expenses, but a few further examples may help to illustrate the possibilities. Court costs, surrogates' fees, accountants' fees, appraisers' fees and expert witnesses' fees are all commonly incurred deductible administration expenses.[133] Brokerage commissions to acquire a new tenant for real estate in the estate during administration of the estate are deductible.[134] Expenses incurred for investment counseling pending administration of the estate have been held deductible.[135]

---

[127] Reg. § 20.2053-3(d)(2). See supra ¶ 5.03[1] text accompanying notes 12–16. See also supra ¶ 5.03[3] text accompanying notes 78–85.

Excise taxes incurred in selling or distributing property also constitute deductible administration expenses if the sale is necessary in order to (1) pay the decedent's debts, expenses of administration, or taxes; (2) preserve the estate; or (3) effect distribution. Reg. § 20.2053-6(e).

Cf. TAM 200444021 (June 21, 2004) (income tax liability on IRA distribution used to pay estate tax not deductible as administration expense).

[128] The underwriters are not purchasers of stock from the estate, but rather brokers on behalf of the estate. Estate of Jenner v. Comm'r, 577 F2d 1100 (7th Cir. 1978); Estate of Joslyn v. Comm'r, 566 F2d 677 (9th Cir 1977). See Gillespie v. United States, 23 F3d 36 (2d Cir. 1994); Rev. Rul. 83-30, 1983-1 CB 224 (both allowing a deduction, but also holding that such fees are not considered in determining a blockage discount). See ¶ 4.02[4][e][ii], especially note 206. Cf. infra ¶ 5.03[6][a] note 273.

[129] Estate of Blossom v. Comm'r, 45 BTA 691, (1941), nonacq. 1966-2 CB 7 (brokerage fees to sell stock to distribute estate); Estate of Allison v. Comm'r, 5 TCM (CCH) 992 (1946) (brokerage fees to sell rather than repair estate property); Ferguson v. United States, 81-1 USTC ¶ 13,409 (D. Ariz. 1981) (selling expenses necessary to preserve estate). Cf. Marcus v. DeWitt, 704 F2d 1227 (11th Cir. 1983) (ruling summary judgment inappropriate on necessity issue).

[130] Estate of Swayne v. Comm'r, 43 TC 190 (1964), acq. 1965-2 CB 6 (no showing of relevant purpose); Estate of Carson v. Comm'r, TC Memo. 1976-73 (1976) (sale for benefit of beneficiary, not the estate); Estate of Posen v. Comm'r, 75 TC 355 (1980) (sale of property not necessary for administration of estate). Cf. Estate of Grant v. Comm'r, TC Memo. 1999-396 (1999) (disallowing deductions for repairs to property to enhance sale where proceeds of sale not for appropriate purposes).

[131] Estate of Smith v. Comm'r, 57 TC 650 (1972), aff'd on other grounds, 510 F2d 479 (2d Cir.), cert. den. sub. nom. 423 US 827 (1975).

[132] Estate of Koss v. Comm'r, TC Memo. 1994-599 (1994).

[133] Reg. § 20.2053-3(d)(1).

[134] Estate of Papson v. Comm'r, 73 TC 290 (1979).

[135] Estate of Lehman v. Comm'r, 39 BTA 17 (1939), acq. 1939-1 CB 20, aff'd on other issues, 109 F2d 99 (2d Cir. 1940), cert. denied, 310 US 637 (1940).

On the grounds that operation of a farm during administration of its owner's estate was a proper matter of maintenance, losses incurred on such operation have been held deductible as administration expenses,[136] but an estate cannot successfully claim expenses incurred in the development of estate property (as opposed to its maintenance) as deductible administration expenses.[137] Expenses allocable to tax-exempt income, for which an estate is denied an income tax deduction under Section 265, are deductible for estate tax purposes.[138] Expenses incurred in defending the decedent's estate against claims described in Section 2053(a)(3)[139] or mortgages described in Section 2053(a)(4)[140] are deductible even if the estate is not ultimately victorious.[141] Such costs include costs related to arbitration, mediation, and reaching a negotiated settlement.[142] However, such costs do not include expenses incurred merely to extend the time for payment or costs not incurred in good faith.[143]

[4] Claims Against the Estate

While Section 2053(a) groups several categories of estate tax deductions, there are sharp philosophical differences in the allowance of previously discussed funeral and administration expenses deductible under Sections 2053(a)(1) and 2053(a)(2) and the allowance of claims under Section 2053(a)(3).[144] The first two paragraphs condition deductions on post-death expenditures that are actually made, and, of course, properly made under local law, to support a reduction in the taxable estate. The deduction under the third paragraph depends on whether there were "personal obligations of the decedent existing at the time of the decedent's death."[145]

---

[136] Estate of Brewer v. Comm'r, 1941 BTA (P-H) ¶ 41,574.

[137] Estate of Hammon v. Comm'r, 10 BTA 43 (1928), acq. 1928 CB 13.

[138] Rev. Rul. 59-32, 1959-1 CB 245 (allowing an estate tax deduction), clarified in Rev. Rul. 63-27, 1963-1 CB 57 (considering allocation of expenses related to exempt and non-exempt income).

[139] See infra ¶ 5.03[4][b] text accompanying note 177, ¶ 5.03[4][c][ii] text accompanying note 219.

[140] See infra ¶ 5.03[5] text accompanying note 253.

[141] Reg. §§ 20.2053-3(d)(3), 20.2053-4(d) Ex. 6.

[142] Reg. §§ 20.2053-3(d)(3).

[143] Reg. §§ 20.2053-3(d)(3).

[144] Deductions of mortgages under Section 2053(a)(4) are similar to claims in that deductibility depends on personal obligations of the decedent at death. See infra ¶ 5.03[5].

[145] Reg. § 20.2053-4(a)(1). See infra ¶¶ 5.03[4][a] and 5.03[4][b]. The claims must be enforceable against the decedent's estate at the time of payment and generally payment must be made by the estate. Reg. §§ 20.2053-4(a) through 20.2053-4(c). See infra ¶ 5.03[4][c][iii]. These requirements often require a post-death examination of events which occur, often along the same lines as the examination of post-death events under Section 2053(a)(1) and 2053(a)(2).

[a] Personal Obligations of Decedent

The required personal obligation exists only if a claim has a substantial economic effect on the person required to pay it. The obligation must be bona fide,[146] not the result of an uncontested family law suit,[147] a collusive law suit,[148] or some other circumstance not constituting a valid personal obligation of the decedent.[149] A successful or settled claim to share in an estate is not a deductible claim against the estate, because it does not represent a personal obligation of the decedent.[150] On the other hand, if there is a valid claim against the estate based on valid consideration,[151] even though the decedent contracted to discharge the debt by a specific provision in the decedent's will, such an arrangement does not convert the creditor's deductible claim to a nondeductible bequest.[152]

See also IRC § 2053(c)(2) generally limiting an allowable deduction for claims to an amount not in excess of the value of estate assets subject to claims, discussed infra ¶ 5.03[6][c][iv].

[146] Reg. § 20.2053-4(a)(1); ¶ 5.03[1][b][ii]; Rev. Rul. 76-498, 1976-2 CB 199 (value of services as trustee of a grantor trust until the time of grantor's death was a bona fide obligation); Estate of Elkins v. United States, 457 F. Supp. 870 (SD Tex. 1978) (bona fide intrafamily loan); Estate of Ribblesdale v. Comm'r, TC Memo. 1964-177 (1964) (same); Bailey v. Comm'r, 741 F2d 801 (5th Cir. 1984) (constructive trust for son was valid claim). Estate of Riese v. Comm'r, TC Memo 2011-60 (2011) (estate of decedent who failed to pay rent on residence following termination of qualified personal residence trust (QPRT) (see, generally, ¶ 19.03[3][d]) entitled to Section 2053(c)(3) deduction for unpaid accrued rent during post-QPRT period). See infra ¶ 5.03[4][a][i], ¶ 5.03[4][a][ii]; text accompanying note 155.

[147] Estate of Bath v. Comm'r, TC Memo. 1975-102 (1975). See infra ¶ 5.03[4][a][i].

[148] Rev. Rul. 83-54, 1983-1 CB 229. See supra ¶ 5.03[1][b][i].

[149] See, e.g., Estate of Gray v. Comm'r, TC Memo. 1997-67 (1997) (payment to decedent by corporation was a dividend not a loan creating a personal obligation of the decedent); Estate of Holland v. Comm'r, TC Memo. 1997-302 (1997) (check to decedent from trust was not a loan creating a personal obligation of the decedent); Estate of Stewart v. Comm'r, TC Memo. 2006-225 (2006) (finding no proof of personal obligation to son); Estate of Olivo, TC Memo. 2011-163 (2011) (uncorroborated testimony by decedent's son that decedent had agreed to pay him $400 a day for the nearly full-time care he provided to her until her death, which amounted to $1.24 million, was insufficient to support an estate tax deduction). Compare Marshall v. United States, 84 AFTR2d ¶ 99-6525, aff'd per curiam 251 F3d 157 (5th Cir. 2001) (obligation under state law where decedent held usufruct interest) with Albritton v. United States, 89 AFTR2d 2002-1764 (MD La. 2001) (no obligation).

[150] Lazar v Comm'r, 58 TC 543 (1972); Estate of Moore v. Comm'r, TC Memo. 1987-587 (1987) (both holding will contest settlements not deductible as Section 2053(a)(3) claims).

[151] See infra ¶ 5.03[4][a][i].

[152] First Nat'l Bank of Amarillo v. United States, 422 F2d 1385 (10th Cir. 1970). Cf. Wolder v. Comm'r, 493 F2d 608 (2d Cir.), cert. denied, 419 US 828 (1974); Rev. Rul. 67-375, 1967-2 CB 60 (both allowing a deductible claim, but properly subjecting to income tax a bequest that was compensation for services, despite the exclusion of "bequests" from gross income under Section 102(a)).

[i] The consideration requirement. A significant limitation on the deduction for claims is codified in Section 2053(c)(1). A claim against the estate that is *"founded on a promise or agreement"* is deductible only to the extent that it was contracted in good faith and for an adequate and full consideration in money or money's worth.[153]

The need for such a rule can be easily understood. Begin with the general proposition that an enforceable claim against the estate gives rise to a deduction. For example, assume that at some time prior to death, Decedent promises to pay Child $100,000 and puts Child in a position to enforce the claim by giving Child an instrument under seal. Perhaps Decedent does the same with other children or other intended beneficiaries. Upon Decedent's death, should such claims operate to reduce the amount of Decedent's estate subject to tax? If so, the estate tax would be subject to very easy avoidance. Therefore, the statute denies a deduction for claims founded on a promise or agreement unless something with a monetary value came into the estate in exchange for the obligation undertaken by the decedent.[154] Because of the tax avoidance possibilities, intrafamily debt is scrutinized carefully to determine, as discussed above, whether a bona fide debt exists and to determine whether the consideration requirement is satisfied.[155] The consideration requirement, which relates

---

[153] IRC § 2053(c)(1)(A). See Reg. § 20.2053-4(d)(5). See also Estate of Fenton v. Comm'r, 70 TC 263 (1978); Estate of Scholl v. Comm'r, 88 TC 1265 (1987); Estate of Wilson v. Comm'r, TC Memo. 1998-309 (1998) (all holding that adequacy of the consideration is made at the time of the promise or agreement).

[154] Latty v. Comm'r, 62 F2d 952 (6th Cir. 1933); Young v. United States, 559 F2d 695 (DC Cir. 1977); Estate of Hughes v. Comm'r, TC Memo. 2005-296 (2005) (holding that note to family corporation not founded on valid consideration). A seal is not a substitute for consideration under Section 2053(c)(1). Estate of Davis v. Comm'r, 57 TC 833 (1972).

See Bank of New York v. United States, 526 F2d 1012 (3d Cir. 1975), (settlement of a claim by a third-party beneficiary against the surviving spouse in a joint and mutual will estate was nondeductible under Section 2053(a)(3) for lack of consideration); Estate of Huntington v. Comm'r, 16 F3d 462 (1st Cir. 1994) (same); Luce v. United States, 444 F. Supp. 347 (WD Mo. 1977) (same). See also Estate of Harden v. Comm'r, TC Memo. 1996-488 (1996) (denying deduction for lack of consideration for nonfamily member obligation). But see Estate of Shapiro v. U.S., No. 08-17491 (9th Cir. 2011), where an estate was entitled to a deduction for a palimony claim filed against the decedent. Although Nevada courts had not yet addressed the sufficiency of homemaking services as consideration for such a contract, other states within the circuit have recognized such services as adequate to form a contract. The Court further held that the estate was not estopped from claiming a deduction in excess of the amount the claim was settled for. In accordance with the version of Regulations § 20.2053-1(b)(3) in effect at the time of the decedent's death, an estate could deduct the value of a claim as of the date of death, even if there were uncertainty about the amount, while contesting the validity of the claim in state court. Compare a surviving spouse's situation under a community property widow's election. See ¶ 4.08[7][c].

[155] See Reg. § 20.2053-1(b)(2) and supra ¶ 5.03[1][b][ii]; Estate of Flandreau v. Comm'r, 994 F2d 91 (Fed. Cir. 1993) (holding that a gift to a family member equal to the annual exclusion amount followed by a loan of the same amount back to donor was a

only to claims founded on a promise or agreement, should not affect the deductibility of claims reflecting liabilities imposed by law or arising out of torts, which do not involve the avoidance possibilities discussed here.[156]

The two most difficult problems with respect to this limitation are: When is a claim founded on a promise or agreement? What is an adequate and full consideration in money or money's worth?

When is a claim founded on a promise or agreement? If a decedent merely made a gratuitous but enforceable promise, any claim resting on it is obviously founded on a promise, and lack of any consideration precludes any deduction for the claim. It is perhaps equally obvious that if the decedent were liable under a judgment based on some tortious act by the decedent during life, a claim under the judgment is not founded on a promise or agreement; thus, the claim is deductible without regard to any question of consideration. The difficult cases arise between these extremes. In the first example, the situation would not be altered merely because the claim was reduced to judgment; the judgment would merely enforce the claim, which would remain founded on a promise.[157] However, some judgments, even though they relate to previously made agreements, do more than enforce the agreements. A claim arising out of a divorce, even if the parties have entered into a separation agreement, will probably not be held to be a claim founded on an agreement.[158]

What is consideration in money or money's worth? A further problem arises out of the requirement that consideration be in money or money's worth.

---

mere promise to pay not founded on consideration when donor died); Estate of Labombarde v. Comm'r, 58 TC 745 (1972), aff'd per curiam, 1973-2 USTC ¶ 12,953 (1st Cir. 1973) (transfers were gifts not loans); Estate of Stewart v. Comm'r, TC Memo. 2006-225 (2006) (son's testimony as to oral agreement was not credible). Compare Estate of Ribblesdale v. Comm'r, TC Memo. 1964-177 (1964) (valid intrafamily loan); Estate of Elkins v. United States, 457 F. Supp. 870 (SD Tex. 1978) (same); Childress v. United States, 1977-1 USTC ¶ 13,181 (ND Ala. 1977) (valid obligation founded on consideration). In Beecher v. United States, 280 F2d 202, 204 (3d Cir. 1960), the court allowed a deduction for a claim by the decedent's children based on the decedent's agreement to leave a portion of his estate to them. The consideration issue was skirted by an unexplained express stipulation that the agreement was for "an adequate and full consideration in money or money's worth."

[156] Cf. Reg. § 20.2053-1(b)(2)(ii).

[157] Estate of Markwell v. Comm'r, 112 F2d 253 (7th Cir. 1940). Other judgments may be nothing more than a mere promise or agreement. See Rev. Rul. 83-54, 1983-1 CB 229 (collusive law suit); Bath v. Comm'r, TC Memo. 1975-102 (1975) (uncontested law suit).

[158] Rev. Rul. 60-160, 1960-1 CB 374, modifying ET 19, 1946-2 CB 166. For a detailed discussion of this issue, see ¶ 4.15[1][b][i] text accompanying notes 40–42. See also Bowes v. United States, 77-2 USTC ¶ 13,212 (ND Ill. 1977), aff'd on another issue, 593 F2d 272 (7th Cir. 1979) (claims founded upon court decree) and Estate of Waters v. Comm'r, 48 F3d 838 (4th Cir. 1995) (agreement not founded on decree but deductible because consideration was provided in the form of vested property rights, not mere marital rights, under Section 2043(b)); Gray v. United States, 541 F2d 228 (9th Cir. 1976) (holding claim not founded on court decree and remanding on adequacy of consideration issue).

If the value the decedent received was less than the value of the obligation the decedent incurred, the deduction is not permitted to exceed the value received. If a decedent was the accommodation endorser of another's note, the consideration requirement is satisfied by the value of the money or money's worth that the borrower received, rather than the value the decedent received.[159] In this connection it should be recalled, however, that the claim against the decedent as an endorser or possibly as comaker is deductible only to the extent that the right against the borrower is valueless.[160]

Support rights are treated as founded on consideration in money or money's worth.[161] However, generally the relinquishment or promised relinquishment of the right to dower or courtesy, or statutory substitutes for either, or of other marital rights in the decedent's property or estate, are not consideration in money or money's worth.[162] Thus, a claim arising out of a prenuptial agreement probably cannot meet the consideration test in order to be deductible.[163] Section 2053(e) creates an exception to the marital rights-consideration rule which treats the relinquishment of such marital rights in the decedent's

---

[159] For example, Comm'r v. Wragg, 141 F2d 638 (1st Cir. 1944), cites numerous cases in which the Commissioner unsuccessfully advanced the contention that nothing was received by the decedent that could satisfy the requirements of Section 2053(c)(1)(A). All these cases, however, were decided prior to the Supreme Court's decision in Comm'r v. Wemyss, 324 US 303, 307 (1945), in which for gift tax purposes the Court said, "[M]oney consideration must benefit the donor to relieve a transfer by him from being a gift...." The estate tax deduction cases regarding accommodation endorsers seem at variance with this concept. On the other hand, some seemingly anomalous results look better under the sharp light of careful analysis. Suppose brother B borrows $11,000 from sister S. Parent P desires to free B of the obligation without making immediate payment. P assumes B's obligation to S who releases B, effecting a novation. P dies and S files a claim. Deductible? Yes. But did P not get anything? Yes, P did. If P has simply borrowed $11,000 from S and made a gift to B, clearly the claim would have been supported by the $11,000 P received. The earlier hypothetical case is not different in principle; what P might do with what P borrowed is not controlling. See Estate of Woody v. Comm'r, 36 TC 900, 904 (1961), acq. 1966-1 CB 3.

[160] See Reg. § 20.2053-4(d)(3).

[161] Rev. Rul. 68-379, 1968-2 CB 414, superseding ET 19, 1946-2 CB 166, which expressed the same principle. See also Estate of Kosow v. Comm'r, 45 F3d 1524 (11th Cir. 1995) (holding that waiver of support rights constituted valid consideration); Leopold v. United States, 510 F2d 617 (9th Cir. 1975) (same).

[162] IRC § 2043(b)(1); ¶ 4.15[1][a].

[163] Sutton v. Comm'r, 535 F2d 254 (4th Cir.), cert. denied, 419 US 1021 (1974); Estate of Morse v. Comm'r, 625 F2d 133 (6th Cir. 1980); Estate of Graegin v. Comm'r, TC Memo. 1988-477 (1988); Estate of Herrmann v. Comm'r, TC Memo. 1995-90 (1995); aff'd, 85 F3d 1023 (2d Cir. 1996). But see Carli v. Comm'r, 84 TC 649 (1985) (prenuptial agreement waiver of community property rights constituted consideration). This problem and cases related to it are discussed with the discussion of Section 2043(b) at ¶ 4.15[1][a].

property or estate as adequate and full consideration in money or money's worth in some divorce situations.[164]

Section 2053(c)(1)(A) expressly provides another important exception to the rule requiring consideration to support a claim based on a promise or agreement. A gratuitous promise to make a gift to a qualified donee for charitable purposes (as defined and specified in Section 2055), if enforceable,[165] is treated as if the promise were, instead, a bequest to charity.[166]

[ii] Community property issues. The personal obligation of the decedent requirement often arises as an issue in community property situations. For example, as manager of community property, one spouse might be personally liable at death for the full amount of community debts. But if the deceased spouse's obligation is accompanied by a right of recovery for half of the amount against the surviving spouse's share of the community property, the deceased spouse has the required personal obligation for only one half of the community obligation.[167] Of course, the Section 2053 deduction is not increased by a will direction that the entire obligation be paid out of the deceased spouse's estate, for then the additional amount is merely an indirect bequest to the surviving spouse and not an obligation.[168]

[iii] Section 2044 claims. Section 2053 allows no deduction for any claim by a remainderperson[169] for property included in a decedent's gross estate under Section 2044.[170] Such a deduction, if allowed, would eliminate the property from the tax base in both the decedent's estate and the estate of the

---

[164] See IRC §§ 2053(e), 2043(b)(2), 2516. This area is discussed in the analysis of Section 2043, see ¶ 4.15[1][b][i] text accompanying notes 43–48.

[165] See Estate of Levin v. Comm'r, TC Memo. 1995-81 (1995) (denying deduction because promise not enforceable under state law); Estate of Sochalski v. Comm'r, TC Memo. 1955-19 (1955) (same).

[166] This paragraph overcomes the decision of the Supreme Court in Taft v. Comm'r, 304 US 351 (1938). See Reg. § 20.2053-5; Priv. Ltr. Rul. 9718031 (Feb. 4, 1997) (pledge to university building fund was deductible). See also Reg. § 20.2053-4(d)(5). However, the restrictive rules of Section 2055, such as Section 2055(e), must be observed to qualify for a Section 2053 deduction. See ¶ 5.05, especially ¶¶ 5.05[4]–5.05[8].

[167] United States v. Stapf, 375 US 118 (1963). Accord Estate of Fulmer v. Comm'r, 83 TC 302 (1984) (allowing deduction as full amount of claim was against decedent's one half of the community property). Cf. Deobald's Estate v. United States, 444 F. Supp. 374 (ED La. 1977) (allowing deduction for surviving spouse's community property claim against one half of property included in decedent's gross estate).

[168] United States v. Stapf, 375 US 118 (1963).

[169] The term "remainderperson" as used in this section should be interpreted broadly to include any person having an interest in the property occurring subsequent to the decedent's qualifying income interest (e.g., a secondary life estate). Cf. ¶ 4.16 text accompanying notes 11 and 12.

[170] IRC § 2053(c)(1)(C). See ¶ 4.16.

decedent's predeceasing spouse,[171] thus eliminating the justification for the previously allowed marital deduction.

[b] Existing at the Time of Death

The debt which is the basis of the claim must be viable at the date of the decedent's death, valid and enforceable under the laws of the jurisdiction in which the estate is administered.[172] An otherwise valid claim barred by the statute of limitations or the doctrine of latches is not an "existing" claim that would support a deduction,[173] assuming that such a claim would not be allowed under local law.[174] Thus, if a claim is unenforceable prior to or at decedent's death or becomes unenforceable during administration of the decedent's estate (if payment was not made while the claim was enforceable),[175] no deduction is allowed even if payment of the claim is made.[176] A deduction may be available as an administrative expense for expenses incurred in establishing the unenforceability of a claim.[177]

[i] Taxes as claims.
The statute under Section 2053 draws specific lines with respect to pre-death accrued taxes which are deductible as claims and post-death taxes which if deductible may only be deductible as administrative expenses.[178] Section 2053(c)(1)(B) expressly precludes any deduction as

---

[171] IRC §§ 2056(b)(7), 2523(f). See ¶¶ 5.06[8][d], 11.03[4][c].

[172] See Greenburg v. Comm'r, 76 TC 680 (1981) (valid claim). Interest accrued at the decedent's death on such a claim is itself a claim. Reg. § 20.2053-4(e)(1).

[173] Reg. §§ 20.2053-4(a)(1), 20.2053-4(d)(4), 20.2053-4(d)(7) Ex. 7; Estate of Honickman v. Comm'r, 58 TC 132 (1972), aff'd in unpub. op. 401 F2d 1398 (3d Cir. 1973); Jones v. United States, 424 F. Supp. 236 (ED Ill. 1976). See also Estate of Ehret v. Comm'r, TC Memo. 1976-315 (1976), (barring deduction of an otherwise valid claim because the claim was not filed in state probate proceedings).

The Service also takes the position that a claim valid under state law is not deductible if allowance of the claim would violate sharply defined public policy. TAM 9207004 (Oct. 21, 1991) (confiscation of illegal drugs). See Turnier, "The Pink Panther Meets the Grim Reaper: Estate Taxation of the Fruits of Crime," 72 NC L. Rev. 163 (1993).

[174] Estate of Horvath v. Comm'r, 59 TC 551 (1973) (decedent's acknowledgment of an obligation precluded its being barred by statute of limitations); Estate of Thompson v. Comm'r, 730 F2d 1071 (7th Cir. 1983) (allowing deduction because executor acknowledged claim even though claim not filed); Estate of Elkins v. United States, 457 F. Supp. 870 (SD Tex. 1978) (allowing claim even though will precluded executor from claiming statute of limitations on intrafamily loan). See Palmquist, "The Estate Tax Deductibility of Unenforced Claims Against a Decedent's Estate," 11 Gonzaga L. Rev. 707 (1976).

[175] To the extent that enforceability is at issue, the claim is a contested claim. Reg. § 20.2053-1(b)(3)(iv). See Reg. § 20.2053-4(d)(4); infra ¶ 5.03[4][c].

[176] Reg. § 20.2053-4(d)(4). See Reg. § 20.2053-4(d)(7) Ex. 7.

[177] Reg. § 20.2053-3(d)(3). See Reg. § 20.2053-4(d)(7) Ex. 7; supra ¶ 5.03[3][c][iii] text accompanying note 139 and 141.

[178] See Reg. § 20.2053-6(a). See also supra ¶ 5.03[3][c].

claims[179] for income taxes on income received after the decedent's death, property taxes not accrued before the decedent's death, and "any[180] estate, succession, legacy, or inheritance taxes."[181] This negative rule seems hardly necessary in light of the personal obligation requirement of Section 2053(a)(3) and the parallel concept under Section 2053(a)(4) discussed later.[182] On the other hand, income taxes on income earned before death[183] and any other taxes, such as unpaid gift taxes on the decedent's lifetime transfers,[184] which are obligations of the decedent at the time of death,[185] represent deductible claims against the estate.[186] Since events occurring after the death of a decedent are considered in

---

[179] See TAM 200444021 (June 21, 2004) (disallowing deduction for income tax liability on an IRA distribution used to pay estate tax).

[180] This preclusion includes a municipal inheritance tax. McFarland v. United States, 80 AFTR2d 8348 (ED La. 1997).

[181] See Reg. § 20.2053-6(c). But see Section 2058 at ¶ 5.09 allowing a deduction for state death taxes and see the limited deduction for foreign death taxes under Section 2053(d) discussed infra ¶ 5.03[4][b][ii].

[182] See infra ¶ 5.03[5].

[183] Reg. § 20.2053-6(f). The regulation contains detailed rules for determining the extent of pre-death tax liability of the decedent where a joint return was filed with the decedent's spouse. See also Johnson v. United States, 742 F2d 137 (4th Cir. 1984) (remanding case to determine if claim for income tax liability not deductible because of a right of recovery of taxes from surviving spouse). Cf. Estate of Sachs v. Comm'r, 856 F2d 1158 (8th Cir. 1988) (no deductible claim for income taxes where Congress retroactively repealed the tax liability).

[184] Reg. § 20.2053-6(d). Estate of O'Neal v. United States, 258 F3d 1265 (11th Cir. 2001) (allowing deduction for donees' claim for reimbursement of gift tax paid as transferees). The regulation contains rules for determining the extent of a decedent's liability where a Section 2513 gift splitting section is made. Reg. § 20.2053-6(d). See also TAM 8837004 (June 2, 1988) (reducing deduction by amount of a surviving spouse's partial payment of a decedent's gift tax obligation, which arose after a post-mortem election to split gifts).

[185] See Estate of Proesel v. United States, 585 F2d 295 (7th Cir. 1978) aff'g 77-2 USTC ¶ 13,217 (ND Ill. 1977), cert. denied, 441 US 961 (1979) (decedent's executor's post-death Section 2513 election to split surviving spouse's pre-death gift was not an obligation of decedent existing at death).

[186] Some states treat state gift tax as a prepayment of state death tax if the property subject to the state gift tax is included in the estate for state death tax purposes. The Commissioner at one time took the position that if the state tax is not paid prior to decedent's death, the tax is a state "estate, inheritance, legacy or succession" tax not qualifying for a Section 2053(a)(3) deduction. Rev. Rul. 71-355, 1971-2 CB 334, revoked by Revenue Ruling 81-302, 1981-2 CB 170. This inappropriate position was repudiated in Lang v. Comm'r, 613 F2d 770 (9th Cir. 1980). Cf. Reg. § 20.2053-6(d); Estate of Gamble v. Comm'r, 69 TC 942 (1978), (rejecting a comparable position taken under Section 2033 in Rev. Rul. 75-63, 1975-1 CB 294). See ¶ 4.05[2][a]. The Commissioner reversed the position in both rulings in Revenue Ruling 81-301, 1981-2 CB 170. However, the Commissioner has appropriately taken the position that such state gift taxes do not qualify for a Section 2011 credit and seemingly will take the position that they will not qualify for a Section 2058 deduction. But see First Nat'l Bank & Trust Co. of Tulsa v. United States, 787 F2d 1393 (10th Cir. 1986), considered at ¶ 3.03[1] note 17; see ¶¶ 3.03[4], 5.09.

determining the amount of a deductible claim,[187] post-death adjustments may be made to the amount of tax liability accrued at death.[188]

Property taxes are deductible if, under local law, they have become obligations[189] of the decedent or liens on the decedent's property[190] at the time of the decedent's death; accrual in the usual accounting sense is not enough.[191] Despite the special problems that sometimes arise with respect to state taxes, an obligation need not have matured to the point of being presently payable to be deductible. It is enough if the decedent's obligation to make the payment at some future time has become fixed by the date of the decedent's death.[192] Again, it will be seen that the guiding thread that runs through the important provisions of Section 2053 seeks to value the decedent's actual net worth (taking account, too, of taxable lifetime transfers), to determine the value of what the decedent can actually transmit to survivors, after costs incurred in transmitting it.

[ii] Section 2053(d): Limited deductibility of certain foreign death taxes. In general, foreign death taxes are permitted to affect the amount of estate tax payable to the federal government only by way of a limited credit against tax provided by Section 2014.[193] Although Section 2053(c)(1)(B) ex-

---

[187] Reg. §§ 20.2053-4(a)(2), 20.2053-1(d)(2). See infra ¶ 5.03[4][c]. In Marshall Naify Revocable Trust v. US, 106 AFTR2d ¶ 2010-6236 (ND Cal. 2010), the court held that the amount an estate could deduct for pre-death state income taxes the estate was contesting was limited to the amount for which the claim was settled after the decedent's death. Since the value of the claim was not ascertainable with reasonable certainty at the time of the decedent's death, it was permissible for the court to consider post-death events in determining the amount of the deduction.

[188] Reg. § 20.2053-6(g). Such adjustments can involve an increase in the amount of tax liability accrued prior to the decedent's death or a decrease in the amount as a result of a tax refund. Id. Administrative expenses related to expenses associated with a determination of the amount may also be deductible. Id. Reg. § 20.2053-3(d)(3). See Reg. § 20.2053-(6)(g) Exs. 1 and 2.

[189] A tax may become a personal obligation and deductible before it becomes a lien on property. Estate of Pardee v. Comm'r, 49 TC 140 (1967) (involving Michigan law).

[190] Reg. § 20.2053-6(b).

[191] Reg. § 20.2053-6(b). Estate of Stewart v. Comm'r, TC Memo. 2006-225 (2006) (disallowing deduction for post-death payment of taxes because no obligation to pay at time of death). See Rev. Rul. 68-335, 1968-1 CB 406 (addressing Wash. property taxes, which accrue proratably over the year); Rev. Rul. 65-274, 1965-2 CB 377 (addressing Calif. property taxes, which accrue on lien date); Rev. Rul. 66-211, 1966-2 CB 439 (addressing Iowa property taxes, which accrue on lien date).

[192] Cf. Rev. Rul. 67-304, 1967-2 CB 224 (Section 642(g) inapplicable because the obligation was a Section 2053(c)(3) claim).

[193] See ¶ 3.06. Prior to the repeal of the Section 2011 state death tax credit in 2004, Section 2053 applied to allow limited deductibility of both state and foreign death taxes. See Stephens, Maxfield, Lind, Calfee & Smith, "Federal Estate and Gift Taxation," ¶ 5.03[8] (8th Ed. 2002). See also Prop. Reg. § 20.2053-9. Under the sunset provisions effective on January 1, 2011, the Section 2011 credit is restored to its status prior to the year 2002, the Section 2058 deduction is eliminated, and Section 2053(d) is restored to its

pressly denies a deduction under Section 2053 for "any estate, succession, legacy or inheritance taxes," which would include foreign death taxes,[194] Section 2053(d)(1) gives the estate an election to adhere to the usual credit provision or, instead, to deduct foreign (subject to special restrictions) death taxes, but only those imposed on charitable bequests. If the deduction is elected,[195] appropriate adjustments must be made in the credit otherwise allowed.[196]

Under Section 2053(d)(2), the provision is severely restricted. The Section 2053(d)(1) deduction can be claimed only if the resulting decrease in tax will inure solely to the benefit of a qualified charity, as defined in Sections 2055 and 2106(a)(2). However, if the financial burden of the federal estate tax is to be apportioned among those interested in the estate, equitably and with reference to interests that qualify for exemptions, credits, or deductions,[197] benefit of the deduction inures "solely" to the charity if its share of the tax is appropriately reduced by reason of the deduction, even though the amount of tax actually to be borne by other beneficiaries is also reduced.[198] If no apportionment provision applies, the entire decrease in tax must inure to the benefit of a qualified charity in order for the deduction to be allowed.[199] The regulations provide a formula for determining the amount of the foreign death tax attributable to the charitable transfer.[200] The significance of this elective provision is more fully explored in Chapter 3.[201]

[c] Contingency of a Claim

[i] **Introduction.** A claim may be deductible from the decedent's gross estate regardless of whether it has matured at the time of the decedent's death. In some instances there is substantial uncertainty whether at the time of the decedent's death the decedent had any personal obligation to another. For example, suppose the decedent was killed in an automobile accident in which

---

prior status. Economic Growth and Tax Relief Reconciliation Act of 2001, Pub. L. No. 107-16, § 901(a)(2), 115 Stat. 38, 150 (2001), reprinted in 2001-3 CB 9, at 122. The sunset provision is discussed more fully at ¶ 8.10[5].

[194] But see Section 2058 at ¶ 5.09 allowing a deduction for state death taxes and see supra ¶ 5.03[4][b][i] text accompanying note 181.

[195] See Reg. § 20.2053-10(c).

[196] See ¶ 3.06[3][b].

[197] See, e.g., "State Statutes" in the discussion of Section 2205, at ¶ 8.04[2].

[198] Reg. §§ 20.2053-10(b)(1)(ii), 20.2053-10(b)(2). Cf. Reg. § 20.2053-9(e) Ex. 2. But also Cf. Reg. § 20.2053-9(e) Exs. 3–5 (benefit did not inure to charity); Estate of Bush v. United States, 618 F2d 741 (Ct. Cl. 1980) (state tax payment not inure to charity).

[199] Reg. § 20.2053-10(b)(1)(i); Watson v. McGinnes, 240 F. Supp. 833 (ED Pa. 1965). Cf. Reg. § 20.2053-9(e) Ex. 1; Estate of Darlington v. Comm'r, 302 F2d 693 (3d Cir. 1962) (state court determination of inurement binding on Tax Court).

[200] Reg. § 20.2053-10(d).

[201] See ¶¶ 3.06[3][b], 3.06[3][c].

another was injured. If the other person presents a claim against the decedent's estate, the decedent's obligation may depend on whether the decedent's negligence caused the injury. In such circumstances, an arm's-length settlement between the claimant and the estate or a judgment calling for payment of the claim is determinative of the existence of the requisite personal obligation and its amount.[202] Similarly, the amount of a decedent's personal obligation may be quite uncertain, even if it is clear there is some obligation, as where at death the decedent's income tax returns for several years are being audited. A post-death arm's-length settlement or actual adjudication again is the amount of the Section 2053 deduction.[203] Post-death events are permitted to affect the deduction;[204] the events mentioned (settlement or adjudication) determine the validity and the amount of the claim as of the date of death.[205]

A decedent's personal obligations at death may be contingent in various respects. For example, the decedent may be secondarily liable as an accommodation endorser of another's note. In a sense, the decedent has an obligation to pay the amount of the note, but in fact neither the decedent nor the decedent's estate may ever be called upon to do so. The settled doctrine in this area is that no deduction will be allowed if at death the estate will not be required to pay anything.[206] However, a deduction will be allowed in full for a claim arising out of the decedent's capacity as a secondary obligor (e.g., as endorser or guarantor) if the decedent's rights against the primary obligor are worthless.[207]

The contingency just mentioned is similar but not identical to another type of claim that clearly exists at death but that is entirely dependent as to amount on future events. The problem has arisen in several cases in which a

---

[202] Reg. § 20.2053-1(b)(3)(iv). See, e.g., Estate of Nilson v. Comm'r, TC Memo. 1972-141 (1972) (allowing deduction for claim based on malicious prosecution that settled pending administration of the estate).

[203] Reg. §§ 20.2053-1(b)(3)(i), 20.2053-1(b)(3)(iv). See Reg. § 20.2053-1(b)(3)(iii). Broadhead Trust v. Comm'r, TC Memo. 1972-196 (1972); Law v. United States, 83-1 USTC ¶ 13,514 (ND Cal. 1983). Cf. Marshall Naify Revocable Trust v. US, 106 AFTR2d ¶ 2010-6236 (ND Cal. 2010). Estate of McMorris v. Comm'r, 243 F3d 1254 (10th Cir. 2001) (since returns not being audited at decedent's death, subsequent change in income tax liability not relevant in determining Section 2053(a)(3) deduction).

[204] Reg. §§ 20.2053-4(a)(2), 20.2053-1(d)(2). Estate of Kyle v. Comm'r, 94 TC 829 (1990) (examining post-death events, taxpayers failed to prove there was a valid claim at death); Estate of Cafaro v. Comm'r, TC Memo. 1989-348 (1989) (same).

[205] But see Estate of Smith v. Comm'r, 198 F3d 515 (5th Cir. 1999), nonacq. 2000-04 (decided prior to the proposed regulations and concluding that a claim existed at death, therefore valuing the claim at death).

[206] See, e.g., Estate of May v. Comm'r, 8 TC 1099 (1947), acq. 1947-2 CB 3; Rev. Rul. 84-42, 1984-1 CB 194. Cf. Reg. § 20.2053-4(d)(3).

[207] Compare Comm'r v. Wragg, 141 F2d 638 (1st Cir. 1944) (citing numerous earlier cases in the same vein) and First Interstate Bank of Ariz. v. United States, 86-1 USTC ¶ 13,665 (D. Ariz. 1986) (looking at post-death events to value the claim) (both allowing a claim) with DuVal's Estate v. Comm'r, 152 F2d 103 (9th Cir. 1945), cert. denied, 328 US 838 (1946), and First Nat'l Bank of Pa. v. United States, 398 F. Supp. 100 (WD Pa. 1975) (neither allowing a claim). Cf. Prop. Reg. § 20.2053-4(b)(3).

decedent's divorced spouse has a deductible claim against the estate for ongoing payment of a fixed monthly or annual amount but the payments are to cease upon the former spouse's death or remarriage. It has never been suggested that these types of contingencies foreclose a Section 2053 deduction. The debated issue is instead whether the occurrence of either terminating event even shortly after the decedent's death is determinative of the amount of the deduction.

The Treasury has argued for almost fifty years that post-death events can affect the deductibility of claims even beyond the contingency of the claim area.[208] Substantial litigation has occurred as a result of the Treasury's position. Early cases in some Circuits were decided on the rationale that the purpose behind Section 2053 is to assure that a tax is imposed on the net estate allowing a deduction only where payment is required.[209] However, more recently, the trend of the cases had been running against the Treasury; several Circuits had not allowed a post-death examination of actual events to effect the amount of the claim.[210] The Treasury has stopped this trend by adopting rules similar to

---

[208] Rev. Rul. 60-247, 1960-2 CB 272, 274. See Rev. Rul. 75-24, 1975-1 CB 306, which is a minor liberalization of Revenue Ruling 60-247 in limited circumstances.

Revenue Ruling 60-247, 1960-2 CB 272, 274, does recognize that if a creditor is sole beneficiary of the estate, the creditor's claim may be allowed as a deduction, without requiring the useless act of the creditor's pressing the claim. See also Estate of Wildenthal v. Comm'r, TC Memo. 1970-119 (1970) (allowing a claim by the beneficiary of the estate).

[209] Jacobs v. Comm'r, 34 F2d 233 (8th Cir. 1929) (disallowing deduction for claim under an ante-nuptial agreement); Estate of Sachs v. Comm'r, 856 F2d 1158 (8th Cir. 1988) (following *Jacobs* even though income tax liability was subsequently forgiven); Comm'r v. Estate of Shively, 276 F2d 372 (2d Cir. 1960) (allowing deduction only for value of spousal support payments actually made before former spouse's remarriage and not value of actuarial payments) as of decedent's death; Estate of Taylor v. Comm'r, 39 TC 371 (1962), aff'd sub nom. Gowetz v. Comm'r, 320 F2d 874 (1st Cir. 1963). See also Estate of Courtney v. Comm'r, 62 TC 317 (1974); Estate of Chesterton v. United States, 551 F2d 278 (Ct. Cl. 1977), cert. denied, 434 US 835 (1977).

[210] Estate of O'Neal v. United States, 258 F3d 1265 (11th Cir. 2001) (claim for transferee gift tax liability reimbursement dependent on valuation of assets); Estate of McMorris v. Comm'r, 243 F3d 1254 (10th Cir. 2001) (reaching similar result with respect to claim for federal and state income tax liabilities); Estate of Smith v. Comm'r, 198 F3d 515, 525 (5th Cir. 1999) (distinguishing its prior decision in Estate of Hoagmann v. Comm'r, 60 TC 465 (1973)}], aff'd per curiam 492 F2d 796 (5th Cir. 1974), nonacq. AOD 2000-04 (rejecting a distinction between claims which are certain at death and mere contingent claims, see supra ¶ 5.03[4][c]; Propstra v. United States, 680 F2d 1248 (9th Cir. 1982) (allowing deduction for full amount of claim at death which were subsequently compromised); Estate of Van Horne v. Comm'r, 78 TC 728 (1982), aff'd, 720 F2d 1114 (9th Cir. 1983), cert. denied, 466 US 980 (1984) (allowing deduction for undisputed spousal support obligation based on actuarial tables). Cf. Succession of McCord v. Comm'r, 461 F3d 614 (5th Cir. 2006) (ruling similarly that post-gift events are off limits in establishing gift tax valuation). But see Marshall Naify Revocable Trust v. US, 106 AFTR2d ¶ 2010-6236 (ND Cal. 2010), where the court cited the Ninth Circuit's Propstra opinion for the comment there that post-death events are relevant when computing the deduction taken for a disputed or contingent claim. Accordingly, the court in Marshall Naify

rules under the other subparts of Section 2053[211] that preclude any deductibility of claims under Section 2053(a)(3) unless at the time of payment the claims are enforceable against the decedent's estate[212] and generally unless the amount of the claim is actually paid by the estate to satisfy the claim.[213] The rules specifically provide that: "[e]vents occurring after the date of a decedent's death shall be considered when determining the amount deductible [as a claim] against a decedent's estate."[214]

[ii] **Types of contingencies.** In effect, the rules limit Section 2053(a)(3) to claims that actually exist at the time of the payment, subject to no contingencies. These contingencies can take a variety of forms at the decedent's death. They include potential and unmatured claims.[215] Similarly, claims which are contested by the decedent's estate at the time of the decedent's death are not deductible until the contest is finally resolved.[216] Claims which are against multiple parties, including the decedent, are not deductible until the decedent's portion of the liability is determined.[217] The portion of the decedent's liability

---

Revocable Trust held that the amount an estate could deduct for pre-death state income taxes the estate was contesting was limited to the amount for which the claim was settled after the decedent's death. Since the value of the claim was not ascertainable with reasonable certainty at the time of the decedent's death, it was permissible for the court to consider post-death events in determining the amount of the deduction. The court also held in the case that the estate was judicially estopped from seeking a higher deduction for the claim given the estate's inconsistent positions in the state income tax proceeding and in the federal estate tax claim. See Aghdami, "Effect of Post-Mortem Facts as Claims Against the Estate," Trusts & Estates 18 (May, 2004).

[211] See supra ¶ 5.03[1][b].

[212] Reg. § 20.2053-4(a)(1).

[213] Reg. § 20.2053-4(a)(1)(i).

[214] Reg. § 20.2053-4(a)(2).

[215] Reg. § 20.2053-4(d)(1). Such claims are not deductible until they are no longer potential and have matured. Id. In a case decided under the prior rules, Marshall Naify Revocable Trust v. US, 106 AFTR2d ¶ 2010-6236 (ND Cal. 2010), the court held that the amount an estate could deduct for pre-death state income taxes the estate was contesting was limited to the amount for which the claim was settled after the decedent's death. Since the value of the claim was not ascertainable with reasonable certainty at the time of the decedent's death, it was permissible for the court to consider post-death events in determining the amount of the deduction. The court also held in the case that the estate was judicially estopped from seeking a higher deduction for the claim given the estate's inconsistent positions in the state income tax proceeding and in the federal estate tax claim. See also Estate of Saunders v. Comm'r, 136 TC No. 18 (2011) (citing *Marshall Naify Revocable Trust* and similarly decided under the prior rules, a malpractice claim against decedent's estate, appraised by the estate at $30 million, was determined to be too uncertain to value and, thus, the estate could only deduct the amount actually paid during administration of the estate – the parties eventually settled for $250,000); and Estate of Foster, TC Memo 2011-95 (2011) (no Section 2053 deduction for lawsuit concerning marital trust assets since estate had failed to establish the value of the claim with reasonable certainty).

[216] Reg. § 20.2053-4(d)(2). See Reg. § 20.2053-4(d)(7) Exs. 1–5.

[217] Reg. § 20.2053-4(d)(3). See Reg. § 20.2053-4(d)(7) Exs. 4 and 5.

must take into consideration the value of any reimbursement from another party, insurance, or by some other means.[218] Expenses incurred in defending or settling a claim may also be deductible but as a Section 2053(a)(2) administrative expense.[219]

Naturally, requiring the deductibility of a claim to be deferred until the claim is enforceable may result in problems with the running of the statute of limitations on the decedent's estate tax return. If the claim is established (and payment made) prior to the expiration of the period for filing a refund claim, a Section 6511 refund claim may be filed.[220] If not, a protective claim for refund may be filed,[221] but it must be filed prior to the expiration of the limitations period for filing a refund claim.[222]

[iii] **Actual payment.** Generally, deductibility of a claim under Section 2053 is also postponed until payment of the claim has been made.[223] This requirement may lead to the same procedural roadblocks that can preclude deductibility until the claim is established;[224] however, the same procedural methods may be used to preclude the estate statute of limitations foreclosing a deduction.[225] There are several exceptions to the claims payment requirement.

Ascertainable amounts. As with other Section 2053 deductions, there is an exception for certain ascertainable amounts.[226]

Claims or Counterclaims in a Related Matter. If a decedent's gross estate includes a particular asset and there are one or more claims against the decedent's estate integrally related to the asset,[227] the current value of the claim or claims may be deducted even though payment has not been made if a series of requirements are met.[228] Several are requirements that are generally applicable

---

[218] Reg. § 20.2053-4(d)(3). See Reg. § 20.2053-4(d)(7) Ex. 4.

[219] Reg. § 20.2053-3(d)(3). See supra ¶ 5.03[3][c][iii] text accompanying note 139. See also Reg. § 20.2053-4(d)(7) Exs. 1–7.

[220] See, e.g., Reg. § 20.2053-4(d)(7) Ex. 1.

[221] See supra ¶ 5.03[1][b][iv].

[222] See Reg. §§ 20.2053-4(d)(1), 20.2053-4(d)(7) Exs. 1 and 6.

[223] Reg. § 20.2053-4(a)(1)(i). See Rev. Rul. 80-260, 1980-2 CB 277 (the foreign exchange rate is the rate of exchange on the date of death if the claim is valued on that date; however, if post-death events are considered in valuing the claim, the rate on the date of payment is used in an automobile accident). Seemingly, under the regulations it should be the payment date in all events.

[224] See supra ¶ 5.03[4][c][ii] text accompanying notes 220–222.

[225] See supra ¶ 5.03[4][c][ii] text accompanying notes 220–222.

[226] Reg. § 20.2053-4(a)(1)(ii), 20.2053-1(d)(4). See supra ¶ 5.03[1][b][iii] text accompanying notes 47 and 48.

[227] See Reg. § 20.2053-4(c)(3) Ex. 3 (involving a claim and counterclaim in an automobile accident).

[228] Reg. § 20.2053-4(b)(1). The purpose of this exception is to provide relief from the need to file a protective claim. TD 9468 (Oct. 16, 2009), Summary of Contents and Explanation of Revisions, Item 5. See Reg. § 20.2053-1(d)(5) and text at notes 52-55 supra.

of deductible claims.[229] To qualify for the exception, the asset included within the gross estate must exceed ten percent of the value of the gross estate.[230] The value of the claim must be validated in a qualified appraisal,[231] be subject to adjustments for post-death events,[232] and is limited to the value of the related claims or particular assets included in the decedent's gross estate.[233]

Unpaid Claims up to $500,000. A second exception for payment allows some claims to be deducted up to a total of $500,000 even though payment has not been made at the time of filing the decedent's return.[234] Several requirements, some of which are generally applicable to claims,[235] apply. The value of each claim must be validated in a qualified appraisal,[236] and must be subject to adjustment for post-death events.[237] Each claim is only deductible in full (not a portion of its value)[238] and the total amount of claims under this exception may not exceed $500,000.[239]

In some circumstances, the estate is required to make recurring payments over a period of time potentially well beyond the limitations period. If the obligation is not subject to any contingencies,[240] the payments may be deducted

---

[229] The requirements of Regulations Section 20.2053-1 are met, the claim represents a personal obligation of the decedent existing at death, and the claim is enforceable against the decedent's estate (and is not unenforceable at death). Reg. §§ 20.2053-4(b)(1)(i) through 20.2053-4(b)(1)(iii).

[230] Reg. § 20.2053-4(b)(1)(vi). The amount of any claim in excess of this limitation may be the subject of a protective claim for refund. Reg. § 20.2053-4(b)(3). See Reg. § 20.2053-1(d)(5) and supra ¶ 5.03[1][b][iv].

[231] Reg. § 20.2053-4(b)(1)(iv). See IRC § 170(f)(11)(E).

[232] Reg. § 20.2053-4(b)(1)(v). See Reg. § 20.2053-4(b)(3).

[233] Reg. § 20.2053-4(b)(2). Cf. Reg. § 20.2053-4(c)(3) Ex. 3.

[234] The purpose of this exception is to provide relief from the need to file a protective claim. TD 9468 (Oct. 16, 2009), Summary of Comments and Explanation of Revisions, Item 5. See Reg. § 20.2053-1(d)(5) and text at notes 52 – 55 supra.

[235] The claims must satisfy the Regulations Section 20.2053-1 requirements, must be personal obligations of the decedent existing at death, and must be enforceable against the decedent's estate (and is not unenforceable when paid). Reg. §§ 20.2053-4(c)(1)(i) through 20.2053-4(c)(1)(iii).

[236] Reg. § 20.2053-4(c)(1)(iv). See IRC § 170(f)(11)(E).

[237] Reg. § 20.2053-4(c)(1)(vii). See Reg. § 20.2053-4(c)(2).

[238] Since the purpose of this exception is to provide relief from the need to file a protective claim, the entire amount of the claim must be deductible and covered by this cap. TD 9468 (Oct. 16, 2009), Summary of Comments and Explanation of Revisions, Item 5.

[239] Reg. §§ 20.2053-4(c)(1)(vi), 20.2053-4(c)(1)(v). These limits are illustrated in the regulations. See Reg. § 20.2053-4(c)(3) Ex. 1 (illustrating both the full deductibility and $500,000 rules), Ex. 2 (same), and Ex. 3 (illustrating the combination of the related matter claim and counterclaim and the full deductibility and $500,000 rules).

[240] If the payment is contingent on the death or remarriage of the claimant, the amount of the otherwise deductible claim is measured according to actuarial principles and is not contingent. Reg. § 20.2053-4(d)(6)(i).

to the extent that the amount may be determined with reasonable certainty.[241] However, if the recurring amounts are subject to a contingency and cannot be determined with reasonable certainty, actual payment is required prior to any deduction.[242] Finally, regardless of the contingency of the claim, if the estate purchases[243] a commercial annuity from an unrelated dealer of such annuities in an arm's-length transaction to satisfy the obligation, a deduction is allowed for any actual payments made (either prior to the annuity purchase or in excess of the annuity amount necessary to satisfy the obligation) and the amount paid for the annuity.[244]

[5] Mortgages

Section 2053(a)(4) allows a deduction for unpaid mortgages or other charges against property, if the value of the decedent's interest in the property is included in the decedent's gross estate without reduction for any such mortgage or charge. If only a portion of the property is included in the decedent's estate, then only that portion of the mortgage qualifies for the Section 2053(a)(4) deduction.[245] Although this provision might appear to afford the estate an election to include the full value and claim the deduction or to include only the value of the equity and claim no deduction, no such election is in fact recognized.[246] It seems to be settled that if the decedent is personally liable for the charge, the inclusion and deduction procedure must be followed;[247] but if the decedent is not personally liable (that is, there is only nonrecourse liability), only the value of the property less the amount of the charge is to be initially included

---

[241] Reg. §§ 20.2053-4(d)(6)(i), 20.2053-1(d)(4). See Reg. § 20.2053-4(d)(7) Ex. 8 (divorce payment terminating on death or remarriage is a noncontingent payment). Cf. Reg. §§ 20.7520-1 through 20.7520-4.

[242] Reg. § 20.2053-4(d)(6)(ii). See supra notes 224 and 225.

[243] The estate is permitted to own the annuity. Reg. §§ 20.2053-4(d)(6)(iii), 20.2053-4(d)(7) Ex. 9.

[244] Reg. § 20.2053-4(d)(6)(iii). See Reg. § 20.2053-4(d)(7) Ex. 9 (annuity for a contingent payment).

[245] Estate of Fawcett v. Comm'r, 64 TC 889 (1975), acq. 1978-2 CB 2 (one half of property included in estate and one half of mortgage deductible where prior transfer of one half of property was subject to the outstanding mortgage); TAM 200104008 (Oct. 17, 2000) (involving a Section 2040(b) inclusion and allowing deduction of one half of the mortgage on property). But see Rev. Rul. 79-302, 1979-2 CB 328 (60 percent of value property included under Section 2040(a) where only 50 percent of mortgage deductible because joint and several liability for the mortgage).

[246] Reg. § 20.2053-7.

[247] Estate of Fawcett v. Comm'r, 64 TC 889 (1975). acq., 1978-2 CB 2 (personal liability); Estate of Crail, 47 BTA 1042 (1942), (decedent and his wife gave their "three-year five percent note" secured by the mortgage in question, which created a personal liability in the decedent supporting a deduction in excess of the value of his interest in the property).

in the gross estate,[248] and then of course no deduction can be claimed.[249] So viewed, Section 2053(a)(4) often operates more as an exclusion than a deduction provision.[250] This provision may not be significant, as a rule, but it could determine the need for filing a return.[251] In some cases, it would be nice to include the low gross value of property and to deduct the charge of a much larger amount of nonrecourse liability against it.[252] However, this would not be in keeping with the purpose of Section 2053 to work toward a realistic taxable estate, for the decedent was not poorer to the full extent of the obligation if the obligation must be satisfied only out of property worth less than the obligation.

With respect to most mortgages, because the amount generally is easily determinable at the time of the decedent's death and, as a result, a post-death examination of events is generally unnecessary[253] and because payment can be anticipated,[254] a deduction generally should be allowed by the time of filing the decedent's estate tax return.[255]

---

[248] See Instructions for Form 706, United States Estate (and Generation-Skipping Transfer) Tax Return (revised Sept. 2009) Instructions for Schedule K. Debts of the Decedent and Mortgages and Liens. See also infra note 256, Comm'r v. Davis, 132 F2d 644 (1st Cir. 1943) (trust termination charge treated as a reduced gross estate inclusion).

[249] The responsive regulation, Regulation Section 20.2053-7, is actually vague. It indicates that if the decedent was not personally liable, only the value of the equity of redemption "need" be included in the gross estate. The word "may" should be substituted for the word "need"; then, as the value of the property "undiminished by the…mortgage" is *not* included, no *deduction* would be allowed under the regulations. In a "taxable estate" sense, one is not poorer to the extent that a charge against property exceeds its value unless the obligor has a personal obligation to the creditor to make up the difference. Cf. Estate of Crail v. Comm'r, 46 BTA 658 (1942), acq. 1946-2 CB 2, nonacq. 1942-2 CB 23, withdrawn (personal liability in excess of value of property).

[250] See, e.g., Estate of Wildenthal v. Comm'r, TC Memo. 1970-119 (1970).

[251] See IRC § 6018. See also Reg. § 20.2032-1(b)(1), on election of the alternate valuation date. Cf. ¶ 6.06[1] note 9 explaining a difference in result in the estate of a nonresident-noncitizen.

[252] Despite the regulations, can Section 2053(a)(4) be read to offer this choice? Cf. Rev. Rul. 83-81, 1983-1 CB 230 (allowing full deductibility of the amount of personal liability, even though Section 2032A special valuation was employed with respect to the underlying property and the mortgage exceeded the special use valuation of the property); Priv. Ltr. Rul. 8423007 (Feb. 22, 1984) (properly allowing deductibility of the full amount of liability even though there was a low rate of interest on the mortgage but stating property encumbered by a below market assumable mortgage is a relevant element in determining fair market value of the property included under Section 2031).

[253] See Reg. §§ 20.2053-1(d)(1), 20.2053-7. If expenses are incurred in determining the validity or amount of a mortgage, such expenses may be deducted as administrative expenses. See supra ¶ 5.03[3][c][iii] text accompanying notes 139–143.

[254] See Reg. § 20.2053-1(d)(4)(i). Such payments are not treated as or subject to the rules applied to recurring payments. Reg. § 20.2053-4(d)(6)(i). See ¶ 5.03[4][c][iii] text accompanying notes 242–244 supra.

[255] Cf. Reg. § 20.2053-1(d)(7) Ex. 1 (involving ascertainable personal representative's commissions).

Beyond these considerations, the charges against property may take many forms and the deduction for such charges is subject to the same qualifications and limitations as the deductions for claims against the estate.[256] For example, if there is a charge against property arising out of the decedent's agreement to put up security for a loan to someone else, the deduction (or exclusion) allowable under Section 2053(a)(4) may be offset by the value of the estate's claim against such other person.[257] The First Circuit accepted this principle in one case, although it held the deduction allowable in full on the ground that the estate's rights against the primary obligor were valueless.[258] Similarly, an employer's right to a portion of the proceeds of a split dollar life insurance policy included in an insured's gross estate under Section 2042 would be allowed as a Section 2053(a)(4) deduction.[259]

[6] Special Rules and Limitations Related to Section 2053 Deductions.

There are several income tax provisions and subparts of Section 2053 which are intended to preclude double deductibility of Section 2053 amounts.[260] Additionally, there are provisions to permit deductibility even though there are insufficient estate assets subject to claims to fund the deductions.[261]

[a] The Section 642(g) Election

The first such provision is Section 642(g). It should be apparent that some of the items deductible for estate tax purposes under Section 2053 are also deductible for income tax purposes under, for example, Section 162 or Section 212. However, Section 642(g) expressly prevents some items from being de-

---

[256] See supra ¶ 5.03[1][b]. See also Estate of Feinberg v. Comm'r, TC Memo. 1976-396 (1976) (mortgage not deductible because there was no Section 2053(c)(1)(A) consideration). See also Rev. Rul. 80-81, 1980-1 CB 203; Estate of Robinson v. Comm'r, 63 TC 717 (1975); Estate of DeVos v. Comm'r, TC Memo. 1975-216 (1975) (all involving deductions allowed under Section 2053(a)(4) where claim founded on a divorce decree).If there is an issue as to a nonrecourse liability, it should also be treated in the same manner as a claim and the full value of the property should be included in the gross estate until the issue is resolved.

[257] Reg. § 20.2053-1(b)(3). Cf. DuVal's Estate v. Comm'r, 152 F2d 103 (9th Cir. 1945), cert. denied, 328 US 838 (1946) (allowing a deduction for claim but holding rights against co-guarantor included as an estate asset); Estate of Theis v. Comm'r, 770 F2d 981 (11th Cir. 1985) (disallowing deduction where others primarily liable for obligation); Estate of Hendrickson v. Comm'r, TC Memo. 1999-357 (1999) (same).

[258] Comm'r v. Wragg, 141 F2d 638 (1st Cir. 1944).

[259] Cf. Rev. Rul. 76-113, 1976-1 CB 276 (claim against insurance proceeds deductible under Section 2053(a)(4)). (See Supplement ¶ 4.14[6] text accompanying notes 103.12, 103.14, 103.17.)

[260] See Reg. § 20.2053-1(d); infra ¶¶ 5.03[6][a], 5.03[6][b].

[261] See infra ¶ 5.03[6][c].

ducted for purposes of both taxes.[262] Section 642(g) applies to estate tax deductions under both Section 2053(a)(2). It also applies to deductions under Section 2054.[263] Affected items are not allowed as income tax deductions in computing taxable income unless a statement is filed indicating that the items have not been allowed as estate tax deductions under Section 2053(a)(2) (or Section 2054) and that the rights to such estate tax deductions are waived.[264]

While the language of Section 642(g) implies that the section is applicable to all four classifications of deductions under Section 2053; in fact, it applies only to administrative expenses under Section 2053(a)(2).[265] The provision is inapplicable to funeral expenses under Section 2053(a)(1) because such expenses are personal expenses that are not deductible under the income tax,[266] and it is also inapplicable to mortgages under Section 2053(a)(4) because they do not generate an income tax deduction.[267] The proscription of double deductions by Section 642(g) is also inapplicable to claims against the estate under Section 2053(a)(3).[268] This "double" deductibility is appropriate so as not to provide an advantage to an accrual method taxpayer over a cash method taxpayer.[269] Of course, many claims that are deductible for estate tax purposes simply fall within no parallel income tax provision.[270]

---

[262] See IRC § 213(c)(2), regarding post-death payment of medical expenses discussed infra ¶ 5.03[6][b].

[263] See ¶ 5.04.

[264] IRC § 642(g). See infra text accompanying notes 273–275.

[265] Reg. § 1.642(g)-1.

[266] IRC § 262.

[267] Cf. IRC § 1014.

[268] Reg. § 1.642(g)-1.

If a claim is in the nature of a deduction in respect of a decedent specified in Section 691(b), it is a deduction to which the Section 642(g) proscription is expressly inapplicable. IRC § 642(g) (last sentence). Reg. § 1.642(g)-2; Rev. Rul. 67-304, 1967-2 CB 224, (allowing a Section 2053(a)(3) deduction for the commuted value of periodic payment due the decedent's divorced spouse, notwithstanding the estate's income tax deduction of periodic payment as distributions under Section 661). While Section 691(b) also applies to a Section 27 foreign tax credit, Section 642(g) refers only to deductions, not credits.

[269] For example, if an accrual method taxpayer had deductible real property taxes which accrued prior to death, they would have been deductible under Section 164(a)(1) during the decedent's life and would also be a Section 2053(a)(3) deductible claim against the decedent's estate. To preclude a cash method taxpayer from taking both a Section 164(a)(1) deduction on payment of the taxes and a Section 2053(a)(3) deductible claim against the estate tax would provide an unfair advantage to accrual method taxpayer. Cf. Rev. Rul. 71-422, 1971-2 CB 255 (appropriately allowing an accrual method taxpayer's estate both a Section 691(b) deduction for predeath interest which was contested and did not accrue until after death and a Section 2053(a)(3) deduction).

[270] Compare a decedent's obligation to repay the principal of a loan, deductible under Section 2053(a)(3) but not for income tax purposes, with the decedent's obligation to pay interest accrued at death on the loan, which may be deductible under both Section 163 (if allowed by Section 163(h)) and Section 2053(a)(3) by virtue of Section 691(b). See IRC § 642(g), Reg. §1.642(g)-2. See also CCA 200836027 (May 12, 2008) (interest accruing

Section 642(g) applies to income tax deductions of the decedent's estate or the taxable income of "any other person."[271] The limitation of Section 642(g) applies not only to deductions but also to reductions.[272] Thus, an estate may deduct the cost of selling securities for estate tax purposes; but the cost, such as a brokerage commission, cannot also be taken into account in the computation of gain or loss for income tax purposes.[273]

A claim of a deduction on the estate tax return does not foreclose the income tax deduction if the estate tax deduction is not finally allowed, although the election of an income tax deduction must be made before the expiration of the statutory period of limitations for the taxable year for which the income

---

on an extension to pay estate tax that was granted under Section 6161 due to the estate's lack of liquid assets is, however, nondeductible personal interest under IRC § 163(h)(2) and cannot be deducted on estate's income tax return).

Similarly, Section 642(g) does not apply to limit double deductibility of state death taxes which are allowed under Section 2058 (see ¶ 5.09) because such taxes are not deductible under the income tax. See IRC § 164, especially IRC § 164(a)(3).

[271] The term "person" as defined in Section 7701(a)(1) includes a trust. See Burrow Trust v. Comm'r, 39 TC 1080 (1963), acq. 1965-2 CB 4, aff'd, 333 F2d 66 (10th Cir. 1964) (Section 642(g) did not prevent both an estate tax and an income tax deduction for a revocable inter vivos trust includible in the settlor's gross estate); Estate of Cohn v. United States, 249 F. Supp. 763 (SDNY 1966), aff'd on other issues, 371 F2d 642 (2d Cir. 1967) (the government followed *Burrow* by stipulation). Both cases were decided prior to the amendment of Section 642(g) by Pub. L. No. 89-621, 80 Stat. 872 (1966), reprinted in 1966-2 CB 604, 605, extending the proscription beyond the estate to "any other person."

[272] Section 642(g) is expressly applicable to "an offset against the sales price of property in determining gain or loss." This rule, added by the Tax Reform Act of 1976, Pub. L. No. 94-455, § 2009(d), 90 Stat. 1520, 1896 (1976), reprinted in 1976-3 CB (Vol. 1) 1, 372, applies to all income taxable years ending after October 4, 1976.

[273] Prior to the 1976 amendment to Section 642(g), see supra note 272, there was substantial contrary authority. Estate of Bray v. Comm'r, 46 TC 577 (1966), acq. 1971-1 CB 1, aff'd, 396 F2d 452 (6th Cir. 1968); Rev. Rul. 71-173, 1971-1 CB 204 (now obsolete, see Rev. Rul. 89-75, 1989-1 CB 319). Conceivably, perhaps where a large block of stock is sold by an estate through underwriters in a "secondary offering" to the public, expenses of the sale may be taken into account in valuing the stock under Section 2031. See ¶ 4.02[4][e][ii] especially note 206. If so, did the *Bray* principle apply to also permit a Section 2053 deduction for the same expenses? The Tax Court has appropriately held it did not, Estate of Joslyn v. Comm'r, 57 TC 722 (1972), but the Ninth Circuit (in *Joslyn*) and Seventh Circuit disagreed, 500 F2d 382 (9th Cir. 1974) and, on reh'g 566 F2d 677 (9th Cir. 1977); Estate of Jenner v. Comm'r, TC Memo. 1977-54 (1977), rev'd, 577 F2d 1100 (7th Cir. 1978). The Service disagrees as to the valuation issue (Rev. Rul. 83-30, 1983-1 CB 224), as does the Second Circuit (Gillespie v. United States, 23 F3d 36 (2d Cir. 1994)) (both allowing a Section 2053 deduction, but also holding that such fees are not considered in determining a blockage discount). Cf. supra ¶ 5.03[3][c][ii] note 115.

tax deduction is claimed.[274] A waiver of estate tax deduction made in the form of the statement required by the regulations[275] is irrevocable.[276]

Obviously, which deduction is more appropriate depends on the facts and circumstances of each situation; in many cases a simple mathematical computation of the respective tax benefits will determine the matter. A portion of a single deduction may be taken under the estate tax and the remaining portion under the income tax.[277] In making the election, an executor should not only compare the relevant estate and income tax rates related to the deduction, but also must recognize that the executor's obligation is to all of the beneficial parties and that their interests may possibly conflict. For example, election of an income tax deduction will usually favor the income beneficiary while increasing the estate tax burden on the remainderpersons.[278]

[b] The Section 213(c)(2) Election

A claim against a decedent's estate for the sometimes considerable medical expenses for the decedent's last illness would usually qualify as a Section 2053(a)(3) deduction. However, Congress has provided under Section 213(c)(1) that if such expenses are paid by an estate within one year of a decedent's death, they may be claimed as income tax deductions of the decedent in

---

[274] Reg. § 1.642(g)-1.

[275] Reg. § 1.642(g)-1. The statement must be filed in duplicate. Id.

[276] Reg. § 1.642(g)-1; Estate of Darby v. Wiseman, 323 F2d 792 (10th Cir. 1963). This prompts the sensible practice of deferring the filing of the waiver until the time of audit of the estate tax return. See McDaniel, Repetti & Caron, "Federal Wealth Transfer Taxation," at 528 (Foundation Press, 5th ed. 2003).

[277] Reg. § 1.642(g)-2; Stack v. United States, 23 F3d 1400 (8th Cir. 1994). See TAM 8022006 (Feb. 15, 1980) (illustrating computation of relative taxes where interest expense depends upon the amount of estate tax). Cf. Rev. Rul. 77-357, 1977-2 CB 328 (the Service, with weak support, states its position that to the extent that if a deduction were taken under the income tax, amounts would not be deductible because of floors such as the floors under Section 213 or Section 67, such amounts are not deductible under Section 2053).

[278] The fiduciary's problem is examined in Blattmachr, "The Tax Effects of Equitable Adjustments: An Internal Revenue Code Odyssey," 18 Miami Inst. on Est. Plan., §§ 1400-1415 (1984); Dobris, "Equitable Adjustments in Postmortem Income Tax Planning: An Unremitting Diet of Worms," 65 Iowa L. Rev. 103 (1979); Wyatt, "Problems of the Fiduciary in Deducting Administration Expenses," 14 Miami Inst. on Est. Plan., § 1300 (1980); Walsh, "Postmortcm Estate Planing," 37 NYU Inst. on Fed. Tax'n Chapter 44 (1979); Wallace, "Current Problems in Postmortem Tax Planning," 3 Notre Dame Est. Plan. Inst. 657, 705 (1979); Fairchild, "Section 642(g) of the Internal Revenue Code: The Executor's Quandary," 24 U. Fla. L. Rev. 106 (1971); Lewis, "Shifting of Deductions From Estate to Income Tax Returns," 97 Trusts & Est. 936 (1958); Fager, "Administrative Expenses Deductible by Estates and Beneficiaries," 25 NYU Inst. on Fed. Tax'n 1167 (1967). More extensive postmortem estate planning is considered in Halbach, "Post-Mortem Estate Planning," 1963 U. Ill. LF 212; Simmons, "Tax Planning of the Administration of an Estate," 15 Vand. L. Rev. 437 (1962); Gallo, "Tax Considerations During Probate," 15 UCLA L. Rev. 1260 (1968).

the decedent's income tax returns for the periods in which the expenses were incurred. This income tax allowance is accompanied by its own special double-deduction limitation rule similar to Section 642(g),[279] which permits the income tax deduction only upon the filing of a statement that the estate tax deduction has not been allowed and a waiver of that deduction.[280]

[c] Special Rules for Property Not Subject to Claims

[i] Introduction. A person's death may necessitate the expenditure of money in the transmission of property that is not a part of the decedent's probate estate and is not subject to claims, but that as a part of the decedent's gross estate figures in the determination of the federal estate tax. If we are thus required to pretend that some property not owned by a decedent was the decedent's property,[281] elementary fairness seems to require the companion pretense that the estate is diminished by Section 2053 obligations incurred with respect to these imaginary assets. However, such expenditures may not be expenses allowable under local law, the test imposed by the last clause of Section 2053(a), because they are not payable out of the estate that is "subject to claims."[282] This is, therefore, what Section 2053(b) and Section 2053(c)(2) are all about.

Suppose, for example, that the decedent had created a revocable living trust[283] taxable under Section 2038 because of the decedent's retention of the right to revoke the trust and that the assets in such trust are not subject to claims under local law. If the property is to be distributed to a remainderperson at the decedent's death, the activities of the trustee in terminating the trust and implementing the appropriate distribution of trust assets are scarcely different from the services performed by the executor with regard to probate assets; and on the termination of the inter vivos trust, there may be a substantial charge by the trustee in the form of principal commissions, which, from an overall estate tax view, are not easily differentiated from executor commissions. In addition, the decedent may have put all of the decedent's assets into

---

[279] IRC § 213(c)(2); Reg. § 1.213-1(d)(2). Medical expenses incurred by the decedent that are paid within one year of death may be deducted on the decedent's estate tax return or on the final income tax return at the executor's option. In Rev. Rul. 77-357, 1977-2 CB 328, the Service, with weak support, states its position that the deduction for estate tax purposes is subject to the same percentage of adjusted gross income limitations as are applied if the executor chooses to take the deduction on the final income tax return.

[280] IRC § 213(c)(2); Reg. § 1.213-1(d)(2). The statement and waiver must be filed in duplicate with or for association with the return, amended return, or claim for credit or refund for the decedent for any taxable year for which such amount is claimed as a deduction. Id. The regulations should (but do not specifically) provide for a portion of the amount to be deducted under both returns. Compare Reg. § 1.642(g)-2.

[281] See IRC §§ 2035, 2036, 2037, 2038, 2039, 2040, 2041, 2042, 2044.

[282] See infra ¶ 5.03[6][c][ii].

[283] See ¶ 4.10[4][a] text accompanying notes 27–28.

the trust, but there will be inevitable funeral expenses and possible other claims against decedent's estate which likely will be paid. In general, Section 2053(b) and Section 2053(c)(2) make these and similar charges deductible but with different requirements imposed under each subsection.[284]

[ii] **Property not subject to claims.** Both Section 2053(b) and Section 2053(c)(2) are applicable to property which is not "subject to claims," against a decedent's estate,[285] and it is temptingly simple to think of this merely in terms of probate and nonprobate assets. However, we know that the tax law is never that simple. Helpfully, Section 2053(c)(2) provides a technical definition of property "subject to claims" which should be employed under Section 2053(b) as well as under Section 2053(c)(2).[286] Section 2053(c)(2) defines property "subject to claims" as that part of the gross estate that under local law will bear the burden of Section 2053 obligations reduced by any casualty loss deduction attributed to such property allowed to the estate under Section 2054.[287]

A decedent's assets not subject to claims may include a broad variety of assets other than those in a revocable living trust,[288] such as the corpus of a Section 2036 trust,[289] property where survivors are in receipt of survivorship annuity payments[290] survivorship rights, jointly held property,[291] property subject to decedent's general power of appointment,[292] life insurance proceeds[293] and other types of property.[294]

Even though the assets listed above are nonprobate assets, those assets may nevertheless be "subject to claims." In each instance, one must examine whether under applicable local law (generally state law) the property involved would bear the burden of the payment of the particular obligation in the final adjustment and settlement of the decedent's estate.[295] Thus, for all nonprobate

---

[284] Compare infra ¶¶ 5.03[6][c][iii] and 5.03[6][c][iv].

[285] IRC §§ 2053(b), 2053(c)(2).

[286] Section 2053(b) refers to "property not subject to claims" while Section 2053(c)(2) refers to "property subject to claims."

[287] IRC § 2053(c)(2).

[288] See ¶ 4.10[4][a] text accompanying notes 27–28.

[289] IRC § 2036(a)(1) or IRC § 2036(a)(2).

[290] IRC § 2039.

[291] IRC §§ 2040(a), 2040(b).

[292] IRC §§ 2041(a)(1), 2041(a)(2).

[293] IRC § 2042(2).

[294] See IRC §§ 2035, 2037, 2044.

[295] IRC § 2053(c)(2). See Reg. § 20.2053-1(c). Estate of Keller, 2010-2 USTC ¶ 60,605 (SD Tex. 2010) (since family trusts were potentially responsible for the payment of the estate tax, they were considered "subject to claims" such that interest payments made by family trusts to family limited partnership after the period of limitation for assessment were deductible under IRC § 2053(a) and, moreover, the payment of interest is an allowable expense under Texas law).

property, the question whether each type of such property is subject to claims may vary between states and even with respect to different types of Section 2053 obligations within a single state.[296] For example, if the decedent had funded a revocable living trust, one must look to applicable local law to determine whether the property in the trust would bear the burden of the particular type of expense[297] involved.[298] If under the applicable local law, the corpus of the trust is responsible for the Sections 2053(a)(1) through 2053(a)(4) expense or liability, then a deduction is allowed under Section 2053(a).[299] If, however, under the applicable law, the corpus of such trusts is not responsible for the Section 2053 amount, then Section 2053(b) or Section 2053(c)(2) may apply.[300]

[iii] **Section 2053(b): Expenses of administering property not subject to claims.** Even though administration expenses are not subject to claims under local law,[301] Section 2053(b) allows administration expenses to be deducted from a decedent's gross estate if certain requirements are met.[302]

---

[296] Compare Estate of Snyder v. United States, 84 AFTR2d 99-5963 (Fed. Cl. 1999) (property in a revocable trust was subject to an EPA liability for environmental clean up under Ohio law) with Wilson v. United States, 372 F2d 232 (3d Cir. 1967) (property in a spendthrift trust with a testamentary general power of appointment was not subject to creditors' claims under Pennsylvania law).

[297] See IRC §§ 2053(a)(1)–2053(a)(4).

[298] Estate of Snyder v. United States, 84 AFTR2d 99-5963 (Ct. Fed. Cl. 1999) (applying this definition for a Section 2053(a)(3) claim and holding that property in a revocable trust was subject to an EPA claim for environmental clean up under Ohio law).

See also Uniform Trust Code § 505(a)(3) subjecting the trust corpus of a trust which is revocable at the settlor's death to claims of settlor's creditors, costs of administration of the settlor's estate, and funeral expenses. Langbein & Waggoner, "Uniform Trust and Estate Statutes" (Foundation Press 2003–2004). See, generally, Scott, "Trusts § 330.12" (Little Brown & Co., 4th ed. 1989); Bogart & Radford, "The Law of Trusts and Trustees," § 1000 (Warren, Gorham & Lamont, 3d ed. 2006).

[299] See, e.g., Snyder v. United States, 84 AFTR2d 99-5963 (Ct. Fed. Cl. 1999) (property in a revocable trust that was subject to a claim for environmental cleanup under local law was a subject to a Section 2053(a)(3) claim).

[300] If the amount is a potentially deductible administration expense, then under Section 2053(b) the expense must be paid before the expiration of the statute of limitations for assessment of the estate tax (see infra ¶ 5.03[6][c][iii]) and if the amount is a potentially deductible funeral expense, administrative expense subject to claims, claim, or mortgage or indebtedness on the property, then under Section 2053(c)(2), the expense must be paid before the date prescribed for filing the estate tax return (see infra ¶ 5.03[6][c][iv]).

[301] If the expenses are subject to claims under local law, they are deductible under Section 2053(a)(2), assuming its requirements are met. See supra ¶ 5.03[3].

[302] Section 2053(b) applies only to Section 2053(a)(2) administrative expenses, but not to Section 2053(a)(1), Section 2053(a)(3), or Section 2053(a)(4) deductions. IRC § 2053(b); Reg. §§ 20.2053-8(a), 20.2053-8(b), 20.2053-8(c). Cf. IRC § 2053(c)(2) discussed infra ¶ 5.03[6][c][iv].

It is possible that some expenses incurred with respect to nonprobate property might be deductible without the assistance of Section 2053(b). Before that subsection was enacted, a trustee's termination charge on artificial gross estate property was allowed under

First, the expenses must be of a type that would be deductible under Section 2053(a)(2) if they related to property that was subject to claims.[303] Thus, all the comments in the segment dealing with administrative expenses[304] are equally applicable here.[305] Second, to be deductible, Section 2053(b) expenses must be paid[306] before the limitation period for assessment of estate tax expires. In general, payment of such expenses is required within three years after the estate tax return is filed.[307] The return is generally due nine months after

what is now Section 2053(a). Estate of Fiske, 45 BTA 52 (1941), nonacq. 1942-1 CB 21, aff'd, 132 F2d 644 (1st Cir. 1942). However, for reasons suggested earlier, the appellate court refused to treat the charge as an administration expense, holding instead that it was deductible (or perhaps more accurately, would support an exclusion) under what is now Section 2053(a)(4). See supra ¶ 5.03[5]. Section 2053(b) might seem now to carry the inference that Section 2053(a) deductions are restricted to charges that fall on property subject to claims, but earlier doctrine regarding charges against gross estate assets is continued in the regulations. Reg. § 20.2053-7, discussed supra ¶ 5.03[5]. In this light, Section 2053(b) might perhaps be viewed as mostly a clarifying change. However, if, for example, a person's entire estate consisted of insurance on that person's life payable to another, includable under Section 2042, or jointly held property, includable under Section 2040, there may be no charges against such nonprobate assets at death and yet the recipients could incur expenses, for items such as the preparation of the federal estate tax return. See IRC §§ 2002, 2203, 6324(a)(1); Reg. § 20.2002-1. See also Reg. § 20.2053-8(d) Ex. 4 (allowing deduction for expenses relating to preparation of an estate tax return). Similarly, expenses might be incurred after death in the determination whether nonprobate assets were includable in the gross estate or with regard to the valuation of nonprobate assets for estate tax purposes. As the *Davis* case held, these are not deductible administration expenses, and they are clearly not indebtedness in respect of estate assets. Thus, these appropriate charges would not reduce estate tax liability except for Section 2053(b), and they are deductible under its provisions. S. Rep. No. 1622, 83d Cong., 2d Sess. 474 (1954). Central Trust of Cincinnati v. Welch, 304 F2d 923 (6th Cir. 1962); Rev. Rul. 68-611, 1968-2 CB 410 (allowing deductible under Section 2053(b) for costs incurred in recovering accident and health policies included in decedent's gross estate).

[303] See Reg. § 20.2053-8(d) Ex. 1 (involving both trustee's commissions and attorney's fees on termination of an irrevocable inter vivos trust included in a decedent's gross estate under Section 2036); Rev. Rul. 76-498, 1976-2 CB 199 (same).

[304] See supra ¶ 5.03[3].

[305] Reg. § 20.2053-8. Note especially that expenses to the extent incurred on behalf of transferees are not deductible. Reg. §§ 20.2053-8(b), 20.2053-8(d) Ex. 2 (some expenses of a Section 2036 trust qualified for Section 2053(b) and others did not), 20.2053-8(d) Ex. 3 (expenses of a Section 2037 trust were for transferee's benefit and nondeductible); Estate of Heckscher v. Comm'r, 63 TC 485 (1975) (attorney's fees incurred for beneficiaries to determine respective interests in trust property not deductible under Section 2053(b)).

[306] Payment should include cash or its equivalent, but not the mere issuance of a note.

[307] IRC § 6501(a).

the decedent's death;[308] however, in some instances, the assessment period is extended[309] and, therefore, the time of payment restriction is also extended.[310]

[iv] Section 2053(c)(2): Limitation based on the value of property subject to claims. Funeral expenses, administration expenses relating to property included in the gross estate and subject to claims,[311] claims against the estate, and charges against estate property are all generally allowed as deductions only to the extent that they do not exceed the value of property subject to claims.[312] "Property subject to claims" is again defined as that part of the gross estate that under local law will bear the burden of such expenses, claims, and charges, reduced by any casualty loss deduction attributed to such property allowed under Section 2054.[313] A person may have a large gross estate for tax purposes, having made lifetime transfers subject to estate tax, and yet the decedent's probate estate and nonprobate property which is liable for such obligations may be hopelessly insolvent. In such a situation, it is not unreasonable to deny a deduction for expenses and claims that cannot be paid by the insolvent estate. If insolvency results from a deductible post-death casualty loss, it is obviously reasonable to reduce correspondingly the general Section 2053(c)(2) ceiling on Section 2053(a) deductions.

However, it is not uncommon for family and friends of an insolvent decedent to discharge a decedent's obligations even if they are not required by law to do so. Seemingly this is most likely to occur where survivors are in receipt of life insurance proceeds, jointly held property with a right of survivorship, property subject to the decedent's general power of appointment, interests in inter vivos trusts or any other property interest acquired from the decedent and taxable as a part of the decedent's gross estate which assume, under local law, is beyond the reach of the decedent's creditors.[314] By way of exception to the usual ceiling on Section 2053(a) deductions, Congress has taken account of the artificiality of the gross estate and allowed additional deductions for expenses,

---

[308] IRC § 6075(a). There may be an extension of the time for such filing which would then also extend the assessment period. See IRC § 6081, ¶ 2.02[1] text accompanying notes 7–11.

[309] E.g., no return, assessment at any time, IRC § 6501(c)(3); false return, same, IRC § 6501(c)(1); substantial omission of items from gross estate, six years, IRC § 6501(e)(2). See Rev. Rul. 61-59, 1961-1 CB 418 (limitations period extended by Section 6503(a)(1)); Rev. Rul. 78-323, 1978-2 CB 240 (clarifying Revenue Ruling 61-59); Gillum v. Comm'r, TC Memo. 1984-631 (1984) (distinguishing Revenue Ruling 61-59).

[310] See also ¶¶ 2.02[3] and 3.07 discussing situations in which the time for payment is extended either automatically or subject to discretion.

[311] Logically, this limitation does not apply to expenses deductible under Section 2053(b) for administration of nonprobate gross estate assets not subject to claims. See supra ¶ 5.03[6][c][iii].

[312] IRC § 2053(c)(2).

[313] IRC § 2053(c)(2). See Reg. § 20.2053-1(c); supra ¶ 5.03[6][c][ii].

[314] See supra ¶ 5.03[6][c][ii].

claims, and charges otherwise deductible, if they are paid[315] before the estate tax return is due.[316] It might appear from the statute that timely payment from any source, including estate assets, works an upward adjustment in the ceiling, as the exception speaks in terms only of when such amounts must be paid. But the regulations appropriately limit the increase over the basic ceiling to timely payments "out of property not subject to claims."[317] Even so, there is neither any statutory requirement that the payment be made by someone who has a beneficial interest in the estate, nor any statutory requirement that the source of the payment be nonprobate property included in the gross estate. Thus, timely payments by a mere volunteer may increase the general ceiling on the Section 2053(a) deductions beyond the value of probate assets.[318]

---

[315] Payment should include cash or its equivalent but not the mere issuance of a note.

[316] IRC § 2053(c)(2). See Reg. § 20.2053-1(c) Ex. 1. Generally, such payment must be made within nine months of the decedent's death (Section 6075), but such payment is regarded as timely within the exception if made within any extension of time granted for filing the return. Reg. § 20.2053-1(c)(2). See IRC § 6081, ¶ 2.02[1] text accompanying notes 7–11.

Note that the time for payment under Section 2053(c)(2) is significantly shorter than the time period under Section 2053(b). See supra ¶ 5.03[6][c][iii] text accompanying notes 306–310.

[317] Reg. § 20.2053-1(c) Ex. 2.

[318] Reg. § 20.2053-1(c) Exs. 1 and 2, fail to reflect these possibilities.

¶ 5.05 SECTION 2055. TRANSFERS FOR PUBLIC, CHARITABLE, AND RELIGIOUS USES

Page 5-43:

Add to note 4.

The Service has revised the general procedures relating to the issuance of written guidance, including letter rulings and determination letters. See Rev. Proc. 2011-1. In addition, see Rev. Proc. 2011-2 for updated general procedures relating to the issuance of technical advice to a director or an appeals area director by the various offices of the Associate Chief Counsel. The Service has also released a revised list of issues on which it will not generally issue letter rulings or determination letters due to the inherently factual nature of the problems involved. Rev. Proc. 2011-3.

[1] Qualified Recipients

[a] In General

Page 5-44:

Add to note 7.

Estate of Engelman v. Comm'r, 121 TC 54 (2003) (discretionary act of executor transferring property to charity did not constitute a transfer by decedent). TAM 200437032 (May 11, 2004) (residuary bequest to decedent's sibling, a member of a religious order who had taken a vow of poverty, did not qualify for an estate tax charitable deduction even though the beneficiary, acting in her capacity as executrix, transferred the assets to the order).

[b] Section 2055(a) Organizations

Page 5-50:

Add to note 41 after Rev. Rul. 74-523, 1974-2 CB 304.

Priv. Ltr. Rul. 200905015 (Oct. 16, 2008) (citing Rev. Rul. 74-523, the Service concluded that decedent's testamentary bequest of (1) money to foreign municipality to be used solely for charitable purposes and (2) paintings to a museum within the foreign municipality both qualified for estate tax charitable deduction). See Estate of Engelman v. Comm'r, 121 TC 54 (2003) (transferor did not limit gift to Israel to charitable uses).

[c] Tainted Organizations

Page 5-52:

Add to note 55.

Priv. Ltr. Rul. 200901023 (Sept. 29, 2008) (donor's proposed lifetime and testamentary transfers to a foreign trust qualify for charitable deduction regardless of whether the trust applies for Section 501(c)(3) status since trust fell under IRC § 4947(a)(1) exception to IRC § 508(d)(2)(B) which generally does not permit a deduction).

Add new paragraph to end of ¶ 5.05[1][c].

A deduction is generally allowed under Section 2055(a) for contributions to "donor advised funds" as defined in Section 4966(d)(2). However, a deduction is denied for contributions to such funds if the sponsoring organization[56.1] is an organization described in Section 2055(a)(3) or Section 2055(a)(4) or if the sponsoring organization is a Section 4943(f)(5)(A) type III supporting organization which is not a functionally integrated organization as defined in Section 4943(f)(5)(B).[56.2] In addition, a deduction is also denied for gifts to other donor advised funds unless the sponsoring organization provides contemporaneous written acknowledgment that it has exclusive legal control over the contributed assets.[56.3]

[56.1] See IRC § 4966(d)(1).

[56.2] IRC § 2055(e)(5)(A).

[56.3] IRC § 2055(e)(5)(B). Cf. IRC § 170(f)(8)(c). The rules are effective to transfers made after the date, which is 180 days after August 17, 2006. Pension Protection Act of 2006, Pub. L. No. 109-280, § 1234(d), __ Stat. __, __ (2006), reprinted in 2006-__ CB __, __.

[2] Transfers to Charity

[a] Outright Transfers

Page 5-52:

In note 58, add the following to end of sentence containing reference to Polster v. Comm'r.

and Priv. Ltr. Rul. 200418002 (Jan. 23, 2004) (bequest of art collection to museum subject to restrictions entitled to charitable deduction since collection will pass to a qualifying charity in any case).

Add to end of note 58.

Technical Advice Memorandum 200252032 (Aug. 22, 2002) concluded that a bequest (and certain lifetime gifts) to a foundation created by a U.S. citizen in a foreign country qualified for the charitable deduction under Section 2055 (Section 2522 as to the gifts) where the foundation was granted, under Regulations Section 301.9100-3, relief from the filing deadline imposed under Section 508.

[b] Indirect Transfers

Page 5-54:

Add to note 68.

Technical Advice Memorandum 200306002 (Sept. 30, 2002) concluded that no charitable deduction should be allowed for amounts paid to a charity in settlement of a will contest brought by the charity and others where the charity was only named as a beneficiary under the first of seven wills the decedent executed over a thirty-five-year span. The Service concluded that the likelihood of the charity establishing a right to any of the decedent's property was virtually nil. See also TAM 201004022 (Sept. 15, 2009) (estate not entitled to a charitable deduction for the amount paid to a charitable trust pursuant to a settlement agreement where charitable trust did not have an enforceable right under applicable state law since extrinsic evidence in the form of decedent's attorney's affidavit was produced in the proceedings that should not have been allowed). But see Estate of Palumbo v. Comm'r, 2011-1 USTC ¶ 60,616 (WD Pa. 2011), where the decedent had previously executed a number of testamentary documents in which the residue of his estate was to pass to a charitable trust. However, in decedent's final will, decedent's attorney forgot to include the residuary clause. Pursuant to a settlement agreement reached with decedent's son, the charitable trust eventually received approximately two-thirds of the residue. The court determined that the amount passing to the charitable trust qualified for a charitable deduction because the settlement between the parties was the product of an arm's length negotiation since trust did have a claim to the residuary estate as evidenced by the attorney's testimony regarding the erroneous omission, the prior wills and the references throughout the effective will to the residuary estate and the charitable trust as residuary beneficiary.

In Jackson Estate v. United States, 96 AFTR2d 2005-7279 (ND W.Va. 2005), non-qualifying split interest trust was terminated in a good faith effort to avoid possible disputes among beneficiaries and charity received an outright distribution of cash calculated using IRS actuarial tables. Court held that IRC § 2055(e)(2) did not apply to prevent estate's charitable deduction for the outright distribution.

Priv. Ltr. Rul. 200825014 (Feb. 28, 2008) (estate entitled to charitable deduction for amounts distributed to two charitable organizations in accordance with a settlement agreement entered into by the organizations under which the assets held in a trust established pursuant to decedent's will would be immediately distributed to the charities).

Estate of Williams v. Comm'r, TC Memo. 2009-5 (2009) (estate was entitled to an additional charitable deduction for the amount paid to charity under a settlement agreement that was attributable to the constructive sale theory utilized by the charities in their litigation against the noncharitable beneficiaries).

Add to note 70.

Priv. Ltr. Rul. 201022001 (Jan. 11, 2010) (court order resolving ambiguity regarding payment of two general legacies that impacted funding of charitable trust).

Add to note 72.

See TAM 200319001 (Dec. 17, 2002) (ruling that a trustee's amendment of a trust after a completed gift was made would be disregarded where the purpose of the amendment was to reduce the amount of the gift). See also TAM 200840008 (June 10, 2008) (the Service cited *Burdick* and *La Meres* and disqualified for an estate tax charitable deduction the property distributed to a charitable trust pursuant to a non-judicial division of decedent's non-qualifying testamentary trust because the only reason provided for dividing the trust was to decrease the federal estate tax liability).

[c] Disclaimers

Page 5-56:

Add to note 81.

But cf. Estate of Christiansen, 130 TC No. 1 (2008) (reviewed), aff'd on other grounds, No. 08-3844 (8th Cir. 2009), where a charitable deduction was disallowed for property passing to a charitable lead trust as a result of daughter's partial disclaimer since daughter retained a contingent remainder interest in the trust which was neither severable property nor an undivided portion of the property as required by Regulations Section 25.2518-2(e)(3).

[e] Lifetime Transfers

Page 5-57:

Add to note 91.

Priv. Ltr. Rul. 200932020 (Apr. 21, 2009) (portion of the charitable remainder of a reformed charitable remainder unitrust (CRUT) was included in the donor's gross estate under Section 2036 because he retained the right to substitute one or more alternate qualified organizations for the charitable remainderman designated in the trust and donor's estate qualified for estate tax charitable deduction equal to the amount included).

[3] The Amount of the Deduction

[a] In General

Page 5-58:

Add to note 95.

As required by Section 7520(c)(3), the Service issued proposed, temporary and final regulations on May 7, 2009, revising Table S and Table U(1), the tables used to value annuities, interests for life or a term of years, and reversionary and remainder interests in property, to reflect the mortality experience from the 2000 census (Life Table 2000CM). Transition rules allow taxpayers to use tables based on either Life Table 90CM or Life Table 2000CM to value gift, charitable and estate transfers made on or after May 1, 2009, but before July 1, 2009, but they must use the appropriate interest rate for the month in which the valuation date falls, regardless of which table is chosen. For charitable deductions, pursuant to the Section 7520(a) election to use a prior month's rate, if the executor or donor elects to use the applicable federal rate (AFR) for March or April, 2009, the Table 90CM valuation tables must be used. If the May or June, 2009, AFR is elected, either the Table 90CM or the Table 2000CM valuation tables may be used and if the valuation occurs after June 30, 2009, the Table 2000CM valuation tables must be used, even if a prior month's interest rate is elected. TD 9448; REG-107845-08. Reg. §§ 1.170A-12T, 1.642(c)-6T, 1.664-4T, 20.2031-7T, 20.2032A-1T, 20.2056A-4T, 25.2512-5T, 25.2522(c)-3, 1.7520-1T, 20.7520-1T, and Reg. § 25.7520-1T. Publications 1457 and 1458 (rev. May 2009), both of which include examples for using the mortality component tables, have been released. On August 10, 2011, the Service issued final regulations that removed the temporary regulations issued in TD 9448 and adopted as final the proposed regulations issued in REG-107845-08. The only substantive change was the deletion of an example in the Section 2032 regulations which the Service anticipates including in a different regulation project under that Code section. TD 9540; Reg. §§ 1.170A-12, 1.642(c)-6, 1.664-4, 20.2031-7, 20.2032-1, 20.2056A-4, 25.2512-5, 25.2522(c)-3, 1.7520-1, 20.7520-1, 25.7520-1.

Page 5-59:

Add to note 97.

TAM 200648028 (Aug. 4, 2006) (although, for estate tax valuation purposes, shares of a corporation owned outright by decedent were aggregated with shares held by a trust included in decedent's estate under Sections 2036 and 2038, the charitable deduction for shares passing to charity from the trust would be valued as a minority interest).

[b] Expenses of an Estate Affecting the Deduction

[i] Death taxes.

Page 5-61:

Add to note 109.

Estate of Bradford v. Comm'r, TC Memo. 2002-238 (2002), held that the decedent's will overrode the North Carolina apportionment statute, placed the burden of estate taxes on the residue of the estate *before* it passed to decedent's revocable trust and was divided into equal charitable and noncharitable shares, and, to the extent the residue was insufficient, on the assets in the revocable trust prior to division between the charitable and noncharitable shares, thus causing the charitable share to bear a portion of the taxes.

See also Hale v. Moore, No. 2005-CA-001895-MR (Ky. Ct. App. 2008) (applying Kentucky law, which governed the pourover will, the Kentucky Court of Appeals affirmed the district court's holding that all beneficiaries of decedent's revocable trust, including two colleges which received a predeceased daughter's share, should bear the death tax burden).

[4] Split Interests: Mixed Private and Charitable Bequests

[a] Background

Page 5-65:

Add to first paragraph of note 128.

Cf. Estate of Petter v. Comm'r, 108 AFTR2d ¶ 2011-5149 (9th Cir. 2011) (reallocation of additional LLC units from noncharitable donees to charitable foundations pursuant to gift tax valuation formula clause, following the Service's audit which resulted in an increase in the value of the gifted units, was not a gift to the foundations subject to a condition precedent and, accordingly, donor was entitled to a charitable deduction on the value of the additional units the foundation would receive).

[b] Present Law

Page 5-67:

Add to note 139 prior to citation to Rev. Rul. 83-45.

Cf. Priv. Ltr. Rul. 201129033 (Apr. 8, 2011) (donor's gifts of nonvoting common stock to charity and transfer of voting shares to a special purpose trust would not result in interests in the same property passing for both charitable and noncharitable purposes). But see Galloway v. United States, 492 F3d 219 (3d Cir. 2007) (no valid split gift).

Page 5-68:

Add to end of first paragraph of note 140.

See Priv. Ltr. Rul. 200505008 (Oct. 15, 2004) (conditions set forth in decedent's trust instrument, including that the charitable beneficiaries would contest decedent's will, were so remote as to be negligible).

Page 5-69:

Add to note 147.

Galloway v. United States, 492 F3d 219 (3d Cir. 2007) (split-interest trust denied estate tax charitable deduction since an interest in the same property, a single trust, passes to both charitable and non-charitable beneficiaries and is not in the form of a CRAT, a CRUT, or a pooled income fund).

[5] Qualified Remainder Interests

Page 5-70:

Add to note 154.

In Revenue Ruling 2008-41 2008-30 IRB 170, the Service ruled that a pro rata division of a qualified charitable remainder trust into two or more separate trusts, if properly effected, will not result in adverse tax consequences for the original trust or the new sub-trusts.

[a] The Charitable Remainder Annuity Trust

Page 5-71:

Replace the second paragraph of note 159 with the following.

CRAT forms are found in Revenue Procedures 2003-53 through 2003-60 at 2003-2 CB __-__. The procedures involve the following forms:

1. Revenue Procedure 2003-53: Sample inter vivos CRAT for one measuring life.
2. Revenue Procedure 2003-54: Sample inter vivos CRAT for a term of years.
3. Revenue Procedure 2003-55: Sample inter vivos CRAT with consecutive interests for two measuring lives.
4. Revenue Procedure 2003-56: Sample inter vivos CRAT with concurrent and consecutive interests for two measuring lives.
5. Revenue Procedure 2003-57: Sample testamentary CRAT for one measuring life.
6. Revenue Procedure 2003-58: Sample testamentary CRAT for a term of years.
7. Revenue Procedure 2003-59: Sample testamentary CRAT with consecutive interests for two measuring lives.
8. Revenue Procedure 2003-60: Sample testamentary CRAT with concurrent and consecutive interests for two measuring lives.

The sample forms supersede Revenue Procedures 89-21, 1989-1 CB 842, and 90-32, 1990-1 CB 546. The Service will not issue determination letters as to the qualification of CRATs substantially similar to the forms set forth in such rulings. Rev. Proc. 90-33, 1990-1 CB 551.

[i] Annuity trust requirements.

Add to note 160 at end of cite to "Atkinson".

, aff'd, 309 F3d 1290 (11th Cir. 2002).

Add to note 161.

In Rev. Rul. 2008-41, the Service ruled that a pro rata division of a CRAT into two or more separate CRATs, if properly effected, will not cause the CRAT or any of the newly created separate CRATs to fail to qualify under IRC § 664.

Page 5-75:

Add to note 187.

See Revenue Procedure 2005-24 for a safe harbor procedure the Service has provided, under which it will disregard a surviving spouse's right of election for purposes of determining whether a CRAT satisfies the requirements of Section 664(d)(1)(B). The surviving spouse must irrevocably waive the right of election to the extent necessary to insure that no part of the CRAT (other than any annuity interest the surviving spouse may be entitled to as a named recipient) can be used to satisfy the elective share. Notwithstanding the grandfather date of June 28, 2005, set forth in the revenue procedure, the Service will disregard the existence of a spouse's right of election, even without the waiver, if the spouse does not exercise the right of election, until further guidance is published regarding the effect of a spousal right of election on a trust's qualification as a CRAT. Notice 2006-15.

Add to note 188.

In Private Letter Ruling 200428013 (Apr. 1, 2004), decedent's estate commenced a judicial proceeding to reform a testamentary trust into a CRAT within ninety days after the due date for filing the decedent's estate tax return and following surviving spouse's disclaimer of her right to receive principal distributions therefrom. The Service ruled that the estate would be allowed a charitable deduction for the present value of the remainder interest and a marital deduction for the value of the spouse's annuity interest.

Add to note 189 at end of cite to "Atkinson".

, aff'd, 309 F3d 1290 (11th Cir. 2002).

Add to note 193.

Priv. Ltr. Rul. 200726005 (Mar. 7, 2007) (qualified reformation of testamentary trust to CRAT for a term of five years (or the earlier death of the beneficiary)—value of remainder interest determined without taking into account the earlier death contingency).

[ii] The amount of the deduction.

Page 5-77:

Add to note 207.

As required by Section 7520(c)(3), the Service issued proposed, temporary and final regulations on May 7, 2009, revising Table S and Table U(1), the tables used to value annuities, interests for life or a term of years, and reversionary and remainder interests in property, to reflect the mortality experience from the 2000 census (Life Table 2000CM). Transition rules allow taxpayers to use tables based on either Life Table 90CM or Life Table 2000CM to value gift, charitable and estate transfers made on or after May 1, 2009, but before July 1, 2009, but they must use the appropriate interest rate for the month in which the valuation date falls, regardless of which table is chosen. For charitable deductions, pursuant to the Section 7520(a) election to use a prior month's rate, if the executor or donor elects to use the applicable federal rate (AFR) for March or April, 2009, the Table 90CM valuation tables must be used. If the May or June, 2009, AFR is elected, either the Table 90CM or the Table 2000CM valuation tables may be used and if the valuation occurs after June 30, 2009, the Table 2000CM valuation tables must be used, even if a prior month's interest rate is elected. TD 9448; REG-107845-08. Reg. §§ 1.170A-12T, 1.642(c)-6T, 1.664-4T, 20.2031-7T, 20.2032A-1T, 20.2056A-4T, 25.2512-5T, 25.2522(c)-3, 1.7520-1T, 20.7520-1T, and Reg. § 25.7520-1T. Publications 1457 and 1458 (rev. May 2009), both of which include examples for using the mortality component tables, have been released. On August 10, 2011, the Service issued final regulations that removed the temporary regulations issued in TD 9448 and adopted as final the proposed regulations issued in REG-107845-08. The only substantive change was the deletion of an example in the Section 2032 regulations which the Service anticipates including in a different regulation project under that Code section. TD 9540; Reg. §§ 1.170A-12,

1.642(c)-6, 1.664-4, 20.2031-7, 20.2032-1, 20.2056A-4, 25.2512-5, 25.2522(c)-3, 1.7520-1, 20.7520-1, 25.7520-1.

[b] The Charitable Remainder Unitrust

Page 5-78:

Delete the first two paragraphs of note 213 and replace with the following.

The Service has issued revised forms meeting the requirements of Section 664(d)(2) and, if applicable, Section 664(d)(3), which include the following:

- Rev. Proc. 2005-52: An inter vivos CRUT for one measuring life.
- Rev. Proc. 2005-53: An inter vivos CRUT for a term of years.
- Rev. Proc. 2005-54: An inter vivos CRUT with consecutive interests for two measuring lives.
- Rev. Proc. 2005-55: An inter vivos CRUT with concurrent and consecutive interests for two measuring lives.
- Rev. Proc. 2005-56: A testamentary CRUT for one measuring life.
- Rev. Proc. 2005-57: A testamentary CRUT for a term of years.
- Rev. Proc. 2005-58: A testamentary CRUT with consecutive interests for two measuring lives.
- Rev. Proc. 2005-59: A testamentary CRUT with concurrent and consecutive interests for two measuring lives.

[i] Unitrust requirements.

Page 5-78:

Add to note 215 at end of cite to "Atkinson."

, aff'd, 309 F3d 1290 (11th Cir. 2002).

Add to note 216.

In Revenue. Ruling 2008-41, the Service ruled that a pro rata division of a CRUT into two or more separate CRUTs, if properly effected, will not cause the CRUT or any of the separate CRUTs to fail to qualify under IRC § 664.

Add to note 218.

Priv. Ltr. Rul. 200832017 (Mar. 21, 2008) (a provision in the governing instrument of a CRUT which gave a special trustee the discretion to allocate a portion of the unitrust amount to charitable organizations did not disqualify the CRUT so long as some portion of the unitrust amount, and not a de minimis amount, be paid to the noncharitable beneficiaries each year).

Page 5-79:

Add to note 227.

Cf. Priv. Ltr. Ruls. 200829015 and 200829016 (Jan. 28, 2008) (judicial reformation of NIMCRUT to strike trust's make-up liability provision so that trust could take additional contributions of property will not cause trust to fail to qualify as a NIMCRUT).

Page 5-81:

Add to note 242.

See Rev. Proc. 2005-24 for a safe harbor procedure the Service has provided, under which it will disregard a surviving spouse's right of election for purposes of determining whether a CRUT satisfies the requirements of Section 664(d)(2)(B). The surviving spouse must irrevocably waive the right of election to the extent necessary to insure that no part of the CRUT (other than any unitrust interest the surviving spouse may be entitled to as a named recipient) can be used to satisfy the elective share. Notwithstanding the grandfather date of June 28, 2005, set forth in the revenue procedure, the Service will disregard the existence of a spouse's right of election, even without the waiver, if the spouse does not exercise the right of election, until further guidance is published regarding the effect of a spousal right of election on a trust's qualification as a CRUT. Notice 2006-15.

Page 5-82:

Add to note 244 at end of cite to Atkinson.

, aff'd, 309 F3d 1290 (11th Cir. 2002).

Add to note 254.

Priv. Ltr. Rul. 200832017 (Mar. 21, 2008) (power held by trustor of a CRUT and his spouse to substitute the named charitable remainder beneficiary with one or more charitable organizations did not disqualify the CRUT). See also Priv. Ltr. Rul. 201016033 (Jan. 12, 2010) (reformation of CRUT to correct scrivener's error which precluded trustor's foundation from qualifying as a charitable remainderman did not disqualify CRUT and, since trustor retained the power to substitute the charitable remainderman with alternate qualified organizations, the charitable remainder was includible in trustor's estate under Section 2036 which then qualified for an estate tax charitable deduction equal to the amount of inclusion).

[ii] The amount of the deduction.

Page 5-84:

Add to note 264.

As required by Section 7520(c)(3), the Service issued proposed, temporary and final regulations on May 7, 2009, revising Table S and Table U(1), the tables used to value annuities, interests for life or a term of years, and reversionary and remainder interests in property, to reflect the mortality experience from the 2000 census (Life Table 2000CM). Transition rules allow taxpayers to use tables based on either Life Table 90CM or Life Table 2000CM to value gift, charitable and estate transfers made on or after May 1, 2009, but before July 1, 2009, but they must use the appropriate interest rate for the month in which the valuation date falls, regardless of which table is chosen. For charitable deductions, pursuant to the Section 7520(a) election to use a prior month's rate, if the executor or donor elects to use the applicable federal rate (AFR) for March or April, 2009, the Table 90CM valuation tables must be used. If the May or June, 2009, AFR is elected, either the Table 90CM or the Table 2000CM valuation tables may be used and if the valuation occurs after June 30, 2009, the Table 2000CM valuation tables must be used, even if a prior month's interest rate is elected. TD 9448; REG-107845-08. Reg. §§ 1.170A-12T, 1.642(c)-6T, 1.664-4T, 20.2031-7T, 20.2032A-1T, 20.2056A-4T, 25.2512-5T, 25.2522(c)-3, 1.7520-1T, 20.7520-1T, and Reg. § 25.7520-1T. Publications 1457 and 1458 (rev. May 2009), both of which include examples for using the mortality component tables, have been released. On August 10, 2011, the Service issued final regulations that removed the temporary regulations issued in TD 9448 and adopted as final the proposed regulations issued in REG-107845-08. The only substantive change was the deletion of an example in the Section 2032 regulations which the Service anticipates including in a different regulation project under that Code section. TD 9540; Reg. §§ 1.170A-12, 1.642(c)-6, 1.664-4, 20.2031-7, 20.2032-1, 20.2056A-4, 25.2512-5, 25.2522(c)-3, 1.7520-1, 20.7520-1, 25.7520-1.

[c] The Pooled Income Fund

[ii] The amount of the deduction.

Page 5-87:

Add to note 291.

As required by Section 7520(c)(3), the Service issued proposed, temporary and final regulations on May 7, 2009, revising Table S and Table U(1), the tables used to value annuities, interests for life or a term of years, and reversionary and remainder interests in property, to reflect the mortality experience from the 2000 census (Life Table 2000CM). Transition rules allow taxpayers to use tables based on either Life Table 90CM or Life Table 2000CM to value gift, charitable and estate transfers made on or after May 1, 2009, but before July 1, 2009, but they must use the appropriate interest rate for the month in which the valuation date falls, regardless of which table is chosen. For charitable deductions, pursuant to the Section 7520(a) election to use a prior month's rate, if the executor or donor elects to use the applicable federal rate (AFR) for March or April, 2009, the Table 90CM valuation tables must be used. If the May or June, 2009, AFR is elected, either the Table 90CM or the Table 2000CM valuation tables may be used and if the valuation occurs after June 30, 2009, the Table 2000CM valuation tables must be used, even if a prior month's interest rate is elected. TD 9448; REG-107845-08. Reg. §§ 1.170A-12T, 1.642(c)-6T, 1.664-4T, 20.2031-7T, 20.2032A-1T, 20.2056A-4T, 25.2512-5T, 25.2522(c)-3, 1.7520-1T, 20.7520-1T, and Reg. § 25.7520-1T. Publications 1457 and 1458 (rev. May 2009), both of which include examples for using the mortality component tables, have been released. On August 10, 2011, the Service issued final regulations that removed the temporary regulations issued in TD 9448 and adopted as final the proposed regulations issued in REG-107845-08. The only substantive change was the deletion of an example in the Section 2032 regulations which the Service anticipates including in a different regulation project under that Code section. TD 9540; Reg. §§ 1.170A-12, 1.642(c)-6, 1.664-4, 20.2031-7, 20.2032-1, 20.2056A-4, 25.2512-5 , 25.2522(c)-3, 1.7520-1, 20.7520-1, 25.7520-1.

[6] Charitable Lead Trusts

[a] Requirements

Page 5-88:

Add to note 304.

In Revenue Procedure 2007-46, 2007-29 IRB ___, the Service provides a sample form for a testamentary charitable lead annuity trust along with annotations and sample alternative provisions. In Revenue Procedure 2008-46, 2008-30 IRB 238, the Service provides a sample form for a testamentary charitable lead unitrust along with annotations and sample alternative provisions.

[ii] Similarities in requirements.

Page 5-92:

Replace the first full paragraph of text and notes 325 and 326 with the following.

The regulations permit a deduction for an otherwise proper charitable lead interest if a noncharitable interest in the form of a guaranteed annuity or unitrust interest either precedes or runs concurrently with a similar charitable interest, so long as the trust instrument does not provide for any preference or priority in the payment of the private interest as opposed to the charitable interest.[325] The regulations were changed (after twenty years) in response to a Tax Court decision holding the predecessor regulations invalid to the extent that they denied a deduction if a private charitable or unitrust interest preceded the charitable interest in time.[326]

---

[325] Reg. §§ 20.2055-2(e)(2)(vi)(f), 20.2055-2(e)(vii)(e).

[326] Estate of Boeshore v. Comm'r, 78 TC 523 (1982), acq. in result only 1987-2 CB 1, AOD 1987-003 (June 15, 1987); Supplementary Information to TD 9068 (July 3, 2003).

[b] The Amount of the Deduction

Page 5-92:

Add to note 327.

As required by Section 7520(c)(3), the Service issued proposed, temporary and final regulations on May 7, 2009, revising Table S and Table U(1), the tables used to value annuities, interests for life or a term of years, and reversionary and remainder interests in property, to reflect the mortality experience from the 2000 census (Life Table 2000CM). Transition rules allow taxpayers to use tables based on either Life Table 90CM or Life Table 2000CM to value gift, charitable and estate transfers made on or after May 1, 2009, but before July 1, 2009, but they must use the appropriate interest rate for the month in which the valuation date falls, regardless of which table is chosen. For charitable deductions, pursuant to the Section 7520(a) election to use a prior month's rate, if the executor or donor elects to use the applicable federal rate (AFR) for March or April, 2009, the Table 90CM valuation tables must be used. If the May or June, 2009, AFR is elected, either the Table 90CM or the Table 2000CM valuation tables may be used and if the valuation occurs after June 30, 2009, the Table 2000CM valuation tables must be used, even if a prior month's interest rate is elected. TD 9448; REG-107845-08. Reg. §§ 1.170A-12T, 1.642(c)-6T, 1.664-4T, 20.2031-7T, 20.2032A-1T, 20.2056A-4T, 25.2512-5T, 25.2522(c)-3, 1.7520-1T, 20.7520-1T, and Reg. § 25.7520-1T. Publications 1457 and 1458 (rev. May 2009), both of which include examples for using the mortality component tables, have been released. On August 10, 2011, the Service issued final regulations that removed the temporary regulations issued in TD 9448 and adopted as final the proposed regulations issued in REG-107845-08. The only substantive change was the deletion of an example in the Section 2032 regulations which the Service anticipates including in a different regulation project under that Code section. TD 9540; Reg. §§ 1.170A-12, 1.642(c)-6, 1.664-4, 20.2031-7, 20.2032-1, 20.2056A-4, 25.2512-5, 25.2522(c)-3, 1.7520-1, 20.7520-1, 25.7520-1.

Add to note 328.

Priv. Ltr. Rul. 200733007 (Apr. 26, 2007) (deduction based on the present value of the guaranteed annuity).

[7] Exceptions to the Split-Interest Rules

[a] Remainders in Residences and Farms

Page 5-93:

Add to note 333.

As required by Section 7520(c)(3), the Service issued proposed, temporary and final regulations on May 7, 2009, revising Table S and Table U(1), the tables used to value annuities, interests for life or a term of years, and reversionary and remainder interests in property, to reflect the mortality experience from the 2000 census (Life Table 2000CM). Transition rules allow taxpayers to use tables based on either Life Table 90CM or Life Table 2000CM to value gift, charitable and estate transfers made on or after May 1, 2009, but before July 1, 2009, but they must use the appropriate interest rate for the month in which the valuation date falls, regardless of which table is chosen. For charitable deductions, pursuant to the Section 7520(a) election to use a prior month's rate, if the executor or donor elects to use the applicable federal rate (AFR) for March or April, 2009, the Table 90CM valuation tables must be used. If the May or June, 2009, AFR is elected, either the Table 90CM or the Table 2000CM valuation tables may be used and if the valuation occurs after June 30, 2009, the Table 2000CM valuation tables must be used, even if a prior month's interest rate is elected. TD 9448; REG-107845-08. Reg. §§ 1.170A-12T, 1.642(c)-6T, 1.664-4T, 20.2031-7T, 20.2032A-1T, 20.2056A-4T, 25.2512-5T, 25.2522(c)-3, 1.7520-1T, 20.7520-1T, and Reg. § 25.7520-1T. Publications 1457 and 1458 (rev. May 2009), both of which include examples for using the mortality component tables, have been released. On August 10, 2011, the Service issued final regulations that removed the temporary regulations issued in TD 9448 and adopted as final the proposed regulations issued in REG-107845-08. The only substantive change was the deletion of an example in the Section 2032 regulations which the Service anticipates including in a different regulation project under that Code section. TD 9540; Reg. §§ 1.170A-12, 1.642(c)-6, 1.664-4, 20.2031-7, 20.2032-1, 20.2056A-4, 25.2512-5, 25.2522(c)-3, 1.7520-1, 20.7520-1, 25.7520-1.

[b] An Undivided Portion of the Property

Page 5-94:

In the first sentence of ¶ 5.05[7][b], after the word statute, *add the following.*
generally[337.1]

[337.1] If a gift is made of an undivided portion of an interest in tangible personal property after August 17, 2006, a deduction generally will be allowed only if the donor, either alone or in conjunction with the charitable donee, holds all interests in the property immediately prior to the contribution. IRC §§ 170(o)(i)(A), 170(f)(3)(B)(ii), 2055(e)(2). See Pension Protection Act of 2006, Pub. L. No. 109-280, § 1218(d), __ Stat. __, __ (2006), reprinted in 2006-__ CB __, __. However, the Treasury may issue regulations to provide an exception to this limitation where all noncharitable donors owning interests in the property make proportionate contributions of undivided portions of such property. IRC § 170(o)(1)(B).

Add to note 338.

Cf. Galloway v. United States, 492 F3d 219 (3d Cir. 2007) (a split-interest trust in which the trust residue was to pass in four equal shares on two separate dates to two charitable and two non-charitable beneficiaries was denied estate tax charitable deduction since an interest in the same property, a single trust, passes to both charitable and non-charitable beneficiaries and is not in the form of a CRAT, a CRUT, or a pooled income fund).

Add the following new paragraph to the end of ¶ 5.05[7][b].

Generally, the amount of a charitable deduction is the fair market value of the property.[341.1] However , a special valuation rule applies if a decedent who has previously made a deductible inter vivos gift of an undivided portion of tangible personal property to charity[341.2] makes a testamentary gift of another undivided portion of the same property.[341.3] Under the valuation rule, the value of the testamentary transfer is limited to the lesser of the proportionate value of the fair market value of the property at the time of the original transfer or at the time of the subsequent contribution.[341.4]

[341.1] See ¶ 5.05[3][a].

[341.2] See IRC §§ 170(o)(1), 2522(e)(1).

[341.3] IRC § 2055(g)(2).

[341.4] IRC § 2055(g)(1). The section is applicable to transfers after August 17, 2006. Pension Protection Act of 2006, Pub. L. No. 109-280, § 1218(d), __ Stat. __, __ (2006), reprinted in 2006-__ CB __, __. Note, however, that the Tax Technical Corrections Act of 2007, Pub. L. No. 110-172, amended Section 2055(g) to remove this valuation rule for an additional charitable contribution of a fractional interest in tangible personal property. Therefore, in practical terms and effect, it is as if the valuation rule never existed for estate and gift tax purposes. The income tax version of this rule is unaffected.

[e] Charitable Gift Annuity

Page 5-96:

Add to note 352.

See Priv. Ltr. Rul. 200847014 (Apr. 9, 2008) (transfer of lump sum to charity pursuant to an agreement between donor and charity that the donor would receive an annual annuity payable to donor for life, that was subsequently funded by a commercial annuity purchased by charity, results in gift tax charitable deduction for donor equal to the amount transferred to the charity less the present value of the annuity).

[8] Curative Amendments Permitted

[b] Reformable and Qualified Interests

Page 5-98:

Add to note 363.

In Estate of Tamulis, No. 06-4141 (7th Cir. 2007), aff'g TC Memo. 2006-183 (2006), the Seventh Circuit affirmed the tax court's conclusion that the remainder interest of a trust failed to meet the criteria for a charitable remainder unitrust and that it failed to qualify as a reformable interest because the noncharitable beneficiaries' interests were not fixed as required by Section 2055(e)(3)(C)(ii). The appellate court also held that the trust could not be saved through the doctrine of "substantial compliance" since the trustee knew that a substantial tax deduction was at stake and did not have an adequate reason for failing to bring the required judicial reform proceeding.

Page 5-99:

Add to note 367.

In Estate of Tamulis, No. 06-4141 (7th Cir. 2007), aff'g TC Memo. 2006-183 (2006), the Seventh Circuit affirmed the tax court's conclusion that the remainder interest of a trust failed to qualify as a reformable interest because a judicial proceeding to reform the trust was not timely commenced as required by Section 2055(e)(3)(C)(iii), notwithstanding attempts by trustee and other interested parties to reform the trust both before and after the issuance of a deficiency notice. The appellate court also held that the trust could not be saved through the doctrine of "substantial compliance" since the trustee knew that a substantial tax deduction was at stake and did not have an adequate reason for failing to bring the required judicial reform proceeding. Accord ESB Fin. v. US, No. 07-1059-JTM (D. Kan. 2008) (charitable deduction disallowed where trustee of non-qualifying split interest trust established by decedent filed a court petition to reform the trust about one year after the deadline to file the estate tax return) and TAM 200840008 (June 10, 2008) (charitable deduction disallowed for non-judicial division of non-qualifying split interest trust under state statute).

See also Private Letter Ruling 200548019 (Aug. 11, 2005) (decedent's estate was not granted an extension of time to commence a judicial reformation of a nonqualifying split-interest trust because the deadline for commencing the judicial proceeding was not a regulatory deadline but was instead prescribed by statute, Section 2055(e)(3)(C)(iii)).

[c] Qualified Reformation

Page 5-100:

Add to note 372.

Priv. Ltr. Rul. 200535006 (May 13, 2005) (qualified disclaimer by decedent's child as to discretionary invasion of testamentary trust principal for medical expenses followed by series of judicial reformations resulting in one severed trust qualifying as a CRUT will be a qualified reformation as to the CRUT) and Priv. Ltr. Rul. 200541038 (June 22, 2005) (following a statutory election against decedent spouse's will and subsequent disclaimer by surviving spouse, residue of decedent's estate was held in a statutory elective share trust which could then be judicially reformed to qualify as a CRUT).

Priv. Ltr. Rul. 200622005 (Feb. 21, 2006) (judicial reformation of CRUT, made within ninety days of the due date of decedent's federal estate tax return, to increase unitrust amount from 4 to 5 percent and make a portion of the unitrust amount payable to charity will be a qualified reformation). Priv. Ltr. Rul. 200927013 (Mar. 18, 2008) (judicial reformation of two CRATs to include provisions under Reg. §§ 1.664-1 and 1.664-2, required for qualification as CRATs, were qualified reformations). Priv. Ltr. Rul. 201115003 (Dec. 13, 2010) (judicial proceeding to reform trust to create two trusts, a CLAT and a CRUT, commenced within 90 days of the due date of decedent's estate tax return, is a qualified reformation since the charitable interests of the trust are presently ascertainable and, hence, severable from the noncharitable interests; accordingly, a charitable deduction will be allowable for the present value of the qualified interests). Priv. Ltr. Rul. 201125007 (Feb. 16, 2011) (judicial reformation of trust, commenced prior to the timely filing of decedent's federal estate tax return, that will convert trust to CRAT and pay a 5 percent annuity, a portion of which will be paid to an elderly family member of decedent and the rest to a foundation, for the life of the elderly family member with the remainder paid to a foundation will be a qualified reformation).

Add to note 377.

Priv. Ltr. Rul. 200726005 (Mar. 7, 2007) (modification to testamentary trust was a qualified reformation).

[d] Additional Rules Related to Reformations

Page 5-102:

Add to note 386.

Priv. Ltr. Rul. 200548019 (Aug. 11, 2005) (decedent's estate was not granted an extension of time to commence a judicial reformation of a nonqualifying split-interest trust because the deadline for commencing the judicial proceeding was not a regulatory deadline but was instead prescribed by statute, Section 2055(e)(3)(C)(iii)).

¶ 5.06 SECTION 2056. TESTAMENTARY TRANSFERS TO SURVIVING SPOUSE

[3] Interests Passing to a Surviving Spouse

Page 5-106:

Add to end of third paragraph of note 17.

Beat v. US, 106 AFTR 2d 2010-5285 (D. Kan. 2010) (no marital deduction for property passing to decedent's companion/executrix, who claimed that she and decedent had a common-law marriage, with the court holding that executrix was estopped from claiming the marital deduction in accordance with the doctrine of consistency – through her marital deduction claim, executrix attempted to change her position regarding her relationship with decedent after the statute of limitations for the income tax returns, in which she and decedent had always filed either as single or head of household, had expired).

Add to the end of note 17.

Cf. Estate of Lee, TC Memo. 2007-371 (2007), in which the tax court held that decedent's estate was not entitled to a marital deduction where decedent's spouse predeceased decedent by forty-six days notwithstanding a will provision that spouse be deemed to have survived decedent if they die within six months of each other. Regulations Section 20.2056(c)-2(e) provides that a presumption supplied by local law or under decedent's will regarding the order of deaths only operates to determine the order of deaths if the actual order cannot be determined.

[a] By Will or Inheritance

Page 5-107:

Add to note 24.

See, e.g. Alan Baer Revocable Trust Dated Feb. 9, 1996 v. United States, No. 8:06-cv-00774 (D. Neb. 2009) where decedent made multiple bequests to individuals contingent upon the sale of decedent's stock in a private equity company for a profit during surviving spouse's lifetime. Decedent's estate claimed the bequests might never be paid out due to the value of the stock and claimed a marital deduction that the Service contested. At trial, the Service filed a motion for summary judgment arguing that there is a possibility that the contingent bequests will be paid and, therefore, cannot be claimed as part of the marital deduction. In denying the Service's motion, the court stated that the stock's valuation was a question of fact and was relevant to the marital deduction if the estate can demonstrate that the contingency on which the bequests depended would never occur. See also TAM 201126030 (Mar. 1, 2011) where the Service construed language in decedent's will stating "it is my desire" to be mandatory which resulted in specific bequests of property to decedent's children that otherwise would have passed with the residue to his surviving spouse thus causing a decrease in the marital deduction.

Page 5-108:

Add to note 30 at end of citation to "Estate of Fung".

, aff'd, 91 AFTR2d 2003-1228 (9th Cir. 2003);

Add to note 31 after citation to Reg. § 20.2056(c)-2(d)(2).

Thus, amounts received in a bona fide adversarial proceeding are treated as received in due course.

Add to note 31 before the last sentence in the first paragraph.

Priv. Ltr. Rul. 200417030 (Jan. 16, 2004) (valid settlement in the form of a transfer to a QTIP trust). Priv. Ltr. Rul. 201046004 (Aug. 17, 2010).

[h] Disclaimers

Page 5-116:

Add to note 81.

Care must also be taken to ensure that a disclaimer by a surviving spouse coupled with a formula clause in the will of the decedent spouse will not cause unintended estate tax consequences. See infra ¶ 5.06[6]. In Estate of Katz, TC Memo. 2004-166 (2004), a residuary trust was funded pursuant to a formula clause in decedent's will that was drafted to minimize tax liability. Decedent's will also provided that the amount passing to the residuary trust would not be reduced by any disclaimer the surviving spouse might make. The surviving spouse's disclaimer of any interest in the residuary trust and also of her interest in numerous shares of stock in decedent's estate caused an overfunding of the residuary trust and an estate tax deficiency. See also Estate of Nix, TC Memo. 1996-109 (1996).

Page 5-117:

Add to end of first paragraph of note 82.

Priv. Ltr. Rul. 200626002 (Mar. 8, 2006) (disclaimers by decedent's children and grandchildren of their interests in trust were qualified disclaimers and the property is treated as passing directly to decedent's surviving spouse thereby qualifying the property for the estate tax marital deduction).

[5] Valuation of Interests Passing

[a] Taxes on Surviving Spouse's Interest

Page 5-120:

Add to note 95.

In Lurie v. Comm'r, 425 F3d 1021 (7th Cir. 2005), the court held that decedent intended to have estate taxes paid by his revocable trust, in the event his probate estate was insufficient, thereby negating default rule of equitable apportionment under state law. Since estate taxes were paid from property otherwise passing to decedent's surviving spouse, the marital deduction was reduced.

Page 5-122:

Add to note 99.

Estate of McCoy v. Comm'r, TC Memo. 2009-61 (2009) (concluding that tax provision in decedent's trust was ambiguous so that the state's equitable apportionment statute governs the allocation of estate taxes and, accordingly, the marital deduction is not reduced).

[b] Encumbrances on Surviving Spouse's Interest

[ii] Administrative expenses.

Page 5-124:

Add to note 109.

Lurie v. Comm'r, 425 F3d 1021 (7th Cir. 2005) (decedent intended administrative expenses to be paid the marital share). In Brown v. United States, 329 F3d 664 (9th Cir. 2003), an imaginative taxpayer theory that would have allowed actual expenses in excess of estimated expenses to be deducted under Section 2053 without reducing the marital deduction was rejected. Although the decision was rendered under the regulations before their amendment in 1999, the result would appear to be the same under the amended regulations.

[7] The Terminable Interest Rule

[b] Identifying Terminable Interests

Page 5-137:

Add in note 174 following citation to Berger v. United States.

Sowder v. United States, 96 AFTR2d 2005-7177 (ED Wash. 2005), aff'd, 2007-2 USTC ¶ 60,550 (9th Cir. 2007); (decedent's residual gift to spouse in self-drafted will construed to qualify for marital deduction despite a provision in will conditioning gift on spouse's survival until distribution of decedent's estate).

Page 5-138:

Add to note 181 after Rev. Ruls. 66-139 *and* 76-199.

Priv. Ltr. Rul. 200417030 (Jan. 16, 2004) (property passing to a QTIP trust pursuant to a settlement agreement from a bona fide adversarial proceeding qualified for an estate tax marital deduction).

[d] The Executor-Purchaser Provision

Page 5-142:

Add to note 197.

As required by Section 7520(c)(3), the Service issued proposed, temporary and final regulations on May 7, 2009, revising Table S and Table U(1), the tables used to value annuities, interests for life or a term of years, and reversionary and remainder interests in property, to reflect the mortality experience from the 2000 census (Life Table 2000CM). Transition rules allow taxpayers to use tables based on either Life Table 90CM or Life Table 2000CM to value gift, charitable and estate transfers made on or after May 1, 2009, but before July 1, 2009, but they must use the appropriate interest rate for the month in which the valuation date falls, regardless of which table is chosen. TD 9448; REG-107845-08. Reg. §§ 1.170A-12T, 1.642(c)-6T, 1.664-4T, 20.2031-7T, 20.2032A-1T,

20.2056A-4T, 25.2512-5T, 25.2522(c)-3, 1.7520-1T, 20.7520-1T, and Reg. § 25.7520-1T. Publications 1457 and 1458 (rev. May 2009), both of which include examples for using the mortality component tables, have been released. On August 10, 2011, the Service issued final regulations that removed the temporary regulations issued in TD 9448 and adopted as final the proposed regulations issued in REG-107845-08. The only substantive change was the deletion of an example in the Section 2032 regulations which the Service anticipates including in a different regulation project under that Code section. TD 9540; Reg. §§ 1.170A-12, 1.642(c)-6, 1.664-4, 20.2031-7, 20.2032-1, 20.2056A-4, 25.2512-5, 25.2522(c)-3, 1.7520-1, 20.7520-1, 25.7520-1.

[8] Terminable Interests That Do Qualify

[b] Life Interests With Powers

[i] The surviving spouse must be entitled for life to all of the income from the entire interest or a specific portion of the entire interest, or to a specific portion of all the income from the entire interest.

Page 5-146:

Replace the sentence containing note 215 with the following.

The income requirement is satisfied if the spouse is entitled to income as defined under applicable state law that provides for a reasonable apportionment between the income and remainder beneficiaries of the total return of the trust.[215]

---

[215] Reg. § 20.2056(b)-5(f)(1). Applicable state law would generally be in the form of a state statute or could be the result of a decision of the highest court of the state applicable to all trusts administered under the state's law. Cf. Reg. § 20.2056(b)-7(d)(1). The applicable state law must also satisfy the requirements of Regulations Section 1.643(b)-1. Regulations Section 1.643(b)-1 is a recognition of state statutes (or court decisions) that change traditional concepts of income and principal in response to investment strategies that seek total positive return on trust assets. Such statutes are designed to ensure that, when a trust invests in assets that may generate little traditional income in the form of dividends, interest, etc., the income and remainder beneficiaries are allocated reasonable amounts of the total return of the trust (traditional income and capital appreciation) so that both classes of beneficiaries are treated impartially. Under the regulations, a reasonable apportionment may be accomplished through a three percent to five percent unitrust definition of income or by giving the trustee the power to make equitable adjustments between income or principal. Reg. § 1.643(b)-1.

Page 5-147:

Add to note 218.

Estate of Davis v. Comm'r, TC Memo. 2003-55 (2003), aff'd, 394 F3d 1294 (9th Cir. 2005) (held that a California trust did not provide the surviving spouse all of the income where the direction to pay the surviving spouse all of the net income from the trust in quarter, annual or more frequent installments was followed by language that seemed to restrict the trustee to distributions that the trustee, in its discretion, determined to be proper for health, education, support, maintenance, comfort and welfare, and there was no express statement of a desire to qualify the trust for the marital deduction); Priv. Ltr. Rul. 200444023 (July 12, 2004) (right of surviving spouse to income of trust was within discretion of trustee and, therefore, was not a qualifying income interest). TAM 200505022 (Nov. 8, 2004).

Page 5-148:

Add to note 220.

TAM 200339003 (May 7, 2003) (shares of non-dividend producing stock in a QTIP trust over which trustee had a limited power to dispose satisfied requirement since, under the trust agreement, surviving spouse had the power to require trustee to make the property productive).

[iii] The surviving spouse must have the power to appoint the entire interest or the specific portion to either surviving spouse or spouse's estate.

Page 5-151:

Add to note 239.

Estate of Posner v. Comm'r, TC Memo. 2004-112 (2004) (decedent did not possess a Section 2041 power of appointment over marital trust property and, accordingly, the property was not includible in decedent's estate even though decedent's predeceased spouse's estate claimed a Section 2056(b)(5) marital deduction. The court rejected the Service's argument that the duty of consistency required inclusion. In order for the duty of consistency to apply, three elements must be present: (1) a representation by the taxpayer; (2) reliance by the Service; (3) an attempt by the taxpayer to change the representation after the statute of limitations on assessment has run. The tax court held that the duty does not apply to a mutual mistake by the taxpayer and the Service over a pure question of law).

Page 5-152:

Add to note 241.

Priv. Ltr. Rul. 200444023 (July 12, 2004) (surviving spouse's power to withdraw entire trust corpus sufficient to qualify decedent spouse's 50 percent interest in trust for Section 2056(b)(5) marital deduction).

Add to note 248.

Technical Advice Memorandum 200244002 (July 16, 2001) ruled that an inferentially granted power to appoint "in the amount and to the extent necessary to qualify the Marital Trust for the marital deduction" was a general power of appointment that required inclusion of the trust property in the surviving spouse's estate under Maryland law.

[d] Election With Respect to Life Estate for Surviving Spouse

[i] The passing requirement.

Page 5-162:

Add to note 307.

In Priv. Ltr. Rul. 200846003 (July 30, 2008), nonqualified disclaimers by decedent's children (see generally ¶ 10.07) of asset which then passed, according to decedent's will, to trust established for the benefit of surviving spouse was a taxable gift of asset by the children to surviving spouse. Accordingly, trust did not qualify for a marital deduction since it did not pass from the decedent to the surviving spouse.

[ii] The qualifying income interest requirement.

Page 5-162:

Add to note 311 immediately after semi-colon.

Estate of Aronson v. Comm'r, TC Memo. 2003-189 (2003) (New York Surrogate Court's reformation ignored and interest held nondeductible where will language provided surviving spouse was to receive as much income from the trust as she "needs");

Add to note 315.

; TAM 200505022 (Nov. 8, 2004).

Page 5-163:

In note 316, replace Prop. Reg. § 20.2056(b)-5(f)(1) *with* Reg. § 20.2056(b)-5(f)(1).

Add to the end of note 316.

In Revenue Ruling 2006-26, the Service described three circumstances, in which a surviving spouse would have a qualifying income interest in an IRA or other qualified retirement plan and the marital deduction trust designated as the IRA or qualified plan beneficiary for purposes of electing QTIP status for both the retirement account and the trust. Two of the situations involve changed concepts of trust accounting income. In one, the trust was governed by state law that provided that the trustee would be authorized to make adjustments between income and principal to fulfill the trustee's duty of impartiality between the income and remainder beneficiaries. In another scenario, the trust was administered pursuant to a state law providing that the trust income would be a certain unitrust amount of the fair market value of the trust assets determined annually. The Service held that both of these situations would meet the requirements of Regulations Section 20.2056(b)-5(f)(1). See also Priv. Ltr. Rul. 201117005 (Jan. 5, 2011) (spouse has qualifying income interest where one fund held by QTIP trust will, among other things, pay surviving spouse a 3 percent to 4 percent unitrust interest).

Page 5-165:

Add to end of first paragraph of note 325.

See Estate of Davis v. Comm'r, TC Memo. 2003-55, aff'd, 394 F3d 1294 (9th Cir. 2005) (trust giving spouse all of the trust's net income as the trustee shall determine to be proper for the spouse's health, education, support, maintenance, comfort and welfare does not qualify for the estate tax marital deduction).

Add to note 328 prior to citation to Priv. Ltr. Rul. 9320015.

Revenue Ruling 2000-2 is modified and, as modified, is superseded by Revenue Ruling 2006-26 where the Service described three circumstances, in which a surviving spouse would have a qualifying income interest in an IRA or other qualified retirement plan and the marital deduction trust designated as the IRA or qualified plan beneficiary for purposes of electing QTIP status for both the retirement account and the trust. In the ruling, the trust provided for the payment of all income to the spouse and the spouse would also have the Revenue Ruling 2000-2 power over the trustee. In the first scenario, the trust was governed by state law that provided that the trustee would be authorized to make adjustments between income and principal to fulfill the trustee's duty of impartiality between the income and remainder beneficiaries. In the second scenario, the trust was administered pursuant to a state law providing that the trust income would be a certain unitrust amount of the fair market value of the trust assets determined annually. Finally, in the third scenario, the trustee would apply applicable state law regarding allocation of receipts and disbursements with no power to allocate between the two. The Service ruled that in all three circumstances, a surviving spouse will be considered to have a qualifying income interest for life for Section 2056(b)(7) QTIP purposes in the IRA, or other qualified retirement plan, and in the marital deduction trust.

Add to end of note 328.

Cf. Estate of Warner v. United States, Doc. 2006-16163 (CD Cal. 2006), in which the court found that surviving spouse had a qualifying income interest for life in trust even though trust instrument specified only that income be paid in convenient installments at the discretion of the trustee. It could be inferred that payments were to be made at least annually given that surviving spouse was co-trustee and had the right to invade principal to supplement her income and there was no provision in the trust instrument regarding the accumulation of income.

Add to note 329.

Estate of Whiting v. Comm'r, TC Memo. 2004-68 (2004) (QTIP trust qualified for marital deduction in a case in which the provisions of marital deduction trust requiring that all income be distributed to a surviving spouse conflicted with disability clause allowing trustee to accumulate income).

Page 5-168:

Add to note 344.

However, under Regulations Section 20.2039-1(e), Section 2039 will not be applicable if a decedent created a trust and retained the right to use property or an annuity, unitrust or other income interest in the trust (other than a trust constituting an employee benefit) where Section 2036 applies. See text in ¶ 4.08[8] accompanying notes 168.1 – 168.9. The regulations are effective on or after July 14, 2008. Reg. § 20.2039-1(f).

Page 5-169:

Add to note 348.

As required by Section 7520(c)(3), the Service issued proposed, temporary and final regulations on May 7, 2009, revising Table S and Table U(1), the tables used to value annuities, interests for life or a term of years, and reversionary and remainder interests in property, to reflect the mortality experience from the 2000 census (Life Table 2000CM). Transition rules allow taxpayers to use tables based on either Life Table 90CM or Life Table 2000CM to value gift, charitable and estate transfers made on or after May 1, 2009, but before July 1, 2009, but they must use the appropriate interest rate for the month in which the valuation date falls, regardless of which table is chosen. TD 9448; REG-107845-08. Reg. §§ 1.170A-12T, 1.642(c)-6T, 1.664-4T , 20.2031-7T, 20.2032A-1T, 20.2056A-4T, 25.2512-5T, 25.2522(c)-3, 1.7520-1T, 20.7520-1T, and Reg. § 25.7520-1T. Publications 1457 and 1458 (rev. May 2009), both of which include examples for using the mortality component tables, have been released. On August 10, 2011, the Service issued final regulations that removed the temporary regulations issued in TD 9448 and adopted as final the proposed regulations issued in REG-107845-08. The only substantive change was the deletion of an example in the Section 2032 regulations which the Service anticipates including in a different regulation project under that Code section. TD 9540; Reg. §§ 1.170A-12, 1.642(c)-6, 1.664-4, 20.2031-7, 20.2032-1, 20.2056A-4, 25.2512-5, 25.2522(c)-3, 1.7520-1, 20.7520-1, 25.7520-1.

In note 353, replace Prop. Reg. § 1.643(b)-1 *with* Reg. § 1.643(b)-1 *and replace* Prop. Reg. § 20.2056(b)-7(d)(1) *with* Reg. § 20.2056(b)-7(d)(1).

Add to note 353.

See Priv. Ltr. Rul. 200919003 (Jan. 14, 2009) (property interest created under decedent's revocable trust, as reformed to correct scrivener's error that had originally provided surviving spouse with a limited power of appointment "during lifetime", constituted qualified terminable interest property).

[iii] The election.

Page 5-172:

Add to note 368.

See also Priv. Ltr. Rul. 200430002 (Apr. 7, 2004) (an estate's QTIP election for 100 percent of reported assets applies to subsequently discovered assets not originally reported on the decedent's estate tax return and to assets whose value was increased pursuant to an audit of the return). Priv. Ltr. Rul. 200450004 (Sept. 1, 2004) (decedent's estate made valid QTIP election for 100 percent of surviving spouse's statutory share of estate despite miscalculation of statutory share amount on return). But see Priv. Ltr. Rul. 200612001 (Nov. 29, 2005) (QTIP election for property listed on Schedule M of estate tax return does not apply to property not listed on Schedule M but that passed to QTIP trust because of disclaimers which were later determined to be invalid).

Page 5-174:

Add to note 383 following citation to "Reg. § 20.2056(b)-7(b)(4)(i)".

Priv. Ltr. Rul. 200825032 (Mar. 4, 2008) (election made on first Form 706 filed after the return's due date is effective).

Add to note 383 before reference to TAM 9411010.

Priv. Ltr. Rul. 200410011 (Nov. 28, 2003); Priv. Ltr. Rul. 200526017 (Mar. 30, 2005); Priv. Ltr. Rul. 200608019 (Nov. 14, 2005) (decedent's estate granted extension of time to make a QTIP election for a fractional or percentage share of a credit shelter trust after attorney belatedly discovered that decedent had made adjusted taxable gifts and election was necessary to keep estate tax at zero); Priv. Ltr. Rul. 201020002 (Jan. 17, 2010) (extension granted where property was discovered after estate tax return was filed). Priv. Ltr. Rul. 201121003 (Feb. 4, 2011).

Add to note 384.

See Priv. Ltr. Rul. 200407016 (Oct. 24, 2003) (citing Revenue Procedure 2001-38, the Service treated a QTIP election made for a surviving spouse's life estate as null and void because the election was unnecessary to eliminate a deceased spouse's estate tax liability); in Private Letter Ruling 200403093 (Sept. 24, 2003), the decedent created a credit shelter trust at his death and left the residue of his estate outright to his surviving spouse who, as executor, made a QTIP election for these assets on the decedent's return. The spouse also transferred a portion of the assets she received from the decedent to a separate credit shelter trust after she discovered that she had underfunded the credit shelter trust. The Service ruled that the QTIP election was null and void and that neither credit shelter trust will be included in the surviving spouse's estate under Section 2044. See also Priv. Ltr. Ruls. 200443027 (July 7, 2004), 200535026 (Apr. 26, 2005), 200603004 (Sept. 30, 2005), 200702018 (Sept. 28, 2006), 200729028 (Apr. 11, 2007). Priv. Ltr. Rul. 200918014 (Dec. 17, 2008), Priv. Ltr. Rul. 201022004 (Jan. 28, 2010), Priv. Ltr. Rul. 201024035 (Jan. 20, 2010), Priv. Ltr. Rul. 201036013 (June 2, 2010). Priv. Ltr. Rul. 201112001 (Nov. 29, 2010), Priv. Ltr. Rul. 201131011 (Apr. 20, 2011). Private Letter Ruling 200219003 (Feb. 5, 2002) illustrates a situation in which Revenue Procedure 2001-38 will not help the taxpayer. In the private letter ruling, the trustee of the marital trust made the QTIP election for more marital trust property than was required to reduce the decedent's estate tax liability to zero, thus underutilizing the decedent's unified credit. The Service ruled that the fact pattern was not within the purview of Revenue Procedure 2001-38 because it assumes that the election was not necessary to reduce the estate tax liability to zero, whereas in the ruling a QTIP election was necessary to reduce the tax to zero, it simply could have been an election as to a smaller amount. The Service also denied relief under Regulations Section 301.9100, which it concluded allows a taxpayer to seek an extension of time to make the QTIP election, but not to partially revoke a QTIP election that has been made. Revenue Procedure 2001-38 was ruled to apply in Private Letter Ruling 200318039 (Jan. 21, 2003). Revenue Procedure 2001-38 is also inapplicable where a partial election was made and a full election was appropriate. Priv. Ltr. Rul. 200540003 (June 20, 2005) (Service ruled that the estate had made a partial election in claiming a marital deduction on the return for just the actuarial value of the surviving spouse's income interest in trust assets and denied the estate's request for an extension of time to make an election for the balance of the trust). See also Priv. Ltr. Rul. 200422050 (Feb. 20, 2004) and Priv. Ltr. Rul. 200612001 (Nov. 29, 2005) (estate denied an extension of time to amend the QTIP election to include property originally not listed on Schedule M of estate tax return but that passed to QTIP trust because of disclaimers which were later determined to be invalid).

But see Priv. Ltr. Rul. 200832011 (Apr. 1, 2008) where estate's attorney, in calculating amount of QTIP election for decedent's estate tax return, made a mathematical error by applying the applicable exclusion amount for the year that the return was filed instead of the year the decedent died which resulted in an underpayment of estate tax. The Service allowed the estate to revise the QTIP election for the amount necessary to reduce the estate tax to zero by using the correct applicable exclusion amount.

Add to note 386.

Priv. Ltr. Rul. 200448038 (Aug. 6, 2004) (QTIP election not made where executor failed to unequivocally communicate QTIP election on estate tax return).

Page 5-175:

Add to note 387.

See Priv. Ltr. Rul. 200618018 (Jan. 12, 2006) (executor granted an extension of time to make a QTIP election with respect to a trust which executor listed as passing to spouse on Schedule M, although no QTIP election was made and a charitable deduction for the trust, which passed to a charity at the death of the surviving spouse, was made on Schedule O).

Add to note 388.

Cf. Priv. Ltr. Rul. 200536015 (May 25, 2005) (election allowed for asset discovered after election previously made). But see Estate of Le Caer v. Comm'r, 135 TC No. 14 (2010) (QTIP protective election untimely where estate filed the election three years after the estate had timely filed its estate tax return and made a QTIP election for other property in the estate).

[e] Special Rules for Charitable Remainder Trusts

Page 5-179:

Add to note 413.

Priv. Ltr. Rul. 200541038 (June 22, 2005) (following a statutory election against decedent spouse's will and subsequent disclaimer by surviving spouse, residue of decedent's estate was held in a statutory elective share trust which could then be judicially reformed to qualify as a CRUT entitling decedent's estate to charitable deduction for present value of remainder interest passing to charities; in addition, present value of surviving spouse's unitrust interest under reformed CRUT will qualify for marital deduction). Priv. Ltr. Rul. 200832017 (Mar. 21, 2008) (creation of a successive unitrust interest in a CRUT, following the trustor's lifetime unitrust interest, in the trustor's spouse for life qualified for the marital deduction pursuant to IRC § 2056(b)(8)). Priv. Ltr. Rul. 201117005 (Jan. 5, 2011) (CRUT that pays one-fifth of the unitrust interest to surviving spouse and remaining four-fifths to surviving spouse and charity in shares determined by the trustees will qualify for a Section 2055 charitable deduction as to the charitable remainder and for a Section 2056(b)(8) marital deduction as to the value of the entire unitrust interest even though the amount paid to surviving spouse from CRUT is unclear; estate will thus be able to deduct the entire value of assets passing to CRUT).

Page 5-180:

Add to note 417.

If the lifetime transfer of the surviving spouse's income interest in a QTIP trust is made to the qualified charity remainder beneficiary of the QTIP trust, there is a merger and the merged interest qualifies for the charitable deduction. See Private Letter Ruling 200438028 (May 12, 2004), where the charitable remainder QTIP trust established by the decedent spouse was judicially divided into two QTIP trusts, and the surviving spouse assigned the entire income interest of one of the QTIP trusts to the remainder beneficiary. The Service determined that a gift tax charitable deduction was allowed for the surviving spouse's transfer of his income interest and for the amount the surviving spouse was deemed to transfer to the charity under Section 2519. The Service also ruled that the surviving spouse's transfer qualified as a charitable contribution under Section 170, limited to the fair market value of the interest.

¶ 5.07 SECTION 2056A. QUALIFIED DOMESTIC TRUSTS

[2] The Passing Requirement

[b] The Surviving Spouse's Transfer to a QDOT

Page 5-189:

Add to note 21.

Priv. Ltr. Rul. 200712010 (Nov. 20, 2006) (estate granted extension of time to assign assets that passed outright to noncitizen spouse under decedent's will and noncitizen spouse's nonprobate property to QDOT and, in addition, an extension of time to make QDOT election with respect to these assets and also as to assets that passed to QDOT created under decedent's will). Priv. Ltr. Rul. 200910019 (Nov. 20, 2009) (estate granted an extension of time to make a protective assignment to QDOT of noncitizen spouse's interest in joint property included in decedent spouse's estate, property passing to noncitizen spouse under decedent spouse's will, and any other property included in decedent spouse's estate and passing to noncitizen spouse outside of will and, in addition, the estate granted an extension of time to make QDOT election).

[c] An Annuity or Other Arrangement Treated as Passing to a QDOT

Page 5-191:

Add to note 33.

Priv. Ltr. Rul. 200445010 (July 12, 2004) (decedent's estate was granted an extension of time to file the Agreement To Pay Section 2056A Estate Tax and the Information Statement).

[3] Requirements of a QDOT

[c] Regulatory Requirements to Ensure Collection of Deferred Tax

Page 5-196:

Add to note 63.

The Service has released revised Form 706-QDT, U.S. Estate Tax Return for Qualified Domestic Trusts (revised February 2007) and Instructions for Form 706-QDT (revised February 2007). The instructions note that the form must now be filed at the Cincinnati Service Center, regardless of whether the decedent's estate (QDOT's grantor) filed Form 706, U.S. Estate (and Generation-Skipping Transfer) Tax Return or Form 706-NA, Estate of Nonresident Not a Citizen of the United States. An automatic six-month extension of time to file the form can be requested on Form 4768, Application for Extension of Time to File a Return and/or Pay U.S. Estate (and Generation-Skipping Transfer) Taxes.

The Service has released revised Form 706–QDT, U.S. Estate Tax Return for Qualified Domestic Trusts (Revised December 2008) and instructions.

[iii] Rules applicable to both classifications of QDOTs.

Page 5-202:

Add to note 112.

The Service has released revised Form 706-QDT, U.S. Estate Tax Return for Qualified Domestic Trusts (revised February 2007) and Instructions for Form 706-QDT (revised February 2007). The instructions note that the form must now be filed at the Cincinnati Service Center, regardless of whether the decedent's estate (QDOT's grantor) filed Form 706, U.S. Estate (and Generation-Skipping Transfer) Tax Return or Form 706-NA, Estate of Nonresident Not a Citizen of the United States. An automatic six-month extension of time to file the form can be requested on Form 4768, Application for Extension of Time to File a Return and/or Pay U.S. Estate (and Generation-Skipping Transfer) Taxes.

The Service has released revised Form 706-QDT, U.S. Estate Tax Return for Qualified Domestic Trusts (Revised December 2008) and instructions.

[d] A QDOT Election

Page 5-202:

Add to note 117.

; and Priv. Ltr. Rul. 200712010 (Nov. 20, 2006) (estate granted extension of time to assign assets that passed outright to noncitizen spouse under decedent's will and noncitizen spouse's nonprobate property to QDOT and, in addition, an extension of time to make QDOT election with respect to these assets and also as to assets that passed to QDOT created under decedent's will); Priv. Ltr. Rul. 200821030 (Jan. 9, 2008) (estate granted extension of time to make QDOT election with respect to decedent's interest in several properties jointly held with surviving spouse and to assign certain property to QDOT); Priv. Ltr. Rul. 200842018 (June 27, 2008) (estate granted extension of time to assign property to QDOT and make QDOT election where CPA had erroneously assumed that, because surviving spouse was a permanent resident, property passing to her from the decedent qualified for the marital deduction without the need of a QDOT); Priv. Ltr. Rul.

201103004 (Sept. 21, 2010) (extension of time granted to make QDOT election with respect to trust and percentage of decedent's residuary trust passing to trust).

Page 5-203:

Add to note 118.

The preamble to the final regulations issued under Section 2032 permits applications to make late QDOT elections so long as the estate tax return is filed no later than one year after the due date of the return, including extensions.

[4] Taxation of QDOT Property

[a] Events Triggering the Tax

Page 5-204:

Add to note 129.

The Service has released revised Form 706-QDT, U.S. Estate Tax Return for Qualified Domestic Trusts (revised February 2007) and Instructions for Form 706-QDT (revised February 2007). The instructions note that the form must now be filed at the Cincinnati Service Center, regardless of whether the decedent's estate (QDOT's grantor) filed Form 706, U.S. Estate (and Generation-Skipping Transfer) Tax Return or Form 706-NA, Estate of Nonresident Not a Citizen of the United States. An automatic six-month extension of time to file the form can be requested on Form 4768, Application for Extension of Time to File a Return and/or Pay U.S. Estate (and Generation-Skipping Transfer) Taxes.

The Service has released revised Form 706–QDT, U.S. Estate Tax Return for Qualified Domestic Trusts (Revised December 2008) and instructions.

[i] Corpus distributions.

Page 5-204:

In note 131, replace Prop. Reg. § 1.643(b)-1 *with* Reg. § 1.643(b)-1.

[ii] The surviving spouse's death.

Page 5-207:

Add to note 146.

The Service has released revised Form 706-QDT, U.S. Estate Tax Return for Qualified Domestic Trusts (revised February 2007) and Instructions for Form 706-QDT (revised February 2007). The instructions note that the form must now be filed at the Cincinnati Service Center, regardless of whether the decedent's estate (QDOT's grantor) filed Form 706, U.S. Estate (and Generation-Skipping Transfer) Tax Return or Form 706-NA, Estate of Nonresident Not a Citizen of the United States. An automatic six-month extension of time to file the form can be requested on Form 4768, Application for Extension of Time to File a Return and/or Pay U.S. Estate (and Generation-Skipping Transfer) Taxes.

The Service has released revised Form 706-QDT, U.S. Estate Tax Return for Qualified Domestic Trusts (Revised December 2008) and instructions.

[c] Liability for and Payment of the Tax

Page 5-211:

Add to note 170.

The Service has released revised Form 706-QDT, U.S. Estate Tax Return for Qualified Domestic Trusts (revised February 2007) and Instructions for Form 706-QDT (revised February 2007). The instructions note that the form must now be filed at the Cincinnati Service Center, regardless of whether the decedent's estate (QDOT's grantor) filed Form 706, U.S. Estate (and Generation-Skipping Transfer) Tax Return or Form 706-NA, Estate of Nonresident Not a Citizen of the United States. An automatic six-month extension of time to file the form can be requested on Form 4768, Application for Extension of Time to File a Return and/or Pay U.S. Estate (and Generation-Skipping Transfer) Taxes.

The Service has released revised Form 706-QDT, U.S. Estate Tax Return for Qualified Domestic Trusts (Revised December 2008) and instructions.

Add to note 172.

The Service has released revised Form 706-QDT, U.S. Estate Tax Return for Qualified Domestic Trusts (revised February 2007) and Instructions for Form 706-QDT (revised February 2007). The instructions note that the form must now be filed at the Cincinnati Service Center, regardless of whether the decedent's estate (QDOT's grantor) filed Form 706, U.S. Estate (and Generation-Skipping Transfer) Tax Return or Form 706-NA, Estate of Nonresident Not a Citizen of the United States. An automatic six-month extension of time to file the form can be requested on Form 4768, Application for Extension of Time to File a Return and/or Pay U.S. Estate (and Generation-Skipping Transfer) Taxes.

The Service has released revised Form 706-QDT, U.S. Estate Tax Return for Qualified Domestic Trusts (Revised December 2008) and instructions.

[5] Exceptions If Surviving Spouse Becomes a U.S. Citizen

Page 5-212:

Add to note 184.

; Priv. Ltr. Rul. 200451024 (Aug. 25, 2004) (the Service grants an extension of time for notifying it that the surviving spouse beneficiary of a QDOT has become a citizen); Priv. Ltr. Rul. 200719002 (Jan. 25, 2007) (same). Priv. Ltr. Rul. 200949009 (Aug. 13, 2009) (same). Priv. Ltr. Rul. 201032022 (Apr. 29, 2010).

The Service has released revised Form 706-QDT, U.S. Estate Tax Return for Qualified Domestic Trusts (revised February 2007) and Instructions for Form 706-QDT (revised February 2007). The instructions note that the form must now be filed at the Cincinnati Service Center, regardless of whether the decedent's estate (QDOT's grantor) filed Form 706, U.S. Estate (and Generation-Skipping Transfer) Tax Return or Form 706-NA, Estate of Nonresident Not a Citizen of the United States. An automatic six-month extension of time to file the form can be requested on Form 4768, Application for Extension of Time to File a Return and/or Pay U.S. Estate (and Generation-Skipping Transfer) Taxes.

The Service has released revised Form 706-QDT, U.S. Estate Tax Return for Qualified Domestic Trusts (Revised December 2008) and instructions.

Page 5-213:

Add to note 187.

The Service has released revised Form 706-QDT, U.S. Estate Tax Return for Qualified Domestic Trusts (revised February 2007) and Instructions for Form 706-QDT (revised February 2007). The instructions note that the form must now be filed at the Cincinnati Service Center, regardless of whether the decedent's estate (QDOT's grantor) filed Form 706, U.S. Estate (and Generation-Skipping Transfer) Tax Return or Form 706-NA, Estate of Nonresident Not a Citizen of the United States. An automatic six-month extension of time to file the form can be requested on Form 4768, Application for Extension of Time to File a Return and/or Pay U.S. Estate (and Generation-Skipping Transfer) Taxes.

The Service has released revised Form 706-QDT, U.S. Estate Tax Return for Qualified Domestic Trusts (Revised December 2008) and instructions.

¶ 5.08 SECTION 2057. FAMILY-OWNED-BUSINESS DEDUCTION

[2] Definition of "Qualified Family-Owned Business Interest"

[a] In General

Page 5-215:

Add to note 16.

In Technical Advice Memorandum 200410002 (Nov. 6, 2003), the Service concluded that a corporation's promissory notes issued to decedent's trust in exchange for cash loaned by the decedent were not an interest in an entity for purposes of Section 2057. Accord Estate of Farnam, 130 TC No. 2 (2008) aff'd, 583 F3d 581 (8th Cir. 2009), where decedents' loans to their family-owned corporation did not qualify as "interest in an entity" and, consequently, the estates failed to meet the 50 percent liquidity test resulting in the disallowance of their claimed qualified family owned business interest deduction. In its analysis, the tax court observed that in Section 6166, see supra ¶ 2.02[3][c], interests in a closely held business are limited to equity or ownership interests and that throughout Section 2057 words expressly denoting equity ownership were used. Accordingly, the court concluded that the definition of an "interest in an entity," for purposes of the 50 percent liquidity test, was limited to equity ownership interests. See also Estate of Artall v. Comm'r, TC Memo. 2008-67 (2008), aff'd, No. 09-60092 (5th Cir. 2010), where the Fifth Circuit cited *Farnam* and held that, for purposes of the liquidity test of Section 2057(b)(1)(c), an "interest" refers only to equity ownership interests and not to decedent's loans to the business.

[c] Additional Requirements With Respect to Entities

[ii] Ownership requirements.

Page 5-221:

Add to note 56.

Priv. Ltr. Rul. 200518011 (Jan. 14, 2005) (noting that Section 2032A qualified use requirements are relevant to qualification under Section 2057(e), the Service ruled that decedent's interest in real property, which he leased to two automobile dealership corporations
he indirectly owned through a trust, is qualified real property because decedent's interests
in the dealership corporations are Section 6166 closely held business interests). But cf. Estate of Farnam, 130 TC No. 2 (2008), aff'd, 583 F3d 581 (8th Cir. 2009), where decedents' loans to their family-owned corporation did not qualify as "interest in an entity"
and, consequently, the estates failed to meet the 50 percent liquidity test resulting in the
disallowance of their claimed qualified family owned business interest deduction. In its
analysis, the tax court observed that in Section 6166, see supra ¶ 2.02[3][c], interests in a
closely held business are limited to equity or ownership interests and that throughout Section 2057 words expressly denoting equity ownership were used. Accordingly, the court
concluded that the definition of an "interest in an entity," for purposes of the 50 percent
liquidity test, was limited to equity ownership interests. See also Estate of Artall v.
Comm'r, TC Memo. 2008-67 (2008), aff'd, No. 09-60092 (5th Cir. 2010), where the Fifth
Circuit cited *Farnam* and held that, for purposes of the liquidity test of Section
2057(b)(1)(c), an "interest" refers only to equity ownership interests and not to decedent's
loans to the business.

[3] Estate Qualifications

[b] Election and Agreement

[i] The election.

Page 5-227:

Add to note 92.

As with other elections, the Service has the limited authority under Regulations Section
301.9100 to grant an extension of time in which to make the election. See, e.g., Priv. Ltr.
Rul. 200234004 (Jan. 18, 2002); Priv. Ltr. Rul. 200505016 (Oct. 28, 2004); and Priv. Ltr.
Rul. 200528019 (Mar. 14, 2005) and Priv. Ltr. Rul. 200743031 (June 27, 2007) ; Priv.
Ltr. Rul. 201015003 (Oct. 26, 2009); Priv. Ltr. Rul. 201022002 (Jan. 7, 2010).

[ii] The agreement.

Page 5-230:

Add to note 99.

In Technical Advice Memorandum 200430030 (Mar. 24, 2004), the Service advised that
an estate's election to deduct the decedent's qualified family-owned business interests was
invalid, since the estate failed to deduct sufficient property to meet the 50 percent test
and, in addition, the recapture agreement was not executed by all parties with an interest
in the property.

[iii] Grace period.

Page 5-230:

Add to note 100.

In Technical Advice Memorandum 200352003 (Aug. 25, 2003), the Service advised that decedent's estate qualified for the Section 2057 deduction even though the agreement was not executed and filed with the decedent's estate tax return but was filed within ninety days of the Service's request for additional information.

[c] The 50 Percent Test

[i] In general.

Page 5-231:

Add to note 101.

In Technical Advice Memorandum 200430030 (Mar. 24, 2004), the Service advised that an estate's election to deduct the decedent's qualified family-owned business interests was invalid, since the estate failed to deduct sufficient property to meet the 50 percent test and, in addition, the recapture agreement was not executed by all parties with an interest in the property.

[iii] Adjusted value of qualified family-owned business interests.

Page 5-234:

Add to note 126.

In Estate of Keeton, TC Memo. 2006-263 (2006), although the value of corporations included in decedent's estate exceeded 50 percent of the adjusted gross estate, as stipulated by the estate and the Service, the "adjusted value" of the corporations was reduced to less than 50 percent because of deductible claims against the estate of $732,000.

[5] The Recapture Rule

[b] Recapture Events

[ii] Dispositions.

Page 5-251:

Add to note 236.

Private Letter Ruling 200252084 (Sept. 18, 2002) ruled that a redemption of all the stock held by a qualified heir triggered recapture tax, concluding that the redemption did not represent a purchase by the other shareholders who were all qualified heirs and that the redeeming corporation itself was not a qualified heir.

Add to note 237 after first sentence.

Private Letter Ruling 200246024 (Aug. 14, 2002) ruled that a statutory merger was not a disposition where qualified heirs owned all the stock of the merged entity and the surviving entity.

In note 237, add the following after "IRC §§ 2057(i)(3)(O), 6166(g)(1)(B)".

; Rev. Rul. 2003-61, 2003-24 IRB 1015 (ruling that a distribution in redemption of stock that qualifies under Section 303 does not affect the initial determination of whether an estate is eligible to elect to treat a business interest as a qualified family owned business interest, nor is it a disposition under Section 2057(f)(1)(B)); Priv. Ltr. Rul. 200327016 (Mar. 20, 2003) (revoking Priv. Ltr. Rul. 200242025 (July 17, 2002)) (ruling that a redemption of stock that qualified under Section 303 was not a disposition under Section 2057).

[c] Measuring the Recapture Tax

[iii] Applicable percentage.

Page 5-255:

Add to note 261.

In October of 2000, the Service issued Form 706-D, United States Additional Estate Tax Return Under Code Section 2057, used for all post-death events requiring a filing with the Internal Revenue Service. If more than one heir is involved in an event requiring filing, each must file a separate Form 706-D. Form 706-D (Rev. Oct. 2006) has been released by the Service with revised instructions which state that the form must be filed at the Cincinnati Service Center and, in addition, note that the provisions concerning qualified charitable conservation contributions were amended by the Pension Protection Act of 2006, Pub. L. No. 109-280, § 1206, __ Stat. __, __ (2006), reprinted in 2006-__ CB __, __.

The Service has released revised Form 706–D, United States Additional Estate Tax Return Under Code Section 2057 (Revised December 2008) and instructions.

CHAPTER **6**

Estates of Nonresident Noncitizens

¶ 6.01	Section 2101. Tax Imposed	S6-2
	[1] Introduction	S6-2
	[2] Computation of the Tax	S6-2
	[3] Citizen or Noncitizen; Resident or Nonresident	S6-2
	[b] Residence	S6-2
	[4] Return Requirements	S6-3
¶ 6.02	Section 2102. Credits Against Tax	S6-3
	[1] Credit for State Death Taxes	S6-3
	[4] Unified Credit	S6-4
¶ 6.03	Section 2103. Definition of "Gross Estate"	S6-4
	[2] Limitation on General Principles	S6-4
	[a] Real Property and Tangible Personal Property	S6-4
¶ 6.04	Section 2104. Property Within the United States	S6-4
	[1] Corporate Stock	S6-4
	[2] Property Subject to Lifetime Transfer	S6-5
¶ 6.05	Section 2105. Property Without the United States	S6-6
	[2] Bank and Similar Deposits	S6-6
	[a] Deposits in Domestic Institutions	S6-6
	[i] Qualifying deposits.	S6-6
	[3] Debt Obligations Treated as Outside the United States	S6-6
	[b] Portfolio Debt Obligations	S6-6
	[5] Stock in Regulated Investment Companies [New]	S6-6
¶ 6.06	Section 2106. Taxable Estate	S6-7
	[1] Expenses, Claims, and Losses	S6-7
	[2] Charitable Bequests	S6-7
¶ 6.07	Expatriation to Avoid Tax [Revised]	S6-8
	[1] Section 2801	S6-9
	[a] Requirements	S6-9
	[b] The Tax Imposed	S6-10

	[c]	Credit	S6-11
[2]		Section 2107	S6-11
	[a]	Requirements	S6-13
	[b]	Special Situs Rule	S6-14
	[c]	Credit	S6-15

¶ 6.01 SECTION 2101. TAX IMPOSED

[1] Introduction

Page 6-2:

Add to note 1.

; Zeydel & Chung, "Estate Planning for Noncitizens and Nonresident Aliens: What Were Those Rules Again?" 106 J. Tax'n 20 (Jan. 2007)

Page 6-3:

Add to note 7.

Section 2102(c), effective for decedents dying before January 1, 2005, is redesignated Section 2102(b), effective for estates of decedents dying on or after this date. See infra ¶ 6.02[4], note 25.

[2] Computation of the Tax

Page 6-4:

In note 15, add "and Section 2501(a)(5)" to the end of first paragraph after "Section 2501(a)(3)".

[3] Citizen or Noncitizen; Resident or Nonresident

Page 6-5:

Add the following as the first paragraph in note 17.

In very limited circumstances, a nonresident noncitizen is treated as a citizen or resident for transfer tax purposes. IRC § 877(g)(1). See ¶ 6.07[1] text accompanying notes 5– 8; ¶ 9.02[1][c].

[b] Residence

Page 6-6:

Add to note 29.

Note that this definition is significantly different from the resident definition for purposes of the income tax found in Section 7701(b).

Page 6-7:

Add to note 33.

Several of the factors and cases are discussed in Heimos, "Non-Citizens—Estate, Gift, and Generation-Skipping Taxation," 837-2d TM, A29–A32 (2005).

[4] Return Requirements

Page 6-7:

Add to note 34.

Revised Form 706-NA, U.S. Estate (and Generation-Skipping Transfer) Tax Return (revised August 2008) has been released by the Service and is to be used for decedents dying after December 31, 2007. A paid preparer signature block has been added to Form 706-NA and, in addition, because the estate and gift tax treaty between the United States and Sweden was terminated on January 1, 2008, the Service deleted Sweden from the list of countries under *Death Tax Treaties* located on page two of the instructions. The Service has released revised Form 706-NA, U.S. Estate (and Generation-Skipping Transfer) Tax Return (revised September 2009), for nonresident noncitizens dying after December 31, 2008. The instructions note that the Emergency Economic Stabilization Act of 2008 extended the provision under IRC ¶ 2105(d), in which a portion of stock in a regulated investment company owned by a nonresident noncitizen is treated as property that is not located within the United States, for two years. The provision which originally expired on January 1, 2008, is now extended through January 1, 2010.

¶ 6.02 SECTION 2102. CREDITS AGAINST TAX

[1] Credit for State Death Taxes

Page 6-9:

Add to fourth sentence of note 7.

and Section 2102(c), effective for decedents dying before January 1, 2005, is redesignated Section 2102(b), effective for estates of decedents dying on or after this date. See infra ¶ 6.02[4], note 25.

Page 6-10:

Add to note 15.

See infra ¶ 6.02[4], note 25, pertaining to the redesignation of Section 2102(c) to Section 2102(b), effective for estates of nonresident noncitizen decedents dying after December 31, 2004.

[4] Unified Credit

Page 6-11:

Add to note 25.

The redesignation of Section 2102(c) to Section 2102(b), effective for estates of nonresident noncitizen decedents dying after December 31, 2004, should be reflected in all references to Section 2102(c) throughout Chapters 6, 7, and 8 of this book.

Page 6-12:

Add to notes 26, 27, and 29.

See supra ¶ 6.02[4], note 25, pertaining to the redesignation of Section 2102(c) to Section 2102(b), effective for estates of nonresident noncitizen decedents dying after December 31, 2004.

¶ 6.03 SECTION 2103. DEFINITION OF "GROSS ESTATE"

[2] Limitation on General Principles

[a] Real Property and Tangible Personal Property

Page 6-15:

Add to the beginning of note 25.

Reg. § 20.2104-1(a)(2).

Add to note 26.

Seemingly, if such real property is owned by a bona fide foreign corporation, it would not be included in the gross estate. See ¶ 6.04[1].

¶ 6.04 SECTION 2104. PROPERTY WITHIN THE UNITED STATES

[1] Corporate Stock

Page 6-17:

Add to note 1.

See CCA 201003013 (Sept. 30, 2009) (a Canadian decedent's RRSP (Registered Retirement Savings Plan, similar to an IRA in the United States), holding shares of Canadian mutual funds, was not includible in his gross estate because the mutual funds were classified as corporations for U.S. tax purposes and, accordingly, were not U.S.-situs property within the meaning of Section 2104(a).

Add to note 6.

See Estate of Charania, 133 TC No. 7 (2009), aff'd, 608 F3d 67 (1st Cir. 2010), (shares of U.S. corporate stock registered in decedent's name were not community property where decedent and spouse did not elect Belgian community property regime following their forced exile from Uganda, a common law nation).

Add to note 9.

See Cassell, Karlin, McCaffrey & Streng, "U.S. Estate Planning for Nonresident Aliens Who Own Partnership Interests," 99 Tax Notes 1683 (June 16, 2003).

Add to note 10 following citation to Rev. Rul. 55-701.

(a partnership's place of business determined its situs for estate tax purposes under a treaty).

Add to end of note 10.

See Martin, "Proposal—Why Section 2104 Must Address When Partnership Interests Owned by Foreign Investors Are (and Are Not) Subject to U.S. Estate Tax," 12 Calif. Tax Law No. 3, at 27 (2003).

[2] Property Subject to Lifetime Transfer

Page 6-18:

Add new note 12.1 to the end of the first paragraph of ¶ 6.04[2].

[12.1] Note, however, that the payment of gift tax by a nonresident/noncitizen made within three years of death under Section 2035(b) is not a transfer within the meaning of Sections 2035-2038 and is, therefore, not property that is deemed situated within the United States at the time of payment under Section 2104(b). CCA 201020009 (Apr. 16, 2010).

Page 6-19:

Add to note 17 at end of parenthetical.

where trust contained only debt obligations of US corporations at decedent's death but had US corporation stocks when decedent originally made the transfer).

Add to note 18 after citation to Comm'r v. Nevius.

(holder of a general power of appointment was deemed to own the underlying assets of the trust).

¶ 6.05 SECTION 2105. PROPERTY WITHOUT THE UNITED STATES

[2] Bank and Similar Deposits

[a] Deposits in Domestic Institutions

[i] Qualifying deposits.

Page 6-23:

In note 16, add the following citation to Rev. Rul. 82-193, 1982-2 CB 219.

(nonresident alien's reversionary interest in a trust holding a bank certificate of deposit was not U.S. situs property because bank deposit not taxable in the United States).

Page 6-24:

Add to note 21.

Priv. Ltr. Rul. 200842013 (June 13, 2008) (annuity proceeds held by the issuing companies at death).

[3] Debt Obligations Treated as Outside the United States

[b] Portfolio Debt Obligations

Page 6-27:

Add to note 40.

Priv. Ltr. Rul. 200752016 (Aug. 27, 2007) (estate of taxpayer who is a U.S. citizen solely from being a resident of a U.S. possession is considered a nonresident noncitizen, see ¶ 8.09, and will not be subject to estate tax on portfolio debt obligations that produce interest described in Section 871(h)(2)).

Page 6-28:

Add new ¶ 6.05[5].

[5] Stock in Regulated Investment Companies [New]

A portion of the value of the decedent's stock in a regulated investment company (RIC) is treated as property located outside the United States and is not therefore included within the gross estate of a nonresident noncitizen.[52.1] A RIC is a domestic company that invests in stocks and securities, commonly referred to as a mutual fund.[52.2]

The portion of the value of the stock in a RIC that is excluded from a nonresident noncitizen's gross estate is the portion of the value of the "qualifying assets" of the RIC to its total assets.[52.3] Qualifying assets are assets that if owned directly by the decedent would have been (1) excluded from decedent's estate under Section 2105(b);[52.4] (2) debt obligations described in the last sentence of Section 2104(c);[52.5] or (3) other property not within the United States.[52.6] The determination of the portion of the qualifying assets is made at the end of the quarter of the RIC's taxable year immediately preceding the decedent's date of death or at such other time as is provided in regulations.[52.7]

[52.1] IRC § 2105(d)(1). The rule is effective for the estates of decedents dying after 2004 and before 2010. IRC § 2105(d)(3); American Jobs Creation Act of 2004, Pub. L. No. 108-357, § 411(d)(2), 118 Stat. 1418, __ (2004), reprinted in 2004-__, __ CB __, __ and the Emergency Economic Stabilization Act of 2008, Pub. L. No. 110-343, § 207, __ Stat. __ (2008), reprinted in 2008-__, __ CB __ (extending the provision which was scheduled to expire on January 1, 2008, for two years, to January 1, 2010).

[52.2] IRC § 851. A complex series of rules define a RIC. See Bittker & Lokken, 4 Federal Taxation of Income, Estates and Gifts, ¶ 99.4 (Warren, Gorham & Lamont, 3d ed. (2003)).

[52.3] IRC § 2105(d)(1).

[52.4] IRC § 2105(d)(2)(A). This includes bank deposits that are exempt from income tax, portfolio debt obligations, and certain original issue discount obligations. See supra ¶¶ 6.05[2], 6.05[3][b], 6.05[3][c].

[52.5] IRC § 2105(d)(2)(B). These are debt obligations of a U.S. corporation that are treated as giving rise to foreign source income. See supra ¶ 6.05[3][a].

[52.6] IRC § 2105(d)(2)(C).

[52.7] IRC § 2105(d)(1).

¶ 6.06 SECTION 2106. TAXABLE ESTATE

[1] Expenses, Claims, and Losses

Page 6-30:

Add to note 9 at the end of the citation to "Fung v. Comm'r".

, aff'd, 91 AFTR2d 2003-1228 (9th Cir. 2003).

[2] Charitable Bequests

Page 6-33:

Add to note 28.

Estate of Silver v. Comm'r, 120 TC No. 14 (2003), held that property not included in the gross estate of a Canadian citizen and that was left to charity did not qualify for a Section 2106(a)(2) deduction.

Page 6-35:

Replace existing ¶ 6.07 with revised ¶ 6.07.

¶ 6.07 EXPATRIATION TO AVOID TAX [REVISED]

Over the years, Congress has enacted a series of provisions whose purpose is to remove incentives to avoid U.S. estate taxes by giving up either U.S. citizenship or U.S. residency.[1] The provisions apply to a U.S. citizen who gives up U.S. citizenship[2] and to any long-term resident[3] of the United States who is not a U.S. citizen and who terminates U.S. residency;[4] both individuals are statutorily referred to as "expatriates." An individual's expatriation date is the date that the individual gives up U.S. citizenship or terminates U.S. residency.[5] Two provisions currently apply to expatriates: (1) Section 2801 which is applicable to individuals who expatriate after June 16, 2008,[6] and (2) Section 2107

---

[1] See Stephens, Maxfield, Lind, Calfee & Smith, Federal Estate and Gift Taxation ¶ 9.02[1] (Warren, Gorham & Lamont 8th ed. 2002).

[2] Section 7701(a)(50)(A) provides that a citizen is treated as losing U.S. citizenship pursuant to Section 877A(g)(4) on the earliest of the date (1) the citizen renounces U.S. nationality before a diplomatic or consular officer (provided the relinquishment is confirmed by issuance of a certificate of loss of nationality); (2) the citizen furnishes the State Department a signed statement of voluntary relinquishment (provided the relinquishment is confirmed by issuance of a certificate of loss of nationality); (3) the State Department issues a certificate of loss of nationality; or (4) a U.S. court cancels the citizen's certificate of naturalization. Cessation may occur earlier for a person who at birth becomes a citizen of the United States and another country. IRC § 7701(a)(50)(B) . See also IRC §§ 2801(f), 877A(g), 2107(a), 877(a).

[3] "Long-term resident" is defined as a noncitizen who has been a lawful permanent resident of the United States in at least eight of the fifteen years ending in the year when U.S. residency was terminated. IRC § 877(e). See IRC §§ 2801(f), 877A(g)(2)(B), 2107(a).

[4] Termination of U.S. residency occurs when either (1) one loses the privilege of residency in the United States (i.e. loses green card status) because the privilege is revoked or administratively or judicially terminated or (2) one commences to be treated as a resident of a foreign country under a tax treaty between the United States and foreign country, does not waive the benefits applicable to residents of the foreign country, and notifies the IRS of the commencement of such treatment. IRC § 7701(b)(6). See IRC §§ 2801(f), 877A(g)(2)(8), 2107(a), 877(e).

[5] IRC § 877(A)(g)(3).

[6] Heroes Earning Assistance and Relief Act of 2008, Pub. L. No. 110-245, § 301(g)(2) __ Stat. __, __ (2008), reprinted in 2008 – __ CB __, __. See Liss,

which is applicable to individuals who expatriate prior to June 17, 2008.[7] Both sections are discussed below.

[1] Section 2801

Section 2801 taxes any "covered bequest" of property to a U.S. citizen or resident made in any calendar year by a "covered expatriate".[8]

[a] Requirements

For estate tax purposes, a "covered expatriate" is an expatriate[9] who expatriates after June 16, 2008 and dies and who meets one of three alternative objective tests at the time of the expatriation date: (1) the decedent's average annual net income tax[10] liability for the five years preceding the expatriation must have exceeded $124,000 (adjusted for inflation after 2004);[11] (2) the decedent's net worth at the time of the expatriation was $2 million or more; or (3) the decedent's personal representative fails to certify, under penalties of perjury, that the decedent has complied with federal tax obligations for the five years preceding the expatriation or fails to provide documentation of such compliance.[12] Even if the decedent exceeds one or both of the two monetary thresholds in items (1) or (2) above,[13] Section 2801 does not apply to certain former dual citizens who did not have substantial U.S. contacts,[14] and it does

---

"HEART-ache: Expatriation Under the New Inheritance Tax," 37 Est. Plan. __ (Apr. 2010).

[7] IRC § 877(h). Section 2107 effectively terminates after June 16, 2018. See infra ¶ 6.07[2][a], note 41.

[8] IRC § 2801(a). The Service has issued Notice 2009-85 (Oct. 15, 2009) which provides guidance regarding the federal tax consequences for citizens who expatriate or cease to be taxed as permanent residents under Sections 877A, 2801 and 6039G. However, separate guidance is yet to be provided for Section 2801. See Section 9 of the Notice.

[9] See supra text accompanying notes 2–5. In general, for income tax purposes, all property of a covered expatriate is treated as sold by the expatriate on the day prior to the expatriate's expatriation date. IRC § 877A(a)(1). See Notice 2009-85 (Oct. 15, 2009).

[10] Section 38(c)(1) defines "net income tax" for this purpose as the "sum of the regular tax liability and the tax imposed by Section 55, reduced by the credits allowable under" Sections 21 through 30A. IRC § 877(a)(2)(A). See IRC §§ 2801(f), 877A(g)(1).

[11] IRC §§ 1(f)(3), 877(a)(2). The inflation adjustment is rounded to the nearest multiple of $1,000. Id. The amount is $139,800 for 2008. Rev. Proc. 2007-66, § 3.29, 2007-2 CB __.

[12] IRC §§ 877(a)(2), 877A(g)(1), 2801(f).

[13] IRC § 877A(g)(1)(B). However, note that such decedents must still satisfy the certification and proof of documentation requirements to avoid Section 2801. IRC § 877(a)(2)(C).

[14] IRC § 877A(g)(1)(B)(i). This is an individual who became at birth a citizen of the United States and another country who continues to be a citizen of and is taxed as a resident of such other country (IRC § 877A(g)(1)(B)(i)(I)) and has been a U.S. resident (under the substantial presence test of Section 7701(b)(1)(A)(ii)) for not more than ten

not apply to certain former citizens who lost their citizenship during their minority.[15]

If any individual who is a covered expatriate subsequently becomes subject to tax as a U.S. citizen or resident for any period after the expatriation date, the individual is not subject to Section 2801; but if the individual again relinquishes citizenship or terminates long-term residency (after subsequently meeting the requirements to become a long-term resident), the Section 2801 rules are retriggered with a new expatriation date.[16]

A "*covered bequest*" is a transfer of property received directly or indirectly by a U.S. citizen or resident by reason of the death of an individual who was a covered expatriate immediately before death.[17] However, a transfer is not a covered bequest if the property was included in the gross estate of the covered expatriate on a timely filed U.S. estate tax return which was filed for the covered expatriate.[18] In addition, a transfer is not a covered bequest to the extent that the transfer would qualify for a charitable deduction[19] or a marital deduction[20] if the covered expatriate were a U.S. person.[21]

Section 2801 makes no specific reference to the Chapter 13 generation-skipping transfer tax and seemingly does not apply to testamentary generation-skipping transfers,[22] although as a policy matter, Section 2801 should apply to such transfers.[23]

[b] The Tax Imposed

The tax under Section 2801 is imposed on the U.S. recipient of the property.[24] It applies only to the extent that the bequest exceeds the dollar amount

---

taxable years during the fifteen-taxable year period ending with the taxable year in which the expatriation date occurs.

[15] IRC § 877A(g)(1)(B)(ii). This exception applies to an individual who became a U.S. citizen at birth, whose loss of citizenship occurred prior to reaching age eighteen and one-half, and who has been a resident of the U.S. (under the substantial presence test of Section 7701(b)(1)(A)(ii) for not more than ten taxable years before the date of relinquishment.)

[16] IRC §§ 2801(f), 877A(g)(1)(C).

[17] IRC § 2801(e)(1)(B). See IRC § 2801(a). Section 2801 also applies to "covered gifts." See ¶ 9.02[1][b][i].

[18] IRC § 2801(e)(2).

[19] See IRC § 2055.

[20] See IRC § 2056.

[21] IRC § 2801(e)(3).

[22] See IRC § 2801(a).

[23] For example, if a covered expatriate makes a testamentary transfer to a skip person, both the estate and the generation-skipping transfer should be taxed to the recipient.

[24] IRC § 2801(b). The tax is imposed on a calendar year basis. The Service has announced that it will issue a new tax form, Form 708, for the purpose of reporting transfers taxable under Section 2801 and also noted its intention to issue guidance under Section 2801 establishing the due date for filing Form 708 and paying the tax. Those dates will be

that qualifies for an annual exclusion under Section 2503(b).[25] If the transfer is made to a domestic trust, the trust is treated as a U.S. citizen, and the trust is required to pay the tax.[26] If the transfer is made to a foreign trust, any distribution by the foreign trust of either income or corpus made to a U.S. citizen or resident which is attributable to the original transfer is treated as if the distribution is a covered bequest.[27]

The amount of tax imposed under Section 2801 is the highest marginal gift tax rate[28] or estate tax rate[29] in effect on the date of the receipt of the covered bequest multiplied by the taxable amount of the value of the covered bequest.[30]

[c] Credit

The amount of tax imposed on the recipient is reduced any transfer tax paid to a foreign country for the covered bequest.[31]

[2] Section 2107

Section 2107 applies to an expatriate whose expatriation date is prior to June 17, 2008[32] and while it employs many of the same definitions and tests as Section 2801, it operates differently from Section 2801. It taxes the estate of the expatriate using the situs rules discussed in the prior sections of this chapter,[33] but it adds some special situs rules as well.

---

contained in future guidance which will allow taxpayers a reasonable amount of time in which to pay the tax and file the return. Ann. 2009-57, 2009-29 IRB 158.

[25] IRC § 2801(c). The amount is $13,000 for 2009. See ¶ 9.04[1].

[26] IRC § 2801(e)(4)(A). Seemingly, the amount of transfer is reduced by the Section 2503(b) dollar amount regardless of whether the entire amount constitutes a present interest under Section 2503(b).

[27] IRC § 2801(e)(4)(B)(i). To the extent the distribution is included in the recipient's gross income, a deduction of the amount of the transfer tax on the distribution is allowed under the income tax (IRC § 164) for the income tax paid. IRC § 2801(e)(4)(B)(ii).

For purposes of these rules, a foreign trust may elect to be treated as a domestic trust; the election may not be revoked without the consent of the IRS. IRC § 2801(e)(4)(B)(iii).

[28] IRC § 2502(a).

[29] IRC § 2001(c).

[30] IRC § 2801(a). See supra text accompanying notes 16–22 and 24–26. The tax applies to covered bequests on or after June 17, 2008 from the estates of transferors whose expatriation date is also on or after June 17, 2008. Heroes Earning Assistance and Relief Tax Act of 2008, Pub. L. No. 110-245, § 301(g)(2), __ Stat. __, __ (2008), reprinted in 2008 __ CB __, __.

[31] IRC § 2801(d).

[32] See IRC § 877(h).

[33] See ¶¶ 6.01–6.06.

Section 2107 was originally enacted in 1966[34] when its principal consequence was to impose estate taxes at rates applicable to citizens on nonresident
noncitizens who expatriated to avoid tax.[35] At that time, the rates applicable to
citizens and residents were considerably higher than the rates applied to nonresident noncitizens. Subsequently, in 1988, the rates applicable to citizens and
residents became applicable to the estates of nonresident noncitizens,[36] thus
taking most of the sting out of Section 2107. In 2004, Congress added some
sting to Section 2107 by treating some nonresident noncitizens as residents or
citizens.[37] If a decedent who would otherwise be subject to Section 2107[38] dies
in a calendar year in which the decedent has spent, with minor exceptions,[39]
more than thirty days in the United States, the decedent is treated as a U.S.
resident or citizen whose worldwide gross estate is subject to the U.S. estate
tax.[40]

---

[34] Foreign Investors Tax Act of 1966, Pub. L. No. 89-809, § 108(f), 80 Stat. 1539,
1573 (1966), reprinted in 1966-2 CB 656, 687.

[35] IRC § 2107(a). Section 2107(a) provides for the tax to be computed "in accordance
with the table contained in Section 2001. . . ." Presumably, this cross-reference is to the
whole method of computing the tax and is not a mere cross-reference to the rate brackets.
Seemingly, the reference in Section 2107(a) to Section 2001 includes the gross-up of the
decedent's estate by inter vivos gifts and a credit for gift taxes paid. See IRC § 2001(b).

[36] See supra ¶ 6.01[2], note 11.

[37] IRC § 877(g). See IRC §§ 877(a), 877(b), 2107. The rule is effective for decedents
dying after June 3, 2004. American Jobs Creation Act of 2004, Pub. L. No. 108-357,
§ 804(f), 118 Stat. 1418, 1573 (2004), reprinted in 2004-__, __ CB __, __.

[38] IRC § 877(g)(1). See infra ¶ 6.07[1][a].

[39] IRC § 877(g)(2). Under the exceptions, a day of physical presence is disregarded if
the decedent was performing services in the United States for an unrelated (IRC §§ 267,
707) employer. IRC § 877(g)(2)(A). No more than thirty days in a calendar year may be
disregarded under this rule. IRC § 877(g)(2)(A). In addition, to satisfy the rule, one's employer must meet any regulations prescribed by the Secretary. IRC § 877(g)(2)(A)(ii).

The exceptions apply only to decedents with certain ties to countries other than the
United States (IRC § 877(g)(2)(B)) or to decedents with minimal physical presence in the
United States (IRC § 877(g)(2)(C)). The first situation applies to decedents who became
(not later than a reasonable time after loss of U.S. citizenship or termination of residency)
a citizen or resident of the country in which the decedent was born, the decedent's spouse
was born, or either of the decedent's parents were born and the decedent became liable
for income taxes in such country. IRC § 877(g)(2)(B). The minimum physical presence
test is satisfied if for each year in the ten-year period ending with the loss of U.S. citizenship or termination of residency, the decedent was physically present in the United States
for thirty days or less. IRC § 877(g)(2)(C). See IRC § 7701(b)(3)(D)(ii).

[40] IRC § 877(g). As a result, the Section 2010 and Section 2014 credits along with
other credits should be applicable. Cf. infra note 65.

[a] Requirements

Section 2107 applies if (a) the decedent's expatriation date occurred within the ten-year period ending with the date of the decedent's death[41] and (b) the objective tests that parallel those under Section 2801 are met.[42] Under the Section 2701 objective test, one of the following three requirements must have been met at the time of the expatriation date: (1) the decedent's average annual net income tax[43] liability for the five years preceding the expatriation must have exceeded $124,000 (adjusted for inflation after 2004);[44] (2) the decedent's net worth at the time of the expatriation was $2 million or more; or (3) the decedent's personal representative fails to certify, under penalties of perjury, that the decedent has complied with federal tax obligations for the five years preceding the expatriating date or fails to provide documentation of such compliance.[45] Even if the decedent exceeds one or both of the two monetary thresholds in items (1) and (2) above,[46] Section 2107 does not apply to certain former dual citizens who did not have substantial U.S. contacts,[47] and it does not apply to certain former citizens who lost their citizenship during their minority.[48]

---

[41] IRC §§ 877(a)(1), 877(b), 2107(a). As a result of the ten-year rule, Section 2107 will be effectively repealed after June 16, 2018.

[42] See supra text accompanying notes 10–15. But compare infra text accompanying note 48 with supra note 15.

[43] Section 38(c)(1) defines "net income tax" for this purpose as the "sum of the regular tax liability and the tax imposed by Section 55, reduced by the credits allowable under" Sections 21 through 30A. IRC § 877(a)(2)(A).

[44] IRC §§ 1(f)(3), 877(a)(2). The inflation adjustment is rounded to the nearest multiple of $1,000. Id. The amount is $139,800 for 2008. Rev. Proc. 2007-66, § 3.29, 2007-2 CB __.

[45] IRC §§ 877(a)(2), 877(b), 2107(a).

[46] IRC § 877(c)(1). However, note that such decedents must still satisfy the certification and proof of documentation requirements to avoid Section 2107. IRC § 877(a)(2)(C).

[47] IRC § 877(c)(2). This is an individual who became at birth a citizen of the United States and another country who continues to be a citizen of such other country. IRC § 877(c)(2)(A). The individual shall be treated as having no substantial contacts if the individual has never been a U.S. resident, held a U.S. passport, and has not been present in the United States for more than thirty days during any calendar year that is one of the ten calendar years preceding the individual's loss of U.S. citizenship. IRC § 877(c)(2)(B).

[48] IRC § 877(c)(3). This exception applies to an individual who became a U.S. citizen at birth, neither of whose parents was a U.S. citizen at such time, whose loss of citizenship occurred prior to reaching age eighteen and one-half and who was not present in the United States for more than thirty days during any calendar year that is one of the ten calendar years preceding the minor's loss of citizenship. Id.

[b] Special Situs Rule

The general effect of Section 2107 is to provide some additional estate tax situs rules to certain expatriates.[49] As previously explained, much of the sting was taken out of Section 2107 with the 1988 rate changes;[50] however, a special situs rule applies to computation of the estate tax under Section 2107 that adds some sting to the section.[51] Although the decedent's gross estate is generally determined using the situs rules previously discussed,[52] under Section 2107(b), the situs rules are expanded to include a portion of the value of the stock of a foreign corporation.[53] Since the gross estate of an expatriate is limited to property situated in the United States, in the absence of Section 2107(b), an expatriate could transfer U.S. assets to a foreign corporation, the stock of which would be property situated outside the United States. But for Section 2107(b), however, a portion of such stock would not be included in the expatriate's gross estate.

The rule applies to the stock of a foreign corporation only if at the time of the decedent's death, the decedent owned:[54]

    1. Directly or indirectly[55] ten percent or more of the total combined voting power of the corporation[56] and

---

[49] IRC § 2107(a). See IRC §§ 877(g), 2107(b), 2107(c). See also Sections 2101 through 2106, which would apply to such decedents in any event, discussed at ¶¶ 6.01–6.06.

[50] See supra text accompanying notes 34–36.

[51] See also IRC § 877(g), discussed supra text accompanying notes 37–40, which adds some additional sting.

[52] See Reg. § 20.2107-1(b)(1)(i); infra ¶¶ 6.03–6.05.

[53] IRC § 2107(b).

[54] In measuring direct or attribution ownership of such corporations, stock will be treated as owned by the decedent at death even if the decedent has made a transfer of the type covered by Sections 2035 through 2038. IRC § 2107(b); Reg. § 20.2107-1(b)(1)(iii)(c). See ¶¶ 4.07–4.10.

[55] In measuring such ownership, Section 2107 employs Section 958(a). Section 958 provides that a shareholder is deemed to own all stock in a foreign corporation that it owns directly. In addition, ownership of stock that is owned by foreign entities, trusts, estates, corporations, or partnerships is attributed proportionately to their beneficiaries, shareholders, and partners. IRC § 958(a).

[56] IRC § 2107(b)(1).

2. Directly or indirectly[57] or by attribution,[58] more than 50 percent of the total combined voting power of the corporation or the total value of the stock of the corporation.[59]

If the Section 2107 decedent owns[60] such stock, then only a portion of the value of the stock is included in the decedent's gross estate. The portion of the stock so included is the portion that the fair market value of the foreign corporation's assets situated in the United States at the time of the decedent's death bears to the fair market value of all the foreign corporation's assets at such time.[61]

[c] Credit

The credit for foreign death taxes is generally inapplicable to the estates of expatriates,[62] because foreign property is not included in their U.S. gross estate.[63] However, since Section 2107(b)[64] is taxing foreign situs property, a limited credit is provided for foreign death taxes imposed on any assets taxed in the decedent's estate as a result of the application of Section 2107(b).

---

[57] See supra note 55 for measurement of indirect ownership.

[58] Section 958(b) provides for such attribution rules. It directs the application of the Section 318(a) stock ownership attribution rules with the following modifications: (1) for purposes of applying Section 318(a)(1)(A), stock owned by a nonresident noncitizen individual, other than a foreign trust or estate, is not owned by a resident or citizen of the United States; (2) an entity that "owns more than 50 percent of the total combined voting power of all classes of stock entitled to vote of a corporation" owns all of the corporation's voting stock for purposes of Sections 318(a)(2)(A), 318(a)(2)(B), and 318(a)(2)(C); (3) 10 percent is substituted for 50 percent in applying Section 318(a)(2)(C); (4) Sections 318(a)(3)(A), 318(a)(3)(B), and 318(a)(3)(C) are not to be applied so that a U.S. person is deemed to own stock that is owned by a non-U.S. person.

Although Section 958(b) directs the application of Section 318 only for purposes of Sections 951(b), 954(3), 956(c)(2), and 957, the specific reference to Section 958(b) in Section 2107(b)(2) renders the attribution rules applicable to Section 2107 as well.

[59] IRC § 2107(b)(2).

[60] The Section 958(a) ownership test is again employed. See IRC § 2107(b) (flush language). See supra note 55.

[61] IRC § 2107(b). The Sections 2104 and 2105 situs rules are employed in measuring such situs. Reg. § 20.2107-1(b)(1)(iii)(b). The fair market value of a foreign corporation's assets, both in the United States and abroad, is determined without reducing the value to reflect any outstanding liabilities. Reg. § 20.2107-1(b)(1)(iii)(a).

[62] See IRC § 2102; supra ¶ 6.02 text accompanying note 5.

[63] See supra ¶ 6.02, text accompanying note 6.

[64] See supra ¶ 6.07[2][b].

CHAPTER 7

Tax Conventions

¶ 7.01   Introduction S7-1
        [1]   Purpose of Treaties S7-1
        [3]   The Basic Patterns of the Treaties S7-2
            [b]   Modern Treaties S7-2
        [4]   Comparison of the Treaties S7-2
¶ 7.02   Early Treaties S7-2
        [3]   Deductions, Unified Credit, and Taxation Based on
            Situs S7-2
¶ 7.03   Modern Treaties S7-3
        [1]   The Organization for Economic Cooperation and
            Development Convention and U.S. Model
            Conventions............................... S7-3
            [c]   Deductions, Exemptions, and Credits S7-3
        [3]   The Canadian Convention S7-3
        [5]   The German Convention S7-4
        [6]   The Netherlands Convention S7-5
        [7]   The Swedish Convention S7-5
        [8]   The United Kingdom and French Conventions S7-5
¶ 7.04   Procedural Provisions........................... S7-6
        [1]   Competent Authority Assistance S7-6

¶ 7.01 INTRODUCTION

[1] Purpose of Treaties

Page 7-4:

Add to note 19.

The Treasury Department announced that on June 7, 2007, the United States delivered to the government of Sweden a notice of termination of the estate, gift, and inheritance tax treaty between the two countries. The treaty was terminated because Sweden eliminated its tax on inheritance and gifts. Treasury Department News Release HP-463 (June 15, 2007).

[3] The Basic Patterns of the Treaties

[b] Modern Treaties

Page 7-10:

Add to note 60.

See supra ¶ 6.02[4], note 25, pertaining to the redesignation of Section 2102(c) to Section 2102(b), effective for estates of nonresident noncitizen decedents dying after December 31, 2004.

Add to note 61.

The Treasury Department announced that on June 7, 2007, the United States delivered to the government of Sweden a notice of termination of the estate, gift, and inheritance tax treaty between the two countries. The treaty was terminated because Sweden eliminated its tax on inheritance and gifts. Treasury Department News Release HP-463 (June 15, 2007).

[4] Comparison of the Treaties

Page 7-11:

Add new note 61.1 after the word No. at end of entry on graph for Sweden.

Country	U.S. Taxes Currently Covered	Entry Into Force	Early/ Modern	Subsequent Protocol No.[61.1]
Sweden	Estate, Gift, and GST	Sept. 5, 1984	Modern	

[61.1] The Treasury Department announced that on June 7, 2007, the United States delivered to the government of Sweden a notice of termination of the estate, gift, and inheritance tax treaty between the two countries. The treaty was terminated because Sweden eliminated its tax on inheritance and gifts. Treasury Department News Release HP-463 (June 15, 2007).

¶ 7.02 EARLY TREATIES

[3] Deductions, Unified Credit, and Taxation Based on Situs

Page 7-26:

Add to note 72.

See supra ¶ 6.02[4], note 25, pertaining to the redesignation of Section 2102(c) to Section 2102(b), effective for estates of nonresident noncitizen decedents dying after December 31, 2004.

Page 7-28:

Add to note 79.

See supra ¶ 6.02[4], note 25, pertaining to the redesignation of Section 2102(c) to Section 2102(b), effective for estates of nonresident noncitizen decedents dying after December 31, 2004.

¶ 7.03 MODERN TREATIES

[1] The Organization for Economic Cooperation and Development Convention and U.S. Model Conventions

[c] Deductions, Exemptions, and Credits

Page 7-38:

Add to note 36.

See supra ¶ 6.02[4], note 25, pertaining to the redesignation of Section 2102(c) to Section 2102(b), effective for estates of nonresident noncitizen decedents dying after December 31, 2004.

[3] The Canadian Convention

Page 7-42:

Add to note 62.

The United States and Canada recently signed a Revised Protocol Amending the Convention With Respect to Taxes on Income and on Capital (Sept. 21, 2007), with Article 26 of the revised protocol amending Article XXIXB. The Senate approved the new protocol on September 23, 2008, and the new protocol entered into force on December 15, 2008. Treasury Department News Release HP-1327.

Add to notes 64 and 66.

See supra ¶ 6.02[4], note 25, pertaining to the redesignation of Section 2102(c) to Section 2102(b), effective for estates of nonresident noncitizen decedents dying after December 31, 2004.

Page 7-44:

Add to notes 77, 78 and 80.

The United States and Canada recently signed a Revised Protocol Amending the Convention With Respect to Taxes on Income and on Capital (Sept. 21, 2007), with Article 26 replacing the current Article XXIXB.5. In the new paragraph 5, an individual and his or her spouse would be considered, for purposes of subsections 70(5.2) and 70(6) of the Canadian Income Tax Act, to have resided in Canada immediately before the individual(s death where the individual was a resident of the United States immediately before death. Upon request, the competent authority of Canada may agree to treat a trust, for purposes of the Canadian Income Tax Act, as residing in Canada for the time and with respect to such property as may be stipulated if that trust would be a trust described in subsection 70(6) of the Canadian Income Tax Act if its U.S. trustees were residents of Canada. The Senate approved the new protocol on September 23, 2008, and the new protocol entered into force on December 15, 2008. Treasury Department News Release HP-1327.

Page 7-45:

Add to note 85.

The United States and Canada recently signed a Revised Protocol Amending the Convention with Respect to Taxes on Income and on Capital (Sept. 21, 2007), with Article 26 replacing the current Article XXIXB.1. In the new paragraph 1, if the property of a U.S. resident passes at death to an organization referred to in art. XXI that is a Canadian resident, the U.S. tax consequences arising out of the passing of the property would apply as if the organization was a resident of the United States. On the other hand, if the property of a Canadian resident passes at death to an organization referred to in Article XXI that is a U.S. resident, the Canadian tax consequences arising out of the passing of the property would apply as if the individual had disposed of the property for proceeds equal to an amount elected on behalf of the individual for this purpose, which would be no less than the individual's cost of the property as determined for Canadian tax purposes and no greater than the fair market value of the property. The Senate approved the new protocol on September 23, 2008, and the new protocol entered into force on December 15, 2008. Treasury Department News Release HP-1327.

[5] The German Convention

Page 7-54:

Add to note 136.

See supra ¶ 6.02[4], note 25, pertaining to the redesignation of Section 2102(c) to Section 2102(b), effective for estates of nonresident noncitizen decedents dying after December 31, 2004.

Page 7-55:

Add to note 137.

See supra ¶ 6.02[4], note 25, pertaining to the redesignation of Section 2102(c) to Section 2102(b), effective for estates of nonresident noncitizen decedents dying after December 31, 2004.

[6] The Netherlands Convention

Page 7-59:

Add to note 162.

See supra ¶ 6.02[4], note 25, pertaining to the redesignation of Section 2102(c) to Section 2102(b), effective for estates of nonresident noncitizen decedents dying after December 31, 2004.

[7] The Swedish Convention

Page 7-60:

Add new note 169.1 following the heading for ¶ 7.03[7].

[169.1] The Treasury Department announced that on June 7, 2007, the United States delivered to the government of Sweden a notice of termination of the estate, gift, and inheritance tax treaty between the two countries. The treaty was terminated because Sweden eliminated its tax on inheritance and gifts. Treasury Department News Release HP-463 (June 15, 2007).

[8] The United Kingdom and French Conventions

Page 7-66:

Add to note 207.

The United States and France signed a protocol on December 8, 2004, which was ratified by the Senate on March 31, 2006, and entered into force on December 21, 2006, that amends several provisions of the treaty. A revised Article 5 (Real Property) provides, in part, that the term "real property" includes shares and other rights in a company the assets of which consist of at least 50 percent of real property situated in one of the two countries. With the exception of paragraph (3) of Article 11 (which is effective after November 10, 1988), the protocol is effective for gifts made and deaths occurring after the date that the protocol enters into force.

Page 7-71:

Add to notes 232, 233, 234.

The United States and France signed a protocol on December 8, 2004, which was ratified by the Senate on March 31, 2006, and entered into force on December 21, 2006, that amends several provisions of the treaty. Article 11 (Community Property and Marital Deduction) is revised to provide new rules on the U.S. taxation of certain property passing to a non-U.S. citizen spouse from a decedent or donor domiciled in France. A new paragraph in Article 11 also sets forth marital deduction qualifications where the surviving spouse was not a U.S. citizen. The marital deduction is equal to the lesser of the value of the "qualifying property" or the applicable exclusion amount. With the exception of paragraph (3) of Article 11 (which is effective afer November 10, 1988), the protocol is effective for gifts made and deaths occurring after the date that the protocol enters into force.

Add to note 235.

See supra ¶ 6.02[4], note 25, pertaining to the redesignation of Section 2102(c) to Section 2102(b), effective for estates of nonresident noncitizen decedents dying after December 31, 2004.

Page 7-72:

Add to notes 238, 239, 240, 241, 242.

The United States and France signed a protocol on December 8, 2004, which was ratified by the Senate on March 31, 2006 and entered into force on December 21, 2006, that amends several provisions of the treaty. Article 12 (Exemptions and Credits) is revised that sets forth rules for determining French and U.S. taxes so as to avoid double taxation. The unified credit available to the estate of a non-U.S. citizen who was domiciled in France at the time of his death is the greater of (1) the amount that bears the same ratio to the credit allowed under U.S. law to the estate of a U.S. citizen as the value of the part of the decedent's entire worldwide gross estate or (2) the unified credit allowed under U.S. law to the estate of a nonresident alien. With the exception of paragraph (3) of Article 12 (which is effective after November 10, 1988), the protocol is effective for gifts made and deaths occurring after the date that the protocol enters into force.

¶ 7.04 PROCEDURAL PROVISIONS

[1] Competent Authority Assistance

Page 7-73:

Add to notes 1 through 7.

Revenue Procedure 96-13, modified each year by the first revenue procedure of the year, was amplified by Revenue Procedure 98-21 and was modified and superseded by Revenue Procedure 2002-52. Revenue Procedure 2002-52 was modified and superseded by Revenue Procedure 2006-54.

Add to note 4.

The Service has revised the general procedures relating to the issuance of written guidance, including letter rulings and determination letters. See Rev. Proc. 2011-1. In addition, see Rev. Proc. 2011-2 for updated general procedures relating to the issuance of technical advice to a director or an appeals area director by the various offices of the Associate Chief Counsel.

CHAPTER **8**

Miscellaneous Estate Tax Provisions

¶ 8.01   Section 2201. Combat Zone–Related Deaths of Members of the Armed Forces and Deaths of Victims of Certain Terrorist Attacks S8-2
    [1]   Qualified Decedents S8-2
       [b]   Specified Terrorist Victims S8-2
       [c]   Astronauts [New] S8-3
    [2]   Effects of the Relief Provision.................. S8-3
       [a]   Rate Relief S8-3
       [b]   Unified Credit Computation S8-3

¶ 8.02   Section 2203. Definition of "Executor" S8-4

¶ 8.03   Section 2204. Discharge of Executor From Personal Liability S8-4
    [1]   Debts Due the United States S8-4
    [2]   Procedure to Gain Release From Personal Liability S8-4

¶ 8.04   Section 2205. Reimbursement Out of Estate S8-5
    [2]   State Statutes S8-5

¶ 8.07   Section 2207A. Right of Recovery in the Case of Certain Marital Deduction Property........................ S8-6
    [1]   Introduction S8-6
    [2]   Estate Tax Recovery........................ S8-6
    [4]   Whose Liability? S8-7
    [5]   The Possibility of Indirect Gifts................ S8-8

¶ 8.08   Section 2207B. Right of Recovery Where Decedent Retained Interest S8-8
    [2]   Estate Tax Recovery........................ S8-8

¶ 8.09   Sections 2208 and 2209. Citizenship and Residence of Certain Residents of Possessions S8-8

¶ 8.10   Section 2210. Estate Tax for the Year 2010 [Revised] S8-9
    [1]   Introduction S8-9
    [2]   The Election S8-10

	[3]	Income Tax Consequences	S8-11
	[a]	Introduction	S8-11
	[b]	Adjustments to the Carry-Over Basis	S8-14
		[i]	Increase in basis regardless of the recipient..........................	S8-15
		[ii]	Increase in basis for surviving spouses.	S8-15
		[iii]	Ownership.	S8-16
		[iv]	Ineligible property.................	S8-18
		[v]	Allocation of the basis adjustments.	S8-19
	[c]	Special Rules for Treatment of Gain	S8-20
		[i]	Character.	S8-20
		[ii]	Pecuniary bequests.	S8-20
		[iii]	Liability in excess of basis...........	S8-20
		[iv]	Sale of residence...................	S8-21
		[v]	Certain foreign transfers.............	S8-21
	[d]	Reporting Requirements	S8-21
		[i]	Lifetime gifts.	S8-22
		[ii]	Transfers at death.	S8-22
		[iii]	Penalties for failure to file required information......................	S8-23
¶ 8.11		The "Sunset" Provision [New]	S8-24
	[1]	The Estate Tax	S8-25
	[2]	The Gift Tax	S8-25
	[3]	The Generation-Skipping Transfer Tax	S8-26

¶ 8.01 SECTION 2201. COMBAT ZONE–RELATED DEATHS OF MEMBERS OF THE ARMED FORCES AND DEATHS OF VICTIMS OF CERTAIN TERRORIST ATTACKS

[1] Qualified Decedents

Page 8-3:

In the text, replace "two" *in the sentence ending with reference to note 6 with* "three".

Add to note 6.

The Military Family Tax Relief Act of 2003 (HR 3365) was signed into law on November 11, 2003, and extends the estate tax relief available under Section 2201 to astronauts who lose their lives in the line of duty. See ¶ 8.01[1][c].

[b] Specified Terrorist Victims

Page 8-6:

Add to note 32.

In Estate of Kalahasthi, No. 2:07-cv-05771 (CD Cal. 2008), the estate of a widow who committed suicide a few weeks after the death of her husband, a passenger in one of the planes that hijackers crashed into the World Trade Center, was not a "specified terrorist victim" and her estate is not eligible for the reduced tax rates under IRC § 2201(b)(2).

Page 8-6:

Add new subparagraph ¶ 8.01[1][c].

[c] Astronauts [New]

Congress has extended the classification of decedents to whom the Section 2201 special estate tax rates apply to include astronauts who lose their lives in the line of duty.[36.1]

[36.1] IRC § 2201(b)(3). The provision is applicable to the estates of decedents dying after December 31, 2002. Pub. L. No. 108-121, § 110(c)(3), 117 Stat. 1342, __ (2003), reprinted in 2003-__ CB __, __.

[2] Effects of the Relief Provision

[a] Rate Relief

Page 8-7:

Add to note 41.

Revenue Ruling 2002-86, 2002-52 IRB 1, provides three sample estate tax calculations for qualified decedents (all terrorist victims) under Section 2201, including for periods of time after the state death tax credit is replaced with a deduction. See also Notices 2002-40, 2002-1 CB 1152; 2001-61, 2001-40 IRB 305; 2001-68, 2001-57 IRB 504; and Ann. 2003-18, 2003-13 IRB 1, all relating to extensions or postponements of due dates and relief from the running of interest and failure to pay penalties.

[b] Unified Credit Computation

Page 8-7:

Add to note 43.

See supra ¶ 6.02[4], note 25, pertaining to the redesignation of Section 2102(c) to Section 2102(b), effective for estates of nonresident noncitizen decedents dying after December 31, 2004.

¶ 8.02 SECTION 2203. DEFINITION OF "EXECUTOR"

Page 8-10:

Add to note 13.

See CCA 200830001 (Feb. 26, 2008) (a statutory executor's liability as a representative within the meaning of the Federal Insolvency Statute, 31 USC § 3713, for a portion of a nonresident alien decedent's estate tax liability relating to property disbursed to decedent's spouse could not be conclusively determined).

¶ 8.03 SECTION 2204. DISCHARGE OF EXECUTOR FROM PERSONAL LIABILITY

[1] Debts Due the United States

Page 8-11:

Add to note 6.

Carroll v. United States, 2009-2 USTC ¶ 60,577 (ND Ala. 2009) (co-executor distributed estate assets to himself, his brother and two closely held corporations and stopped making Section 6166 installment payments of the estate tax; he was, therefore, personally liable for the unpaid estate tax and, since he intentionally attempted to avoid the estate tax due, his debt was not dischargeable through bankruptcy).

Page 8-12:

Add to note 10.

But see United States v. Russell, 93 AFTR2d 2003-484 (ED Mich. 2003) (condominium association fees do not have priority pursuant to state law and, accordingly, the personal representative was personally liable for the decedent's unpaid income taxes because her transfer of estate's sole asset rendered the estate insolvent).

[2] Procedure to Gain Release From Personal Liability

Page 8-12:

Add to note 14.

Carroll v. United States, 2009-2 USTC ¶ 60,577 (ND Ala. 2009) (co-executor distributed estate assets to himself, his brother and two closely held corporations and stopped making Section 6166 installment payments of the estate tax; he was, therefore, personally liable for the unpaid estate tax and, since he intentionally attempted to avoid the estate tax due, his debt was not dischargeable through bankruptcy).

Add to note 24.

United States v. Bevan, No. 102 AFTR2d 2008-7268 (ED Cal. 2008) (transferees of decedent's estate and trustee of decedent's trust were each personally liable for the estate's outstanding estate tax liability).

¶ 8.04 SECTION 2205. REIMBURSEMENT OUT OF ESTATE

Page 8-15:

Add to end of first paragraph of note 4.

United States v. Bevan, No. 2:07-cv-1944 (ED Cal. 2008) (transferees of decedent's estate and trustee of decedent's trust were each personally liable for the estate's outstanding estate tax liability). Upchurch v. Comm'r, TC Memo 2010-169 (2010) (estate beneficiaries who received property from the estate pursuant to a settlement agreement were considered transferees pursuant to IRC § 6901(a)(1)(A)(ii) and were thus liable for an estate tax deficiency plus interest).

Add to note 4.

Saigh v. Comm'r, TC Memo. 2005-20 (2005) (citing *R. Baptiste*, the tax court held that transferee was liable for interest accruing on the obligation from the due date of the decedent's estate tax return).

In CCA 201129037 (July 22, 2011), the Chief Counsel advised that the provisions of Section 6324(a)(2) do not apply to a transferee who received decedent's partnership interest to which a lien was attached. Transferee liability under Section 6324(a)(2) extends only to those who receive assets that are includible in a decedent's estate for federal estate tax purposes under the provisions of Sections 2034 to 2042 as assets that pass outside decedent's probate estate. The partnership interest in this case passed through the probate estate and was includible in decedent's estate under Section 2033 and thus was probate property not subject to Section 6324(a)(2). The Chief Counsel advised, however, that probate property to which a Section 6324(a)(1) estate tax lien has attached is transferred subject to that lien unless the estate's fiduciary was discharged from personal liability pursuant to Section 2204. Section 6324(a)(2) provides that upon the transfer of non-probate property to a purchaser, the property is divested of the federal estate tax lien whereas, if the property is part of decedent's probate estate, Section 6324(a)(3) provides that such property is divested of its estate tax lien upon transfer to a subsequent purchaser only if the estate's fiduciary is discharged from personal liability pursuant to Section 2204.

[2] State Statutes

Page 8-16:

Add to note 13.

See, e.g., Patrick v. Patrick, No. 03-04-00375-CV (Tex. Ct. App. 2005) (estate taxes should be apportioned to both probate assets and also to several individual retirement accounts not included in decedent's probate estate since decedent's will did not override Texas law apportioning taxes among all assets).

Page 8-17:

Add to note 15.

For a discussion of the constitutionality of state apportionment statutes in light of federal apportionment provisions, see Litman, "Apportionment of the Federal Estate Tax—Effect of Selective Federal Apportionment and Need for Reform," 33 Real Prop. Prob. & Tr. J. 327, 384–386 (1998).

Add new note 15.1 to sentence following reference to note 15.

[15.1] In Green Estate v. Comm'r, TC Memo. 2003-348 (2003), after concluding that the decedent's will lacked a clear expression of intent as to the payment of estate taxes, the court held that Missouri law controls as to the apportionment of estate tax and that no portion of the estate tax is allocable to the charitable residuary.

Add to note 16.

Boulis v. Blackburn, 4D08-2307 (Fla. App. 4th Dist. 2009) (elective share of surviving spouse, which is not entitled to a marital deduction, must bear a proportionate share of federal estate tax under the Florida estate tax apportionment statute).

Add to note 17.

Estate of Thornhill v. Bloom, No. 02A04-0908-CV-489 (Ind. Ct. App. 2010) (apportionment of estate taxes pursuant to statute where pour-over will's apportionment clause was in conflict with revocable trust's silence as to the apportionment of taxes).

¶ 8.07 SECTION 2207A. RIGHT OF RECOVERY IN THE CASE OF CERTAIN MARITAL DEDUCTION PROPERTY

[1] Introduction

Page 8-24:

Add to note 7.

State law controls the apportionment of state estate taxes and, in Colorado, Section 2207A governs the apportionment of state estate taxes in the absence of a contrary provision in the surviving spouse's testamentary instrument(s). Katz, Look & Moison, P.C. v. Shirley, 113 P3d 150 (Colo. 2005). Alabama, on the other hand, allocates the burden of state estate taxes attributable to QTIP property included in the surviving spouse's estate to the residue with no right of recovery from the beneficiaries of the QTIP trust unless decedent directs otherwise. Hollis v. Forrester, 2005 WL 797405 (Ala. 2005).

[2] Estate Tax Recovery

Page 8-25:

Add to note 9 after "Id."

Priv. Ltr. Rul. 200452010 (Sept. 13, 2004) (boilerplate tax apportionment clause in decedent's will did not waive estate's Section 2207A right of recovery because it did not contain specific language waiving that right). But see Eisenbach v. Schneider, 166 P3d 858 (Wash. App. Ct. 2007) (settlors of pre-1997 trust clearly intended that estate taxes be allocated pro rata between two funds described in the trust notwithstanding failure to specifically refer to Section 2207A or the QTIP trust).

Add to note 9 immediately before the last sentence.

If the right to recover is given up, the transfer of the recoverable tax is considered made when the right of recovery is no longer enforceable under applicable law. Reg. § 20.2207A-1(a)(2). A delay in the exercise of the right of recovery without payment of sufficient interest is treated as a below-market loan under Section 7872. Id.

[4] Whose Liability?

Page 8-28:

In the second paragraph of text, seventh line, replace the words "should be" *with* "is".

Replace note 34 with the following.

[34] The Section 2519 transfer resulting in a taxable gift is treated as a "net gift," with the amount of the gift reduced by the amount recoverable under Section 2207A(b). Reg. § 25.2519-1(c)(4). Thus, Section 2207A(b) is viewed as a statutory "net gift" agreement between the spouse making the Section 2519 transfer and the person or persons receiving the property. The spouse has the primary liability for the tax because the spouse is making the taxable transfer, but Section 2207A(b) allows the spouse to shift the liability, like a net gift agreement between a donor or donee. If the spouse recovers part or all of the Section 2207A(b) amount such that there is a net gift, the value of the remainder interest transferred requires an interdependent variable computation because the amount of the tax recovered affects the amount of the gift, which in turn determines the amount of the tax.

Although Section 2207A(b) allows a shifting of the tax liability from the transferring spouse to the person or persons receiving the property, the shift is not mandatory. Cf. Rev. Rul. 80-111, 1980-1 CB 208. See Priv. Ltr. Rul. 201118007 (Jan. 25, 2011) (QTIP trust divided into two sub-trusts with the sub-trust renounced by surviving spouse funded with sufficient assets to make gifts to couple's children and also to pay any gift tax attributable to the gifts). See also Priv. Ltr. Rul. 201119004 (Jan. 24, 2011). If the transferring spouse makes a written waiver of the right of recovery or allows it to become unenforceable under applicable law, an additional gift is made of the amount that could have been recovered. Reg. § 25.2207A-1(b). If a written waiver is executed, the transfer of the unrecovered amount is deemed to occur on the later of the date the waiver renders the right of recovery unenforceable or the date the tax is paid. A delay in the recovery of the tax without sufficient interest being paid is a below-market loan subject to Section 7872. Id. The transfer of the unrecovered amount of a gift tax transfer is considered to be made on the later of (1) the date of the valid and irrevocable waiver rendering the right of recovery no longer enforceable or (2) the date of the payment of the tax by the transferor. Priv. Ltr. Rul. 200530014 (Apr. 12, 2005).

[5] The Possibility of Indirect Gifts

Page 8-30:

Replace the last sentence of text on the page and existing note 43 with the following.

The regulations also treat a failure to recover gift tax due on a Section 2519 transfer as an indirect gift.[43]

---

   [43] Regulations Section 25.2207A-1(b) provides that the failure to exercise the right of recovery is a gift of the unrecovered amounts that is made when the right of recovery is no longer enforceable. The gift occurs even if recovery of the tax amount is impossible. Any delay in the exercise of the right of recovery is treated as an interest-free loan with corresponding gift tax consequences.

¶ 8.08 SECTION 2207B. RIGHT OF RECOVERY WHERE DECEDENT RETAINED INTEREST

[2] Estate Tax Recovery

Page 8-32:

Add to note 7.

In Estate of Sheppard, 2010-1 USTC ¶ 60,593 (Wis. 2010), the Wisconsin Supreme Court held that an estate has no right of recovery for estate taxes attributable to two payable-on-death (POD) accounts. Under applicable state law, the creator of a POD account has complete control over the account until his death and, since Section 2036 is only applicable when a decedent makes a transfer and retains an interest, Section 2207B's right of recovery does not apply to such accounts because no interest is transferred to the beneficiary of a POD account during the creator's lifetime.

¶ 8.09 SECTIONS 2208 AND 2209. CITIZENSHIP AND RESIDENCE OF CERTAIN RESIDENTS OF POSSESSIONS

Page 8-35:

Add to note 2.

   Priv. Ltr. Rul. 200603011 (Oct. 12, 2005) (decedent who derived her U.S. citizenship solely from being a resident of Puerto Rico was not a citizen or resident for estate tax purposes). Priv. Ltr. Rul. 200848014 (Aug. 18, 2008) (resident of Puerto Rico with U.S. citizenship is treated as nonresident noncitizen (1) for purposes of Section 2501(c) so long as he remains a resident of Puerto Rico, and (2) for purposes of Section 2209 at the time of his death provided that at such time he is a resident of Puerto Rico or another posses-sion of the United States). In Private Letter Ruling 200752016 (Aug. 27, 2007), estate of taxpayer who is a U.S. citizen solely due to taxpayer being a resident of a U.S. possession will not be subject to estate tax on portfolio debt obligations that produce interest de-scribed in Section 871(h)(2). See ¶ 6.05[3][b].

Page 8-35:

Replace existing ¶ 8.10 with revised ¶ 8.10.

¶ 8.10 SECTION 2210. ESTATE TAX FOR THE YEAR 2010 [REVISED]

[1] Introduction

In the year 2001, Congress enacted now-repealed Section 2210, which pro-vided that decedents dying after December 31, 2009, and before January 1, 2011, were not subject to the Chapter 11 federal estate tax.[1] However, property transferred by decedents during this period was subject to a modified carry-over basis system under the income tax.[2] The estate tax termination was itself scheduled to be terminated in 2011, and the estate tax provisions applica-ble in 2001 were scheduled to be resurrected.[3]

---

[1] Congressional thinking was that the estate tax is unduly burdensome to all taxpay-ers, especially those owning businesses, and more specifically small, family-owned, and farming businesses. HR Rep. No. 37, 107th Cong., 1st Sess. 25 (2001).

Section 2664 was also enacted, and it provided for the termination of the genera-tion-skipping transfer tax for generation-skipping transfers occurring during the period. See Supplement ¶ 18.04. Many states passed laws protecting beneficiaries from the unin-tended consequences of Sections 2210 and 2664 on formula clauses in testamentary docu-ments. See, e.g., Fla. Stat. §§ 733.1051, 736.04114.

Although the estate tax and the generation-skipping transfer tax were terminated, the gift tax continued to apply after 2009. Seemingly out of a concern for abusive assign-ments of income that could occur if the gift tax were repealed and the possibility that a donor would have a window of opportunity to make significant inter vivos gifts in the year 2010 (a year when the estate tax did not apply prior to the "sunset" provision taking effect in the year 2011, see infra ¶ 8.11), the gift tax was not repealed in the year 2010 or thereafter. See ¶ 9.01. See Blattmachr & Gans, "Wealth Transfer Tax Repeal: Some Thoughts on Policy and Planning," 140 No. 2 Tr. & Est. 49 (Feb. 2001). The gift tax con-tinued with a $1 million applicable exclusion amount under the Section 2505 credit; how-ever, the gift tax was imposed at a flat 35 percent rate, equal to the maximum income tax rate imposed at that time. See Supplement ¶ 9.03[2].

Several provisions of Chapter 11 had continued viability with respect to the estates of decedents who died prior to January 1, 2010.

[2] See infra ¶ 8.10[3].

[3] See Supplement ¶ 8.11 for a discussion of that resurrection, which is now sched-uled for the year 2013.

On December 17,2010, as the year 2010 was closing, a Congressional compromise[4] was reached on the transfer taxes.[5] The estate tax was restored for three years and the sunset provision postponed until 2013,[6] but with, in general, a $5 million applicable exemption amount,[7] a 35 percent tax rate,[8] and the basis in property acquired from the decedent determined under Section 1014.[9] Since the legislation was passed so late in 2010, Congress was left with a decision how to treat the estates of decedents who died in 2010. In a generous, but perhaps practical action, Congress allowed the estates of 2010 decedents an alternative. The executors of these estates could elect to not be subject to the estate tax[10] and could use the modified carryover basis rules of Section 1022 to determine the basis of property acquired from the decedent.[11]

[2] The Election

The executor[12] of the estate of a decedent dying after December 31, 2009, and before January 1, 2011, could elect to treat the estate tax as terminated.[13] If such an election was made, property acquired from the decedent in the estate

---

[4] See Gravelle, Estate Tax Options, CRS Report R41203 (Dec. 23, 2010).

[5] Tax Relief Act of 2010, Pub. L. No. 111-312, 124 Stat. 3296 (2010). The compromise also imposed a zero tax rate on generation-skipping transfers occurring in the year 2010. Tax Relief Act of 2010, Pub. L. No. 111-312 § 301(c), 124 Stat. 3296, 3300 (2010). See ¶ 16.01 text accompanying note 11. It restored the generation-skipping transfer tax in 2011 with a $5 million GST exemption (adjusted for inflation in 2012) (see IRC §§ 2631(c), 2010(c), Supplement ¶ 15.02) and a 35 percent maximum tax rate (see IRC §§ 2641(a)(1), 2001(c), Supplement ¶ 16.01). However, even if an executor elects out of applying the estate tax to the estate of a decedent dying in 2010, the decedent is treated as the transferor of property transferred at death to a generation-skipping trust. Tax Relief Act of 2010, Pub. L. No. 111-312 § 301(c), 124 Stat. 3296, 3300 (2010). See Supplement ¶ 17.02[1][a] text accompanying notes 6 and 7. The transferor decedent may allocate a maximum $5 million GST exemption to such trusts. IRC § 2631(c).

The compromise also extended the time for decedents dying between January 1, 2010, and December 16, 2010, to file their estate tax returns and make estate tax payments to September 17, 2011, and allowing persons acquiring property interests from such decedents to disclaim until September 17, 2011. Tax Relief Act of 2010, Pub. L. No. 111-312 § 301(d), 124 Stat. 3296, 3300 (2010).

[6] Tax Relief Act of 2010, Pub. L. No. 111-312 §§ 101(a)(1), 304, 124 Stat. 3296, 3298, 3304 (2010). See infra ¶ 8.11.

[7] IRC § 2010. See Supplement ¶ 3.02.

[8] IRC § 2001(c). See Supplement ¶ 2.01[1][c].

[9] IRC § 1014.

[10] Tax Relief Act of 2010, Pub. L. No. 111-312 § 301(c), 124 Stat. 3296, 3300 (2010).

[11] Tax Relief Act of 2010, Pub. L. No. 111-312 § 301(c), 124 Stat. 3296, 3300 (2010). See infra ¶ 8.10[3].

[12] IRC § 2203. See ¶ 8.02.

[13] Tax Relief Act of 2010, Pub. L. No. 111-312 § 301(c), 124 Stat. 3296, 3300 (2010).

took a modified carryover basis as provided in Section 1022.[14] The election was made in a manner that the Treasury prescribes, and it is revocable only with the consent of the Treasury.[15]

Generally, estates of decedents having a taxable estate and adjusted taxable gifts not in excess of the $5 million applicable exclusion amount will not have made the election as they did not owe any estate tax, and the property acquired from the decedent would take a basis determined under Section 1014. Whereas, very large estates seemingly will make the election to avoid an immediate 35 percent tax at death and, to the extent that the property does not take a fair market value basis, postpone income tax that will likely be taxed primarily at capital gain rates and not taxed, even on ordinary income, beyond a 35 percent rate. In estates between the two extremes, planning becomes more difficult.

---

[14] Tax Relief Act of 2010, Pub. L. No. 111-312 § 301(c), 124 Stat. 3296, 3300 (2010). See infra ¶ 8.10[3].

[15] Tax Relief Act of 2010, Pub. L. No. 111-312 § 301(c), 124 Stat. 3296, 3300 (2010). Guidance with regard to the time and manner in which the executor of the estate of a decedent who died in 2010 elects to apply the carryover basis rules under Section 1022, rather than the estate tax, has been issued by the Service. Notice 2011-66. Such executors will need to file Form 8939, Allocation of Increase in Basis for Property Acquired From a Decedent, to make such an election. Although Notice 2011-66 stated the due date for the filing of Form 8939 to be November 15, 2011, the Service pushed back the due date for filing Form 8939 to January 17, 2012. Notice 2011-76. In addition, safe harbor procedures applicable to executors of the estates of decedents who died in 2010, and recipients of property acquired from a 2010 decedent if the carryover basis election under Section 1022 is made, have also been provided by the Service. Revenue Procedure 2011-41. If the executor makes the election and follows the provisions of § 4 of Revenue Procedure 2011-41 and takes no return position contrary to the provisions of § 4, the Service will not challenge the taxpayer's reliance on § 4 on either Form 8939 or any other tax return.

[3] Income Tax Consequences

[a] Introduction

The benefits of electing out of the estate tax for the year 2010 were not granted without exacting potential income tax detriments to the recipients of the decedent's property. When the estate tax applies, the income tax basis for most assets included in an individual's gross estate at the individual's death is automatically adjusted, *up or down*, according to the fair market value of the assets on the date of the individual's death.[16] If an election is made for decedents dying in 2010 to avoid the estate tax,[17] Section 1014 was replaced by

---

[16] IRC § 1014(a)(1). But see several exceptions to this rule under Sections 1014(a)(2), 1014(a)(3), 1014(a)(4), 1014(c), and 1014(e).

[17] See supra ¶ 8.10[2].

Section 1022 providing for a modified "carry-over" basis system.[18] This carry-over basis regimen is similar in many respects to the basis determined under Section 1015 for lifetime gifts.[19]

The modified carry-over basis regimen is applicable only to "property acquired from a decedent" after December 31, 2009, and before January 1, 2011.[20] The term "acquired from a decedent" is broadly defined to encompass any " *property*"[21] that would have been included in the decedent's gross estate under the current estate tax if termination had not been elected.[22] Thus, it includes property acquired by the decedent's estate from the decedent or property acquired from the decedent by bequest, devise, or inheritance.[23] It also includes property transferred inter vivos by the decedent to a qualified revocable trust[24] or to any trust with respect to which the decedent has reserved the right to make any change in enjoyment through the power to alter, amend, or

---

[18] Tax Relief Act of 2010, Pub. L. No. 111-312 § 301(c), 124 Stat. 3296, 3300 (2010). The Service has released Publication 4895, Basis of Inherited Property Held by Decedents Who Died in 2010, which explains that if the executor of an estate of a decedent who died in 2010 elects to avoid the estate tax, such election could affect beneficiaries' 2010 income tax returns if inherited property was sold in 2010. Because beneficiaries may not yet know whether the executor intends to elect for the estate to be subject to the modified carryover basis regime, Publication 4895 notes such beneficiaries may need to request an extension of time by filing Form 4868, Application for Automatic Extension of Time To File U.S. Income Tax Return, by April 18, 2011, and estimate any gain or loss from such a sale.

[19] However, because no estate tax is paid, there will be no increase in the basis of the transferred property that is directly related to transfer taxes paid as can occur with respect to gifts. See IRC §§ 1015(d)(1), 1015(d)(6).

For some, this conjures up memories of the short-lived 1976 congressional experimentation with a carry-over basis at death under then Section 1023. Tax Reform Act of 1976, Pub. L. No. 94-455, § 2005(a)(2), 90 Stat. 1520, 1872 (1976), reprinted in 1976-3 CB (Vol. 1) 1, 348. Section 1023 is distinguishable from the current Section 1022 legislation, because when Section 1023 was enacted, the estate tax continued in existence. After a public outcry, that provision was retroactively repealed in 1980, when Congress resurrected Section 1014. Crude Oil Windfall Profit Tax Act of 1980, Pub. L. No. 96-223, § 401, 94 Stat. 229, 299 (1980), reprinted in 1980-3 CB 1, 71.

[20] IRC § 1022(a)(1). Section 1022 may only apply to decedents dying in 2010.

[21] The provision applies only to "property," so any cash received, especially the receipt of life insurance proceeds, would not be subject to these rules. Cf. IRC §§ 101(a), 2042. Similarly, cash payments included in a decedent's gross estate under Section 2035(b) (see ¶ 4.07[3]) would not be included. Cash would also include annuity payments in cash (cf. IRC § 2039); but see also IRC § 1022(f), which makes Section 1022 inapplicable to items of income in respect of a decedent. Cf. infra ¶ 8.10[3][b][iv].

[22] IRC § 1022(e). It also encompasses property that would have been subject to the Section 2031(c) exclusion. IRC § 1022(e)(3). See infra text accompanying note 26. See ¶ 4.02[7].

Compare infra ¶ 8.10[3][b][iii] more narrowly defining "ownership," which is required in order to make any basis adjustments to such property. See infra ¶ 8.10[3][b].

[23] IRC § 1022(e)(1).

[24] IRC § 645(b)(1). Cf. IRC § 2038.

terminate the trust.[25] Finally, the term broadly encompasses any other property passing from the decedent by reason of death, to the extent that such property passed without consideration.[26] This would include property held as joint tenants with a right of survivorship or as tenants by the entirety[27] or property held in an inter vivos trust created by a decedent where the decedent held an interest in the property in the trust, even though the decedent held no powers over the trust.[28] It is unclear whether it includes property subject to a general power of appointment created by another person and held by the decedent.[29] The rules are specifically inapplicable to any items of income in respect of a decedent.[30]

Although the carry-over basis rules apply to the broad range of property "acquired from a decedent," the advantageous rules allowing an upward adjustment to the carry-over basis apply only if the decedent " *owned*" such property, a term that is much more narrowly defined.[31]

Under the carry-over basis regimen, the income-tax basis of an asset passing at death will generally be the *lesser* of the adjusted basis of the asset in the hands of the decedent or the fair market value of the asset on the date of the decedent's death.[32] Once the estate tax is eliminated, and the carry-over basis system applies to transfers of property at death, the decedent's estate or beneficiaries may incur an income tax upon sale of assets acquired from the decedent that had appreciated in value prior to the decedent's death. Property that has depreciated in value that is acquired from a decedent will have its basis adjusted downward to the property's fair market value on the date of the dece-

---

[25] IRC § 1022(e)(2). Cf. IRC § 2038; ¶ 4.08. Seemingly, in order to qualify for the adjustments considered infra ¶ 8.10[3][b], such property must be held in either type of such trusts at the date of the decedent's death. See infra ¶ 8.10[3][b] text accompanying note 66.

[26] IRC § 1022(e)(3).

[27] Cf. IRC § 2040; ¶ 4.12.

[28] Cf. IRC §§ 2035, 2036, 2037; ¶¶ 4.07, 4.08, 4.09.

[29] IRC § 2041. Theoretically it would include such property, but statutorily such property might not be included. The question is academic because such property does not qualify for any basis adjustments (see infra ¶ 8.10[3][b] text accompanying notes 66–69), and such property will simply be allowed a carry-over basis in any event.

[30] IRC § 1022(f). See ¶ 4.05[4]. To the extent an item is an item of income in respect of a decedent, it is accorded a zero basis.

[31] IRC § 1022(d)(1)(A). See infra ¶ 8.10[3][b], especially ¶ 8.10[3][b][iii].

[32] IRC § 1022(a)(2). Recipients of assets from the estates of 2010 decedents may have a dilemma. Since these recipients may not yet know whether the executor will make the Section 1022 carryover basis election (or the basis, character, or holding period of such assets) at the time they file their income tax returns, such recipients must make good faith estimates based on the available facts and circumstances. As relief for these recipients, the Service has stated that to the extent the recipient's tax liability is increased by the application of Section 1022, the recipient's reasonable cause and good faith will be presumed and, accordingly, penalties under Sections 6651(a)(2) and 6662(a) will not be imposed on these recipients. Notice 2011-76.

dent's death, precluding the decedent's estate or beneficiaries from deducting the loss on sale of the property.[33]

[b] Adjustments to the Carry-Over Basis

The executor[34] or administrator of the decedent's estate may increase the adjusted basis of a decedent's appreciated assets under two separate rules, in effect exempting an amount of unrealized gain from the income tax.[35] Under the first adjustment, the aggregate adjusted basis of the decedent's assets may generally be increased by an amount of $1.3 million, regardless of who is the recipient of the property.[36] In addition, the adjusted basis of assets transferred to a surviving spouse either outright or in certain other ways, may be increased by an additional $3 million.[37] The result is that, if the decedent is survived by the decedent's spouse, $4.3 million of basis increase is potentially available to assets acquired from the decedent. Adjustments are made on an asset-by-asset basis, for example, a block of stock or a single share of stock.[38] However, the adjusted basis of an asset may not be increased above its fair market value as of the date of the decedent's death (thus making it impossible to create artifi-

---

[33] However, such losses may be indirectly allowed. See IRC § 1022(b)(2)(C)(ii), infra ¶ 8.10[3][b] text accompanying note 45.

[34] IRC § 7701(a)(47). Cf. IRC § 2203; ¶ 8.02.

[35] IRC §§ 1022(b), 1022(c), 1022(d).

[36] IRC § 1022(b)(2). See infra ¶ 8.10[3][b][i]. Form 8939, Allocation of Increase in Basis for Property Acquired from a Decedent, is an informational return used to establish basis for income tax purposes of property acquired from a person who died in 2010 whose estate elects to apply Section 1022. On March 31, 2011, the Treasury Department and IRS announced in IR-2011-33 that the April 18 deadline for filing Form 8939 has been extended and the form should not be filed with the decedent's final income tax return, which must still be filed by April 18, 2011. The news release indicates that the Service plans to issue guidance explaining how to make the Section 1022 election, to provide deadlines for making the election and filing Form 8939 and to make the Form 8939 available on the IRS website. Guidance with regard to the time and manner in which the executor of the estate of a decedent who died in 2010 elects to apply the carryover basis rules under Section 1022, rather than the estate tax, has been issued by the Service. Notice 2011-66. Such executors will need to file Form 8939, Allocation of Increase in Basis for Property Acquired From a Decedent, to make such an election. Although Notice 2011-66 stated the due date for the filing of Form 8939 to be November 15, 2011, the Service pushed back the due date for filing Form 8939 to January 17, 2012. Notice 2011-76. In addition, safe harbor procedures applicable to executors of the estates of decedents who died in 2010, and recipients of property acquired from a 2010 decedent if the carryover basis election under Section 1022 is made, have also been provided by the Service. Revenue Procedure 2011-41. If the executor makes the election and follows the provisions of § 4 of Revenue Procedure 2011-41 and takes no return position contrary to the provisions of § 4, the Service will not challenge the taxpayer's reliance on § 4 on either Form 8939 or any other tax return.

[37] IRC § 1022(c). See infra ¶ 8.10[3][b][ii].

[38] See infra ¶ 8.10[3][b][v].

cial losses).[39] The basis adjustment rules are subject to some other limitations. They apply only to property "acquired from the decedent"[40] only if the property was "owned" by the decedent at death.[41] Furthermore, the adjustment rules are inapplicable to some types of property.[42]

[i] **Increase in basis regardless of the recipient.** Potentially an executor may increase the adjusted basis of the decedent's assets transferred to anyone generally by $1.3 million.[43] The $1.3 million amount is increased by the amount of the decedent's unused capital loss carryover at death under Section 1212(b) and the amount of any of the decedent's unused net operating loss carryover under Section 172, either of which would (but for the event of death) be carried from the decedent's last taxable year to a later taxable year.[44] The $1.3 million amount is also increased by the amount of any losses that would have been deductible under Section 165 if the property acquired from the decedent had been sold at fair market value immediately before the decedent's death.[45]

[ii] **Increase in basis for surviving spouses.** An executor may also increase the adjusted basis of property transferred to a surviving spouse[46] by a total of $3 million, if the property is "qualified spousal property," that is, property that passes "outright" to the spouse or passes as "qualified terminable interest property."[47] Outright bequests to a surviving spouse qualify only if they are not terminable interests under a test identical to the terminable interest rule applicable under the estate tax marital deduction provision.[48] Transfers qualify-

---

[39] IRC § 1022(d)(2). In determining fair market value, valuation discounts should be applicable.

[40] See supra ¶ 8.10[3][a] text accompanying notes 20–30.

[41] IRC § 1022(d)(1)(A). See infra ¶ 8.10[3][b][iii].

[42] See infra ¶ 8.10[3][b][iv].

[43] IRC § 1022(b)(2)(B). Nonresidents who are not U.S. citizens may increase the basis of their property by only up to $60,000. IRC § 1022(b)(3)(A). The Section 1022(b)(2)(C) adjustments discussed infra text accompanying notes 45, 46 are inapplicable to the potential $60,000 adjustment available to a nonresident noncitizen. IRC § 1022(b)(3)(B).

[44] IRC § 1022(b)(2)(C)(i).

[45] IRC § 1022(b)(2)(C)(ii). The effect of this Section 165 rule is to allocate the amount of any reduction in the basis of assets, which have declined in value prior to the decedent's death and whose sale would result in a deduction under Section 165(c) because they are business or investment assets (see IRC §§ 165(c)(1), 165(c)(2)), to any other assets that have appreciated in value. The adjustment would not apply to any potential losses under Section 165(c)(3).

[46] The $3 million adjustment does not apply to a nonresident, noncitizen surviving spouse. IRC § 1022(b)(3)(B).

[47] IRC § 1022(c).

[48] IRC § 1022(c)(4)(B). See IRC § 2056(b)(1); ¶ 5.06[7]. Property transferred to a surviving spouse in a marital deduction estate trust that does not violate the terminable in-

ing for the Section 2056(b)(3) condition on survival for a limited period exception to the terminable interest rule are generally treated as outright transfers.[49] However, property passing to a surviving spouse in a trust subject to a general power of appointment held by the spouse or a similar interest[50] is not treated as an outright transfer.[51] Qualified terminable interest property does qualify for the $3 million basis adjustment.[52] Qualified terminable interest property is similar to Section 2056(b)(7) property[53] in that it is property that passes from the decedent,[54] from which the spouse is entitled for life to all the income payable annually or at more frequent intervals,[55] and no portion of which may be appointed to anyone other than the surviving spouse during the surviving spouse's lifetime.[56] The $3 million amount is not adjusted for any income tax carryovers or potential losses.[57]

[iii] **Ownership.** To qualify for either type of increase in basis, the property must be "owned" or treated as owned by the decedent at the time of

---

terest rule (see ¶ 5.06[7][c] text accompanying notes 194, 195) should be treated as an "outright" transfer qualifying for the adjustment. For estate tax purposes, one's estate is essentially treated the same as oneself and consequently a transfer to a surviving spouse's estate should be treated as a transfer to the surviving spouse under Section 1022(c)(4)(A). Cf. IRC § 2056(b)(1)(A); ¶ 5.06[7][c] note 194.

[49] IRC § 1022(c)(4)(C). See IRC § 2056(b)(3); ¶ 5.06[8][a]. If there is such a clause and, as a result, the property does not pass to the surviving spouse, then there is no potential $3 million adjustment.

[50] IRC §§ 2056(b)(5), 2056(b)(6). See ¶¶ 5.06[8][b], 5.06[8][c]. See also supra ¶ 8.10[3][a] text accompanying note 29.

[51] IRC §§ 1022(c)(3), 1022(c)(4), 1022(c)(5). As a policy matter, it is questionable why such trusts do not qualify for the adjustment.

[52] IRC § 1022(c)(5).

[53] See ¶ 5.06[8][d]. However, no election is required. Cf. IRC § 2056(b)(7)(B)(i)(III).

[54] IRC § 1022(c)(5)(A)(i).

[55] IRC §§ 1022(c)(5)(A)(ii), 1022(c)(5)(B)(i). A usufruct interest in the property for life also qualifies. Id. To the extent provided in regulations, an annuity shall be treated similarly to an income interest in property (regardless of whether the property from which the annuity is payable can be separately identified). IRC § 1022(c)(5)(B) (flush language). See IRC § 2056(b)(7)(B)(ii) (flush language); ¶ 5.06[8][d][ii].

[56] IRC §§ 1022(c)(5)(A)(ii), 1022(c)(5)(B)(ii). See IRC § 2056(b)(7)(B)(ii)(II); ¶ 5.06[8][d][ii]. The definition of qualified terminable interest property also incorporates two other rules from Section 2056(b)(7). The term "property" includes an interest in property. IRC § 1022(c)(5)(C). See IRC § 2056(b)(7)(B)(iii). Furthermore, a specific portion of property is treated as separate property. IRC § 1022(c)(5)(D). See IRC § 2056(b)(7)(B)(iv); ¶ 5.06[8][d][ii]. Property passing from a decedent to a trust qualifying for the marital deduction under Section 2056 (b)(5) where the surviving spouse is granted only a testamentary general power of appointment should satisfy the statutory definition of qualified terminable interest property.

[57] See supra text accompanying notes 45, 46. Any such adjustment would provide a double benefit of such attributes to the recipients of property.

death.[58] "Ownership" is defined more narrowly than the current gross estate ownership inclusion provisions, and thus, it does not include all properties "acquired from the decedent" that are described earlier.[59] The statute provides some specific rules of ownership,[60] but it does not specifically define the term "owned" as that term is used under the statute. Congress needs to tighten up the statute by specifically defining the term "owned." It is arguable that any property "acquired from a decedent"[61] would be treated as "owned" by the decedent, unless the statute otherwise provides some special rule under the special rules that are discussed next:

Joint Tenancy with Spouse. In the case of property held as joint tenants or tenants by the entireties with the surviving spouse, when Section 2040(b) applies, and only one half of the property is treated as having been owned by the decedent and thus being eligible for the basis increase.[62]

Joint Tenancy with Others. In the case of property held as joint tenants with right of survivorship with a person other than the surviving spouse, the statute is patterned after Section 2040(a). The portion of the property attributable to the consideration furnished by the decedent is treated as having been owned by the decedent and is eligible for a basis increase.[63] If the property was acquired by the joint tenants by gift, bequest, devise, or inheritance, and their interests are not otherwise specified or fixed by law, the decedent shall be treated as the owner to the extent of the value of a fractional part, which is to be determined by dividing the value by the number of joint tenants.[64]

Revocable Trust. The decedent is treated as the owner of property if the property was transferred by the decedent during life to a qualified revocable trust (as defined in Section 645(b)(1)).[65] It makes sense that the property must be held in the trust at the time of the decedent's death to qualify for the adjustments under this provision, although the statute is not that specific.

Powers of Appointment. The decedent is not treated as owning any property solely by reason of holding a power of appointment with respect to such property (whether a general or nongeneral power of appointment).[66] Thus, such property is not provided any basis adjustments. Therefore, property held in a Section 2056(b)(5) general power marital deduction trust[67] does not qual-

---

[58] IRC § 1022(d)(1).

[59] See supra ¶ 8.10[3][a] text accompanying notes 20–30.

[60] IRC § 1022(d)(1)(B).

[61] See supra ¶ 8.10[3][a] text accompanying notes 20–30.

[62] IRC § 1022(d)(1)(B)(i)(I). Cf. IRC § 2040(b); ¶ 4.12[10].

[63] IRC § 1022(d)(1)(B)(i)(II). Cf. IRC § 2040(a); ¶¶ 4.12[1]–4.12[8].

[64] IRC § 1022(d)(1)(B)(i)(III). Cf. IRC § 2040(a); ¶ 4.12[6].

[65] IRC § 1022(d)(1)(B)(ii). Cf. ¶ 4.10. Seemingly, a trust over which a decedent has a Section 2038 power under the current law (see ¶ 4.10[4]) other than a power to revoke the trust is not treated as "owned" by the decedent. Cf. supra text accompanying note 62.

[66] IRC § 1022(d)(1)(B)(iii). Cf. supra ¶ 8.10[3][a] text accompanying note 29.

[67] See ¶ 5.06[8][b].

ify for a basis increase at the surviving spouse's death.[68] Presumably, if the surviving spouse held and exercised a general power in favor of the surviving spouse's estate, the property would be eligible for the basis adjustment.[69]

Community Property.   The decedent is treated as owning the surviving spouse's one-half share of community property (which will be eligible for a basis increase) if at least one-half share of the whole of the community interest is treated as owned by, and acquired from, the decedent.[70] This rule applies to property that is not currently included in the decedent spouse's gross estate and it is therefore distinguishable from the special rules, noted earlier. However, it is similar to the generally beneficial rule of Section 1014(b)(6), and it allows basis adjustments to the surviving spouse's one half of the community property, even though such property was not actually owned by the decedent.[71]

Qualified Terminal Interest Property.   The statute does not provide any special rules with respect to a surviving spouse's ownership of qualified terminable interest property that is included in the surviving spouse's gross estate under Section 2044.[72] Without a special rule similar to Section 2044, it appears that property held in a QTIP trust at the death of the surviving spouse is ineligible for the *surviving spouse's* $1.3 million basis adjustment.[73]

[iv] **Ineligible property.** Certain types of property are made specifically ineligible for any of the adjustments to basis.[74]

Property Acquired Within Three Years of Death. Property that was acquired by the decedent by gift or by an inter vivos transfer for less than adequate and full consideration during the three-year period ending on the date of the decedent's death is ineligible for any adjustments.[75] There is an exception to this three-year rule for property acquired from the decedent's spouse, unless

---

[68] See supra text accompanying notes 50- 57.

[69] However, there may be nontax reasons, such as creditor issues, why making such an exercise would not be desirable.

[70] IRC § 1022(d)(1)(B)(iv). The surviving spouse's one-half share is also treated as acquired from the decedent. Id. Cf. IRC § 1014(b)(6).

[71] For example, if Decedent and Spouse own community property with an adjusted basis of $1.7 million that is worth $6 million (each owns $3 million of community property) and the decedent's estate qualifies for a total of $4.3 million in adjustments, the basis of both halves of the community property are stepped-up to $3 million at Decedent's death, even though only one-half is actually owned by Decedent.

[72] See ¶ 4.16. But see ¶ 4.16 text accompanying notes 20–23 not aggregating the interest with other property owned by the surviving spouse for valuation purposes.

[73] Seemingly, the result would be different if the trustee of the QTIP trust distributed the property out of the QTIP trust to the surviving spouse before the surviving spouse's death.

[74] Because property that constitutes a right to receive income in respect of a decedent is not within Section 1022 (IRC § 1022(f)), such property does not qualify for a basis adjustment.

[75] IRC § 1022(d)(1)(C)(i). This rule is similar to Section 1014(e) except that it involves a three-year (rather than one-year) time frame and it does not require a transfer of

the decedent's spouse also acquired the property during such three-year period in whole or in part by gift or by inter vivos transfer for less than adequate and full consideration.[76]

Foreign Personal Holding Company. Stock or securities of a foreign personal holding company are ineligible for any basis adjustments.[77]

Domestic International Sales Corporation. Stock of a domestic international sales corporation (or former domestic international sales corporation) is also ineligible.[78]

Foreign Investment Companies. Stocks of a foreign investment company and stock of a passive foreign investment company (except that for which a decedent shareholder had made a qualified electing fund election) are similarly ineligible.[79]

[v] Allocation of the basis adjustments. The executor of the decedent's estate[80] is permitted to allocate both the potential $1.3 million and the $3 million adjustments to any qualifying property;[81] however, the adjustments may not increase the basis of any asset above its fair market value.[82] The allocation is made on an asset-by-asset basis, with the result that generally an executor has a broad amount of discretion to decide which appreciated assets will receive a basis adjustment and the extent of the increase. The allocation is made on an informational return required by Section 6018.[83] Once made, the allocation may be changed only as allowed by the Service.[84]

---

the property by the decedent back to the donor of the property. The purpose of the rule is to preclude near-death transfers of property taking advantage of the basis increases.

[76] IRC § 1022(d)(1)(C)(ii). This is consistent with the income tax policy of allowing tax-free interspousal transfers. See IRC § 1041. However, it precludes an interspousal transfer where the transferor spouse transfers property that violates the Section 1022(d)(1)(C)(i) rule. IRC § 1022(d)(1)(C)(ii). Thus, a surviving spouse may make a transfer to a decedent spouse (during that spouse's life) to take advantage of the $3 million adjustment (as the property is transferred back at decedent spouse's death to the surviving spouse) as long as the surviving spouse had not acquired the property by gift (in whole or in part) from a third person within three years of the decedent's death.

[77] IRC § 1022(d)(1)(D)(i).

[78] IRC § 1022(d)(1)(D)(ii).

[79] IRC §§ 1022(d)(1)(D)(iii), 1022(d)(1)(D)(iv). See IRC § 1295.

[80] IRC § 7701(a)(47). Cf. IRC § 2203; ¶ 2.02.

[81] IRC § 1022(d)(3)(A). Although the federal law allows such discretion, state fiduciary law may impose important fairness restrictions with the respect to the allocation of such adjustments. If local law imposes a fiduciary duty to treat beneficiaries impartially, the fiduciary would have to allocate basis in a manner that benefits the beneficiaries proportionately. It is advisable for the fiduciary to allocate the adjustment first to ordinary income property in hands of distributee, which otherwise would be taxed at higher rates.

[82] IRC § 1022(d)(2).

[83] IRC § 1022(d)(3)(A). This is the return relating to large transfers at death. See infra ¶ 8.10[3][d][ii].

[84] IRC § 1022(d)(3)(B).

[c] Special Rules for Treatment of Gain

Several of the post-estate tax termination provisions deal with the treatment of gains under the income tax law.

[i] Character. The character of gain on the sale of property received from a decedent generally is treated the same as if the property had been acquired by gift.[85] Thus, the character of gain is normally determined by the character of the property in the donee's hands.[86] However, for example, real estate that has been depreciated and would be subject to ordinary income recapture gain if sold by the decedent would be subject to recapture gain if sold by the recipient of the property.[87]

[ii] Pecuniary bequests. A nonrecognition rule provides that gain on the transfer of property by an executor in satisfaction of a pecuniary bequest is recognized only to the extent that the fair market value of the property at the time that the pecuniary bequest is satisfied exceeds the fair market value of the property on the date of the decedent's death (not the property's carry-over basis).[88] These same rules apply to trusts to the extent provided by regulations.[89] The adjusted basis of property acquired in an exchange to which the pecuniary bequest rule applies is the adjusted basis of the property held before the transfer appropriately increased by the amount of gain recognized on the transfer.[90]

[iii] Liability in excess of basis. Another nonrecognition rule provides that gain is not recognized at the time of death when an estate or beneficiary, other than a tax-exempt beneficiary,[91] acquires property from the decedent that is subject to a liability greater than the decedent's adjusted basis in that property.[92] Similarly, no gain is recognized by the estate on the distribution of such

---

[85] IRC § 1022(a)(1).

[86] However, the tacking of holding periods would apply. IRC § 1223(2).

[87] See IRC §§ 1245(a)(2), (b)(1), 1250(b)(1), 1250(b)(3), 1250(d)(1).

[88] IRC § 1040(a). Prior to 2010, a similar rule applies to transfers of property to a qualified heir if the property was valued under Section 2032A. IRC § 1040(a).

[89] IRC § 1040(b). Until regulations are promulgated, a Section 645 election might be prudent with respect to a qualified revocable trust.

[90] IRC § 1040(c). The adjusted basis would include any Section 1022(b) or Section 1022(c) adjustments.

[91] Under Section 1022(g)(2), a tax-exempt beneficiary includes (1) the United States, any state or political subdivision thereof, any U.S. possessions, any Indian tribal government, or any agency or instrumentality of the above; (2) any organization exempt from tax (other than a Section 521 farmers' cooperative); or (3) any foreign person or entity (see IRC § 168(h)(2)). Section 1022(g)(2)(D) extends the definition to include, to extent provided in regulations, any person to whom property is transferred for the principal purpose of tax avoidance.

[92] IRC § 1022(g)(1)(A).

property to a beneficiary of the estate other than to a tax-exempt beneficiary.[93] Thus, except with respect to a tax-exempt beneficiary,[94] in determining whether gain is recognized and in determining the adjusted basis of such property, liabilities in excess of basis are disregarded.[95]

[iv] **Sale of residence.** The benefit of the decedent's income tax exclusion of up to $250,000 of gain on the sale of a principal residence[96] is extended to the decedent's estate, other recipients of the residence, or to a trust that immediately before death was a qualified revocable trust established by the decedent.[97] If the decedent's estate or a person who acquired the residence from the decedent or a qualified revocable trust sells the decedent's principal residence, up to $250,000 of gain may be excluded provided that the decedent owned and used the property as a principal residence for two or more years during the five-year period prior to the sale.[98] In addition, if an heir or a beneficiary occupies the property as a principal residence, the decedent's period of ownership and use is tacked on to the recipient's subsequent ownership and use in determining whether the property was owned or used for two or more years as a principal residence during the five-year period prior to the sale.[99] As a result of this rule, an executor might not want to allocate a decedent's potential increase in basis adjustments to a principal residence.

[v] **Certain foreign transfers.** Gain is recognized on the transfer of an asset by a U.S. person to a foreign estate or trust or to a nonresident noncitizen.[100] The amount of gain is the difference between the fair market value of the property transferred and its adjusted basis.[101]

[d] Reporting Requirements

New reporting rules and penalties for failure to satisfy such rules are applicable to estates that elect out of the estate tax.

---

[93] IRC § 1022(g)(1)(B).

[94] In the case of a transfer to a tax-exempt beneficiary, gain would be recognized to the extent of the excess of the liabilities over the adjusted basis of the property, because it represents the last opportunity for the government to capture such gain.

[95] IRC § 1022(g).

[96] IRC § 121.

[97] IRC §§ 121(d)(9)(A), 121(d)(9)(B), 121(d)(9)(C). See also IRC §§ 645(b)(1), 1022(e).

[98] IRC §§ 121(a), 121(b)(1), 121(d)(11).

[99] IRC §§ 121(a), 121(b)(1), 121(d)(11) (flush language), 121(d)(9)(B). As a result of this rule, an executor may want to give close consideration to which heir or beneficiary to whom the residence is distributed.

[100] IRC § 684. Prior to 2010, Section 684 provided the same rule; however, it was inapplicable to a nonresident citizen.

[101] IRC § 684.

[i] Lifetime gifts. A donor who is required to file a gift tax return under Section 6019(a)[102] is, in addition, required to furnish certain information by written statement to each recipient of such property.[103] The statement must show the name, address, phone number of the donor,[104] and the information required on the gift tax return with respect to the property received by the person (e.g., a description of the property, the adjusted basis of the property, and the value of the property).[105] This information must be furnished to the recipient of the property not later than thirty days after the date the gift tax return is filed.[106]

[ii] Transfers at death. Where transfers of property acquired from a decedent[107] of noncash assets exceeding $1.3 million[108] or transfers of appreciated property received by a decedent within three years of death that is ineligible for any basis adjustment[109] and which was required to be reported on a gift tax return,[110] the executor of the estate[111] is required to file an informational return.[112] The informational return must provide the following: (1) the name and

---

[102] See ¶ 9.04[5].

[103] IRC § 6019(b).

[104] IRC § 6019(b)(1).

[105] IRC § 6019(b)(2).

[106] IRC § 6019(b) (flush language).

[107] IRC §§ 1022(e), 6018(d). See supra ¶ 8.10[3][a] text accompanying notes 20–30.

[108] IRC § 6018(b)(1). See IRC § 1022(b)(2)(B); supra ¶ 8.10[3][b][i].

[109] See IRC § 1022(d)(1)(C).

[110] IRC § 6018(b)(2). See IRC § 1022(d)(1)(C), discussed supra ¶ 8.10[3][b] text accompanying notes 75-76; IRC § 6019(a), discussed ¶ 9.04[5].

[111] IRC § 7701(a)(47). Thus, the term executor would include the trustee of a revocable trust. Id. Cf. IRC § 2203; ¶ 8.02.

[112] IRC § 6018(a). Form 8939, Allocation of Increase in Basis for Property Acquired from a Decedent, is an informational return used to establish basis for income tax purposes of property acquired from a person who died in 2010 whose estate elects to apply Section 1022. On March 31, 2011, the Treasury Department and IRS announced in IR-2011-33 that the April 18 deadline for filing Form 8939 has been extended and the form should not be filed with the decedent's final income tax return, which must still be filed by April 18, 2011. The news release indicates that the Service plans to issue guidance explaining how to make the Section 1022 election, to provide deadlines for making the election and filing Form 8939 and to make the Form 8939 available on the IRS website. The provision also applies to a nonresident noncitizen decedent where tangible property situated in the United States and other property acquired from the decedent by a U.S. person has a value exceeding $60,000. IRC §§ 1022(b)(3), 6018(b)(3). Guidance with regard to the time and manner in which the executor of the estate of a decedent who died in 2010 elects to apply the carryover basis rules under Section 1022, rather than the estate tax, has been issued by the Service. Notice 2011-66. Such executors will need to file Form 8939, Allocation of Increase in Basis for Property Acquired From a Decedent, to make such an election. Although Notice 2011-66 stated the due date for the filing of Form 8939 to be November 15, 2011, the Service pushed back the due date for filing Form 8939 to January 17, 2012. Notice 2011-76.

taxpayer identification number of the recipient of the property; (2) an accurate description of the property; (3) the adjusted basis of the property in the hands of the decedent and its fair market value at the time of death; (4) the decedent's holding period for the property; (5) sufficient information to determine whether any gain on the sale of the property would be treated as ordinary income; (6) the amount of basis increase allocated to the property under Section 1022(b) or Section 1022(c);[113] and (7) any other information as the Treasury Secretary may prescribe.[114] If the executor is unable to make a complete return as to any property, the executor is to include in the return a description of the property and the name of every person holding a legal or beneficial interest therein.[115] Similar information (including the name, address, and phone number of the person filing the return) is required to be provided to each recipient of such property within thirty days after the date the return is filed.[116]

[iii] Penalties for failure to file required information. Any person required to report to beneficiaries and donees under Section 6018(e) or Section 6019(b)[117] will incur a penalty of $50 for each failure to report such information to a beneficiary.[118] Any person required to furnish any information under Section 6018 for transfers at death who fails to do so timely would be liable for a penalty of $10,000 for the failure to report such information[119] (or $500 in the case of each failure to furnish information in accordance with Section 6018(b)(2) relating to gifts received by the decedent within three years of death).[120] No penalty is imposed with respect to any failure that is due to rea-

---

[113] See supra ¶ 8.10[3][b].

[114] IRC § 6018(c).

[115] IRC § 6018(b)(4). Upon notification from the Service, such persons shall file a similar return with respect to such property. Id.

[116] IRC § 6018(e). Guidance with regard to the time and manner in which the executor of the estate of a decedent who died in 2010 elects to apply the carryover basis rules under Section 1022, rather than the estate tax, has been issued by the Service. Notice 2011-66. Such executors will need to file Form 8939, Allocation of Increase in Basis for Property Acquired From a Decedent, to make such an election. Although Notice 2011-66 stated the due date for the filing of Form 8939 to be November 15, 2011, the Service pushed back the due date for filing Form 8939 to January 17, 2012. Notice 2011-76. In addition, safe harbor procedures applicable to executors of the estates of decedents who died in 2010, and recipients of property acquired from a 2010 decedent if the carryover basis election under Section 1022 is made, have also been provided by the Service. Revenue Procedure 2011-41. If the executor makes the election and follows the provisions of § 4 of Revenue Procedure 2011-41 and takes no return position contrary to the provisions of § 4, the Service will not challenge the taxpayer's reliance on § 4 on either Form 8939 or any other tax return.

[117] See supra ¶¶ 8.10[3][d][i], 8.10[3][d][ii].

[118] IRC § 6716(b).

[119] IRC § 6716(a). See supra ¶ 8.10[3][d][ii].

[120] IRC § 6716(a) (parenthetical). See supra ¶ 8.10[3][d][ii].

sonable cause.[121] If any failure to report to the Service or a beneficiary is due to intentional disregard of the rules, then the penalty is 5 percent of the fair market value of the property for which reporting was required, determined at the date of the decedent's death (for property passing at death) or determined at the time of gift (for a lifetime gift).[122]

---

[121] IRC § 6716(c). Cf. ¶ 2.02[1] text accompanying notes 17–19.

[122] IRC § 6716(d). The deficiency procedures of subchapter B of Chapter 63 do not apply to the assessment or collection of any of the previously stated penalties. IRC § 6716(e).

Page 8-53:

Add new ¶ 8.11 following revised ¶ 8.10.

¶ 8.11 THE "SUNSET" PROVISION [NEW]

It is no understatement that in this century the federal estate tax law has been and continues to be in a state of flux. Under the legislation enacted in 2001,[1] the estate tax was to terminate for the year 2010,[2] then in the year 2011 was to "sunset" (be resurrected) to the year 2001 status.[3] Congress hedged on the 2010 termination, allowing decedent's executors to either use a more generous exemption and rates ($5 million and 35 percent) than applied in 2009 ($3.5 million and 45 percent)[4] or to elect to pay no estate tax but to transfer property with a modified tax deferred carryover income tax basis.[5] Congress continued the more generous estate tax exemption and rules laws for 2011 and 2012, but only for those two years. In 2013, the estate tax law (along with the gift tax and the generation-skipping transfer tax) is scheduled to revert to its year 2001 status.[6] In effect, Congress postponed the 2011 sunset provision to the year 2013.

---

[1] Economic Growth and Tax Relief Reconciliation Act of 2001, Pub. L. No. 107-16, 115 Stat. 38 (2001), reprinted in 2001-3 CB 9.

[2] Now-repealed IRC § 2210(a). Now-repealed Section 2664 was also enacted and it provided for the termination of the generation-skipping transfer tax for generation-skipping transfers during 2010. See Supplement ¶ 18.04[1]. However, the gift tax was not terminated in 2010. See Supplement ¶ 8.10[1] note 1.

[3] Economic Growth and Tax Relief Reconciliation Act of 2001, Pub. L. No. 107-16, § 901, 115 Stat. 38, 150 (2001), reprinted in 2001-3 CB 9, 122.

[4] See Supplement ¶ 8.10[1].

[5] Tax Relief Act of 2010; Pub. L. No. 111-312 § 301(c), 124 Stat. 3296, 3300 (2010). See Supplement ¶ 8.10[1].

[6] Tax Relief Act of 2010; Pub. L. No. 111-312 § 304, 124 Stat. 3296, 3304 (2010). See Economic Growth and Tax Relief Reconciliation Act of 2001, Pub. L. No. 107-16 § 901, 115 Stat. 38, 150 (2001), reprinted in 2001-3 CB 9, 122.

The reasons for the original "sunset" provision were apparently both procedural[7] and political. The same can be said for the 2010 two-year extension of the sunset provision. With multiple new Congresses, a Presidential election year, and a constantly changing economic situation, it is futile to try to predict whether a future Congress and administration will either retain the transfer taxes in their 2011 and 2012 form for 2013 and later years, retain the transfer taxes in some other form,[8] or allow the sunset provision to take effect in 2013. Total inaction will result in a sunsetting, although such inaction seems unlikely. For that reason we provide only a cursory summary of the sunsetted provisions under each of the three taxes.

[1] The Estate Tax

Under the sunset provision reverting to 2001 levels, the estate tax applicable exclusion amount will be $1 million,[9] and the maximum tax rate will be 55 percent (plus the 5 percent surtax, if applicable).[10] Several estate tax provisions will return to their 2001 status. The Section 2011 credit for state death taxes will be restored, and Section 2058 will be eliminated.[11] The Section 2057 deduction for qualified family-owned business interests will be restored.[12] The Section 2031(c) conservation easement exclusion qualification requirements[13] and the rules under Section 6166[14] return to their original form.

[2] The Gift Tax

Even though the gift tax was not terminated in 2010,[15] nevertheless the gift tax will revert to its 2001 status with an applicable exclusion amount of $1 mil-

---

[7] The provisions were sunset to ensure compliance with the Byrd Rule. 2 USC § 644. The Byrd Rule imposes a ten-year limit on spending increases and (as here) revenue decreases enacted under procedural rules that preclude the possibility of a filibuster (i.e., may be broken only by a vote of sixty senators). 2 USC § 644. See Economic Growth and Tax Relief Reconciliation Act of 2001, Pub. L. No. 107-16, §§ 901(a)(2), 901(b), 115 Stat. 38, 150 (2001), reprinted in 2001-3 CB 9, 122.

[8] The Obama budget proposals would revert to the 2009 levels of a $3.5 million exemption and a 45 percent rate.

[9] This is the applicable exclusion amount that under the pre-2001 law was to be phased-in to $1 million in the year 2006. See Supplement ¶ 3.02[1] note 11.

[10] See Supplement ¶ 2.01[1][b] text accompanying note 52.

[11] See ¶¶ 3.03, 5.09. Thus, the pick-up tax system enacted by many states again becomes effective. See ¶ 3.03.

[12] IRC § 2057. See ¶ 5.08.

[13] See ¶ 4.02[7][b] text accompanying note 287.

[14] See ¶ 2.02[3][c] text accompanying notes 64, 66, 87-88, notes 93–99.

[15] See Supplement ¶ 8.10[1] note 1.

lion,[16] and maximum gift tax rates under the unified tax rates of 55 percent with a possible 5 percent surtax.[17]

[3] The Generation-Skipping Transfer Tax

Reverting to its 2001 levels, the GST exemption will be $1 million (adjusted for inflation after 1998)[18] and the maximum generation-skipping transfer tax rate will be 55 percent.[19] Changes made by the legislation to the generation-skipping transfer tax rules since 2001 are also sunsetted. The Section 2604 credit for state death taxes will be restored.[20] The Section 2632(c) automatic allocation of GST exemption to indirect skips,[21] the Section 2632(d) retroactive allocation of GST exemption,[22] the Section 2642(a)(3) qualified severing of trusts rule,[23] the clarification of the Section 2642(b) valuation rules,[24] and the relief provisions of Section 2642(g)[25] were not in existence in 2001 and are all eliminated in the year 2013.

---

[16] See Supplement ¶ 9.06 note 17.

[17] See Supplement ¶ 9.03[2] text accompanying note 17.

[18] See Supplement ¶ 15.02 note 7.

[19] See Supplement ¶ 16.01 note 10.

[20] See ¶ 12.04.

[21] See ¶ 15.03[4].

[22] See ¶ 15.03[5].

[23] See ¶ 15.03[5][c][ii].

[24] See ¶ 16.02[4][d].

[25] See ¶ 16.02[9].

PART III

The Gift Tax

CHAPTER **9**

Gift Tax: Determination of Liability

¶ 9.02		Section 2501. Imposition of Tax	S9-2
	[1]	Imposition of the Gift Tax on Nonresident Noncitizens [Revised]	S9-2
		[a] General Rules for Nonresident Noncitizens . . .	S9-2
		[b] Gift Taxation of Some Expatriates	S9-3
		[i] Section 2801.	S9-4
		[ii] Section 2501(a)(3).	S9-6
	[2]	Transfers to Political Organizations	S9-10
¶ 9.03		Section 2502. Rate of Tax [Revised]	S9-10
	[1]	Periodic Accounting for Gifts	S9-11
	[2]	Rates	S9-11
	[3]	Method of Computation	S9-13
	[4]	Liability for the Gift Tax	S9-15
¶ 9.04		Section 2503. Taxable Gifts	S9-15
	[1]	The Annual Exclusion	S9-15
		[b] Identification of Donees	S9-16
		[ii] Gifts to other entities.	S9-16
		[iii] Gift by an entity.	S9-16
		[iv] Gifts to charitable organizations.	S9-16
		[v] Straw person.	S9-16
	[3]	Definition of "Future Interests"	S9-17
		[a] Separate Interests Tested	S9-17
		[b] Non-Income-Producing Property	S9-17
		[e] Right to Enjoyment Suffices	S9-18
		[f] *Crummey* Powers	S9-19
		[g] Qualified Tuition Programs and Education Savings Accounts	S9-19
	[5]	Special Statutory Rule for Minor Donees	S9-20
		[a] First Requirement	S9-20
		[b] Second Requirement	S9-21
	[6]	Medical Expenses and Tuition	S9-21

	[9]	Gift Tax Returns	S9-21
	[10]	Limitations on Assessment	S9-22
		[a] Commencement of Limitations Period	S9-22
	[11]	Donee and Fiduciary Liability	S9-23
¶ 9.05		Section 2504. Taxable Gifts for Preceding Calendar Periods	S9-23
	[2]	Valuation for Prior Years	S9-23
		[a] Gifts Made Through August 5, 1997	S9-23
¶ 9.06		Section 2505. Unified Credit Against the Gift Tax [Revised]	S9-23
	[1]	Amount of the Credit	S9-25
	[2]	Relation to the Section 2010 Credit	S9-28

¶ 9.02 SECTION 2501. IMPOSITION OF TAX

Page 9-5:

Replace existing ¶ 9.02[1] with revised ¶ 9.02[1].

[1] Imposition of the Gift Tax on Nonresident Noncitizens [Revised]

In general, the Chapter 12 gift tax rules dealing with persons who are treated as nonresident noncitizens[4] and with the situs of property[5] parallel the Chapter 11 estate tax rules.

[a] General Rules for Nonresident Noncitizens

As a general rule, nonresident noncitizens are subject to gift tax only on transfers of property situated within the United States.[6] However, Section 2501(a)(2) provides an overriding exemption under which the gratuitous transfer of intangibles by nonresident noncitizens are not taxed, even if they are located in the United States.

This exemption first appeared in the 1954 Code. Two factors seem to have motivated its adoption. First, under prior law, nonresident noncitizens may have been able to avoid the tax on transfers of intangibles, such as bonds, by moving the bonds outside the United States prior to making the gifts. If the tax was so easily avoided,[7] there was little reason for its imposition.[8] Second,

---

[4] See ¶ 6.01[3]. See also ¶ 6.07.

[5] See ¶¶ 6.03–6.05, 6.07[2].

[6] IRC § 2511(a). Priv. Ltr. Rul. 201032021 (Apr. 28, 2010) (nonresident noncitizen donor's transfers of naked title to shares of an entity that is not a U.S. corporation to her resident noncitizen child and U.S. citizen grandchildren are not subject to gift tax). Even property situated in the United States may not be subject to gift tax if a gift tax convention with a foreign country exempts it. Reg. § 25.0-1(a)(1).

[7] But see De Goldschmidt-Rothschild v. Comm'r, 168 F2d 975 (2d Cir. 1948).

[8] S. Rep. No. 1622, 83d Cong., 2d Sess. 126 (1954).

efforts to avoid the tax tended to deny "United States financial institutions business as depositories for property" of nonresident noncitizens.[9] This business is encouraged by the present rule.[10] Section 2511(b) and Section 2105(a) provide rules for the location of intangibles, but since they are not subject to taxation under the general rule, this location is irrelevant for purposes of Section 2501(a)(2) and their location becomes relevant only to certain nonresident noncitizens who are subject to a special rule described below.[10.1]

Section 2501(c) provides a special rule to determine whether persons are potentially subject to the general rules above.[10.2] The section provides that a citizen of the United States who is a resident of a U.S. possession will be considered a nonresident noncitizen if the person acquired U.S. citizenship solely because the person was a citizen of such possession or because of birth or residence within such possession.[10.3]

[b] Gift Taxation of Some Expatriates

Over the years, Congress has enacted several special provisions whose purpose is to remove incentives to avoid U.S. gift taxes by giving up U.S. citizenship or residency.[10.4] The provisions currently apply to a U.S. citizen who gives up U.S. citizenship[10.5] and to any long-term resident[10.6] of the United

---

[9] S. Rep. No. 1622, 83d Cong., 2d Sess. 126 (1954).

[10] Until 1966, the exemption applied only if the nonresident noncitizen donor was not engaged in business in the United States. Elimination of this qualification is a further inducement to foreign investment in U.S. securities.

[10.1] See infra ¶ 9.02[1][b][ii].

[10.2] The rule is precisely parallel to Section 2209, which is discussed at ¶ 8.09.

[10.3] IRC § 2501(c). Section 2501(b) provides the flip side of the rule stating the circumstances in which such persons will be considered U.S. citizens. Both rules are discussed with historical detail at ¶ 8.09.

[10.4] See Stephens, Maxfield, Lind, Calfee & Smith, Federal Estate and Gift Taxation ¶ 9.02[1] (Warren, Gorham & Lamont 8th ed. 2002).

[10.5] Section 7701(a)(50)(A) provides that a citizen is treated as losing U.S. citizenship pursuant to Section 877A(g)(4) on the earliest of the date (1) the citizen renounces U.S. nationality before a diplomatic or consular officer (provided the relinquishment is confirmed by issuance of a certificate of loss of nationality); (2) the citizen furnishes the State Department a signed statement of voluntary relinquishment (provided the relinquishment is confirmed by issuance of a certificate of loss of nationality); (3) the State Department issues a certificate of loss of nationality; or (4) a U.S. court cancels the citizen's certificate of naturalization. Cessation may occur earlier for a person who at birth becomes a citizen of the U.S. and another country. IRC § 7701(a)(50)(B). See also IRC §§ 2801(f), 877A(g), 2501(a)(3), 877(a).

[10.6] A "long-term resident" is defined as a noncitizen who has been a lawful permanent resident of the United States in at least eight of the fifteen years ending in the year when U.S. residency was terminated. IRC § 877(e)(2). See IRC §§ 2801(f), 877A(g)(2)(B), 2501(a)(3).

States who is not a U.S. citizen and who terminates U.S. residency;[10.7] both individuals are statutorily referred to as "expatriates." An individual's expatriation date is the date that the individual gives up U.S. citizenship or terminates U.S. residency.[10.8] Two provisions currently apply to expatriates: (1) Section 2801, which is applicable to individuals who expatriate after June 16, 2008,[10.9] and (2) Section 2501(a)(3), which is applicable to individuals who expatriate prior to June 17, 2008.[10.10] Both sections are discussed below.

[i] Section 2801. Section 2801 taxes any "covered gift" of property made in any calendar year to a U.S. citizen or resident by a "covered expatriate."[10.11]

Requirements. For gift tax purposes, a *"covered expatriate"* is an expatriate[10.12] who expatriates after June 16, 2008 and makes inter vivos gifts and who meets one of three alternative tests at the time of the expatriation date: (1) the donor's average annual net income tax[10.13] liability for the five years preceding expatriation date exceeded $124,000 (adjusted for inflation after 2004);[10.14] (2) the donor's net worth at the time of the expatriation date was $2 million or more; or (3) the donor fails to certify, under penalties of perjury, that the donor has complied with federal tax obligations for the five years preceding the expatriation date or fails to provide documentation of such compliance.[10.15] Even if the donor exceeded the monetary thresholds in items (1) or

---

[10.7] Termination of U.S. residency occurs when either (1) one loses the privilege of residing in the U.S. (i.e. loses green card status) because the privilege is revoked or administratively or judicially terminated or (2) one commences to be treated as a resident of a foreign country under a tax treaty between the United States and a foreign country, does not waive the benefits applicable to residents of the foreign country, and notifies the IRS of the commencement of such treatment. IRC § 7701(b)(6). See IRC §§ 2801(f), 877A(g)(2)(B), 2501(a)(3), 877(e).

[10.8] IRC § 877(A)(g)(3).

[10.9] Heroes Earning Assistance and Relief Act of 2008, Pub. L. No. 110-245, § 301(g)(2) __ Stat. __, __ (2008), reprinted in 2008- __ CB __, __.

[10.10] IRC § 877(h). Section 2501(a)(3) effectively terminates after June 16, 2018. See infra ¶ 9.02[1][b][ii] note 10.38.

[10.11] IRC § 2801(a). The Service is requesting comments on Notice 2008-XX, which has not yet been fully published and provides guidance regarding the federal tax consequences for citizens who expatriate or cease to be taxed as permanent residents under IRC §§ 877A, 2801 and 6039G.

[10.12] See supra text accompanying notes 10.5–10.8.

[10.13] Section 38(c)(1) defines "average net income tax" for this purpose as the "sum of the regular tax liability and the tax imposed by Section 55, reduced by the credits allowable under" Sections 21 through 30A. IRC § 877(a)(2)(A). See IRC §§ 2801(f), 877A(g)(1).

[10.14] IRC §§ 1(f)(3), 877(a)(2). The inflation adjustment is rounded to the nearest multiple of $1,000. Id. The amount is $139,800 for 2008. Rev. Proc. 2007-66, § 3.29, 2007-2 CB __.

[10.15] IRC §§ 877(a)(2), 877A(g)(1), 2801(f).

(2), above,[10.16] Section 2801 is inapplicable to certain former dual citizens who did not have substantial U.S. contacts[10.17] and is inapplicable to certain former citizens who lost their citizenship during their minority.[10.18]

If any individual who is a covered expatriate subsequently becomes subject to tax as a U.S. citizen or resident for any period after the expatriation date, the individual is not subject to Section 2801, but if the individual again relinquishes citizenship or terminates long-term residency (after subsequently meeting the requirements to become a long-term resident), the Section 2801 rules are retriggered with a new expatriation date.[10.19]

Section 2801 applies to a "covered gift."[10.20] A covered gift is a gift acquired by a U.S. citizen or resident directly or indirectly from an individual who is a covered expatriate at the time of the acquisition.[10.21] However, a transfer is not a covered gift if the property is shown on a timely filed U.S. gift tax return filed by the covered expatriate.[10.22] In addition, a transfer is not a covered gift to the extent that the transfer would qualify for a charitable deduction[10.23] or a marital deduction[10.24] if the covered expatriate were a U.S. person.[10.25]

Section 2801 makes no specific reference to Chapter 13 generation-skipping transfer tax and seemingly does not apply to inter vivos generation-skipping transfers,[10.26] although, as a policy matter, Section 2801 should apply to such transfers.[10.27]

[10.16] IRC § 877A(g)(1)(B). However, note that the certification and proof of documentation requirements still must be met for the exceptions to apply. IRC § 877(a)(2)(C).

[10.17] IRC § 877A(g)(1)(B)(i). This is an individual who became at birth a citizen of the United States and another country who continues to be a citizen of and is taxed as a resident of such other country (IRC § 877A(g)(1)(B)(i)(I)) and has been a U.S. resident (under the substantial presence test of Section 7701(b)(1)(A)(ii)) for not more than ten taxable years during the fifteen-taxable year period ending with the taxable year in which the expatriation date occurs. IRC § 877A(g)(1)(B)(i)(II).

[10.18] IRC § 877A(g)(1)(B)(ii). This exception applies to an individual who became a U.S. citizen at birth, whose loss of citizenship occurred prior to reaching age eighteen and one-half, and (under the substantial presence test of Section 7701(b)(1)(A)(ii)) who has been a resident of the U.S. for not more than ten taxable years before the date of relinquishment.

[10.19] IRC §§ 2801(f), 877(g)(1)(C).

[10.20] It also applies to "covered bequests." IRC § 2801(e)(1)(B). See ¶ 6.07[1][a].

[10.21] IRC § 2801(e)(1)(A). See IRC § 2801(a).

[10.22] IRC § 2801(e)(2).

[10.23] See IRC § 2522.

[10.24] See IRC § 2523.

[10.25] IRC § 2801(e)(3).

[10.26] See IRC § 2801(a).

[10.27] For example, if a covered expatriate makes an inter vivos transfer to a skip person, both the gift transfer and the generation-skipping transfer should be taxed.

The Tax Imposed. The tax under Section 2801 is imposed on the U.S. recipient of the property.[10.28] It applies only to the extent that the gift exceeds the dollar amount that qualifies for an annual exclusion under Section 2503(b).[10.29] If the transfer is made to a domestic trust, the trust is treated as a U.S. citizen, and the trust is required to pay the tax.[10.30] If the transfer is made to a foreign trust, any distribution by the foreign trust of either income or corpus made to a U.S. citizen or resident which is attributable to the original transfer is treated as if the distribution is a covered gift.[10.31]

The amount of tax imposed under Section 2801 is the highest marginal gift tax rate[10.32] or estate tax rate[10.33] in effect on the date of the receipt of the covered gift multiplied by the taxable amount of the value of the covered gift.[10.34]

Credit. The amount of tax imposed on the recipient is reduced any gift tax paid to a foreign country for the covered gift.[10.35]

[ii] Section 2501(a)(3). Section 2501(a)(3) is applicable to expatriate donors who expatriated prior to June 17, 2008.[10.36] It operates in a manner different from Section 2801 because it imposes a tax on the expatriate using the situs rules discussed above, but when Section 2501(a)(3) applies, it adds some special situs rules applicable to intangibles that tax otherwise nontaxable gifts.[10.37]

[10.28] IRC § 2801(b). The tax is imposed on a calendar year basis. The Service has announced that it will issue a new tax form, Form 708, for the purpose of reporting transfers taxable under Section 2801 and also noted its intention to issue guidance under Section 2801 establishing the due date for filing Form 708 and paying the tax. Those dates will be contained in future guidance which will allow taxpayers a reasonable amount of time in which to pay the tax and file the return. Ann. 2009-57, 2009-29 IRB 158.

[10.29] IRC § 2801(c). The amount is $12,000 for 2008. See ¶ 9.04[1].

[10.30] IRC § 2801(e)(4)(A). Seemingly the amount of transfer is reduced by the Section 2503(b) dollar amount regardless of whether the entire amount constitutes a present interest under Section 2503(b).

[10.31] IRC § 2801(e)(4)(B)(i). To the extent the distribution is included in the recipient's gross income, a deduction of the amount of the transfer tax on the distribution is allowed under the income tax (IRC § 164) for the income tax paid. IRC § 2801(e)(4)(B)(ii).

For the purposes of these rules, a foreign trust may elect to be treated as a domestic trust; the election may not be revoked without the consent of the IRS. IRC § 2801(e)(4)(B)(iii).

[10.32] IRC § 2502(a).

[10.33] IRC § 2001(c).

[10.34] IRC § 2801(a). See supra text accompanying notes 10.21–10.27 and 10.29–10.31. The tax applies to covered gifts on or after June 17, 2008, from transferors whose expatriation date is also on or after June 17, 2008. Heroes Earning Assistance and Relief Tax Act of 2008, Pub. L. No. 110-245, § 301(g)(2), __ Stat. __, __ (2008), reprinted in 2008 __ __ CB __, __.

[10.35] IRC § 2801(d).

[10.36] IRC § 877(h).

[10.37] See infra text accompanying notes 10.47–10.53.

Expatriates who are subject to the rule. If a donor expatriated within a ten-year period ending with the date of a gift of intangible property treated as located in the United States[10.38] and if certain other objective requirements paralleling those under Section 2801 are met, the Section 2501(a)(2) exemption does not apply and the transfer is subject to U.S. gift taxation.[10.39] The objective requirement is satisfied if one of the following three tests was met at the time of the expatriation date[10.40] (1) the donor's average annual income tax[10.41] liability for the five years preceding the loss of the expatriation date exceeded $124,000 (adjusted for inflation after 2004);[10.42] (2) the donor's net worth at the time of the expatriation date was $2 million or more; or (3) the donor fails to certify, under penalties of perjury, that the donor has complied with federal tax obligations for the five years preceding the expatriation date or fails to provide documentation of such compliance.[10.43] Even if the donor exceeded the monetary thresholds in test (1) or test (2), above,[10.44] Section 2501(a)(3) is inapplicable to certain former dual citizens who did not have substantial U.S. contacts[10.45] and is inapplicable to certain former citizens who lost their citizenship during their minority.[10.46]

Intangible property subject to taxation. If the requirements above are met, Section 2501(a)(3) subjects some intangible property situated in the United States to Chapter 12 taxation on its transfer by the expatriate. Congress under-

---

[10.38] See IRC §§ 2501(a)(5), 2511(b); infra text accompanying notes 10.47–10.53; ¶ 10.01[11]. Thus Section 2501(a)(3) is effectively repealed after June 16, 2018.

[10.39] IRC §§ 877(a), 877(b), 2501(a)(3)(A). However, compare supra note 10.18 with infra note 10.46.

[10.40] IRC §§ 877(a)(2), 877(b), 2501(a)(3)(A). In addition, the donor must be subject to the alternative nonresident, noncitizen income tax under Section 877(b) in the year of the gift. IRC §§ 877(b), 2501(a)(3)(A).

[10.41] Section 38(c)(1) defines "average net income tax" for this purpose as the "sum of the regular tax liability and the tax imposed by Section 55, reduced by the credits allowable under" Sections 21 through 30A. IRC § 877(a)(2)(A).

[10.42] IRC §§ 1(f)(3), 877(a)(2). The inflation adjustment is rounded to the nearest multiple of $1,000. Id. The amount is $139,000 for 2008. Rev. Proc. 2007-66, § 3.29, 2007-2 CB __.

[10.43] IRC §§ 877(a)(2), 877(b), 2501(a)(3)(A).

[10.44] IRC § 877(c)(1). However, note that the certification and proof of documentation requirements still must be met for the exceptions to apply. IRC § 877(a)(2)(C).

[10.45] IRC § 877(c)(2). This is an individual who became at birth a citizen of the United States and another country who continues to be a citizen of such other country. IRC § 877(c)(2)(A). The individual is treated as having no substantial contacts if the individual has never been a U.S. resident, held a U.S. passport, and has not been present in the United States for more than thirty days during any calendar year that is one of the ten calendar years preceding the individual's loss of U.S. citizenship. IRC § 877(c)(2)(B).

[10.46] IRC § 877(c)(3). This exception applies to an individual who became a U.S. citizen at birth, neither of whose parents was a U.S. citizen at such time, whose loss of citizenship occurred prior to reaching age eighteen and one-half, and who was not present in the United States for more than thirty days during any calendar year that is one of the ten calendar years preceding the minor's loss of citizenship. Id.

takes in Sections 2511(b) and 2501(a)(5) to spell out what intangible property is to be treated as situated in the United States.

Stock issued by U.S. corporations has long been treated as property situated in the United States and is expressly so classified now by Section 2511(b)(1). In addition, sometimes stock issued by a foreign corporation is treated as U.S. situs property. In the absence of such a rule, an expatriate could transfer U.S. assets to a foreign corporation, the stock of which would be property situated outside the United States. Under Section 2501(a)(5), however, a portion of such stock is treated as having a U.S. situs.[10.47] Section 2501(a)(5) applies only if at the time of the donor's gift, the donor owned

1. Directly or indirectly[10.48] ten percent or more of the total combined voting power of the corporation;[10.49] and
2. Directly or indirectly[10.50] or by attribution,[10.51] more than 50 percent of the total combined voting power of the corporation or the total value of the stock of the corporation.[10.52]

The portion of the foreign corporation stock treated as U.S. situs property is the "U.S.-asset value" of the stock.[10.53] This is the portion that the fair market value of the foreign corporation's assets situated in the United States at the

---

[10.47] IRC §§ 2501(a)(5)(A)(ii), 2501(a)(5)(C). The Section 2511 situs rules should be employed in measuring such situs. The fair market value of a foreign corporation's assets, both in the United States and abroad, is likely determined without reducing the value to reflect any outstanding liabilities. Cf. Reg. § 20.2107-1(b)(1)(iii)(a).

[10.48] In measuring such ownership, Section 2501(a)(5) employs Section 958(a). Section 958 provides that a shareholder is deemed to own all stock in a foreign corporation that it owns directly. In addition, ownership of stock that is owned by foreign entities, trusts, estates, corporations, or partnerships is attributed proportionately to their beneficiaries, shareholders, and partners. IRC § 958(a).

[10.49] IRC § 2501(a)(5)(B)(i).

[10.50] See supra note 10.48 for measurement of indirect ownership.

[10.51] Section 958(b) provides for such attribution rules. It directs the application of the Section 318(a) stock ownership attribution rules with the following modifications: (1) for purposes of applying Section 318(a)(1)(A), stock owned by a nonresident noncitizen individual, other than a foreign trust or estate, is not owned by a resident or citizen of the United States; (2) an entity that "owns more than 50 percent of the total combined voting power of all classes of stock entitled to vote of a corporation" owns all of the corporation's voting stock for purposes of Sections 318(a)(2)(A), 318(a)(2)(B), and 318(a)(2)(C); (3) 10 percent is substituted for 50 percent in applying Section 318(a)(2)(C); (4) Sections 318(a)(3)(A), 318(a)(3)(B), and 318(a)(3)(C) are not to be applied so that a U.S. person is deemed to own stock that is owned by a non-U.S. person.

Although Section 958(b) directs the application of Section 318 only for purposes of Sections 951(b), 954(d)(3), 956(c)(2), and 957, the specific reference to Section 958(b) in Section 2501(a)(5)(B)(ii) renders the attribution rules applicable to Section 2501(a)(5) as well.

[10.52] IRC § 2501(a)(5)(B)(ii).

[10.53] IRC § 2501(c)(5)(A)(ii).

time of the gift bears to the fair market value of all of the foreign corporation's assets at such time.[10.54]

At one time "bonds issued by United States persons, unlike other debt obligations, [were] considered to be situated where the instrument [was] located."[10.55] Section 2511(b)(2) alters that rule so that any debt obligation of a "United States person"[10.56] or of the United States, a state and its political subdivisions, and the District of Columbia, if owned by an expatriate, also is deemed to be situated in the United States.[10.57]

Credit for foreign gift taxes. A credit is allowed for any foreign gift tax actually paid with respect to a gift subject to tax solely by reason of Section 2501(a)(3).[10.58] Since the effect of Section 2501(a)(3) is to potentially trigger Sections 877(g),[10.59] 2501(a)(5), and 2511(b)(1), the credit should apply to taxes imposed as a result of any of those sections.

Special Rule Treating Expatriates as Residents or Citizens. If an expatriate *to whom Section 2501(a)(3)* applies[10.60] makes gifts in a year in which, with minor exceptions,[10.61] the donor spends more than thirty days in the

---

[10.54] IRC §§ 2501(a)(5)(A)(ii), 2501(a)(5)(C).

[10.55] S. Rep. No. 1707, 89th Cong., 2d Sess. (1966), reprinted in 1966-2 CB 1059, 1099.

[10.56] Section 7701(a)(30) defines "United States person" as (1) a citizen or resident of the United States; (2) a domestic partnership; (3) a domestic corporation; and (4) any estate or trust other than a foreign estate or trust as defined in Section 7701(a)(31).

[10.57] Fitting this rule together with the rules of Section 2501(a) on the gift taxation of nonresident noncitizens, it will be seen that the situs of intangibles is rarely relevant. Citizens and residents are taxed on gifts of any property wherever situated; nonresident noncitizens are taxed on gifts of tangible property situated in the United States but generally escape tax on gifts of intangibles wherever situated. However, when the special provisions of Section 2501(a)(3) come into play, certain expatriates who are nonresident noncitizens become taxable on gifts, not only of tangible property within the United States, but also of intangibles if they are located here. It is then that the special situs rule of Section 2511(b)(2) on debt obligations may exact its toll.

[10.58] IRC § 2501(a)(3)(B).

[10.59] See infra text accompanying notes 10.60–10.62.

[10.60] IRC §§ 877(a), 877(g), 2501(c)(3)(A). See supra text accompanying notes 10.38–10.46.

[10.61] IRC § 877(g)(2). Under the exceptions, a day of physical presence is disregarded if the donor was performing service in the United States for an unrelated (IRC §§ 267, 707) employer. IRC § 877(g)(2)(A). No more than thirty days in a calendar year may be disregarded under this rule. IRC § 877(g)(2)(A). In addition, to satisfy the rule, one's employer must meet regulations prescribed by the Secretary. IRC § 877(g)(2)(A)(ii). However, the exceptions apply only to donors with certain ties to countries other than the United States (IRC § 877(g)(2)(B)) or donors with minimal physical presence in the United States (IRC § 877(g)(2)(C)). The first situation applies to donors who became (not later than a reasonable time after loss of U.S. citizenship or termination of residency) a citizen or resident of the country in which the donor was born, the donor's spouse was born, or either of the donor's parents were born and the donor became liable for income taxes in such country. IRC § 877(g)(2)(B). The minimum physical presence test is satisfied if for each year in the ten-year period ending with the loss of U.S. citizenship or ter-

United States, the donor is treated as a resident or citizen of the United States and all of the donor's gifts in the year located anywhere in the world are subject to gift taxation.[10.62]

---

mination of residency, the donor was physically present in the United States for thirty days or less. IRC § 877(g)(2)(C). See IRC § 7701(b)(3)(D)(ii).

[10.62] IRC §§ 877(g)(1), 2501. This rule is effective for donors after June 3, 2004. American Jobs Creation Act of 2004, Pub. L. No. 108-357, § 804(f), 118 Stat. 1418, 1573 (2004), reprinted in 2004- __, __ CB __, __. It does not apply to donors who expatriate after June 17, 2008. IRC § 877(h).

[2] Transfers to Political Organizations

Page 9-7:

In first full paragraph, replace references to "2501(a)(5)" with "2501(a)(4)".

¶ 9.03 SECTION 2502. RATE OF TAX [REVISED]

Replace existing ¶ 9.03 with the following revised ¶ 9.03.

Section 2502 specifies the method of computation to be used in the determination of gift tax liability. A two-step computation is required, as will be explained. However, it should be observed at the outset that the rates are always applied to "taxable gifts," a term that is akin to the "taxable estate" for estate tax purposes and "taxable income" for income tax purposes. The term "taxable gifts," which is defined in Section 2503, represents a net figure to be arrived at by determining what gifts are generally within the scope of the tax, by possibly taking advantage of the Section 2503(b) exclusion,[1] and finally, by taking into account certain deductions allowed by the statute.

It should also be observed that while one must follow the complicated statutory process described below, as a practical matter when one combines the Section 2505 unified gift tax credit[2] and the tax rates applicable under this section,[3] taxable gifts made after 2009 and before 2013[4] taxation are taxed at a flat rate of 35 percent.[5]

---

[1] See also IRC §§ 2503(e), 2503(f), 2503(g), which treat some transfers as nontransfers.

[2] See Supplement ¶ 9.06.

[3] See infra ¶ 9.03[2].

[4] See infra note 17 for the consequences in 2013.

[5] See infra note 17 for the differences in the amount taxed in 2010.

[1] Periodic Accounting for Gifts

Imposition of a gift tax based on taxable gifts for the year gives this tax a superficial resemblance to the federal income tax, which is based on taxable income for the year. One obvious difference is that gift tax liability is always determined with reference to the calendar year, whereas in determining income tax liability, the taxpayer may adopt a fiscal year.[6] There is another fundamental difference. Income tax rates are determined with reference only to the taxable income figure for the taxable period in question;[7] gift tax rates depend on the donor's aggregate sum of taxable gifts since June 6, 1932.[8] This cumulative method of applying rates is the reason for the rather involved language of Section 2502(a).

[2] Rates

The Section 2001(c) rate schedule, which also applies to the estate tax, is the rate schedule for "taxable gifts."[9] Thus the rate brackets applicable to gifts are identical to the rate brackets applicable to estates. Prior to 2002, the maximum gift tax rate was 55 percent,[10] and it was increased by a 5 percent surtax on gifts over $10 million.[11] Beginning in the year 2002, the maximum rate declined to 50 percent with no surtax.[12] The top marginal rate was gradually reduced from 50 percent to 45 percent in years 2003 through 2009.[13] In 2010,

---

[6] See IRC §§ 441, 2501(a)(1).

[7] But see IRC § 1341.

[8] A decedent's taxable gifts made after December 31, 1976, not includible in the decedent's gross estate, also affect the amount of estate tax incurred by a decedent's estate. IRC § 2001(b).

[9] IRC § 2502(a)(1).

[10] See IRC § 2001(c)(1), prior to its amendment by the Economic Growth and Tax Relief Reconciliation Act of 2001, Pub. L. No. 107-16, § 511(a), 115 Stat. 38, 70 (2001), reprinted in 2001-3 CB 9, 42. See Supplement ¶ 2.01[1][c] text accompanying note 48.

[11] See IRC § 2001(c)(2), prior to its repeal by the Economic Growth and Tax Relief Reconciliation Act of 2001, Pub. L. No. 107-16, § 511(b), 115 Stat. 38, 70 (2001), reprinted in 2001-3 CB 9, 42. The 5-percent surtax was imposed on gifts in excess of $10 million. IRC § 2001(c)(2), prior to its repeal by the Economic Growth and Tax Reconciliation Act of 2001, Pub. L. No. 107-16, § 511(b), 115 Stat. 38, 70 (2001), reprinted in 2001-3 CB 9, 42. The surtax was phased out at $17,184,000, the point at which the rate of tax on all gifts was a flat 55 percent rate. See Supplement ¶ 2.01[1][c] note 49.

[12] IRC §§ 2001(c), 2502(a)(1). See Supplement ¶ 2.01[1][c] text accompanying note 50.

[13] IRC §§ 2001(c), 2502(a)(1). See Supplement ¶ 2.01[1][c] text accompanying note 51.

the maximum gift tax rate was reduced to 35 percent.[14] As previously stated,[15] the interrelationship of the Section 2505 unified gift tax credit[16] and the Section 2502 rates results in a flat 35 percent gift tax rate on taxable gifts made after 2009 through 2012.[17]

Prior to 1976, the gift tax rates were exactly 75 percent of the corresponding estate tax rates. As a justification for equalizing the rates, the House Committee Report states:

> The tax burden imposed on transfers of the same amount of wealth should be substantially the same whether the transfers are made both during life and at death or made only upon death. As a practical matter, the preferences for lifetime transfers are available only for wealthier individuals who are able to afford lifetime transfers....[P]references for lifetime transfers principally benefit the wealthy and result in eroding the transfer tax base.[18]

The Committee Report recognizes that some advantages still exist with respect to inter vivos giving.[19] However, an objection can be made to the rate equalization.[20] When one makes a gift tax payment, the government immedi-

---

[14] See IRC § 2502(a)(2) as amended by the Economic Growth and Tax Relief Reconciliation Act of 2001, Pub. L. No. 107-16, § 511(d), 115 Stat. 38, 70 (2001), reprinted in 2001-3 CB 9, 42, for the year 2010. See IRC § 2502(a) for the years 2011 and 2012. The 35 percent rate is also the maximum income tax rate. IRC § 1(a)-(e).

[15] See supra text accompanying notes 2-5.

[16] See Supplement ¶ 9.06.

[17] However, since the exclusion amount related to the credit was increased from $1 million in 2010 to $5 million in 2011 and $5 million adjusted for inflation in 2012 (see Supplement ¶ 9.06[1]) and assuming a donor has made no prior taxable gifts, a $5 million taxable gift in 2010 would have generated $1,400,000 of gift tax liability, while, again assuming no prior taxable gifts, a $5 million taxable gift in 2011 or 2012 would result in no gift tax liability. Cf. infra note 30.

In 2013, the rates are sunsetted to their 2001 level. Under the sunset provision effective January 1, 2013, the top gift tax rate of 55 percent is restored, as is the 5-percent surtax on transfers in excess of $10 million, which eliminates the graduated tax rates. See text accompanying supra notes 10 and 11. See also the Economic Growth and Tax Relief Reconciliation Act of 2001, Pub. L. No. 107-16 § 901(a)(2), 115 Stat. 38, 150 (2001), reprinted in 2001-3 CB 9, 122, as amended by the Tax Relief Act of 2010, Pub. L. No. 111-312, §§ 101(a)(1), 304, 124 Stat. 3296, 3298, 3304 (2010). The sunset provision is discussed more fully at Supplement ¶ 8.11.

[18] HR Rep. No. 1380, 94th Cong., 2d Sess. 11 (1976), reprinted in 1976-3 CB (Vol. 3), 735, 745.

[19] HR Rep. No. 1380, 94th Cong., 2d Sess. 12 (1976), reprinted in 1976-3 CB (Vol. 3) 735, 746. See Supplement ¶ 2.01[3].

[20] In addition, while Congress provided for transfer tax rate equalization, it currently fails to provide for income tax basis equalization. Compare Section 1014, generally providing a fair market value basis at death for property taxed under the estate tax, with Section 1015, generally providing a carryover of the donor's basis for property taxed under the gift tax. In 1976, Congress enacted a modified carryover basis rule for property taxed under the estate tax, but the rule was retroactively repealed in 1980. See IRC § 1023 as

ately has the use of money that would otherwise be producing more wealth for the donor until the donor's death. That additional cost to the donor's overall wealth was seemingly overlooked by Congress in its rate "equalization." Avoidance of this additional cost was a justification for the previous rate discrepancy. Conceivably, a modest credit against the estate tax could be allowed, figured with regard to interest on what are in effect prepayments of estate tax with a view to the time elapsed between payment of the gift tax and the donor's death. Such a credit would encourage lifetime gifts, probably a desirable consequence of the abandoned rate differential.

After 1976, it is less likely than it was before 1977 that it is better to give than to bequeath,[21] but as indicated in the introduction to Chapter 2, there are still advantages to inter vivos giving.[22]

[3] Method of Computation

To simplify the explanation of the gift tax computation, disregard for the moment the problem of determining taxable gifts and assume that the statute simply taxes all gifts. Section 2502 requires that (1) a tentative tax figure be determined by applying the current tax rates to all gifts made since June 6, 1932,[23] including gifts made in the current year for which tax liability is being determined and (2) a second tentative tax figure be determined by applying the *current tax rates*[24] to all gifts made since June 6, 1932, but not including gifts made in the current year. The excess of the first tentative figure over the second is the tax on gifts for the current year.[25]

Reference to the computation of a tax on gifts in preceding periods may make it appear that in some fashion the earlier gifts are again being subjected to tax. The statute has neither that purpose nor that effect; instead, the effect is

---

enacted by the Tax Reform Act of 1976, Pub. L. No. 94-455 § 2005(a), 90 Stat. 1520, 1872 (1976), reprinted in 1976-3 CB (vol. 1) 1, 348, prior to repeal by the Windfall Profit Tax Act of 1980, Pub. L. No. 96-223 § 401, 94 Stat. 229, 299 (1980), reprinted in 1980-3 CB 1, 71. In the year 2010 when the estate tax could electively be terminated, Congress reenacted a similar modified carryover basis provision. Now-repealed IRC § 1022. See Supplement ¶ 8.10[3].

[21] For an analysis of this issue under pre-1977 law, see Stephens, Maxfield & Lind, Federal Estate and Gift Taxation 8-8–8-10 (Warren, Gorham & Lamont, 3d ed. 1974).

[22] See Supplement ¶ 2.01[3].

[23] Section 2502(b) establishes the June 6, 1932, cut-off date.

[24] Section 2502(a)(2) uses the language "computed under such section" which references the current Section 2001(c) rates.

[25] With the exception of Section 2505, there are no statutory credits against the gift tax, such as those against the estate tax discussed in Chapter 3; but in rare circumstances a treaty may provide a credit if the gift is subject to tax by the United States and a foreign country as well. See Form 709, "United States Gift (and Generation-Skipping Transfer) Tax Return" (2010), Part 2, Tax Computation, Line 13; Chapter 7. A few states impose gift taxes. This practice raises the question of whether there should be a federal deduction for state gift taxes, as is provided for state death taxes against the federal estate tax by Section 2058. See ¶ 5.08.

only to fix the rates applicable to the current year's gifts by reference to the total of all gifts made since 1932. Similarly, while the post-1976 rates are being used in both computations, only the current year's gifts are actually being taxed at those rates. This may be more readily understood by a comparison with the computation of tax liability under the graduated income tax rates. With regard to that tax, the taxpayer may be viewed as beginning each year with an empty container marked off with the graduated rates. As income pours in, additional amounts become subject to higher tax rates,[26] but at the end of the year the container is emptied and the process starts all over again.

In the case of the gift tax, the container is never emptied.[27] Instead, any gift made since June 6, 1932, stays in the container and gifts made in later periods are poured in on top of earlier years' gifts to form a layer that is subject to higher rates than if the entire computation were begun afresh for each taxable period.[28]

The effect of Section 2502 in this respect can best be illustrated by the use of numbers that correspond to the Section 2505 credit. Suppose an individual has made taxable gifts in the total amount of $5 million in the year 2011 and then makes taxable gifts of $1 million in the year 2012. The computation would be as follows:

Tax on all gifts, including current year ($6 million)	$2,080,800
Less tax on gifts made in prior periods ($5 million)[29]	
taxed at current rates[30]	-1,730,800
Tax on current year's gifts	$ 350,000

The same result is reached if the 35 percent rate, applicable to gifts above $500,000, is applied directly to the $1 million amount of taxable gifts for the current year.[31]

---

[26] IRC § 1.

[27] See, however, Section 2001(b), under which the container is emptied at the end of 1976 for purposes of computing *estate* tax liability under the unified rate table.

[28] See Supplement ¶ 9.06.

[29] Since the prior years' gifts were made in 2011, the gift tax liability on those gifts would have been eliminated by the Section 2505 credit discussed at ¶ 9.06. See infra note 30.

[30] If the prior taxable gifts had been made in years prior to 2010, the tax rates were higher for those years, but the current year's 35 percent rate is nevertheless employed to again properly reach a $350,000 tax on the current year's gifts. If the prior years' higher rates were used under Section 2502(a)(2), there would be a reduction or elimination of the current year's Section 2502(a) tax. For example, if the taxable gifts had been made in 2009, when the maximum rate was 45 percent, the tax on the prior gifts would have been $2,130,800, in effect eliminating any tax in the current year since $2,130,800 exceeds $2,080,800.

[31] Even though the donor had used the donor's $5 million Section 2505 applicable exclusion amount in 2011, the donor might have had some additional credit in 2012 because of inflation adjustments to the basic exclusion amount (see IRC § 2010(c)(3)(C)) or

Section 2502(b) defines "preceding calendar period" to make it plain that gifts made on or before June 6, 1932, are to be disregarded in the computation of the tax. The critical date is the date of first enactment of the current gift tax law; by making the tax inapplicable to gifts made on or before that date, Congress escaped constitutional difficulties previously encountered under the earlier 1924 statute.[32] The definition also makes it clear that calendar quarters, used from 1971 to 1981 (inclusive) for purposes of gift tax administration, have been replaced by a return to the calendar year.[33]

[4] Liability for the Gift Tax

Section 2502(c) provides that the tax shall be paid by the donor. This fastens the primary liability for the tax on the donor; the donee's secondary liability for the tax is explained at the end of the discussion of Section 2503.[34] As between donor and donee, the ultimate financial burden may be shifted by an agreement that the donee will pay the tax.[35] Of course, such an agreement does not affect the right of the Commissioner to collect the tax from either donor or donee in accordance with established procedures.

---

because of a deceased spouse's unused exclusion amount (see IRC § 2010(c)(4)). See Supplement ¶ 9.06[1].

[32] See ¶ 9.01.

[33] See ¶ 9.02 note 22.

[34] See ¶ 9.04[11].

[35] An incidental effect of these agreements is to reduce the amount of the gift and consequently the amount of the gift tax. See the discussion of Section 2512 at ¶ 10.02[6][d]. The income tax ramifications of such agreements are also discussed at ¶ 10.02[6][d] note 181.

¶ 9.04 SECTION 2503. TAXABLE GIFTS

[1] The Annual Exclusion

Page 9-14:

Add to note 5.

For gifts made in 2006, the annual gift tax exclusion increases to $12,000. Rev. Proc. 2005-70. For gifts made in 2007, the annual gift tax exclusion remains at $12,000. Rev. Proc. 2006-53. For gifts made in 2008, the annual gift tax exclusion remains at $12,000. Rev. Proc. 2007-66, 2007-__ IRB __. For gifts made in 2009, the annual gift tax exclusion increases to $13,000. Rev. Proc. 2008-66, IRB 2008-45. For gifts made in 2010, the annual gift tax exclusion remains at $13,000. Rev. Proc. 2009-50. For gifts made in 2011, the annual gift tax exclusion remains at $13,000. Rev. Proc. 2010-40.

Add to note 9.

For gifts made in 2006, the annual gift tax exclusion increases to $12,000. Rev. Proc. 2005-70. For gifts made in 2007, the gift tax exclusion remains at $12,000. Rev. Proc. 2006-53. For gifts made in 2008, the annual gift tax exclusion remains at $12,000. Rev. Proc. 2007-66, 2007-__ IRB __. For gifts made in 2009, the annual gift tax exclusion increases to $13,000. Rev. Proc. 2008-66, IRB 2008-45. For gifts made in 2010, the annual gift tax exclusion remains at $13,000. Rev. Proc. 2009-50. For gifts made in 2011, the annual gift tax exclusion remains at $13,000. Rev. Proc. 2010-40.

Add the following to the second paragraph of note 10 after reference to "§ 2523(i)(2)."

In 2003, the amount is $112,000. Rev. Proc. 2002-70, 2002-36 IRB 1. In 2004, the amount is $114,000. Rev. Proc. 2003-85, 2003-49 IRB 1104. In 2005, the amount is $117,000. Rev. Proc. 2004-71, 2004-50 IRB 970. In 2006, the amount is $120,000. Rev. Proc. 2005-70, 2005-47 IRB 979. In 2007, the amount is $125,000. Rev. Proc. 2006-53, 2006-48 IRB 996. In 2008, the amount is $128,000. Rev. Proc. 2007-66, 2007-__ IRB __. In 2009, the amount is $133,000. Rev. Proc. 2008-66, IRB 2008-45. In 2010, the amount is $134,000. Rev. Proc. 2009-50. In 2011, the amount is $136,000. Rev. Proc. 2010-40.

[b] Identification of Donees

[ii] Gifts to other entities.

Page 9-18:

Add the following to end of the first sentence of note 29.

See ¶ 10.01[2][b][ii] note 25.1.

[iii] Gift by an entity.

Add to note 30:

See also Priv. Ltr. Rul. 200608011 (Nov. 15, 2005) (gift to a social club organized as a nonprofit mutual benefit corporation exempt under Section 501(c)(7) is a gift to the entity, not to the other members of the club individually, and only one gift tax annual exclusion will apply).

[iv] Gifts to charitable organizations.

Add to note 33.

Priv. Ltr. Rul. 200533001 (May 9, 2005).

[v] Straw person.

Page 9-19:

Add to note 35 after citation to "Estate of Schuler".

, aff'd, 282 F3d 575 (8th Cir. 2002)

In note 36 replace "78 TCM (CCH) 456 (1999)" *with* "251 F3d 1168 (8th Cir. 2001)".

[3] Definition of "Future Interests"

Page 9-21:

Add to note 46.

By statute, a transfer of cash to a qualified state tuition plan is not a transfer of a future interest. IRC § 529(c)(2)(A)(i); Prop. Reg. § 1.529-5(b)(1).

[a] Separate Interests Tested

Page 9-21:

Add to note 48.

Notice 2009-18 provides supplements to the actuarial tables prescribed under IRC § 7520 by providing factors for interest rates below 2.2 percent. As required by Section 7520(c)(3), the Service issued proposed, temporary and final regulations on May 7, 2009, revising Table S and Table U(1), the tables used to value annuities, interests for life or a term of years, and reversionary and remainder interests in property, to reflect the mortality experience from the 2000 census (Life Table 2000CM). Transition rules allow taxpayers to use tables based on either Life Table 90CM or Life Table 2000CM to value gift, chari-table and estate transfers made on or after May 1, 2009, but before July 1, 2009, but they must use the appropriate interest rate for the month in which the valuation date falls, re-gardless of which table is chosen. TD 9448; REG-107845-08. Reg. §§ 1.170A-12T, 1.642(c)-6T, 1.664-4T, 20.2031-7T, 20.2032A-1T, 20.2056A-4T, 25.2512-5T, 25.2522(c)-3, 1.7520-1T, 20.7520-1T, and Reg. § 25.7520-1T. Publications 1457 and 1458 (rev. May 2009), both of which include examples for using the mortality component ta-bles, have been released. On August 10, 2011, the Service issued final regulations that re-moved the temporary regulations issued in TD 9448 and adopted as final the proposed regulations issued in REG-107845-08. The only substantive change was the deletion of an example in the Section 2032 regulations which the Service anticipates including in a dif-ferent regulation project under that Code section. TD 9540; Reg. §§ 1.170A-12, 1.642(c)-6, 1.664-4, 20.2031-7, 20.2032-1, 20.2056A-4, 25.2512-5, 25.2522(c)-3, 1.7520-1, 20.7520-1, 25.7520-1.

[b] Non-Income-Producing Property

Page 9-24:

Add to note 61.

Notice 2009-18 provides supplements to the actuarial tables prescribed under IRC § 7520 by providing factors for interest rates below 2.2 percent.

Page 9-25:

In note 64, replace Prop. Reg. §§ 20.2056(b)-5(f)(1), 20.2056(b)-7(d)(1), 25.2523(e)-1(f)(1) *with* Reg. §§ 20.2056(b)-5(f)(1), 20.2056(b)-7(d)(1), 25.2523(e)-1(f)(1) *and replace* Proposed Regulation Section 1.643(b)-1 *with* Regulations Section 1.643(b)-1.

[e] Right to Enjoyment Suffices

Page 9-29:

In note 88, replace reference to the "Hackl" *case with the following.*

  In Hackl v. Commissioner, 118 TC 279 (2002) aff'd, 335 F3d 664 (7th Cir. 2003), the Tax Court (Judge Nimms) held that various gifts of ownership units in a limited liability company controlled by the donor did not qualify the annual gift tax exclusion. The donor had purchased two tree farms and placed them, together with cash and publicly traded securities, in a limited liability company. The donor and his wife both had 50 percent interests in the limited liability company voting and nonvoting units and under the operating agreement the donor was designated as the manager of the limited liability company for life or until resignation, removal, or incapacity. As manager, the donor had control over distributions, transfers of ownership interests, and other actions pertaining to the limited liability company. The donor and his wife claimed annual exclusions for gifts of membership units in the limited liability company and the Service disallowed the exclusions. The Court rejected the donor's argument that where a gift takes the form of an outright transfer of an equity interest in property no further analysis is required or permitted. Although not as analytically clear as might be desired, the opinion effectively concluded that the donees did not receive the right to the use, possession, or enjoyment of the property because of the absence of an income stream and the degree of control over economic benefit from the property retained by the donor in his position as manager of the limited liability company. Applying *Hackl's* methodology, the Tax Court in Price v. Comm'r, TC Memo. 2010-2 (2010), concluded that a couple's gifts to their children of limited partnership interests in FLP failed to qualify for the annual gift tax exclusion because the children did not have the unrestricted right to the immediate use, possession or enjoyment of the transferred property or the income therefrom. The court noted the restrictions in the FLP on the donee's ability to transfer or liquidate their interests, the fact that the donees were not even properly characterized as partners of the FLP and were effectively only assigned a right to receive profits, and that no ascertainable portion of the FLP's income would flow steadily to them. See also Fisher v. United States, 2010-1 USTC ¶ 60,588 (SD Ind. 2010) (citing *Hackl*, the Court held that gifts of interests in an LLC, whose primary asset is beach front property on Lake Michigan, did not qualify for the annual gift tax exclusion due to restrictions in the operating agreement preventing the donees from presently realizing any substantial financial or economic benefit from the gifted interests—the LLC's general manager had complete discretion over distribution of any potential proceeds, the right to use the LLC's primary asset is a non-pecuniary benefit and limitations on the donees' ability to transfer their interests made it impossible for them to realize a present economic benefit from a sale of their interests).

Add to note 89.

The regulations provide that a transfer to a corporation that operates for "charitable, public, political or similar" purposes may constitute a gift to the organization as a single entity. Reg. § 25.2511-1(h)(1). In that situation, the gift qualifies for the gift tax annual exclusion. See Priv. Ltr. Rul. 200533001 (May 9, 2005).

[f] *Crummey* Powers

Page 9-30:

Add to note 96.

In Estate of Turner v. Comm'r, TC Memo. 2011-209 (2011), the Tax Court held that decedent's payments of life insurance premiums on policies that were held in a Crummey trust for the benefit of his children and grandchildren were present interest gifts that qualified for the annual exclusion since the terms of the trust gave the beneficiaries the right to demand withdrawals from the trust after each direct or indirect transfer.

Page 9-31:

Add to note 101.

In Estate of Turner v. Comm'r, TC Memo. 2011-209 (2011), the Tax Court held that decedent's payments of life insurance premiums on policies that were held in a Crummey trust for the benefit of his children and grandchildren were present interest gifts that qualified for the annual exclusion. The Court noted that the fact that transfers were made to the trust through the payment of insurance premiums and that not all beneficiaries were notified of the transfers was irrelevant since the beneficiaries had the legal right under the trust to withdraw the same payments that were used to pay the insurance premiums.

Page 9-32:

Add to note 110.

Cf. TAM 200341002 (June 5, 2003) (*Crummey* power given to charity held invalid because it would be a breach of charity's fiduciary obligation to not exercise the power which went unexercised on forty-four different occasions).

Page 9-34:

Add to first paragraph of note 119 prior to cf. cite.

Priv. Ltr. Ruls. 200426005, 200426006, 200426007 (Mar. 22, 2004) (estate tax impact of severance of trust established for each of grantor's children into two separate trusts on a fractional basis, one trust holding the assets from the original trust attributable to the first $5,000 of the grantor's original contribution and the other trust holding the assets from the original trust attributable to grantor's original contribution in excess of $5,000).

[g] Qualified Tuition Programs and Education Savings Accounts

Page 9-35:

Add to note 124.

The Pension Protection Act of 2006 has added Section 529(f) to permit the Service to prescribe any estate, gift or GST tax regulations necessary to carry out the purposes of Section 529 or to prevent abuse of such purposes. Pension Protection Act of 2006, Pub. L. No. 109-280, § 1304(b), __ Stat. __, __ (2006), reprinted in 2006-__ CB __, __.

Acting under such authority, the Service, in an Advanced Notice of Proposed Rulemaking, seeks comments from the public regarding rules it proposes on the transfer tax treatment of Section 529 accounts in Qualified Tuition Programs and, in addition, the Service seeks to provide a general anti-abuse rule that applies when 529 accounts are established or used to avoid or evade transfer tax, or for other purposes inconsistent with Section 529. REG-127127-05.

Page 9-36:

Add to note 130.

In Private Letter Ruling 200743001 (June 15, 2007), donor failed to make the election on Line B of Schedule A of Form 709 but substantially complied with the requirements for making an election by attaching a statement to the return indicating her intent to prorate her contributions over a five-year period.

Replace the sentence after reference to note 135 with the following.

However, if, under either type of plan, there is a change in the designation of the beneficiary or a rollover from the account of one beneficiary to another beneficiary and the new beneficiary is not a family member of the old beneficiary[136] or is assigned by the generation assignment rules of the generation-skipping transfer tax to a generation below the old beneficiary,[137] there is a taxable transfer from the old beneficiary to the new beneficiary.[137.1]

---

[136] IRC §§ 529(c)(5)(B)(ii), 530(d)(3); Prop. Reg. § 1.529-5(b)(3)(i).

[137] IRC §§ 529(c)(5)(B)(i), 530(d)(3); Prop. Reg. §§ 1.529-5(b)(3)(ii), 1.529-5(b)(3)(iii) Ex. See IRC § 2651. See ¶ 17.01. Such transfer may also constitute a generation-skipping transfer if the new beneficiary is a skip person in relation to the old beneficiary. Prop. Reg. § 1.529-5(b)(3)(ii).

[137.1] The five-year spreading rule also applies to such transfers by beneficiaries. Prop. Reg. § 1.529-5(b)(3)(ii). See supra text accompanying notes 130-134.

[5] Special Statutory Rule for Minor Donees

[a] First Requirement

Page 9-39:

Add to note 145.

Priv. Ltr. Rul. 200633015 (May 12, 2006) (a couple's transfers to three irrevocable trusts for the benefit of their minor grandchildren are excluded for gift tax purposes pursuant to Section 2503(c) from the date of their creation).

[b] Second Requirement

Page 9-40:

Add to note 150.

Priv. Ltr. Rul. 200633015 (May 12, 2006) (interest qualifies for exclusion where minor has the right to terminate trust upon reaching age 21 and, if not exercised within sixty days after receiving notice, the right to terminate will lapse and the trust will then continue).

[6] Medical Expenses and Tuition

Page 9-44:

Add to note 180.

Priv. Ltr. Rul. 200602002 (Sept. 6, 2005) (prepayments of tuition for each of six grandchildren pursuant to written agreements with school that payments would not be refundable and would not give the grandchildren any additional rights or privileges over other students will qualify for Section 2503(e) unlimited gift tax exclusion).

[9] Gift Tax Returns

Page 9-46:

Add to note 197.

As part of a compliance initiative aimed specifically at taxpayers who transfer real property for little or no consideration, the Service filed, on December 27, 2010, a petition seeking leave to file a John Doe summons on the California Board of Equalization to obtain information on taxpayers who failed to file a gift tax return after transferring real property to a family member. The court, in an action entitled In Re the tax liabilities of John Does, No. 2:10-mc-00130-MCE-EFB (ED Cal. 2011), denied the petition because the Service had failed to establish that it had exhausted other available remedies within the BOE and the various county assessors. Previously, the Service has sought and received information at the state or county level in Connecticut, Florida, Hawaii, Nebraska, New Hampshire, New Jersey, New York, North Carolina, Ohio, Pennsylvania, Tennessee, Texas, Virginia, and Washington.

Page 9-47:

Add to note 204.

The Service has released the final version of Form 709, U.S. Gift (and Generation-Skipping Transfer) Tax Return for gifts made in 2010 and several versions of related instructions. The instructions note the following changes for the 2010 version of the form: (1) the annual exclusion for gifts of present interests remains at $13,000 per donee; (2) the annual exclusion for gifts to non-citizen spouses has increased to $134,000; (3) the generation-skipping transfer tax rate for 2010 is zero; (4) the top rate on gifts decreased to 35 percent, which caused the unified credit to drop to $330,800; and (5) any unified credit previously allocated to gifts made in past years shall be redetermined under current gift tax rates. On March 30, the Service released its third version of the instructions which include the Table of Unified Credits (as Recalculated for 2010 Rates), which provides the unified credits for all tax periods beginning in 1977, as recalculated using the 2010 maximum gift tax rate of 35 percent.

Add to note 206.

In email advice, CCA 201116018 (Apr. 22, 2011), the Service's Chief Counsel determined that a late-filing penalty against a donor for failure to file a gift tax return was proper even though donor suffered from an illness. Although illness may be evidence of reasonable cause, the Service found in this case that the donor had been competent enough during the time period the gift tax return was to be filed to conduct a real estate transaction. Consequently, it was not improper to assert the failure-to-file penalty.

Add to note 209.

See also IRC § 7508A which was added by the Taxpayer Relief Act of 1997, Pub. L. No. 105-34, 111 Stat. 788, 877-78 (1997) and final regulations issued thereunder, TD 9443, 74 FR 2370-2373 (Jan. 15, 2009), relating to the postponement of certain tax-related acts by reason of a federally declared disaster or terroristic or military action.

Add to note 210.

If a donor does not obtain an extension of time to file his or her income tax return, the donor will be allowed an automatic six-month extension to file his or her federal gift tax return by submitting a complete application on Form 8892, Payment of Gift/GST Tax and/or Application for Extension of Time to File Form 709. Reg. § 25.6081-1. An automatic extension of time for filing Form 709 will not extend the time for payment of any tax due on the return. Reg. § 25.6081-1(c). In general, Form 8892 must be filed by the gift tax return's due date.

[10] Limitations on Assessment

[a] Commencement of Limitations Period

Page 9-49:

Add to note 219.

In CCA 200916022 (Dec. 18, 2008), the Office of Chief Counsel, in a highly redacted analysis, discussed whether certain exchanges of family LLC interests in return for annuities were adequately disclosed on a gift tax return. In its recommendation, the Office of Chief Counsel notes what information is necessary for a reported property transfer to be "adequately disclosed" under Section 6501(c)(9) and, as a result, subject to the statute of limitations. Three primary concerns were raised: (1) Regulations Section 25.2702-3(b) which prohibits the use of the mortality component of the actuarial tables to calculate the present value of an annuity if the measuring life is considered to have at least a 50 percent probability of dying within one year of the date the gift was completed; (2) Regulations Section 301.6501(c)-1(f)(2)(iv) which requires a detailed description of the method used to determine the fair market value of transferred property, the Office of Chief Counsel noting that the taxpayer bears the burden of demonstrating the appropriateness of any discounted valuation; and (3) Regulations Section 301.6501(c)-1(f)(4) which provides that any transfer reported as not constituting a gift will only be deemed adequately disclosed if the return contains an explanation of why the transfer is not a gift under the Internal Revenue Code.

Add to note 220.

In CCA 201024059 (May 11, 2010), the Office of Chief Counsel ruled, in email advice, that the failure by a donor of closely held stock to disclose on the Form 709 any information regarding either the method used to value the stock or a description of the discounts taken appeared to indicate that the gift tax imposed on the transfer could be assessed at any time.

[11] Donee and Fiduciary Liability

Page 9-52:

Add to note 245.

In United States v. Davenport, Doc. No. 06-40466 (5th Cir. 2007), the Fifth Circuit determined that res judicata binds donee to the Tax Court's determination of value of the gifted property, an issue which had been litigated in the donor's estate, and precludes donee from litigating other issues established therein. Accordingly, donee is liable under Section 6324(b) for all gift tax owed by the donor's estate up to the value of the gift donee received.

¶ 9.05 SECTION 2504. TAXABLE GIFTS FOR PRECEDING CALENDAR PERIODS

[2] Valuation for Prior Years

[a] Gifts Made Through August 5, 1997

Page 9-57:

Add to note 19.

E.g., Priv. Ltr. Rul. 200334020 (May 13, 2003) (adjustment in previous year's taxable gifts and Section 2505 credit allowed since state court determination that gifts from marital trust with spendthrift provision were null and void and involved an issue other than valuation).

¶ 9.06 SECTION 2505. UNIFIED CREDIT AGAINST THE GIFT TAX [REVISED]

Replace existing ¶ 9.06 with the following revised ¶ 9.06.

Citizens and residents[1] of the United States are allowed a credit against the gift tax on transfers made after 1976.[2] The gift tax credit is unified with the estate tax credit.[3] Both credits are based upon an "applicable credit amount,"[4] which is a mechanism whereby the amount of dollars shielded from the gift tax by an "applicable exclusion amount"[5] set forth in Section 2010(c) and cross-referenced in Section 2505 is converted to a credit amount. The estate tax return filing requirements are related to the applicable exclusion;[6] however, the gift tax return filing requirements are not related in any way to the amount of the Section 2505 credit.[7] Congress sometimes seems inclined to state the obvious; Section 2505(c) makes it clear that no refund is allowed if the amount of the credit exceeds the gift tax liability imposed under Section 2501.[8]

Use of the gift tax credit is mandatory;[9] failure to use the credit, when available, will result in denial of the credit to the extent it is not used.[10] Statutorily, the denial occurs because Section 2505(a)(2) provides that the amount

---

[1] Nonresident noncitizens are allowed no gift tax credit. HR Rep. No. 1380, 94th Cong., 2d Sess. 17 (1976), reprinted in 1976-3 CB (Vol. 3) 735, 751.

[2] IRC §§ 2505, 2010. Prior to 1977, a $30,000 specific lifetime exemption was allowed under now-repealed Section 2521 but as part of the Tax Reform Act of 1976, Congress eliminated both the gift tax and estate tax exemptions that were deductions and replaced them with credits. See Supplement ¶ 3.02 note 1. Section 2521 was repealed by the Tax Reform Act of 1976, Pub. L. No. 94-455, § 2001(b)(3), 90 Stat. 1520, 1849 (1976), reprinted in 1976-3 CB (Vol. 1) 1, 325. Section 2521 is discussed in detail in Stephens, Maxfield & Lind, "Federal Estate and Gift Taxation" ¶¶ 10.01-10.04 (WG&L 3d ed. 1974). Since a flat rate tax is imposed on taxable transfers after the applicable exemption amount is taken into consideration, if Congress retains the current law beyond 2012 it would simplify the statutory process by returning to an exemption of the applicable exclusion amount for taxable gifts rather than pursuing the complicated credit mechanism. The credit mechanism was appropriate when transfers were taxed atgraduated rates.

[3] See infra ¶ 9.06[2].

[4] IRC § 2505(a)(1). See IRC §§ 2010(c), 2505(a).

[5] See IRC §§ 2010(c)(1), 2010(c)(2).

[6] See IRC § 6018(a)(1); Supplement ¶ 3.02[3].

[7] See IRC §§ 6019, 6075(b), which are discussed at ¶ 9.04[5].

[8] See IRC § 2010(d), providing an identical rule for the estate tax unified credit.

[9] See Staff of Joint Comm. On Tax'n, 94th Cong. 2d Sess., General Explanation of the Tax Reform Act of 1976, at 531 (1976), reprinted in 1976-3 CB (Vol. 2) 1, 543 and Rev. Rul. 79-160, 1979-1 CB 313, illustrating the use of the Section 2505 credit.

Cf. IRC § 2521 (prior to repeal by the Tax Reform Act of 1976, Pub. L. No. 94-455, § 2001(b)(3), 90 Stat. 1520, 1849 (1976), reprinted in 1976-3 CB (Vol. 1) 1,325), under which use of the $30,000 lifetime exemption was elective. The exemption could be used at any time in a taxpayer's gift-giving career.

[10] Rev. Rul. 79-398, 1979-2 CB 338; Rev. Rul. 79-160, 1979-1 CB 313. Failure to use the gift tax credit indirectly precludes use of the estate tax credit. See Supplement ¶ 3.02 text accompanying notes 62 and 63.

of credit available for any subsequent gift must take account of a reduction for the credit "allowable" for preceding gifts.[11]

[1] Amount of the Credit

The gift tax credit was enacted for the year 1977,[12] and it has been increased in varying amounts over the years.[13] In the year 2011, the applicable exclusion amount (which shields taxable gifts from taxation) is generally $5 million[14] which using current tax rates results in an applicable credit amount of $1,730,800.[15] The $5 million applicable exclusion amount may be adjusted for

---

[11] One might want to postpone the credit in order to pay gift tax on the first $500,000 of gifts at rates less than 35 percent; but the statute precludes this.

[12] See supra note 2.

[13] The amount of the credit from the years 1977 to 2010 was as follows:

Year of gift	Credit Amount	Exclusion Amount
1977 (before July 1)	$ 6,000	$ 30,000
1977 (after June 30)	30,000	120,667
1978	34,000	134,000
1979	38,000	147,333
1980	42,500	161,563
1981	47,000	175,625
1982	62,800	225,000
1983	79,300	275,000
1984	96,300	325,000
1985	121,800	400,000
1986	155,800	500,000
1987–1997	192,800	600,000
1998	202,050	625,000
1999	211,300	650,000
2000 and 2001	220,550	675,000
2002–2010	345,800	1,000,000

The applicable credit amounts for the gift tax and the estate tax were equal until the year 2003. Thereafter, until 2010, the gift tax applicable exclusion amount was $1 million, while the estate tax applicable exclusion amount increased in varying phases to $3.5 million in 2009. See Supplement ¶ 3.02 note 12. In 2011 the amounts were again equalized.

[14] IRC §§ 2505(a)(1), 2010(c). But see infra notes 15 and 18–21.

[15] The credit amount reflects the maximum 35 percent rate. See IRC § 2001(c), Supplement ¶ 3.02[1] note 19.

The credit amount is sometimes subject to a minor reduction. If a decedent made inter vivos gifts between September 8, 1976, and January 1, 1977, and used the Section 2521 $30,000 specific lifetime exemption to reduce such gifts (see supra note 2), Section 2505(b) requires a reduction in the amount of the Section 2505 credit by 20 percent of the amount of exemption so used. This results in a maximum Section 2505 credit reduction of $6,000 if the full $30,000 specific exemption was used during such period. Between the adoption of the Tax Reform Act of 1976 and December 31, 1976, there were substantial tax incentives for taxpayers with large estates to make inter vivos gifts at lower tax rates. Although Congress condoned a full use of the $30,000 exemption against gifts made before September 8, 1976, with no reduction in the Section 2505 credit, a credit reduction

inflation in 2012;[16] however, the amount is currently scheduled to "sunset" to the year 2006 level of $1 million in the year 2013.[17] A donor's gift tax applicable exclusion amount includes the "transported" amount of a predeceased spouse's unused exclusion amount.[18] Since, other than inflation adjustments,[19] the ceiling on the transported amount is $5 million,[20] the maximum applicable exclusion amount is $10 million.[21]

The amount of the maximum credit in a year is reduced by the amount of credit allowable in prior years.[22] Since the gift tax rates have been reduced over the years,[23] the amount of the credit allowable in prior years is adjusted to reflect the tax rate reduction to protect the full applicable exclusion amount.[24]

---

in the amount indicated was considered a proper cost for last-minute use of the exemption. A potential donor's prior gift history was an obvious factor in the decision whether to elect to use the Section 2521 exemption during that period. See IRC § 2010(b) which requires an identical reduction in the estate tax credit.

[16] IRC §§ 2505(a)(1), 2010(c)(2)(B). The amount of the inflationary adjustment is determined by multiplying the cost-of-living adjustment determined under a modified version of Section 1(f)(3) for the calendar year by $5 million. IRC § 2010(c)(3)(B). The Section 1(f)(3) cost-of-living adjustment for 2012 is modified by taking into consideration the amount of inflation between 2010 and 2011. IRC § 2010(c)(3)(b)(ii). Inflationary adjustments will be made only in multiples of $10,000, rounded to the next lowest multiple of $10,000. IRC § 2010(c)(3) flush language.

[17] Under the "sunset" provision effective January 1, 2013, the $1 million applicable exclusion amount for the year 2006 will apply to the estates of decedents dying after the year 2012. Economic Growth and Tax Relief Reconciliation Act of 2001, Pub. L. No. 107-16 § 901(a)(2), 115 Stat. 38, 150 (2001), reprinted in 2001-3 CB 9, 122, as amended by the Tax Relief Act of 2010, Pub. L. No. 111-312, §§ 101(a)(1), 304, 124 Stat. 3296, 3298, 3304 (2010). The "sunset" provision is discussed more fully at Supplement ¶ 8.11.

[18] See Supplement ¶ 3.02[1][b].

[19] In 2012, a donor's $5 million "basic" exclusion amount is adjusted for inflation as is a predeceased spouse's unused exclusion amount prior to being transported to a surviving spouse donor. IRC §§ 2010(c)(3), 2010(c)(4)(B)(i). However, once transported, the predeceasing spouse's unused exclusion amount is not adjusted for inflation. Thus, if a predeceasing spouse dies in 2011, there is no inflation adjustment to the unused exclusion amount; whereas if the predeceasing spouse dies in 2012, an inflation adjustment may be made to the basic exclusion amount prior to its being transported to the surviving spouse. IRC §§ 2010(c)(3), 2010(c)(4).

[20] IRC § 2010(c)(4). See Supplement ¶ 3.02 text accompanying note 33.

[21] The Secretary is to provide regulations applicable to the portability rule. IRC § 2010(c)(6).

See infra ¶ 9.06[2] for the interrelationship of the Section 2505 and Section 2010 credits.

[22] IRC § 2505(a)(2). Cf. supra note 15.

[23] See Supplement ¶ 9.03[2].

[24] IRC §2505(a) flush language. Thus, if Donor having made no prior taxable gifts, had made a $1 million taxable gift in 2009, which was allowed a $345,800 credit using 2009 tax rates, and if in 2011 Donor makes a $4 million taxable gift, Donor will have a Section 2505 credit in 2011 of $1,730,800 under Section 2505(a)(1) reduced under Section 2505(a)(2) by $330,800 (not $345,800) or a 2011 credit of $1,400,000 which equals the Section 2502 tax on the $4 million taxable gift. Note that Donor would owe $15,000

Because of the increases in the applicable exclusion amounts,[25] a donor could be required to pay tax on a "taxable gift" in a year before the credit was increased and yet be required to pay no tax on a transfer of a "taxable gift" in a subsequent year when the credit was larger. For example, if a donor, having made no prior gifts, made $1.5 million of "taxable gifts" in 2009 and makes $3 million of "taxable gifts" in 2011, the 2009 transfer would have generated a gift tax of $555,800 that was reduced by a $345,800 Section 2505 credit, resulting in $210,000 of gift tax liability for 2009.[26] The year 2011 transfer of $3 million of "taxable gifts" results in no actual gift tax liability, because the gift tax on that transfer is $1,050,000,[27] but that liability is eliminated by the remaining Section 2505 credit computed at 2011 rates which is $1,400,000 ($1,730,800 reduced by the $330,800 credit previously allowable).[28] Thus, no tax is due. However, no refund of the prior $210,000 of taxes properly paid is allowed.[29]

While the Section 2505 credit has only been in existence since 1977,[30] the gift tax has been in existence since 1932 and even though there was a different exemption regime in existence for pre-1977 years,[31] gifts between 1932 and 1977 effectively use up a portion of a donor's current credit amount.[32]

---

more in gift taxes in 2011 if the Section 2505(a)(2) adjustment reflecting current rates was not made.

[25] See supra note 13.

[26] This would also constitute an amount of gift tax "payable" under Section 2001(b)(2), although the reduction would have to reflect the changes in rates under Section 2001(c). See Supplement ¶ 2.01[2], text accompanying notes 48-62.

[27] Under Section 2502, this $1,050,000 amount of tax is the difference between the tax on aggregate transfers of $4.5 million equal to $1,555,800 of tax at the year 2011 tax rate, less the $505,800 of tax on preceding transfers of $1.5 million at the 2011 rates.

[28] IRC §§ 2505(a)(1), 2505(a)(2). The donor still has a remaining Section 2505 credit amount of $350,000 ($1,730,800 less $330,800 and $1,050,000). As a result, if the donor makes up to another $1 million of taxable gifts in 2012, no gift tax is incurred.

[29] Cf. IRC § 2505(c).

[30] See supra text accompanying note 1.

[31] See supra note 2.

[32] For example, if Donor made a $30,000 taxable gift in 1975 (and paid no gift tax because of the $30,000 exemption under now-repealed Section 2501, see supra note 2) and Donor made a $5 million gift in 2011, Donor's Section 2502(a) tax (using the year 2011 rates) would be:

Section 2502(a)(1)	$1,741,300
Section 2502(a)(2)	-6,000
	$1,735,300
Section 2505 credit	-1,730,800
	$ 4,500

If $30,000 was taxed at 35 percent, it would result in $10,500 of tax. However because the now-repealed Section 2521 exemption generally does not reduce the Section

[2] Relation to the Section 2010 Credit

Section 2505 provides a credit against gift tax liability for inter vivos transfers that is almost identical to the estate tax credit under Section 2010.[33] Although the credit is referred to as unified, use of the Section 2505 gift tax credit does not reduce the amount of the Section 2010 estate tax credit. At first glance, it may appear that a donor-decedent is allowed the double advantage of both credits; however, as previously explained, the donor-decedent is not provided a double benefit.[34] Under the system, the two credits are effectively used only once.[35] Thus if a decedent, who had never made any prior gifts, made a $5 million taxable gift in 2011 and died later that year with a $5 million taxable estate, the decedent would incur $1,750,000 of estate tax liability.[36]

2505 credit (see supra note 15) an additional $6,000 (20 percent of $30,000) goes untaxed.

[33] See supra ¶ 9.06[1]. The credits are currently equal in amount. Note that while portability of a predeceased spouse's unused exclusion amount is allowed at death (IRC § 2010(c)(4)) no inter vivos transfer of an unused exclusion amount is permitted during a spouse's life. However, a transported unused exclusion amount from a predeceased spouse may be used in an inter vivos transfer by a donor surviving spouse. See supra ¶ 9.06[1] text accompanying note 18.

[34] See Supplement ¶ 3.02 text accompanying notes 54–56.

[35] See Supplement ¶ 3.02 text accompanying note 55. The amount of the estate tax, before credits, is the tentative tax on the sum of the taxable estate and adjusted taxable gifts, reduced by gift taxes payable on post-1976 gifts. Inter vivos use of the gift tax credit reduces taxes payable on post-1976 gifts and correspondingly reduces that reduction in estate tax liability. Because the lifetime use of the credit merely neutralizes gifts that otherwise would have generated gift tax, thereby reducing the estate tax reduction under Section 2001(b)(2), the credit has not been used in an estate tax sense when applied to lifetime gifts. In the end, the Section 2505 and Section 2010 credits result in a single reduction for gift and estate tax purposes.

[36] Under Section 2001(b)(1) there would be a tentative tax on $10 million of $3,480,800 reduced by zero, the gift taxes payable on post-1976 gifts under Section 2001(b)(2) and further reduced by the $1,730,800 estate tax Section 2010 credit amount, resulting in an estate tax liability of $1,750,000. Cf. IRC § 2035(b) discussed at ¶ 4.07[3].

CHAPTER 10

Gift Tax: Transfers Subject to Tax

¶ 10.01		Section 2511. Transfers in General	S10-2
	[2]	Indirect Gifts	S10-2
		[b] Transfers to Entities	S10-3
		[ii] Partnerships or limited liability companies.	S10-3
		[c] Gifts by Entities	S10-4
		[d] Nature of the Transfer	S10-4
		[h] Gift by an Incompetent	S10-4
	[3]	Property Interests Covered	S10-4
		[c] Uncertain Interests	S10-5
		[e] Savings and Formula Clauses	S10-5
		[g] Insurance and Annuities	S10-7
	[5]	Revocable Transfers	S10-11
		[d] Transfers of Community Property	S10-12
	[6]	Power to Change Beneficiaries	S10-12
	[8]	Donor's Power Exercisable Only With Third Persons	S10-13
	[10]	Relationship of the Gift Tax to the Income Tax and the Estate Tax	S10-13
		[e] Powers Held by the Transferor	S10-13
	[11]	Nonresident Noncitizens [Revised]	S10-15
¶ 10.02		Section 2512. Valuation of Gifts	S10-15
	[1]	Time of Valuation	S10-15
		[a] Valuation on Completion	S10-16
	[2]	Methods of Valuation	S10-16
		[b] Special Approaches to Valuation	S10-16
		[ii] Insurance policies.	S10-16
		[iii] Temporal property interests.	S10-16
		[c] Premiums and Discounts for Interests in Property	S10-17
		[ii] Minority interest discount.	S10-17
		[iii] Discount for lack of marketability.	S10-18

		[iv]	Other discounts.	S10-19
		[v]	Discount resulting from a gift on formation.	S10-20
	[d]		Statutes Applicable to Gift Tax Valuation	S10-20
		[iii]	Section 7477.	S10-20
	[3]		Consideration for a Transfer	S10-21
	[4]		Transfers in the Ordinary Course of Business	S10-22
	[5]		Family Obligations	S10-22
		[d]	Elective Share Marital Rights	S10-22
	[6]		Other Receipts of Money's Worth	S10-22
		[c]	Reciprocal Trusts	S10-23
		[d]	Donee's Payment of Gift Tax	S10-23
¶ 10.03			Section 2513. Gifts by Husband or Wife to Third Party . . .	S10-23
	[1]		Introduction	S10-23
	[3]		Signifying Consent	S10-24
		[a]	Manner	S10-24
¶ 10.04			Section 2514. Powers of Appointment	S10-24
	[4]		Treatment of Post-1942 Powers	S10-24
		[a]	In General	S10-24
		[c]	Lapse of Power	S10-24
¶ 10.05			Section 2515. Treatment of Generation-Skipping Transfer Tax	S10-25
¶ 10.06			Section 2516. Certain Property Settlements	S10-25
	[2]		Statutory Requirements	S10-25
		[a]	Type of Transfer	S10-25
	[3]		Comparative Estate Tax Treatment	S10-26
¶ 10.07			Section 2518. Disclaimers	S10-26
	[2]		Definition of "Qualified Disclaimer"	S10-26
		[b]	Disclaimer Must Be Timely	S10-27
		[c]	Disclaimer May Not Follow an Acceptance . . .	S10-29
		[d]	Persons to Whom the Interest Must Pass	S10-29
		[i]	Disclaimer by a surviving spouse.	S10-31
		[ii]	Disclaimers ineffective under local law.	S10-31
	[3]		Effective Date	S10-32
¶ 10.08			Section 2519. Disposition of Certain Life Estates	S10-32
	[1]		The General Rule	S10-32
		[a]	Disposition of a Portion of the Transferee Spouse's Qualifying Income Interest	S10-32
		[b]	Section 2519 Transfer	S10-33
	[2]		Meaning of "Disposition"	S10-34
	[3]		Gift Tax Liability	S10-34

¶ 10.01 SECTION 2511. TRANSFERS IN GENERAL

[2] Indirect Gifts

Page 10-5:

Add to note 13 just after the parenthetical description of "Estate of Maggos".

, rev'd on another issue, 89 AFTR2d (RIA) 2002-1691 (9th Cir. 2002) (unpublished per curiam opinion)

Page 10-6:

Add to end of note 13.

Some events that may appear to be indirect transfers are not, due to long-recognized principles of state law. Where, with proper proof, a trust is reformed to conform to the grantor's original intent, the reformation relates back to the date of the trust's creation and thus what may appear to be changes in legal rights and possible indirect transfers are not. See, for example, Priv. Ltr. Rul. 200318064 (Jan. 28, 2003) (ruling that the reformation of a trust to allow afterborn children of the grantor to share in all transfers made to the trust, including transfers made before their birth, did not result in a gift by the child living at the trust's creation to the afterborn children). See also Priv. Ltr. Rul. 200334025 (May 14, 2003) (the Service ruled that the exercise of the independent trustees' statutory power to make adjustments between principal and income of a trust did not cause the remaindermen trustees to be treated as having made a gift to the income beneficiary).

[b] Transfers to Entities

[ii] Partnerships or limited liability companies.

Page 10-8:

Add the following to the end of ¶ 10.01[2][b][ii].

The situation here where a donor makes a transfer to a pre-existing entity should be compared with that in which a donor transfers property to a new entity and immediately transfers interests in the entity to donees. In the latter situation, the courts have in essence applied the step transaction doctrine and treated it as a transfer of assets by the donor to the donees followed by the donees' transfer to the entity thus reducing the discounts allowed on the transfer.[25.1]

[25.1] Shepherd v. Comm'r, 283 F3d 1258 (11th Cir. 2002). See also Senda v. Comm'r, 433 F3d 1044 (8th Cir. 2006) (taxpayers' transfers of assets to family limited partnerships, coupled with gifts by taxpayers of limited partnership interests to children, effectively were gifts of assets to the children); Heckerman v. United States, 2009-2 USTC ¶ 60,578 (D. Wash. 2009) (same). Compare Holman v. Comm'r, 130 TC 170 (2008) , aff'd, Doc. No. 08-3774 (8th Cir. 2010) (separate transfers with discounts, distinguishing *Senda*, where contribution of stock to the family limited partnership occurred six days before the taxpayers' gifts of limited partnership interests for the benefit of their children) and Gross v. Comm'r, TC Memo. 2008-221 (2008) (gifts to daughters were of interests in FLP rather than indirect gifts of the securities donor had contributed to the FLP because donor's contributions were properly credited to the parties' capital accounts and, citing *Holman*, the step transaction doctrine did not apply because the donor bore a real economic risk of a change in the value of the FLP for the eleven-day period between the donor's contributions to the FLP and the gifts). See also Linton v. United States, 638 F. Supp. 2d 1277 (WD Wash. 2009), aff'd in part, rev'd in part and remanded, Linton v. United States, Doc. No. 09-35681 (9th Cir. 2011) (reversing the district court's use of the step-transaction doctrine in awarding summary judgment to the government by holding that such doctrine did not apply in this case).

The Service recently cited *Senda* in its Appeals Settlement Guidelines: Family Limited Partnerships and Family Limited Liability Corporations, effective October 20, 2006. The guidelines address, among other things, whether there is an indirect gift of the entity's underlying assets, rather than the FLP interests, where the funding of the FLP and the gifting of the FLP interests are effectively integrated. The settlement guidelines provide the positions of both the government and the taxpayer and include a discussion of the applicable case law with respect to each issue the Service addresses. The full text of the settlement guidelines is available on the Service's website. See also ¶ 9.04[1][b][ii] note 29, ¶ 10.02[2][c][v] notes 118 and 119.

[c] Gifts by Entities

Page 10-9:

In note 30, replace all references to "Section 2501(a)(5)" with "Section 2501(a)(4)".

[d] Nature of the Transfer

Page 10-9:

Add to note 32.

But cf. Priv. Ltr. Rul. 200842007 (June 24, 2008) (grantor's substitution of stock he personally owns for assets of equal value held in grantor trust he created, and under which he holds a power of substitution, will not constitute a gift to the trust for gift tax purposes if the fair market value of assets transferred to the trust equals the fair market value of assets transferred from the trust).

[h] Gift by an Incompetent

Page 10-15:

Add to note 69.

Generally, an attorney-in-fact is not authorized to make gifts for the principal where the power of attorney is silent on the issue. See, e.g., Cal. Prob. Code § 4264 and Barnett v. United States, 2009-2 USTC ¶ 60,576 (WD Penn. 2009) (Pennsylvania law limits the attorney-in-fact's power to make gifts to only those instances where such language is specifically provided in the power of attorney).

[3] Property Interests Covered

Page 10-16:

Add to note 76.

See Priv. Ltr. Rul. 200618003 (Jan. 19, 2006) (execution of a trust construction agreement by a trust's beneficiaries, court approval of that agreement and trustee's creation of a separate trust funded by a distribution of assets from the original trust will not result in a taxable gift by the trust beneficiaries or the trustee).

Add new note 78.1 to the end of sentence following note 78.

[78.1] The receipt of community property one half by each spouse from the earnings of either results in no gift as each owns one half of such property and makes no transfer. This includes receipts by registered domestic partners under California law. Priv. Ltr. Rul. 201021048 (May 5, 2010).

[c] Uncertain Interests

Page 10-18:

Add to note 97.

Priv. Ltr. Rul. 200917004 (Dec. 16, 2008) (court-ordered modification of irrevocable trust to increase the number of contingent beneficiaries by including legally adopted children in the trust's definition of "issue" and "descendants" results in taxable gifts from existing beneficiaries of trust to the new contingent beneficiaries).

[e] Savings and Formula Clauses

Page 10-19:

Replace existing ¶ 10.01[3][e] with new ¶ 10.01[3][e].

In a case[104] in which the donor sought to make a donative transfer void to the extent that it was held to be taxable, the court concluded that the condition was void as contrary to public policy and upheld the Commissioner's assertion of a deficiency. The court refused to condone "this sort of trifling with the judicial process,"[105] pointing out, among other things, that when the transfer was held taxable the condition would operate to set the decree aside. The holding of the case has been extended to other cases to void what are commonly referred to as "safety clauses" where there are valuation questions in a donative transfer made on the condition that a portion of the transfer will be void (returned to the donor) to the extent that, after valuation, it results in a taxable

---

[104] {{Comm'r v. Procter, 142 F2d 824 (4th Cir.)}}, cert. denied, {{323 US 756 (1944)}}.

[105] {{Comm'r v. Procter, 142 F2d 824, 827 (4th Cir.)}}, cert denied {{323 US 756 (1944)}}.

transfer.[106] A savings clause in a sale in the ordinary course of business where there are valuation questions is not a void provision.[107] [^The Service has also attempted to void "formula clauses" as contrary to public policy. A formula clause is a provision in a donative transfer that, like a safety clause, is triggered by valuation questions. Instead of a reversion to the donor, however, the formula clause results in a reallocation of the transfer among the donees. The courts have not agreed with the Service and have refused to void formula clauses as contrary to public policy.[107.1] [^Cases involving either savings clauses or formula clauses should reach a result by applying the regular dominion and control tests on completed transfers under the gift tax.[107.2] Thus, if under the clause the property may return to the donor or if the donor can directly or indirectly control which donee will receive the property (by having control over the valuation decision), the clause should be ruled void. In all other events, where the donor has no direct or indirect dominion or control, a clause should be upheld.[107.4]

---

[106] {{Ward v. Comm'r, 87 TC 78 (1986)}}; {{Knight v. Comm'r, 115 TC 506 (2000)}}. Cf. {{Harwood v. Comm'r, 82 TC 239 (1984)}}, aff'd in unpub. op. {{786 F2d 1174 (9th Cir.)}}, cert. denied {{479 US 1007 (1986)}} (no void transfer because no price adjustment was made). The Commissioner has applied the Procter result in regular and private rulings. See, e.g., Rev. Rul. 86-41, 1986-1 CB 300. Cf. Rev. Rul. 65-144, 1965-1 CB 442 (invalid savings clause sought to negate broad fiduciary powers); {{Estate of McLendon v. Comm'r, TC Memo 1993-459 (1993)}}, rev'd on other grounds, {{135 F3d 1017 (5th Cir. 1998)}} (void savings clause involving an adjustment to purchase price of a private annuity).

[107] {{King v. United States, 545 F2d 700 (10th Cir. 1976)}}. Compare {{Estate of McLendon v. Comm'r, TC Memo 1993-459 (1993)}}, rev'd on other grounds, {{135 F3d 1017 (5th Cir. 1998)}} (consideration transfer was not free from donative intent). Cf. Reg. § 25.2512-8.The Service disagrees with the King result. Rev. Rul. 86-41, 1986-1 CB 300; TAM 9309001 (Sept. 30, 1992); TAM 9133001 (Jan. 31, 1990); Priv. Ltr. Rul. 8549005 (Aug. 30, 1985); TAM 200337012 (May 6, 2003).

[107.1] Succession of {{McCord v. Comm'r, 461 F3d 614 (5th Cir. 2006)}}; {{Estate of Christiansen v. Comm'r, 586 F3d 1061 (8th Cir. 2008)}} (holding Reg. § 25.2522(c)-3(b)(1) inapplicable to the transfer); {{Estate of Petter v. Comm'r, TC Memo. 2009-280 (2009)}}, aff'd {{___ F3d ___ (9th Cir. 2011)}} (holding Reg. § 25.2522(c)-3(b)(1) inapplicable to the transfer); {{Hendrix v. Comm'r, ___ TCM(CCH) ___ (2011)}}. These cases all involve transfers where any excess amount was to pass to a charity. The Service disagrees with these results. FSA 200122011 (Feb. 20, 2001), TAM 200245053 (Nov. 8, 2002).

The Service by regulations and rulings condones formula clauses in numerous other situations which the Tax Court in {{Estate of Petter v. Comm'r, TC Memo. 2009-280 (2009)}}, aff'd {{___ F3d ___ (9th Cir. 2011)}}, refused to find distinguishable: Reg. § 1.664-2(a)(1)(iii) (formula clause in a valid charitable remainder annuity trust); Rev. Proc. 64-19, 1964-1 CB (pt. 1) 682 (formula clauses in marital bequests); Reg. § 26.2632-1(d)(1) (formula clauses allocating GST exemption); Reg. § 25.2518-3(d) Ex. 20 (formula disclaimer in marital deduction situation); Reg. § 25.2702-3(b)(1)(ii)(B) (formula clause related to a grantor retained annuity trust).

[107.2] See infra ¶¶ 10.01[4], 10.01[5], 10.01[6], and 10.01[8].

[107.4] Thus, in the cases cited in supra note 107.1, the result would be the same regardless of whether the excess amount passed to another individual or a charity.For a discussion of this area, see Bowman, "McCord v. Commissioner: Defined Value Clauses Redefined," 33 ACTEC Journal 169 (2008) and B.K. Duffey & P.J. Duffey, "Valuation Formula Clauses for the Noncharitably Inclined," 38 Estate Planning, No. 6, 30 (June 2011).

[g] Insurance and Annuities

Page 10-22:

Insert in text after note 115.

The Treasury has issued final regulations with respect to split dollar life insurance arrangements.[115.1] Generally, a split dollar life insurance arrangement involves the ownership arrangement of a life insurance policy where there is a splitting of the interest in the life insurance policy through either a sharing of the costs or of the benefits of the policy or both. Over the years, some of the gift tax consequences with respect to such arrangements have been determined by revenue rulings,[115.2] and more recently other gift tax consequences have been provided in the recently finalized regulations. The regulations primarily involve the income tax consequences of such split dollar life insurance arrangements.[115.3] However, they also provide rules for some of the gift tax consequences of *premium payments* on such arrangements.[115.4] Established gift tax principles determine the gift tax consequences of *other premium payments* and of a transfer of an interest in the *policy* that is involved in a split dollar life insurance arrangement.[115.5]

Split dollar life insurance arrangements include a policy held jointly by private parties, an employer and employee, or a corporation and a share-

---

[115.1] Reg. §§ 1.61-22, 1.83-3(e), 1.83-6(a)(5), 1.301-1(q), 1.7872-15. The regulations apply to any split dollar arrangement entered into after September 17, 2003. Reg. §§ 1.61-22(j)(1)(i), 1.7872-15(n)(1).

[115.2] See, e.g., Rev. Rul. 81-198, 1981-2 CB 188; Rev. Rul. 78-420, 1978-2 CB 67 (now obsolete, see Rev. Rul. 2003-15, 2003-2 CB __).

[115.3] Reg. §§ 1.61-22, 1.7872-15. See also Reg. §§ 1.83-3(e), 1.83-6(a)(5), 1.301-1(q). The regulations defer to the general estate tax rules to determine the estate tax consequences of such arrangements. See ¶ 4.14 notes 103.11–103.25.

[115.4] See ¶ 10.01 text accompanying notes 115.9–115.25. These final regulations are inapplicable in analyzing policy premiums paid pursuant to split-dollar arrangements executed prior to September 17, 2003, which are governed by Revenue Ruling 64-328, 1964-2 CB 11, and Revenue Ruling 66-110, 1966-1 CB 12, to the extent provided in Notice 2002-8, 2002-1 CB 398. Priv. Ltr. Rul. 200728015 (Apr. 9, 2007), Priv. Ltr. Rul. 200747011 (Aug. 7, 2007). Priv. Ltr. Rul. 200822003 (Jan. 28, 2008), Priv. Ltr. Rul. 200848002 (Sept. 19, 2008), Priv. Ltr. Rul. 200851013 (Sept. 9, 2008). Priv. Ltr. Rul. 200925003 (Dec. 16, 2008).

[115.5] Supplementary Information, 68 Fed. Reg. 54,336, 54,343 (adopted Sept. 17, 2003). See ¶ 10.01 text accompanying notes 115.27–115.35.

holder.[115.6] If the arrangement involves private parties and there is a gift, there is a direct Section 2511 transfer from the transferor to the third-party transferee, generally an individual or a life insurance trust transferee.[115.7] If there is an employer-employee arrangement or a corporate-shareholder arrangement and the employee or shareholder has transferred an interest in the policy to a third party, there are income tax consequences between the employer and the employee or the corporation and the shareholder and, in addition, there is a deemed Section 2511 transfer from the employee or shareholder to the third-party transferee.[115.8]

Premium Payments. The gift tax consequences of premium payments under the regulatory rules generally[115.9] depend in part upon who is the "owner" of the policy held in the split dollar arrangement.[115.10] Once the owner of the policy is determined, one of two mutually exclusive regimes applies,[115.11] either a "loan" regime[115.12] or an "economic benefit" regime.[115.13] The "loan" regime involves a collateral assignment arrangement[115.14] where the person who "owns" the policy is effectively being loaned the premium payments by the nonowner of the policy who has a security interest in some portion of the policy.[115.15] Assuming the loan is a below market loan,[115.16] the rules of Section 7872 apply to determine the income tax and gift tax consequences. If, as is generally the case, the loan is repayable on the death of the insured, the term of the loan is the insured's life expectancy[115.17] determined as of the date of the premium payment.[115.18] The amount of the income and gift is the amount of the

---

[115.6] Reg. §§ 1.61-22(b)(1), 1.61-22(b)(2). See Amoia, Simmons & Slane, "Private Split Dollar—What's New About an Old Opportunity," NAEPC Journal of Estate & Tax Planning, (June, 2009).

[115.7] See ¶ 10.01 text accompanying notes 115.22, 115.30, 115.34.

[115.8] Reg. §§ 1.61-22(d)(1), 1.7872-15(e)(2). See ¶ 10.01 text accompanying notes 115.23–115.25, 115.31, 115.34.

[115.9] See ¶ 10.01 text accompanying note 115.20.

[115.10] Reg. § 1.61-22(c)(1). Generally, the person named as the policy owner of the contract is the owner. Reg. § 1.61-22(c)(1)(i). If two or more persons are named owners, then the contract is treated as two contracts if each has all incidents of ownership in an undivided portion of the contract. If not, the first named owner is the owner. Id. There are some deemed owner exceptions. See Reg. § 1.61-22(c)(1)(ii); ¶ 10.01 note 115.20.

[115.11] Reg. § 1.61-22(b)(3).

[115.12] See Reg. § 1.7872-15.

[115.13] See Reg. § 1.61-22.

[115.14] Under a collateral assignment arrangement, the owner of the policy files a collateral assignment of the policy to protect the nonowner's interest in the policy.

[115.15] See Reg. § 1.7872-15.

[115.16] Reg. § 1.7872-15(a)(1). For a discussion of Section 7872, see Carlson, "Personal and Business Planning: The Impact of a Low Interest Loan," 44 NYU Tax Inst. 35-1 (1986); Hartigan "From *Dean* and *Crown* to the Tax Reform Act of 1984: Taxation of Interest-Free Loans," 60 Notre Dame L. Rev. 31 (1984).

[115.17] See Reg. § 1.72-9.

[115.18] Reg. §§ 1.7872-15(e)(4)(iii)(D), 1.7872-15(e)(5)(ii)(C), 1.7872-15(e)(5)(iv)(D).

Section 7872 forgone interest resulting from the loan of the premium payment arrangement.[115.19] For example, if a third party donee is the owner of the policy[115.20] and a transferor is reasonably expected to recover an amount equal to the transferor's premium payments, those premium payments are treated as loans made by the transferor.[115.21] The loan may be made directly between private persons, in which case if there is forgone interest, Section 7872 applies and there is a direct Section 2511 transfer.[115.22] In the alternative,[115.23] the loan may be made to the third party from an employer who, if there is Section 7872 forgone interest, makes a compensatory interest payment to the employee who then makes a deemed gift of interest to the third party. Similarly, the loan may be made indirectly to the third party by a corporation which, if there is Section 7872 forgone interest, makes a dividend interest payment to the shareholder who then makes a deemed gift of interest to the third party. In the latter two situations, when the employee and the shareholder make a deemed Section 2511 transfer to the third party,[115.24] each deemed loan is treated as having the same provisions as the original loan.[115.25]

If the nonowner of the policy makes a premium payment where no repayments of the premiums are to be made, the transaction is not in the nature of a loan and general gift tax principles apply to determine the gift tax consequences of the premium payment.[115.26]

If, instead, a private party donor, an employer, or a corporation is treated as the "owner" of the policy, an "economic benefit" regime applies[115.27] under which there is an endorsement arrangement[115.28] where the owner of the policy is providing benefits to the nonowner because of the endorsement relationship and the owner is immediately transferring some rights in the policy to the nonowner. Under the economic benefit regime, the gift tax consequences of the

---

[115.19] See Reg. § 1.7872-15(e)(4)(ii), 1.7872-15(e)(4)(iv), 1.7872-15(e)(5)(iv)(D).

[115.20] There is a limited situation in which the donor is treated as the owner of the policy even though the donee is named as owner of the policy if at all times the only economic benefits available to the donee would be the value of current life insurance protection. In such circumstances the economic benefit rules apply. Reg. §§ 1.61-22(c)(1)(ii)(A)(2), 1.61-22(d)(3). See ¶ 10.01 accompanying notes 115.27–115.35.

[115.21] Reg. § 1.7872-15(a)(2)(i).

[115.22] Reg. § 1-7872-15(e)(5)(iv). Cf. ¶ 10.01 note 115.30.

[115.23] Reg. §§ 1.7872-15(e)(4), 1.7872-15(e)(5)(iv)(D).

[115.24] Reg. §§ 1.7872-15(e)(2)(i), 1.7872-15(e)(2)(iv) Exs. Cf. note 115.31.

[115.25] Reg. § 1.7872-15(e)(2)(ii).

[115.26] Reg. §§ 1.7872-15(a)(2)(iii), 1.61-22(b)(5), 1.61-2(d)(2)(ii)(A). Cf. ¶ 10.01 text accompanying notes 115.29–115.32.

[115.27] See Reg. § 1.61-22.

[115.28] Under the endorsement arrangement, the owner of the policy files an endorsement with the insurance company setting out the split of ownership in the policy, its cash value, and death proceeds.

premium payments are consistent with general gift tax principles.[115.29] If the premium payments are made in a private party arrangement, the transfer is a direct Section 2511 transfer from the donor to the third party donee.[115.30] However, if the split dollar arrangement arises out of an employer-employee relationship or a corporate-shareholder relationship, the employee or shareholder has income in the form of compensation or a dividend and, in addition, then makes a deemed Section 2511 transfer of the compensation or dividend amount to the third party.[115.31] The amount of each Section 2511 transfer is the amount of the premium paid by the transferor private person, employer, or corporation, reduced by the amount of any economic benefits related to the payment retained by the transferor. The amount of any gift is further reduced by any consideration paid by the transferee or deemed transferee to the transferor or deemed transferor.[115.32]

Policy Transfers. The gift tax consequences of the transfer of an interest in the policy involved in a split dollar life insurance arrangement are determined by established gift tax principles regardless of the owner of the pol-

---

[115.29] Reg. § 1.61-22(d)(1) (last sentence); Rev. Rul. 81-198, 1981-2 CB 188; Rev. Rul. 78-420 (Situation 2), 1978-2 CB 67 (employer-employee premium payments were indirect Section 2511 transfers to the third party); TAM 9604001 (Sept. 8, 1995) (same). See also ¶ 9.04[3].

[115.30] Reg. § 1.61-22(d)(1). Priv. Ltr. Rul. 200825011 (Feb. 5, 2008) (husband and wife who established life insurance trust are treated as owners of second-to-die policy purchased by trust pursuant to split-dollar life insurance agreement because the only economic benefit provided under the agreement is current life insurance protection, see ¶ 10.01 note 115.20; accordingly, the amount of the annual gift made by husband and wife is the full cost of current life insurance protection provided to the trust). Cf. Priv. Ltr. Rul. 200910002 (Sept. 30, 2008) (where the irrevocable trust pays the portion of the premium equal to the cost of current life insurance protection and husband and wife pay the balance, no gift by trust settlors).

[115.31] Reg. § 1.61-22(d)(1) (last sentence); Rev. Rul. 81-198, 1981-2 CB 188; Rev. Rul. 78-420 (Situation 2), 1978-2 CB 67 (employer-employee premium payments were indirect Section 2511 transfers to the third party) (now obsolete, see Rev. Rul. 2003-105, 2003-2 CB __); TAM 9604001 (Sept. 8, 1995) (same).

In both the loan and economic benefit situations above, general gift tax principles apply to determine whether the transfer qualifies for an annual exclusion. If the policy is owned outright by the donee, the transfer qualifies as a present interest qualifying for an annual exclusion. See Reg. § 25.2503-3(c) Ex. 6. If the policy is owned by a trust where there is currently no present interest no annual exclusion is allowed. Reg. § 25.2503-3(c) Ex. 2. The latter result may be altered if the beneficiaries of the trust are given *Crummey* powers. See ¶ 9.04[3][f]. However, *Crummey* powers may be complex in split dollar arrangements when no funds are actively transferred to the trust, because of a need to fund the *Crummey* power. Cf. Rev. Rul. 76-490, 1976-2 CB 490 (premiums on a group term policy held by an irrevocable trust qualify for an annual exclusion); Rev. Rul. 79-47, 1979-1 CB 312 (premiums paid on a policy held by a trust where income not paid until insured's death did not qualify for an annual exclusion). See also ¶ 9.04[3].

[115.32] Reg. § 1.61-22(d)(1).

icy.[115.33] Again, there is a direct Section 2511 transfer of an interest in the policy in a private party arrangement or there is compensation to an employee or a dividend to a shareholder followed by a deemed Section 2511 transfer of the same amount to the third-party donee.[115.34] The amount of the transfer is the gift tax value of the policy reduced by any interest in the policy retained by the employer, corporation, or donor.[115.35]

[115.33] See Supplementary Information, 68 Fed. Reg. 54,336, 54,343 (adopted Sept. 17, 2003). The consequences are consistent with Reg. § 1.61-22(d). A transfer occurs when one owning a partial interest in a policy transfers one's interest in the policy to a third person, often a life insurance trust.

[115.34] See Rev. Rul. 81-198, 1981-2 CB 188 (employer-employee arrangement with a deemed Section 2511 transfer of the policy to employee's child); TAM 9604001 (Sept. 8, 1995) (similar result). Reg. § 1.61-22(g).

Established gift tax principles also apply in determining whether the transfer of the policy qualifies for an annual exclusion. If there is an outright transfer of the policy, the transfer qualifies for an annual exclusion (Cf. Reg. § 25.2503-3(c) Ex. 6), whereas, if the transfer is to a trust, it will generally not qualify as a present interest. See Reg. § 25.2503-3(c) Ex. 2, but see ¶ 9.04[3][f] involving *Crummey* powers given to beneficiaries to essentially cash in the policy.

[115.35] See IRC § 2512; Reg. 25.2512-6(a); ¶ 10.01[2][b]; Rev. Rul. 81-198, 1981-2 CB 188.

Add to note 119.

Note that the Service has issued proposed regulations under Sections 72 and 1001 that would eliminate the income tax advantages of transferring appreciated property in exchange for a private annuity by causing the transferor's gain to be recognized in the year the transaction is effected rather than as payments are received. Prop. Reg. §§ 1.72-6(e), 1.1001-1(j). The proposed regulations would apply for transactions entered into after October 18, 2006, with certain transactions effected before April 19, 2007, subject to the current rules. In addition, the Service proposes to declare Rev. Rul. 69-74 obsolete effective contemporaneously with the effective date of these regulations. REG-141901-05. For a transfer of property that is in part a sale and in part a gift, the proposed regulations would apply the same rules as for any other such exchange under Section 1001. Prop. Reg. § 1.1001-1(j)(1).

[5] Revocable Transfers

Page 10-27:

Add to note 144.

Private Letter Ruling 200324018 (Feb. 24, 2003) rules that a settlor's power to revoke, together with an express provision allowing a court appointed guardian or an attorney-in-fact specifically granted the power to revoke at any time the settlor is incapacitated, prevented a completed gift.

Add to note 146.

In Private Letter Ruling 200210051 (Dec. 10, 2001) the Service ruled that the donor's transfer of assets into a joint revocable trust created with the donor's spouse was an incomplete gift until the death of the donor's spouse at which time, pursuant to the joint revocable trust document, the assets were divided into a family trust to utilize the unified credit of the deceased spouse and a marital trust. The Service ruled that upon the death of the donor's spouse, the donor's gift transfer to the spouse became complete because the donor's power to revoke terminated at that time, and further held that the transfer qualified for the marital deduction (which raises the question whether one can make a gift to a decedent). The Service also ruled that the assets deemed transferred from the donor to the deceased spouse as a gift would not get a stepped up basis in the deceased spouse's estate due to Section 1014(e).

Page 10-28:

Add to note 150.

See, e.g., Priv. Ltr. Rul. 200816008 (Dec. 14, 2007) (income beneficiary of trust did not make a gift to trust by paying federal income taxes on mineral revenues erroneously reported as income because beneficiary enforced her right to recover the erroneously paid tax and the trust agreed to reimburse her).

[d] Transfers of Community Property

Page 10-31:

Delete the first full paragraph of ¶ 10.01[5][d] and replace with the following.

Generally, if a third party is made the owner of a life insurance policy that was purchased with community property funds, it is treated as a transfer of one half of the value of the policy by each spouse.[169.1] However, if the community property policy is not transferred to the third party, but the proceeds are paid to the third party at the insured's death, there has been a revocable transfer of community property that becomes complete upon the death of the insured spouse and the transfer of the survivor's interest may become a completed lifetime transfer at that time. The regulations contain an example of a possible gift arising out of the transaction.

[169.1] Cf. Perkins v. Comm'r, 1 TC 982 (1943).

[6] Power to Change Beneficiaries

Page 10-34:

Add to note 185 prior to citation to Priv. Ltr. Rul. 200148028.

See also Reg. § 25.2511-2(b);

Add to note 185.

; Priv. Ltr. Rul. 200502014 (Sept. 17, 2004) (taxpayer's transfer of property to trust will not be a completed gift because he will retain power to change beneficiaries − gift will be complete if and when taxpayer exercises or releases retained distribution power or when trust makes a distribution). Priv. Ltr. Rul. 200612002 (Nov. 23, 2005) (a donor's transfer to a trust is not a completed gift where donor retains a limited testamentary power to appoint trust corpus and income). Priv. Ltr. Rul. 200637025 (June 5, 2006) (donor's contribution of property to a trust was not a completed gift because of the donor's retained testamentary limited power of appointment); Priv. Ltr. Rul. 200647001 (Aug. 7, 2006) (same). Priv. Ltr. Rul. 200647001 (Aug. 7, 2006) (same); Priv. Ltr. Rul. 200715005 (Jan. 3, 2007) (same); Priv. Ltr. Rul. 200729025 (Apr. 10, 2007) (same).

[8] Donor's Power Exercisable Only With Third Persons

Page 10-36:

Add to note 192.

Priv. Ltr. Rul. 200612002 (Nov. 23, 2005) (a donor's transfer to a trust is not a completed gift where the trust provides that income and principal of the trust would be distributed pursuant to the unanimous direction of a power of appointment committee created by the trust or by agreement of the donor and one member of that committee to appoint the property to one or more members of a class which includes the donor, donor's descendants, committee members, a named beneficiary, and a named private foundation). See also Priv. Ltr. Rul. 200647001 (Aug. 7, 2006); Priv. Ltr. Rul. 200715005 (Jan. 3, 2007); Priv. Ltr. Rul. 200729025 (Apr. 10, 2007). See also ¶ 4.13[4][c], supplement note 41. The Service announced that it is reconsidering the gift tax consequences in a series of private letter rulings issued under Sections 2511 and 2514 which involved trusts that used distribution committees comprised of trust beneficiaries who direct distributions of trust income and principal. The Office of Chief Counsel has discovered that its rulings on the application of Section 2514 may not be consistent with Revenue Ruling 76-503, 1976-2 CB 275 and Revenue Ruling 77-158, 1977-1 CB 285 which provide that such committee members would be treated as possessing general powers of appointment because the committee members are replaced if they resign or die. IR-2007-127 (July 9, 2007). Priv. Ltr. Rul. 200731019 (May 1, 2007).

Add to note 193.

; Priv. Ltr. Rul. 200715005 (Jan. 3, 2007); Priv. Ltr. Rul. 200729025 (Apr. 10, 2007). See also ¶ 4.13[4][c], supplement note 41. The Service announced that it is reconsidering the gift tax consequences in a series of private letter rulings issued under Sections 2511 and 2514 which involved trusts that used distribution committees comprised of trust beneficiaries who direct distributions of trust income and principal. The Office of Chief Counsel has discovered that its rulings on the application of Section 2514 may not be consistent with Revenue Ruling 76-503, 1976-2 CB 275 and Revenue Ruling 77-158, 1977-1 CB 285 which provide that such committee members would be treated as possessing general powers of appointment because the committee members are replaced if they resign or die. IR-2007-127 (July 9, 2007). Priv. Ltr. Rul. 200731019 (May 1, 2007).

[10] Relationship of the Gift Tax to the Income Tax and the Estate Tax

[e] Powers Held by the Transferor

Page 10-43:

Delete the sentence ending with note 233 and replace with the following.

Ironically, not only are there differences in the gift and estate tax rules for determining the degree of control which results in a completed gift transfer or results in property not being included within the decedent's gross estate but, in addition, the income tax adds a third set of rules for determining the degree of control over trust property which results in the grantor of the trust being treated as the owner of the property for income tax purposes.[233] None of the three sets of rules are identical to any other set. In some circumstances although a transferor may have made a completed transfer of property for both gift and estate tax purposes, the transferor will be treated as continuing to own the property for income tax purposes.[233.1] Thus, the transferor sometimes will be treated as the owner of and liable for income taxes on property that is the subject of a completed gift and that will not be included in the transferor's gross estate at death. Of course, assuming the transferor is forewarned of the transferor's potential income tax liability, this will not necessarily result in adverse *transfer* tax consequences, because to the extent that the transferor incurs income tax liability in respect of the transferred property, payment of that liability is not a gift to the transferees.[233.2] Such situations are commonly known as "defective" grantor trusts.[233.3] The Service has issued a predominantly taxpayer-friendly revenue ruling providing that the transferor's payment of the income tax liability on a "defective" grantor trust's income will not result in a taxable gift by the transferor.[233.4] While the ruling was a welcome sight for gift tax purposes, it contained some potentially ominous Section 2036(a)(1) consequences.[233.5]

---

[233] See IRC §§ 671, 672, 674–678. See also S. Rep. No. 1622, 83d Cong., 2d Sess. 364–372 (1954).

[233.1] See, e.g., IRC §§ 671, 673(c) (power held by an independent trustee), 675(3), 675(4)(c), 676(a) (power held by an independent trustee), 677(a) (power held by an independent trustee). A more complete list of such circumstances is found in Henkel, Estate Planning and Wealth Preservation, Strategies and Solutions ¶ 6.06[3] (Warren, Gorham & Lamont (1997)).

[233.2] The Service originally argued that the income tax payment constituted a gift by the transferor. Priv. Ltr. Rul. 9444033 (Aug. 5, 1994). However, the ruling was withdrawn and reissued without the gift transfer statement. Priv. Ltr. Rul. 9543049 (Aug. 3, 1995). See Huffaker, Kessel & Sindoni, "Is Income Tax Payment by Grantor-Owner of a Subpart E Trust a Taxable Gift?" 82 J. Tax'n 202 (1995).

[233.3] Defective grantor trusts are discussed in more detail at Henkel, Estate Planning and Wealth Preservation, Strategies and Solutions ¶ 6.06 (Warren, Gorham & Lamont (1997)); Price, Price on Contemporary Estate Planning § 10.32 (Little Brown & Co. (1992)); Weinstock, Planning an Estate § 8.44 (Sheppard's McGraw-Hill 4th ed. (1995)); van Hoften, "Planning for Flexibility With Intentionally Defective Grantor Trusts," 9 Prac. Tax Law. No. 3, at 31 (1995).

[233.4] Rev. Rul. 2004-64, 2004-27 IRB 7.

[233.5] See ¶ 4.08[4][b] note 28.

Page 10-43:

Replace current ¶ 10.01[11] with revised ¶ 10.01[11].

[11] Nonresident Noncitizens [Revised]

Section 2511(b) provides rules for the situs of certain intangible property owned by nonresident noncitizens. It is a relatively insignificant provision which is misplaced in its location in the Code. It should be in Section 2501 accompanying Section 2501(a)(5) which is also an intangible property situs rule.[235] As a general rule, intangible property, wherever it is located, owned by nonresident noncitizens is not subject to U.S. gift taxation.[236] The Section 2511(b) intangible situs rule applies only to gifts made by certain limited[237] nonresident noncitizens who expatriated prior to June 17, 2008.[238] Section 2511(b) treats stock issued by U.S. corporations and certain debt obligations as U.S. situs property and it, along with Section 2501(a)(5) which treats certain foreign stock as U.S. situs property, taxes those limited nonresident noncitizens on transfers of such property. The provisions are discussed in more detail elsewhere in this treatise.[239]

---

[235] Section 2501(a)(5) is discussed at ¶ 9.02[1][b][ii].

[236] IRC § 2501(a)(2). See ¶ 9.02[1][a].

[237] See ¶ 9.02[1][b][ii] text accompanying notes 10.38–10.46.

[238] "Covered gifts" of property wherever located made by a "covered expatriate" who expatriated after June 17, 2008, to a U.S. resident or citizen are taxed under Section 2801. See ¶ 9.02[1][b][i]. See also ¶ 6.07[1].

[239] See ¶ 9.02[1][b][ii].

¶ 10.02 SECTION 2512. VALUATION OF GIFTS

[1] Time of Valuation

Page 10-45:

Add note 5.1 to end of ¶ 10.02[1].

[5.1] Okerlund v. Comm'r, 365 F3d 1044 (Fed. Cir. 2004) (refusal to consider post-gift earnings of a corporation which were reduced because of a death of a key employee and a salmonella outbreak was not legal error, citing Krapf v. United States, 977 F2d 1454 (Fed. Cir. 1992) – valuation must be as of the donative date relying primarily on ex ante information and using ex post data sparingly); Polack v. Comm'r, 366 F3d 608 (8th Cir. 2004) (rejection of taxpayer's argument that the financial statements of a corporation whose shares had previously been gifted should be considered in establishing valuation, holding that post-gift statements were simply not relevant). McCord v. Comm'r, 120 TC 358 (2003), rev'd sub nom., Succession of McCord v. Comm'r, 461 F3d 614 (5th Cir. 2006) (in its reversal of the tax court the Fifth Circuit took the tax court to task for its violation of the "firmly-established maxim" that post-gift events are "off limits." In its valuation of limited partnership interests, the tax court had erroneously relied on an agreement executed by the donees two months following the gift that the donors were not even a party to. See a discussion of this principle in the valuation of a decedent's estate at ¶ 5.03[5][b].

[a] Valuation on Completion

Page 10-46:

Add to note 9.

In Priv. Ltr. Rul. 200918006 (Jan. 9, 2009), an attorney mistakenly placed provisions generally included in a "supplemental needs trust" (by which the trustee has the absolute discretion to distribute income and/or principal for the beneficiary's needs) in trusts created for grantor's grandchildren. Correction deeds filed to correct these errors will cause the transfers of property to the trusts to be completed gifts on the date the original deeds were executed, in the percentages described in the original deeds.

[2] Methods of Valuation

[b] Special Approaches to Valuation

[ii] Insurance policies.

Page 10-53:

Add to note 51.

But see Priv. Ltr. Rul. 200603002 (Oct. 24, 2005) (mere reformation of an insurance policy and assignment of the policy to trust in order to reflect the original intent of the transferors regarding ownership of the policy will not be a gift nor will it cause inclusion of the policy proceeds in estate if a transferor dies within three years of the reformation and assignment). See ¶ 4.07[2].

[iii] Temporal property interests.

Pages 10-54 and 10-55:

Add to notes 55 and 60.

Notice 2009-18 provides supplements to the actuarial tables prescribed under IRC § 7520 by providing factors for interest rates below 2.2 percent.

Add to note 56.

As required by Section 7520(c)(3), the Service issued proposed, temporary and final regulations on May 7, 2009, revising Table S and Table U(1), the tables used to value annuities, interests for life or a term of years, and reversionary and remainder interests in property, to reflect the mortality experience from the 2000 census (Life Table 2000CM). Transition rules allow taxpayers to use tables based on either Life Table 90CM or Life Table 2000CM to value gift, charitable and estate transfers made on or after May 1, 2009, but before July 1, 2009, but they must use the appropriate interest rate for the month in which the valuation date falls, regardless of which table is chosen. TD 9448; REG-107845-08. Reg. §§ 1.170A-12T, 1.642(c)-6T, 1.664-4T, 20.2031-7T, 20.2032A-1T, 20.2056A-4T, 25.2512-5T, 25.2522(c)-3, 1.7520-1T, 20.7520-1T, and Reg. § 25.7520-1T.

Publications 1457 and 1458 (rev. May 2009), both of which include examples for using the mortality component tables, have been released. On August 10, 2011, the Service issued final regulations that removed the temporary regulations issued in TD 9448 and adopted as final the proposed regulations issued in REG-107845-08. The only substantive change was the deletion of an example in the Section 2032 regulations which the Service anticipates including in a different regulation project under that Code section. TD 9540; Reg. §§ 1.170A-12, 1.642(c)-6, 1.664-4, 20.2031-7, 20.2032-1, 20.2056A-4, 25.2512-5, 25.2522(c)-3, 1.7520-1, 20.7520-1, 25.7520-1.

Page 10-55:

Add to note 62.

Priv. Ltr. Rul. 200551013 (Aug. 11, 2005) (Service provided special actuarial factor to be used in valuing gifts of life estate interests by terminally ill donor).

[c] Premiums and Discounts for Interests in Property

Page 10-57:

Add new note 74.1 to the end of the sentence following note 74.

[74.1] In a case involving a single-member LLC organized under New York law, where donor had not elected to treat the LLC as a corporation under the "check-the-box" regulations, transfers of LLC interests to trusts were to be valued as transfers of interests in the LLC, subject to valuation discounts for lack of marketability and control, and not as transfers of proportionate shares of the LLC's underlying assets. Pierre v. Comm'r, 133 TC No. 2 (2009). See John A. Bogdanski, "Much Ado About (A Tax) Nothing: *Pierre v. Commissioner*," 36 Est. Plan. 38 (Dec. 2009). The Tax Court had bifurcated the issues in *Pierre* and, subsequently, in TC Memo 2010-106 (2010), the Tax Court ruled in *Pierre II* that the step transaction doctrine applied to collapse donor's gift of a 9.5 percent LLC interest and her sale of a 40.5 percent LLC interest made to each of two trusts established for the benefit of her son and granddaughter into two gifts of 50 percent interests. The Court determined that the gifts and sales were part of an integrated plan to transfer donor's entire interest in the LLC. The Court also held that the lack of control discount for the gifts was reduced from 10 percent to 8 percent because of the powers each 50 percent interest-holder would possess as a non-minority owner.

Add to note 75.

See, e.g., Ludwick v. Comm'r, TC Memo 2010-104 (2010), in which a husband and wife who owned a vacation home in Hawaii as tenants in common transferred their undivided interest in the home to a qualified personal residence trust (see ¶ 19.03[3][d]). In valuing each donor's fractional interest in the property, the Court rejected each party's valuation experts and concluded that a buyer would be willing to pay half of the fair market value of the entire property less the costs associated with selling the property, which could include the cost of partition. The Court then calculated that a 17 percent discount was appropriate.

[ii] Minority interest discount.

Page 10-58:

Add new note 83.1 to the end of the second sentence of the second paragraph of ¶ 10.02[2][c][ii].

[83.1] In Astleford v. Comm'r, TC Memo. 2008-128 (2008), the donor had transferred a 50 percent general partnership interest to a family limited partnership that was the subject of gifts made by donor to her children. In valuing the gifted FLP interests, the donor discounted the general partnership interest transferred to the FLP by five percent because, under state law, the holder of an assignee interest would have an interest only in the profits of the general partnership and no influence over management. The Tax Court, however, applied the substance over form doctrine, and disallowed the discount explaining that because the donor was the FLP's general partner, she was essentially in the same management position relative to the transferred general partnership interest both before and after the transfer.

Add to note 84.

Dallas v. Comm'r, TC Memo. 2006-212 (2006) (the court found the Service's expert's opinion more convincing and thorough; accordingly it accepted the Service's minority interest discount of 20 percent on nonvoting stock for operating assets of the corporation over the taxpayer's objection that the discount was too low and it accepted the Service's lack of marketability discount of 20 percent for the stock rejecting the taxpayer's lack of marketability discount of 40 percent).

Page 10-59:

Add to note 85.

Hess v. Comm'r, TC Memo. 2003-251 (the court criticized the valuation approaches taken by both the taxpayer's expert and the Service's expert on a gift of closely held stock and, after applying a 15 percent minority interest and a 25 percent marketability discount, found that the stock's value fell somewhere in the middle of the parties' respective values). Accord Lappo v. Comm'r, TC Memo. 2003-258 and Peracchio v. Comm'r, TC Memo. 2003-280 (two recent tax court memorandum decisions where the courts have seemed to reach a valuation based on discounts which were at the midpoint between the taxpayers' and government's valuation of the two FLPs). See also Kelley Estate v. Comm'r, TC Memo. 2005-235 (2005). In McCord v. Comm'r, 120 TC 358 (2003), rev'd sub nom., Succession of McCord v. Comm'r, 461 F3d 614 (5th Cir. 2006), the tax court repeatedly selected minority discount rates for various asset classes that, as the Fifth Circuit noted in its reversal of the tax court, "split this . . . baby precisely halfway between the expert's respective values."

Add to note 86.

See also Temple v. United States, 2006-1 USTC ¶ 60,523 (ED Tex. 2006) (donor's gift of 76.6 percent of LLC to daughter entitled to discount for lack of control).

[iii] Discount for lack of marketability.

Page 10-60:

Add a new note 93.1.

[93.1] McCord v. Comm'r, 120 TC 358 (2003), rev'd sub nom. Succession of McCord v. Comm'r, 461 F3d 614 (5th Cir. 2006), provides a close discussion of the analyses of competing experts and of the factors that may affect marketability and of factors that may have been confused with marketability.

Page 10-62:

Add to note 100.

Temple v. United States, 2006-1 USTC ¶ 60,523 (ED Tex. 2006) (donor's gifts of limited partnership interests to son and LLC interests to grandchildren entitled to a combined lack of marketability and lack of control discount of 33 percent and an additional incremental lack of marketability discount of 7.5 percent because of their status as private and nonregistered interests).

[iv] Other discounts.

Page 10-62:

Add to note 102 after citation to "Shepherd".

, aff'd, 283 F3d 1258 (11th Cir. 2002)

Page 10-63:

Add to note 104.

As noted in ¶ 4.02[4][e][ii], for assets other than business interests, the corollary term often used instead of blockage discount is "market absorption discount." In Astleford v. Comm'r, TC Memo. 2008-128 (2008), the Tax Court applied a 10 percent market absorption discount to 3,000 acres of Minnesota real property used largely for farming that donor had transferred to a family limited partnership she had created which she used to make gifts to her children.

Add to note 108 after citation to "Dunn".

, rev'd, 301 F3d 339 (5th Cir. 2002) (holding that in an asset-based valuation the amount of the discount is the entire amount of the potential capital gains tax). See also Estate of Jensen v. Comm'r, TC Memo 2010-182 (2010) (although the Tax Court applied a present-value approach to determine a range of values for the estate's discount for built-in capital gains, instead of the dollar for dollar reduction adopted by the Fifth and Eleventh Circuits, it nonetheless accepted the estate's 100 percent discount for the built-in capital gains as falling within that range).

Page 10-64:

Add to note 109.

Temple v. United States, 2006-1 USTC ¶ 60,523 (ED Tex. 2006).

Add new paragraph to note 114.

In Revenue Ruling 2008-35, 2008-29 IRB 116, the Service ruled that an interest in a restricted management account (RMA) will be valued for transfer tax purposes without any reduction or discount for the restrictions imposed by the RMA agreement. Compare with CCA 200941016 (Aug. 26, 2008) where the IRS Chief Counsel ruled that the account owner of an RMA was limited to a discount for potential damages for breach of contract for transfer tax purposes.

[v] Discount resulting from a gift on formation.

Page 10-65:

Add to note 118.

The Shepherd decision was affirmed by the Eleventh Circuit, Shepherd v. Comm'r, 115 TC 376 (2000), aff'd 283 F3d 1258 (11th Cir. 2002).

In note 119, replace ¶ 10.01[1][b] text accompanying note 22 with the following.

¶ 10.01[2][b][ii] note 25.1.

Add to note 120.

The Tax Court's ruling in *Strangi* was reversed on another issue on appeal to the Fifth Circuit. Gulig v. Comm'r, 293 F3d 279 (5th Cir. 2002). The case was remanded to the Tax Court (Estate of Albert Strangi, TC Memo. 2003-145 (2003) which was affirmed in 96 AFTR2d 2005-5230 (5th Cir. 2005). See ¶ 4.08[4][c] note 49.

Add to note 121.

See also Gross v. Comm'r, TC Memo. 2008-221 (2008) (gifts to daughters were of interests in FLP rather than indirect gifts of the securities donor had contributed to the FLP because donor's contributions were properly credited to the parties' capital accounts and the step transaction doctrine did not apply).

[d] Statutes Applicable to Gift Tax Valuation

Page 10-66:

Replace ¶ 10.02[2][d][iii] with the following.

[iii] Section 7477. Section 7477 provides that the donor[127.1] of a gift who has exhausted the donor's administrative remedies[128] may seek a declaratory

---

[127.1] IRC § 7477(b)(1). See Reg. § 301.7477-1(a).

[128] IRC § 7477(b)(2). See Reg. §§ 301.7477-1(b)(3), 301.7477-1(d)(4), and 301.7477-1(e) Exs. 1 and 3 (administrative remedies exhausted) and Ex. 2 (administrative remedies not exhausted).

judgment in the Tax Court as to the value of a gift[129] where there is an actual controversy[130] regarding the amount of a gift shown on a return or disclosed on a statement attached to the return[130.1] even though there is no actual gift tax deficiency or no refund will result (for example, where the gift is offset by the Section 2505 credit).[130.2] The donor's pleading must be filed within ninety days of the secretary's mailing of the notice of determination of value with respect to the gift.[130.3] The court's determination has the same effect as a decision rendered by the Tax Court and is reviewable.[130.4]

---

[129] The issue as to valuation may involve the interpretation or application of the gift tax law which indirectly affects valuation. Reg. §§ 301.7477-1(c), 301.7477-1(e) Ex. 4.

[130] See Reg. § 301.7477-1(e) Ex. 5 (only a part of the gift in controversy).

[130.1] IRC §§ 7477(a), 7477(b)(2). The adequate disclosure requirements of Section 6501(c)(9) and Reg. §§ 301.6501(c)-1(e) or 301.6501(c)-1(f) do not need to be met to satisfy this requirement. Reg. § 301.7477-1(d)(2). Section 7477 is applicable to gifts made after August 5, 1997. Taxpayer Relief Act of 1997, Pub. L. No. 105-34, § 506(e)(1), 111 Stat. 788, 856 (1997), reprinted in 1997-4 CB (Vol. 1) 1, 70. Regulations § 301.7477-1 is effective for civil proceedings filed on or after September 9, 2009. Reg. § 301.7477-1(f).

[130.2] Reg. § 301.7477-1(a). See HR Conf. Rep. No. 220, 105th Cong., 1st Sess. 408 (1997), reprinted in 1997-4 CB (Vol. 2) 1457, 1878. If there is a proposed tax deficiency or a potential refund these procedures do not apply. Reg. § 301.7477-1(a).

[130.3] IRC § 7477(b)(3), Reg. § 301.7477-1(d)(5). See Prop. Reg. § 301.7477-1(b)(2). Notice of such determination is made in a Preliminary Determination Letter, generally Letter 3569. Reg. §§ 301.7477-1(b)(1), 301.7477-1(d)(3).

[130.4] IRC § 7477(a).

[3] Consideration for a Transfer

Page 10-67:

Add to note 131 after citation to "Estate of Powell".

, aff'd sub nom. Lane v. United States, 286 F3d 723 (4th Cir. 2002)

Page 10-68:

Add to note 132.

Priv. Ltr. Rul. 200603002 (Oct. 24, 2005) (transfer of life insurance policies by parents to trust revocable by children in exchange for promissory note, which was forgiven the year following the transfer without any payments made on the note, was part of a prearranged plan and was ruled to be not for adequate and full consideration). See also Pierre v. Comm'r, TC Memo. 2010-106 (2010), where the Court held that the step transaction doctrine applied to collapse donor's gift of a 9.5 percent LLC interest and her sale of a 40.5 percent LLC interest made to each of two trusts established for the benefit of her son and granddaughter into two gifts of 50 percent interests. The Court determined that the gifts and sales were part of an integrated plan to transfer donor's entire interest in the LLC noting that the transfers all occurred on the same day, that the donor intended to transfer her entire interest in the LLC to the trusts, and that the transfers were originally recorded by donor's attorney as two gifts of 50 percent interests in the LLC.

[4] Transfers in the Ordinary Course of Business

Page 10-68:

In note 135, replace all references to "Section 2501(a)(5)" *with* "Section 2501(a)(4)".

Page 10-69:

Add to note 141 just after the parenthetical description of "Estate of Maggos".

, rev'd on another issue, 89 AFTR2d (RIA) 2002-1691 (9th Cir. 2002) (unpublished per curiam opinion); TAM 200648028 (Aug. 4, 2006) (settlement agreement under which trust beneficiary received selected properties in exchange for relinquishment of inheritance rights was made in the ordinary course of business in accordance with Regulations Section 25.2512-8, but a portion of the settlement attributable to the relinquishment would be subject to gift tax).

Add to penultimate sentence of note 141.

; Estate of Amlie v. Comm'r, TC Memo. 2006-76 (2006) (a payment made to decedent's son prior to decedent's death to reimburse him for expenses incurred in negotiating a family settlement agreement was not a gift but rather consideration paid for son to enter into the agreement and was, hence, a transfer in the ordinary course of business within the meaning of Regulations Section 25.2512-8). Priv. Ltr. Rul. 200707158 (Dec. 19, 2006) (no taxable gift as a result of taxpayer, who had been named as decedent's attorney-in-fact, entering into settlement agreement with estate beneficiary that resolved litigation surrounding decedent's estate).

[5] Family Obligations

[d] Elective Share Marital Rights

Page 10-74:

Add to note 167.

See, e.g., TAM 200648028 (Aug. 4, 2006) (settlement agreement under which trust beneficiary received selected properties in exchange for relinquishment of inheritance rights was made in the ordinary course of business in accordance with Regulations Section 25.2512-8, but a portion of the settlement attributable to the relinquishment would be subject to gift tax).

[6] Other Receipts of Money's Worth

Page 10-74:

Add to note 171.

Note that the Service has issued proposed regulations that would make significant changes to the income tax impact of transferring appreciated property in exchange for a private annuity and also would make Revenue Ruling 69-74 obsolete effective contemporaneously with the effective date of the regulations. REG-141901-05. See ¶ 4.11[5].

[c] Reciprocal Trusts

Page 10-76:

Add to note 180.

See also Priv. Ltr. Rul. 200919002 (Dec. 23, 2008) which involve the sale of a remainder interest in a residence held in a qualified personal residence trust, see infra ¶ 19.03[3][d], by a married couple who hold life interests in the trust. In its ruling, the Service cites Revenue Ruling 69-505 and notes there is no gift by either spouse to the other in the sale so long as sufficient consideration is exchanged between them to reflect the difference in value between the contingent life estates the husband and wife will be exchanging in the transaction.

[d] Donee's Payment of Gift Tax

Page 10-77:

In the third line of text delete the words "should be" *and replace them with* "is".

In note 185, last sentence, change "gifted to" *to* "gifted too".

Page 10-78:

Add to note 187.

In Succession of McCord v. Comm'r, 461 F3d 614 (5th Cir. 2006), the Fifth Circuit held that transferred limited partnership interests were properly valued by applying, among other discounts, the actuarially determined date-of-gift present value of the obligation assumed by the donees to pay any increased estate tax that would occur if the donors were to die within three years of the gifts.

¶ 10.03 SECTION 2513. GIFTS BY HUSBAND OR WIFE TO THIRD PARTY

[1] Introduction

Page 10-80:

Add to note 13.

Priv. Ltr. Rul. 200345038 (July 28, 2003) (gifts made by a husband to irrevocable trusts that included a wife as a primary beneficiary were eligible for Section 2513 gift splitting since wife's interest was limited to an ascertainable standard). Priv. Ltr. Ruls. 200422051 (Feb. 20, 2004), 200616022 (Dec. 26, 2005) and 200620003 (Feb. 3, 2006).

[3] Signifying Consent

[a] Manner

Page 10-85:

Add to note 40.

Priv. Ltr. Rul. 200616022 (Dec. 26, 2005) (where wife consented to splitting gifts on husband's return but failed to sign husband's return and also failed to file gift tax return for herself, Section 2513 gift splitting was permitted because the couple had evidenced their intent to split the gifts).

¶ 10.04 SECTION 2514. POWERS OF APPOINTMENT

[4] Treatment of Post-1942 Powers

[a] In General

Page 10-95:

Add to note 33 just before "200144018 (Aug. 3, 2001)".

200311020 (Dec. 9, 2002) and

Add to end of note 33.

 Priv. Ltr. Rul. 201020001 (Dec. 31, 2009) (judicial reformation of trust to correct scrivener's error will not be treated as the exercise or release of a general power of appointment by trustor's son and daughter-in-law). Priv. Ltr. Rul. 200335015 (May 16, 2003) (no taxable exercise or release of general power of appointment where a taxpayer enters into a divorce settlement agreeing to treat one of his daughters no less favorably than his other issue in exercising his general power over the trust).

[c] Lapse of Power

Page 10-96:

Add to note 47.

Priv. Ltr. Rul. 200637021 (June 2, 2006) (citing Rev. Proc. 94-44, the Service noted that a state statute which provides that the invasion power of the trustee-beneficiary is limited by an ascertainable standard within the meaning of Sections 2041 and 2514 will not cause the lapse of a general power of appointment).

¶ 10.05 SECTION 2515. TREATMENT OF GENERATION-SKIPPING TRANSFER TAX

Page 10-99:

After second paragraph, add the following paragraph.

The rationale for the provision would appear to be an attempt to equate inter vivos direct skips with testamentary direct skips. If there is a testamentary direct skip, the estate tax is a "tax-inclusive" tax because the estate tax is paid out of the tax base, whereas the gift tax on an inter vivos direct skip is "tax-exclusive" because the tax is paid from a separate source-the donor.[8.1] The generation-skipping transfer tax on both an inter vivos and testamentary direct skip is tax-exclusive.[8.2] Section 2515 creates a hybrid tax-inclusive, tax-exclusive situation under which the gift tax becomes tax-inclusive with respect to the tax imposed on the generation-skipping transfer but remains tax exclusive with respect to the generation-skipping transfer tax.

[8.1] Cf. ¶ 12.02 text accompanying notes 24–25.

[8.2] See ¶ 12.02 text accompanying notes 24 and 28–30.

¶ 10.06 SECTION 2516. CERTAIN PROPERTY SETTLEMENTS

[2] Statutory Requirements

Page 10-102:

Add to note 14.

In Private Letter Ruling 200408015 (Nov. 12, 2003), a former husband sought to establish an irrevocable trust for the benefit of a former wife which would fully satisfy the former husband's spousal support payment obligation. The Service ruled that the transfer to the trust will be a transfer for full and adequate consideration under Section 2516 to the extent of the former wife's annuity interest, but that the former husband will make a Section 2511 taxable gift of the remainder interest in the trust to the former spouses' children. Similarly, in Private Letter Ruling 201116006 (Dec. 27, 2010), former spouse's transfer of cash to an irrevocable trust, made in settlement of the divorcing parties' property and marital rights, with decedent receiving all trust income for life and holding a limited power of appointment to appoint the trust remainder to her surviving issue, constituted a transfer for full and adequate consideration under Section 2516. A taxable gift did occur upon the transfer of the trust remainder to decedent's surviving issue, upon decedent's failure to exercise power of appointment, with former spouse as the transferor. See also Priv. Ltr. Rul. 200616008 (Jan. 12, 2006) (division of CRUT established by wife during marriage for the lifetime benefit of both spouses into two CRUTs pursuant to divorce, one for the benefit of each divorcing spouse, are transfers made for full and adequate consideration under Section 2516).

[a] Type of Transfer

Page 10-103:

Add to note 21.

Priv. Ltr. Rul. 200442003 (June 22, 2004) (ex-husband's lump-sum payment to ex-wife in exchange for her interest in his retirement plan was a transfer for full and adequate consideration under IRC § 2516). Priv. Ltr. Rul. 200832021 (May 6, 2008) (divorced couple's termination of a charitable remainder unitrust (CRUT) and transfer of the CRUT's assets to two separate trusts, with each former spouse being the principal non-charitable beneficiary of their respective trust, were not subject to gift tax).

[3] Comparative Estate Tax Treatment

Page 10-105:

Add to note 33.

See Priv. Ltr. Rul. 200709014 (Nov. 16, 2006) (a lifetime transfer of stock by ex-husband to ex-wife in exchange for the release of one half of her claim under an original separation agreement, which provided for a testamentary transfer of stock from her ex-husband's estate should she survive him, comes within the purview of Section 2516 and would be treated as made for full and adequate consideration).

¶ 10.07 SECTION 2518. DISCLAIMERS

[2] Definition of "Qualified Disclaimer"

Page 10-108:

Add to note 12.

; Priv. Ltr. Rul. 200428013 (Apr. 1, 2004) (involving surviving spouse's valid disclaimer of her right to receive principal distributions from a testamentary trust established by decedent spouse that the estate later commenced a judicial proceeding to reform into a charitable remainder annuity trust—see generally ¶ 5.05[8]).

In the first sentence of note 13, replace Reg. § 25.2518-3(a)(1) Ex. 11 *with* Reg. § 25.2518-3(d) Ex. 11.

Page 10-109:

Add to note 15.

Priv. Ltr. Rul. 200832018 (Mar. 17, 2008) (wife's disclaimer of portion of her deceased husband's interest in two brokerage accounts that were then distributed into a marital and family trust over which the wife held a testamentary non-general power of appointment, which she also disclaimed, were qualified disclaimers of the accounts).

Add to note 18.

Priv. Ltr. Rul. 200503024 (Oct. 5, 2004) (surviving spouse's disclaimer of portion of her survivorship interest in joint brokerage account was qualified disclaimer because cash and securities were severable assets).

Page 10-110:

Add to note 21.

In Revenue Ruling 2005-36, 2005-1 CB 1368, the Service ruled that a beneficiary's disclaimer of an interest in a decedent's individual retirement account (IRA) is qualified even though the disclaimant received the required minimum distribution (RMD) from the IRA for the year of the decedent's death. Receipt of the RMD, however, constitutes acceptance of that portion of the corpus of such account, plus the income attributable to that amount. See, e.g., Priv. Ltr. Rul. 201125009 (Mar. 10, 2011) (wife's disclaimer of her husband's retirement benefits, effected by her daughter as administratrix of her estate, was a qualified disclaimer of those benefits other than the RMDs wife was deemed to have accepted when they were automatically deposited into her bank account).

Add to note 23.

The validity of this regulation has been upheld by the Eighth Circuit in Walshire v. United States, 288 F3d 342 (8th Cir. 2002) (upholding the regulation and applying it to determine that the decedent's estate included the one fourth of his predeceased brother's residuary estate as to which the decedent had disclaimed the remainder while retaining an income interest).

See also Estate of Christiansen, 130 TC No. 1 (2008) (reviewed), aff'd on other grounds, No. 08-3844 (8th Cir. 2009), citing *Walshire*, in which a charitable deduction was disallowed for property passing to a charitable lead trust as a result of daughter's partial disclaimer since undisclaimed portion passed to disclaimant, see infra ¶ 10.07[2][d], which rendered disclaimer invalid since undisclaimed portion was neither severable property nor an undivided portion of the property as required by Regulations Section 25.2518-2(e)(3).

Page 10-111:

Add to note 26.

In Private Letter Ruling 200303020 (Sept. 30, 2002), the Service ruled that disclaimers on behalf of minor grandchildren by a court appointed guardian were valid. See also Priv. Ltr. Rul. 200616041 (Jan. 25, 2006) (disclaimer of an interest in decedent's IRA made on behalf of decedent spouse, who died shortly after decedent, by decedent's spouse's personal representative (one of the couple's daughters) within nine months of decedent's death was a qualified disclaimer).

[b] Disclaimer Must Be Timely

Page 10-112:

Add to note 30.

Final regulations relating to the manner for establishing *prima facie evidence* of delivery of documents having a filing deadline in the absence of actual delivery, have been adopted by the Service. TD 9543. The final regulations, which are intended to resolve conflicts among the courts as to whether Section 7502 provides the only means to establish such evidence, note that that proper use of registered or certified mail, or a designated private delivery service (PDS) will constitute *prima facie* evidence of delivery but does not purport to limit other delivery options offered by the United States Postal Service or a PDS for purposes of satisfying the timely mailing rule of Section 7502(a).

Add to end of first paragraph of note 35.

Priv. Ltr. Rul. 200339021 (June 19, 2003) (surviving spouse's disclaimer of contingent interest in trust more than nine months after the trust was established by decedent spouse did not qualify as a Section 2518 disclaimer and resulted in a taxable gift).

Add to note 36.

See, e.g., Breakiron v. Gudonis, 2010-2 USTC ¶ 60,597 (D. Mass. 2010) where a putative disclaimant of remainder interests in two QPRTs, see ¶ 19.03[3][d], was able to rescind the disclaimers because they were executed based on a mistake that frustrated the purpose of the transfer. The putative disclaimant had consulted with an attorney who advised him that he could disclaim such property within nine months of the expiration of the QPRTs' terms without incurring gift tax. Regulations § 25.2518-2(c)(3)(i) provides, however, that disclaimers must be made within nine months of the date on which the individual has a contingent, not a vested, interest in the property. Under applicable state law, disclaimers may be rescinded in cases where the disclaimer was based on a mistake that frustrated the purpose of the transfer. The court then noted that, in accordance with Dodge v. US, 413 F2d 1239, 1243 (5th Cir. 1969), the transferor should not be subject to gift tax for the reformed transfer because the disclaimers were based on a mistake and the transferor had the right to rescind the transfers under state law. Furthermore, the fact that the transferor had named the Service as a party to the case prevented collusion and gave the Service the opportunity to dispute that the transferor had made a mistake. Accordingly, the rescission of the disclaimer was conclusive of the federal tax liability.

Page 10-114:

Add to the end of first paragraph of note 46.

Priv. Ltr. Rul. 200618017 (Jan. 24, 2006) (surviving spouse's qualified disclaimer within nine months of decedent's death of surviving spouse's interest in the decedent's share of joint financial accounts with right of survivorship which were established by decedent during his life).

In the first sentence of note 49, replace Reg. § 25.2518-2(c)(5) Exs. 7, 8 *with* Reg. § 25.2518-2(c)(5) Exs. 7, 8, and 10.

Page 10-116:

Add to note 61.

Priv. Ltr. Rul. 200953010 (Sept. 14, 2009) (disclaimer of a contingent remainder beneficiary's right to receive a distribution from a pre-1977 trust upon its termination, made within nine months of the beneficiary attaining the age of majority, would not constitute a transfer subject to gift tax and, in addition, the beneficiary's retained right to receive discretionary distributions of trust corpus and income during the term of the trust and prior to its termination will not invalidate the disclaimer of the remainder interest). Priv. Ltr. Rul. 201001007 (Sept. 14, 2009) and Priv. Ltr. Rul. 201004006 (Oct. 21, 2009) (same). Cf. Priv. Ltr. Rul. 200333023 (May 8, 2003) (disclaimer filed by person more than nine months after decedent's death but within nine months after person's twenty-first birthday must still comply with requirements of local law to be effective). See also Priv. Ltr. Ruling 200435006 (Apr. 26, 2004) (qualified disclaimer of tribal gaming revenue payments made before record dates of payments, as required by tribal law).

[c] Disclaimer May Not Follow an Acceptance

Page 10-118:

Add to end of first paragraph of note 66.

Priv. Ltr. Rul. 200503024 (Oct. 5, 2004) (surviving spouse's disclaimer of portion of her survivorship interest in joint brokerage account was qualified disclaimer despite retitling of the account in her name); Priv. Ltr. Rul. 200832018 (Mar. 17, 2008) (wife's disclaimer of her deceased husband's interest in two brokerage accounts, except for post-death distributions she had received from one account and new securities she had purchased in the other account, was a qualified disclaimer despite the retitling of the accounts in her name). In Revenue Ruling 2005-36, 2005-1 CB 1368, the Service ruled that a beneficiary's disclaimer of an interest in a decedent's IRA is qualified even though the disclaimant received the RMD from the IRA for the year of the decedent's death. Receipt of the RMD, however, constitutes acceptance of that portion of the corpus of such account, plus the income attributable to that amount. See, e.g., Priv. Ltr. Rul. 201125009 (Mar. 10, 2011) (wife's disclaimer of her husband's retirement benefits, effected by her daughter as administratrix of her estate, was a qualified disclaimer of those benefits other than the RMDs wife was deemed to have accepted when they were automatically deposited into her bank account).

Add to note 66.

Priv. Ltr. Rul. 200406038 (Oct. 24, 2003) (heir's execution of amendment to LLC in her capacity as co-personal representative of decedent's estate will not be considered as the acceptance of any benefits of the LLC interest previously disclaimed by heir). Priv. Ltr. Ruls. 201032002, 201032010 (Apr. 27, 2010) (trust beneficiary's actions in her capacity as trustee did not constitute acceptance of disclaimed property).

Add to note 69.

Priv. Ltr. Rul. 200953010 (Sept. 14, 2009) (disclaimer of a contingent remainder beneficiary's right to receive a distribution from a pre-1977 trust upon its termination, made within nine months of the beneficiary attaining the age of majority, would not constitute a transfer subject to gift tax and, in addition, the beneficiary's retained right to receive discretionary distributions of trust corpus and income during the term of the trust and prior to its termination will not invalidate the disclaimer of the remainder interest). Priv. Ltr. Rul. 201001007 (Sept. 14, 2009) and Priv. Ltr. Rul. 201004006 (Oct. 21, 2009) (same).

Add to note 71.

See Estate of Engelman v. Comm'r, 121 TC 54 (2003) (testamentary exercise of a general power of appointment by decedent is an acceptance which may not be disclaimed by the administrator of decedent's estate under the relation-back doctrine).

[d] Persons to Whom the Interest Must Pass

Page 10-119:

Add to note 76.

Priv. Ltr. Rul. 200616041 (Jan. 25, 2006) (disclaimer of an interest in decedent's IRA made on behalf of decedent spouse, who died shortly after decedent, by decedent's spouse's personal representative (one of the couple's daughters) within nine months of decedent's death was a qualified disclaimer even though a portion of the disclaimed interest passed to the daughter). Estate of Tatum, AFTR2d ¶ 2011-5159 (5th Cir. 2011) (distribution of property to disclaimant's children did not result in a taxable gift by disclaimant since state's anti-lapse statute directs that, to the extent disclaimer results in lapsed bequest, disclaimed interest passes without any direction on disclaimant's part and, furthermore, testator's intent, which is the most important consideration under state law, was that any property not going to disclaimant should go to disclaimant's children).

But see Priv. Ltr. Rul. 200846003 (July 30, 2008) (no qualified disclaimer by decedent's children, named beneficiaries of IRA, who disclaimed their interests in IRA, which then passed to trust established in favor of surviving spouse — children failed to disclaim interest in a second trust established for them which would be the distributee of IRA upon death of surviving spouse).

Add to end of first paragraph of note 78.

Priv. Ltr. Rul. 200616026 (Dec. 22, 2005) (qualified disclaimer of pecuniary amount that passes to private foundation which will amend its bylaws to provide that disclaimant, a director and president of the foundation, cannot make decisions on distributions of the disclaimed property).

Page 10-120:

Add to note 80 following reference to Priv. Ltr. Rul. 199903019.

Priv. Ltr. Rul. 200420007 (Jan. 23, 2004) (valid disclaimer of property in favor of charitable foundation of which disclaimant was fiduciary where disclaimed property was maintained in a separate account over which disclaimant would have no power); Priv. Ltr. Rul. 200519042 (Feb. 3, 2005) (valid disclaimer of property by decedent's child in favor of charitable foundation, which will qualify decedent's estate for estate tax charitable deduction, so long as disclaimed property is maintained in a segregated fund by a committee over which disclaimant has no influence); Priv. Ltr. Rul. 200518012 (Dec. 17, 2004) (valid disclaimer by decedent's grandchildren in favor of charitable foundation to which disclaimant may make advisory recommendations that may be accepted or rejected by the foundation will qualify decedent's estate for estate tax charitable deduction). Priv. Ltr. Rul. 200503024 (Oct. 5, 2004) (surviving spouse's disclaimer of property which passed to credit shelter trust of which surviving spouse was beneficiary and co-trustee was qualified disclaimer since surviving spouse's power to direct beneficial enjoyment of the disclaimed property was limited by an ascertainable standard). Priv. Ltr. Rul. 200649023 (Aug. 23, 2006) (valid disclaimer of property in favor of private foundation of which disclaimant was fiduciary where property went into segregated fund over which disclaimant had no authority); Priv. Ltr. Rul. 200744005 (June 28, 2007) (same); Priv. Ltr. Rul. 200802010 (Sept. 12, 2007) (same). Priv. Ltr. Ruls. 201032002, 201032010 (Apr. 27, 2010) (same).

Page 10-121:

Add to note 81.

In Estate of Christiansen, 130 TC No. 1 (2008) (reviewed), aff'd on other grounds, No. 08-3844 (8th Cir. 2009), a charitable deduction was disallowed for property passing to a charitable lead trust as a result of daughter's partial disclaimer since daughter retained a contingent remainder interest in the trust which was neither severable property nor an undivided portion of the property as required by Regulations Section 25.2518-2(e)(3).

Add to note 82.

Priv. Ltr. Rul. 200616041 (Jan. 25, 2006) (disclaimer of interest in decedent's IRA, reformed consistent with applicable state law to designate decedent's daughters as the IRA's contingent beneficiaries, which was made on behalf of decedent spouse by decedent's spouse's personal representative (one of the daughters) was a qualified disclaimer and the proceeds of the IRA passed to daughters). Estate of Tatum, AFTR2d ¶ 2011-5159 (5th Cir. 2011) (distribution of property to disclaimant's children did not result in a taxable gift by disclaimant since state's anti-lapse statute directs that, to the extent disclaimer results in lapsed bequest, disclaimed interest passes without any direction on disclaimant's part and, furthermore, testator's intent, which is the most important consideration under state law, was that any property not going to disclaimant should go to disclaimant's children).

[i] Disclaimer by a surviving spouse.

Page 10-122:

Add to note 87.

Priv. Ltr. Rul. 200442027 (June 21, 2004) (series of proposed disclaimers by grantor's spouse whereby trust assets would pass to four additional trusts for the benefit of grantor's spouse and issue).

Add to note 88.

See also Priv. Ltr. Rul. 200443030 (July 7, 2004) (valid disclaimer where the surviving spouse disclaimed the decedent spouse's community property interest in trust, her lifetime and testamentary power to appoint the disclaimed interest, and her power to amend the trust) and Priv. Ltr. Rul. 200832018 (Mar. 17, 2008) (wife's disclaimer of portion of her deceased husband's interest in two brokerage accounts that were then distributed into a marital and family trust over which the wife held a testamentary non-general power of appointment, which she also disclaimed, were qualified disclaimers of the accounts).

[ii] Disclaimers ineffective under local law.

Page 10-123:

Add to note 93.

Cf. Priv. Ltr. Rul. 200437032 (May 11, 2004) (a vow of poverty made by a member of a religious order who was the residuary estate beneficiary does not constitute a qualified disclaimer; in addition, the transfer of assets by the estate beneficiary to the religious order is not a qualified disclaimer pursuant to Section 2518(c)(3)).

[3] Effective Date

Page 10-123:

Replace existing note 98 with the following.

   [98] See Reg. §§ 25.2518-1(a)(1), 25.2518-1(a)(2).

¶ 10.08 SECTION 2519. DISPOSITION OF CERTAIN LIFE ESTATES

[1] The General Rule

Page 10-124:

Add to note 3.

Citing Revenue Procedure 2001-38, the Service in Private Letter Ruling 200407016 (Oct. 24, 2003) treated a QTIP election made for a surviving spouse's life estate as null and void because the election was unnecessary to eliminate deceased spouse's estate tax liability; Priv. Ltr. Rul. 200603004 (Sept. 30, 2005) (estate's QTIP election for credit shelter trust is null and void because election was not necessary to reduce estate tax liability to zero), Priv. Ltr. Rul. 201131011 (Apr. 20, 2011).

Page 10-125:

In note 7 delete everything after the fourth period and insert the following.

Final regulations (issued by TD 9077 and effective July 18, 2003) treat the exercise of the spouse's right to recovery as resulting in a net gift that reduces the value of the gift of the remainder interest. Reg. § 25.2519-1(c)(4). Priv. Ltr. Rul. 200628007 (Mar. 22, 2006), Priv. Ltr. Rul. 200717016 (Dec. 19, 2006), Priv. Ltr. Rul. 200801009 (Aug. 7, 2007). See ¶¶ 8.07[4] text accompanying note 34, 10.02[6][d]. In Priv. Ltr. Rul. 201118007 (Jan. 25, 2011), however, surviving spouse severed QTIP trust into two sub-trusts and funded sub-trust spouse intended to renounce with sufficient assets to both make gifts to couple's children and also to pay any gift tax attributable to the gifts. See also Priv. Ltr. Rul. 201119004 (Jan. 24, 2011).

[a] Disposition of a Portion of the Transferee Spouse's Qualifying Income Interest

Page 10-126:

Add to note 13.

In Priv. Ltr. Rul. 201118007 (Jan. 25, 2011), surviving spouse severed QTIP trust into two sub-trusts and renounced his interest in one sub-trust. Renunciation of that sub-trust resulted in a Section 2511 taxable gift of spouse's income interest in that trust and, in addition, a Section 2519 transfer of the entire fair market value of the trust assets in the renounced sub-trust less the value of the spouse's income interest. Renounced sub-trust was funded with sufficient assets to both make gifts to third parties and also to pay any gift tax attributable to the gifts. See also Priv. Ltr. Rul. 201119004 (Jan. 24, 2011).

Page 10-127:

In note 16, delete the entire second paragraph and replace it with the following.

If the transferee spouse asserts the Section 2207A(b) right to recover the gift tax incurred on the Section 2519 transfer a net gift occurs, reducing the amount of the Section 2519 transfer. Reg. § 25.2519-1(c)(4). The transferee spouse's failure to exercise the right of recovery is an additional gift. Reg. § 25.2207A-1(b). See Priv. Ltr. Rul. 200530014 (Apr. 12, 2005), and Priv. Ltr. Rul. 201024008 (Feb. 4, 2010).

Add to note 21 after Reg. § 25.2519-1(c)(2).

Similar results occur where a single trust is legally severed into separate trusts. See Priv. Ltr. Rul. 200628007 (Mar. 22, 2006) and Priv. Ltr. Rul. 200717016 (Dec. 19, 2006).

Page 10-128:

Add to note 22 just before the cite to Priv. Ltr. Ruls. 200122025.

Priv. Ltr. Rul. 200324023 (Feb. 26, 2003) (also holding that an apparently nonqualified renunciation by the beneficiary spouse of her interest in one QTIP accelerated the transfer of the property in that QTIP to a charitable remainder trust and that the spouse's transfer qualified for the gift tax charitable deduction to the extent of the charitable interest); see also Priv. Ltr. Rul. 200530014 (Apr. 12, 2005);

Add to end of note 22.

, Priv. Ltr. Rul. 200717016 (Dec. 19, 2006), Priv. Ltr. Rul. 200844010 (June 13, 2008) (involving division of QTIP trust on a pro-rata basis into five QTIP trusts, each providing a remainder interest for each of five children—a termination of one such separate QTIP trust does not result in the application of Section 2519 to the other four QTIP trusts).

[b] Section 2519 Transfer

Page 10-130:

Add to note 29.

Compare this with the situation in which the lifetime transfer of the surviving spouse's income interest in a QTIP trust is made to the qualified charity remainder beneficiary of the QTIP trust. That would also result in a merger and the merged interest would qualify for the charitable deduction. See Private Letter Ruling 200438028 (May 12, 2004), where the charitable remainder QTIP trust established by the decedent spouse was judicially divided into two QTIP trusts, and the surviving spouse assigned the entire income interest of one of the QTIP trusts to the remainder beneficiary. The Service determined that a gift tax charitable deduction was allowed for the surviving spouse's transfer of his income interest and for the amount the surviving spouse was deemed to transfer to the charity under Section 2519. The Service also ruled that the surviving spouse's transfer qualified as a charitable contribution under Section 170, limited to the fair market value of the interest.

[2] Meaning of "Disposition"

Page 10-130:

Add to end of first sentence of note 30.

and Priv. Ltr. Rul. 200604006 (Sept. 30, 2005) (same).

Page 10-111:

Add to note 30.

Final regulations relating to the manner for establishing *prima facie* evidence of delivery of documents having a filing deadline in the absence of actual delivery have been adopted by the Service. TD 9543. The final regulations, which are intended to resolve conflicts among the courts as to whether Section 7502 provides the only means to establish such evidence, note that that proper use of registered or certified mail, or a designated private delivery service (PDS) will constitute *prima facie* evidence of delivery but does not purport to limit other delivery options offered by the United States Postal Service or a PDS for purposes of satisfying the timely mailing rule of Section 7502(a).

Page 10-130:

Add to note 31.

See Priv. Ltr. Rul. 201119003 (Jan. 12, 2011) (settlement agreement between surviving spouse and children of predeceased spouse whereby the QTIP trust and the children would make several exchanges of property interests that would unwind their co-ownership of multiple entities does not constitute a Section 2519 disposition of QTIP property).

Add to note 33.

Cf. TAM 200602033 (Sept. 19, 2005) (decedent did not make a Section 2519 disposition of assets improperly withdrawn from a QTIP trust established for his benefit and placed in decedent's individual account).

[3] Gift Tax Liability

Page 10-133:

Add to note 49.

In Estate of Morgens v. Comm'r, 133 TC No. 17 (2009), surviving spouse transferred her income interest in QTIP trust to the remainder beneficiaries who agreed to pay the associated gift tax. Following surviving spouse's death less than three years later, the Tax Court held that her estate was required to include the amount of gift tax paid by the remainder beneficiaries on the deemed Section 2519 transfers of the remainder interest. Citing Sachs v. Comm'r, 88 TC 769 (1987), aff'd in part and rev'd in part on another ground, 856 F2d 1158 (8th Cir. 1988), where the court held that the gift tax paid by the donee of a "net gift" was includible in the donor's gross estate under Section 2035(b) if paid within three years of the donor's death, the Tax Court in Morgens stated that a donee's liability for the gift tax paid under Section 2207A is no different from a net gift, and decedent's primary liability for the gift tax was sufficient for Section 2035(b) inclusion.

CHAPTER 11

Gift Tax Deductions

¶ 11.02		Section 2522. Charitable and Similar Gifts		S11-1
	[1]	Charitable Transfers in General		S11-1
		[a]	Qualified Recipients	S11-1
		[b]	The Amount of the Deduction	S11-2
		[c]	Timing of the Deduction	S11-3
	[2]	Mixed Private and Charitable Gifts		S11-3
		[a]	Introduction	S11-3
		[b]	Qualified Remainder Interests	S11-3
			[i] The charitable remainder annuity trust.	S11-3
		[c]	Temporary Interests Gifted to Charity:	
			Charitable Lead Trusts	S11-4
		[d]	Exceptions to the Split-Gift Rules	S11-5
		[e]	Curative Amendments Permitted	S11-5
¶ 11.03		Section 2523. Gifts to Spouse		S11-6
	[2]	Basic Requirements		S11-6
	[4]	Exceptions to the Terminable Interest Rule		S11-6
		[c]	Qualified Terminable Interest Property	S11-6
			[i] Other QTIP consequences.	S11-7
		[d]	Special Rule for Charitable Remainder Trusts	S11-8
	[5]	Noncitizen Donee Spouses		S11-8

¶ 11.02 SECTION 2522. CHARITABLE AND SIMILAR GIFTS

[1] Charitable Transfers in General

[a] Qualified Recipients

Page 11-4:

In note 12, replace reference to "Section 2501(a)(5)" *with* "Section 2501(a)(4)" *in second paragraph.*

Page 11-6:

Add to end of ¶ 11.02[1][a].

Restrictions are also imposed on donations to donor-advised funds.[23.1]

[23.1] IRC § 2522(c)(5). See ¶ 5.05[1][c] text accompanying ns. 56.1–56.3.

[b] The Amount of the Deduction

Page 11-6:

Add to note 25.

Priv. Ltr. Rul. 200630006 (Apr. 14, 2006) (husband and wife each entitled to gift tax charitable deduction following their renunciation of their interests in a charitable remainder unitrust and the husband's irrevocable designation of the charitable remainder beneficiary of the trust); Priv. Ltr. Rul. 200631006 (Apr. 14, 2006) (same); Priv. Ltr. Rul. 200633011 (Apr. 14, 2006) (same); Priv. Ltr. Rul. 200802024 (Sept. 14, 2007) (transfer of couple's interests in two charitable remainder unitrusts to the trusts' charitable remainder beneficiaries entitled them to a Section 2522(a) gift tax charitable deduction); Priv. Ltr. Rul. 200808018 (Nov. 7, 2007) (taxpayer's division of charitable remainder unitrust into two trusts with identical terms combined with the contribution of his interest in one of the CRUTs to the charitable beneficiary entitles him to a Section 2522 gift tax charitable deduction to the extent of the present value of the transferred unitrust interest). Priv. Ltr. Rul. 200834013 (Apr. 15, 2008) (surviving spouse's transfer of her income interest in a charitable remainder trust to the charitable remainder beneficiaries entitles her to a Section 2522 gift tax charitable deduction; moreover, if such transfer occurs within three years of surviving spouse's death, the Service concluded that surviving spouse's estate would be entitled to an estate tax charitable deduction equal to the amount included in her estate pursuant to IRC § 2035 — see supra ¶ 4.07).

Add to note 27.

As required by Section 7520(c)(3), the Service issued proposed, temporary and final regulations on May 7, 2009, revising Table S and Table U(1), the tables used to value annuities, interests for life or a term of years, and reversionary and remainder interests in property, to reflect the mortality experience from the 2000 census (Life Table 2000CM). Transition rules allow taxpayers to use tables based on either Life Table 90CM or Life Table 2000CM to value gift, charitable and estate transfers made on or after May 1, 2009, but before July 1, 2009, but they must use the appropriate interest rate for the month in which the valuation date falls, regardless of which table is chosen. TD 9448; REG-107845-08. Reg. §§ 1.170A-12T, 1.642(c)-6T, 1.664-4T, 20.2031-7T, 20.2032A-1T, 20.2056A-4T, 25.2512-5T, 25.2522(c)-3, 1.7520-1T, 20.7520-1T, and Reg. § 25.7520-1T. Publications 1457 and 1458 (rev. May 2009), both of which include examples for using the mortality component tables, have been released. On August 10, 2011, the Service issued final regulations that removed the temporary regulations issued in TD 9448 and adopted as final the proposed regulations issued in REG-107845-08. The only substantive change was the deletion of an example in the Section 2032 regulations which the Service anticipates including in a different regulation project under that Code section. TD 9540; Reg. §§ 1.170A-12, 1.642(c)-6, 1.664-4, 20.2031-7, 20.2032-1, 20.2056A-4, 25.2512-5, 25.2522(c)-3, 1.7520-1, 20.7520-1, 25.7520-1.

Add to first paragraph of note 28.

Priv. Ltr. Rul. 200847014 (April 9, 2008) (transfer of lump sum to charity pursuant to an agreement between donor and charity that the donor would receive an annual annuity payable to donor for life, that was subsequently funded by a commercial annuity purchased by charity, results in gift tax charitable deduction for donor equal to the amount transferred to the charity less the present value of the annuity).

[c] Timing of the Deduction

Page 11-7:

Add to note 36.

Private Letter Ruling 200241044 (July 9, 2002) applied this and related concepts to a labyrinthine set of facts involving a donation to a university.

[2] Mixed Private and Charitable Gifts

[a] Introduction

Page 11-9:

At the end of the second sentence of the first full paragraph add new note 47.1.

[47.1] In his concurring opinion in McCord v. Comm'r, 120 TC 358 (2003), rev'd sub nom., Succession of McCord v. Comm'r, 461 F3d 614 (5th Cir. 2006), Judge Swift indicates that where donors transfer assignee interests in a limited partnership to charity, he would hold that the gifts were gifts of partial interests that do not meet the Section 2522(c)(2) requirements and are thus not deductible. Cf. Priv. Ltr. Ruls. 200445023, 200445024 (July 12, 2004) (donors entitled to gift tax deduction for contributions to college notwithstanding donors' agreement with college to manage the investments made with the contributions).

[b] Qualified Remainder Interests

[i] The charitable remainder annuity trust.

Page 11-10:

Replace the second paragraph of note 56 with the following.

Inter vivos CRAT forms are found in Revenue Procedure 2003-53 through 2003-56 at 2003-2 CB ___–___. The procedures involve the following forms:

1. Revenue Procedure 2003-53: Sample inter vivos CRAT for one measuring life.
2. Revenue Procedure 2003-54: Sample inter vivos CRAT for a term of years.
3. Revenue Procedure 2003-55: Sample inter vivos CRAT with consecutive interests for two measuring lives.
4. Revenue Procedure 2003-56: Sample inter vivos CRAT with concurrent and consecutive interests for two measuring lives.

The sample forms supersede Revenue Procedure 89-21, 1989-1 CB 842, and Revenue Procedure 90-32, 1990-1 CB 546. The Service will not issue determination letters as to the qualification of CRATs substantially similar to the forms set forth in such rulings. Rev. Proc. 90-33, 1990-1 CB 551.

Delete the third paragraph of note 56.

[c] Temporary Interests Gifted to Charity: Charitable Lead Trusts

Page 11-15:

Add to note 90.

In Revenue Procedure 2007-45, 2007-29 IRB ___, the Service provides sample forms for inter vivos grantor and nongrantor charitable lead annuity trusts along with annotations for each trust and sample alternative provisions. In Revenue Procedure 2008-45, 2008-30 IRB 224, the Service provides sample forms for inter vivos grantor and nongrantor charitable lead unitrusts along with annotations for each trust and sample alternative provisions.

Add to note 91.

See, e.g., Priv. Ltr. Rul. 200404009 (Oct. 21, 2003) (donor entitled to gift tax charitable deduction for present value of four twenty-one-year charitable lead annuity trusts, each paying a $70,000 annual charitable annuity) and Priv. Ltr. Rul. 200516005 (Nov. 30, 2004) (husband and wife each are entitled to a gift tax charitable deduction equal to one half of the present value of the guaranteed annuity interest in a charitable lead trust created by the couple).

Add to note 92.

TAM 200341002 (June 5, 2003) (no charitable deduction was allowed for transfers made to a trust over which several individual beneficiaries and charities each held withdrawal powers since the trust did not satisfy the statutory requirements for a mixed bequest). Priv. Ltr. Rul. 200537020 (June 2, 2005) (husband and wife who created a CLUT were each allowed a gift tax charitable deduction for the present value of the unitrust amount payable to a charitable foundation on which the couple served as two of the initial five directors).

Page 11-16:

Add to note 96.

Several special rules apply to a gift of an undivided portion of an interest in tangible personal property made after August 17, 2006. First, generally, a charitable deduction will be allowed only if the donor and the charitable donee hold all interests in the property immediately prior to the contribution. IRC § 2522(e)(1)(A). However, the Treasury may issue regulations to provide an exception where all noncharitable donors owning interests in the property make proportionate contributions of individual portions of such property. IRC § 2522(e)(1)(B). Second, if a donor who has previously made a deductible contribution of an undivided portion of tangible personal property after the enactment of these provisions makes an additional contribution of an undivided portion of such property (see Section 2522(e)(4)), the value of the subsequent gift is limited to the lesser of the fair market value of the proportionate share of the property at the time of the original transfer or at the time of the subsequent transfer. IRC § 2522(e)(2). Note, however, that the Tax Technical Corrections Act of 2007, Pub. L. No. 110-172, amended Section 2522(e) to remove this valuation rule for an additional charitable contribution of a fractional interest in tangible personal property. Therefore, in practical terms and effect, it is as if the valuation rule never existed for estate and gift tax purposes. The income tax version of this rule is unaffected. Third, there is a recapture of a prior charitable deduction (plus interest) of a prior gift of an undivided portion of tangible personal property after the enactment of these provisions, if the donor's remaining interest in the property is not contributed to the charity (or another Section 170(c) charity if it is no longer in existence) by the earlier of the date ten years subsequent to the original gift or the date of the donor's death. IRC § 2522(e)(3)(A)(i). The recapture rule also applies even if a subsequent gift is made within the above time period, if during the time period the charitable donee has not had substantial physical possession of the property or has not used the property in a use related to the charity's purpose or function constituting the basis for its charitable exemption. IRC § 2522(e)(3)(A)(ii). The recapture seemingly would involve only the Section 2522 deduction taken in prior years (after consideration of the Section 2503(b) annual exclusion) plus interest. In addition, there is a penalty equal to the percent of the recapture amount. IRC § 2522(e)(3)(B).

[d] Exceptions to the Split-Gift Rules

Page 11-17:

Add to note 102.

Priv. Ltr. Rul. 200847014 (Apr. 9, 2008) (transfer of lump sum to charity pursuant to an agreement between donor and charity that the donor would receive an annual annuity payable to donor for life, that was subsequently funded by a commercial annuity purchased by charity, results in gift tax charitable deduction for donor equal to the amount transferred to the charity less the present value of the annuity).

[e] Curative Amendments Permitted

Page 11-17:

Add to note 103.

In Private Letter Ruling 200818003 (Jan. 28, 2008), the Service ruled that a judicially reformed trust does not qualify as a valid charitable remainder unitrust for estate or gift tax purposes. Although Section 2522(c)(4) permits an intervivos trust to be reformed to qualify for the gift tax charitable deduction, the statute requires that the reformation be accomplished under rules similar to those in Section 2055(e)(3). Because the trust was created prior to 1969, it could not be reformed to qualify as a charitable remainder unitrust. See ¶ 5.05[4][b], note 134.

¶ 11.03 SECTION 2523. GIFTS TO SPOUSE

[2] Basic Requirements

Page 11-18:

In note 12, add "2501(a)(5)" *after* "2501(a)(3)".

[4] Exceptions to the Terminable Interest Rule

[c] Qualified Terminable Interest Property

Page 11-29:

Add to note 56.

Private Letter Ruling 200314012 (Dec. 17, 2002) ruled that because the time for filing the election is prescribed by statute, the Service could not give Section 9100 relief to a taxpayer that failed to file a Form 709 for the year of transfer to a trust otherwise eligible for QTIP treatment. Although the Service appeared to take a contrary position to that of Private Letter Ruling 200314012 in Private Letter Ruling 201025021 (Feb. 19, 2010) by granting the donor an extension of time to make a Section 2523(f) gift tax QTIP election on a supplemental Form 709, the Service subsequently revoked Private Letter Ruling 201025021 in Private Letter Ruling 201109012 (Nov. 15, 2010), determining that it was erroneous since the time for filing an inter vivos QTIP election is expressly prescribed by statute and the Service does not have the discretion to grant an extension of time to make a QTIP election.

In note 58, replace Prop. Reg. §§ 20.2056(b)-5(f)(1), 20.2056(b)-7(d)(1) *with* Reg. §§ 20.2056(b)-5(f)(1), *and replace* Prop. Reg. § 20.2056(b)-7(d)(1) *with* Reg. § 20.2056(b)-7(d)(1).

Add to note 58 immediately after third sentence.

Wells Fargo Bank v. United States, 91 AFTR2d 2003-857 (10th Cir. 2003), held that once the donor had given up dominion and control of the property transferred to a trust that she intended to be a lifetime QTIP, but as to which no election was ever made, state law was irrelevant and the transfer was taxable, reversing the trial court which seemed to have found the donor's transfer to have been conditional on its qualifying for the marital deduction.

Add to end of note 58.

See ¶ 5.06[8][b][i] note 215.

[i] Other QTIP consequences.

Page 11-31:

Add to end of note 75.

See also Gans, Blattmachr & Zeydel, "Supercharged Credit Shelter Trust," 21 Prob. & Prop. No. 4, at 52 (July/Aug. 2007).

Add to note 76.

In Private Letter Ruling 200406004 (Oct. 31, 2003), the donor proposed to transfer property to an irrevocable marital trust that would pay the net income to the spouse for life and, if the donor survives the spouse, the net income would be paid to the donor for life. The Service ruled that if the donor makes a valid QTIP election, each transfer to the trust will qualify for the gift tax marital deduction. The Service also ruled that, if the donor survives spouse, no portion of the trust will be includible in the donor's gross estate except to the extent that the spouse's executor had made a QTIP election.

See Priv. Ltr. Rul. 200413011 (Dec. 3, 2003) (assets of a trust will qualify for the gift tax marital deduction upon termination of the donor's special power of appointment over the trust and nullification of the prenuptial agreement between donor and spouse on disposition of trust property in the event of a divorce).

Page 11-32:

Add to note 78.

Cf. the consequences to donor and spouse if donor grants spouse a revocable general power of appointment over a portion of donor's assets. See, e.g., Private Letter Ruling 200604028 (Sept. 30, 2005), in which husband and wife each intend to amend their respective revocable living trusts. Under the proposed reformation of wife's trust, if husband predeceases her, husband will have a testamentary general power of appointment over the assets in the trust equal to his unused applicable exclusion amount. Husband plans to sign a new will appointing this property to his trust. The Service ruled that if husband predeceases wife, the assets in wife's trust subject to husband's general power of appointment will be included in husband's estate and, if husband exercises power, wife will make a Section 2501 completed gift to husband that qualifies for the Section 2523 marital deduction. See also Priv. Ltr. Rul. 200403094 (Sept. 24, 2003). See supra ¶ 11.03[4][c][i] note 76.

Add to note 79.

See supra ¶ 11.03[4][c][i] note 76.

[d] Special Rule for Charitable Remainder Trusts

Page 11-35:

Add to note 102.

Priv. Ltr. Rul. 200832017 (Mar. 21, 2008) (creation of a successive unitrust interest in a CRUT, following the trustor's lifetime unitrust interest, in the trustor's spouse for life qualified for the marital deduction pursuant to IRC § 2523(g)).

[5] Noncitizen Donee Spouses

Page 11-35:

Add to note 105.

Private Letter Ruling 200240020 (June 25, 2002) ruled that a gift by a U.S. citizen of the entire remainder of a fifty-year residential leasehold to the donor's noncitizen spouse did not qualify for the marital deduction due to Section 2523(i). While not certain, it appears the donor's estate may have argued that Section 2036 caused the leasehold to be included in his estate because the donor continued to live in the residence until his death. Presumably, this would have permitted the surviving spouse to take steps to qualify the property as a "qualified domestic trust" under Section 2056(d)(2)(B). The asserted basis of inclusion was rejected, resulting in a taxable gift.

Add to note 107.

In 2003, the amount is $112,000. Rev. Proc. 2002-70, 2002-36 IRB 1. In 2004, the amount is $114,000. Rev. Proc. 2003-85, 2003-49 IRB 1104. In 2005, the amount is $117,000. Rev. Proc. 2004-71, 2004-50 IRB 970. In 2006, the amount is $120,000. Rev. Proc. 2005-70, 2005-47 IRB 979. In 2007, the amount is $125,000. Rev. Proc. 2006-53, 2006-48 IRB 996. In 2008, the amount is $128,000. Rev. Proc. 2007-66, 2007-__ IRB __. In 2009, the amount is $133,000. Rev. Proc. 2008-66, IRB 2008-45. In 2010, the amount is $134,000. Rev. Proc. 2009-50. In 2011, the amount is $136,000. Rev. Proc. 2010-40.

PART

Generation-Skipping
Transfers

Imposition of the Generation-Skipping Transfer Tax

¶ 12.03   Section 2603. Liability for Tax S12-1

         [1]   General Rules S12-1

¶ 12.03 SECTION 2603. LIABILITY FOR TAX

[1] General Rules

Page 12-11:

Add to note 4.

In Green Estate v. Comm'r, TC Memo. 2003-348, the court applied Section 2603(b) and held that the decedent's will expressly provided that no generation-skipping transfer tax on a direct skip should be paid from the direct skip transfer and, as a result, that all generation-skipping transfer tax should be apportioned to the charitable residuary's share. But see Estate of Denman, 270 SW3d 639 (Tex. Ct. App. 2008) where will's tax provision which apportions "transfer, estate, inheritance, succession and other death taxes" to the residue did not refer to the GST tax in an unambiguous manner. The court cited Monroe Estate v. Comm'r, 104 TC 352 (1995), rev'd in part on other grounds, 124 F3d 699 (5th Cir. 1997), and concluded that a reference to transfer taxes is insufficient for IRC § 2603(b) purposes and, accordingly, GST taxes were properly chargeable to property constituting a generation-skipping transfer and not to the residue.

CHAPTER 13

Generation-Skipping Transfers

¶ 13.01	Section 2611. "Generation-Skipping Transfer" Defined	S13-1
	[2] Transfers Excluded by Section 2611(b)	S13-1
	[a] Transfers for Educational and Medical Expenses	S13-1
¶ 13.02	Section 2612. Taxable Terminations, Taxable Distributions, and Direct Skips	S13-2
	[4] Direct Skips	S13-2
	[b] General Rule	S13-2
	[i] First requirement: transfer subject to estate or gift tax.	S13-2
	[ii] Second requirement: transfer of an interest to a skip person.	S13-2

¶ 13.01 SECTION 2611. "GENERATION-SKIPPING TRANSFER" DEFINED

[2] Transfers Excluded by Section 2611(b)

[a] Transfers for Educational and Medical Expenses

Page 13-4:

Add to note 9.

See Priv. Ltr. Rul. 200602002 (Sept. 6, 2005) (prepayments of tuition for each of six grandchildren pursuant to written agreements with school that payments would not be refundable and would not give the grandchildren any additional rights or privileges over other students will qualify for Section 2503(e) unlimited gift tax exclusion and, accordingly, are not treated as generation-skipping transfers).

¶ 13.02 SECTION 2612. TAXABLE TERMINATIONS, TAXABLE DISTRIBUTIONS, AND DIRECT SKIPS

[4] Direct Skips

[b] General Rule

[i] First requirement: transfer subject to estate or gift tax.

Page 13-50:

In note 258, add "2501(a)(5)" *after* "2501(a)(3)".

[ii] Second requirement: transfer of an interest to a skip person.

Page 13-54:

Add to note 289.

See also Prop. Reg. §§ 26.2651-1(a)(3), 26.2651-1(c) Ex. 3. Cf. Prop. Reg. § 26.2651-1(c) Ex. 4.

CHAPTER 14

Taxable Amount

¶ 14.02	Section 2621. Taxable Amount in Case of Taxable Distributions	S14-1
	[2] Valuation of Property Received by the Transferee . . .	S14-1
	[3] Reductions	S14-1
¶ 14.05	Section 2624. Valuation	S14-2
	[3] Reduction for Consideration	S14-2

¶ 14.02 SECTION 2621. TAXABLE AMOUNT IN CASE OF TAXABLE DISTRIBUTIONS

[2] Valuation of Property Received by the Transferee

Page 14-3:

Add to note 6.

In Robertson v. United States, 97 AFTR2d 2006 (ND Tex. 2006), the court determined the value of limited partnership units distributed by the trustees of several charitable lead non-exempt trusts to the grantor's grandchildren who were the remainderpersons of the trusts. The court concluded that the partnership units were entitled to a 19 percent lack of control discount and a 12.5 percent lack of marketability discount in determining the taxable amount of the distribution under Section 2621(a)(1).

[3] Reductions

Page 14-4:

Add to note 19.

See Robertson v. United States, 97 AFTR2d 2006 (ND Tex. 2006), where certain payments made to various attorneys, accountants, and appraisers in connection with distributions made by severable charitable lead non-exempt trusts to the grantor's grandchildren trusts had been erroneously deducted on income tax returns filed by the trusts and one or more of the grandchildren. The court allowed these expenses as deductions to offset the value of the taxable distributions under Section 2621(a)(2) so long as amended income tax returns were filed to remove the previously claimed deductions.

¶ 14.05　SECTION 2624. VALUATION

[3]　Reduction for Consideration

Page 14-17:

Insert reference to new note 38 at end of sentence that precedes sentence containing note 39.

Add new note 38.

   [38] See ¶ 4.08[1][a]. Cf. IRC § 2702; ¶ 19.03[4][e][iii].

CHAPTER 15

The Generation-Skipping Transfer Exemption

¶ 15.02	Section 2631. The GST Exemption [Revised]	S15-2
	[1] Individual Allocation	S15-3
	[2] Use of the Exemption	S15-6
	[3] The Transferor Requirement	S15-8
	[4] Duration of the Exemption	S15-9
¶ 15.03	Section 2632. Special Rules for Allocation of the GST	
	Exemption	S15-12
	[2] Actual Allocation to Inter Vivos Transfers	S15-12
	[b] Manner of Allocation	S15-12
	[3] Deemed Allocation to Inter Vivos Direct Skips	S15-13
	[a] The Deemed Allocation	S15-13
	[b] Delayed Direct Skips	S15-13
	[c] Opting Out of the Deemed Allocation	S15-13
	[4] Deemed Allocation to Inter Vivos Indirect Skips	S15-14
	[d] The Amount Deemed Allocated	S15-14
	[e] Elections	S15-15
	[i] Preventing automatic allocation.	S15-15
	[ii] Elective GST trusts.	S15-16
	[5] Retroactive Allocations	S15-17
	[b] Consequences of a Retroactive Allocation	S15-17
	[ii] Inclusion ratio valuation.	S15-17
	[6] Allocations Made at or After Death	S15-17
	[c] Inter Vivos Trusts Not Included in the Gross	
	Estate	S15-17
	[7] Allocation of Residual Exemption	S15-18
	[a] In General	S15-18
	[b] Allocation Between Categories	S15-18
	[ii] Trusts with generation-skipping transfer	
	potential.	S15-18
	[c] Apportionment Within Categories	S15-18

[i]   Direct skips and trusts with
        generation-skipping transfer potential. . . .   S15-18

¶ 15.02 SECTION 2631. THE GST EXEMPTION [REVISED]

Replace existing ¶ 15.02 with the following revised ¶ 15.02.

Every individual is allowed a GST exemption.[1] The GST exemption amount equals the estate tax *basic* exclusion amount under Section 2010(c)(3).[2] Since the GST exemption equals only the basic exclusion amount, there is no spousal portability of unused GST exemption.[3] The GST exemption amount has steadily increased over the years since the enactment of the generation-skipping transfer tax.[4] The GST exemption amount is $5 million for years 2010 and 2011,[5] and that amount is adjusted upward for inflation in 2012.[6] The GST exemption amount currently sunsets in 2013 and reverts to the 2001 exemption amount.[7]

---

[1] IRC § 2631(a).

[2] IRC § 2631(c). See IRC §§ 2010(c)(2)(A), 2010(c)(3).

[3] IRC §§ 2631(c), 2010(c)(2), 2010(c)(3), 2010(c)(4). See Supplement ¶ 3.02[1][b]. Cf. Supplement ¶ 9.06[1] text accompanying notes 18–21.

[4] The GST exemption amount is as follows:

Year	Exclusion Amount
1987–1998	$1 million
1999	$1,010,000 (Rev. Proc. 98-61, 1998-2 CB 811, 816)
2000	$1,030,000 (Rev. Proc. 99-42, 1999-2 CB 568, 572)
2001	$1,060,000 (Rev. Proc. 2001-13, 2001-1 CB 337, 341)
2002	$1,100,000 (Rev. Proc. 2001-59, 2001-2 CB 623, 627)
2003	$1,120,000 (Rev. Proc. 2002-70, 2002-2 CB 845, 850)
2004 and 2005	$1,500,000
2006–2008	$2,000,000
2009	$3,500,000
2010 and 2011	$5,000,000
2012	$5,000,000 (adjusted for inflation)

[5] IRC §§ 2631(c), 2010(c)(3).

[6] IRC §§ 2631(c), 2010(c)(3)(B). The amount of the inflationary adjustment is determined by multiplying the cost-of-living adjustment determined under a modified version of Section 1(f)(3) for the calendar year by $5 million. IRC § 2010(c)(3)(B). The Section 1(f)(3) cost-of-living adjustment is modified by adjusting for inflation after 2010 (rather than 1992). IRC § 2010(c)(3)(B)(ii). Inflationary adjustments to the GST exemption will be made only in multiples of $10,000, rounded to the next lowest multiple of $10,000. IRC § 2010(c)(3)(B) (flush language).

[7] Economic Growth and Tax Relief Reconciliation Act of 2001, Pub. L. No. 107-16 § 901(a)(2), 115 Stat. 38, 150 (2001), reprinted in 2001-3 CB 9, 122, as amended by the Tax Relief Act of 2010, Pub. L. No. 111-312, §§ 101(a)(1), 304, 124 Stat. 3296, 3298, 3304 (2010). The "sunset" provision is discussed more fully at ¶ 8.11. The 2001 GST exemption amount was $1 million adjusted for inflation after 1998. See supra notes 4 and 6.

The GST exemption provided by Section 2631 is an important factor in the determination of the applicable rate of tax to be imposed on any generation-skipping transfer. The applicable rate of tax[8] is the product of the maximum Section 2001(c) federal estate tax rate[9] and the inclusion ratio.[10] The amount of the inclusion ratio is dependent on the amount of the transferor's GST exemption allocated to the transfer. The inclusion ratio is equal to one minus the applicable fraction.[11] The GST exemption allocated[12] to a transfer is the numerator of the applicable fraction,[13] and the value of the property transferred is generally the denominator of the fraction.[14] In general, if the amount of exemption allocated to a transfer is equal to the value of the property involved in the transfer, the applicable fraction is one, both the inclusion ratio and the applicable rate of tax are zero, and no generation-skipping transfer tax will be imposed on the property until there is a new transferor.[15]

[1] Individual Allocation

An individual may allocate GST exemption generally to any property transferred with respect to which the individual is the transferor.[16] The allocation of the exemption, if not made by the individual before death, may be made by the executor of the individual's estate[17] until the date for filing the individual's federal estate tax return.[18] As the GST exemption is cumulative over life and

---

[8] IRC § 2641(a). See ¶ 16.01.

[9] IRC § 2641(b).

[10] IRC § 2642(a)(1). See ¶ 16.02.

[11] IRC § 2642(a)(2). See ¶ 16.02.

[12] See IRC § 2632; infra ¶ 15.03.

[13] IRC § 2642(a)(2)(A). But see IRC § 2642(e)(2); ¶ 16.02[6].

[14] IRC § 2642(a)(2)(B)(i). However, Section 2642(a)(2)(B)(ii) provides for potential reductions in the denominator, and Section 2642(c) provides for an exclusion of nontaxable gifts from the denominator. See ¶¶ 16.02[2][b], 16.02[3][b][ii].

[15] But see supra notes 13, 14. In the alternative, if no GST exemption is allocated to a generation-skipping transfer, the applicable fraction is zero, the inclusion ratio is one, and the estate is taxed at the maximum federal transfer tax rate.

[16] IRC §§ 2631(a), 2652(a). But see IRC § 2642(f); infra ¶ 15.03[3][b], ¶ 16.02[7]. Use of the exemption allows a major planning opportunity under the generation-skipping transfer tax. See Slade, "Lifetime Planning Under the GSTT Rules," 137 Tr. & Est. 46 (Dec. 1998); Gallo, "Estate Planning and the Generation-Skipping Transfer Tax," 33 Real Prop. Prob. & Tr. J. 457 (Fall 1998); Pennell & Williamson, "The Economics of Prepaying Wealth Transfer Tax," 136 Tr. & Est. 52 (Aug. 1997); Kalik & Schneider, "Generation-Skipping Transfer Taxes Under the Tax Reform Act of 1986," 21 U. Miami Inst. Est. Plan. 9-1, at ¶ 907 (1987); US Trust and Practical Drafting, "Generation-Skipping Transfers," 1149, 1255 (1987). See also Lang, "Allocating the GST Exemption Under the Generation-Skipping Transfer Tax," 41 Me. L. Rev. 43 (1989).

[17] See IRC § 2203; ¶ 8.02.

[18] IRC § 2632(a)(1), discussed infra ¶ 15.03. This date applies regardless of whether a federal estate tax return is required to be filed. Reg. § 26.2632-1(a). Regardless of whether a federal estate tax return is ultimately required to be filed, the deadline includes

may be allocated to transfers made at death, the individual or the individual's executor may choose to allocate all, a part, or none of the available GST exemption to a particular transfer. An allocation, once made, becomes irrevocable.[19] The allocation of GST exemption may be made by means of a formula.[20] If the allocation of GST exemption is made to property held in trust, the allocation is made to the entire trust rather than specific trust assets or a fractional

---

extensions actually granted. Reg. § 26.2632-1(a). See IRC § 6018(a); infra ¶ 15.03[6][a] text accompanying note 231. But see IRC § 2642(g); ¶ 16.02[9].

[19] IRC § 2631(b). A timely allocation of GST exemption becomes irrevocable after the due date of the return. Reg. § 26.2632-1(b)(4)(i). Priv. Ltr. Rul. 200816007 (Dec. 11, 2007) (request to reallocate GST exemption denied). Reg. § 26.2632-1(b)(4). Thus, the allocation of GST exemption to property transferred inter vivos by the transferor may be modified by a subsequent allocation on an amended return filed on or before the date the Form 709 reporting the transfer is due, or would be due if no return is required to be filed. Reg. § 26.2632-1(b)(4)(ii)(A)(1) . The later allocation must clearly identify the transfer and the nature and extent of the modification. Id. See Reg. §§ 26.2632-1(b)(4)(iii) Exs. 1, 2.

Sections 2632(b) and 2632(c) automatically allocate GST exemption to inter vivos direct and indirect skips. IRC §§ 2632(b), 2632(c). The transferor may elect to prevent the automatic allocation of GST exemption to direct or indirect skips. IRC §§ 2632(b)(3), 2632(c)(5)(A). An election to prevent the automatic allocation of GST exemption to an inter vivos direct or indirect skip should also be subject to modification on an amended return filed on or before the due date of the Form 709 reporting the transfer. See Reg. § 26.2632-1(b)(1)(ii); infra ¶ 15.03[3][c] text accompanying notes 76, 77. See also IRC § 2642(g); ¶ 16.02[9]. Likewise, any timely allocation of GST exemption on Form 706 should be subject to modification by filing an amended Form 706 on or before the date prescribed for filing the return, including extensions actually granted. See Reg. § 26.2632-1(d)(1). A late allocation of GST exemption is irrevocable when made. Reg. § 26.2632-1(b)(2)(ii)(A)(2).

[20] Reg. §§ 26.2632-1(b)(4)(i), 26.2632-1(d)(1). The allocation may be expressed as the amount necessary to yield an inclusion ratio of zero for the trust after the transfer. Reg. § 26.2632-1(b)(4)(i). See also IRC § 2642(g)(2); ¶ 16.02[9][b].

When a transferor desires to prevent the automatic allocation of GST exemption to an inter vivos direct or indirect skip, a formula should be effective in describing the extent to which the automatic allocation is not to apply. See Reg. § 26.2632-1(b)(1)(i). However, a formula allocation of GST exemption with respect to a charitable lead annuity trust is invalid except to the extent the formula allocation is dependent on values as finally determined for federal estate or gift tax purposes. Reg. § 26.2632-1(b)(4)(i). See infra ¶ 15.03[6] text accompanying note 227. See also ¶ 16.02[6].

share of the trust.[21] Generally,[22] an allocation of GST exemption is void to the extent the amount allocated exceeds the amount necessary to yield an inclusion ratio of zero for the trust.[23] An allocation of GST exemption to a trust is also void if, at the time of the allocation, the trust has no potential to yield generation-skipping transfers attributed to the transferor whose GST exemption is allocated to the trust.[24] Any portion of an individual's GST exemption not allocated by the individual or the individual's executor is deemed allocated in a manner prescribed by Section 2632.[25]

Allocation of the GST exemption is needed only for potentially taxable generation-skipping transfers. It is not needed, for example, to protect transfers of property to grandchildren who are treated under the statutory scheme as the transferor's children,[26] transfers to grandchildren before 1990 that did not exceed $2 million,[27] transfers excluded by Section 2611(b),[28] transfers of certain

---

[21] Reg. § 26.2632-1(a). Even where the transfer is a direct skip to a trust, any of the transferor's GST exemption allocated to the transferred property is an allocation to the trust that is used in the computation of the applicable rate of generation-skipping transfer tax imposed on subsequent generation-skipping transfers from the trust attributed to that transferor, rather than an allocation of GST exemption to specific assets transferred in the direct skip. Id. If the GST exemption allocated is less than the total value of the assets in the trust, the result is that the trust has an inclusion ratio greater than zero, but less than one, as opposed to a fraction of the trust having an inclusion ratio of zero and the remaining portion of the trust having an inclusion ratio of one. Cf. IRC § 2642(a)(3), discussed ¶ 16.02[5][e] text accompanying notes 372–380.

[22] An exception is provided for allocation of GST exemption to charitable lead annuity trusts. Reg. § 26.2632-1(b)(4)(i). See Reg. § 26.2642-3(c) Ex. See also infra ¶ 15.03[6][a] note 237.

[23] Reg. § 26.2632-1(b)(4), Reg. § 26.2632-1(b)(4)(i). See Reg. § 26.2642-4(b) Ex. 3. This provision voiding excessive GST exemption allocations is intended to prevent a transferor from wasting GST exemption. TD 8644, Supplementary Information, 60 Fed. Reg. 66,898, 66,900 (1995).

[24] Reg. § 26.2632-1(b)(4)(i). This provision is intended to prevent a transferor from wasting GST exemption with respect to a testamentary or inter vivos transfer. TD 8644, Supplementary Information, 60 Fed. Reg. 66,898, 66,900 (1995). Priv. Ltr. Rul. 199929040 (Apr. 15, 1999) (allocation by settlor to qualified terminable interest property (QTIP) trust without reverse QTIP election void). A trust is considered to have the potential to yield generation-skipping transfers with respect to the transferor whose GST exemption is allocated to the trust, even if the possibility of a generation-skipping transfer is so remote as to be negligible. Reg. § 26.2632-1(b)(4)(i) .

[25] See IRC §§ 2632(b), 2632(c), 2632(e). Sections 2632(b) and 2632(c) require the GST exemption to be allocated to inter vivos direct and indirect skips unless the transferor elects to the contrary, and Section 2632(e) provides a rule allocating the GST exemption if the transferor and the transferor's executor do not totally deplete the transferor's GST exemption. These sections are discussed more fully infra ¶¶ 15.03[3], 15.03[4], 15.03[7].

[26] See IRC § 2651(e); ¶ 17.01[2][a][ii].

[27] See ¶ 13.02[4][c][ii].

[28] See ¶ 13.01[2].

nontaxable gifts under Section 2642(c),[29] or transfers that are grandfathered under the transitional rules.[30]

[2] Use of the Exemption

In general, an individual may allocate the GST exemption to any completed inter vivos transfer[31] or any testamentary transfer of property,[32] even though no immediate generation-skipping transfer occurs.[33] However, if an inter vivos transfer is potentially includible in the gross estate of the transferor or the transferor's spouse, other than by reason of Section 2035, if such individual were to die immediately after the transfer, the allocation generally is not effective until the termination of the "estate tax inclusion period" (ETIP).[34]

Once the GST exemption allocated to property held in a trust is effective,[35] the applicable fraction structure effectively permits it to appreciate and depreciate with fluctuations in the value of the corpus of the trust to which it is allocated.[36] For example, assume A in 2011 transfers property worth $5 million to an irrevocable inter vivos trust[37] and immediately allocates $5 million GST exemption to the property. The trust provides for income to A's child for life, then income to A's grandchildren for life, with a remainder to A's

-----

[29] See ¶ 16.02[2][b].

[30] See ¶ 18.05[2].

[31] See IRC § 2652(a)(1)(B). But see IRC § 2642(f), discussed infra ¶ 15.03[3][b], ¶ 16.02[7].

[32] See IRC § 2652(a)(1)(A).

[33] Instructions for Form 709, United States Gift (and Generation-Skipping Transfer) Tax Return (2010) Schedule C, Part 2, Line 5, at 14; Instructions for Form 706, United States Estate (and Generation-Skipping Transfer) Tax Return (Rev. Sept. 2009) How to Complete Schedule R, Part 1, Line 9, at 26. See IRC § 2632(c); infra ¶ 15.03[4].

[34] IRC §§ 2642(f)(1), 2642(f)(3), 2642(f)(4). The estate tax inclusion period is generally the period after the inter vivos transfer during which, should death occur, the property transferred would be included in the transferor's or the transferor's spouse's gross estate, other than by reason of Section 2035. Reg. § 26.2632-1(c)(2)(i). There are three exceptions to the general rule: (1) possible inclusion in the transferor's spouse's gross estate is disregarded if a Section 2652(a)(3), reverse QTIP, election is made (Reg. § 26.2632-1(c)(2)(ii)(C)); (2) possible inclusion is so remote as to be negligible (Reg. § 26.2632-1(c)(2)(ii)(A)); or (3) where the spouse holds a five-or-five power that expires within sixty days of the transfer (Reg. § 26.2632-1(c)(2)(ii)(B)). See ¶ 16.02[7][b][ii]. This period will not extend beyond the earlier of the generation-skipping transfer, the time at which no portion of the property is potentially includible in the gross estate of the transferor or the transferor's spouse, other than under Section 2035, or the death of the transferor or the transferor's spouse. IRC § 2642(f)(3); Reg. § 26.2632-1(c)(3). The estate tax inclusion period and other Section 2642(f) rules are more fully discussed infra ¶ 15.03[3][b] and at ¶ 16.02[7].

[35] This includes any trust equivalent. See IRC §§ 2652(b)(1), 2652(b)(3); ¶ 17.02[2].

[36] HR Rep. No. 426, 99th Cong., 1st Sess. 1, 826 (1986), reprinted in 1986-3 CB (vol. 2) 1, 826.

[37] The same principles would apply if the trust were a testamentary trust.

great-grandchildren. Assuming no application of the Rule Against Perpetuities[38] and no addition to the trust corpus, the property held in the trust is shielded from the Chapter 13 tax throughout the duration and termination of the trust.[39] No Chapter 13 tax will be imposed on the taxable terminations occurring at the deaths of A's child and grandchildren, even if the trust corpus appreciates in value to tens of millions of dollars by the time the generation-skipping transfers occur because regardless of the value of the trust corpus, generation-skipping transfers are taxed at an applicable rate of zero.[40]

Alternatively, if A allocates $2.5 million of GST exemption to the $5 million worth of property transferred to the trust, the trust's inclusion ratio will be 0.500.[41] Assuming that the trust is not severed in a qualified severance[42] and that there are no corpus additions or additional GST exemption allocations to the property held in trust, a generation-skipping transfer from this trust will be taxed at one-half the maximum federal estate tax rate; in effect, one half of the

---

[38] The remainder interest under this trust would violate the common-law Rule Against Perpetuities. If the trust had provided instead for income to be paid to A's child, then income to specifically named children of A's child who were living at the time the trust was created, with a remainder to those of A's great-grandchildren who are children of the grandchildren who are the income beneficiaries of the trust, there would be no violation of the Rule Against Perpetuities. We chose to use the looser provisions of the trust in our example, but technicians who prefer a common-law perpetuities-proper trust should substitute the above provisions for those in the text. See generally Gray, The Rule Against Perpetuities § 201 (Little Brown & Co., 4th ed. 1942).

A number of states have modified the Rule Against Perpetuities. See Bloom, "The Generation-Skipping Transfer Tax Tail Is Killing the Rule Against Perpetuities," 87 Tax Notes 569 ns. 22, 23 (2000).

[39] HR Rep. No. 426, 99th Cong., 1st Sess. 1, 826 (1986), reprinted in 1986-3 CB (vol. 2) 1, 826.

[40] The Section 2642 inclusion ratio and the Section 2641 applicable rate of tax are both zero in this example: one minus ($5 million/$5 million is 1) one = zero.

As an alternative to the example in the text, consider the following example that results in both a generation-skipping transfer (a direct skip) at the creation of the trust and another generation-skipping transfer (a taxable termination or a taxable distribution) at a later time. Assuming an adequate allocation of the GST exemption, both generation-skipping transfers to and from the trust are shielded from the Chapter 13 tax.

For example, assume A transfers $5 million to an irrevocable trust. The trust agreement provides that the income is to be paid to A's grandchild for life with a remainder to the grandchild's children (A's great-grandchildren) and permits the nongrantor trustee to invade corpus for the great-grandchildren. A's child, the parent of the grandchild, is alive at the time of the transfer to the trust. See IRC § 2651(e). If A allocates $5 million of GST exemption to the property transferred, the trust's inclusion ratio and the applicable tax rate are zero. The transfer to the trust, as well as any generation-skipping transfers from the trust, assuming no corpus additions are made, will not generate any tax under Chapter 13 notwithstanding any increases or decreases in the value of the trust assets.

[41] The applicable fraction is 0.500 (IRC § 2642(a)(2)), and one minus 0.500 results in an inclusion ratio of 0.500. IRC § 2642(a)(1). See ¶ 16.02[1] note 6.

[42] A "qualified severance" of the trust would result in one trust with an inclusion ratio of one and another with an inclusion ratio of zero. See IRC § 2642(a)(3); ¶ 16.02[5][e].

property transferred to the trust will be taxed and one-half will not, regardless of whether the property appreciates or depreciates in value.[43]

Should *A* subsequently allocate an additional amount of GST exemption to the property held in the trust, the applicable fraction must be recomputed,[44] resulting in the recomputation of the inclusion ratio and the rate of tax imposed on any subsequent generation-skipping transfer.[45]

[3] The Transferor Requirement

An individual's GST exemption may be allocated only to property with respect to which the individual is the transferor.[46] When there are multiple transferors and a single trust, each transferor's transfers must be segregated and each transferor treated as creating a separate trust for purposes of both allocation of the GST exemption and computation of the generation-skipping transfer tax.[47]

An individual may not assign GST exemption to property when another person is the transferor and may not apply the exemption of another person to property for which the individual is the transferor. However, when a transferor and the transferor's spouse elect under Section 2513 to split gifts for gift tax purposes,[48] that election also applies to transfers of property for generation-skipping transfer tax purposes.[49] Under these rules, each spouse is treated

---

[43] Assuming a maximum federal tax rate of 35 percent, a generation-skipping transfer from the trust would be taxed at a rate of 17.5 percent. This is the same as taxing one half of any generation-skipping transfer at a tax rate of 35 percent and the other one-half at a tax rate of zero.

The inclusion ratio for the trust must be recomputed after the initial generation-skipping transfer at the child's death to take into account the generation-skipping transfer tax borne by the trust. IRC § 2653(b)(1). See infra note 44. Under Section 2653(b)(1), assuming the $5 million corpus has not appreciated in value at the child's death, the generation-skipping transfer tax of $875,000 would be paid out of the trust corpus, leaving a $4,125,000 corpus, an applicable fraction of $2,500,000/$4,125,000 or 0.606, and an inclusion ratio of 0.394. Under Section 2653(b)(1), the generation-skipping transfer tax is treated as paid from the nonexempt portion of the trust. See ¶ 17.03[2][a].

[44] IRC § 2642(d)(4). The recomputation process is prescribed by Section 2642(d)(2). See ¶¶ 16.02[5][b][i], 16.02[5][b][iii]. The applicable fraction is also recomputed when additional property is transferred to the trust (see IRC § 2642(d)(1); ¶¶ 16.02[5][b][ii], 16.02[5][b][iii]), and when only a portion of the trust is shielded from tax and the trust is involved in a taxable termination without any substitution of transferor. See IRC § 2653(b)(1); supra note 43; ¶¶ 16.02[5][d], 17.03[2][a]. The applicable fraction also may be recomputed where separate trusts are consolidated. See Reg. § 26.2642-4(a)(2); ¶ 16.02[5][c]. Additionally, a recomputation of the applicable fraction may be necessary if additional estate tax is imposed under Section 2032A. See Reg. § 26.2642-4(a)(4)(i); ¶ 16.02[5][f].

[45] IRC §§ 2641(a), 2642(a); see ¶ 16.02[5].

[46] IRC § 2631(a). See also IRC § 2652(a).

[47] IRC § 2654(b)(1). See ¶ 17.04[2].

[48] See ¶ 10.03.

[49] IRC § 2652(a)(2). See ¶ 17.02[1][c][ii]. Reg. § 26.2632-1(b)(4). See also Reg. § 26.2632-1(b)(4)(iii) Ex. 5.

as a transferor to a single trust and each spouse is able to allocate GST exemption to the trust, thus effectively permitting an interspousal assignment of the GST exemption to the extent that the spouse is treated as a transferor.[50]

[4] Duration of the Exemption

Once the amount of GST exemption allocated to a transfer of property equals the value of the property transferred, the GST exemption effectively protects that property from the imposition of the generation-skipping transfer tax whether it appreciates or depreciates in value.[51] However, the allocation effectively protects the property from Chapter 13 tax only as long as the individual who transferred the property and allocated GST exemption to it continues as the Chapter 13 transferor of the property.[52] When property held in trust is subject to taxation under the Chapter 11 estate tax or the Chapter 12 gift tax and the decedent or the donor is someone other than the original transferor, the decedent or the donor generally[53] becomes the transferor of the property for purposes of Chapter 13.[54] That new transferor must allocate GST exemption to the property to shield it from the imposition of tax under Chapter 13.

When property that qualifies for the marital deduction as qualified terminable interest property (QTIP) is transferred in a generation-skipping transfer, the donee spouse usually replaces the donor spouse as the transferor of the property.[55] However, Section 2652(a)(3) permits the donor spouse or the donor spouse's executor to make an election, referred to as a reverse QTIP election, that retains the donor spouse as the Chapter 13 transferor and prevents the do-

---

[50] The election also requires the trust to be treated as two trusts for computational purposes. See supra text accompanying note 47. For example, assume Transferor transfers $10 million to a trust with income to Child for life and a remainder to Grandchild. Transferor and Transferor's Spouse, both of whom have exhausted any available annual exclusion for gifts to Child in the year the trust is established, elect to use Section 2513 gift splitting, and each allocates $5 million of GST exemption to the transfer. As a result, the trust is treated as two separate trusts for computational purposes, with each trust having a zero inclusion ratio. In effect, Transferor's Spouse's GST exemption has been allocated to Transferor's transfer.

[51] See supra ¶ 15.02[2] text accompanying notes 35–40.

[52] Cf. IRC § 2652(a)(1). See ¶ 17.02[1].

[53] See infra text accompanying note 56.

[54] IRC § 2652(a)(1). See, e.g., IRC §§ 2041, 2514. For example, assume transferor T creates a trust that provides income to child C for life with a remainder to grandchild GC, but gives C a general power of appointment over the corpus. Even if C fails to appoint the corpus, it is included in C's gross estate under Section 2041(a)(2), and C becomes the Section 2652(a)(1) transferor of the property. See infra text accompanying notes 57–64.

[55] Under Section 2652(a)(1), the donee spouse would be the transferor of any property once that property is included in the donee spouse's gross estate under Section 2044, or once the donee spouse makes a gift of the qualifying income interest and under Section 2511 and Section 2519 the property held in trust is subject to the gift tax. See IRC §§ 2044, 2511, 2519. See also ¶¶ 4.16, 10.08.

nee spouse from becoming the Chapter 13 transferor of the property.[56] Use of this reverse QTIP election permits the donor spouse to allocate GST exemption to a transfer that otherwise eventually would be attributable to the donee spouse and would require use of the donee spouse's GST exemption.

An allocation of an individual's GST exemption to a transfer that will not eventually be the subject matter of a generation-skipping transfer while the individual is the transferor of the trust is void.[57] For example, assume that grantor *G* transfers $1 million to a trust with income to child *C* for life, then income to grandchild *GC*, who is living at the creation of the trust, for life, and a remainder to grandchild's child *GGC*.[58] *G* allocates $1 million of GST exemption to the property held in the trust, shielding it from any Chapter 13 tax.[59] *G* also gives *C* a general power to appoint the entire corpus by will. At *C*'s death, the property held in the trust is included in *C*'s gross estate.[60] *C* becomes the transferor of the property held in trust,[61] and there is no generation-skipping transfer attributed to *G*.[62] Even if *C* fails to exercise the general power of appointment and, by default, the property remains in the trust created by *G*, *C* still becomes the Chapter 13 transferor of the trust and there is no generation-skipping transfer.[63] *G*'s GST exemption allocation is void because it was made with respect to a trust that had no generation-skipping transfer tax potential for the grantor at the time of the allocation of GST exemption by *G*.[64] Assuming *GC* survives *C*, *C*'s GST exemption must be allocated to the property held in trust to prevent the imposition of the generation-skipping transfer tax on any generation-skipping transfer with respect to the property held in the trust.

---

[56] See ¶¶ 16.02[7][b] text accompanying notes 472–475, 17.02[1][c][i]. The election creates several tax-planning opportunities. See ¶ 17.02[1][c] text accompanying notes 56–60.

[57] Reg. § 26.2632-1(b)(4), Reg. §§ 26.2632-1(b)(4)(i), 26.2632-1(d)(1), 26.2632-1(d)(2).

[58] See generally supra ¶ 15.02[2] note 38.

[59] See supra ¶ 15.02[2] text accompanying notes 35–40.

[60] IRC § 2041(a)(2).

[61] See IRC § 2652(a)(1)(A); ¶¶ 13.02[2][e][ii], 17.02[1].

[62] Although *C*'s interest terminates, the property is deemed to pass to *C* (see ¶ 13.02[2][e] text accompanying notes 95, 96; see also Reg. § 26.2612-1(b)(1)), and as a result, there is no taxable termination, both because *C* is not a skip person in relation to *G* and there is a transfer subject to federal estate tax that occurs with respect to the property held in the trust at the time of the termination. See ¶ 13.02[2][d].

[63] See supra text accompanying note 61. Because *GC* is a non–skip person in relation to *C*, there is no direct skip on *C*'s deemed transfer of the property back to the trust.

[64] Reg. § 26.2632-1(b)(4)(i). See Priv. Ltr. Rul. 200838022 (Apr. 28, 2008). See also Reg. § 26.2632-1(d)(1). Similarly, automatic allocation of GST exemption after death under Section 2632(e) does not occur if the entire trust will have a new transferor prior to the occurrence of any generation-skipping transfer. Reg. § 26.2632-1(d)(2). See infra ¶ 15.03[7].

Assume the facts change and that instead C is granted only a noncumulative annual general power of appointment over 5 percent of the corpus. If, in any year, C exercises the general power and appoints the property to GGC, whose parents are still alive,[65] C (not G) is the Chapter 13 transferor of the direct skip generation-skipping transfer to GGC.[66] For this direct skip generation-skipping transfer to escape tax, C must allocate GST exemption to the transfer.[67] If, instead, C allows the power to lapse each year, the entire amount of the lapse would come within the Section 2514(e) exception, and there would be no new transferor during C's life.[68] At C's death, however, five percent of the value of the property held in the trust would be included in C's gross estate,[69] and that five percent of the corpus would thereafter be considered C's transfer to the trust.[70] An allocation of C's GST exemption would be needed to protect the five percent portion of the trust property that was included in C's gross estate from the imposition of the generation-skipping transfer tax on the taxable termination that occurs at GC's death.[71] Alternatively, if the trust instrument had not granted the general power of appointment to C, the property ultimately would have passed to GGC without imposition of

---

[65] See IRC § 2612(c)(2).

[66] IRC §§ 2612(c)(1), 2652(a)(1)(B). See IRC § 2514(b). See also ¶ 13.02[2][e][ii]. However, to the extent that the exercise of the power results in outright transfers excluded under Section 2503(b)(1) of the gift tax, the transfers are also exempted from Chapter 13 taxation. See IRC §§ 2642(c)(1), 2642(c)(3), discussed ¶ 16.02[2][b]. See also ¶ 13.02[4][b] text accompanying notes 261–264.

[67] See supra note 66. See also Section 2632(b)(1) (which would make a deemed allocation here in the absence of an election out of such deemed allocation under Section 2632(b)(3)); infra ¶ 15.03[3].

[68] IRC § 2514(e). In addition, each year's lapse of the power would not constitute a taxable termination. See ¶ 13.02[2][e] text accompanying notes 118, 129.

[69] IRC § 2041(a)(2). Inclusion of 5 percent of the value of the property held in the trust in C's gross estate could possibly be avoided by limiting the time during the year when C holds and could exercise the 5 percent power. See ¶ 13.02[2][e] note 142.

[70] IRC § 2652(a)(1)(A). There is no immediate Section 2612(c) direct skip of that 5 percent of the corpus to the trust because the trust is not a skip person, due to the fact GC is not a skip person in relation to C. IRC § 2613. Cf. ¶ 13.02[2][e][ii]. Because there are now two transferors, the trust must be separated into two trusts. IRC § 2654(b)(1); see supra ¶ 15.02[3] text accompanying note 47. The first trust contains 5 percent of the original corpus and C is its transferor. A taxable termination of that trust occurs at GC's death. IRC § 2612(a)(1). The second trust contains the remaining 95 percent of the original corpus with G as its transferor. There will be taxable terminations with respect to second trust at C's death and again at GC's death. IRC § 2612(a)(1). Cf. IRC § 2653(b)(1).

[71] See supra note 70. See Austin W. Bramwell, "Generation-Skipping Transfer Tax Consequences of GRATs: Finding the Answers," 114 J. Tax'n 260 (May 2011).

any generation-skipping transfer tax by virtue of *G*'s GST exemption having been allocated to the property held in the trust.[72]

---

[72] See supra ¶ 15.02[2] text accompanying notes 35–40. This would also occur if *C* made a qualified disclaimer under Section 2518 of the general power of appointment. See ¶ 10.07.

¶ 15.03   SECTION 2632. SPECIAL RULES FOR ALLOCATION OF THE GST EXEMPTION

[2] Actual Allocation to Inter Vivos Transfers

Page 15-14:

In note 8 change citation Reg. § 26.2632-1(b)(2) *to the following.*

Reg. § 26.2632-1(b)(4)

[b] Manner of Allocation

Page 15-15:

In note 15 change citation Reg. § 26.2632-1(b)(2) *to the following.*

Reg. § 26.2632-1(b)(4)

Add to end of note 15.

Priv. Ltr. Rul. 200510026 (Nov. 30, 2004) (trust agreement attached to federal gift tax return contained sufficient information to constitute substantial compliance with the requirements for making a valid allocation). Priv. Ltr. Rul. 200550006 (Aug. 25, 2005) (although deceased donor had not complied with the federal gift tax return instructions by misidentifying the actual donee of a gift on the return, the information on the return constituted substantial compliance with the requirements for making a timely allocation of the decedent's available GST exemption).

Page 15-16:

In notes 17 and 18, change citations Reg. § 26.2632-1(b)(2) *to the following.*

Reg. § 26.2632-1(b)(4)

Page 15-17:

In note 21, change citations Reg. § 26.2632-1(b)(2)*to the following.*

Reg. § 26.2632-1(b)(4)

Page 15-18:

In notes 24, 25, 26, and 28, change citations Reg. § 26.2632-1(b)(2) to the following.

Reg. § 26.2632-1(b)(4)

Page 15-19:

In notes 30, 31, 32, and 33, change citations Reg. § 26.2632-1(b)(2) to the following.

Reg. § 26.2632-1(b)(4)

[3] Deemed Allocation to Inter Vivos Direct Skips

[a] The Deemed Allocation

Page 15-19:

Add to note 38 after citation "Reg. § 26.2632-1(a)".

Priv. Ltr. Rul. 200633015 (May 12, 2006) (all of couple's previous and future contributions to irrevocable trusts established by them for the benefit of their minor grandchildren are direct skips and couple's unused GST exemption is automatically allocated to these contributions necessary to make the inclusion ratio for each trust equal to zero).

[b] Delayed Direct Skips

Page 15-22:

In note 50, replace the fourth sentence with the following:

Regulations Section 26.2632-1(c)(1)(ii) provides "[a]n affirmative allocation of GST exemption cannot be revoked, but becomes effective as of (and no earlier than) the date of the close of the ETIP with respect to the trust."

[c] Opting Out of the Deemed Allocation

Page 15-25:

Add to note 70.

For *inter vivos* direct skips occurring in 2010, where the donor wishes to pay tax at the zero-percent rate, an election out of the automatic allocation can be made in two ways. Notice 2011-66. The donor may affirmatively elect out of the automatic allocation on a timely filed Form 709 or pay the GST tax shown on the return. Because a donor would never want to allocate GST exemption to a direct skip not in trust, the Service will interpret the reporting of an *inter vivos* direct skip not in trust occurring in 2010 on a timely filed Form 709 as payment of the tax, at zero percent, and an election out of the automatic allocation rules. See Supplement ¶ 18.04.

Page 15-26:

Add to note 75.

See Harrington, McCaffrey, Leva Plaine & Schneider, "Generation-Skipping Transfer Tax Planning After the 2001 Act—Mostly Good News," 95 J. Tax'n 143 (Sept. 2001).

[4] Deemed Allocation to Inter Vivos Indirect Skips

[d] The Amount Deemed Allocated

Page 15-37:

Replace the text beginning with the first full paragraph on the page to end of ¶ 15.03[4] with the following.

If an indirect skip transfer occurs with respect to a pre-existing trust, which has an inclusion ratio greater than zero, the amount of the deemed allocation is not as clear. It is arguable that under the provisions dealing generally with GST exemption allocation, when an allocation of GST exemption is made for property held in a trust, the inclusion ratio for the trust is determined, not an inclusion ratio for the property transferred.[163] Under this argument it would be more appropriate to read the statute to provide that the inclusion ratio of the trust, not the value of the property transferred, controls the amount of the unused GST exemption to be allocated upon an indirect skip transfer to the trust in order to give the property transferred to the trust an inclusion ratio of zero.[164] However, it is also arguable that the statute should be interpreted as allocating GST exemption equal to the value of the property transferred in the indirect skip and the regulations have adopted that approach.[165]

The automatic allocation is effective whether or not a gift tax return is filed reporting the transfer and is effective as of the date of the transfer to which it relates.[166] For an indirect skip to which the Section 2642(f) ETIP period does not apply, an automatic allocation is irrevocable after the due date of

---

[163] IRC § 2642(a)(1)(A); Reg. § 26.2642-1(b).

[164] The legislative history does not provide an answer to this issue. It provides that "any unused portion of such individual's generation-skipping transfer tax exemption is allocated to the property transferred to the extent necessary to produce the lowest possible inclusion ratio for such property." HR Conf. Rep. No. 84, 107th Cong., 1st Sess. 198 (2001), reprinted in 2001—CB —, —. Possibly a trust may be severed or treated as severed to get an inclusion ratio of zero for the value of the property transferred with an allocation of GST exemption equal in value to the property transferred. See IRC §§ 2642(a)(3), 2654(b).

[165] Reg. § 26.2623-1(b)(2)(i), referring to an automatic allocation to an indirect skip provides that "the transferor's unused GST exemption is automatically allocated to the property transferred (but not in excess of the fair market value of the property on the date of the transfer)."

[166] Reg. § 26.2632-1(b)(2)(i). Priv. Ltr. Rul. 201115005 (Dec. 15, 2010) (GST exemption automatically allocated to portion of transfers to trust represented by child's with-

the gift tax return for the calendar year in which the transfer is made.[167] Where there is an indirect skip to which the ETIP rules apply, the indirect skip and the automatic allocation of GST exemption occur at the termination of the ETIP period.[168]

[e] Elections

[i] Preventing automatic allocation. The statute specifically provides that an individual may elect to prevent the automatic allocation of unused GST exemption to an indirect skip[169] or to any or all transfers to a particular trust.[170] The Treasury has broadened the scope of this preventive election to permit an election out for designated future transfers to any trust (regardless of whether the trust exists at the time of the transfer).[171] The rules potentially alleviate the burden of having to make numerous elections with respect to numerous transfers to the same or other trusts.[172] If the transfer is not one to which the ETIP rules apply, the election is to be made on a timely filed gift tax return for the calendar year in which the indirect skip is made.[173] If the transfer is an indirect

---

drawal right and, in addition, to additional transfers to trust inadvertently unreported on donors' gift tax returns).

[167] Reg. § 26.2632-1(b)(2)(i). Cf. Reg. § 26.2632-1(b)(4)(iii) Exs. 1 and 2. The Section 642(f) ETIP rules are discussed at ¶ 16.02[7].

[168] Reg. §§ 26.2632-1(b)(2)(i), 26.2632-1(c)(1)(i). However, any affirmative allocation of GST exemption may not be revoked even if the transfer is subject to Section 2642(f), the ETIP rules, prior to the close of the ETIP. Reg. § 26.2632-1(c)(1)(ii). See generally Reg. § 26.2632-1(c)(1), which applies to transfers made after June 29, 2005. Reg. § 26.2632-1(e)(2).

[169] IRC § 2632(c)(5)(A)(i)(I).

[170] IRC § 2632(c)(5)(A)(i)(II).

[171] Reg. § 26.2632-1(b)(2)(iii). Regulations Section 26.2632-1(b)(2) is applicable to elections made for transfers on or after July 13, 2004. Reg. § 26.2632-1(e)(1).

[172] One may terminate an election preventing an automatic allocation under Section 2632(c)(1) to the extent that the election out applied to future transfers or was made to one or more transfers subject to Section 2642(f), the ETIP rules. Reg. § 26.2632-1(b)(2)(iii)(E). Thus, an automatic allocation would occur on subsequent transfers. Furthermore, a subsequent election out can be made for future transfers and for prior year transfers subject to the ETIP rules prior to the termination of the ETIP period. Reg. § 26.2632-1(b)(2)(iii)(E).

[173] IRC § 2632(c)(5)(B)(i). An election to prevent the automatic allocation of GST exemption to an indirect skip is subject to modification on an amended return filed on or before the due date of the Form 709 reporting the transfer. Reg. § 26.2632-1(b)(2)(iii)(C)(2). See Reg. § 26.2632-1(b)(4)(iii) Exs. 1 and 2; see also ¶ 15.02[1] note 25. Priv. Ltr. Rul. 201115005 (Dec. 15, 2010) (although donors had elected not to have GST exemption automatically allocated to transfers to trust, donors timely allocated GST exemption to these transfers).

The manner of making the election out is described in Reg. § 26.2632-1(b)(2)(iii)(B). See also Regulations Section 26.2632-1(b)(4)(iv) Ex. for illustrations of appropriate language to be used in electing to have automatic allocation rules not apply. The time and manner rules for electing out of indirect skips are identical to those rules for electing out

skip, which under Section 2642(f) is treated as made at the end of the estate tax inclusion period, the election is to be made on a timely filed gift tax return for the calendar year in which the estate tax inclusion period ends.[174]

If a transferor elects to use Section 2513 to treat the transfer as made one-half by the transferor and one-half by the transferor's spouse, each spouse is treated as a separate transferor who must separately make an election out.[175] If a transferor makes an indirect skip and affirmatively allocates GST exemption in an amount that is less than the value of the property transferred, the allocation will be deemed to be an election out for the value of the property not covered by the exemption amount affirmatively allocated.[176]

[ii] Elective GST trusts. Even though a trust is not treated as a GST trust owing to the statutory exceptions,[177] an individual may elect to treat the trust as a GST trust for purposes of Section 2632(c).[178] The election may be made with respect to a current year transfer to a trust, to all current year transfers to a trust, to all future transfers to a trust, or to selected future transfers to a trust.[179] The election to treat a trust as a GST trust is generally to be made on a timely filed gift tax return for the calendar year in which the election is to become effective.[180]

---

of an automatic allocation to a direct skip. See Reg. § 26.2632-1(b)(1)(ii); supra ¶ 15.03[3][c].

[174] IRC § 2632(c)(5)(B)(i). See Reg. §§ 26.2632-1(c)(1)(i), 26.2632-1(c)(5) Ex. 5. However, if an affirmative allocation of GST exemption has been made to a GST trust that is subject to an estate tax inclusion period, it may not be revoked after the last date on which a timely filed Form 709 may be filed for the transfer. Reg. § 26.2632-1(c)(1)(ii).

The manner of making the election out is described in Regulations Section 26.2632-1(b)(2)(iii)(B). If the election out applies to a transfer made in a prior year, the election out statement must specifically describe the prior-year transfers to be covered. Reg. § 26.2632-1(b)(2)(iii)(B).

With respect to either type of election out, the Secretary is authorized to prescribe later dates for an individual to make a valid election preventing the automatic allocation of unused GST exemption to an indirect skip. IRC § 2632(c)(5)(B)(i). The time to make the election may also be extended under Section 2642(g)(1). See IRC § 2642(g)(1)(A)(ii), at ¶ 16.02[9][a].

[175] Reg. § 26.2632-1(b)(2)(iii)(A).

[176] Reg. § 26.2632-1(b)(2)(ii). See Reg. § 26.2632-1(b)(4)(iii) Ex. 6.

[177] IRC § 2632(c)(3)(B). See supra ¶ 15.03[4][b][iii].

[178] IRC § 2632(c)(5)(A)(ii).

[179] IRC § 2632(c)(5)(A)(ii). The regulations clarify the scope of possible elections. Reg. § 26.2632-1(b)(3)(i). The election may be made without regard to whether the trust is subject to Section 2642(f). Reg. § 26.2632-1(b)(3)(i). A transferor may terminate the election to treat the trust as a GST trust to the extent that it applies to future transfers or to a transfer subject to Section 2642(f), an ETIP transfer. Reg. § 26.2632-1(b)(3)(iv). Regulations Section 26.2632-1(b)(3) is applicable to transfers on or after July 13, 2004. Reg. § 26.2632-1(e)(1).

[180] IRC § 2632(c)(5)(B)(ii). The time to make this election may be extended under Section 2642(g)(1). See IRC § 2642(g)(1)(A)(ii); ¶ 16.02[9][a].

The effect of the election is to treat a trust as a GST trust with the result that the transferor's unused GST exemption may be automatically allocated to transfers to the trust.[181] Even though such an election is made, the transferor may prevent the automatic allocations of unused GST exemption to the trust.[182]

The manner of making the election is described in the regulations. Reg. § 26.2632-1(b)(3)(ii).

[181] Reg. § 26.2632-1(b)(3)(iii). See supra ¶ 15.03[4][e][i].

One may terminate an election to treat a trust as a GST trust to the extent that the election applied to future transfers or to a transfer subject to Section 2642(f). Reg. § 26.2632-1(b)(3)(iv). Thus, the trust will not be treated as a GST trust until a subsequent election to treat it as a GST trust is made. Reg. § 26.2632-1(b)(3)(iv).

[182] Reg. § 26.2632-1(b)(3)(iii). See supra ¶ 15.03[4][e][i].

[5] Retroactive Allocations

[b] Consequences of a Retroactive Allocation

[ii] Inclusion ratio valuation.

Page 15-42:

Add to note 208.

The following example illustrates the interrelationship of Sections 2632(d)(2)(A) and 2632(d)(2)(B). Assume transferor made a $1.5 million transfer to a trust in a year prior to 2003 and that an unnatural order of deaths occurred in the year 2004 so that transferor appropriately makes a retroactive allocation of of GST exemption under Section 2632(d) when the trust corpus was valued at $2.5 million. The allocation occurs in 2004 when the GST exemption amount is $1.5 million. IRC §§ 2631(c), 2632(d)(2)(B). Nevertheless, the allocation is deemed to be made at the time of the $1.5 million transfer to the trust. IRC § 2632(d)(2)(A). As a result of Section 2632(d) the trust has a zero inclusion ratio.

[6] Allocations Made at or After Death

Page 15-45:

In note 227, change citation Reg. § 26.2632-1(b)(2) to the following.

Reg. § 26.2632-1(b)(4).

Add to end of note 227.

Priv. Ltr. Rul. 200848009 (Sept. 19, 2008) (decedent's formula bequest to GST trust of an amount equal to decedent's remaining GST tax exemption was pecuniary in nature rather than a fractional share so that GST trust did not share in the post-death appreciation of decedent's estate, other than interest due under state law, as a result of the delay in funding the GST trust).

[c] Inter Vivos Trusts Not Included in the Gross Estate

Page 15-48:

In note 246, change citations to Reg. § 26.2632-1(b)(2) to the following.

Reg. § 26.2632-1(b)(4)

[7] Allocation of Residual Exemption

[a] In General

Page 15-50:

Add to note 256.

Priv. Ltr. Rul. 200910004 (Nov. 14, 2009) (allocation of GST tax exemption to exempt marital trust void to the extent that it exceeded the portion of the trust that could potentially be subject to the GST tax and decedent's remaining GST tax exemption was then automatically allocated to subtrust with GST potential); Priv. Ltr. Rul. 200924006 (Feb. 9, 2009) (allocation of GST tax exemption to marital trust void to the extent that it exceeded the amount required to obtain an inclusion ration of zero; the balance of the exemption was automatically allocated to another trust with GST potential, established pursuant to decedent's will, equal to the amount passing to that trust so that the inclusion ratio for each of these trusts was zero).

[b] Allocation Between Categories

[ii] Trusts with generation-skipping transfer potential.

Page 15-53:

Add to note 269.

Priv. Ltr. Rul. 200825032 (Mar. 4, 2008) (effective QTIP and reverse QTIP elections made on late filed Form 706 resulted in automatic allocation of GST exemption to trusts for which decedent is considered the transferor, including the GST-exempt marital trust).

Add to note 270.

Priv. Ltr. Rul. 200932026 (Apr. 29, 2009) (since there was no allocation of GST exemption by decedent or her estate and there were no direct skips from decedent's estate, unused GST exemption is automatically allocated to trust benefiting decedent's grandchildren).

[c] Apportionment Within Categories

[i] Direct skips and trusts with generation-skipping transfer potential.

Page 15-56:

Add to note 287.

Priv. Ltr. Rul. 200838022 (Apr. 28, 2008) (voided allocation of decedent's entire GST exemption made on decedent's estate tax return to a trust that had no GST potential with respect to decedent resulted in automatic allocation of GST exemption to two other trusts established by decedent that did have GST potential based on the respective values of each trust on decedent's date of death).

CHAPTER **16**

Applicable Rate and Inclusion Ratio

¶ 16.01   Section 2641. The Applicable Rate [Revised] S16-2

¶ 16.02   Section 2642. The Inclusion Ratio S16-5

    [3]   Calculation of the Inclusion Ratio for Taxable
           Terminations and Taxable Distributions S16-5

           [b]   Applicable Fraction S16-5

                   [ii]   The denominator. S16-5

    [4]   Valuation Rules S16-5

           [c]   Allocation to Other Inter Vivos Transfers S16-5

    [5]   Redetermination of the Applicable Fraction S16-5

           [a]   In General S16-5

           [b]   Additional Exemption Allocations and
                Transfers to a Trust S16-6

                 [iii]   Additional transfers and exemption
                         allocations. S16-6

           [c]   Consolidation of Separate Trusts S16-6

           [e]   Trust Severance [Revised] S16-7

           [f]   Recapture Tax Imposed Under Section 2032A   S16-11

                 [ii]   Section 2032A property valued at fair
                      market value in the denominator of the
                      applicable fraction. S16-11

    [6]   Special Rules for Charitable Lead Annuity Trusts . . .   S16-11

    [7]   Deferral of the Effect of Generation-Skipping
           Transfer Exemption Allocation and Direct and
           Indirect Skips on Certain Inter Vivos Transfers S16-12

           [a]   Introduction S16-12

           [b]   General Rules of Deferral S16-12

                 [i]   Inclusion in the transferor's gross estate.   S16-12

           [c]   Termination of the Estate Tax Inclusion Period   S16-13

                 [i]   Potential inclusion in the transferor's
                      gross estate. S16-13

    [9]   Statutory Relief Provisions S16-13

[a] Election Relief S16-13
[b] Substantial Compliance S16-17

Page 16-3:

Replace existing ¶ 16.01 with the following revised ¶ 16.01.

¶ 16.01 SECTION 2641. THE APPLICABLE RATE [REVISED]

The Internal Revenue Code sections discussed in this chapter provide the formula to determine the rate of tax on any generation-skipping transfer.[1] The rate, statutorily titled the "applicable rate,"[2] is the product of the "maximum Federal estate tax rate"[3] and the "inclusion ratio"[4] with respect to the transfer.[5]

Unlike some other taxes, such as the income and estate taxes, the generation-skipping transfer tax does not have its own independent rate schedule.[6] Instead, it relies on the maximum rate of the federal estate tax schedule.[7] That maximum rate is determined at the time of the generation-skipping transfer.[8] The maximum federal estate tax rate[9] has generally declined over the years to a current 35 percent rate.[10] However, for the year 2010, the rate was zero with

---

[1] Under Section 2602, the amount of generation-skipping transfer tax imposed on a generation-skipping transfer is the "taxable amount" (see IRC §§ 2621, 2622, 2623, and 2624, which are discussed in Chapter 14) multiplied by the "applicable rate" (see IRC § 2641(a)).

[2] IRC § 2641(a).

[3] IRC § 2641(b). This is also the maximum federal gift tax rate, as the gift and estate taxes are derived from the use of a unified rate table. See IRC §§ 2001(c), 2502.

[4] IRC § 2641(a)(2). This term is defined in Section 2642, which is discussed at ¶ 16.02. The inclusion ratio is one minus the applicable fraction. See IRC § 2642(a)(1).

[5] The inclusion ratio is stated in a decimal fraction rounded to the nearest one-thousandth, because it is derived by subtracting the applicable fraction, which is required to be rounded to the nearest one-thousandth, from one. See Reg. § 26.2642-1; ¶ 16.02[1] text accompanying note 6. The regulations do not provide for any rounding of the applicable rate of tax, which is the maximum federal estate tax rate times the inclusion ratio. The product of the inclusion ratio, expressed as a decimal fraction to the nearest one-thousandth, and the maximum federal estate tax rate, expressed as a decimal fraction in one-hundredths, results in a decimal fraction to the nearest one hundred-thousandth.

[6] See, e.g., IRC §§ 1 (income tax rates for noncorporate taxpayers), 11 (corporate income tax rates), 2001(c) (estate tax rates). But see IRC § 2502, which adopts the estate tax rates for computation of the gift tax.

[7] IRC § 2641(a)(1).

[8] IRC § 2641(b).

[9] IRC § 2001(c).

[10] IRC § 2001(c). From 2002 to 2012 the maximum federal estate tax rate under Section 2001(c) is:

Calendar Year   *Maximum Rate*

the result that there was no tax on any generation-skipping transfers in that year.[11]

Prior to the Tax Reform Act of 1986, the generation-skipping transfer tax employed graduated rates.[12] In repealing and reenacting Chapter 13, Congress

2002	50%
2003	49%
2004	48%
2005	47%
2006	46%
2007	45%
2008	45%
2009	45%
2010	zero
2011–2012	35%

In 2013, the "sunset" provision restores the 55 percent maximum federal estate tax rate and the generation-skipping transfer tax. Economic Growth and Tax Relief Reconciliation Act of 2001, Pub. L. No. 107-16 § 901(a)(2), 115 Stat. 38, 150 (2001), reprinted in 2001-3 CB 9, 122, as amended by the Tax Relief Act of 2010, Pub. L. No. 111-312, §§ 101(a)(1), 304, 124 Stat. 3296, 3298, 3304 (2010). The "sunset" provision is discussed more fully at Supplement ¶ 8.11.

[11] Tax Relief Act of 2010, Pub. L. No. 111-312 § 302(c), 124 Stat. 3296, 3302 (2010). Applying an applicable rate of zero to any generation-skipping transfer results in zero tax regardless of the size or type of generation-skipping transfer. Thus in 2010, any inter vivos or testamentary direct skips in the year were subject to no generation-skipping transfer tax. In addition, in 2010, any taxable terminations or taxable distributions from trusts were subject to no tax. Furthermore, with the disclaimer period extended to September 17, 2011, for disclaimers of property passing by reason of the death of a decedent between January 1, 2010 and December 16, 2010 (see Supplement ¶ 17.04[3] note 79), the opportunities for post-mortem avoidance of the generation-skipping transfer tax were significant. However, any trust created in 2010, while subject to a potential $5 million GST exemption (see Supplement ¶ 15.02 text accompanying note 5), is subject to tax on any generation-skipping transfers in years after 2010. (See Supplement ¶ 17.02 text accompanying notes 6 and 7.)

[12] Prior to its repeal, old Section 2602(a) used the rate schedule of Section 2001(c) to determine the tax imposed on a generation-skipping transfer. See IRC § 2602(a) prior to its repeal by Tax Reform Act of 1986, Pub. L. No. 99-514, § 1431(a), 100 Stat. 2085, 2718 (1986), reprinted in 1986-3 CB (Vol. 1) 1, 635. The tax imposed on the transfer was computed in a manner similar to the computation employed under the current gift tax by taxing the transfer at the deemed transferor's top rate based on the deemed transferor's prior wealth transfers. Under the prior generation-skipping transfer tax, a tentative tax was computed on an amount that included all current and prior generation-skipping transfers and gifts and, if the transferor was deceased, the transferor's taxable estate. IRC § 2602(a)(1) prior to its repeal by Tax Reform Act of 1986, Pub. L. No. 99-514, § 1431(a), 100 Stat. 2085, 2718 (1986), reprinted in 1986-3 CB (Vol. 1) 1, 635. A second tentative tax was then computed on an amount that included all prior generation-skipping transfers and gifts and, if applicable, the transferor's taxable estate. IRC § 2602(a)(2) prior to its repeal by Tax Reform Act of 1986, Pub. L. No. 99-514, § 1431(a), 100 Stat. 2085, 2718 (1986), reprinted in 1986-3 CB (Vol. 1) 1, 635. The amount of the tax on the current generation-skipping transfer was the difference between the two tentative tax computations. IRC § 2602(a) prior to repeal by Tax Reform Act of 1986, Pub. L. No. 99-514, § 1431(a), 100 Stat. 2085, 2718 (1986), reprinted in 1986-3 CB (Vol. 1) 1, 635. Under

opted for a flat rate of tax seemingly for the purpose of tax simplification and ease of administration.[13]

The second factor in computing the applicable rate is the inclusion ratio, which is defined in Section 2642(a). The role of the inclusion ratio is to integrate the amount of the Section 2631(a) GST exemption allocated to a transfer with the maximum federal estate tax rate to arrive at the applicable rate. The inclusion ratio is considered in detail in the next section.[14] Suffice it to say that if no GST exemption is allocated to a transfer, the inclusion ratio generally[15] is 100 percent and the transfer is taxed at the maximum federal estate tax rate. If the amount of the GST exemption allocated to a transfer is equal to the amount of the transfer, the inclusion ratio is zero and no generation-skipping transfer tax is imposed on the transfer.[16] If only part of a transfer is exempted, the inclusion ratio will be a fraction greater than zero and less than one.[17] The fraction when multiplied by the maximum federal estate tax rate yields the applicable rate of tax to be imposed on the generation-skipping transfer.[18]

---

this system, the tax rate imposed under the now-repealed tax on generation-skipping transfers ranged from a low of 18 percent to a high of 65 percent.

[13] HR Rep. No. 426, 99th Cong., 2d Sess. 1, 824 (1985), reprinted in 1986-3 CB (Vol. 2) 1, 824. Using the maximum Section 2001 rate schedule eliminates any need to maintain an independent Chapter 13 rate schedule and provides a readily identifiable rate that can be used without regard to prior transfers made by the transferor. Future amendments of the Section 2001 rate schedule also effectively amend the rate of tax imposed under Chapter 13.

[14] See ¶ 16.02.

[15] Certain nontaxable gifts are assigned a zero inclusion ratio, thereby negating the necessity of allocating any GST exemption to the transfer to reduce the tax rate to zero. See IRC § 2642(c), discussed at ¶ 16.02[2][b].

[16] Again, to the extent that the transfer is a nontaxable gift, no allocation of GST exemption is required to reduce the inclusion ratio to zero. See IRC § 2642(c), discussed at ¶ 16.02[2][b].

[17] When the transfer is to a trust and the trust has an inclusion ratio greater than zero but less than one, it may be possible to sever the trust into multiple trusts with inclusion ratios of zero and one. See IRC § 2642(a)(3); ¶ 16.02[5][e].

[18] If property transferred will eventually be subject to generation-skipping transfer tax and will not be shielded from tax by the Section 2631 GST exemption (see supra text accompanying notes 15, 16), it may be beneficial not to skip a generation but, instead, to have the estate tax apply at the level of the generation immediately below the transferor. For example, assume grantor G who has $1 million of unused GST exemption transfers $3 million to a trust with a life estate to child C and a remainder to grandchildren or the grandchildren's estates. Unless C has a very substantial estate, G, if tax-motivated, most likely will prefer to transfer $1 million (using the unused GST exemption) to the trust and $2 million either outright to C, or to a second trust providing a life estate to C and giving C a testamentary general power of appointment with the grandchildren or their estates as takers in default of appointment. The $2 million transfer will ensure inclusion of that property in C's gross estate under Section 2033 or Section 2041(a)(2) and avoid a taxable termination under Section 2612(a)(1). In this fashion, any of C's unused applicable exclusion amount under Section 2010 can be used to avoid the transfer tax burden on the $2 million.

¶ 16.02 SECTION 2642. THE INCLUSION RATIO

[3] Calculation of the Inclusion Ratio for Taxable Terminations and Taxable Distributions

[b] Applicable Fraction

[ii] The denominator.

Page 16-29:

Add to note 177 after citation to IRC § 2642(a)(2)(B)(ii)(I).

See Priv. Ltr. Rul. 200343019 (July 11, 2003) (denominator of the applicable fraction is net of amount trust paid for federal estate and state death taxes and also trust expenses that would not have been incurred, but for the decedent's death).

[4] Valuation Rules

[c] Allocation to Other Inter Vivos Transfers

Page 16-37:

In note 244, replace Reg. § 26.2632-1(b)(2)(ii)(A). with the following.

Reg. § 26.2632-1(b)(4)(ii)(A). See Reg. § 26.2632-1(b)(4)(iii) Ex. 3.

In note 245, replace Reg. § 26.2632-1(b)(2)(i). with the following.

Reg. § 26.2632-1(b)(4)(i). See Reg. § 26.2632-1(b)(4)(iii) Ex. 4.

[5] Redetermination of the Applicable Fraction

[a] In General

Page 16-47:

Add to note 301.

Seemingly all of the modifications that will not cause a GST exempt trust to lose its exempt status, see infra ¶ 18.05[2][e], should not cause a GST trust that is exempt because it has a zero inclusion ratio to lose its exempt status and the Service appears to agree. In Private Letter Ruling 200715002 (November 30, 2006), the Service cites Regulations Section § 26.2601-1(b)(4)(1)(E) Example 6, which involves a pre-September 25, 1985 trust, in a case involving a trust exempt from GST tax because it has a zero inclusion ratio noting that "[a]t a minimum, a change that would not affect the GST tax status of a trust that was irrevocable on September 25, 1985, should similarly not affect the exempt status of a trust that is exempt from GST tax because sufficient GST exemption was allocated to the trust to result in an inclusion ratio of zero." See also Priv. Ltr. Rul. 201134017 (May 26, 2011).

[b] Additional Exemption Allocations and Transfers to a Trust

[iii] Additional transfers and exemption allocations.

Page 16-52:

In notes 332 and 333, change citation Reg. § 26.2632-1(b)(2) *to the following.*

Reg. § 26.2632-1(b)(4)

Page 16-53:

In notes 334, 337, 338, and 339, change citation Reg. § 26.2632-1(b)(2) *to the following.*

Reg. § 26.2632-1(b)(4)

Page 16-54:

In notes 345 and 347, change citation Reg. § 26.2632-1(b)(2) *to the following.*

Reg. § 26.2632-1(b)(4)

Page 16-55:

In notes 348 and 351, change citation Reg. § 26.2632-1(b)(2) *to the following.*

Reg. § 26.2632-1(b)(4)

Page 16-56:

In note 356, change citation Reg. § 26.2632-1(b)(2) *to the following.*

Reg. § 26.2632-1(b)(4)

[c] Consolidation of Separate Trusts

Page 16-57:

Add to note 357.

Priv. Ltr. Rul. 200547010 (Aug. 15, 2005) (consolidation of three GST trusts all with inclusion ratios of zero into one GST trust with a zero inclusion ratio will not change the inclusion ratio); Priv. Ltr. Rul. 200548018 (Aug. 15, 2005) (same).

Page 16-60:

Replace existing ¶ 16.02[5][e] with revised ¶ 16.02[5][e].

[e] Trust Severance [Revised]

Severance of a single trust into two or more trusts for generation-skipping transfer tax purposes has long been recognized in limited circumstances.[363] Section 2642(a)(3) is an additional severance rule designed to make severance of a single trust into multiple trusts for generation-skipping transfer tax purposes less burdensome and less complex.[364] This provision not only provides additional opportunities for severing trusts, but it also provides planning opportunities for more effective use of a transferor's GST exemption.[365]

Under Section 2642(a)(3), a trust may be severed with the resulting trusts recognized as separate trusts for purposes of Chapter 13 if there is a "qualified severance" of the trust.[366] A "qualified severance" is the division of a single

---

[363] Reg. §§ 26.2654-1(a)(3), 26.2654-1(b). A single trust treated as a separate trust under Section 2654(b)(1) (multiple transferors) or Section 2654(b)(2) (separate and independent shares) may be divided into separate trusts where the new trusts are severed on a fractional basis and satisfy the funding requirements specified in the regulations. Reg. §§ 26.2654-1(a)(3), 26.2654-1(b)(1)(ii)(C). Additionally, a trust included in the transferor's gross estate or created under the transferor's will may be divided into two or more trusts that are recognized under Chapter 13 if certain requirements are satisfied. Such divisions are effective retroactively to the date of the transferor's death. Reg. § 26.2654-1(b). See ¶ 17.04[2][b].

[364] See HR Rep. No. 37, 107th Cong., 1st Sess. 38 (2001). In addition, a Section 2642(a)(3) severance is not a taxable exchange under the income tax. Reg. § 1.1001-1(h). Section 2642(a)(3) also makes the application of the generation-skipping transfer tax less complex by allowing the severance of an existing trust with an inclusion ratio greater than zero and less than one into separate trusts with inclusion ratios of zero and one. HR Rep. No. 107-37, 107th Cong., 1st Sess. 38 (2001). See infra text accompanying notes 373-378.

Cf. Reg. § 26.2642-6(g)(2) providing the interrelationship of Section 2642(a)(3) qualified severance of trusts where a pre–September 25, 1985, irrevocable trust receives a post–September 25, 1985, addition to its corpus. See Reg. § 26.2601-1(b)(4); ¶ 18.05[2][e].

[365] For example, see Reg. § 2642-6(j) Exs. 8 and 10 and see the combination of a qualified severance and a retroactive allocation discussed at ¶ 15.03[5][c][ii]. See also Harrington, McCaffrey, Plaine & Schneider, "Generation-Skipping Transfer Tax Planning After the 2001 Act: Mostly Good News," 95 J. Tax'n 143, 150–156 (2001) and Heilbron, "The Complete Guide to Trust Severances for GST Tax Purposes," 36 Est. Plan., Nos. 6, 8 (2009). Priv. Ltr. Rul. 200508001 (Nov. 16, 2005).

[366] IRC § 2642(a)(3)(A). See Reg. § 26.2642-6. A qualified severance is not a division described in Section 2654. See Reg. § 26.2642-6(b). The regulations also recognize as separate trusts, for generation-skipping transfer tax purposes, resulting trusts from a nonqualified severance, provided that the trusts resulting from the nonqualified severance are recognized as separate trusts under the applicable state law. Reg. § 26.2642-6(h). Resulting trusts from a nonqualified severance will have the same inclusion ratio as the original trust. Id. The resulting trusts in such instances are treated as separate trusts for generation-skipping transfer tax purposes from the date of the severance. Id. Reg.

trust and the creation of *two or more* trusts if several requirements are met.[367] Either the governing instrument of the trust or a provision of local law must permit the severance of the trust.[368] In addition, the severance must be effective under local law.[369] The trust must be divided on a fractional basis.[370] The terms of the new trusts, in the aggregate, must provide for the same succession of interests of beneficiaries as are provided in the original trust.[371] For example, a

---

§ 26.2642-6(j) Ex. 12. A trust resulting from a nonqualified severance may later be severed in a qualified severance. Reg. § 26.2642-6(j) Ex. 13. See also Reg. § 26.2654-1.

[367] IRC § 2642(a)(3)(B). See Reg. § 26.2642-6(d) for a list of the requirements.

[368] IRC § 2642(a)(3)(B)(i). The statute specifies the severance may be made by any means available under the governing instrument or local law. A single trust may be divided into multiple trusts pursuant to locals law authorizing trust severance (see, e.g., Fla. Stat. Chapter 736.0417), judicial modification of a trust (see, e.g., Fla. Stat. Chapter 736.01113, 736.04115), or non-judicial modification of a trust (see, e.g., Fla. Stat. Chapter 736.0412). A severance may be accomplished under a broad power in the instrument to distribute in further trust held by the trustee or by the exercise of a non-general power of appointment, rather than under a power expressly referencing severance for generation-skipping transfer tax purposes. See Reg. § 26.2642-6(j) Ex. 2.

[369] Reg. § 26.2642-6(d)(2).

[370] IRC § 2642(a)(3)(B)(i)(I). Each new trust must be funded with a fraction or percentage of the original trust, which may be determined by means of a formula. Reg. § 26.2642-6(d)(4). See Reg. 26.2642-6(j) Ex. 4. Severance of a trust based on a pecuniary amount does not satisfy this requirement. Reg. § 26.2642-6(d)(4). Each resulting trust may be funded with a pro rata portion of each asset held by the original trust. Id. The trusts also may be funded on a non-pro rata basis with each trust funded by applying the appropriate fraction or percentage to the total fair market value of the trust assets at the date of the severance. Id. See Reg. § 26.2642-6(j) Ex. 5. Thus the assets must be valued without taking into account any discount or premium arising from the severance. Reg. § 26.2642-6(d)(4). See Reg. § 26.2642-6(j) Ex. 6.

[371] IRC § 2642(a)(3)(B)(i)(II). The regulations provide that:

> [t]his requirement is satisfied if the beneficiaries of the separate resulting trusts and the interests of the beneficiaries with respect to the separate trusts, when the separate trusts are viewed collectively, are the same as the beneficiaries and their respective beneficial interests with respect to the original trust before severance. [Reg. § 26.2642-6(d)(5). See Reg. § 26.2642-6(j) Ex. 1 (qualified severance); Reg. § 26.2642-6(j) Ex. 3 (not a qualified severance). Ed.] With respect to trusts from which discretionary distributions may be made to any one or more beneficiaries on a non-pro rata basis, this requirement is satisfied if -

> (i) The terms of each of the resulting trusts are the same as the terms of the original trust (even though each permissible distributee of the original trust is not a beneficiary of all of the resulting trusts);

> (ii) Each beneficiary's interest in the resulting trusts (collectively) equals the beneficiary's interest in the original trust, determined by the terms of the trust instrument or, if none, on a per-capita basis. For example, in the case of the severance of a discretionary trust established for the benefit of A, B and C and their descendants with the remainder to be divided equally among those three families, this requirement is satisfied if the trust is divided into three separate trusts of equal value with one trust established for the benefit of A and A's descendants, one trust for the benefit of B and B's descendants, and one trust for the benefit of C and C's descendants;

trust that provides income to *Child C* for life with the remainder split 75 percent to a skip person and 25 percent to a non-skip person could be the subject of a qualified severance. This trust could be severed into two trusts both providing income to the child for life, but one with a remainder to the skip person and the other with a remainder to the non-skip person.[372]

Although trusts with inclusion ratios of zero and one may be severed under Section 2642(a)(3),[373] a principal purpose of the statute is to eliminate complexity when an existing trust with an inclusion ratio of between zero and one is severed.[374] However, in that circumstance, an additional requirement must be satisfied to have a "qualified severance."[375] A single trust with an inclusion ratio greater than zero but less than one may be divided into two or more trusts with one or more trusts receiving a fractional share of the total value of all trust assets equal to the applicable fraction of the single trust immediately before the severance.[376] The trust or trusts receiving the fractional share of assets based on the applicable fraction will have an inclusion ratio of zero.[377] The other trust or trusts will receive the balance of the trust's assets

---

(iii) The severance does not shift a beneficial interest in the trust to any beneficiary in a lower generation (as determined under section 2651) than the person or persons who held the beneficial interest in the original trust; and

(iv) The severance does not extend the time for the vesting of any beneficial interest in the trust beyond the period provided in (or applicable to) the original trust.

Reg. § 26.2642-6(d)(5). See Reg. § 26.2642-6(j) Ex. 2.

[372] See Reg. § 26.2642-6(j) Ex. 1.

[373] IRC §§ 2642(a)(3)(A), 2642(a)(3)(B). See Reg. § 2642-6(d)(6). In this situation, the resulting trusts will have an inclusion ratio of one or zero just like the original trust.

[374] See supra text accompanying note 363. Under the regulations, a single existing trust treated as multiple trusts after the application of Section 2654(b)(1) (multiple transferors) or Section 2654(b)(2) (separate and independent shares) may be divided into separate trusts where the new trusts are severed on a fractional basis and satisfy the funding requirements specified in the regulations. Reg. §§ 26.2654-1(a)(3), 26.2654-1(b)(1)(ii)(C). However, under Regulations Section 26.2654-1(a)(3) "a trustee cannot establish inclusion ratios of zero and one by severing a trust that is subject to the generation-skipping transfer tax after the trust has been created." HR Conf. Rep. No. 84, 107th Cong., 1st Sess. 200 (2001), reprinted in 2001-3 CB 123, 323.

[375] IRC § 2642(a)(3)(B)(ii).

[376] IRC § 2642(a)(3)(B)(ii). See Reg. § 26.2642-6(d)(7). Each one of the two resulting trusts may be further divided in a qualified severance. Reg. §§ 26.2642-6(d)(7), 26.2642-6(j) Ex. 7. The regulations provide that a trust with an exclusion ratio that is greater than zero and less than one may be severed into more than two resulting trusts. Reg. § 26.2642-6(d)(7)(iii). See Reg. § 26.2642-6(j) Ex. 9.

[377] IRC § 2642(a)(3)(B)(ii). See Reg. § 26.2642-6(d)(7), Reg. § 26.2642-6(j) Exs. 4 and 5.

Under the regulations, where there are more than two resulting trusts, one or more of the resulting trusts in the aggregate must receive that fractional share of the total value of the original trust equal to the applicable fraction. Reg. § 26.2642-6(d)(7)(iii). See Reg. § 26.2642-6(j) Ex. 9.

and have an inclusion ratio of one.[378] For example, under the preceding example, assume that the trust with income to *Child C* for life and remainder 75 percent to a skip person and 25 percent to a non-skip person had an inclusion ratio of 0.250.[379] If this trust is severed in a qualified severance, one trust with 75 percent of the trust corpus would have an inclusion ratio of zero and the other trust with 25 percent of the corpus would have an inclusion ratio of one.[380] The allocation works nicely where the inclusion ratio and the corpus divisions are equal; however, even if they are not equal, a qualified severance may still be made and a further division of the trust may be made under Section 2642(a)(3).[381] In a similarly lenient mode, a qualified severance is allowed in the case of a trust with an inclusion ratio of between zero and one where the beneficiary is granted a contingent testamentary general power of appointment that is dependent upon the trust's inclusion ratio.[382]

A qualified severance may occur any time after December 31, 2000,[383] and prior to the termination of the trust,[383.1] and is deemed to occur before a

---

[378] IRC § 2642(a)(3)(B)(ii). See Reg. § 26.2642-6(d)(7), Reg. § 26.2642-6(j) Exs. 4 and 5.

Under the regulations, where there are more than two resulting trusts, more than one resulting trust may have an inclusion ratio of one. Reg. § 26.2642-6(j) Ex. 9.

[379] The trust would have an applicable fraction of 0.750.

[380] Cf. Reg. § 26.2642-6(j) Exs. 1 and 8. This, of course, is advantageous to the recipients of the property constituting the trust remainder. Had there been no qualified severance of the trust, there would have been generation-skipping transfer tax imposed on the taxable termination occurring at the death of the non-skip person for the value of the remainder passing to the skip person. However, because the trust severed with the remainder passing to the skip person has a zero inclusion ratio no generation-skipping transfer tax is imposed.

[381] Reg. § 26.2642-6(d)(7). See Reg. § 26.2642-6(j) Ex. 7. For example, if the original trust had provided that 80 percent of the remainder go to a skip person and 20 percent to a non-skip person and the inclusion ratio was 0.250, the trust would still be severed with one trust having 75 percent of the corpus and an inclusion ratio of zero providing income to Child C and a remainder to the skip person. The second trust would provide income to Child C and 20 percent of the remainder of the second trust to the skip person and 80 percent of the remainder of the second trust to the non-skip person. The second trust would have an inclusion ratio of one and the second trust could be severed into two trusts, one with 80 percent of the corpus income to Child C and a remainder to a skip person and the other with 20 percent of the corpus income to Child C and a remainder to a non-skip person. Cf. Reg. § 26.2642-6(j) Ex. 7. A qualified severance in this instance would result in a 75 percent reduction of the generation-skipping transfer tax imposed on the taxable termination occurring upon the death of Child C. See Reg. §§ 26.2642-6(d)(7)(iii), 26.2642-6(j) Ex. 9.

[382] Reg. § 26.2642-6(j) Ex. 10.

[383] Economic Growth and Tax Relief Reconciliation Act of 2001, Pub. L. No. 107-16, § 562(b), 115 Stat. 38, 90 (2001), reprinted in 2001-3 CB 9, 62. Section 2642(a)(3) is subject to a "sunset" provision contained in the Economic Growth and Tax Relief Reconciliation Act of 2001, Pub. L. No. 107-16, § 901(a)(2), 115 Stat. 38, 150 (2001), reprinted in 2001-3 CB 9, 122. See ¶ 18.04. See also ¶ 8.10[5].

[383.1] IRC § 2642(a)(3)(C); Reg. § 26.2642-6(f)(1).

taxable termination or taxable distribution that occurs as a result of the qualified severance.[382.2] The date of a qualified severance may be selected by the trustee or may be determined by a court order.[383.3]

The regulations provide rules for the reporting of a qualified severance,[383.4] and may provide for additional instances where a severance of the trust will be classified as a "qualified severance" and the resulting trusts recognized for purposes of Chapter 13.[383.5]

[382.2] Reg. § 26.2642-6(f)(2). See Reg. § 26.2642-6(j) Ex. 8.

[383.3] Reg. § 26.2642-6(d)(3). The funding of the trusts must occur within a reasonable time (and not more than 90 days) after the selected valuation date. Id. See Reg. § 26.2642-6(j) Ex. 11.

Most of the final regulations under Section 2642(a)(3) are effective to severances occurring on or after August 2, 2007; some are effective after September 2, 2008. Reg. § 26.2642-6(k)(1). See Reg. § 26.2642-6(k)(2).

[383.4] Reg. § 26.2642-6(e). Form 706-GS(T), "Generation-Skipping Transfer Tax Returns for Termination" is generally to be filed by April 15 of the year following the year of the qualified severance. Reg. § 26.2642-6(e)(1). It should include the words "Qualified Severance" at the top of Form 706-GS(T) and it must be accompanied by a Notice of Qualified Severance. Reg. § 26.2642-6(e).

[383.5] IRC § 2642(a)(3)(B)(iii).

[f] Recapture Tax Imposed Under Section 2032A

[ii] Section 2032A property valued at fair market value in the denominator of the applicable fraction.

Page 16-65:

In note 397, change citations to Reg. § 26.2632-1(b)(2) to the following.

Reg. § 26.2632-1(b)(4)

[6] Special Rules for Charitable Lead Annuity Trusts

Page 16-67:

Add to end of first paragraph of note 409.

As required by Section 7520(c)(3), the Service issued proposed, temporary and final regulations on May 7, 2009, revising Table S and Table U(1), the tables used to value annuities, interests for life or a term of years, and reversionary and remainder interests in property, to reflect the mortality experience from the 2000 census (Life Table 2000CM). Transition rules allow taxpayers to use tables based on either Life Table 90CM or Life Table 2000CM to value gift, charitable and estate transfers made on or after May 1, 2009, but before July 1, 2009, but they must use the appropriate interest rate for the month in which the valuation date falls, regardless of which table is chosen. TD 9448; REG-107845-08. Reg. §§ 1.170A-12T, 1.642(c)-6T, 1.664-4T, 20.2031-7T, 20.2032A-1T, 20.2056A-4T, 25.2512-5T, 25.2522(c)-3, 1.7520-1T, 20.7520-1T, and Reg. § 25.7520-1T. Publications 1457 and 1458 (rev. May 2009), both of which include examples for using the mortality component tables, have been released. On August 10, 2011, the Service issued final regulations that removed the temporary regulations issued in TD 9448 and adopted as final the proposed regulations issued in REG-107845-08. The only substantive change was the deletion of an example in the Section 2032 regulations which the Service anticipates including in a different regulation project under that Code section. TD 9540; Reg. §§ 1.170A-12, 1.642(c)-6, 1.664-4, 20.2031-7, 20.2032-1, 20.2056A-4, 25.2512-5, 25.2522(c)-3, 1.7520-1, 20.7520-1, 25.7520-1.

Add to notes 409 and 412.

Notice 2009-18 provides supplements to the actuarial tables prescribed under IRC § 7520 by providing factors for interest rates below 2.2 percent.

[7] Deferral of the Effect of Generation-Skipping Transfer Exemption Allocation and Direct and Indirect Skips on Certain Inter Vivos Transfers

[a] Introduction

Page 16-70:

In note 428, change citation Reg. § 26.2632-1(b)(2) to the following.

Reg. § 26.2632-1(b)(4)

Replace the second sentence of note 430 with the following.

However, pursuant to the authority granted in the introductory clauses of Section 2642(f), Regulations § 26.2632-1(c)(1)(ii) provides "[a]n affirmative allocation of GST exemption cannot be revoked, but becomes effective as of (and no earlier than) the date of the close of the ETIP with respect to the trust."

[b] General Rules of Deferral

[i] Inclusion in the transferor's gross estate.

Page 16-72:

In note 445, change citation Reg. § 26.2632-1(c)(1) with the following.

Reg. § 26.2632-1(c)(1)(iii)

Page 16-73:

In note 451, change citation Reg. § 26.2632-1(c)(1) with the following.

Reg. § 26.2632-1(c)(1)(iii)

Page 16-74:

In note 454, change citation Reg. § 26.2632-1(c)(1) with the following.

Reg. § 26.2632-1(c)(1)(iii)

[c] Termination of the Estate Tax Inclusion Period

[i] Potential inclusion in the transferor's gross estate.

Page 16-76:

Add to note 476.

Priv. Ltr. Rul. 200419011 (Jan. 12, 2004) (transfers to irrevocable trusts for the benefit of grandchildren were subject to the estate tax inclusion period until donors resigned from the trusts' advisory committee whose consent was required for any distribution of trust principal).

[9] Statutory Relief Provisions

[a] Election Relief

Page 16-89:

Add to note 565.

Priv. Ltr. Rul. 200439001 (Apr. 2, 2004).

Add to note 568.

See Priv. Ltr. Ruls. 200407003, 200407005 (Nov. 6, 2003).

Page 16-90:

Delete the last paragraph on page 16-90 and replace with the following.

Regulations prescribing the circumstances and procedures under which extensions will be granted under Section 2642(g)(1) to allocate GST exemption to a transfer,[573] to elect out of an automatic allocation of GST exemption under Sections 2632(b)(3) and 2632(c)(5)(A)(i), or to treat a trust as a GST trust under Section 2632(c)(5)(A)(ii) have been proposed.[574] The time pre-

---

[573] An alternative simplified method to obtain an extension to an intervivos transfer which qualified for a Section 2503(b) annual exclusion but not a Section 2642(c)(1) zero inclusion ratio because of failure to satisfy Section 2642(c)(2) is provided in Rev. Proc. 2004-46, 2004-2 CB 142.

[574] Prop. Reg. § 26.2642-7. Until such regulations are final, relief will be granted under Reg. § 301.9100-3. Prop. Reg. § 26.2642-7(i). See Notice 2001-50, 2001-2 CB 189 and the following private letter rulings:

Extensions of Time to make Allocations of GST Exemption: See, e.g., Priv. Ltr. Rul. 200443010 (July 9, 2004) (extension of time to allocate GST exemption given to grantor's spouse for Section 2513 split gift to trust); Priv. Ltr. Rul. 200616022 (Dec. 26, 2005) (husband and wife each granted an extension of time to allocate GST exemption for Section 2513 split gifts to trust) and Priv. Ltr. Rul. 200620003 (Feb. 3, 2006) (executor of husband's estate and surviving spouse). Priv. Ltr. Ruls. 200440019, 200440020 (June 4, 2004) (late and revised GST exemption allocations for gifts to irrevocable life insurance trust). Priv. Ltr. Rul. 200513006 (Nov. 30, 2004) (donor who had relied upon her financial advisor, attorney and accountant to advise her on necessary tax filings granted extension of time to allocate GST exemption to transfers made to irrevocable trust); Priv. Ltr. Rul. 200512006 (Dec. 3, 2004) (donors, husband and wife, who had relied upon their accountants and attorney regarding available elections and allocations granted extension of time to allocate GST exemption to transfers made over a fifteen-year period to nine separate subtrusts for the benefit of their children and descendants); Priv. Ltr. Rul. 200513008 (Dec. 8, 2004) (donor's accountant inadvertently failed to allocate GST exemption); Priv. Ltr. Rul. 200538023 (June 21, 2005) (tax professionals relied upon by spouses who had elected to split gifts made to trusts inadvertently failed to properly allocate GST exemption to transfers); Priv. Ltr. Rul. 200542030 (July 6, 2005) (couple's attorney did not file gift tax returns with respect to trust transfers made during a two year period and did not fully allocate GST exemption for trust transfers made during another year); Priv. Ltr. Rul. 200606002 (Sept. 30, 2005) (couple's attorney failed to advise them to file gift tax returns allocating their GST exemption to transfers made of community property to an irrevocable trust). Priv. Ltr. Rul. 200519006 (Jan. 27, 2005) (extensions of time granted to allocate available GST exemption to qualified personal residence trust). Priv. Ltr. Rul. 200652042 (Sept. 20, 2006) (couple's accounting firm failed to allocate any of their GST exemption to Section 2513 split gifts made to irrevocable trust); Priv. Ltr. Rul. 200704003 (Oct. 16, 2006) (couple's accounting firm failed to allocate any of their GST exemption to transfers each spouse made to an irrevocable trust); Priv. Ltr. Rul. 200905002 (Sept. 30, 2008) (same). Priv. Ltr. Rul. 200715002 (Nov. 30, 2006) (estate granted extension of time to sever single GST nonexempt CLUT into GST exempt CLUT and GST nonexempt CLUT); Priv. Ltr. Rul. 200735006 (Apr. 13, 2007) (CPA neglected to allocate GST exemption to transfers); Priv. Ltr. Rul. 200736011 (May 15, 2007) (decedent's death after accountant's preparation of decedent's gift tax return with GST exemption allocated to transfer of assets into irrevocable trust but before return was signed); Priv. Ltr. Rul. 200815011 (Dec. 3, 2007) (law firm failed to allocate a portion of couple's respective GST exemptions to transfers made to trust that had GST potential). Priv. Ltr. Rul. 200919013 (Feb. 3, 2009) (attorney who prepared the Form 706 failed to advise the executor concerning decedent's GST exemption and inadvertently failed to allocate the exemption). Priv. Ltr. Rul. 200921007 (Jan. 27, 2009) (accounting firm omitted gifts to trusts from Form 709). Priv. Ltr. Ruls. 200924007 (Feb. 4, 2009), 200925015 (Feb. 24, 2009), 200925018 (Mar. 3, 2009), 200925028 (Mar. 16, 2009), 200927015 (Mar. 17, 2009), 200930032 (Apr. 14, 2009), 200931009 (Mar. 30, 2009), 200931010 (Apr. 13, 2009), 200931011 (Mar. 31, 2009), 200934023 (Apr. 26, 2009), 200934024 (Apr. 23, 2009), 200934025 (Apr. 27, 2009), 200934027 (May 4, 2009), 200944003 (July 15, 2009), 200944004 (July 14, 2009), 200944009 (July 20, 2009), Priv. Ltr. Rul. 200944003 (July 15, 2009), Priv. Ltr. Rul. 200944004 (July 14, 2009), Priv. Ltr. Rul. 200944009 (July 20, 2009), Priv. Ltr. Rul. 200945003 (July 15, 2009), Priv. Ltr. Ruls. 200946001, 200946002 (July 7, 2009), Priv. Ltr. Ruls. 200947003, 200947031 (Aug. 10, 2009), Priv. Ltr. Ruls. 200949006, 200949008 (Aug. 10, 2009), Priv. Ltr. Rul. 200949021 (Aug. 13, 2009), Priv. Ltr. Rul. 200953002 (Sept. 3, 2009), Priv. Ltr. Rul. 200953003 (Sept. 2, 2009), Priv. Ltr. Rul. 200953004 (Sept. 18, 2009), Priv. Ltr. Rul. 200953017 (Sept. 2, 2009), Priv. Ltr. Ruls. 201001003, 201001004 (Sept. 4, 2009), Priv. Ltr. Rul. 201002010 (Sept. 22, 2009), Priv. Ltr. Ruls. 201006008 (Oct. 30, 2009), 201006009 (Oct. 30, 2009), Priv. Ltr. Rul. 201006009 (Oct. 30, 2009), Priv. Ltr. Rul. 201010003 (Nov. 16, 2009), Priv. Ltr. Rul. 201010004 (Nov. 19, 2009), Priv. Ltr. Rul. 201010005 (Nov. 6, 2009), Priv. Ltr. Rul. 201010016 (Nov. 16, 2009), Priv. Ltr. Rul. 201014032 (Nov. 16, 2009), Priv. Ltr. Rul. 201021012 (Jan. 12, 2010), Priv. Ltr. Rul. 201022003 (Jan. 15, 2010). Priv. Ltr. Ruls. 201024006 (Jan. 20, 2010), 201024009 (Feb. 12, 2010), 201025019 (Dec. 8, 2009), 201026020, 201026021 (Mar. 17, 2010), 201027005 (Mar. 29, 2010), 201026019 (Mar. 23, 2010), 201032024 (May 5, 2010), 201034008, 201034009 (May 10, 2010), 201034013

(May 19, 2010), 201035001, 201035008 (May 24, 2010), 201036010, 201036011 (June 3, 2010), 201037002 (June 7, 2010), 201039004 (June 24, 2010), Priv. Ltr. Rul. 201049012 (Aug. 24, 2010), Priv. Ltr. Rul. 201102053 (Sept. 17, 2010), Priv. Ltr. Rul. 201103016 (Sept. 15, 2010), Priv. Ltr. Ruls. 201103023 and 201103024 (Sept. 29, 2010), Priv. Ltr. Rul. 201103039 (Sept. 15, 2010), Priv. Ltr. Rul. 201104022 (Oct. 13, 2010). Priv. Ltr. Ruls. 201108002, 201108005 (Nov. 2, 2010), Priv. Ltr. Rul. 201108010 (Nov. 5, 2010), Priv. Ltr. Rul. 201109005 (Nov. 5, 2010), Priv. Ltr. Ruls. 201109009, 010 (Nov. 15, 2010), Priv. Ltr. Ruls. 201110004, 201110005 (Nov. 22, 2010), Priv. Ltr. Rul. 201118006 (Dec. 20, 2010), Priv. Ltr. Rul. 201124006 (Mar. 4, 2011), Priv. Ltr. Rul. 201128016 (Apr. 8, 2011), Priv. Ltr. Rul. 201125016 (Mar. 15, 2011), Priv. Ltr. Ruls. 201131012– 201131013 (Apr. 27, 2011), Priv. Ltr. Rul. 201133005 (May 16, 2011), Priv. Ltr. Rul. 201135024 (May 25, 2011), Priv. Ltr. Rul. 201137001 (June 13, 2011), Priv. Ltr. Rul. 201137009 (June 13, 2011). But see Priv. Ltr. Rul. 200710001 (Nov. 28, 2006) (although decedent's spouse granted an extension of time to allocate her available GST exemption to gifts made to two trusts established by the couple in previous years, decedent's estate denied an extension since his remaining GST exemption was "affirmatively and automatically" allocated at his death and Section 2631(b) provides that allocations of GST exemption are irrevocable once made). See also Priv. Ltr. Rul. 200746006 (Aug. 7, 2007) (even though accounting firm had neglected to allocate GST exemption to transfers to trust on couple's gift tax returns, couple was denied an extension where assets transferred were limited partnership interests on which a substantial valuation discount had been taken). Priv. Ltr. Rul. 200816007 (Dec. 11, 2007) (decedent's estate's request to reallocate GST exemption that had been affirmatively allocated by estate's attorney denied).

Extensions of Time to Elect Out of the Automatic Allocation of GST Exemption: Priv. Ltr. Rul. 200504024 (Oct. 5, 2004). Priv. Ltr. Rul. 200512003 (Nov. 17, 2004) (donors, husband and wife, who had intended to elect out of the automatic allocation of GST tax exemption for transfers to a trust and did not want trust treated as a "GST trust" were each granted an extension of time to make an election out of the automatic allocation of GST exemption because they had relied on their accountant and attorney who inadvertently failed to realize that a written election out of the automatic allocation of GST exemption was required); Priv. Ltr. Rul. 200528015 (Mar. 30, 2005) (grantor given an extension of time to elect out of the automatic allocation rules because he had relied on his counsel who had erroneously advised him that the trust was not a GST trust); Priv. Ltr. Rul. 200613006 (Nov. 28, 2005) (grantor given an extension of time to elect out of the automatic allocation of GST exemption to a transfer made to a qualified personal residence trust established for the benefit of grantor's daughter and her descendants where grantor did not intend to allocate GST exemption to the transfer and existing law at the time of the transfer did not provide for automatic allocation of GST exemption to such transfers). Priv. Ltr. Rul. 200703002 (Sept. 22, 2006) (donor granted extension of time to elect out of automatic allocation of GST exemption to two trusts and to allocate donor's GST exemption to transfers made to two other trusts). Priv. Ltr. Rul. 200627017 (Mar. 22, 2006) (decedent and decedent's spouse each granted an extension of time to elect out of the automatic allocation of GST tax exemption with respect to transfers made to a trust); Priv. Ltr. Rul. 200644001 (June 16, 2006) (taxpayer granted extension of time to elect out of the automatic allocation of GST tax exemption for transfers made to grantor retained annuity trust prior to termination of the estate tax inclusion period); Priv. Ltr. Rul. 200835021 (Apr. 10, 2008) (couple were each granted an extension of time to elect out of the automatic allocation of GST tax exemption to transfers made to two trusts where couple's accountant had failed to advise them that it was necessary to file gift tax returns for the year in which the ETIP with respect to the transfers ended). Priv. Ltr. Rul. 200906017 (Oct. 28, 2009) (decedent's estate granted an extension of time to elect out of the automatic allocation of GST tax exemption to a transfer decedent had earlier made to

scribed by statute for making the allocation or election is to be disregarded and determined as if the statute did not provide any time for making the election or allocation.[575] The requests for an extension under Section 2642(g)(1) are to follow the same procedures as a request for a private letter ruling.[576] If an extension of time to allocate GST exemption is granted, the allocation is effective as of the date of the transfer and the property is valued as of that date.[577] Similarly, an election out under Section 2632(b)(3) or Section 2632(c)(5) is effective on the date of the transfer[578] and an election under Section 2632(c)(5)(A)(ii) is effective as of the date of the first (or each) transfer covered by the election.[579]

Relief is granted under the proposed regulations if it is established that the taxpayer acted reasonably and in good faith and that the grant of an extension under Section 2642(g)(1) will not prejudice the interests of the government.[580] In determining whether the taxpayer acted reasonably and in good faith the Service will consider several nonexclusive factors.[580.1] In determining whether the allowance of relief would be prejudicial to the interests of the

---

a trust where the decedent's attorney did not advise him that a gift tax return needed to be filed for the year that the ETIP closed in order to elect out of automatic allocation). Priv. Ltr. Ruls. 200930033 (Apr. 15, 2009), 200931026 (Apr. 10, 2009), 200938013-16 (May 26, 2009), 200939012-13 (May 26, 2009), 200942035-36 (June 1, 2009), Priv. Ltr. Rul. 201003003 (Oct. 9, 2009), Priv. Ltr. Rul. 201025036 (Mar. 11, 2010), Priv. Ltr. Rul. 201042005 (July 7, 2010), Priv. Ltr. Rul. 201104012 (Oct. 13, 2010), Priv. Ltr. Rul. 201123007 (Mar. 3, 2011), Priv. Ltr. Rul. 201124003 (Mar. 10, 2011).

[575] IRC § 2642(g)(1)(B).

[576] Prop. Reg. § 26.2642-7(h). See Rev. Proc. 2008-1 CB ___ or its successor. The transferor or the executor of the transferor's estate must submit a detailed affidavit with respect to the request. Prop. Reg. § 26.2642-7(h)(2). Other persons may also be required to submit an affidavit. Prop. Reg. § 26.2642-7(h)(3). The Service has revised the general procedures relating to the issuance of written guidance, including letter rulings and determination letters. See Rev. Proc. 2011-1. In addition, see Rev. Proc. 2011-2 for updated general procedures relating to the issuance of technical advice to a director or an appeals area director by the various offices of the Associate Chief Counsel.

[577] Prop. Reg. § 26.2642-7(b). The amount of GST exemption allowed is limited to the amount available on the date of the transfer. Prop. Reg. § 26.2642-7(c).

[578] Prop. Reg. § 26.2642-7(b).

[579] Prop. Reg. § 26.2642-7(b).

[580] Prop. Reg. § 26.2642-7(d)(1).

[580.1] Prop. Reg. § 26.2642-7(d)(2). Those factors are: (1) the intent at the time of the transfer to timely allocate the GST exemption as evidenced by the trust instrument, instrument of transfer, tax returns or correspondence; (2) the occurrence of intervening events beyond the control of the transferor (see IRC § 2653(a)) or the executor of the transferor's estate (see IRC § 2203); (3) the lack of awareness of the transferor or executor of the need to allocate GST exemption considering their experience and the complexity of the issue; (4) evidence of consistency in allocating or not allocating GST exemption; and (5) reasonable reliance by the transferor or executor on a qualified tax professional. Prop. Reg. § 26.2642-7(d)(2)(i)-(v).

government, the Service will consider several nonexclusive factors.[580.2] Relief under Section 2642(g)(1) will not be granted when the standard of reasonableness, good faith, and lack of prejudice to the interests of the government is not met.[580.3]

[580.2] Prop. Reg. § 26.2642-7(d)(3). Those factors are: (1) whether the use of hindsight would produce an economic advantage or benefit that otherwise would not have been available; (2) whether the delay of the request was an attempt to deprive the Service of sufficient time to challenge the transfer in some manner; (3) whether the granting of relief would cause disruptions or difficulties in adjusting the GST consequences of intervening taxable terminations or taxable distributions. Prop. Reg. § 26.2642-7(d)(3)(i)-(iii).

The request does not affect the period of limitations under Section 6501 [Prop. Reg. § 26.2642-7(f)] and does not constitute a claim for a refund or extend the period of limitations under Section 6511 [Prop. Reg. § 26.2642-7(g)].

[580.3] Prop. Reg. § 26.2642-7(e). The standard is not met in the following situations, where: (1) granting relief would decrease or revoke a timely allocation of GST exemption or revoke a timely election; (2) the transferor or executor delayed the request to deprive the Service of sufficient time to challenge the identity of the transferor or valuation of the property; (3) the transferor or executor failed to act after receiving accurate information by a qualified tax professional; (4) the request is an attempt to benefit from hindsight. Prop. Reg. § 26.2642-7(e)(1)-(4).

[b] Substantial Compliance

Page 16-91:

Add to note 584.

Priv. Ltr. Rul. 200622029 and 2006220030 (Feb. 23, 2006) (information contained in gift tax return filed by donor for gifts to trusts demonstrates taxpayer's intent to allocate GST exemption which would result in inclusion ratios of zero for the trusts such that tax return substantially complies with Section 2642(g)(2)) and Priv. Ltr. Rul. 200622015 (Feb. 8, 2006) (information provided on a couple's gift tax returns for a split gift to a trust constituted substantial compliance with the requirements of making a timely allocation of GST exemption). Priv. Ltr. Rul. 200717002 (Jan. 9, 2007) (Notices of Allocation that couple attached to their gift tax returns for split gift to trust constituted substantial compliance under Section 2642(g) such that each spouse was deemed to have timely allocated their respective GST exemption to produce an inclusion ration of zero in the trust). Priv. Ltr. Rul. 201027034 (Apr. 12, 2010) (allocation of a portion of decedent's GST exemption to trusts on estate tax return was sufficient to produce a zero inclusion ratio for the trusts and constituted substantial compliance under IRC § 2642(g) notwithstanding accountant's failure to list GST trusts on Part 1 of Schedule R; decedent's remaining GST exemption was automatically allocated to a separate trust for the benefit of decedent's daughter and her descendants).

CHAPTER 17

Other Definitions and Special Rules

¶ 17.01	Section 2651. Generation Assignment		S17-2
	[2]	Classes of Beneficiaries	S17-2
		[a] Related Beneficiaries	S17-2
		[ii] Predeceased parent rule.	S17-2
		[iii] Overlapping related beneficiaries.	S17-3
¶ 17.02	Section 2652. Other Definitions		S17-4
	[1]	Transferor	S17-4
		[a] Introduction [Revised]	S17-4
		[b] General Rules	S17-5
		[c] Special Rules	S17-5
		[i] Qualified terminable interest property.	S17-5
		[ii] Gift-splitting by married couples.	S17-7
	[2]	Trusts and Trustees	S17-7
	[3]	Interest	S17-7
		[b] Present Right to or Permissible Noncharitable Current Recipient of Income or Corpus	S17-7
¶ 17.04	Section 2654. Special Rules		S17-8
	[2]	Single Trust Treated as or Divided Into Multiple Trusts	S17-8
		[a] Single Trust Treated as Multiple Trusts	S17-8
		[b] Division of a Single Trust Into Multiple Trusts	S17-8
	[3]	Disclaimers	S17-9

¶ 17.01 SECTION 2651. GENERATION ASSIGNMENT

[2] Classes of Beneficiaries

[a] Related Beneficiaries

[ii] Predeceased parent rule.

Page 17-6:

Add to end of first paragraph of note 18.

If a transferor contributes additional property to a pre-1998 trust after December 31, 1997, the additional property is treated as a separate trust for purposes of Section 2651(e). Reg. § 26.2651-1(a)(4).

Add to the end of note 18.

The Treasury has issued final regulations explaining the Section 2651(e) predeceased parent rule. See Reg. §§ 26.2651-1, 26.2651-2. The rules are applicable for terminations, distributions, and transfers occurring on or after July 18, 2005. Reg. § 26.2651-3(a).

Add to note 20.

See Reg. § 26.2651-1(a)(1).

Add to note 21.

If an individual's generation assignment is adjusted as a result of Section 2651(e), a corresponding adjustment with respect to that transfer is made to the generation assignment of that individual's spouse or former spouse, that individual's descendants, and the spouse or former spouse of each of that individual's descendants. Reg. § 26.2651-1(a)(2)(i).

Add to note 22.

Cf. Reg. § 26.2651-1(c) Ex. 7 (same result even though predeceased child's spouse remarried and successor spouse adopts grandchild).

Page 17-7:

Add to note 26.

See Reg. § 26.2651-1(c) Ex. 1.

Insert new note 26.1 to text at end of first runover paragraph on page.

26.1 See Reg. §§ 26.2651-1(a)(2)(ii), 26.2651-1(c) Ex. 1.

Add to note 28.

Any individual who dies no later than ninety days after a transfer is treated as having predeceased the transferor. Reg. § 26.2651-1(a)(2)(iii). However, a living descendant is not treated as having predeceased the transferor solely by reason of a provision of applicable local law. Reg. § 26.2651-1(a)(2)(iv).

Add to note 29.

See Reg. § 26.2651-1(b).

Add to note 30.

See Reg. § 26.2651-1(c) Ex. 5. But compare Reg. § 26.2651-1(c) Ex. 6.

Page 17-8:

Add to note 36.

See Reg. § 26.2651-1(c) Ex. 2.

Insert the following at beginning of note 37.

Reg. § 26.2651-1(a)(4). If a transferor contributes additional property to a pre-1998 trust after December 31, 1997, the additional property is treated as a separate trust for purposes of Section 2651(e). Id.

Page 17-9:

Add new note 37.1 at end of first complete sentence on page.

[37.1] Reg. §§ 26.2651-1(a)(3), 26.2651-1(c) Ex. 4.

Add new note 37.2 at end of second complete sentence on page.

[37.2] Reg. §§ 26.2651-1(a)(3), 26.2651-1(c) Ex. 3.

[iii] Overlapping related beneficiaries.

Page 17-10:

Add to text following reference to note 45 and run into the next sentence.

For example, regulations provide that when a transferor adopts a descendant of a parent of the transferor (or the transferor's spouse or former spouse) who is under age 18 at the time of the adoption, and tax avoidance is not a primary motive,[45.1] the adopted individual is treated as a member of the generation that

---

[45.1] Reg. § 26.2651-2(b). The determination whether tax avoidance is a primary motive is made based on all the facts and circumstances. Reg. § 26.2651-2(b)(4). The most

is one generation below the adoptive parent.[45.2] Other exceptions may apply, although other possible

---

significant factor is whether there is a bona fide parent/child relationship between the parties. Id. See also Reg. §§ 26.2651-2(b)(4)(i) and 26.2651-2(b)(4)(ii) for other factors.

[45.2] Reg. § 26.2651-2(b).

¶ 17.02 SECTION 2652. OTHER DEFINITIONS

[1] Transferor

Page 17-15:

Replace existing ¶ 17.02[1][a] with the following revised ¶ 17.02[1][a].

[a] Introduction [Revised]

Anyone who lived through the first congressional frolic with a tax on generation-skipping transfers may recall with a certain weird fondness the "Deemed Transferor," who was supposed to play a very large role in that nonstatute, which retroactively self-destructed when Congress enacted the current generation-skipping tax in the Tax Reform Act of 1986. The Deemed Transferor, always ephemeral, was nevertheless tenacious. Although the Deemed Transferor is still not always real, his ghost stalks the paragraphs of the current statute. Playing a different role, the Deemed Transferor is still often *deemed*, but with a lowercase "d." How is the deemed transferor identified? Section 2652(a) undertakes this task.

For every generation-skipping transfer, a transferor must be identified. A transferor is needed to ascertain the generation assignment of most individuals possessing interests in property subject to the tax,[1] to classify individuals as skip or non-skip persons,[2] and to ascertain whether special generation assignment rules may apply to individuals whose parent is deceased.[3]

The term "transferor" includes a decedent who transfers any property in a manner that is subject to the estate tax and a donor who transfers any property in a manner that is subject to the gift tax.[4] The determination of the transferor of property is fleeting, not permanent. Generally, anytime the property is again subjected to either the gift tax or the estate tax, a new transferor is recognized. There are two exceptions to the general rule. The first, discussed later, in-

---

[1] IRC § 2651.

[2] IRC § 2613. See ¶¶ 13.03[1]–13.03[5]. Reg. § 26.2612-1(d).

[3] IRC § 2651(e); discussed ¶ 17.01[2][a][ii].

[4] IRC § 2652(a)(1).

volves a special election for QTIP.[5] The second exception treats a decedent, who died in the year 2010 and whose executor elected out of applying the estate tax for that year,[6] as a transferor under the generation-skipping transfer tax even though the decedent's property was not subject to the estate tax imposed by Chapter 11.[7] The initial phrase of Section 2652(a)(1) is deceptive, indicating that Section 2653(a) provides an exception to the general definition of "transferor." Actually, Section 2653(a) does no more than affect the generation level of the transferor in certain situations.[8] The transferor is not changed by Section 2653(a).

---

[5] IRC § 2652(a)(3), discussed infra ¶ 17.02[1][c][i].

[6] See Supplement ¶¶ 8.10[1] and 8.10[2]. The election also results in a modified carryover basis in the decedent's property for income tax purposes. See IRC § 1022, Supplement ¶ 8.10[3].

[7] Tax Relief Act of 2010, Pub. L. No. 111-312 § 301(c), 124 Stat. 3296, 3300 (2010). While generation-skipping transfers made in 2010 were not subject to the generation-skipping transfer tax because they were taxed at a zero tax rate (see Tax Relief Act of 2010, Pub. L. No. 111-312 § 302(c), 124 Stat. 3296, 3302 (2010) and supplement ¶ 16.01 note 11), this transferor rule potentially subjects any post-2010 generation-skipping transfers from trusts created in 2010 to the generation-skipping transfer tax. If the executor of the estate of a decedent who died in 2010 makes the Section 1022 carryover basis election, decedent's available GST exemption can be allocated by attaching Schedule R or R-1 to Form 8939, Allocation of Increase in Basis for Property Acquired From a Decedent, which will be considered timely if filed by January 17, 2012. Notice 2011-76. See Supplement ¶¶ 8.10[1] and 8.10[2].

[8] IRC § 2653(a), discussed ¶ 17.03[1].

[b] General Rules

Page 17-17:

In note 18, add ", 2501(a)(5)" *immediately after* "2501(a)(3)".

In note 18, in the penultimate citation, replace "§ 2501(a)(5)" *with* "§ 2501(a)(4)".

Page 17-19:

Add to note 32.

Priv. Ltr. Rul. 201013002 (Nov. 4, 2009) (exercise of a limited power of appointment by donor's children over GST exempt trust will not cause inclusion of the property in children's gross estates nor will such exercise be treated as a gift by the children and children will not become transferors of the property).

[c] Special Rules

[i] Qualified terminable interest property.

Page 17-21:

Add to note 42.

Citing Revenue Procedure 2001-38, the Service in Private Letter Ruling 200407016 (Oct. 24, 2003) treated a QTIP election made for a surviving spouse's life estate as null and void, because the election was unnecessary to eliminate the deceased spouse's estate tax liability; Priv. Ltr. Rul. 200603004 (Sept. 30, 2005) (estate's QTIP election for credit shelter trust is null and void because election was not necessary to reduce estate tax liability to zero); Priv. Ltr. Rul. 201022004 (Jan. 28, 2010); Priv. Ltr. Rul. 201131011 (Apr. 20, 2011).

Page 17-23:

Add to end of note 52.

Priv. Ltr. Rul. 200925008 (Feb. 19, 2009) (extension of time granted to make an election to treat marital trust as two separate trusts, a GST exempt portion and a GST nonexempt portion, and for reverse QTIP election to apply to the GST exempt portion); Priv. Ltr. Ruls. 200926021 (Mar. 3, 2009), 200934036 (Apr. 29, 2009); Priv. Ltr. Rul. 200946027 (Aug. 10, 2009).

Page 17-24:

Add to first paragraph of note 54.

Priv. Ltr. Rul. 200825032 (Mar. 4, 2008) (effective QTIP and reverse QTIP elections made on first return filed which was not timely).

Add to note 54 after reference to Priv. Ltr. Rul. 9611011.

Priv. Ltr. Rul. 200411004 (Dec. 3, 2003) (same) and Priv. Ltr. Rul. 200548017 (Aug. 22, 2005) (decedent's estate granted an extension of time to make a reverse QTIP election); Priv. Ltr. Rul. 200835022 (Apr. 10, 2008) (same); Priv. Ltr. Rul. 201002008 (Sept. 22, 2009); Priv. Ltr. Rul. 201023007 (Jan. 22, 2010); Priv. Ltr. Rul. 201109016 (Dec. 2, 2010). Revenue Procedure 2004-47, 2004-2 CB ___, provides a simplified alternative method to make a late reverse QTIP election in lieu of the normal letter ruling process. It follows several prior letter rulings and is applicable only to testamentary transfers. It is inapplicable to noncitizen spouses, and does not apply to a late severance of a trust or to a late allocation of GST exemption. To qualify for the extension of time, the taxpayer: (1) must have made a valid QTIP election; (2) not made the reverse QTIP election on the return as filed because the taxpayer relied on the advice and counsel of a qualified tax professional and the tax professional failed to advise the taxpayer of the need, advisability, or proper method to make a reverse QTIP election; (3) a zero inclusion ratio would have resulted for the reverse QTIP trust or property; (4) the estate is not eligible for Regulations Section 301.9100-2(b) automatic six-month extension; (5) the surviving spouse has not disposed of any part of the qualifying income interest for life in the QTIP assets or trust; (6) the surviving spouse is alive or no more than six months have passed since the death of the surviving spouse; and (7) the executor requests relief in the manner outlined in the revenue procedure.

Add to note 54.

In Private Letter Ruling 200439036 (June 2, 2004), a decedent's estate was granted an extension of time to sever a marital trust for GST tax purposes and to make a reverse QTIP election. See also Priv. Ltr. Rul. 200443027 (July 7, 2004), Priv. Ltr. Rul. 200522002 (Feb. 18, 2005), Priv. Ltr. Rul. 200625014 (Feb. 23, 2006), and Priv. Ltr. Rul. 200626010 (Feb. 13, 2006). Priv. Ltr. Rul. 200719003 (Jan. 19, 2007). Priv. Ltr. Ruls. 200908002 (Oct. 20, 2008), 200916002 (Nov. 12, 2008), and 200919005 (Jan. 22, 2009). Priv. Ltr. Ruls. 200930031 (Apr. 10, 2009), 200936014 (May 21, 2009), and 200941010 (July 10, 2009); Priv. Ltr. Rul. 201116004 (Dec. 27, 2010).

Delete the first paragraph of note 57 and insert the following replacement paragraph.

IRC § 2631(a). Before 2004, the amount of the Section 2010 applicable exclusion amount was less than the GST exemption amount with the result that a Section 2652(a)(3) election was frequently made. After 2003 and before 2010, where a decedent has made an inter vivos transfer to a non-skip person using the Section 2505 credit, but not the GST exemption, the GST exemption amount will exceed the Section 2010 applicable credit amount and a Section 2652(a)(3) election may be beneficial. A Section 2652(a)(3) election will be beneficial if no GST exemption was allocated to the inter vivos transfer and the inter vivos transfer is not pulled into the decedent's gross estate.

[ii] Gift-splitting by married couples.

Page 17-25:

Add to note 62.

In Private Letter Ruling 200345038 (July 28, 2003), gifts made by the husband to irrevocable trusts that included the wife as a primary beneficiary were eligible for Section 2513 gift splitting since the wife's interest was limited to an ascertainable standard; accordingly, the wife is the transferor for GST tax purposes of one half of the entire value of the property transferred by the husband. Priv. Ltr. Rul. 200422051 (Feb. 20, 2004) (donor's spouse treated as transferor of one half of the value of the gifts made to an irrevocable trust by donor regardless of the interest donor's spouse was actually deemed to have transferred under Section 2513). See ¶ 10.03[1] note 13.

[2] Trusts and Trustees

Add to note 79.

If a decedent died between January 1, 2010, and December 16, 2010, the decedent's executor had until September 17, 2011, (not just nine months) to make a disclaimer, regardless of the date of death. Tax Relief Act of 2010, Pub. L. No. 111-312 § 301(d)(1)(C), 124 Stat. 3296, 3300 (2010). Since the generation-skipping transfer tax rate was zero for the year 2010 (Tax Relief Act of 2010, Pub. L. No. 111-312 § 302(c), 124 Stat. 3296, 3302 (2010)), this provided an opportunity to avoid the generation-skipping transfer tax by means of a disclaimer of property transferred by a decedent dying in 2010 but only dying prior to December 17, 2010.

[3] Interest

[b] Present Right to or Permissible Noncharitable Current Recipient of Income or Corpus

Page 17-35:

Add new note 130.1 at end of fifth sentence of the first paragraph.

    [130.1] See Priv. Ltr. Rul. 200814016 (Dec. 19, 2007) (decedent's transfers to nonexempt trusts, established for the benefit of beneficiaries two or more generations below decedent, over which each beneficiary's parent holds a testamentary general power of appointment were direct skips since parent does not have a present right to receive trust income or principal and is not a permissible recipient of same).

¶ 17.04 SECTION 2654. SPECIAL RULES

[2] Single Trust Treated as or Divided Into Multiple Trusts

[a] Single Trust Treated as Multiple Trusts

Page 17-60:

Add to note 49.

Priv. Ltr. Rul. 200804013 (Sept. 26, 2007) (although two qualified personal residence trusts, one established by each of husband and wife, were consolidated with two other irrevocable trusts they had established into a single trust, the qualified personal residence trusts would continue to be treated as separate trusts following the consolidation).

Replace note 51 with the following.

IRC § 2654(b)(2). See Reg. § 26.2654-1(a)(5) Exs. 1 and 2. Generally, a portion of a trust that is a separate and independent share must exist from the creation of the trust and at all times thereafter. Reg. § 26.2654-1(a)(1)(i). A trust for this purpose is treated as created at the date of the tranferor's death if the entire trust is included in the transferor's gross estate as defined in Section 2031. See Private Letter Rulings 201116003, 201116008 and 201118003 (Jan. 3, 2011) (death of non-skip trust beneficiary results in share of trust income passing to beneficiary's children and, since trust is comprised of substantially separate and independent shares, a taxable termination then occurred because no non-skip person continued to be a beneficiary of that separate share). Reg. § 26.2654-1(a)(1)(i). However, if there is a mandatory severance of a trust which is effective under state law, but it is not a qualified severance under Section 2642(a)(3) (see ¶ 16.05[5][e]), the separate and independent share rule does not apply and the separate shares need not exist on the creation of the trust in order to sever the trust. Each trust with a separate and independent share at the time of the mandatory severance is treated as a separate trust and subsequent allocations of GST exemption may be made separately to the separate trusts. Prop. Reg. § 26.2654-1(a)(1)(iii). See Prop. Reg. § 26.2654-1(a)(5) Ex. 8.

[b] Division of a Single Trust Into Multiple Trusts

Page 17-63:

Add to end of first paragraph of note 69.

See also Priv. Ltr. Rul. 200715002 (Nov. 30, 2006) (severance of single GST nonexempt CLUT into GST exempt CLUT and GST nonexempt CLUT).

Add to note 70.

Cf. ¶ 16.02[5][e] note 370.

Add to note 72.

See, however, Priv. Ltr. Rul. 200715002 (Nov. 30, 2006) (estate granted extension of time under Regulation Section 301.9100-3 to sever single GST nonexempt CLUT into GST exempt CLUT and GST nonexempt CLUT).

[3] Disclaimers

Page 17-65:

Add to note 79.

If a decedent died between January 1, 2010, and December 16, 2010, the decedent's executor had until September 17, 2011, (not just nine months) to make a disclaimer, regardless of the date of death. Tax Relief Act of 2010, Pub. L. No. 111-312 § 301(d)(1)(C), 124 Stat. 3296, 3300 (2010). Since the generation-skipping transfer tax rate was zero for the year 2010 (Tax Relief Act of 2010, Pub. L. No. 111-312 § 302(c), 124 Stat. 3296, 3302 (2010)), this provided an opportunity to avoid the generation-skipping transfer tax by means of a disclaimer of property transferred by a decedent dying in 2010 prior to December 17, 2010.

Add to note 81.

Priv. Ltr. Rul. 200901013 (Sept. 12, 2008) (trust beneficiaries making nonqualified disclaimers of interests in trust are subject to gift tax but passing of disclaimed interest to beneficiaries' children, the settlors' grandchildren, as a result of disclaimers not subject to GST tax).

CHAPTER **18**

Administrative and Miscellaneous Matters

¶ 18.01	Section 2661. Administration	S18-2
	[2] Deferral of Payment	S18-2
	[a] Transfers at Death	S18-2
¶ 18.02	Section 2662. Return Requirements	S18-2
	[2] Returns Required	S18-2
	[a] Taxable Distributions and Taxable	
	Terminations	S18-2
	[b] Direct Skips	S18-3
	[4] When to File	S18-3
	[b] Extensions of Time to File	S18-3
	[5] Where to File	S18-3
	[6] Information Returns	S18-3
¶ 18.03	Section 2663. Regulations	S18-4
	[1] Recapture Tax Under Section 2032A	S18-4
	[b] Other Testamentary Transfers	S18-4
	[2] Nonresident Noncitizen Transferor	S18-4
	[b] Transfer of Property Situated in the United	
	States	S18-4
	[c] Trusts Partially Subject to Chapter 13	S18-4
¶ 18.04	The Generation-Skipping Transfer Tax in 2010, 2013 and	
	Thereafter [Revised]	S18-5
	[1] The Generation-Skipping Transfer Tax in the Year	
	2010	S18-5
	[2] The Generation-Skipping Transfer Tax in the Year	
	2013 and Thereafter	S18-6
¶ 18.05	Effective Dates	S18-6
	[2] Transitional Rules	S18-6
	[b] Trusts Irrevocable on September 25, 1985	S18-6
	[ii] Additions to corpus.	S18-6
	[iii] Consequences when tainted corpus is	
	added.	S18-8

[d]   Mental Disability S18-9
[e]   Permissible Modifications to Exempt Trusts   S18-9
       [i]   Trustee's discretionary powers. S18-9
       [ii]   Settlement. S18-10
       [iii] Judicial construction. S18-11
       [iv]   Other changes. S18-12

¶ 18.01 SECTION 2661. ADMINISTRATION

[2] Deferral of Payment

[a] Transfers at Death

Page 18-6:

Add to note 29.

, and Priv. Ltr. Rul. 200939003 (June 23, 2009) (Section 6166 applies to direct skips pursuant to IRC § 6661(i) but does not apply to the GST tax imposed on taxable terminations).

¶ 18.02 SECTION 2662. RETURN REQUIREMENTS

[2] Returns Required

[a] Taxable Distributions and Taxable Terminations

Page 18-8:

Add to note 11.

The Service has released revised instructions for Form 706-GS(D) (revised Mar. 2007) to be used with Form 706-GS(D), Generation-Skipping Transfer Tax Return for Distributions (revised Feb. 2006).

Add to note 12.

The Service has released the final version of Form 706-GS(D), Generation-Skipping Transfer Tax Return for 2010 Distributions and related instructions.

Add to note 13.

The Service has released revised instructions for Form 706-GS(D-1), Notification of Distribution From a Generation-Skipping Trust, which notes that trustees should file the October 2008 version of the form and that the due date for Form 706-GS(D-1) is September 19, 2011, for distributions made after December 31, 2009, but before December 17, 2010. Otherwise, the form is due by April 18, 2011.

Add to note 14.

The Service has released the final version of Form 706-GS(T), Generation-Skipping Transfer Tax Return for 2010 Terminations, and related instructions.

[b] Direct Skips

Page 18-10:

In note 25, replace "Section 2501(a)(5)" *with* "Section 2501(a)(4)".

[4] When to File

[b] Extensions of Time to File

Page 18-16:

Delete final three sentences of note 60 and replace with the following.

Revised Form 4768 and related instructions have been released by the Service (revised July 2008). The Service revised Form 4768 to add Part V – Notice to Applicant, which will be used to notify an executor whether the request for an extension has been accepted, denied or requires additional information.

A skip person distributee required to file Form 706-GS(D) or a trustee required to file Form 706-GS(T) will be allowed an automatic six-month extension of time to file the return by filing Form 7004, Application for Automatic 6-Month Extension of Time to File Certain Business Income Tax, Information, and Other Returns. Reg. § 26.6081-1. An automatic extension of time for filing Form 706-GS(D) or Form 706-GS(T) will not extend the time for payment of any tax due on the return. Reg. § 26.6081-1(c). In general, Form 7004 must be filed by the due date of the tax return to which it pertains.

[5] Where to File

Page 18-18:

Add to note 63.

The Service has released a new version of Form 706-GS(D-1), Notification of Distribution From a Generation-Skipping Trust (revised January 2007). The instructions note that Form 706-GS(D-1) is to be filed at the Cincinnati Service Center, regardless of the settlor's residency or citizenship status. The Service has released revised instructions for Form 706-GS(D-1), Notification of Distribution From a Generation-Skipping Trust which notes that trustees should file the October 2008 version of the form and that the due date for Form 706-GS(D-1) is September 19, 2011, for distributions made after December 31, 2009, but before December 17, 2010. Otherwise, the form is due by April 18, 2011.

[6] Information Returns

Page 18-18:

Add to note 66.

The Service has released a new version of Form 706-GS(D-1), Notification of Distribution From a Generation-Skipping Trust (revised January 2007). The instructions note that Form 706-GS(D-1) is to be filed at the Cincinnati Service Center, regardless of the settlor's residency or citizenship status. The Service has released revised instructions for Form 706-GS(D-1), Notification of Distribution From a Generation-Skipping Trust which notes that trustees should file the October 2008 version of the form and that the due date for Form 706-GS(D-1) is September 19, 2011, for distributions made after December 31, 2009, but before December 17, 2010. Otherwise, the form is due by April 18, 2011.

¶ 18.03　SECTION 2663. REGULATIONS

[1]　Recapture Tax Under Section 2032A

[b]　Other Testamentary Transfers

Page 18-23:

In note 26, change citation to Reg. § 26.2632-1(b)(2) to the following.

Reg. § 26.2632-1(b)(4).

[2]　Nonresident Noncitizen Transferor

[b]　Transfer of Property Situated in the United States

Page 18-25:

In note 42, add "2501(a)(5)," after "2501(a)(3)".

Add to the end of note 42.

Priv. Ltr. Rul. 201032021 (Apr. 28, 2010) (nonresident noncitizen donor's transfers of naked title to shares of an entity that is not a U.S. corporation to her U.S. citizen grandchildren are not subject to gift tax and, accordingly, are not subject to the GST tax).

[c]　Trusts Partially Subject to Chapter 13

Page 18-26:

Add to note 49.

In Private Letter Ruling 200817009 (Dec. 28, 2007), nonresident noncitizen's transfer of assets to trust was not subject to gift tax because assets transferred did not have a situs in the United States or were securities in a U.S. corporation that were not subject to gift tax.

When nonresident noncitizen died, however, the trust included securities in a U.S. corporation and that portion of his estate was not exempt from Chapter 13 and nonresident noncitizen's GST exemption was automatically allocated to this nonexempt portion.

Replace existing ¶ 18.04 with the following revised ¶ 18.04

¶ 18.04 THE GENERATION-SKIPPING TRANSFER TAX IN 2010, 2013 AND THEREAFTER [REVISED]

[1] The Generation-Skipping Transfer Tax in the Year 2010

The generation-skipping transfer tax was scheduled to terminate as to generation-skipping transfers after December 31, 2009.[1] Late in the year 2010, Congress passed legislation that, seemingly because of its tardiness, provided generous rules for the generation-skipping transfer tax.[2]

Under those rules, the applicable rate of tax imposed on all generation-skipping transfers occurring in 2010 is zero.[3] Thus any direct skips, taxable terminations, or taxable distributions occurring in 2010 did not incur generation-skipping transfer tax.[4] Congress also allowed an extended disclaimer rule related to the estates of decedents who died between January 1, 2010 and December 17, 2010.[5] Disclaimers of interests in property transferred during this period may be made until September 17, 2011.[6]

However, individuals who have elected not to be subject to Chapter 11 estate tax are treated as making transfers subject to Chapter 11 when determining the 2652(a) transferor for generation skipping transfer tax purposes.[7]

---

[1] IRC § 2664 (repealed by the Tax Relief Act of 2010). The estate tax was also scheduled to terminate on that date. IRC § 2210 (repealed by the Tax Relief Act of 2010). The termination was to be short-lived and a sunset provision restored both taxes to their 2001 status. Economic Growth and Tax Relief Reconciliation Act of 2001, Pub. L. No. 107-16, § 901, 115 Stat. 150 (2001), reprinted in 2001-3 CB 9, 122. See infra Supplement ¶ 18.04[2], Supplement ¶ 8.11.

[2] Tax Relief Act of 2010, Pub. L. No. 111-312, 124 Stat. 3296 (2010).

[3] Tax Relief Act of 2010, Pub. L. No. 111-312, § 302(c), 124 Stat. 3296, 3302 (2010). See Supplement ¶ 16.01 text accompanying note 11.

[4] Even though generation-skipping transfers occurred, since the applicable rate was zero, the tax was zero. For *inter vivos* direct skips occurring in 2010, where the donor wishes to pay tax at the zero-percent rate, an election out of the automatic allocation rule of Section 2632 can be made. Notice 2011-76. See ¶ 15.03[3][c] note 70.

[5] Tax Relief Act of 2010, Pub. L. No. 111-312, § 301(d)(1)(C), 124 Stat. 3296, 3300 (2010).

[6] This provision provides an opportunity for beneficiaries of generation-skipping trusts or recipients of direct skips to do post-mortem estate planning. See Supplement ¶ 17.04 note 79.

[7] Tax Relief Act of 2010, Pub. L. No. 111-312, § 301(c), 124 Stat. 3296, 3300 (2010). See Supplement ¶¶ 8.10[1], 8.10[2], 17.02 text accompanying notes 6 and 7.

[2] The Generation-Skipping Transfer Tax in the Year 2013 and Thereafter

In the year 2013, all three Federal transfer taxes are sunsetted and are to be taxed as they were before the enactment of the Economic Growth and Tax Relief Reconciliation Act of 2001[8] As a result, the generation skipping transfer tax will revert to the rules that existed in 2001,[9] and the amount of the GST exemption under Section 2631 will be $1 million (as adjusted for inflation occurring after 1998),[10] the maximum tax rate under Section 2001(c) for purposes of Section 2641 will be 55 percent[11] and the Section 2604 credit for state generation-skipping transfer taxes will be restored.[12] In addition, the Section 2632(c) automatic allocation of GST exemption to indirect skips,[13] the Section 2632(d) retroactive allocation of GST exemption,[14] the Section 2642(a)(3) severance rules,[15] the clarification of the Section 2642(b) valuation rules,[16] and the relief provisions of Section 2642(g)[17] will disappear.

---

[8] Economic Growth and Tax Relief Reconciliation Act of 2001, Pub. L. No. 107-16, 115 Stat. 150 (2001), reprinted in 2001-3 CB 9, as amended by the Tax Relief Act of 2010, Pub. L. No. 111-312, §§ 101(a)(1), 304, 124 Stat. 3296, 3298, 3304 (2010).

[9] See Supplement ¶ 8.11[3].

[10] See Supplement ¶ 15.02 note 7.

[11] See ¶ 16.01 note 10.

[12] See ¶ 12.04.

[13] See ¶ 15.03[4].

[14] See ¶ 15.03[5].

[15] See ¶ 15.03[5][c][ii].

[16] See ¶ 16.02[4][d].

[17] See ¶ 16.02[9].

¶ 18.05 EFFECTIVE DATES

[2] Transitional Rules

[b] Trusts Irrevocable on September 25, 1985

[ii] Additions to corpus.

Page 18-35:

Add to note 34.

Priv. Ltr. Rul. 200530002 (Apr. 19, 2005) (beneficiary's renunciation of one-fifth of remainder interest in trust created prior to January 1, 1977, is taxable gift of one-fifth of entire value of trust corpus and constructive addition to trust which will cause one-fifth of trust corpus to become subject to GST tax); Priv. Ltr. Rul. 200532024 (May 9, 2005) (renunciation of interests in exempt trust by grandchildren resulting in trust termination and distribution of trust corpus to great-grandchildren constituted a constructive addition to trust by grandchildren). But cf. Priv. Ltr. Rul. 200908003 (Oct. 28, 2008) (distributions from an exempt trust created by decedent spouse prior to the effective date, to which were added marital trust assets included in the estate of the surviving spouse, were not subject to the GST tax because, at surviving spouse's death, her executor allocated her entire GST tax exemption to the marital trust).

Replace Chapter 13 *with* Chapter 11 *in the third sentence of the second paragraph of note 38.*

Page 18-36:

Replace the contents of note 38 after citation to Priv. Ltr. Rul. 199923028 with the following.

. Priv. Ltr. Rul. 200540004 (June 2, 2005) (an inter vivos failure to exercise a general power of appointment cumulative withdrawal right does not constitute a constructive addition to grandfathered trust); Priv. Ltr. Rul. 200541031 (June 2, 2005) (same).

The transfer of property for federal transfer tax purposes pursuant to the exercise, release, or lapse of a general power of appointment that is to any extent taxable under Chapter 11 or 12 where the general power of appointment was created in a pre-September 25, 1985, trust should not be treated as a transfer "under the exempt trust," but rather a transfer by the power holder occurring when the taxable exercise, release, or lapse of the power becomes effective for purposes of determining whether or not the transfer is subject to the tax imposed by Chapter 13. See Reg. § 26.2601-1(b)(1)(i).

Replace note 39 with the following.

These rules have been upheld in Estate of Gerson v. Comm'r, 507 F3d 435 (6th Cir. 2007) cert. denied sub. nom. Kleinman v. Comm'r, No. 07-1064 (2008) (exercise of general power of appointment); Estate of Timken v. United States, 601 F3d 431 (6th Cir. 2010) cert. denied, No. 10-363 (2011); (lapse of general power of appointment); Peterson Marital Trust v. Comm'r, 78 F.3d 795 (2d Cir. 1996) (lapse). But see Bachler v. United States, 281 F3d 1078 (9th Cir. 2002) (exercise) and Simpson v. United States, 183 F3d 812 (8th Cir. 1999) (exercise) both inappropriately reaching the opposite result and treating the trust as an exempt trust under a prior regulation.

Page 18-37:

Add to note 41.

Priv. Ltr. Rul. 200745015 (June 6, 2007) (release of testamentary nongeneral power of appointment over shares of stock in conjunction with release of all interest in such shares). Priv. Ltr. Rul. 200812022 (Nov. 7, 2007) (beneficiary's exercise of testamentary limited power of appointment over grandfathered trust, created pursuant to a pre–September 25, 1985, partial release of a general power of appointment, that was made in favor of living issue, per stirpes, is not deemed a constructive addition to the trust).

Add to note 43.

Priv. Ltr. Rul. 200511013 (Nov. 29, 2004) (exercise of special power of appointment over exempt trusts did not constitute a constructive addition to the trusts and did not cause trusts to lose their exempt status); Priv. Ltr. Rul. 200535009 (May 10, 2005) (exempt trust beneficiary's exercise of nongeneral testamentary power of appointment over exempt trust was not deemed to be a constructive addition to the trust since power was not exercised in a manner that postponed or suspended vesting beyond the perpetuities period); Priv. Ltr. Rul. 200535022 (May 5, 2005) (same). Priv. Ltr. Rul. 200928013 (Mar. 12, 2009) (same). Priv. Ltr. Rul. 201029011 (Apr. 12, 2010) (decedent's exercise of her nongeneral power of appointment over exempt trust to create a power of appointment in each of her children to appoint property at the child's death among decedent's descendants living at the time of decedent's death did not postpone or suspend vesting of the trust assets beyond the perpetuities period and, therefore, did not cause trust to lose its exempt status). Priv. Ltr. Rul. 200541035 (June 27, 2005) (beneficiary's partial release of limited power of appointment is not a constructive addition to trust and trustees' consent to an electing small business trust (ESBT) election will not cause exempt trust to lose its GST exempt status). Priv. Ltr. Rul. 200712008 (Oct. 26, 2006) (surviving spouse's exercise of limited power of appointment over exempt trust in favor of testamentary trust established under her will, which does not postpone vesting beyond the prohibited period, will not constitute a constructive addition to either trust; testamentary trust will be exempt from GST tax except for a non-exempt portion, which is subject to an estate tax inclusion period, resulting from surviving spouse's prior tainted addition to exempt trust). Priv. Ltr. Rul. 201136017 (June 8, 2011) (beneficiary's exercise of nongeneral powers of appointment over three exempt trusts to appoint the trusts to several family trusts did not postpone or suspend the vesting of the trusts' assets beyond the perpetuities period and did not cause these assets to lose their GST-exempt status). Private Letter Ruling 200243026 (July 24, 2002) ruled, however, that a proposed exercise of an inter vivos limited power of appointment would cause the power holder to become the transferor of the value of his income and principal interests in the trust to the extent to which the power holder was making a gift under Section 2511. Income and principal of the trust were distributable to the power holder for "care, support, maintenance, education, advancement in life and comfortable living," and the power was to be exercised in such a way as to cause a direct skip.

Page 18-38:

Add to note 44.

Cf. Priv. Ltr. Rul. 200816008 (Dec. 14, 2007) (income beneficiary did not make a constructive tainted addition to a grandfathered GST trust by paying federal income taxes on mineral revenues erroneously reported as income because beneficiary enforced her right to recover the erroneously paid tax and the trust agreed to reimburse her).

[iii] Consequences when tainted corpus is added.

Add to note 47.

In Private Letter Ruling 200210018 (Nov. 28, 2001), the Service ruled that an addition to a grandfathered trust would occur where a transferor's surviving spouse made a nonqualified disclaimer of her rights to receive trust income and corpus. The ruling concluded that the spouse was making an addition to the trust of an amount equal to the value of the interests in the trust that the spouse relinquished. However, the same ruling had held that because the beneficiaries of the disclaimer had agreed to pay the federal and income taxes incurred by the spouse, the amount of the gift transferred by the spouse would be reduced by the consideration received. The ruling does not address whether the same reduction should apply for purposes of determining the amount of the addition to the trust by the spouse. Priv. Ltr. Rul. 200532024 (May 9, 2005) (renunciation of interests in exempt trust by grandchildren which would result in trust termination and distribution of trust corpus to great-grandchildren constituted a constructive addition to trust by grandchildren, but so long as trust distributions were made to individuals who were not two or more generations below the grandchildren the distributions would not be subject to GST tax).

[d] Mental Disability

Page 18-42:

Add to note 80.

Priv. Ltr. Rul. 200728040 (Mar. 26, 2007) (extension of time granted under Regulations Section 301.9100-3 (see ¶ 16.02[9][a], note 577) to file qualified doctor's certification that decedent was mentally incompetent at all times on or after October 22, 1986, until his death). Priv. Ltr. Rul. 200944017 (July 21, 2009) (same). Priv. Ltr. Ruls. 201027026, 201027027 (Mar. 26, 2010).

[e] Permissible Modifications to Exempt Trusts

Page 18-42:

Add to note 83.

Currently, no guidance has been issued concerning changes that may affect the status of GST trusts that are exempt from GST tax because they have a zero inclusion ratio. However, the Service found in Priv. Ltr. Rul. 200715002 (Nov. 30, 2006) and in Priv. Ltr. Rul. 200841027 (May 30, 2008), both involving modifications made to such GST trusts, that, at a minimum, a change that would not affect the GST tax status of a trust that was irrevocable on September 25, 1985, should similarly not affect the exempt status of a trust that is exempt from GST tax because sufficient GST exemption was allocated to the trust to result in a zero inclusion ratio.

Page 18-43:

Add to note 84.

Priv. Ltr. Rul. 201023050 (Jan. 25, 2010) (trustees' division of an IRA held by exempt trust with one portion of the IRA used to fund annual distributions to a trust beneficiary deemed to be the individual for whose benefit the IRA is maintained for required distributions will not cause the trust to lose its exempt status).

[i] Trustee's discretionary powers.

Page 18-44:

Add to note 96.

Priv. Ltr. Ruls. 200539001, 200539010, 200539011 (June 24, 2005) (trustee's exercise of limited power of appointment in trusts and modifications of certain administrative provisions). See also Priv. Ltr. Rul. 200551001 (Sept. 6, 2005) (trustees' distribution of assets from exempt trust to another trust and trustees' modification of the second trust's administrative provisions); Priv. Ltr. Rul. 200608007 (Nov. 16, 2005) (trustee's proposed exercise of discretion in allocating receipts from mineral royalties pursuant to the authority granted in the exempt trust and state law). Priv. Ltr. Rul. 200924008 (Feb. 12, 2009) (trustees' distribution of principal from six trusts to six identical trusts with modified trust terms that do not improperly extend the time for vesting of any beneficial interest will not affect the exempt status of the trusts). Priv. Ltr. Rul. 201013027, 032 (Nov. 9, 2010) (transfers of exempt trust assets to individual trusts for trust beneficiary's children that do not extend the time for vesting of beneficial interests will not cause the trusts to lose their tax-exempt status). Priv. Ltr. Rul. 201134017 (May 26, 2011) (transfer of trust assets to receiving trust won't alter inclusion ratio of receiving trust which will have an inclusion ratio of zero).

[ii] Settlement.

Page 18-44:

Add to note 99.

See Priv. Ltr. Rul. 200435008 (Apr. 21, 2004) (a settlement agreement that modified the terms of two trusts was a settlement of a bona fide issue, the product of arm's-length negotiations, and within the range of reasonable outcomes under the governing instrument and local law and, accordingly, did not cause the trusts to lose their GST exempt status) and Priv. Ltr. Rul. 200543015 (July 5, 2005) (implementation of a settlement agreement that modified a trust due to an ongoing controversy over whether a grandchild was actually a descendant of one of the grantor's children did not cause the trust to lose its GST exempt status). See also Priv. Ltr. Rul. 200634004 (May 3, 2006) (court-approved settlement agreement that appointed a corporate trustee for an exempt trust, modified the trust to permit certain investments, included various administrative provisions and caused the resignation of the existing trustee did not affect the trust's GST exempt status) and Priv. Ltr. Rul. 200638020 (June 15, 2006) (division of exempt trust into two separate trusts and an allocation of assets between the trusts pursuant to a court-approved settlement agreement did not cause the trusts to lose their tax-exempt status). Priv. Ltr. Rul. 200936008 (Apr. 27, 2009) (early termination of exempt trust pursuant to settlement agreement among beneficiaries and trustees over bona fide issues regarding the trust's administration and construction, that is the product of arm's length negotiations, represents a compromise reflecting the parties' assessments of the relative strengths of their positions, and is within the range of reasonable outcomes under the governing instrument and applicable law does not cause distributions from the trust to be subject to GST tax). Priv. Ltr. Rul. 201006005 (Oct. 27, 2009) (settlement agreement which clarified the identity of trust beneficiaries will not cause the trust to lose its tax-exempt status); Priv. Ltr. Rul. 201013017, 018 (Nov. 30, 2009) (subdivision of exempt trusts and equitable adjustments to subtrusts to account for certain state tax savings pursuant to a settlement agreement will not cause the trusts to lose their tax-exempt status); Priv. Ltr. Ruls. 201021003–201021011 (Nov. 24, 2009) (division of exempt trust pursuant to settlement agreement that concluded litigation among beneficiaries and change in corporate trustee); Priv. Ltr. Ruls. 201023001– 201023006 (Nov. 24, 2009) (division of exempt trust pursuant to settlement agreement that concluded litigation among beneficiaries). Priv. Ltr. Ruls. 201051002, 201051003, 201051004 and 201051023 (July 29, 2010) (proposed settlement agreement to resolve litigation among decedent's descendants arising from trust terms set forth in decedent's will that could have led to a violation of the applicable rule against perpetuities will not cause trust to lose its exempt status); Priv. Ltr. Ruls. 201052002 (July 29, 2010); 201101001 – (July 29, 2010); 201102004 – 201102024 (July 29, 2010); 201102051 – 201102052 (July 29, 2010); Priv. Ltr. Rul. 201104001 (July 29, 2010) (same). Priv. Ltr. Rul. 201121002 (Jan. 28, 2011) (settlement agreement providing that grandchild born out of wedlock is issue of grantor in order to settle litigation among beneficiaries). Priv. Ltr. Rul.

201123014 (Mar. 4, 2011) (settlement agreement that attempted to resolve bona fide issues regarding the administration of an exempt trust and later court order that settled continued negotiations and litigation following the settlement agreement will not cause trust to lose its exempt status).

[iii] Judicial construction.

Page 18-44:

Add to note 100.

Priv. Ltr. Rul. 200618004 (Jan. 26, 2006) (judicial construction of exempt trust that remedies ambiguity, maintains grantor's intent and implements a proposed plan to fund routine trust expenses will not cause trust to lose its exempt status). Priv. Ltr. Rul. 201049016 (Aug. 30, 2010) (reformation of trust to correct scrivener's error that creates patent ambiguity regarding trust disposition if beneficiary dies testate without exercising limited power of appointment will not cause trust to lose its exempt status). The Service has concluded that the same rules should apply to a judicial reformation of a post-September 25, 1985, GST trust with a zero inclusion ratio. Priv. Ltr. Rul. 200527008 (Mar. 16, 2005). Seemingly, all of the types of modifications listed in ¶ 18.05[2][e] should be permitted with respect to GST trusts that are exempt because they have a zero inclusion ratio and the Service appears to agree. In Private Letter Ruling 200715002 (November 30, 2006), the Service cites Regulations Section 26.2601-1(b)(4)(i)(E) Example 6, which involves a pre–September 25, 1985 trust, in a case involving a trust exempt from GST tax because it has a zero inclusion ratio noting that "[a]t a minimum, a change that would not affect the GST tax status of a trust that was irrevocable on September 25, 1985, should similarly not affect the exempt status of a trust that is exempt from GST tax because sufficient GST exemption was allocated to the trust to result in an inclusion ration of zero."

Page 18-45:

Add to note 102.

See Priv. Ltr. Rul. 200303030 (Oct. 8, 2002) (ruling that a state court decision construing a will to include adopted descendants within the class of beneficiaries was consistent with the decisions of the state supreme court on the treatment of adopted persons) and Priv. Ltr. Rul. 200712029 (Nov. 30, 2006) (reformation of trust to clarify a drafting ambiguity as to whether a child's spouse at the time of a child's death was entitled to receive trust income, regardless of whether that spouse was named in the trust instrument, resolved a bona fide issue and was consistent with applicable state law).

Add to note 103.

Priv. Ltr. Rul. 200910003 (Nov. 17, 2008) (judicial reformation of trust to clarify the grantor's intent that a power of appointment provision in a GST tax-exempt trust was a limited power of appointment was consistent with applicable state law and did not result in adverse GST tax consequences); Priv. Ltr. Ruls. 201006005, 201006023 (Oct. 27, 2009) (judicial modification of son's general power of appointment as a limited power of appointment is consistent with trust grantor's intent and applicable state law and will not cause trust to lose its GST-exempt status). Priv. Ltr. Ruls. 201026014, 201026024, 201026027 (Feb. 24, 2010) (judicial construction of spendthrift clause to permit proposed sales of remainder interests will not cause trust to lose its exempt status); Priv. Ltr. Rul. 201136011 (June 7, 2011) (same); Priv. Ltr. Ruls. 201121007–201121009, 201121011 (Feb. 14, 2011) (judicial modification to trust to clarify treatment of accumulated income consistent with settlor's intent).

[iv] Other changes.

Page 18-45:

In note 105, replace "Prop. Reg. § 26.2601-1(b)(4)(i)(D)(2)" *with* "Reg. § 26.2601-1(b)(4)(i)(D)(2)".

Add to note 106.

Priv. Ltr. Rul. 200441005 (May 26, 2004) (exempt status of grandfathered trust not lost by judicial modification to extend term of trust for the rest of the beneficiary's life or until beneficiary's mental disability was removed). A modification may also occur as a result of change in state law. Priv. Ltr. Rul. 200530020 (Apr. 6, 2005) (enactment of state statute converting beneficiary/trustee's general power of appointment over trust income to a limited power is not considered a modification resulting in a proscribed shift of a beneficial interest). Priv. Ltr. Rul. 200902008 (Sept. 29, 2008) (contribution of GST exempt trust assets to a new limited partnership and operation and management of those assets under the limited partnership and a limited liability company agreements and the state trust code will not cause trust to lose its exempt status). Priv. Ltr. Rul. 200917004 (Dec. 16, 2008) (court-ordered modification of exempt trust to increase the number of contingent beneficiaries by including legally adopted children in the trust's definition of "issue" and "descendants" will not cause the trust to lose its exempt status since the amendment did not shift a beneficial interest in the trust to any beneficiary who occupied a lower generation than the person who held the interest prior to the modification). Priv. Ltr. Rul. 200917015 (Dec. 16, 2008) (court-ordered reformation of exempt trust to limit the time in which a beneficiary may exercise his annual withdrawal right will not cause the trust to lose its exempt status).

Add to note 107.

Priv. Ltr. Ruls. 200839025 through 200839027 (May 30, 2008) (trustee's administrative modification to trust that moves the situs of the trust from one state to another will not cause the trust to have a non-zero inclusion ratio). Priv. Ltr. Rul. 200841027 (May 30, 2008) (involving a change of trust situs in a GST trust exempt from GST tax because it has a zero inclusion ratio).

Add to note 108.

Priv. Ltr. Rul. 200516001 (Dec. 14, 2004) (division of exempt trust into separate trusts for each trust beneficiary with a pro rata allocation of common stock, which is the sole asset of the trust, into each separate trust will not cause the trust to lose its exempt status); Priv. Ltr. Rul. 200520003 (Feb. 14, 2005) (pro rata division of single trust into four trusts, one for each of four beneficiaries); Priv. Ltr. Rul. 200539024 (June 9, 2005) (severance of trust, previous resignation of trustee and modification of trust to (1) liberalize investment requirements; (2) allow each successor trustee to pick a successor; and (3) allow principal distributions); Priv. Ltr. Rul. 200601010 (Sept. 29, 2005) (judicial modification to exempt trust to create two new trusts along with other judicial modifications). Priv. Ltr. Rul. 200645005 (Aug. 4, 2006) (division of exempt trust into nine separate trusts); Priv. Ltr. Rul. 200703031 (Sept. 26, 2006) (division of exempt trust into three separate trusts and modification of the trusts to give the beneficiary of each trust testamentary limited powers of appointment); Priv. Ltr. Rul. 200708054 (Sept. 26, 2006) (exchange of property interests held by exempt trust with property interests held by nonexempt trust and the partition of the exempt trust into two separate trusts); Priv. Ltr. Rul. 200738005 (May 29, 2007) (implementation of settlement agreement which divided exempt trust in order to resolve ambiguity in trust will not cause trust distributions to be subject to the GST tax); Priv. Ltr. Rul. 200736023 (May 14, 2007) (proposed division of exempt trust into three trusts, one for each of the grantor's grandsons and their issue); Priv. Ltr. Rul. 200736002 (May 22, 2007) (proposed division of exempt trust into three trusts, one for each of the grantor's children and their respective issue). Priv. Ltr. Rul. 200913002 (Nov. 24, 2008) (proposed division of electing small business trust because a potential current beneficiary of the trust was a resident alien). Priv. Ltr. Rul. 201003015 (Sept. 14, 2009) (proposed division of exempt trust into five separate trusts for different family lines, and possible change of trustees with respect to each separate trust). Priv. Ltr. Ruls. 201011002 and 201011008 (Nov. 6, 2009) (modification and division of exempt trusts into separate and equal trusts). Priv. Ltr. Rul. 201013030 (Nov. 6, 2009) (division of exempt trusts into separate trusts, one for the benefit of each child and his or her family). Priv. Ltr. Ruls. 201024026, 201024027, 201024029 (Mar. 8, 2010), 201026018 (Mar. 22, 2010), 201032026 (Apr. 28, 2010), 201039003 (June 25, 2010). Priv. Ltr. Rul. 201049008 (Aug. 26, 2010) (modification and division of trust, exempt due to the allocation of the grantor's GST exemption, into four subtrusts did not cause trust to lose its GST inclusion ratio of zero); Priv. Ltr. Rul. 201104003 (Oct. 8, 2010) (amendment of trust to provide for the creation of two new trusts intended to receive income distributions from the original trust for the benefit of separate beneficiaries, will not cause the original trust or the new trusts to lose their exempt status); Priv. Ltr. Rul. 201109004 (Nov. 9, 2010) (division of trust to create separate trusts for each family line and modifications to distribution, termination and administrative provisions to allow each family to more efficiently control its separate trust); Priv. Ltr. Rul. 201131014 (Apr. 19, 2011) (division of trust into subtrusts); Priv. Ltr. Rul. 201133007 (May 17, 2011) (division of two trusts into subtrusts).

Add to note 109.

Priv. Ltr. Ruls. 200513003, 200513004, 200513005 (Nov. 22, 2004) (citing Regulations Section 26.2601-1(b)(4)(i)(E) Example 6, the Service ruled that the mergers of three exempt trusts into "S trusts" for which an electing small business trust (ESBT) election could be made did not cause the trusts to lose their exempt status). Priv. Ltr. Rul. 200715002 (Nov. 30, 2006) (merger of two GST exempt CLUTs with identical dispositive provisions). Priv. Ltr. Rul. 200923012-16 (Feb. 2, 2009) (proposed consolidation of series of trusts for the benefit of grantors' grandchildren for administrative convenience will not result in loss of GST tax exemption). Priv. Ltr. Ruls. 201024014, 201024015, 201024016 (Feb. 26, 2010), 201024017–201024024 (Mar. 2, 2010), 201024043, 201024044 (Mar. 2, 2010), 201025026 (Feb. 26, 2010). Priv. Ltr. Rul. 201042004 (July 20, 2010) (merger of exempt trusts with substantially similar terms). Priv. Ltr. Ruls. 201050005, 201050006 and 201050008 (Sept. 8, 2010) (same).

Add to note 110.

In Private Letter Ruling 200403031 (October 1, 2003), the Service ruled that proposed reformations of exempt trusts that would restrict distributions of income and principal to higher generation beneficiaries in order to qualify trusts as qualified subchapter S trusts will not affect the trusts' exempt status. Priv. Ltr. Rul. 200714009 (Dec. 19, 2006) (court-ordered modification of exempt trust's distributions due to circumstances not known or anticipated by the grantor when the trust was established which did not shift a beneficial interest in the trust to any lower-generation-level beneficiary nor extend the time for vesting of any beneficial interest in the trust did not result in the loss of trust's exempt status).

Priv. Ltr. Ruls. 200839025 through 200839027 (May 30, 2008) (court-ordered reformation of trust to increase discretionary distributions of trust assets to trust beneficiaries as a group, with no limitation on the amount of such discretionary distributions, done to insure that the original intentions of the grantor be carried out will not cause the trust to have a non-zero inclusion ratio).

Priv. Ltr. Rul. 200841027 (May 30, 2008) (involving a restatement of a GST trust, exempt from GST tax because it has a zero inclusion ratio, to remove percentage limitation placed on discretionary distributions in the trust agreement). Priv. Ltr. Rul. 201122007 (Feb. 24, 2011) (court-ordered shift of a portion of trust principal to remainder beneficiaries following submission of affidavits that primary beneficiary's financial resources prevented her from receiving any trust income or principal under the terms of the trust did not cause the trust to lose its exempt status).

In note 111, replace "Prop. Reg. § 26.2601-1(b)(4)(i)(E) Ex. 11" *with* "Reg. § 26.2601-1(b)(4)(i)(E) Ex. 11".

Add to the end of note 111.

Priv. Ltr. Ruls. 200447002 (July 15, 2004), 200507010 (Oct. 25, 2004), and Priv. Ltr. Rul. 200609003 (Nov. 21, 2005). Priv. Ltr. Rul. 200705025 (Oct. 20, 2006). Priv. Ltr. Rul. 201025030 (Mar. 10, 2010). Priv. Ltr. Rul. 201049008 (Aug. 26, 2010) (division of trust, exempt due to the allocation of the grantor's GST exemption, into four subtrusts, three of which were to be unitrusts, did not cause trust to lose its GST inclusion ratio of zero); Priv. Ltr. Rul. 201104003 (Oct. 8, 2010) (proposed conversion of exempt trust to unitrust, pursuant to applicable state law, and amendment of trust to provide for the creation of two new trusts intended to receive income distributions from the original trust for the benefit of separate beneficiaries, will not cause the original trust or the new trusts to lose their exempt status).

In note 112, replace "Prop. Reg. § 26.2601-1(b)(4)(i)(E) Ex. 12" *with* "Reg. § 26.2601-1(b)(4)(i)(E) Ex. 12".

Add to the end of note 112.

Priv. Ltr. Rul. 200533006 (April 20, 2005) (equitable adjustment between principal and income of trusts in accordance with state statutes). Priv. Ltr. Rul. 201128011 (Mar. 23, 2011) (judicial reformation of exempt trust to clarify and amend trustees' investment responsibilities and to allow trustees to make equitable adjustments between principal and income of trusts in accordance with state law will not cause trust to lose its exempt status).

Add to note 113.

See, e.g., Priv. Ltr. Ruls. 200410014 (Oct. 10, 2003), 200410015 (Oct. 10, 2003), 200341011 (July 3, 2003). In Private Letter Ruling 200430009 (Mar. 22, 2004), a judicial modification of a trust agreement that would allow separate trustees for separate trusts did not cause the separate trusts to lose their exempt status. Priv. Ltr. Rul. 200507002 (Oct. 28, 2004) (settlement agreement dividing a trust and exercising beneficiary's power of appointment did not cause original trust to lose its GST-tax exempt status and did not subject the separate trusts to the GST tax). Priv. Ltr. Rul. 200841027 (May 30, 2008) (involving a restatement of a GST trust, exempt from GST tax because it has a zero inclusion ratio, to increase the number of trustees).

Priv. Ltr. Ruls. 200520021, 200520022, 200520023 (Jan. 28, 2005) (proposed distribution of exempt trust into further trust combined with a change in trustee and inclusion of a spendthrift clause in the new trust will not affect the exempt status of the assets since the proposed modification and distribution in further trust will not result in a shift of any beneficial interest to any beneficiary who occupies a generation lower than the persons holding the beneficial interests and will not extend the time for vesting of any beneficial interest in the new trust beyond the period provided for in the original trust).

Cf. Priv. Ltr. Ruls. 200536011 and 200536012 (May 12, 2005) (neither the execution of shareholder agreements nor the exercise of any purchase option provided thereunder by the trustees of exempt trusts will cause the exempt trusts to lose their GST exempt status); Priv. Ltr. Rul. 200541035 (June 27, 2005) (beneficiary's partial release of limited power of appointment and trustees' consent to an ESBT election will not cause exempt trust to lose its GST exempt status); Priv. Ltr. Ruls. 200546052–200546055 (Aug. 2, 2005) (trustee and firewall provisions prevent appointment of family's trust company as independent trustee to cause exempt trust to lose GST exempt status); Priv. Ltr. Ruls. 200548035 (Aug. 2, 2005) (same); 200549005 (Aug. 18, 2005) (proposed modification of exempt trust that adds an additional successor trustee, pursuant to procedure outlined under state law, is administrative in nature); 200551020 (Sept. 21, 2005) (proposed modification of trustee provisions will not cause exempt trust to lose its GST exempt status); 200944013 (July 20, 2009) (same), Priv. Ltr. Rul. 201015025 (Dec. 30, 2009) (modify provisions relating to the removal, resignation and replacement of trustees and trustee compensation, and to authorize appointment of an investment adviser will not cause exempt trust to lose its GST exempt status). Priv. Ltr. Rul. 200601010 (Sept. 29, 2005) (judicial modification to exempt trust to create two new trusts, to provide that a deceased beneficiary's siblings (or their issue) will receive the corpus of a deceased beneficiary share if he or she dies without issue, to define issue to include certain adopted persons, to allow different trustees to be elected for different shares and to specify that the trustees must distribute all the income of the separate trust shares will not cause trust to lose its status as GST exempt); Priv. Ltr. Ruls. 200622042 and 200620021 (Jan. 31, 2006) (resignation of members of an advisory committee and appointment of successor advisors with respect to an exempt trust in accordance with decedent's will was a modification that was administrative in nature). Priv. Ltr. Rul. 200637021 (June 2, 2006) (resignation of original cotrustee and beneficiary's appointment as sole trustee will not cause trust to lose its exempt status since the modification of the trust is administrative in nature). Priv. Ltr. Rul. 200726008 (Mar. 22, 2007) (modification of trust to limit beneficiary's annual withdrawal right to the month of January did not cause the trust to lose its exempt status). Priv. Ltr. Rul. 200734010 (Apr. 19, 2007) (corporate board resolution appointing a bank or trust company designated by the trust beneficiaries as successor trustee would not cause trust to lose its GST exempt status since resolution required that such bank or trust company not be subordinate to any trust beneficiary). Priv. Ltr. Ruls. 200839025 through 200839027 (May 30, 2008) (court-ordered reformation of trust to increase the number of trustees so that trust powers can be segregated to provide a clear delineation of responsibility among the Investment Trustee, the Benefits Trustee, and the Administrative Trustee will not cause the trust to have a non-zero inclusion ratio). Priv. Ltr. Rul. 200919008 (Jan. 12, 2009) (court-ordered modification to administrative provisions of a trust with a zero inclusion ratio will not cause the trust to lose its GST tax-exempt status). Priv. Ltr. Rul. 200922013-22027 (Sept. 15, 2008) (court-ordered early termination of exempt charitable remainder trusts in order to accelerate distributions to charitable remainder beneficiaries where trust corpus far exceeds amount needed to fund remaining annuity interests will not cause trusts to lose their GST tax-exempt status).

Priv. Ltr. Ruls. 200936017–200936019, 200936023 (May 14, 2009) (modification of trusts to require grantor's grandchildren to execute premarital agreements before marrying or entering into any legally recognizable union in order to protect trust assets will not cause the trusts to lose their exempt status). Priv. Ltr. Rul. 201039008-09 (June 29, 2010) (procedures for the removal and designation of trustees and the payment of trust principal for a beneficiary's health, education, support and maintenance). Priv. Ltr. Rul. 201042004 (July 20, 2010) (court-ordered modification of exempt trusts to limit trust beneficiary's annual five percent principal withdrawal right to the month of January will not cause the trusts to lose their exempt status).

In Notice 2008-63, 2008-31 IRB, the Service proposed a revenue ruling that would allow families to use private trust companies as trustees of family trusts without adverse gift, estate or generation-skipping transfer tax consequences for either the grantor(s) of the trust or trust beneficiaries in carefully defined situations.

Page 18-46:

Add to note 114.

See Priv. Ltr. Rul. 200314003 (Apr. 4, 2003) (ruling that a trust reformation granting income beneficiaries of a trust who die leaving no descendants, or whose descendants predecease the other income beneficiaries, a limited testamentary power of appointment over the income which could not be exercised to appoint to a person in a generation lower than the person that held the beneficial interest prior to the reformation would not cause the trust to lose its exempt status); to similar effect is Priv. Ltr. Rul. 200314011 (Apr. 4, 2003). Priv. Ltr. Rul. 201023050 (Jan. 25, 2010) (trustees' division of IRA held by exempt trust with one portion of the IRA used to fund annual distributions to trust beneficiary deemed to be the individual for whose benefit the IRA is maintained for required distributions will not cause the trust to lose its exempt status—such action will not cause property to pass to a lower generation nor will it extend the time for vesting of any beneficial interest).

PART V

Special Valuation Rules

CHAPTER **19**

Special Valuation Rules

¶ 19.02	Section 2701. Special Valuation Rules		S19-2
	[3]	Exceptions	S19-2
		[b] Interests of the Same Class and Interests Proportionate to the Class	S19-2
	[4]	Section 2701 Valuation Rules	S19-2
		[c] Distribution Rights	S19-2
		[i] Qualified payment rights.	S19-2
	[5]	Special Rules Under Section 2701	S19-3
		[a] Section 2701(d)	S19-3
		[ii] Qualified payment elections.	S19-3
		[d] Open Statute of Limitations	S19-3
¶ 19.03	Section 2702: Special Valuation Rules for Transfers of Interests in Trusts		S19-4
	[1]	Introduction	S19-4
	[2]	The General Rule	S19-4
		[a] The Requirements of Section 2702	S19-4
		[ii] Family members.	S19-4
		[iv] A retained interest.	S19-5
	[3]	Exceptions	S19-5
		[a] Incomplete Gifts	S19-5
		[b] Qualified Interests	S19-5
		[i] Qualified income interests.	S19-5
		[d] Personal Residence Trusts	S19-7
		[i] Requirements applicable to both types of personal residence trusts.	S19-8
		[iii] A qualified personal residence trust.	S19-8
		[iv] The two personal residence trusts limitation.	S19-10
	[4]	Special Rules Under Section 2702	S19-10
		[a] The Joint Purchase Rule	S19-10
		[d] The Open Statute of Limitations	S19-11
		[e] The Relationship of Section 2702 to Other Taxes	S19-11
		[i] The estate tax.	S19-11

	[f]	Effective Dates..........................	S19-12
¶ 19.04	Section 2703. Certain Rights and Restrictions Disregarded		S19-12
	[2]	The General Rule of Section 2703..............	S19-12
	[3]	The Section 2703(b) Statutory Exception	S19-13
	[a]	Bona Fide Business Arrangement..........	S19-13
	[b]	Not a Device to Transfer Property to Members of Decedent's Family for Less Than Full and Adequate Consideration..................	S19-14
		[i] Not a family device................	S19-14
		[ii] Full and adequate consideration.	S19-14
	[c]	Similar Arrangement Test	S19-14
	[4]	Deemed Satisfaction	S19-15
	[6]	Establishing Valuation When a Right or Restriction Is Excepted From Section 2703	S19-15
	[a]	Estate Tax Valuation...................	S19-15
		[i] Restrictions on lifetime dispositions. ...	S19-15
		[ii] Obligation of the estate to sell.	S19-16
	[7]	Effective Dates and Substantial Modification	S19-16

¶ 19.02 SECTION 2701. SPECIAL VALUATION RULES

[3] Exceptions

[b] Interests of the Same Class and Interests Proportionate to the Class

Page 19-33:

Add new note 174.1 for the sentence following the text containing note 174.

Priv. Ltr. Rul. 200407006 (Nov. 5, 2003) (Section 2701 inapplicable where two companies were merged into a single company and, as part of the consolidation, the shareholders of the original two companies received voting stock in the single company which, following the consolidation, was then exchanged for both voting and non-voting common stock).

[4] Section 2701 Valuation Rules

[c] Distribution Rights

[i] Qualified payment rights.

Page 19-37:

Add to note 204.

In Priv. Ltr. Rul. 200839029 (May 15, 2008) a dividend right held by a family member who had received preferred stock in a closely held corporation in exchange for voting common stock is a retained distribution right subject to IRC § 2701. Because the preferred stock is non-cumulative, the distribution right is not a qualified payment right and, accordingly, the value of the preferred stock held by the family member is deemed to be zero. Family member must make an election, pursuant to IRC § 2701(c)(3)(C)(ii), in order to treat that distribution right as a qualified payment right. The Service ruled that such election, which was not made on family member's originally filed Form 709, may be made on an amended return.

In Priv. Ltr. Rul. 200934013 (May 20, 2009) a family member's right of return from preferred stock in an LLC was an applicable retained interest subject to IRC § 2701 because it was an equity interest in a controlled entity in which the family member had a distribution right. The right of return was not, however, a qualified payment right under Reg. § 25.2701-2(b)(6) since it was not payable at a fixed rate or in a fixed amount. In accordance with Reg. § 25.2701-2(c), the Service granted the family member's election to treat the distribution right as a qualified payment right so long as the election was timely made.

[5] Special Rules Under Section 2701

[a] Section 2701(d)

[ii] Qualified payment elections.

Page 19-53:

Add to note 316.

In Private Letter Ruling 200839029 (May 15, 2008) a dividend right held by a family member who had received preferred stock in a closely held corporation in exchange for voting common stock is a retained distribution right subject to IRC § 2701. Because the preferred stock is non-cumulative, the distribution right is not a qualified payment right and, accordingly, the value of the preferred stock held by the family member is deemed to be zero. Family member failed to make an election, pursuant to IRC § 2701(c)(3)(C)(ii), to treat that distribution right as a qualified payment right on family member's originally filed Form 709. The Service ruled, however, that such election may be made on an amended return.

[d] Open Statute of Limitations

Page 19-75:

Add to end of first paragraph of note 491.

But see CCA 201024059 (May 11, 2010), where the Office of Chief Counsel ruled, in email advice, that the failure by a donor of closely held stock to disclose on the Form 709 any information regarding either the method used to value the stock or a description of the discounts taken appeared to indicate that the gift tax imposed on the transfer could be assessed at any time under Regulations § 301.6501(c)-1(f). In its ruling, the Chief Counsel's office also noted that if the gift was subject to the special valuation rules under IRC § 2701, the gifts must be "adequately shown" on the gift tax return under Regulations § 301.6501(c)-1(e) for the period of limitations on assessment to begin to run. Although the Regulations § 301.6501(c)-1(e) adequately shown standard may differ somewhat from the Regulations § 301.6501(c)-1(f) adequate disclosure standard, the Chief Counsel's office advised that similar disclosure requirements are imposed as to the particular method the donor used for gift valuation purposes.

¶ 19.03 SECTION 2702: SPECIAL VALUATION RULES FOR TRANSFERS OF INTERESTS IN TRUSTS

[1] Introduction

Page 19-81:

Add to note 3.

As required by Section 7520(c)(3), the Service issued proposed, temporary and final regulations on May 7, 2009, revising Table S and Table U(1), the tables used to value annuities, interests for life or a term of years, and reversionary and remainder interests in property, to reflect the mortality experience from the 2000 census (Life Table 2000CM). Transition rules allow taxpayers to use tables based on either Life Table 90CM or Life Table 2000CM to value gift, charitable and estate transfers made on or after May 1, 2009, but before July 1, 2009, but they must use the appropriate interest rate for the month in which the valuation date falls, regardless of which table is chosen. TD 9448; REG-107845-08. Reg. §§ 1.170A-12T, 1.642(c)-6T, 1.664-4T, 20.2031-7T, 20.2032A-1T, 20.2056A-4T, 25.2512-5T, 25.2522(c)-3, 1.7520-1T, 20.7520-1T, and Reg. § 25.7520-1T. Publications 1457 and 1458 (rev. May 2009), both of which include examples for using the mortality component tables, have been released. On August 10, 2011, the Service issued final regulations that removed the temporary regulations issued in TD 9448 and adopted as final the proposed regulations issued in REG-107845-08. The only substantive change was the deletion of an example in the Section 2032 regulations which the Service anticipates including in a different regulation project under that Code section. TD 9540; Reg. §§ 1.170A-12, 1.642(c)-6, 1.664-4, 20.2031-7, 20.2032-1, 20.2056A-4, 25.2512-5, 25.2522(c)-3, 1.7520-1, 20.7520-1, 25.7520-1.

[2] The General Rule

[a] The Requirements of Section 2702

[ii] Family members.

Page 19-89:

Add to note 59.

See Priv. Ltr. Rul. 201116006 (Dec. 27, 2010), in which a former spouse's transfer of cash to an irrevocable trust, made in settlement of the divorcing parties' property and marital rights, with decedent receiving all trust income for life and holding a limited power of appointment to appoint the trust remainder to her surviving issue, constituted a transfer for full and adequate consideration under IRC § 2516. A taxable gift did occur upon the transfer of the trust remainder to decedent's surviving issue, upon decedent's failure to exercise power of appointment, with former spouse as the transferor. As a result, decedent was not the transferor, settlor, or donor of the trust for purposes of Section 2702.

[iv] A retained interest.

Page 19-91:

Add to note 68.

However, a transfer with respect to one trust while continuing to have an interest in a separate but related trust does not cause the latter interest to be treated as a retained interest. Private Letter Ruling 200250033 (Sept. 10, 2002) ruled that where a trustee divided a marital deduction trust into two trusts, and the spouse beneficiary made a nonqualified disclaimer of the income interest in one, her interest in the other was not treated as a retained interest because the two trusts were separate trusts. Thus, Section 2702 did not apply to cause her to be treated as having made a gift equal to the value of both trusts.

[3] Exceptions

[a] Incomplete Gifts

Page 19-97:

Delete the phrase in note 109 beginning with Technically *and ending in note 268, and replace with the word* See.

[b] Qualified Interests

Page 19-98:

Add to note 112.

As required by Section 7520(c)(3), the Service issued proposed, temporary and final regulations on May 7, 2009, revising Table S and Table U(1), the tables used to value annuities, interests for life or a term of years, and reversionary and remainder interests in property, to reflect the mortality experience from the 2000 census (Life Table 2000CM). Transition rules allow taxpayers to use tables based on either Life Table 90CM or Life Table 2000CM to value gift, charitable and estate transfers made on or after May 1, 2009, but before July 1, 2009, but they must use the appropriate interest rate for the month in which the valuation date falls, regardless of which table is chosen. TD 9448; REG-107845-08. Reg. §§ 1.170A-12T, 1.642(c)-6T, 1.664-4T, 20.2031-7T, 20.2032A-1T, 20.2056A-4T, 25.2512-5T, 25.2522(c)-3, 1.7520-1T, 20.7520-1T, and Reg. § 25.7520-1T. Publications 1457 and 1458 (rev. May 2009), both of which include examples for using the mortality component tables, have been released. On August 10, 2011, the Service issued final regulations that removed the temporary regulations issued in TD 9448 and adopted as final the proposed regulations issued in REG-107845-08. The only substantive change was the deletion of an example in the Section 2032 regulations which the Service anticipates including in a different regulation project under that Code section. TD 9540; Reg. §§ 1.170A-12, 1.642(c)-6, 1.664-4, 20.2031-7, 20.2032-1, 20.2056A-4, 25.2512-5, 25.2522(c)-3, 1.7520-1, 20.7520-1, 25.7520-1.

[i] Qualified income interests.

Page 19-99:

Add to note 118.

Although specifically providing a sample of a qualified personal residence trust, see ¶ 19.03[3][d][iii], Rev. Proc. 2003-42, 2003-23 IRB 1, essentially provides a sample GRAT also since the sample instrument contemplates the conversion of the qualified personal residence trust to a GRAT upon sale of the residence.

Add to note 120.

See text in ¶ 4.08[8] accompanying notes 168.1–168.9

Page 19-101:

Add to note 133 just before reference to the article by McCaffrey, Plaine and Schneider.

In Notice 2003-72, 2003-44 IRB 964, the Service acquiesced to the Tax Court's decision in *Walton*, holding that Example 5 of Regulations Section 25.2702-3(e) is invalid.

The Service has proposed regulations to address the results in the *Walton* decision. See Prop. Reg. §§ 25.2702-2(a)(5), 25.2702-3(d)(4), 25.2702-3(e) Exs. 5, 6, and 25.2702-7. The principal changes are found in Proposed Regulations Section 25.2702-3(e) Ex. 5, which now treats *A*'s (and *A*'s estate's) interests as a qualified interest and in Proposed Regulations Section 25.2702-3(e) Ex. 6, which treats *A*'s or *A*'s estate's interest for ten years as a qualified interest, but the payment for the remaining balance of the additional thirty-five-year period as a contingent interest which is not a qualified interest. The proposed regulations are generally effective for trusts created after July 25, 2004, although the Service will not change any prior application of the changes to Examples 5 and 6. Prop. Reg. § 25.2702-7. The proposed regulations revising Regulations Section 25.2702-3(e) Exs. 5 and 6 were finalized. Under the final regulations, a unitrust or annuity interest payable for a specified term of years to the grantor, or to the grantor's estate if the grantor dies before the term expires, is a qualified interest for the specified term.

Page 19-102:

Add to note 134 at end of second paragraph.

It would appear the Ninth Circuit Court of Appeals would disagree with the first sentence of this paragraph. See its reversal of the Tax Court at Schott v. Comm'r, 319 F3d 1203 (9th Cir. 2003), holding that a revocable spousal annuity interest that would take effect only if the donor died during the term of a fifteen-year retained annuity without having revoked the spouse's interest was a qualified interest under Regulations Section 25.2702-2(d)(1) Ex. 7.

In Technical Advice Memorandum 200319001 (Dec. 17, 2002), the Service followed *Cook* and *Schott* (before its reversal) and held a spouse's interest to be a nonqualified contingent revocable interest. The Service also rejected as ineffective the purported reformation of the trust (effected by the trustee under a power to amend), which changed its terms to be consistent with *Walton*, on the basis that the gift was complete before the amendment was made. If the Ninth Circuit's opinion in *Schott* (described below) governs these taxpayers, and the Service is correct that the effort to reform the trust is ignored for gift tax purposes, query whether the taxpayers may still be entitled to the result they were seeking. But see Estate of Focardi v. Commissioner, TC Memo. 2006-56 (2006), where the court held that contingent revocable spousal interests in GRATs were not qualified interests because such interests were not fixed and ascertainable at GRATs inception. According to the court, the Ninth Circuit's opinion in *Schott* distinguished the GRAT at issue there from the GRAT in *Cook* on the ground that *Cook* involved "an expressed contingency that the spouses remain married" at the grantor's death. Since Mr. Focardi's GRATs reveal a strong implicit understanding of a marriage contingency, and *Schott* did not mention a marital trust, the court concluded that *Cook* applied to these GRATs with greater "force and vigor" than *Schott.* The Service has issued proposed regulations in response to the *Schott* case. Prop. Reg. §§ 25.2702-2(a)(6), 25.2702-3(d)(2), 25.2702-3(e) Ex. 8, and 25.2702-3(e) Ex. 9. The proposed regulations clarify that the exception treating a spouse's revocable successor interest as a retained qualified interest would apply only if the spouse's annuity or unitrust interest, standing alone, would constitute a qualified interest that meets the requirements of Regulations Section 25.2702-3(d)(3), but for the grantor's revocation power. Prop. Reg. § 25.2702-2(a)(6). See Prop. Reg. § 25.2702-3(e) Ex. 8 and 25.2702-3(e) Ex. 9. The proposed regulations are generally effective for trusts created after July 25, 2004. Prop. Reg. § 25.2702-7.

The proposed regulations amending Regulations Section 25.2702-2 were finalized with limited changes. The exception treating a spouse's revocable successor interest as a retained qualified interest applies only if the spouse's annuity or unitrust interest, standing alone, constitutes a qualified interest satisfying the requirement of Regulations Section 25.2702-3(d)(3), but for the grantor's revocation power. New Example 8 is added to the final regulations in Regulations Section 25.2702-3(e) to clarify that the grantor makes a completed gift to the spouse when the revocation right lapses on the expiration of the grantor's retained term.

Page 19-103:

Add to note 141.

However, a power to substitute property of equal value in a fiduciary capacity does not disqualify the GRAT. Priv. Ltr. Rul. 200846001 (July 31, 2008).

[d] Personal Residence Trusts

Page 19-106:

Add to note 162.

As required by Section 7520(c)(3), the Service issued proposed, temporary and final regulations on May 7, 2009, revising Table S and Table U(1), the tables used to value annuities, interests for life or a term of years, and reversionary and remainder interests in property, to reflect the mortality experience from the 2000 census (Life Table 2000CM). Transition rules allow taxpayers to use tables based on either Life Table 90CM or Life Table 2000CM to value gift, charitable and estate transfers made on or after May 1, 2009, but before July 1, 2009, but they must use the appropriate interest rate for the month in which the valuation date falls, regardless of which table is chosen. TD 9448; REG-107845-08. Reg. §§ 1.170A-12T, 1.642(c)-6T, 1.664-4T, 20.2031-7T, 20.2032A-1T, 20.2056A-4T, 25.2512-5T, 25.2522(c)-3, 1.7520-1T, 20.7520-1T, and Reg. § 25.7520-1T. Publications 1457 and 1458 (rev. May 2009), both of which include examples for using the mortality component tables, have been released. On August 10, 2011, the Service issued final regulations that removed the temporary regulations issued in TD 9448 and adopted as final the proposed regulations issued in REG-107845-08. The only substantive change was the deletion of an example in the Section 2032 regulations which the Service anticipates including in a different regulation project under that Code section. TD 9540; Reg. §§ 1.170A-12, 1.642(c)-6, 1.664-4, 20.2031-7, 20.2032-1, 20.2056A-4, 25.2512-5, 25.2522(c)-3, 1.7520-1, 20.7520-1, 25.7520-1.

[i] Requirements applicable to both types of personal residence trusts.

Page 19-108:

Add to note 173 following citation to Priv. Ltr. Rul. 9741004.

, 200617035 (Dec. 22, 2005) (two parcels of land that were a portion of a larger tract of land owned by the grantor with a residence, bathhouse and pavilion). Priv. Ltr. Rul. 200626043 (Feb. 23, 2006) (home used as grantor's second residence, detached garage, artist studio, and bunk house). Priv. Ltr. Rul. 200822011 (Feb. 9, 2008) (multiacre residence which includes a barn, two closed sheds and an open shed is comparable in size to that of other residential properties in the vicinity).

Add to note 177.

See also Priv. Ltr. Rul. 200814011 (Dec. 6, 2007) in which a parent who had deeded her interest in her residence to a qualified personal residence trust for a ten-year term with remainder to her children stayed on in the residence following the term and began leasing the residence from her children. In the ruling, the children intend to create a new qualified personal residence trust that will hold the residence with the parent holding a one-year term at the termination of which the trust will liquidate by distribution of the entire trust estate to the children. The Service ruled that said trust qualified for the personal residence trust exception; Priv. Ltr. Rul. 200816025 (Dec. 5, 2007) (same). In Priv. Ltr. Rul. 200848003 (Aug. 18, 2008), following the term interest held by parent in qualified personal residence trust, and pursuant to a modification previously made to that trust which allows remainder beneficiaries (the children) to make a gift of a term interest in the trust's residence, the children propose to transfer property to another qualified personal residence trust which will give parent the right to occupy and possess the property for a stated term. The Service concluded that Sections 2702(a)(1) and 2702(a)(2) will not apply to the children's proposed transfer of the residence to the second qualified personal residence trust. No opinion was made on whether the transfer of the residence to the second qualified personal residence trust would cause the residence to be included in the parents' estates under IRC § 2036. See infra text accompanying note 230.1. See also Priv. Ltr. Rul. 200751022 (Sept. 5, 2007) (relying on Regulations Section 25.2702-5(d), Example 2, the Service ruled that property qualifies as personal residence even if caretaker house is rented to third party since the primary use of the trust property is as the term holder's residence). In Estate of Riese v. Comm'r, TC Memo 2011-60 (2011), decedent had neither executed a rental agreement nor paid rent for the six month period between termination of the QPRT which held the residence and decedent's death. The Tax Court noted, however, that on multiple occasions the payment of rent was discussed between decedent and her daughter and her attorney and, in addition, daughter expressed her interest in enforcing decedent's payment of rent by contacting decedent's attorney and inquiring about the calculation of fair market rent. The court also recognized that decedent's execution of the QPRT agreement and payment of gift taxes as evidence of decedent's intent to comply with the terms of the agreement, including the payment of rent upon expiration of the term. Accordingly, the court held that the residence was not includible in decedent's gross estate since there was evidence of decedent's intent to pay rent following termination of the QPRT.

[iii] A qualified personal residence trust.

Page 19-112:

Add to note 209.

Revenue Procedure 2003-42, 2003-23 IRB 1, provides a sample governing instrument for a qualified personal residence trust (QPRT). The Service will recognize a trust as a QPRT if the trust instrument is substantially similar to the sample or properly integrates one or more of the offered alternative provisions, the trust is operated in a manner consistent with the terms of the instrument, and is a valid trust under local law. In general, the Service will no longer issue private letter rulings on whether a trust with one term holder qualifies as a QPRT, but will rule on the effect of substantive provisions, other than those contained in the revenue procedure, on the qualification of a trust as a QPRT.

Page 19-114:

Add to note 226.

In Private Letter Ruling 200617002 (Jan. 10, 2006) the husband and wife grantors of two QPRTs each containing a one-half undivided interest in their principle residence conveyed the residence held by the QPRTs into their respective revocable trusts eight months before the end of the QPRTs' term and in violation of the QPRTs' provisions. When the remainder beneficiaries (the couple's daughters) discovered this several years after the QPRTs expired during the time the spouses were in the process of selling the residence, they sued the grantors and demanded the sales proceeds. The Service ruled that the remainder beneficiaries did not make taxable gifts to the grantors upon grantors' unauthorized withdrawal of the residence from the QPRT and the grantors did not make gifts to the remainder beneficiaries upon payment of the sales proceeds to the remainder beneficiaries.

Add to note 230.

Priv. Ltr. Rul. 200822011 (Feb. 9, 2008) (citing Estate of Barlow v. Comm'r, 55 TC 666 (1971), the Service noted that when a grantor is obligated to pay fair market rent after the QPRT's term ends and he continues to live in the residence and there is no express or implied agreement that the grantor could occupy the residence whether or not rent is paid, the property will not be includible in the grantor's gross estate).

Add to text following note 230.

A relatively new twist involves a modification of the qualified personal residence trust's governing instrument after the trust term has begun which would allow the remainder beneficiaries of the trust, following the expiration of the term interest, to transfer the real property in the trust to another qualified personal residence trust which will give the original grantor the right to occupy and possess the property for a stated term. Although Section 2702 does not apply (and regular Section 7520 rules govern valuation of the gifted term interest in the second trust), the Service has specifically stated in its rulings that no opinion is expressed or implied as to whether the transfer of the residence to the second qualified personal residence trust will cause the residence to be included in the grantor's estate under Section 2036.[230.1]

[230.1] Priv. Ltr. Ruls. 200848003 (Aug. 18, 2008), 200901019 (Sept. 26, 2008), 200904022 (Sept. 30, 2008), 200920033 (Feb. 3, 2009), 200935004-200935005 (May 19, 2009), 201006012 Oct. 30, 2009), 201014044 (Dec. 16, 2009), 201019006-201019007 (Dec. 16, 2009), 201019012 (Jan. 14, 2010), 201024012 (Feb. 3, 2010), 201039001 (June

28, 2010). See also Priv. Ltr. Ruls. 200814011 (Dec. 6, 2007), 200816025 (Dec. 5, 2007), 201118014 (Jan. 13, 2011) and Priv. Ltr. Rul. 201131006 (Apr. 13, 2011) (modification of qualified personal residence trust to give settlor's children a power of appointment over the trust at the trust's expiration to, among other things, extend the settlor's term interest in the trust).

[iv] The two personal residence trusts limitation.

Page 19-118:

Add to note 257.

In Ludwick v. Comm'r, TC Memo. 2010-104 (2010), a husband and wife who owned a vacation home in Hawaii as tenants in common transferred their undivided interest in the home to a qualified personal residence trust. In valuing each donor's fractional interest in the property (see, generally, ¶ 10.02[2][c]), the Court rejected each party's valuation experts and concluded that a buyer would be willing to pay half of the fair market value of the entire property less the costs associated with selling the property, which could include the cost of partition. The Court then calculated that a 17 percent discount was appropriate.

[4] Special Rules Under Section 2702

[a] The Joint Purchase Rule

Page 19-120:

Delete the notes and the text sentences at notes 268 and 269 and provide the following explanation.

The transfers illustrated are not joint purchases because there is no Section 2702(c)(2) family acquisition by the original transferor of the property.

Page 19-122:

Add to note 282 after initial citation to Priv. Ltr. Rul. 200112023.

Cf. Priv. Ltr. Ruls. 200728018 (Mar. 19, 2007), 200840038 (June 10, 2008) and 200919002 (Dec. 23, 2008) each of which involved an irrevocable trust ("Purchasing Trust") grantor had previously established for the benefit of grantor's issue and funded with cash and/or marketable securities. In the rulings, the grantor proposes to create a qualified personal residence trust ("QPRT") with the grantor holding the term interest for his or her life and the Purchasing Trust entitled to the remainder. Grantor then proposes to transfer his or her residence to the qualified personal residence trust coupled with the sale of the remainder interest in the QPRT to the Purchasing Trust for cash and/or marketable securities held by the Purchasing Trust. The consideration provided by the Purchasing Trust would have an aggregate fair market value equal to the value of the remainder interest in the QPRT as of the date of transfer based upon a fair market value of the residence and the actuarial tables prescribed under Section 7520. The Service ruled in each case that no gift occurs on grantor's transfer of the residence.

Add to note 282 prior to See also Blattmachr.

Private Letter Rulings 200728018 and 200840038 expressly provide that no opinion is made regarding whether the trust property is includible in the transferors' gross estates under Section 2036. Priv. Ltr. Rul. 200919002 (Dec. 23, 2008) (same).

[d] The Open Statute of Limitations

Page 19-132:

Add to note 354.

But see CCA 201024059 (May 11, 2010), where the Office of Chief Counsel ruled, in email advice, that the failure by a donor of closely held stock to disclose on the Form 709 any information regarding either the method used to value the stock or a description of the discounts taken appeared to indicate that the gift tax imposed on the transfer could be assessed at any time under Regulations § 301.6501(c)-1(f). In its ruling, the Chief Counsel's office also noted that if the gift was subject to the special valuation rules under IRC § 2702, the gifts must be "adequately shown" on the gift tax return under Regulations § 301.6501(c)-1(e) for the period of limitations on assessment to begin to run. Although the Regulations § 301.6501(c)-1(e) adequately shown standard may differ somewhat from the Regulations § 301.6501(c)-1(f) adequate disclosure standard, the Chief Counsel's office advised that similar disclosure requirements are imposed as to the particular method the donor used for gift valuation purposes.

[e] The Relationship of Section 2702 to Other Taxes

[i] The estate tax.

Page 19-134:

Replace note 367 with the following.

[367] Even without regard to Section 2702, there is controversy over what amount is an adequate and full consideration for Section 2036 purposes. One line of cases requires consideration equal to the full value of the transferred corpus in order to avoid Section 2036. See, e.g., Estate of Gradow v. United States, 897 F2d 516 (Fed. Cir. 1990). The other line of cases requires consideration equal only to the value of the remainder interest. See Estate of D'Ambrosio v. Comm'r, 101 F3d 309 (3d Cir. 1996); Wheeler v. United States, 116 F3d 749 (5th Cir. 1997); Estate of Magnin v. Comm'r, 184 F3d 1074 (9th Cir. 1999). See ¶ 4.08[1][a], ¶ 4.08[7][c], text accompanying notes 140–146. The cases may be reconcilable on the grounds of whether a bona fide sale occurred. See ¶ 4.08[7][c], text accompanying notes 145–146. The enactment of Section 2702 does not alter the outcome of the controversy. Assuming the *D'Ambrosio* line of cases is correct, the joint purchase of an interest in a GRAT, GRUT, or QPRT in a bona fide transaction with adequate and full consideration should avoid a gift (see Priv. Ltr. Ruls. 9841017 (Oct. 9, 1998), 200112023 (Dec. 18, 2000)) and any inclusion of the property in the term interest holder's gross estate. See also Priv. Ltr. Rul. 200728018 (Mar. 19, 2007) (transfer of parcel by husband and wife to personal residence trust followed by a sale of the remainder interest in the trust to a purchasing trust, established by husband for the benefit of the couple's issue, for fair market value, as determined in accordance with the general actuarial valuation rules set forth in Section 7520, will not constitute a taxable gift). Private Letter Ruling 200840038 (June 10, 2008) (same). Note that in Private Letter Rulings 9841017 and 200112023, the remainder interests were purchased using independent funds provided by

the QPRTs' remainder beneficiaries. Since, in Private Letter Ruling 200728018 and Private Letter Ruling 200840038, the remainder interest was purchased with funds presumably supplied by the transferors, the question of whether a bona fide sale occurred for Section 2036 purposes is closer. See also Jordan "Sale of Remainder Interests: Reconciling *Gradow v. United States* and Section 2702," 14 Va. Tax. Rev. 671 (1995); Jensen, "Estate and Gift Effects of Selling a Remainder: Have *D'Ambrosio, Wheeler,* and *Magnin* Changed the Rules?" 4 Fla. Tax Rev. 537 (1999).

[f] Effective Dates

Page 19-136:

Add to note 385.

See Priv. Ltr. Rul. 200502008 (Sept. 30, 2004) (pre–October 8, 1990, transfer).

¶ 19.04 SECTION 2703. CERTAIN RIGHTS AND RESTRICTIONS DISREGARDED

[2] The General Rule of Section 2703

Page 19-140:

Add to note 19.

In Sidney Smith III, 94 AFTR2d 2004-5627 (D. Pa. 2004), the court held that Section 2703(a) applied to a provision in an FLP agreement that limited the price and terms upon which the FLP would be obligated to purchase a partner's limited partnership interest if the FLP exercised its right of first refusal. The court characterized the case as one of first impression and ruled that the restrictive provision in the agreement fell within the plain language of Section 2703(a), noting that Regulations Section § 25.2703-1(a)(3) provides that such a restriction could be contained in a partnership agreement. The court also held that the issue of whether the "safe harbor" of Section 2703(b) applied was not appropriate for resolution at the summary judgment stage. Subsequently, in 96 AFTR2d, ¶ 2005-6549 (WD Pa. 2005), the court granted the Service's motion for partial summary judgment. Adopting a magistrate's report and recommendation, the court found that a threshold issue existed as to whether the restrictive provision met the requirements of pre-existing pre-Section 2703 law, which continues to apply. Specifically, the court determined that the restrictive provision was not binding on the donor both during life and after death, as required by Regulations Section 20.2031-2(h) in order for the restrictive provision to control the determination of value. Because the donor retained the unilateral authority during his life to amend or modify the FLP agreement, the terms of the agreement should be disregarded for determining value for gift tax purposes.

Add new paragraph to note 21.

In Revenue Ruling 2008-35, 2008-29 IRB 116, the Service ruled that an interest in a restricted management account (RMA) will be valued for transfer tax purposes without any reduction or discount for the restrictions imposed by the RMA agreement. In its analysis, the Service ruled that the legislative history of Section 2703 confirms that it is to have a broad application and Reg. § 25.2703-1(a)(3) further clarifies that a right or restriction may be contained in a partnership agreement, articles of incorporation, bylaws, shareholders' agreement, or any other agreement, or may be implicit in the capital structure of an entity.

Page 19-141:

Add to note 25 after citation to "Strangi".

, rev'd sub nom. (on another issue) Gulig v. Comm'r, 293 F3d 279 (5th Cir. 2002)

Add to note 26 after citation to "Strangi".

, rev'd sub nom. (on another issue) Gulig v. Comm'r, 293 F3d 279 (5th Cir. 2002)

Add to note 26.

The Service successfully attacked the restrictions on transferability of a buy-sell provision found in a limited partnership agreement in Holman v. Comm'r, Doc. No. 08-3774 (8th Cir. 2010). Restrictive sale agreements are disregarded in valuing gifts of limited partnership units unless the taxpayer can establish that the restriction satisfies the three-part exception under Section 2703(b). The Eighth Circuit held that the provision failed the first part of the exception in that the donors' stated purposes for creating the limited partnership, i.e. estate planning, tax reduction, wealth transference, protection against dissipation and wealth management education, were not bona fide business purposes. See infra ¶ 19.04[3] notes 48 and 80.

[3] The Section 2703(b) Statutory Exception

Page 19-144:

Add to note 44 after citation to "True".

, aff'd, 390 F3d 1210 (10th Cir. 2004).

[a] Bona Fide Business Arrangement

Page 19-144:

Add to note 48.

But see Holman v. Comm'r, 601 F3d 763 (8th Cir. 2010), where the restrictions on transferability of a buy-sell provision found in a limited partnership agreement were disregarded in valuing gifts of limited partnership units. The Eighth Circuit held that the provision failed the first part of the exception in that the donors' stated purposes for creating the limited partnership, i.e. estate planning, tax reduction, wealth transference, protection against dissipation and wealth management education, were not bona fide business purposes. See also 2010-2 USTC ¶ 60,601 (SD Ind. 2010) (with facts analogous to those of Holman, transfer restrictions were ignored in valuing gifts of LLC membership interests because such restrictions were not a bona fide business arrangement – the LLC had no investment strategy and neither the parents nor the children made any efforts to increase the value of the property or to expand the property holdings).

Page 19-145:

Add to note 54.

Estate of Amlie v. Comm'r, TC Memo. 2006-76 (2006) (in holding that a buy-sell agreement controlled the value of decedent's stock for federal estate tax purposes, the tax court found that the agreement was a bona fide business arrangement because it secured a guaranteed price and buyer for the stock and was useful in planning for the estate's liquidity needs).

[b] Not a Device to Transfer Property to Members of Decedent's Family for Less Than Full and Adequate Consideration

[i] Not a family device.

Page 19-146:

Add to note 62.

The *True* case has been affirmed by the Tenth Circuit, aff'd, 390 F3d 1210 (10th Cir. 2004). The case turned on the bonafide business arrangement question which the court held was not met. The court looked at a number of factors to conclude that the transaction was a testamentary device to pass decedent's interest for less than adequate and full consideration including whether the price term in a buy-sell agreement is reached in an arbitrary manner, whether the price term in a buy-sell agreement excluded the value of intangible assets and whether the buy-sell agreement contained within its provisions a mechanism by which to reevaluate the price terms.

Page 19-148:

Add to note 80.

In Holman v. Comm'r, Doc. No. 08-3774 (8th Cir. 2010), the Eighth Circuit held that restrictions on transferability of a buy-sell provision found in a limited partnership agreement failed the first part of the exception in that the donors' stated purposes for creating the limited partnership, i.e., estate planning, tax reduction, wealth transference, protection against dissipation and wealth management education, were not bona fide business purposes.

[ii] Full and adequate consideration.

Page 19-149:

Add to note 90.

, aff'd, 390 F3d 1210 (10th Cir. 2004).

[c] Similar Arrangement Test

Page 19-149:

Add to note 91.

Blount Estate v. Comm'r, TC Memo. 2004-116 (2004), aff'd, 428 F3d 1338 (11th Cir. 2005), (agreement did not meet this requirement).

Add to note 93.

In Estate of Amlie v. Comm'r, TC Memo. 2006-76 (2006), the court observed that the buy-sell agreement for decedent's stock was comparable to similar arm's-length arrangements since the price established therein was used in an earlier arm's-length agreement concerning decedent's stock that was based on a survey of comparable transactions.

Page 19-150:

Add to note 97 after citation to "True".

, aff'd, 390 F3d 1210 (10th Cir. 2004).

[4] Deemed Satisfaction

Page 19-150:

Add to note 99.

Priv. Ltr. Rul. 200746012 (July 17, 2007) (stock transfer restriction contained in amendment to option agreement between taxpayer and company satisfied both requirements and was therefore excepted from Section 2703(b) and said restriction would be considered in valuation of stock).

    Priv. Ltr. Rul. 200852029 (Sept. 19, 2008) (Section 2703(a) did not apply to valuation of the transferor's interest where there was "a substantial modification" to a pre-October 8, 1990, buy-sell agreement that nevertheless fell under the Reg. § 25.2703-1(b)(3) exception).

[6] Establishing Valuation When a Right or Restriction Is Excepted From Section 2703

[a] Estate Tax Valuation

Page 19-152:

Add to note 116.

In Estate of Amlie v. Comm'r, TC Memo. 2006-76 (2006), the tax court determined that a buy-sell agreement controlled the value of stock for estate tax purposes because the agreement satisfied the Section 2703(b) requirements as well as prior law which Section 2703 supplements but does not replace.

[i] Restrictions on lifetime dispositions.

Page 19-152:

Add to note 117.

Estate of Blount v. Comm'r, TC Memo. 2004-116 (2004), aff'd, 428 F3d 1338 (11th Cir. 2005) (buy-sell agreement is disregarded in valuing decedent's closely held stock because the agreement was not binding on the decedent during his life); Sidney Smith III, 96 AFTR2d, ¶ 2005-6549 (WD Pa. 2005) (a restrictive provision in a FLP agreement was disregarded in determining the value of gifted interests because the donor retained the unilateral authority during his life to amend or modify the agreement).

[ii] Obligation of the estate to sell.

Page 19-154:

Add to note 128.

In Estate of True, 390 F3d 1210 (10th Cir. 2004), the Tenth Circuit noted that Brodrick "no longer represents controlling authority for our circuit on the question of when the price terms in buy-sell agreements set estate tax values."

[7] Effective Dates and Substantial Modification

Page 19-157:

Add to note 143.

See Blount Estate v. Comm'r, TC Memo. 2004-116 (2004), aff'd, 428 F3d 1338 (11th Cir. 2005) (lowering price and changing agreement terms was a substantial modification).

Add to note 146.

, 200625011 (Mar. 2, 2006) (amendment to restrictive sales agreement merely clarified the original agreement and did not affect the quality, value or timing of any rights under the original agreement).

Cumulative Table of IRC Sections

*[Text references are to paragraphs and notes (9"n.");
references to the supplement are preceded by "S."]*

IRC §

1 . . . . . 9.03[2] n.10; 9.03[3] n.18; S9.03[3] &
n.26; 16.01 n.6; S16.01 n.6
1(a)–1(e) . . . . S9.03[2] n.14
1(a) . . . . 4.03[1] ns. 9, 12; 5.06[1] n.1
1(b) . . . . 4.03[1] ns. 9, 12
1(c) . . . . 4.03[1] ns. 9, 12
1(d) . . . . 4.03[1] ns. 9, 12
1(e) . . . . .4.03[1] ns. 9, 12; 17.02[2] n.80
1(f)(3) . . . . . S3.02[1][a] n.20; S6.07[1][a] n.11;
S6.07[2][a] n.44; S9.02[1][b][i] n.10.4;
S9.02[1][b][ii] n.10.32; S9.06[1] n.51;
15.02 n.2; S15.02 n.6
1(g) . . . . 4.03[1] ns. 9, 12
1(h) . . . . 4.03[1] ns. 9, 12
1(i)(2) . . . . 4.03[1] n.9
2 . . . . 5.06[1] n.1
11 . . . . 16.01 n.6
21–30A . . . . . 6.07[1] n.11; S6.07[1][a] n.10;
S6.07[2][a] n.43; S9.02[1][b][i] n.10.3;
S9.02[1][b][ii] n.10.31
25A . . . . 9.04[3][g] n.121; 9.04[6] n.183
27 . . . . S5.03[6][a] n.268
38(c)(1) . . . . . . 6.07[1] n.11; S6.07[1][a] n.10;
S6.07[2][a] n.43; S9.02[1][b][i] n.10.3;
S9.02[1][b][ii] n.10.31
55 . . . . 6.07[1] n.11; S6.07[1][a] n.10;
S6.07[2][a] n.43; S9.02[1][b][i] n.10.3;
S9.02[1][b][ii] n.10.31
59(a)(2) 7.06 n.17
61 . . . . 4.02 n.3; 4.05[5][c]; S5.03[3][a] n.87;
10.01[2][f] ns. 46, 51, 58
67 . . . . S5.03[6][a] n.277
71 . . . . 4.15[1][a] n.22; 10.06[4]
72 . . . . S4.11[5] n.54; 4.15[1][a] n.22; 9.04[3][g]
n.123; S10.01[3][g] n.119
72(b)(2) . . . . 4.11[5] n.54
72(b)(3) . . . . 4.11[5] n.54
79 . . . . S4.14[6] n.103.2
84(a) . . . . 9.02[2] n.18
101(a) . . . . . . 8.10[3][a] n.29; S8.10[3][a] n.21
101(a)(2) . . . . 4.14[4][d] n.61
101(c) . . . . 4.14[7][a] n.106
101(d) . . . . 4.14[7][a] n.106

IRC §

102 . . . . 5.03[3][a] n.50; 5.03[5][b] n.127;
5.06[3][a] n.33; 10.01[2][e] n.34;
10.01[10][b] n.219; 10.02[3] n.131;
10.07[2][b] n.63; 12.01[1] n.11
102(a) . . . . S5.03[3][a] n.90; S5.03[4][a] n.152
109 . . . . 4.04[5][a][i] n.183
112 . . . . 8.01[1][a][iii] n.26
112(c)(2) . . . . 8.01[1][a][iii]
112(c)(3) . . . . 8.01[1][a][iii]
121 . . . . . 5.07[3][c] n.59; 8.10[3][c][iv] n.106;
S8.10[3][c][iv] n.96; 19.03[3][d][i] n.169
121(a) . . . . .8.10[3][c][iv] ns. 108, 109;
S8.10[3][c][iv] ns. 98, 99
121(b)(1) . . . . 8.10[3][c][iv] ns. 108, 109;
S8.10[3][c][iv] ns. 98, 99
121(d)(9) . . . . 8.10[3][c][iv] ns. 108, 109
121(d)(9)(A) . . . . 8.10[3][c][iv] n.107;
S8.10[3][c][iv] n.97
121(d)(9)(B) . . . . .8.10[3][c][iv] ns. 107, 109;
S8.10[3][c][iv] n.99
121(d)(9)(C) . . . . 8.10[3][c][iv] n.107;
S8.10[3][c][iv] n.97
121(d)(11) . . . . . . S8.10[3][c][iv] ns. 98, 99;
S8.10[3][c][iv] ns. 107–109
151(c)(4) . . . . 4.04[7][b][ii] n.308; 5.08[5][b][i]
n.231
152 . . . . 5.08[3][c][iii]; 19.03[3][d][i]
162 . . . . 4.04[3][b][iv]; 5.03[3][d]; S5.03[6][a];
5.08[2][b][i] n.23
162(a) . . . . 5.03[1] n.12; S5.03[1][a] n.12
162(a)(1) . . . . 5.03[1] n.12; S5.03[1][a] n.12
163 . . . . . 5.03[5][c] n.132; S5.03[6][a] n.270;
10.01[2][f] ns. 46, 51, 58
163(f)(2)(B) . . . . 6.05[3][b] n.43
163(h) . . . . S5.03[6][a] n.270; 10.01[2][f] n.51;
19.03[3][d][iv] n.250
163(h)(2) . . . S2.02[3][b][i] n.39; S5.03[3][c][i]
n.119; S5.03[6][a] n.270
163(h)(2)(E) . . . . 2.02[3][c][v] n.132
163(h)(3) . . . . . 5.08[3][c][iii]; 5.08[4][a][iii]
163(h)(4)(A)(i) . . . . 19.03[3][d][iv] n.250
163(h)(4)(A)(i)(II) . . . . . 19.03[3][d][i] n.170
163(h)(4)(A)(iii) . . . . 19.03[3][d][i] n.184

[Text references are to paragraphs and notes (9"n.");
references to the supplement are preceded by "S."]

IRC §

163(k) . . . . 2.02[3][c][v] ns. 131, 132
164 . . . . . . S5.03[6][a] n.270; S6.07[1][b] n.27;
                    S9.02[1][b][i] n.10.21
164(a)(1) . . . . S5.03[6][a] n.269
164(a)(3) . . . . S5.03[6][a] n.270
164(a)(4) . . . . . 12.03[1] n.1; 13.02[3][c] n.232;
                    14.02[4] n.21
164(b)(4) . . . . 12.03[1] n.1; 14.02[4] n.21
165 . . . . 5.04 n.3; 8.10[3][b][i] n.53;
            S8.10[3][a][i]; 14.02[3] ns. 18, 19;
                    14.03[3] n.23
165(b) . . . . 4.03[4][a] n.56
165(c) . . . . 4.03[4][a] n.56; 5.04[4] n.24;
            5.06[6][a] n.146; 8.10[3][b][i] n.53;
                    S8.10[3][b][i] n.45
165(c)(1) . . . . 8.10[3][b][i] n.53; S8.10[3][b][i]
                    n.45; 10.02[4] n.138
165(c)(2) . . . . 8.10[3][b][i] n.53; S8.10[3][b][i]
                    n.45
165(c)(3) . . . . 5.04[2] n.12; 5.04[4] n.22;
            8.10[3][b][i] n.53; S8.10[3][b][i]n.45
                    17.02[2] n.75
165(e) . . . . 5.04[3] n.15
166 . . . . 5.04[3] n.21
167 . . . . 4.04[3][b][iv]
167(a) . . . . 17.04[1][a] n.8
167(a)(1) . . . . 10.02[4] n.138
167(c) . . . . 17.04[1][a] n.8
167(d) . . . . 17.04[1][a] n.8
167(e) . . . . 17.04[1][a] n.8
168 . . . . 17.04[1][a] n.8
168(h)(2) . . . . 8.10[3][c][iii] n.101;
                    S8.10[3][c][iii] n.91
170 . . . . . . 4.02[7][a]; 4.02[7][b][ii] & ns. 314,
            315; 4.02[7][d][i] ns. 324, 326; 5.05;
            5.05[1][a] n.16; 5.05[2][c] n.85;
            5.05[7][b] n.341; S5.06[8][e] n.417;
            10.02[2][b][iii] n.57; S10.08[1][b] n.29;
            11.02 ns. 2, 5; 11.02[2][b][ii] n.82;
            17.02[3][c] ns. 145–147; 19.02[5][f][ii]
                    n.511
170(a)(3) . . . . 4.08[4][a] n.24
170(b) . . . . 5.05 n.3; 11.02[1][b] n.30
170(b)(1)(A) . . . . 5.05[5][c][i] n.271;
            11.02[2][b][ii] n.82; 11.02[2][b][iii] n.88
170(b)(1)(A)(ii) . . . 4.04[7][b][ii] n.308; 9.04[6]
                    n.172
170(b)(1)(A)(vii) . . . . 5.05[5][c][i] n.271;
                    11.02[2][b][iii] n.88
170(b)(1)(A)(viii) . . . . . . 5.05[5][c][i] n.271;
                    11.02[2][b][iii] n.88
170(c) . . . . . . 5.05[5][a][i] & ns. 187, 196;
            5.05[5][b][i] & ns. 242, 252; 5.06[8][e]
            n.410; 11.02[2][b][i] & n.60;
            11.02[2][b][iii] n.88; S11.02[2][c] n.96
170(c)(1) . . . . 5.05[1][a] n.18
170(c)(2) . . . . 5.05[1][a] n.18
170(c)(3) . . . . . 5.05[1][a] n.18; 5.05[1][b] n.40
170(c)(4) . . . . 5.05[1][a] n.18
170(e) . . . . . 5.05 n.3; 11.02[1][b] n.30; 9.04[8]
                    n.192

IRC §

170(e)(2) . . . . 4.15[2] n.69
170(f) . . . . . 5.05[4][a] n.133; 5.05[4][b] n.144;
                    5.05[8][a] n.354
170(f)(3)(B) . . . 5.05[7] n.329; 5.05[7][a] n.333
170(f)(3)(B)(i) . . . . 11.02[2][d] n.97
170(f)(3)(B)(ii) . . . 5.05[7][b] n.339; S5.05[7][b]
                    n.337.1; 11.02[2][d] n.98
170(f)(3)(B)(iii) . . . 5.05[7][c] n.342; 11.02[2][d]
                    n.99
170(f)(4) . . . . 11.02[2][d] n.97
170(f)(7) . . . . 5.05[8][a] n.356
170(f)(8)(C) . . . . S5.05[1][c] n.56.3
170(f)(11)(E) . . . . S5.03[4][c][iii] ns. 231, 236
170(h) . . . . 5.05[7][c] n.342; 5.08[5][b][ii]
170(h)(1)(A) . . . . 5.05[7][c] n.343
170(h)(1)(B) . . . . 5.05[7][c] n.346
170(h)(1)(C) . . . . . 4.02[7][b][ii] ns. 294, 301;
                    5.05[7][c] n.347
170(h)(2) . . . 4.02[7][b][ii] n.297; 5.05[7][c] ns.
                    343, 345
170(h)(2)(A) . . . . 5.05[7][c] n.344
170(h)(2)(C) . . . . 4.02[7][b][ii] n.295; 19.04[2]
                    ns. 30, 31
170(h)(3) . . . . . 4.02[7][b][ii] n.296; 5.05[7][c]
                    n.346; 19.04[2] ns. 30, 31
170(h)(3)(A) . . . . 5.05[7][c] n.346
170(h)(3)(B)(i) . . . . 5.05[7][c] n.346
170(h)(3)(B)(ii) . . . . 5.05[7][c] n.346
170(h)(4) . . . . 5.05[7][c] n.347
170(h)(4)(A) . . . 5.05[7][c] n.348; 19.04[2] n.33
170(h)(4)(A)(i) . . . . 4.02[7][b][ii] ns. 294, 299
170(h)(4)(A)(ii) . . . 4.02[7][b][ii] ns. 294, 300
170(h)(4)(A)(iii) . . . . 4.02[7][b][ii] ns. 294, 301
170(h)(4)(A)(iv) . . . . 4.02[7][b][ii] n.302
170(h)(5)(A) . . . . 5.05[7][c] n.347; 19.04[2] ns.
                    30, 31
170(h)(5)(B) . . . . 5.05[7][c] n.344
170(h)(6) . . . . 5.05[7][c] n.344
170(o)(1) . . . . S5.05[7][b] n.341.2
170(o)(1)(A) . . . . S5.05[7][b] n.337.1
170(o)(1)(B) . . . . S5.05[7][b] n.337.1
172 . . . . 8.10[3][b][i]; S8.10[3][a][i]
183 . . . . 4.04[3][b][iv] n.65
212 . . . . 5.03[3][d]; S5.03[6][a]
212(2) . . . . 14.02[3] ns. 18, 19
212(3) . . . . . 5.03[3][a] n.46; 14.02[3]; 14.03[3]
            n.15; 14.04[3]; 14.05[1] ns. 8, 10
213 . . . . . . S5.03[6][a] n.277; 9.04[6] & n.177
213(a) . . . . 9.04[6] n.177
213(c)(1) . . . . S5.03[6][b]
213(c)(2) . . . . . . 5.03[3][d] n.74; 5.03[5][d] &
            n.133; S5.03[6][a] n.262; S5.03[6][b] &
                    ns. 279, 280
213(d) . . . . 9.04[6] & n.172
215 . . . . 10.06[4]
262 . . . . S5.03[6][a] n.266
265 . . . 5.03[3][c]; S5.03[3][c][iii]; 6.05[2][a][i]
                    n.20
267 . . . . . S6.07[2] n.39; S9.02[1][b][ii] n.10.51
267(b) . . . . 19.05[3][b] n.60
267(b)(13) . . . . 5.06[6][a] n.146

*[Text references are to paragraphs and notes (9"n.");
references to the supplement are preceded by "S."]*

IRC §

267(c) . . . . 4.14[5][a] n.89
267(c)(4) . . . . 2.02[3][c][ii] & n.69;
   2.02[3][c][vi] n.142; 5.07[3][c][ii] n.92
267(f)(1) . . . . 5.08[2][c][i] n.54
269B(d) 7.06 n.14
273 . . . . 4.08[7][c] n.134
280A(c)(1) . . . . . 19.03[3][d][i] & ns. 181, 182
280A(c)(4) . . . . 19.03[3][d][i] & n.182
280A(d)(1) . . . . 19.03[3][d][i] & n.184
280A(d)(2) . . . . 19.03[3][d][i] n.184
291 . . . . 6.05[2][a][i] n.20
303 . . . . . 2.02[3][c][i]; 2.02[3][c][vi] & n.143;
   4.02[7][e][iii]; 5.07[4][a][ii] & n.142;
   5.08[5][b][ii] n.237; S5.08[5][b][ii] n.237
303(a) . . . . 4.02[7][e][iii] n.405
303(a)(1) . . . . 5.07[4][a][ii] n.142
303(b) . . . . 4.07[2][d]
303(b)(2)(A) . . . . . . 4.02[7][e][iii] ns. 405, 407
304 . . . . . 2.02[3][c][vi] & n.143; 5.08[5][b][ii]
   n.237
305(b)(4) . . . . 19.02[1][b] n.10
316(a) . . . . 4.03[2][c] n.32
318 . . . 4.08[6][d] & ns. 95, 97; 4.14[5][a] n.89;
   6.07[2] n.25; S6.07[2][b] n.58;
   S9.02[1][b][ii] n.10.41
318(a) . . . . . . 6.07[2] n.25; S6.07[2][b] n.58;
   S9.02[1][b][ii] n.10.41
318(a)(1)(A) . . . 6.07[2] n.25; S6.07[2][b] n.58;
   S9.02[1][b][ii] n.10.41
318(a)(2)(A) . . . 6.07[2] n.25; S6.07[2][b] n.58;
   S9.02[1][b][ii] n.10.41; 17.01[2][c][i]
   n.56
318(a)(2)(B) . . . 6.07[2] n.25; S6.07[2][b] n.58;
   S9.02[1][b][ii] n.10.41
318(a)(2)(C) . . . 6.07[2] n.25; S6.07[2][b] n.58;
   S9.02[1][b][ii] n.10.41
318(a)(3)(A) . . . 6.07[2] n.25; S6.07[2][b] n.58;
   S9.02[1][b][ii] n.10.41
318(a)(3)(B) . . . 6.07[2] n.25; S6.07[2][b] n.58;
   S9.02[1][b][ii] n.10.41
318(a)(3)(C) . . . 6.07[2] n.25; S6.07[2][b] n.58;
   S9.02[1][b][ii] n.10.41
351 . . . . . . 2.02[3][c][vi]; 4.04[3][c][i] n.113;
   4.04[7][b][i]; 4.05[4] n.33; 5.08[3][d]
   n.150; 10.01[2][b][i] n.16; 19.02[2][c]
   n.133; 19.02[5][c][iii] n.447
351(a) . . . . 10.01[2][g] n.63
351(b) . . . . 4.04[7][b][i] n.278
355 . . . . 2.02[3][c][vi]; 5.08[5][b][ii] n.237
356 . . . . 5.08[5][b][ii] n.237
368 . . . . 19.02[5][c][iii] n.447
368(a)(1) . . . 2.02[3][c][vi]; 5.08[5][b][ii] n.237
368(a)(1)(A) . . . . 2.02[3][c][vi] n.144
368(a)(1)(B) . . . . 2.02[3][c][vi] n.144
368(a)(1)(C) . . . . 2.02[3][c][vi] n.144
368(a)(1)(D) . . . . 2.02[3][c][vi]
368(a)(1)(E) . . . . 2.02[3][c][vi]; 19.02[1][a] n.6
368(a)(1)(F) . . . . 2.02[3][c][vi]
401(a)(11) . . . . 9.04[7] n.184
408(a) . . . . 5.07[2][c] n.28
417 . . . . 9.04[7] n.184

IRC §

417(b) . . . . . 5.06[8][d][ii] n.341; 11.03[4][c][ii]
   n.87
441 . . . . 9.03[1] n.2; S9.03[1] n.6
453B . . . . 10.08[2] n.30
469 . . . . . . 4.04[3][c][ii] n.127; S4.04[3][c][ii]
   n.127; S4.04[3][c][iii] n.144; S4.04[4]
   n.165
469(c)(1)(B) . . . . 2.02[3][c][ii] n.79
469(h)(1) . . . . 2.02[3][c][ii] n.79
469(i)(1) . . . . 2.02[3][c][ii] n.79
483 . . . . 10.02[3] n.132
501(a) . . . . . . 5.05[1][a] n.15; 5.05[2][a] n.66
501(c) . . . . 5.05[1][a] n.15; 5.05[1][b]
501(c)(3) . . . . 5.05[1][a] n.18; 5.05[1][b] n.35;
   5.05[1][c] n.56; S5.05[1][c] n.55;
   5.05[2][a] n.66; 5.05[7][d] n.350;
   11.02[1][a]; 16.02[3][b][ii] & n.186
501(c)(6) . . . . 5.05[1][a] n.17
501(c)(7) . . . . 5.05[1][a] n.17; S9.04[1][b][iii]
   n.30
501(c)(8) . . . . 5.05[1][a] n.17
501(j)(2) . . . . 5.05[1][b] n.22; 11.02[1][a] n.13
507(a) . . . . 5.05[1][c] n.53
507(a)(2) . . . . 5.05[1][c] n.51
507(c) . . . . 5.05[1][c] ns. 51, 53
508 . . . . S5.05[2][a] n.58
508(a) . . . . 5.05[1][c] n.56
508(c) . . . . 5.05[1][c] n.56
508(d) . . . . 5.05[1][c]
508(d)(1) . . . . 5.05[1][c] n.53
508(d)(2) . . . . 5.05[1][c] ns. 53, 55
508(d)(2)(A) . . . . 5.05[1][c] n.53
508(d)(2)(B) . . . . . 5.05[1][c] n.56; S5.05[1][c]
   n.55
508(e) . . . . 5.05[1][c] ns. 53, 55
509 . . . . 5.05[1][c] n.46; 5.05[7][d] n.350
511(a)(2) . . . . . 17.01[2][c] n.51; 17.01[2][c][ii]
511(b)(2) . . . . . 17.01[2][c] n.51; 17.01[2][c][ii]
512(b)(7) . . . . 5.05[1][b] n.31
512(b)(8) . . . . 5.05[1][b] n.31
512(b)(9) . . . . 5.05[1][b] n.31
513 . . . . 4.04[3][b][iv]
514(b) . . . . 4.02[7][d][i] n.336
521 . . . . 8.10[3][c][iii] n.101
527(e)(1) . . . . 9.02[2] & n.18; 17.02[1][b] n.18
529 . . . . 9.04[3][g] ns. 122, 129, 136; S9.04[3]
   n.46; S9.04[3][g] n.124; 9.04[6] n.180;
   10.01[3][j] n.135
529(a) . . . . 9.04[3][g] n.122
529(b)(1) . . . . 9.04[3][g] n.122
529(b)(6) . . . . 9.04[3][g] n.129
529(c)(2) . . . . 9.04[3][g] ns. 124, 125; 9.04[6]
   n.183
529(c)(2)(A)(i) . . . . 9.04[3][g] n.126; S9.04[3]
   n.46; 10.01[3][j] n.133
529(c)(2)(A)(ii) . . . . 9.04[3][g] n.127
529(c)(2)(B) . . . . 9.04[3][g] n.132
529(c)(3)(A) . . . . 9.04[3][g] n.122
529(c)(3)(B) . . . . 9.04[3][g] n.122
529(c)(4) . . . . 9.04[3][g] n.125

*[Text references are to paragraphs and notes (9"n.");
references to the supplement are preceded by "S."]*

IRC §

529(c)(4)(A) . . . . . 4.08[5] n.54; 9.04[3][g] ns.
                        133, 134
529(c)(4)(B) . . . . 4.08[5] n.54; 9.04[3][g] n.134
529(c)(4)(C) . . . . 4.08[5] n.54; 9.04[3][g] n.133
529(c)(5) . . . . 9.04[3][g] n.125
529(c)(5)(A) . . . . . 9.04[3][g] n.135; 10.01[3][j]
                        n.134
529(c)(5)(B) . . . . . 9.04[3][g] n.137; 10.01[3][j]
                        n.137
529(c)(5)(B)(i) . . . . S9.04[3][g] n.137
529(c)(5)(B)(ii) . . . . S9.04[3][g] n.136
529(f) . . . . S9.04[3][g] n.124
530 . . . . 9.04[3][g] n.123
530(a) . . . . 9.04[3][g] n.123
530(b)(1)(A)(iii) . . . . 9.04[3][g] n.128
530(b)(2) . . . . 9.04[3][g] n.123
530(d)(2)(A) . . . . 9.04[3][g] n.123
530(d)(3) . . . 4.08[5] n.54; 9.04[3][g] ns. 125–
                127, 132–137; S9.04[3][g] n.136;
                10.01[3][j] ns. 133–135, 137
542(c)(2) . . . 5.08[2][b][iii] n.31; 5.08[2][b][iv]
                n.44
543(a) . . . . . 5.08[2][b][iii] n.28; 5.08[2][b][iv]
                n.36
543(a)(2)(B) . . . . 5.08[2][b][iii] n.28;
                5.08[2][b][iv] n.36
543(b)(2) . . . . 5.08[2][b][iii] n.26
581 . . . . 5.07[3][c][i] ns. 68, 76; 5.08[2][b][iii]
                n.29; 5.08[2][b][iv] n.42; 19.05[3][b]
                n.60
591 . . . . 6.05[2][a][i] n.20
641(b) . . . . 5.04[4] n.22
642 . . . . 10.02[2][b][iii] n.57
642(c) . . . . 5.05[1][a] n.11
642(c)(5)   5.05[5] ns. 151, 154; 5.05[5][c] ns.
                268, 269; 5.05[5][c][ii] ns. 287, 289,
                290; 5.05[8][b] n.371; 8.08[2] n.13;
                11.02[2][b][iii] ns. 84, 88; 13.02[2][b][i]
                n.36; 13.03[3][a] n.44; 17.02[3][c] n.147;
                19.03[3][c] n.156
642(c)(5)(A) . . . . . . 5.05[5][c][i] ns. 271–273;
                11.02[2][b][iii] n.88
642(c)(5)(B) . . . . 5.05[5][c][i] n.277;
                11.02[2][b][iii] n.86
642(c)(5)(C) . . . . 5.05[5][c][i] n.280;
                11.02[2][b][iii] n.88
642(c)(5)(D) . . . . 5.05[5][c][i] n.278;
                11.02[2][b][iii] n.88
642(c)(5)(E) . . . . . . 5.05[5][c][i] ns. 281, 283;
                11.02[2][b][iii] ns. 85, 87
642(c)(5)(F) . . . . 5.05[5][c][i] n.284;
                11.02[2][b][iii] n.88
642(d)(1) . . . . 5.05[6][a] n.299
642(d)(2) . . . . 5.05[6][a] n.299

IRC §

642(g)   2.02[3][c][ii] n.104; 4.03[4][a] ns. 56,
                57; S5.03[3] n.74; 5.03[3][d] & ns. 75,
                78; S5.03[4][b][i] n.192; 5.03[5][c] &
                n.132; 5.03[5][d] n.133; S5.03[6][a] &
                ns. 264, 268, 270–273; S5.03[6][b];
                5.04[4]; 5.05[3][b][ii] & n.115;
                5.06[5][b][ii]; 5.08[4][a][iii] & ns. 184,
                188; 8.07[2] n.15; 11.02 n.4; 14.02[3] &
                ns. 19, 20; 14.02[4] n.33; 14.03[3] &
                n.20
643(b) . . . . . . 5.05[5][b][i] n.223; 5.07[4][a][i]
                n.131; 11.02[2][b][ii] n.74
643(e) . . . . 17.04[1][b] n.19
643(e)(3) . . . . 17.04[1][b] ns. 17–19
644(a) . . . . 18.02[4][a] n.50
645 . . . . . 8.10[3][c][ii] n.99; S8.10[3][a] n.24;
                S8.10[3][a][iii]; S8.10[3][c][iv] n.97;
                17.04[2][a] n.48
645(b)(1) . . . . . 8.10[3][a] n.32; 8.10[3][b][iii];
                8.10[3][c][iv] n.107
651 . . . . 14.02[4] ns. 22, 31
652 . . . . 10.01[10][c] n.223; 12.01[1] n.11;
                14.02[4] ns. 22, 31
661 . . . . 4.04[7][c][iv] n.331; 5.03[5][c] n.131;
                S5.03[6][a] n.268; 14.02[4] ns. 22, 31;
                17.04[2][a] n.53
662 . . . 4.04[7][c][iv] n.331; 10.01[10][c] n.223;
                12.01[1] n.11; 14.02[4] ns. 22, 31;
                17.04[2][a] n.53
663 . . . . 14.02[4] ns. 22, 31
663(a) . . . . 12.01[1] n.11
663(c) . . . . 17.04[2][a] n.53
664 . . . . S5.05[5][a][i] n.161; S5.05[5][b][i]
                n.216; 8.08[2] n.13; 10.02[2][b][iii] n.57;
                11.02[2][b][ii] n.81; 19.03[3][b] n.112;
                19.03[3][c] n.155
664(a) . . . . 14.02[4] n.27
664(b) . . . . 5.05[5] n.154
664(b)(1) . . . . 5.05[5][a][i] n.174; 5.05[5][b][i]
                n.233
664(b)(2) . . . . 5.05[5][a][i] n.174; 5.05[5][b][i]
                n.233
664(b)(3) . . . . 5.05[5][a][i] n.174; 5.05[5][b][i]
                n.233
664(c) . . . . 5.05[5] n.154; 5.05[5][a][i]
664(d) . . . . . . 5.05[5] ns. 151, 154; 5.05[8][b]
                n.371; 5.06[8][e] n.409; 11.03[4][d]
                n.101
664(d)(1) . . . . 5.05[5][a]; 5.05[5][b] n.210;
                11.02[2][b] n.53; 11.02[2][b][i];
                13.02[2][b][i] n.36; 13.03[3][a] n.42;
                15.03[4][b][iii] n.129; 17.02[3][c] n.145;
                19.03[3][c] n.157
664(d)(1)(A) . . . . . . 5.05[5][a][i] ns. 163, 165,
                168–170, 175, 177, 179, 180;
                5.05[6][a][ii] n.320; 11.02[2][b][i] n.58
664(d)(1)(B) . . . . . . 5.05[5][a][i] ns. 163, 187;
                S5.05[5][a][i] n.187; 11.02[2][b][i] n.59
664(d)(1)(C) . . . 5.05[5][a][i] ns. 163, 186, 197;
                11.02[2][b][i] n.60

[Text references are to paragraphs and notes (9"n.");
references to the supplement are preceded by "S."]

IRC §

664(d)(1)(D) . . . 5.05[5][a][i] ns. 163, 201, 202;
5.05[6][a][ii] n.320; 5.05[8][d] n.383;
11.02[2][b][i] n.61
664(d)(2) . . . . 5.05[5][b] & n.210; S5.05[5][b]
n.213; 11.02[2][b][ii] n.68; 13.02[2][b][i]
n.36; 13.03[3][a] n.43; 15.03[4][b][iii]
n.130; 16.02[3][b][ii] n.185; 19.03[3][c]
ns. 158, 159
664(d)(2)(A) . . . 5.05[5][b][i] ns. 216, 218–220,
222, 229, 234, 236, 238, 239;
5.05[6][a][ii] n.320; 11.02[2][b][ii] n.70;
19.03[3][c] n.158
664(d)(2)(B) . . . . . . 5.05[5][b][i] ns. 216, 242;
S5.05[5][b][i] n.242; 11.02[2][b][ii] n.71
664(d)(2)(C) . . . 5.05[5][b][i] ns. 216, 241, 252;
11.02[2][b][ii] n.71
664(d)(2)(D) . . . . 5.05[5][b] n.211; 5.05[5][b][i]
ns. 216, 256, 257; 5.05[6][a][ii] n.320;
5.05[8][d] n.383; 11.02[2][b][ii] n.71
664(d)(3) . . . . . . S5.05[5][b] n.213; 19.03[3][c]
n.159
664(d)(3)(A) . . . . 5.05[5][b][i] n.224;
11.02[2][b][ii] n.75
664(d)(3)(B) . . . . 5.05[5][b][i] n.225;
11.02[2][b][ii] n.76
664(d)(4) . . . . . . 5.05[5][b] n.211; 5.05[5][b][i]
n.259
664(e) . . . . 11.02[2][b][ii] n.76
664(f) . . . . 5.05[8][b] n.371
664(f)(1) . . . . 5.05[5][a][i] n.192; 5.05[5][b][i]
n.247
664(f)(2) . . . . 5.05[5][a][i] n.193; 5.05[5][b][i]
n.248
664(f)(3) . . . . 5.05[5][a][i] n.192; 5.05[5][b][i]
n.247
664(g)(1)(A) . . . . 5.05[1][b] n.42
664(g)(2)(A) . . . . 5.05[1][b] n.42
665 . . . . 4.09[3] n.14
666 . . . . . . 4.09[3] n.14; 12.03[1] n.1; 14.02[4]
n.21
667 . . . . 4.09[3] n.14
668 . . . . 4.09[3] n.14
671–677 . . . . 9.04[3][f] n.118
671–679 . . . . 4.05[5][c] n.63; 4.14[5][a] n.82;
10.01[8] n.191; 19.02[2][d][iii] n.162
671 . . . . 5.05[5][a][i] n.178; 5.05[5][b][i] n.237;
8.10[4] n.135; 10.01[10][e] n.233;
S10.01[10][e] ns. 233, 233.1; 10.02[6][d]
n.183; 19.03[2][a][iv] n.71
672 . . . . . S4.14[4][e] n.69; 5.05[5][a][i] n.178;
5.05[5][b][i] n.237; 8.10[4] n.135;
10.01[10][e] n.233; S10.01[10][e] n.233
672(c) . . . . 4.08[4][b] n.32; 4.08[5][a] & n.61;
5.05[5][a][ii] n.205; 5.05[5][b][ii] n.262;
11.02[2][b][ii] n.78; 19.03[2][a][iv] n.72
672(c)(1) . . . . 4.08[6][e] n.112
672(c)(2) . . . . 4.08[6][e] n.113
672(e) . . . . 4.07[2][b][ii] n.51; 4.10[4][g] n.54;
4.10[8] n.87

IRC §

673 . . . . . . 4.08[6][c] n.84; 5.05[5][a][i] n.178;
5.05[5][b][i] n.237; 8.10[4] n.135;
19.02[2][a][i] n.57
673(a) . . . . . 4.08[2] n.18; 4.09[4] n.24; 8.10[4]
n.139; 10.01[10][d] n.225
673(c) . . . . S10.01[10][e] n.233.1
674–678 . . . 10.01[10][e] n.233; S10.01[10][e]
n.233
674 . . . . . . 4.10[4][g] n.54; 5.05[5][a][i] n.178;
5.05[5][b][i] n.237; 8.10[4] n.135;
10.01[10][c] n.223; 19.02[2][a][i] n.52;
19.03[2][a][iv] n.71
674(a) . . . . 11.02[2][b][ii] n.78
674(b) . . . . 11.02[2][b][ii] n.78
674(c) . . . . 11.02[2][b][ii] n.78; 19.03[2][a][iv]
n.72
674(d) . . . . 11.02[2][b][ii] n.78
675 . . . . 5.05[5][a][i] n.178; 5.05[5][b][i] n.237;
8.10[4] n.135; 19.03[2][a][iv] n.71
675(3) . . . . S10.01[10][e] n.233.1
675(4)(c) . . . . S4.08[4][c] n.53.1; S10.01[10][e]
n.233.1; 19.02[2][a][i] n.57
676 . . . 4.07[2][b][ii]; 4.10[4][g] n.54; 4.10[8] &
n.87; 5.05[5][a][i] n.178; 5.05[5][b][i]
n.237; 8.10[4] n.135; 19.02[2][a][i] n.52
676(a) . . . . S10.01[10][e] n.233.1
676(b) . . . . 8.10[4] n.142
677 . . . . . . 4.10[4][g] n.54; 5.05[5][a][i] n.178;
5.05[5][b][i] n.237; 8.10[4] n.135;
10.01[10][c] n.223; 19.02[2][a][i] n.57
677(a) . . . . S10.01[10][e] n.233.1
677(a)(2) . . . . 8.10[4] n.139
677(b) . . . . . . 4.08[4][b] n.35; 4.10[4][f] n.52;
9.04[5][c] n.166
678 . . . . 5.05[5][a][i] n.178; 5.05[5][b][i] n.237;
8.10[4] n.135; 9.04[3][f] n.120;
19.02[2][a][i] n.49; 19.02[2][d][iii] n.163
678(a)(1) . . . . 19.02[2][a][i] n.62
678(a)(2) . . . . . 9.04[3][f] n.118; 19.02[2][a][i]
n.62
678(d) . . . . 10.07[2][b] n.62
679 . . . . 8.10[4] n.135
682 . . . . 10.06[4]
684 . . . . 8.10[3][c][v] ns. 110, 111;
S8.10[3][c][v] ns. 100, 101
691 . . . . 4.03[1] n.8; 4.05[4]; 4.11[5] n.53;
5.03[3][d] n.78; 5.05[2][a] n.63;
17.04[1][c] n.41; 19.02[5][a][iii] n.335
691(a) . . . . 5.05[2][a] n.65
691(a)(5) . . . . 4.07[2][b][i] n.40
691(b) . . . . 5.03[5][c] & n.132; S5.03[6][a] ns.
268–270
691(c) . . . . S4.02[4][e][iii] n.219; 4.05[4] n.35;
4.05[7][b] n.85
691(c)(2)(C) . . . . 19.02[5][c][ii] n.425
692(d)(4) . . . . 8.01[1][b] ns. 31, 35, 36
692(d)(4)(A) . . . . 8.01[1][b] ns. 32, 33
692(d)(4)(B) . . . . 8.01[1][b] n.34
704(b) . . . . 19.02[3][b] n.174
704(e) . . . . 10.07[2][b] n.63
707 . . . . . S6.07[2] n.39; S9.02[1][b][ii] n.10.51

*[Text references are to paragraphs and notes (9"n.");
references to the supplement are preceded by "S."]*

IRC §

707(a) . . . . 17.01[2][c][i] n.56
707(a)(2)(B) . . . . 4.04[7][b][i] n.278
707(b) . . . . 4.14[5][a] n.89; 17.01[2][c][i] n.56
707(c) . . . 19.02[2][b][ii] & ns. 92, 93, 96, 123
721–723 . . . . 19.02[1][a] n.6
721 . . . . . . 2.02[3][c][vi] & n.144; 4.04[3][c][i]
n.113; 4.04[7][b][i]; 4.05[4] n.33;
5.08[3][d] n.150; 10.01[2][g] n.63;
19.02[2][c] n.133; 19.02[5][c][iii] n.447
731–733 . . . . 19.02[1][a] n.6
731 . . . . 4.04[7][b][i] n.278
736(b) . . . . 4.05[7][b] n.80
741 . . . . 4.05[7][b] n.80
751 . . . . 4.05[7][b] n.80
754 . . . . . . 4.02[4][e][iii] n.216; 10.02[2][c][iv]
761(b) . . . . 4.05[7][a] n.79
802 . . . . 8.09 n.1
851 . . . . S6.05[5] n.52.2
861(a)(1)(A) . . . . 6.05[3][a] ns. 38, 39
864(c) . . . . 7.02[2][c]
861(c)(1) . . . . 6.05[3][a] n.39
864(c)(2) . . . . 6.05[2][a][ii] ns. 23, 29, 30
871(a)(1) . . . . 6.05[3][b] n.40
871(a)(1)(C) . . . . 6.05[3][c] n.49
871(g)(1)(A) . . . . 6.05[3][c] n.48
871(g)(1)(B)(i) . . . . 6.05[3][c] ns. 48, 49
871(h)(1) . . . . 6.05[3][b] n.40
871(h)(2) . . . 6.05[3][b] ns. 40, 43; S6.05[3][b]
n.40; S8.09 n.2
871(h)(2)(A)(ii) . . . . 6.05[3][b] n.43
871(h)(3) . . . . 6.05[3][b] n.42
871(h)(4) . . . . 6.05[3][b] n.45
871(h)(4)(A) . . . . 6.05[3][b] n.46
871(i)(1) . . . . 6.05[2][a] n.11
871(i)(2)(A) . . . . 6.05[2][a][ii] ns. 22, 23
871(i)(3) . . . . 6.05[2][a] n.10
871(i)(3)(A) . . . . 6.05[2][a][i] n.13
871(i)(3)(B) . . . . 6.05[2][a][i] n.20
871(i)(3)(C) . . . . 6.05[2][a][i] n.21
875(1) . . . . 6.04[1] n.10
877 . . . . 5.08[5][b][iii] & ns. 241, 242
877(a) . . . S6.07 n.2; S6.07[2] n.37; S9.02[1][b]
n.5; S9.02[1][b][ii] ns. 10.29, 10.30,
10.50
877(a)(1) . . . . 5.08[5][b][iii] n.241; S6.07[2][a]
n.41
877(a)(2) . . . 5.08[5][b][iii] n.241; 6.07[1] n.12;
S6.07[1][a] ns. 11, 12; S6.07[2][a] ns.
44, 45; S9.02[1][b][i] ns. 10.4, 10.5;
S9.02[1][b][ii] ns. 10.32, 10.33
877(a)(2)(A) . . . 6.07[1] n.11; S6.07[1][a] n.10;
S6.07[2][a] n.43; S9.02[1][b][i] n.10.3;
S9.02[1][b][ii] n.10.31
877(a)(2)(C) . . . . S6.07[1][a] n.13; S6.07[2][a]
n.46; S9.02[1][b][i] n.10.6;
S9.02[1][b][ii] n.10.34
877(b) . . . S6.07[2] n.37; S6.07[2][a] ns. 41, 45;
S9.02[1][b][ii] ns. 10.29, 10.30, 10.33
877(c) . . . . 5.08[5][b][iii] n.241
877(c)(1) . . . . . 6.07[1] n.15; S6.07[2][a] n.46;
S9.02[1][b][ii] n.10.34

IRC §

877(c)(2) . . . . . 6.07[1] n.13; S6.07[2][a] n.47;
S9.02[1][b][ii] n.10.35
877(c)(2)(A) . . . . . S6.07[2][a] n.47; S9.02[1][b][ii]
n.10.35
877(c)(2)(A)(i) . . . . 6.07[1] n.13
877(c)(2)(A)(ii) . . . . 6.07[1] n.13
877(c)(2)(B) . . . 6.07[1] n.13; S6.07[2][a] n.47;
S9.02[1][b][ii] n.10.35
877(c)(2)(C) . . . . 6.07[1] n.13
877(c)(2)(D) . . . . 6.07[1] n.13
877(c)(3) . . . . S6.07[2][a] n.48; S9.02[1][b][ii]
n.10.36
877(e) . . . 6.07 n.1; S6.07 ns. 3, 4; S9.02[1][b]
n.7
877(e)(1) . . . . 5.08[5][b][iii] & n.242
877(e)(1)(A) . . . . 5.08[5][b][iii] & n.242
877(e)(1)(B) . . . . 5.08[5][b][iii] & n.242
877(e)(2) . . . . 5.08[5][b][iii] n.242; 6.07[1] n.7;
S9.02[1][b] n.6
877(e)(3)(A) . . . . 6.07[1] n.14
877(e)(4) . . . . 6.07[1] n.14
877(g) . . . . S6.07[2] ns. 37, 40; S6.07[2][b] ns.
49, 51; S9.02[1][b][ii] & n.10.50
877(g)(1) . . . . . . S6.01[3] n.17; S6.07[2] n.38;
S9.02[1][b][ii] n.10.52
877(g)(1)(C) . . . . S9.02[1][b][i] n.10.9
877(g)(2) . . . . . S6.07[2] n.39; S9.02[1][b][ii]
n.10.51
877(g)(2)(A) . . . . S6.07[2] n.39; S9.02[1][b][ii]
n.10.51
877(g)(2)(A)(ii) . . . . S6.07[2] n.39;
S9.02[1][b][ii] n.10.51
877(g)(2)(B) . . . . S6.07[2] n.39; S9.02[1][b] ns.
6, 7; S9.02[1][b][ii] n.10.51
877(g)(2)(C) . . . . S6.07[2] n.39; S9.02[1][b][ii]
n.10.51
877(h) . . . S6.07 n.7; S6.07[2] n.32; S9.02[1][b]
n.10; S9.02[1][b][ii] ns. 10.26, 10.52
877A . . . . S6.07[1] n.8; S9.02[1][b][i] n.10.11
877A(a)(1) . . . . S6.07[1][a] n.9
877A(g) . . . . S6.07 n.2; S9.02[1][b] n.5
877A(g)(1) . . . . S6.07[1][a] ns. 10, 12;
S9.02[1][b][i] ns. 10.3, 10.5
877A(g)(1)(B) . . . . S6.07[1][a] n.13;
S9.02[1][b][i] n.10.6
877A(g)(1)(B)(i) . . . . S6.07[1][a] n.14;
S9.02[1][b][i] n.10.7
877A(g)(1)(B)(i)(I) . . . . . . S6.07[1][a] n.14;
S9.02[1][b][i] n.10.7
877A(g)(1)(B)(i)(II) . . . . . S9.02[1][b][i] n.10.7
877A(g)(1)(B)(ii) . . . . S6.07[1][a] n.15;
S9.02[1][b][i] n.10.8
877A(g)(1)(C) . . . . S6.07[1][a] n.16
877A(g)(2)(B) . . . . S6.07 ns. 3, 4
877A(g)(3) . . . . S6.07 n.5; S9.02[1][b] n.8
877A(g)(4) . . . . S6.07 n.2; S9.02[1][b] n.5
894 . . . . 7.06 & n.11
894(b) 7.06 n.14
897 . . . . 7.06 n.14
901(f) 7.06
904(f) 7.06 n.17

[Text references are to paragraphs and notes (9"n.");
references to the supplement are preceded by "S."]

IRC §

905(c) 3.08
907 . . . . 7.06
911(d)(3) . . . . 5.07[3][a] n.44; 5.07[4][b] n.159
939(a) 8.01 n.2
951(b) . . . . 6.07[2] n.25; S6.07[2][b] n.58; S9.02[1][b][ii] n.10.41
954(c)(1)(B)(ii) . . . . 5.08[2][b][iv] n.37
954(c)(1)(B)(iii) . . . . 5.08[2][b][iv] n.38
954(c)(1)(C) . . . . 5.08[2][b][iv] n.39
954(c)(1)(D) . . . . 5.08[2][b][iv] n.39
954(c)(1)(E) . . . . 5.08[2][b][iv] n.40
954(c)(1)(F) . . . . 5.08[2][b][iv] n.41
954(c)(1)(G) . . . . 5.08[2][b][iv] n.41
954(d)(3) . . . . . 6.07[2] n.25; S6.07[2][b] n.58; S9.02[1][b][ii] n.10.41
956(c)(2) . . . . . 6.07[2] n.25; S6.07[2][b] n.58; S9.02[1][b][ii] n.10.41
957 . . . . . 6.07[2] ns. 23, 25; S6.07[2][b] n.58; S9.02[1][b][ii] n.10.41
958 . . . . 6.07[2] n.23; S6.07[2][b] ns. 55; S9.02[1][b][ii] n.10.38
958(a) . . . . . 6.07[2] ns. 23, 27; S6.07[2][b] ns. 55, 60; S9.02[1][b][ii] n.10.38
958(b) . . . . 6.07[2] n.25; S6.07[2][b] n.58; S9.02[1][b][ii] n.10.41
1001 . . . . S4.11[5] n.54; 4.12[7][a] ns. 42, 47; S10.01[3][g] n.119; 17.04[1][a] n.7
1001(e) . . . . 4.08[7][c] n.134
1001(e)(1) . . . . 4.08[7][c] n.151
1001(e)(3) . . . . 4.08[7][c] n.151
1011(b) . . . . 11.02[1][b] n.28
1012 . . . . 4.02[7][e][iii]; 10.02[2][a] n.23; 17.04[1][a] n.1; 19.02[5][f][ii] n.515; 19.03[4][e][ii]
1014 . . . . 3.02 n.30; S3.02[3] n.66; 4.02[3][g]; 4.02[4][e][iii]; 4.03[1] n.8; 4.03[4][a] n.56; 4.07[2][a][ii] & ns. 27, 36; 4.12[10] ns. 84, 85; 4.16 n.19; S5.03[6][a] n.267; 5.05 n.3; 5.08[1] n.11; 8.10[3][a] & n.40; 8.10[5]; S8.10 n.9; S8.10[2]; S8.10[3][a] n.19; S8.11; 9.03[2] n.13; S9.03[2] n.20; 10.02[2][a] n.23; 17.04[1][b]; 19.02[5][a][iii] n.335; 19.02[5][f][i] n.509; 19.03[4][e][i] n.366; 19.04[2] n.17
1014(a) . . . . 4.12[8] n.60; 5.05[2][a] & ns. 64, 66; 5.06[6][a] n.145; 17.04[1][a]; 17.04[1][d]
1014(a)(1) . . . . . . 4.02[7][e][iii] n.397; 4.12[2] n.12; 8.10[3][a] n.23; S8.10[3][a] n.16; S8.10[3][c][i] n. 85; 17.04[1][a] ns. 5, 6; 17.04[1][b]; 17.04[1][c] ns. 26, 27
1014(a)(2) . . . . . . 4.03[1] n.7; 8.10[3][a] n.23; S8.10[3][a] n.16; 17.04[1][a] ns. 5, 6; 17.04[1][b]; 17.04[1][c] & n.33
1014(a)(3) . . . . 4.04[7][h] n.362; 5.06[5] n.89; 8.10[3][a] n.23; S8.10[3][a] n.16; 17.04[1][a] ns. 5, 6; 17.04[1][b]; 17.04[1][c] & n.32

IRC §

1014(a)(4) . . . . . . 4.02[7][e][i] n.354; 4.02[7][e][iii] & ns. 393, 398; S8.10[3][a] n.16; 17.04[1][a] n.4; 17.04[1][b] & n.21; 17.04[1][c] & n.39; 17.04[1][d] n.43
1014(b) . . . . 4.04[3][b][i] n.40; 4.04[3][b][viii]; 5.08[3][c][ii] & ns. 108, 110
1014(b)(6) . . . . . . 4.12[2] n.12; 4.12[10] n.84; 8.10[3][b][iii] & n.80; S8.10[3][a][ii]; S8.10[3][b][iii] n.70
1014(b)(9) . . . . 4.04[3][b][i] n.40; 4.12[8] n.60
1014(b)(10) 4.16 n.19
1014(c) . . . 4.03[1] n.8; 4.07[2][a][ii] n.35; 5.05 n.3; 5.05[2][a] n.64; 8.10[3][a] n.23; S8.10[3][a] n.16; 17.04[1][c] & n.41; 19.02[5][a][iii] n.335
1014(e) . . . . . . 4.03[1] n.8; 4.07[2][a][ii] n.35; 8.10[3][a] n.23; 8.10[3][b][iv] n.85; S8.10[3][a] n.16; S10.01[5] n.146
1014(e)(1) . . . . 4.03[1] n.8
1014(e)(2)(A) . . . . 4.03[1] n.8
1014(e)(2)(B) . . . . 4.03[1] n.8
1015 . . . . . . 4.02[4][e][iii] n.213; 4.03[1] n.8; 4.07[2][a][ii] & n.27; 4.12[7][a] ns. 41, 42; 5.07[4][a][i] n.130; 8.10[3][a]; S8.10[3][a]; 9.03[2] n.13; S9.03[2] n.20; 10.02[2][a] n.23; 17.04[1][a]; 17.04[1][b] & n.24; 19.02[5][f][ii] & ns. 512, 514; 19.03[4][e][ii]
1015(a) . . . . 17.04[1][a] n.2; 19.02[5][f][ii] ns. 513, 514; 19.03[4][e][ii]
1015(d) . . . . 17.04[1][a]; 17.04[1][b] & ns. 14, 24; 19.02[5][a][iii] ns. 338, 348; 19.02[5][f][ii] & ns. 514, 515; 19.03[4][e][ii]
1015(d)(1) . . . . . 5.07[4][a][i] n.130; 8.10[3][a] n.25; S8.10[3][a] n.19; 19.02[5][f][ii] n.514; 19.03[4][e][ii] ns. 370, 371
1015(d)(6) . . . . . 5.07[4][a][i] n.130; 8.10[3][a] n.25; S8.10[3][a] n.19; 17.04[1][a] & n.3; 17.04[1][b] ns. 14, 24; 19.02[5][f][ii] n.514; 19.03[4][e][ii] ns. 370, 371
1016(c) . . . . . . 4.04[7][h]; 17.04[1][c] & n.37
1016(c)(1) . . . . 4.04[7][h] & n.364; 17.04[1][a] n.6
1016(c)(2)(A) . . . . . . 4.04[7][h] ns. 365, 366; S8.10[3][a] n.43
1016(c)(2)(B) . . . . 4.04[7][h] n.365
1016(c)(3) . . . . 4.04[7][h] n.370
1016(c)(4) . . . . 4.04[7][h] n.369
1016(c)(5)(B) . . . 4.04[7][c][i] n.312; 4.04[7][h] n.373; 17.04[1][a] n.6; 17.04[1][c] n.37
1022 . . . . . . S8.10; S8.10[1]; S8.10[2] & n.15; 8.10[3][a] & ns. 26, 29; S8.10[3][a] ns. 20, 21, 32; S8.10[3][b] n.36; 8.10[3][b][iv] n.84; S8.10[3][b][iv] n.66; S8.10[3][d][ii] ns. 112, 116; 8.10[5]; 9.03[2] n.13; S9.03[2] n.20; S17.02[1][a] ns. 6, 7
1022(a)(1) . . . . . . 8.10[3][a] n.28; 8.10[3][c][i] n.95; S8.10[3][a] n.20

[Text references are to paragraphs and notes (9"n.");
references to the supplement are preceded by "S."]

IRC §

1022(a)(2) . . . 8.10[3][a] n.40; S8.10[3][a] n.32
1022(b) . . . 8.10[3][b] n.43; 8.10[3][c][ii] n.100;
 8.10[3][d][ii]; S8.10[3][b] n.35;
 S8.10[3][d][ii]; S8.10[3][d][ii] n.90
1022(b)(1)(C)(i) . . . . 8.10[3][a] n.41
1022(b)(2) . . . 8.10[3][b] n.44; S8.10[3][b] n.36
1022(b)(2)(B) . . . . 8.10[3][b][i] n.51;
 8.10[3][d][ii] n.118; S8.10[3][a][i] n.43;
 S8.10[3][d][ii] n.108
1022(b)(2)(C) . . . . 8.10[3][b][i] n.51;
 S8.10[3][a][i] n.43
1022(b)(2)(C)(i) . . . . 8.10[3][b][i] n.52
1022(b)(2)(C)(ii) . . . . 8.10[3][b][i] n.53;
 S8.10[3][b] n.45;
1022(b)(3) . . . . 8.10[3][d][ii] n.122;
 S8.10[3][d][ii] n.112
1022(b)(3)(A) . . . 8.10[3][b][i] n.51; S8.10[3][a]
 n.43
1022(b)(3)(B) . . . 8.10[3][b][i] n.51; S8.10[3][a]
 n.43; S8.10[3][a][ii] n.46; 8.10[3][b][ii]
 n.55
1022(c) . . . 8.10[3][b] ns. 43, 45; 8.10[3][b][ii]
 n.56; 8.10[3][c][ii] n.100; 8.10[3][d][ii];
 S8.10[3][b] ns. 35, 37; S8.10[3][d][ii]
 n.90;
1022(c)(3) 8.10[3][b][ii] n.60; S8.10[3][b][ii]
 n. 51
1022(c)(4) 8.10[3][b][ii] n.60; S8.10[3][b][ii]
 n. 51
1022(c)(4)(A) . . . . 8.10[3][b][ii] n.57;
 S8.10[3][b][ii] n. 48
1022(c)(4)(B) . . . . 8.10[3][b][ii] n.57;
 S8.10[3][b][ii] n. 48
1022(c)(4)(C) . . . . 8.10[3][b][ii] n.58;
 S8.10[3][b][ii] n. 49
1022(c)(5) . . . . 8.10[3][b][ii] ns. 60, 61
1022(c)(5)(A)(i) . . . . 8.10[3][b][ii] n.63;
 S8.10[3][b][ii] n.51, 52
1022(c)(5)(A)(ii) . . . . 8.10[3][b][ii] ns. 64, 65;
 S8.10[3][b][ii] ns. 55, 56
1022(c)(5)(B) . . . . 8.10[3][b][ii] n.64;
 S8.10[3][b][ii] n.55
1022(c)(5)(B)(i) . . . . 8.10[3][b][ii] n.64;
 S8.10[3][b][ii] n.55
1022(c)(5)(B)(ii) . . . . 8.10[3][b][ii] n.65;
 S8.10[3][b][ii] n.56
1022(c)(5)(C) . . . . 8.10[3][b][ii] n.65;
 S8.10[3][b][ii] n.56
1022(c)(5)(D) . . . . 8.10[3][b][ii] n.65;
 S8.10[3][b][ii] n.56
1022(d) . . . . . 8.10[3][b] n.43; S8.10[3][b] n.35
1022(d)(1) . . . . 8.10[3][b][iii] n.68;
 S8.10[3][b][iii] n.58
1022(d)(1)(A) . . . . . 8.10[3][a] n.39; 8.10[3][b]
 n.49; S8.10[3][a] n.31; S8.10[3][b] n.41
1022(d)(1)(B) . . . . 8.10[3][b][iii] n.70;
 S8.10[3][b][iii] n.60
1022(d)(1)(B)(i)(I) . . . . . . 8.10[3][b][iii] n.72;
 S8.10[3][b][iii] n.62
1022(d)(1)(B)(i)(II) . . . . . . 8.10[3][b][iii] n.73;
 S8.10[3][b][iii] n.63

IRC §

1022(d)(1)(B)(i)(III) . . . . . 8.10[3][b][iii] n.74;
 S8.10[3][b][iii] n.64
1022(d)(1)(B)(ii) . . . . 8.10[3][b][iii] n.75;
 S8.10[3][b][iii] n.65
1022(d)(1)(B)(iii) . . . . . . 8.10[3][b][iii] n.76;
 S8.10[3][b][iii] n.66
1022(d)(1)(B)(iv) . . . . 8.10[3][b][iii] n.80;
 S8.10[3][b][iii] n.70
1022(d)(1)(C) . . . . 8.10[3][d][ii] ns. 119, 120;
 S8.10[3][d][ii] ns. 109, 110;
1022(d)(1)(C)(i) . . . . 8.10[3][b][iv] ns. 85, 86;
 S8.10[3][b][iv] ns. 75, 76
1022(d)(1)(C)(ii) . . . . 8.10[3][b][iv] n.86;
 S8.10[3][b][iv] n.76
1022(d)(1)(D)(i) . . . . 8.10[3][b][iv] n.87;
 S8.10[3][b][iv] n.77
1022(d)(1)(D)(ii) . . . . 8.10[3][b][iv] n.88;
 S8.10[3][b][iv] n.78
1022(d)(1)(D)(iii) . . . . . . 8.10[3][b][iv] n.89;
 S8.10[3][b][iv] n.79
1022(d)(1)(D)(iv) . . . . . . 8.10[3][b][iv] n.89;
 S8.10[3][b][iv] n.79
1022(d)(2) . . . . . 8.10[3][b] n.47; 8.10[3][b][v]
 n.92; S8.10[3][b] n. 39; S8.10[3][b][v]
 n.82
1022(d)(3)(A) . . . . . 8.10[3][b][v] ns. 91, 93;
 S8.10[3][b][v] ns. 81, 83
1022(d)(3)(B) . . . . 8.10[3][b][v] n.94;
 S8.10[3][b][v] n. 84
1022(d)(4) . . . . . . 8.10[3][d][ii] ns. 118, 122
1022(d)(4)(A) . . . . 8.10[3][b][i] n.54;
 8.10[3][b][ii] n.66
1022(d)(4)(B) . . . . 8.10[3][b][i] n.54
1022(d)(4)(B)(iii) . . . . 8.10[3][b][ii] n.66
1022(e) 8.10[3][a] n.30; 8.10[3][c][iv] n.107;
 8.10[3][d][ii] n.117; S8.10[3][c][iv] n.97;
 S8.10[3][d][ii] n.107
1022(e)(1) . . . 8.10[3][a] n.31; S8.10[3][a] n.23
1022(e)(2) . . . 8.10[3][a] n.33; S8.10[3][a] n.25
1022(e)(3) 8.10[3][a] ns. 30, 34; S8.10[3][a]
 ns. 22, 26
1022(f) . . . 8.10[3][a] ns. 29, 38; 8.10[3][b][iv]
 n.84; S8.10[3][a] ns. 21, 30;
 S8.10[3][b][iv] n.74
1022(g) . . . 8.10[3][c][iii] n.105; S8.10[3][c][iii]
 n.95
1022(g)(1)(A) . . . . 8.10[3][c][iii] n.102;
 S8.10[3][c][iii] n.92
1022(g)(1)(B) . . . . 8.10[3][c][iii] n.103;
 S8.10[3][c][iii] n.93
1022(g)(2) . . . . 8.10[3][c][iii] n.101;
 S8.10[3][c][iii] n.91
1022(g)(2)(D) . . . . S8.10[3][c][iii] n.101;
 S8.10[3][c][iii] n.91
1023 . . . . 8.10[3][a] & n.26; 9.03[2] n.13;
 S9.03[2] n.20; S9.03[2] n.20
1031 . . . . . 4.04[3][c][i]; 4.04[7][b][i] & n.274;
 4.04[7][g]; 4.04[7][h]; 4.12[7][a] n.41;
 5.08[3][d] n.150; 5.08[3][e] n.156;
 5.08[5][b][i] n.225; 5.08[5][b][ii]

[Text references are to paragraphs and notes (9"n.");
references to the supplement are preceded by "S."]

IRC §

1031(a)(2)(B) . . . . 5.08[3][d] n.150; 5.08[3][e] n.156
1031(a)(2)(D) . . . . 5.08[3][d] n.150; 5.08[3][e] n.156
1033 . . . . 4.04[3][c][i]; 4.04[7][b][i]; 4.04[7][b][ii] n.294; 4.04[7][g]; 4.04[7][h]; 5.08[3][d] n.150; 5.08[3][e] n.156; 5.08[5][b][i] n.225; 5.08[5][b][ii]; 5.08[5][c][iii] n.261; 19.03[3][d][ii] n.197; 19.03[3][d][iii] n.232
1033(a)(2)(B) . . . . 4.04[7][b][ii] & n.295; 19.03[3][d][iii] n.234
1033(a)(2)(B)(i) . . . . 4.04[7][a] & n.259
1033(g) . . . . 4.04[7][b][i] n.274
1034 . . . . 5.07[3][c] n.59; 19.03[3][d][iii] n.222
1034(b)(1) . . . . 5.07[3][c] n.62
1040(a) . . . . 4.04[3][b][viii] n.93; 8.10[3][c][ii] n.98; S8.10[3][c][ii] n.88
1040(b) . . . . 4.04[3][b][viii] n.93; 8.10[3][c][ii] n.99; S8.10[3][c][ii] n.89
1040(c) . . . . . . 4.04[3][b][viii] n.93; 4.04[7][h] n.364; 8.10[3][c][ii] n.100; S8.10[3][c][ii] n.90
1041 . . . . 8.10[3][b][iv] n.86; 10.06[4]
1041(a)–1041(c) . . . . 10.06[4] n.36
1041(a)(2) . . . . 10.06[2][c] n.29
1041(b)(2) . . . . 17.04[1][a] n.2
1041(c)(2) . . . . 10.06[2][c] n.29
1212(b) . . . . 8.10[3][b][i]
1221 . . . . 10.07[2][b] n.63; S8.10[3][a][i]
1222(11) . . . . 4.03[1] ns. 9, 12
1223(2) . . . . . 8.10[3][c][i] n.96; S8.10[3][c][i] ns.86
1223(11) . . . . 5.06[6][a] n.146
1231(b) . . . . 10.02[4]
1239 . . . . 10.07[2][b] n.63
1245 . . . . 4.04[7] n.251; S8.10[3][c][i] n.87
1245(b)(1) . . . . S8.10[3][c][i] n.87
1250 . . . . 4.04[7] n.251
1250(b)(1) . . . . S8.10[3][c][i] n.87
1250(b)(3) . . . . S8.10[3][c][i] n.87
1250(d)(1) . . . . S8.10[3][c][i] n.87
1273 . . . . 6.05[3][c] n.48
1274(d)(1) . . . . . 4.02[5]; 10.02[2][b][iii] n.59; 16.02[4][d][iii] n.277; 16.02[6] n.409
1274(d)(1)(B) . . . . 10.01[2][f] n.45
1274(d)(1)(C) . . . . 10.01[2][f] n.45
1295 . . . . 8.10[3][b][iv] n.89
1341 . . . 5.03[5][a] n.116; 9.03[1] n.3; S9.03[1] n.7
1361(b)(1)(D) . . . . 19.02[3][b] n.172
1374 . . . . . 4.02[4][e][iii] n.218; 10.02[2][c][iv] n.108
1401 . . . . 4.04[3][c][iii]
1402(a)(1) . . . 2.02[3][c][ii] n.79; 4.04[3][c][ii] & n.129
1504 . . . . 2.02[3][c][ii] n.95
1504(b)(3) . . . . 2.02[3][c][ii] n.95

IRC §

2001 . . . . . 2.01; S2.01; 2.01[3] n.68; 3.02 n.2; S3.02 n.7; 3.03[3][a]; 3.03[3][b]; 3.03[3][c]; 3.04 n.1; 3.06[3][a]; 4.04[7][c][ii]; 4.04[7][e]; 5.06[9] n.443; 5.07[4][b] & n.157; 5.08[5][c][ii]; 5.08[5][d][i]; 6.01[2] ns. 11, 16; 6.07 n.3; S6.07[2] n.35; 7.01[1] n.1; 8.01[2][b] n.42; 8.07[2] ns. 16, 17; 8.09; 9.01 n.12; 16.01 n.12; S16.01 n.13; 18.01[1] & n.2
2001(a) . . . . . 2.01 & n.9; S2.01; 6.01[1] n.1; 7.01[1] n.27; 13.01[2][b][i] n.26; 13.02[4][b][i] n.255; 17.02[1][b] n.14
2001(a)(4) S3.02 n.1
2001(b) . . . . 1.02[1]; 2.01 & ns. 11, 12; S2.01; 2.01[1][b]; S2.01[1][b]; S3.02 n.3; 3.04 ns. 2, 3; 4.07[2][a][ii] n.34; 4.12[3] n.28; 5.04; 5.08[3][c][iv] n.138; 6.07 n.3; S6.07[2] n.35; 7.03[5] n.134; 8.01[2][a]; 9.03[1] n.4; S9.03[1] n.8; 9.03[3] n.19; S9.03[3] n.27; 12.01[1] n.8; 19.02[5][c][i] & ns. 405, 418; 19.02[5][c][iii] n.443; 19.03[1] & n.11; 19.03[4][c][i] n.321; 19.03[4][c][ii] & ns. 329, 332, 347
2001(b)(1) . . . S2.01; 2.01[1] n.13; S2.01[1] ns. 8, n.10; S2.01[2] n.60; 3.02 n.19; S3.02[1][b][i] n.35; S3.02[2] n.56; 4.04[7][c][ii] n.325; 4.07[3][a] n.81; 5.01 ns. 3, 4; 8.01[2][a]; S9.06[2] n.71; 9.06[3] n.32
2001(b)(1)(A) . . . 2.01 n.10; S2.01; S2.01[1] ns. 6, 11; 2.01[1][b] n.19; 2.01[2] ns. 46, 51; S2.01[2] ns. 56, 573.02 n.3; 3.04 n.4; 4.07[2][b][i]; 19.02[5][c][i] n.405; 19.03[4][c][ii] & ns. 338, 339
2001(b)(1)(B) . . . . . S2.01; S2.01[1] ns. 7, 12; 2.01[2] n.51; S2.01[2] n.57; 3.02 n.3; 4.07[3][a] n.81; 4.12[9] n.74; 5.08[3][c][iv] & ns. 137, 138; 9.01 n.1; 9.05[2] n.10; 10.08[1][a] n.19; 10.08[3] n.46; 19.02[5][c][i] ns. 405, 407; 19.02[5][c][ii] n.422; 19.02[5][c][iii] n.443; 19.02[5][c][iv] n.454; 19.02[5][c][v] ns. 479, 485; 19.03[4][c][ii] & ns. 332, 336, 338, 340
2001(b)(2) . . . S2.01 n.9; 2.01[2] ns. 46, 48, 49, 59, 64; S2.01[2]; 2.01[3] n.72; 3.02 n.19; S3.02[2] ns. 55, 56; 3.04 n.7; 4.04[7][c][ii] n.325; 4.07[3][a] n.81; 4.09[3] n.9; 4.12[3] n.25; 5.01 n.5; 8.01[2][a]; 9.06[1] n.18; S9.06[1] n.61; S9.06[2] ns. 70, 71; 9.06[3] ns. 30, 32; 10.01[10][b] n.217; 10.03[2] & n.35; 10.08[3] n.46; 19.02[1][c] n.23; 19.02[5][c][v] ns. 480, 486; 19.03[4][c][ii]

*[Text references are to paragraphs and notes (9"n.");
references to the supplement are preceded by "S."]*

IRC §

2001(c) . . . . 1.02[4]; 2.01 & n.5; S2.01 & n.5;
  2.01[1]; S2.01[1]; S2.01[1][c]; 2.01[2] &
  ns. 47, 52; S2.01[2] n.66; 2.01[3] & ns.
  66, 67, 73; 3.01 n.2; 3.02 ns. 2, 5, 6;
  S3.02 n.6; S3.02[1]; 3.03[3][d] n.39;
  5.01; 5.07[3][c][i] n.70; 5.07[4][b] &
  n.159; 5.07[4][b] ns. 160, 162, 165;
  5.08[4][b] n.210; 5.09[3] n.33; 6.01[1];
  6.01[2] & n.11; 6.02[4] n.28; 6.06;
  S6.07[1][b] n.29; 6.08; 7.01[3][b];
  7.03[6] ns. 159, 162; 7.03[7] n.182;
  7.03[8] n.233; 8.01[2][a]; 8.01[2][b]
  n.42; S8.10[1] ns. 5, 8; S9.03[2] ns. 12,
  13; S9.03[3] n.24; 9.01 n.1; 9.02;
  S9.02[1][b][i] n.10.23; 9.03[2] & ns. 8–
  10; S9.03[2] & ns. 12, 13; S9.03[3]
  n.24; S9.06[1] ns. 50, 61; 10.03[2];
  10.05 n.10; 12.01[2]; 12.02 & n.11;
  15.02; 16.01 ns. 3, 6, 11; S16.01 ns. 3,
  6, 9, 10, 12; 16.02[1] ns. 1, 11;
  18.01[2][a] n.23; 18.04 n.6; S18.04[2]
2001(c)(1) . . . . S2.01[1][c] n.49; 2.01[2] n.53;
  2.01[3] ns. 66, 68, 69; 6.01[2] n.13;
  6.02[4] n.26; 9.03[2] n.6; S9.03[2] n.11;
  9.06[1] n.9; 12.01[2] n.23; 12.02 n.10;
  16.01 n.9; 19.02[5][f][iii] n.525
2001(c)(2) . . . . S2.01[1][c] ns. 47, 50; 2.01[2]
  ns. 53, 54; 2.01[3] ns. 66, 68, 70; 3.02
  n.6; 5.07[4][b] n.159; 6.01[2] n.13;
  9.03[2] n.7; S9.03[2] n.11; 9.06[1] ns. 9,
  12; 16.01 n.10
2001(c)(2)(B) . . . . 3.03[1] n.15; 19.02[5][f][iii]
  n.525
2001(d)   S2.01[1][c] n.54; 2.01[2] ns. 59, 60;
  S2.01[2] n.77; 2.01[3] n.72; 4.07[3][a]
  n.81; 6.01[2] n.12; 10.03[2];
  19.02[5][c][v] n.474
2001(d)(2) . . . . 10.03[2] n.30
2001(e) . . . . 2.01[1][b] n.20; S2.01[1][b] n.20;
  2.01[2] n.59; S2.01[2] n.77; 4.07[3][a]
  n.81; 10.03[2]; 19.02[5][c][v] n.481;
  19.03[4][c][ii] n.349
2001(e)(2) . . . 2.01[1][b] n.20; S2.01[1][b] n.20
2001(f)   2.01[1][b][ii] ns. 28, 30, 41; 2.01[2];
  S2.01[2]; 9.04[10][a] n.219
2001(f)(1)(B) . . . . 2.01[1][b][ii] n.27;
  S2.01[1][b][ii] n.27
2001(f)(2) . . . . 2.01[1][b][ii] ns. 25, 26;
  S2.01[1][b][ii] ns. 25, 26, 31; 3.05[3][b]
  n.34; 9.05[2][b] ns. 23, 27; 16.02[4][a]
  ns. 219, 236
2001(f)(2)(A) . . . . . . 2.01[1][b][ii] ns. 27, 42;
  S2.01[1][b][ii] ns. 27, 42; 9.05[2][b] n.28
2001(f)(2)(B) . . . . . . 2.01[1][b][ii] n.43;
  S2.01[1][b][ii] n.43; 9.05[2][b] n.29
2001(f)(2)(C) . . . . . . 2.01[1][b][ii] ns. 44, 45;
  S2.01[1][b][ii] ns. 44, 45; 9.05[2][b] ns.
  30, 31
2001(g) . . . . S2.01[2] n.61
2001(g)(1) . . . . S2.01[2] ns. 62, 64
2001(g)(2) . . . . S2.01[2] ns. 63, 68

IRC §

2002 . . . . 2.02; 5.03[4][a] n.89; S5.03[6][c][iii]
  n.302; 8.02; 8.03 n.1; 8.03[2] n.15; 8.04
  & n.2; 12.03[1] n.11
2005(c) . . . . 5.07[4][b] n.162
2010–2016 . . . . 2.01[2]; 2.01[3] & n.68; 3.01
  n.1; 5.01
2010 . . . . S2.01[1][c]; 2.01[2]; S2.01[2];
  S2.01[3] n.89; 3.02 & ns. 2, 5, 6, 13, 17,
  19; S3.02; S3.02[1]; S3.02[1][a] n.18;
  S3.02[1][b] & n.22; S3.02[2] & ns. 53,
  56; S3.02[3]; 3.03[1] n.10; 3.03[3][a]
  n.31; 3.03[3][b] n.33; 3.04[2][a];
  S3.05[2] n.22.1; 3.05[4][a] n.53;
  3.06[3][a]; 4.02[7][e][ii] n.380; 4.03[1]
  n.13; 4.04[1] n.10; 4.04[7][c][ii] n.325;
  4.08[7][c] n.138; 4.13[8][a] n.119; 5.02
  n.2; 5.06[5] n.94; 5.06[6] & ns. 137,
  138; 5.07[4][b] ns. 160, 162; 5.07[5] &
  n.183; 5.08[1] n.2; 5.08[4][b] & n.203;
  5.08[6][b] & n.281; S6.07[2] n.40;
  7.02[3] n.74; 7.02[4][a] n.83; 7.02[4][b]
  & n.89; 7.03[3] & ns. 63, 65, 67;
  7.03[5] & n.134; 7.03[6] n.168;
  8.01[2][b] & n.42; 8.07[2] & ns. 16, 17;
  S8.10[1] n.7; 9.06 n.2; S9.06 n.37;
  S9.06[1] n.56; S9.06[2] & ns. 70, 71;
  9.06[3] & ns. 28, 30, 32; 10.07[2][d][i]
  n.87; 16.01 n.18; S16.01 n.18;
  17.02[1][c][i] n.57; S17.02[1][c][i] n.57
2010(a) . . . . 3.02 ns. 8, 9
2010(b) . . . S2.01[1][c] n.54; 2.01[3] n.72; 3.02
  & ns. 13, 27; S3.02[1][a] n.18; 9.06[1]
  n.15; S9.06[1] n.56
2010(c) . . . . . . S2.01[1][c] n.55; 2.01[3] n.73;
  2.02[3][c][v] n.127; 3.02 ns. 2, 4, 8, 9,
  11; S3.02[1][b] n.29; 3.03[1] ns. 10, 15;
  5.02 n.2; 5.08[4][b]; 6.02[4] & n.29;
  7.02[3] & n.73; 7.03[5] & n.133;
  8.01[2][b] n.42; 8.10[3][a] n.40; 9.06
  n.4; S9.06 & ns. 39, 43; 9.06[1] & n.11;
  S9.06[1] n.49; 9.06[3] ns. 31, 32;
  12.01[2] ns. 23, 24; 15.02 & n.11;
  S15.02; 15.03[5][c][ii] n.220; 16.01 n.10;
  18.01[2][a] n.23; 18.03[2][a] n.31;
  19.04[2] n.17
2010(c)(1) . . . . . . S3.02[1][b] n.28; S9.06 n.40
2010(c)(2)–2010(c)(4) . . . . S3.02 n.5; S3.02[1]
  n.13
2010(c)(2) . . . . . S3.02[1][b] ns. 27, 28; S9.06
  n.40; S15.02 n.3
2010(c)(2)(A) . . . . . S3.02[1] n.14; S15.02 n.2
2010(c)(2)(B) . . . . . S3.02[1] n.15; S3.02[1][b]
  n.24; S9.06[1] n.51
2010(c)(3) . . . S3.02[1] ns. 12, 14; S3.02[1][a]
  n.20; S3.02[1][b] ns. 26, 30;
  S3.02[1][b][i] n.33; S3.02[3]; S9.06[1]
  ns. 51, 54; S15.02 & ns. 2, 3, 5
2010(c)(3)(A) . . . S3.02[1][a] n.17; S3.02[1][b]
  n.32; S3.02[2] n.52
2010(c)(3)(B) . . . . . S3.02[1][a] n.20; S9.06[1]
  n.51; S15.02 n.6

*[Text references are to paragraphs and notes (9"n.");
references to the supplement are preceded by "S."]*

IRC §

2010(c)(3)(B)(ii) . . . S3.02[1][a] n.20; S9.06[1] n.51; S15.02 n.6
2010(c)(3)(C) . . . . S9.03[3] n.31
2010(c)(4) . . . S3.02[1] ns. 12, 15; S3.02[1][b] ns. 24, 25, 31, 32; S3.02[1][b][i] ns. 33, 37, 38; S9.03[3] n.31; S9.06[1] ns. 54, 55; S9.06[2] n.68; S15.02 n.3
2010(c)(4)(A) . . . . . . S3.02[1][b][i] ns. 34, 38
2010(c)(4)(B) . . . . S3.02[1][b] n.32; S3.02[1][b][i] ns. 35, 38
2010(c)(4)(B)(i) . . . . S3.02[1][b] n.32; S3.02[1][b][i] ns. 34, 38, 39, 41, 43; S9.06[1] n.54
2010(c)(4)(B)(ii) . . . . S3.02[1][b][i] ns. 35, 43
2010(c)(5) . . . S2.02[1] n.7; S3.02[1][b] ns. 24, 25, 32
2010(c)(5)(A) . . . S3.02[1][b][i]; S3.02[1][b][ii] ns. 45–47; S3.02[3] n.63
2010(c)(5)(B) . . . . S3.02[1][b][ii] n.49
2010(c)(6) . . . S3.02[1][b] n.32; S3.02[1][b][ii] n.50; S9.06[1] n.56
2010(d) . . . . S3.02 n.7; 7.03[3] n.68
2011–2016 . . . . 2.01[2] n.63
2011 . . . S3.02 n.1; 3.03; 3.03[1] & ns. 1, 3, 9, 10, 16; 3.03[2] ns. 17, 29; 3.03[3][b]; 3.03[3][c] & n.37; 3.03[3][d] ns. 38, 40; 3.03[5]; 3.04[2][a] & n.25; 3.05[4][a] n.54; 3.06[3][a] & n.20; 3.06[4] & ns. 25, 33; 3.08 n.2; 4.04[7][c][ii] ns. 324, 325; 4.05[2][a] n.9; S5.03[4][b][ii] n.193; 5.03[5][a] n.105; 5.03[8]; 5.07[4][a][ii] & n.143; 5.07[4][b] n.160; 5.09[1] & ns. 2, 5; 5.09[2] & ns. 10, 12, 31; 5.09[3] & n.34; 6.02 & n.2; 6.02[1] & ns. 7, 14; 7.02[4][b] & n.89; 7.03[6] n.168; 8.07[2] & ns. 16, 17; 8.10[5]; S8.11[1]; 9.03[3] n.17; 9.06 n.7; 12.04 & ns. 1, 10
2011(a) . . . . 3.03[1] & n.7; 3.03[3][b]; 6.06[4] n.39
2011(b) . . . 3.03[1]; 3.03[3][c]; 3.03[3][d] n.39; 4.04[7][c][ii] n.324; 5.07[4][a][ii] n.143; 6.02[1]; 6.06[4] n.45; 8.01[2][a] n.38; 12.04
2011(b)(1) . . . . . 3.03[3][b] & n.35; 3.03[3][d] n.38; 4.04[7][c][ii] n.325; 8.01[2][a] n.38; 8.07[2] ns. 16, 17
2011(b)(2) . . . . . 3.03[1] n.12; 3.03[3][d] n.38; 5.07[4][a][ii] n.143; 6.02[1] n.17; 8.07[2] ns. 16, 17; 12.04 n.10
2011(b)(2)(B) . . . . 3.03[1] n.15
2011(b)(3) . . . . 3.03[3][b] & ns. 33, 35; 3.03[3][d] n.38; 8.01[2][a] n.38
2011(c) . . . . . 3.03[2]; 3.06[4]; 3.07 & ns. 1, 6
2011(c)(1) . . . . 3.03[2]
2011(c)(2) 3.03[2]; 3.06[4] n.30; 3.07 & n.7; 4.02[7][a] n.278
2011(c)(3) . . . . 3.03[2]; 3.06[4] n.27
2011(d) . . . . 3.03[3][c]
2011(d)(1) . . . . 3.03[3][c]
2011(d)(2) . . . . 3.03[3][c]

IRC §

2011(e) . . . . . . 3.03[1] n.10; 3.03[3][a] n.32; 6.02[1] n.15
2011(f) . . . . 3.03[1] n.1; 3.03[3][d] n.39; 3.05[4][a] n.54; 3.06[3][a] n.20; 3.06[4] n.25; 3.07 ns. 1, 7; 3.08 n.2; 4.04[7][c][ii] n.324; 5.07[4][a][ii] n.143; 6.02 n.2; 6.02[1] n.7
2011(g) . . . . 5.03[8] n.167; 12.04 n.10
2012–2016 . . . . S2.01[2] n.81
2012 2.01[2] ns. 46, 64; S2.01[2] ns. 56, 77, 82; 3.04 & n.9; 3.04[1][b] n.16; 3.04[1][c] n.22; 3.04[2][b] & ns. 26, 27; 3.05; 3.05[3][a] & n.23; 3.05[4][a] n.54; 3.06[3][a]; 4.07[3][a] n.75; 4.08[7][d] n.165; 4.12[3] n.25; 6.02; 6.02[2]; 10.01[5][b] n.166; 10.01[10][b] n.217; 10.03[2] n.35; 12.01[1] n.8
2012(a) . . . . . 2.01[2] n.46; S2.01[2] n.56; 3.04 n.9; 3.04[1]; 3.04[2] & n.24; 3.04[2][c] n.36
2012(b)(1) . . . . 3.04[2][b]
2012(b)(2) . . . . 3.04[2][b]
2012(b)(3) . . . . 3.04[2][b]
2012(c) . . . . 3.04[1][a] n.15
2012(c)(2) . . . . 3.04[2][b]
2012(d)(1) . . . . 3.04[1]; 3.04[1][c]
2012(d)(2) . . . . 3.04[1][b]
2012(e) . . . . . 2.01[2] n.46; S2.01[2] n.56; 3.04 n.6; 3.04[1][b] n.16; 4.09[3] n.9; 6.02[2] n.21
2013 . . . . . 3.05 & n.2; 3.05[1] n.4; 3.05[1][a]; 3.05[1][b]; 3.05[1][c]; 3.05[2] n.22; S3.05[2] n.22; 3.05[3][a]; 3.05[3][b] & n.46; 3.05[5]; 3.06 n.9; 3.06[3][a]; 4.02[5] n.254; 4.08[7][c] n.141; 4.12[10] & n.94; 5.03[3][c] n.71; S5.03[3][c][i] n.113; 5.06[1]; 5.06[9] & ns. 444, 446, 447; 5.07[2][b] n.26; 5.07[4][a][i] n.135; 5.07[4][a][ii] & n.139; 5.07[4][b] n.160; 6.02; 6.02[3]; 7.03[5] n.141; 13.01[2][b][i] n.29; 13.01[2][b][iii] n.42
2013(a) . . . . . 3.05[1]; 3.05[1][c]; 3.05[2] n.22; S3.05[2] n.22; 3.05[4][b]; 6.02[3] n.24
2013(b) . . . . 3.05[2]; S3.05[2] n.22; 3.05[3][a]; 3.05[4][a]; 5.06[9] n.444
2013(c) . . . . S3.05[2] n.22; 3.05[4][a]; 5.06[9] n.444
2013(c)(1) . . . . . 3.05[4][a] n.57; 5.06[9] n.447
2013(c)(2) . . . . 3.05[4][a]
2013(d) . . . . 3.05[3][b]; 5.06[9] n.444
2013(e) . . . . 3.05[1][b]
2013(f) . . . . 3.05[5] n.63
2013(f)(1) . . . . 3.05[5] n.64
2013(f)(2) . . . . 3.05[5] n.66
2014 3.05[4][a] n.54; 3.06 & n.9; 3.06[3][a]; 3.06[4] n.27; S5.03[4][b][ii]; 5.03[8]; 5.07[4][a][ii] & n.144; 5.07[4][b] n.160; 6.02; 6.07[2] n.31; S6.07[2] n.40; 7.01[1]; 7.01[3][a]; 7.02[4][a]; 7.02[4][b] n.89; 7.03[8] & n.244; 7.06
2014(a) . . . . . . 3.06; 3.06[2] n.13; 7.01[1] n.4

[Text references are to paragraphs and notes (9"n.");
references to the supplement are preceded by "S."]

IRC §

2014(b) . . . . 3.06[1]
2014(b)(2) . . . . 3.06[3][a] n.20; 3.06[3][c] n.23
2014(c) . . . . 3.06[2]; 3.06[3][b]
2014(d) . . . . 3.06[4]
2014(e) . . . . 3.06[4]; 3.07 & n.6
2014(e)(1) . . . . 3.06[4]
2014(e)(2) . . . . 3.06[4] & n.30; 3.07
2014(f) . . . . . . 3.06[3][b] n.21; 3.06[3][c] n.23
2014(g) 3.06 n.10
2014(h) 3.06 n.5
2015 . . . . 3.07; 6.02 n.3
2016 . . . . 3.08 & ns. 2, 5; 6.02 n.3
2025(b)(1)(A) . . . . 5.06[7][c] n.194
2031–2046 . . . 2.01; S2.01 n.4; 5.01; 9.02 n.2
2031 . . . . . . 2.01[1][a]; S2.01[1][a]; 3.05[3][b]
    n.29; 3.06[1] n.12; 4.01; 4.02; S4.02;
    4.02[7][d][i] ns. 323, 324; 4.02[7][e][ii]
    n.364; 4.02[7][e][iv] n.417; 4.04[7][h]
    n.363; 4.05[1]; 4.05[4] n.45; 4.05[7][b]
    n.81; 4.07[2][c] n.55; 4.10[9] n.93;
    4.11[4][a]; 4.12[1] n.9; 4.13[6][a] n.73;
    4.16 n.19; S5.03[1][b] n.17; 5.03[3][d]
    n.78; S5.03[5] n.252; S5.03[6][a] n.273;
    5.05[5][a][ii] n.205; 5.05[5][b][ii] n.262;
    5.06[8][d][ii] n.348; 5.08[3][c][iii] ns.
    122, 124; 6.02[1]; 6.06[1] n.13; 7.01[1]
    n.2; 8.08[2] n.10; 10.02[2][a];
    10.02[2][b][iii] n.59; 10.02[2][d][ii];
    11.03[4][c][i] n.71; 14.05[2][a] n.14;
    15.03[7][b][i] ns. 262, 264;
    15.03[7][b][ii] ns. 275, 277;
    16.02[4][d][i] n.253; 16.02[4][d][ii]
    n.271; 16.02[4][e] n.292; 16.02[7][e][ii]
    n.514; 17.02[1][b]; 17.04[2][a] n.51;
    19.02[5][f][i] n.509; 19.03[4][e][i] n.366
2031(a) . . . . 4.01 n.1; 4.02[1]; 4.02[2][a];
    4.14[9][b] n.133; 7.01[1] n.27; 7.06 n.14;
    10.02[2][a] n.24
2031(b) . . . . 4.02[1] n.5; 4.02[3][f] n.111
2031(c) . . . . 2.01 n.6; 2.02[3][c][ii] n.100; 4.02
    n.2; 4.02[7][a] ns. 273, 278;
    4.02[7][b][i]; 4.02[7][b][ii] & ns. 298,
    308, 312–315; 4.02[7][c]; 4.02[7][d];
    4.02[7][d][i] & ns. 325, 327;
    4.02[7][d][ii] & n.346; 4.02[7][d][iii];
    4.02[7][d][iv]; 4.02[7][e]; 4.02[7][e][i] &
    n.354; 4.02[7][e][ii] & ns. 360, 369, 380;
    4.02[7][e][iii]; 4.02[7][e][iv] & ns. 412,
    416, 417; 4.02[7][f] & n.419; 5.05[7][c]
    n.342; 5.06[4] n.84; 5.08[3][c][ii] n.105;
    5.08[3][c][iii] n.121; 5.08[3][c][v] n.142;
    5.08[6][a] & n.277; 5.08[6][b] ns. 287,
    290; 6.03[1]; 8.10[2][b][iii]; 8.10[3][a]
    n.22; S8.11[1]; 11.02[2][d] n.99;
    17.04[1][a] & n.4; 17.04[1][b] n.21;
    17.04[1][c] & ns. 27, 38; 17.04[1][d]
    n.43

IRC §

2031(c)(1) . . . . . 4.02[7][a] n.272; 4.02[7][b]
    n.279; 4.02[7][c] n.316; 4.02[7][d][iii]
    n.351; 4.02[7][e][i] n.354
2031(c)(1)(A) . . . . 4.02[7][a] n.275; 4.02[7][b][ii]
    n.293; 4.02[7][d] n.321; 4.02[7][d][i] ns.
    325–327; 4.02[7][d][iii] n.349;
    4.02[7][e][i] & ns. 354–357;
    4.02[7][e][iii] n.361
2031(c)(1)(B) . . . . 4.02[7][d] n.322;
    4.02[7][d][iii] n.350; 4.02[7][e][i] & ns.
    354–357
2031(c)(2) . . . 4.02[7][d][i] n.340; 4.02[7][d][ii]
    ns. 344–346; 4.02[7][e][ii] n.361
2031(c)(3) . . . . 4.02[7][a] n.278
2031(c)(4) . . . . 4.02[7][d][i] n.328
2031(c)(4)(A) . . . . 4.02[7][d][i] n.331
2031(c)(4)(B)(i) . . . . 4.02[7][d][i] n.333
2031(c)(4)(B)(ii)(I) . . . . . . 4.02[7][d][i] n.334
2031(c)(4)(B)(ii)(II) . . . . . . 4.02[7][d][i] n.335
2031(c)(4)(B)(ii)(III) . . . . . 4.02[7][d][i] n.336
2031(c)(4)(B)(ii)(IV) . . . . . 4.02[7][d][i] n.337
2031(c)(5)(A) . . . . . 4.02[7][d][i] ns. 330, 338
2031(c)(5)(B) . . . . . 4.02[7][d][i] ns. 340, 341
2031(c)(5)(C) . . . . 4.02[7][d][i] n.342;
    8.10[2][b][iii] & n.18
2031(c)(5)(D) . . . . . 4.02[7][d][i] ns. 329, 339
2031(c)(6) . . . . 4.02[7][b] n.284; 4.02[7][c] ns.
    317, 318
2031(c)(7) . . . . 4.02[7][d][i] n.343
2031(c)(8)(A) . . . . 4.02[7][a] n.272; 4.02[7][b]
    n.279
2031(c)(8)(A)(i) . . . . 4.02[7][b] n.280;
    4.02[7][b][i] ns. 286, 287
2031(c)(8)(A)(i)(I) . . . . . . 4.02[7][b][i] n.287
2031(c)(8)(A)(i)(II) . . . . . . 4.02[7][b][i] n.287
2031(c)(8)(A)(i)(III) . . . . . 4.02[7][b][i] n.287
2031(c)(8)(A)(ii) . . . . 4.02[7][b] n.281;
    4.02[7][b][i] ns. 289, 292
2031(c)(8)(A)(iii) . . . . 4.02[7][b] ns. 282–284;
    4.02[7][b][i] n.292; 4.02[7][b][ii] ns. 303,
    306, 309, 310
2031(c)(8)(B) . . . . . 4.02[7][b][ii] ns. 293, 296,
    298, 301, 302; 4.02[7][d][iii] n.345
2031(c)(8)(C) . . . . 4.02[7][b] ns. 283, 284;
    4.02[7][b][ii] n.306
2031(c)(8)(C)(i) . . . . 4.02[7][b][ii] n.304
2031(c)(8)(C)(ii) . . . . 4.02[7][b][ii] n.305
2031(c)(8)(C)(iii) . . . . 4.02[7][b][ii] n.306
2031(c)(8)(C)(iv) . . . . 4.02[7][b][ii] n.307
2031(c)(8)(D) . . . . 4.02[7][b][i] n.290;
    4.02[7][b][ii] n.305
2031(c)(9) . . . . . . 4.02[7][b][ii] ns. 310, 315;
    4.02[7][d][i] n.326
2031(c)(10) . . . . . . 4.02[7][b][i]]ns. 291, 292

[Text references are to paragraphs and notes (9"n.");
references to the supplement are preceded by "S."]

IRC §

2032 . . . 1.04[4][a][i]; 1.04[4][a][ii]; 2.01[1][a];
S2.01[1][a]; 2.02[3][c][ii]; 3.05[3][b]
n.29; S3.05[3][b] n.29; 4.01 & n.2;
4.02[2][a]; 4.02[5] n.245; S4.02[5] ns.
244, 247; 4.02[7][d][i] ns. 323, 324;
4.02[7][e][ii] n.364; 4.03; 4.03[1] & ns.
2, 10; S4.03[1] ns. 2, 3; 4.03[2];
4.03[2][d]; 4.03[3][a] n.39; S4.03[3][a]
n.40; 4.03[3][b] & n.48; S4.03[3][c];
4.03[4][b] & n.59; 4.04[1] & n.4;
4.04[7][h] n.363; 4.05[1]; 4.05[4] n.39;
4.07[2][c] ns. 55, 60; S4.08[1][a] n.5;
4.09[3] n.8; 4.09[6]; 4.10[9] n.93;
4.10[10][f] & n.109; 4.11[4][a];
4.13[6][a] n.73; 4.14[1] n.2; 4.16 n.19;
S5.03[1][b] n.17; 5.03[5][b] n.122;
5.04[1]; 5.04[4] n.24; 5.05[2][e] n.93;
5.05[3][a] & n.95; S5.05[3][a] n.95;
5.05[5][a][ii] n.205; S5.05[5][a][ii] n.207;
5.05[5][b][ii] n.262; S5.05[5][b][ii]
n.264; 5.05[5][c][ii] n.288; S5.05[5][c][ii]
n.291; S5.05[6][b] n.327; S5.05[7][a]
n.333; 5.06[5] n.88; 5.06[7][b];
S5.06[7][d] n.197; S5.06[8][d][ii] n.348;
5.06[9] n.437; S5.07[3][d] n.118;
5.07[4][a][ii] & n.145; 5.07[4][b] n.158;
5.08[3][c][iii] n.123; 8.06 n.10; 8.08[2]
n.10; S9.04[3][a] n.48; 10.02[1] n.5;
S10.02[2][b][iii] n.56; S11.02[1][b] n.27;
11.03[4][c][i] n.71; 14.02[2] n.10;
14.03[1] n.6; 14.03[2]; 14.04[2];
14.05[2][a] & n.15; 14.05[2][b] & n.26;
15.03[6][a] n.235; 15.03[7][b][i] n.265;
15.03[7][b][ii] n.277; 15.03[7][c][i]
n.292; 16.02[4][d][i] n.254; 16.02[4][e]
n.292; S16.02[6] n.409; 16.02[7][e][ii]
n.514; 17.04[1][a] n.6; 17.04[1][c] & ns.
27, 29, 34; 17.04[1][d]; 18.02[4][a];
18.03[1][a] n.10; 19.02[5][f][i] n.509;
S19.03[1] n.3; S19.03[3][b] n.112;
S19.03[3][d] n.162 19.03[4][e][i] n.366
2032(a) . . . 4.03[3]; S4.03[3][a] n.40; 4.14[9][b]
n.133; 14.05[2][a] n.15; 14.05[2][b] n.24
2032(a)(1) . . . . 4.03[3][a] & ns. 40, 47;
14.05[2][a] n.16
2032(a)(2) . . . 4.03[3][a] ns. 46, 47; 14.05[2][a]
n.16
2032(a)(3) . . . . . . 4.03[3][b]; 14.05[2][a] n.16
2032(b) . . . . 4.03[1]; 4.03[4]; 5.05[3][a] ns. 95,
98 – 100; 5.06[5]; 14.05[2][b] n.27
2032(b)(1) . . . . 4.03[4][b]
2032(b)(2) . . . . 4.03[4][b]; 5.06[3][b] n.45
2032(c) . . . . 4.03[1] & ns. 10, 14, 15;
5.07[4][a][ii] n.145; 14.05[2][a] n.17;
15.03[7][b][ii] n.270
2032(c)(2) . . . . . 4.03[1] n.14; 14.05[2][a] n.17
2032(d) . . . . 4.03[1] n.2; S4.03[1] n.3
2032(d)(1) . . . . 4.03[1] n.2; S4.03[1] n.2
2032(d)(2) . . . . . 4.03[1] n.3; 14.05[2][b] n.26
2032A . . . 1.02[2][c]; 1.04[4][a][i]; S2.01[1][a];
2.01[1][a]; 2.02[3][c][i]; 2.02[3][c][ii];

IRC §

3.05[3][b] n.29; 3.05[5] & n.61; 4.01 &
n.3; 4.02[3][b] ns. 62, 83; 4.02[7][d][i]
ns. 323, 324; 4.02[7][e][ii] & ns. 360,
364, 369, 372, 374; 4.02[7][e][iii];
4.03[1] ns. 2, 8; S4.03[1] n.2; 4.04;
4.04[1] & ns. 4, 10, 12, 19; S4.04[1]
n.11; 4.04[2]; 4.04[3][a]; 4.04[3][b][i] &
n.40; 4.04[3][b][ii]; 4.04[3][b][iii] n.53;
4.04[3][b][iv]; 4.04[3][b][v] & ns. 66,
67, 69, 71; 4.04[3][b][vi] n.79;
4.04[3][b][viii] & ns. 93, 100; 4.04[3][c];
4.04[3][c][ii] & n.127; 4.04[3][c][iii]
n.143; 4.04[4]; 4.04[5] & ns. 171, 172,
174; S4.04[5] n.171; 4.04[5][a] n.176;
S4.04[5][a] n.176; 4.04[5][a][v];
4.04[5][a][vi] n.203; 4.04[5][b] n.205;
4.04[6] & ns. 214, 233, 239, 245;
S4.04[6] n.215; 4.04[7] & n.254;
4.04[7][a] & n.265; 4.04[7][b][i] &
n.270; S4.04[7][b][i] ns. 272, 273;
4.04[7][b][ii] & n.282; S4.04[7][b][ii]
n.284; 4.04[7][c][i] & n.315;
4.04[7][c][ii] & ns. 324, 325;
4.04[7][c][iii]; 4.04[7][c][iv]; 4.04[7][h]
& n.366; 4.05[1]; 4.07[2][c] n.55;
S4.08[5][a] n.56; 4.07[2][d]; 4.10[9]
n.94; 4.16 n.19; S5.03[1][b] n.17;
S5.03[5] n.252; 5.03[6] n.151; 5.04[1]
n.5; 5.06[5] & ns. 87, 89, 90; 5.06[9]
n.437; 5.07[4][a][ii] & n.146; 5.07[4][b]
n.158; 5.08[1] & ns. 11, 13; 5.08[2][a]
n.20; 5.08[2][c][ii] n.56; S5.08[2][c][ii]
n.56; 5.08[3]; 5.08[3][b]; 5.08[3][b][i]
n.94; 5.08[3][c][iii] ns. 124, 125;
5.08[3][e] n.159; 5.08[5][a]; 5.08[5][b][i]
n.224; 5.08[6][b] & ns. 281, 292; 6.03[1]
n.1; 8.06 n.10; 8.08[2] n.10;
8.10[2][b][i]; 8.10[3][c][ii] n.98;
11.03[4][c][i] n.71; 14.02[2] n.8;
14.03[2] n.10; 14.04[2] & n.9;
14.05[2][a] & n.21; 14.05[2][b] & n.31;
15.02[2] n.50; S15.02[2] n.44;
15.03[6][a] & ns. 235, 237; 15.03[6][b]
n.242; 15.03[7][a] & n.260;
15.03[7][b][i] & n.263; 15.03[7][b][ii] &
n.276; 15.03[7][b][iii] & n.284;
15.03[7][c][i] n.292; 15.03[7][c][ii] &
n.296; 16.02[1]; 16.02[2][c][ii] n.153;
16.02[3][b][ii] n.174; 16.02[3][b][iii];
16.02[4][d][i] & ns. 250, 255;
16.02[4][d][ii] & ns. 270, 271;
16.02[4][e] n.292; 16.02[5][a];
16.02[5][c] ns. 358, 360; 16.02[5][f];
16.02[5][f][i] & ns. 385 – 387;
16.02[5][f][ii] & n.396; 16.02[7][e][ii]
n.514; 16.02[8][b] n.559; 17.04[1][a] n.6;
17.04[1][c] & ns. 27, 34, 36;
17.04[1][d]; 18.03[1]; 18.03[1][a] & ns.
10 – 12; 18.03[1][b] & ns. 16, 22;
19.02[5][f][i] n.509; 19.03[4][e][i] n.366
2032A(a)(1) . . . . 5.06[5] n.89

[Text references are to paragraphs and notes (9"n.");
references to the supplement are preceded by "S."]

IRC §

2032A(a)(1)(A) . . . . 4.04[2] n.20; 6.03[1] n.1
2032A(a)(1)(B) . . . . 4.04[1] ns. 13, 14; 4.04[6]
          n.212
2032A(a)(2)   4.04[1] ns. 2, 10; 4.04[5] n.171;
          4.04[6] n.244; 4.04[7][c][i] n.311;
          5.07[4][a][ii] n.146; 5.08[6][b] n.279
2032A(a)(3) . . . . 4.04[1] n.11
2032A(b) . . . . 4.04[1] n.3; 18.03[1] n.5
2032A(b)(1) . . . . 4.02[7][e][ii]; 4.04[2] ns. 25–
     27; 4.04[3][c][ii] n.124; 4.04[4] ns. 152,
          153, 156, 159
2032A(b)(1)(A) . . . . 4.02[7][e][ii] ns. 362, 365,
          368; 4.04[2] n.21; 4.04[3][b] n.31;
          4.04[3][b][vi]; 5.08[6][b] ns. 283, 293
2032A(b)(1)(A)(i) . . . . 4.04[2] n.22; 4.04[3][b]
     n.32; 4.04[3][b][ii] n.48; 4.04[3][b][v]
     n.70; 4.04[3][b][vii] n.85; 4.04[3][c][iii]
          n.143
2032A(b)(1)(A)(ii) . . . . 4.04[2] ns. 23, 24;
          4.04[3][b] n.33; 4.04[3][c] n.104
2032A(b)(1)(B) . . . . 4.02[7][e][ii] ns. 362, 366,
     368; 4.04[2] n.24; 4.04[3][c] n.104;
     4.04[3][c][i] n.112; 4.04[6] & n.241;
          5.08[6][b] ns. 283, 293
2032A(b)(1)(C) . . . . 4.04[2] ns. 24, 28;
     4.04[3][b][vi] n.78; 4.04[3][c] n.104;
          4.04[3][c][ii] n.123
2032A(b)(1)(C)(i) . . . . 4.04[3][b][ii] n.48;
     4.04[3][c][i] n.112; 4.04[3][c][iii] n.143;
          4.04[4] n.163
2032A(b)(1)(C)(ii) . . . . 2.02[3][c][ii] n.79;
     4.04[3][c][i] n.112; S4.04[3][c][ii] n.127;
     4.04[3][c][iii] n.143; S4.04[3][c][iii]
     n.144; 4.04[4] n.165; S4.04[4] n.165
2032A(b)(1)(D) . . . 4.04[2] n.29; 4.04[4] n.166;
          4.04[6] ns. 222, 240
2032A(b)(2) . . . . 18.03[1] n.7
2032A(b)(2)(A) . . . . 4.04[3][b][ii] n.41;
          4.04[7][b][ii]
2032A(b)(2)(B) . . . . 4.04[3][b][ii] n.42;
          4.04[3][b][iv]; 4.04[7][b][ii]
2032A(b)(3) . . . . 2.01[1][b][ii] n.39; 5.08[6][b]
          n.294
2032A(b)(3)(A) . . . . 4.02[7][e][ii] n.367;
          4.04[3][b][i] n.35; 4.04[6] n.243
2032A(b)(3)(B) . . . . 4.04[3][b][i] n.36; 4.04[6]
          n.242
2032A(b)(4) . . . . 4.04[2] ns. 24, 28;
     4.04[3][b][vi] n.78; 4.04[3][c] n.104;
     S4.04[3][c][ii] n.127; 4.04[3][c][iii]
     n.144; S4.04[3][c][iii] n.144; 4.04[4]
     n.165; S4.04[4] n.165; 5.08[3][e] n.160
2032A(b)(4)(A) . . . . 4.04[3][c][i] n.112;
     4.04[3][c][ii] n.124; 5.08[5][b][i] n.222
2032A(b)(4)(B) . . . . 4.04[3][c][ii] n.125;
     4.04[7][b][ii] n.307; 5.08[3][e] n.158;
          5.08[5][b][i] n.230
2032A(b)(4)(C) . . . . 5.08[5][b][i] n.222

IRC §

2032A(b)(5) . . . . 4.04[3][b][vi] n.78; 4.04[3][c]
     n.104; 4.04[3][c][ii] n.128; S4.04[3][c][ii]
          n.127; 4.04[3][c][iii] n.144;
     S4.04[3][c][iii] n.144; S4.04[4] n.165;
     5.08[3][e] n.162; 5.08[5][b][i] n.228
2032A(b)(5)(A) . . . . 4.04[3][c][iii] ns. 143, 144
2032A(b)(5)(B) . . . . 4.04[3][c][iii] n.142
2032A(b)(5)(C) . . . . 4.04[3][c][iii] n.144
2032A(c) . . . . 3.05[5] & n.61; 4.02[7][e][ii] &
     n.360; 4.04[1] n.12; 4.04[5][a][vi] n.203;
     4.04[5][b] n.206; 4.04[6] & n.223;
          4.04[7] n.254; 4.04[7][c][i] n.319;
     4.04[7][e] & n.344; 4.04[7][g]; 5.03[3][c]
     n.71; S5.03[3][c][i]; 5.08[5][a] n.216;
     8.10[2][b][i] n.13; 14.05[2][a] ns. 20, 21;
     15.03[6][a] n.237; 15.03[7][b][ii];
     16.02[4][d][i] n.255; 16.02[4][d][ii]
     n.270; 16.02[4][e] n.292; 16.02[5][c]
     n.358; 16.02[5][f] n.384; 16.02[5][f][i] &
          ns. 386, 387; 16.02[7][e][ii] n.514;
     16.02[8][a]; 16.02[8][b] n.559;
     17.04[1][c]; 18.03[1]; 18.03[1][a] & ns.
     11, 12; 18.03[1][b] & n.19; 19.03[3][d]
          n.165
2032A(c)(1) . . . . . . 4.04[7] ns. 250, 252, 255;
     4.04[7][a] n.256; 4.04[7][b][i] n.271;
          4.04[7][g] n.360; 4.04[7][h];
     15.03[7][c][ii] n.295; 17.04[1][a] n.6;
          18.03[1] ns. 6, 8
2032A(c)(1)(A) . . . . 4.04[7] n.253; 4.04[7][b][i]
     n.270; 4.04[7][b][ii] n.286; 4.04[7][d];
          4.04[7][f] n.349
2032A(c)(1)(B) . . . 4.04[7] n.254; 4.04[7][b][ii]
     ns. 282, 291; 4.04[7][d]; 18.03[1] n.8
2032A(c)(2) . . . . . 4.04[7][g]; 5.08[6][b] n.295;
          18.03[1] n.9
2032A(c)(2)(A) . . . . 4.04[7][c][v] n.338
2032A(c)(2)(A)(i) . . . . 4.04[7][c][i] n.314
2032A(c)(2)(A)(ii)   4.04[7][c][i] ns. 315, 316;
     4.04[7][d] n.342; 15.03[7][c][ii] n.296
2032A(c)(2)(B) . . . . 4.04[7][c][i] n.322
2032A(c)(2)(C) . . . . 4.04[7][c][ii] ns. 323, 324
2032A(c)(2)(D) . . . . 5.08[5][b][ii] n.233
2032A(c)(2)(D)(i) . . . . 4.04[7][c][i] n.315;
          4.04[7][c][iii] n.327
2032A(c)(2)(D)(ii) . . . . . . 4.04[7][c][iii] n.329
2032A(c)(2)(E) . . . . 4.04[7][b][i] n.276;
          4.04[7][c][v] ns. 335, 340
2032A(c)(2)(E)(ii)(I) . . . . . 4.04[7][c][v] n.336
2032A(c)(2)(E)(ii)(II) . . . 4.04[7][c][v] ns. 337,
          339
2032A(c)(3) . . . . 4.04[7][d] ns. 341, 343;
          5.08[5][c][ii] n.255
2032A(c)(4) . . . . 4.04[7][e] n.344; 5.08[5][d][i]
          n.262
2032A(c)(5) . . . 4.04[6] n.228; 4.04[7][f] n.348;
     5.08[2][b][v] n.52; 5.08[5][b][iii] n.246;
     5.08[5][d][iii] ns. 267, 270; 18.03[1] n.9
2032A(c)(6)(A) . . . . 4.04[7][b][iii] ns. 289, 290
2032A(c)(6)(B) . . . . 2.02[3][c][ii] n.79;
     4.04[7][b][ii] n.297; 5.08[5][b][i] n.225

[Text references are to paragraphs and notes (9"n.");
references to the supplement are preceded by "S."]

IRC §

2032A(c)(6)(B)(i) . . . . . . 5.08[5][b][i] n.222
2032A(c)(7) . . . . 5.08[5][b][i] n.221
2032A(c)(7)(A) . . . . 4.04[7][a] n.257; 4.04[7][f]
n.348; 5.08[5][b] n.218
2032A(c)(7)(A)(i)   4.04[7][b][ii] ns. 292, 301
2032A(c)(7)(A)(ii) . . . . . . 5.08[5][b][i] n.221;
5.08[5][b][iii] n.243
2032A(c)(7)(B) . . . . 4.04[7][b][ii] ns. 303, 304,
309; 5.08[5][b][i] ns. 226, 227, 232
2032A(c)(7)(B)(i) . . . 5.08[5][b][i] ns. 229, 230
2032A(c)(7)(C)(i) . . . . . 4.04[7][b][ii] n.305;
5.08[5][b][i] n.228
2032A(c)(7)(C)(ii) . . . . . 4.04[7][b][ii] n.306;
5.08[5][b][i] n.229
2032A(c)(7)(C)(iii) . . . . 4.04[7][b][ii] n.307;
5.08[5][b][i] n.230
2032A(c)(7)(C)(iv) . . . . 4.04[7][b][ii] n.308;
5.08[5][b][i] n.231
2032A(c)(7)(D) . . . . 4.04[7][b][ii] n.308;
5.08[5][b][i] n.231
2032A(c)(7)(E) . . . . 4.04[3][c][iii] n.143;
4.04[7][b][ii] n.288
2032A(c)(8) . . . . 4.02[7][e][ii] n.360;
4.04[7][b][i] n.272; S4.04[7][b][i] n.272
2032A(d)(1) . . . 4.04[1] n.13; 4.04[6] ns. 214–
216; 5.08[3] n.74; 5.08[3][b] n.89;
5.08[3][b][i] ns. 92, 94–96
2032A(d)(2) . . . . . . 4.04[1] n.14; 4.04[2] n.29;
4.04[6] ns. 223–225; 14.05[2][a] n.21;
15.03[7][b][ii]; 16.02[4][d][ii] n.270;
16.02[4][e] n.292; 18.03[1][a] n.11
2032A(d)(3) . . . 4.04[6] & ns. 233, 239; 5.08[3]
n.74; 5.08[3][b] ns. 89, 90; 5.08[3][b][iii]
n.100
2032A(d)(3)(B) . . . . 4.04[6] n.232
2032A(e)(1) . . . . 4.04[3][b][viii] n.90;
4.04[3][b][ix] n.101; 4.04[7][a] ns. 261,
268; 4.04[7][b][i] n.269; 4.04[7][f]
n.350; 5.08[3][c][ii] n.113; 5.08[5][d][iii]
n.269; 18.03[1] n.4
2032A(e)(2) . . . . S2.01[1][b][ii] n.39;
4.02[7][b][i] n.290; 4.02[7][b][ii] n.305;
4.04[2] n.22; 4.04[3][b][vii] n.87;
4.04[3][b][ix] n.103; 4.04[7][b][i] n.269;
5.08[2][c][ii] ns. 59–61; 5.08[3][c][ii]
ns. 114, 115; 5.08[3][c][iv] n.136;
5.08[3][d] n.149; 5.08[5][b][i] n.223;
9.04[10][a] n.228; 9.04[10][b] n.232
2032A(e)(2)(C) . . . . 5.08[2][c][ii] n.60
2032A(e)(3) . . . . 4.04[3][b][v] n.72;
4.04[3][b][vi] ns. 73, 75, 77–79;
4.04[5][a][iii] n.198
2032A(e)(4) . . . . 4.04[1] n.6; 4.04[3][b][iii] ns.
50–52
2032A(e)(5) . . . 4.02[7][d][i] n.339; 4.04[1] n.7;
4.04[3][b][iii] n.53
2032A(e)(5)(A) . . . . 4.04[3][b][iii] n.54
2032A(e)(5)(B) . . . . . 4.04[3][b][iii] ns. 55, 56
2032A(e)(5)(C)(i) . . . . . . 4.04[3][b][iii] n.57
2032A(e)(5)(C)(ii) . . . . . . 4.04[3][b][iii] n.58

IRC §

2032A(e)(6)   2.02[3][c][ii] n.79; 4.04[3][c][ii]
n.127; 5.08[3][e] ns. 151, 152, 154, 155
2032A(e)(7) . . . 4.04[1] n.1; 4.04[3][b][ii] n.44;
4.04[3][b][iii] n.59; 4.04[5] ns. 167, 168;
4.04[5][b] n.205
2032A(e)(7)(A) . . . . 4.04[5][a] n.178
2032A(e)(7)(A)(i) . . . . 4.04[5][a] n.175;
4.04[5][a][iii] n.198
2032A(e)(7)(A)(ii) . . . . 4.04[5][a] n.176;
4.04[5][a][v] n.200
2032A(e)(7)(B) . . . . 4.04[5][a][i] n.184;
4.04[5][a][ii] n.187
2032A(e)(7)(B)(i) . . . . 4.04[5][a] n.177
2032A(e)(7)(B)(ii) . . . . . . 4.04[5][a][ii] n.188
2032A(e)(7)(C)(i) . . . . 4.04[5][a] n.180;
4.04[5][a][iii] n.196
2032A(e)(7)(C)(ii) . . . 4.04[5] n.169; 4.04[5][a]
n.181; 4.04[5][b] n.205
2032A(e)(8) . . . 4.04[1] n.1; 4.04[3][b][ii] n.44;
4.04[3][b][iii] n.59; 4.04[5] n.167;
4.04[5][b] ns. 204, 205
2032A(e)(8)(A) . . . . 4.04[5][b] n.206
2032A(e)(8)(B) . . . . 4.04[5][b] n.207
2032A(e)(8)(C) . . . . 4.04[5][b] n.208
2032A(e)(8)(D) . . . . 4.04[5][b] n.209
2032A(e)(8)(E) . . . . 4.04[5][b] n.210
2032A(e)(9)(A) . . . . 4.04[3][b][i] n.40;
4.04[3][b][viii] n.88; 5.08[3][c][ii] ns.
108, 110
2032A(e)(9)(B) . . . . 4.04[3][b][viii] n.91;
5.08[3][c][ii] n.111
2032A(e)(9)(C) . . . . 4.04[3][b][viii] n.92;
5.08[3][c][ii] n.112
2032A(e)(10) . . . . . . 4.04[3][d] ns. 149, 150;
4.04[6] n.244; 5.08[3][c][i] n.102
2032A(e)(11) . . . . 4.04[6] n.228; 4.04[7][f] ns.
348, 352–354; 5.08[5][b][iii] n.246;
5.08[5][d][iii] n.267
2032A(e)(12)   4.04[3][c][iii] n.145; 5.08[3][e]
n.161; 5.08[5][b][i] n.226
2032A(e)(13) . . . . 4.04[3][b][vi] n.82;
4.04[5][a][iii]
2032A(e)(13)(A) . . . 4.04[7][b][i]; 4.04[7][c][v]
n.334
2032A(e)(13)(B) . . . . 4.04[3][c] n.108;
4.04[7][c][v] n.333
2032A(e)(13)(C) . . . . 4.04[3][c] n.108
2032A(e)(13)(D) . . . . 4.04[3][c] n.107
2032A(e)(14) . . . . 4.04[3][c][i] n.115; 5.08[3][d]
n.150; 5.08[3][e] n.156
2032A(e)(14)(B) . . . . 4.04[3][c][i] n.119
2032A(e)(14)(C) . . . . 4.04[3][c][i] n.118
2032A(e)(14)(C)(i) . . . . . . 4.04[3][c][i] n.116
2032A(e)(14)(C)(ii) . . . . . 4.04[3][c][i] n.117
2032A(f)(1) . . . . 4.04[7][g] ns. 356, 359;
5.08[5][d][iv] n.273
2032A(f)(2) . . . . 4.04[7][g] n.355
2032A(g) . . . . 4.04[1] n.8; 4.04[3][b][v] ns. 66,
69; 4.04[3][b][viii] n.100; 4.04[5] n.171;
5.08[2][a] n.20; 5.08[2][c][ii] ns. 56, 59,
70; 5.08[3][d] n.150; 5.08[3][f] n.165

*[Text references are to paragraphs and notes (9"n.");
references to the supplement are preceded by "S."]*

IRC §

2032A(h) . . . . . . 4.04[7][b][i] n.274; 4.04[7][g]
   n.358; 5.08[5][b] n.218; 5.08[5][b][ii]
   n.240
2032A(h)(1)(A)(i) . . . . 4.04[7][c][i] n.319
2032A(h)(1)(B) . . . . . 4.04[7][c][i] ns. 320, 321
2032A(h)(2)(A) . . . . . . 4.04[7][a] ns. 258, 259;
   5.08[5][c][iii] n.261
2032A(h)(2)(C)(i)   4.04[7][b][ii] ns. 295, 300
2032A(h)(3) . . . . 4.04[7][h] n.367
2032A(h)(3)(A) . . . . 4.04[7][b][ii] ns. 294, 298
2032A(h)(3)(B) . . . . 4.04[7][a] n.258;
   4.04[7][b][ii] n.299; 4.04[7][c][i] n.317
2032A(i) . . . . . . 4.04[7][b][i] n.274; 4.04[7][g]
   n.357; 5.08[5][b][ii] n.240
2032A(i)(1)(A) . . . . 4.04[7][c][i] n.319
2032A(i)(3) . . . . 4.04[7][c][i] n.318; 4.04[7][h]
   n.368
2033–2046 . . . . 4.01; 4.02; 6.03[1] n.1

IRC §

2033 . . . . . . 2.01 n.6; S2.01[1][a] n.14; 3.03[2]
   n.17; 3.04 n.9; 3.05[1][c]; 3.05[3][b]
   n.35; 3.07; 4.02 n.3; 4.02[2][a] n.16;
   4.02[3][g] n.117; 4.02[3][i]; 4.02[5];
   S4.02[5] n.244; 4.02[7][e][i] n.354;
   4.03[2] n.17; 4.05; 4.05[1] & n.1;
   4.05[2]; 4.05[2][a] & n.5; S4.05[2][a]
   n.6; 4.05[2][b] & n.13; 4.05[3] & ns. 28,
   32; 4.05[4] & ns. 37, 39, 41, 45;
   S4.05[4] n.40; 4.05[5][a] & n.47;
   4.05[5][b] & n.50; 4.05[5][c]; 4.05[6] &
   ns. 67, 70, 76; 4.05[7][a]; 4.05[7][b] &
   n.81; 4.05[8] & ns. 94, 95; 4.06 & ns. 4,
   15; 4.07[2][a][ii] & n.28; 4.08;
   S4.08[4][c] n.49; 4.08[7][c] ns. 133, 135,
   137; 4.09[3] ns. 5, 6; 4.10[10][f]; 4.11
   n.2; S4.11[4][a] n.40; 4.11[5] & n.53;
   4.11[7]; 4.12[1]; 4.12[3] ns. 24, 27;
   4.12[4] n.30; 4.12[9] n.73; 4.12[10] n.94;
   4.13[1] & n.2; 4.13[2][b]; 4.13[3] n.24;
   4.13[5]; 4.13[7][a] n.86; 4.13[7][b];
   4.13[8][a] & n.116; 4.13[10]; 4.14[1] &
   n.2; 4.14[2] & n.20; 4.14[3][b] n.28;
   4.14[3][c]; 4.14[4][d]; 4.14[5][b];
   S4.14[6] ns. 103.10, 103.23, 103.24;
   4.14[7][a] & n.104; 4.14[8]; 4.16 n.22;
   5.03[1] n.14; S5.03[1][a] n.14; 5.03[2][b]
   n.31; S5.03[4][b][i] n.186; 5.03[5][a]
   n.105; 5.06[3][d] n.53; 5.06[7][a] n.161;
   5.06[7][c] n.194; 5.06[8][b][iii] n.252;
   5.06[8][d][i] n.308; 5.06[8][d][ii] &
   n.338; 5.06[9] n.443; 5.07[4][a][ii] n.140;
   5.09[2] n.10; 6.03[1]; 6.05[1] ns. 2, 7;
   S8.04 n.4; 9.02 n.3; 9.04[8] n.194; 10.01
   n.7; 10.01[3]; 10.01[3][h] n.122;
   10.02[1][b] n.18; 10.04[1] n.1;
   10.07[2][b] n.46; 10.08[2] & n.41;
   10.08[3] n.49; 11.03[3][a] n.24;
   11.03[3][b] n.40; 11.03[4][a] n.43;
   11.03[4][c][i]; 13.02[4][b][ii] n.276;
   16.01 n.18; S16.01 n.18; 16.02[2][b][iii]
   n.69; 16.02[4][d][i]; 19.02[1][a] n.7;
   19.02[1][b] n.15; 19.02[5][a][iii] n.335;
   19.02[5][a][iv] n.383; 19.02[5][c][i]
   n.404; 19.02[5][f][i] n.508; 19.03[1] ns.
   9, 18, 19; 19.03[3][b][i] n.133;
   19.03[4][a] n.282; S19.03[3][d][iii];
   19.03[4][c][ii] & ns. 336, 343
2033A . . . . 4.02[7][e][ii] n.388; 5.08[1];
   5.08[4][b] & n.203; 5.08[6][b] n.278;
   5.08[6][c] n.298; 5.08[7] n.304
2034–2042 . . . . 4.17; S8.04 n.4
2034 . . . 4.03[2] n.17; 4.06 & n.4; 4.15[1] n.2;
   4.15[1][a]; 4.15[1][a][ii]; 4.17; 6.03[1];
   8.03[2] n.24; 10.02[5][d] n.168
2035–2037 . . . . 4.13[8][b]

[Text references are to paragraphs and notes (9"n.");
references to the supplement are preceded by "S."]

IRC §

2035–2038 .... S4.07[3][a] n.76; 4.09[1] n.2;
4.10[1]; 4.10[10]; 4.11[7]; 4.13[1];
4.13[6][a]; 4.13[7][b]; 4.13[7][c]; 4.15;
4.15[1][a][ii]; 4.15[1][b][ii]; 6.03[2];
6.04[2]; S6.04[2] n.12.1; 6.07[2] n.22;
S6.07[2][b] n.54; 10.02[1][a] n.9;
13.02[4][b][i] n.265; S6.07[2][b] n.54;
17.02[1][b] n.26; 19.02[1][a] n.8
2035–2041 .... 4.17
2035–2042 .... 3.05[1][c] n.14; 4.03[2] n.18;
8.04[2] n.14
2035–2044 .... 2.01 n.7
2035 ...... 2.01[1][b] n.20; S2.01[1][b] n.18;
2.01[2] n.59; S2.01[2] n.77; 3.02 n.13;
S3.02[1][a] n.18; 4.02[7][b][i] n.292;
4.04[3][b][i] n.40; 4.05[8] n.108; 4.07;
4.07[1] & ns. 1, 6; 4.07[2][a][i] & n.21;
4.07[2][a][ii] & ns. 27, 28, 32, 36, 38;
4.07[2][b][i] & n.42; 4.07[2][b][ii] &
n.52; 4.07[2][c] & ns. 59, 67; 4.07[3][a]
& n.81; 4.07[4]; 4.08[1][a] n.3;
4.08[6][d] n.100; 4.08[8][b] & n.183;
4.09[2] & n.3; 4.09[3] n.6; 4.10[8] &
n.85; 4.10[10][d] n.101; 4.10[10][e] &
n.108; 4.10[10][f]; 4.11[7]; 4.12[3] n.23;
4.12[7][a] n.34; 4.12[9]; 4.13[6][a] n.71;
4.13[7][b] n.88; 4.14[1] n.3; 4.14[5][a]
ns. 84, 87; 4.14[8] n.126; 4.14[9][b] &
ns. 134, 136, 138; S4.14[9][b] n.137;
4.15[1] n.11; 4.15[1][a][ii] n.30;
4.15[1][b][ii] & ns. 59, 61; 4.17;
S5.03[6][c][i] n.281; S5.03[6][c][ii]
n.294; 5.05[2][e] n.91; 5.06[4] n.85;
6.03[1] & n.2; 6.04[2] n.15; 6.05[1] &
n.4; 8.03[2] n.24; 8.10[3][a] n.36;
S8.10[3][a] n.28; 10.01[10][b] n.219;
10.03[2] ns. 27, 30; S11.02[1][b] n.25;
12.01[1] n.3; 13.02[4][d]; 15.02[2] &
n.40; S15.02[2] & n.34; 15.03[2][a] &
n.11; 15.03[3][b]; 16.02[4][b];
16.02[4][c] n.246; 16.02[4][d][i] ns. 258,
261; 16.02[7][a] n.426; 16.02[7][b][i] &
ns. 442, 448, 449; 16.02[7][c][i] & ns.
479, 481; 16.02[7][c][ii]; 16.02[7][c][iii];
16.02[7][e][ii] n.514; 16.02[7][e][iii] &
ns. 523, 551; 18.03[2][d]; 19.02[5][a][iii]
& n.339; 19.02[5][c][v] n.481;
19.02[5][f][i] n.506; 19.03[4][c][ii] ns.
328, 336

IRC §

2035(a) .... 2.01[1][b] n.20; S2.01[1][b] n.20;
2.02[3][c][ii]; 4.02[4][b][ii]; 4.03[2][c]
n.32; 4.03[3][a]; 4.04[3][b][i] n.40;
4.05[6] n.71; 4.07[1] & n.2; 4.07[2];
4.07[2][a]; 4.07[2][a][i]; 4.07[2][a][ii] &
n.38; 4.07[2][b]; 4.07[2][b][i];
S4.07[2][b][i] n.40.1; 4.07[2][b][ii] &
n.53; 4.07[2][c]; 4.07[2][d]; 4.07[4];
4.08[4][b] n.39; 4.08[8][b] & n.181;
4.09[5] & n.46; 4.10[8] ns. 83, 91;
4.10[10][e] n.107; 4.12[9] n.74;
4.14[5][a] n.87; 4.14[6]; S4.14[6];
4.14[9][b] & ns. 134, 137, 138, 142;
S4.14[9][b] n.136; 4.15[1][a][ii];
5.06[3][f] n.64; 6.03[1] n.2; 6.05[1] &
ns. 1, 4; 9.01 n.6; 10.01[10][b];
16.02[7][b][i] n.442
2035(a)(1) ... S4.02[4][g] n.241; 4.07[1] n.10;
4.07[2][a] ns. 16, 20; 4.07[2][a][i];
4.08[4][b] n.39; 4.17 n.1; 10.03[2] ns.
27, 30
2035(a)(2) .... 4.04[3][b][i] n.37; 4.07[1] n.11;
4.07[2][a] ns. 18–20; 4.07[2][a][ii] & ns.
28, 32, 36, 38; 4.07[2][b][ii] n.49;
4.07[2][c]; 4.07[2][d]; 4.08[4][b] n.33;
4.08[6][d] ns. 100, 106; 4.09[3] n.6;
4.10[2] n.9; 4.12[7][a] n.34; 4.12[9]
n.74; 10.03[2] ns. 27, 30; 16.02[7][b][i]
n.449; 18.05[2][b][i] n.13
2035(b) .... S2.01[3] n.84; 2.01[4] n.75;
3.04[2][b] n.26; 4.07[1]; 4.07[2][a][ii]
n.26; 4.07[3]; 4.07[3][a] & ns. 76, 80,
81; S4.07[3][a] ns. 76, 83; 4.07[3][b];
4.12[3] n.28; 4.12[9] n.74; 4.14[9][b]
n.135; 4.17 n.1; S6.04[2] n.12.1;
S8.10[3][a] n.21; 8.04 n.4; 8.07[3] n.26;
8.10[3][a] n.29; S9.06[2] n.71;
10.01[10][b] n.218; 10.02[6][d] n.183;
10.03[2] & n.26; 10.08[3] & n.49;
S10.08[3] n.49; 12.02 n.29; 19.02[1][c]
n.23
2035(c)–2035(e) .... 4.07[1]
2035(c) .... 4.07[3][a]
2035(c)(1) .... 4.07[2][d]
2035(c)(1)(A) .... 4.07[2][d] n.71
2035(c)(1)(B) ..... 4.04[3][b][i] n.37; 4.04[6]
n.244; 4.07[2][d] n.72
2035(c)(1)(C) .... 4.07[2][d] n.73
2035(c)(2) .... 2.02[3][c][ii] n.108; 4.07[2][d]
2035(c)(3) .... 4.07[1] n.10; 4.07[2][d] n.74
2035(d) .... 4.07[1] n.9; 4.07[2][a] n.17;
4.07[2][b][i]; S4.07[2][b][i] n.40.1;
4.07[2][d] n.69; 4.08[1][a] n.3; 14.05[3]
n.37
2035(e) ... 4.07[2][b][ii] & ns. 50, 52; 4.10[2]
n.9; 4.10[8] & ns. 83, 85, 87, 88;
4.10[10][d] n.101; 4.10[10][e] n.108;
6.04[2] n.16; 16.02[2][b][iii] n.79;
16.02[7][c][i] n.485

[Text references are to paragraphs and notes (9"n.");
references to the supplement are preceded by "S."]

IRC §

2036–2038 . . . . . 2.01[1][b] n.20; S2.01[1][b]
n.20; 4.07[2][c] & n.59; 4.10[10][e];
4.14[4][e]; 13.02[4][d]; 16.02[7][b][i];
19.03[2][a][iv] n.71

IRC §

2036   2.01 n.7; 2.02 n.2; 3.04 n.4; 3.05[1][c];
4.02[4][g] n.241; 4.02[7][b][i] n.292;
4.05[1] n.1; 4.05[5][c] n.59; 4.05[6]
n.73; 4.07[2][a]; 4.07[2][a][i] n.21;
4.07[2][a][ii] & n.36; 4.07[2][b][i] n.46;
4.07[2][c] n.60; 4.08; 4.08[1][a] & n.11;
4.08[1][b] & n.13; 4.08[2] & ns. 15, 17;
4.08[4]; 4.08[4][a]; 4.08[4][b] & n.32;
4.08[4][c] & ns. 51, 53; S4.08[4][c] &
n.49; 4.08[5] & n.55; S4.08[5][a] n.56;
4.08[5][c] & n.64; 4.08[6][a] & n.76;
S4.08[6][a] n.76; 4.08[6][c]; 4.08[6][d]
& n.100; 4.08[7] & ns. 114, 117;
4.08[7][a] & n.124; 4.08[7][c] & ns. 137,
138; 4.08[7][d] & n.153; 4.08[8] &
n.171; S4.08[8]; 4.08[8][a] & ns. 173,
177; 4.08[8][b] & ns. 180, 183; 4.08[9];
4.09[1]; 4.09[2]; 4.09[3] ns. 6, 13;
4.09[4][a] & ns. 26, 29; 4.09[5]; 4.10[1];
4.10[3] n.15; 4.10[4][a] n.21; 4.10[4][f]
n.52; 4.10[7] & n.77; 4.10[8] & ns. 81,
82; 4.10[9][b]; 4.10[10][a]; 4.10[10][b];
4.10[10][c]; 4.10[10][d] & n.102;
4.10[10][e]; 4.10[10][f] & n.113;
4.11[2][b] & n.13; 4.11[3][b] & n.23;
4.11[3][c]; 4.11[5]; 4.11[6]; 4.11[7];
4.12[1] ns. 1, 7; 4.12[3] n.23; 4.12[9];
4.13[1] n.3; 4.13[2][a] & n.9; 4.13[4][a]
n.25; 4.13[4][c][i]; 4.13[6][a] & ns. 71,
72; 4.13[7][b] n.88; 4.13[7][c];
4.13[7][e]; 4.13[7][f]; 4.14[1] n.3;
4.14[4][e]; 4.14[9][a] & n.131; 4.14[9][b]
n.146; 4.15[1] ns. 11, 12; 4.15[1][b][ii]
& ns. 59, 61; 4.15[2] n.75; 4.16 n.22;
5.03[4]; 5.05[2][e] & n.91; S5.03[6][c][i]
n.281; S5.03[6][c][ii]; S5.03[6][c][iii] ns.
303, 305; S5.05[2][e] n.91; S5.05[3][a]
n.97; S5.05[5][b][i] n.254; 6.03[1]; 8.02
n.12; 8.03[2] n.24; 8.04; 8.08[1] & n.3;
8.08[2] & ns. 6, 11; S8.08[2] n.7;
8.10[3][a] n.36; S8.10[3][a] n.28
9.04[5][c] n.168; 10.01[5][b] n.166;
10.01[6] n.183; 10.01[10][c] n.223;
10.02[1][a] n.8; 10.02[5][b] n.161;
10.02[6][d] n.183; 10.08[1][a] n.15;
11.03[4][c][i]; S11.03[5] n.105;
13.02[1][b]; 13.02[2][d] & n.80;
13.02[4][d] n.339; 16.02[3][b][ii] n.179;
16.02[4][d][i] n.261; 16.02[4][e] n.288;
16.02[7][b][ii]; 16.02[7][c][i]; 17.02[1][b]
n.40; 17.02[1][c][i] n.48; 17.03[2][a]
n.30; 19.02[1][b] n.14; 19.02[5][f][i]
n.506; 19.03[1] & n.19; 19.03[3][b][i]
n.120; 19.03[3][d] n.163; S19.03[3][d][i]
n.177; 19.03[3][d][iii] n.222;
S19.03[3][d][iii]; 19.03[4][a] n.282;
S19.03[4][a] n.282; 19.03[4][c][i] ns.
319, 321; 19.03[4][c][ii] & n.343;
19.03[4][e][i] & ns. 366, 369;
S19.03[4][e][i] n.367

*[Text references are to paragraphs and notes (9"n.");
references to the supplement are preceded by "S."]*

IRC §

2036(a) . . . 3.04[1][b] n.18; 4.08[1][a] & ns. 3,
10; 4.08[3]; 4.08[4][b] ns. 31, 39;
S4.08[4][c] & n.49; 4.08[6][c];
4.08[6][d]; 4.08[7][c] & ns. 138, 141,
144; 4.08[8] n.166; 4.08[9]; 4.11 n.3;
4.15[1][b][ii] n.61; 5.05[4][b] n.145;
8.08[2] n.5; 10.07[2][b] n.42; 10.08[1][a]
& n.15; 10.08[1][b] n.27; 14.05[3] n.37;
16.02[7][b][i] n.450; 16.02[7][e][iii];
19.02[1][b] & n.14

2036(a)(1) . . . 3.04[2][b] n.27; 3.05[1][d] n.21;
4.02[4][g]; S4.02[4][g] n.241;
4.07[2][a][ii] & n.32; 4.07[2][b][i]; 4.08;
4.08[4] ns. 21, 22; 4.08[4][b] & n.38;
S4.08[4][b] n.28; 4.08[4][c] & ns. 44,
46–50, 52, 53; S4.08[4][c] n.49; 4.08[5];
S4.08[5][c] n.64; 4.08[6][a] ns. 74, 78;
4.08[6][b] & n.82; 4.08[6][c] & n.86;
S4.08[6][c] n.86; 4.08[6][d] & ns. 94,
98; 4.08[7][b]; 4.08[7][c] & ns. 134,
142; S4.08[8]; 4.09[3] n.6; 4.10[4][a]
n.23; 4.10[4][g] n.55; 4.10[10][e] n.107;
4.11[5] n.47; 4.15[1][a][ii]; 4.16;
S5.03[6][c][ii] n.289; 5.06[3][d] n.59;
5.06[5] n.94; 5.06[8][d][ii] n.344;
5.07[2][b] n.26; 8.08[2] ns. 5, 13;
S10.01[10][e]; 10.08[1][a] n.22; 10.08[2]
n.39; 16.02[4][e] n.284; 19.01[1];
19.02[1][b]; 19.03[1] n.6

2036(a)(2) . . . . S4.02[4][g] n.241; 4.08;
4.08[4][b] n.34; 4.08[5]; 4.08[5][a] & ns.
58, 61; 4.08[5][b]; 4.08[5][c] & ns. 64,
65; S4.08[5][c] ns. 64, 69; 4.08[6][a]
n.76; 4.08[6][d] n.94; 4.08[8][b];
4.09[4][a] n.26; 4.10[4][c] n.35;
4.10[4][d] n.46; 4.10[5] ns. 59, 64;
4.10[9][b] & n.100; 4.10[10][d] & ns.
101, 102, 104–106; S5.03[6][c][ii]
n.289; 10.01[10][e] & ns. 228, 230;
19.03[2][a][iv] n.71; 19.03[4][c][ii] n.336

2036(b) . . . 4.08; 4.08[4][a] n.26; 4.08[6][d] &
ns. 92, 108; 4.08[9] n.188; 8.08[2] n.5;
19.02[1][a] n.8; 19.02[1][b] n.14

2036(b)(1) . . . . 4.08[6][d] n.94

2036(b)(2) . . . . 4.08[6][d] n.97

2036(b)(3) . . . . 4.08[6][d] ns. 98, 100, 106

2036(c) . . . 4.08 n.2; 4.08[1][b] n.13; 4.08[4][a]
n.27; 4.08[6][d]; 4.08[9]; 4.09[4][a] n.26;
19.01[1]; 19.01[2]; 19.01[2]; 19.01[3];
19.02[1][b] & ns. 12–14; 19.02[1][c] &
n.22; 19.03[1] n.15

2036(c)(1) . . . . 19.01[1] n.3

2036(c)(4) . . . . . 19.01[1] n.3; 19.02[1][b] n.12

2037 . . . 3.04 n.4; 3.07 n.5; 4.02[7][b][i] n.292;
4.05[1] n.1; 4.05[4] n.37; 4.05[5][c]
n.59; 4.07[2][a]; 4.07[2][a][i] n.21;
4.07[2][a][ii]; 4.07[2][b][i] n.46;
4.07[2][c]; 4.08[8][b] n.183; 4.09;
4.09[1]; 4.09[2]; 4.09[3] & ns. 12, 13,
18; 4.09[4][a] & n.26; 4.09[4][c] & n.32;
4.09[4][e] n.35; 4.09[4][g]; 4.09[5];
4.09[6]; 4.09[7]; 4.10[8] n.83;
4.10[10][a]; 4.10[10][b]; 4.10[10][d] &
n.102; 4.10[10][e]; 4.11[7] & n.68;
4.12[1] ns. 1, 7; 4.12[3] n.23; 4.12[11]
n.96; 4.13[1] n.3; 4.13[6][a] & ns. 71,
72; 4.13[7][b] n.88; 4.14[1] n.3;
4.14[4][b] & n.47; 4.14[4][e]; 4.14[9][a];
4.15[1] n.11; 4.15[1][b][ii] ns. 59, 61;
4.17; S5.03[6][c][i] n.281; S5.03[6][c][ii]
n.294; S5.03[6][c][iii] n.305; 5.05[2][e]
n.91; 6.03[1]; 8.03[2] n.24; 8.08[2] n.6;
8.10[3][a] n.36; S8.10[3][a] n.28
10.01[10][d]; 11.03[4][c][i] & n.82;
16.02[4][d][i] n.261; 16.02[7][b][i];
16.02[7][c][i]; 19.02[5][f][i] n.506;
19.03[1] n.18; 19.03[2][a][ii] n.59;
19.03[4][c][ii] ns. 328, 336

2037(a) . . . . . . 4.09[4]; 4.09[4][c]; 4.17 n.2;
14.05[3] n.37

2037(a)(1) . . . . 4.09[3]

2037(a)(2) . . . . . . 4.09[3] n.18; 4.10[7] n.75

2037(b) . . . . . . 4.05[5][b] n.58; 4.09[3] n.10;
4.09[4][a]; 4.09[4][d]; 4.09[4][e] & n.36;
4.09[4][g] n.44; 4.14[4][b]

2037(b)(2) . . . . 4.07[2][a] n.19; 19.03[4][c][ii]
n.336

*[Text references are to paragraphs and notes (9"n.");
references to the supplement are preceded by "S."]*

IRC §

2038 . . . 3.04 n.4; 3.04[1][b] n.18; 4.02[7][b][i]
n.292; 4.05[4] ns. 37, 40; 4.07[2][a] &
n.19; 4.07[2][a][i] n.21; 4.07[2][a][ii] &
n.38; 4.07[2][b][ii] & ns. 50, 53;
4.07[2][c] & n.60; 4.08[2] n.17;
4.08[4][b] ns. 32, 41; S4.08[4][c] n.49;
4.08[5][c] & n.64; 4.08[6][a] n.80;
4.08[7][d] n.153; 4.08[8][a] n.173;
4.08[8][b] n.183; 4.09[1]; 4.09[2];
4.09[3] n.6; 4.09[4][a] n.26; 4.10;
4.10[1] & n.2; 4.10[2] & n.9; 4.10[3] &
n.15; 4.10[4]; 4.10[4][a] & ns. 21, 24,
25; 4.10[4][b]; S4.10[4][b] n.30;
4.10[4][c] & n.39; S4.10[4][c] n.40;
4.10[4][e]; 4.10[4][f] & n.52; 4.10[4][g]
& ns. 53, 55, 57; 4.10[5] & n.64;
4.10[6] & n.67; 4.10[7]; 4.10[8] & ns.
81, 82, 85; 4.10[9]; 4.10[9][a];
4.10[9][b]; 4.10[10][a]; 4.10[10][b];
4.10[10][d] & ns. 101, 102, 104–106;
4.10[10][e] & n.108; 4.11 n.3; 4.11[7];
4.12[1] n.1; 4.12[3] n.23; 4.13[1] n.3;
4.13[2][a] & ns. 8, 9; 4.13[4][a] ns. 25,
29; 4.13[4][c][i]; 4.13[6][a] & n.71;
4.13[7][a]; 4.13[7][b] n.88; 4.13[8][b]
n.120; 4.14[1] n.3; 4.14[4][e] & n.68;
4.14[9][a]; 4.15[1] n.11; 4.15[1][b][ii] &
ns. 59, 61; 4.15[2] n.72; 4.16 n.22;
S5.03[6][c][i] & n.281; S5.05[3][a] n.97;
6.04[2] n.15; 8.02 n.12; 8.03[2] n.24;
8.07[1] n.7; 8.08[2] n.6; 8.10[3][a] ns.
32, 33; 8.10[3][b][iii] n.75; S8.10[3][a]
ns. 24, 25; 9.04[5][c] n.168; 10.01[5]
n.146; 10.01[5][b] n.166; 10.01[6] n.183;
10.01[7] n.189; 10.01[10][e] & ns. 228,
230; 10.02[1][a] n.8; 10.08[1][b] & n.27;
13.02[4][d] n.339; 15.03[3][b] & n.55;
16.02[4][d][i] n.261; 16.02[7][c][i];
16.02[7][d]; 16.02[7][e][ii]; 18.05[2][b][i]
& ns. 13, 15, 17; 19.02[5][a][iii] n.339;
19.02[5][f][i] n.506; 19.03[1] n.13;
19.03[2][a][iv] n.71; 19.03[4][c][ii] ns.
328, 336

2038(a) . . . 4.07[2][b][ii] n.53; 4.10[7]; 4.10[8]
& n.91; 14.05[3] n.37

2038(a)(1) . . . . 4.07[2][a][ii] n.38; 4.10[2];
4.10[4][e] n.47; 4.10[4][g] n.53; 4.10[6]
n.65; 4.10[7]; 4.10[8]; 4.10[10][e] n.108;
4.14[4][e] n.68; 16.02[7][c][i] n.485;
18.05[2][b][i] n.13

2038(a)(2) . . . . 4.07[2][a][ii] n.38; 4.10[2];
4.10[4][e] n.47; 4.10[6] n.65; 4.10[7];
4.10[8]; 4.10[10][e] n.108

2038(b) . . . . . . 4.10[8]; 4.10[9][a]; 4.10[10][d]
n.102

2038(c) . . . . 4.10[8] n.83

IRC §

2039 . . . . . . S4.02[5] n.244; 4.03[3][b] n.51;
4.05[1] n.1; 4.05[3] n.32; 4.05[4] ns. 37,
40; S4.05[4] n.40; 4.05[6] n.73; 4.05[8]
n.105; 4.07[2][a][ii]; 4.08[8] n.168;
S4.08[8]; 4.11 & n.3; S4.11 n.3; 4.11[1];
4.11[2][a]; 4.11[2][b] & n.13; 4.11[3];
4.11[3][a]; 4.11[3][b] & n.23; 4.11[3][c];
4.11[3][d] & n.34; 4.11[4]; 4.11[4][a];
S4.11[4][a] n.40; 4.11[4][b]; 4.11[5];
4.11[6]; 4.11[7]; 4.12[1] n.1; 4.14[2] &
ns. 5, 20; 4.14[4][e] n.63; 4.14[9][a];
4.17; S5.03[6][c][i] n.281; S5.03[6][c][ii]
n.290; 5.06[3][g] n.69; 5.06[8][d][ii];
6.03[1]; 8.03[2] n.24; 8.08[2] n.6;
8.10[3][a] n.29; S8.10[3][a] n.21;
11.03[4][c][ii] & n.99; 13.02[4][d];
16.02[7][b][i]; 19.03[3][b][i] n.120;
19.03[4][a] n.282

2039(a) . . . . 4.11[1]; 4.11[2]; 4.11[2][a] & n.7;
4.11[2][b]; 4.11[3][a]; 4.11[3][c];
4.11[4]; 4.11[4][b]; 4.11[5] n.49;
S4.11[6] n.60

2039(b) . . . . 4.11[1]; 4.11[3][a]; 4.11[4];
4.11[4][b]

2039(c) . . . 4.05[4] n.37; 4.11[6] ns. 55–57, 60

2039(d) . . . . 4.11[6] n.55

2039(e) . . . . .4.11[6] ns. 55, 56

2039(f) . . . . .4.11[6] ns. 55, 57

2039(g) . . . . 4.11[6] n.58

2040 . . . . 4.02[3][e] n.99; 4.02[4][e][i];
4.03[2][c] n.32; 4.05[1] n.1; 4.05[3] &
n.30; 4.05[5][a] ns. 47, 48; 4.06;
4.07[2][a][ii]; 4.08[8] n.171; 4.08[8][a]
n.177; 4.12; 4.12[1] & n.10; 4.12[2] ns.
16, 21; 4.12[3]; 4.12[4]; 4.12[7][a];
4.12[9]; S4.12[9]; 4.12[11]; 4.14[4][e]
n.63; 4.14[9][a]; 5.03[4][a];
S5.03[6][c][i] n.281; S5.03[6][c][iii]
n.302; 5.06[3][d]; 6.03[1]; 8.03[2] n.24;
8.08[2] n.6; 8.10[3][a] n.35; S8.10[3][a]
n.27; 10.07[2][b] & n.46; 13.02[4][d];
15.03[3][b] n.65; 16.02[7][b][i];
16.02[7][d]; 17.02[1][d]

2040(a) . . . . 4.04[7][a] n.267; 4.08[8][a];
4.11[4][b]; 4.12[1] ns. 6–9; 4.12[3] ns.
24, 27; 4.12[4] & n.30; 4.12[5]; 4.12[6];
4.12[7][a] & n.37; 4.12[7][b]; 4.12[8] &
n.64; 4.12[9] & ns. 71, 74; 4.12[10] &
ns. 87, 88, 94; 4.14[5][a] n.82; S5.03[5]
n.245; S5.03[6][c][ii] n.291; 5.06[9]
n.428; 5.06[10] n.452; 8.10[3][b][iii] &
ns. 73, 74; S8.10[3][a][iii];
S8.10[3][b][iii] ns.63, 64; 10.01[3][f]
n.112; 10.07[2][b] n.52; 11.03[5] n.106;
17.02[2] n.106

[Text references are to paragraphs and notes (9"n.");
references to the supplement are preceded by "S."]

IRC §

2040(b) . . . 4.06 n.12; 4.08[8][a] n.179; 4.12[1]
& ns. 5, 7–9; 4.12[2]; 4.12[5]; 4.12[6];
4.12[7][a]; 4.12[8]; 4.12[9] n.71;
4.12[10] & ns. 82, 84–86; 4.14[4][e]
n.63; S5.03[5] n.245; 5.03[6] n.146;
S5.03[6][c][ii] n.291; 5.06[3][d] ns. 52–
54; 5.06[4] n.86; 5.06[5][b][i] n.104;
5.06[9] & ns. 428, 435; 5.07[1] n.1;
5.07[5] n.180; 8.10[3][b][iii] & n.72;
S8.10[3][a][iii]; 10.07[2][b] n.52;
11.03[4][a] n.43; 11.03[5] n.106
2040(b)(1) . . . . 4.12[10]
2040(b)(2) . . . . 4.12[10]
2040(b)(2)(B) . . . . 4.12[10] n.83
2040(c) . . . . 4.12[8] n.64; 4.12[10] n.82
2040(d) . . . . 4.12[10] n.82
2040(e) . . . . 4.12[10] n.82
2041 . . . . 3.05[1][b]; 3.05[1][c] n.12; 4.04[7][a]
n.265; 4.05[4] ns. 37, 41; S4.05[5][b]
n.57; 4.05[5][c] n.65; 4.05[6] n.76;
4.05[8] ns. 95, 96; 4.07[2][a][ii] & n.28;
4.07[2][c] & n.67; 4.08[8][a]; 4.09[3]
n.12; 4.10[2] n.9; 4.12[1] n.1; 4.13;
4.13[1]; 4.13[2] & n.4; 4.13[2][a] & ns.
8, 9; 4.13[2][b] & ns. 12, 15; 4.13[3];
S4.13[3] ns. 20, 22; 4.13[4][a] & n.25;
S4.13[4][a] n.35; 4.13[4][c][ii] n.42;
4.13[5]; 4.13[6][a]; 4.13[6][d] n.76;
4.13[7][a] ns. 81, 82, 86; S4.13[7][a]
n.78; 4.13[7][b]; 4.13[7][d]; 4.13[8][b];
4.13[9]; 4.13[10]; 4.14[3][c] n.32;
4.14[4][e] & n.64; 4.14[9][a]; 4.15;
4.15[1] n.11; 4.15[1][a][ii]; 4.15[1][b][ii];
4.16 n.22; S5.03[6][c][i] n.281;
5.05[2][d] & n.87; 5.06[3][e]; 5.06[7][c]
n.194; 5.06[8][b][iii]; S5.06[8][b][iii]
n.239; 5.06[8][d][ii] ns. 356, 362;
5.06[8][d][iv] n.401; 6.03[1]; 6.04[2];
6.05[1] n.7; 8.03[2] n.24; 8.06 & n.3;
8.10[3][a] n.37; S8.10[3][a] n.29;
10.04[1] & n.1; 10.04[2][b] n.8;
10.04[3][b] n.15; S10.04[4][c] n.47;
10.07[2][b] n.62; 12.01[1] ns. 3, 11;
13.02[2][e][ii]; 15.02[4] n.60; S15.02[4]
n.54; 16.02[4][d][i] & ns. 260, 261;
16.02[7][b][i]; 16.02[7][c][i];
16.02[7][e][ii] n.514; 17.02[1][b] ns. 31,
40; 18.05[2][b][ii] n.38; 19.03[1] n.13
2041(a) . . . . 13.02[4][b][i] n.271
2041(a)(1) . . . . 4.13[6][d] n.76; 4.13[7][c];
S5.03[6][c][ii] n.292; 13.02[2][e][ii] ns.
93, 95, 107; 13.02[4][b][i] n.265;
16.02[4][d][i] n.261; 17.02[1][b] n.26
2041(a)(1)(A) . . . . 16.02[4][d][i] n.261
2041(a)(1)(B) . . . 4.07[2][a][ii] n.28; 4.13[6][a]
& n.71; 16.02[7][c][i] n.486

IRC §

2041(a)(2) . . . . 4.07[2][a][ii] n.28; S4.13[2][b]
n.14; 4.13[7]; 4.13[7][b] n.88; 4.13[7][c];
4.13[7][d] n.99; 4.13[7][f] n.109;
4.13[8][a] n.117; S5.03[6][c][ii] n.292;
5.06[9] n.443; 5.07[4][a][ii] n.140;
13.02[2][e][ii] ns. 93, 95, 105, 107, 114,
122, 132, 142; 13.02[4][b][i] n.265;
13.03[4][a] n.82; 15.02[4] ns. 60, 66, 75;
S15.02[4] ns. 54, 60, 69; 15.03[4][b][iii];
16.01 n.18; S16.01 n.18; 16.02[2][b][iii]
ns. 68, 69; 16.02[4][d][i] n.261;
16.02[7][b][ii] n.458; 16.02[7][c][i]
n.486; 17.02[1][b] ns. 11, 26, 39, 40
2041(a)(3) . . . . . 4.13[3] n.17; 4.13[8][b] & ns.
122, 123; 13.02[2][e][iii] n.171;
13.02[4][b][i] n.272; 17.02[1][b] ns. 31,
33
2041(a)(3)(B) . . . . 16.02[7][c][i] n.486
2041(b) . . . . . . 4.09[3] n.12; 4.13[1]; 4.13[3];
4.14[4][e] ns. 65, 70; 5.06[8][b][iii];
15.03[4][b][iii] n.144; 17.02[3][b] ns.
128, 133
2041(b)(1) . . . . 4.13[3]; 4.13[8][a] n.118;
13.02[2][b][i] n.47; 13.02[2][e][i] n.88;
13.02[4][b][i] n.271; 16.02[4][d][i] n.260;
17.02[1][b] n.10
2041(b)(1)(A) . . . 4.13[4][a] & n.25; 4.13[8][a]
n.115; 5.06[8][d] n.294
2041(b)(1)(B) . . . . 4.13[4][b]; 4.13[4][c]
2041(b)(1)(C) . . . . 4.13[4][c]; 4.13[4][c][iii] &
n.49; 5.06[8][b][iv] n.261
2041(b)(1)(C)(ii) . . . . 4.13[4][c][ii] n.43;
4.13[4][c][iii] n.49
2041(b)(1)(C)(iii) . . . . . 4.13[4][c][iii] & n.49
2041(b)(2) . . . . . 4.13[7][e] & n.104; 4.13[8][a]
n.116; 13.02[4][b][i] ns. 265, 267, 269;
16.02[7][b][ii] n.457; 17.02[1][b] n.39;
18.05[2][b][ii] n.38
2041(b)(2)(B) . . . . 4.09[6] n.48; 4.13[7][f]
2041(b)(3) . . . . 4.13[5] n.56
2042 . . . . 4.02[3][h] n.140; 4.05[1] n.1; 4.05[6]
& n.67; 4.05[8] n.94; 4.07[2][a];
4.07[2][a][ii]; 4.07[2][c]; 4.10[10][e];
4.11[2][a]; 4.12[1] n.1; 4.14; 4.14[1] &
n.4; 4.14[2] & n.20; 4.14[3][c];
4.14[4][a] n.44; 4.14[4][d]; S4.14[6] &
n.103.24; 4.14[8]; 4.14[9]; 4.14[9][a];
4.14[9][b] & n.138; 4.14[10]; 4.17;
5.03[4][a]; S5.03[5]; S5.03[6][c][i] n.281;
S5.03[6][c][iii] n.302; 5.04[3] n.19;
5.06[3][f]; 6.03[1]; 6.05[1] & n.4;
8.03[2] n.24; 8.10[3][a] n.29; S8.10[3][a]
n.21; 12.03[2] n.27; 16.02[4][d][i];
18.05[2][b][i]
2042(1) . . . . 4.14[3] & n.21; 4.14[3][a];
4.14[3][b]; 4.14[3][c] & n.32; 4.14[4][a]
n.44; S4.14[6]; 4.14[7][b]; 4.14[8];
16.02[4][d][i] n.259

[Text references are to paragraphs and notes (9"n.");
references to the supplement are preceded by "S."]

IRC §

2042(2) . . . . . . 4.14[3][a]; 4.14[3][b]; 4.14[4];
4.14[4][a] & n.35; 4.14[4][a] n.44;
4.14[4][b] & n.46; 4.14[4][e]; 4.14[4][f]
n.78; 4.14[5][a] & ns. 80, 83; 4.14[5][b]
& ns. 92, 93; 4.14[6] n.102; S4.14[6] &
ns. 103.22, 103.23; 4.14[7][b]; 4.14[8];
4.14[9][a]; 4.14[9][b] & n.142;
S5.03[6][c][ii] n.293; 16.02[4][d][i]
n.259; 16.02[7][b][i]; 16.02[7][c][i]
2043 . . . . . 4.08[1][a] n.10; 4.15; S5.03[4][a][i]
n.164; 5.03[5][e]; 10.01[10][b] n.219;
10.06[1] n.1
2043(a) . . . . . . 4.07[2][b][i] & ns. 41, 45, 47;
4.08[1][a] n.11; 4.08[7][c] n.130;
4.08[7][c] ns. 141, 142; 4.08[8] n.170;
4.14[9][b] n.134; 4.15; 4.15[1][a][ii] &
n.35; 4.15[2] & n.70; 14.05[3] n.40
2043(b) . . . . 4.06 n.16; 4.08[4][b] n.41;
4.10[10][d] n.101; 4.12[8] n.64; 4.15;
4.15[1] n.1; 4.15[1][a] ns. 24, 26;
4.15[1][b]; 4.15[1][b][i]; S5.03[4][a][i]
ns. 158, 163; 5.03[5][e] ns. 139, 140;
6.06[1] n.16; 10.06[1] n.7
2043(b)(1) . . . . 4.15[1] & ns. 3, 8, 12;
4.15[1][a]; 4.15[1][a][i]; 4.15[1][a][ii] &
n.32; S5.03[4][a][i] n.162; 10.02[5][d]
n.166
2043(b)(2) . . . . 4.15[1][b][i] & n.46;
4.15[1][b][ii] ns. 52, 59–61;
S5.03[4][a][i] n.164; 5.03[5][e];
10.02[5][d] n.166; 10.06[3] n.33
2044 . . . . 2.02[3][c][ii] n.107; S3.02[1][b] n.22;
4.02[4][b][ii]; 4.03[2] n.18; 4.08[7][c]
n.138; 4.16 & ns. 1, 11, 12, 14, 20;
4.17; S5.03[4][a][iii]; 5.03[5][a];
S5.03[6][c][i] n.281; S5.03[6][c][ii]
n.294; 5.06[5] n.94; 5.06[8][d] & n.301;
5.06[8][d][ii] & ns. 320, 323, 362;
S5.06[8][d][iii] n.384; 5.06[8][e] &
n.415; 5.06[8][f] n.421; 5.06[9] n.443;
5.07[4][a][ii] ns. 140, 150; 6.03[1];
8.04[2] n.14; 8.07[1] & n.7; 8.07[2] &
ns. 8, 9, 12, 15; 8.07[4] & n.31; 8.07[5]
& n.43; 8.10[3][b][iii]; S8.10[3][a][iii];
10.07[2][b] n.59; 10.08[1]; 10.08[1][a]
n.11; 10.08[1][b] n.27; 10.08[2] ns. 39,
41; 10.08[3] n.44; 11.03[4][c][i] & n.71;
11.03[4][c][ii] & ns. 86, 97; 13.02[2][d]
n.84; 13.02[4][b][i]; 13.02[4][b][ii]
n.290; 15.02[4] n.61; S15.02[4] n.55;
15.03[4][b][iii] n.150; 16.02[4][e] & ns.
284, 292; 16.02[7][b][ii] n.472;
17.01[2][a][ii]; 17.02[1][c][i] & n.48;
18.05[2][b][iii]
2044(a) . . . . 4.16; 5.06[8][d][iii] n.384
2044(b)(2) . . . . 4.16 ns. 9, 15; 8.07[1] n.7;
8.07[2] n.8; 10.08[1] n.5; 10.08[1][a]
n.11; 10.08[1][b] n.27; 10.08[2] n.39

IRC §

2044(c) 4.16 n.17
2045 . . . . . . 4.08[1][b] n.13; 4.13[4][d] n.51;
4.13[6] n.58; 4.17 & n.5; 5.05[2][c] ns.
78, 81
2046 . . . 4.03[4][b] n.61; 4.13[7][d] n.94; 4.18;
5.06[1] n.9; 5.06[3][h] & n.82; 5.06[7][e]
n.201; 10.01[2][g] n.67; 10.07[1] n.2;
17.04[3] n.75
2051–2058 . . . . 2.01 n.8; 3.01 n.1; 5.01; 5.02
2051 . . . . . . 2.01; S2.01 & n.6; S2.01[1] n.11;
S3.02 n.4; 3.05[3][c]; 5.02
2052 . . . . 2.01[2] n.62; S2.01[2] n.80; 3.02 n.2;
S3.02 n.1; 3.03[3][b] n.33; 3.05[3][c]
n.52; 4.04[1] n.10; 5.02 n.2
2053–2054 . . . . 6.06[1]
2053–2058 . . . . 5.06[2] n.14
2053 . . . . . . 1.04[4][a][ii]; 2.02[3][b][i] n.39;
2.02[3][c][ii] & ns. 104, 106;
2.02[3][c][iv] n.118; 2.02[3][c][v] &
n.132; 3.03[2] n.17; 3.03[3][c];
3.05[3][c] n.51; 3.05[4][a] & n.57;
4.02[4][e][ii] n.206; 4.03[2][d] n.34;
4.04[3][b][viii] n.100; 4.04[5]; 4.14[3] &
n.24; 4.14[7][b] n.109; 4.15[1] & ns. 8,
12; 4.15[1][a][i]; 4.15[1][a][ii] n.30;
4.15[1][b]; 4.15[1][b][i]; 4.15[1][b][ii] &
ns. 52, 59, 61; 5.02; 5.03; S5.03; 5.03[1]
& n.l; S5.03[1] & n.1; S5.03[1][a];
S5.03[1][b] & n.24; S5.03[1][b][ii] &
n.32; S5.03[1][b][iv] & ns. 52, 54;
S5.03[1][b][iv]; 5.03[3] ns. 35, 38;
S5.03[3] n.80; 5.03[3][a] n.46;
5.03[3][b]; S5.03[3][b]; 5.03[3][c] & ns.
71, 72; S5.03[3][c][i] & ns. 113, 124;
5.03[3][d] & n.78; S5.03[4][a][i] n.166;
S5.03[4][a][ii]; S5.03[4][a][iii];
S5.03[4][b][i]; S5.03[4][b][ii] & n.193;
S5.03[4][c][i]; S5.03[4][c][ii] n.215;
S5.03[4][c][iii]; S5.03[5]; 5.03[5][a];
5.03[5][b]; 5.03[6]; S5.03[6]; S5.03[6][a]
& ns. 273, 277; S5.03[6][c][i];
S5.03[6][c][ii]; 5.05[3][b][ii] & ns. 115,
117, 125, 126; 5.05[2][a]; 5.06[2] n.14;
5.06[5][b][i] & ns. 102–104;
5.06[5][b][ii] & ns. 128, 129;
S5.06[5][b][ii] n.109; 5.06[10];
5.08[4][a][iii] n.183; 5.09[2] n.10; 6.06;
6.06[1]; 7.03[5]; 8.07[2] n.15;
10.02[2][b][i] ns. 30, 41; 10.02[5] n.143;
10.03[2]; 12.02; 14.02[3] ns. 18, 19;
14.03[1]; 14.03[3] & ns. 15, 19;
14.04[3]; 14.05[1] & n.11; 14.05[2][b]
n.27; 17.02[1][b] n.19; 18.05[2][b][iii]
n.49

*[Text references are to paragraphs and notes (9"n.");
references to the supplement are preceded by "S."]*

IRC §

2053(a) . . . . . . 5.03[1] & n.4; S5.03[1] & n.5;
S5.03[1][a]; S5.03[1][b] n.22; 5.03[2][b];
S5.03[2][b]; 5.03[3][a]; S5.03[3][a];
5.03[3][d]; 5.03[4]; S5.03[4]; 5.03[4][a];
5.03[4][b]; 5.03[5]; 5.03[5][b] n.124;
5.03[5][d]; 5.03[5][e]; S5.03[6][c][i];
S5.03[6][c][ii] & n.295; S5.03[6][c][iii]
n.302; S5.03[6][c][iv]; 5.03[7];
5.06[8][d][iv]; 5.08[6][b] n.286
2053(a)(1)–2053(a)(4) . . . . . S5.03[6][c][ii] &
n.297
2053(a)(1) . . . . 5.03[1] & n.3; S5.03[1] & n.4;
5.03[2][a]; S5.03[2][a]; S5.03[2][b] &
n.72; S5.03[4] & n.145; 5.03[5];
5.03[5][b] n.122; 5.03[5][e] & n.135;
S5.03[6][a]; S5.03[6][c][iii] n.302;
5.08[3][b][i] n.94; 5.08[4][a][iii] & n.180
2053(a)(2) . . . . 2.02[3][b][i] n.39; 2.02[3][c][v]
n.131; 5.03[1] n.3; S5.03[1] n.4; 5.03[3]
& n.38; S5.03[3] & ns. 74, 83;
5.03[3][c] n.652; S5.03[3][c] n.109;
S5.03[4] & n.145; S5.03[4][c][ii];
5.03[5]; 5.03[5][b] n.122; S5.03[6][a];
S5.03[6][c][iii] & ns. 301, 302;
5.08[3][b][i] n.94; 5.08[4][a][iii] &
n.181; 8.08[2] n.11; 14.03[3] n.16
2053(a)(3)   4.15[1] n.3; 5.03[1] n.3; S5.03[1]
ns. 3, 4; 5.03[3][c]; S5.03[3][c] n.109;
S5.03[3][c][i] n.111; S5.03[3][c][iii];
S5.03[4]; S5.03[4][a] n.150;
S5.03[4][a][i] n.154; S5.03[4][b][i] &
n.186; S5.03[4][c][i] & n.203;
S5.03[4][c][ii]; 5.03[5]; 5.03[5][a] &
n.105; 5.03[5][c] ns. 131, 132; 5.03[5][e]
n.135; S5.03[6][a] & ns. 268–270;
S5.03[6][b]; S5.03[6][c][ii] ns. 298, 299;
S5.03[6][c][iii] n.302; 5.08[3][b][i] n.94;
5.08[3][c][iii] & n.126; 5.08[3][c][v];
5.08[4][a][iii] & n.183; 5.08[6][b] n.286;
10.02[2][b][i] n.35; 14.03[3] n.18
2053(a)(4) . . . 4.02[7][d][i] n.332; 4.04[3][b][i]
& n.35; S4.14[6] & ns. 103.16, 103.23;
5.03[1] n.3; S5.03[1] n.4; 5.03[3][c];
S5.03[3][c][i] n.111; S5.03[3][c][iii];
S5.03[4] n.144; 5.03[4][a];
S5.03[4][b][i]; S5.03[5] & ns. 252, 256,
259; 5.03[5][a]; 5.03[5][b] n.128; 5.03[6]
& n.151; S5.03[6][a]; S5.03[6][c][iii]
n.302; 5.07[3][c] n.53; 5.08[3][b][i] n.94;
5.08[3][c][iii] & n.127; 5.08[3][c][v];
5.08[4][a][iii] & n.183; 5.08[6][b] n.286;
6.06[1] n.9; 14.03[3] n.17

IRC §

2053(b) . . . . . 5.03[1] & ns. 3, 4; S5.03[1] n.5;
S5.03[1][b] n.22; S5.03[3] n.74;
S5.03[3][b] n.106; 5.03[4]; 5.03[4][a];
5.03[4][b]; S5.03[6][c][ii]; S5.03[6][c][iii]
& ns. 285, 286, 300; S5.03[6][c][iii] &
ns. 302, 305; S5.03[6][c][iv] ns. 311,
316; 5.03[7] n.156; 5.08[4][a][iii] ns.
180, 181
2053(c) . . . . 5.03[1] n.4
2053(c)(1)   S4.15[1][b][i] n.49; S5.03[4][a][i]
& n.154; 5.06[8][d][iv] n.397
2053(c)(1)(A) . . . . .4.06 n.16; 4.15[1] n.3;
4.15[1][b][i] ns. 37, 43; S4.14[6] ns.
103.12, 103.14; S5.03[4][a][i] & ns. 153,
159; S5.03[5] n.256; 5.03[5][e] n.143;
6.06[1] ns. 16, 17; 10.02[1][b] n.18;
10.02[2][b][i] n.33; 10.06[3] n.32
2053(c)(1)(B) . . . . . . 5.03[1] n.5; S5.03[1] n.6;
S5.03[4][b][i]; S5.03[4][b][ii]; 5.03[5][a]
& n.103; 5.03[8]; 5.05[3][b][i] n.104
2053(c)(1)(C) . . . . S5.03[4][a][iii] n.170
2053(c)(1)(D) . . . . . 2.02[3][c][v] ns. 130, 132;
5.03[3][c] n.72; S5.03[3][c][i] ns. 114,
124
2053(c)(2) . . . . S5.03[1] n.5; 5.03[2][b];
S5.03[2][b]; 5.03[3][d]; 5.03[4] n.84;
S5.03[4] n.145; S5.03[6][c][ii];
S5.03[6][c][ii] & ns. 285–287, 295, 300;
S5.03[6][c][iii] n.302; S5.03[6][c][iv] &
ns. 312, 313, 316; 5.03[7] & ns. 156,
158
2053(c)(3) . . . S5.03[4][a] n.146; S5.03[4][b][i]
n.192
2053(d) . . . . 3.03[1] n.14; 3.03[3][c] & ns. 36,
37; 3.06[3][b] n.21; 3.06[3][c] n.23;
5.03[1] n.5; S5.03[1] n.6; S5.03[4][b][i]
n.181; S5.03[4][b][ii] & n.193;
5.03[5][a]; 5.03[8]; 5.09[3] n.37
2053(d)(1) . . . . S5.03[4][b][ii]
2053(d)(2) . . . . S5.03[4][b][ii]; 5.03[8]
2053(e) . . . 4.15[1][b][i] n.47; S5.03[4][a][i] &
n.164; 5.03[5][e]; 10.06[3] n.33
2054 . . . . 2.02[3][c][ii] & ns. 104, 106;
2.02[3][c][iv] n.118; 3.05[4][a] & n.58;
4.03[4][a]; 4.04[5] n.174; 5.02;
5.03[3][d]; S5.03[6][a]; S5.03[6][c][ii];
S5.03[6][c][iv]; 5.03[7]; 5.04 & n.2;
5.04[1]; 5.04[2]; 5.04[3]; 5.06[2] n.14;
5.06[10]; 5.08[3][b][i] n.94;
5.08[4][a][iii] & n.182; 6.06; 6.06[1];
7.03[5]; 14.02[3] ns. 18, 19; 14.03[3];
14.05[2][b] n.27; 17.02[1][b] n.19

[Text references are to paragraphs and notes (9"n.");
references to the supplement are preceded by "S."]

IRC §

2055 . . . . 2.02[3][c][iv] n.118; 3.06[3][b] n.21;
    3.06[3][c]; 4.02[7][a]; 4.02[7][d][i] & ns.
    325–327; 4.03[4][b] & n.59; 4.04[5]
    n.174; 4.16; 5.02; S5.03[1][b] n.18;
    S5.03[1][b][ii] n.39; 5.03[3][c] n.71;
    S5.03[3][c][i] n.113; S5.03[4][a][i] &
    n.166; S5.03[4][b][ii]; 5.03[5][e] &
    n.145; 5.03[8]; 5.05; S5.05; 5.05[1][a]
    ns. 11, 16; 5.05[1][b] & n.22; 5.05[1][c];
    5.05[2][a] & n.63; S5.05[2][a] n.58;
    5.05[2][e] & ns. 90, 91; 5.05[3][b][i]
    n.106; 5.05[3][b][ii]; 5.05[4]; 5.05[4][a];
    5.05[4][b]; 5.05[5][a] n.159; 5.05[5][a][i]
    n.161; 5.05[5][c][ii]; 5.05[6] n.295;
    5.06[2] n.14; 5.06[5] n.91; 5.06[8][e] &
    ns. 405, 414; S5.06[8][e] n.413;
    5.07[4][a][ii]; 5.07[4][a][ii] n.150;
    5.08[3][b][i] n.94; 5.08[4][a][ii];
    5.08[4][a][iii] & n.183; 6.06; 6.06[2]
    n.20; S6.07[1][a] n.19; 8.05[4] n.15;
    8.08[2] n.13; 10.02[2][b][iii] n.57; 11.02
    & ns. 1, 5; 11.02[1][a] & ns. 10, 15;
    11.02[2][a]; 13.02[2][b][i]; 13.03[3][a]
    n.41; 16.02[1]; 16.02[2][c][i] & n.137;
    16.02[3][b][ii] n.183; 16.02[5][b][i] &
    ns. 316, 319; 16.02[5][b][ii] ns. 327,
    328; 16.02[5][c] ns. 359, 360; 16.02[6]
    n.399; 17.02[1][b] n.19; 17.02[3][c] ns.
                                      145–147
2055(a) . . . . . . 4.02[7][b][ii] & ns. 314, 315;
    4.02[7][d][i] n.325; 4.03[4][b] n.61;
    5.03[5][b] n.122; 5.05[1][a]; 5.05[1][b]
    & n.22; S5.05[1][c]; 5.05[2] & n.57;
    5.05[2][c] n.77; 5.05[2][e]; 5.05[3][b][i]
    n.106; 5.05[4][b] ns. 134, 143;
    5.05[5][a][i] n.196; 5.05[5][b][i] n.251;
    5.05[5][c][i] n.271; 5.05[8][a];
    5.05[8][b]; 6.06[2] n.24; 11.02[1][a];
    13.02[2][b][i] ns. 35, 38; 13.03[3][a] &
    n.44; 16.02[6] n.398; 17.02[3][a];
                                      17.02[3][c]
2055(a)(1)   5.05[1][a] n.12; 5.05[1][b] ns. 19,
                                       28, 36
2055(a)(2) . . . 5.05[1][a] n.18; 5.05[1][b] & ns.
                               21, 22, 26, 29, 34, 41
2055(a)(3) . . . 5.05[1][a] n.18; 5.05[1][b] & ns.
    39, 41; S5.05[1][c]; 11.02[1][a] n.17
2055(a)(4) . . . . S5.05[1][c]; 6.06[2]
2055(a)(5) . . . . 5.05[1][b] & n.42
2055(b) . . . . 5.05[2][d]; 6.06[2] n.23; 10.07[1]
                                           n.9
2055(b)(2) . . . . 5.05[2][d] n.89
2055(c) . . . . 5.05[3][b][i] & ns. 105, 106;
    5.08[4][a][ii] n.177; 6.06[2] n.25
2055(d) . . . 5.05[2][a] n.60; 5.05[2][e]; 6.06[2]
                          n.27; 19.04[2] n.29
2055(e) . . . . 4.03[4][b] n.60; S5.03[4][a][i]
    n.166; 5.03[5][e] n.145; 5.06[8][e] &
                          n.407; 6.06[2] n.26
2055(e)(1) . . . . . . 5.05[1][c] & ns. 53, 55, 56;
                              11.02[1][a] n.23

2055(e)(2) . . . . S5.05[2][b] n.68; 5.05[4];
    5.05[4][b] ns. 135, 146, 147, 150;
    5.05[6][a][ii] n.322; 5.05[7] n.329;
    5.05[7][a] n.333; 5.05[7][b] n.339;
    S5.05[7][b] n.337.1; 5.05[7][c] n.342;
    5.05[7][e]; 5.05[8][a]; 5.05[8][b] &
    n.371; 16.02[3][b][ii] n.184;
                   16.02[5][b][i] n.316
2055(e)(2)(A) . . . . 5.05[4][b] n.148; 5.05[5] ns.
    151, 154; 5.05[5][c] n.269; 5.05[6][a]
    n.299; 5.05[7] n.329; 8.08[2] n.13
2055(e)(2)(B) . . . . . . 5.05[4][b] n.149; 5.05[6]
    n.295; 5.05[6][a] ns. 296, 297;
    5.05[6][a][i] ns. 306, 311; 5.05[6][a][ii]
    n.320; 5.05[7] n.329; 16.02[3][b][ii]
             n.193; 16.02[6] n.400
2055(e)(3)   5.05[2][b] n.71; 5.05[4][a] n.128;
    5.05[4][b] n.134; 5.05[5] n.156;
    5.05[6][a] n.303; 5.05[8][a] & ns. 355,
    356; 5.05[8][b]; 5.05[8][d]; 11.02[2][e]
         & n.103; S11.02[2][e] n.103
2055(e)(3)(A) . . . . 5.05[8][a] n.356
2055(e)(3)(B) . . . . 5.05[8][b] n.366; 5.05[8][c]
    ns. 372, 375; 5.05[8][d] n.385
2055(e)(3)(B)(i) . . . . 5.05[8][c] n.374
2055(e)(3)(B)(ii)(I) . . . 5.05[8][c] ns. 374, 376
2055(e)(3)(B)(iii) . . . . 5.05[8][c] n.377
2055(e)(3)(C) . . . . 5.05[8][a] n.358
2055(e)(3)(C)(i) . . . . 5.05[8][b] ns. 361, 363
2055(e)(3)(C)(ii) . . . . 5.05[8][b] n.363;
                              S5.05[8][b] n.363
2055(e)(3)(C)(iii) . . . . . 5.05[8][b] ns. 363, 366,
    367; S5.05[8][b] n.367; 5.05[8][d] n.386;
                              S5.05[8][d] n.386
2055(e)(3)(C)(iv) . . . . 5.05[8][b] n.363
2055(e)(3)(D) . . . . 5.05[8][a] n.359; 5.05[8][b]
                                           n.371
2055(e)(3)(E) . . . . . 5.05[2][b] n.76; 5.05[8][b]
    n.370; 5.05[8][c] ns. 374, 380
2055(e)(3)(F) . . 5.05[2][c] n.82; 5.05[8][d] ns.
                                       381, 382
2055(e)(3)(G) . . . . 5.05[8][d] n.387
2055(e)(3)(H) . . . . 5.05[8][d] n.388
2055(e)(3)(I) . . . . 5.05[8][d] n.388
2055(e)(3)(J) . . . . 5.05[5][a][i] n.204;
    5.05[5][b][i] n.260; 5.05[8][d] n.384
2055(e)(3)(J)(i) . . . . 5.05[8][d] n.384
2055(e)(3)(J)(ii) . . . . 5.05[8][d] ns. 385, 386
2055(e)(4) . . . . 5.05[7][d] & n.349; 11.02[2][d]
                                           n.101
2055(e)(4)(A) . . . . 5.05[7][d] ns. 350, 351
2055(e)(4)(C) . . . . 5.05[7][d] ns. 350, 351
2055(e)(4)(D) . . . . 5.05[7][d] n.350
2055(e)(5)(A) . . . . S5.05[1][c] n.56.2
2055(e)(5)(B) . . . . S5.05[1][c] n.56.3
2055(f)   4.02[7][d][i] ns. 325, 326; 5.05[7][c]
    n.348; 19.04[2] & ns. 29, 31, 32
2055(g) . . . 5.05[1][b] n.20; S5.05[7][b] n.341.4
2055(g)(1) . . . . S5.05[7][b] n.341.4
2055(g)(2) . . . . S5.05[7][b] n.341.3

[Text references are to paragraphs and notes (9"n.");
references to the supplement are preceded by "S."]

IRC §

2056 . . . . . . 2.02[3][c][iv] n.118; S3.02[1][b][i]
n.37; 3.04[2][b] & ns. 31, 33; 3.05[3][b]
n.35; 3.06[3][b] n.21; 3.06[3][c];
4.02[7][e][ii]; 4.03[4][b] & n.59; 4.05[4]
n.40; 4.05[5][a] n.47; 4.05[8] n.94; 4.06
& n.15; 4.08[7][c] ns. 137, 138; 4.12[10]
n.84; 4.15[1] & ns. 8, 9, 12;
4.15[1][a][i]; 4.16; 5.02; 5.03[3][c] n.71;
S5.03[3][c][i] n.113; 5.03[5][b] n.122;
5.05[2][b] n.68; 5.05[4][b] n.138; 5.06;
5.06[1]; 5.06[2] n.14; 5.06[3] & n.17;
5.06[3][b] n.37; 5.06[5] n.94; 5.06[7][a];
5.06[7][c] n.194; 5.06[8][d][iii] n.389;
5.06[8][d][iv]; 5.06[8][e]; 5.06[8][f];
5.06[9]; 5.06[10]; 5.07[2][b] n.18;
5.07[3][e]; 5.07[4][a][i] n.135;
5.07[4][a][ii]; 5.08[1] n.11; 5.08[4][a]
n.172; 5.08[4][a][i] & n.174;
5.08[4][a][ii]; 5.08[4][a][iii]; 6.06;
6.06[3] & n.35; S6.07[1][a] n.20;
7.01[3][a]; 7.03[5] n.130; 8.05[2]; 8.06;
8.08[2] n.13; S8.10[3][a][ii]; 10.03[1]
n.10; 10.08[1] n.3; 10.08[1][a]; 11.03[1]
n.1; 11.03[3] n.20; 11.03[3][b] n.40;
11.03[4][b]; 11.03[4][d] n.103;
17.02[1][b] n.19; 17.02[1][c][i] n.42;
19.02[5][a][iii] & n.357
2056(a) . . . . 4.02[7][e][ii] ns. 376, 379;
4.03[4][b]; 4.15[1][b] n.36; 5.03[5][b]
n.122; 5.06[2] n.13; 5.06[3][e] n.61;
5.06[4]; 5.06[5][b][ii] n.117;
5.06[8][d][i]; 5.07[3][e] n.122;
5.07[4][a][ii] n.149; 7.03[8] ns. 230, 232
2056(b) . . . 4.15[1] n.11; 5.06[8][d][ii] ns. 353,
356
2056(b)(1) . . . . . 4.03[4][b] n.63; 4.15[1] n.12;
5.06[7][a]; 5.06[7][b] & n.165; 5.06[7][c]
n.194; 5.06[8][d] n.295; 5.06[8][e] n.406;
5.07[1] n.6; 8.05[2] n.6; 8.10[3][b][ii]
n.57; S8.10[3][b][ii] n.48; 11.03[3][a]
n.21
2056(b)(1)(A) . . . 5.06[3][a] n.24; 5.06[7][c] &
n.194; 5.06[8][d][i] n.310; 8.10[3][b][ii]
n.57; S8.10[3][b][ii] n.48; 11.03[3][b]
n.39
2056(b)(1)(C) . . . . 5.06[7][d]
2056(b)(2) . . . . 5.06[7][e]
2056(b)(3) . . . . 5.06[8][a]; 5.06[8][b][iv] n.262;
5.06[8][f] & n.420; 8.10[3][b][ii] & n.58;
S8.10[3][b][ii] n.49
2056(b)(3)(B) . . . . 5.07[4][a][i] n.132
2056(b)(4) . . . . 5.06[5]
2056(b)(4)(A) . . . . 5.06[5][a] & n.95;
5.08[4][a][ii] n.178
2056(b)(4)(B) . . . . . 5.06[5][b]; 5.06[5][b][i] &
n.105; 5.06[5][b][ii] n.109;
5.06[5][b][iii]; 10.02[2][b][i] ns. 32, 36

IRC §

2056(b)(5)   S4.13[7][a] n.78; 5.06[3][e] n.63;
5.06[5] n.94; 5.06[7][c] n.194; 5.06[8][b]
& n.206; 5.06[8][b][i] & ns. 224, 230,
232, 234; 5.06[8][b][iii] & ns. 241, 242;
S5.06[8][b][iii] ns. 239, 241;
5.06[8][b][iv] & n.260; 5.06[8][b][v];
5.06[8][c]; 5.06[8][d][ii] & ns. 344, 356;
5.06[8][d][iv] & n.400; 5.06[8][f] & ns.
420, 422; 5.07[2][b] n.18; 5.07[3][b]
n.46; 5.07[3][e]; 5.07[4][a][i] n.135;
5.07[4][a][ii] ns. 149, 150; 8.10[3][b][ii]
n.59; 8.10[3][b][iii]; S8.10[3][b][ii] ns.
50, 56; 11.03[4][b]; 16.02[2][b][iii] n.63;
19.02[5][a][iii] n.357
2056(b)(6) . . . 4.03[4][b] n.63; 5.06[3][e] n.63;
5.06[8][b][i] ns. 223, 231; 5.06[8][c] &
n.277; 5.06[8][d][ii] n.344; 5.06[8][f];
5.07[3][b] n.47; 5.07[3][e] n.126;
8.10[3][b][ii] n.59; S8.10[3][b][ii] n.50;
19.02[5][a][iii] n.357
2056(b)(7)   3.05[3][b] n.46; 4.08[7][c] n.138;
4.15[1] n.12; 4.16 & ns. 2, 11;
S5.03[4][a][iii] n.171; 5.05[4][b] n.148;
5.06[1]; 5.06[3][g] n.69; 5.06[5] n.94;
5.06[7][d]; 5.06[8][b] ns. 206, 208;
5.06[8][b][i] ns. 223, 232, 234;
5.06[8][b][iii] n.246; 5.06[8][c] n.278;
5.06[8][d] & n.296; 5.06[8][d][ii] & ns.
325, 344, 353, 354, 356; S5.06[8][d][ii]
n.328; 5.06[8][d][iii] & ns. 372, 383,
384; 5.06[8][d][iv]; 5.06[8][e] & ns. 410,
413, 414; 5.06[8][f] & ns. 421, 422;
5.07[2][b] n.18; 5.07[3][b] n.46;
5.07[3][d]; 5.07[3][e]; 5.07[4][a][ii] &
n.150; 8.07[1] n.1; 8.10[3][b][ii] & n.65;
S8.10[3][b][ii] n.56; 10.07[2][b] n.58;
10.08[1] & ns. 2, 3; 10.08[1][a];
11.03[4][d] n.103; 13.02[2][d] & n.81;
13.02[4][b][ii]; 17.02[1][c][i] n.43;
18.05[2][b][i] n.24; 19.02[2][a][i] n.45;
19.02[5][a][iii]; 19.03[2][a][iv] n.65
2056(b)(7)(A)(i) . . . . 5.06[8][d] n.298
2056(b)(7)(A)(ii) . . . . 5.06[8][d] n.297
2056(b)(7)(B)(i)(I) . . . . 5.06[8][d] n.303;
5.06[8][d][i] ns. 307, 309; 5.06[8][d][ii]
n.347
2056(b)(7)(B)(i)(II) . . . . . . 5.06[8][d] n.304;
S8.10[3][b][ii] ns. 55, 56
2056(b)(7)(B)(i)(III) . . . . . . 5.06[8][d] n.305;
5.06[8][d][ii] n.347; 5.06[8][d][iii] n.364;
8.10[3][b][ii] n.62; 17.02[1][c][i] n.50
2056(b)(7)(B)(ii) . . . . 4.08[7][c] n.138; 4.16 ns.
5, 8; 5.06[8][b] n.208; 5.06[8][d][ii] ns.
337, 341, 342, 344, 359; 8.07[1] n.4;
8.10[3][b][ii] n.64; 10.08[1] n.3;
11.03[4][c] n.58; 11.03[4][c][i] n.68;
11.03[4][c][ii] n.84
2056(b)(7)(B)(ii)(I) . . . . 5.06[8][d][ii] ns. 311,
325, 328, 336, 344; 5.06[8][f] n.420;
11.03[4][c] ns. 62, 63; 19.03[4][a] n.265

*[Text references are to paragraphs and notes (9"n.");
references to the supplement are preceded by "S."]*

IRC §

2056(b)(7)(B)(ii)(II) . . . . . 5.06[8][d][ii] n.312;
   5.06[8][d][ii] ns. 353, 355; 8.10[3][b][ii]
   n.65; 11.03[4][c] n.64
2056(b)(7)(B)(iii) . . . . 8.10[3][b][ii] n.65;
   S8.10[3][b][ii] ns. 55, 56
2056(b)(7)(B)(iv) . . . 5.06[8][d][ii] ns. 327, 344;
   5.06[8][d][iii] ns. 369, 372; 8.10[3][b][ii]
   n.65; S8.10[3][b][ii] ns. 55, 56;
   11.03[4][c] n.62
2056(b)(7)(B)(v) . . . 5.06[8][d][iii] ns. 367, 384
2056(b)(7)(C) . . . 4.05[4] n.40; 5.06[3][g] n.69;
   5.06[8][d][ii] & ns. 337–339, 341, 344;
   5.07[3][e]; 11.03[4][c][ii] ns. 91, 97
2056(b)(7)(C)(i) . . . . 5.06[8][d][ii] n.340
2056(b)(7)(C)(ii) . . . . 5.06[8][d][ii] n.341;
   11.03[4][c][ii] n.92
2056(b)(8) . . . . 5.05[4][b] n.148; 5.06[8][d][ii]
   n.335; 5.06[8][e] & ns. 409, 410, 417;
   S5.06[8][e] n.413; 5.07[2][b] n.18;
   5.07[3][e]; 5.07[4][a][ii]; 11.03[4][d]
   n.103; 19.02[5][a][iii] n.353
2056(b)(8)(A) . . . . 5.06[8][e] n.410
2056(b)(8)(B)(i) . . . . 5.06[8][e] n.410
2056(b)(8)(B)(ii) . . . . 5.06[8][e] n.410
2056(b)(9) . . . . . 4.15[1] n.8; 5.05[3][b][ii] ns.
   114, 117; 5.05[4][b] n.148; 5.06[2] n.14;
   5.06[5][b][i] n.104; 5.06[5][b][ii] ns. 110,
   120; 5.06[8][e] n.414; 5.06[8][f] n.424;
   5.08[4][a][i] n.174; 5.08[4][a][iii] &
   n.179; 5.09[3] n.39
2056(b)(10) . . . . 5.06[8][b][i] & n.232;
   5.06[8][b][iii] n.256; 5.06[8][c] n.282;
   5.06[8][d][ii] ns. 326, 344; 5.06[8][d][iii]
   ns. 368, 371, 373; 10.08[1][a] n.20;
   11.03[4][c] n.61
2056(c) . . . . . 5.06[3]; 5.06[3][c]; 5.06[3][g] &
   n.69; 5.06[3][h]; 5.06[6][b]; 5.06[8][d][i]
2056(c)(1) . . . . 5.06[3][a] n.24; 5.06[3][d]
2056(c)(2) . . . . 5.06[3][a] & n.24
2056(c)(3) . . . . . 4.06 n.9; 5.06[3][b] & n.36;
   5.06[7][b]
2056(c)(4) . . . . 5.06[3] n.23; 5.06[3][c]
2056(c)(5) . . . . . . 5.06[3][d] & n.53; 5.06[4]
2056(c)(6) . . . . 5.06[3][e]
2056(c)(7) . . . . 5.06[3][f]
2056(d) . . . . 5.06[1] n.4; 5.07[2]; 5.06[9] & ns.
   426, 427; 5.07[4][b] n.157; 5.07[5];
   6.06[3]; 7.03[4] n.100; 7.03[8] ns. 230,
   232, 233; 7.06; 17.04[3] n.76
2056(d)(1)(A) . . . . . 4.12[10] n.94; 5.06[9] &
   n.427; 5.07[1] n.1; 5.07[2][b] n.15;
   5.07[2][c]; 5.07[4][a] n.127; 6.06[3]
   n.32; 11.03[5] n.105
2056(d)(1)(B)   4.12[10] ns. 87, 88; 5.06[3][d]
   n.52; 5.06[4] n.86; 5.06[9] n.428; 5.07[1]
   n.1; 6.03[1] n.3; 10.01[3][f] n.112;
   11.03[5] n.106
2056(d)(2)   4.12[10] n.93; 5.06[3] ns. 21, 22;
   5.07[1] n.1; 10.01[3][f] n.112; 10.07[1]
   n.4; 11.03[5] n.105

2056(d)(2)(A) . . . 4.12[10] n.94; 5.06[9] n.435;
   5.07[1] n.5; 5.07[2] n.8; 5.07[3][e]
   n.122; 6.06[3] n.34
2056(d)(2)(B) . . . 5.07[2][b] n.17; 6.06[3] n.34;
   S11.03[5] n.105
2056(d)(2)(B)(i) . . . . . . 5.07[2][b] ns. 20, 21
2056(d)(3) . . . . 3.05 n.1; 4.12[10] n.94; 5.06[9]
   ns. 442, 444–446; 5.07[1] n.1;
   5.07[4][a][ii] n.139; 11.03[5] n.105
2056(d)(3)(B) . . . . 5.06[9] n.441
2056(d)(3)(C) . . . . 5.06[9] n.443
2056(d)(4) . . . . . . 4.12[10] n.89; 5.06[3] n.21;
   5.07[1] n.1; 5.07[5] n.180; 6.06[3] n.33
2056(d)(4)(A) . . . . 5.06[9] n.431
2056(d)(4)(B) . . . . 5.06[9] n.433
2056(d)(5) . . . . 5.07[1] n.1
2056(d)(5)(A) . . . . 5.07[2][a] n.9
2056(d)(5)(A)(i) . . . . 5.07[2][a] n.11
2056(d)(5)(A)(ii) . . . . 5.07[2][a] n.12
2056(d)(5)(B) . . . . 5.07[2][a] n.13
2056A . . . . . 4.12[10] n.94; 5.06[1] n.4; 5.06[3]
   n.21; 5.06[9] & ns. 426, 444; 5.07;
   5.07[1] n.7; 5.07[2][c] n.33; S5.07[2][c]
   n.33; 5.07[3][c][i]; 5.07[4][a][i] & n.132;
   5.07[4][a][ii] & n.150; 5.07[4][a][iii]
   n.154; 5.07[4][b] & ns. 157, 160, 162;
   5.07[4][c] n.177; 5.07[5] n.181;
   5.08[2][b][v] n.50; 5.08[5][b][iii] n.246;
   6.06[3] & ns. 34, 35; 7.03[4] n.100;
   7.03[5] n.130; 7.03[8] ns. 230, 232;
   11.03[5] n.105; 19.03[3][c] n.154
2056A(a) . . . 5.06[9] n.439; 5.07[1] n.3; 5.07[3]
   n.37; 5.07[3][e] n.122; 6.06[3] n.35
2056A(a)(1)(A) . . . . 5.07[3][a] n.44
2056A(a)(1)(B) . . . . 5.07[3][b] n.46
2056A(a)(2) . . . . 5.07[3][c] n.49
2056A(a)(3) . . . . 5.07[3][d] n.117
2056A(b) . . . . 5.07[1] ns. 6, 7; 5.07[3][c] n.49;
   5.07[3][c][i]; 6.06[3] n.36
2056A(b)(1) . . . 5.07[4][a] n.129; 5.07[4][a][ii]
   n.138; 5.07[4][b] n.156; 5.07[4][b] n.161;
   5.07[5] n.181; 6.06[3] n.36
2056A(b)(1)(A) . . . . . 5.06[9] n.444; 5.07[3][b]
   n.46; 5.07[4][a][i] n.130; 5.07[4][a][ii]
   n.150; 5.07[4][a][iii] n.154; 5.07[4][b]
   n.158; 5.07[4][c] n.171; 5.07[5] & ns.
   183, 186; 8.10[2][a] n.12
2056A(b)(1)(B) . . . . . 4.12[10] n.94; 5.06[9] ns.
   436, 444; 5.07[4][a][ii] ns. 137, 142;
   5.07[4][a][iii] n.154; 5.07[4][b] n.158;
   5.07[4][c] n.169; 8.10[2][a] n.11
2056A(b)(2) . . . . 4.12[10] n.94
2056A(b)(2)(A) . . . . . 5.06[9] n.438; 5.07[4][b]
   n.159; 6.06[3] n.36
2056A(b)(2)(A)(i) . . . . . . 5.07[4][a][ii] n.143;
   5.07[4][b] n.159
2056A(b)(2)(A)(i)(II) . . . . 5.07[4][b] n.162
2056A(b)(2)(A)(ii) . . . . 5.07[4][b] ns. 160, 162
2056A(b)(2)(B) . . . . 6.06[3] n.34
2056A(b)(2)(B)(i) . . . . 5.07[4][b] n.165
2056A(b)(2)(B)(ii) . . . . 5.07[4][b] n.166

*[Text references are to paragraphs and notes (9"n.");
references to the supplement are preceded by "S."]*

IRC §

2056A(b)(2)(C) . . . . 5.07[4][b] n.159; 6.06[3]
　　　　　　n.34
2056A(b)(3)(A) . . . . 5.07[4][a][i] n.131
2056A(b)(4) . . . 5.07[4][a] n.129; 5.07[4][a][ii]
　　n.138; 5.07[4][a][iii] n.154; 5.07[4][c]
　　　　　　n.174
2056A(b)(5) . . . . 5.07[4][c] n.168
2056A(b)(5)(A) . . . . 5.07[4][a][iii] n.154;
　　　　　5.07[4][c] ns. 172, 173
2056A(b)(5)(B) . . . . 5.07[4][a][iii] n.154;
　　　　　　5.07[4][c] n.170
2056A(b)(6) . . . 5.06[9] n.439; 5.07[3][a] n.45;
　　　　　　5.07[4][c] n.176
2056A(b)(7) . . . 5.07[4][a][ii] n.139; 5.07[4][b]
　　　　　　n.157
2056A(b)(8) . . . . 5.07[4][c] n.177
2056A(b)(9) . . . . . 5.07[4][a] n.129; 5.07[4][c]
　　　　　　n.167
2056A(b)(10)　5.06[9] n.437; 5.07[4][a][ii] &
　　　n.143; 5.07[4][a][iii] n.154
2056A(b)(10)(A) . . . 5.07[4][a][ii] ns. 149, 150;
　　5.07[4][a][iii] n.154; 5.07[4][b] n.158
2056A(b)(10)(B) . . . . 5.07[4][a][ii] n.142
2056A(b)(10)(C) . . . . 5.07[4][a][ii] n.147
2056A(b)(11) . . . . 5.07[4][a][i] n.136
2056A(b)(12) . . . . 5.07[5] n.181
2056A(b)(12)(A) . . . . 5.07[5] n.182
2056A(b)(12)(B) . . . . 5.07[5] n.183
2056A(b)(12)(C) . . . . . . 5.07[5] ns. 183, 185
2056A(b)(12)(C)(i) . . . . 5.07[5] n.186
2056A(b)(12)(C)(ii)　5.07[4][b] n.160; 5.07[5]
　　　　　　n.187
2056A(b)(13) . . . . 5.07[4][a][i] n.130;
　　　　　5.07[4][a][iii] n.154
2056A(b)(14) . . . . 5.07[3][b] n.46; 5.07[3][e]
　　　　　　n.126
2056A(b)(15) . . . . 5.07[4][a][i] n.133
2056A(c)(1) . . . . 5.07[1] n.6
2056A(c)(2) . . . . 5.07[4][a][i] n.131
2056A(c)(3) . . . . 5.07[3] n.40
2056A(d) . . . . 5.07[3][d] ns. 117, 118
2056A(e) . . . . 5.07[1] n.7

IRC §

2057 . . . . . . 2.02[3][c][i]; 2.02[3][c][ii] n.100;
　　2.02[3][c][iv] n.118; 3.05[5] n.67;
　　4.02[7][e][ii]; 4.04[1] & ns. 18, 19;
　　4.04[7] n.251; 4.15[1][a][i] n.28; 5.02;
　　5.06[2] n.14; 5.07[4][a][ii]; 5.08; 5.08[1]
　　& ns. 1, 2, 11, 13; 5.08[2][a] n.20;
　　S5.08[2][a] n.16; 5.08[2][b][iv];
　　5.08[2][b][v] & n.50; 5.08[2][c][ii] ns.
　　56, 59, 70; S5.08[2][c][ii] n.56; 5.08[3];
　　5.08[3][a]; 5.08[3][b]; 5.08[3][b][i] & ns.
　　94, 96; 5.08[3][b][ii] & ns. 98, 99;
　　S5.08[3][b][iii] n.100; 5.08[3][c][ii] &
　　n.107; 5.08[3][c][iii] n.121; 5.08[3][d] &
　　n.150; 5.08[3][e] & ns. 152, 156;
　　5.08[3][f] & n.164; 5.08[4]; 5.08[4][a] &
　　n.172; 5.08[4][a][i] & n.174;
　　5.08[4][a][ii] & n.176; 5.08[4][a][iii] &
　　ns. 179, 183; 5.08[4][b] & n.212;
　　5.08[5][a]; 5.08[5][b][i] n.225;
　　5.08[5][b][ii]; S5.08[5][b][ii] n.237;
　　5.08[5][b][iii] ns. 241, 242, 246;
　　S5.08[5][c][iii] n.261; 5.08[5][d][iii] &
　　n.267; 5.08[6]; 5.08[6][a] & n.277;
　　5.08[6][b] & ns. 278, 281; 5.08[6][c] &
　　n.301; 5.08[7] & n.305; 6.06 n.1;
　　8.10[2][b][ii]; 8.10[5] n.155; S8.11[1]
　　n.12; 17.02[1][b] n.19
2057(a) . . . . 5.08[1] n.4; 5.08[3] n.76
2057(a)(1)　5.08[4][a][ii] n.176; 5.08[4][a][iii]
　　　n.193; 5.08[4][b] n.200
2057(a)(2) . . . . 5.08[1] n.2; 5.08[4] n.69;
　　　　　5.08[4][b] n.201
2057(a)(3) . . . . 5.08[1] n.2
2057(a)(3)(A) . . . . 5.08[4][b] n.202
2057(a)(3)(B) . . . . 5.08[4][b] ns. 204, 205
2057(b)(1)(A) . . . 5.08[3] n.79; 5.08[3][a] n.85;
　　　　　　6.06 n.1
2057(b)(1)(B) . . . 5.08[3] ns. 74, 75; 5.08[3][b]
　　n.88; 5.08[3][b][i] ns. 92, 95, 96;
　　5.08[3][b][ii] n.97; 5.08[3][b][iii] n.100;
　　　　　5.08[3][f] n.163
2057(b)(1)(C) . . . . S5.08[2][a] n.16;
　　S5.08[2][c][ii] n.56; 5.08[3] n.81;
　　5.08[3][c][i] n.101; 5.08[3][c][iv] n.135;
　　5.08[3][c][v] n.141; 5.08[6][b] ns. 278,
　　　　284, 285, 289, 292
2057(b)(1)(C)(i) . . . 5.08[3] n.80; 5.08[3][c][iv]
　　　　　　n.132
2057(b)(1)(C)(ii) . . . 5.08[3][c][iv] ns. 131, 133
2057(b)(1)(D) . . . . . 5.08[3] n.78; 5.08[3][c][ii]
　　　　　　n.107
2057(b)(1)(D)(i) . . . . 5.08[3][d] n.150
2057(b)(1)(D)(ii) . . . . 2.02[3][c][ii] n.79;
　　5.08[3][e] ns. 151, 152, 154–157
2057(b)(2) . . . . . 5.08[3] n.80; 5.08[3][c][ii] ns.
　　103, 107; 5.08[3][c][iv] n.132; 5.08[3][d]
　　n.150; 5.08[3][e] n.152; 5.08[4][a][ii]
　　n.176; 5.08[5][c][ii]; 5.08[6][b] n.278
2057(b)(2)(A) . . . . 4.02[7][e][ii] n.382;
　　5.08[3][c][ii] n.105; 5.08[3][c][iii] n.121;
　　　5.08[6][a] n.277; 5.08[6][b]

[Text references are to paragraphs and notes (9"n.");
references to the supplement are preceded by "S."]

IRC §

2057(b)(2)(B) . . . . . 5.08[3][c][ii] ns. 106, 108,
    110; 5.08[3][f] n.163; 5.08[4][a][ii] n.176
2057(b)(3) . . . 5.08[3][c][iv] ns. 131, 137, 140;
    5.08[3][c][v] n.145
2057(b)(3)(A) . . . . . 5.08[3][c][iv] ns. 133, 138
2057(b)(3)(B) . . . . . 5.08[3][c][iv] ns. 133, 138,
    139
2057(c) . . . . 5.08[3][c][v] ns. 142, 147;
    5.08[6][b] ns. 278, 285−287
2057(c)(1) . . . . 5.08[3][c][v] n.143
2057(c)(2) . . . . 5.08[3][c][v] n.144
2057(c)(2)(A)(i) . . . 5.08[3][c][v] ns. 145, 146
2057(c)(2)(A)(ii) . . . . 5.08[3][c][v] n.146
2057(c)(2)(A)(iii) . . . . 5.08[3][c][v] n.147
2057(d) . . . . 5.08[1] n.3; 5.08[3] n.80;
    5.08[3][c][iii] ns. 118, 119, 121;
    5.08[4][a][ii] n.176
2057(d)(1) . . . 5.08[3][c][iii] ns. 120, 126, 127;
    5.08[4][a][iii] n.194
2057(d)(2)   5.08[3][c][iii] n.120; 5.08[3][c][v]
    n.143; 5.08[4][a][iii] n.183
2057(d)(2)(A) . . . . 5.08[3][c][iii] n.128;
    5.08[4][a][iii] n.195
2057(d)(2)(B) . . . . 5.08[3][c][iii] n.129;
    5.08[4][a][iii] n.196
2057(d)(2)(C) . . . . 5.08[3][c][iii] n.130;
    5.08[4][a][iii] n.197
2057(e) . . . . . . 5.08[1] n.4; 5.08[2][b][iv] n.35;
    5.08[2][c][ii] n.56; S5.08[2][c][ii] n.56;
    5.08[3][c][ii] n.103; 5.08[3][d] n.150;
    5.08[3][e] n.152
2057(e)(1) . . . 5.08[2][a] ns. 17, 20; 5.08[3][d]
    ns. 148, 150; 5.08[3][e] ns. 152, 156
2057(e)(1)(A) . . . . 5.08[2][a] n.15
2057(e)(1)(B) . . . 5.08[2][a] n.16; 5.08[2][c][ii]
    ns. 56, 59, 70; 5.08[3][d] n.148
2057(e)(1)(B)(i)(I) . . . . 5.08[2][c][ii] ns. 57, 59
2057(e)(1)(B)(i)(II) . . . 5.08[2][c][ii] ns. 56, 58,
    59
2057(e)(1)(B)(i)(III) . . . 5.08[2][c][ii] ns. 56, 59
2057(e)(1)(B)(ii) . . . 5.08[2][c][ii] ns. 58, 59
2057(e)(1)(C) . . . . 5.08[2][a] n.20
2057(e)(2)   5.08[2][b][iii] n.32; 5.08[2][b][iv]
    ns. 36, 45
2057(e)(2)(A) . . . . 5.08[2][b][ii] n.24
2057(e)(2)(B) . . . . 5.08[2][c][i] n.55
2057(e)(2)(C) . . . 5.08[2][b][iii] ns. 25, 27, 28,
    31; 5.08[2][b][iv] n.36
2057(e)(2)(D) . . . . 5.08[2][b][iv] n.33
2057(e)(2)(D)(i) . . . . 5.08[2][b][iv] n.34
2057(e)(2)(D)(ii) . . . . 5.08[2][b][iv] ns. 35, 36,
    44
2057(e)(3)(A) . . . . 4.02[7][b][i] n.291;
    5.08[2][c][ii] n.70
2057(e)(3)(A)(i) . . . . 4.02[7][b][i] n.291;
    5.08[2][c][ii] ns. 62, 70
2057(e)(3)(A)(ii) . . . . 4.02[7][b][i] n.291;
    5.08[2][c][ii] ns. 64, 70
2057(e)(3)(B) . . . . 4.02[7][b][i] n.291;
    5.08[2][c][ii] ns. 65, 66
2057(e)(3)(B)(i) . . . . 5.08[2][c][ii] n.67

IRC §

2057(e)(3)(C) . . . . . . 5.08[2][c][ii] ns. 69, 70;
    5.08[3][d] n.150; 5.08[3][e] n.156;
    5.08[3][f] ns. 164, 165
2057(f) . . . . 5.08[3][b][ii] n.99; 5.08[5][a] ns.
    214, 215; 5.08[5][b][i] n.221;
    5.08[5][b][ii] n.237; 5.08[5][d][iii];
    5.08[5][d][iv] n.272; 8.10[2][b][ii] n.16;
    19.03[3][d] n.165
2057(f)(1)   5.08[3][f] n.163; 5.08[5][b] n.217;
    5.08[5][b][iii] n.243
2057(f)(1)(A) . . . 2.02[3][c][ii] n.79; 5.08[5][a]
    n.216; 5.08[5][b][i] ns. 221, 225
2057(f)(1)(B) . . . . . 5.08[5][b][ii] ns. 235−237,
    239; S5.08[5][b][ii] n.237; 5.08[5][d][iii]
    n.268
2057(f)(1)(C) . . . . 5.08[5][b][iii] ns. 241, 242,
    245
2057(f)(1)(D) . . . . 5.08[5][b][iv] n.247
2057(f)(2) . . . . 5.08[5][d][iv] n.274; 5.08[6][b]
    n.296
2057(f)(2)(A) . . . . 5.08[5][c][i] n.251
2057(f)(2)(A)(i) . . . . 5.08[5][c][i] ns. 248, 249;
    5.08[5][c][iii] n.257
2057(f)(2)(A)(ii) . . . . 5.08[5][d][ii] n.266
2057(f)(2)(B) . . . . 5.08[5][b][i] n.221;
    5.08[5][c][i] ns. 249, 250; 5.08[5][c][iii]
    ns. 256, 259−261; 5.08[6][b]
2057(f)(2)(C) . . . . 5.08[5][c][i] n.248
2057(f)(2)(C)(i) . . . . 5.08[5][c][ii] n.254
2057(f)(2)(C)(ii) . . . 5.08[5][c][ii] ns. 252, 253
2057(f)(3) . . . . 5.08[3][e] n.152; 5.08[5][b][iii]
    n.236
2057(g) . . . . . 5.08[5][b][iii] ns. 241, 242, 245
2057(g)(1) . . . . . . 5.08[2][b][v] ns. 47−49, 52;
    5.08[5][b][iii] ns. 244, 246
2057(g)(2) . . . . 5.08[5][b][iii] n.246
2057(g)(2)(A) . . . . 5.08[2][b][v] n.50
2057(g)(2)(B) . . . . 5.08[2][b][v] n.51
2057(h) . . . . . . 5.08[3] n.74; 5.08[3][b] n.88;
    5.08[3][b][ii] ns. 97−99; 5.08[3][f]
    n.163; 5.08[5][d][iii] n.271
2057(i) . . . . 5.08[1] n.13
2057(i)(1) . . . . 5.08[5][b][i] n.220
2057(i)(1)(A) . . . . 5.08[3][c][ii] n.113;
    5.08[5][d][iii] n.269
2057(i)(1)(B) . . . . 5.08[3][c][ii] ns. 116, 117
2057(i)(2) . . . 5.08[2][c][ii] ns. 59−61; 5.08[3]
    n.77; 5.08[3][c][iii] ns. 114, 115;
    5.08[3][c][iv] n.136; 5.08[3][d] n.149;
    5.08[5][b][i] n.223
2057(i)(3) . . . . 5.08[5][a] n.216
2057(i)(3)(A) . . . . 5.08[3][e] ns. 158−160;
    5.08[5][b][i] n.222
2057(i)(3)(B) . . . . . . 5.08[3][e] ns. 161, 162;
    5.08[5][b][i] n.228
2057(i)(3)(C) . . . . 5.08[5][b][ii] n.233
2057(i)(3)(D) . . . . 5.08[5][c][ii] n.255
2057(i)(3)(E) . . . . 5.08[5][d][i] n.262
2057(i)(3)(F) . . . . 5.08[2][b][v] n.52;
    5.08[5][b][iii] n.246; 5.08[5][d][iii] n.267

[Text references are to paragraphs and notes (9"n.");
references to the supplement are preceded by "S."]

IRC §

2057(i)(3)(G) . . . 5.08[5][b] n.218; 5.08[5][b][i]
ns. 221, 226, 227; 5.08[5][b][iii] n.243
2057(i)(3)(H) . . . 5.08[3] n.74; 5.08[3][b] n.91;
5.08[3][b][i] ns. 92, 94–96;
5.08[3][b][iii] n.100
2057(i)(3)(I) . . . . 5.08[3][c][i] n.102
2057(i)(3)(J) . . . . . 5.08[3][d] n.150; 5.08[3][e]
n.156
2057(i)(3)(K) . . . . 5.08[5][d][iv] n.273
2057(i)(3)(L) . . . 5.08[2][a] n.20; 5.08[2][c][ii]
ns. 56, 59, 70; 5.08[3][d] n.150;
5.08[3][f] n.165
2057(i)(3)(M) 5.08[5][b] n.218; 5.08[5][b][ii]
n.240; 5.08[5][c][iii] n.261
2057(i)(3)(N) . . . . 5.08[3][c][ii] n.104
2057(i)(3)(O) . . . . 5.08[5][b][ii] n.237
2057(i)(3)(P) . . . . 5.08[3][b][i] n.92;
5.08[3][b][ii] n.99; 5.08[5][b][ii] n.235
2057(j) . . . 4.04[1] n.18; 5.08[1] n.1; 5.08[4][b]
n.212; 5.08[7] n.305; 8.10[2][b][ii] n.15
2058 . . . . . S3.02 n.1; 3.03[1]; 3.03[3][d] n.40;
3.03[4]; 3.08 n.2; 5.02; S5.03[4][b][i] ns.
181, 186; S5.03[4][b][ii] n.194;
5.03[5][a] n.105; S5.03[6][a] n.270;
5.07[4][a][ii] n.143; 5.09[2] & n.10;
5.09[3]; 6.02[1] n.7; 6.06; 8.10[5];
8.11[11]; 9.03[3] n.17; S9.03[3] n.25;
9.06 n.7; 12.04 n.11; 17.02[1][b] n.19;
5.09; 5.09[1] & ns. 1, 2
2058(a) . . . 3.03[4] ns. 43–46; 5.09[1] & ns. 1,
9; 5.09[2] n.10
2058(b) . . . . 3.06[4] n.25; 3.07 n.1; 5.09[2] &
ns. 30, 31
2058(b)(2)(A) . . . . 5.09[2] n.17
2058(b)(2)(B) . . . . 3.07 n.7; 5.09[2] n.22
2058(b)(2)(C) . . . . 5.09[2] n.25
2058(b)(2)(C)(i) . . . . 5.09[2] n.26
2058(b)(2)(C)(ii) . . . . 5.09[2] n.27
2058(b)(2)(C)(iii) . . . . 5.09[2] n.28
2077A . . . . 5.06[8][d] n.302
2101–2106 . . . . 6.07[2]; S6.07[2][b] n.49
2101–2108 2.01 n.1; S2.01; 3.06; 6.01[1] &
n.9; 7.01
2101 . . . . . 5.06[9] n.443; 6.01; 6.01[1] & n.6;
6.01[2] & ns. 11, 16; 6.02; 6.02[1];
6.02[2]; 6.02[4]; 6.08; 7.01[1] n.2; 8.09;
9.02[1] n.5; 10.01[11] n.235;
19.02[5][c][i] n.405
2101(a) . . . . 7.01[2] n.28; 13.02[4][b][i] n.257;
17.02[1][b] n.16
2101(b) . . . . . 7.01[3][b] n.59; 7.03[6] ns. 159,
162; 7.03[7] n.182; 8.01[2][a];
19.02[5][c][i] n.418
2101(b)(1) . . . . . . 6.02[4] n.28; 7.03[8] n.233;
8.01[2][a]
2101(b)(1)(B) . . . . 6.02[2] n.22; 19.02[5][c][ii]
n.422; 19.02[5][c][iii] n.443;
19.02[5][c][iv] n.454; 19.02[5][c][v] ns.
479, 485
2101(b)(2) . . . . 6.01[2] n.12; 8.01[2][a];
19.02[5][c][v] ns. 480, 486

IRC §

2101(c) . . . . 7.03[5] n.134; S8.10[1] n.5
2101(c)(1) . . . . . . 6.01[2] n.15; 6.02[2] n.22;
19.02[5][c][iii] n.443
2101(c)(2) . . . . 6.01[2] n.12
2102 . . . . 5.07[4][b] n.160; 6.02; S6.02; 6.02[1]
& n.19; 6.02[2]; 6.02[3]; 6.06[4] & ns.
37, 38; 6.07[2] n.29; S6.07[2][c] n.62;
6.08
2102(a) . . . . 6.02[1] ns. 15, 16, 18; 6.02[2] ns.
20, 21; 6.02[3] n.23
2102(b) . . . . S6.01[1] n.7; 6.02 n.4; 6.02[1] &
n.7; S6.02[1] ns. 7, 15; 6.02[4] n.25;
S6.02[4] ns. 25–27, 29; 6.06[4] n.41;
S7.01[3][b] n.60; S7.02[3] ns. 72, 79;
S7.03[1][c] n.36; S7.03[3] ns. 64, 66;
S7.03[5] ns. 136, 137; S7.03[6] n.162;
S7.03[8] n.235; S8.01[2][b] n.43
2102(c) . . . . S6.01[1] n.7; 6.02 & n.4; 6.02[1];
S6.02[1] ns. 7, 15; 6.02[4] n.25;
S6.02[4] ns. 25–27, 29; 7.01[3][b] n.60;
S7.01[3][b] n.60; 7.02[3] n.72; S7.02[3]
ns. 72, 79; S7.03[1][c] n.36; S7.03[3] ns.
64, 66; S7.03[5] ns. 136, 137; S7.03[6]
n.162; S7.03[8] n.235; 8.01[2][b];
S8.01[2][b] n.43
2102(c)(1) 6.01[1] n.7; 6.01[4] n.36; 6.02[4]
n.26; 7.03[1][c] n.36; 7.03[5] n.136;
7.03[6] n.162; 7.03[8] n.235
2102(c)(2) . . . . 6.02[4] ns. 26, 27
2102(c)(3) . . . . 7.03[3] n.66; 7.03[5] n.137
2102(c)(3)(A) . . . 6.02[4] n.29; 7.02[3] & n.79;
7.03[3]; 7.06 n.25
2102(c)(3)(B) . . . . 6.02[4] n.26
2102(c)(4) . . . . 6.02[1] n.15
2102(c)(5) . . . . 6.02[1] n.15
2103–2106 . . . . 6.01[2] n.14
2103 . . . . . 4.12[10] ns. 87, 94; 5.06[3] n.22;
6.01[1] n.3; 6.01[2] n.15; 6.02[1]; 6.03;
S6.03; 6.03[1]; 6.04[2] n.18; 6.05[1] &
n.2; 6.06[2] n.28; 6.06[4]; 7.01[1] n.2;
7.01[2] n.28; 17.02[1][b] & n.15
2104–2105 . . . . 7.03[8]
2104 . . . . . 5.06[3] n.22; 6.01[1] n.4; 6.03[2] &
n.18; 6.04; 6.07[2] n.28; S6.07[2][b]
n.61; 17.02[1][b] n.15
2104(a) . . . . 6.03[2] n.11; 6.03[2][b] n.27;
6.04[1]; S6.04[1] n.1; 6.04[2] & n.18;
6.05[2][a][ii]; 7.02[2][c] n.21
2104(b) . . . S4.07[3][a] n.76; 6.03[2] ns. 7, 12;
6.04[2] & n.17; S6.04[2] n.12.1; 6.05[1]
2104(c) . . . . 6.03[2] n.13; 6.03[2][b] n.28;
6.04[3] & n.22; 6.05[2][b] ns. 31, 32;
6.05[3]; 6.05[3][a] n.38; S6.05[5];
6.06[1] n.12; 7.02[2][c] ns. 24, 28, 38
2104(c)(1) . . . . 6.01[2] n.15
2105 . . . . . 5.06[3] n.22; 6.01[1] n.4; 6.03[2] &
n.18; 6.04[3]; 6.05; 6.05[3]; 6.07[2] n.28;
S6.07[2][b] n.61
2105(a) . . . . 6.03[1]; 6.03[2] n.14; 6.03[2][b]
n.29; 6.05[1]; 7.02[2][c] n.46;
S9.02[1][a]

[Text references are to paragraphs and notes (9"n.");
references to the supplement are preceded by "S."]

IRC §

2105(b) . . . . . 6.03[2] ns. 13, 15; 6.03[2][b] ns.
 28, 30; 6.05[3][b] n.45; S6.05[5]; 6.06[1]
 n.12
2105(b)(1) . . . 6.05[2][a] & n.9; 6.05[2][a][i] &
 ns. 13, 20, 21; 6.05[2][a][ii]; 6.05[2][b]
 n.32; 7.02[2][c] n.33
2105(b)(2) . . . . 6.05[2][c] n.34; 7.02[2][c] n.34
2105(b)(3) . . . . . 6.04[2] n.17; 6.05[2][b] n.32;
 6.05[3][b] n.40
2105(b)(4) . . . 6.05[2][b] n.32; 6.05[3][c] n.49
2105(c) . . . . 6.03[2] n.16; 6.03[2][a] n.21;
 6.05[4] & n.52
2105(c)(1) . . . . 6.05[4] n.51
2105(c)(2) . . . . 6.05[4] n.50
2105(c)(3) . . . . 6.05[4] n.52
2105(d) . . . . S6.02[4] n.34
2105(d)(1) . . . . . . S6.05[5] ns. 52.1, 52.3, 52.7
2105(d)(2)(A) . . . . S6.05[5] n.52.4
2105(d)(2)(B) . . . . S6.05[5] n.52.5
2105(d)(2)(C) . . . . S6.05[5] n.52.6
2105(d)(3) . . . . S6.05[5] n.52.1
2106 . . . . 5.01 n.7; 6.01[1] n.5; 6.06; 6.08;
 7.02[3] n.65; 13.02[4][b][i] n.256;
 16.02[1]; 16.02[2][c][i]; 16.02[3][b][ii]
 n.183; 16.02[5][b][i] & ns. 316, 319;
 16.02[5][b][ii] ns. 327, 328; 16.02[5][c]
 ns. 359, 360; 17.02[1][b] n.15;
 17.02[3][c] ns. 145–147
2106(a) . . . . . . 5.06[3] n.22; 6.06 n.1; 7.03[5]
 n.121; 8.06 n.6
2106(a)(1) . . . 3.05[4][a] n.57; 6.06 ns. 2, 3, 7;
 6.06[1] & ns. 11, 13; 7.03[1][c] n.30;
 7.03[8] n.222
2106(a)(2) . . . 3.05[4][a] n.57; 4.03[4][b] n.58;
 S5.03[4][b][ii]; 5.03[8]; 5.05 n.2;
 5.05[1][b] n.41; 6.06 ns. 4, 7; 6.06[1];
 6.06[2] & ns. 24, 28; S6.06[2] n.28
2106(a)(2)(A)(ii) . . . . 6.06[2] n.21
2106(a)(2)(A)(iii) . . . . 6.06[2] n.22
2106(a)(2)(B) . . . . 6.06[2] n.23
2106(a)(2)(C) . . . . 6.06[2] n.25
2106(a)(2)(D) . . . . 6.06[2] n.27
2106(a)(2)(E) . . . . . 6.06[2] n.26; 16.02[5][b][i]
 n.316
2106(a)(3) . . . . . . 4.03[4][b] n.58; 5.06[1] n.4;
 5.06[3] ns. 20, 22; 6.06 n.5; 6.06[3]
 n.30; 7.03[5] n.126; 11.03[2] n.13;
 19.02[5][a][iii] & n.357
2106(a)(4) . . . . . 6.02[1] & ns. 7, 19; 6.06 n.6;
 6.06[4] & ns. 37, 39, 40, 42
2106(b) . . . . 6.06 & n.7
2107 . . . . . 6.01[1] n.4; 6.01[3][a] n.28; 6.07 &
 n.1; S6.07 & n.7; 6.07[1] & n.16;
 6.07[2] & ns. 23, 25; S6.07[2] & n.37;
 S6.07[2][a] & ns. 41, 46; S6.07[2][b] &
 ns. 55, 58; 9.02[1] n.7
2107(a) . . . . . 6.07 n.3; S6.07 ns. 2–4; 6.07[1]
 n.9; 6.07[2] n.18; S6.07[2] n.35;
 S6.07[2][a] ns. 41, 45; S6.07[2][b] n.49

2107(a)(1) . . . . 6.07[1] n.6
2107(a)(2)(A) . . . . 6.07[1] n.12
2107(a)(2)(B) . . . . 6.07[1] n.15
2107(b)   6.03[2] n.9; 6.04[1] ns. 1, 7; 6.07[1]
 n.16; 6.07[2] & ns. 18, 21, 22, 27, 28;
 S6.07[2][b] & ns. 49, 53, 54, 60, 61;
 S6.07[2][c]
2107(b)(1) . . . . . 6.07[2] n.23; S6.07[2][b] n.56
2107(b)(2) . . . . 6.07[2] ns. 25, 26; S6.07[2][b]
 ns. 58, 59
2107(c) . . . . . . 6.07[2] n.18; S6.07[2][b] n.49
2107(c)(2) . . . . 6.02 n.5; 6.07[2] n.31
2107(c)(2)(B) . . . . 6.07[2] n.31
2107(c)(2)(C) . . . . 6.07[2] n.31
2107(d) . . . . 6.07[1] ns. 16, 17
2108 . . . . 6.08
2108(a) . . . . 6.08 ns. 1, 4
2108(a)(2) 6.08 n.3
2108(a)(3) 6.08 n.2
2108(b) 6.08 n.4
2108(c) 6.08 n.4
2156(b)(6) . . . . 5.06[8][f] n.420
2201 . . . . S2.01[1] n.13; S2.01[1][c] n.46; 8.01
 & n.1; 8.01[1]; S8.01[1] n.6;
 8.01[1][a][iii] & n.26; 8.01[1][b];
 S8.01[1][c]; 8.01[2][a]; S8.01[2][a] n.41
2201(a) . . . 8.01 n.4; 8.01[1] n.5; 8.01[2][a] ns.
 39, 40; 8.01[2][b] n.42
2201(b) . . . . 8.01[1]
2201(b)(1) . . . . 8.01[1] n.6; 8.01[1][a] ns. 7, 8
2201(b)(1)(A) . . . . 8.01[1][a][iii] n.15
2201(b)(1)(B) . . . . 8.01[1][a][iv] n.29
2201(b)(2) . . . . . . 8.01[1] n.6; 8.01[1][b] n.31;
 S8.01[1][b] n.32
2201(b)(3) . . . . S8.01[1][c] n.36.1
2201(c) . . . . . 8.01[2][a] & n.38; 8.01[2][b] &
 n.42
2201(d) . . . . 8.01[2][b] n.42
2203 . . . 2.02 n.1; 4.14[3][a] & n.25; 5.03[4][a]
 n.89; S5.03[6][c][iii] n.302;
 5.06[8][d][iii] n.366; 5.08[3] n.73;
 5.08[3][b] n.87; 6.01[4] n.37; 8.02;
 8.03[2]; 8.10[3][b] n.42; 8.10[3][b][v]
 n.90; 8.10[3][d][ii] n.121; S8.10[2] n.12;
 S8.10[3][b][iv] n.79; S8.10[3][d][ii]
 n.111; 12.03[1] n.9; 15.02[1] n.23;
 S15.02[1] n.17; S16.02[9][a] n.580.1
2204 . . . . . 2.02 n.4; 2.02[3][c][iii] n.116; 8.02;
 8.03; 8.03[1] n.12; 8.03[2] & n.16; S8.04
 n.4; 9.04[11] & n.249; 12.03[1] n.11
2204(a) . . . . 8.03; 8.03[2] & ns. 17, 26
2204(b) . . . . 8.03[2] & n.26
2204(c) . . . . 8.03[2]
2204(d) . . . . 8.03[2]
2205 . . . . 3.05[3][b] n.41; 4.07[2][c] n.56;
 5.03[8] n.163; 5.05[3][b][i] ns. 107, 108;
 5.06[5][a] ns. 95, 98; 8.04 & n.8;
 8.04[1]; 8.04[2]; 8.05[4]; 8.06; 8.08[2]
 n.7

[Text references are to paragraphs and notes (9"n.");
references to the supplement are preceded by "S."]

IRC §

2206 . . . . 3.05[3][b] n.42; 5.04[3] n.20;
5.06[5][a] ns. 95, 98; 8.04 & n.1;
8.04[1] n.11; 8.05; 8.05[1]; 8.05[2] &
n.7; 8.05[3] n.10; 8.05[4] & n.13; 8.06
& ns. 1, 7, 8; 8.08[1] n.1; 8.08[2] ns. 7,
8, 11–13; 17.02[2] n.104

2207 . . . 3.05[3][b] n.42; 5.06[5][a] ns. 95, 98;
8.04 & n.1; 8.04[1] n.11; 8.05[4] &
n.11; 8.06 & ns. 6, 8; 8.08[1] n.1;
8.08[2] ns. 7, 8, 11–13

2207A . . . . 3.05[3][b] n.42; 4.16; 5.06[5][a] ns.
95, 98; 5.06[8][f] n.421; 8.04 & ns. 1,
10; 8.05[4]; 8.06; 8.07; 8.07[1]; S8.07[1]
n.7; 8.07[2] ns. 9, 10; S8.07[2] n.9;
8.07[3] n.26; 8.07[4] & ns. 32, 34, 37;
8.07[5] n.44; 8.07[6]; 8.08[2] ns. 7, 13;
10.02[6][d]; 10.07[2] n.27; 10.08[1][b]
n.27; S10.08[3] n.49; 11.03[4][c][i] &
n.70; 13.02[4][b][i] n.273; 16.02[4][e];
17.02[1][c][i] & n.48; 17.02[1][d] &
n.73; 18.05[2][b][ii] & n.46

2207A(a) . . . 8.07[1] n.7; 8.07[4] n.38; 8.07[5];
8.08[1] n.1; 10.08[3] n.44; 17.02[1][c][i]
n.45

2207A(a)(1) . . . . 8.07[2] ns. 12, 14
2207A(a)(2) . . . . . . 8.07[2] n.9; 8.07[3] n.27;
8.07[5] n.40; 8.08[2] n.8
2207A(b) . . . . . 4.07[3][a]; 5.06[8][d][ii] n.330;
8.04 n.10; 8.07[1] n.7; 8.07[3] ns. 18,
20, 21, 23; 8.07[4] ns. 34, 35; S8.07[4]
n.34; 10.08[1] n.7; 10.08[1][a] ns. 16,
22; S10.08[1][a] n.16; 10.08[3] & ns. 44,
47; 17.02[1][c][i] n.44
2207A(c) . . . . 8.07[4] n.28
2207A(d) . . . . 8.07[2] n.13; 8.07[3] n.21
2207B . . . 3.05[3][b] n.42; 8.04 & n.1; 8.05[4];
8.06; 8.08; S8.08; 8.08[1]; 8.08[2] & ns.
6, 8; S8.08[2] n.7; 18.05[2][b][ii] n.45
2207B(a) . . . . 8.08[1] n.3
2207B(a)(1) . . . . 8.08[2] ns. 6, 7, 13
2207B(a)(2) . . . . 8.08[2] ns. 8, 9
2207B(a)(3) . . . . 8.08[2] n.7
2207B(b) . . . . 8.08[1] n.2
2207B(c) . . . . 8.08[1] n.4; 8.08[2] n.13
2207B(d) . . . . 8.08[2] n.13
2208 . . . . 2.01 n.1; S2.01 n.1; 4.02[7][b][i]
n.285; 4.04[3][a] n.30; 5.08[3][a] n.86;
6.01[3]; 8.04 & n.1; 8.09; 9.02[1] n.5
2209 . . . . 2.01 n.1; S2.01 n.1; 4.02[7][b][i]
n.285; 4.04[3][a] n.30; 5.08[3][a] n.86;
6.01[3]; 6.02[4]; 8.09 & n.2; S8.09 n.2;
9.02[1] n.5; S9.02[1][a] n.10.2
2210 . . . 3.02 n.10; 6.01[1] n.9; 8.10; 8.10[1] &
n.1; S8.10; S8.11; 9.01 n.14; 9.03[2]
n.13; 18.04 n.3; S18.04[1] n.1
2210(a) . . . . . 2.01[4] n.74; 4.02[7][d][i] n.342;
4.04[1] n.15; 5.07[4][a][i] n.130; 6.01[1]
n.8; 8.10[1] n.2; 8.10[2]; 8.10[3][a] n.24;
S8.11 n.2; 10.05 n.16; 12.01[3] n.33
2210(b) . . . . . . 8.10[2][a] n.10; 8.10[5] n.162

IRC §

2210(b)(1) . . . . 5.07[4][a][i] n.130; 8.10[2][a]
n.12
2210(b)(2) . . . . 5.07[4][a][ii] n.137; 8.10[2][a]
n.11
2501–2524 . . . . 10.02 n.1
2501 . . . . S4.13[7][a] n.87; 6.01[2] n.15; 9.02;
S9.02[1][b][ii] n.10.52; 9.06; S9.06;
S9.06[1] n.67; 10.01; 10.01[2][g] n.61;
10.01[3][i] n.126; 10.01[11] n.235;
S10.01[11]; S11.03[4][c][i] n.78;
16.02[2][b][v] n.114; 17.02[3][e][i]
n.162; 18.01[1]; 18.03[2][b]
2501(a) . . . S9.02[1][b][ii] n.10.47; 10.01[2][c]
n.27; 10.01[11]; 13.01[2][a] n.11;
13.01[2][b][i]; 13.02[4][b][i] n.270;
15.03[4][b][i] n.98; 17.02[1][b];
18.03[2][b] & ns. 42, 46
2501(a)(1) . . . . 9.02; 9.02[3] n.22; 9.03[1] n.2;
S9.03[1] n.6; 9.04[1][b] n.30; 10.01[11]
n.236; 13.02[4][b][i] ns. 258, 263, 268;
17.02[1][b] ns. 18, 21, 23, 29, 37
2501(a)(2) . . . . 6.01[2] n.15; 9.02[1] n.4;
S9.02[1][a]; S9.02[1][b][ii]; 10.01[11]
n.236; S10.01[11] n.236; 11.03[2] n.12;
13.02[4][b][i] n.258; 17.02[1][b] n.18;
18.03[2][b] n.42
2501(a)(3) . . . . . . 6.01[2] n.15; S6.01[2] n.15;
9.02[1] n.7; S9.02[1][b] & ns. 5–7,
10.10; S9.02[1][b][ii] & ns. 10.28, 10.47;
10.01[11] & n.237; 11.03[2] n.12;
13.02[4][b][i] n.258; 17.02[1][b] n.18;
18.03[2][b] n.42
2501(a)(3)(A)   9.02[1] n.7; S9.02[1][b][ii] ns.
10.29, 10.30, 10.33
2501(a)(3)(B) . . . . . 9.02[1] n.7; S9.02[1][b][ii]
n.10.48
2501(a)(3)(D) . . . . 9.02[1] n.7
2501(a)(4) . . . . 9.02[1] n.7; S9.02[2];
S10.01[2][c] n.30; 10.01[11] n.237;
S10.02[4] n.135; S11.02[1][a] n.12;
S17.02[1][b] n.18; S18.02[2][b] n.25
2501(a)(5) . . . S6.01[2] n.15; S9.02[1][b][ii] &
ns. 10.28, 10.38, 10.41; 9.02[2];
10.01[2][c] n.30; S10.01[11] & n.235;
10.02[4] n.135; 11.02[1][a] n.12;
S11.03[2] n.12; S13.02[4][b][i] n.258;
17.02[1][b] n.18; S17.02[1][b] n.18;
18.02[2][b] n.25; S18.03[2][b] n.42
2501(a)(5)(A)(ii) . . . . S9.02[1][b][ii] ns. 10.37,
10.44
2501(a)(5)(B)(i) . . . . . . S9.02[1][b][ii] n.10.39
2501(a)(5)(B)(ii) . . . . S9.02[1][b][ii] ns. 10.41,
10.42
2501(a)(5)(C) . . . . . . S9.02[1][b][ii] ns. 10.37,
10.44
2501(b) . . . 8.09 & n.2; 9.02[1] n.5; S9.02[1][a]
n.10.3
2501(c) . . . 8.09 & n.2; S8.09 n.2; 9.02[1] n.5;
S9.02[1][a] & n.10.3
2501(c)(3)(A) . . . . S9.02[1][b][ii] n.10.50
2501(c)(5)(A)(ii) . . . . . . S9.02[1][b][ii] n.10.43

IRC §

2502 . . . . 3.04 ns. 1, 2; 8.06 n.6; 8.07[3] n.19;
9.01 & n.1; 9.02; 9.02[3]; 9.03; S9.03;
S9.03[3]; 9.03[3]; S9.03[3]; 9.05;
9.05[3]; 9.06[1] n.19; S9.06[1] ns. 59,
62; 9.06[2]; 10.03[2]; 10.08[3] n.45;
11.03[4][c][i] n.70; 16.01 ns. 3, 6;
S16.01 ns. 3, 6
2502(a) . . . . . S2.01[2] n.71; S6.07[1][b] n.28;
S9.02[1][b][i] n.10.22; 9.03[1]; S9.03[1];
9.03[2] n.10; S9.03[2] ns. 14, 30;
S9.03[3] n.30; S9.06[1] n.67; 10.03[2]
n.19; 10.05 n.10; 19.02[5][c][i];
19.02[5][c][ii] n.421; 19.02[5][c][iii];
19.02[5][c][v] n.478
2502(a)(1)   S2.01[1][c] n.46; S2.01[2] ns. 69,
71; 9.03[2] ns. 5, 8, 9; S9.03[2] ns. 9,
12, 13; S9.06[1] n.67; 9.06[2] n.27;
9.06[3] ns. 31, 32; 19.03[4][c][i] & ns.
315, 321
2502(a)(2)   S2.01[2] ns. 69, 71; 9.03[2] n.10;
S9.03[2] n.14; S9.03[3] ns. 24, 30;
S9.06[1] n.67; 9.06[2] n.27
2502(b) . . . . . . 9.03[3] & n.16; S9.03[3]; 9.05
2502(c) . . . . . . 9.02[3] n.23; 9.03[4]; S9.03[4];
10.05 n.6
2503 . . . . 2.01[1][b]; S2.01[1][b]; 3.04[1][b] &
n.16; 3.04[1][c]; 5.08[3][c][iv] n.138;
6.01[2] & n.15; 9.03; S9.03; 9.03[4];
S9.03[4]; 9.04; 9.04[9]; 11.04 n.1
2503(a) . . . 9.04; 10.06[1] n.10; 19.02[5][a][iii]
n.338

IRC §

2503(b) . . . . 2.01[1][b] n.17; S2.01[1][b] n.18;
S2.01[3]; 2.01[4] & n.76; 4.02[7][e][iv]
n.417; 4.10[4][a] n.26; 4.11[5] n.51;
4.14[8] n.119; 4.16 n.10; 5.08[2][c][ii]
n.70; 5.08[3][c][iv] & n.137;
5.08[3][c][v]; 5.08[3][f] n.165;
S6.07[1][b] & n.26; 9.01 n.1;
S9.02[1][b][i] & n.10.20; 9.03; S9.03;
9.04; 9.04[1] & n.11; 9.04[2]; 9.04[3][a]
n.50; 9.04[3][c]; 9.04[3][f] & ns. 96,
113, 115; 9.04[3][g]; 9.04[4]; 9.04[5][c];
9.04[9]; 10.01[2]; 10.01[3][a] n.82;
10.01[3][f] n.112; 10.01[9] n.202;
10.03[2] & n.19; 10.05 ns. 2, 11;
10.08[1][a] n.13; 10.08[1][b] & n.28;
11.02[1][b]; S11.02[2][c] n.96; 11.03[5];
12.03[3] n.32; 13.02[2][e][ii] n.122;
13.02[4][b][i] & ns. 261, 262, 264;
15.03[4][b][i] n.99; 15.03[4][b][iii] & ns.
119, 124, 147; 16.02[2][b][i] n.38;
16.02[2][b][ii] & ns. 42, 44;
16.02[2][b][iii] & ns. 63–65, 77, 78;
16.02[2][b][iv] ns. 84, 86; 16.02[2][b][v]
n.112; 16.02[2][c][i] & n.139;
16.02[3][b][ii] & n.194; S16.02[9][a]
n.573; 17.02[1][b] & n.25; 17.04[1][b]
n.23; 17.04[4]; 18.02[2][b] & n.21;
19.02[2][a][iii] n.76; 19.02[5][a][iii] &
n.338; 19.02[5][c][iii] n.436; 19.02[5][e];
19.03[2][a] ns. 31, 32; 19.03[2][c] & ns.
91, 95
2503(b)(1) . . . . . 4.10[3] n.11; 11.03[5] n.107;
15.02[4] n.72; S15.02[4] n.66
2503(b)(2)   9.04[1] ns. 6, 8; 9.04[3][g] n.131;
9.05[3] n.36; 10.03[2] n.19; 11.03[5]
n.107
2503(b)(2)(B) . . . . 9.04[1] n.7
2503(c) . . . . . . 3.04[1][b] n.17; 4.09[3] n.12;
4.10[4][a] n.26; 4.10[4][f] n.51;
9.04[3][a] n.50; 9.04[3][f] n.113; 9.04[4];
9.04[5] & n.144; 9.04[5][a]; S9.04[5][a]
n.145; 9.04[5][b]; 9.04[5][c] & n.165;
16.02[2][b][i] n.38; 16.02[2][b][iii] n.77;
16.02[7][b][i] n.450
2503(c)(1) . . . . 9.04[5][a] n.147
2503(c)(2)(A) . . . . 9.04[5][c] n.165
2503(c)(2)(B) . . . . 9.04[5][b]
2503(e) . . . . 1.04[3][d]; 2.01[1][b] n.17;
S2.01[1][b] n.18; S2.01[3]; 2.01[4] &
n.78; 4.02[7][e][iv] n.417; 9.01 n.1; 9.03
n.1; S9.03 n.1; 9.04[3][g] & n.124;
9.04[6] & n.172; S9.04[6] n.180;
9.04[9]; 10.02[5]; 11.01 n.1; 13.01[2][a]
& ns. 11, 14, 16; S13.01[2][a] n.9;
13.02[4][b][i] ns. 260, 264; 15.03[3][a]
n.44; 16.02[2][b][i] n.39; 16.02[2][b][ii]
& ns. 51, 54, 57; 16.02[2][b][iii];
16.02[2][b][iv] n.84; 17.02[1][b] & ns.
22, 25; 17.04[4]; 18.02[2][b] n.25;
19.02[5][c][iii] n.436

*[Text references are to paragraphs and notes (9"n.");
references to the supplement are preceded by "S."]*

IRC §

2503(e)(1) . . . . . 9.04[6] n.174; 13.02[4][b][i];
    17.02[1][b] n.24
2503(e)(2) . . . . 9.04[6] n.174; 13.01[2][a] n.19
2503(e)(2)(A) . . . . 13.01[2][a]
2503(f) . . . 9.03 n.1; S9.03 n.1; 9.04[7] n.185;
    9.04[9] n.198
2503(g) . . . . . . 9.03 n.1; S9.03 n.1; 9.04[8] &
    n.188; 9.04[9] n.198
2503(g)(1) . . . . 9.04[8] n.189
2503(g)(1)(A) . . . . 9.04[8] n.191
2503(g)(1)(B) . . . . 9.04[8] n.192
2503(g)(2)(A) . . . . 9.04[8] n.190
2504 . . . . S2.01[1][b] n.21; 9.01; 9.05
2504(a) . . . . 9.05[4] n.49
2504(a)(1) 9.05 n.1
2504(a)(3) . . . . 9.05[4]
2504(b) . . . . 9.04[1] n.10; 9.05[3]
2504(c) . . . . . 2.01[1][b][i] n.21; S2.01[1][b][i]
    n.21; 9.04[10][a] n.219; 9.05[2] & n.10;
    9.05[2][a] & n.14; 9.05[2][b] & ns. 21,
    23, 24, 27; 10.02[2][d][i] & n.123
2504(c)(2) . . . . 9.05[2][b] n.20
2504(d) . . . . 9.05[4]
2505 . . . . . . 2.01[2] & ns. 50, 57; S2.01[1][c];
    S2.01[3] & n.89; 2.01[4]; 3.02 & ns. 15,
    17, 19–21; S3.02[2] & ns. 52, 53, 57,
    58; 4.04[1] n.10; 5.07[5]; 6.02[4] n.26;
    7.03[3] & n.67; 8.07[3] n.24; 8.10[1]
    n.5; 8.10[5]; S8.11; 9.01 n.1; S9.03;
    9.03[2] ns. 7, 10; S9.03[2]; 9.03[3] ns.
    17, 20; S9.03[3] & ns. 25, 29, 31;
    9.05[2][a] n.14; S9.05[2][a] n.19; 9.05[4]
    n.52; 9.06 & n.2; S9.06 & ns. 37, 44;
    9.06[1] & ns. 10, 16, 20; S9.06[1] & ns.
    50, 56, 59, 63, 67; 9.06[2]; S9.06[2] &
    n.709.06[3] & ns. 28, 30; 10.02[2][d][iii]
    n.129; S10.02[2][d][iii]; 10.02[5][a]
    n.157; 10.03[2] & n.37; 10.08[3]; 11.01
    ns. 3, 4; 11.03[4][c][i] n.70; 14.05[2][a]
    n.17; 15.03[4][b][i] & n.103;
    17.02[1][c][i] n.57; S17.02[1][c][i] n.57;
    18.02[2][a] n.11; 18.02[2][b] n.18;
    19.02[5][e]; 19.03[1] ns. 10, 12;
    19.03[2][c]
2505(a) . . . . 6.02[4] n.26; S9.06 n.39; S9.06[1]
    n.59
2505(a)(1) . . . . . . 3.02 n.17; S3.02[1][b] n.28;
    S3.02[2] n.53; 9.06 n.3; S9.06 n.39;
    9.06[1] ns. 110, 11, 20; S9.06[1] ns. 49,
    51, 59, 63
2505(a)(2) . . . . . . 2.01[2] n.57; S2.01[2] n.75;
    S9.06; 9.06[1] ns. 12, 20; S9.06[1] ns.
    57, 59, 63; 9.06[2]
2505(b) . . . . 9.06[1]; S9.06[1] n.50
2505(c) . . . . 9.05[4] n.49; 9.06; S9.06; 9.06[1]
    n.21; S9.06[1] n.64

IRC §

2508 . . . . S9.03[3] n.25
2511–2519 . . . . 9.02; 9.04
2511 . . . . 4.05[3] n.32; 4.07[2][a][i] n.22;
    4.07[3][b] n.85; S4.13[4][c][ii] ns. 41,
    50; 5.03[5][b] n.124; 5.06[8][d] n.300;
    5.06[8][d][ii] & ns. 330, 362; 5.06[8][e]
    ns. 417, 418; 5.07[5] n.182; 6.01[2]
    n.15; 8.07[1] n.7; 8.07[4]; 8.07[5];
    8.10[4]; 9.02 n.1; S9.02[1][b][ii] n.10.37;
    9.02[2] n.11; 10.01; 10.01[1];
    10.01[3][a]; S10.01[3][g] & ns. 115.29,
    115.34; S10.01[8] ns. 192, 193;
    10.01[10][b] n.219; 10.02; 10.02[1][a];
    10.04[1] n.1; 10.05 & n.2; S10.06[2]
    n.14; 10.08[1]; 10.08[1][a] & ns. 13, 16,
    19, 22; S10.08[1][a] n.13; 10.08[1][b]
    n.25; 10.08[2] & ns. 30, 36, 41;
    11.03[4][c][i]; 11.03[4][c][ii];
    13.02[2][e][ii] n.108; 13.02[2][e][iii]
    n.167; 13.02[4][a] n.250; 13.02[4][b][i]
    ns. 268, 272; 13.02[4][b][ii] n.276;
    15.02[4] n.61; S15.02[4] n.55;
    15.03[3][a] n.39; 16.02[4][e] ns. 283,
    288; 16.02[7][b][i] n.452; 17.01[2][a][iii]
    n.32; 17.02[1][c][i]; 17.02[3][e][i] n.162;
    S18.05[2][b][ii] n.43; 19.02[2][a][i] &
    ns. 52, 55; 19.02[2][b][ii] n.83;
    19.02[5][c][ii] n.432; 19.03[2][a][iv] n.71
2511(a)   8.10[4]; 9.02[1] n.6; S9.02[1][a] n.3;
    9.02[2]; 10.01 & n.5; 10.01[11] n.236;
    13.02[2][e][iii] n.167; 17.02[1][b] n.18;
    17.02[3][e][i] n.170
2511(b) . . . . S9.02[1][a]; S9.02[1][b][ii] &
    n.10.28; 10.01 n.5; 10.01[11];
    S10.01[11]; 11.03[2] n.12; 18.03[2][b]
    n.42
2511(b)(1) . . . . S9.02[1][b][ii]; 10.01[11]
2511(b)(2) . . . . S9.02[1][b][ii] & n.10.47;
    10.01[11]
2511(c) . . . . . . 8.10[4] & ns. 136, 138, 141;
    S8.10[4] n.138; 8.10[5] n.162
2512 . . . . . . 3.05[3][b] n.44; 4.08[7][c] n.129;
    9.03[4]; S9.03[4] n.35; 10.01 n.6;
    10.01[2][b][i] n.16; S10.01[3][g]
    n.115.35; 10.01[10][b] n.219; 10.02;
    10.02[2][a] n.20; 10.02[3]; 10.06[1] n.6;
    10.08[2] n.36; 11.02[1][b] n.28;
    19.03[2][a][ii] n.57; 19.03[2][c]
2512(a) . . . . 10.02[1]; 10.02[2][a] n.25
2512(b) . . . . 10.01[5][b] n.162; 10.01[5][d]
    n.176; 10.02[3] & n.131; 10.02[4];
    10.02[6]; 19.02[2][a][i] n.29;
    19.02[4][d][iv] n.275; 19.03[2][a] n.30;
    19.03[2][c]; 19.03[4][a] n.262
2513–2519 . . . . 10.01; 10.02

*[Text references are to paragraphs and notes (9"n.");
references to the supplement are preceded by "S."]*

IRC §

2513 . . . . 2.01[1][b] ns. 17, 20; S2.01[1][b] ns.
18, 20; 2.01[2]; S2.01[2]; 3.04[1][a] &
n.14; 3.04[2][b]; 4.07[3][a] & n.81;
4.08[7] n.114; 4.10[1] n.2; S5.03[4][b][i]
ns. 184, 185; 5.06[1] n.1; 5.08[3][c][iv]
n.138; 6.01[2] n.12; 9.01 n.1; 9.04[1][a]
n.15; 9.04[3][f] n.116; 9.04[3][g] n.130;
9.04[9] n.215; 9.04[10][b] n.236; 9.05[4]
n.52; 10.02[2][b][i] n.40; 10.02[5][c]
n.163; 10.03; S10.03 n.13; 10.03[1] &
ns. 4, 10, 16; 10.03[2] & ns. 29, 37;
10.03[3][a] ns. 38, 40; S10.03[3][a] n.40;
10.03[4]; 10.05 n.2; 10.08[3] n.45;
13.02[4][c][ii] n.328; 15.02[3] & n.56;
S15.02[3] & n.50; S15.03[4][e][i];
16.02[2][b][ii]; 16.02[2][b][iv] n.84;
16.02[7][b][ii]; 16.02[7][c][ii];
S16.02[9][a] n.574; S17.02[1][a] n.2;
17.02[1][c][ii] & ns. 61, 64;
S17.02[1][c][ii] n.62; 17.02[1][d];
19.02[2][a][i] n.60; 19.02[5][c][i];
19.02[5][c][ii] n.420; 19.02[5][c][iv]
n.465; 19.02[5][c][v]; 19.02[5][e];
19.03[2][c]; 19.03[4][c][i]
2513(a) . . . . 10.03[1]
2513(a)(1) . . . . 10.03[1]
2513(a)(2) . . . . 10.03[1]
2513(b) . . . . 10.03[1]; 10.03[3][a]
2513(b)(2) . . . . 10.03[3][b]
2513(b)(2)(B) . . . . 10.03[3][b] n.45
2513(c) . . . . 10.03[3][c]
2513(c)(1) . . . . 10.03[3][c] n.49
2513(c)(2) . . . . 10.03[3][c] n.50
2513(d) . . . . 10.01[2][e] n.38; 10.03[2]
2514 . . . 3.05[1][b]; 4.07[2][a][ii] n.28; 4.13[1];
S4.13[4][a] n.35; S4.13[4][c][ii] ns. 41,
50; 4.13[6][a] n.67; 5.06[7][c] n.194;
5.06[8][d][ii] ns. 356, 362; 5.07[5]
n.182; S10.01[8] ns. 192, 193; 10.04;
10.04[1]; 10.04[3][a]; 10.04[3][b];
10.04[3][c]; 10.04[3][e]; S10.04[4][c]
n.47; 11.02[1][d] n.37; 11.03[3][a] n.32;
11.03[3][b]; 13.02[2][e][ii]; 13.02[4][b][i]
n.272; 15.02[4] n.60; S15.02[4] n.54;
16.02[4][d][i] n.260; 18.05[2][b][ii] n.38;
19.02[2][a][i] & n.64; 19.03[2][a][i] n.36
2514(a) . . . . 10.04[3]; 10.04[3][a]; 10.04[3][b];
13.02[2][e][ii] ns. 92, 94; 13.02[4][b][i]
n.266; 17.02[1][b] n.28; 19.02[2][a][i]
n.62; 19.03[2][a][i] n.36
2514(b) . . . 4.13[7][c] & n.89; 4.13[7][d] n.97;
10.01[8] n.200; 10.04[4][a];
13.02[2][e][ii] ns. 92, 94, 101, 103, 108,
113, 126, 143, 151; 13.02[4][b][i] ns.
267, 270; 15.02[4] n.72; S15.02[4] n.66;
15.03[4][b][iii] n.119; 16.02[2][b][v]
n.114; 17.02[1][b] ns. 28, 32, 35, 37;
19.02[2][a][i] n.62

2514(c) . . . . 10.04[1]; 10.04[2][b]; 10.04[3][a]
n.11; 13.02[2][b][i] n.47; 13.02[2][e][i]
n.88; 16.02[4][d][i] n.260; 17.02[1][b]
n.32; 17.02[3][b] ns. 128, 133
2514(c)(3) . . . . 5.06[8][b][iv] n.261
2514(d) . . . 10.04[1] n.3; 13.02[2][e][iii] n.171;
13.02[4][b][i] n.272; 17.02[1][b] n.33
2514(e) . . . . . 9.04[3][f] ns. 117, 119; 10.01[8]
n.200; 10.04[4][c] & n.50; 10.07[2][d][i]
n.89; 12.01[1] n.9; 13.02[2][e][ii] & ns.
92, 94, 108, 113, 116, 122, 126, 143,
146, 151; 13.02[4][b][i] ns. 267, 269,
270; 15.02[4] n.74; S15.02[4] & n.68;
15.03[4][b][iii] ns. 119, 123;
16.02[2][b][iii] n.72; 16.02[2][b][v]
n.114; 16.02[7][b][iii] n.457; 17.02[1][b]
ns. 35, 37, 40; 18.05[2][b][ii] n.38;
19.02[2][a][i] & n.61; 19.03[2][a][i] ns.
34–36
2514(f) . . . . 10.04[1] n.4
2515 . . . 4.08[8] n.171; 4.12[3] n.26; 4.12[7][b]
n.52; 4.12[10] n.88; 4.12[11] n.97;
5.06[9] n.428; 9.04[1][b] ns. 41, 42;
9.05[1] n.2; 10.03[1] n.16; 10.05 & n.8;
S10.05; 11.03[5] n.106; 12.02 & ns. 24,
33; 13.02[2][e][ii] n.103; 13.02[4][a] &
n.250; 17.02[1][c][ii] n.61; 17.04[1][b]
ns. 14, 23
2515(c) . . . . 10.01[3][f] n.112
2515A . . . . 4.12[3] n.26; 4.12[10] n.88; 5.06[9]
n.428; 11.03[5] n.106
2516 . . . S4.08[7] n.114; 4.15[1][b][i] & ns. 45,
46; 4.15[1][b][ii] & ns. 59, 61;
S5.03[4][a][i] n.164; 9.04[9] n.215;
10.02[4] n.135; 10.02[5][c]; 10.06;
10.06[1] & n.7; 10.06[2] & n.15;
S10.06[2] n.14; 10.06[2][a]; 10.06[2][b];
10.06[2][c] & n.30; S10.06[2][c] n.29;
10.06[3]; 11.03[2] & n.11;
19.02[5][c][iii] n.445; 19.03[2][a][ii] &
ns. 54, 57, 59; S19.03[2][a][ii] n.59;
19.03[2][c]
2517 . . . . 4.11[6]
2518 . . . . 4.03[4][b] n.61; 4.13[4][d] n.51;
4.13[6] n.58; 4.13[7][d] & ns. 93, 95,
101; 4.18; 5.05[2][c] & ns. 78, 81, 85;
5.06[1] n.9; 5.06[3][h]; 5.06[7][e] n.201;
5.06[8][d][ii] ns. 325, 354; 5.06[8][e]
n.410; 10.01[2][g] & n.67; 10.02 n.3;
10.04[1]; 10.04[3][d]; 10.04[4][b] &
n.43; 10.07; 10.07[1] & ns. 2–5;
10.07[2] & n.26; 10.07[2][b];
10.07[2][c]; 10.07[3]; 11.02[1][d] n.39;
13.02[2][b][ii] n.60; 15.02[4] n.78;
S15.02[4] n.72; 17.02[3][a] n.120;
17.04[3]; 19.02[5][e]; 19.03[2][a][i];
19.03[2][c]
2518(a) . . . . 5.05[2][c] n.79; 10.04[4][b] n.39;
10.07[2]; 10.07[2][d] n.80; 13.02[2][b][ii]
n.61; 17.04[3] n.79

[Text references are to paragraphs and notes (9"n.");
references to the supplement are preceded by "S."]

IRC §

2518(b) . . . . 5.06[3][h] n.82; 10.04[4][b] & ns.
　　　38, 44; 10.07[2] & n.27; 19.02[5][e]
　　　n.500
2518(b)(1)–2518(b)(4) . . . . 10.07[2] n.20
2518(b)(1) . . . . . 4.13[7][d] n.102; 10.04[4][b]
　　　n.42; 10.07[2][a] n.28; 17.04[3] n.80
2518(b)(2) . . . . . . 10.04[4][b] n.42; 10.07[2][a]
　　　n.29; 10.07[2][b] n.31; 10.07[2][d][ii]
　　　n.95; 17.04[3] n.80
2518(b)(2)(A) . . . . . 10.07[2][b] n.32; 17.04[3]
　　　n.80
2518(b)(2)(B) . . . . . . 10.07[2][b] & ns. 32, 34;
　　　17.04[3] n.80
2518(b)(3)　　　5.05[2][c] n.85; 10.04[4][b] n.41;
　　　10.07[2][c] ns. 65, 70; 10.07[2][d][ii]
　　　n.97; 17.04[3] n.82
2518(b)(4) . . . . 5.05[2][c] n.86; 10.07[2] n.16;
　　　10.07[2][d] ns. 74, 80; 10.07[2][d][i]
2518(b)(4)(A) . . . . . 3.05[3][b] n.46; 5.06[3][h]
　　　n.80; 10.07[1] n.7; 10.07[2][d] n.75;
　　　10.07[2][d][i] ns. 83, 84
2518(b)(4)(B) . . . . 5.06[3][h] n.78; 10.07[2][d]
　　　n.76
2518(c)(1) . . . . . . 10.04[4][b] n.46; 10.07[2];
　　　10.07[2][c]
2518(c)(2) . . . 4.13[7][d] n.98; 5.05[2][c] n.77;
　　　10.01[2][g] n.66; 10.04[4][b] ns. 38, 39,
　　　45; 10.07[1]; 10.07[2] ns. 12, 13;
　　　17.04[3] n.79
2518(c)(3) . . . . 10.04[4][b]; 10.07[1] n.10;
　　　10.07[2]; 10.07[2][d] n.77; 10.07[2][d][ii]
　　　& ns. 93, 94; S10.07[2][d][ii] n.93;
　　　10.07[3]
2518(c)(3)(A) . . . . . . 10.07[2][d][ii] ns. 95, 97
2518(c)(3)(B)　　　5.05[2][c] n.86; 10.07[2][d][ii]
　　　n.96
2519 . . . . . . 4.16 & n.15; 5.06[8][d] & n.300;
　　　5.06[8][d][ii] ns. 330, 362; 5.06[8][d][iii]
　　　n.384; 5.06[8][e] n.419; S5.06[8][e]
　　　n.417; 5.06[8][f] n.421; 5.07[5] n.182;
　　　8.07[1] & n.7; 8.07[2] n.8; 8.07[3];
　　　8.07[4] & n.34; S8.07[4] n.34; 8.07[5] &
　　　n.44; 8.08[1] n.2; 10.02[6][d];
　　　10.07[2][b] n.59; 10.08; 10.08[1] & ns.
　　　1, 6, 7; 10.08[1][a] & ns. 11, 13, 15, 16,
　　　21, 22; S10.08[1][a] ns. 13, 16, 22;
　　　10.08[1][b] & n.27; S10.08[1][b] n.29;
　　　10.08[2] & ns. 30, 39; S10.08[2] ns. 31,
　　　33; 10.08[3] & n.47; 10.08[4] & ns. 50,
　　　51; 11.03[4][c][i]; 11.03[4][c][ii] & ns.
　　　86, 97; 13.02[4][b][i]; 13.02[4][b][ii]
　　　n.290; 15.02[4] n.61; S15.02[4] n.55;
　　　16.02[4][e] & ns. 283, 288;
　　　16.02[7][b][ii] n.472; 17.02[1][c][i] &
　　　n.48
2519(a) . . . 10.08[1] ns. 3, 6, 7; 10.08[1][a] ns.
　　　11, 12; 11.03[4][c][i] n.69

IRC §

2521　　　2.01[2] n.57; S2.01[2] n.75; 3.02 & ns.
　　　13, 28; S3.02[1][a] n.18; S3.02[3] n.64;
　　　3.04[1][c] & n.22; 4.04[1] n.10; 6.01[4]
　　　n.36; 9.05[4] & n.43; 9.06 n.5; S9.06 ns.
　　　37, 44; 9.06[1]; S9.06[1] ns. 50, 67;
　　　9.06[2] n.22; 10.03[2] n.31; 11.01 n.3
2522 . . . . . . 2.01[1][b] n.18; S2.01[1][b] n.18;
　　　3.04[1][b]; 5.05[1][a] n.16; S5.05[2][a]
　　　n.58; 5.05[2][c] n.85; 5.07[4][a][ii]
　　　n.150; S9.02[1][b][i] n.10.13; 9.04;
　　　9.04[1][b] n.32; 9.04[9] & n.196;
　　　10.02[2][b][iii] n.57; 11.02 & n.3;
　　　11.02[1][a]; 11.02[1][b] n.24;
　　　S11.02[1][b] n.25; 11.02[1][e];
　　　11.02[2][b][ii] ns. 76, 82; S11.02[2][c]
　　　n.96; 11.03[2] n.18; 15.03[4][b][i] n.101;
　　　15.03[4][b][iii] n.132; 16.02[1];
　　　16.02[2][c][i]; 16.02[3][b][ii] & ns. 183,
　　　194, 195; 16.02[5][b][i] & ns. 316, 319;
　　　16.02[5][b][ii] ns. 327, 328; 16.02[5][c]
　　　ns. 359, 360; 16.02[6] n.399; 17.02[1][b]
　　　n.20; 17.02[3][c] ns. 145–147;
　　　19.03[3][c] & n.160; 19.04[2] n.29
2522(a) . . . 9.04[9] n.202; 11.02[1][a] & ns. 8,
　　　13; 11.02[1][b] n.24; S11.02[1][b] n.25;
　　　11.02[1][c] n.33; 11.02[1][e] & n.44;
　　　11.02[2][b][ii] & n.82; 16.02[6] n.398
2522(a)(1) . . . . 11.02[1][a] n.12
2522(a)(2) . . . . 11.02[1][a] n.14
2522(a)(3) . . . . 11.02[1][a] ns. 16, 17
2522(a)(4) . . . . 5.05[1][b] n.40; 11.02[1][a] n.18
2522(b) . . . . 9.04[9] n.202; 11.02[1][a];
　　　11.02[1][b] n.24; 11.02[1][c] n.33;
　　　11.02[1][e] & n.45
2522(b)(2) . . . . 11.02[1][a] n.19
2522(b)(3) . . . . 11.02[1][a] n.21
2522(b)(4) . . . . 11.02[1][a] n.21
2522(c) . . . . 5.05[4][a] n.133; 5.05[8][a] n.354
2522(c)(1) . . . . 11.02[1][a]
2522(c)(2) . . . 5.05[4][b] n.144; 9.04[9] n.202;
　　　11.02[2][a] & n.47; S11.02[2][a] n.47.1;
　　　11.02[2][d] ns. 97–99; 16.02[3][b][ii]
　　　n.184; 16.02[5][b][i] n.316; 19.02[5][e]
　　　n.499
2522(c)(2)(A) . . . . 5.06[8][e] n.419; 11.02[2][b]
　　　ns. 53, 55; 11.02[2][b][ii] n.68;
　　　11.02[2][b][iii] n.84; 16.02[3][b][ii] ns.
　　　185, 186
2522(c)(2)(B) . . . 9.04[8] n.187; 11.02[2][c] ns.
　　　91, 92, 94; 16.02[3][b][ii] n.193;
　　　16.02[6] ns. 400, 418
2522(c)(3) . . . . 11.02[2][d] & n.101
2522(c)(4) . . . . . 5.05[8][a] n.356; 11.02[2][e];
　　　S11.02[2][e] n.103
2522(c)(5) . . . . S11.02[1][a] n.23.1
2522(d) . . . 11.02[1][e]; 11.02[2][d]; 19.04[2] &
　　　ns. 30, 32
2522(e)(1) . . . . S5.05[7][b] n.341.2
2522(e)(1)(A) . . . . S11.02[2][c] n.96
2522(e)(1)(B) . . . . S11.02[2][c] n.96
2522(e)(2) . . . . S11.02[2][c] n.96

[Text references are to paragraphs and notes (9"n.");
references to the supplement are preceded by "S."]

IRC §

2522(e)(3)(A)(i) . . . . S11.02[2][c] n.96
2522(e)(3)(A)(ii) . . . . S11.02[2][c] n.96
2522(e)(3)(B) . . . . S11.02[2][c] n.96
2522(e)(4) . . . . S11.02[2][c] n.96
2523 . . . . . . 2.01[1][b] n.17; S2.01[1][b] n.18;
   3.04[1][b]; S4.13[7][a] n.87; 4.14[8]
   n.119; 4.15[1] n.10; 5.06[1] ns. 1, 3;
   5.06[4] n.85; S9.02[1][b][i] n.10.14;
   9.04; 9.04[9] & n.196; 9.05[1]; 9.05[4]
   n.42; 10.01[3][f] ns. 108, 110;
   10.02[5][a] ns. 156, 159; 10.03[1] n.10;
   10.08[1] n.3; 10.08[1][a]; 11.03; 11.03[1]
   & n.6; 11.03[2]; 11.03[3][a] n.27;
   11.03[4][b]; S11.03[4][c][i] n.78;
   11.03[5]; 11.04[2]; 15.03[4][b][i] n.100;
   17.02[1][b] n.20; 17.02[1][c][i] n.42;
   19.02[5][a][iii]; 19.02[5][e] n.499;
   19.03[2][c] n.83
2523(a) . . . . . . 3.04[2][b] n.33; 10.06[1] n.9
2523(a)(2) . . . . 11.03[3][b]
2523(b)–2523(f) . . . . 10.06[1] n.8
2523(b) . . . . 11.03[3]; 11.03[3][a]; 19.03[2][c]
   n.83
2523(b)(1) . . . 11.03[3][a]; 11.03[3][b] & n.38;
   11.03[4][c][ii]
2523(b)(2) . . . . 11.03[3][b] & n.33; 11.03[4][c]
   n.58
2523(c) . . . . 11.03[3][c]
2523(d)–2523(g) . . . . 16.02[7][b][ii] n.467
2523(d) . . . . 11.03[3]; 11.03[4][a]
2523(e) . . . 11.03[3]; 11.03[4][b] & ns. 48, 50;
   11.03[5] n.109; 16.02[2][b][iii] n.63;
   16.02[7][d]
2523(f) . . . . . 4.16 & ns. 2, 11; S5.03[4][a][iii]
   n.171; 8.07[1] n.2; 9.04[9] n.200;
   10.07[2][b] n.58; 10.08[1] & ns. 2, 3;
   10.08[1][a]; 11.03[2] n.18; 11.03[3];
   11.03[3][b] n.33; 11.03[4][c] & n.55;
   S11.03[4][c] n.56; 11.03[4][c][i] & ns.
   68, 74; 11.03[4][d] ns. 100, 103;
   13.02[2][d] & n.81; 13.02[4][b][ii];
   15.03[4][b][iii] & ns. 142, 148;
   16.02[7][b][ii]; 17.02[1][c][i] n.43;
   18.05[2][b][i] n.24; 19.03[2][a][iv] ns.
   62, 65; 19.03[4][a] n.265
2523(f)(2) . . . . 4.16 n.8; 11.03[4][c] ns. 57, 58
2523(f)(2)(B) . . . . 4.16 n.5; 10.08[1] n.3;
   11.03[3][b] n.33; 11.03[4][c][ii] n.84;
   19.03[4][a] n.265
2523(f)(2)(C) . . . . . 11.03[1] n.8; 17.02[1][c][i]
   n.50
2523(f)(3) . . . . . 4.16 n.8; 5.06[8][b][i] n.232;
   8.07[1] n.4; 10.08[1][a] n.20; 11.03[4][c]
   ns. 58, 61–64
2523(f)(4) . . . 11.03[4][c] n.56; 11.03[5] n.111
2523(f)(4)(A) . . . . 11.03[4][c][ii] n.92
2523(f)(5) . . . . 11.03[4][c][ii] n.86
2523(f)(5)(A) . . . . . 11.03[4][c][i] ns. 75, 76;
   11.03[4][c][ii] n.93
2523(f)(5)(A)(i) . . . . 11.03[4][c][i] n.78

IRC §

2523(f)(5)(A)(ii) . . . . 11.03[4][c][i] n.77;
   11.03[4][c][ii] n.94
2523(f)(5)(B) . . . . 11.03[4][c][i] n.79
2523(f)(6)   5.06[8][d][ii] n.341; 11.03[1] n.8;
   11.03[4][c][ii] & n.92; 11.03[5] n.105
2523(f)(6)(A) . . . . 5.06[8][d][ii] n.341;
   11.03[4][c][ii] n.89
2523(f)(6)(B) . . . . 5.06[8][d][ii] n.341;
   11.03[4][c][ii] ns. 91, 92
2523(f)(6)(C) . . . . . 11.03[4][c][ii] ns. 94, 95
2523(f)(6)(D) . . . . 11.03[4][c][ii] ns. 90, 91, 98
2523(g) . . . . 11.02[2][b] n.55; 11.03[3];
   11.03[4][d] & n.103; S11.03[4][d] n.102;
   19.02[5][a][iii] n.361
2523(h) . . . . 11.03[2]; 11.03[4][d] n.103
2523(h)(1) . . . . 19.03[2][a] ns. 31, 32
2523(i) . . . 11.03[4][c][ii] n.91; 11.03[5] n.105;
   S11.03[5] n.105
2523(i)(1) . . . . 10.01[3][f] n.112; 11.03[1] n.6;
   11.03[2] n.14; 11.03[5] n.105
2523(i)(2) . . . . 9.04[1] n.10; 10.01[3][f] n.112;
   11.03[5] ns. 107, 110
2523(i)(3) . . . . . . 4.12[10] ns. 88, 94; 5.06[9]
   n.428; 10.07[2][b] n.46; 11.03[5] n.106
2524 . . . . . . 2.01[1][b] n.18; S2.01[1][b] n.18;
   4.14[8] n.119; 9.04[1][b] n.32; 9.04[9]
   ns. 199, 201; 11.02[1][b] & ns. 24, 28,
   32; 11.02[1][e] & n.42; 11.03[1] & ns.
   6, 9; 11.03[2]; 11.04; 11.04[1]; 11.04[2];
   16.02[3][b][ii] & ns. 194, 195;
   19.02[5][a][iii] ns. 361, 362; 19.03[2][a]
   ns. 31, 32
2601 . . . . 3.03[1] n.1; 4.09[3] n.14; 10.05 n.13;
   12.01; 12.01[2] & ns. 15, 16; 12.02;
   12.03[1] n.1; 13.02[1][a] n.1; 13.03[1]
   n.3; 14.02[4] n.21; 16.02[3][b][ii] n.189;
   18.01[1]
2602 . . . . . . 10.05 ns. 10, 13; 12.01[2] & n.19;
   12.02; 12.04 ns. 5, 8; 13.02[1][a] n.4;
   14.01 n.1; 16.01 n.1; S16.01 n.1;
   16.02[1] ns. 1, 16; 16.02[2][b][i] n.40;
   16.02[2][c][ii] n.159; 16.02[3][a] n.163;
   16.02[6] n.424; 16.02[7][e][iii] n.542
2602(a) 16.01 n.11; S16.01 n.12
2602(a)(1) 12.02 n.11; 16.01 n.11; S16.01
   n.12
2602(a)(2) 16.01 n.11; S16.01 n.12
2602(c)(5)(A) . . . . 14.03[3] n.21
2602(c)(5)(B) 12.04 n.5
2602(1) . . . . 12.01[2] n.20
2603   12.03; 12.03[1] & n.1; 18.02[3][a] n.34
2603(a) . . . . . . 12.03[1] n.3; 13.02[1][b] n.20;
   13.02[2][f] n.188; 18.02[1] n.3; 18.02[3]
2603(a)(1) . . . . 12.02 n.20; 12.03[1] n.5;
   13.02[3][c] n.232; 14.02[4] ns. 21, 24,
   30; 14.05[1] n.8; 17.03[2][b] n.44
2603(a)(2) . . . . . . 12.02 n.20; 12.03[1] n.15;
   13.02[4][a] n.249; 14.04[3] n.15;
   14.05[1] n.10; 14.05[2][b] n.25; 17.02[2]
   ns. 91, 94; 17.03[2][b] n.46; 18.02[3][a]
   n.34; 18.03[3] n.67

[Text references are to paragraphs and notes (9"n.");
references to the supplement are preceded by "S."]

IRC §

2603(a)(3) .... 10.05 n.7; 12.02 n.21; 12.03[1]
n.7; 13.02[4][a] n.249; 14.04[3] n.15;
14.05[1] n.10; 18.02[3][a] n.35
2603(b) ...... 12.02 n.20; 12.03[1] ns. 4, 18;
S12.03[1] n.4; 12.03[2]; 12.03[3] n.36;
17.02[2] n.104
2604   3.03[1] n.3; 8.10[5]; S8.11[3]; 12.03[1]
n.1; 12.04 & ns. 2, 5, 8–10; 14.02[4]
n.21; 17.04[1][b]; 18.04 n.6; S18.04[2]
2604(a) ...... 3.03[1] ns. 1, 3; 12.04 ns. 3–5
2604(b) 12.04 n.6
2604(c) .... 3.03[1] n.1; 12.04 ns. 2, 9
2611 .... 12.02 n.4; 13.01
2611(a) .... 12.01[2] ns. 16, 17; 12.03[1] n.2;
13.02[1][a] n.2; 13.03[1] n.4; 17.01[1]
n.1
2611(a)(1) ...... 13.01[1] n.1; 16.02[3][b][ii]
n.189; 17.02[2] n.86
2611(a)(2) .... 13.01[1] n.2
2611(a)(3) ... 13.01[1] n.3; 13.01[2][a] ns. 12,
22; 13.02[4][a] n.239
2611(b)   12.01[2] n.18; 13.01[2]; 13.02[1][a];
13.02[3][a] n.207; 13.02[4][a] & n.253;
13.02[4][c][ii] n.326; 15.02[1];
S15.02[1]; 18.02[2][a] n.10
2611(b)(1) .... 13.01[2] n.6; 13.01[2][a] & ns.
8–10, 14, 16, 17, 20; 13.02[3][a] n.207;
13.02[4][a] n.253; 15.03[3][a] n.44;
17.02[2] n.85; 18.02[2][a] n.10
2611(b)(2)   13.01[2] n.7; 13.01[2][b][i] & ns.
31, 32, 35; 13.01[2][b][ii];
13.01[2][b][iii] & n.42; 13.02[2][e][ii]
n.101; 13.02[2][g] n.204; 13.02[3][a]
n.207; 13.02[4][a] n.253; 17.02[2] n.85;
17.02[3][b]; 17.02[3][e][i] n.166;
17.02[3][e][ii] n.177; 17.03[1] ns. 3, 6,
7, 24; 17.04[1][b]; 18.02[2][a] n.10
2611(b)(2)(A) .... 13.01[2][b][i] n.23
2611(b)(2)(B) .... 13.01[2][b][i] n.24
2611(b)(2)(C) .... 13.01[2][b][i] n.25;
13.01[2][b][ii] & n.38; 13.01[2][b][iii]
n.41; 13.02[2][e][ii] n.101; 17.03[1] n.24
2612 .... 5.08[1] n.11; 12.02 n.4; 13.01[1] n.4;
13.02; 13.03[1] n.5
2612(a) ...... 12.01[1] n.13; 12.01[2] n.17;
12.03[1] n.2; 13.01[1] n.5; 13.01[2][b][ii]
n.36; 13.02[1][b] n.8; 13.02[2][b][i] n.44;
13.02[2][d] n.82; 13.02[3][a] n.211;
13.02[3][b][ii] n.231; 13.02[4][b][iii]
n.302; 13.03[1] n.5; 14.05[2][b] n.27;
15.03[2][b] n.23; 15.03[4][b][iii] n.108;
15.03[5][b][i] n.205; 16.02[3][b][iii]
n.204; 17.01[1] n.1; 17.02[1][b] n.11;
17.03[2][b] n.46; 17.04[1][d]; 18.02[2][a]
n.10

IRC §

2612(a)(1) .... 4.02[7][e][iv] n.413; 4.08[7][b]
n.128; 13.01[2][a] n.17; 13.01[2][b][i]
n.35; 13.02[2][a] ns. 23, 24, 26;
13.02[2][b][i] n.31; 13.02[2][b][ii] ns. 55,
58, 63; 13.02[2][e][ii] ns. 98, 99, 101,
102, 105, 108, 122, 128, 131, 137, 143,
150, 153; 13.02[2][e][iii] ns. 162, 163,
165, 168, 170, 173, 177, 178; 13.02[2][f]
& n.188; 13.02[4][a] n.242;
13.02[4][c][i] n.322; 13.03[3][b] n.71;
14.03[1] n.1; 15.02[4] n.76; S15.02[4]
n.70; 16.01 n.18; S16.01 n.18;
16.02[4][a] n.238; 17.02[1][c][i] n.58;
17.02[2] ns. 82, 85, 89; 17.02[3][a]
n.121; 17.02[3][d]; 17.02[3][e][i] n.166;
17.02[3][e][ii] ns. 175, 182, 183;
17.03[1] ns. 5, 7, 10, 12, 14; 17.03[2][a];
18.02[3][a] n.32
2612(a)(1)(A) .... 13.01[2][a] n.17; 13.02[1][b]
n.16; 13.02[2][a] n.28; 13.02[2][b][i]
n.38; 13.02[2][b][ii] n.55; 13.02[2][c] ns.
66, 67, 74; 13.02[2][e][ii] ns. 126, 129,
134; 13.02[2][e][iii] n.179; 13.02[2][f] &
ns. 184, 188, 191, 193, 196;
13.02[3][b][ii] n.226; 13.02[4][b][ii]
n.279; 13.02[4][b][iii] n.303;
17.01[2][c][ii] & n.65; 17.02[3][c] ns.
152, 153; 17.02[3][e][i] n.166;
17.02[3][e][ii] n.180; 17.03[1] ns. 11, 17,
23; 17.04[3] n.81
2612(a)(1)(B) .... 13.02[2][a] n.28; 13.02[2][c]
n.72; 13.02[2][f] n.185; 13.02[4][b][iii]
n.303; 17.02[3][e][i] n.166
2612(a)(2)   13.02[2][c] ns. 65, 67; 13.02[2][f]
& ns. 188, 192, 194; 13.02[3][b][ii]
n.231; 14.03[2] n.8; 17.04[2][a] n.62
2612(a)(3) .... 13.02[1][b] n.13
2612(b) ..... 3.03[1] n.3; 4.02[7][e][iv] n.414;
4.13[4][a] n.26; 12.01[1] n.13; 12.01[2]
n.17; 12.02 n.4; 12.03[1] ns. 2, 3;
13.01[2][a] ns. 15, 16; 13.02[1][b] ns. 9,
11, 12; 13.02[2][b][i] n.38; 13.02[2][d]
ns. 79, 82; 13.02[2][e][ii] ns. 100, 128,
134, 156; 13.02[2][e][iii] ns. 162, 173,
176, 177; 13.02[2][f] ns. 187, 188, 191,
192; 13.02[3][a] ns. 210, 211;
13.02[3][b] ns. 213, 214; 13.02[3][b][ii]
ns. 220, 222, 226; 13.02[3][c];
13.02[4][a] ns. 246, 247; 13.02[4][b][iii]
ns. 301, 304; 13.03[1] n.5; 13.03[3][a]
ns. 44, 57; 13.03[3][b] n.71; 14.02[1]
n.1; 15.03[4][b][iii] n.108; 16.02[3][b][ii]
n.189; 16.02[7][e][iii] n.540; 17.01[1]
n.1; 17.02[3][c] ns. 151, 153; 17.02[3][d]
ns. 155, 156; 17.02[3][e][ii] ns. 176,
177; 17.03[1] ns. 6, 13; 17.03[2][b];
17.04[1][b] n.17; 18.02[2][a] n.10;
18.02[3][a] n.31

[Text references are to paragraphs and notes (9"n.");
references to the supplement are preceded by "S."]

IRC §

2612(c) . . . . 12.01[1] n.14; 12.01[2] n.17;
12.03[1] n.2; 13.01[2][a] n.11;
13.02[1][b] ns. 10, 11; 13.02[3][a] n.210;
13.02[4][b][i] n.260; 13.03[1] n.5;
13.03[4][a] n.81; 14.04[1] n.1; 15.02[4]
n.76; S15.02[4] n.70; 15.03[2][b] n.22;
16.02[2][b][i] n.34; 16.02[2][b][iii] n.65;
16.02[2][c][i] ns. 137, 140; 17.01[1] n.1;
17.02[2] n.105; 17.02[3][a] n.109;
17.04[2][a] n.57; 18.02[2][b] ns. 21, 23;
19.03[4][e][iii] & ns. 375, 378
2612(c)(1) . . . 3.03[1] n.3; 4.02[7][e][iv] n.415;
10.05 ns. 3, 14; 13.01[2][a] ns. 11, 18,
21; 13.01[2][b][i] n.28; 13.02[1][b] n.17;
13.02[2][e][ii] ns. 103, 111, 112, 122,
125, 126, 130, 136, 143, 145, 158;
13.02[2][e][iii] n.172; 13.02[2][f] n.187;
13.02[3][b][i] n.218; 13.02[3][b][ii] &
n.221; 13.02[4][a] ns. 240, 241;
13.02[4][b] n.254; 13.02[4][b][ii] ns.
274, 278, 279, 285–288; 13.02[4][b][iii]
ns. 292, 298, 300; 13.02[4][c][i] ns. 309,
315; 13.02[4][d] ns. 331, 345;
13.03[4][a] ns. 80, 82; 13.03[4][b];
15.02[4] n.72; S15.02[4] n.66;
16.02[2][b][ii] n.56; 16.02[2][b][iii] n.63;
16.02[3][b][ii] n.188; 16.02[4][e] n.295;
17.01[2][a][ii] ns. 22, 26, 35, 36;
17.01[2][c][i] n.59; 17.01[2][c][ii] n.63;
17.02[1][b] ns. 13, 25; 17.02[1][c][i]
n.58; 17.02[3][a] n.122; 17.02[3][c] ns.
150, 153; 17.02[3][d]; 17.02[3][e][i] ns.
160, 163, 164; 17.03[1] n.15; 17.04[2][a]
n.61; 18.02[3][a] ns. 33–35;
19.02[5][f][iii] n.520; 19.03[4][e][iii]
2612(c)(2) . . . . 13.02[3][b][ii] n.224;
13.02[4][b][iii] & ns. 293, 304;
13.02[4][c][i] & ns. 305–308, 311, 313–
315, 317–320, 323; 13.02[4][c][ii]
n.327; 13.03[3][a] n.58; 13.03[3][b] n.65;
13.03[4][b] n.87; 15.02[4] n.71;
S15.02[4] n.65; 17.01[2][a][ii] ns. 18,
37; 17.01[2][c][ii] ns. 64, 66
2612(e)(1) . . . . 17.01[2][a][ii] n.34
2613 . . . . 13.02[2][e][ii] n.126; 13.03;
13.03[3][a] n.46; 13.03[4][a] n.79;
15.02[4] n.76; S15.02[4] n.70;
16.02[3][b][ii] n.188
2613(a) . . . . 12.01[1] n.13; 13.01[1] n.5;
13.02[2][a] n.29; 13.02[2][e][iii] n.164;
13.02[2][f] n.185; 13.02[3][a] n.209;
13.02[3][b] n.213; 13.02[4][a] n.240;
13.02[4][b] n.254; 13.02[4][b][iii] n.280;
13.02[4][b][iii] & n.295; 13.03[1] n.1;
13.03[2] n.14; 15.03[4][b][iii] n.127;
17.01[1] ns. 1, 2; 17.01[2][c] n.53;
17.02[1][a] n.2; 17.02[2] n.84;
17.02[3][e][i] n.164; 17.02[3][e][ii]
n.177; 19.03[4][e][iii] n.377

IRC §

2613(a)(1) . . . . 13.01[1] n.5; 13.02[2][c] n.70;
13.02[2][e][ii] ns. 100, 112, 122, 123,
126, 134, 140, 143; 13.02[2][e][iii]
n.168; 13.02[3][b][i] & n.215;
13.02[4][a] n.245; 13.02[4][b][ii] n.281;
13.02[4][b][iii] ns. 299, 300;
13.02[4][c][i] n.309; 13.03[1] n.6;
13.03[2] n.17; 13.03[3] ns. 21, 33;
13.03[3][b] n.63; 13.03[4][a] n.76;
13.03[4][b] ns. 85, 86; 17.01[2][a][i] ns.
10, 11; 17.01[2][a][ii] n.22;
17.01[2][c][ii] n.64; 17.02[2] n.90;
17.02[3][e][i] n.171; 17.03[1] ns. 2, 5–7,
13, 14, 17, 23
2613(a)(2) . . . 13.02[2][e][ii] ns. 124, 145, 150,
158; 13.02[2][e][iii] n.170; 13.02[3][b][i]
n.216; 13.02[4][a] n.245; 13.02[4][b][ii]
n.287; 13.02[4][b][iii] ns. 296, 303;
13.02[4][c][i] n.311; 13.03[1] n.7;
13.03[3] ns. 33, 35; 13.03[3][a] & ns.
38, 44, 60; 13.03[3][b] ns. 64, 65;
13.03[3][c]; 15.03[4][b][iii] n.108;
16.02[2][c][i] n.137; 17.01[2][a][ii] ns.
25, 33
2613(a)(2)(A) . . . . 13.02[2][e][ii] ns. 136, 145;
13.02[2][e][iii] n.175; 13.02[2][f] n.194;
13.02[3][b][i] n.216; 13.02[4][b][ii]
n.283; 13.02[4][b][iii] n.299; 13.03[3] ns.
23, 32; 13.03[3][a] ns. 37, 47, 48, 50,
59, 60; 13.03[4][b] n.87; 17.02[3][c]
n.150; 17.03[1] n.15
2613(a)(2)(B) . . . . 13.02[2][e][iii] n.175;
13.02[3][b][i] n.216; 13.02[4][b][ii]
n.284; 13.02[4][b][iii] ns. 299, 303;
13.03[3] ns. 24, 32; 13.03[3][b] n.69;
13.03[4][a] n.83
2613(a)(2)(B)(i) . . . . . . 13.03[3][b] ns. 61, 68
2613(a)(2)(B)(ii) . . . . 13.03[3] ns. 35, 36;
13.03[3][b] ns. 62, 69–71; 13.03[4][a]
ns. 82, 83
2613(b) . . . . 12.01[1] n.13; 13.01[1] n.5;
13.02[2][a] n.27; 13.02[2][b][ii] n.55;
13.02[2][c] & n.68; 13.02[2][e][ii] ns.
123, 126, 134, 145; 13.02[2][f] n.183;
13.02[4][b][iii] ns. 295, 299, 303;
13.03[1] ns. 2, 10; 13.03[3][b] n.70;
13.03[5] n.88; 15.03[2][b] n.22;
15.03[4][b][iii] ns. 127, 149; 15.03[5]
n.184; 15.03[5][a][i] n.191; 17.01[1] ns.
1, 3; 17.01[2][a][ii] n.24; 17.02[1][a] n.3;
17.02[3][c] n.149
2613(b)(7)(B) . . . . 13.01[2][b][iii] n.39
2613(c)(1) . . . . 13.03[4][b] n.87
2621–2623 . . . . 16.02[1] n.1
2621–2642 . . . . 13.02[1][a] n.4
2621 . . . . 12.01[2] n.20; 12.02 ns. 1, 3, 6;
13.02[1][b] n.19; 14.01 n.7; 14.02;
14.05[1] n.1; 16.01 n.1; S16.01 n.1;
16.02[1] n.15; 19.03[4][e][iii] n.382
2621(a) . . . . 14.02[3]

[Text references are to paragraphs and notes (9"n.");
references to the supplement are preceded by "S."]

IRC §

2621(a)(1) . . . . 14.02[1] n.2; 14.02[2] n.6;
    S14.02[2] n.6; 14.05[1] ns. 4, 8
2621(a)(2) . . . 14.02[1] n.4; 14.02[3] & ns. 12,
    16; S14.02[3] n.19; 14.02[4] n.33;
    14.03[3] n.15; 14.05[1] n.10
2621(b) . . . . 5.07[4][a][i] n.136; 12.02 n.5;
    12.03[1] n.6; 13.02[3][c] & ns. 233, 237,
    238; 14.02[1] n.5; 14.02[4] n.22;
    18.01[2][a] n.28
2622 . . . . . . 12.01[2] n.20; 12.02 ns. 1, 3, 7;
    13.02[1][b] n.19; 14.01 n.8; 14.03;
    14.05[1] n.1; 14.05[2][b] n.27; 16.01 n.1;
    S16.01 n.1; 16.02[1] n.15; 16.02[6]
    n.424; 19.03[4][e][iii] n.382
2622(a)(1) . . . . 14.03[1] n.2; 14.03[2] n.7;
    14.05[1] n.4; 14.05[1] n.11
2622(a)(2) . . . . . . 14.03[1] n.3; 14.03[3] n.15;
    14.05[1] & n.11
2622(b) . . . . 5.03[1] n.1; S5.03[1] n.1;
    13.02[3][a] n.212; 14.03[1] n.3; 14.03[3]
    n.15; 14.05[1] n.11
2623 . . . 10.05 n.13; 12.01[2] n.20; 12.02 ns. 1,
    3, 8; 13.02[1][b] n.19; 14.01 n.9; 14.04;
    14.04[1] n.2; 14.05[1] ns. 1, 4; 14.05[1]
    n.10; 16.01 n.1; S16.01 n.1; 16.02[1]
    n.15; 16.02[2][c][i] ns. 135, 141;
    16.02[2][c][ii] n.159; 19.02[5][f][iii]
    n.520; 19.03[4][e][iii] n.382
2624 . . . . . 4.02[7][e][iv] n.412; 10.02[2][b][iii]
    n.57; 12.01[2] n.20; 14.01 n.10; 14.02[2]
    n.8; 14.03[2] n.13; 14.05; 16.01 n.1;
    S16.01 n.1; 16.02[1] n.15
2624(a) . . . 14.02[2] n.9; 14.03[1] n.5; 14.03[2]
    n.11; 14.04[2] n.4; 14.05[1] & n.2;
    17.04[1][b] n.16; 17.04[1][c] ns. 28, 40
2624(b) . . . . 14.02[2] ns. 8, 10; 14.04[2] ns. 8,
    9; 14.05[1] n.9; 14.05[2][a] & ns. 12,
    21; 14.05[2][b] n.31; 15.03[7][b][i]
    n.263; 16.02[5][f][i] n.390; 17.02[1][c][i]
    n.60; 17.04[1][c] & ns. 29, 30;
    17.04[1][d]; 18.03[1][a] & ns. 10, 11;
    18.03[1][b] n.16
2624(c) . . . . 14.02[2] n.10; 14.03[1] n.6;
    14.03[2] n.12; 14.05[2][b] & ns. 22, 23;
    14.05[2][b] n.27; 17.02[1][c][i] n.60;
    17.04[1][d]; 18.02[4][a]
2624(d) . . . . 14.02[1] n.3; 14.02[3] n.11;
    14.03[1] n.4; 14.03[3] n.14; 14.04[1] n.3;
    14.04[3] & ns. 13, 14; 14.05[1]; 14.05[3]
    n.32
2631 . . . . . . 4.13[8][a] n.119; 10.05 ns. 5, 12;
    12.01[2] n.24; 12.02 ns. 13, 26;
    13.02[3][c] ns. 237, 238; 14.01 n.4;
    14.05[2][a] n.17; 15.01; 15.02; S15.02;
    15.03[1] n.1; 15.03[7][b][ii] n.270; 16.01
    n.18; S16.01 n.18; 16.02[1] n.21;
    17.02[1][c][ii] n.64; 18.03[2][a] n.31;
    18.04 n.6; S18.04[2]

IRC §

2631(a) . . . . . 15.02 n.1; S15.02 n.1; 15.02[1]
    n.22; S15.02[1] n.16; 15.02[3] n.52;
    15.03[4][c] n.152; 15.03[5] ns. 185, 186;
    15.03[6] n.226; 16.01 n.13; S16.01;
    16.02[2][c][i] n.124; 16.02[3][b][i] n.170;
    16.02[6] n.424; 17.02[1][c][i] n.57;
    S17.02[1][c][i] n.57
2631(b) . . . . . . 15.02[1] n.25; S15.02[1] n.19;
    15.03[2][b] n.21; S16.02[9][a] n.574
2631(c) . . . . . S3.02[1][b] n.30; S3.02[2] n.52;
    15.02 ns. 2, 10; 15.02 ns. 3, 12;
    S8.10[1] n.5; S15.02 ns. 2, 3, 5, 6;
    S15.03[5][b][ii] n.208; 15.03[5][c][ii]
    n.220; 15.03[6][c] n.243; 18.03[2][a]
    n.31
2631(c)(1)
2631(c)(1)(B) 15.02 n.2
2631(c)(2) . . . . 15.02 ns. 8, 9
2632 . . . 12.02 n.16; 15.01; 15.02 n.18; S15.02
    n.12; 15.02[1]; S15.02[1]; 15.03;
    15.03[1]; 16.02[2][c][i] n.149;
    16.02[3][a] n.167; 16.02[4] n.208;
    16.02[9][b]; 17.02[1][c][ii] n.64;
    S18.04[1] n.4
2632(a) . . . . 15.03[3][a] n.36; 15.03[3][c] n.81;
    15.03[4][c] n.153; 15.03[6] n.226;
    15.03[6][d] n.253; 16.02[2][b][iii] ns. 47,
    50; 16.02[2][c][i] n.145; 16.02[4] n.208;
    18.03[1][a] n.13; 18.03[1][b] n.22
2632(a)(1) . . . . 15.02[1] n.24; S15.02[1] n.18;
    15.03[1] n.2; 15.03[2] ns. 6, 7;
    15.03[2][a] n.10; 15.03[2][b] n.20;
    15.03[3][b] n.51; 15.03[5] n.186;
    15.03[5][a][ii] n.199; 15.03[6][a] n.231;
    15.03[6][b] n.240; 16.02[2][c][i] n.124;
    16.02[3][b][i] n.171; 16.02[3][b][ii]
    n.191; 16.02[4][a] ns. 223, 234;
    16.02[4][c] n.243
2632(a)(2) . . . . . . 15.03[2][b] n.14; 15.03[6][a]
    n.233
2632(b) . . . . . . 10.05 n.5; 15.02[1] ns. 25, 31;
    S15.02[1] ns. 19, 25; 15.03[1] n.3;
    15.03[3][a] & n.38; 15.03[3][b] ns. 50,
    57; 15.03[3][c] & ns. 71, 75; 15.03[4]
    n.85; 15.03[4][b] n.97; 15.03[4][b][ii] &
    n.106; 15.03[4][c] n.154; 15.03[5] n.186;
    15.03[5][a][ii] n.200; 15.03[6][d] n.250;
    16.02[2][b][ii] ns. 47, 50; 16.02[2][c][i]
    n.145; 16.02[3][b][i] n.172; 16.02[4][c]
    n.243; 16.02[9][a]; 17.04[2][a] n.58
2632(b)(1) . . . . 15.02[4] n.73; S15.02[4] n.67;
    15.03[2] n.5; 15.03[3][a] ns. 34, 36, 39,
    40; 15.03[3][b] n.51; 15.03[3][c] ns. 80,
    82; 15.03[4][d] n.161; 15.03[6][d] n.254;
    16.02[2][b][iv] n.92; 16.02[2][c][i] n.127;
    16.02[4] n.208; 16.02[4][a] n.227;
    16.02[7][d] ns. 501, 503, 504
2632(b)(2) . . . . . . 15.03[3][a] n.37; 15.03[6][d]
    n.254; 16.02[2][c][i] n.126

IRC §

2632(b)(3) . . . . 15.02[1] n.25; S15.02[1] n.19;
    15.02[4] n.73; S15.02[4] n.67; 15.03[2]
    n.5; 15.03[3][a] n.41; 15.03[3][c] ns. 66,
    68, 71, 75, 83; 15.03[6][c] n.243;
    15.03[6][d] n.252; 16.02[2][b][iv] n.92;
    16.02[2][c][i] n.128; 16.02[4] n.208;
    16.02[4][a] n.237; 16.02[9][a];
    S16.02[9][a]; 19.02[5][f][iii] n.524
2632(c) . . . . . . S8.11[3]; 15.02[1] ns. 25, 31;
    S15.02[1] ns. 19, 25; 15.02[2] n.39;
    S15.02[2] n.33; 15.03[1] n.3; 15.03[3][a]
    n.38; 15.03[4] & ns. 84, 87;
    15.03[4][b][ii] & n.106; 15.03[4][b][iii]
    ns. 108, 119, 124, 137, 147; 15.03[4][d]
    & ns. 166, 168; 15.03[4][e][ii];
    S15.03[4][e][ii]; 15.03[5] n.186;
    15.03[5][a][ii] n.200; 15.03[6][d] n.250;
    15.03[7][b][ii] n.270; 16.02[3][b][i]
    n.172; 16.02[3][b][ii] n.191; 16.02[4][a]
    n.235; 16.02[4][c] n.243; 16.02[7][a]
    n.436; 16.02[9][a]; 18.04 n.6; S18.04[2]
2632(c)(1) . . . . 15.03[2] n.5; 15.03[3][a] n.36;
    15.03[4][a] n.93; 15.03[4][b] n.96;
    15.03[4][d] ns. 160, 162; S15.03[4][e][i]
    n.172; 15.03[6][d] n.254; 16.02[4] n.208;
    16.02[4][a] ns. 228, 234
2632(c)(2) . . . . . . 15.03[4][a] n.92; 15.03[6][d]
    n.254
2632(c)(2)(A) . . . . 15.03[4][c] n.153
2632(c)(2)(B) . . . . 15.03[4][c] n.155
2632(c)(2)(C) . . . . . . 15.03[4][c] ns. 156, 158
2632(c)(3)(A) . . . . 15.03[4][a] n.90; 15.03[4][b]
    n.97; 15.03[4][b][ii] n.104
2632(c)(3)(B) . . . . 15.03[4][b][iii] ns. 109, 118,
    120, 125, 140, 141, 146, 147;
    15.03[4][e][ii] n.179; S15.03[4][e][ii]
    n.177; 15.03[5] n.186; 15.03[7][b][ii]
    n.270
2632(c)(3)(B)(i) . . . . 15.03[4][b][iii] ns. 111–
    113, 115–117, 126, 134, 137
2632(c)(3)(B)(i)(I) . . . . . . 15.03[4][b][iii] n.113
2632(c)(3)(B)(i)(II) . . . . . 15.03[4][b][iii] n.113
2632(c)(3)(B)(i)(III) . . . 15.03[4][b][iii] ns. 113,
    134
2632(c)(3)(B)(ii) . . . . 15.03[4][b][iii] ns. 112,
    114, 117, 126, 135
2632(c)(3)(B)(iii) . . . . . 15.03[4][b][iii] ns. 117,
    134–137
2632(c)(3)(B)(iv) . . . . 15.03[4][b][iii] ns. 138,
    139, 145, 147
2632(c)(3)(B)(v) . . . . . . 15.03[4][b][iii] n.131;
    16.02[3][b][ii] n.191
2632(c)(3)(B)(vi) . . . . . 15.03[4][b][iii] ns. 111,
    133
2632(c)(4) . . . 15.03[4][b][ii] n.104; 15.03[4][c]
    n.157; 15.03[4][d] ns. 170, 171;
    16.02[4][b] n.242; 16.02[7][a] n.436
2632(c)(5)   15.03[7][b][ii] n.270; 16.02[9][a];
    S16.02[9][a]
2632(c)(5)(A)   15.02[1] n.25; S15.02[1] n.19;
    15.03[5] n.186; 16.02[9][a]

2632(c)(5)(A)(i)   15.03[2] n.5; 15.03[4][b][iii]
    n.112; 15.03[6][c] n.243; 15.03[6][d]
    n.252; 16.02[4] n.208; 16.02[4][a] n.235;
    S16.02[9][a]
2632(c)(5)(A)(i)(I) . . . . 15.03[4][a] n.94;
    15.03[4][e][i] n.173; S15.03[4][e][i]
    n.169
2632(c)(5)(A)(i)(II) . . . . . . 15.03[4][a] n.95;
    15.03[4][e][i] n.177; S15.03[4][e][i]
    n.170
2632(c)(5)(A)(ii) . . . . . 15.03[4][b][iii] ns. 110,
    137; 15.03[4][e][ii] ns. 178, 179;
    S15.03[4][e][ii] ns. 180–182;
    16.02[3][b][ii] n.191; S16.02[9][a]
2632(c)(5)(B)(i)   15.03[4][e][i] ns. 174–176;
    S15.03[4][e][i] ns. 173, 174
2632(c)(5)(B)(ii) . . . . . 15.03[4][b][iii] n.110;
    15.03[4][e][i] n.178; 15.03[4][e][ii]
    n.182; S15.03[4][e][ii] n.180
2632(d) . . . . S8.11[3]; 15.03[1] n.2; 15.03[5] &
    ns. 189, 190; 15.03[5][b]; 15.03[5][b][i]
    n.205; S15.03[5][b][ii] n.208;
    15.03[5][b][iii] n.209; 15.03[5][b][iv];
    15.03[5][c]; 16.02[4][a] & n.230;
    16.02[5][b][i] n.317; 16.02[7][a] n.433;
    18.04 n.6; S18.04[2]
2632(d)(1)   15.03[5][b][iii] n.210; 16.02[4][a]
    n.226
2632(d)(1)(A) . . . . 15.03[5][a][i] n.193
2632(d)(1)(B)(i) . . . . 15.03[5][a][i] n.194
2632(d)(1)(B)(ii) . . . . 15.03[5][a][i] n.194
2632(d)(1)(C) . . . . 15.03[5][a][i] n.196
2632(d)(2) . . . . 15.03[5][a][iii] n.203
2632(d)(2)(A) . . . . 15.03[5][b][ii] n.208;
    S15.03[5][b][ii] n.208; 15.03[5][c][i]
    n.214; 15.03[5][c][ii] ns. 221, 225;
    16.02[4][a] n.226
2632(d)(2)(B) . . . . 15.03[5][b][i] n.205;
    S15.03[5][b][ii] n.208; 15.03[5][c][i]
    n.213
2632(d)(2)(C) . . . . . 15.03[5][a][ii] ns. 197, 201
2632(d)(3) . . . . 15.03[5][a][i] n.193
2632(e) . . . . . . 15.02[1] n.31; S15.02[1] n.25;
    15.02[4] n.70; S15.02[4] n.64; 15.03[1]
    n.4; 15.03[2][b] n.20; 15.03[3][b] n.51;
    15.03[4] n.86; 15.03[6] n.228;
    15.03[6][a] ns. 231, 232; 15.03[7][b][i]
    ns. 267, 268; 15.03[7][b][ii];
    16.02[3][b][i] n.172; 16.02[4] n.208;
    16.02[6] n.424; 16.02[9][a] & n.570;
    18.03[1][a] n.14
2632(e)(1) . . . . 15.03[7][a] n.256
2632(e)(1)(A) . . . . . . 15.03[7][a] ns. 257, 259;
    15.03[7][b][i] n.261; 16.02[2][c][i] n.129
2632(e)(1)(B) . . . . . . 15.03[7][a] ns. 258, 259;
    15.03[7][b][ii] ns. 269, 270
2632(e)(2) . . . . 15.03[7][b][ii] n.280
2632(e)(2)(A) . . . . 15.03[3][a] n.40;
    15.03[7][c][i] ns. 286, 287, 289
2632(e)(2)(B) . . . . 15.03[7][a] n.258;
    15.03[7][c][i] n.288

*[Text references are to paragraphs and notes (9"n.");
references to the supplement are preceded by "S."]*

IRC §

2641 . . . S2.01[1][c] n.46; 2.01[3] n.65; 4.03[1]
n.13; 10.05 n.13; 12.01[2] n.22; 12.02 &
ns. 2, 14; 15.01; 15.02[2] n.46;
S15.02[2] n.40; 15.03[1] n.3; 16.01;
S16.01; 16.02[1] ns. 1, 11, 13, 16;
16.02[2][c][ii] n.159; 16.02[3][a] n.163;
16.02[3][b][ii] n.192; 16.02[6] ns. 406,
424; 16.02[7][e][iii] n.542; 17.03[2][a]
n.35; 18.02[2][b] n.24; 18.04 n.6;
S18.04[2]
2641(a) 14.01 n.2; 15.02 n.14; S15.02 n.8;
15.02[2] n.51; S15.02[2] n.45; 16.01 &
ns. 1, 2; S16.01 ns. 1, 2; 16.02[1] n.1;
16.02[2][b][i] n.40; 16.02[3][b][iii]
n.206; 16.02[4][c] n.249; 16.02[5][b]
n.311; 17.03[2][b] n.44; 19.02[5][f][iii]
n.525
2641(a)(1) 10.05 n.10; 12.02 n.11; 14.01
n.6; 16.01 ns. 4, 7; S16.01 n.7
2641(a)(2) . . . 14.01 n.3; 16.01 n.4; S16.01 n.4
2641(a)(2)(B)(ii) 14.01 n.5
2641(b) . . . . . 12.01[2] n.23; 12.02 ns. 10, 11;
14.01 n.6; 15.02 n.15; S15.02 n.9; 16.01
ns. 3, 8; S16.01 ns. 2, 8; 16.02[2][c][i]
n.130
2641(c) . . . . S8.10[1] n.5
2642 . . . 12.01[2] n.25; 12.02 n.14; 14.05[2][a]
n.13; 15.01; 15.02[2] n.46; S15.02[2]
n.40; 15.03[1] n.3; 16.01 n.4; S16.01
n.4; 16.02; 16.02[1] & ns. 1, 11, 13;
16.02[3][a] n.163; 16.02[3][b][ii] n.192;
16.02[7][e][iii] n.542; 19.02[5][f][iii]
n.519
2642(a) . . . . 12.03[3] n.33; 14.02[2] n.10;
15.02[2] n.51; S15.02[2] n.45; S16.01;
16.02[4][e] n.292; 16.02[5][b] n.310;
16.02[6]; 17.02[1][c][i] n.58; 17.04[1][d]
2642(a)(1) 12.02 n.15; 15.02 n.16; S15.02
n.10; 15.02[2] n.47; S15.02[2] n.41;
15.03[5][c][ii] ns. 221, 225; S16.01 n.4;
16.02[1] ns. 6, 14; 16.02[2][a] n.30;
16.02[2][b][iv] ns. 98, 107; 16.02[2][c]
n.122; 16.02[2][c][i] n.144;
16.02[2][c][ii] n.157; 16.02[3][a] n.165;
16.02[3][b][ii] n.182; 16.02[4] n.210;
16.02[5][b] n.310; 16.02[6] ns. 424, 425;
17.03[2] n.26; 17.03[2][a] n.34
2642(a)(1)(A) . . . . 15.03[4][d] n.163;
S15.03[4][d] n.163; 16.02[1] n.19
2642(a)(1)(B) . . . . . 16.02[1] n.17; 16.02[2][a]
n.29
2642(a)(2)   15.02 n.17; S15.02 n.11; 15.02[2]
n.47; S15.02[2] n.41; 15.03[5][c][ii] ns.
221, 225; 16.02[2][b][iv] ns. 100, 105,
106; 16.02[2][c][ii] n.156; 16.02[3][a]
n.164; 16.02[3][b][ii] n.181; 16.02[4]
n.209; 16.02[5][a] n.300; 17.03[2][a]
n.34

IRC §

2642(a)(2)(A) 12.02 n.17; 15.02 n.19;
S15.02 n.13; 16.02[1] ns. 2, 7;
16.02[2][a] n.31; 16.02[2][b][iv] n.92;
16.02[2][c][i] ns. 123, 125, 146;
16.02[3][b][i] n.169
2642(a)(2)(B) . . . 12.02 n.18; 16.02[2][a] n.32;
16.02[2][b][iv] ns. 84, 93; 16.02[2][c][i]
n.146
2642(a)(2)(B)(i) 15.02 n.20; S15.02 n.14;
16.02[1] n.8; 16.02[2][c][i] n.131;
16.02[3][b][iii] n.174
2642(a)(2)(B)(ii) 15.02 n.20; S15.02 n.14;
16.02[1] n.9; 16.02[3][b][iii] n.175
2642(a)(2)(B)(ii)(I) . . . . 16.02[1] n.3;
16.02[2][c][i] n.133; 16.02[3][b][ii]
n.177; 16.02[5][f][i] n.391; 16.02[5][f][ii]
n.396
2642(a)(2)(B)(ii)(II) . . . . 16.02[1] n.4;
16.02[2][c][i] n.134; 16.02[3][b][ii] ns.
183, 194, 195; 16.02[5][b][i] n.316;
16.02[6] n.405
2642(a)(3) . . . 8.10[5]; S8.11[3]; 15.02[1] n.27;
S15.02[1] n.21; 15.02[2] n.48; S15.02[2]
n.42; 15.03[4][d] n.164; S15.03[4][d]
n.164; 15.03[5][c]; 15.03[5][c][ii]; 16.01
n.17; S16.01 n.17; 16.02[1] ns. 14, 27;
16.02[3][a] n.166; 16.02[3][b][iii] n.201;
16.02[5][a] n.306; 16.02[5][e] & ns. 364,
383; S16.02[5][e] & ns. 364, 383, 383.3;
17.02[1][c][i] n.49; 17.04[2][a] n.47;
S17.04[2][a] n.51; 17.04[2][b] n.65;
18.04 n.6; S18.04[2]
2642(a)(3)(A) . . . . . . 16.02[5][e] ns. 367, 372;
S16.02[5][e] ns. 366, 373
2642(a)(3)(B) . . . . . 16.02[5][e] ns. 367, 372;
S16.02[5][e] ns. 367, 373
2642(a)(3)(B)(i) . . . . 16.02[5][e] n.368;
S16.02[5][e] n.368
2642(a)(3)(B)(i)(I) . . . . 16.02[5][e] n.369;
S16.02[5][e] n.370
2642(a)(3)(B)(i)(II) . . . . 16.02[5][e] n.370;
S16.02[5][e] n.371
2642(a)(3)(B)(ii) . . . . 15.03[3][c] n.82;
15.03[5][c][ii] ns. 222, 223; 16.02[5][e]
ns. 374–377; S16.02[5][e] ns. 375–378
2642(a)(3)(B)(iii) . . . . 16.02[5][e] n.381;
S16.02[5][e] n.383.5
2642(a)(3)(C) . . . . 16.02[5][e] n.382;
S16.02[5][e] n.383.1
2642(b) . . . . S8.11[3]; 15.03[2][a] n.12;
15.03[4][d] n.168; 15.03[7][b][ii] n.280;
15.03[7][c][i] n.290; 16.02[1] ns. 8, 12;
16.02[2][a] n.32; 16.02[3][b][ii] n.174;
16.02[4] & n.213; 18.03[1][a] & n.11;
18.04 n.6; S18.04[2]; 19.03[4][e][iii] ns.
383, 384
2642(b)(1) . . . 15.03[2][b] n.17; 16.02[4] n.214;
16.02[4][a] ns. 219, 234, 236;
16.02[4][d][i] n.258; 16.02[4][e] ns. 290,
296; 16.02[9][a] & ns. 566, 569

*[Text references are to paragraphs and notes (9"n.");
references to the supplement are preceded by "S."]*

IRC §

2642(b)(1)(A) . . . . 15.03[2][b] ns. 17, 25;
    15.03[5][c][i] n.216; 15.03[6][c] n.247;
    16.02[4][a] n.222; 16.02[4][b] n.242;
    16.02[7][e][iii] n.523; 19.02[5][f][iii] &
    ns. 519, 523, 524
2642(b)(1)(B) . . . . 15.03[2][b] ns. 17, 25;
    15.03[5][c][i] n.215; 15.03[6][c] n.246;
    16.02[4][a] n.218
2642(b)(2) . . . 15.03[7][a] n.255; 15.03[7][b][ii]
    n.280; 16.02[4] n.214; 16.02[4][d][i] &
    ns. 257–259, 261; 16.02[9][a] & n.569
2642(b)(2)(A) . . . . . . 4.03[1] n.13; 15.03[6][a]
    n.235; 15.03[6][b] ns. 239, 242;
    15.03[7][b][i] n.266; 15.03[7][c][i] ns.
    291–293; 16.02[4] n.215; 16.02[4][d][i]
    ns. 250–252, 254, 257; 16.02[4][d][ii]
    n.265; 16.02[4][e] n.292; 16.02[5][f][i]
    n.390; 16.02[5][f][ii] n.395; 16.02[9][a]
    n.569; 18.03[1][a] n.11; 18.03[1][b] n.15
2642(b)(2)(B) . . . 15.03[6][a] n.234; 15.03[6][b]
    n.241; 15.03[7][b][ii] n.282; 16.02[4][e]
    n.293
2642(b)(3) . . . . . 15.03[7][b][ii] n.280; 16.02[4]
    n.215; 16.02[4][d][i] n.258; 16.02[4][e]
    ns. 290, 296; 16.02[9][a] n.567
2642(b)(3)(A) . . . . 15.03[2][b] ns. 18, 26;
    15.03[3][c] n.80; 15.03[6][c] n.249;
    16.02[4][a] n.237; 16.02[4][c] n.245
2642(b)(3)(B) . . . . 15.03[2][b] ns. 18, 26;
    16.02[4][c] n.244
2642(b)(4)   16.02[4] n.214; 16.02[4][e] n.292
2642(c) . . . . 9.04[3][g] n.124; 12.03[3] & n.32;
    13.01[2][a] n.11; 13.02[4][b][i] ns. 260,
    262; 15.02 n.20; S15.02 n.14; 15.02[1];
    S15.02[1]; 15.03[3][a] ns. 40, 44; 16.01
    ns. 15, 16; S16.01 ns. 15, 16; 16.02[1]
    ns. 11, 12; 16.02[2][a] n.33;
    16.02[2][b][i] n.39; 16.02[2][b][iii] ns.
    63, 64; 16.02[2][b][iv] & n.84;
    16.02[5][b][i] n.319; 17.02[1][b] n.25;
    17.04[4]; 18.02[2][b] & n.21;
    19.02[5][f][iii] n.525
2642(c)(1) . . . . 13.01[2][a] n.16; 15.02[4] n.73;
    S15.02[4] n.66; 15.03[3][a] n.44;
    16.02[1] ns. 5, 8; 16.02[2][b][i] n.36;
    16.02[2][b][ii] ns. 42, 54; 16.02[2][b][iv]
    ns. 84, 88, 98; 16.02[2][c][i] n.143;
    S16.02[9][a] n.573; 17.02[1][c][ii] n.64;
    18.02[2][b] n.24
2642(c)(2) . . . 9.04[3][f] n.95; 9.04[3][g] n.126;
    12.03[3] n.32; 13.02[4][b][i] n.261;
    16.02[2][b][i] n.37; 16.02[2][b][ii] n.53;
    16.02[2][b][iii] & ns. 61, 63, 65, 72, 74,
    78; 16.02[2][b][iv] ns. 84, 85, 87;
    16.02[2][b][v] n.119; 16.02[2][c][ii]
    n.154; 16.02[3][b][ii] n.190; S16.02[9][a]
    n.573; 17.04[4] & n.87; 18.02[2][b] n.21
2642(c)(2)(A) . . . . . 16.02[2][b][iii] ns. 61, 71;
    16.02[2][b][iv] ns. 84, 89, 103;
    16.02[2][b][v] n.116

2642(c)(2)(B) . . . 16.02[2][b][iii] ns. 62, 64, 67,
    71, 72; 16.02[2][b][iv] ns. 84, 88, 101,
    104; 16.02[2][b][v] n.114
2642(c)(3) . . . . . 13.02[4][b][i] n.262; 15.02[4]
    n.73; S15.02[4] n.66; 16.02[2][b][i] n.35;
    16.02[2][b][iv] ns. 84, 96; 16.02[2][b][v]
    n.115
2642(c)(3)(A) . . . . 13.02[4][b][i] n.262;
    13.02[4][d] n.345; 16.02[2][b][i] n.38;
    16.02[2][b][ii] ns. 42, 50; 16.02[2][b][iv]
    n.84; 16.02[2][b][v] n.113; 16.02[2][c][i]
    n.142; 17.02[1][c][ii] n.64
2642(c)(3)(B) . . . . 13.01[2][a] ns. 11, 16;
    13.02[4][b][i] n.260; 16.02[2][b][i] n.39;
    16.02[2][b][ii] ns. 54, 57; 16.02[2][b][iii]
    n.81; 16.02[2][b][iv] ns. 84, 86;
    17.02[1][b] n.25
2642(d) . . . . 16.02[2][b][iv] & n.106;
    16.02[2][b][v] n.120; 16.02[3][b][i]
    n.169; 16.02[5][a] n.301; 16.02[7][a]
    n.432; 17.03[2] n.25; 17.03[2][b] & n.38
2642(d)(1) . . . . . 15.02[2] n.50; S15.02[2] n.44;
    16.02[1] n.24; 16.02[2][b][v] n.117;
    16.02[3][b][iii] n.198; 16.02[5][a] n.303;
    16.02[5][b] n.309; 16.02[5][b][ii] ns.
    322, 329; 16.02[5][b][iii] n.331
2642(d)(2)–2642(d)(4) . . . . . 15.03[6][c] n.244
2642(d)(2) . . . . 15.02[2] n.50; S15.02[2] n.44;
    16.02[3][b][ii] n.174; 17.03[2][b] n.45
2642(d)(2)(A) . . . . 16.02[1] n.7; 16.02[2][b][iv]
    n.97
2642(d)(2)(A)(i) . . . . 16.02[5][b][i] n.313
2642(d)(2)(A)(ii) . . . . 16.02[5][b][i] n.314;
    16.02[5][b][ii] n.323
2642(d)(2)(B) . . . . 16.02[2][b][iv] n.99;
    16.02[5][b][ii] ns. 326, 328; 17.03[2][b]
    n.45
2642(d)(2)(B)(i) . . . . 16.02[5][b][i] n.318
2642(d)(2)(B)(ii) . . . . 16.02[5][b][i] n.316
2642(d)(3) . . . . 16.02[2][b][iv] n.98;
    16.02[5][b][i] n.316; 16.02[5][b][ii]
    n.325; 17.03[2][b] n.45
2642(d)(3)(A) . . . . 16.02[5][b][i] n.316
2642(d)(3)(B) . . . . 16.02[5][b][i] n.315
2642(d)(4) . . . . 15.02[2] n.50; S15.02[2] n.44;
    16.02[1] n.23; 16.02[3][b][iii] n.199;
    16.02[4][c] n.248; 16.02[5][a] n.302;
    16.02[5][b] n.309; 16.02[5][b][i] n.312;
    16.02[5][b][iii] n.330
2642(e) . . . . 5.05[6][a][i] n.312; 16.02[1] n.12;
    16.02[3][b][i] n.169; 16.02[3][b][ii] &
    n.184; 16.02[4] & n.211; 16.02[4][f]
    n.297; 16.02[6] & ns. 403, 404, 419, 425
2642(e)(1)(A) . . . . . . 16.02[1] n.7; 16.02[4][f]
    n.299; 16.02[6] ns. 414, 420
2642(e)(1)(B) . . . . 16.02[3][b][ii] n.174;
    16.02[4][f] n.298; 16.02[6] ns. 416, 423
2642(e)(2)   15.02 n.19; S15.02 n.13; 16.02[6]
    ns. 415, 422
2642(e)(3)(A) . . . . 15.03[4][b][iii] n.128;
    16.02[6] n.401

[Text references are to paragraphs and notes (9"n.");
references to the supplement are preceded by "S."]

IRC §

2642(e)(3)(B) . . . . 16.02[6] n.401
2642(e)(4) . . . . 16.02[5][a] n.301
2642(f)   13.02[2][e][ii] n.106; 13.02[4][d] ns.
     333, 338, 339, 342, 346; 14.04[2];
     15.02[1] n.22; S15.02[1] n.16; 15.02[2]
     ns. 37, 40; S15.02[2] ns. 31, 34;
     15.03[1] n.1; 15.03[2][a] n.11;
     15.03[3][b] ns. 46, 50; 15.03[4][b][ii]
     n.104; 15.03[4][d] & n.169; S15.03[4][d]
     ns. 167, 168; 15.03[4][e][i];
     S15.03[4][e][i] & n.172; 15.03[4][e][ii]
     n.181; S15.03[4][e][iii] ns. 179, 181;
     15.03[5][c]; 15.03[5][c][i] & ns. 212–
     214; 15.03[6][a] n.229; 15.03[6][b]
     n.238; 15.03[7][a] n.257; 16.02[1] n.12;
     16.02[2][a] n.32; 16.02[3][a] n.167;
     16.02[4] & n.212; 16.02[4][b] n.239;
     16.02[4][d][i] & ns. 257, 259, 261;
     16.02[4][e] ns. 288, 290, 296;
     16.02[7][a] & ns. 427, 430, 432;
     16.02[7][b][i] & n.448; 16.02[7][b][ii];
     16.02[7][c][i] n.479; 16.02[7][d];
     16.02[7][e][ii]; 16.02[7][e][iii];
     17.02[1][b] ns. 30, 36; 17.02[2] n.105;
     17.03[2][a] n.30; 18.02[2][b] n.15;
     18.03[2][d] n.62; 19.03[4][e][iii] n.376
2642(f)(1) . . . . 13.02[2][e][ii] n.106;
     13.02[4][b][ii] n.288; 13.02[4][d] & ns.
     333, 341, 345, 346; 14.04[2] ns. 6, 7;
     15.02[2] n.40; S15.02[2] n.34;
     15.03[2][a] n.11; 15.03[3][b] ns. 48–50,
     56, 65; 15.03[5][c][i] ns. 215, 217;
     16.02[1] n.18; 16.02[2][a] n.31;
     16.02[3][b][ii] n.178; 16.02[4][b] &
     n.239; 16.02[4][c]; 16.02[7][a] ns. 426,
     430, 435; 16.02[7][b] n.440;
     16.02[7][b][i] & ns. 444, 446–449;
     16.02[7][b][ii] & n.464; 16.02[7][c][i] &
     n.479; 16.02[7][c][ii]; 16.02[7][d] & ns.
     490, 493–495, 502; 16.02[7][e][iii] ns.
     525, 534; 17.02[1][c][i] n.58; 19.02[1][c]
     n.22; 19.02[5][a][iii] n.339
2642(f)(1)(A) . . . . 15.03[3][b] n.45;
     16.02[7][b][i]
2642(f)(1)(B)   15.03[3][b] n.47; 16.02[7][b][i]
     n.451
2642(f)(2) . . . . 15.03[5][c][i] ns. 214, 216;
     16.02[4][b] n.242; 19.03[1] n.8
2642(f)(2)(A) . . . . 13.02[4][d] n.342;
     16.02[4][d][i] n.257; 16.02[7][e][ii] ns.
     514, 519
2642(f)(2)(B) . . . . 16.02[7][e][iii] ns. 523, 527,
     528
2642(f)(3) . . . . . 13.02[4][d] ns. 334, 337, 344;
     14.04[2] n.7; 15.02[2] n.40; S15.02[2]
     n.34; 15.03[2][a] n.11; 15.03[3][b] ns.
     49, 51; 16.02[4][b] n.240; 16.02[7][a]
     n.431; 16.02[7][b] n.440; 16.02[7][c][i]
     & n.479; 16.02[7][d] ns. 490, 493, 499,
     502; 16.02[7][e][iii] n.524;
     19.02[5][a][iii] n.339

IRC §

2642(f)(3)(A) . . . . 13.02[4][d] n.345;
     16.02[7][c][i] n.477; 16.02[7][d] ns. 492,
     496
2642(f)(3)(B) . . . . 13.02[4][d] n.342;
     16.02[7][c][i] n.478; 16.02[7][d] n.491;
     16.02[7][e][ii] n.511
2642(f)(4) . . . . . 13.02[4][d] ns. 332, 335, 336;
     15.02[2] n.40; S15.02[2] n.34;
     15.03[2][a] n.11; 15.03[3][b] n.46;
     16.02[7][a] n.427; 16.02[7][b][ii] ns. 455,
     464; 17.02[1][c][i] n.58; 17.02[1][c][ii]
     n.63
2642(f)(5) . . . . 16.02[1] n.7; 16.02[5][a] n.301;
     16.02[7][a] n.432
2642(g) . . . . S8.11[3]; 15.02[1] ns. 24, 25;
     S15.02[1] n.18; 16.02[9][a]; S16.02[9][b]
     n.584; 18.04 n.6; S18.04[2]
2642(g)(1) . . . . 15.03[2][b] ns. 17, 26;
     15.03[3][c] ns. 69, 71, 75, 83;
     15.03[4][e][i] n.178; S15.03[4][e][i]
     n.174; 15.03[4][e][ii] n.182;
     S15.03[4][e][ii] n.180; 16.02[4][a] & ns.
     229, 234; 16.02[9] n.562; 16.02[9][a] &
     n.564; S16.02[9][a]
2642(g)(1)(A) . . 15.03[7][a] n.255; 16.02[4][a]
     n.225; 16.02[9][a] ns. 573, 580
2642(g)(1)(A)(i) . . . 15.03[3][c] ns. 69, 71, 75,
     83; 15.03[7][a] n.255; 16.02[9][a] n.565
2642(g)(1)(A)(ii) . . . . . . 15.03[4][b][iii] n.112;
     15.03[4][e][i] n.178; S15.03[4][e][i]
     n.174; 15.03[4][e][ii] n.182;
     S15.03[4][e][ii] n.180; 16.02[4][a] n.235;
     16.02[9][a] ns. 568, 571, 572
2642(g)(1)(B) . . . . 16.02[9][a] n.574;
     S16.02[9][a] n.575
2642(g)(2) . . . . 15.02[1] n.26; S15.02[1] n.20;
     15.03[3][c] n.71; 16.02[9] n.563;
     16.02[9][b] & ns. 584, 585; S16.02[9][b]
     n.584
2644 . . . . 10.05 n.16
2651 . . . . . 9.04[3][g] n.137; 10.01[3][j] n.136;
     13.01[1] n.5; 13.02[4][b][ii] n.282;
     13.03[1] n.12; 13.03[2] n.15;
     S16.02[5][e] n.371; 17.01; 17.01[2][a][i]
     n.5; 17.01[2][c][ii]; 17.02[1][a] n.1;
     S17.02[1][a] n.1; 17.03[1] ns. 4, 9;
     19.04[7] n.151
2651(b) . . . 13.02[2][c] ns. 68, 70; 13.03[2] ns.
     18, 19; 17.01[2][a][iii]; 17.01[2][b] &
     n.46; 17.01[2][c][i] n.58
2651(b)(1) . . . 13.02[4][c][i] n.310; 13.03[3][a]
     n.52; 17.01[2][a][i] ns. 6, 10;
     17.01[2][a][ii] n.23; 17.01[2][a][iii] n.40
2651(b)(2) . . . . 17.01[2][a][i] ns. 7, 8
2651(b)(3)(A) . . . . 17.01[2][a][i] n.16
2651(b)(3)(B) . . . . 17.01[2][a][i] n.17
2651(c) . . . 13.03[2] ns. 18, 19; 17.01[2][a][iii];
     17.01[2][b] & n.46
2651(c)(1) . . . 14.05[2][b] n.27; 15.03[4][b][iii]
     n.149; 17.01[2][a][i] ns. 13, 15;
     17.01[2][a][ii] n.36; 17.02[1][c][ii] n.63

*[Text references are to paragraphs and notes (9"n.");
references to the supplement are preceded by "S."]*

IRC §

2651(c)(2) . . . . 17.01[2][a][i] ns. 14, 15;
    17.01[2][a][iii] n.42
2651(d) . . . 13.03[2] ns. 14, 18, 20; 17.01[2][b]
    & n.50
2651(d)(1) . . . . 17.01[2][b] n.47
2651(d)(2) . . . . 17.01[2][b] n.48
2651(d)(3) . . . . 17.01[2][b] n.49
2651(e) . . . . . 10.05 ns. 3, 9; 13.01[2][a] n.14;
    13.01[2][b][i] ns. 27, 30; 13.02[1][b]
    n.15; 13.02[2][d] n.86; 13.02[2][e][ii]
    n.112; 13.02[3][b][i] n.218;
    13.02[3][b][ii] n.224; 13.02[4][b][ii] ns.
    285–289; 13.02[4][c][i] n.305;
    13.02[4][c][ii] n.327; 13.03[2] n.18;
    13.03[3][a] n.49; 15.02[1] n.32;
    S15.02[1] n.26; 15.02[2] n.46; S15.02[2]
    n.40; 15.03[3][b] n.52; 15.03[3][c] n.79;
    15.03[5][a][i] n.194; 16.02[2][b][ii] n.45;
    16.02[7][d] n.491; 17.01[2][a][i] n.10;
    17.01[2][a][iii] n.18; S17.01[2][a][ii] ns.
    18, 21, 37; 17.02[1][a] n.4; S17.02[1][a]
    n.3; 17.03[2][b] n.43; 17.04[3] n.77;
    18.02[2][b] & n.23
2651(e)(1) . . . 17.01[2][a][i] ns. 20, 21, 34, 35
2651(e)(1)(A) . . . . 17.01[2][a][ii] n.27
2651(e)(1)(B) . . . . 17.01[2][a][i] ns. 28, 31, 38,
    39
2651(e)(2) . . . . 17.01[2][a][i] ns. 29, 30
2651(f)(1) . . . . 17.01[2][a][i] n.14;
    17.01[2][a][iii] & ns. 43–45; 17.01[2][b]
2651(f)(2) . . . . 13.02[2][b][i] n.39;
    13.02[4][b][iii] & ns. 292, 303, 304;
    13.03[1] ns. 6, 9; 13.03[3] ns. 33, 34;
    13.03[3][a] ns. 58, 59; 13.03[3][b] n.65;
    13.03[4][a] n.78; 17.01[2][c] n.51;
    17.01[2][c][i] & ns. 54, 55;
    17.01[2][c][ii] & ns. 60, 61, 65;
    17.02[3][a] n.111
2651(f)(3)   5.05[5] n.152; 13.02[2][b][i] n.38;
    13.02[2][c] n.75; 13.03[3][a] n.44;
    14.05[2][b] n.27; 15.03[4][b][iii] n.127;
    16.02[2][c][i] n.136; 16.02[3][b][ii]
    n.188; 17.01[2][c] n.51; 17.01[2][c][ii]
    ns. 67, 68
2651(f)(3)(A) . . . . 17.02[3][c] n.148
2651(f)(3)(B) . . . . 17.02[3][c] n.148
2652 . . . . 17.02
2652(a) . . . . . 5.06[8][d][iii] n.384; 13.02[2][d]
    n.82; 13.03[1] n.11; 13.03[2] n.16;
    14.05[3]; 15.02[1] n.22; S15.02[1] n.16;
    15.02[3] n.52; 15.03[4][b][iii] n.107;
    15.03[5] n.183; 16.02[2][b][iii] n.62;
    17.01[2][a][i] n.5; 17.02[1][a];
    S17.02[1][a]; 17.02[1][c][i] n.42;
    S18.04[1]; 18.05[2][b][ii] n.38

IRC §

2652(a)(1) . . . . 12.02 n.19; 13.02[2][d] n.87;
    13.02[2][e][ii] ns. 96, 120, 147;
    13.02[2][e][iii] n.164; 13.03[3][b] n.71;
    15.02[4] ns. 58, 60, 61; S15.02[4] ns.
    52, 54, 55; 16.02[1] n.21; 16.02[4][e] ns.
    285, 294; 16.02[7][b][ii] ns. 470, 472;
    17.02[1][a]; S17.02[1][a] & n.4;
    17.02[1][b] & ns. 9, 36; 17.02[1][c][i]
    n.41; 17.02[2] n.90; 17.03[2][a] n.32
2652(a)(1)(A) . . . . 4.02[7][e][iv] n.418;
    13.02[2][c] n.75; 13.02[2][e][iii] ns. 111,
    122, 136; 15.02[2] n.38; S15.02[2] n.32;
    15.02[4] ns. 67, 76; S15.02[4] ns. 61,
    70; 16.02[4][e] n.291; 16.02[7][b][ii]
    n.465; 17.02[1][a] n.5; 17.02[1][b] ns.
    12, 27, 40
2652(a)(1)(B)   15.02[2] n.37; S15.02[2] n.31;
    15.02[4] n.72; S15.02[4] n.66;
    15.03[4][b][iii] n.119; 16.02[4][e]
    n.114; 16.02[4][e] n.289; 17.02[1][a] n.6;
    17.02[1][b] ns. 12, 30, 36; 17.04[3] n.81;
    18.02[3][a] n.33
2652(a)(2) . . . . 15.02[3] n.55; S15.02[3] n.49;
    16.02[2][b][ii] n.49; 16.02[3][b][ii] n.170;
    16.02[7][b][ii] n.461; 17.02[1][c][ii] ns.
    61, 62; 17.04[2][a] n.49
2652(a)(3) . . . . 5.06[8][b] n.206; 5.06[8][d][iii]
    ns. 365, 383; 5.07[2][b] n.27; 10.07[2][b]
    n.59; 10.08[1] n.6; 11.03[4][c][i] n.80;
    13.02[2][d] & ns. 77, 83, 87;
    13.02[4][b][i]; 13.02[4][b][ii] n.289;
    15.02[2] n.40; S15.02[2] n.34; 15.02[4];
    S15.02[4]; 15.03[4][b][iii]; 16.02[4][e];
    16.02[7][a] n.429; 16.02[7][b][ii] &
    n.472; 17.01[2][a][ii]; 17.02[1][a] n.7;
    S17.02[1][a] n.5; 17.02[1][c][i] & ns.
    47–48, 51–53, 56–58, 60;
    S17.02[1][c][i] n.57; 17.02[1][d] & n.73;
    17.04[2][b] n.69; 18.05[2][b][i] ns. 25,
    26; 18.05[2][b][ii] & ns. 31, 46;
    18.05[2][d] n.71
2652(a)(3)(B) . . . . 15.03[4][b][iii] n.151
2652(b) . . . . . 12.03[2] n.21; 17.02[2] & n.95;
    18.03[3] & ns. 66, 67
2652(b)(1) . . . 12.03[1] n.12; 12.03[2] & n.20;
    13.01[1] n.5; 13.02[1][b] ns. 6, 7;
    13.02[2][a] n.26; 13.02[3][a] n.206;
    13.03[1] n.8; 13.03[3] ns. 25, 29;
    13.03[3][c] n.72; 13.03[4][a] ns. 77, 82;
    15.02[2] n.41; S15.02[2] n.35; 16.02[1]
    n.17; 16.02[2][b][iii] n.74; 17.02[2] ns.
    74, 80, 87; 17.02[3][a] ns. 110, 112,
    114; 17.02[3][e][i] n.165; 18.02[3][b]
    n.36; 18.05[2][b] n.8; 18.05[2][b][i] n.19;
    18.05[2][d] n.70
2652(b)(2) . . . . 12.03[2] n.22; 17.02[2] ns. 92,
    93, 96; 18.02[3][b] n.38

[Text references are to paragraphs and notes (9"n.");
references to the supplement are preceded by "S."]

IRC §

2652(b)(3) . . . . . 12.03[1] n.12; 12.03[2] n.20;
13.01[1] n.5; 13.02[1][b] n.7; 13.02[2][a]
n.26; 13.02[3][a] n.208; 13.03[1] n.8;
13.03[3] n.30; 13.03[3][c] n.72; 13.03[5]
n.90; 15.02[2] n.41; S15.02[2] n.35;
16.02[1] n.17; 17.02[2] & ns. 76, 97;
17.02[3][a] ns. 110, 114; 17.02[3][e][i]
n.165; 18.02[2][b] n.17; 18.02[3][b] n.36;
18.05[2][b] n.8; 18.05[2][b][i] n.19;
18.05[2][d] n.70
2652(c) . . . . 13.01[1] n.5; 13.02[1][b] n.5;
13.02[2][a] n.25; 13.02[2][b][i] & ns. 31,
44; 13.02[4][b][ii] ns. 276, 278, 279;
13.02[4][b][iii] n.294; 13.03[1] n.13;
13.03[3] & n.31; 13.03[3][a] & ns. 38,
41, 55; 13.03[3][b] n.61; 15.03[2][b]
n.22; 15.03[3][b] n.53; 15.03[5][a][i];
16.02[2][c][i] & n.137; 16.02[4][e]
n.288; 17.01[2][a][ii] n.33; 17.02[2][c][ii]
& n.62; 17.02[3][a] & n.107; 17.02[3][b]
ns. 141, 142; 17.02[3][c] n.150;
17.02[3][e][i]; 17.02[3][e][ii]; 17.03[1]
ns. 1, 5, 7, 11, 15; 19.03[4][e][iii]
2652(c)(1) . . . . 13.02[2][b][i] ns. 32, 54;
13.02[2][e][ii] n.126; 17.02[2] n.81;
17.02[3][a] ns. 108, 113; 17.02[3][e][i]
ns. 159, 167–169; 17.02[3][e][ii] n.179
2652(c)(1)(A) . . . 13.02[2][b][i] ns. 33, 40, 41,
45, 52, 53; 13.02[2][b][ii] n.64;
13.02[2][e][i] n.88; 13.02[2][e][ii] ns. 99,
117, 123, 125, 140, 143, 144, 148, 153;
13.02[2][e][iii] n.179; 13.02[2][f] n.181;
13.02[2][g] n.202; 13.03[3][a] ns. 39, 51,
53, 56; 13.03[3][b] n.68; 17.02[3][a]
n.115; 17.02[3][b] ns. 123, 124, 129,
131, 135, 137, 140; 17.02[3][e][i] n.161;
19.03[4][e][iii] ns. 374, 376, 378, 380
2652(c)(1)(B) . . . 13.02[2][b][i] ns. 34, 46, 49–
51, 53; 13.02[2][e][i] n.89;
13.02[2][e][ii] ns. 99, 117;
13.02[2][e][iii] ns. 161, 174, 179;
13.02[2][f] n.181; 13.02[2][g] n.203;
13.03[3][a] ns. 40, 54, 57; 13.03[3][b]
n.68; 17.02[3][a] n.116; 17.02[3][b] ns.
127, 130, 131, 135–138
2652(c)(1)(C) . . . . 5.05[5] n.152; 13.02[2][b][i]
ns. 36, 38, 41; 13.03[3][a] n.41;
13.03[3][b] n.68; 16.02[2][c][i] ns. 136,
137; 16.02[3][b][ii] n.188; 17.02[3][a]
n.118; 17.02[3][c] ns. 144, 148
2652(c)(2)   13.02[2][b][i] n.37; 13.02[2][e][ii]
& ns. 123, 144, 160; 13.02[2][e][iii]
n.175; 13.03[3][a] n.45; 13.03[3][b] ns.
61, 62; 17.02[3][a] n.119; 17.02[3][d]
n.154; 17.03[1] & n.24
2652(c)(3) . . . . 13.02[2][b][i] n.46;
16.02[2][b][iii] n.61; 17.02[3][a] n.117
2653 . . . . 17.03

IRC §

2653(a)   13.01[2][b][i] & n.35; 13.02[2][e][ii]
n.140; 13.02[2][e][iii] ns. 169, 173, 177;
13.02[2][g] n.204; 13.02[3][b][i];
13.02[3][b][ii]; 13.02[4][c][i] & ns. 322,
324; 15.03[3][b]; S16.02[9][a] n.580.1;
17.01[2][a][i] n.5; 17.02[1][a] & n.8;
S17.02[1][a] & n.8; 17.02[3][b];
17.02[3][d] n.157; 17.02[3][e][i] n.163;
17.03[1] & ns. 2, 4, 8, 13, 16, 24;
17.03[2] ns. 27, 28; 17.03[2][a] n.30
2653(b)(1) . . . . S15.02[2] ns. 43, 44; 15.02[4]
n.76; S15.02[4] n.70; 16.02[1] & ns. 20,
22, 26; 16.02[2][c][ii] n.153;
16.02[3][b][iii] n.17; 16.02[3][b][iii] ns.
203, 207; 16.02[5][a] n.305; 16.02[5][d]
ns. 361, 362; 17.03[2] ns. 25, 27;
17.03[2][a] n.29; 17.03[2][b] n.46
2653(b)(2)   17.03[2] n.28; 17.03[2][a] ns. 30,
31; 17.03[2][b] & ns. 39, 45
2653(b)(2)(A) . . . . 17.03[2][b] ns. 40, 46
2653(b)(2)(B) . . . . 17.03[2][b] ns. 41, 46
2654 . . . S16.02[5][e] n.366; 17.04; 17.04[1][c]
2654(a) . . . . 8.10[3][a] n.22; 17.04[1][c]
2654(a)(1)   17.04[1][a] n.9; 17.04[1][b] & ns.
12–14, 18, 19, 22, 24; 17.04[1][c] & ns.
27, 34
2654(a)(2) . . . 17.04[1][a] n.11; 17.04[1][d] ns.
42, 45
2654(b) . . . . 13.02[3][b][ii] ns. 228, 231;
14.05[2][b] n.30; 15.03[4][d] n.164;
S15.03[4][d] n.164; 17.04[2][a] ns. 47,
48
2654(b)(1) . . . . . . 13.02[2][e][ii] ns. 121, 142;
14.03[2] n.8; 15.02[2] ns. 49, 50;
15.02[3] n.53; 15.02[4] n.76; S15.02[4]
n.70; 15.03[3][b] n.62; 16.02[1] n.21;
16.02[2][b][v] n.114; 16.02[5][e] ns. 363,
373; S16.02[5][e] ns. 363, 374;
17.01[2][a][ii] n.37; 17.02[1][d] ns. 65,
67; 17.04[2][a] ns. 48, 49; 18.05[2][b][ii]
n.38
2654(b)(2) . . . . 13.02[2][e][ii] & n.160;
13.02[2][f] & ns. 188, 197, 199; 14.03[2]
n.8; 15.03[5][c][ii] n.224; 16.02[5][e] ns.
363, 373; S16.02[5][e] ns. 363, 374;
17.04[2][a] ns. 48, 51; S17.04[2][a] n.51
2654(c) . . . . 4.13[7][d] n.96; 10.01[2][g] n.67;
10.07[1] n.3; 13.02[2][b][ii] n.60;
17.02[3][a] n.120; 17.04[3] & n.75
2654(d)   12.03[3] & n.34; 17.04[4] & ns. 86,
90
2654(d)(1) . . . . . 12.03[3] n.32; 17.04[4] n.85
2654(d)(2) . . . . . 12.03[3] n.33; 17.04[4] n.89
2661 . . . . 12.03[3] n.35; 14.02[4] n.27;
16.02[8][a] n.558; 18.01; 18.01[1] & ns.
1, 11; 18.02[4][b] n.54
2661(1) . . . . 12.03[1] n.8; 18.01[1] n.3;
18.02[4][a] ns. 45, 52; 18.02[4][b] n.60
2661(2) . . . . 12.03[1] n.14; 18.01[1] n.2;
18.01[2][a]; 18.02[4][a] ns. 43, 52
2662 . . . . 18.02; 18.02[1]

IRC §

2662(a) . . . 13.02[2][f] n.188; 16.02[2][b][ii] &
    n.53; 18.02[1] n.2; 18.02[3] & n.28;
    18.02[4][a] & ns. 39, 52
2662(a)(1) . . . . 12.03[1] n.1; 13.02[1][b] n.21;
    18.02[1] n.4; 18.02[3] n.29
2662(a)(2) . . . . 14.05[2][b] n.26
2662(a)(2)(A) . . . . 18.02[1] n.5; 18.02[4][a] ns.
    40, 52
2662(a)(2)(B) . . . . . . 13.02[3][c] ns. 234, 236;
    14.02[4] n.27; 18.02[1] n.6; 18.02[4][a]
    ns. 47, 50, 52
2662(b) . . . . . . 18.02[2][b] n.27; 18.02[6] n.64
2663 . . . . 18.03
2663(1) . . . . . 17.04[1][c] n.36; 18.03[1] & n.2
2663(2) . . . 13.02[4][b][i] n.257; 17.02[1][b] ns.
    14, 16, 18; 18.03[2][a] n.27
2663(3) . . . . . . 12.03[2]; 17.02[2] ns. 95, 104;
    18.02[3][b] n.38; 18.03[3] & ns. 65, 67
2664 . . . . . 8.10[1] n.2; 8.10[3][a] n.22; S8.10;
    S8.11 n.2; 9.01 n.14; 10.05 n.17;
    12.01[2] n.15; 12.01[3] n.33; 15.02 n.13;
    16.01 n.10; 16.02[3][b][iii] n.206; 18.04
    & ns. 3, 4; S18.04[1] n.1; 18.05[1] n.1
2701–2704 . . . . 19.02[1][b]

IRC §

2701 . . . . 9.04[10][a] n.218; 10.01[2] n.13;
    19.01[1] & ns. 6, 10; 19.02; 19.02[1];
    19.02[1][a] & ns. 1, 7; 19.02[1][c] & ns.
    18, 22, 23; 19.02[2] & n.24; 19.02[2][a];
    19.02[2][a][i] & ns. 27, 31, 40, 45, 48,
    49, 52, 55–57; 19.02[2][a][ii] & n.68;
    19.02[2][a][iii] & ns. 72, 76; 19.02[2][b];
    19.02[2][b][ii] & ns. 81, 83, 84, 91, 93;
    19.02[2][c]; 19.02[2][d]; 19.02[2][d][iii]
    n.152; 19.02[2][d][iv] & n.168; 19.02[3];
    19.02[3][a]; 19.02[3][b] & ns. 172, 174,
    175; 19.02[3][c] & ns. 180, 182, 184,
    185; 19.02[4]; 19.02[4][a]; 19.02[4][c][i];
    S19.02[4][c][i] n.204; 19.02[4][d] & ns.
    216, 217, 232; 19.02[4][d][i] & n.236;
    19.02[4][d][ii] & n.247; 19.02[4][d][iii];
    19.02[4][d][iv] & ns. 263, 269, 274;
    19.02[4][d][v] & n.290; 19.02[4][e] &
    n.294; 19.02[4][f] & n.301; 19.02[5];
    19.02[5][a][i] & ns. 309, 313;
    19.02[5][a][ii] & n.321; S19.02[5][a][ii]
    n.316; 19.02[5][a][iii] & ns. 364, 367;
    19.02[5][a][iv] n.392; 19.02[5][b] &
    n.400; 19.02[5][c][i] & ns. 403, 405,
    407, 412, 413; 19.02[5][c][ii] & ns. 420,
    424, 425, 427, 428, 432; 19.02[5][c][iii]
    & ns. 435, 436, 438, 444, 449, 453;
    19.02[5][c][iv] & ns. 455, 456, 464, 465;
    19.02[5][c][v] & ns. 469, 472, 473, 476;
    19.02[5][d] & n.491; S19.02[5][d] n.491;
    19.02[5][e] & ns. 499, 501; 19.02[5][f]
    & n.504; 19.02[5][f][i]; 19.02[5][f][ii] &
    ns. 511, 512, 514; 19.02[5][f][iii] & ns.
    516, 519; 19.02[5][g]; 19.03[2][a][ii]
    n.50; 19.03[2][a][iii] n.60; 19.03[4][d] &
    n.353; 19.03[4][e] & ns. 359, 362;
    19.03[4][e][iii] n.381; 19.05[2][b];
    19.05[2][b][iv]; 19.05[2][c] & n.42;
    19.05[3][a] n.48
2701(a) . . . . . . 9.05[2][a] n.15; 19.01[1] n.7;
    19.02[5][d]; 19.02[5][e]; 19.02[5][f][i]
    n.510; 19.03[4][d]
2701(a)(1) . . . . 19.02[2][a] n.26; 19.02[2][a][ii]
    n.68; 19.02[2][a][iii] n.73; 19.02[2][c]
    n.131; 19.02[3][a] n.171; 19.02[5][e]
    n.499; 19.02[5][f] ns. 503, 504
2701(a)(1)(B) . . . . 19.02[2][b] n.78;
    19.02[2][b][ii] n.83
2701(a)(2) . . . . 19.01[1] n.7; 19.02[3][a] n.171;
    19.02[3][b] ns. 175, 176, 179
2701(a)(2)(B) . . . . 19.02[2][a][ii] n.68;
    19.02[3][b] ns. 173, 174; 19.02[5][b]
    n.401
2701(a)(2)(C) . . . . 19.02[2][a][i] n.45;
    19.02[3][b] ns. 174, 179; 19.02[3][c]
    n.180
2701(a)(3) . . . . . . 19.01[1] n.7; 19.01[3] n.15;
    19.02[2][b][ii] n.91; 19.02[4][a] n.186;
    19.02[5][a][i] n.310

[Text references are to paragraphs and notes (9"n.");
references to the supplement are preceded by "S."]

IRC §

2701(a)(3)(A)   19.02[2][b][ii] ns. 84, 88, 130;
    19.02[4][b] n.191; 19.02[4][c] n.194;
    19.02[4][c][i] ns. 196, 206, 207;
    19.02[4][d] n.212; 19.02[4][d][ii] n.252;
    19.02[4][d][v] & n.285; 19.02[4][f]
    n.301; 19.02[5][a][ii] n.323
2701(a)(3)(B) . . . . . 19.02[2][b][ii] ns. 88, 104,
    110, 129; 19.02[4][c][ii] n.209;
    19.02[4][d][ii] n.253; 19.02[4][f] n.307
2701(a)(4) . . . . 19.02[4][d] ns. 211, 232;
    19.02[5][a][iv] n.387
2701(a)(4)(A) . . . 19.02[4][a] n.188; 19.02[4][f]
    n.302
2701(a)(4)(B)(i) . . . . 19.02[2][b][ii] n.89;
    19.02[4][f] n.300
2701(a)(4)(B)(ii) . . . . 19.02[2][a][ii] n.69
2701(b) . . . . 19.02[2] n.24; 19.02[2][a][i] n.38;
    19.02[2][b][i] n.79; 19.02[4][d][ii] n.242
2701(b)(1) . . . . 19.02[2][b][ii] n.82
2701(b)(1)(A) . . . 19.02[2][b][ii] ns. 86, 87, 94,
    98, 100, 101
2701(b)(2) . . . . 19.05[2][b][iv] n.37
2701(b)(2)(A) . . . . 19.02[2][b][ii] n.95;
    19.05[2][b][iv] n.38
2701(b)(2)(B)(i) . . . . 19.02[2][b][ii] n.96
2701(b)(2)(B)(ii) . . . . 19.02[2][b][ii] n.97
2701(b)(2)(C) . . . . 19.02[2][b][i] n.79;
    19.02[2][b][ii] ns. 100, 101, 127
2701(c)(1) . . . . 19.02[4][c] n.192
2701(c)(1)(A)(i) . . . . 19.02[2][b][ii] n.85
2701(c)(1)(A)(ii) . . . . 19.02[2][b][ii] n.85
2701(c)(1)(B)(i) . . . . 19.02[2][b][ii] n.89
2701(c)(1)(B)(ii) . . 19.02[2][b][ii] ns. 90, 103
2701(c)(1)(B)(iii) . . . . 19.02[2][b][ii] n.93
2701(c)(2) . . . . 19.02[2][b][ii] n.119
2701(c)(2)(A) . . . . 19.02[2][b][ii] n.103;
    19.02[4][b] n.190
2701(c)(2)(B)(i) . . . . 19.02[2][b][ii] ns. 106,
    110–112
2701(c)(2)(B)(ii) . . . . . . 19.02[2][b][ii] n.110
2701(c)(2)(C) . . . . 19.02[2][b][ii] ns. 107, 113
2701(c)(2)(C)(i) . . . . 19.02[2][b][ii] n.116
2701(c)(2)(C)(ii) . . . . 19.02[2][b][ii] n.115
2701(c)(2)(C)(iii) . . . . 19.02[2][b][ii] n.117
2701(c)(2)(C)(iv) . . . . 19.02[2][b][ii] n.118
2701(c)(3)   19.02[2][b][ii] n.88; 19.02[5][a][i]
    n.310
2701(c)(3)(C)(ii) . . . . . . S19.02[4][c][i] n.204;
    19.02[4][c][ii] n.208; S19.02[5][a][ii]
    n.316
2701(c)(3)(C)(iii) . . . . 19.02[5][a][ii] n.325
2701(c)(3)(A) . . . . . 19.02[4][c][i] ns. 200, 202;
    19.02[4][d] n.215; 19.02[4][d][iv] n.271
2701(c)(3)(B) . . . . 19.02[4][b] n.191;
    19.02[4][c][i] n.199
2701(c)(3)(C) . . . . 19.01[3] n.17; 19.02[4][c][i]
    n.198
2701(c)(3)(C)(i) . . . 19.02[4][c][i] ns. 203, 204;
    19.02[5][a][i] n.309; 19.02[5][a][ii] ns.
    320–322

IRC §

2701(c)(3)(C)(ii) . . . 19.02[4][c][i] ns. 204, 205;
    19.02[5][a][i] n.309; 19.02[5][a][ii] ns.
    316, 317
2701(c)(4) . . . . 19.02[1][c] n.21
2701(d) . . . . 2.01[1][b][ii] n.27; S2.01[1][b][ii]
    n.27; 9.04[10][a] n.218; 9.05[2][a] ns.
    13, 15; 9.05[2][b] n.20; 19.01[3] n.16;
    19.02[2][b][ii] ns. 93, 118, 122;
    19.02[4][c][i] ns. 204, 207;
    19.02[4][d][iv] n.271; 19.02[5][a];
    19.02[5][a][i] & ns. 311, 313;
    19.02[5][a][ii] & n.321; 19.02[5][a][iii]
    & ns. 327, 362; 19.02[5][a][iv] & n.381;
    19.02[5][c][i] n.403; 19.02[5][d] &
    n.491; 19.02[5][e] n.496; 19.02[5][f][ii]
    n.511; 19.03[4][d]
2701(d)(1) . . . . 19.02[5][a][iii] n.327
2701(d)(1)(A) . . . . 19.02[5][a][iii] n.334
2701(d)(1)(B) . . . . 19.02[5][a][iii] ns. 337, 346,
    365, 368; 19.02[5][a][iv] n.394
2701(d)(2)(A) . . . . 19.02[5][a][iv] ns. 369, 372
2701(d)(2)(A)(i)   19.02[5][a][iv] ns. 376, 397
2701(d)(2)(A)(i)(II) . . . . . 19.02[5][a][i] n.313;
    19.02[5][a][iv] n.377
2701(d)(2)(A)(ii) . . . . . 19.02[5][a][iv] ns. 378,
    381
2701(d)(2)(B) . . . . 19.02[5][a][iii] n.349;
    19.02[5][a][iv] n.370; 19.02[5][a][iv]
    n.386; 19.05[2][b][iv] n.39
2701(d)(2)(B)(i) . . . . . . 19.02[5][a][iv] n.390
2701(d)(2)(B)(i)(I) . . . . . 19.02[5][a][iv] n.387
2701(d)(2)(B)(i)(II) . . . . . 19.02[5][a][iv] n.389
2701(d)(2)(B)(ii) . . . . . . 19.02[5][a][iv] n.391
2701(d)(2)(C) . . . . . 19.02[5][a][i] ns. 311, 312;
    19.02[5][a][iii] ns. 343–345;
    19.02[5][a][iv] ns. 379, 393
2701(d)(3)(A) . . . . 19.02[5][a][iii] n.327
2701(d)(3)(A)(i) . . . . . 19.02[5][a][iii] ns. 328,
    334, 357; 19.02[5][a][iv] n.371
2701(d)(3)(A)(ii) . . . . . 19.02[5][a][iii] ns. 329,
    337, 365, 368; 19.02[5][a][iv] n.371
2701(d)(3)(A)(iii) . . . . 19.02[5][a][iii] ns. 330,
    346, 349; 19.02[5][a][iv] ns. 385, 386,
    394, 397
2701(d)(3)(B) . . . . 19.02[5][a][iii] n.363;
    19.02[5][e] n.499
2701(d)(3)(B)(i)   19.02[5][a][iii] ns. 351, 354
2701(d)(3)(B)(ii) . . . . 19.02[5][a][iii] ns. 351,
    362, 363
2701(d)(3)(B)(iii) . . . . 19.02[5][a][iii] ns. 352,
    355, 362
2701(d)(4)(A) . . . . 19.02[5][a][iii] n.327
2701(d)(4)(B) . . . . 19.02[5][a][iii] ns. 365, 366,
    368; 19.02[5][a][iv] ns. 374, 389
2701(d)(4)(C) . . . . 19.02[5][a][iii] ns. 365, 366,
    368
2701(d)(5) . . . . . . 19.02[5][a][iii] ns. 340, 341
2701(e) . . . . 19.02[5][f][iii] n.521

[Text references are to paragraphs and notes (9"n.");
references to the supplement are preceded by "S."]

IRC §

2701(e)(1) . . . . . 19.02[2][a][iii]; 19.02[2][b][i]
n.79; 19.02[2][b][ii] n.127;
19.02[4][d][ii] n.249; 19.02[5][e] n.501;
19.03[2][a][ii] n.50
2701(e)(1)(A) . . . . 19.02[5][e] n.498
2701(e)(2) . . . . 10.01[3][b] n.93; 19.02[2][a][i]
n.37; 19.02[2][b][i] n.79; 19.02[2][b][ii]
n.127; 19.02[4][d][ii] n.243;
19.03[2][a][iii] n.60; 19.03[2][a][iv] n.75
2701(e)(3) . . . 19.02[2][b][ii] n.99; 19.02[2][d]
n.135; 19.05[2][b][iv] n.37
2701(e)(3)(A) . . . . 19.05[2][b][iv] n.40
2701(e)(4) . . . . 19.02[2][a][iii] n.71;
19.02[2][b][i] n.80; 19.02[2][b][ii] n.102
2701(e)(5) . . . 19.02[2][a][i] ns. 27, 30, 31, 36,
45
2701(e)(5)(A) . . . . 19.02[2][a][i] n.33
2701(e)(5)(B) . . . . 19.02[2][a][i] n.34
2701(e)(6)   19.02[2][b][ii] n.83; 19.02[5][a][i]
n.311; 19.02[5][c]; 19.02[5][c][i] ns. 403,
405, 406; 19.02[5][f][i] & n.510;
19.02[5][f][ii] n.511; 19.02[5][g] n.528;
19.03[4][c] n.305
2701(e)(7) . . . . 19.02[3][b]; 19.02[3][c] n.185;
19.02[5][b] & n.400

IRC §

2702 . . . . . . 3.04[2][b] n.27; 4.08[1][a] n.11;
4.08[7][c] & n.147; 4.08[8][b] ns. 180,
186; 4.11[5] n.50; 5.05[4][a] n.133;
5.06[5] n.94; 5.06[8][d] n.300;
5.06[8][d][ii] n.330; 5.07[2][b] ns. 25,
26; 8.10[4] ns. 140, 141; 9.04[3][f]
n.118; 9.04[10][a] n.218; 9.05[2][a] n.15;
10.01[3][b] & n.94; 10.01[5][d];
10.01[10][c] n.222; 10.01[10][d] n.226;
10.02[6][b]; 10.04[4][c] n.55; 10.06[2]
n.15; 10.08[1][a] & ns. 21, 22; 10.08[2]
& n.39; 11.02[2][b][ii]; 11.03[2] n.16;
11.03[3][a] ns. 23, 30; 11.03[3][b] n.37;
12.01[1] n.3; S14.05[3] n.38; 16.02[4][e]
n.288; 16.02[7][b][i] n.452;
17.01[2][a][ii] n.32; 17.02[1][b] n.40;
19.01[1] & ns. 6, 10; 19.02[2][a][i] ns.
29, 55, 56; 19.02[2][b][ii] n.83;
19.02[4][d] & n.216; 19.02[4][d][iv] &
n.269; 19.02[5][c][iii] n.436; 19.02[5][d]
n.489; 19.02[5][f] n.502; 19.02[5][f][iii]
n.516; 19.03; 19.03[1] & ns. 4, 16, 18,
23; 19.03[2][a] & n.29; 19.03[2][a][i] &
ns. 35, 40; 19.03[2][a][ii] & ns. 51, 55–
57, 59; 19.03[2][a][iii] & n.60;
19.03[2][a][iv] & ns. 70, 71;
S19.03[2][a][iv] n.68; 19.03[2][b] &
n.80; 19.03[2][c] & ns. 83, 84, 87, 93;
19.03[3]; 19.03[3][a] & n.99;
19.03[3][b]; 19.03[3][b][i] ns. 127, 133,
143; 19.03[3][c] & ns. 154, 155;
19.03[3][d] & n.162; 19.03[3][d][i];
19.03[3][d][iii] & ns. 214, 237, 247;
S19.03[3][d][iii]; 19.03[3][d][iv] n.250;
19.03[4]; 19.03[4][a] & ns. 272, 282;
19.03[4][b]; 19.03[4][c] & n.303;
19.03[4][c][i] & ns. 308, 309, 317, 318,
320, 324, 326; 19.03[4][c][ii] & ns. 331,
336, 340, 346; 19.03[4][d] & ns. 353,
354; S19.03[4][d] n.354; 19.03[4][e] &
n.361; S19.03[4][e]; 19.03[4][e][i] &
n.367; S19.03[4][e][i] n.367;
19.03[4][e][ii] & ns. 370–372;
19.03[4][e][iii]; 19.03[4][f]; 19.05[2][b];
19.05[2][b][iii] n.36
2702(a) . . . . 19.03[1]; 19.03[4][a]
2702(a)(1) . . . 4.08[7][c] n.149; 10.01[3][b] ns.
92, 93; 10.08[1][a] n.14; 19.02[2][b][ii]
n.83; 19.03[2][a]; 19.03[2][a][i] n.45;
19.03[2][a][iii] n.60; 19.03[2][a][iv] ns.
64, 75; 19.03[3][a] n.107; S19.03[3][d][i]
n.177; 19.03[4][e] ns. 360, 361
2702(a)(2) . . . . S19.03[3][d][i] n.177;
19.03[4][c][ii]
2702(a)(2)(A) . . . . . . 4.08[7][c] ns. 147, 149;
10.01[3][b] n.94; 10.02[6][b] n.177;
10.08[1][a] n.17; 19.01[3] n.15;
19.02[4][d][iv] n.268; 19.03[1] n.22;
19.03[2][a][i] n.45; 19.03[2][c] n.86;
19.03[3][b][ii] n.150; 19.03[4][a] n.263;
19.03[4][c][ii] n.336

*[Text references are to paragraphs and notes (9"n.");
references to the supplement are preceded by "S."]*

IRC §

2702(a)(2)(B) . . . . 4.08[1][a] n.11; 10.01[3][b]
n.94; 19.01[3] n.16; 19.02[4][d][iv] ns.
270, 271; 19.03[3][b] ns. 110–112;
19.03[3][c] n.155; 19.03[4][a] n.279;
19.03[4][b] n.298
2702(a)(3) . . . . 10.01[3][b] n.94
2702(a)(3)(A)(i)   19.03[1] n.24; 19.03[2][a][i]
n.44; 19.03[3][a] ns. 99, 105
2702(a)(3)(A)(ii) . . . 4.08[1][a] n.11; 4.08[4][c]
n.47; 4.08[7][c] n.147; 19.03[1] n.27;
19.03[2][a][i] n.40; 19.03[3][d] & ns.
164, 167; 19.03[3][d][iv]
2702(a)(3)(A)(iii) . . . . 19.03[1] n.26;
19.03[2][a][ii] n.55; 19.03[2][a][iv] n.73;
19.03[2][c] n.88; 19.03[3][c]
2702(a)(3)(B)   19.02[2][a][i] n.29; 19.03[2][a]
n.30; 19.03[2][a][i] n.44; 19.03[2][a][iv]
ns. 66, 67; 19.03[2][c] n.85; 19.03[3][a]
n.108
2702(b) . . . . . . 4.08[1][a] n.11; 19.01[3] n.16;
19.02[4][d][iv] n.270; 19.03[1] n.25;
19.03[4][a] n.279
2702(b)(1) . . . 4.08[7][c] n.147; 19.02[4][d][iv]
n.273; 19.03[2][a][iv] n.78; 19.03[3][b][i]
n.121
2702(b)(2) . . . 4.08[7][c] n.147; 19.02[4][d][iv]
n.273; 19.03[2][a][iv] n.78; 19.03[3][b][i]
n.123
2702(b)(3) . . . . . . 19.03[3][b][ii] ns. 148, 149
2702(c) . . . . 19.03[4][a]
2702(c)(1) . . . 19.03[2][a][i] ns. 38, 40, 43, 48;
19.03[2][a][ii] n.58; 19.03[2][a][iv] n.68;
19.03[3][d][ii] & n.202; 19.03[3][d][iii];
19.03[4][a] n.273
2702(c)(2) . . . . . 4.08[1][a] n.11; 19.02[2][a][i]
n.29; 19.03[1] ns. 20–22; 19.03[2][a][i]
n.48; 19.03[2][c] n.86; 19.03[4][a] & ns.
260–262, 274; 19.03[4][c][ii];
19.03[4][e][i] n.368; S19.03[4][a]
2702(c)(3) . . . 19.03[2][a][i] ns. 39, 40, 43, 48;
19.03[2][a][iv] n.69
2702(c)(4) . . . 19.03[3] n.98; 19.03[4][a] n.283;
19.03[4][b] ns. 287–289; 19.03[4][c]
n.304; 19.03[4][c][i] n.307;
19.03[4][c][ii] ns. 335, 341
2702(d)   10.08[1][a] n.18; 19.03[2][b] ns. 79,
80; 19.03[2][c] n.84; 19.03[3][a] &
n.104; 19.03[3][b][ii] n.147; 19.03[4][a]
n.277
2702(e) . . . . 4.08[1][a] n.11; 10.01[3][b] n.92;
10.02[6][b] n.176; 10.08[1][a] n.14;
19.03[2][a][ii] ns. 50, 53; 19.03[4][a]
n.260; 19.05[2][b][iii] n.36

IRC §

2703 . . . . 4.02[1] n.5; 4.02[2][c] & n.48;
4.02[4][g] n.238; 4.05[7][b] n.81;
10.02[2][b][vi]; 12.01[1] n.3; 19.01[1] &
n.6; 19.02[2][b][ii] n.112; 19.04;
19.04[1][a]; 19.04[1][c] & ns. 12, 14;
19.04[2] & n.29; S19.04[2] n.19;
19.04[3]; 19.04[3][a]; 19.04[3][b] n.55;
19.04[3][b][i] & n.62; 19.04[3][b][ii];
19.04[3][c]; 19.04[4] n.105; 19.04[6];
19.04[7] & ns. 140, 141; 19.05[3][b]
2703(a) . . . . . . 4.02[2][c] n.48; 19.01[3] n.15;
19.04[1][c] & n.14; 19.04[2] & ns. 17,
18, 26; S19.04[2] n.19; 19.04[4];
S19.04[4] n.99; 19.04[6]
2703(a)(1) . . . . 19.04[2] ns. 17, 20
2703(a)(2) . . . . 19.04[2] ns. 18, 20
2703(b) . . . . 4.02[2][c] n.52; S4.02[4][g] n.238;
10.02[2][b][vi]; 19.04[1][c]; 19.04[2]
n.21; S19.04[2] n.19; 19.04[3] & n.35;
19.04[3][b] n.56; 19.04[3][b][i] n.57;
19.04[4]; S19.04[4] n.99; 19.04[5];
19.04[6]; 19.04[6][a] n.116; S19.04[6][a]
n.116; 19.04[7]
2703(b)(1)   19.04[1][c] n.10; 19.04[3] ns. 37,
40; 19.04[3][a] n.45
2703(b)(2) . . . . 19.04[1][c] n.10; 19.04[2] n.17;
19.04[3] ns. 38, 40; 19.04[3][b] n.56;
19.04[3][b][i] ns. 57, 58, 62;
19.04[3][b][ii] n.88
2703(b)(3)   19.04[1][c] n.11; 19.04[3] ns. 39,
42; 19.04[3][c] n.91
2703(e)(1) . . . . 19.04[4] n.105
2703(e)(2) . . . . 19.04[4] n.105
2704 . . . . 12.01[1] n.3; 19.01[1] & n.6;
19.02[3][b] n.174; 19.05; 19.05[1] & ns.
1, 2; 19.05[2][b][iv]; 19.05[3][b] n.56
2704(a) . . . . . . 19.01[1] n.7; 19.05[1] & n.3;
19.05[2]; 19.05[2][a]; 19.05[2][b];
19.05[2][b][i] & n.27; 19.05[2][b][ii];
19.05[2][c]; 19.05[2][d] & n.45
2704(a)(1) . . . 19.05[1] n.4; 19.05[2][a] ns. 18–
21
2704(a)(1)(B) . . . . 19.05[2][c] n.41
2704(a)(2) . . . . 19.05[2][d] n.45
2704(a)(3) . . . . 19.05[2][b][i] n.27
2704(b) . . . . . . 4.02[4][g] n.238; 19.02[4][d][i]
n.238; 19.05[1] & ns. 3, 9; 19.05[2][b];
19.05[2][c] n.41; 19.05[3]; 19.05[3][a] &
n.48; 19.05[3][b] & n.53
2704(b)(1) . . . . 19.05[1] n.4
2704(b)(2)(A) . . . . 19.05[3][b] n.53
2704(b)(2)(B)(i) . . . . 19.05[3][b] n.55
2704(b)(2)(B)(ii) . . . . 19.05[3][b] n.56
2704(b)(3)(A) . . . . 19.05[3][b] n.61
2704(b)(3)(B) . . . . 19.05[3][b] ns. 54, 57
2704(b)(4) . . . . 19.05[3][b] n.64
2704(c)(1) . . . . . . 19.05[2][b][iv] ns. 37–39
2704(c)(2) . . . 8.10[4] n.141; 10.01[3][b] n.92;
10.02[6][b] n.176; 10.08[1][a] n.14;
11.03[3][a] n.30; 19.03[2][a][ii] n.50;
19.03[4][a] n.260; 19.05[2][b][iii] n.36

*[Text references are to paragraphs and notes (9"n.");
references to the supplement are preceded by "S."]*

IRC §

2704(c)(2)(A) . . . . 19.03[2][a][ii] n.53
2704(c)(3) . . . . 19.05[2][b][iv] n.40
2704(c)(4) . . . . 19.03[4][b] ns. 298, 302;
                        19.03[4][c][ii] n.335
2801 . . . . S6.07; S6.07[1] & n.8; S6.07[1][a] &
        ns. 13, 17; S6.07[1][b] & n.24; S6.07[2];
        S6.07[2][a]; S9.02[1][b]; S9.02[1][b][i] &
        ns. 10.11, 10.27; S9.02[1][b][ii];
                        S10.01[11] n.238
2801(a)   S6.07[1] n.8; S6.07[1][a] ns. 17, 22;
        S6.07[1][b] n.30; S9.02[1][b][i] ns. 10.1,
                        10.11, 10.16, 10.24
2801(b) . . . . . S6.07[1][b] n.24; S9.02[1][b][i]
                        n.10.18
2801(c) . . . . . S6.07[1][b] n.25; S9.02[1][b][i]
                        n.10.19
2801(d) . . . . . S6.07[1][b] n.31; S9.02[1][b][i]
                        n.10.25
2801(e)(1)(A) . . . . S9.02[1][b][i] n.10.11
2801(e)(1)(B) . . . . S6.07[1][a] n.17;
                        S9.02[1][b][i] n.10.10
2801(e)(2) . . . . S6.07[1][a] n.18; S9.02[1][b][i]
                        n.10.12
2801(e)(3) . . . S6.07[1][a] n.21; S9.02[1][b][i]
                        n.10.15
2801(e)(4)(A) . . . . S6.07[1][b] n.26;
                        S9.02[1][b][i] n.10.20
2801(e)(4)(B)(i) . . . . S6.07[1][b] n.27;
                        S9.02[1][b][i] n.10.21
2801(e)(4)(B)(ii) . . . . S6.07[1][b] n.27;
                        S9.02[1][b][i] n.10.21
2801(e)(4)(B)(iii) . . . . S6.07[1][b] n.27;
                        S9.02[1][b][i] n.10.21
2801(f) . . . . S6.07 ns. 2–4; S6.07[1][a] ns. 10,
        12, 16; S9.02[1][b] ns. 5–7;
        S9.02[1][b][i] ns. 10.3, 10.5, 10.9
3032A . . . . S4.04[5][a] n.176
4940 . . . . 5.05[1][c] n.47
4941 . . . . 5.05[1][c] n.52
4942 . . . . 5.05[1][c] n.48
4942(j)(3) . . . . 5.05[7][d] n.350
4943 . . . . 5.05[1][c] n.49
4943(f)(5)(A) . . . . S5.05[1][c]
4943(f)(5)(B) . . . . S5.05[1][c]
4944 . . . . . 5.05[1][c] n.50; 5.05[6][a][ii] n.319
4945 . . . . 5.05[1][c] n.51
4947 . . . . 5.05[1][c] n.55
4947(a)(1)   S5.05[1][c] n.55; 5.05[8][d] n.381
4947(a)(2) . . . . 5.05[6][a][ii] n.319
4947(b)(3) . . . . 5.05[6][a][ii] n.319
4948(c)(4) . . . . 5.05[1][c] & n.56
4966(d)(1) . . . . S5.05[1][c] n.56.1
4966(d)(2) . . . . S5.05[1][c]
4980A(d) . . . 2.01[5] & n.82; 5.03[5][a] n.103;
                        5.05[3][b][i] n.104
6001–7873 . . . . 18.01[1]
6007(e)(2)(B) . . . . S2.01[1][b][ii] n.41
6012(b) . . . . 18.02[3] n.30
6013 . . . . 5.06[1] n.1; 10.01[2][e] n.35
6013(d)(3) . . . . 10.01[2][e] n.38

IRC §

6018 . . . . . S2.01[1][c] n.53; 2.01[3] n.71; 3.02
        n.23; 4.03[1] n.10; S5.03[5] n.251;
        5.03[6] n.150; 5.06[8][e] n.416; 6.08;
        8.02; 8.10[3][b][v]; 8.10[3][d][iii];
        S8.10[3][a][v]; S8.10[3][d][ii]; 10.08[1]
                        n.3; 18.02[2][b] n.15
6018(a) . . . . 3.02 & n.24; S3.02[3] n.61;
        8.10[3][d][ii] n.122; S8.10[3][d][ii]
        n.112; 9.06[3] n.28; 15.02[1] n.24;
        S15.02[1] n.18; 15.03[6][a] n.231
6018(a)(1) . . . . S3.02[3]; 5.02 n.2; S9.06 n.41
6018(a)(2) . . . . 6.01[4] ns. 36, 37
6018(a)(3) . . . . 6.01[4] n.36
6018(a)(3)(A) . . . . . . 3.02 n.25; S3.02[3] n.62
6018(a)(3)(B) . . . . . . 3.02 n.26; S3.02[3] n.64
6018(b) . . . . S8.10[3][d][iii]
6018(b)(1) . . . . 8.10[3][d][ii] n.118;
        S8.10[3][d][ii] n.108; S8.10[3][d][iii]
6018(b)(2) . . . . 8.10[3][d][ii] n.120;
        S8.10[3][d][ii]; S8.10[3][d][iii]
6018(b)(3) . . . . 8.10[3][d][ii] n.122;
        S8.10[3][d][ii] n.112
6018(b)(4) . . . . 8.10[3][d][ii] n.125;
        S8.10[3][d][ii] n.115
6018(c) . . . 8.10[3][d][ii] n.124; S8.10[3][d][ii]
                        n.114
6018(d) . . . 8.10[3][d][ii] n.117; S8.10[3][d][ii]
                        n.107
6018(e) . . . 8.10[3][d][ii] n.126; 8.10[3][d][iii];
        S8.10[3][d][ii] n.116; S8.10[3][d][iii]
6019 . . . . 9.04[9] & n.198; S9.06 n.42; 9.06[3]
        n.28; 16.02[4][a] n.224; 17.02[1][b] n.25;
                        18.02[2][b] n.20
6019(a) . . . . 8.10[3][d][i]; 8.10[3][d][ii] n.120;
        S8.10[3][d][i]; S8.10[3][d][ii] n.110;
                        9.04[8] n.193
6019(a)(1) . . . 9.04[9] n.198; 16.02[2][b][ii] ns.
                        51, 52
6019(a)(2) . . . . . 9.04[9] n.200; 10.06[1] n.11
6019(b) . . . . 8.10[3][d][i] ns. 113, 116;
        8.10[3][d][iii]; S8.10[3][c][v] ns. 103,
                        106
6019(b)(1)   8.10[3][d][i] n.114; S8.10[3][c][v]
                        n.104
6019(b)(2) . . . . 8.10[3][d][i] n.115;
        8.10[3][d][iii]; S8.10[3][c][v] n.105
6019(1) . . . . 4.07[2][d]; 11.02[1][e] n.43;
                        18.02[2][b] n.22
6019(2) . . . 4.07[2][d] n.74; 11.02[1][e] n.43;
                        11.03[1] n.9
6019(3) . . . . . 4.07[2][d] n.74; 9.04[9] n.203;
                        11.02[1][e] n.42
6019(3)(A) . . . . 9.04[9] n.202; 11.02[1][e] n.45
6019(3)(A)(ii) . . . . . 9.04[9] n.202; 11.02[1][e]
                        n.43
6019(3)(B) . . . . 9.04[9] n.203; 11.02[1][e] n.46
6036 . . . . 2.02[1] n.17
6039G . . . . S6.07[1] n.8; S9.02[1][b][i] n.10.11
6072(a) . . . . 9.04[9] n.207

[Text references are to paragraphs and notes (9"n.");
references to the supplement are preceded by "S."]

IRC §

6075 . . . . 4.03[1] & n.5; 4.04[7][h] n.373;
　　　S5.03[6][c][iv] n.316; 5.03[7] n.158;
　　　6.01[4] n.38; 11.03[4][c] n.56;
　　　16.02[7][e][iii] n.523; 16.02[8][b] n.560
6075(a) . . . . 2.02[1] n.7; 5.03[4][b] n.93;
　　　S5.03[6][c][iii] n.308; 18.02[4][a] ns. 42,
　　　46
6075(b) . . . . S9.06 n.42; 9.06[3] n.28;
　　　15.03[2][b] n.16; 15.03[5][a][iii] n.202;
　　　16.02[4][a] n.224
6075(b)(1) . . . 9.04[9] ns. 206, 211; 15.03[6][d]
　　　n.251; 16.02[4][a] n.231; 18.02[4][a] ns.
　　　44, 46
6075(b)(2) . . . 9.04[9] n.210; 16.02[4][a] n.232;
　　　18.02[4][b] n.60
6075(b)(3) . . . 9.04[9] n.211; 15.03[6][d] n.251;
　　　16.02[4][a] n.231; 18.02[4][a] ns. 46, 52;
　　　18.02[4][b] n.60
6081 . . . 2.02[1]; 2.02[3][b][i]; 3.05[3][b] n.46;
　　　4.03[1] n.4; S5.03[6][c][iii] n.308;
　　　S5.03[6][c][iv] n.316; 5.03[7] n.158;
　　　5.07[5] ns. 184, 187; 6.01[4] n.38;
　　　16.02[4][a] n.232; 18.02[4][a] ns. 43, 45,
　　　46, 48; 18.02[4][b] n.54
6081(a) . . . 2.02[1] n.8; 5.07[4][c] ns. 170, 172;
　　　9.04[9] n.208
6081(a)(1) . . . . S3.02[1][b] n.30
6091 . . . . 18.02[5] ns. 61, 62
6091(b) . . . . 9.04[9] n.212
6091(b)(1)(A) . . . . 18.02[5] n.61
6091(b)(1)(A)(ii) . . . . 9.04[9] n.212
6091(b)(3) . . . . 2.02[1] n.19; 18.02[5] n.62
6091(b)(4) . . . . 2.02[1] ns. 19, 22
6114 . . . . 7.01[1] n.1; 7.06 n.15
6151 . . . . 2.02[2]; 14.02[4] n.27
6151(a) . . . . 2.02[3][c][ii] n.98; 2.02[3][c][iii];
　　　9.04[9] n.213; 18.01[2] n.12; 18.01[2][a]
　　　n.22
6151(c) . . . . 18.01[2] n.12
6159 . . . . 2.02[3]; 2.02[3][a] & ns. 28, 32;
　　　9.04[9] n.213; 18.01[2]; 18.01[2][b] n.32
6159(a) . . . . 2.02[3][a] n.28
6159(b)(1) . . . . 2.02[3][a] n.29
6159(b)(2)(A) . . . . 2.02[3][a] n.30
6159(b)(2)(B) . . . . 2.02[3][a] n.31
6159(b)(3) . . . . 2.02[3][a] n.35
6159(b)(4)(A) . . . . 2.02[3][a] n.32
6159(b)(4)(B) . . . . 2.02[3][a] n.33
6159(b)(4)(C) . . - - . - . . . . 2.02[3][a] n.34
6159(b)(5) . . . . 2.02[3][a] n.35
6161 . . . . . . S2.02[1] n.11; 2.02[3]; 2.02[3][b];
　　　2.02[3][b][i] n.39; S2.02[3][b][i] ns. 38,
　　　39; S2.02[3][b][ii] n.41; 2.02[3][c][ii] &
　　　n.58; S2.02[3][c][vi] n.137; 3.03[2];
　　　3.05[2] n.22; 3.06[4]; S5.03[3][c][i]
　　　n.119; S5.03[6][a] n.270; 5.09[2]
6161(a) . . . . . 2.02[3][b][ii] n.44; 9.04[9] n.213

IRC §

6161(a)(1) . . . 2.02[3][b][i] n.36; 2.02[3][b][ii];
　　　5.07[4][a][i] n.130; 5.07[4][a][ii] ns. 137,
　　　147; 5.07[4][c] ns. 170, 172; 18.01[1]
　　　n.2; 18.01[2]; 18.01[2][a] n.15;
　　　18.01[2][b] n.31
6161(a)(2) . . . . . 2.02[3][b][ii]; 3.03[2] n.24;
　　　3.06[4] n.29; 4.04[7][e] n.346;
　　　5.07[4][a][ii] & n.147; 5.07[4][c] n.170;
　　　5.08[5][d][i] n.263; 5.09[2] n.20;
　　　18.01[2][a] n.16; 18.01[2][b] n.31
6161(a)(2)(A) . . . . . . 4.04[7][e]; 5.08[5][d][i]
6161(a)(2)(B) . . . . . 3.03[2] n.24; 3.06[4] n.29;
　　　5.09[2] n.20
6161(b) . . . . . . 18.01[2] n.13; 18.01[2][b] n.31
6161(b)(2) . . . . 3.03[2] n.25; 3.06[4] n.30;
　　　5.09[2] n.21
6163 . . . . . . 2.02[3] & n.26; 2.02[3][b][i] n.39;
　　　3.05[2] n.22; 3.07; 4.04[7][c][iv]
6163(a) . . . 3.07; 4.02[5] n.243; 8.07[4] ns. 33,
　　　35, 38; 18.01[1] n.2; 18.01[2][a] n.17
6163(b) . . . . 3.07 n.3; 18.01[2][a] n.18
6165 . . . . 2.02[3][c][iii] n.116; S2.02[3][c][iii]
　　　n.116; 3.07 n.3
6166 . . . . S2.02[1] ns. 7, 8; 2.02[3];
　　　2.02[3][b][ii] & n.41; S2.02[3][b][ii]
　　　n.41; 2.02[3][c]; 2.02[3][c][i] n.46;
　　　2.02[3][c][ii] & ns. 55, 64, 107, 111;
　　　S2.02[3][c][ii] ns. 55, 57, 82;
　　　2.02[3][c][iii] & ns. 115, 116;
　　　S2.02[3][c][iii] & ns. 115, 116;
　　　2.02[3][c][iv]; 2.02[3][c][v] & ns. 127,
　　　131, 132; 2.02[3][c][vi] & n.151;
　　　S2.02[3][c][vi] n.142; 2.02[3][c][vii] &
　　　ns. 153, 155; S2.02[3][c][vii] & n.156;
　　　3.03[2] & n.24; 3.05[2] n.22; 3.06[4]
　　　n.30; 3.07 n.12; 4.02[7][e][ii] & n.388;
　　　4.02[7][e][iii]; 4.04[1]; 4.04[3][b][v]
　　　n.66; 4.04[7][e]; 4.16; 5.03[3][c] & ns.
　　　71, 72; S5.03[3][c][i] & ns. 114, 124,
　　　125; 5.07[4][a][i] n.130; 5.07[4][a][ii];
　　　5.08[1] & n.11; S5.08[2][a] n.16;
　　　S5.08[2][c][ii] n.56; 5.08[5][d][i];
　　　5.08[6][c] & ns. 298, 301; 5.09[2] &
　　　n.20; S8.03[1] n.6; 8.03[2]; S8.03[2]
　　　n.14; 8.10[2][b][iv]; 8.10[5]; S8.11[1];
　　　18.01[2][a] & ns. 28, 29
6166(a) . . . . S2.02[3][c][vi] n.142
6166(a)(1) . . . . 2.02[3][c][i] n.47; 2.02[3][c][ii]
　　　ns. 52–54, 62, 100, 106, 111, 112, 114;
　　　2.02[3][c][iii] n.115; 4.02[7][e][ii] ns.
　　　385, 387; 4.04[7][e] n.347; 4.07[2][d];
　　　5.08[5][d][i] n.264; 5.08[6][c] ns. 300,
　　　302, 303; 18.01[1] n.2; 18.01[2][a] n.22
6166(a)(2) . . . . 2.02[3][c][iv] ns. 118, 120
6166(a)(3) . . . . 2.02[3][c][i] n.47; 2.02[3][c][ii]
　　　n.98; 2.02[3][c][iii] ns. 115, 116;
　　　8.10[2][b][iv] n.21; 18.01[2][a] ns. 21,
　　　22
6166(b) . . . . . 4.04[3][b][v] n.66; 4.04[7][b][i];
　　　5.08[2][a] n.20; 5.08[2][c][ii] n.56

IRC §

6166(b)(1) . . . 2.02[3][c][ii] n.60; 4.02[7][e][ii] n.384; 4.04[1] n.8; 4.04[3][b][v] & ns. 66–68; 4.04[3][c][i] n.113; 4.04[5] n.170; 5.08[2][a] n.20; 5.08[2][c][ii] ns. 56, 59; 5.08[3][d] n.150; 5.08[6][c] ns. 298, 299

6166(b)(1)(A) . . . . . . 2.02[3][c][ii] ns. 63, 78
6166(b)(1)(A)(i) . . . . 2.02[3][c][ii] n.71
6166(b)(1)(B) . . . . . . 2.02[3][c][ii] ns. 64, 78; 4.04[7][b][i] n.279; 5.08[2][c][ii] n.56
6166(b)(1)(B)(i)   2.02[3][c][ii] & ns. 71, 111
6166(b)(1)(C) . . . . 2.02[3][c][ii] ns. 65, 71, 78; S2.02[3][c][ii] n.71; 4.04[3][b][v] n.66; 4.04[3][c][i] n.113; 4.04[7][b][i] n.279; 5.08[2][c][ii] ns. 56, 59; 5.08[3][d] n.150
6166(b)(1)(C)(i) . . . 2.02[3][c][ii] & ns. 71, 84
6166(b)(1)(D) . . . . 2.02[3][c][ii] n.71
6166(b)(2)(A) . . . . 2.02[3][c][ii] n.66
6166(b)(2)(A)(i) . . . . 2.02[3][c][ii] n.71
6166(b)(2)(B) . . . . 2.02[3][c][ii] n.67
6166(b)(2)(C) . . . . . . 2.02[3][c][ii] ns. 68, 71
6166(b)(2)(D) . . . . . . 2.02[3][c][ii] ns. 70, 71; 5.08[2][c][ii] n.59
6166(b)(3) . . . 2.02[3][c][ii] n.83; 4.04[3][b][vi] n.75; 5.08[3][c][ii] n.104
6166(b)(4) . . . . 2.02[3][c][ii] n.101
6166(b)(5) . . . . 2.02[3][c][iv] n.119
6166(b)(6) . . . . 2.02[3][c][ii] ns. 105, 114; 2.02[3][c][iv] n.122; 4.02[7][e][ii] ns. 386, 389; 5.08[6][c] ns. 301, 303
6166(b)(7) . . . . . . 2.02[3][c][ii] & ns. 71, 111
6166(b)(7)(A) . . . . 2.02[3][c][ii]; 5.08[2][c][ii] n.59
6166(b)(7)(A)(i) . . . . 2.02[3][c][ii] ns. 73, 74, 110, 111
6166(b)(7)(A)(ii) . . . . 2.02[3][c][ii] n.76; 2.02[3][c][iii] n.117
6166(b)(7)(A)(iii) . . . . . . 2.02[3][c][ii] n.75; 2.02[3][c][v] n.129
6166(b)(8) . . . . 2.02[3][c][ii] n.84; 18.01[2][a] n.22
6166(b)(8)(A) . . . . . 2.02[3][c][vi] ns. 145, 149
6166(b)(8)(A)(ii) . . . . 2.02[3][c][ii] ns. 86, 88; 2.02[3][c][iii] n.117; 18.01[2][a] n.22
6166(b)(8)(A)(iii) . . . 2.02[3][c][ii] ns. 86, 88; 2.02[3][c][v] n.129; 18.01[2][a] n.22
6166(b)(8)(B)(i) . . . . 2.02[3][c][ii] n.85
6166(b)(8)(B)(ii) . . . . 2.02[3][c][ii] ns. 87, 88; 18.01[2][a] n.21
6166(b)(8)(C) . . . . 2.02[3][c][ii] n.85
6166(b)(9) . . . . 2.02[3][c][ii] n.61
6166(b)(9)(A) . . . . . . 2.02[3][c][ii] ns. 77, 80
6166(b)(9)(B)(i) . . . . 2.02[3][c][ii] n.81
6166(b)(9)(B)(ii) . . . . 2.02[3][c][ii] n.89
6166(b)(9)(B)(ii)(I) . . . . . 2.02[3][c][ii] n.92; 2.02[3][c][v] n.129
6166(b)(9)(B)(iii)(I) . . . . . . 2.02[3][c][ii] n.90
6166(b)(9)(B)(iii)(II) . . . . . 2.02[3][c][ii] n.91
6166(b)(10) . . . 8.10[5] n.162; 18.01[2][a] n.22
6166(b)(10)(A) . . . . . . 2.02[3][c][ii] ns. 93, 94

IRC §

6166(b)(10)(A)(ii) . . . . . . 2.02[3][c][ii] n.98; 18.01[2][a] n.21
6166(b)(10)(A)(iii) . . . . 2.02[3][c][ii] n.99
6166(b)(10)(B)(i)(I) . . . . . . 2.02[3][c][ii] n.96
6166(b)(10)(B)(i)(II) . . . . . . 2.02[3][c][ii] n.97
6166(b)(10)(B)(ii) . . . . 2.02[3][c][ii] n.95
6166(b)(10)(B)(iii) . . . . 2.02[3][c][ii] n.95
6166(c) . . . . . 2.02[3][c][ii] & ns. 72, 113, 114
6166(d) . . . . 2.02[3][c][ii] n.57
6166(e) . . . . . 2.02[3][c][ii] n.57; 3.03[2] n.25; 5.09[2] n.21
6166(f)(1) . . . . 2.02[3][c][v] n.123
6166(f)(2) . . . . 2.02[3][c][v] n.124
6166(f)(3) . . . . 2.02[3][c][ii] n.57
6166(f)(4) . . . . 2.02[3][c][v] n.123
6166(g) . . . . .2.02[3][c][vi] ns. 133, 142; 8.10[2][b][iv] ns. 20, 21
6166(g)(1)(A) . . . . S2.02[3][c][iii] n.115; 2.02[3][c][vi] & ns. 141, 144
6166(g)(1)(A)(i)(I) . . 2.02[3][c][vi] n.138
6166(g)(1)(A)(i)(II) . . . . . 2.02[3][c][vi] n.139
6166(g)(1)(A)(ii) . . . . 2.02[3][c][vi] n.140
6166(g)(1)(B) . . . . 2.02[3][c][vi] n.143; 5.08[5][b][ii] n.237
6166(g)(1)(C) . . . . 2.02[3][c][vi] n.144; 5.08[5][b][ii] n.237
6166(g)(1)(D) . . . . 2.02[3][c][vi] n.142; 5.08[5][b][ii] n.237
6166(g)(1)(E) . . . . 2.02[3][c][vi] n.146
6166(g)(1)(F) . . . . 2.02[3][c][vi] n.147
6166(g)(2)(A) . . . . 2.02[3][c][vi] n.149
6166(g)(2)(B) . . . . 2.02[3][c][vi] n.148
6166(g)(2)(C) . . . . 2.02[3][c][vi] n.149
6166(g)(3) . . . . 2.02[3][c][vi] n.149
6166(g)(3)(A) . . . . 2.02[3][c][vi] n.134
6166(g)(3)(B)(i) . . . . 2.02[3][c][vi] n.135
6166(g)(3)(B)(ii) . . . . 2.02[3][c][vi] n.136
6166(g)(3)(B)(iii) . . . . 2.02[3][c][vi] n.137
6166(h) . . . 4.04[7][e] n.347; 5.08[5][d][i] n.264
6166(h)(1) . . . . 2.02[3][c][ii] n.59
6166(h)(2) . . . . 2.02[3][c][ii] n.59
6166(h)(3) . . . . 2.02[3][c][ii] n.59
6166(i) . . . 2.02[3][c][i] n.46; 18.01[2][a] n.25
6166(j) . . . . 2.02[3][c][ii] n.105
6166(j)(3) . . . . 2.02[3][c][v] n.126
6166(j)(3)(B) . . . . 2.02[3][c][v] n.126
6166(k)(1) . . . . S2.02[3][c][iii] n.116
6166(k)(2) . . . . S2.02[3][c][iii] n.116
6166A . . . . 2.02[3][c][i] n.46
6201–6255 . . . . 18.01[1] n.5
6211–6216 . . . . 18.01[1] n.8
6212(a) . . . . 10.03[3][b] n.46
6213(a) . . . . 5.09[2] n.16
6214(b) . . . . 9.05[1] n.6
6301–6344 . . . . 18.01[1] n.6
6312 . . . . 4.02[3][e] n.98
6321–6326 . . . . 4.07[2][d]
6321 . . . . 10.07[2][d] n.82; 18.01[1] n.7
6323(f) . . . . 4.04[6] n.248
6324 . . . . 4.04[6] n.248; 5.07[4][c] n.177; 12.03[3] n.35; 18.01[1] n.7

[Text references are to paragraphs and notes (9"n.");
references to the supplement are preceded by "S."]

IRC §

6324(a)(1) . . . S2.02[3][c][iii] n.116; 5.03[4][a]
n.89; S5.03[6][c][iii] n.302; 8.04 n.3;
S8.04 n.4
6324(a)(2)   8.02 n.15; 8.03[2] n.24; 8.04 n.4;
S8.04 n.4
6324(a)(3) . . . 8.03[2] n.23; 8.04 n.3; S8.04 n.4
6324(b) . . . . . 9.04[11] ns. 245, 248; S9.04[11]
n.245; 12.03[1] n.8
6324(c) . . . . 12.03[1] n.8
6324A . . . . 2.02[3][c][iii] n.116; S2.02[3][c][iii]
n.116; 2.02[3][c][vi] n.133; 8.03[2];
18.01[1] n.7
6324A(b) . . . . S2.02[3][c][iii] n.116
6324A(b)(1)(B) . . . . S2.02[3][c][iii] n.116
6324A(b)(2) . . . . S2.02[3][c][iii] n.116
6324A(b)(3) . . . . 2.02[3][c][iii] n.116
6324A(d)(1) . . . . 4.04[6] n.248
6324A(d)(3) . . . . 4.04[6] n.248
6324A(d)(4) . . . . S2.02[3][c][iii] n.116
6324A(d)(5) . . . . 2.02[3][c][vi] n.133
6324B . . . . 4.04[6]; 4.04[7][c][ii] n.324;
5.08[3][b][i] n.92; 5.08[3][b][ii] n.99;
18.01[1] n.7
6324B(a) . . . . 4.04[6] n.245
6324B(b) . . . . 4.04[6] n.247
6324B(c)(1) . . . . 4.04[6] n.248
6324B(d) . . . . 4.04[6] n.246
6325 . . . . 6.01[4] n.36
6401–6408 . . . . 18.01[1] n.8
6402 . . . . 2.02[3][c][vi]
6403 . . . . . 2.02[3][c][vi] n.150; S2.02[3][c][vi]
n.142
6501–6515 . . . . 18.01[1] n.11
6501 . . . . . 3.02; S3.02[1][b][ii] n.48; S3.02[3];
3.08; 5.07[4][b] n.163; 8.03[2];
9.05[2][b] n.21; S5.03[1][b][iv] n.50;
16.02[8][a] n.558; 16.02[8][b] n.560
6501(a) . . . . . . 5.03[4][b] n.92; S5.03[6][c][iii]
n.307; 9.04[10][b] n.240; 18.01[1] n.11
6501(b)(1) . . . . 9.04[10][b] n.241
6501(c)(1) . . . . 5.03[4][b] n.94; S5.03[6][c][iii]
n.309; 9.04[10][b] n.243
6501(c)(2) . . . . 9.04[10][b] n.243
6501(c)(3) . . . . 5.03[4][b] n.94; S5.03[6][c][iii]
n.309; 9.04[10][b] n.243
6501(c)(9) . . . . . . 2.01[1][b][ii] ns. 25, 30, 31;
S2.01[1][b][ii] ns. 25, 30, 31; 9.04[10][a]
n.219; S9.04[10][a] n.219; 9.05[2][a]
n.13; 9.05[2][b] n.21; S10.02[2][d][iii]
n.130.1; 19.02[5][a][i] n.311; 19.02[5][d]
ns. 489, 491; 19.03[4][d] ns. 351, 354
6501(d) . . . . 8.03[2] n.13
6501(e)(2) . . . . 5.03[4][b] n.94; S5.03[6][c][iii]
n.309; 9.04[10][b] n.242
6503 . . . . S2.02[3][c][iii] n.115
6503(a)(1) . . . . S5.03[6][c][iii] n.309
6503(d) . . . . 2.02[3][c][iii] n.115
6511 . . . . S5.03[1][b][iv] ns. 51, 52; 5.03[3][c]
n.71; S5.03[3][c][i] n.125;
S5.03[4][c][ii]; 18.06 n.6

IRC §

6511(a) . . . . 3.03[2] n.30; 3.06[4] n.34;
4.07[3][a] n.81; 5.06[8][d][ii] n.320;
5.09[2] n.32; 9.04[10][b] n.240
6532(a)(3) . . . . 5.09[2]
6651 . . . . 9.04[9] n.206
6651(a)(1) . . . . 2.02[1] & ns. 13, 14
6651(a)(2) . . . . 2.02[1] n.12
6601–6631 . . . . 18.01[1] n.9
6601 . . . . 2.02[3][a] n.28
6601(a) . . . . . 2.02[3][b][i] n.40; 2.02[3][b][ii]
n.45; 2.02[3][c][v] ns. 123, 132; 3.07
n.9; 18.01[2][a] ns. 19, 24
6601(b) 3.07 n.8
6601(b)(1) . . . . 2.02[3][b][i] n.40
6601(j) . . . S2.02[3][c][iii] n.116; 2.02[3][c][v]
n.132; 3.07 n.12; 5.03[3][c] n.72;
S5.03[3][c][i] n.124; 18.01[2][a] n.23
6601(j)(1) . . . . 2.02[3][c][v] ns. 125, 127
6601(j)(1)(A) . . . . 18.01[2][a] n.23
6601(j)(2) . . . . . . 2.02[3][c][v] ns. 127, 132;
18.01[2][a] n.23
6601(j)(3) . . . . 2.02[3][c][v] n.126; 18.01[2][a]
n.23
6601(j)(4) . . . . 2.02[3][c][v] n.128
6621 . . . . . 2.02[3][a] n.28; 2.02[3][b][ii] n.45;
3.07; 5.08[5][d][ii] n.265
6621(a)(2) . . . . 18.01[2][a] ns. 19, 24
6621(b) . . . . 2.02[3][b][i] n.39
6621(b)(1) . . . . 18.01[2][a] ns. 19, 24
6651–6751 . . . . 18.01[1] n.10
6651 . . . . . S5.03[3][c][i] n.119; 18.01[1] n.10
6651(a)(2) . . . . S8.10[3][a] n.32
6662 . . . . . 4.02[6][a]; S4.02[6][a] & n.261
6662(a)   4.02[6][a] n.257; S4.02[6][a] ns.257,
261; S8.10[3][a] n.32
6662(b)(5) . . . . . 4.02[6][a] n.256; S4.02[6][a]
n.256
6662(d)(2)(B)(ii)(I) . . . . . . S4.02[6][b] n.264.9
6662(g)(1) . . . . . 4.02[6][a] n.259; S4.02[6][a]
n.259
6662(g)(2) . . . . . 4.02[6][a] n.258; S4.02[6][a]
n.258
6662(h)(1) . . . . . 4.02[6][a] n.260; S4.02[6][a]
n.260
6662(h)(2)(C) . . . . 4.02[6][a] n.260; S4.02[6][a]
n.260
6664 . . . . 4.02[6][a]; S4.02[6][a]
6664(c) . . . . 4.02[6][a] & n.261
6664(c)(1) . . . . S4.02[6][a] n.261
6684 . . . . 5.05[1][c] n.51
6694 . . . S4.02[6][b] & ns. 264.1, 264.5, 264.17
6694(a) . . . . S4.02[6][b] ns. 264.1, 264.5
6694(a)(1) . . . . S4.02[6][b] ns. 264.5, 264.11
6694(a)(1)(A) . . . . S4.02[6][b] n.264.6
6694(a)(1)(B) . . . . S4.02[6][b] n.264.7
6694(a)(2) . . . . S4.02[6][b] n.264.6
6694(a)(2)(A) . . . . S4.02[6][b] n.264.8
6694(a)(2)(B) . . . . S4.02[6][b] n.264.10
6694(a)(3) . . . . S4.02[6][b] n.264.12
6694(b)(1) . . . . S4.02[6][b] ns. 264.5, 264.14
6694(b)(2) . . . . S4.02[6][b] n.264.13

[Text references are to paragraphs and notes (9"n.");
references to the supplement are preceded by "S."]

IRC §

6694(b)(3) . . . . S4.02[6][b] n.264.15
6694(d) . . . . S4.02[6][b] n.264.1
6695 . . . . S4.02[6][b] n.264.1
6695A . . . . S4.02[6][b]
6716(a) . . . . 8.10[3][d][iii] ns. 129, 130;
                        S8.10[3][d][iii] ns. 119, 120
6716(b) . . 8.10[3][d][iii] n.128; S8.10[3][d][iii]
                                                    n.118
6716(c) . . . 8.10[3][d][iii] n.131; S8.10[3][d][iii]
                                                    n.121
6716(d) . . . . 8.10[3][d][iii] n.132
6716(e) . . 8.10[3][d][iii] n.132; S8.10[3][d][iii]
                                                    n.122
6901 . . . 8.02 ns. 14, 15; S8.10[3][d][iii] n.122
6901(a)(1)(A)(ii) S8.04 n.4
6901(a)(1)(A)(iii) . . . . 9.04[11] n.246
6901(c)(1) . . . . . 9.04[11] n.247; 12.03[1] n.8
6901(c)(3) . . . . 8.03[2] n.19
6903 . . . . 2.02[1] n.18
6905 . . . . 9.04[11]; 12.03[1] n.10
6905(a) . . . . 12.03[1] n.14
7101 . . . . 5.07[3][c][i] n.73
7121   2.01[1][b][ii] n.45; S2.01[1][b][ii] n.45;
                5.07[3][c] n.52; 5.07[4][b] n.164;
                5.08[3][b][ii] n.99; 9.05[2][b] n.31
7122   2.01[1][b][ii] n.45; S2.01[1][b][ii] n.45;
                                          9.05[2][b] n.31
7430 . . . . . . 5.03[3][a] n.46; 10.03[3][b] n.47
7430(c)(4)(A)(iii) . . . . 5.03[3][a] n.46
7477 . . . . 10.02[2][d][iii] & n.128;
                        S10.02[2][d][iii] & n.130.1
7477(a) . . . . 10.02[2][d][iii] ns. 128, 130;
                        S10.02[2][d][iii] ns. 130.1, 130.4
7477(b)(1) . . . . S10.02[2][d][iii] n.127.1
7477(b)(2) . . . . 10.02[2][d][iii] n.128;
                        S10.02[2][d][iii] ns. 128, 130.1
7477(b)(3) . . . . 10.02[2][d][iii] n.129;
                                S10.02[2][d][iii] n.130.3
7479 . . . . 2.02[3][c][vii] & ns. 152, 155;
                            S2.02[3][c][vii] n.156
7479(a) . . . . 2.02[3][c][vii]
7479(a)(1) . . . . 2.02[3][c][vii] n.153
7479(a)(2) . . . . 2.02[3][c][vii] n.154
7479(b)(1) . . . . 2.02[3][c][vii] n.156
7479(b)(1)(B) . . . . 2.02[3][c][vii] n.156
7479(b)(2) . . . . 2.02[3][c][vii] n.156
7479(b)(3) . . . . 2.02[3][c][vii] n.155
7491 . . . . 4.02[6][b] & n.266
7491(a) . . . . 4.02[6][b] n.265
7491(a)(2) . . . . 4.02[6][b] n.268
7491(b) . . . . 4.02[6][b] n.265
7502 . . . . 2.02[1] n.22; 10.07[2][b] n.30;
                                S10.07[2][b] n.30
7502(a) . . . . S10.07[2][b] n.30
7508 . . . . 9.04[9] n.209
7508A . . . . S9.04[9] n.209
7517 . . . . 4.02[6][c]; 10.02[2][d][ii]
7517(a) . . . 4.02[6][c] n.269; 10.02[2][d][ii] ns.
                                                125, 126
7517(b) . . . . 4.02[6][c] n.270
7517(c) . . . . 4.02[6][c] n.271

IRC §

7520 . . .   3.05[3][b] n.29; 4.02[3][h]; 4.02[5] &
                ns. 244–246, 253; S4.02[5] ns. 244,
                247; S4.08[8]; 4.10[9] n.94; S4.11[4][a]
                n.40; 5.05[3][a] n.95; 5.05[5][a][i] n.201;
                5.05[5][a][ii] n.207; 5.05[5][b][i] n.256;
                5.05[5][b][ii]; 5.05[5][c][ii]; 5.05[7][a]
                n.333; 5.06[7][b] n.190; 5.06[7][d] ns.
                197, 198; 5.06[8][d][ii] n.348; 9.04[3][a]
                ns. 48, 51, 53; S9.04[3][a] n.48;
                S9.04[3][b] n.61; 10.01[3][c] n.97;
                10.02[2][b][iii] & ns. 52, 57, 58;
                S10.02[2][b][iii] ns. 55, 60; 10.02[6][c]
                n.180; 11.02[1][b]; 14.05[3] n.36;
                16.02[3][b][ii] n.186; 16.02[4][d][iii] ns.
                274, 277; 16.02[6] n.409; S16.02[6] ns.
                409, 412; 19.03[1] ns. 1, 3;
                19.03[2][a][iv] n.70; 19.03[3];
                19.03[3][b] & n.112; 19.03[3][c] n.155;
                19.03[3][d]; 19.03[3][d][iii] n.246;
                S19.03[3][d][iii]; 19.03[4][a];
                S19.03[4][a] n.282; 19.03[4][b] & ns.
                296, 299; S19.03[4][e][i] n.367
7520(a) . . . . .   4.02[5] n.245; 5.05[3][a] n.95;
                5.05[5][a][ii] n.207; S5.05[5][a][ii] n.207;
                5.05[5][b][i] n.265; S5.05[5][b][ii]
                n.264; S5.05[5][c][ii] n.291; S5.05[6][b]
                n.327; S5.05[7][a] n.333; 10.02[2][b][iii]
                                              ns. 52, 57, 58
7520(a)(2) . . . . 4.02[5] ns. 245, 247; 5.05[4][a]
                n.130; 10.02[2][b][iii] ns. 58, 59
7520(c)(3) . . . . . S3.05[3][b] n.29; S4.02[5] ns.
                244, 247; S4.08[1][a] n.5; S4.11[4][a]
                n.40; S5.05[3][a] n.95; S5.05[5][a][i]
                n.207; S5.05[5][b][ii] n.264;
                S5.05[5][c][ii] n.291; S5.05[6][b] n.327;
                S5.05[7][a] n.333; S5.06[7][d] n.197;
                S5.06[8][d][ii] n.348; S9.04[3][a] n.48;
                10.02[2][b][iii] n.56; S10.02[2][b][iii]
                n.56; S11.02[1][b] n.27; S16.02[6] n.409;
                S19.03[1] n.3; S19.03[3][b] n.112;
                                        S19.03[3][d] n.162
7701 . . . . . . S8.10[3][b][v] n.83; 13.03[3] n.26
7701(a)(1) . . . . S5.03[6][a] n.271; 5.05[5][a][i]
                n.175; 5.05[5][b][i] n.234; 6.05[2][a][i]
                n.12; 13.02[2][b][i] n.39; 13.02[4][b][ii]
                n.275; 13.03[3] n.34; 13.03[4][a] n.75
7701(a)(2) . . . . 19.02[2][a][ii] n.67
7701(a)(3) . . . . 5.05[1][b] n.24; 19.02[2][a][ii]
                                                    n.67
7701(a)(4) . . . . . . 5.07[3][a] n.44; 6.04[1] n.2
7701(a)(9) . . . . . 4.04[4] ns. 152, 153; 6.03[2]
                                    n.19; 9.02[1] n.5
7701(a)(10) 12.04 n.5
7701(a)(15) . . . . 8.01[1][a][ii] n.11
7701(a)(19) . . . . 5.08[2][b][iii] n.30;
                                    5.08[2][b][iv] n.43
7701(a)(30) . . . . 6.04[3] n.21; S9.02[1][b][ii]
                            n.10.46; 10.01[11] n.239
7701(a)(31) . . . . S9.02[1][b][ii] n.10.46;
                                    10.01[11] n.239
7701(a)(36) . . . . S4.02[6][b] n.264.4

*[Text references are to paragraphs and notes (9"n.");
references to the supplement are preceded by "S."]*

IRC §

7701(a)(45) . . . . 19.02[5][c][iii] n.447
7701(a)(47) . . . . 2.02 n.1; 8.02 n.1; 8.10[3][b]
    n.42; 8.10[3][b][v] n.90; 8.10[3][d][ii]
    n.121; S8.10[3][d][ii] n.111
7701(a)(50)(A) . . . . S6.07 n.2; S9.02[1][b] n.5
7701(a)(50)(B) . . . . S6.07 n.2; S9.02[1][b] n.5
7701(b) . . . . 5.06[9] n.432; 6.01[3] n.17;
    S6.01[3][b] n.29
7701(b)(1) . . . . 6.01[3] n.17
7701(b)(1)(A)(ii) . . . . . . S6.07[1][a] ns. 14, 15;
    S9.02[1][b][i] ns. 10.7, 10.8
7701(b)(3)(D)(ii) . . . . S6.07[2] n.39;
    S9.02[1][b][ii] n.10.51
7701(b)(6) . . . . 5.08[5][b][iii] n.242; S6.07 n.4;
    S9.02[1][b] n.7
7805 . . . . 10.06[2][c]; 18.03
7806(b) . . . . . 19.02[5][f] n.504; 19.02[5][f][iii]
    n.516; 19.03[4][e] n.361
7851(a)(2)(A) . . . . . . 4.11[2][b] n.12; 4.17 n.3
7851(a)(2)(B) 9.01 n.13
7852(d) . . . . 7.06 & ns. 12, 14, 17
7852(d)(2) 4.17 n.4; 7.06 n.12

IRC §

7872 . . . . . S8.07[2] n.9; S8.07[4] n.34; 8.07[5]
    n.40; 9.04[8] n.186; 10.01[2][f] & ns.
    44, 46–48; S10.01[3][g]
7872(a) . . . . 10.01[2][f] ns. 52, 55, 56;
    13.02[3][b][i] n.219
7872(a)(1)(A) . . . . 10.01[2][f] n.54
7872(a)(2) . . . . 10.01[2][f] n.52
7872(b)(1) . . . . 10.01[2][f] n.50
7872(c) . . . . 10.01[2][f] n.47
7872(c)(2)(A) . . . . 10.01[2][f] n.59
7872(c)(2)(B) . . . . 10.01[2][f] n.60
7872(d)(1) . . . . 10.01[2][f] n.60
7872(d)(1)(B) . . . . 10.01[2][f] n.60
7872(d)(2) . . . . 10.01[2][f] n.50
7872(e)(2) . . . . 10.01[2][f] ns. 46, 52, 55
7872(f)(1) . . . . 10.01[2][f] n.49
7872(f)(2)(B) . . . . 10.01[2][f] n.45
7872(f)(3) . . . . 10.01[2][f] n.47
7872(f)(5) . . . . 10.01[2][f] n.53
7872(f)(6) . . . . 10.01[2][f] n.48
9100 . . . . 'S11.03[4][c]

Cumulative Table of
Treasury Regulations

[Text references are to paragraphs and notes (9"n.");
references to the supplement are preceded by "S."]

Reg. §

105 . . . . 5.06[3][a] n.29
1.61-8(c) . . . . 4.04[5][a][i] n.183
1.61-22 . . . . S4.14[6] ns. 103.1, 103.8;
    S10.01[3][g] ns. 115.1, 115.3, 115.13,
               115.27
1.61-22(b)(1) . . . . . S4.14[6] ns. 103.6, 103.7;
               S10.01[3][g] n.115.6
1.61-22(b)(1)(iii) . . . . S4.14[6] n.103.2
1.61-22(b)(2)   S4.14[6] n.103.6; S10.01[3][g]
                   n.115.6
1.61-22(b)(3) . . . . S10.01[3][g] n.115.11
1.61-22(b)(5) . . . . S10.01[3][g] n.115.26
1.61-22(c)(1) . . . . S10.01[3][g] n.115.10
1.61-22(c)(1)(i) . . . . . . S10.01[3][g] n.115.10
1.61-22(c)(1)(ii) . . . . . . S10.01[3][g] n.115.10
1.61-22(c)(1)(ii)(A)(2)   S10.01[3][g] n.115.20
1.61-22(d) . . . . S10.01[3][g] n.115.33
1.61-22(d)(1)   S10.01[3][g] ns. 115.8, 115.29,
                 115.30–115.32
1.61-22(d)(2)(ii)(A) . . . . S10.01[3][g] n.115.26
1.61-22(d)(3) . . . . S10.01[3][g] n.115.20
1.61-22(g) . . . . S10.01[3][g] n.115.34
1.61-22(j)(1)(i) . . . . S4.14[6] n.103.1;
               S10.01[3][g] n.115.1
1.72-9 . . . . S10.01[3][g] n.115.17
1.79-0 . . . . 4.14[5][a] n.84
1.79-1 . . . . 4.14[5][a] n.84
1.83-3(e) . . . . S4.14[6] ns. 103.1, 103.8;
             S10.01[3][g] ns. 115.1, 115.3
1.83-6(a)(5) . . . . . S4.14[6] ns. 103.1, 103.8;
             S10.01[3][g] ns. 115.1, 115.3
1.112-1(b)(1) . . . . 8.01[1][a][i] n.10
1.112-1(e) . . . . 8.01[1][a][iii] n.24
1.112-1(e)(2) . . . . 8.01[1][a][iii] n.24
1.112-1(f) . . . . 8.01[1][a][iv] n.30
1.165-7(b)(1) . . . . 4.03[4][a] n.57; 5.04[1] n.4;
             5.04[3] n.17; 5.04[4] n.24
1.165-7(b)(1)(ii) . . . . 4.03[4][a] n.57
1.165-8(b) . . . . 5.04[3] n.17
1.170-1(a)(2) . . . . 10.01[2][g] n.62

Reg. §

1.170A-12 . . . . . S3.05[3][b] n.29; S4.02[5] ns.
    244, 247; S4.08[1][a] n.5; S5.05[3][a]
        n.95; S5.05[5][a][ii] n.207;
    S5.05[5][b][ii] n.264; S5.05[5][c][ii]
    n.291; S5.05[6][b] n.327; S5.05[7][a]
    n.333; S5.06[7][d] n.197; S5.06[8][d][ii]
    n.348; S9.04[3][a] n.48; S10.02[2][b][iii]
    n.56; S11.02[1][b] n.27; S16.02[6] n.409;
       S19.03[1] n.3; S19.03[3][b] n.112;
            S19.03[3][d] n.162
1.212-1(l)   14.02[3] ns. 13, 15; 14.03[3] n.15
1.213-1(d)(2) . . . 5.03[5][d] n.133; S5.03[6][b]
               ns. 279, 280
1.267(c)-1(a)(4) . . . . 2.02[3][c][ii] n.69
1.301-1(q) . . . . . . S4.14[6] ns. 103.1, 103.8;
        S10.01[3][g] ns. 115.1, 115.3
1.351-1(a)(1)(i) . . . . 4.05[4] n.33
1.401(k)-1(d)(2)(i) . . . . 5.07[4][a][i] n.132
1.501(c)(3)-1(d)(5) . . . . 5.05[1][b] n.31
1.513-1(b) . . . . 4.04[3][b][iv] n.61
1.527-2 . . . . 9.02[2] n.18
1.641(b)-3(a) . . . . 17.02[2] n.80
1.642(c)-5 . . . . 11.02[2][b][iii] n.84
1.642(c)-5(a)(4) . . . . 17.02[3][c] n.147
1.642(c)-5(b)(1) . . . . 5.05[5][c][i] ns. 271, 272
1.642(c)-5(b)(2) . . . 5.05[5][c][i] ns. 274–276
1.642(c)-5(b)(3) . . . 5.05[5][c][i] ns. 277, 278
1.642(c)-5(b)(4) . . . . 5.05[5][c][i] n.280
1.642(c)-5(b)(5) . . . . 5.05[5][c][i] n.281
1.642(c)-5(b)(6) . . . . 5.05[5][c][i] n.283
1.642(c)-5(b)(7) . . . . 5.05[5][c][i] n.285
1.642(c)-5(b)(8) . . . . 5.05[5][c][i] n.275
1.642(c)-5(c) . . . . 5.05[5][c][i] n.284
1.642(c)-6 . . . . . S3.05[3][b] n.29; S4.02[5] ns.
    244, 247; S4.08[1][a] n.5; S5.05[3][a]
        n.95; S5.05[5][a][ii] n.207;
    S5.05[5][b][ii] n.264; 5.05[5][c][ii]
    n.287; S5.05[5][c][ii] n.291; S5.05[6][b]
    n.327; S5.05[7][a] n.333; S5.06[7][d]
    n.197; S5.06[8][d][ii] n.348; S9.04[3][a]
    n.48; S10.02[2][b][iii] n.56; S11.02[1][b]
    n.27; S16.02[6] n.409; S19.03[1] n.3;
     S19.03[3][b] n.112; S19.03[3][d] n.162

*[Text references are to paragraphs and notes (9"n.");
references to the supplement are preceded by "S."]*

Reg. §

1.642(c)-6(a)(2) . . . . 5.05[5][c][ii] n.288
1.642(c)-6(b) . . . . 5.05[5][c][ii] n.293
1.642(c)-6(b)(2) . . . . . 5.05[5][c][ii] n.290
1.642(c)-6(e)(1) . . . . 5.05[5][c][ii] n.291
1.642(c)-6(e)(3) . . . . 5.05[5][c][ii] n.290
1.642(c)-6(e)(4) . . . . 5.05[5][c][ii] n.293
1.642(c)-6(e)(5) . . . . 5.05[5][c][ii] ns. 291, 292
1.642(g)-1   5.03[3][d] ns. 79–81; S5.03[6][a]
ns. 265, 268, 274–276
1.642(g)-2 . . . . . 5.03[3][d] n.76; 5.03[5][c] ns.
131, 132; S5.03[6][a] ns. 268, 270, 277;
S5.03[6][b] n.280; 14.02[3] n.19
1.643(b)-1 . . . . . S4.02[5] n.251; S5.06[8][b][i]
n.215; S5.06[8][d][ii] n.353;
S5.07[4][a][i] n.131; S9.04[3][b] n.64
1.661(a)-2(e) . . . . 4.05[3] n.22
1.661(a)-2(f)(3) . . . . 4.04[3][b][viii] n.93
1.663(c)-1(a) . . . . 17.04[2][a] n.53
1.663(c)-3 . . . . 17.04[2][a] n.50
1.664-1 . . . . S5.05[8][c] n.372
1.664-1(a)(1)(iii) . . . . 17.02[3][c] ns. 145, 146
1.664-1(a)(2) . . . . 5.05[5] n.155
1.664-1(a)(3) . . . . 5.05[5] n.154
1.664-1(a)(4) . . . . 5.05[5][a][i] n.160;
5.05[5][b][i] n.215
1.664-1(a)(5) . . . . 5.05[5][a][i] n.160;
5.05[5][b][i] ns. 215, 255
1.664-1(a)(5)(i) . . . . 5.05[5][a][i] ns. 160, 177,
200; 5.05[5][b][i] ns. 215, 236
1.664-1(a)(7) . . . . 5.05[5][a][ii] n.205;
5.05[5][b][ii] n.262
1.664-1(a)(7)(ii) . . . . 5.05[5][b][i] n.228
1.664-1(d)(5) . . . . 5.05[5][a][i] n.164;
5.05[5][b][i] n.224
1.664-2 . . . . . . 5.05[5][a][i] n.163; S5.05[8][c]
n.372; 11.02[2][b] n.53; 11.02[2][b][i]
n.58
1.664-2(a)(1)(i) . . . . 5.05[5][a][i] n.171
1.664-2(a)(1)(i)(a) . . . 5.05[5][a][i] ns. 171, 174
1.664-2(a)(1)(i)(b) . . . . . . 5.05[5][a][i] n.174
1.664-2(a)(1)(i)(c) . . . . . . 5.05[5][a][i] n.173
1.664-2(a)(1)(ii) . . . . 5.05[5][a][i] n.166
1.664-2(a)(1)(iii) . . . . 5.05[5][a][i] n.167;
S10.01[3][e] n.107.1; 19.03[3][b][i] n.123
1.664-2(a)(1)(iv) . . . . 5.05[5][a][i] n.169;
19.03[3][b][i] n.138
1.664-2(a)(2)(ii) . . . 5.05[5][a][i] ns. 166, 168;
19.03[3][b][i] n.138
1.664-2(a)(3)(i) . . . . . 5.05[5][a][i] ns. 175, 176
1.664-2(a)(3)(ii) . . . 5.05[5][a][i] ns. 178, 199;
11.02[2][b][ii] ns. 78, 79
1.664-2(a)(4)   5.05[5][a][i] ns. 187, 190, 192,
199; 11.02[2][b][i] n.59; 11.02[2][b][ii]
n.77
1.664-2(a)(5)(i) . . . . 5.05[5][a][i] ns. 179–182,
184
1.664-2(a)(5)(ii) . . . . 5.05[5][a][i] n.185
1.664-2(a)(5)(ii)(b) . . . . 5.05[5][a][i] n.181
1.664-2(a)(5)(ii)(c) . . . . . . 5.05[5][a][i] n.183
1.664-2(a)(5)(ii)(e) . . . . . . 5.05[5][a][i] n.168

Reg. §

1.664-2(a)(6) . . . . 5.05[5][a][i] n.197;
11.02[2][b][i] n.60
1.664-2(a)(6)(i) . . . . 5.05[5][a][i] ns. 195, 198
1.664-2(a)(6)(iii) . . . . 5.05[5][a][i] n.198
1.664-2(a)(6)(iv) . . . . 5.05[5][a][i] ns. 187, 195
1.664-2(b) . . . . . . 5.05[5][a][i] ns. 161, 162;
5.05[6][a][i] n.312; 11.02[2][b][i] ns. 65,
66
1.664-2(c) . . . 5.05[5][a][i] n.170; 5.05[5][a][ii]
ns. 205–207; 19.03[3][b] n.112
1.664-3 . . . . 5.05[5][b][i] n.216; 11.02[2][b][ii]
ns. 68, 70
1.664-3(a)(1)(i)(a) . . . . . . 5.05[5][b][i] n.230
1.664-3(a)(1)(i)(b)(1) . . . . 5.05[5][b][i] n.224
1.664-3(a)(1)(i)(b)(2) . . . . 5.05[5][b][i] n.225
1.664-3(a)(1)(i)(b)(3) . . . . 5.05[5][b][i] n.223
1.664-3(a)(1)(i)(c)(1) . . . . 5.05[5][b][i] n.228
1.664-3(a)(1)(i)(c)(3) . . . . 5.05[5][b][i] n.228
1.664-3(a)(1)(i)(d) . . . . . . 5.05[5][b][i] n.228
1.664-3(a)(1)(i)(f)(1) . . . . . 5.05[5][b][i] n.228
1.664-3(a)(1)(i)(f)(2) . . . . . 5.05[5][b][i] n.228
1.664-3(a)(1)(i)(f)(3) . . . . . 5.05[5][b][i] n.228
1.664-3(a)(1)(i)(g) . . . 5.05[5][b][i] ns. 231, 233
1.664-3(a)(1)(i)(h) . . . . . . 5.05[5][b][i] n.233
1.664-3(a)(1)(i)(j) . . . . . . 5.05[5][b][i] n.233
1.664-3(a)(1)(i)(k) . . . . . . 5.05[5][b][i] n.232
1.664-3(a)(1)(i)(l) . . . . . . 5.05[5][b][i] n.230
1.664-3(a)(1)(ii) . . . . 5.05[5][b][i] n.217
1.664-3(a)(1)(iii) . . . . 5.05[5][b][i] n.221
1.664-3(a)(1)(iv) . . . . 5.05[5][b][i] n.221
1.664-3(a)(1)(v) . . . . 5.05[5][b][i] n.222;
19.03[3][b][i] n.123
1.664-3(a)(2)(ii) . . . . 5.05[5][b][i] ns. 219, 221
1.664-3(a)(3)(i) . . . . . 5.05[5][b][i] ns. 234, 235
1.664-3(a)(3)(ii) . . . . 5.05[5][b][i] n.237;
11.02[2][b][ii] ns. 78, 79
1.664-3(a)(4)   5.05[5][b][i] ns. 242, 245, 247,
254; 11.02[2][b][ii] ns. 71, 77
1.664-3(a)(5)(i) . . . . . 5.05[5][b][i] ns. 238, 239
1.664-3(a)(5)(ii) . . . . 5.05[5][b][i] n.240
1.664-3(a)(5)(ii)(e) . . . . 5.05[5][b][i] n.221
1.664-3(a)(6) . . . . 5.05[5][b][i] n.252;
11.02[2][b][ii] n.71
1.664-3(a)(6)(i) . . . . 5.05[5][b][i] n.250
1.664-3(a)(6)(iii) . . . . 5.05[5][b][i] n.253
1.664-3(a)(6)(iv) . . . . 5.05[5][b][i] ns. 242, 250
1.664-3(b) . . . 5.05[5][b] n.211; 11.02[2][b][ii]
n.73
1.664-4 . . . S3.05[3][b] n.29; S4.02[5] ns. 244,
247; S4.08[1][a] n.5; S5.05[3][a] n.95;
S5.05[5][a][ii] n.207; S5.05[5][b][ii]
n.264; S5.05[5][c][ii] n.291; S5.05[6][b]
n.327; S5.05[7][a] n.333; S5.06[7][d]
n.197; S5.06[8][d][ii] n.348; S9.04[3][a]
n.48; S10.02[2][b][iii] n.56; S11.02[1][b]
n.27; S16.02[6] n.409; S19.03[1] n.3;
19.03[3][b] n.112; S19.03[3][b] n.112;
S19.03[3][d] n.162
1.664-4(a)(1) . . . . 5.05[5][b][ii] n.264
1.664-4(a)(2) . . . . 5.05[5][b][ii] n.265

*[Text references are to paragraphs and notes (9"n.");
references to the supplement are preceded by "S."]*

Reg. §

1.664-4(a)(3) . . . . 5.05[5][b][i] n.226;
        5.05[5][b][ii] ns. 266, 267;
        11.02[2][b][ii] n.76
1.664-4(c) . . . . 5.05[5][b][ii] n.261
1.664-4(d)(6) . . . . 5.05[5][b][ii] n.263
1.664-4(e)(4) . . . . 16.02[3][b][ii] ns. 186, 187
1.664-4(e)(6)(F) . . . . 5.05[5][b][i] n.229;
        5.05[6][a][ii] n.316
1.671-3(b)(2) . . . . 8.10[4] ns. 139, 142
1.691(c)-1(d) . . . . 4.05[4] n.39
1.707-1(c) . . . . 19.02[2][b][ii] n.92
1.721-1(b)(1) . . . . 4.05[4] n.33
1.761-1(a) . . . . 4.05[7][a] n.79
1.882-5 . . . . 7.06 n.10
1.1001-1(e) . . . . 19.02[5][f][ii] n.515
1.1001-1(h) . . . . S16.02[5][e] n.364
1.1001-3 . . . . 18.05[2][e] n.88
1.1014-2(b)(2) . . . . 4.04[3][b][i] n.40
1.1014-2(b)(3) . . . . 4.04[3][b][i] n.40
1.1015-4 . . . 10.02[6][d] n.181; 17.04[1][a] n.3;
        19.02[5][f][ii] n.515
1.1015-4(a) . . . . 4.15[2] n.69
1.1015-4(a)(1) . . . . 19.02[5][f][ii] n.515
1.1015-4(a)(2) . . . . 19.02[5][f][ii] n.515
1.1015-5(c) . . . . 17.04[1][a] n.3
1.1033(a)-2(c)(3) . . . . 4.04[7][a] n.259
1.1034-1(c)(3)(i) . . . . . . 19.03[3][d][i] n.172
1.1402(a)-4 . . . . 4.04[3][c][ii] n.130
1.1402(a)-4(b)(3)(ii) . . . . . 4.04[3][c][ii] n.131
1.1402(a)-4(b)(3)(iii) . . . . 4.04[3][c][ii] n.133
1.6662-3(b)(3) . . . . S4.02[6][b] n.264.10
1.6662-4(d) . . . . S4.02[6][b] n.264.8
1.6662-4(d)(3)(i) . . . . S4.02[6][b] n.264.8
1.6662-4(d)(3)(ii) . . . . . . S4.02[6][b] n.264.8
1.6662-4(d)(3)(iii) . . . . . . S4.02[6][b] n.264.8
1.6662-4(d)(3)(iv)(B) . . . . S4.02[6][b] n.264.8
1.6662-4(d)(3)(iv)(C) . . . . S4.02[6][b] n.264.8
1.6664-4(b) . . . . 5.07[3][c][i] n.86
1.6664-4(b)(1) . . . . . 4.02[6][a] ns. 262, 263
1.6664-4(c)(1) . . . . 4.02[6][a] n.264; S4.02[6][a]
        n.264
1.6694-1(b) . . . . S4.02[6][b] n.264.5
1.6694-1(d) . . . . S4.02[6][b] n.264.1
1.6694-1(e) . . . . S4.02[6][b] n.264.10
1.6694-1(f) . . . . S4.02[6][b] n.264.11
1.6694-2(d)(2) . . . . S4.02[6][b] n.264.10
1.6694-2(d)(3) . . . . S4.02[6][b] n.264.9
1.6694-2(e) . . . . S4.02[6][b] n.264.12
1.6694-2(e)(5) . . . . S4.02[6][b] n.264.10
1.6694-3(b) . . . . S4.02[6][b] n.264.13
1.6694-3(c) . . . . S4.02[6][b] n.264.13
1.7520-1   S3.05[3][b] n.29; S4.02[5] ns. 244,
        247; S4.08[1][a] n.5; S5.05[3][a] n.95;
        S5.05[5][a][ii] n.207; S5.05[5][b][ii]
        n.264; S5.05[5][c][ii] n.291; S5.05[6][b]
        n.327; S5.05[7][a] n.333; S5.06[7][d]
        n.197; S5.06[8][d][ii] n.348; S9.04[3][a]
        n.48; S10.02[2][b][iii] n.56; S11.02[1][b]
        n.27; S16.02[6] n.409; S19.03[1] n.3;
        S19.03[3][b] n.112; S19.03[3][d] n.162

Reg. §

1.7872-15 . . . . . . S4.14[6] ns. 103.1, 103.8;
        S10.01[3][g] ns. 115.1, 115.3, 115.12,
        115.15
1.7872-15(a)(1) . . . . . . S10.01[3][g] n.115.16
1.7872-15(a)(2)(i) . . . . . S10.01[3][g] n.115.21
1.7872-15(a)(2)(iii) . . . . S10.01[3][g] n.115.26
1.7872-15(e)(2) . . . . S10.01[3][g] n.115.8
1.7872-15(e)(2)(i) . . . . . S10.01[3][g] n.115.24
1.7872-15(e)(2)(ii) . . . . . S10.01[3][g] n.115.25
1.7872-15(e)(2)(iv) Exs. . . . . . . S10.01[3][g]
        n.115.24
1.7872-15(e)(4) . . . . S10.01[3][g] n.115.23
1.7872-15(e)(4)(ii) . . . . . S10.01[3][g] n.115.19
1.7872-15(e)(4)(iii)(D)   S10.01[3][g] n.115.18
1.7872-15(e)(4)(iv) . . . . S10.01[3][g] n.115.19
1.7872-15(e)(5)(ii)(C) . . . S10.01[3][g] n.115.18
1.7872-15(e)(5)(iv) . . . . S10.01[3][g] n.115.22
1.7872-15(e)(5)(iv)(D) . . . . . S10.01[3][g] ns.
        115.18, 115.19, 115.23
1.7872-15(n)(1) . . . . S4.14[6] n.103.1;
        S10.01[3][g] n.115.1
20.0-1(b) . . . . 6.03[2] n.19
20.0-1(b)(1) . . . 5.06[9] n.432; 5.08[3][a] n.84;
        6.01[3][b] ns. 29–31; 7.01[2] ns. 40, 41;
        7.03[8] ns. 194, 196
20.0-2(b)(4) 5.01 n.5
20.0-2(b)(5) 5.01 n.6
20.0-2(c) . . . . 6.03[2] n.10
20.2001-1(a) . . . . 2.01[1][b][i] ns. 22, 23;
        S2.01[1][b][i] ns. 22, 23
20.2001-1(b) . . . . 2.01[1][b][ii] ns. 27, 28;
        S2.01[1][b][ii] ns. 27, 28
20.2001-1(c)(1) . . . . 2.01[1][b][ii] n.25;
        S2.01[1][b][ii] n.25
20.2001-1(d) . . . . . . 2.01[1][b][ii] ns. 44, 45;
        S2.01[1][b][ii] ns. 44, 45; 9.05[2][b] ns.
        30, 31
20.2001-1(f) . . . . 2.01[1][b][ii] n.24;
        S2.01[1][b][ii] n.24
20.2002-1 . . . . . 2.02 ns. 2, 5; 5.03[4][a] n.89;
        S5.03[6][c][iii] n.302; 8.02 n.13; 8.03[1]
        n.6; 12.03[1] n.11
20.2011-1(a) . . . . . 3.03[1] n.2; 5.09[1] ns. 4, 5;
        6.06[4] n.39
20.2011-1(c)(2) . . . . 3.03[2] n.19; 5.09[2] n.12
20.2012-1 . . . . 3.04[2][d] n.37
20.2012-1(a) . . . . 3.04[1][a] n.13
20.2012-1(b) . . . . 3.04[2] n.24
20.2012-1(d)(2)(i) . . . . 3.04[2][b] n.30
20.2012-1(e) . . . . 3.04[1] n.11
20.2013-1 – 20.2013-6 . . . . . 3.05[4][b] n.60
20.2013-1(a) . . . . 3.05[1][a] n.6
20.2013-2 . . . . 5.06[9] n.444
20.2013-3 . . . . 5.06[9] n.444
20.2013-4 . . . . 5.06[9] n.444
20.2013-4(a) . . . . 3.05[3][b] n.29
20.2013-4(b)(3)(i)   3.05[3][b] n.47; 5.03[3][c]
        n.71; S5.03[3][c][i] n.113
20.2013-5(b) . . . . 3.05[1][c] n.15
20.2014-1(a)(1)   3.06 n.11; 3.06[2] ns. 16, 17
20.2014-1(a)(3) . . . . 3.06 ns. 2, 3; 3.06[2] n.15

[Text references are to paragraphs and notes (9"n.");
references to the supplement are preceded by "S."]

Reg. §

20.2014-1(c)(2)(iii) 3.06 n.6
20.2014-3(b) . . . . 3.06[3][b] n.22
20.2014-3(d) . . . . 3.06[2] n.18
20.2014-4 . . . . 3.06 n.9
20.2014-4(a)(1) . . . . 7.02[4][a] n.86; 7.06 n.16
20.2014-4(a)(2) 3.06 n.9
20.2014-5 . . . . 3.06[4] n.24
20.2014-6 . . . . 3.06[4] n.26
20.2015-1(a)(1) 3.07 n.6
20.2016-1 . . . . 3.08 n.3
20.2031-1(b) . . . 4.02[2][a] ns. 7, 15; 4.02[3][a]
    n.57; 4.02[3][b] n.65; 4.02[3][g] n.118;
    4.04[1] n.4; 4.10[9] n.94; 4.11[4][a]
    n.37; 5.08[3][c][iii] n.124; 10.02[2][a] ns.
    22, 23; 14.02[2] n.7; 14.04[2] n.11;
    14.05[1] n.3; 16.02[4][d][i] n.253;
    17.04[1][b] n.15; 17.04[1][c] n.26
20.2031-1(c) 4.02 n.1
20.2031-2 – 20.2031-9 . . . . 4.10[9] n.94
20.2031-2(b) . . . . 4.02[3][e] n.96
20.2031-2(b)(1) . . . . 4.02[3][c] n.87
20.2031-2(b)(2) . . . . 4.02[3][c] n.88
20.2031-2(b)(3) . . . . 4.02[3][c] n.88
20.2031-2(c) . . . . 4.02[3][c] n.89
20.2031-2(d) . . . . 4.02[3][c] n.89
20.2031-2(e) . . . . . 4.02[3][c] n.89; 4.02[4][b][i]
    n.148; 4.02[4][e][ii] n.206
20.2031-2(f) . . . . . . 4.02[3][c] n.89; 4.02[3][f]
    n.111; 4.05[7][a] n.78; 4.14[5][a] n.80;
    S4.14[6] ns. 103.20, 103.21
20.2031-2(f)(1) . . . . 4.02[3][e] n.96; 4.02[3][f]
    n.101
20.2031-2(f)(2) . . . 4.02[3][f] n.102; S4.02[3][f]
    n.102
20.2031-2(h) . . . . 10.02[2][b][vi] n.72;
    19.04[1][b] & ns. 1, 4; 19.04[1][c];
    19.04[2] n.17; S19.04[2] n.19; 19.04[3]
    & n.40; 19.04[3][b][i] ns. 59, 62;
    19.04[3][c] n.97; 19.04[4] n.102;
    19.04[6][a] n.116; 19.04[6][a][i] n.118;
    19.04[6][b] n.138; 19.04[7] n.140
20.2031-2(i) . . . . . 4.03[2] n.20; 4.05[4] n.45
20.2031-3 . . . . 4.05[7][a] n.78; 4.05[7][b] n.84
20.2031-4 . . . . 4.02[3][g] ns. 120, 121
20.2031-5 . . . . 4.05[3] n.28
20.2031-6(a) . . . . 4.02[3][a] n.56
20.2031-6(b) . . . . 4.02[3][a] n.58
20.2031-7 . . . . . S3.05[3][b] n.29; S4.02[5] ns.
    244, 247; S4.08[1][a] n.5; 4.11[4][a]
    n.40; S5.05[3][a] n.95; S5.05[5][a][ii]
    n.207; S5.05[5][b][ii] n.264;
    S5.05[5][c][ii] n.291; 5.05[6][a][ii] n.317;
    S5.05[6][b] n.327; S5.05[7][a] n.333;
    S5.06[7][d] n.197; 5.06[8][d][ii] n.348;
    S5.06[8][d][ii] n.348; S9.04[3][a] n.48;
    S10.02[2][b][iii] n.56; S11.02[1][b] n.27;
    S16.02[6] n.409; S19.03[1] n.3;
    S19.03[3][b] n.112; S19.03[3][d] n.162
20.2031-7(a) . . . . 4.05[5][b] n.57
20.2031-7(d) . . . . 4.05[5][b] n.57
20.2031-7(d)(1) . . . . 4.02[5] n.244

Reg. §

20.2031-7(d)(2)(ii) . . . . 4.02[5] n.248
20.2031-7(d)(2)(iii) . . . . 4.02[5] ns. 247, 248
20.2031-7(d)(2)(iv) . . . . 4.02[5] n.248
20.2031-7(d)(2)(v) . . . . 4.02[5] n.248
20.2031-7(d)(4) . . . . . 4.02[5] n.247; 4.09[4][f]
    n.39; 16.02[6] n.409
20.2031-7(d)(6) . . . . 4.02[5] ns. 247, 248;
    5.05[5][a][i] n.170; 5.05[6][a][ii] n.316;
    9.04[3][a] ns. 51, 53; 10.02[2][b][iii] ns.
    55, 60; 16.02[6] ns. 409, 412
20.2031-7(d)(7) . . . 4.08[1][a] n.5; 5.06[7][d] ns.
    197, 198; 9.04[3][a] n.48; 9.04[3][b]
    n.61; 19.03[1] n.14
20.2031-8 . . . . . 4.05[6] ns. 68, 70; 4.11[4][a];
    5.05[6][b] n.328
20.2031-8(a) . . . . . 4.02[3][h] n.139; 4.14[7][a]
    n.104; 4.14[8] n.118
20.2031-8(a)(1) . . . . 4.02[3][h] n.141
20.2031-8(a)(2) . . . . 4.02[3][h] n.142
20.2031-8(a)(3) . . . 4.02[3][h] ns. 137, 141, 142
20.2032-1 . . . . . S3.05[3][b] n.29; S4.02[5] ns.
    244, 247; S4.08[1][a] n.5; S5.05[3][a]
    n.95; S5.05[5][a][ii] n.207;
    S5.05[5][b][ii] n.264; S5.05[5][c][ii]
    n.291; S5.05[6][b] n.327; S5.05[7][a]
    n.333; S5.06[7][d] n.197; S5.06[8][d][ii]
    n.348; S9.04[3][a] n.48; S10.02[2][b][iii]
    n.56; S11.02[1][b] n.27; S16.02[6] n.409;
    S19.03[1] n.3; S19.03[3][b] n.112;
    S19.03[3][d] n.162
20.2032-1(b) . . . . S4.03[1] n.3
20.2032-1(b)(1) . . . . 4.03[1] n.10; S4.03[1] n.2;
    S5.03[5] n.251; 5.03[6] n.150
20.2032-1(b)(2) . . . . S4.03[1] n.2
20.2032-1(b)(3) . . . . S4.03[1] n.3
20.2032-1(c)(1) . . . . 4.03[3][a] ns. 41, 42;
    S4.03[3][a] n.40
20.2032-1(c)(2) . . . . 4.03[3][a] n.39
20.2032-1(c)(3) . . . . 4.03[3][a] n.44
20.2032-1(d)(1) . . . . 4.03[2][a] ns. 24, 25;
    4.05[4] n.44
20.2032-1(d)(2) . . . . 4.03[2][a] ns. 23, 24
20.2032-1(d)(3) . . . . 4.03[2][a] n.22
20.2032-1(d)(4) . . . . . 4.03[2] n.21; 4.03[2][a]
    n.24; 4.03[2][c] ns. 29, 30; 4.05[4] n.45;
    4.07[2][c] n.62
20.2032-1(f) . . . . 4.03[3][b] n.49
20.2032-1(f)(2) . . . . 4.03[3][b] n.49
20.2032-1(g) . . . . . 4.03[4][a] n.56; 5.04[1] n.5
20.2033-1
20.2032A-3(a) . . . . 5.08[3][e] n.154
20.2032A-3(b) . . . 4.04[3][b][iv] ns. 60, 62–65;
    4.04[3][b][v] ns. 67–69; 4.04[3][b][viii]
    n.100
20.2032A-3(b)(1) . . . . . . 4.04[7][b][ii] n.286;
    5.08[2][a] n.20; 5.08[2][c][ii] n.56;
    5.08[3][d] n.150
20.2032A-3(c)(2) . . . 4.04[3][c][ii] ns. 121, 122;
    4.04[7][a] ns. 260, 264; 5.08[3][e] ns.
    153, 156

*[Text references are to paragraphs and notes (9"n.");
references to the supplement are preceded by "S."]*

Reg. §

20.2032A-3(d) . . . . 4.04[3][b][v] n.66;
    4.04[3][c][i] n.113; 5.08[3][d] n.150
20.2032A-3(e)(1) . . . . . . 4.04[3][c][ii] ns. 120,
    135–139
20.2032A-3(e)(2) . . 4.04[3][c][ii] ns. 132, 134;
    5.08[3][e] n.155
20.2032A-3(f)(1) . . . 4.04[3][c][ii] ns. 140, 141
20.2032A-3(f)(2) . . . . 4.04[3][b][v] n.66
20.2032A-3(g) . . . . 4.04[3][c][ii] ns. 139, 140
20.2032A-4(b) . . . . 4.04[5][a][i] n.185
20.2032A-4(b)(1) . . . . . . 4.04[5][a][i] n.183
20.2032A-4(b)(2)(ii) . . . . . . 4.04[5][a][i] n.185
20.2032A-4(b)(2)(iii) . . . . 4.04[5][a][i] ns. 182,
    184; 4.04[5][a][iii] n.192
20.2032A-4(b)(2)(iv) . . . . . . 4.04[5][a] n.179;
    4.04[5][a][iii] n.193
20.2032A-4(b)(2)(v) . . . . . 4.04[5][a][i] n.186
20.2032A-4(c) . . . . 4.04[5][a][iv] n.199
20.2032A-4(d) . . . . 4.04[5][a] n.175;
    4.04[5][a][iii] ns. 194–198
20.2032A-4(e) . . . . 4.04[5][a][v] n.201
20.2032A-8 . . . . 4.04[6] n.239
20.2032A-8(a)(1) . . . . 5.08[3][b][i] n.92
20.2032A-8(a)(2) . . . 4.04[3][b][viii] ns. 94, 95,
    100; 4.04[3][c] n.104; 4.04[6] n.241;
    4.04[7][a] n.263
20.2032A-8(a)(3) . . . 4.04[6] ns. 213, 214, 217,
    221, 223; 5.08[3][b][i] ns. 92, 94
20.2032A-8(b) . . . . 4.04[6] ns. 218–221;
    5.08[3][b][i] n.96
20.2032A-8(c)(1) . . . . 4.04[6] ns. 229, 230
20.2032A-8(c)(2) . . . . 4.04[6] n.224; 4.04[7][a]
    n.265
20.2032A-8(c)(4) . . . . 4.04[6] n.230
20.2032A-8(d)(2) . . . . 4.04[3][b][viii]
    n.1004.05[3] n.22
20.2033-1(a) . . . 4.05[2] n.2; 4.05[3] ns. 21, 30
20.2033-1(b) . . . . . 4.03[2] n.20; 4.05[3] ns. 23,
    24, 32; 4.05[4] ns. 42, 45
20.2035-1(b) . . . . 4.10[10][d] n.101
20.2035-1(e) . . . . 4.07[2][c] ns. 55, 64
20.2036-1(a) . . . 4.08[8] n.169; 4.14[7][b] n.113
20.2036-1(a)(2) . . . . 4.08[5][b] n.63
20.2036-1(a)(3)(ii) . . . . 4.08[5][b] n.62
20.2036-1(b)(1) . . . . 4.08[2] n.16
20.2036-1(b)(1)(ii) . . . . 4.08[2] n.17
20.2036-1(b)(2) . . . . 4.08[4][b] n.30
20.2036-1(b)(3) . . . . 4.08[5][a] n.57; 4.08[5][b]
    n.63; 4.10[10][d] ns. 103–105
20.2036-1(c) . . . . S4.08[8] n.168.6
20.2036-1(c)(1)(ii) Ex. 2 . . S4.08[8] ns. 168.4,
    168.8
20.2036-1(c)(2)(i) . . . . S4.08[8] n.168.7
20.2036-1(c)(2)(iii) Ex. 1 . . . . S4.08[8] n.168.8
20.2036-1(c)(2)(iii) Ex. 2 . . . . S4.08[8] n.168.8
20.2036-1(c)(2)(iii) Ex. 3 . . . . S4.08[8] n.168.8
20.2036-1(c)(2)(iii) Ex. 4 . . . . S4.08[8] n.168.8
20.2036-1(c)(2)(iii) Ex. 5 . . . . S4.08[8] n.168.8
20.2036-1(c)(3) . . . . S4.08[8] n.168.6
20.2037-1(b) . . . . 4.09[3] n.15
20.2037-1(b)(3) . . . . 4.09[4][a] n.29

Reg. §

20.2037-1(c)(2) . . . . 4.09[4][a] n.27
20.2037-1(c)(3) . . . . 4.09[4][f] n.39; 4.09[4][g]
    n.43
20.2037-1(c)(4)   4.09[4][g] n.43; 4.09[6] n.51
20.2037-1(e) . . . . 4.09[3] ns. 11, 16; 4.09[4][b]
    n.31; 4.09[6] n.50
20.2038-1(a) . . . 4.08[5][c] n.70; 4.10[3] ns. 10,
    14; 4.10[4][g] n.53; 4.10[6] n.65; 4.10[9]
    n.95; 10.01[7] n.187
20.2038-1(a)(2) . . . . 4.10[6] n.70
20.2038-1(a)(3) . . . . 4.10[2] n.7; 4.10[4][g] ns.
    54, 55; 10.01[5] n.149
20.2038-1(b) . . . 4.10[8] n.79; 4.13[7][a] ns. 86,
    87
20.2038-1(b)(3)(iii) . . . . 4.10[8] n.81
20.2038-1(d) . . . . 4.10[6] n.67
20.2038-1(e)(1) . . . . 4.10[8] n.85
20.2038-1(e)(2) . . 4.10[2] n.9; 4.10[8] n.86
20.2038-1(f) . . . . 4.10[8] n.83
20.2039-1(a) . . . . . . S4.08[8] n.168.9; 4.11 n.3
20.2039-1(b)(1) . . . . 4.11[3][a] n.14; 4.11[3][c]
    ns. 25–27; 4.11[3][d] n.34
20.2039-1(b)(2) . . . . 4.11[3][a] ns. 17, 18;
    4.11[3][d] n.35; 4.14[2] n.15
20.2039-1(d) . . . 4.11[2][a] ns. 6, 9–11; 4.14[2]
    n.5
20.2039-1(e) . . . . . S4.08[8] ns. 168.6, 168.9;
    S4.11 n.3
20.2039-1(f) . . . . . S4.08[8] n.168.6; S4.11 n.3
20.2040-1(a) . . . . 4.12[2] n.11
20.2040-1(a)(2) . . 4.12[7][b] & ns. 49, 50, 56
20.2040-1(b) . . . . . . 4.12[1] n.2; 4.12[2] n.16
20.2040-1(c)(2) . . . . 4.12[1] n.9
20.2040-1(c)(4) . . . . 4.12[7][a] ns. 39, 43
20.2040-1(c)(5) . . . . 4.12[7][a] n.36
20.2041-1(b)(1) . . . 4.13[2] n.6; 4.13[2][a] n.7
20.2041-1(b)(2) . . . . 4.13[2][a] ns. 8, 9;
    4.13[2][b] & n.11; 19.03[1] n.13
20.2041-1(c)(1) . . . . 4.13[8][a] n.118
20.2041-1(c)(2) . . . . 4.13[4][a] & ns. 27–32
20.2041-1(d) . . . . 4.13[6] ns. 57, 60; 4.13[6][a]
    n.65
20.2041-1(e) . . . . 4.08[1][b] n.13; 4.13[5] n.55
20.2041-2(c) . . . . 4.13[6][a] n.72
20.2041-2(d) . . . . 4.13[6][c] n.75
20.2041-2(e) . . . . 4.13[6][d] n.77
20.2041-2(f) . . . . 4.13[6] n.68
20.2041-3(b) . . . . 4.13[7][a] ns. 83, 84
20.2041-3(c)(2) . . . . 4.13[4][c][ii] n.44
20.2041-3(c)(3) . . . . 4.13[4][c][iii] n.50
20.2041-3(d)(1) . . . . 5.06[8][b][iv] n.259
20.2041-3(d)(3) . . . . 4.13[7][e] n.106; 4.13[7][f]
    n.108; 9.04[3][f] n.118
20.2041-3(d)(4) . . 4.13[7][f] n.110; 10.04[4][c]
    n.56
20.2041-3(d)(5) . . . . 10.04[4][c] n.56
20.2041-3(d)(6) . . . . 4.13[7][d] n.99
20.2041-3(d)(6)(ii) . . . . 10.07[1] n.4
20.2042-1(a)(1) . . . . 4.14[2] n.12
20.2042-1(a)(2) . . . . 4.14[9][b] n.139
20.2042-1(a)(3) . . . . . 4.14[7][a] ns. 104, 105

[Text references are to paragraphs and notes (9"n.");
references to the supplement are preceded by "S."]

Reg. §

20.2042-1(b)(1) . . . . . . 4.14[3] ns. 21, 23, 24;
4.14[7][b] n.110
20.2042-1(b)(2) . . . . 4.14[8] n.115
20.2042-1(c) . . . . 18.05[2][b][i] n.20
20.2042-1(c)(2) . . . . 4.14[4][a] n.41; 4.14[4][f]
n.77; 4.14[5][a] ns. 79, 83
20.2042-1(c)(3) . . . . . 4.14[4][b] & ns. 48, 49
20.2042-1(c)(5) . . . . 4.14[7][b] n.113; 4.14[8]
n.116
20.2042-1(c)(6) . . . . 4.14[4][d] n.62; 4.14[4][f]
n.78; 4.14[5][a] ns. 79, 80, 82, 84, 87;
S4.14[6] n.103.19
20.2043-1(a) . . . . 4.15[2] ns. 66, 67
20.2044-1(a) 4.16 n.10
20.2044-1(b) . . . . . 2.02[3][c][ii] n.107; 4.16 ns.
17–19
20.2044-1(c) 4.16 n.11
20.2044-1(d) 4.16 n.10
20.2044-1(d)(1) 4.16 n.13
20.2044-1(d)(2) . . . . . 4.16 n.12; 5.06[8][d][ii]
n.323
20.2044-1(d)(3) 4.16 n.14
20.2044-1(d)(3)(iii) 4.16 n.14
20.2044-1(d)(4) 4.16 n.10
20.2044-1(e) . . . . . 4.16 ns. 10, 13, 14, 16, 17;
10.08[1][a] ns. 11, 15, 19; 10.08[1][b]
n.27; 17.02[1][c][i] n.48
20.2053 . . . . S5.03[1][b] n.25
20.2053-1 . . . . 5.03[1] n.6; S5.03[1] n.7;
S5.03[4][c][iii] ns. 229, 235
20.2053-1(a)(1) . . . 5.03[2][b] n.25; S5.03[2][b]
n.66
20.2053-1(b)(1) . . . 5.03[2][b] n.24; S5.03[1][a]
n.15; S5.03[1][b] ns. 28, 29;
S5.03[1][b][iii] n.46; S5.03[2][b] ns. 61,
65; S5.03[3][a] n.96
20.2053-1(b)(2) . . . . 5.03[1] n.15; S5.03[4][a][i]
n.155
20.2053-1(b)(2)(i) . . . . . . S5.03[1][b][ii] n.39;
S5.03[1][b][iv] n.50
20.2053-1(b)(2)(ii)   S5.03[1][b][ii] ns. 40, 45;
S5.03[4][a][i] n.156
20.2053-1(b)(2)(iii)(A) . . . . S5.03[1][b][ii] n.42
20.2053-1(b)(2)(iii)(B) . . . . S5.03[1][b][ii] n.43
20.2053-1(b)(2)(iii)(C) . . . . S5.03[1][b][ii] n.44
20.2053-1(b)(3) . . . . S5.03[1][b] n.29;
S5.03[1][b][i] n.32; S5.03[1][b][iii] n.49;
5.03[3][c] n.70; S5.03[4][a][i] n.154;
S5.03[5] n.257; 14.02[3] n.17; 14.03[3]
n.19
20.2053-1(b)(3)(i) . . . . S5.03[1][b][i] n.33;
S5.03[4][c][i] n.203
20.2053-1(b)(3)(ii) . . . . S5.03[1][b][i] n.34
20.2053-1(b)(3)(iii)   S5.03[1][b][i] ns. 35, 36;
S5.03[4][c][i] n.203
20.2053-1(b)(3)(iv)   S5.03[1][b][i] ns. 37, 38;
S5.03[4][b] n.175; S5.03[4][c][i] ns. 202,
203
20.2053-1(b)(3)(v) . . . . S5.03[1][b][i] n.32
20.2053-1(b)(4) Ex. 1   . . . S5.03[1][b][i] ns. 33,
36

Reg. §

20.2053-1(b)(4) Ex. 2   . . . . S5.03[1][b][i] n.34
20.2053-1(b)(4)(i) . . . . . . S5.03[1][b][iii] n.47
20.2053-1(b)(4)(ii) . . . . . . S5.03[1][b][iv] n.52
20.2053-1(b)(7) Ex. 3   . . . S5.03[1][b][iv] n.55
20.2053-1(c) . . . . S5.03[6][c][ii] n.295;
S5.03[6][c][iv] n.313; 5.03[7] n.160
20.2053-1(c) Ex. 1   . . . S5.03[6][c][iv] ns. 315,
318
20.2053-1(c) Ex. 2   . . . S5.03[6][c][iv] ns. 317,
318
20.2053-1(c)(1) . . . . S5.03[3][a] n.96
20.2053-1(c)(2) . . . . S5.03[6][c][iv] n.316;
5.03[7] ns. 158, 159
20.2053-1(d) . . . . S5.03[6] n.260
20.2053-1(d)(1) . . . . S5.03[2][b] n.63; S5.03[5]
n.253
20.2053-1(d)(2) . . . . S5.03[1][b] n.27;
S5.03[4][b][i] n.187; S5.03[4][c][i] n.204
20.2053-1(d)(2)(i) . . . . . . S5.03[1][b][iii] n.50
20.2053-1(d)(3) . . . . S5.03[1][b][iii] n.49
20.2053-1(d)(4) . . . . S5.03[2][b] n.63;
S5.03[3][a] ns. 97, 102; S5.03[4][c][iii]
ns. 226, 241
20.2053-1(d)(4)(i) . . . . . S5.03[1][b][iii] n. 48;
S5.03[3][c][i] n.114; S5.03[5] n.254
20.2053-1(d)(4)(ii) . . . . . S5.03[1][b][iv] n.51;
S5.03[3][c][i] n.117
20.2053-1(d)(5)(i) . . . S5.03[1][b][iv] ns. 52, 53
20.2053-1(d)(5) . . . . S5.03[3][a] n.97;
S5.03[3][c][i] n.117; S5.03[4][c][iii] ns.
228, 230, 234
20.2053-1(d)(5)(i) . . . . . . S5.03[1][b][iv] n.52
20.2053-1(d)(5)(ii) . . . . . . S5.03[1][b][iv] n.55
20.2053-1(d)(7) Ex. 1 . . . . . S5.03[2][b] n.63;
S5.03[3][a] n.97; S5.03[5] n.255
20.2053-1(d)(7) Ex. 2   . . . S5.03[1][b][iv] n.52
20.2053-1(f) . . . . S5.03[1][b] n.25
20.2053-2   5.03[2][a] ns. 16–18; S5.03[2][a]
ns. 56–58; 5.03[2][b] n.22; S5.03[2][b]
n.62
20.2053-3 . . . . 14.03[3] n.19
20.2053-3(a) . . . 5.03[3] ns. 35, 38; S5.03[3] ns.
74, 78; 5.03[3][a] n.53; S5.03[3][a] ns.
92, 94; 5.03[3][c] ns. 68, 71; S5.03[3][c]
n.109; S5.03[3][c][i] ns. 110, 113, 118
20.2053-3(b) . . . . . 5.03[3] n.36; S5.03[3] n.75;
S5.03[3][a] n.86; 14.02[3] n.17
20.2053-3(b)(1) . . . . 5.03[2][b] n.22; 5.03[3][a]
ns. 41, 42; S5.03[3][a] ns. 96, 97
20.2053-3(b)(2) . . . 5.03[3][a] n.49; S5.03[3][a]
n.97
20.2053-3(b)(3) . . . . S5.03[1][b][iv] n.50;
5.03[3][a] n.55; S5.03[3][a] n.97;
5.03[3][b] ns. 57, 60
20.2053-3(b)(4) . . . . S5.03[3][a] n.89
20.2053-3(b)(5) . . . . S5.03[3][a] n.94;
S5.03[3][b] ns. 103, 106
20.2053-3(c) . . . . . 5.03[3] n.36; S5.03[3] n.75;
5.03[3][a] ns. 41, 42; S5.03[3][a] n.86;
14.03[3] n.15
20.2053-3(c)(1) . . . . S5.03[3][a] ns. 96, 97, 102

[Text references are to paragraphs and notes (9"n.");
references to the supplement are preceded by "S."]

Reg. §

20.2053-3(c)(2) . . . 5.03[3][a] n.43; S5.03[3][a]
n.98
20.2053-3(c)(3) . . . . . . 5.03[3][a] ns. 53, 55;
S5.03[3][a] ns. 92, 94, 97
20.2053-3(d) . . . . . 5.03[3] n.37; S5.03[3] n.76;
14.03[3] n.15
20.2053-3(d)(1) . . . . S5.03[3][c][i] n.113;
S5.03[3][c][iii] n.133
20.2053-3(d)(2) . . . . 5.03[3][c] n.63;
S5.03[3][c][ii] n.127
20.2053-3(d)(3) . . . . . . S5.03[3][a] ns. 97, 99;
S5.03[3][c][iii] ns. 141–143; S5.03[4][b]
n.177; S5.03[4][b][i] n.188;
S5.03[4][c][ii] n.219
20.2053-3(d)(4) . . . . S5.03[4][b] n.173
20.2053-3(e) . . . . S5.03[1][b] n.25
20.2053-4 . . . . 5.03[5] n.96; 5.03[5][e] n.137;
14.05[3] n.34
20.2053-4(a)–20.2053-4(c) . . . S5.03[4] n.145
20.2053-4(a)(1) . . . S5.03[4] n.145; S5.03[4][a]
n.146; S5.03[4][b] n.173; S5.03[4][c][i]
n.212
20.2053-4(a)(1)(i) . . . . . S5.03[4][c][i] n.213;
S5.03[4][c][iii] n.223
20.2053-4(a)(1)(ii) . . . . . S5.03[4][c][iii] n.226
20.2053-4(a)(2) . . . . S5.03[1][b] n.27;
S5.03[4][b][i] n.187; S5.03[4][c][i] ns.
204, 214
20.2053-4(b)(1) . . . . S5.03[4][c][iii] n.228
20.2053-4(b)(1)(i)–20.2053-4(b)(1)(iii) . . . . . .
. . . . S5.03[4][c][iii] n.229
20.2053-4(b)(1)(iv) . . . . . S5.03[4][c][iii] n.231
20.2053-4(b)(1)(v) . . . . . S5.03[4][c][iii] n.232
20.2053-4(b)(1)(vi) . . . . . S5.03[4][c][iii] n.230
20.2053-4(b)(2) . . . . S5.03[4][c][iii] n.233
20.2053-4(b)(3) . . . . S5.03[4][c][i] n.207;
S5.03[4][c][iii] ns. 230, 232
20.2053-4(c)(1)(i)–20.2053-4(c)(2)(i) . . . .
. . . . S5.03[4][c][iii] n.235
20.2053-4(c)(1)(iii) . . . . . S5.03[4][c][iii] n.235
20.2053-4(c)(1)(iv) . . . . . S5.03[4][c][iii] n.236
20.2053-4(c)(1)(v) . . . . . S5.03[4][c][iii] n.239
20.2053-4(c)(1)(vi) . . . . . S5.03[4][c][iii] n.239
20.2053-4(c)(1)(vii) . . . . . S5.03[4][c][iii] n.237
20.2053-4(c)(2) . . . . S5.03[4][c][iii] n.237
20.2053-4(c)(3) Ex. 1 . . . . S5.03[4][c][iii] n.239
20.2053-4(c)(3) Ex. 2 . . . . S5.03[4][c][iii] n.239
20.2053-4(c)(3) Ex. 3 . . . . . S5.03[4][c][iii] ns.
227, 233, 239
20.2053-4(d) Ex. 6 . . . . . S5.03[3][c][iii] n.141
20.2053-4(d) Ex. 7   S5.03[4][b] ns. 173, 176,
177
20.2053-4(d)(1) . . . S5.03[4][c][ii] ns. 215, 222
20.2053-4(d)(2) . . . . S5.03[4][c][ii] n.216
20.2053-4(d)(3) . . . . S5.03[4][a][i] n.160;
S5.03[4][c][i] n.206; S5.03[4][c][ii] ns.
217, 218
20.2053-4(d)(4) . . . . S5.03[4][b] n.219
20.2053-4(d)(5) . . . . S5.03[4][a][i] ns. 153, 166
20.2053-4(d)(6)(i) . . . . S5.03[4][c][iii] ns. 240,
241; S5.03[5] n.254

Reg. §

20.2053-4(d)(6)(ii) . . . . . . S5.03[4][c][iii] n.242
20.2053-4(d)(6)(iii) . . . S5.03[4][c][iii] ns. 243,
244
20.2053-4(d)(7) Exs. 1–7 . . . . . S5.03[4][c][ii]
n.219
20.2053-4(d)(7) Exs. 1–5 . . . . S5.03[4][c][ii]
n.216
20.2053-4(d)(7) Ex. 1 . . . . S5.03[4][c][ii] ns.
220, 222
20.2053-4(d)(7) Ex. 4 . . . . S5.03[4][c][ii] ns.
217, 218
20.2053-4(d)(7) Ex. 5 . . . S5.03[4][c][ii] n.217
20.2053-4(d)(7) Ex. 6 . . . S5.03[4][c][ii] n.222
20.2053-4(d)(7) Ex. 7 . . . . S5.03[4][b] n.177
20.2053-4(d)(7) Ex. 8 . . S5.03[4][c][iii] n.241
20.2053-4(d)(7) Ex. 9 . . . S5.03[4][c][iii] ns.
243, 244
20.2053-4(e)(2) . . . . S5.03[3][c][i] n.111
20.2053-4(f) . . . . S5.03[1][b] n.25
20.2053-5 . . . . S5.03[4][a][i] n.166; 5.03[5][e]
n.145; 5.05[2][a] n.61
20.2053-6(a) . . . . S5.03[4][b][i] n.178
20.2053-6(b) . . . . S5.03[4][b][i] ns. 190, 191;
5.03[5][a] ns. 107, 108
20.2053-6(c) . . . . S5.03[4][b][i] n.181
20.2053-6(d) . . . . S5.03[4][b][i] ns. 184, 186;
5.03[5][a] n.105
20.2053-6(e) . . . . S5.03[3][c][ii] n.127
20.2053-6(f) . . . . . . 5.03[1] n.9; S5.03[1] n.10;
S5.03[4][b][i] n.183; 5.03[5][a] n.104
20.2053-6(g) . . . . S5.03[4][b][i] n.188
20.2053-6(g) Ex. 1 . . . . . S5.03[4][b][i] n.188
20.2053-6(g) Ex. 2 . . . . . S5.03[4][b][i] n.188
20.2053-6(h) . . . . S5.03[1][b] n.25
20.2053-7   4.02[3][b] n.75; 4.04[3][b][i] n.35;
4.04[5] n.172; 5.03[3][c] n.73;
S5.03[3][c][i] n.111; 5.03[4][a] n.88;
S5.03[5] ns. 246, 249, 253; 5.03[6] ns.
147, 148; S5.03[6][c][iii] n.302;
5.06[5][b][i] n.103; 5.07[3][c] n.53;
6.06[1] n.9; 10.02[2][b][i] ns. 35, 41;
14.05[1] n.6; 14.05[3] n.35
20.2053-8 . . . . . . 5.03[4] n.85; S5.03[6][c][iii]
n.305
20.2053-8(a) . . . . S5.03[6][c][iii] n.302
20.2053-8(b) . . . . . S5.03[6][c][iii] ns. 302, 305
20.2053-8(c) . . . . S5.03[6][c][iii] n.302
20.2053-8(d) . . . . . 5.03[4] n.85; 5.03[4][a] n.91
20.2053-8(d) Ex. 1 . . . . . S5.03[3][a] n.96;
S5.03[3][b] n.107; S5.03[6][c][iii] n.303
20.2053-8(d) Ex. 2 . . . . . . S5.03[3][b] n.107;
S5.03[6][c][iii] n.303
20.2053-8(d) Ex. 3 . . . . . S5.03[6][c][iii] n.305
20.2053-8(d) Ex. 4 . . . . . . S5.03[3][b] n.107;
S5.03[6][c][iii] n.302
20.2053-9(b)(1) . . . . 5.03[8] n.164
20.2053-9(d) . . . . 5.03[8] n.165
20.2053-9(e) Ex. 1 . . . . S5.03[4][b][ii] n.199
20.2053-9(e) Ex. 2 . . . . S5.03[4][b][ii] n.198
20.2053-9(e) Exs. 3–5 . . S5.03[4][b][ii] n.198
20.2053-9(f) . . . . S5.03[1][b] n.25

[Text references are to paragraphs and notes (9"n.");
references to the supplement are preceded by "S."]

Reg. §

20.2053-10(b)(1)(ii) . . . . . S5.03[4][b][ii] n.198
20.2053-10(b)(2) . . . . S5.03[4][b][ii] n.198
20.2053-10(c) . . . . S5.03[4][b][ii] n.195
20.2053-10(d) . . . . S5.03[4][b][ii] n.200
20.2053-10(e) . . . . S5.03[1][b] n.25
20.2054-1 . . . . 5.04 ns. 2, 3
20.2055-1(a) . . . . 5.05[2][e] n.90
20.2055-1(a)(2) . . . 5.05[1][b] ns. 22, 25, 26, 29
20.2055-1(a)(3) . . . . 5.05[1][b] n.39
20.2055-2(b) . . . . 5.05[5][a][i] n.202;
                  5.05[5][b][i] n.257; 5.05[7][a] n.335
20.2055-2(b)(1) . . . 5.05[4][a] n.128; 5.05[4][b]
                                            n.140
20.2055-2(c) . . . . 5.05[2][c] n.85
20.2055-2(e)(1) . . . 5.05[4][b] n.146; 11.02[2][a]
                                            n.49
20.2055-2(e)(1)(i) . . . . 5.05[4][b] ns. 138–140
20.2055-2(e)(1)(ii) . . . . 5.05[7][d] n.349;
                                    11.02[2][d] n.101
20.2055-2(e)(2)(i) . . . . 5.05[7][b] ns. 339, 340
20.2055-2(e)(2)(ii) . . . . 5.05[7][a] ns. 330, 331
20.2055-2(e)(2)(iii) . . . 5.05[7][a] ns. 330, 332
20.2055-2(e)(2)(vi) . . . . . . 5.05[5][a][i] n.163;
                     5.05[6][a] ns. 296, 300, 301
20.2055-2(e)(2)(vi)(a) . . 5.05[6][a][i] ns. 306–
           308, 312; 5.05[6][a][ii] ns. 313, 315,
                                        317, 318
20.2055-2(e)(2)(vi)(b) . . . . . 5.05[6][a][ii] n.322
20.2055-2(e)(2)(vi)(c) . . . . . 5.05[6][a][ii] n.314
20.2055-2(e)(2)(vi)(d) . . . . . 5.05[6][a][ii] n.321
20.2055-2(e)(2)(vi)(e) . . . 5.05[6][a][ii] n.319
20.2055-2(e)(2)(vi)(f) . . . 5.05[6][a][ii] ns. 325,
                      326; S5.05[6][a][ii] n.325
20.2055-2(e)(2)(vii) . . . . . . 5.05[5][b][i] n.216;
                      5.05[6][a] ns. 297, 300, 301
20.2055-2(e)(2)(vii)(a) . . . 5.05[6][a][i] ns. 310,
           312; 5.05[6][a][ii] ns. 313, 315, 317, 318
20.2055-2(e)(2)(vii)(b) . . . . 5.05[6][a][ii] n.322
20.2055-2(e)(2)(vii)(c) . . . . 5.05[6][a][ii] n.314
20.2055-2(e)(2)(vii)(d) . . . . 5.05[6][a][ii] n.321
20.2055-2(e)(2)(vii)(e) . . . 5.05[6][a][ii] ns. 325,
                      326; S5.05[6][a][ii] n.325
20.2055-2(e)(3) . . . . 5.05[4][b] n.134
20.2055-2(e)(3)(i) . . . . 5.05[4][b] n.134
20.2055-2(e)(3)(i)(a) . . . . . . 5.05[4][b] n.134
20.2055-2(e)(3)(ii) . . . . 5.05[4][b] n.134;
                                  5.05[6][a][ii] n.317
20.2055-2(e)(4) . . . . 5.05[4][b] n.134
20.2055-2(f)(2) . . . . 19.03[3][b] n.112
20.2055-2(f)(2)(i) . . . 5.05[5][a][ii] ns. 205–207
20.2055-2(f)(2)(iv) . . . . . . 5.05[6][a][ii] n.325;
                                      5.05[6][b] n.328
20.2055-2(f)(2)(v) . . . . 5.05[6][b] n.327
20.2055-3(a) . . . . 5.05[3][b][i] n.106
20.2055-3(b) . . . . 5.05[3][b][ii] n.115;
                                  5.08[4][a][iii] n.185
20.2055-3(b)(1)(i) . . . . . 5.05[3][b][ii] ns. 120,
                      121; 5.08[4][a][iii] n.189
20.2055-3(b)(1)(ii) . . . . . 5.05[3][b][ii] ns. 122–
                      124; 5.08[4][a][iii] n.187

Reg. §

20.2055-3(b)(1)(iii) . . . . 5.05[3][b][ii] ns. 111,
                                            116
20.2055-3(b)(2) . . . . 5.05[3][b][ii] n.125;
                                  5.08[4][a][iii] n.188
20.2055-3(b)(3) . . . . 5.03[3][c] n.71;
           S5.03[3][c][i] n.113; 5.05[3][b][ii] ns.
           117, 126; 5.08[4][a][iii] ns. 190, 191
20.2055-3(b)(4) . . . . 5.05[3][b][ii] n.119;
                                  5.08[4][a][iii] n.192
20.2055-3(b)(5) . . . . 5.05[3][b][ii] n.125
20.2055-3(b)(6) . . . . 5.03[3][c] n.71;
           S5.03[3][c][i] n.113; 5.05[3][b][ii] ns.
                            116, 117, 126
20.2055-3(b)(7) . . . . 5.05[3][b][ii] n.115
20.2055-4(d) . . . . 5.05[1][c] n.45
20.2055-5(b) . . . . 5.05[1][c] n.45
20.2055-5(c) . . . . 5.05[1][c] n.45
20.2055-6   5.05[4][b] n.148; 5.06[8][e] n.414;
                                      5.06[8][f] n.424
20.2056-2(d)(1)(i)(B) . . . . 5.07[3][c][i] n.70
20.2056(a)-1(c) . . . . 5.06[1] n.3; 5.06[10] n.459
20.2056(a)-1(c)(1) . . . . 5.06[10] n.456
20.2056(a)-1(c)(2) . . . . 5.06[10] n.457
20.2056(a)-1(c)(3) . . . . 5.06[10] n.457
20.2056(a)-2(a) . . . . 5.06[2] n.12
20.2056(a)-2(b) . . . . 5.06[8][c] n.276
20.2056(a)-2(b)(1) . . . . . 4.02[7][e][ii] ns. 376,
                            379; 5.06[5] n.89
20.2056(a)-2(b)(2) . . . . 5.06[2] n.14
20.2056(a)-2(b)(3) . . . . 5.06[2] n.14
20.2056(a)-2(b)(4) . . . . 5.06[2] n.15
20.2056(b)-1(b) . . . . 5.06[7][c] n.191
20.2056(b)-1(e)(1) . . . . 5.06[3][d] n.58
20.2056(b)-1(g) . . . . 5.06[3][g] n.74; 5.06[7][b]
           ns. 168, 169; 5.06[7][d] n.196
20.2056(b)-2(d) . . . . 5.06[7][e] n.200
20.2056(b)-3(b) . . . . 5.06[8][a] n.204
20.2056(b)-4(a) . . . . 5.05[3][b][ii] n.115;
           5.06[5][b][ii] ns. 109, 112, 114;
                            5.06[8][b][i] n.216
20.2056(b)-4(b) . . . . 5.06[5][b][i] ns. 103, 106;
           5.06[5][b][ii] n.109; 5.06[5][b][iii] & ns.
                  130, 133; 10.02[2][b][i] n.37
20.2056(b)-4(c) . . . . 5.06[8][e] n.412
20.2056(b)-4(d) . . . . 3.05[3][b] n.47;
           5.06[5][b][ii] n.116; 5.06[7][b] n.190;
                                  5.08[4][a][iii] n.185
20.2056(b)-4(d)(1)(i) . . . . . 3.05[3][b] n.47;
           5.06[5][b][ii] ns. 123, 124; 5.08[4][a][iii]
                                            n.189
20.2056(b)-4(d)(1)(ii) . . . . 3.05[3][b] n.47;
           5.06[5][b][ii] ns. 125–127; 5.08[4][a][iii]
                                            n.187
20.2056(b)-4(d)(1)(iii) . . . . 5.06[5][b][ii] n.117
20.2056(b)-4(d)(2) . . . . 5.03[3][c] n.71;
           S5.03[3][c][i] n.113; 5.06[5][b][ii] ns.
           119, 128; 5.08[4][a][iii] n.188
20.2056(b)-4(d)(3) . . . . 3.05[3][b] n.48;
           5.03[3][c] n.71; S5.03[3][c][i] n.113;
           5.06[5][b][ii] ns. 119, 129; 5.08[4][a][iii]
                                      ns. 190, 191

[Text references are to paragraphs and notes (9"n.");
references to the supplement are preceded by "S."]

Reg. §

20.2056(b)-4(d)(4) . . . . 3.05[3][b] n.48;
S5.03[4][b] ns. 175, 176; 5.06[5][b][ii]
n.122; 5.08[4][a][iii] n.192
20.2056(b)-4(d)(5) . . . . 3.05[3][b] n.48;
5.03[3][c] n.71; 5.05[3][b][ii] ns. 116,
117, 119, 126; 5.06[5][b][ii] ns. 117,
119, 122, 128, 129
20.2056(b)-4(d)(5) Ex. 4   S5.03[3][c][i] n.113
20.2056(b)-4(d)(6) . . . . . . 5.06[5][b][ii] n.116
20.2056(b)-5(a)(1) . . . . 5.06[8][b] n.208
20.2056(b)-5(a)(2) . . . . 5.06[8][b] n.208
20.2056(b)-5(a)(3) . . . . 5.06[8][b] n.208
20.2056(b)-5(a)(4) . . . . 5.06[8][b] n.208
20.2056(b)-5(a)(5) . . . . 5.06[8][b] n.208
20.2056(b)-5(b) . . . . 5.06[8][b][i] n.235
20.2056(b)-5(c) . . . . 5.06[8][b][i] ns. 225, 228;
11.03[4][b] n.50
20.2056(b)-5(c)(2)   5.06[8][b][i] ns. 233, 234;
5.06[8][c] n.282
20.2056(b)-5(c)(3)(i) . . . . 5.06[8][b][i] n.233
20.2056(b)-5(c)(3)(iii) . . . . 5.06[8][b][i] n.233
20.2056(b)-5(c)(3)(iv) . . . . 5.06[8][b][i] n.233
20.2056(b)-5(c)(5) . . . 5.06[8][b][i] ns. 233, 234
20.2056(b)-5(e) . . . . 5.06[8][b][i] ns. 219, 221;
5.06[8][b][ii] n.236
20.2056(b)-5(f) . . . . 5.06[8][d][ii] n.315;
5.06[8][d][ii] n.333
20.2056(b)-5(f)(1) . . . . . . 5.06[8][b][i] n.212;
S5.06[8][b][i] n.215; S5.06[8][d][ii]
n.316; S9.04[3][b] n.64; S11.03[4][c]
n.58
20.2056(b)-5(f)(3) . . . . . . 5.06[8][b][i] n.213
20.2056(b)-5(f)(4)   5.06[8][b][i] ns. 217, 220;
5.06[8][d][ii] ns. 316, 325
20.2056(b)-5(f)(5) . . . . . . 5.06[8][b][i] n.220;
5.06[8][d][ii] ns. 316, 325
20.2056(b)-5(f)(7)   5.06[8][b][i] ns. 214, 218;
5.06[8][d][ii] n.331
20.2056(b)-5(f)(8) . . . . . 5.06[8][b][ii] n.237;
5.06[8][f] n.420
20.2056(b)-5(f)(9) . . . . . . 5.06[5][b][ii] n.117;
5.06[8][b][i] n.216; 5.06[8][d][ii] n.313;
5.06[8][f] ns. 420, 424
20.2056(b)-5(g)(1)(i) . . . . 5.06[8][b][iv] n.263
20.2056(b)-5(g)(3) . . . . 5.06[8][b][iii] ns. 245,
246; 5.06[8][b][iv] n.262
20.2056(b)-5(g)(4) . . . . . . 5.06[8][b][iv] n.262
20.2056(b)-5(g)(5) . . . . . . 5.06[8][b][iv] n.258
20.2056(b)-5(h) . . . . 5.06[8][b][iv] n.262
20.2056(b)-5(j) . . . . 5.06[8][b][v] ns. 268, 270,
272; 5.06[8][d][ii] n.355
20.2056(b)-6(a) . . . . 5.06[8][c] n.278
20.2056(b)-6(a)(1) . . . . 5.06[8][c] n.279
20.2056(b)-6(a)(2) . . . . 5.06[8][c] n.279
20.2056(b)-6(a)(3) . . . . 5.06[8][c] n.279
20.2056(b)-6(a)(4) . . . . 5.06[8][c] n.279
20.2056(b)-6(a)(5) . . . . 5.06[8][c] n.279
20.2056(b)-6(c)(1) . . . . 5.06[8][c] n.283
20.2056(b)-6(e)(4) . . . . 5.06[8][c] n.284
20.2056(b)-7 . . . . 11.03[4][c] n.65
20.2056(b)-7(a) . . . . 5.06[8][d] n.296

Reg. §

20.2056(b)-7(b)(1)(i) . . . . . 5.06[7][d] n.199;
5.06[8][d][ii] n.344
20.2056(b)-7(b)(1)(ii) . . . . . 5.06[8][d][ii] n.326
20.2056(b)-7(b)(2) . . . . . . 5.06[8][d][iii] n.369
20.2056(b)-7(b)(2)(i)   5.06[8][d][iii] ns. 373–
375, 379
20.2056(b)-7(b)(2)(ii) . . . 4.16 n.10; 10.08[1][a]
n.13
20.2056(b)-7(b)(2)(ii)(A) . . . . 5.06[8][d][iii] ns.
376, 377
20.2056(b)-7(b)(2)(ii)(B) . . . . 5.06[8][d][iii] ns.
378, 380; 17.04[2][b] n.73
20.2056(b)-7(b)(2)(ii)(C) . . . . . . 5.06[8][d][iii]
n.381; 17.04[2][b] n.73
20.2056(b)-7(b)(3) . . . . 5.06[8][d][iii] n.366
20.2056(b)-7(b)(4)(i) . . . . 5.06[8][d][iii] n.383
20.2056(b)-7(b)(4)(ii) . . . . 5.06[8][d][iii] n.385
20.2056(b)-7(c)(1) . . . . . 5.06[8][d][iii] n.388
20.2056(b)-7(c)(2) . . . . . 5.06[8][d][iii] n.389
20.2056(b)-7(d)(1) . . . . . . S5.06[8][b][i] n.215;
5.06[8][d][ii] n.352; S5.06[8][d][ii]
n.353; S9.04[3][b] n.64; S11.03[4][c]
n.58
20.2056(b)-7(d)(2) . . . . 5.06[8][b] n.208;
5.06[8][d][ii] ns. 313, 315, 331–333
20.2056(b)-7(d)(3) . . . . . 5.06[8][d][ii] ns. 314,
317
20.2056(b)-7(d)(3)(i) . . . . . . 5.06[6][a] n.155;
5.06[8][d][ii] n.320
20.2056(b)-7(d)(3)(ii) . . . . 5.06[8][d][ii] n.320
20.2056(b)-7(d)(4) . . . . . 5.06[8][d][ii] ns. 321–
323
20.2056(b)-7(d)(5) . . . . . . 5.06[8][d][ii] n.335;
5.06[8][e] n.409
20.2056(b)-7(d)(6) . . . . . 5.06[8][d][ii] ns. 353,
355, 357, 358
20.2056(b)-7(e) . . . . 5.06[8][d][ii] ns. 343, 344
20.2056(b)-7(e)(1) . . . . . . 5.06[8][d][ii] n.345
20.2056(b)-7(e)(2) . . . . . 5.06[8][d][ii] ns. 349–
351
20.2056(b)-7(e)(3) . . . . . . 5.06[8][d][ii] n.346
20.2056(b)-7(e)(4) . . . . . . 5.06[8][d][ii] n.348
20.2056(b)-7(e)(5) . . . . 5.06[8][e] n.410
20.2056(b)-7(e)(5)(ii) . . . . 5.06[8][d][ii] n.343
20.2056(b)-7(e)(5)(iii) . . . . 5.06[8][d][ii] n.343
20.2056(b)-7(f) . . . 5.06[8][d][ii] ns. 341, 344
20.2056(b)-7(g) . . . . 5.06[8][d][ii] n.329
20.2056(b)-7(h) . . . . 5.06[8][d][ii] ns. 314, 316,
317, 334, 335, 341, 349–351, 353–355,
363; 5.06[8][d][iii] ns. 370–372, 375,
379, 381; 5.06[8][e] n.409; 11.03[4][c]
ns. 59, 65
20.2056(b)-8(a)(1) . . . . 5.06[8][e] n.413
20.2056(b)-8(a)(2) . . . . 5.06[8][e] n.411
20.2056(b)-8(a)(3) . . . . 5.06[8][e] n.412
20.2056(b)-8(b) . . . . 5.06[8][e] n.410
20.2056(b)-9 . . . . . 5.05[4][b] n.148; 5.06[8][e]
n.414
20.2056(c)-1 . . . . 5.06[3] n.23
20.2056(c)-1(a)(6) . . . . 5.06[3][g] n.69
20.2056(c)-2 . . . . 5.06[3] n.23

*[Text references are to paragraphs and notes (9"n.");
references to the supplement are preceded by "S."]*

Reg. §

20.2056(c)-2(a) . . . . 5.06[3][a] n.27; 5.06[3][c]
n.50; 5.06[3][g] n.71
20.2056(c)-2(b) . . . . 5.06[3][a] n.27
20.2056(c)-2(b)(1)(i) . . . . . 5.06[7][c] n.194;
5.07[3][e] n.126
20.2056(c)-2(b)(1)(ii) . . . . . . 5.06[7][c] n.194;
5.07[3][e] n.126
20.2056(c)-2(b)(1)(iii) . . . . . 5.07[3][e] n.126
20.2056(c)-2(b)(2)(ii) . . . . . . 11.03[3][b] n.39
20.2056(c)-2(b)(3) . . . . . 5.06[3][f] ns. 66, 67;
5.06[8][c] n.276
20.2056(c)-2(c) . . . . 5.06[3][b] n.38
20.2056(c)-2(d) . . . . 5.06[3][a] n.28
20.2056(c)-2(d)(1) . . . . 5.06[3][a] n.29
20.2056(c)-2(d)(2) . . . . 5.06[3][a] n.31;
5.06[3][b] ns. 43, 44; 5.06[7][b] n.181
20.2056(c)-2(e) . . . 5.06[3] n.17; S5.06[3] n.17
20.2056(d)-2(a) . . . . 5.06[3][h] n.76
20.2056(d)-2(b) . . . . 5.06[3][h] n.82
20.2056A-4 . . . . S3.05[3][b] n.29; S4.02[5] ns.
244, 247; S4.08[1][a] n.5; S5.05[3][a]
n.95; S5.05[5][a][ii] n.207;
S5.05[5][b][ii] n.264; S5.05[5][c][ii]
n.291; S5.05[6][b] n.327; S5.05[7][a]
n.333; S5.06[7][d] n.197; S5.06[8][d][ii]
n.348; S9.04[3][a] n.48; S10.02[2][b][iii]
n.56; S11.02[1][b] n.27; S16.02[6] n.409;
S19.03[1] n.3; S19.03[3][b] n.112;
S19.03[3][d] n.162
20.2101-1 . . . . 6.01[2] n.11
20.2102-1 . . . . 6.02 n.3
20.2102-1(a) . . . 3.06 n.8; 6.02 ns. 3, 5; 6.02[1]
n.15
20.2102-1(b) . . . . . . 6.02[1] n.10; 6.06[4] n.43
20.2102-1(b)(1) . . . . . 6.02[1] n.11; 6.06[4] n.44
20.2102-1(b)(2) . . . . 6.02[1] ns. 11, 13; 6.06[4]
n.44
20.2103-1 . . . . 6.06[1] n.14
20.2104-1(a)(1) . . . . 6.03[2][a] ns. 20, 26;
7.01[1] n.5
20.2104-1(a)(2) . . . 6.03[2][a] n.20; S6.03[2][a]
n.25
20.2104-1(a)(3) . . . . 7.02[2][c] ns. 18, 23
20.2104-1(a)(4) . . . . 6.03[2][b] n.33
20.2104-1(a)(5) . . . . 7.02[2][c] ns. 18, 21
20.2104-1(a)(7) . . . . . 6.04[3] n.20; 6.05[2] n.8
20.2105-1(e) . . . . 6.03[2][b] n.34
20.2105-1(g) . . . . 6.05[1] n.3
20.2105-1(k) . . . . 6.04[3] n.19
20.2106-1(b) 6.06 n.7
20.2106-1(a)(2)(i) . . . . 6.06[2] ns. 21, 22
20.2106-1(a)(2)(ii) . . . . 6.06[2] n.24
20.2106-2(a)(1) . . . . 6.06[1] n.19
20.2106-2(a)(2) . . . . 6.06[1] n.11
20.2107-1(b)(1)(i) . . . 6.07[2] n.20; S6.07[2][b]
n.52

20.2107-1(b)(1)(iii)(a) . . . . 6.07[2] n.28;
S6.07[2][b] n.61; S9.02[1][b][ii] n.10.37
20.2107-1(b)(1)(iii)(b) . . . . 6.07[2] n.28;
S6.07[2][b] n.61
20.2107-1(b)(1)(iii)(c) . . . . 6.07[2] n.22;
S6.07[2][b] n.55
20.2201-1(a)(2) . . . . 8.01[1][a][iv] n.29
20.2201-1(c)(1) . . . . 8.01[1][a][iii] n.16
20.2201-1(c)(2) . . . . 8.01[1][a][iii] n.17
20.2201-1(d) . . . . 8.01[1][a][iv] n.29
20.2201-1(e) . . . . 8.01[1][a][i] ns. 9, 10;
8.01[1][a][iii] n.14
20.2203-1 . . . . 8.02 n.2
20.2204-1 . . . . 8.03[2] n.15
20.2204-3 . . . . 2.02[3][c][iii] n.116
20.2205-1 . . . . 8.04[3] & n.21
20.2206-1 . . . . 8.05[4] n.17
20.2207-1 . . . . 8.06 n.9
20.2207A-1(a)(2) . . . . S8.07[2] n.9
20.2208-1 . . . . 8.09 n.2
20.2209-1 . . . . 8.09 n.2
20.6018-1(a) 5.02 n.2
20.6018-2 . . . . . 6.01[4] n.37; 8.02 ns. 11, 13
20.6018-3(b) . . . . 6.01[4] n.37
20.6018-4 . . . . 2.02[1] n.25
20.6018-4(a) . . . . 2.02[1] n.23
20.6075-1 . . . . . 2.02[1] n.7; 18.02[4][a] n.46
20.6081-1 . . . . 18.02[4][b] n.56
20.6081-1(a) . . . . 2.02[1] n.8; 18.02[4][b] n.58
20.6081-1(b) . . . . . 2.02[1] ns. 9, 10; 3.05[3][b]
n.46; 4.03[1] n.4; 18.02[4][b] ns. 57, 59,
60
20.6081-1(c) . . . . . 2.02[1] n.10; 18.02[4][b] ns.
57, 60
20.6081-1(e) . . . . 2.02[1] n.11; 18.02[4][b] ns.
55, 59
20.6091-1(a) . . . . 2.02[1] n.22
20.6091-1(a)(1) . . . . 18.02[5] n.62
20.6091-1(b) . . . . . . 2.02[1] n.19; 18.02[5] n.62
20.6161-1(a)(1) . . . . 2.02[3][b][i] n.37;
2.02[3][b][ii] n.44; 3.07 n.3; 18.01[2][a]
ns. 15, 16
20.6161-1(a)(2)(ii) . . . . 2.02[3][b][ii] n.44
20.6161-1(a)(2)(ii)(2) . . . . . . 2.02[3][b][ii] n.44
20.6161-1(b) . . . . 2.02[3][c][ii] n.58
20.6163-1 . . . . 3.07 n.3
20.6163-1(a)(1) 3.07 n.5
20.6163-1(b) 3.07 n.4
20.6163-1(c) 3.07 n.2
20.6166-1(b) . . . . 2.02[3][c][ii] n.56
20.6166-1(c)(1) . . . . 2.02[3][c][ii] n.59
20.6166-1(c)(2) . . . . 2.02[3][c][ii] n.57
20.6166-1(d) . . . . 2.02[3][c][ii] n.57
20.6324A-1(a) . . . . S2.02[3][c][iii] n.116
20.6325-1(b)(1) . . . . 6.01[4] n.36
20.7520-1 – 20.7520-4 . . . . S5.03[4][c][iii] n.241

[Text references are to paragraphs and notes (9"n.");
references to the supplement are preceded by "S."]

Reg. §

20.7520-1   3.05[3][b] n.29; S3.05[3][b] n.29;
S4.02[5] ns. 244, 247; S4.08[1][a] n.5;
S5.05[3][a] n.95; S5.05[5][a][ii] n.207;
S5.05[5][b][ii] n.264; S5.05[5][c][ii]
n.291; S5.05[6][b] n.327; 5.05[7][a]
n.333; S5.05[7][a] n.333; S5.06[7][d]
n.197; 5.06[8][d][ii] n.348;
S5.06[8][d][ii] n.348; S9.04[3][a] n.48;
S10.02[2][b][iii] n.56; S11.02[1][b] n.27;
S16.02[6] n.409; S19.03[1] n.3;
S19.03[3][b] n.112; S19.03[3][d] n.162
20.7520-1(a)(1) . . . . . . 4.02[5] n.244; 16.02[6]
n.409
20.7520-1(a)(2) . . . . 5.05[5][c][ii] n.291
20.7520-1(a)(3) . . . . 5.05[5][a][ii] n.207
20.7520-1(b) . . . . 4.02[5] n.244
20.7520-1(b)(1) . . . . . 4.02[5] n.245; 5.05[4][a]
n.130; 16.02[4][d][iii] n.277
20.7520-1(b)(1)(i) . . . . 4.02[5] n.245
20.7520-1(b)(1)(ii) . . . . 4.02[5] n.245
20.7520-1(c) . . . . 4.02[5] ns. 244, 247
20.7520-1(c)(1) . . . . 4.02[5] n.246
20.7520-2   3.05[3][b] n.29; 4.02[5] n.245;
5.05[7][a] n.333
20.7520-2(a)(1) . . . . 5.05[4][a] n.130
20.7520-2(a)(2) . . . . 5.05[5][a][ii] n.207;
5.05[5][b][ii] n.265; 5.05[6][b] ns. 327,
328; 5.05[7][a] n.333
20.7520-3   3.05[3][b] n.29; 5.05[4][a] n.130;
5.05[7][a] n.333
20.7520-3(a) . . . . 4.02[5] n.249
20.7520-3(a)(7) . . . . 4.02[5] n.249
20.7520-3(a)(8) . . . . 4.02[5] n.249
20.7520-3(b) . . . . . S4.02[5] n.244; S4.11[4][a]
n.40
20.7520-3(b)(1)(ii) . . . . 4.02[5] n.250
20.7520-3(b)(2) . . . . 4.02[5] n.250
20.7520-3(b)(2)(iv) . . . . . . 5.05[5][c][ii] n.291
20.7520-3(b)(2)(v) . . . . 4.02[5] n.251
20.7520-3(b)(3) . . . . . 4.02[5] n.253; 4.11[4][a]
n.40; 5.05[5][b][ii] n.264; 5.05[5][c][ii]
n.291; 5.05[7][a] n.333
20.7520-3(b)(3)(i) . . . 3.05[3][b] ns. 31–33, 46;
4.02[5] ns. 254, 255; 5.05[5][a][ii] n.208
20.7520-3(b)(3)(ii) . . . . . 3.05[3][b] ns. 35, 36;
4.02[5] n.254; 4.09[4][d] n.34; 4.09[4][e]
n.35
20.7520-3(b)(3)(iii) . . . 3.05[3][b] n.37; 4.02[5]
n.252; 5.05[5][a][ii] n.209
20.7520-3(b)(4) . . . 3.05[3][b] n.37; 4.02[5] ns.
252–254
20.7520-3(c) . . . . 3.05[3][b] ns. 33, 37
20.7520-4 . . . . 3.05[3][b] n.29
25.0-1(a)(1) . . . . . 9.02[1] n.6; S9.02[1][a] n.6;
18.03[2][a] n.32
25.0-1(b) . . . . 9.04[1][b] n.30; 10.01[2][c] n.27
25.2207A-1 . . . . S8.07[5] n.43
25.2207A-1(b) . . . S8.07[4] n.34; S10.08[1][a]
n.16
25.2501-1(a)(3) . . . . 18.03[2][b] n.42
25.2501-1(a)(5) . . . . 9.02[2] n.18

Reg. §

25.2501-1(b) . . . 5.06[9] n.433; 7.03[8] ns. 194,
196; 9.02[1] n.5
25.2502-1(c)(1) . . . . 10.03[1] n.15
25.2502-1(d) . . . . . 9.04[1][b] n.31; 11.02[1][b]
n.31
25.2502-2 . . . . 8.03[1] n.6
25.2503-2 . . . . . 9.04[1] n.12; 9.04[1][b] n.17
25.2503-2(a) . . . . 16.02[2][b][ii] n.46
25.2503-3(a) . . . . . 4.14[8] n.119; 9.04[3] n.44;
9.04[3][e] ns. 84, 85; 13.02[2][b][i] n.42;
19.03[2][c] n.96; 19.03[4][c][ii] n.312
25.2503-3(b) . . . . 9.04[3][a] ns. 50, 54;
9.04[3][e] n.75; 19.03[2][c] n.91
25.2503-3(c) . . . 4.14[8] n.119; 9.04[3][a] n.49;
9.04[3][e] ns. 76, 80; 9.04[3][f] n.96;
13.02[2][e][ii] n.143
25.2503-3(c) Ex. (2) . . . . S10.01[3][g] ns.
115.31, 115.34
25.2503-3(c) Ex. (6) . . . . S10.01[3][g] ns.
115.31, 115.34
25.2503-4(b) . . . . 9.04[5][b] ns. 152, 153
25.2503-4(b)(1) . . . . . . 9.04[5][a] ns. 145, 147
25.2503-4(b)(2) . . . . 9.04[5][b] n.148
25.2503-4(b)(3) . . . . 9.04[5][b] n.154
25.2503-4(c) . . . . 9.04[5][c] n.170
25.2503-6(a) . . . . 9.04[6] n.175
25.2503-6(b)(1)(i) . . . . 9.04[6] n.183
25.2503-6(b)(1)(ii) . . . . 9.04[6] n.178
25.2503-6(b)(2) . . . . 9.04[6] ns. 181, 182
25.2503-6(b)(3) . . . . 9.04[6] n.176
25.2503-6(c) . . . . . 9.04[6] ns. 178, 179, 183;
13.01[2][a] n.20
25.2504-1(a) . . . . 9.05[3] n.34
25.2504-1(b) . . . . 9.05[4] n.46
25.2504-1(d) . . . . 9.05[1] n.6; 9.05[2][a] ns. 13,
18
25.2504-2(a) . . . 9.05[2] n.11; 9.05[2][a] ns. 13,
14, 18
25.2504-2(b) . . . 9.05[2] n.12; 9.05[2][b] ns. 21,
22, 24, 26
25.2504-2(c) . . . . . 2.01[1][b][i] n.22; 9.05[2][a]
ns. 14, 19; 9.05[2][b] ns. 24–26
25.2504-2(c) Ex. 3 . . . . . . S2.01[1][b][i] n.22
25.2504-2(d) . . . . 9.05[2][b] n.20
25.2511-1(a) . . . . . 10.01[2][e] n.34; 10.01[2][f]
n.39
25.2511-1(d) . . . . . 4.07[3][a] n.79; 10.01[2][e]
n.37; 10.02[2][b][i] n.40; 10.03[2] n.23
25.2511-1(e) . . . . 10.01[3][b] n.90; 19.03[1] n.1
25.2511-1(g)(1) . . . . 10.01[3] n.76
25.2511-1(g)(2) . . . . 10.01[3] n.76
25.2511-1(h)(1) . . . . . 9.04[1][b] ns. 21, 22, 30,
33; 9.04[3][e] n.89; S9.04[3][e] n.89;
10.01[2][b][i] n.20; 10.01[2][c] & ns. 26,
29; 10.02[6][a] n.173; 13.03[4][b] n.84;
17.01[2][c][i] n.56; 19.02[2][a][i] n.27
25.2511-1(h)(2) . . . 9.04[1][b] n.34; 10.01[2][d]
n.32; 10.01[3][g] n.118
25.2511-1(h)(3) . . . . 10.01[2][d] n.32
25.2511-1(h)(4) . . . . 10.01[3][f] n.109;
10.01[5][c] n.167; 10.07[2][b] n.45

[Text references are to paragraphs and notes (9"n.");
references to the supplement are preceded by "S."]

Reg. §

25.2511-1(h)(5) . . . . 10.01[3][f] n.109
25.2511-1(h)(8) . . . . . 10.01[3][g] ns. 113, 114
25.2511-1(h)(9)   4.14[8] n.117; 10.01[5][d] &
                                                    n.170
25.2511-2 . . . . 10.08[1][b] n.26; 14.04[2] n.5;
                        16.02[4][a] n.221
25.2511-2(b) . . . . . 10.01[3][c] n.97; S10.01[6]
        n.185; 10.01[9] n.203; 15.03[2][a] n.9;
        17.02[1][b] n.29; 19.02[2][a][i] n.52
25.2511-2(c) . . . 13.01[2][a] n.16; 19.02[2][a][i]
                        n.52; 19.03[2][a][iv] n.71
25.2511-2(d) . . . . . 10.01[7] n.188; 10.01[10][e]
        n.229; 13.02[4][d] n.339; 15.03[3][b]
                                                    n.54
25.2511-2(e) . . . . . . 10.01[8] ns. 192, 197, 198
25.2511-2(f) . . . 10.01[4] ns. 145, 146; 10.01[6]
        n.185; 10.01[8] n.200; 10.01[9] n.20;
        10.02[1][b] n.16; 10.04[3][a] n.14;
                        19.03[2][a][iv] n.71
25.2511-2(h) . . . . 10.01[4] n.140
25.2512-1 . . . . 10.02[2][a] n.23; 10.02[2][b][v]
        n.67; 16.02[4][a] n.220; 19.02[4][d][i]
                                                    n.233
25.2512-5 . . . . . S3.05[3][b] n.29; S4.02[5] ns.
        244, 247; S4.08[1][a] n.5; S5.05[3][a]
        n.95; S5.05[5][a][ii] n.207;
        S5.05[5][b][ii] n.264; S5.05[5][c][ii]
        n.291; S5.05[6][b] n.327; S5.05[7][a]
        n.333; S5.06[7][d] n.197; S5.06[8][d][ii]
        n.348; S9.04[3][a] n.48; 10.01[3][g]
        n.117; 10.02[2][b][iii] ns. 54, 55, 60;
        S10.02[2][b][iii] n.56; S11.02[1][b] n.27;
        S16.02[6] n.409; S19.03[1] n.3;
        S19.03[3][b] n.112; S19.03[3][d] n.162
25.2512-5(a) . . . . 4.02[5] n.247; 16.02[6] n.409
25.2512-5(d) . . . . 10.02[2][b][iii] n.56
25.2512-5(d)(2)(iii)   9.04[3][a] ns. 48, 51, 53;
                        9.04[3][b] n.61
25.2512-5(d)(2)(iv) . . . 4.02[5] n.248; 16.02[6]
                                                    n.409
25.2512-5(d)(4) . . . . 16.02[6] n.409
25.2512-6 . . . . 10.01[3][g] n.117
25.2512-6(a) . . . . S10.01[3][g] n.115.35;
                        10.02[2][b][ii] ns. 50, 51
25.2512-7 . . . . 10.02[2][b][iv] n.65
25.2512-8 . . . 9.02[2] n.12; S10.01[3][e] n.107;
        10.02[2][b][i] n.43; 10.02[4] n.134;
        S10.02[4] n.141; S10.02[5][d] n.167;
                        10.06[1] n.4
25.2512-9 . . . . 10.01[3][g] n.117
25.2512-9(a)(1)(i) . . . . 19.02[4][d] n.216
25.2513-1(a) . . . . 10.03[1] n.5
25.2513-1(b) . . . . 10.03[1] n.17
25.2513-1(b)(1) . . . . 10.03[1] ns. 5, 6
25.2513-1(b)(2) . . . . 10.03[1] n.4
25.2513-1(b)(4) . . . . 10.03[1] ns. 12, 14
25.2513-1(b)(5) . . . . 10.03[1] n.16
25.2513-2(a)(1) . . . 10.03[1] n.15; 10.03[3][a] &
                                                    n.39
25.2513-2(c) . . . . 10.03[3][a] ns. 41, 42;
                        19.03[4][c][i] n.322

Reg. §

25.2513-3 . . . . 10.03[3][c] n.48
25.2513-4 . . . . 4.07[3][a] n.79
25.2514-1(b)(2) . . . . . 4.13[7][c] n.92; 10.01[9]
        n.207; 10.04[3][a] n.11; 10.04[3][e] n.29;
                        13.02[2][e][iii] n.167
25.2514-1(c)(1) . . . . 10.04[2][a] n.7
25.2514-1(c)(2) . . . . 10.04[2][b] n.8
25.2514-1(d) . . . 10.04[3][d] & n.23; 10.04[3][f]
        & ns. 31, 32; 10.04[4][a] n.34
25.2514-1(e) . . . . 10.04[1] n.4
25.2514-2(c) . . . . . . 10.04[3][b] ns. 16, 18;
                        10.04[4][a] n.37
25.2514-2(d) . . . . 10.04[3][b] n.15
25.2514-2(e) . . . . 10.04[3][c] n.19
25.2514-3(c)(2) . . . . 10.04[4][a] n.35
25.2514-3(c)(3) . . . . 10.04[4][a] n.36
25.2514-3(c)(4) . . . . . . 5.06[8][b][iv] n.259;
        10.04[4][c] & ns. 47, 52
25.2514-3(c)(5) . . . . . . 10.04[4][b] ns. 40, 43
25.2514-3(c)(6) . . . . 10.04[4][b] n.43
25.2515-1(c)(2) . . . 4.08[8] n.171; 4.12[7][b] ns.
                        50, 52
25.2515-2(b)(1) . . . . 9.04[1][b] n.41
25.2515-2(b)(2) . . . . 4.08[8][a] n.179; 4.12[2]
        n.14; 4.12[9] n.74; 9.04[1][b] n.42
25.2516-1(a) . . . . 10.06[2] ns. 17, 19
25.2516-2 . . . 10.06[2] n.18; 10.06[2][b] n.23
25.2518-1(a) . . . 4.13[7][d] n.101; 10.07[3] n.98
25.2518-1(a)(1) . . . . . 10.07[2] n.27; S10.07[3]
                        n.98
25.2518-1(a)(2) . . . . S10.07[3] n.98
25.2518-1(b) . . . . 10.07[1] ns. 6, 7
25.2518-1(c)(1)(i) . . . . 10.07[3] n.99
25.2518-1(c)(1)(ii) . . . . . . 10.07[2][d][iii] n.93
25.2518-1(c)(2) . . . . 10.07[1] n.6
25.2518-1(c)(3) . . . . 10.07[3] n.99
25.2518-2(c)(3)(l) . . . . S10.07[2][b] n.36
25.2518-2(b)(1) . . . . 10.07[2] n.27; 10.07[2][a]
                        n.29
25.2518-2(b)(2) . . . . 10.07[2][b] n.30
25.2518-2(c)(1) . . . . 10.07[2][b] n.32
25.2518-2(c)(2) . . . . 10.07[2][b] n.30
25.2518-2(c)(3) . . . . 10.07[2][b] n.34
25.2518-2(c)(3)(i)   10.07[2][b] ns. 32, 35, 36,
        39, 42–44, 53–57, 60
25.2518-2(c)(3)(ii) . . . . 10.07[2][b] n.35
25.2518-2(c)(4)(i)   10.07[2][b] ns. 48, 49, 51,
                        52
25.2518-2(c)(4)(ii) . . . . 10.07[2][b] n.46
25.2518-2(c)(4)(iii) . . . . 10.07[2][b] n.46
25.2518-2(c)(4)(iv) . . . . 10.07[2][b] n.49
25.2518-2(c)(5) . . . 10.07[2][b] ns. 34–36, 38,
        39, 46, 49, 51–54, 56, 57; 10.07[2][c]
                        n.66
25.2518-2(c)(5) Ex. 7 . . . . . . S10.07[2][b] n.49
25.2518-2(c)(5) Ex. 8 . . . . . . S10.07[2][b] n.49
25.2518-2(c)(5) Ex. 10 . . . . . S10.07[2][b] n.49
25.2518-2(d) . . . . 5.05[2][c] ns. 84, 85;
        10.07[2][b] n.41
25.2518-2(d)(1) . . . . . 10.07[2][c] & ns. 66, 68,
                        70, 71, 73

[Text references are to paragraphs and notes (9"n.");
references to the supplement are preceded by "S."]

Reg. §

25.2518-2(d)(2) . . . . 10.07[2][c] n.66
25.2518-2(d)(3) . . . . 10.07[2][c] n.69
25.2518-2(d)(4) . . . . 10.07[2][c] ns. 66, 68–70, 73; 17.04[3] n.82
25.2518-2(e)(1) . . . . . . 10.07[2][d] ns. 78–80
25.2518-2(e)(1)(i) . . . . 10.07[2][d] ns. 78, 80
25.2518-2(e)(1)(ii) . . . . 10.07[2][d] n.82
25.2518-2(e)(2) . . . . . 10.07[2][d][i] ns. 84, 88
25.2518-2(e)(3) . . . S5.05[2][c] n.81; S10.07[2] n.23; 10.07[2][d] n.81; S10.07[2][d] n.81
25.2518-2(e)(4) . . . . 10.07[2][d] n.78
25.2518-2(e)(5) . . . . . 10.07[2][d] ns. 78, 80, 82; 10.07[2][d][i] ns. 85, 88, 89, 91
25.2518-3(a)(1) . . . . 10.04[4][b] n.45; 10.07[2] n.13
25.2518-3(a)(1)(i) . . . . 10.07[2] ns. 11, 12, 14
25.2518-3(a)(1)(ii) . . . . 10.07[2] n.18
25.2518-3(a)(1)(iii) . . . 3.05[3][b] n.46; 10.07[2] ns. 12, 15, 16
25.2518-3(a)(1)(iv) . . . . 10.07[2] n.14
25.2518-3(a)(2) . . . . 10.07[2] n.19
25.2518-3(b) . . . . 10.07[2] ns. 22, 23
25.2518-3(c) . . . . 10.07[2] n.24
25.2518-3(d) . . . . . 10.07[2] ns. 13, 14, 17–19, 21–24
25.2518-3(d) Ex. 11 . . . . S10.07[2] n.13
25.2518-3(d) Ex. 20 . . . . . S10.01[3][e] n.107.1
25.2519-1 . . . . 11.03[4][c][i] n.69
25.2519-1(a) . . . 4.16 n.16; 8.07[1] n.7; 10.08[1] ns. 6, 7; 10.08[1][a] ns. 11, 14, 15, 19; 16.02[4][e] ns. 284, 288
25.2519-1(b) . . . . 10.08[1] n.3
25.2519-1(c)(1) . . . 10.08[1][a] n.13; 10.08[1][b] n.29
25.2519-1(c)(2) . . . . 10.08[1][a] n.21
25.2519-1(c)(3) . . . . 10.08[1][a] n.23
25.2519-1(c)(4) . . . 8.07[4] ns. 34, 37; S8.07[4] n.34; 10.08[1] n.7; S10.08[1] n.7; S10.08[1][a] n.16
25.2519-1(c)(5) . . . . 10.08[1][a] n.13
25.2519-1(d) . . . . 10.08[1][a] n.22
25.2519-1(e) . . . . 10.08[2] n.30
25.2519-1(f) . . . . 10.08[2] ns. 31–33, 37, 40
25.2519-1(g) . . . . 4.16 n.16; 10.08[1][a] ns. 11, 14, 15, 18, 19, 21–23; 10.08[2] ns. 34, 36, 38, 40; 10.08[4] n.51; 16.02[4][e] ns. 284, 288; 17.02[1][c][i] n.48
25.2519-2 . . . . 10.08[4] n.51
25.2521-1(a) . . . . . 2.01[2] n.57; S2.01[2] n.75
25.2522(a)-1(a) . . . . 11.02[1][a] n.17
25.2522(a)-2(a) . . . . 11.02[2][a] n.47
25.2522(a)-2(b) . . . . 11.02[2][a] n.47
25.2522(a)-2(c) . . . . 11.02[2][a] n.47
25.2522(a)-1 . . . . 11.02[1][a] n.12
25.2522(b)-1(a)(1) . . . . 11.02[1][a] n.20
25.2522(c)-2 . . . . 11.02[1][a] n.23

Reg. §

25.2522(c)-3 . . . . S3.05[3][b] n.29; S4.02[5] ns. 244, 247; S4.08[1][a] n.5; S4.11[4][a] n.40; S5.05[3][a] n.95; S5.05[5][a][ii] n.207; S5.05[5][b][ii] n.264; S5.05[5][c][ii] n.291; S5.05[6][b] n.327; S5.05[7][a] n.333; S5.06[7][d] n.197; S5.06[8][d][ii] n.348; S9.04[3][a] n.48; S10.02[2][b][iii] n.56; S11.02[1][b] n.27; S16.02[6] n.409; S19.03[1] n.3; S19.03[3][b] n.112; S19.03[3][d] n.162
25.2522(c)-3(b)(1) . . . . 11.02[2][a] n.47
25.2522(c)-3(b)(2) . . . . 11.02[2][a] n.47
25.2522(c)-3(c) . . . . 11.02[2][a] n.48
25.2522(c)-3(c)(1)(ii) . . . . . 11.02[2][d] n.101
25.2522(c)-3(c)(2)(i) . . . . 11.02[2][d] n.98
25.2522(c)-3(c)(2)(ii) . . . . 11.02[2][d] n.97
25.2522(c)-3(c)(2)(iii) . . . . 11.02[2][d] n.97
25.2522(c)-3(c)(2)(iv) . . . . 11.02[2][d] n.98
25.2522(c)-3(c)(2)(v) . . . 11.02[2][b] ns. 53, 55; 11.02[2][b][ii] ns. 68, 77; 11.02[2][b][iii] n.84
25.2522(c)-3(c)(2)(vi) . . . . . . 11.02[2][c] n.91
25.2522(c)-3(c)(2)(vi)(c) . . . . 11.02[2][c] n.95
25.2522(c)-3(c)(2)(vii) . . . . 11.02[2][c] n.92; 19.03[3][b][i] n.122
25.2522(c)-3(c)(2)(vii)(b) . . . . 11.02[2][c] n.92
25.2522(c)-3(c)(2)(vii)(c) . . . . 11.02[2][c] n.95
25.2522(c)-3(d) . . . . 11.02[1][b] n.27
25.2522(c)-3(d)(2)(i) . . . . . . 11.02[2][b] n.54
25.2522(c)-3(d)(2)(ii) . . . . . . 11.02[2][b] n.54
25.2522(c)-3(d)(2)(iii) . . . . . . 11.02[2][b] n.54
25.2522(c)-3(d)(2)(iv) . . . . . 11.02[2][c] n.96
25.2522(c)-3(d)(2)(v) . . . . . 11.02[2][c] n.96
25.2523(a)-1(a) . . . . 11.03[2] n.13
25.2523(a)-1(b)(3)(ii)   11.03[2] n.15; 11.04[2] n.2
25.2523(a)-1(c) . . . . 11.03[1] n.6
25.2523(a)-1(d) . . . 11.03[1] n.6; 11.03[2] n.15; 11.04[2] n.2
25.2523(a)-1(e) . . . . 11.03[2] n.16
25.2523(b)-1(b) . . . . 11.03[3][a] n.28
25.2523(b)-1(b)(2) . . . . 11.03[3][a] n.30
25.2523(b)-1(b)(3)(i) . . . . . 11.03[3][a] n.31
25.2523(b)-1(b)(6)(v) . . . . . 11.03[3][a] n.30
25.2523(b)-1(c) . . . . 11.03[3][a] n.23
25.2523(b)-1(d)(2) . . . . 11.03[3][b] n.34
25.2523(b)-1(d)(3) . . . . 11.03[3][b] ns. 33, 36
25.2523(c)-1(c) . . . . 11.03[3][c] n.42
25.2523(d)-1 . . . . 11.03[4][a] ns. 45, 47
25.2523(e)-1 . . . . 11.03[4][b] n.51
25.2523(e)-1(c) . . . . 11.03[4][b] n.50
25.2523(e)-1(f) . . . . 11.03[4][b] n.54
25.2523(e)-1(f)(1) . . . . S9.04[3][b] n.64
25.2523(f)-1 . . . . 11.03[4][c] n.65
25.2523(f)-1(a) . . . . 11.03[4][c] n.58
25.2523(f)-1(a)(1) . . . . 11.03[3][b] n.33; 11.03[4][c] n.55
25.2523(f)-1(a)(2) . . . . 11.03[4][c][i] ns. 75, 76
25.2523(f)-1(b)(4) . . . . 9.04[9] n.200; 11.03[1] n.9
25.2523(f)-1(b)(3)(i) . . . . 11.03[4][c] n.61

*[Text references are to paragraphs and notes (9"n.");
references to the supplement are preceded by "S."]*

Reg. §

25.2523(f)-1(b)(3)(ii) . . . 4.16 n.10; 10.08[1][a]
            n.13; 11.03[4][c] n.62
25.2523(f)-1(b)(4)(i) . . . . 11.03[4][c] n.56
25.2523(f)-1(b)(4)(ii) . . . . . . 11.03[4][c] n.56
25.2523(f)-1(c) . . . . 11.03[4][c] n.59
25.2523(f)-1(c)(1)(i) . . . . . . 19.03[4][a] n.265
25.2523(f)-1(c)(2) . . . . 11.03[4][c] n.60
25.2523(f)-1(c)(3) . . . . 11.03[4][c] n.62;
        11.03[4][c][ii] n.86; 11.03[4][d] n.100
25.2523(f)-1(c)(4) . . . . 11.03[4][c] n.62;
            11.03[4][c][ii] n.86
25.2523(f)-1(d)(1) . . . 11.03[4][c][i] ns. 78, 80,
                                81
25.2523(f)-1(d)(2) . . . .11.03[4][c][i] ns. 79, 82
25.2523(f)-1(e) . . . . 11.03[4][c] n.58
25.2523(f)-1(f) . . . 11.03[4][c] ns. 59, 60, 62,
        65; 11.03[4][c][i] ns. 78, 79, 81, 82;
        11.03[4][c][ii] n.86; 11.03[4][d] n.100
25.2523(g)-1(a) . . . . 11.03[4][d] n.102
25.2523(g)-1(b) . . . . 11.03[4][d] n.100
25.2523(h)-1 . . . . 11.03[2] n.18
25.2523(i)-1(a) . . . . . . 11.03[5] ns. 104, 105
25.2523(i)-1(b) . . . . 11.03[4][c][ii] n.91
25.2523(i)-1(c)(1) . . . . 11.03[5] n.110
25.2523(i)-1(c)(2) . . . . 11.03[5] n.107
25.2523(i)-1(d)   11.03[4][c][ii] n.91; 11.03[5]
                            ns. 104, 109–111
25.2523(i)-2(b)(1) . . . . 10.01[3][f] n.112
25.2523(i)-2(b)(2)(i) . . . . . . 10.01[3][f] n.112
25.2523(i)-2(b)(2)(ii) . . . . . 10.01[3][f] n.112
25.2523(i)-2(b)(4) . . . . 10.01[3][f] n.112
25.2523(i)-2(c)(1) . . . . 10.01[3][f] n.112
25.2523(i)-2(c)(2) . . . . 10.01[3][f] n.112
25.2701-1(a)(1) . . . . 19.03[2][c] n.83
25.2701-1(a)(2)(i) . . . . 19.02[4][d] n.212
25.2701-1(a)(2)(ii) . . . . 19.02[4][d] n.212
25.2701-1(a)(3) . . . . 19.02[2][c] n.131;
                        19.02[4][d] n.217
25.2701-1(b)(1) . . . . . . 19.02[2][a][i] ns. 28, 29
25.2701-1(b)(2) . . . . 19.02[4][d][v] n.286
25.2701-1(b)(2)(i)(A) . . . 19.02[2][a][i] ns. 30–
        32, 34; 19.02[4][e] ns. 294, 299
25.2701-1(b)(2)(i)(B) . . . . 19.02[2][a][i] ns. 32,
        35, 36; 19.02[2][c] n.132; 19.02[4][e]
                                n.294
25.2701-1(b)(2)(i)(B)(1) . . . 19.02[2][a][i] n.39
25.2701-1(b)(2)(i)(B)(2) . . . 19.02[2][a][i] n.42
25.2701-1(b)(2)(i)(B)(3) . . . 19.02[2][a][i] n.43
25.2701-1(b)(2)(i)(C) . . . . 19.02[2][a][i] ns. 30,
        57; 19.02[2][d][iii] n.152
25.2701-1(b)(2)(i)(C)(1) . . . . 19.02[2][a][i] ns.
                        49, 50, 58, 62
25.2701-1(b)(2)(i)(C)(2) . . . . 19.02[2][a][i] ns.
                            48, 58
25.2701-1(b)(3)(i) . . . 19.02[2][a][i] ns. 31, 44,
                                45
25.2701-1(b)(3)(ii) . . . . . . 19.02[2][a][i] n.65
25.2701-1(b)(3)(iii) . . . . . 19.02[2][a][i] n.63
25.2701-1(c)(1) . . . . 19.02[3][a] n.169
25.2701-1(c)(2) . . . . 19.02[3][a] n.170

Reg. §

25.2701-1(c)(3) . . . . 19.02[3][b] ns. 174–176,
                                179
25.2701-1(c)(4) . . . . 19.02[3][c] ns. 180–184
25.2701-1(c)(8) . . . . 19.03[3][c] n.154
25.2701-1(d)(1) . . . . 19.02[5][a][iii] n.347
25.2701-1(d)(3) . . . . 19.02[2][a][iii] n.71
25.2701-1(e) . . . . 19.02[2][c] n.131; 19.02[4][b]
        n.191; 19.02[4][c] n.195; 19.02[4][c][i]
        n.198; 19.02[4][d] n.215; 19.02[4][d][ii]
                                n.254
25.2701-2 . . . 19.02[4][d][ii] n.250; 19.02[4][e]
                                n.296
25.2701-2(a)(1) . . . . 19.02[4][d][ii] n.252
25.2701-2(a)(2) . . . . 19.02[4][d][ii] n.252
25.2701-2(a)(3) . . . . 19.02[2][b][ii] n.83;
        19.02[4][c][ii] n.209; 19.02[4][d][ii]
                                n.253
25.2701-2(a)(4) . . . . 19.02[4][c][i] ns. 196, 198,
        207; 19.02[4][d] n.215; 19.02[4][d][ii]
        n.254; 19.02[4][d][iii] n.259
25.2701-2(a)(5) . . . . 19.02[4][b] n.191;
                19.02[4][c][ii] n.210
25.2701-2(b)(1) . . . . 19.02[2][b][ii] n.82
25.2701-2(b)(2) . . . . 19.02[2][b][ii] ns. 82, 103;
                    19.02[4][b] n.190
25.2701-2(b)(3) . . . . . 19.02[2][b][ii] ns. 82, 85
25.2701-2(b)(3)(i) . . . . . . 19.02[2][b][ii] n.89
25.2701-2(b)(3)(ii) . . . . . . 19.02[2][b][ii] n.90
25.2701-2(b)(3)(iii)   19.02[2][b][ii] ns. 91, 93
25.2701-2(b)(4) . . . . 19.02[2][b][ii] ns. 91, 105
25.2701-2(b)(4)(i) . . . . 19.02[2][b][ii] ns. 106,
                            110–112
25.2701-2(b)(4)(ii) . . . . 19.02[2][b][ii] ns. 109,
                        127, 129
25.2701-2(b)(4)(iii) . . . . 19.02[2][b][ii] ns. 93,
                96, 108, 124, 125
25.2701-2(b)(4)(iv) . . . . 19.02[2][b][ii] n.107
25.2701-2(b)(4)(iv)(A) . . . . . 19.02[2][b][ii] ns.
                            114, 116
25.2701-2(b)(4)(iv)(B) . . . 19.02[2][b][ii] n.120
25.2701-2(b)(4)(iv)(C) . . . . 19.02[2][b][ii] ns.
                            117, 121
25.2701-2(b)(4)(iv)(D) . . . . . 19.02[2][b][ii] ns.
                            118, 122
25.2701-2(b)(5) . . . . 19.04[3][b][i] n.57
25.2701-2(b)(5)(i) . . . . 19.02[2][b][ii] ns. 100,
        101; 19.02[4][d][i] n.236; 19.04[4] n.105
25.2701-2(b)(5)(ii) . . . . . . 19.02[2][b][ii] n.95
25.2701-2(b)(5)(ii)(A) . . . . 19.05[2][b][iv] n.38
25.2701-2(b)(5)(ii)(B) . . . . . 19.02[2][b][ii] n.95
25.2701-2(b)(5)(iii) . . . . . 19.02[2][b][ii] n.96;
                19.05[2][b][iv] n.39
25.2701-2(b)(6)(i)(A) . . . 19.02[4][c][i] n.201
25.2701-2(b)(6)(i)(B) . . . . . 19.02[4][c][i] n.202
25.2701-2(b)(6)(i)(C) . . . . 19.02[4][c][i] n.204
25.2701-2(b)(6)(ii) . . . . . . 19.02[4][c][i] n.199
25.2701-2(c) . . . . 19.02[4][d][i] n.238
25.2701-2(c)(1) . . . .19.02[4][c][i] ns. 203, 205;
                19.02[5][a][ii] n.324
25.2701-2(c)(2) . . . .19.02[4][c][i] ns. 204, 205;
                19.02[5][a][ii] ns. 318, 324

[Text references are to paragraphs and notes (9"n.");
references to the supplement are preceded by "S."]

Reg. §

25.2701-2(c)(2)(ii) . . . . . . 19.02[5][a][ii] n.317
25.2701-2(c)(3) . . . . 19.02[5][a][ii] n.325
25.2701-2(c)(4) . . . . 19.02[4][c][i] ns. 204, 205;
      19.02[5][a][ii] ns. 321, 322, 324;
      19.02[5][a][iii] n.327
25.2701-2(c)(5) . . . . 19.02[5][a][ii] n.316
25.2701-2(d) . . . . 19.02[2][b][ii] n.127;
      19.02[4][c] n.195; 19.02[4][c][i] n.201;
      19.02[4][c][ii] n.210; 19.02[4][d][i]
      n.238; 19.02[4][d][iv] n.279;
      19.02[5][a][ii] n.318
25.2701-2(d)(1) . . . . 19.03[3][a] n.105
25.2701-2(d)(2) . . . . 19.03[4][a] n.285
25.2701-3(a) . . . . 19.02[4][d] n.211
25.2701-3(a)(2)(i) . . . . . 19.02[4][d][i] n.236;
      19.02[4][d][ii] n.245
25.2701-3(a)(2)(ii) . . . . 19.02[2] n.25;
      19.02[2][a][i] n.60; 19.02[4][d] n.222
25.2701-3(a)(2)(iii) . . . . 19.02[2] n.24;
      19.02[2][a][ii] n.70; 19.02[4][d] n.226;
      19.02[4][f] n.300; 19.05[2][b][ii] n.30
25.2701-3(b) . . . . 19.02[4][d] ns. 211, 218
25.2701-3(b)(1) . . . . 19.02[4][d][v] n.282
25.2701-3(b)(1)(i) . . . . 19.02[4][d] n.220;
      19.02[4][d][i] ns. 234, 238
25.2701-3(b)(1)(ii) . . . . 19.02[4][e] n.295
25.2701-3(b)(2) . . . . 19.02[4][d][ii] n.240
25.2701-3(b)(2)(i) . . . . 19.02[4][d] n.221;
      19.02[4][d][ii] n.241
25.2701-3(b)(2)(i)(A) . . . . . 19.02[4][d] n.224;
      19.02[4][d][ii] ns. 243, 248
25.2701-3(b)(2)(i)(B) . . . . . 19.02[4][d] n.225;
      19.02[4][d][ii] ns. 247, 250, 251;
      19.02[4][d][v] n.291
25.2701-3(b)(2)(ii) . . . . 19.02[4][e] n.297
25.2701-3(b)(2)(ii)(A) . . . . . 19.02[4][d] n.223
25.2701-3(b)(3) . . . . 19.02[4][d] n.227;
      19.02[4][d][iii] ns. 255, 259, 260;
      19.02[4][d][v] ns. 287, 292
25.2701-3(b)(4)(i) . . . . . 19.02[4][d][iv] n.261
25.2701-3(b)(4)(ii) . . . . 19.02[4][d] n.228;
      19.02[4][d][i] n.239; 19.02[4][d][iv] ns.
      262, 263; 19.02[4][d][v] n.283;
      19.02[4][f] n.302
25.2701-3(b)(4)(iii) . . . . . . 19.02[4][d] n.229;
      19.02[4][d][iv] ns. 272, 274
25.2701-3(b)(4)(iv) . . . . . . 19.02[4][d] n.230;
      19.02[4][d][iv] ns. 275–277, 281;
      19.02[4][d][v] ns. 288, 293; 19.02[4][e]
      n.298
25.2701-3(b)(5) . . . 19.02[4][d][ii] ns. 240, 244
25.2701-3(b)(5)(i) . . . . . 19.02[4][d][ii] n.247
25.2701-3(b)(5)(ii) . . . . . 19.02[4][d][ii] n.246
25.2701-3(c)(1) . . . . 19.02[4][f] n.302
25.2701-3(c)(2) . . . . 19.02[4][f] n.300
25.2701-3(c)(3)(i)(A) . . . . . . 19.02[4][f] n.303
25.2701-3(c)(3)(i)(B) . . . . . . 19.02[4][f] n.304
25.2701-3(c)(3)(i)(C) . . . . . . 19.02[4][f] n.305
25.2701-3(c)(3)(ii) . . . . 19.02[4][f] n.306

Reg. §

25.2701-3(d) . . . . . . 19.02[2][a][i] ns. 29, 40;
      19.02[2][c] n.132; 19.02[4][c][ii] n.210;
      19.02[4][d] n.211; 19.02[4][d][ii] ns.
      247, 252, 253; 19.02[4][d][iii] ns. 257,
      258; 19.02[4][d][iv] n.263; 19.02[4][d][v]
      ns. 284, 287, 289, 290
25.2701-4(a) . . . . 19.02[4][c][i] n.204;
      19.02[5][a][i] n.309
25.2701-4(b)(1) . . . 19.02[5][a][iii] ns. 341, 342
25.2701-4(b)(2) . . . . 19.02[5][a][iii] n.339
25.2701-4(b)(2)(ii) . . . . . . 19.02[5][a][iii] n.339
25.2701-4(b)(3)(i) . . . . 19.02[5][a][iii] ns. 364,
      365, 368
25.2701-4(b)(3)(ii) . . . . . . 19.02[5][a][iii] n.352
25.2701-4(b)(3)(ii)(A) . . . . 19.02[5][a][iii] ns.
      353, 361
25.2701-4(b)(3)(ii)(B) . . . . 19.02[5][a][iii] n.359
25.2701-4(b)(3)(ii)(B)(1) . . . . . 19.02[5][a][iii]
      n.360
25.2701-4(b)(3)(ii)(B)(2) . . . . . 19.02[5][a][iii]
      n.360
25.2701-4(b)(3)(ii)(C) . . . . 19.02[5][a][iii] ns.
      357, 360
25.2701-4(c)(1) . . . . 19.02[5][a][iv] n.372
25.2701-4(c)(1)(i) . . . . 19.02[5][a][iv] ns. 376,
      378
25.2701-4(c)(1)(i)(A) . . . . 19.02[5][a][iv] n.374
25.2701-4(c)(1)(i)(B) . . . . 19.02[5][a][iv] n.397
25.2701-4(c)(1)(ii)(C) . . . . 19.02[5][a][iv] n.382
25.2701-4(c)(1)(ii)(C)(1) . . . . . 19.02[5][a][iv]
      n.383
25.2701-4(c)(1)(ii)(C)(2) . . . . 19.02[5][a][iv] ns.
      381, 384
25.2701-4(c)(1)(ii)(C)(3) . . . . . 19.02[5][a][iv]
      n.385
25.2701-4(c)(2) . . . . . . 19.02[5][a][iii] n.345;
      19.02[5][a][iv] n.375
25.2701-4(c)(3) . . . . 19.02[5][a][iv] n.377
25.2701-4(c)(4) . . . . 19.02[5][a][iii] n.347;
      19.02[5][a][iv] ns. 380, 396
25.2701-4(c)(5) . . . 19.02[5][a][iii] ns. 331, 336,
      343, 365; 19.02[5][a][iv] ns. 373, 379,
      381
25.2701-4(c)(6)(i) . . . . . 19.02[5][a][iv] n.389
25.2701-4(c)(6)(i)(A)(1) . . . . . 19.02[5][a][iv]
      n.387
25.2701-4(c)(6)(i)(A)(2) . . . . . 19.02[5][a][iv]
      n.388
25.2701-4(c)(6)(i)(B) . . . . 19.02[5][a][iv] n.389
25.2701-4(c)(6)(ii) . . . . . 19.02[5][a][iv] n.387
25.2701-4(c)(6)(iii) . . . 19.02[5][a][iv] ns. 391,
      392
25.2701-4(d)(1) . . . 19.02[5][a][iii] ns. 346, 347;
      19.02[5][a][iv] ns. 385, 393, 395, 399
25.2701-4(d)(2) . . . . 19.02[5][a][iii] n.349;
      19.02[5][a][iv] ns. 386, 398
25.2701-4(d)(3) . . . . 19.02[5][a][iii] n.349
25.2701-4(d)(3)(i) . . . . . 19.02[5][a][iii] n.349
25.2701-4(d)(3)(ii) . . . . . 19.02[5][a][iii] n.349
25.2701-4(d)(3)(iii) . . . . 19.02[5][a][iii] n.346

[Text references are to paragraphs and notes (9"n.");
references to the supplement are preceded by "S."]

Reg. §

25.2701-4(d)(4) . . . . . .   19.02[5][a][iii] n.347;
19.02[5][a][iv] ns. 380, 385, 395–397,
399
25.2701-5   19.02[2][b][ii] n.83; 19.02[5][c][i]
n.407; 19.02[5][f][iii] n.521; 19.02[5][g]
& n.528
25.2701-5(a)(1) . . . . 19.02[5][c][i] ns. 409, 410,
416, 417; 19.02[5][c][iii] n.443;
19.02[5][c][iv] ns. 454, 466
25.2701-5(a)(2) . . . . 19.02[5][c][i] ns. 415, 416;
19.02[5][c][iii] ns. 434, 437, 439, 441–
443, 449, 450; 19.02[5][c][iv] ns. 457,
466; 19.02[5][c][v] ns. 470, 471
25.2701-5(a)(3) . . . . 19.02[5][c][i] ns. 417, 419;
19.02[5][c][iii] n.443; 19.02[5][c][iv] ns.
455, 460, 464, 465
25.2701-5(a)(4) . . . .   19.02[5][c][i] ns. 411, 412
25.2701-5(b)(1) . . . .   19.02[5][c][ii] n.423;
19.02[5][c][iii] n.436
25.2701-5(b)(2) . . . .   19.02[5][c][ii] n.424
25.2701-5(c)(1) . . . . 19.02[5][c][ii] ns. 426, 429
25.2701-5(c)(2) . . . .   19.02[5][c][ii] n.425
25.2701-5(c)(3)(i) . . . 19.02[5][c][iii] ns. 444,
445, 451; 19.02[5][c][iv] ns. 458–460
25.2701-5(c)(3)(ii) . . . .   19.02[5][c][iv] ns. 461,
463, 464
25.2701-5(c)(3)(iii) . . .   19.02[5][c][iii] ns. 447,
448
25.2701-5(c)(3)(iv) . . . . .   19.02[5][c][ii] n.420;
19.02[5][c][iii] ns. 444, 452, 453;
19.02[5][c][iv] n.456; 19.02[5][c][v]
n.469
25.2701-5(c)(3)(v) . . . . .   19.02[5][c][ii] n.424
25.2701-5(c)(3)(vi) . . . . .   19.02[5][c][ii] n.430
25.2701-5(d) . . . . . . 19.02[5][c][i] ns. 413, 415,
419; 19.02[5][c][ii] ns. 426, 429;
19.02[5][c][iii] ns. 437, 438, 441, 442,
453; 19.02[5][c][iv] ns. 455, 460, 463
25.2701-5(e) . . . .   19.02[5][c][ii] n.420;
19.02[5][c][v] n.468
25.2701-5(e)(2) . . . .   19.02[5][c][v] n.469
25.2701-5(e)(3)(i) . . . . . 19.02[5][c][v] ns. 473,
474
25.2701-5(e)(3)(ii)(A) . . . .   19.02[5][c][v] n.481
25.2701-5(e)(3)(ii)(B) . . . .   19.02[5][c][v] n.477
25.2701-5(e)(3)(iii) . . . . .   19.02[5][c][v] ns. 483,
484, 487
25.2701-5(e)(3)(iv) . . . . .   19.02[5][c][v] n.476
25.2701-5(f) . . . .   19.02[5][c][ii] n.420;
19.02[5][c][v] ns. 469–471, 474, 476,
481
25.2701-5(g) . . . .   19.02[5][c][iv] n.462
25.2701-5(g)(1) . . . .   19.02[5][c][i] n.405
25.2701-5(g)(2) . . . .   19.02[5][c][i] n.405
25.2701-5(h) . . . .   19.02[5][c][i] n.407;
19.02[5][g] n.528
25.2701-6   19.02[2][a][i] n.46; 19.02[2][a][iii]
n.74; 19.02[2][b][ii] ns. 99, 128;
19.02[2][d] n.136; 19.02[2][d][iii] n.152;
19.02[3][c] n.181; 19.02[5][c][iii] n.434;
19.04[4] n.108

Reg. §

25.2701-6(a)(1) . . . . . 19.02[2][d] ns. 137–139;
19.02[2][d][i] n.147; 19.02[2][d][ii] n.150
25.2701-6(a)(2) . . . .   19.02[2][a][i] n.47;
19.02[2][d][i] ns. 145, 146; 19.04[4]
n.106
25.2701-6(a)(3) . . . .   19.02[2][a][i] n.47;
19.02[2][d][ii] ns. 148, 149; 19.04[4]
n.107
25.2701-6(a)(4) . . . 19.02[2][a][i] n.47; 19.04[4]
n.108
25.2701-6(a)(4)(i) . . . .   19.02[2][a][i] n.53;
19.02[2][a][iii] n.75; 19.02[2][d][iii] ns.
151, 152, 155, 156, 159–161
25.2701-6(a)(4)(ii)(A) . . . . 19.02[2][d][iii] n.153
25.2701-6(a)(4)(ii)(B) . . . 19.02[2][d][iii] n.154
25.2701-6(a)(4)(ii)(C) . . . . 19.02[2][a][i] ns. 49,
53; 19.02[2][d][iii] ns. 161, 164
25.2701-6(a)(5) . . . .   19.04[4] n.109
25.2701-6(a)(5)(i) . . . . 19.02[2][d][iv] n.165;
19.02[4][d][iv] n.269
25.2701-6(a)(5)(i)(A)–25.2701-6(a)(5)(i)(D) . . .
. . . .   19.02[2][d][iii] n.166
25.2701-6(a)(5)(i)(A) . . . 19.02[4][d][iv] n.266
25.2701-6(a)(5)(ii) . . . .   19.02[2][a][i] n.54;
19.02[2][a][iii] n.75; 19.02[2][d][iv]
n.167; 19.02[5][f][i] n.507
25.2701-6(a)(5)(ii)(A)–25.2701-6(a)(5)(ii)(F)
. . . .   19.02[2][d][iv] n.168
25.2701-6(b) . . . .   19.02[2][a][iii] n.75;
19.02[2][d][i] n.146; 19.02[2][d][iii] ns.
157, 158; 19.02[2][d][iv] ns. 165, 167
25.2701-6(b)(2) . . . .   19.02[5][c][iii] n.436
25.2701-7 . . . . . 19.02[3][c] n.185; 19.02[5][b]
n.400
25.2701-8 . . . .   19.02[5][g] n.529
25.2702-1(a) . . . .   19.03[2][c] n.83
25.2702-1(c)(1) . . . 19.03[3][a] ns. 99, 104, 108
25.2702-1(c)(3)(i) . . . .   19.03[3][c] n.160
25.2702-1(c)(3)(ii) . . . .   19.03[3][c] n.160
25.2702-1(c)(5) . . . .   19.03[3][c] n.161
25.2702-1(c)(6) . . . .   19.03[2][a][iv] n.73;
19.03[3][c] n.154
25.2702-1(c)(7)   10.06[2] n.15; 19.03[2][a][ii]
ns. 55, 59; 19.03[2][c] n.88; 19.03[3][c]
n.154
25.2702-1(c)(8) . . . . . .   5.07[2][b] ns. 25, 26;
19.03[2][a][i] n.33; 19.03[3][c] n.154
25.2702-2 . . . .   S19.03[3][b][i] n.134
25.2702-2(a)(1) . . . .   19.05[2][b][iii] n.36
25.2702-2(a)(2) . . . .   19.03[2][a][i] n.33
25.2702-2(a)(2)(i) . . . .   19.03[2][a][i] n.36
25.2702-2(a)(2)(ii) . . . .   19.03[2][a][i] n.37
25.2702-2(a)(3) . . . .   19.03[2][a][iv] ns. 61, 63,
78
25.2702-2(a)(4) . . . .   11.02[2][b][ii] n.81;
19.03[2][a][ii] n.59; 19.03[2][a][iv] n.70;
19.03[3][a] ns. 101, 102, 106;
19.03[3][b][i] n.134; 19.03[3][b][ii]
n.151; 19.03[4][c][ii] n.336
25.2702-2(a)(5) . . . .   19.03[3][b][i] n.134
25.2702-2(a)(9) . . . .   19.03[3][d][ii] n.188

[Text references are to paragraphs and notes (9"n.");
references to the supplement are preceded by "S."]

Reg. §

25.2702-2(b)(1) . . . . 19.03[4][b] n.302
25.2702-2(b)(2) . . . . 19.03[3][b] n.112
25.2702-2(c) . . . . 19.03[4][c][ii] n.335
25.2702-2(c)(1) . . . . . 19.03[4][b] ns. 295, 297, 298
25.2702-2(c)(2) . . . . 19.03[4][b] n.291
25.2702-2(c)(2)(i)(A) . . . . . . 19.03[4][b] n.286
25.2702-2(c)(2)(ii) . . . . 19.03[4][b] n.286
25.2702-2(c)(3) . . . . 19.03[4][b] n.296
25.2702-2(c)(4)(i) . . . . 19.03[4][b] n.299
25.2702-2(c)(4)(ii) . . . . 19.03[4][b] n.299
25.2702-2(c)(4)(iii) . . . . . . 19.03[4][b] n.300;
    19.03[4][c][i] n.307
25.2702-2(c)(5)(i) . . . . 19.03[4][b] n.301
25.2702-2(c)(5)(ii) . . . . 19.03[4][b] n.302
25.2702-2(d) . . . . 19.02[4][d][iv] n.270;
    19.03[2][a] n.29; 19.03[2][a][iv] n.70
25.2702-2(d)(1) . . . . 19.03[2][a][iv] n.62;
    19.03[2][c] n.94; 19.03[3][a] ns. 100,
    102–104; 19.03[3][b][i] n.134;
    S19.03[3][b][i] n.134
25.2702-2(d)(2) . . . . . 19.03[4][b] ns. 290, 292, 297, 299
25.2702-3 . . . . 19.03[3][d][iii] n.245
25.2702-3(b) . . . . S9.04[10][a] n.219;
    19.03[3][b][i] n.117
25.2702-3(b)(1)(i) . . . . . 19.03[3][b][i] ns. 121, 137–140
25.2702-3(b)(1)(ii) . . . . . 19.03[3][b][i] ns. 121, 125, 126
25.2702-3(b)(1)(ii)(B) . . . . S10.01[3][e] n.107.1
25.2702-3(b)(1)(iii) . . . . . 19.03[3][b][i] n.128
25.2702-3(b)(2) . . . . 19.03[3][b][i] n.123
25.2702-3(b)(3) . . . . 19.03[3][b][i] ns. 123, 138
25.2702-3(b)(4) . . . . 19.03[3][b][i] ns. 123, 141
25.2702-3(c) . . . . 19.03[3][b][i] n.118
25.2702-3(c)(1)(i) . . . . . 19.03[3][b][i] ns. 123, 137–140
25.2702-3(c)(1)(ii) . . . . . 19.03[3][b][i] ns. 125, 126
25.2702-3(c)(1)(iii) . . . . . 19.03[3][b][i] n.128
25.2702-3(c)(2) . . . . 19.03[3][b][i] n.123
25.2702-3(c)(3) . . . . 19.03[3][b][i] ns. 123, 138
25.2702-3(c)(4) . . . . 19.03[3][b][i] n.123
25.2702-3(d) . . . . . . 19.03[3][b][i] ns. 117, 118
25.2702-3(d)(1) . . . 19.03[3][b][i] ns. 130, 131, 135
25.2702-3(d)(2) . . . . 19.03[3][b][i] n.136
25.2702-3(d)(3) . . . 19.03[3][b][i] ns. 132, 134;
    S19.03[3][b][i] n.134
25.2702-3(d)(4) . . . . 19.03[3][b][i] n.143
25.2702-3(d)(5)(i) . . . . . . 19.03[3][b][i] n.140
25.2702-3(d)(5)(ii) . . . . . . 19.03[3][b][i] n.140
25.2702-3(e) . . . . . 19.03[3][b][i] ns. 124, 126, 128, 129, 133, 134, 136
25.2702-3(e) Ex. 5 . . . . . S19.03[3][b][i] n.133
25.2702-3(e) Ex. 6 . . . . . S19.03[3][b][i] n.133
25.2702-3(e) Ex. 8 . . . . . S19.03[3][b][i] n.134
25.2702-3(f)(1)(ii) . . . . . . 19.03[3][b][ii] n.145
25.2702-3(f)(1)(iii) . . . . 19.03[3][b][ii] ns. 148, 149

Reg. §

25.2702-3(f)(1)(iv) . . . . 19.03[3][b][ii] ns. 146, 152
25.2702-3(f)(2) . . . 19.03[3][b][ii] ns. 144, 147
25.2702-3(f)(3) . . . 19.03[3][b][ii] ns. 146, 147, 151, 153
25.2702-4(a) . . . . . . 19.03[2][a][i] ns. 41, 42;
    19.03[2][a][iv] n.69; 19.03[4][a] n.267
25.2702-4(b) . . . . 19.03[2][a][i] ns. 46, 47
25.2702-4(c) . . . . 19.03[1] n.20; 19.03[4][a] ns.
    270, 272, 275, 279; 19.03[4][e][i] n.365
25.2702-4(d) . . . 19.03[2][a] n.30; 19.03[2][a][ii]
    ns. 56, 59; 19.03[2][a][iv] n.67;
    19.03[3][a] n.109; 19.03[4][a] ns. 264,
    266, 268, 269, 271, 279
25.2702-5 . . . . 19.03[3][d][ii] n.201
25.2702-5(a)(1) . . . . 19.03[3][d] n.164;
    19.03[3][d][iii] n.203; 19.03[3][d][iv] ns.
    250, 252–256
25.2702-5(a)(2) . . . . 19.03[3][d] n.168;
    19.03[3][d][ii] n.202; 19.03[3][d][iii]
    n.210
25.2702-5(a)(9) . . . . 19.03[3][d][iii] n.209
25.2702-5(b) . . . . 19.03[3][d] n.167;
    19.03[3][d][ii] n.201; 19.03[3][d][iii]
    n.204
25.2702-5(b)(1) . . . 19.03[3][d][i] ns. 186, 187;
    19.03[3][d][ii] ns. 190–194, 196, 198, 201
25.2702-5(b)(2) . . . . 19.03[4][a] n.281
25.2702-5(b)(2)(i) . . . . 19.03[3][d][iv] ns. 251, 254
25.2702-5(b)(2)(i)(A) . . . . 19.03[3][d][i] n.169
25.2702-5(b)(2)(i)(B) . . . 19.03[3][d][i] ns. 170, 183, 184
25.2702-5(b)(2)(i)(C) . . . . 19.03[3][d][i] n.171
25.2702-5(b)(2)(ii) . . . . 19.03[3][d][i] ns. 173–175
25.2702-5(b)(2)(iii) . . . 19.03[3][d][i] ns. 177–180, 185
25.2702-5(b)(2)(iv) . . . 19.03[3][d][iv] ns. 257, 258
25.2702-5(b)(3) . . . 19.03[3][d][ii] ns. 198, 199;
    19.03[3][d][iii] n.234
25.2702-5(c) . . . . 19.03[3][d] n.167;
    19.03[3][d][iii] ns. 203, 204
25.2702-5(c)(1) . . . . 19.03[3][d][ii] n.201;
    19.03[3][d][iii] n.209
25.2702-5(c)(2)(i) . . . 19.03[3][d][iv] ns. 251, 254
25.2702-5(c)(2)(i)(A) . . . . 19.03[3][d][i] n.169
25.2702-5(c)(2)(i)(B) . . . 19.03[3][d][i] ns. 170, 183, 184
25.2702-5(c)(2)(i)(C) . . . . 19.03[3][d][i] n.171
25.2702-5(c)(2)(ii) . . . . 19.03[3][d][i] ns. 173–175
25.2702-5(c)(2)(iii) . . . 19.03[3][d][i] ns. 177–180, 185
25.2702-5(c)(2)(iv) . . . 19.03[3][d][iv] ns. 257, 258
25.2702-5(c)(3) . . . . 19.03[3][d][iii] n.218

[Text references are to paragraphs and notes (9"n.");
references to the supplement are preceded by "S."]

Reg. §

25.2702-5(c)(4) . . . . 19.03[3][d][ii] n.198;
    19.03[3][d][iii] ns. 219, 236, 237, 242
25.2702-5(c)(5) . . . . 19.03[3][d][iii] n.205
25.2702-5(c)(5)(ii) . . . . . 19.03[3][d][iii] n.224
25.2702-5(c)(5)(ii)(A)(1) . . . . . . 19.03[3][d][iii]
    n.211
25.2702-5(c)(5)(ii)(A)(1)(i) . . . . 19.03[3][d][iii]
    ns. 212, 231
25.2702-5(c)(5)(ii)(A)(1)(ii) . . . . 19.03[3][d][iii]
    n.212
25.2702-5(c)(5)(ii)(A)(1)(iii) . . . 19.03[3][d][iii]
    n.213
25.2702-5(c)(5)(ii)(A)(1)(iv) . . . 19.03[3][d][iii]
    n.213
25.2702-5(c)(5)(ii)(A)(2) . . . 19.03[3][d][iii] ns.
    216, 217
25.2702-5(c)(5)(ii)(B) . . . . . 19.03[3][d][iii] ns.
    207, 214
25.2702-5(c)(5)(ii)(C) . . . . . 19.03[3][d][iii] ns.
    206, 221, 222, 226, 229
25.2702-5(c)(5)(ii)(D) . . 19.03[3][d][iii] n.232
25.2702-5(c)(5)(iii) . . . . . 19.03[3][d][iii] n.224
25.2702-5(c)(5)(iii)(B) . . 19.03[3][d][iii] n.234
25.2702-5(c)(5)(iv)(D) . . . 19.03[3][d][iii] n.215
25.2702-5(c)(6) . . . . 19.03[3][d][iii] n.235
25.2702-5(c)(7) . . . . 19.03[3][d][iii] n.206
25.2702-5(c)(7)(i) . . . . . 19.03[3][d][i] ns. 186,
    187; 19.03[3][d][iii] n.238
25.2702-5(c)(7)(ii) . . . . 19.03[3][d][iii] ns. 222,
    223, 234
25.2702-5(c)(7)(ii)(B) . . . . . 19.03[3][d][iii] ns.
    222, 234
25.2702-5(c)(8) . . . . . . 19.03[3][d][iii] n.239;
    19.03[4][b] n.300; 19.03[4][c][i] n.307
25.2702-5(c)(8)(i) . . . . . 19.03[3][d][iii] n.241
25.2702-5(c)(8)(i)(A) . . . . 19.03[3][d][iii] n.242
25.2702-5(c)(8)(i)(B) . . . 19.03[3][d][iii] ns. 208,
    243
25.2702-5(c)(8)(i)(C) . . . . 19.03[3][d][iii] n.244
25.2702-5(c)(8)(i)(A) . . . . 19.03[3][d][iii] n.245
25.2702-5(c)(8)(ii)(B) . . . 19.03[3][d][iii] n.246
25.2702-5(c)(8)(ii)(C)(1) . . . . . . 19.03[3][d][iii]
    n.247
25.2702-5(c)(8)(ii)(C)(2) . . . . . . 19.03[3][d][iii]
    n.248
25.2702-5(c)(8)(ii)(C)(3) . . . . . . 19.03[3][d][iii]
    n.249
25.2702-5(c)(9) . . . 19.03[3][d][iii] ns. 206, 225,
    226, 229
25.2702-5(d) . . . . . 19.03[3][d][i] ns. 173, 180,
    184, 187; 19.03[3][d][iii] n.249
25.2702-5(d), Ex. 2 . . . . . S19.03[3][d][i] n.177
25.2702-6 . . . . . . 10.08[1][a] n.19; 19.03[4][c]
    n.306
25.2702-6(a) . . . 19.03[2][a] n.29; 19.03[4][c][i]
    n.320; 19.03[4][c][ii] n.336
25.2702-6(a)(1) . . . . 19.03[4][c][i] ns. 307, 308;
    19.03[4][e][i] ns. 363, 364
25.2702-6(a)(2) . . . 19.03[4][c][ii] ns. 334, 335,
    341

Reg. §

25.2702-6(a)(2)(i) . . . . 19.03[4][c][ii] ns. 335,
    342, 343
25.2702-6(a)(2)(ii) . . . . 19.03[4][c][ii] ns. 335,
    336
25.2702-6(a)(3) . . . 19.03[4][c][i] ns. 322–326
25.2702-6(b) . . . . 19.03[4][c][i] n.307
25.2702-6(b)(1) . . . . 19.03[4][c][i] ns. 308, 310,
    311; 19.03[4][c][ii] ns. 333, 336, 340,
    347, 348; 19.03[4][e][i] ns. 363, 364
25.2702-6(b)(1)(i) . . . . . 19.03[4][c][i] ns. 309,
    315, 321, 323, 324
25.2702-6(b)(1)(ii) . . . . 19.03[4][c][i] ns. 315,
    324; 19.03[4][c][ii] n.333
25.2702-6(b)(2) . . . . 19.03[4][c][i] n.313
25.2702-6(b)(3) . . . . 19.03[4][c][ii] ns. 337, 349
25.2702-6(c) . . . . 19.03[2][a][iv] n.71;
    19.03[2][c] n.82; 19.03[4][a] n.273;
    19.03[4][c][i] ns. 310, 313, 315–317,
    322, 324; 19.03[4][c][ii] ns. 345, 349
25.2702-7 . . . . 19.03[4][f] n.385
25.2703-1(a)(1) . . . . 19.04[1][c] n.13
25.2703-1(a)(2) . . . . 19.04[1][c] n.14
25.2703-1(a)(3) . . . . . 4.02[2][c] n.51; 19.04[2]
    n.19; S19.04[2] n.19
25.2703-1(a)(4) . . . . 19.04[2] n.27
25.2703-1(b) . . . . 19.04[3][a] n.46
25.2703-1(b)(1)(i) . . . . 19.04[3] n.37
25.2703-1(b)(1)(ii) . . . . 19.04[3] n.38;
    19.04[3][b][i] n.58; 19.04[3][b][ii] n.88
25.2703-1(b)(1)(iii) . . . . 19.04[3] n.39
25.2703-1(b)(2) . . . . 19.04[3] n.35
25.2703-1(b)(3) . . . . 19.04[1][c] n.15; 19.04[3]
    n.36; 19.04[3][b][i] n.57; 19.04[4] ns.
    99–101, 103, 105–109; S19.04[4] n.99;
    19.04[6] n.114; 19.04[6][a] n.116
25.2703-1(b)(4)(i) . . . . 19.04[3][c] ns. 92, 93, 95
25.2703-1(b)(4)(ii) . . . . 19.04[3][c] ns. 93, 94, 96
25.2703-1(b)(5) . . . . . . 19.04[5] ns. 112, 113
25.2703-1(c) . . . . . . 19.04[3] n.44; 19.04[7] ns.
    140, 142
25.2703-1(c)(1) . . . 19.04[7] ns. 143, 145, 147,
    150, 151
25.2703-1(c)(2)(i) . . . . 19.04[7] n.144
25.2703-1(c)(2)(ii) . . . . 19.04[7] n.146
25.2703-1(c)(2)(iii) . . . . 19.04[7] n.149
25.2703-1(c)(2)(iv) . . . . 19.04[7] n.148
25.2703-1(d) . . . 19.04[2] n.18; 19.04[3][c] n.91;
    19.04[7] ns. 146, 151
25.2703-2 . . . . 19.04[7] ns. 140, 142
25.2704-1(a) . . . . 19.05[2][a] n.13
25.2704-1(a)(1) . . . . 19.05[1] n.7
25.2704-1(a)(2)(i) . . . 19.05[2][b][iv] ns. 38, 39
25.2704-1(a)(2)(ii) . . . . . 19.05[2][b][iii] n.36
25.2704-1(a)(2)(iii) . . . . 19.05[2][a] n.13
25.2704-1(a)(2)(iv) . . . 19.05[2][b][i] ns. 22–24
25.2704-1(a)(2)(v) . . . 19.05[2][b][i] ns. 24, 25;
    19.05[3][b] n.53
25.2704-1(a)(2)(vi) . . . . . . 19.05[2][b][ii] n.30
25.2704-1(a)(3) . . . . 19.05[2][b][ii] n.35
25.2704-1(a)(4) . . . . 19.05[2][b][i] n.26;
    19.05[2][b][ii] n.33

*[Text references are to paragraphs and notes (9"n.");
references to the supplement are preceded by "S."]*

Reg. §

25.2704-1(b) . . . . . . 19.05[2][b][ii] ns. 28, 34
25.2704-1(c)(1) . . . . . 19.05[2][b][ii] ns. 28, 29,
31, 34
25.2704-1(c)(2)(i)(A) . . . . . . 19.05[2][c] n.41
25.2704-1(c)(2)(i)(B) . . . . 19.05[2][c] n.41
25.2704-1(c)(2)(ii) . . . 19.01[1] n.9; 19.05[2][c]
n.43
25.2704-1(c)(2)(iii) . . . . 19.05[2][c] n.44
25.2704-1(d) . . . . 19.05[2][d] n.45
25.2704-1(e) . . . . 19.05[2][b][i] n.27
25.2704-1(f) . . . 19.05[2][a] n.18; 19.05[2][b][ii]
ns. 29, 31, 35; 19.05[2][c] ns. 41, 42;
19.05[2][d] ns. 45, 46
25.2704-2(a) . . . . 19.05[1] n.10
25.2704-2(b) . . . . 19.05[3][b] ns. 53, 54, 60, 63
25.2704-2(c) . . . . 19.05[3][a] ns. 48, 52
25.2704-2(d) . . . . 19.05[2][c] n.41; 19.05[3][a]
ns. 48, 52; 19.05[3][b] ns. 53, 56, 61
25.2704-3 . . . . 19.05[4] ns. 65–67
25.6019-1(a) . . . . 9.04[9] n.214
25.6019-3(a) . . . . 9.04[9] n.205
25.6019-3(b) . . . . 10.06[2] & ns. 16, 19
25.6075-1(b)(2) . . . . 18.02[4][a] n.46
25.6081-1 . . . . 9.04[9] ns. 208, 213; S9.04[9]
n.210; 18.02[4][b] ns. 55–58, 60
25.6081-1(c) . . . . S9.04[9] n.210
25.6091-1(b) . . . . 9.04[9] n.212; 18.02[5] n.61
25.6091-1(c) . . . . 18.02[5] n.61
25.6161-1 . . . . 9.04[9] n.213
25.7520-1 . . . . . S3.05[3][b] n.29; S4.02[5] ns.
244, 247; S4.08[1][a] n.5; S5.05[3][a]
n.95; S5.05[5][a][ii] n.207;
S5.05[5][b][ii] n.264; S5.05[5][c][ii]
n.291; S5.05[6][b] n.327; S5.05[7][a]
n.333; S5.06[7][d] n.197; S5.06[8][d][ii]
n.348; S9.04[3][a] n.48; 10.02[2][b][iii]
n.57; S10.02[2][b][iii] n.56; 11.02[1][b]
n.27; S11.02[1][b] n.27; S16.02[6] n.409;
S19.03[1] n.3; S19.03[3][b] n.112;
S19.03[3][d] n.162
25.7520-1(a)(1) . . . . 10.02[2][b][iii] n.57
25.7520-1(b) . . . . 10.02[2][b][iii] n.54
25.7520-1(b)(1) . . . . 10.02[2][b][iii] n.59
25.7520-1(b)(2) . . . . 10.02[2][b][iii] n.56
25.7520-1(c) . . . . 10.02[2][b][iii] n.52
25.7520-2 . . . . 11.02[1][b] n.27
25.7520-2(a)(2) . . . . 5.05[3][a] n.95;
10.02[2][b][iii] n.58; 11.02[1][b] n.27
25.7520-3 . . . . 11.02[1][b] n.27
25.7520-3(b) . . . . 10.02[2][b][iii] n.61
25.7520-3(b)(2) . . . . 10.02[2][b][iii] n.61
25.7520-3(b)(3) . . . . . 4.11[5] n.52; 10.01[3][b]
n.89; 10.02[2][b][iii] n.62
25.7520-3(b)(4) . . . . 10.02[2][b][iii] n.62
26.2601-1(a)(1) . . . 10.05 n.8; 18.03[2][a] n.28;
18.05[1] n.1
26.2601-1(a)(2) . . . . 10.05 n.8; 18.05[2][a] n.4
26.2601-1(a)(2)(ii) . . . . 18.05[2][a] n.7
26.2601-1(a)(3) . . . . 18.05[2][a] ns. 5–7
26.2601-1(a)(4) . . . . 18.05[2][a] n.3
26.2601-1(b)(1) . . . . 18.05[2][b][ii] n.35

26.2601-1(b)(1)(i) . . . . 18.05[2][b] n.9;
18.05[2][b][i] n.15; 18.05[2][b][ii] ns. 36,
38; S18.05[2][b][ii] n.38
26.2601-1(b)(1)(ii)(B) . . . 18.05[2][b][i] ns. 13–
15
26.2601-1(b)(1)(ii)(C) . . . . 18.05[2][b][i] ns. 21,
22
26.2601-1(b)(1)(ii)(D) . . 18.05[2][b][i] ns. 14,
15, 18, 23
26.2601-1(b)(1)(iii)(A) . . . 18.05[2][b][i] ns. 25,
27; 18.05[2][b][ii] n.46
26.2601-1(b)(1)(iii)(B) . . . . 18.05[2][b][i] n.27
26.2601-1(b)(1)(iv) . . . . 18.05[2][a] n.6;
18.05[2][b] ns. 11, 12; 18.05[2][b][iii]
n.47
26.2601-1(b)(1)(iv)(A) . . . 18.05[2][b][iii] n.47
26.2601-1(b)(1)(iv)(C) . . . 18.05[2][b][iii] n.48
26.2601-1(b)(1)(iv)(C)(1) . . . 18.05[2][b][iii] ns.
48–54
26.2601-1(b)(1)(iv)(C)(2) . . . 18.05[2][b][iii] ns.
50, 54
26.2601-1(b)(1)(v) . . . . . . 18.05[2][b][ii] n.36
26.2601-1(b)(1)(v)(A) . . . . . . 17.02[1][b] n.40;
18.05[2][b][ii] ns. 37–39
26.2601-1(b)(1)(v)(B) . . . 18.05[2][b][ii] ns. 37,
40–43
26.2601-1(b)(1)(v)(B)(1) . . . 18.05[2][b][ii] n.41
26.2601-1(b)(1)(v)(B)(2) . . . 18.05[2][b][ii] n.42
26.2601-1(b)(1)(v)(C) . . . 18.05[2][b][ii] ns. 44,
45
26.2601-1(b)(1)(v)(D) . . . . . . 17.02[1][b] n.40;
18.05[2][b][ii] ns. 36–39, 42
26.2601-1(b)(1)(vi) . . . . 18.05[2][b][ii] ns. 29,
30; 18.05[2][c] n.67
26.2601-1(b)(2) . . . . . 18.05[2][b][ii] ns. 31, 33
26.2601-1(b)(2)(i) . . . . 18.05[2][c] n.55
26.2601-1(b)(2)(i)(A) . . . . 18.05[2][c] n.58
26.2601-1(b)(2)(i)(B) . . . . 18.05[2][c] n.59
26.2601-1(b)(2)(ii) . . . . . . 18.05[2][b][i] n.16;
18.05[2][c] n.56
26.2601-1(b)(2)(iii) . . . . 18.05[2][c] n.55
26.2601-1(b)(2)(iv) . . . . 18.05[2][c] n.60
26.2601-1(b)(2)(iv)(A) . . . . . . 18.05[2][c] n.61
26.2601-1(b)(2)(v) . . . . . 18.05[2][b][iii] n.50;
18.05[2][c] n.64
26.2601-1(b)(2)(vi) . . . 18.05[2][c] ns. 66, 67
26.2601-1(b)(2)(vii)(A) . . . . 18.05[2][c] ns. 57,
58, 62, 63, 65
26.2601-1(b)(2)(vii)(B) . . . . 18.05[2][c] ns. 58,
65
26.2601-1(b)(3) . . . . 18.05[2][b][ii] n.33
26.2601-1(b)(3)(i) . . . . . 18.05[2][d] ns. 69, 77
26.2601-1(b)(3)(i) . . . . . 18.05[2][d] ns. 69, 77
26.2601-1(b)(3)(i)(A) . . . 18.05[2][d] ns. 70, 71,
74
26.2601-1(b)(3)(i)(B) . . . . 18.05[2][d] n.72
26.2601-1(b)(3)(ii) . . . 18.05[2][d] ns. 68, 75, 76
26.2601-1(b)(3)(iii)(A) . . . . . . 18.05[2][d] n.79
26.2601-1(b)(3)(iii)(A)(1) . . . . . 18.05[2][d] n.80
26.2601-1(b)(3)(iii)(A)(2) . . . . 18.05[2][d] n.81
26.2601-1(b)(3)(iii)(A)(3) . . . . 18.05[2][d] n.82

[Text references are to paragraphs and notes (9"n.");
references to the supplement are preceded by "S."]

Reg. §

26.2601-1(b)(3)(iii)(B) . . . . . . 18.05[2][d] n.82
26.2601-1(b)(3)(iv) . . . . 18.05[2][d] n.78
26.2601-1(b)(3)(v) . . . . 18.05[2][d] n.73
26.2601-1(b)(3)(vi) . . . . 18.05[2][d] n.73
26.2601-1(b)(4) . . . . S16.02[5][e] n.364;
    18.05[2][b][ii] n.36
26.2601-1(b)(4)(i) . . . . 18.05[2][e] n.88
26.2601-1(b)(4)(i)(A) . . . . . . 18.05[2][e] n.84;
    18.05[2][e][i] n.90
26.2601-1(b)(4)(i)(A)(1) . . . 18.05[2][e][i] n.93
26.2601-1(b)(4)(i)(A)(1)(i) . . . . . 18.05[2][e][i]
    n.91
26.2601-1(b)(4)(i)(A)(1)(ii) . . . . 18.05[2][e][i]
    n.92
26.2601-1(b)(4)(i)(A)(2) . . . . 18.05[2][e][i] ns.
    94, 95
26.2601-1(b)(4)(i)(B) . . . . . . 18.05[2][e] n.85;
    18.05[2][e][ii] n.99
26.2601-1(b)(4)(i)(B)(1) . . . 18.05[2][e][ii] n.98
26.2601-1(b)(4)(i)(B)(2) . . . 18.05[2][e][ii] n.97
26.2601-1(b)(4)(i)(C) . . . . . . 18.05[2][e] n.86;
    18.05[2][e][iii] n.100
26.2601-1(b)(4)(i)(C)(1) . . . . . . 18.05[2][e][iii]
    n.101
26.2601-1(b)(4)(i)(C)(2) . . . . . . 18.05[2][e][iii]
    n.102
26.2601-1(b)(4)(i)(D) . . . . . . 18.05[2][e] n.87;
  18.05[2][e][i] n.90; 18.05[2][e][iv] n.114
26.2601-1(b)(4)(i)(D)(1) . . . . 18.05[2][e][iv] ns.
    104–106
26.2601-1(b)(4)(i)(D)(2) . . . . . . 18.05[2][e][iv]
    n.105
26.2601-1(b)(4)(i)(E) . . . . 18.05[2][e][i] ns. 90,
  96; 18.05[2][e][iii] n.102; 18.05[2][e][iv]
    ns. 107–113, 115
26.2601-1(b)(4)(i)(E) Ex. 6 . . . . . S16.02[5][a]
  n.301; S18.05[2][e][iii] n.100;
    S18.05[2][e][iv] n.109
26.2601-1(b)(4)(i)(E) Ex. 11   S18.05[2][e][iv]
    n.111
26.2601-1(b)(4)(i)(E) Ex. 12   S18.05[2][e][iv]
    n.112
26.2601-1(b)(5) . . . . 18.05[2][b][ii] n.31
26.2601-1(b)(5)(i) . . . 18.05[2][b][ii] ns. 31, 32
26.2601-1(b)(5)(ii) . . . 18.05[2][b][ii] ns. 31, 32,
    34, 39
26.2601-1(c) . . . . 16.02[1] n.6
26.2611-1 . . . . 13.02[1][a] n.2
26.2612-1(a)(1) . . . 13.02[4][b][i] ns. 263, 268,
    273
26.2612-1(a)(2) . . . . 13.02[4][c][i] ns. 307, 308,
    317, 318
26.2612-1(a)(2)(i) . . . . . 13.02[4][c][i] ns. 306,
    307, 316, 319
26.2612-1(a)(2)(ii) . . . . . 13.02[4][c][i] ns. 321,
    323; 17.01[2][a][ii] n.37
26.2612-1(b)(1) . . . . 13.02[2][e][iii] n.166;
  15.02[4] n.68; S15.02[4] n.62; 17.02[2]
    ns. 83, 88; 17.03[1] n.5

Reg. §

26.2612-1(b)(1)(i) . . . . . 3.03[1] n.3; 12.02 n.4;
  12.03[1] n.3; 13.01[1] n.5; 13.02[1][b]
    ns. 10, 14, 18; 13.02[2][a] n.30;
  13.02[2][d] ns. 77, 85; 13.02[2][e][ii] ns.
    108, 122, 139, 149; 13.02[2][e][iii]
    n.165; 13.02[2][f] ns. 182, 190;
    13.02[4][a] n.248; 13.03[1] n.5;
    13.03[3][b] n.71
26.2612-1(b)(1)(iii) . . . . 13.02[2][c] n.72
26.2612-1(b)(2) . . . . 13.02[2][f] n.190
26.2612-1(b)(3) . . . . . 13.02[2][g] ns. 201, 204,
    206
26.2612-1(c) . . . . 14.02[4] ns. 26, 27
26.2612-1(c)(1) . . . . 13.02[2][e][ii] ns. 96, 101,
  108; 13.02[3][c] ns. 234, 235;
    13.03[3][b] n.71
26.2612-1(c)(2) . . . . 13.02[3][b][i] n.216;
  13.02[4][b][iii] ns. 293, 297, 304;
    13.03[3][a] n.58
26.2612-1(d) . . . 13.02[2][a] n.29; 13.02[4][b][ii]
  n.274; 17.02[1][a] n.2; S17.02[1][a] n.2
26.2612-1(d)(1) . . . . 13.03[2] n.17
26.2612-1(d)(2)(i)   13.03[3] n.23; 13.03[3][a]
    n.37
26.2612-1(d)(2)(ii) . . . . . . 13.02[3][b][i] n.216;
  13.02[4][b][ii] n.284; 13.03[3] ns. 24,
    36; 13.03[3][b] ns. 66, 70
26.2612-1(e) . . . . 13.02[1][b] n.5; 13.02[2][b][i]
    n.31; 17.02[3][a] n.108
26.2612-1(e)(1) . . . . 13.02[2][b][i] n.32
26.2612-1(e)(1)(i) . . . 13.02[2][b][i] ns. 33, 40;
    17.02[3][b] n.123
26.2612-1(e)(1)(ii)   13.02[2][b][i] ns. 34, 49–
    51; 17.02[3][b] n.127
26.2612-1(e)(1)(iii) . . . . . . 13.02[2][b][i] n.36;
    17.02[3][c] n.144
26.2612-1(e)(2)(i) . . . 13.02[2][b][i] ns. 45, 46;
  13.02[2][e][ii] n.144; 17.02[3][b] ns.
    140–142
26.2612-1(e)(2)(ii) . . . . . . 13.02[2][b][i] n.37;
  13.02[2][e][ii] n.123; 13.03[3][a] n.57;
    17.02[3][d] n.154
26.2612-1(e)(3) . . . . 13.02[2][b][ii] n.61;
  13.02[4][b][iii] n.295; 17.02[3][a] n.120
26.2612-1(f) . . . . 12.02 n.4; 12.03[1] n.3;
  13.02[2][b][i] ns. 40, 41, 46;
  13.02[2][b][ii] ns. 56, 57, 62, 63;
  13.02[2][c] n.71; 13.02[2][d] ns. 85, 86;
  13.02[2][e][ii] ns. 96, 99; 13.02[2][e][iii]
    ns. 169, 179, 180; 13.02[2][f] ns. 190,
    195; 13.02[2][g] ns. 205, 206;
  13.02[3][b][ii] n.227; 13.02[4][a] n.244;
  13.02[4][b][ii] ns. 279, 285, 290;
    13.02[4][b][iii] ns. 296, 299;
  13.02[4][c][i] n.312; 13.03[3][b] n.71;
  16.02[2][b][iii] ns. 71, 73; 17.02[1][c][i]
  n.58; 17.02[3][b] ns. 124, 126, 140–142
26.2623-1(b)(2)(i) . . . . S15.03[4][d] n.165
26.2632-1 . . . 16.02[5][b][i] n.312; 18.03[2][c]
    n.50

*[Text references are to paragraphs and notes (9"n.");
references to the supplement are preceded by "S."]*

Reg. §

26.2632-1(a) . . . 15.02[1] ns. 24, 27; S15.02[1]
   ns. 18, 21; 15.03[2][a] n.10; 15.03[3][a]
   n.38; 15.03[3][b] n.64; 15.03[6][a] n.231;
   16.02[2][c][i] n.124; 16.02[3][a] n.166;
   16.02[3][b][i] n.171; 16.02[5][b][iii]
   n.344; 16.02[7][e][iii] n.532
26.2632-1(b)(1) . . . . 15.03[3][c] ns. 70, 71;
   19.02[5][f][iii] n.524
26.2632-1(b)(1)(i) . . . 15.02[1] n.26; S15.02[1]
   n.20; 15.03[3][a] ns. 36, 39, 42;
   15.03[3][b] n.63; 15.03[3][c] ns. 66–69,
   74, 83; 16.02[2][c][i] n.128; 17.04[2][a]
   n.59
26.2632-1(b)(1)(ii) . . . 15.02[1] n.25; S15.02[1]
   n.19; 15.03[2][b] ns. 16, 21; 15.03[3][a]
   ns. 35, 43; 15.03[3][c] ns. 69, 72, 73,
   75–77; S15.03[4][e][i] n.173
26.2632-1(b)(1)(iii) . . . . 15.03[3][c] n.77
26.2632-1(b)(2) . . . . S15.03[4][e][i] n.171
26.2632-1(b)(2)(i) . . . 15.02[1] ns. 25, 26, 28–
   30; 15.02[4] ns. 63, 70; 15.03[2] n.8;
   15.03[2][b] ns. 15, 18, 21, 24, 33;
   S15.03[4][d] ns. 166–168; 15.03[6]
   n.227; 16.02[4][c] n.245; 16.02[5][b][iii]
   ns. 337, 339, 356; 16.02[5][f][ii] n.397;
   18.03[1][b] n.26
26.2632-1(b)(2)(ii) . . . . . S15.03[4][e][i] n.176
26.2632-1(b)(2)(ii)(A) . . . . . 16.02[4][c] n.244
26.2632-1(b)(2)(ii)(A)(1) . . . . . . 15.02[1] n.25;
   15.03[2][b] ns. 17, 18, 21, 25, 26;
   15.03[6][c] n.246; 16.02[5][b][iii] ns.
   332, 333, 338, 347, 348; 16.02[7][a]
   n.428
26.2632-1(b)(2)(ii)(A)(1)(i)   15.03[2][b] n.30;
   16.02[5][b][iii] n.345
26.2632-1(b)(2)(ii)(A)(1)(ii) . . . . . . 15.03[2][b]
   n.31; 16.02[5][b][iii] n.347
26.2632-1(b)(2)(ii)(A)(1)(iii) . . . 15.03[2][b] ns.
   28, 32; 16.02[5][b][iii] ns. 334, 351
26.2632-1(b)(2)(ii)(A)(2) . . . . . . 15.02[1] n.25;
   S15.02[1] n.19; 15.03[2][b] ns. 18, 21
26.2632-1(b)(2)(ii)(B) . . . 15.03[2][b] ns. 30–32
26.2632-1(b)(2)(iii) . . . 15.02[1] n.25; 15.02[3]
   n.56; 15.03[2][b] ns. 17, 18, 21;
   S15.03[4][e][i] n.171
26.2632-1(b)(2)(iii)(A) . . . S15.03[4][e][i] n.175
26.2632-1(b)(2)(iii)(B) . . . . S15.03[4][e][i] ns.
   173, 174
26.2632-1(b)(2)(iii)(C)(2) . . . . . S15.03[4][e][i]
   n.173
26.2632-1(b)(2)(iii)(E) . . . S15.03[4][e][i] n.172
26.2632-1(b)(3) . . . . S15.03[4][e][ii] n.179
26.2632-1(b)(3)(i) . . . . . S15.03[4][e][ii] n.179
26.2632-1(b)(3)(ii) . . . . . S15.03[4][e][ii] n.180
26.2632-1(b)(3)(iii) . . . S15.03[4][e][ii] ns. 181,
   182
26.2632-1(b)(3)(iv) . . . S15.03[4][e][ii] ns. 179,
   181

Reg. §

26.2632-1(b)(4) . . . . S15.02[1] ns. 19, 23;
   S15.02[3] n.49; S15.02[4] n.57;
   S15.03[2] n.8; S15.03[2][b] ns. 15, 17,
   18, 21, 24–26, 28, 30–33;
   S16.02[5][b][iii] ns. 332–334, 337–339,
   345, 347, 348, 351; S18.03[1][b] n.26
26.2632-1(b)(4)(i)   S15.02[1] ns. 19, 20, 22–
   24; S15.02[4] ns. 57, 64; S16.02[4][c]
   n.245
26.2632-1(b)(4)(ii)(A) . . . . S16.02[4][c] n.244
26.2632-1(b)(4)(ii)(A)(1) . . . . . . S15.02[1] n.19
26.2632-1(b)(4)(iii) Ex. 1 . . . . S15.02[1] n.19;
   S15.03[4][d] n.167; S15.03[4][e][i] n.173
26.2632-1(b)(4)(iii) Ex. 2 . . . . S15.02[1] n.19;
   S15.03[4][d] n.167; S15.03[4][e][i] n.173
26.2632-1(b)(4)(iii) Ex. 3   S16.02[4][c] n.244
26.2632-1(b)(4)(iii) Ex. 4   S16.02[4][c] n.245
26.2632-1(b)(4)(iii) Ex. 5 . . . . . S15.02[3] n.49
26.2632-1(b)(4)(iii) Ex. 6 . . . . . S15.03[4][e][i]
   n.176
26.2632-1(b)(4)(iv) Ex. . . . . S15.03[4][e][i] n.173
26.2632-1(c) . . . . . 16.02[7][e][iii] ns. 531, 534;
   18.03[2][d] n.61
26.2632-1(c)(1) . . . . 13.02[2][e][ii] n.106;
   15.03[2][a] n.11; 15.03[3][b] n.50;
   S15.03[4][d] n.168; 15.03[5][c][i] ns.
   213, 217; 16.02[7][a] ns. 428, 430, 433;
   16.02[7][b][i] ns. 445, 451, 454;
   16.02[7][e][i] n.510; 16.02[7][e][ii]
   n.518; 16.02[7][e][iii] ns. 522, 535
26.2632-1(c)(1)(i) . . . . . . S15.03[4][d] n.168;
   S15.03[4][e][i] n.174
26.2632-1(c)(1)(ii) . . . . S15.03[3][b] n.50;
   S15.03[4][d] n.168; S15.03[4][e][i]
   n.174; S16.02[7][a] n.430
26.2632-1(c)(1)(iii) . . . S16.02[7][b][i] ns. 445,
   451, 454
26.2632-1(c)(2) . . . . 15.03[2][a] n.11
26.2632-1(c)(2)(i) . . . 15.02[2] n.40; S15.02[2]
   n.34; 16.02[7][b] n.440; 16.02[7][b][i]
   n.444
26.2632-1(c)(2)(i)(B)   16.02[7][b][ii] ns. 455,
   463, 468, 474; 16.02[7][c][iii] n.489;
   16.02[7][d] n.509
26.2632-1(c)(2)(ii)(A) . . . . . . 13.02[4][d] n.338;
   15.02[2] n.40; S15.02[2] n.34;
   16.02[7][b] n.441; 16.02[7][b][ii] n.443;
   16.02[7][b][ii] n.456
26.2632-1(c)(2)(ii)(B) . . . . 15.02[2] n.40;
   S15.02[2] n.34; 16.02[7][b][ii] n.459
26.2632-1(c)(2)(ii)(C) . . . . 15.02[2] n.40;
   S15.02[2] n.34; 16.02[7][b][ii] ns. 473,
   475; 17.02[1][c][i] n.60
26.2632-1(c)(3) . . . 13.02[4][d] n.337; 15.02[2]
   n.40; S15.02[2] n.34; 15.03[2][a] n.11;
   16.02[7][d] n.493
26.2632-1(c)(3)(i) . . . . . . 16.02[7][c][i] n.478;
   16.02[7][c][ii] n.488; 16.02[7][e][ii] ns.
   513, 518

*[Text references are to paragraphs and notes (9"n.");
references to the supplement are preceded by "S."]*

Reg. §

26.2632-1(c)(3)(ii) . . . . . 16.02[7][c][i] ns. 476,
    479, 480; 16.02[7][c][ii] n.488;
    16.02[7][e][iii] ns. 520, 521, 524, 535,
    551
26.2632-1(c)(3)(iii) . . . . 15.03[3][b] n.59;
    16.02[7][c][i] n.477; 16.02[7][c][ii]
    n.488; 16.02[7][e][iii] ns. 529, 541, 546
26.2632-1(c)(3)(iv) . . . . 16.02[4][b] n.241;
    16.02[7][c][iii] n.489
26.2632-1(c)(3)(iv)(A) . . . 16.02[7][e][ii] n.513
26.2632-1(c)(3)(iv)(B) . . . . 16.02[7][e][iii] ns.
    520, 521, 524
26.2632-1(c)(4) . . . 15.03[3][a] n.39; 15.03[3][b]
    ns. 49, 50, 60; 15.03[7][a] n.257
26.2632-1(c)(5) . . . . 15.03[3][b] ns. 50, 59;
    16.02[7][a] ns. 430, 433; 16.02[7][c][i]
    n.477; 16.02[7][e][i] n.511;
    16.02[7][e][iii] ns. 533, 540;
    17.02[1][c][ii] n.62; 17.03[2][a] n.30
26.2632-1(c)(5) Ex. 5 . . . . S15.03[4][e][i] n.174
26.2632-1(d)(1) . . . . 15.02[1] ns. 25, 26;
    S15.02[1] ns. 19, 20; 15.02[4] ns. 63,
    70; S15.02[4] ns. 57, 64; 15.03[2][b] ns.
    19, 20, 24, 26; 15.03[6] n.227;
    15.03[6][a] ns. 231, 234; 15.03[6][b]
    n.241; 15.03[6][c] ns. 245, 248;
    16.02[4][c] n.246; 16.02[5][b][i] n.317;
    16.02[7][e][iii] n.523
26.2632-1(d)(2) . . . . 15.02[4] ns. 63, 70;
    S15.02[4] ns. 57, 64; 15.03[2][b] n.20;
    15.03[7][a] ns. 255–259; 15.03[7][b][i]
    ns. 261, 268; 15.03[7][b][ii] ns. 269,
    272–274, 280, 281; 15.03[7][c][i] ns.
    287, 290, 291, 293, 294; 16.02[2][c][i]
    n.129
26.2632-1(e)(1) . . . . . . S15.03[4][e][i] n.171;
    S15.03[4][e][ii] n.179
26.2632-1(e)(2) . . . . S15.03[4][d] n.168
26.2641-1 . . . . 12.02 n.10
26.2642-1 . . . . 16.01 n.5; S16.01 n.5
26.2642-1(a) . . . 16.02[1] n.6; 16.02[2][c][i] ns.
    150–152; 16.02[2][c][ii] n.153;
    17.03[2][a] n.34; 17.03[2][b] n.45
26.2642-1(b) . . . 15.03[4][d] n.163; S15.03[4][d]
    n.163; 16.02[2][c][i] n.123
26.2642-1(b)(1) . . . . 16.02[3][b][i] n.169;
    16.02[7][e][iii] n.535
26.2642-1(b)(2) . . . . 15.03[3][b] n.50; 16.02[1]
    n.7; 16.02[3][b][i] n.169; 16.02[7][e][iii]
    ns. 530, 531, 547, 552
26.2642-1(b)(2)(i) . . . . . . 16.02[7][e][iii] n.547
26.2642-1(b)(2)(i)(A) . . . . . 16.02[7][e][iii] ns.
    538, 544, 549, 552
26.2642-1(b)(2)(i)(B) . . . . 16.02[7][e][iii] n.538
26.2642-1(b)(2)(ii) . . . . . . 16.02[7][e][iii] n.549
26.2642-1(b)(2)(ii)(1) . . . . . 16.02[7][e][iii] ns.
    539, 544
26.2642-1(c) . . . . 16.02[2][c][i] n.131;
    16.02[3][b][ii] n.174; 16.02[4][d][i]
    n.255; 18.03[1][b] n.19

Reg. §

26.2642-1(c)(1) . . . . 16.02[3][b][ii] n.174;
    16.02[7][e][iii] n.535; 18.03[2][c] n.60
26.2642-1(c)(1)(i) . . . . . . 16.02[2][c][i] n.133;
    16.02[5][f][i] ns. 391, 392; 16.02[5][f][ii]
    n.396; 18.03[1][b] n.25
26.2642-1(c)(1)(ii) . . . . 16.02[1] n.9;
    16.02[2][c][i] n.134; 16.02[3][b][ii]
    n.183; 16.02[5][b][i] n.316
26.2642-1(c)(1)(iii) . . . . . . 16.02[2][c] n.121;
    16.02[2][c][i] ns. 132, 147
26.2642-1(d) . . . . 13.02[4][b][i] n.263;
    16.02[2][b][i] n.41; 16.02[2][b][ii] ns. 47,
    50; 16.02[2][b][iii] ns. 60, 70, 71;
    16.02[2][b][v] n.113; 16.02[3][a] n.168
26.2642-2(a)(1) . . . . 15.03[6][c] n.247;
    19.02[5][f][iii] ns. 519, 523; 19.04[6][c]
    n.139
26.2642-2(a)(2) . . . . 15.03[6][c] n.249;
    16.02[4][a] n.237; 16.02[4][c] ns. 246,
    247; 16.02[7][e][iii] ns. 523, 528
26.2642-2(b) . . . . 15.03[6][a] n.235;
    15.03[7][b][i] n.261; 15.03[7][b][ii]
    n.274; 15.03[7][c][i] ns. 290, 291
26.2642-2(b)(1) . . . 14.05[2][a] n.21; 15.03[6][a]
    ns. 235, 237; 15.03[6][b] n.242;
    15.03[7][b][i] n.263; 15.03[7][b][ii]
    n.278; 15.03[7][b][iii] n.285;
    16.02[4][d][i] ns. 250, 252, 255, 256;
    16.02[4][d][ii] n.270; 16.02[4][e] n.292;
    16.02[5][c] n.358; 16.02[5][f][i] ns. 386,
    394; 16.02[5][f][ii] n.395; 16.02[7][e][iii]
    n.514; 17.04[1][c] n.36; 18.03[1][a] ns.
    11, 12; 18.03[1][b] ns. 15, 16, 24;
    19.04[6][c] n.139
26.2642-2(b)(2) . . . . 15.03[6][a] n.235;
    15.03[6][b] n.239; 15.03[7][b][i] n.266;
    16.02[4][d][i] n.250
26.2642-2(b)(2)(i) . . . . 16.02[4][d][ii] ns. 262,
    263
26.2642-2(b)(2)(i)(A) . . . . 16.02[4][d][ii] n.264
26.2642-2(b)(2)(i)(B) . . . . 16.02[4][d][ii] ns. 265,
    269
26.2642-2(b)(2)(ii) . . . . . . 16.02[4][d][ii] n.266
26.2642-2(b)(3) . . . . 15.03[6][a] n.235;
    15.03[6][b] n.239; 15.03[7][b][i] n.266;
    16.02[4][d][i] n.250; 16.02[4][d][iii]
    n.272
26.2642-2(b)(3)(i) . . . . 16.02[4][d][iii] ns. 273,
    276, 277, 279
26.2642-2(b)(3)(ii) . . . . 16.02[4][d][iii] ns. 273,
    279, 282
26.2642-2(b)(3)(ii)(A) . . . 16.02[4][d][iii] n.280
26.2642-2(b)(3)(ii)(B) . . . . 16.02[4][d][iii] n.281
26.2642-2(b)(4) . . . 17.04[2][a] n.52; 17.04[2][b]
    ns. 67, 74
26.2642-2(b)(4)(i) . . . . . 16.02[4][d][iii] n.274
26.2642-2(b)(4)(i)(A)(1) . . . . . . 16.02[4][d][iii]
    n.274
26.2642-2(b)(4)(i)(A)(2) . . . . . . 16.02[4][d][iii]
    n.274
26.2642-2(b)(4)(i)(B) . . . . 16.02[4][d][iii] n.274

[Text references are to paragraphs and notes (9"n.");
references to the supplement are preceded by "S."]

Reg. §

26.2642-2(b)(4)(ii) . . . . . . 16.02[4][d][iii] n.275
26.2642-2(b)(4)(ii)(A) . . . . 16.02[4][d][iii] ns.
        275, 278
26.2642-2(b)(4)(ii)(B) . . . . 16.02[4][d][iii] n.275
26.2642-2(c) . . . 16.02[1] n.6; 16.02[4][c] n.246
26.2642-3 . . . . 16.02[3][b][i] n.169;
        16.02[5][b][iii] n.336; 16.02[6] n.402
26.2642-3(a)(2) . . . . 16.02[3][b][ii] n.174
26.2642-3(b) . . . . 16.02[6] ns. 415, 425
26.2642-3(c) . . . . 15.02[1] n.28; 16.02[6] n.425
26.2642-3(c) Ex. . . . . S15.02[1] n.22
26.2642-4 . . . . 16.02[2][b][v] n.120;
        16.02[3][b][i] n.169; 16.02[3][b][ii]
        n.174; 16.02[5][a] n.301; 18.03[2][c]
        n.58
26.2642-4(a) . . . . . . 16.02[1] n.23; 16.02[5][a]
        n.302; 16.02[5][b][i] n.316
26.2642-4(a)(1) . . . . 16.02[1] n.24; 16.02[5][a]
        n.303; 16.02[5][c] n.358
26.2642-4(a)(2) . . . . . 15.02[2] n.50; S15.02[2]
        n.44; S15.02[2] n.44; 16.02[1] n.25;
        16.02[3][b][iii] n.200; 16.02[5][a] n.304;
        16.02[5][c] n.357
26.2642-4(a)(3) . . . . 16.02[1] n.23; 16.02[5][a]
        n.302
26.2642-4(a)(4) . . . . 14.05[2][a] n.21;
        15.03[7][b][iii] n.285; 16.02[1] n.28;
        16.02[3][b][iii] n.202; 16.02[5][a] n.307;
        16.02[5][c] n.358; 17.04[1][c] n.36;
        18.03[1][a] n.12; 18.03[1][b] n.16
26.2642-4(a)(4)(i) . . . 15.02[2] n.50; S15.02[2]
        n.44; 15.03[7][a] n.260; 15.03[7][b][iii]
        ns. 283, 284; 16.02[4][d][i] n.255;
        16.02[5][f][i] ns. 387–391, 393;
        16.02[5][f][ii] n.395; 18.03[1][a] ns. 12,
        14; 18.03[1][b] ns. 17–19, 23, 25
26.2642-4(a)(4)(ii) . . . . . . 16.02[4][d][i] n.255;
        16.02[5][f][i] n.394; 18.03[1][b] ns. 20,
        21
26.2642-4(a)(4)(iii) . . . . . . 15.03[6][b] n.242;
        16.02[4][d][i] n.255
26.2642-4(b) . . . . 15.02[1] n.29; 15.03[2][b] ns.
        28, 29; 15.03[3][b] n.50; 16.02[5][b][iii]
        ns. 335, 340, 346, 350, 352–354;
        16.02[7][a] ns. 430, 433; 16.02[7][e][i]
        n.511; 16.02[7][e][iii] ns. 533, 540
26.2642-4(b) Ex. 3 . . . . S15.02[1] n.23
26.2642-5(a) . . . . 16.02[8][a] ns. 556, 557
26.2642-5(b) . . . . 16.02[8][b] n.560
26.2642-5(b)(1) . . . . 16.02[8][b] n.559
26.2642-5(b)(2) . . . . 16.02[8][b] n.560
26.2642-6 . . . . S16.02[5][e] n.366
26.2642-6(b) . . . . S16.02[5][e] n.366
26.2642-6(d) . . . . S16.02[5][e] n.367
26.2642-6(d)(2) . . . . S16.02[5][e] n.369
26.2642-6(d)(3) . . . . S16.02[5][e] n.383.3
26.2642-6(d)(4) . . . . S16.02[5][e] n.370
26.2642-6(d)(5) . . . . S16.02[5][e] n.371
26.2642-6(d)(6) . . . . S16.02[5][e] n.373
26.2642-6(d)(7) . . . . S16.02[5][e] ns. 376–378,
        381

Reg. §

26.2642-6(d)(7)(ii) . . . . . S16.02[5][e] ns. 376,
        377, 381
26.2642-6(e) . . . . S16.02[5][e] n.383.4
26.2642-6(e)(1) . . . . S16.02[5][e] n.383.4
26.2642-6(e)(2) . . . . S16.02[5][e] n.383.4
26.2642-6(f)(1) . . . . S16.02[5][e] n.383.1
26.2642-6(f)(2) . . . . S16.02[5][e] n.383.2
26.2642-6(g)(2) . . . . S16.02[5][e] n.364
26.2642-6(h) . . . . S16.02[5][e] n.366
26.2642-6(j) Ex. 1 . . . . . . S16.02[5][e] ns. 371,
        372, 380
26.2642-6(j) Ex. 2 . . . S16.02[5][e] ns. 368, 371
26.2642-6(j) Ex. 3 . . . . . S16.02[5][e] n.371
26.2642-6(j) Ex. 4 . . . . . . S16.02[5][e] ns. 370,
        377, 378
26.2642-6(j) Ex. 5 . . . . . . S16.02[5][e] ns. 370,
        377, 378
26.2642-6(j) Ex. 6 . . . . S16.02[5][e] n.370
26.2642-6(j) Ex. 7 . . . S16.02[5][e] ns. 376, 381
26.2642-6(j) Ex. 8 . . . . . . S16.02[5][e] ns. 365,
        380, 383.2
26.2642-6(j) Ex. 9 . . . . . S16.02[5][e] ns. 376,
        377, 381
26.2642-6(j) Ex. 10 . . . . S16.02[5][e] ns. 365,
        382
26.2642-6(j) Ex. 11 . . . . . S16.02[5][e] n.383.3
26.2642-6(j) Ex. 12 . . . . S16.02[5][e] n.366
26.2642-6(j) Ex. 13 . . . . . S16.02[5][e] n.366
26.2642-6(k) . . . . S16.02[5][e] n.383.3
26.2651-1–26.2651-2 . . . . S17.01[2][a][ii] n.18
26.2651-1(a)(1) . . . . S17.01[2][a][ii] n.20
26.2651-1(a)(2)(i) . . . . . . S17.01[2][a][ii] n.21
26.2651-1(a)(2)(ii) . . . . . S17.01[2][a][ii] n.26.1
26.2651-1(a)(2)(iii) . . . . . S17.01[2][a][ii] n.28
26.2651-1(a)(2)(iv) . . . . . S17.01[2][a][ii] n.28
26.2651-1(a)(3) . . . . . S17.01[2][a][ii] ns. 37.1,
        37.2
26.2651-1(a)(4) . . . . S17.01[2][a][ii] ns. 18, 37
26.2651-1(b) . . . . S17.01[2][a][ii] n.29
26.2651-1(c) Ex. 1 . . . S17.01[2][a][ii] ns. 26,
        26.1
26.2651-1(c) Ex. 2 . . . . . S17.01[2][a][ii] n.36
26.2651-1(c) Ex. 3 . . . . S17.01[2][a][ii] n.37.2
26.2651-1(c) Ex. 4 . . . . S17.01[2][a][ii] n.37.1
26.2651-1(c) Ex. 5 . . . . . S17.01[2][a][ii] n.30
26.2651-1(c) Ex. 6 . . . . . S17.01[2][a][ii] n.30
26.2651-1(c) Ex. 7 . . . . . S17.01[2][a][ii] n.22
26.2651-2(b) . . . . S17.01[2][a][iii] ns. 45.1, 45.2
26.2651-2(b)(4) . . . . . . S17.01[2][a][iii] n.45.1
26.2651-2(b)(4)(i) . . . . S17.01[2][a][iii] n.45.1
26.2651-2(b)(4)(ii) . . . . S17.01[2][a][iii] n.45.1
26.2651-3(a) . . . . S17.01[2][a][ii] n.18
26.2652-1(a) . . . . 17.02[1][b] n.12
26.2652-1(a)(1) . . . . 13.02[2][e][ii] n.120
26.2652-1(a)(2) . . . . 4.02[7][e][iv] n.417;
        13.01[1] n.5; 13.01[2][b][i] ns. 23, 25;
        13.02[4][a] n.241; 13.02[4][b][i] ns. 257,
        263, 268; 15.03[4][b][i] ns. 98, 102;
        16.02[2][b][ii] n.56; 17.02[1][b] ns. 13,
        17, 20, 21, 25, 29

[Text references are to paragraphs and notes (9"n.");
references to the supplement are preceded by "S."]

Reg. §

26.2652-1(a)(3) . . . . 13.02[4][b][i] n.273;
    16.02[4][e] n.286; 17.02[1][c][i] ns. 47,
    48; 17.02[1][d] n.73; 18.05[2][b][ii] n.46
26.2652-1(a)(4) . . . . . 17.02[1][c][ii] ns. 61, 62
26.2652-1(a)(5) . . . . . 13.02[2][e][ii] ns. 96, 120,
    141; 13.02[4][b][i] ns. 270, 273;
    13.02[4][b][iii] n.297; 13.03[3][b] n.71;
    15.03[4][b][iii] n.119; 16.02[2][b][iii] ns.
    71, 73; 16.02[2][b][iv] n.108;
    16.02[2][b][v] ns. 114, 118; 17.02[1][b]
    n.21; 17.02[1][b] ns. 36, 37;
    17.02[1][c][i] ns. 46, 48; 17.02[1][c][ii]
    n.62; 17.02[1][d] ns. 72, 73;
    17.02[3][e][i] ns. 162, 166;
    17.02[3][e][ii] n.173; 18.05[2][b][ii] n.46
26.2652-1(b) . . . . 18.05[2][b] n.8
26.2652-1(b)(1) . . . . . 17.02[2] ns. 78, 79, 97
26.2652-1(b)(2) . . . . 16.02[2][b][iii] n.74;
    17.02[2] ns. 77–79
26.2652-1(c) . . . . 17.02[2] ns. 92, 96
26.2652-1(d) . . . . 12.03[1] n.9
26.2652-1(e) . . . 13.02[2][b][i] n.31; 17.02[3][a]
    n.108
26.2652-2(a) . . . . 16.02[4][e] n.286;
    17.02[1][c][i] ns. 49, 51, 52, 55
26.2652-2(b) . . . . 17.02[1][c][i] ns. 53, 54
26.2652-2(c) . . . . 17.02[1][c][i] n.52
26.2652-2(d) . . . . 13.02[2][d] ns. 76, 87;
    16.02[4][e] ns. 285–287, 291;
    17.02[1][c][i] ns. 48, 58
26.2653-1 . . . . 17.03[1] n.2
26.2653-1(a) . . . . 17.03[1] ns. 4, 14
26.2653-1(b) . . . . 17.03[1] ns. 2, 4, 14
26.2654-1 . . . . S16.02[5][e] n.366
26.2654-1(a) . . . . 17.04[2][a] n.55
26.2654-1(a)(1)(i) . . . 13.02[2][f] ns. 197, 199;
    17.04[2][a] ns. 50, 51, 53, 54;
    S17.04[2][a] n.51
26.2654-1(a)(1)(ii) . . . . . 17.04[2][a] ns. 48, 52
26.2654-1(a)(1)(ii)(A) . . . . 17.04[2][a] n.52
26.2654-1(a)(1)(ii)(B) . . . . 17.04[2][a] n.52
26.2654-1(a)(2) . . . . 17.01[2][a][ii] n.37;
    17.02[1][d] n.65; 17.04[2][a] ns. 49, 54
26.2654-1(a)(2)(i) . . . . . . 13.02[2][e][ii] n.121;
    16.02[2][b][v] n.114; 17.02[1][d] ns. 66,
    67
26.2654-1(a)(2)(ii) . . . . . 17.02[1][d] ns. 66, 69;
    17.04[2][a] n.54
26.2654-1(a)(3) . . . . . 16.02[5][e] ns. 363, 369,
    373; S16.02[5][e] ns. 363, 374;
    17.04[2][b] ns. 65, 67
26.2654-1(a)(4)(i) . . . . 17.04[2][a] n.56
26.2654-1(a)(4)(ii) . . . . 17.04[2][a] ns. 58–60
26.2654-1(a)(5) . . . . 16.02[5][e] n.371;
    17.02[1][d] ns. 68, 70; 17.04[2][a] ns.
    49, 51, 52
26.2654-1(a)(5) Ex. 1 . . . . . . S17.04[2][a] n.51
26.2654-1(a)(5) Ex. 2 . . . . . . S17.04[2][a] n.51
26.2654-1(b) . . . . . . 16.02[5][e] ns. 363, 369;
    S16.02[5][e] n.363; 17.02[1][c][i] n.49
26.2654-1(b)(1) . . . . 18.02[6] n.66

26.2654-1(b)(1)(i) . . . . 17.04[2][b] n.68
26.2654-1(b)(1)(ii) . . . . 17.04[2][b] n.69
26.2654-1(b)(1)(ii)(A) . . . . . 16.02[5][e] n.370;
    17.04[2][b] ns. 67, 70, 74
26.2654-1(b)(1)(ii)(B) . . . 17.04[2][b] ns. 67, 72,
    74
26.2654-1(b)(1)(ii)(C) . . . . 5.06[8][d][iii] n.381;
    16.02[5][e] ns. 363, 373; S16.02[5][e]
    ns. 363, 374
26.2654-1(b)(1)(ii)(C)(1) . . . . 16.02[5][e] n.369;
    17.04[2][b] ns. 66, 73
26.2654-1(b)(1)(ii)(C)(2) . . . 17.04[2][b] ns. 67,
    74
26.2654-1(b)(2) . . . . 17.04[2][b] n.71
26.2654-1(b)(4) . . . . 17.04[2][b] n.69
26.2662-1 . . . . 18.02[1] n.7
26.2662-1(b)(1) . . . 18.02[2][a] ns. 8, 10, 12, 13
26.2662-1(b)(2) . . . . 18.02[2][a] ns. 9, 10, 14
26.2662-1(b)(3) . . . . 18.02[2][b] n.15
26.2662-1(b)(3)(i) . . . . . 16.02[2][b][iii] n.53;
    18.02[2][b] ns. 16, 21
26.2662-1(b)(3)(ii)(A) . . . . . . 18.02[2][b] n.17
26.2662-1(b)(3)(ii)(B) . . . . . . 18.02[2][b] n.17
26.2662-1(c) . . . . 18.02[3] n.30
26.2662-1(c)(1) . . . . . 12.03[1] n.3; 13.02[1][b]
    n.21
26.2662-1(c)(1)(i) . . . 12.02 n.20; 12.03[1] n.5;
    18.02[3][a] n.31; 18.02[6] n.65
26.2662-1(c)(1)(ii) . . . . . 12.02 n.20; 12.03[1]
    n.15; 18.02[3][a] n.32
26.2662-1(c)(1)(iii) . . . . . . 12.02 n.21; 12.03[1] n.7;
    18.02[3][a] n.33
26.2662-1(c)(1)(iv) . . . . . 12.02 n.22; 12.03[1]
    n.15; 18.02[3][a] n.34
26.2662-1(c)(1)(v) . . . . . 12.02 n.23; 12.03[1] n.12;
    18.02[3][a] n.35
26.2662-1(c)(2) . . . . 12.03[2] ns. 21, 27;
    13.02[1][b] n.21; 18.02[3][b] n.36
26.2662-1(c)(2)(i) . . . . 17.02[2] n.100
26.2662-1(c)(2)(ii) . . . . . 12.03[1] n.17; 12.03[2]
    ns. 19, 25; 18.02[2][b] n.17; 18.02[3][b]
    n.36; 18.03[3] n.66; 18.05[2][b] n.8
26.2662-1(c)(2)(iii) . . . 12.03[1] n.12; 12.03[2]
    ns. 21, 27, 28, 30; 14.04[3] n.15;
    17.02[2] ns. 99, 100; 18.02[2][b] n.17;
    18.02[3][b] n.37; 18.03[3] n.67
26.2662-1(c)(2)(iv) . . . 12.03[1] n.12; 12.03[2]
    ns. 21, 27, 28, 30; 17.02[2] n.99;
    18.02[3][b] n.37
26.2662-1(c)(2)(v) . . . . . 12.03[2] ns. 26, 28;
    14.04[3] n.15; 17.02[2] ns. 101, 102,
    104; 18.02[3][b] n.37; 18.03[3] n.67
26.2662-1(c)(2)(vi) . . . 12.03[2] ns. 23, 26, 27,
    29; 13.03[3][c] & n.74; 17.02[2] ns. 98,
    99, 102; 18.02[3][b] ns. 36–38; 18.03[3]
    n.67
26.2662-1(c)(3)(i) . . . . 12.03[3] n.32
26.2662-1(c)(3)(ii) . . . . 12.03[3] n.33
26.2662-1(c)(3)(iii) . . . . 12.03[3] n.34
26.2662-1(c)(4)(i) . . . . 18.02[3] n.30
26.2662-1(c)(4)(ii) . . . . 18.02[3] n.30

*[Text references are to paragraphs and notes (9"n.");
references to the supplement are preceded by "S."]*

Reg. §

26.2662-1(d)(1)(i)   18.02[4][a] ns. 41, 42, 44,
46
26.2662-1(d)(1)(ii) . . . . 13.02[3][c] n.234;
18.02[4][a] ns. 49, 52
26.2662-1(d)(2) . . . . 18.02[4][a] n.53
26.2662-1(e) . . . . 18.02[5] ns. 61, 62
26.2662-1(f) . . . . . . 12.03[1] n.8; 18.01[1] n.7
26.2663-1 . . . . 17.04[1][c] n.36; 18.03[1] n.2;
18.03[1][a] n.12; 18.03[1][b] n.16
26.2663-2 . . . . 18.03[2][a] n.27
26.2663-2(a) . . . . 18.03[2][a] ns. 29, 31;
18.03[2][c] n.50
26.2663-2(b) . . . 18.03[2][b] ns. 36, 38, 39, 41,
42, 44
26.2663-2(b)(2) . . . . 18.03[2][b] ns. 40, 45, 46;
18.03[2][c] n.47
26.2663-2(c)(1) . . . . 18.03[2][c] n.48
26.2663-2(c)(1)(i) . . . . . 18.03[2][c] ns. 51, 55
26.2663-2(c)(1)(ii) . . . . 18.03[2][c] n.59
26.2663-2(c)(2) . . . . 18.03[2][c] ns. 51–54
26.2663-2(c)(3) . . . 18.03[2][c] n.49; 18.03[2][d]
ns. 61, 63
26.2663-2(d) . . . . 18.03[2][b] ns. 43, 45;
18.03[2][c] ns. 47–49, 54, 57;
18.03[2][d] n.61
26.6081-1 . . . . S18.02[4][b] n.60
26.6081-1(c) . . . . S18.02[4][b] n.60
81.47(a) . . . . 5.06[3][a] n.29
81.47(g) . . . . 5.06[3][a] n.29
301.6114-1(b)(8) . . . . 7.01[1] n.1
301.6159-1 . . . . S2.02[3][a] n.28
301.6159-1(e)(1) . . . . S2.02[3][a] n.31
301.6159-1(e)(2) . . . . S2.02[3][a] n.34
301.6159-1(e)(3) . . . . S2.02[3][a] n.35
301.6324A-1(e) . . . . S2.02[3][c][iii] n.116
301.6501(c)-1(e) . . . . S10.02[2][d][iii] n.130.1;
19.02[5][d] n.491; S19.02[5][d] n.491;
19.03[4][d] n.354; S19.03[4][d] n.354
301.6501(c)-1(e)(2)   9.04[10][a] ns. 218, 220;
19.02[5][d] ns. 491, 492; 19.03[4][d] ns.
354, 355
301.6501(c)-1(e)(2)(i) . . . . . . 19.02[5][d] n.493;
19.03[4][d] n.356
301.6501(c)-1(e)(2)(ii) . . . . . 19.02[5][d] n.494;
19.03[4][d] n.357
301.6501(c)-1(e)(2)(iii) . . . . . 19.02[5][d] n.495;
19.03[4][d] n.358
301.6501(c)-1(e)(3) . . . . 9.04[10][a] n.220
301.6501(c)-1(f) . . . . S10.02[2][d][iii] n.130.1;
S19.02[5][d] n.491; S19.03[4][d] n.354
301.6501(c)-1(f)(2)   2.01[1][b][ii] ns. 32, 33;
S2.01[1][b][ii] ns. 32, 33; 9.04[10][a] ns.
220, 222; 19.02[5][d] n.491; 19.03[4][d]
n.354
301.6501(c)-1(f)(2)(i) . . . . . 2.01[1][b][ii] n.34;
S2.01[1][b][ii] n.34; 9.04[10][a] n.223
301.6501(c)-1(f)(2)(ii) . . . . 2.01[1][b][ii] n.35;
S2.01[1][b][ii] n.35; 9.04[10][a] n.224
301.6501(c)-1(f)(2)(iii) . . . . 2.01[1][b][ii] n.36;
S2.01[1][b][ii] n.36; 9.04[10][a] n.225

Reg. §

301.6501(c)-1(f)(2)(iv) . . . 2.01[1][b][ii] ns. 37,
39; S2.01[1][b][ii] ns. 37, 39; 9.04[10][a]
ns. 226, 228; S9.04[10][a] n.219
301.6501(c)-1(f)(2)(v) . . . . 2.01[1][b][ii] n.40;
S2.01[1][b][ii] n.40; 9.04[10][a] n.229
301.6501(c)-1(f)(3)   2.01[1][b][ii] ns. 32, 33,
39; S2.01[1][b][ii] ns. 32, 33, 39;
9.04[10][a] ns. 220, 222, 228;
19.02[5][d] n.491; 19.03[4][d] n.354
301.6501(c)-1(f)(3)(i) . . . . . 2.01[1][b][ii] n.39;
S2.01[1][b][ii] n.39; 9.04[10][a] n.228
301.6501(c)-1(f)(3)(i)(B) . . . . 9.04[10][a] n.227
301.6501(c)-1(f)(3)(ii) . . . . 2.01[1][b][ii] n.38;
S2.01[1][b][ii] n.38; 9.04[10][a] n.227
301.6501(c)-1(f)(4) . . . . . . 2.01[1][b][ii] n.30;
S2.01[1][b][ii] n.30; S9.04[10][a] n.219;
9.04[10][b] ns. 232, 233
301.6501(c)-1(f)(4)(i) . . . . . . 9.04[10][b] n.230
301.6501(c)-1(f)(4)(ii) . . . . 9.04[10][b] n.231
301.6501(c)-1(f)(5) . . . . . 2.01[1][b][ii] n.30;
S2.01[1][b][ii] n.30; 9.04[10][b] ns. 234,
235
301.6501(c)-1(f)(6) . . . . . . 2.01[1][b][ii] n.30;
S2.01[1][b][ii] n.30; 9.04[10][b] n.237
301.6501(c)-1(f)(7)   2.01[1][b][ii] ns. 28, 30,
37, 38; 9.04[10][a] ns. 221, 226, 228;
9.04[10][b] n.233
301.6501(c)-1(f)(7) Ex. 1 . . . . . S2.01[1][b][ii]
n.37
301.6501(c)-1(f)(7) Ex. 2 . . . . . S2.01[1][b][ii]
n.28
301.6501(c)-1(f)(7) Ex. 3 . . . . . S2.01[1][b][ii]
n.37
301.6501(c)-1(f)(7) Ex. 4 . . . . . S2.01[1][b][ii]
n.37
301.6501(c)-1(f)(7) Ex. 5 . . . S2.01[1][b][ii] ns.
37, 38
301.6501(c)-1(f)(7) Ex. 6 . . . . . S2.01[1][b][ii]
n.30
301.6501(c)-1(f)(8) . . . . . . 2.01[1][b][ii] n.32;
S2.01[1][b][ii] n.32; 9.04[10][a] n.220
301.6903-1(a) . . . . 2.02[1] n.18
301.6903-1(b) . . . . 2.02[1] n.18
301.6905-1 . . . . 9.04[11] n.250
301.7101-1 . . . . 5.07[3][c][i] n.73
301.7477-1 . . . . S10.02[2][d][iii] n.130.1
301.7477-1(a) . . . . . S10.02[2][d][iii] ns. 127.1,
130.2
301.7477-1(b)(1) . . . . S10.02[2][d][iii] n.130.3
301.7477-1(b)(2) . . . . S10.02[2][d][iii] n.130.3
301.7477-1(b)(3) . . . . . S10.02[2][d][iii] n.128
301.7477-1(c) . . . . S10.02[2][d][iii] n.129
301.7477-1(d)(2) . . . . S10.02[2][d][iii] n.130.1
301.7477-1(d)(3) . . . . S10.02[2][d][iii] n.130.3
301.7477-1(d)(4) . . . . . S10.02[2][d][iii] n.128
301.7477-1(d)(5) . . . . S10.02[2][d][iii] n.130.3
301.7477-1(e) Ex. 1 . . . . S10.02[2][d][iii] n.128
301.7477-1(e) Ex. 2 . . . . S10.02[2][d][iii] n.128
301.7477-1(e) Ex. 3 . . . . S10.02[2][d][iii] n.128
301.7477-1(e) Ex. 4 . . . . S10.02[2][d][iii] n.129
301.7477-1(e) Ex. 5 . . . . S10.02[2][d][iii] n.130

Reg. §

301.7477-1(f) . . . . . S10.02[2][d][iii] n.130.1
301.7502-1(c)(1) . . . . 10.07[2][b] n.30
301.7502-1(c)(2) . . . . 10.07[2][b] n.30
301.7502-1(d)(3)(ii) . . . . 10.07[2][b] n.30
301.7502-1(e) . . . . 10.07[2][b] n.30
301.7503-1(b) . . . . 10.07[2][b] n.30
301.7517-1 . . . . 4.02[6][c] n.269; 10.02[2][d][ii]
ns. 125, 126
301.7701-1(a)(1) . . . . 4.05[7][c] n.88
301.7701-2 . . . . . . 5.07[3] n.39; 19.02[2][a][ii]
n.67; 19.02[2][d][i] n.145;
19.02[2][d][iii] n.151
301.7701-2(a) . . . . 4.05[7][c] n.88
301.7701-2(b)(8) . . . . 6.04[1] n.9
301.7701-3 . . . . . 5.07[3] n.39; 5.08[2][c] n.53;
19.02[2][a][ii] n.67; 19.02[2][d][ii] n.148;
19.02[2][d][iii] n.151
301.7701-3(a) . . . . 4.05[7][c] n.88
301.7701-3(b)(1) . . . . 4.05[7][c] n.88
301.7701-4 . . . . . . 5.07[3] n.39; 13.03[3] n.27;
19.02[2][d][iii] n.151
301.7701-4(a) . . . . 5.07[3] n.39; 12.03[1] n.17;
13.03[3] n.28; 18.02[3][b] n.36
301.7701-4(b) . . . . 13.03[3] n.28
301.7701-4(c) . . . . 13.03[3] n.28
301.7701-4(d) . . . . 13.03[3] n.28
301.7701-4(e) . . . . 13.03[3] n.28
301.7701-15 . . . . S4.02[6][b] n.264.4
301.7701(b)-7(c) . . . . 7.01[1] n.1
301.9001-1(a) . . . . 5.06[8][d][iii] n.383
301.9100 . . . S5.06[8][d][iii] n.384; 5.07[3][c][i]
ns. 75, 82; S5.08[3][b][i] n.92;
16.02[9][a] n.576; 17.02[1][c][i] n.54
301.9100-1 . . . . S4.03[1] n.3; 17.02[1][c][i] ns.
52, 54
301.9100-1(a) . . . . 5.07[3][d] n.117
301.9100-1(c) . . . . 5.03[2][b] n.18
301.9100-2(b) . . . . S17.02[1][c][i] n.54
301.9100-3 . . . S2.02[3][c][ii] n.57; 4.03[1] n.3;
S4.03[1] n.3; 4.04[6] n.214; S5.05[2][a]
n.58; 5.06[8][d][iii] n.369; 5.07[5] n.184;
16.02[9][a] n.577; S16.02[9][a] n.574;
17.02[1][c][i] ns. 52, 54; S17.04[2][b]
n.72; S18.05[2][b][iii] n.80
301.9200-2 . . . . 4.04[6] n.215

TEMPORARY
REGULATIONS

Temp. Reg. §

1.25A-5(a)(1) . . . . 9.04[6] n.183
1.25A-5(a)(2) . . . . 9.04[6] n.183
1.170A-1(h)(2)(i) . . . . 5.05[7][b] n.339
1.170A-7(b)(1)(i) . . . . 5.05[7][b] n.339

Temp. Reg. §

1.170A-12T . . . . S3.05[3][b] n.29; S4.02[5] ns.
244, 247; S4.08[1][a] n.5; S4.11[4][a]
n.40; S5.05[3][a] n.95; S5.05[5][a][ii]
n.207; S5.05[5][b][ii] n.264;
S5.05[5][c][ii] n.291; S5.05[6][b] n.327;
S5.05[7][a] n.333; S5.06[7][d] n.197;
S5.06[8][d][ii] n.348; S9.04[3][a] n.48;
S10.02[2][b][iii] n.56; S11.02[1][b] n.27;
S16.02[6] n.409; S19.03[1] n.3;
S19.03[3][b] n.112; S19.03[3][d] n.162
1.170A-13(c)(3) . . . . . . 5.05[5][a][ii] n.205;
5.05[5][b][ii] n.262
1.170A-13(c)(5) . . . . . . 5.05[5][a][ii] n.205;
5.05[5][b][ii] n.262
1.170A-14   5.05[7][c] n.342; 11.02[2][d] n.99
1.170A-14(h)(3)(iii) . . . . 4.02[7][e][iii] ns. 395,
400, 403
1.170A-14(h)(4)   4.02[7][e][iii] ns. 395, 400,
403
1.642(c)-6T . . . . S3.05[3][b] n.29; S4.02[5] ns.
244, 247; S4.08[1][a] n.5; S4.11[4][a]
n.40; S5.05[3][a] n.95; S5.05[5][a][ii]
n.207; S5.05[5][b][ii] n.264;
S5.05[5][c][ii] n.291; S5.05[6][b] n.327;
S5.05[7][a] n.333; S5.06[7][d] n.197;
S5.06[8][d][ii] n.348; S9.04[3][a] n.48;
S10.02[2][b][iii] n.56; S11.02[1][b] n.27;
S16.02[6] n.409; S19.03[1] n.3;
S19.03[3][b] n.112; S19.03[3][d] n.162
1.642(c)-6A . . . . 5.05[5][c][ii] n.287
1.664-4T   S3.05[3][b] n.29; S4.02[5] ns. 244,
247; S4.08[1][a] n.5; S4.11[4][a] n.40;
S5.05[3][a] n.95; S5.05[5][a][ii] n.207;
S5.05[5][b][ii] n.264; S5.05[5][c][ii]
n.291; S5.05[6][b] n.327; S5.05[7][a]
n.333; S5.06[7][d] n.197; S5.06[8][d][ii]
n.348; S9.04[3][a] n.48; S10.02[2][b][iii]
n.56; S11.02[1][b] n.27; S16.02[6] n.409;
S19.03[1] n.3; S19.03[3][b] n.112;
S19.03[3][d] n.162
1.664-4T(d) . . . . 5.05[5][b][ii] n.263
1.664-4T(e) . . . 5.05[5][b][ii] n.263; 5.05[6][b]
n.327
1.664-4T(e)(4) . . . . 5.05[5][b][ii] n.264
1.664-4T(e)(5) . . . . 5.05[5][b][ii] n.264
1.664-4T(e)(6) . . . . 5.05[5][b][ii] n.264
1.664-4T(e)(7) . . . . 5.05[5][b][ii] n.264
1.1041-1T(b) . . . . 10.06[2][c] n.29
1.7520-1T . . . . . S3.05[3][b] n.29; S4.02[5] ns.
244, 247; S4.08[1][a] n.5; S4.11[4][a]
n.40; S5.05[3][a] n.95; S5.05[5][a][ii]
n.207; S5.05[5][b][ii] n.264;
S5.05[5][c][ii] n.291; S5.05[6][b] n.327;
S5.05[7][a] n.333; S5.06[7][d] n.197;
S5.06[8][d][ii] n.348; S9.04[3][a] n.48;
S10.02[2][b][iii] n.56; S11.02[1][b] n.27;
S16.02[6] n.409; S19.03[1] n.3;
S19.03[3][b] n.112; S19.03[3][d] n.162
15A.453-1(d)(2)(iii) . . . . 10.02[1][b] n.13

[Text references are to paragraphs and notes (9"n.");
references to the supplement are preceded by "S."]

Temp. Reg. §

20.2031-7T . . . . S3.05[3][b] n.29; S4.02[5] ns.
 244, 247; S4.08[1][a] n.5; S4.11[4][a]
 n.40; S5.05[3][a] n.95; S5.05[5][a][ii]
 n.207; S5.05[5][b][ii] n.264;
 S5.05[5][c][ii] n.291; S5.05[6][b] n.327;
 S5.05[7][a] n.333; S5.06[7][d] n.197;
 S5.06[8][d][ii] n.348; S9.04[3][a] n.48;
 S10.02[2][b][iii] n.56; S11.02[1][b] n.27;
 S16.02[6] n.409; S19.03[1] n.3;
 S19.03[3][b] n.112; S19.03[3][d] n.162
20.2031-7A . . . 4.02[5] n.244; 4.05[5][b] n.57;
 4.11[4][a] n.40; 5.05[6][b] n.328;
 5.06[8][d][ii] n.348
20.2031-7A(d)(6) . . . . 19.03[1] n.10
20.2031-7A(e)(4) . . . . 4.08[1][a] n.5
20.2032A-1T . . . . n.29; S4.02[5] ns. 244, 247;
 S4.08[1][a] n.5; S4.11[4][a] n.40;
 S5.05[3][a] n.95; S5.05[5][a][ii] n.207;
 S5.05[5][b][ii] n.264; S5.05[5][c][ii]
 n.291; S5.05[6][b] n.327; S5.05[7][a]
 n.333; S5.06[7][d] n.197; S5.06[8][d][ii]
 n.348; S9.04[3][a] n.48; S10.02[2][b][iii]
 n.56; S11.02[1][b] n.27; S16.02[6] n.409;
 S19.03[1] n.3; S19.03[3][b] n.112;
 S19.03[3][d] n.162
20.2056A . . . . 5.08[5][b][iii] n.248
20.2056A-1 – 20.2056A-13 . . . . . . 5.07[1] n.7
20.2056A-1(a) . . . . 5.06[9] n.429
20.2056A-1(a)(1) . . . . 5.06[1] n.4
20.2056A-1(a)(1)(i) . . . 5.07[1] n.4; 5.07[2] n.8
20.2056A-1(a)(1)(ii) . . . . 5.07[2][a] n.9
20.2056A-1(a)(1)(iii) . . . 5.07[2][b] ns. 17, 20;
 5.07[3][d] n.118
20.2056A-1(a)(1)(iv) . . . . 5.07[2][c] n.30
20.2056A-1(b)   5.06[9] ns. 431, 432; 5.07[5]
 ns. 178, 180
20.2056A-1(c) . . . . 5.06[9] n.426
20.2056A-2 . . . . 5.07[3][c] n.49
20.2056A-2(a) . . . . 5.07[3] ns. 38, 39
20.2056A-2(b) . . . . 5.07[3] n.37
20.2056A-2(b)(1) . . . . 5.07[3][e] ns. 122, 126
20.2056A-2(b)(2) . . . . . . 5.07[2][b] ns. 17, 20
20.2056A-2(b)(3) . . . . 5.07[2][c] n.30
20.2056A-2(c) . . . . 5.07[3][a] n.44
20.2056A-2(d) . . . . . 5.07[1] n.7; 5.07[3] n.37
20.2056A-2(d)(1) . . . . 5.07[3][c][i] n.66;
 5.07[3][c][iv] n.116
20.2056A-2(d)(1)(i) . . . . 5.07[3][c] ns. 48, 53;
 5.07[3][c][i] n.65; 5.07[3][c][ii] n.99
20.2056A-2(d)(1)(i)(A) . . . . 5.07[3][c][i] ns. 68,
 69
20.2056A-2(d)(1)(i)(B) . . . . 5.07[3][c][i] ns. 70,
 71, 80
20.2056A-2(d)(1)(i)(B)(1) . . . . 5.07[3][c][i] ns.
 72, 73
20.2056A-2(d)(1)(i)(B)(2) . . . 5.07[3][c][i] n.74
20.2056A-2(d)(1)(i)(B)(3) . . . 5.07[3][c][i] n.72
20.2056A-2(d)(1)(i)(B)(4) . . . 5.07[3][c][i] n.75

Temp. Reg. §

20.2056A-2(d)(1)(i)(C) . . . 5.07[3][c][i] ns. 76–
 78, 80
20.2056A-2(d)(1)(i)(C)(1) . . . . 5.07[3][c][i] ns.
 79, 80
20.2056A-2(d)(1)(i)(C)(2) . . . 5.07[3][c][i] n.81
20.2056A-2(d)(1)(i)(C)(3) . . . 5.07[3][c][i] n.81
20.2056A-2(d)(1)(i)(C)(4) . . . 5.07[3][c][i] n.80
20.2056A-2(d)(1)(i)(C)(5) . . . 5.07[3][c][i] n.82
20.2056A-2(d)(1)(i)(D)(1) . . . . 5.07[3][c][i] ns.
 83–85
20.2056A-2(d)(1)(i)(D)(2) . . . 5.07[3][c][i] n.86
20.2056A-2(d)(1)(ii) . . . . 5.07[3][c] ns. 52, 53;
 5.07[3][c][ii] ns. 89, 90
20.2056A-2(d)(1)(ii)(A) . . . . . 5.07[3][c] n.54
20.2056A-2(d)(1)(ii)(B) . . . . . 5.07[3][c][ii] ns.
 92–94
20.2056A-2(d)(1)(ii)(C) . . . . 5.07[3][c][ii] n.95
20.2056A-2(d)(1)(i)(C) . . . 5.07[3][c][ii] n.101
20.2056A-2(d)(1)(iii) . . . . 5.07[3][c] n.52
20.2056A-2(d)(1)(iv)(A) . . . . 5.07[3][c] ns. 55,
 61; 5.07[3][c][i] n.85
20.2056A-2(d)(1)(iv)(B) . . . . . 5.07[3][c] n.63;
 5.07[3][c][i] ns. 70, 77
20.2056A-2(d)(1)(iv)(C) . . . . . 5.07[3][c] n.57;
 5.07[3][c][ii] n.91
20.2056A-2(d)(1)(iv)(D) . . . 5.07[3][c] ns. 59–
 61
20.2056A-2(d)(1)(iv)(E) . . . . . . 5.07[3][c] n.58
20.2056A-2(d)(1)(iv)(F) . . . . . 5.07[3][c] n.63
20.2056A-2(d)(1)(iv)(G) . . . . . 5.07[3][c] n.62
20.2056A-2(d)(1)(v) . . . . 5.07[2][a] n.12;
 5.07[3][c][iii] ns. 113–115
20.2056A-2(d)(2) . . . . 5.07[3][a] n.44
20.2056A-2(d)(3)(i)(A) . . . . . 5.07[3][c][iii] ns.
 102, 104, 105
20.2056A-2(d)(3)(i)(B) . . . . . . 5.07[3][c] n.63;
 5.07[3][c][iii] n.106
20.2056A-2(d)(3)(i)(C) . . . . 5.07[3][c][iii] ns.
 102, 104, 105
20.2056A-2(d)(3)(ii) . . . . 5.07[3][c][iii] ns. 112,
 113, 115
20.2056A-2(d)(3)(iii)(A)   5.07[3][c][iii] n.109
20.2056A-2(d)(3)(iii)(B)   5.07[3][c][iii] n.110
20.2056A-2(d)(3)(iii)(C)   5.07[3][c][iii] n.111
20.2056A-2(d)(3)(iii)(D)   5.07[3][c][iii] n.111
20.2056A-2(d)(4) . . . . 5.07[3][c][iv] n.116
20.2056A-2(d)(5) . . . . . . 5.07[3][c] ns. 51, 56
20.2056A-2(d)(6)(i) . . . . 5.07[1] n.7; 5.07[3][c]
 n.48
20.2056A-2(d)(6)(ii) . . . . 5.07[1] n.7; 5.07[3][c]
 n.48
20.2056A-2(d)(6)(iii) . . . 5.07[1] n.7; 5.07[3][c]
 n.48
20.2056A-3(a) . . . . 5.07[3][d] n.118
20.2056A-3(b) . . . . . . 5.07[3][d] ns. 119, 120
20.2056A-3(c) . . . . 5.07[3][d] n.121
20.2056A-3(d) . . . . 5.07[3][d] n.117

[Text references are to paragraphs and notes (9"n.");
references to the supplement are preceded by "S."]

Temp. Reg. §

20.2056A-4T . . . S3.05[3][b] n.29; S4.02[5] ns.
    244, 247; S4.08[1][a] n.5; S4.11[4][a]
    n.40; S5.05[3][a] n.95; S5.05[5][a][ii]
    n.207; S5.05[5][b][ii] n.264;
    S5.05[5][c][ii] n.291; S5.05[6][b] n.327;
    S5.05[7][a] n.333; S5.06[7][d] n.197;
    S5.06[8][d][ii] n.348; S9.04[3][a] n.48;
    S10.02[2][b][iii] n.56; S11.02[1][b] n.27;
    S16.02[6] n.409; S19.03[1] n.3;
    S19.03[3][b] n.112; S19.03[3][d] n.162
20.2056A-4(a)(1) . . . . . . 5.07[2][a] ns. 9–11
20.2056A-4(a)(2) . . . . 5.07[2][a] n.12;
    5.07[3][c][iii] n.115
20.2056A-4(b)(1) . . . 5.07[2][b] ns. 16, 18, 20
20.2056A-4(b)(2) . . . . . 5.07[2][b] ns. 19, 23
20.2056A-4(b)(2)(i) . . . . 4.04[5][b] n.205
20.2056A-4(b)(3) . . . . 5.07[2][b] n.22
20.2056A-4(b)(4)(i) . . . . 5.07[2][b] n.23
20.2056A-4(b)(4)(ii) . . . . 5.07[2][b] n.23
20.2056A-4(b)(5) . . . . . 5.07[2][b] ns. 25–27
20.2056A-4(b)(6) . . . . 5.07[2][b] n.21
20.2056A-4(b)(7)   5.07[2][b] n.14; 5.07[2][c]
    n.29
20.2056A-4(b)(8) . . . . 5.07[2][b] n.24
20.2056A-4(c) . . . . . . 5.07[2][c] ns. 29, 30
20.2056A-4(c)(1) . . . . . . 5.07[2][c] ns. 28, 29
20.2056A-4(c)(2) . . . . 5.07[2][c] n.32
20.2056A-4(c)(2)(i) . . . . 5.07[2][c] ns. 33, 36
20.2056A-4(c)(2)(ii) . . . . 5.07[2][c] n.33
20.2056A-4(c)(2)(iii) . . . . 5.07[2][c] n.33
20.2056A-4(c)(2)(iv) . . . . 5.07[2][c] n.33
20.2056A-4(c)(3) . . . . . 5.07[2][c] ns. 32, 34;
    5.07[4][a][i] n.133
20.2056A-4(c)(3)(i) . . . . 5.07[2][c] ns. 34, 36
20.2056A-4(c)(3)(ii) . . . . 5.07[2][c] n.34
20.2056A-4(c)(3)(iii) . . . . 5.07[2][c] n.34
20.2056A-4(c)(3)(iv) . . . . 5.07[2][c] n.34
20.2056A-4(c)(3)(v) . . . . 5.07[2][c] n.34
20.2056A-4(c)(4) . . . . 5.07[2][c] n.31
20.2056A-4(c)(5) . . . . . . 5.07[2][c] ns. 33, 34
20.2056A-4(c)(6) . . . . 5.07[2][c] n.33
20.2056A-4(c)(6)(i) . . . . 5.07[4][c] n.172
20.2056A-4(c)(7) . . . . 5.07[2][c] n.34
20.2056A-4(d) . . . . . 5.07[2][b] ns. 23, 26, 27;
    5.07[2][c] n.31
20.2056A-5(b)(1) . . . . 5.07[4][a][i] n.136
20.2056A-5(b)(2) . . . . . . 5.07[4][a][ii] n.137
20.2056A-5(b)(3) . . . . . . 5.07[4][a][iii] n.154
20.2056A-5(c)(1) . . . . 5.07[4][a][i] n.132
20.2056A-5(c)(2) . . . . 5.07[4][a][i] n.131
20.2056A-5(c)(3)(i) . . . . . . 5.07[4][a][i] n.134
20.2056A-5(c)(3)(ii) . . . . . . 5.07[4][a][i] n.134
20.2056A-5(c)(3)(iii) . . . . . 5.07[4][a][i] n.134
20.2056A-5(c)(3)(iv) . . . . . . 5.07[2][c] n.34;
    5.07[4][a][i] n.133
20.2056A-6(a) . . . . . 5.07[4][b] ns. 159, 160
20.2056A-6(b)(1) . . . . 5.07[4][a][ii] n.141
20.2056A-6(b)(2) . . . . 5.07[4][a][ii] n.141
20.2056A-6(b)(3)   5.07[4][a][ii] ns. 141, 151
20.2056A-6(b)(4)   5.07[4][a][ii] ns. 141, 143,
    144
20.2056A-6(b)(5) . . . . . . 5.07[4][a][ii] n.141

Temp. Reg. §

20.2056A-6(b)(5)(i) . . . . 5.07[4][a][ii] ns. 145,
    146
20.2056A-6(b)(5)(ii) . . . . . . 5.07[4][a][ii] n.145
20.2056A-6(b)(5)(iii) . . . . 5.07[4][a][ii] n.146
20.2056A-6(d) . . . . 5.07[4][a][ii] n.143;
    5.07[4][b] n.160
20.2056A-7 . . . . 5.06[9] n.444
20.2056A-7(a)(1) . . . . 5.06[9] n.444
20.2056A-7(a)(2) . . . . 5.06[9] n.444
20.2056A-7(a)(3) . . . . 5.06[9] n.445
20.2056A-7(b) . . . . . . 5.06[9] ns. 441, 445
20.2056A-7(c) . . . . . . 5.06[9] ns. 444, 445
20.2056A-8 . . . . 4.12[10] n.93
20.2056A-8(a)(1) . . . . 4.12[10] ns. 87, 93
20.2056A-8(a)(2) . . . . 4.12[10] n.88
20.2056A-8(a)(3) . . . . 4.12[10] n.93
20.2056A-8(b) . . . . 4.12[10] n.89
20.2056A-8(c) . . . . 4.12[10] n.88
20.2056A-9 . . . . 5.07[4][b] n.159
20.2056A-10(a)(2) . . . . 5.07[5] n.184
20.2056A-10(b)(1) . . . . 5.07[5] n.186
20.2056A-10(b)(2) . . . . 5.07[5] n.187
20.2056A-10(b)(3) . . . . 5.07[5] n.187
20.2056A-11 . . . . 5.07[4][a] n.129
20.2056A-11(a) . . . . 5.07[4][c] n.172
20.2056A-11(b) . . . . 5.07[4][c] n.170
20.2056A-11(c)(1)   5.07[4][a][ii] ns. 147, 148
20.2056A-11(c)(2) . . . . . . 5.07[4][a][i] n.130;
    5.07[4][a][ii] ns. 137, 147; 5.07[4][c]
    n.172
20.2056A-11(d) . . . . . 5.07[4][c] ns. 176, 177
20.2056A-12 . . . . 5.07[4][a][i] n.130
20.2056A-13 . . . . 5.07[1] n.7
20.2207A-1 . . . . 8.07[6] n.47
20.2207A-1(a)(1) . . . 8.07[2] ns. 12, 15; 8.07[5]
    n.41
20.2207A-1(a)(2) . . . . . 8.07[5] ns. 40, 42, 43
20.2207A-1(a)(3) . . . . 8.07[2] ns. 9, 10; 8.07[5]
    n.39
20.2207A-1(b) . . . . 8.07[2] ns. 13–15
20.2207A-1(c) . . . 8.07[2] n.14; 8.07[4] ns. 30,
    31
20.2207A-1(d) . . . 8.07[2] n.11; 8.07[4] ns. 32,
    36, 38
20.2207A-1(e) . . . . 8.07[2] n.14; 8.07[4] n.32
20.2207A-2 . . . . 8.07[6] ns. 46, 47
20.6324B-1(c) . . . . 4.04[6] n.246
20.7520-1T . . . . S3.05[3][b] n.29; S4.02[5] ns.
    244, 247; S4.08[1][a] n.5; S4.11[4][a]
    n.40; S5.05[3][a] n.95; S5.05[5][a][ii]
    n.207; S5.05[5][b][ii] n.264;
    S5.05[5][c][ii] n.291; S5.05[6][b] n.327;
    S5.05[7][a] n.333; S5.06[7][d] n.197;
    S5.06[8][d][ii] n.348; S9.04[3][a] n.48;
    S10.02[2][b][iii] n.56; S11.02[1][b] n.27;
    S16.02[6] n.409; S19.03[1] n.3;
    S19.03[3][b] n.112; S19.03[3][d] n.162
25.2207A-1 . . . . . S8.07[5] n.43; 8.07[6] n.47
25.2207A-1(a) . . . . 8.07[3] ns. 18, 26, 27;
    8.07[4] n.34
25.2207A-1(b) . . . 8.07[4] n.37; S8.07[4] n.34;
    8.07[5] n.43

*[Text references are to paragraphs and notes (9"n.");
references to the supplement are preceded by "S."]*

Temp. Reg. §

25.2207A-1(c) . . . . 8.07[3] ns. 21, 23
25.2207A-1(d) . . . . 8.07[3] n.23; 8.07[4] n.30
25.2207A-1(e) . . . . 8.07[3] n.22; 8.07[4] n.36
25.2207A-1(f) . . . . . 8.07[3] n.23; 8.07[4] n.34
25.2207A-2 . . . . 8.07[6] ns. 46, 47
25.2512-5T . . . . S3.05[3][b] n.29; S4.02[5] ns.
    244, 247; S4.08[1][a] n.5; S4.11[4][a]
    n.40; S5.05[3][a] n.95; S5.05[5][a][ii]
    n.207; S5.05[5][b][ii] n.264;
    S5.05[5][c][ii] n.291; S5.05[6][b] n.327;
    S5.05[7][a] n.333; S5.06[7][d] n.197;
    S5.06[8][d][ii] n.348; S9.04[3][a] n.48;
    S10.02[2][b][iii] n.56; S11.02[1][b] n.27;
    S16.02[6] n.409; S19.03[1] n.3;
    S19.03[3][b] n.112; S19.03[3][d] n.162
25.2512-5A . . . . 10.02[2][b][iii] n.54
25.2512-5A(d)(1) . . . . 19.03[1] n.10
25.2512-5A(d)(6) . . . . 19.03[1] n.10
25.7520-1T . . . . S3.05[3][b] n.29; S4.02[5] ns.
    244, 247; S4.08[1][a] n.5; S4.11[4][a]
    n.40; S5.05[3][a] n.95; S5.05[5][a][ii]
    n.207; S5.05[5][b][ii] n.264;
    S5.05[5][c][ii] n.291; S5.05[6][b] n.327;
    S5.05[7][a] n.333; S5.06[7][d] n.197;
    S5.06[8][d][ii] n.348; S9.04[3][a] n.48;
    S10.02[2][b][iii] n.56; S11.02[1][b] n.27;
    S16.02[6] n.409; S19.03[1] n.3;
    S19.03[3][b] n.112; S19.03[3][d] n.162
26.2601-1(d)(1) . . . . 13.02[4][c][i] n.314
26.2662-1(d)(2)(i) . . . . 18.02[4][a] n.44
26.2662-1(d)(2)(ii) . . . . 18.02[4][a] n.51
26.2662-1(d)(2)(iii) . . . . 18.02[4][a] n.42
301.6324A-1 . . . . 8.03[2] n.26
301.6324A-1(d) . . . . 2.02[3][c][iii] n.116
301.9100-3T . . . . 5.06[8][d][iii] n.383
301.9100-6T . . . . 4.03[1] n.2
301.9100-7T(a)(3)(i) . . . . . . 15.03[3][c] n.71

PROPOSED REGULATIONS

Prop. Reg. §

1.72-6(e) . . . S4.11[5] n.54; S10.01[3][g] n.119
1.121-1(b) . . . . 5.07[3][c] n.59
1.529-5(a) . . . . 9.04[3][g] n.124
1.529-5(b) . . . . 9.04[3][g] n.126
1.529-5(b)(1) . . . . S9.04[3] n.46
1.529-5(b)(2)(i) . . . . . 9.04[3][g] ns. 130, 132
1.529-5(b)(2)(ii) . . . . 9.04[3][g] n.130
1.529-5(b)(2)(iii) . . . . 9.04[3][g] n.130
1.529-5(b)(2)(iv) . . . . 9.04[3][g] n.131
1.529-5(b)(2)(v) . . . . 9.04[3][g] n.131
1.529-5(b)(3)(i)   9.04[3][g] n.136; S9.04[3][g]
    n.136; 10.01[3][j] n.135
1.529-5(b)(3)(ii)   9.04[3][g] n.137; 10.01[3][j]
    n.137
1.529-5(b)(3)(iii) . . . . 9.04[3][g] n.137;
    10.01[3][j] n.137
1.529-5(c) . . . . 9.04[3][g] n.124

Prop. Reg. §

1.529-5(d)(1) . . . . 9.04[3][g] n.133
1.529-5(d)(2) . . . . 4.08[5] n.54
1.529-5(d)(3) . . . . 9.04[3][g] n.134
1.643(a)-3(e) . . . . 5.06[8][b][i] n.215
1.643(a)-8 . . . . 5.05[5][a][i] n.203
1.643(b)-1   4.02[5] n.251; 5.06[8][b][i] n.215;
    5.06[8][d][ii] n.353; 5.07[4][a][i] n.131;
    9.04[3][b] n.64
1.643(b)-1(a) . . . . 5.06[8][b][i] n.215
1.664-1(d)(1)(iii) . . . . 5.05[5][a][i] n.203
1.1001-1(j) . . . . . . S4.11[5] n.54; S10.01[3][g]
    n.119
1.1001-1(j)(1) . . . . S10.01[3][g] n.119
1.7872-1(b)(1) . . . . 10.01[2][f] n.44
1.7872-3(b) . . . . 10.01[2][f] n.45
1.7872-4(b) . . . . 10.01[2][f] n.47
1.7872-4(c)–1.7872-4(g) . . . . 10.01[2][f] n.47
1.7872-6(b)(3) . . . . 10.01[2][f] n.56
1.7872-6(c) . . . . 10.01[2][f] n.55
1.7872-7(a) . . . . 10.01[2][f] n.49
1.7872-7(a)(1) . . . . 10.01[2][f] n.50
1.7872-8 . . . . 10.01[2][f] n.59
1.7872-8(b)(3) . . . . 10.01[2][f] n.60
1.7872-10(a)(1) . . . . 10.01[2][f] n.53
1.7872-10(a)(2) . . . . . . 10.01[2][f] ns. 48, 53
20.2001-1(b)–20.2001-1(g) . . . . . 2.01[1][b][ii]
    n.24
20.2001-1(b) . . . . 2.01[1][b][ii] n.28;
    S2.01[1][b][ii] n.28
20.2001-1(d) . . . . 2.01[1][b][ii] n.28;
    S2.01[1][b][ii] n.28
20.2001-1(f) . . . . 2.01[1][b][ii] n.28
20.2001-1(f) Ex. 2 . . . . S2.01[1][b][ii] n.28
20.2032-1(f)(1) . . . . S4.03[3][c] ns. 54.2, 54.3
20.2032-1(f)(3)(i)   S4.03[3][c] ns. 54.4–54.7
20.2032-1(f)(3)(ii) Ex. 1 . . . . . . S4.03[3][c] ns.
    54.1, 54.5
20.2032-1(f)(3)(ii) Ex. 2 . . . S4.03[3][c] n.54.4
20.2032-1(f)(3)(ii) Ex. 3 . . . . . . S4.03[3][c] ns.
    54.1, 54.5
20.2032-1(f)(3)(ii) Ex. 4 . . . . . . S4.03[3][c] ns.
    54.1, 54.4, 54.7
20.2032-1(f)(3)(ii) Ex. 5 . . . . S4.03[3][c] ns.
    54.1, 54.4, 54.7
20.2036-1(b)(1)(ii) . . . . S4.08[8] n.168.11
20.2036-1(c)(1)(ii), Ex. 1 . . S4.08[8] n.168.11
20.2036-1(c)(2)(ii) . . . . S4.08[8] n.168.10
20.2036-1(c)(2)(iii), Ex. 7 . . . S4.08[8] n.168.10
20.2036-2(a) . . . . 4.08[6][d] n.108
20.2036-2(b) . . . . 4.08[6][d] ns. 100, 105
20.2036-2(c) . . . . 4.08[6][d] ns. 96, 97, 99, 101
20.2036-2(d)(1) . . . . 4.08[6][d] n.97
20.2036-2(d)(2) . . . . 4.08[6][d] n.97
20.2036-2(d)(2)(iii) . . . . 4.08[6][d] n.97
20.2036-2(e) . . . . 4.08[6][d] n.104
20.2036-2(e)(1) . . . . 4.08[6][d] n.103
20.2036-2(e)(2) . . . . 4.08[6][d] ns. 103, 104
20.2036-2(e)(3) . . . . 4.08[6][d] n.105
20.2036-2(e)(4) . . . . 4.08[6][d] ns. 103, 104
20.2040-1(a)(2) . . . . 4.12[7][a] n.38
20.2041-3(b) . . . . 4.13[7][a] n.79
20.2043-1(b) . . . . 4.15[2] n.73

[Text references are to paragraphs and notes (9"n.");
references to the supplement are preceded by "S."]

Prop. Reg. §

20.2053-4(e)(1) . . . . S5.03[3][c][i] n.111
20.2053-9 . . . . S5.03[4][b][ii] n.193
20.2056(b)-5(c)(3) . . . . . . 5.06[8][b][i] n.231
20.2056(b)-5(c)(5) . . . . . . 5.06[8][b][i] n.231
20.2056(b)-5(f)(1) . . . . . . 5.06[8][b][i] n.215;
    5.06[8][d][ii] n.316; 9.04[3][b] n.64;
    11.03[4][c] n.58
20.2056(b)-7(d)(1) . . . . . . 5.06[8][d][ii] n.353;
    9.04[3][b] n.64; 11.03[4][c] n.58
20.2056(b)-7(e) . . . . 5.06[8][d][ii] n.344
20.6166A-3(d)(2) . . . . . . 2.02[3][c][vi] n.140
20.6166A-3(d)(3) . . . . . . 2.02[3][c][vi] n.140
20.6166A-3(e)(2) . . . . 2.02[3][c][vi] n.144
25.2504-2(b) . . . . 9.05[2][b] n.20
25.2511-1(f)(1) . . . . 10.02[5] & n.142;
    10.02[5][a] n.154
25.2512-4 . . . . 10.01[3][h] n.120
25.2512-8 . . . . 10.02[5][b] n.160
25.2519-1(a) . . . . 8.07[4] n.34
25.2523(e)-1(f)(1) . . . . 9.04[3][b] n.64
25.2701-5 . . . . 19.02[5][c][i] n.407
25.2701-5(a) . . . . 19.02[5][c][i] n.407
25.2702-1(c)(3) . . . . 19.03[2][c] n.93
25.2702-2(a)(5) . . . . S19.03[3][b][i] n.133
25.2702-2(a)(6) . . . . S19.03[3][b][i] n.134
25.2702-3(d)(2) . . . . S19.03[3][b][i] n.134
25.2702-3(d)(3) . . . . S19.03[3][b][i] n.134
25.2702-3(d)(4) . . . . S19.03[3][b][i] n.133
25.2702-3(e) Ex. 5 . . . . . S19.03[3][b][i] n.133
25.2702-3(e) Ex. 6 . . . . . S19.03[3][b][i] n.133
25.2702-3(e) Ex. 8 . . . . . S19.03[3][b][i] n.134
25.2702-3(e) Ex. 9 . . . . . S19.03[3][b][i] n.134
25.2702-5(b)(1) . . . . 19.03[4][f] n.385
25.2702-5(c)(1) . . . . 19.03[4][f] n.385
25.2702-5(c)(9) . . . . 19.03[4][f] n.385

Prop. Reg. §

25.2702-7 . . . . . S19.03[3][b][i] ns. 133, 134;
    19.03[4][f] n.385
25.2702-7 Ex. 5 . . . . . . S19.03[3][b][i] n.133
25.2702-7 Ex. 6 . . . . . . S19.03[3][b][i] n.133
25.7872-1 . . . . 10.01[2][f] n.44
26.2601-1(b)(4)(i)(D)(2) . . . . . . 18.05[2][e][iv]
    n.105
26.2601-1(b)(4)(i)(E)   18.05[2][e][iv] ns. 111,
    112
26.2613-1(f)(1) . . . . 13.02[3][b][i] n.219
26.2642-2(a)(1) . . . . 19.02[5][f][iii] n.519
26.2642-2(a)(2) . . . . 15.03[6][c] n.249
26.2642-6(k) . . . . S16.02[5][e] n.383.3
26.2642-7 . . . . S16.02[9][a] n.574
26.2642-7(b) . . . . . S16.02[9][a] ns. 577-579
26.2642-7(c) . . . . . S16.02[9][a] ns. 577, 580.3
26.2642-7(d)(1) . . . . S16.02[9][a] n.580
26.2642-7(d)(2) . . . . S16.02[9][a] n.580.1
26.2642-7(d)(2)(i)-26.2642-7(d)(2)(v) . . . . . .
    . . . . S16.02[9][a] n.580.1
26.2642-7(d)(3) . . . . S16.02[9][a] n.580.2
26.2642-7(d)(3)(i)-26.2642-7(d)(3)(iii) . . . . . .
    . . . . S16.02[9][a] n.580.2
26.2642-7(e)(1)-26.2642-7(e)(3) . . . .
    . . . . S16.02[9][a] n.580.3
26.2642-7(h) . . . . S16.02[9][a] n.576
26.2642-7(i) . . . . S16.02[9][a] n.574
26.2651-1(a)(3) . . . . . . S13.02[4][b][ii] n.289
26.2651-1(c) Ex. 3 . . . . S13.02[4][b][ii] n.289
26.2651-1(c) Ex. 4 . . . . S13.02[4][b][ii] n.289
26.2654-1(a)(1)(iii) . . . . . . S17.04[2][a] n.51
26.2654-1(a)(5) Ex. 8 . . . . . . S17.04[2][a] n.51
301.6501(c)-1(f)(2)-301.6501(c)-1(f)(6) . . . . . .
    . . . . 9.04[10][a] n.220

Cumulative Table of Revenue Rulings, Revenue Procedures, and Other IRS Releases

[Text references are to paragraphs and notes (9"n.");
references to the supplement are preceded by "S."]

REVENUE RULINGS

Rev. Rul.

188 . . . . 10.03[3][a] n.40
53-83 . . . . . . 5.06[3][g] n.71; 5.06[7][b] n.170
53-146 . . . . 10.03[1] ns. 9, 16
53-157 . . . . 19.04[6][a][i] n.117
53-158 . . . . 4.11[7] n.69
53-187 . . . . 6.03[2][a] n.24
53-189 . . . . 19.04[6][b] n.138
53-243 . . . . 4.13[3] n.23
53-260 . . . . 4.11[7] n.70
53-279 . . . . 5.06[7][b] n.179
54-6 . . . . 10.03[3][a] n.40
54-19 . . . . . . 4.05[8] ns. 93, 96; 4.14[2] n.9
54-30 . . . . 10.03[2] n.22
54-91 . . . . 9.04[4] n.140
54-114 . . . . 6.05[2][a][i] n.19
54-121 . . . . 5.06[8][a] n.204
54-135 . . . . 4.07[3][b] n.88
54-153 . . . . 4.13[3] n.23
54-344 . . . . 9.04[3][e] n.78
54-400 . . . . . 9.04[4] n.138; 9.04[5][c] n.171
54-407 . . . . 6.03[2] n.17
54-410 . . . . 11.03[4][b] n.48
54-444 . . . . 4.03[3][a] n.41
54-465 . . . . 11.02[1][c] n.35
54-470 . . . . 11.03[3][b] ns. 37, 40
54-537 . . . . 10.01[5] n.147
55-71 . . . . 10.02[2][b][iv] n.65
55-87 . . . . S5.03[2][b] n.72
55-119 . . . . 4.11[5] n.54
55-123 . . . . . . 4.03[3][a] n.41; 4.05[4] n.39
55-143 . . . . 6.05[2][a][i] n.18
55-163 . . . . 6.03[2][b] n.32; 6.04[1] n.6
55-178 . . . . 5.06[3] n.17
55-241 . . . . 10.03[1] n.18

Rev. Rul.

55-277 . . . . . . 4.05[6] n.76; 5.06[8][c] n.287
55-301 . . . . 4.02[3][e] n.100
55-333 . . . . 4.03[1] n.10
55-334 . . . . . . 10.03[1] n.7; 10.03[2] n.24;
10.03[3][a] n.41
55-335 . . . . 5.05[1][a] n.9
55-379 . . . . . . 4.03[2][d] n.36; 4.05[6] n.68
55-381 . . . . 4.05[8] n.104
55-419 . . . . 5.06[3][a] n.25
55-438 . . . . 4.05[5][b] n.50
55-486 . . . . 4.13[6][a] n.65
55-506 . . . . 10.03[1] n.6
55-518 . . . . 4.13[7][a] n.79
55-678 . . . . 9.04[3][c] n.68
55-679 . . . . 9.04[3][c] n.68
55-683 . . . . 4.10[6] n.69
55-701 . . . . 6.04[1] n.10
56-52 . . . . 6.05[2][a][ii] n.26
56-60 . . . . 4.03[1] n.10
56-86 . . . . 9.04[5][c] n.165
56-251 . . . . 7.02[4][b] n.91
56-329 . . . . 11.02[1][a] n.15
56-397 . . . . 4.14[5][b] & n.96
56-439 . . . . 10.03[1] n.14
56-519 . . . . 4.12[7][a] n.46
56-637 . . . . 4.05[8] n.100
57-54 . . . . 4.14[2] ns. 8, 11
57-315 . . . 10.01[3][a] n.84; 10.01[10][a] n.210
57-366 . . . . 4.10[4][f] n.49
57-368 . . . . 5.06[3] n.17
57-424 . . . . 8.02 n.3
57-506 . . . . . . 10.06[2] n.14; 10.06[4] n.35
57-530 . . . . S5.03[2][a] n.59
58-13 . . . . 10.01[3] n.79
58-167 . . . . 3.05[3][b] n.46
58-436 . . . . 4.03[2][d] n.34

[Text references are to paragraphs and notes (9"n.");
references to the supplement are preceded by "S."]

Rev. Rul.

58-576 . . . . 4.03[2][a] n.25
59-9 . . . . 3.05[1][a] n.6; 3.05[4][a] n.56
59-32 . . . 5.03[3][c] n.67; S5.03[3][c][iii] n.138
59-57 . . . . 9.02[2] n.11; 11.02[1][a] n.12
59-60 . . . . . 4.02[2][b][i] n.39; 4.02[3][f] & ns.
103–112; S4.02[3][f]; 4.02[4][g];
4.05[7][a] n.78; 19.04[6][a][i] n.117
59-73 . . . . 3.05 n.3; 3.05[3][a] n.25
59-78 . . . . 9.04[5][c] n.171
59-123 . . . 3.05[1] n.4; 3.05[3][b] n.46; 5.06[1]
n.8; 5.06[3][h] n.77
59-144 . . . . 9.04[5][b] n.149
59-152 . . . . 5.05[1][b] n.28
59-310 . . . . 5.05[1][b] ns. 31, 33
59-357 . . . . 4.08[4][b] n.34; 4.10[4][f] n.49;
9.04[5][c] ns. 165–167
60-70 . . . . 4.05[8] n.101; 4.11[3][a] n.16
60-87 . . . . 5.06[6][a] n.145
60-88 . . . . . . 3.03[1] ns. 5, 6; 5.09[1] ns. 7, 8
60-160 . . . . . 4.15[1][b][i] n.40; S5.03[4][a][i]
n.158; 5.03[5][e] n.139; 10.06[3] n.32
60-218 . . . . 9.04[5][b] n.149
60-247 . . . 3.05[1][c] ns. 16, 17; S5.03[4][c][i]
n.208; 5.03[5][b] & ns. 123, 124
60-367 . . . . 11.02[1][a] n.14
61-58 . . . . . 3.03[2] n.29; 3.06[4] n.33; 5.09[2]
n.31
61-59 . . . . S5.03[6][c][iii] n.309
61-208 . . . . 3.05[4][a] n.57
62-13 . . . . 10.01[9] n.205
62-102 . . . . 10.07[2][b] n.63
62-245 . . . . 6.05[2][a][i] n.15
63-27 . . . 5.03[3][c] n.67; S5.03[3][c][iii] n.138
63-52 . . . 4.03[2][d] n.37; 4.05[6] n.68; 4.14[1]
n.2
63-232 . . . . 5.04[2] n.13
64-328 . . . . S4.14[6] ns. 103.2, 103.3;
S10.01[3][g] n.115.4
65-57 . . . . 4.14[2] n.19
65-144 . 10.01[3][e] n.106; S10.01[3][e] n.105
65-186 . . . . 8.03[2] n.16
65-193 . . . . 4.02[3][f] n.109
65-217 . . . . . 4.05[4] n.38; 4.14[2] ns. 17, 18
65-222 . . . . 4.14[2] n.12
65-274 . S5.03[4][b][i] n.191; 5.03[5][a] n.108
66-20 . . . . 4.05[7][b] n.82
66-38 . . . 3.05[1][c] n.12; 5.06[8][b][iv] n.267
66-39 . . . . 5.06[8][b][i] ns. 217, 220
66-60 . . . . 4.05[5][b] n.54; 4.12[4] n.30;
5.06[8][a] n.203
66-85 . . . . 4.02[3][c] n.87
66-87 . . . . 4.09[6] n.48; 4.13[7][f] n.111;
9.04[3][f] n.119
66-110 . . . . S10.01[3][g] n.115.4
66-139 . . . . 5.06[7][b] n.181
66-167 . . . . 5.03[3][a] n.51; S5.03[3][a] n.91;
10.01[2][g] n.65
66-211 . . . . S5.03[4][b][i] n.191
66-234 . . . 5.03[2][b] n.33; S5.03[2][b] ns. 71,
72

Rev. Rul.

66-271 . . . . 3.05[1][a] n.6
66-286 . . . . 8.02 ns. 7, 9
66-307 . . . . . 3.05[3][b] n.33; 4.09[4][e] n.35
67-53 . . . . 3.05[3][b] ns. 38, 39
67-55 . . . . 10.03[3][a] n.41
67-110 . . . . 3.05[4][a] n.55
67-170 . . . . 5.05[1][b] n.36
67-172 . . . . 9.04[3][a] n.50
67-228 . . . . 4.05[6] n.72; 4.14[8] ns. 118, 123
67-230 . . . . 10.02[2][b][iv] n.66
67-255 . . . . 4.04[7][b][i] n.274
67-270 . . . . 9.04[5][a] n.147
67-276 . . . . 4.02[3][g] n.123
67-277 . . . . 4.05[8] n.99
67-280 . . . . 10.01[2][h] ns. 69, 71
67-304 . . . . . S5.03[4][b][i] n.192; 5.03[5][a]
n.109; 5.03[5][c] n.131; S5.03[6][a]
n.268
67-319 . . . . 3.04[2][b] n.28
67-325 . . . . 5.05[1][b] n.34
67-370 . . . . . 4.05[5][b] n.57; 4.09[4][c] n.32
67-375 . . S5.03[4][a] n.152; 5.03[5][b] n.127
67-384 . . . . . 9.04[3][a] n.50; 9.04[3][c] n.68
67-396 . . . . 10.01[3][h] ns. 122, 123
67-442 . . . . . 5.06[3] n.17; 11.03[2] n.11
67-463 . . . . 4.14[9][b] n.143
68-88 . . . . 4.05[8] n.94; 4.14[2] n.10
68-269 . . . . . 4.12[2] n.16; 10.01[5][c] n.168
68-271 . . . . 5.06[3][b] n.36
68-272 . . . . 4.02[3][c] n.87
68-335 . S5.03[4][b][i] n.191; 5.03[5][a] n.108
68-379 . . 4.15[1][a] n.24; S5.03[4][a][i] n.161;
5.03[5][e] n.141; 10.02[5][d] n.169;
10.02[6][d] n.188; 10.06[1] n.6; 10.06[2]
n.18
68-459 . . . . 5.05[1][a] n.7
68-538 . . . . 4.10[8] n.81
68-554 . . . . . 5.06[7][c] n.195; 16.02[7][b][ii]
n.467
68-558 . . . . 10.02[4] ns. 136, 137
68-609 . . . . . 4.02[3][f] n.109; 4.05[7][a] n.78;
4.05[7][b] n.84
68-611 . . . . S5.03[6][c][iii] n.302
68-670 . . . . 9.04[5][b] n.158
69-8 . . . . 4.05[8] n.98
69-54 . . . . 4.14[6] ns. 98, 100
69-56 . . . . . 5.06[8][b][i] n.212; 5.06[8][b][v]
n.269; 11.03[4][b] n.49
69-74 . . . . . 4.11[5] ns. 50, 54; S4.11[5] n.54;
10.01[3][g] n.119; S10.01[3][g] n.119;
10.02[6] n.171; S10.02[6] n.171
69-148 . . . . 10.01[5][c] n.169
69-164 . . . . 4.05[2][a] ns. 5, 6
69-165 . . . . 4.02 n.1
69-193 . . . . 5.03[2][b] n.27; S5.03[2][b] n.68
69-285 . . . . . 4.13[4][a] n.36; 5.05[1][a] n.11
69-341 . . . . 4.03[3][b] n.54
69-342 . . . . 4.13[2][b] n.14
69-344 . . . . . 9.04[3][b] n.63; 9.04[3][e] n.79
69-345 . . . . 9.04[5][a] n.147

[Text references are to paragraphs and notes (9"n.");
references to the supplement are preceded by "S."]

Rev. Rul.

69-346   10.01[3][i] n.127; 10.01[5][d] n.174;
10.01[5][e] n.178; 10.01[10][a] n.212;
10.02[1][b] ns. 16, 17
69-347   10.01[3][i] n.127; 10.01[5][d] n.174;
10.01[10][a] n.212
69-402 . . . 5.03[3][c] n.69; S5.03[3][c][i] n.120
69-411 . . . . 5.04[3] n.21
69-505 . . . . 10.02[6][c] n.180
69-545 . . . . 5.05[1][b] n.35
69-551 . . . . 5.03[3][a] n.52; S5.03[3][a] n.87
69-577 . . . . . . 4.08[8][a] n.179; 4.12[9] n.75
69-596 . . . . 6.05[2][a][i] ns. 16, 18
70-84 . . . . 4.08[7][b] n.128
70-155 . . . . 4.08[4][c] ns. 44, 45
70-156   5.03[2][b] ns. 26, 27; S5.03[2][b] ns.
67, 68
70-272 . . . . 3.03[1] n.6; 5.09[1] n.8
70-292 . . . . 3.05[1][a] n.6
70-348 . . . . . 4.10[4][f] n.49; 4.10[7] & n.76
70-401 . . . . 10.01[3][b] n.89
70-452 . . . . 5.05[5][a][i] n.202; 5.05[5][b][i]
n.257
70-513 . . . . . . 4.08[5][b] n.62; 4.10[3] n.13;
4.10[4][e] n.48; 4.10[9] n.96
70-527 . . . . 4.03[4][b] n.59
70-537 . . . . 8.01[1][a][ii] n.13
70-600 . . . . 10.03[2] n.28
70-621 . . . . 8.01[1][a][iii] n.24
71-51 . . . . 5.06[3][d] ns. 54, 59
71-67 . . . . 4.15[1][a][ii] n.31
71-168 . . . . . 5.03[2][b] n.27; S5.03[2][b] n.68
71-173 . . . . 5.03[3][d] n.78; S5.03[6][a] n.273
71-200 . . . . 5.05[1][a] n.11
71-317 . . . . . . 4.03[2][d] n.35; 4.03[3][a] n.41
71-355 . . . . 3.03[2] n.17; S5.03[4][b][i] n.186;
5.03[5][a] n.105; 5.09[2] n.10
71-422 . . . 5.03[5][c] n.131; S5.03[6][a] n.269
71-441 . . . . 5.05[1][a] n.10
71-443 . . . . . 9.04[1][b] n.27; 9.04[3][e] n.90;
10.01[2][b][i] ns. 19, 21; 11.03[3][a]
n.27
71-480 . . . . 3.05[1][c] n.20
71-497 . . . 4.07[3][b] n.91; 4.14[9][b] ns. 134,
138; 10.02[2][b][ii] n.49
71-507 . . . . 4.11[3][a] n.21
72-6 . . . . 3.06 n.7
72-7 . . . . 4.06 n.10; 5.06[3][b] n.48; 5.06[7][b]
n.179
72-8 . . . . . . 4.05[8] n.94; 4.06 n.10; 5.06[3][b]
n.48; 5.06[7][b] n.183
72-33 . . . . 5.06[7][c] n.194
72-153 . . . . 5.06[7][b] ns. 170, 177, 188
72-154 . . . . 5.06[8][b][iii] n.240; 5.06[8][b][v]
n.271
72-188 . . . . 2.02[3][c][vi] n.143
72-196 . . . . 5.05[5][c][i] n.286; 11.02[2][b][iii]
n.83
72-282 . . . . . 4.03[3][a] n.45; 4.07[2][c] n.58
72-283 . . . . 5.06[8][b][ii] n.238
72-307 . . . . . . 4.14[4][a] n.41; 4.14[6] n.101
72-333 . . . . 5.06[8][b][v] n.275

Rev. Rul.

72-355 . . . . 9.02[2] n.14
72-395   5.05[5][a] n.159; 5.05[5][a][i] n.187;
5.05[5][b] n.213; 5.05[5][b][i] n.242;
11.02[2][b][i] ns. 56, 65; 11.02[2][b][ii]
n.77
72-419 . . . . 5.05[7][b] n.341
72-442 . . . . 5.05[1][a] n.10
72-443 . . . . 6.03[2] n.8
72-525 . . . . 3.08 n.4
72-552 . . . . 5.05[2][e] n.91
72-571 . . . . 10.01[3][d] n.103; 10.01[6] n.186;
10.01[8] n.195
72-583 . . . . . . 9.02[2] n.12; 10.02[4] n.135
72-592 . . . . 5.04[2] n.14
72-611 . . . . 4.08[7] n.117
72-612 . . . . . 5.06[5][a] n.100; 8.05[4] n.13
73-21 . . . . . 4.08[5][a] n.58; 4.10[4][g] n.55
73-47 . . . . 3.05[1] n.4
73-61 . . . 10.01[2][f] n.40; 10.01[10][a] n.212
73-74 . . . . 5.05[1][b] n.32
73-97 . . . . 4.03[3][a] n.39
73-98 . . . . 5.06[5][b][i] n.105
73-142 . . . . 4.05[2][b] n.13
73-143 . . . . 4.10[5] n.62
73-207 . . . . 10.03[1] ns. 3, 6
73-240 . . . . 3.08 n.1
73-287 . . . . 9.04[5][c] n.165
73-316 . . . . 4.05[8] n.101
73-339 . . . 5.05[7][b] n.339; 5.05[7][c] n.348
73-405   9.04[3][f] n.94; 9.04[4] ns. 140, 142
73-612 . . . . 10.01[2][h] n.69
74-19 . . . . 5.05[5][b][i] n.219
74-25 . . . . 8.09 n.2
74-43 . . . . 9.04[5][b] n.150
74-120 . . . . 5.06[8][b][iii] n.251
74-132 . . . . 5.05[5][c][i] n.281
74-149 . . . . 11.02[2][b][ii] n.69
74-199 . . . . 9.02[2] n.14
74-247 . . . . 5.05[5][c][i] n.281
74-260 . . . . 4.03[1] n.1
74-284 . . . . 4.05[5][a] n.47
74-345 . . . . 9.04[1][b] n.37
74-363 . . . . 3.04[1] n.11
74-364 . . . . 6.01[3][b] n.32
74-365 . . . . 10.01[5] n.150
74-424 . . . . 4.02[3][c] n.87
74-491 . . . . 3.04[2][b] n.28
74-492 . . . . 4.05[5][b] n.52; 4.13[7][d] n.100
74-509 . . . . S5.03[3][a] n.92
74-523 . . . . S5.05[1][b] n.41
74-533 . . . . . 3.04[1] n.11; 4.08[7][d] n.165;
5.05[1][b] n.41
74-556   4.08[7] n.114; 4.10[1] n.2; 4.10[4][f]
n.49; 9.04[5][c] n.167
75-8 . . . . 9.04[1][b] n.37
75-24 . . . S5.03[4][c][i] n.208; 5.03[5][b] n.123
75-63 . . . . . . 3.03[2] n.17; 4.05[2][a] ns. 7, 9;
S5.03[4][b][i] n.186; 5.03[5][a] n.105;
5.09[2] n.10
75-70 . . . . 4.14[4][a] n.37
75-72 . . . . 10.02[6][d] ns. 181, 186

*[Text references are to paragraphs and notes (9"n.");
references to the supplement are preceded by "S."]*

Rev. Rul.

75-73 . . . . . 10.06[2][a] n.22; 10.06[2][b] n.25
75-100 . . . . 4.14[8] n.118
75-116 . . . . 5.05[5][c][i] n.281
75-126 . . . . 4.05[8] n.97
75-127 . . . . 4.05[8] ns. 97, 98
75-128   5.06[7][c] n.194; 5.06[8][b][v] n.275
75-145 . . . . 4.05[8] n.99
75-239 . . . . 5.03[3][c] n.71
75-257 . . . . 4.08[6][b] n.82
75-258 . . . . 4.08[6][b] n.82
75-259 . . . . 4.08[6][b] n.82
75-260 . . . . 4.08[6][b] n.82
75-350 . . . . 5.06[8][b][iv] n.265
75-351 . . . . 4.13[7][a] n.79
75-357 . . . . 6.01[3][a] n.27
75-360 . . . . 9.04[3] n.46
75-365 . . . 2.02[3][c][ii] n.82; S2.02[3][c][ii]
n.82
75-366 . . . 2.02[3][c][ii] n.82; S2.02[3][c][ii]
n.82
75-367 . . . 2.02[3][c][ii] n.82; S2.02[3][c][ii]
n.82
75-395 . . . . 4.15[1][b][i] n.40
75-414 . . . . 5.05[7][b] n.339
75-415 . . . . 9.04[3][d] n.74
75-439 . . . . 3.06[2] n.14
75-440 . . . . 5.06[8][b][i] n.217
75-505 . . . . . 4.05[8] n.105; 4.11[3][a] n.17
75-506 . . . . 9.04[3][a] n.56
75-509 . . . . 5.03[3][a] n.53
75-550 . . . . 3.05[3][b] n.39
76-7 . . . 5.05[5][a][i] n.199; 5.05[5][b][i] n.254
76-8 . . 5.05[5][a][i] n.199; 11.02[2][b][ii] n.81
76-49 . . . . 10.02[6][d] n.186
76-57 . . . . 10.02[6][d] n.186
76-102 . . . . . 4.05[8] n.102; 4.11[3][a] n.16
76-103 . . . . . 4.10[4][a] n.23; 10.01[5] n.153
76-112 . . . . 4.02[3][g] n.121
76-113 . . . S4.14[6] n.103.16; S5.03[5] n.259
76-114 . . . . 8.03[2] n.14
76-155 . . . . . 5.06[3] n.17; 5.06[7][b] n.181
76-165 . . . . 5.05[7][a] n.331
76-166 . . . 5.06[7][b] ns. 170, 188; 5.06[8][a]
n.205
76-179 . . . . 9.04[3][a] n.57; 9.04[5][b] n.160
76-199 . . . 5.06[7][b] n.181; 10.01[3][e] n.106;
S10.01[3][e] n.105
76-200 . . . . 10.01[3][g] n.113
76-225 . . . . 5.05[6][a][ii] n.325
76-234 . . . . 4.03[2] n.21
76-273 . . . . . 4.08[8] n.168; S4.08[8] n.168.5;
4.11[5] n.47; 5.06[8][d][ii] n.344;
19.03[3][b][i] n.120
76-274 . . . . 4.14[5][a] n.83; S4.14[6] n.103.24
76-275 . . . 10.01[3][d] n.103; 10.01[9] n.205
76-291 . . . . 5.05[5][a][i] n.180; 5.05[5][b][i]
n.239; 11.02[2][b][ii] n.69
76-303 . . . . . 4.05[5][b] n.54; 4.12[4] n.30;
5.06[3][d] n.53
76-304 . . . . 4.05[4] ns. 37, 40
76-307 . . . 5.05[1][a] n.18; 11.02[2][b][ii] n.82

Rev. Rul.

76-310 . . . . 5.05[5][b][i] n.227; 11.02[2][b][ii]
n.76
76-348 . . . . 4.12[9] n.79
76-357 . . . . 5.05[7][a] n.330
76-358 . . . . . . 5.05[3][b][i] ns. 109, 111
76-359 . . . . . . 5.05[3][b][i] ns. 109, 111
76-369 . . . 5.03[2][b] n.29; S5.03[2][b] n.70
76-371 . . . . 5.05[5][a][i] n.199; 11.02[2][b][ii]
n.82
76-376 . . . . 5.05[7][c] n.348
76-404 . . . . 5.06[7][c] n.192
76-421 . . . . 4.14[4][b] n.46
76-446 . . . . 5.06[8][b][iv] n.262
76-451 . . . . 9.05[2][a] n.18
76-470 . . . . 3.04 n.9
76-471 . . . . 3.04 n.8; 3.04[1] n.11
76-473 . . . . 11.02[2][d] n.97
76-490 . . . . . 10.01[3][g] n.113; S10.01[3][g]
n.115.31
76-498 . . . . 5.03[4] n.85; S5.03[4][a] n.146;
5.03[5] n.96; S5.03[6][c][iii] n.303
76-501 . . . . 4.05[8] n.104; 4.11[3][a] n.15
76-502 . . . . 4.13[3] n.20
76-503 . . . . S4.13[4][c][ii] ns. 41, 50;
4.13[4][c][iii] n.50; S10.01[8] ns. 192,
193
76-504 . . . . 5.05[2][d] n.88
76-543 . . . . 5.05[7][a] n.336
76-544 . . . . 5.05[7][a] n.334
76-545 . . . . 5.05[8][d] n.382
76-546 . . . . 5.05[2][c] n.83; 5.05[4][b] n.143
76-547 . . . . 4.13[4][a] n.37; 10.04[2][b] n.8;
10.04[4][a] n.33
77-30 . . . . 5.06[8][b][iv] n.257
77-58   5.05[5][a][i] n.188; 5.05[5][b][i] n.243
77-73   5.05[5][a][i] n.178; 5.05[5][b][i] n.237
77-97 . . . . 5.05[7][b] n.338
77-98 . . . . 5.06[7][b] n.164
77-99 . . . . 10.01[3][d] n.103; 10.01[9] n.205
77-130 . . . . 5.06[8][c] ns. 289, 293
77-131 . . . . 9.02[2] n.14
77-156 . . . . 3.05[1][b] n.11
77-158 . . . . S4.13[4][c][ii] ns. 41, 50;
4.13[4][c][iii] n.50; S10.01[8] ns. 192,
193
77-169 . . . . 5.05[7][a] n.336
77-170 . . . . 5.06[7][c] n.194
77-181 . . . 4.02[3][h] n.142; 4.05[6] n.70
77-182 . . . . 4.08[5][a] n.60
77-183 . . . . 4.11[3][a] ns. 20, 22
77-193 . . . . . 4.08[4] n.22; 4.11[5] n.47
77-194 . . . . 4.13[4][a] n.37
77-232 . . . . 5.05[1][b] n.28
77-287 . . . . 4.02[4][e][iv] n.221
77-299 . . . . 9.04[1] n.13
77-300   5.05[6][a][ii] n.322; 11.02[2][c] n.92
77-314 . . . 10.02[5][c] n.162; 10.06[1] n.6
77-327 . . . . 11.02[2][c] n.91
77-345 . . . . 5.06[5][a] n.97
77-346 . . . . 5.06[8][b][i] n.216; 5.06[8][b][ii]
n.238

*[Text references are to paragraphs and notes (9"n.");
references to the supplement are preceded by "S."]*

Rev. Rul.

77-357 . . . 5.03[5][d] n.133; S5.03[6][a] n.277;
S5.03[6][b] n.279
77-358 . . . . 9.04[3][e] n.81
77-359 . . . . 10.01[3][f] n.108
77-374   5.05[4][a] n.128; 5.05[5][a][i] n.202;
5.05[5][b][i] n.257; 5.05[8][b] n.361
77-378 . . . . . 4.08[4][c] n.53; 4.10[4][a] n.23;
10.01[9] ns. 204, 205; 19.03[2][a][iv]
n.74
77-385 . . . . 5.05[1][b] n.36
77-404 . . . . 5.06[7][c] n.193
77-411 . . . . 3.07 n.11
77-460 . . . . 4.13[3] n.18
77-461 . . . 5.03[3][c] ns. 68, 73; S5.03[3][c][i]
n.110
77-732 . . . . 10.01[2][d] n.32
78-15 . . . . 4.05[4] n.37; 4.09[2] n.4
78-16 . . . . 4.10[6] n.67
78-26 . . . . 4.08[4][b] n.28
78-27 . . . 10.03[3][a] n.40; 10.03[3][b] n.44
78-58 . . . . 3.05[3][b] n.44
78-101 . . . . 11.02[2][b][ii] n.82
78-105 . . . . 5.05[5][a][i] ns. 175, 180;
5.05[5][b][i] ns. 234, 239
78-106 . . . . 9.05[4] n.49
78-125 . . . 5.03[3][c] ns. 71, 72; S5.03[3][c][i]
n.124
78-137 . . . . 4.02[3][h] n.141
78-152 . . . . 5.05[2][b] n.69
78-168 . . . . 9.04[3][a] n.59
78-303 . . . . 5.05[7][a] n.334
78-323 . . . 5.03[3][a] ns. 44, 47; S5.03[3][a]
n.100; S5.03[6][c][iii] n.309
78-360 . . . . 4.02[2][a] n.14
78-362 . . . . 10.01[3][f] n.109
78-366 . . . . 5.05[1][a] n.7
78-378 . . . . 4.03[3][a] n.39
78-409 . . . . 4.08[4][c] ns. 42, 46
78-418 . . . . 4.12[7][a] n.35
78-419 . . . . 5.06[5][a] n.101
78-420 . . . 10.01[3][g] n.113; S10.01[3][g] ns.
115.2, 115.29, 115.31
78-431 . . . . 4.03[3][a] n.39
78-445 . . . . 5.05[3][b][i] n.110
79-7 . . . . 4.02[4][b][iii] ns. 155, 156
79-14 . . . . 5.06[5][a] n.95
79-46 . . . . 4.14[4][a] n.41
79-47 . . . . . 9.04[3][a] n.49; 10.01[3][g] n.113;
S10.01[3][g] n.115.31
79-50 . . . . S4.14[6] n.103.5
79-54 . . . . 9.04[1][b] n.37
79-61 . . . . 5.05[5][c][i] n.273
79-62 . . . . 4.09[5] n.46
79-63 . . . . . 4.13[4][c][ii] ns. 41, 48
79-86 . . . . 5.06[8][b][i] n.224
79-94 . . . . 4.08[8] n.170
79-109 . . . 4.08[4][c] n.42; 4.08[8] n.167;
S4.08[8] n.167
79-118 . . . . 10.06[2] n.13
79-129 . . . . 4.14[4][a] n.40; 4.14[7][b] n.112
79-159 . . . . . . 4.13[3] n.18; 5.05[1][b] n.36

Rev. Rul.

79-160 . . . 3.02 n.20; S3.02[2] n.57; S9.06 ns.
44, 45; 9.06[2] n.23
79-177 . . . . 4.08[5] n.55
79-211 . . . . 3.05[1][c] n.12
79-219 . . . 3.03[2] n.29; 3.06[4] n.33; 5.09[2]
n.31
79-224 . . . . 5.06[7][c] n.193
79-243 . . 10.01[5] n.148; 11.02[2][b][ii] n.77
79-252 . . . 5.03[3][c] n.71; S5.03[3][c][i] n.119
79-295 . . . 5.05[4][b] n.137; 5.05[7][b] n.340
79-302   4.12[8] n.67; S5.03[5] n.245; 5.03[6]
n.146
70-303 . . . . 4.14[8] n.117
79-312 . . . . 10.02[5][d] n.165
79-317 . . . . 3.05[3][c] n.52
79-327 . . . 10.01[3][a] n.83; 10.04[3][e] n.29
79-353 . . . 4.08[5][a] n.60; 18.05[2][b][i] n.17
79-354 . . . . . 5.06[3] n.17; 5.06[3][c] n.49
79-372 . . . . 4.12[7][a] n.41
79-373 . . . . 4.13[7][f] n.109
79-383 . . . . 5.06[3][a] n.26
79-384 . . . . 10.01[3][i] n.127
79-387 . . . . 5.05[5][c][i] n.279
79-397 . . . . 4.05[8] n.103; 4.11[3][a] n.16
79-398 . . . . S2.01[2] n.75; 3.05[1] n.4; S9.06
n.45; 9.06[2] n.23
79-420 . . . . 5.06[7][c] n.193
79-421   10.01[3][c] n.100; 10.01[3][d] n.103;
10.02[1][b] n.12; 10.04[4][a] n.33
80-66 . . . . 5.05[2][c] n.79; 5.05[3][b][i] n.104
80-80 . . . . . 3.05[3][b] n.33; 4.02[5] n.253;
4.09[4][e] n.35
80-81 . . . . S5.03[5] n.256; 5.03[6] n.153
80-82 . . . . 10.02[5][c] n.162; 10.06[1] n.12
80-83 . . . . 11.02[2][b][ii] n.73
80-111 . . . . 8.07[4] n.34; S8.07[4] n.34;
10.02[6][d] n.181
80-112 . . . . 8.03[1] n.10
80-123 . . . 5.05[5][a] n.159; 5.05[5][b] n.213;
11.02[2][b][i] n.56
80-142 . . . . . 4.03[2][c] n.31; 4.12[7][a] n.37
80-159 . . . . 5.06[5][b][ii] n.111
80-185 . . . . 3.04[1][b] n.21; 3.04[2][b] n.32
80-186 . . . . 10.01[3][a] n.86
80-196 . . . . 10.02[4] n.140
80-201 . . . . 7.06 n.17
80-202 . . . 2.02[3][c][ii] n.106; 2.02[3][c][iv]
n.119
80-209 . . . . 6.01[3][b] n.30
80-223 . . . . 7.06 n.20
80-224 . . . . 10.03[3][b] n.44
80-241 . . . . 4.12[2] n.18
80-242 . . . . . 4.05[6] n.72; 4.14[8] n.116
80-250 . . . 2.02[3][c][v] n.132; 5.03[3][c] ns.
71, 72, 117
80-255 . . . . 4.10[4][b] n.30
80-260 . . . 3.06[2] n.14; 5.03[3] n.35; S5.03[3]
n.83; S5.03[4][c][iii] n.223; 5.03[5][b]
n.120
80-261 . . . . 9.04[3][f] n.114
80-281 . . . 11.02[1][b] n.28; 11.02[2][d] n.102

*[Text references are to paragraphs and notes (9"n.");
references to the supplement are preceded by "S."]*

Rev. Rul.

80-289 . . . . 4.14[6] n.103
80-319 . . . . 4.02[3][b] n.68
80-336 . . . . 4.07[2][c] n.62
80-346 . . . . 4.08[6][d] n.99
80-347 . . . . 8.02 ns. 8, 10
80-363 . . . . 6.01[3][b] n.32
81-7 . . . . 9.04[3][f] & ns. 100, 101, 119
81-15 . . . . 4.08[6][d] n.108
81-20 . . . . 5.05[4][a] n.128
81-31 . . . 10.01[5][b] n.164; 10.02[1][b] ns. 16,
17
81-51 . . . . 4.08[5][a] n.60; 18.05[2][b][i] n.17
81-63 . . . . 4.05[3] n.30
81-85 . . . 2.01[2] n.59; S2.01[2] n.77; 4.07[3][a]
n.81; 10.03[2] n.36
81-110 . . . 10.01[3][i] n.127; 11.02[1][c] n.36;
11.02[1][d] n.40
81-118 . . . . 3.05[3][b] n.29
81-128 . . . . 4.14[4][e] n.69
81-154 . . . . S5.03[3][c][i] n.119
81-166 . . . . 4.08[7][a] n.125; 4.14[4][a] n.35
81-179 . . . . 4.04[3][b][ix] n.103; 5.08[2][c][ii]
n.61
81-182 . . . . 4.05[8] n.99; 4.11[3][a] n.16
81-183 . . . . 4.12[8] n.67
81-184 . . . . 4.12[8] n.67
81-198 . . . . . S10.01[3][g] ns. 115.2, 115.29,
115.31, 115.34, 115.35
81-220 . . . . 4.04[3][b][viii] n.94
81-221 . . . . 4.08[4][b] n.29
81-223 . . . . 10.02[6][d] n.181
81-230 . . . . 4.04[7][b][i] n.270
81-236 . . . . 4.04[3][b][ix] n.102; 5.08[2][c][ii]
n.60; 5.08[3][c][ii] n.114
81-237 . . . . 2.02[1] n.12
81-253 . . . . 10.02[2][c][ii] n.90
81-256 . . . 5.03[3][c] n.71; S5.03[3][c][i] n.122
81-260 . . . . 3.07 n.10
81-263 . . . . 3.03[2] n.30; 3.06[4] n.34; 5.09[2]
n.32
81-264 . . . . 10.01[2][e] n.34
81-286 . . . . 4.05[3] n.32
81-287 . . . 5.03[3][c] n.71; 5.03[3][c][i] n.124
81-301 . . . . S5.03[4][b][i] n.186
81-302 . . . . . . 3.03[2] n.17; 4.05[2][a] & n.9;
S5.03[4][b][i] n.186; 5.03[5][a] n.105;
5.09[2] n.10
81-303 . . . . 7.02[3] n.74
82-5 . . . . 4.05[8] n.93
82-6 . . . . 5.06[5][b][ii] n.111
82-35 . . . . 4.04[7][c][ii] n.324
82-38 . . . . . 5.05[5][c][i] n.286; 11.02[2][b][iii]
n.83
82-39 . . . . 5.05[1][a] n.18
82-97 . . . . 5.05[8][d] n.382
82-98 . . . . 9.04[6] n.178
82-105 . . . . . 4.08[8] n.168; S4.08[8] n.168.5;
4.11[5] n.47; 5.06[8][d][ii] n.344;
19.03[3][b][i] n.120

Rev. Rul.

82-128 . . . . 5.05[5][a] n.159; 5.05[5][a][i] n.189;
5.05[5][b] n.213; 5.05[5][b][i] n.244;
11.02[2][b][i] n.56
82-140 . . . . . . 4.04[3][b][viii] ns. 89, 94, 95;
4.04[7][a] n.263; 5.08[3][c][ii] n.109
82-141 . . . . 4.07[2][a][ii] n.29; 4.14[5][a] ns. 84,
87
82-143 . . . . 9.04[6] n.183
82-145 . . . . 4.14[5][a] n.83; S4.14[6] ns. 103.22,
103.24
82-156 . . . . . 4.13[4][c][ii] n.42; 5.06[8][b][iv]
n.260
82-165 . . . . 5.05[5][a] n.159; 5.05[5][b] n.213;
11.02[2][b][i] n.56
82-184 . . . . 5.06[7][b] n.185
82-193 . . . . 6.05[2][a][i] n.16; S6.05[2][a][i] n.16
82-198 . . . . 4.07[3][a] ns. 78, 81; 10.03[2] ns.
29, 36
82-216 . . . . 9.02[2] n.18
83-24 . . . . 5.03[3][c] n.71; S5.03[3][c][i] n.123
83-26 . . . . 5.06[8][d][ii] n.325
83-30 . . . . 4.02[4][e][ii] n.206; 5.03[3][c] n.62;
S5.03[3][c][ii] n.128; 5.03[3][d] n.78;
S5.03[6][a] n.273
83-31 . . . . 4.04[1] n.4; 4.04[3][b][i] n.34
83-32 . . . . 4.04[3][c][ii] n.138
83-45 . . . . 5.05[4][b] n.139
83-51 . . . . 19.02[2][a][i] n.52
83-54 . . . . . S5.03[4][a] n.148; S5.03[4][a][i]
n.157; 5.03[5] n.96
83-81 . . . 4.04[5] n.172; S5.03[5] n.252; 5.03[6]
n.151
83-96 . . . . 4.04[3][d] n.150; 5.08[3][c][i] n.102
83-107 . . . 5.06[3][a] ns. 30, 31; 5.06[7][b] ns.
179, 181
83-108 . . . . 9.04[3][f] ns. 101, 102
83-119 . . . . 19.02[1][b] n.10
83-120 . . . . 19.02[1][b] n.10
83-147 . . . . 4.14[5][b] n.92
83-148 . . . . 4.14[5][a] n.84
83-158 . . . . 5.05[7][a] n.337
83-180 . . . . 9.04[1] n.13
84-11 . . . . 9.05[2][a] n.14
84-25 . . . . . 2.01[1][b] n.20; S2.01[1][b] n.20;
10.01[3][h] n.124; 10.01[3][i] n.127
84-42 . . . S5.03[4][c][i] n.206; 5.03[5][a] n.117
84-75 . . . . 5.03[3][c] ns. 70, 71; S5.03[3][c][i]
n.116
84-97 . . . . 5.05[7][a] n.337
84-105 . . . . 5.06[5] n.94; 10.01[2] n.13
84-130 . . . . 4.14[6] n.102
84-140 . . . . 11.02[1][a] n.18
84-147 . . . . 10.02[2][b][ii] n.49
84-162 . . . . 4.11[4][a] n.40
84-179 . . . . 3.05[1][b] n.11; 4.08[6][d] n.104;
4.10[7] n.74; 4.14[4][e] n.73
85-13 . . . . 19.03[3][b][i] n.121
85-23 . . . . 5.05[7][a] n.335; 5.05[8][b] n.362
85-24 . . . . 9.04[1][b] n.36; 9.04[3][f] ns. 114,
118
85-35 . . . . 5.06[8][b][i] n.212

[Text references are to paragraphs and notes (9"n.");
references to the supplement are preceded by "S."]

Rev. Rul.

85-49 . . . . 11.02[2][c] n.94
85-66 . . . . 4.04[7][b][i] n.269
85-84 . . . . 4.04[6] n.235
85-87 . . . . . 5.05[5][c][i] n.286; 11.02[2][b][iii]
n.83
85-88 . . . . . 9.04[3][f] n.118; 10.04[4][c] n.54
85-100 . . . . 5.06[7][b] n.172
85-111 . . . . 3.05[3][b] n.40
85-148 . . . . 4.04[6] ns. 225, 235
85-168 . . 4.04[3][b][ii] n.43; 4.04[3][c] n.111
86-38 3.03[2] ns. 26, 27; 3.06[4] ns. 31, 32;
5.09[2] ns. 23, 24
86-39 . . . . . 4.13[7][c] n.91; 10.04[4][a] n.33
86-41 10.01[3][e] ns. 106, 107; S10.01[3][e]
ns. 105, 106
86-54 . . . . 2.02[3][c][vi] n.143
86-60 . . . . 11.02[1][b] n.25
86-99 . . . . 4.04[5][a][iii] n.196
86-117 . . . . 3.03[2] n.18; 5.09[2] n.11
87-37 . . . . 5.05[7][a] n.334
87-98 . . . . .4.12[2] n.12; 4.12[10] n.84
88-12 . . . . 5.06[5][a] n.98
88-27 . . . 5.05[6][a][ii] n.323; 11.02[2][c] n.94
88-59 . . . . 4.04[5][a][v] n.201
88-76 . . . . 4.05[7][c] n.88
88-81 . . . . 5.05[5][a] n.159; 5.05[5][b] n.213;
11.02[2][b][i] n.56
88-82 . . . . 5.05[6][a][ii] n.321
88-89 . . . . 4.04[1] n.4
88-90 . . . . 5.06[7][b] n.172
89-22 . . . . 4.04[7][b][i] n.269
89-30 . . . . 4.04[5][b] n.210
89-31 . . . . 5.05[2][b] n.68
89-75 . . . 5.03[3][d] n.78; S5.03[6][a] n.273
90-2 . . . . 3.05[4][a] n.57
90-3 . . . . . 5.05[4][a] n.128; 5.06[6][a] n.154
90-8 . . . . . 5.03[3][c] n.71; S5.03[3][c][i] n.126
90-21 . . . . 4.14[5][a] n.87
90-45 . . . . . 10.07[2][b] n.35; 10.07[2][c] n.66
90-101 . . . . 7.02[3] ns. 74, 79
90-103 . . . . 5.05[5][c][i] n.286; 11.02[2][b][iii]
n.83
90-110 . . . . 10.07[2][d][ii] n.96
92-26 . . . . 12.02 n.4; 12.03[1] n.3; 13.02[1][b]
n.14; 13.02[2][d] n.78
92-57 . . . . . 5.05[5][a] n.159; 5.05[5][b] n.213;
11.02[2][b][i] n.56
92-68 . . . 10.01[5][b] n.164; 10.02[1][b] ns. 16,
17
92-109 . . . . 9.02[1] n.7
93-12 . . . . 4.02[4][b][ii] nw. 151, 153;
4.02[4][b][iv] n.168; 10.02[2][c][i] ns.
77, 78; 10.02[2][c][ii] n.90
93-48 . . . . . 5.06[5][b][i] n.105; 5.06[5][b][ii]
n.111
94-69 . . . . . 4.14[8] n.120; 10.01[5][d] n.170
95-58 4.08[4][b] n.32; 4.08[5][a] ns. 60, 61;
4.10[4][g] n.56; 4.13[2] n.6; S4.13[2]
n.6; 18.05[2][b][i] n.17
96-1 . . . . 5.05[5][c][ii] n.290
96-3 . . . . 4.02[5] n.253; 4.09[4][e] n.35

Rev. Rul.

96-38 . . . . 5.05[5][c][i] n.281
96-56 . . . . . 4.05[3] n.28; 10.01[3][h] n.122
98-8 . . . . 4.16 n.10; 10.08[2] n.41
98-21 . . . . 10.01[3][a] n.86
2000-2 . . . . 5.06[8][d][ii] ns. 328, 341;
S5.06[8][d][ii] n.328
2001-21 . . . . . . 4.04[5][a] n.176; 4.04[5][a][v]
n.201
2001-22 . . . . 2.02[3][b][i] n.39
2002-86 . . . . S8.01[2][a] n.41
2003-15 . . . . S10.01[3][g] n.115.2
2003-40 . . . . S4.14[8] n.125
2003-53 . . . . S4.04[5][a] n.176
2003-61 . . . . S5.08[5][b][ii] n.237
2003-105 . . . . S4.14[6] ns. 103.2, 103.3, 203.5;
S10.01[3][g] n.115.31
2004-63 . . . . S4.04[5][a] n.176
2004-64 . . . . . S4.08[4][b] n.28; S10.01[10][e]
n.233.4
2005-36 . . . . S10.07[2] n.21; S10.07[2][c] n.66
2005-41 . . . . S4.04[5][a] n.176
2006-26 . . . . S5.06[8][d][ii] n.316
2006-32 . . . . S4.04[5][a] n.176
2006-34 . . . . S2.02[3][c][ii] n.82
2007-45 . . . . S4.04[5][a] n.176
2008-22 . . . . . S4.08[4][c] n.53.1; S4.08[6][a]
n.76; S4.10[4][a] n.23.1; S4.10[4][c] n.40
2008-35 . . . . S4.02[4][a] n.146; S10.02[2][c][iv]
n.114
2008-41 . . . . . . S5.05[5] n.154; S5.05[5][a][i]
n.161; S5.05[5][b][i] n.216
2008-44 . . . . S4.04[5][a] n.176
2008-46 . . . . S5.05[6][a] n.304
2009-21 . . . . S4.04[5][a] n.176
2011-17 . . . . S4.04[5][a] n.176

REVENUE PROCEDURES

Rev. Proc.

60-17 . . . . 3.08 n.6
62-27 . . . . 3.08 n.5
64-19 5.06[3][b] n.46; 5.06[6][a] & ns. 147,
152, 154; 5.06[8][d][iii] n.381; 5.07[2][b]
n.23; 8.03[1] n.7; 10.07[2] n.24;
16.02[4][d][ii] n.265; 17.04[2][b] n.67
70-10 . . . . 8.03[2] n.20
75-39 . . . . 4.02[3][f] n.104
78-21 . . . . 10.02[2][b][iii] n.52
79-24 . . . . 4.02[3][b] n.70
79-55 . . . . 2.02[3][c][ii] n.55
79-398 . . . . 2.01[2] n.57
80-250 . . . . 2.02[3][b][i] n.39
80-255 . . . . 4.08[5][c] n.64
81-14 . . . . 4.04[6] n.212
81-27 . . . 2.02[3][b][i] n.39; 5.03[3][c] n.71;
S5.03[3][c][i] n.124
81-154 . . . . 2.02[3][b][i] n.39
81-164 . . . . 4.08[4][c] n.42
83-7 . . . . 2.02[3][b][i] n.39

*[Text references are to paragraphs and notes (9"n.");
references to the supplement are preceded by "S."]*

Rev. Proc.

83-15 . . . . 3.05[2] n.22
83-44 . . . . 4.14[2] ns. 6, 11
84-17 . . . . 4.02[3][c] n.88
88-3 . . . . 5.05[6][a][ii] n.323; 11.02[2][c] n.94
88-53 . . . . . 5.05[5][c][i] n.286; 11.02[2][b][iii]
                                                n.83
88-54 . . . . 5.05[5][c][i] n.286; 11.02[2][b][iii]
                                                n.83
89-20 . . . 5.05[5][b] n.213; 11.02[2][b][ii] n.67
89-21 . . . . 5.05[5][a] n.159; S5.05[5][a] n.159;
                                   S11.02[2][b][i] n.56
89-23 . . . . 11.02[2][b][i] n.56
90-30 . . . 5.05[5][b] n.213; 11.02[2][b][iii] n.67
90-31 . . . 5.05[5][b] n.213; 11.02[2][b][ii] n.67
90-32 . . . 5.05[5][a] n.159; S5.05[5][a] n.159;
            11.02[2][b][i] n.56; S11.02[2][b][i] n.56
90-33 . . . . 5.05[5][a] n.159; S5.05[5][a] n.159;
              5.05[5][b] n.213; 11.02[2][b][i] n.56;
              S11.02[2][b][i] n.56; 11.02[2][b][ii] n.67
91-14 . . . . 4.02 n.4
94-44 . . . . . . 4.13[3] n.24; S4.13[4][a] n.25;
            4.13[7][e] n.104; 10.04[4][c] n.47;
                                    S10.04[4][c] n.47;
95-3 . . . . 9.04[3][f] n.96
95-17 . . . . 2.02[3][b][i] n.39
96-13 . . . 7.04[1] & ns. 1–7; S7.04[1] ns. 1–7
96-54 . . . . 5.07[3][c] n.48
98-15 . . . . 2.02[3][c][v] n.132
98-21 . . . . S7.04[1] ns. 1–7
98-34 . . . . 10.02[2][b][v] ns. 69, 70
98-54 . . . . 10.03[3][b] n.46
98-61 . . . . . 2.02[3][c][v] n.126; 4.04[1] n.11;
              9.04[1] n.7; 15.02 n.4; S15.02 n.4;
                                    18.01[2][a] n.23
99-42 . . . . . 2.02[3][c][v] n.126; 4.04[1] n.11;
                          15.02 n.5; S15.02 n.4
2000-34 . . . . 9.04[10][b] n.238
2001-13 . . . . 2.02[3][c][v] n.126; S4.04[1] n.11;
                          15.02 n.6; S15.02 n.4
2001-38 . . . . 4.16 n.10; S4.16 n.10;
            5.06[8][d][iii] n.384; S5.06[8][d][iii]
            n.384; 10.08[1] n.3; S10.08[1] n.3;
            17.02[1][c][i] n.42; S17.02[1][c][i] n.42
2001-59 . . . 2.02[3][c][v] n.126; S4.04[1] n.11;
              9.04[1] n.7; 9.05[3] n.36; 13.02[4][b][i]
              n.261; 15.02 n.7; S15.02 n.4; 18.02[2][b]
                                                n.21
2002-1 . . . . . 4.02 n.4; 5.05 n.4; 7.04[1] n.4;
                          16.02[9][a] n.578
2002-3 . . . 4.02 n.4; 4.02[1] n.6; 4.02[2][a] n.8;
                                          5.05 n.4
2002-7 . . . . 4.02 n.4; 5.05 n.4
2002-70 . . . S2.02[3][c][v] n.126; S4.04[1] n.11;
            S9.04[1] n.10; S11.03[5] n.107; S15.02
                                                n.4
2003-42 . . . . S19.03[3][b][i] n.118;
                          S19.03[3][d][iii] n.209
2003-53 – 2003-56 . . . . . . S11.02[2][b][i] n.56
2003-53 – 2003-60 . . . . S5.05[5][a] n.159
2003-53 . . . . S5.05[5][a] n.159; S11.02[2][b][i]
                                                n.56

Rev. Proc.

2003-54 . . . . S5.05[5][a] n.159; S11.02[2][b][i]
                                                n.56
2003-55 . . . . S5.05[5][a] n.159; S11.02[2][b][i]
                                                n.56
2003-56 . . . . S5.05[5][a] n.159; S11.02[2][b][i]
                                                n.56
2003-57 . . . . S5.05[5][a] n.159
2003-58 . . . . S5.05[5][a] n.159
2003-59 . . . . S5.05[5][a] n.159
2003-60 . . . . S5.05[5][a] n.159
2003-85 . . . S2.02[3][c][v] n.127; S4.04[1] n.11;
              S9.04[1] n.10; S11.03[5] n.107
2004-46 . . . . S16.02[9][a] n.573
2004-47 . . . . S17.02[1][c][i] n.54
2004-71 . . S2.02[3][c][v] n.126; S4.04[1] n.11;
              S9.04[1] n.10; S11.03[5] n.107
2005-24 . . . . S5.05[5][a][i] n.187; S5.05[5][b][i]
                                                n.242
2005-33 . . . . S2.02[3][c][vii] n.156
2005-52 . . . . S5.05[5][b] n.213
2005-53 . . . . S5.05[5][b] n.213
2005-54 . . . . S5.05[5][b] n.213
2005-55 . . . . S5.05[5][b] n.213
2005-56 . . . . S5.05[5][b] n.213
2005-57 . . . . S5.05[5][b] n.213
2005-58 . . . . S5.05[5][b] n.213
2005-59 . . . . S5.05[5][b] n.213
2005-70 . . . . S9.04[1] ns. 5, 9; S9.04[1][b][ii]
                          n.29; S11.03[5] n.107
2006-52 . . . . S7.04[1] ns. 1–7
2006-53 . . . S2.02[3][c][v] n.126; S4.04[1] n.11;
              S9.04[1] ns. 5, 9, 10; S11.03[5] n.107
2006-54 . . . . S7.04[1] ns. 1–7
2007-45 . . . . S11.02[2][c] n.90
2007-46 . . . . S5.05[6][a] n.304
2007-66 . . . . . . S2.02[3][c][iii] n.126; S4.04[1]
            n.11; S6.07[1][a] n.11; S6.07[2][a] n.44;
            S9.02[1][b][i] n.10.4; S9.02[1][b][ii]
            n.10.32; S9.04[1] ns. 5, 9, 10; S11.03[5]
                                                n.107
2008-1 . . . . S16.02[9][a] n.576
2008-45 . . . . S11.02[2][c] n.90
2008-66 . . . S2.02[3][c][v] n.126; S4.04[1] n.11;
              S9.04[1] ns. 5, 9, 10; S11.03[5] n.107
2009-11 . . . . S4.02[6][b] n.264.5
2009-50 . . . . . . S2.02[3][c][iii] n.116; S4.04[1]
            n.11; S9.04[1] ns. 5, 9, 10; S11.03[5]
                                                n.107
2010-40 . . . S2.02[3][c][v] n.126; S4.04[1] n.11;
              S9.04[1] ns. 5, 9, 10; S11.03[5] n.107
2011-1 . . . S4.02 n.4; S5.05 n.4; S7.04[1] n.4;
                                    S16.02[9][a] n.576
2011-2 . . . S4.02 n.4; S5.05 n.4; S7.04[1] n.4;
                                    S16.02[9][a] n.576
2011-3 . . . . S4.02 n.4; 4.02[1] n.6; 4.02[2][a]
                          n.8; S5.05 n.4
2011-41 . . . . . S8.10[2] n.15; S8.10[3][b] n.36;
                          S8.10[3][d][ii] n.116
2011-48 . . . . S5.03[1][b][iv] ns. 52, 54

*[Text references are to paragraphs and notes (9"n.");
references to the supplement are preceded by "S."]*

PRIVATE LETTER RULINGS

Priv. Ltr. Rul.

7735002	5.05[7][b] n.338
7809043	5.05[2][c] n.84
7826050	9.04[3][f] ns. 96, 101
7833062	10.01[9] n.204
7917006	2.02[3][c][ii] n.82
7937010	3.02 n.13; S3.02[1][a] n.18
7944009	10.01[5][e] n.179
7947066	9.04[3][f] n.118
8004172	9.04[3][f] n.101
8006109	9.04[3][f] ns. 96, 119
8022006	5.03[3][d] n.81
8022048	9.04[3][f] n.102
8045010	5.05[7][e] n.352
8047131	9.04[3][f] ns. 96, 101
8103130	10.01[3][d] n.103
8106022	5.05[4][b] n.136
8141037	5.05[7][a] n.337
8142008	10.07[2][c] n.71
8213074	9.04[3][f] n.95
8222018	4.04[6] n.216
8229097	9.04[3][f] n.118
8239002	10.07[2] n.25
8239004	5.06[3][d] n.53
8240012	10.07[2] n.27
8240015	4.04[7][b][ii] n.292
8244001	4.04[3][b][viii] n.100
8244003	2.02[3][c][ii] n.82
8251015	2.02[3][c][ii] n.82
8314001	4.04[5] n.173
8314005	4.04[5] n.173; 5.06[5] n.90
8320007	9.04[5][b] n.151
8321007	4.04[3][b][viii] n.94
8326110	10.07[2][d] n.76
8331005	4.08[8][a] n.179
8337015	4.04[3][b][viii] n.94
8339004	4.13[4][a] n.36
8342106	9.02[1] n.4
8346006	4.04[3][b][viii] n.94; 4.13[4][a] n.36
8350035	4.04[7][c][ii] n.325
8403001	4.04[7][c][i] n.311
8403010	10.01[2] n.13
8407005	4.04[6] n.218
8412014	4.04[3][b][ix] n.102
8416016	4.04[7][b][i] n.277
8418005	5.06[8][d][iii] n.385
8422008	4.04[6] n.228
8422011	4.04[5] n.173; 5.06[5] ns. 89, 90
8423007	S5.03[5] n.252; 5.03[6] n.151
8428088	2.02[3][c][ii] n.71; 5.08[2][c][ii] n.59
8429058	4.04[7][b][ii] n.297
8429085	5.06[8][d][ii] n.353
8434071	9.04[5][b] n.150
8434085	4.04[7][c][iii] n.328
8441006	4.04[3][b][viii] n.94
8443005	5.06[8][d][ii] n.353

Priv. Ltr. Rul.

8451014	2.02[3][c][ii] n.82
8512003	2.02[3][c][ii] n.57
8514032	4.04[3][b][i] n.40
8515001	5.08[3][c][iv] n.138
8515005	10.07[2] n.27
8515010	2.02[3][c][ii] n.82
8516011	4.13[7][a] n.83
8516012	4.04[3][b][iv] n.64
8520006	4.04[6] n.235
8523006	5.06[8][d][iii] n.385
8526032	4.04[7][b][i] n.274
8527007	4.04[6] n.235
8528003	4.04[6] n.235
8528007	5.06[6][b] n.157
8531004	4.04[7][c][iii] n.328
8532003	4.04[6] n.218
8532007	4.04[3][b][viii] n.100
8532010	4.04[6] n.235
8536004	4.04[6] n.227
8538007	4.05[5][b] n.54
8539004	10.07[2] n.27
8540003	4.04[6] n.235
8541005	19.04[3][a] n.53
8546001	10.01[5] n.147
8548007	5.06[6][b] n.157
8549005	10.01[3][e] n.106; S10.01[3][e] n.107
8601005	2.02[3][c][ii] n.82
8602007	4.04[6] n.235
8614006	4.04[6] n.235
8617005	4.04[6] n.235
8617007	4.04[6] n.235
8623004	4.10[4][a] n.22
8625005	2.02[3][c][ii] \n.82
8632001	4.04[6] n.235
8637001	4.04[6] n.235
8643005	4.04[3][b][viii] n.94
8645004	4.04[6] n.226
8646007	4.04[6] n.235
8647002	4.04[6] n.235
8650002	4.04[6] n.235
8651001	4.05[3] n.23
8703069	5.05[8][b] n.369
8704002	4.04[6] n.235
8704005	4.13[4][c][ii] n.42
8705002	5.06[8][b][ii] n.236
8706006	4.04[6] n.220
8708001	5.06[5] n.90
8711003	4.04[6] n.235
8713001	4.04[6] n.235
8714001	3.05[2] n.22
8717003	9.04[1][b] n.36
8723007	10.01[2] n.13
8725002	4.04[6] n.235
8730004	5.06[8][d][ii] n.344
8742001	5.05[7][a] n.330
8745002	5.05[6][a][ii] n.323; 11.02[2][c] n.94
8746004	5.06[8][d][iii] n.385
8747001	2.01[1][b] n.20; S2.01[1][b] n.20
8809003	5.06[8][a] n.205

[Text references are to paragraphs and notes (9"n.");
references to the supplement are preceded by "S."]

Priv. Ltr. Rul.

8810002	5.06[8][a] n.205
8812003	5.05[2][a] n.58
8814002	5.06[8][d][iii] n.369
8816001	5.06[8][a] n.205
8819001	4.14[4][b] n.47
8820002	4.04[3][b][iv] n.65
8820003	4.05[5][b] n.51
8823001	5.06[5][b][iii] n.135
8826002	5.06[6][b] n.157
8826003	5.03[3] n.38; 5.03[3][c] n.62
8832001	5.06[6][b] n.157
8834005	5.06[6][b] n.157
8837002	5.06[6][b] n.157
8837004	5.03[5][a] n.104
8838009	5.03[2][b] n.30
8924003	5.06[8][b][iv] n.262
8948023	5.05[5][a][i] n.191; 5.05[5][b][i] n.246
9001046	19.03[3][d][i] n.173
9017015	5.07[2][a] n.12
9021001	5.06[8][d][ii] n.344
9021037	5.06[9] n.433
9026041	S4.14[6] ns. 103.4, 103.15
9034004	9.04[3][f] n.118
9036028	10.07[2][c] n.66
9109032	13.01[2][a] n.16
9109033	19.03[1] n.16
9113009	5.06[5][b][i] n.103; 5.06[8][d][ii] n.353; 10.01[3][h] n.124
9114023	9.04[1][b] n.28
9121002	5.03[5] n.96
9126020	5.06[8][d][ii] n.334; 17.04[2][b] n.69
9126025	17.04[2][b] n.69
9135043	10.07[2][c] n.70; 10.07[2][d][ii] n.93
9141043	19.04[7] n.146
9146002	4.08[6][c] n.88
9147065	5.06[8][b][v] n.269
9151045	4.05[7][b] n.81
9152031	19.04[7] ns. 146, 148
9203028	10.07[2] n.21
9203037	10.07[2] n.12
9206006	4.08[8] n.171
9218074	19.04[7] n.146
9222043	19.04[4] n.105
9226051	19.04[7] n.146
9229028	19.05[4] n.65
9241002	2.02[3][b][i] n.39
9241014	19.02[2][a][i] n.45; 19.04[7] n.146
9242006	5.06[8][b][i] n.220; 5.06[8][d][ii] n.333
9248026	19.02[3][c] n.180; 19.04[7] n.146
9250004	2.01[2] n.50; S2.01[2] n.67
9304020	4.13[3] n.19
9309018	19.02[2][a][i] n.45; 19.05[2][b][ii] n.28
9310003	19.04[7] n.151
9314050	18.01[2][a] n.29; 18.01[2][b] n.31
9317025	5.06[8][d][ii] n.341

9320015	5.06[8][d][ii] ns. 325, 328; 10.07[2] n.17; 10.07[2][d][i] n.91
9321046	19.02[2][a][i] n.45; 19.02[2][d][iv] ns. 165, 167
9322035	19.04[7] n.148
9324018	19.04[7] n.151
9325002	5.06[8][d][ii] n.325
9329025	10.07[2] n.12
9332006	10.01[9] n.204
9333028	16.02[2][b][iii] n.79
9335004	18.05[2][d] n.82
9337006	17.02[1][c][i] n.52; 17.04[2][b] n.69
9345035	19.03[3][b][i] n.128
9347002	5.05[4][b] n.139
9350016	19.04[3][c] n.98
9352001	19.05[2][b][ii] n.31
9352012	19.05[4] n.65
9403004	2.02[3][c][ii] n.82
9409005	5.06[8][d][ii] n.344
9409018	5.06[8][d][ii] n.353
9410011	2.02[3][c][ii] n.82
9412036	4.08[8] n.168; S4.08[8] n.168.5; 19.03[3][b][i] n.120
9415007	9.04[3][e] n.86; 19.02[2][b][ii] n.89
9417007	19.04[7] n.147
9418013	10.08[2] n.31
9419021	5.05[5][a][i] n.175; 5.05[5][b][i] n.234
9422052	2.02[3][c][ii] n.82
9427023	19.02[2][a][i] ns. 31, 45
9432017	19.04[7] n.148
9436005	4.02[4][b][iv] n.167
9436006	19.02[2][b][ii] n.81
9437037	18.05[2][d] n.82
9441031	19.03[3][b][i] n.128
9442019	19.03[3][d][i] n.173
9443004	5.05[4][a] n.128
9444016	18.05[2][d] n.82
9444033	S10.01[10][e] n.233.2; 19.03[3][b][i] n.128
9447036	19.03[3][d] n.162
9448035	19.03[3][d][i] ns. 172, 177
9449017	19.04[7] n.147
9451050	19.02[3][b] n.179; 19.04[7] n.146; 19.05[2][b][ii] n.28
9451051	19.02[3][b] n.179
9503025	19.03[3][d][i] n.173
9504004	4.02[5] n.253
9505007	5.07[3][d] n.117
9507028	19.04[7] n.147
9510065	10.04[4][c] n.47
9511028	19.02[2][a][i] n.45
9517020	11.02[2][b][ii] n.81
9532006	13.03[3][a] n.41; 16.02[2][c][i] n.137; 17.02[3][c] n.148
9534001	15.03[6][b] n.240
9543049	S10.01[10][e] n.233.2
9547005	5.07[3][d] n.117
9602010	4.14[4][e] n.71
9602017	2.02[3][c][ii] n.82

[Text references are to paragraphs and notes (9"n.");
references to the supplement are preceded by "S."]

Priv. Ltr. Rul.

9604003	5.06[8][b][i] n.220
9604015	5.05[6][a][ii] n.319
9604018	4.04[7][b][i] n.274
9606003	19.03[3][d][i] n.171
9606008	5.06[7][c] n.192
9609015	19.03[3][d][i] n.180
9609018	4.05[2][b] n.13
9609052	10.07[2][d][i] n.86
9610018	5.06[3][a] n.31
9611011	17.02[1][c][i] n.54
9613016	5.06[8][b][i] n.212
9620017	19.04[7] n.151
9621007	2.02[3][c][ii] n.82
9622036	19.04[1][c] n.14
9623024	4.14[5][b] n.93
9623063	5.07[2][b] n.17
9625033	10.07[2][b] n.44
9623019	5.05[8][d] n.382
9626041	19.03[3][d][i] n.171
9627020	18.05[2][b][ii] n.46
9630008	5.05[1][a] n.5
9631021	5.05[6][a][ii] ns. 318, 324
9633004	10.07[2] n.12
9634019	5.05[5][a] n.159; 5.05[5][b] n.213
9634020	5.06[7][c] n.195
9635011	5.05[2][c] n.81
9636033	S4.14[6] n.103.4
9639053	S4.14[6] n.103.25
9639056	10.01[2][h] n.69; 10.01[5] n.153; 10.01[9] n.205
9643013	4.08[7][d] n.161
9644053	2.02[3][c][ii] n.71
9644057	18.05[2][b][ii] n.34
9645010	19.03[3][d][i] n.173
9646003	4.05[2][a] n.6
9646010	10.07[2][d][i] n.87
9646021	4.08[4][c] n.53
9651004	4.14[9][b] n.137
9651017	4.14[5][a] n.83
9651030	4.14[5][a] n.83; S4.14[6] n.103.24
9652010	19.04[7] n.148
9702006	5.06[8][d][iii] n.383
9704029	5.06[8][d][ii] n.328
9705011	18.05[2][b][ii] n.31
9705017	19.03[3][d][i] n.173
9709015	13.02[4][c][i] n.307
9710021	9.04[3][e] n.86; 9.04[3][f] n.99; 19.02[3][b] n.174; 19.05[2][b][i] n.23
9711017	19.04[7] n.146
9716023	5.05[6][a] n.304
9718031	S5.03[4][a][i] n.166; 5.03[5][e] n.145
9718032	5.05[6][a] n.304
9719001	4.02[2][a] n.21
9719014	19.04[7] ns. 147, 148
9720029	9.02[1] n.5
9721006	5.05[6][a] n.304
9721009	15.03[2][b] ns. 15, 18
9722022	19.02[3][b] n.173
9723028	10.07[2][d][i] n.86
9723038	5.05[2][a] n.63; 5.05[3][b][i] n.104

Priv. Ltr. Rul.

9724016	5.06[8][d][iii] n.375
9724021	6.07[1] n.15
9725005	10.07[2] n.19
9725014	18.05[2][b][i] n.25; 18.05[2][d] n.71
9725031	10.04[4][a] n.33
9725032	10.01[3][a] n.86
9707026	17.04[2][b] n.69
9710021	4.08[6][d] n.108; 19.05[3][b] n.54
9711017	19.05[4] n.66
9713008	4.13[4][a] ns. 30, 37
9725032	19.02[3][a] n.170
9729015	5.06[3][g] n.69
9729024	5.05[7][b] n.339
9729040	5.07[2][c] n.34
9730004	19.04[2] n.21; 19.04[3][b] n.56; 19.04[3][b][i] n.81; 19.05[3][b] n.54
9731003	10.01[2][h] n.70
9731009	11.03[4][c][i] n.75
9731029	5.06[6][b] n.157
9731030	12.03[1] n.4
9732025	6.07[1] n.15
9733017	5.06[3][a] n.31
9734057	5.05[6][a][ii] n.323
9735025	4.08[7][d] n.161
9735029	18.05[2][b][i] n.25; 18.05[2][d] n.71
9737026	18.05[2][b][i] n.15
9738006	18.05[2][b][i] ns. 15, 18
9739015	5.06[8][b][i] n.212
9741004	19.03[3][d][i] ns. 173, 180
9741009	4.13[2] n.6
9741040	10.04[4][a] n.34
9743033	4.13[3] n.22
9745019	4.14[4][a] n.38
9746004	4.14[5][a] n.82
9748004	6.05[3][b] n.40
9752022	5.06[8][d][iii] n.383
9752072	10.07[2][d][i] n.86
9801009	2.02[3][c][ii] n.82
9801013	5.05[6][a][ii] n.324
9801025	13.02[2][e][ii] n.126
9801026	16.02[5][c] n.357
9801049	6.07[1] n.15
9802004	19.02[3][b] n.173; 19.05[4] n.65
9802013	6.07[1] n.15
9802031	10.02[2][b][iii] n.52
9803017	5.07[3][c][i] n.75
9804001	19.05[2][b][ii] n.33
9804012	4.08[7][d] n.161
9804047	19.03[2][a][i] n.35
9808010	19.02[2][b][ii] n.93
9808024	S4.14[6] n.103.24
9815023	4.08[8][b] n.181
9816010	5.07[2][b] n.21
9818008	10.07[2][d][i] n.89
9818009	5.05[2][a] n.63
9818042	9.04[1][b] n.33
9818053	10.07[2][b] n.56
9821030	10.01[6] n.186
9822014	10.07[2] n.24

[Text references are to paragraphs and notes (9"n.");
references to the supplement are preceded by "S."]

Priv. Ltr. Rul.

9822031 . . . . 5.06[8][d][ii] n.341
9823006 . . . . . 13.01[2][a] n.20; 17.03[1] n.13
9831005 . . . . 10.01[2][h] n.69
9832039 . . . . 4.14[4][e] n.69
9837007 . . . . 10.01[9] n.204
9839003 . . . . 18.05[2][b][ii] n.43
9839018 . . . . 4.10[4][a] n.24
9840008 . . . . . 16.02[3][b][ii] n.193; 16.02[6]
n.404
9840036 . . . . . 16.02[3][b][ii] n.193; 16.02[6]
n.404
9841017 . . . . 19.03[4][a] n.282; 19.03[4][e][i]
n.367; S19.03[4][e][i] n.367
9842003 . . . . 19.04[2] n.21; 19.04[3][b] n.56;
19.04[3][b][i] n.81; 19.05[3][b] n.54
9842060 . . . . 10.07[2][b] n.56; 18.05[2][b][ii]
n.38
9843024 . . . . 4.14[5][b] n.93
9845019 . . . . 10.07[2] n.19
9847026 . . . . 10.07[2][d][i] n.86
9848006 . . . . 19.02[2][b][ii] n.103
9848018 . . . . 18.05[2][b][ii] n.43
9852031 . . . . 4.13[7][e] n.104
9852034 . . . . 10.07[2] n.12
9903038 . . . . S5.03[3][c][i] n.116
9952039 . . . . S5.03[3][c][i] n.116
199901023 . . . . 5.05[2][a] n.63
199903019 . . . . 10.07[2][d] n.80
199903025 . . . . 4.08[6][a] n.77
199903038 . . . . 2.02[3][c][v] n.131
199904001 . . . . 4.13[8][a] n.118; 18.05[2][b][ii]
n.41
199905009 . . . . 15.03[2][b] n.18
199906003 . . . . 18.05[2][b][ii] n.41
199908022 . . . 10.01[3][c] n.97; 19.03[2][a][iv]
n.70
199908024 . . . . 17.02[1][c][i] n.54
199908033 . . . . 10.08[2] n.41
199908060 . . . . 10.01[3][c] n.97
199909034 . . . . 15.03[2][b] n.15
199911008 . . . . 18.05[2][b][ii] n.41
199912014 . . . . 6.07[1] n.14
199912027 . . . . 10.01[2][a] n.14
199913022 . . . . 17.02[1][c][i] n.52
199915015 . . . . 5.06[8][d][iii] n.369
199915052 . . . . 10.08[2] n.31
199917068 . . . . 16.02[6] n.404
199918006 . . . . 19.03[2][a][iv] n.70
199918039 . . . . 5.07[2][b] n.22
199919027 . . . . 15.03[2][b] n.15
199922038 . . . . 6.05[4] n.52
199922045 . . . 15.03[3][b] n.50; 16.02[7][a]
n.428
199922062 . . . . 4.08[4][b] n.31
199923028 . . . . 18.05[2][b][ii] n.38
199924014 . . . . 4.13[6][a] n.62
199924015 . . . . 19.04[7] n.147
199926019 . . . . 10.08[1][a] n.22
199927002 . . . . 10.01[3][a] n.86
199929027 . . . . 10.07[2][d] n.80
199929040 . . . . . 15.02[1] n.30; S15.02[1] n.24

Priv. Ltr. Rul.

199930019 . . . . 6.07[1] n.15
199932001 . . . . 5.06[8][d][ii] n.328
199932042 . . . . 10.07[2][c] n.66
199933002 . . . . 19.02[3][b] n.179
199933020 . . . . 4.13[4][c][ii] ns. 44, 48;
4.13[7][f] n.109; S4.13[7][f] n.109
199935003 . . . . 4.08[8][b] n.181
199936036 . . . . 10.08[1] n.7
199936052 . . . . . . 4.13[3] n.18; 5.06[8][b][ii]
n.237; 5.06[8][b][iv] n.263
199937026 . . . . . 15.03[6][b] n.238; 15.03[7][a]
n.256; 15.03[7][c][i] n.286
199939039 . . . . 5.05[2][a] n.63
199941013 . . . . 9.04[6] n.180
199942015 . . . . 4.03[1] n.2; S4.03[1] n.2
199944003 . . . . 9.04[3][e] n.87
199945046 . . . . 4.04[7][b][i] n.274
199947034 . . . 19.01[1] n.10; 19.02[2][a][i] n.45
199951032 . . . . 19.03[3][b][i] n.134
199952012 . . . 10.01[3][a] n.86; 19.02[2][a][ii]
n.69
199952039 . . . . 5.03[3][c] n.70
199952044 . . . . 5.05[6][a][i] n.308
200000634 . . . . 2.02[3][c][ii] n.82
200001010 . . . . 5.05[1][b] n.22
200001013 . . . . 19.03[3][b][i] n.128
200002011 . . . . 5.05[2][a] n.63
200010015 . . . . 19.04[7] n.146
200013015 . . . . 10.08[2] n.40
200014002 . . . . 4.13[3] n.23
200014013 . . . . 4.02[7][d][i] n.340
200015012 . . . . 19.04[7] n.148
200017013 . . . . 15.03[2][b] n.15
200017051 . . . . 4.14[5][b] n.92
200018036 . . . . 17.02[1][c][i] n.54
200022014 . . . . 5.05[8][d] n.385
200022031 . . . . . 10.08[1] n.7; 10.08[2] n.30
200024007 . . . . 4.13[2] n.6
200024016 . . . . 5.05[1][b] n.41
200025032 . . . . 5.06[3][a] n.29
200027001 . . . . 10.08[1] n.7
200027002 . . . . 17.01[2][a][ii] n.30
200027009 . . . . 15.03[2][b] n.18
200027015 . . . . 5.05[2][b] n.70
200028021 . . . . 17.02[1][c][i] n.54
200030012 . . . . 5.06[8][d][ii] n.325
200032010 . . . . 5.05[2][b] n.68
200040010 . . . . 17.04[2][a] n.50
200043031 . . . . 2.02[3][c][vi] n.142
200043036 . . . . 4.13[3] n.22
200044034 . . . . 10.08[1][a] n.22
200045004 . . . . 4.13[3] n.22
200105048 . . . . 8.09 n.2
200106008 . . . . 5.06[8][d][ii] n.312
200107015 . . . . . 16.02[6] n.425; 17.02[3][e][i]
n.168; 17.02[3][e][ii] n.179
200111038 . . . . 4.14[5][b] n.93
200112023 . . . 19.03[4][a] n.282; S19.03[4][e][i]
n.367
200114004 . . . . 19.02[4][c][i] n.202
200114005 . . . . 2.02[3][c][ii] n.82

[Text references are to paragraphs and notes (9"n.");
references to the supplement are preceded by "S."]

Priv. Ltr. Rul.

200114026	16.02[2][b][iii] n.68
200116006	10.08[1][a] n.22
200116007	5.05[2][a] n.58
200117021	19.03[3][d][i] n.184
200120021	4.08[4][b] n.31; 4.08[4][c] n.51
200122024	19.04[7] n.146
200127007	8.07[2] n.9; 10.07[2] ns. 11, 27
200127027	5.06[3][a] n.31
200128021	4.05[2][a] n.6
200129018	2.02[3][c][vi] n.144
200132013	5.07[5] n.184
200138028	19.02[4][c][ii] n.210
200143014	4.04[6] n.214
200144018	10.04[4][a] n.33
200148028	10.01[6] n.185
200148034	18.05[2][e][iv] n.111
200150016	18.05[2][e][iv] n.111
200201020	18.05[2][e][iii] n.100
200202032	5.05[3][a] n.97
200203031	4.03[1] n.3
200203045	4.08[7] n.114
200204022	5.06[8][e] n.410
200210018	S18.05[2][b][iii] n.47
200210038	S4.13[3] n.22
200210051	S10.01[5] n.146
200219003	S5.06[8][d][iii] n.384
200229013	S4.13[2] n.6
200234004	S5.08[3][b][i] n.92
200240018	S4.08[7][a] n.121
200240020	S11.03[5] n.105
200241044	S11.02[1][c] n.36
200242025	S5.08[5][b][ii] n.237
200243026	S18.05[2][b][ii] n.43
200246024	S5.08[5][b][ii] n.237
200247037	S4.10[6] n.70
200250033	S19.03[2][a][iv] n.68
200252084	S5.08[5][b][ii] n.236
200303020	S10.07[2] n.26
200303030	S18.05[2][e][iii] n.102
200311020	S4.13[3] n.22; S10.04[4][a] n.33
200314003	S18.05[2][e][iii] n.114
200314009	S4.14[4][e] n.69
200314011	S18.05[2][e][iii] n.114
200314012	S11.03[4][c] n.56
200318039	S5.06[8][d][iii] n.384
200318064	S10.01[2] n.13
200324018	S10.01[5] n.144
200324023	S10.08[1][a] n.22
200327016	S5.08[5][b][ii] n.237
200333023	S10.07[2][b] n.61
200334020	S9.05[2][a] n.19
200334025	S10.01[2] n.13
200335015	S10.04[4][a] n.33
200339021	S10.07[2][b] n.35
200339043	S2.02[3][c][ii] n.82
200339047	S2.02[3][c][ii] n.82
200340012	S2.02[3][c][ii] n.82
200341011	S18.05[2][e][iv] n.113
200343019	S16.02[3][b][ii] n.177
200345038	S10.03 n.13; S17.02[1][c][ii] n.62

Priv. Ltr. Rul.

200350009	S4.08[5][a] n.56; S4.10[4][b] n.30
200350010	S4.08[5][a] n.56; S4.10[4][b] n.30
200403031	S18.05[2][e][iv] n.110
200403093	S5.06[8][d][iii] n.384
200403094	S4.13[7][a] n.87; S11.03[4][c][i] n.78
200404009	S11.02[2][c] n.91
200404013	S4.14[4][e] n.73
200406004	S3.02[1][b] n.22; S11.03[4][c][i] n.76
200406038	S10.07[2][c] n.66
200407003	S16.02[9][a] n.568
200407005	S16.02[9][a] n.568
200407006	S19.02[3][b] n.174.1
200407016	S4.16 n.10; S5.06[8][d][iii] n.384; S10.08[1] n.3; S17.02[1][c][i] n.42
200408015	S10.06[2] n.14
200410011	S5.06[8][d][iii] n.383
200410014	S18.05[2][e][iv] n.113
200410015	S18.05[2][e][iv] n.113
200411004	S17.02[1][c][i] n.54
200413011	S11.03[4][c][i] n.76
200417030	S5.06[3][a] n.31; S5.06[7][b] n.181
200418002	S5.05[2][a] n.58
200419011	S16.02[7][c][i] n.476
200420007	S10.07[2][d] n.80
200422050	S5.06[8][d][iii] n.384
200422051	S10.03[1] n.13; S17.02[1][c][ii] n.62
200426005	S9.04[3][f] n.119
200426006	S9.04[3][f] n.119
200426007	S9.04[3][f] n.119
200426008	S4.08[7][d] n.163
200428013	S5.05[5][a][i] n.188; S10.07[2] n.12
200430002	S5.06[8][d][iii] n.368
200430009	S18.05[2][e][iv] n.113
200435006	S10.07[2][b] n.61
200435008	S18.05[2][e][iii] n.99
200437032	S10.07[2][d][ii] n.93
200438014	S4.03[1] n.2
200438028	S5.06[8][e] n.417; S10.08[1][b] n.29
200438036	S4.04[6] n.215
200439001	S16.02[9][a] n.565
200439036	S17.02[1][c][i] n.54
200440019	S16.02[9][a] n.574
200440020	S16.02[9][a] n.574
200441005	S18.05[2][e][iv] n.106
200442003	S10.06[2][a] n.21
200442027	S10.07[2][d][i] n.87
200443010	S16.02[9][a] n.574
200443027	S5.06[8][d][iii] n.384; S17.02[1][c][i] n.54
200443030	S10.07[2][d][i] n.88
200444023	S5.06[8][b][i] n.218; S5.06[8][b][iii] n.241

*[Text references are to paragraphs and notes (9"n.");
references to the supplement are preceded by "S."]*

Priv. Ltr. Rul.

200445010 . . . . S5.07[2][c] n.33
200445023 . . . . S11.02[2][a] n.47.1
200445024 . . . . S11.02[2][a] n.47.1
200447002 . . . . S18.05[2][e][iv] n.111
200448006 . . . . S4.04[5] n.171
200448038 . . . . S5.06[8][d][iii] n.386
200450004 . . . . S5.06[8][d][iii] n.368
200450033 . . . . S4.13[3] n.22
200451024 . . . . S5.07[5] n.184
200452010 . . . . S8.07[2] n.9
200502008 . . . . S19.03[4][f] n.385
200502014 . . . . S10.01[6] n.185
200503024 . . . . . S10.07[2] n.18; S10.07[2][c]
n.66; S10.07[2][d] n.80
200504024 . . . . S16.02[9][a] n.574
200505008 . . . . S5.05[4][b] n.140
200505016 . . . . S5.08[3][b][i] n.92
200507002 . . . . S18.05[2][e][iii] n.99
200507010 . . . . S18.05[2][e][iv] n.111
200508001 . . . . S16.02[5][e] n.365
200510026 . . . . S15.03[2][b] n.15
200511013 . . . . S18.05[2][b][ii] n.43
200512003 . . . . S16.02[9][a] n.574
200512006 . . . . S16.02[9][a] n.574
200513006 . . . . S16.02[9][a] n.574
200513008 . . . . S16.02[9][a] n.574
200513014 . . . . S4.04[6] n.215
200516001 . . . . S18.05[2][e][iv] n.108
200516005 . . . . S11.02[2][c] n.91
200518005 . . . . S4.14[4][e] n.73
200518011 . . . . S2.02[3][c][ii] n.82;
S5.08[2][c][ii] n.56
200518012 . . . . S10.07[2][d] n.80
200518047 . . . . S2.02[3][c][ii] n.82
200519006 . . . . S16.02[9][a] n.574
200519042 . . . . S10.07[2][d] n.80
200520003 . . . . S18.05[2][e][iv] n.109
200520021 . . . . S18.05[2][e][iv] n.113
200520022 . . . . S18.05[2][e][iv] n.113
200520023 . . . . S18.05[2][e][iv] n.113
200521014 . . . . S2.02[3][c][ii] n.82
200522002 . . . . S17.02[1][c][i] n.54
200523003 . . . . . S4.08[5][a] n.56; S4.10[4][b]
n.30; S18.05[2][e][iv] n.109
200523004 . . . . S18.05[2][e][iv] n.109
200523005 . . . . S18.05[2][e][iv] n.109
200523015 . . . . S4.04[6] n.215
200526017 . . . . S5.06[8][d][iii] n.282
200527008 . . . . S18.05[2][e][iii] n.100
200528015 . . . . S16.02[9][a] n.574
200528019 . . . . . S4.04[6] n.215; S5.08[3][b][i]
n.92
200529006 . . . . S2.02[3][c][ii] n.71;
S2.02[3][c][v] n.128
200530002 . . . . S18.05[2][b][ii] n.34
200530014 . . . . S8.07[4] n.34; S10.08[1][a] ns.
16, 22
200530020 S4.13[4][a] n.25; S18.05[2][e][iv]
n.106
200531004 . . . . . S4.08[5][a] n.56; S4.10[4][g]
n.56

Priv. Ltr. Rul.

200532024 . . . . S18.05[2][b][ii] n.34;
S18.05[2][b][iii] n.47
200533001 . . . S9.04[1][b][iv] n.33; S9.04[3][e]
n.89
200533006 . . . . S18.05[2][e][iv] n.112
200535006 . . . . S5.05[8][c] n.372
200535009 . . . . S18.05[2][b][ii] n.43
200535022 . . . . S18.05[2][b][ii] n.43
200535026 . . . . S5.06[8][d][iii] n.384
200536012 . . . . S18.05[2][e][iv] n.113
200536015 . . . . S5.06[8][d][iii] n.386
200537020 . . . . S11.02[2][c] n.92
200538023 . . . . S16.02[9][a] n.574
200539001 . . . . S18.05[2][e][i] n.96
200539010 . . . . S18.05[2][e][i] n.96
200539011 . . . . S18.05[2][e][i] n.96
200539024 . . . . S18.05[2][e][iv] n.109
200540003 . . . . S5.06[8][d][iii] n.384
200540004 . . . . S18.05[2][b][ii] n.38
200541031 . . . . S18.05[2][b][ii] n.38
200541035 . . . . S18.05[2][b][ii] n.43;
S18.05[2][e][iv] n.113; S18.05[2][e][iv]
n.113
200541038 . . . . . S5.05[8][c] n.372; S5.06[8][e]
n.413
200542030 . . . . S16.02[9][a] n.574
200543015 . . . . S18.05[2][e][ii] n.99
200543037 . . . . S4.05[2][b] n.13
200546052–200546055 . . . . . S18.05[2][e][iv]
n.113
200547010 . . . . S16.02[5][c] n.357
200548017 . . . . S17.02[1][c][i] n.54
200548018 . . . . S16.02[5][c] n.357
200548019 . . . . S5.05[8][b] n.367; S5.05[8][d]
n.386
200548035 . . . . . S4.08[5][a] n.56; S4.10[4][b]
n.30; S4.13[3] n.20; S18.05[2][e][iv]
n.113
200549005 . . . . S18.05[2][e][iv] n.113
200550006 . . . . S15.03[2][b] n.15
200551001 . . . . S18.05[2][e][i] n.96
200551013 . . . . S10.02[2][b][iii] n.62
200551020 . . . . S18.05[2][e][iv] n.113
200601010 . . . . . S18.05[2][e][iv] ns. 108, 113
200602002 . . S9.04[6] n.180; S13.01[2][a] n.9
200602033 . . . . S10.08[2] n.33
200603002 . . . . S10.02[2][b][ii] n.51; S10.02[3]
n.132
200603004 . . . . . . S4.16 n.10; S5.06[8][d][iii]
n.384; S10.08[1] n.3; S17.02[1][c][i]
n.42
200603011 . . . . S8.09 n.2
200603040 . . . . . S4.08[6][a] n.76; S4.10[4][c]
n.40
200604006 . . . . S10.08[2] n.30
200604028 . . . . . S4.05[5][b] n.57; S4.13[7][a]
n.87; S11.03[4][c][i] n.78
200606002 . . . . S16.02[9][a] n.574
200606006 . . . . S4.10[4][c] n.40
200608007 . . . . S18.05[2][e][i] n.96
200608011 . . . . S9.04[1][b][iii] n.30

[Text references are to paragraphs and notes (9"n.");
references to the supplement are preceded by "S."]

Priv. Ltr. Rul.

200608012 . . . . S4.04[7][b][i] n.273;
           S4.04[7][b][ii] n.284
200608019 . . . . S5.06[8][d][iii] n.383
200609003 . . . . S18.05[2][e][iv] n.111
200612001 . . . . . . S5.06[8][d][iii] ns. 368, 384
200612002 . . . . S4.13[4][c][ii] ns. 41, 50;
        S10.01[6] n.185; S10.01[8] n.192
200613006 . . . . S16.02[9][a] n.574
200613020 . . . . S2.02[3][c][vi] n.142
200615025 . . . . S4.05[2][b] n.17
200616008 . . . . S10.06[2] n.14
200616022 . . . . . S10.03[1] n.13; S10.03[3][a]
        n.40; S16.02[9][a] n.574
200616026 . . . . S10.07[2][d] n.78
200616041 . . . S10.07[2] n.26; S10.07[2][d] ns.
        76, 78, 82
200617002 . . . . S19.03[3][d][iii] n.226
200617008 . . . . . S4.14[4][e] n.73; S4.14[9][b]
        n.136
200617035 . . . . S19.03[3][d][i] n.173
200618003 . . . . S10.01[3] n.76
200618004 . . . . S18.05[2][e][iii] n.100
200618017 . . . . S10.07[2][b] n.46
200618018 . . . . S5.06[8][d][iii] n.387
200620003 . . . . . S10.03[1] n.13; S16.02[9][a]
        n.574
200620021 . . . . S18.05[2][e][iv] n.113
200622005 . . . . S5.05[8][c] n.372
200622015 . . . . S16.02[9][b] n.584
200622029 . . . . S16.02[9][b] n.584
200622030 . . . . S16.02[9][b] n.584
200622042 . . . . S18.05[2][e][iv] n.113
200625011 . . . . S19.04[7] n.146
200625014 . . . . S17.02[1][c][i] n.54
200626002 . . . . S5.06[3][h] n.82
200626010 . . . . S17.02[1][c][i] n.54
200626043 . . . . S19.03[3][d][i] n.173
200627016 . . . . . S3.06[3][b] n.22; S3.06[3][b]
        n.22
200627017 . . . . S16.02[9][a] n.574
200628007 . . . S10.08[1] n.7; S10.08[1][a] n.21
200630006 . . . . S11.02[1][b] n.25
200631006 . . . . S11.02[1][b] n.25
200633011 . . . . S11.02[1][b] n.25
200633015 . . . . S9.04[5][a] n.145; S9.04[5][b]
        n.150; S15.03[3][a] n.38
200634004 . . . . S18.05[2][e][ii] n.99
200637021 . . . . . S4.13[4][a] n.35; S10.04[4][c]
        n.47; S18.05[2][e][iv] n.113
200637025 . . . . S4.13[4][c][ii] ns. 41, 50;
        S10.01[6] n.185
200638020 . . . . S18.05[2][e][ii] n.99
200644001 . . . . S16.02[9][a] n.574
200645005 . . . . S18.05[2][e][iv] n.106
200647001 . . . . S4.13[4][c][ii] ns. 41, 50;
        S10.01[6] n.185; S10.01[8] n.192;
200649023 . . . . S10.07[2][d] n.80
200652042 . . . . S16.02[9][a] n.574
200702018 . . . . S5.06[8][d][iii] n.384
200703002 . . . . S16.02[9][a] n.574
200703031 . . . . S18.05[2][e][iv] n.106

Priv. Ltr. Rul.

200704003 . . . . S16.02[9][a] n.574
200705025 . . . . S18.05[2][e][iv] n.111
200707158 . . . . S10.02[4] n.141
200708054 . . . . S18.05[2][e][iv] n.106
200709014 . . . S4.15[1][b][i] n.49; S10.06[2][c]
        n.29
200710001 . . . . S16.02[9][a] n.574
200712008 . . . . S18.05[2][b][ii] n.43
200712010 . . . . . S5.07[2][b] n.21; S5.07[3][d]
        n.117
200712029 . . . . S18.05[2][e][iii] n.102
200714009 . . . . S18.05[2][e][iv] n.110
200715002 . . . S16.02[5][a] n.301; S16.02[9][a]
        n.574; S17.04[2][b] ns. 69, 72;
        S18.05[2][e] n.83; S18.05[2][e][iii]
        n.100; S18.05[2][e][iv] n.109
200715005 . . . . S4.13[4][c][ii] ns. 41, 50;
        S10.01[6] n.185; S10.01[8] ns. 192, 193
200717002 . . . . S16.02[9][b] n.584
200717016 . . . . S10.08[1] n.7; S10.08[1][a] ns.
        21, 22
200719002 . . . . S5.07[5] n.184
200719003 . . . . S17.02[1][c][i] n.54
200721006 . . . . S2.02[3][c][ii] n.57
200726005 . . . S5.05[5][a][i] n.193; S5.05[8][c]
        n.377
200726008 . . . . S18.05[2][e][iv] n.113
200728015 . . . . S10.01[3][g] n.115.4
200728018 . . . . S19.03[4][a] n.282;
        S19.03[4][e][i] n.367
200728040 . . . . S18.05[2][b][iii] n.80
200729025 . . . . S4.13[4][c][ii] ns. 41, 50;
        S10.01[6] n.185; S10.01[8] ns. 192, 193
200729028 . . . . S5.06[8][d][iii] n.384
200730015 . . . . S4.05[2][b] n.17
200731019 . . . . S4.13[4][c][ii] n.41;
        S4.13[4][c][iii] n.50; S10.01[8] ns. 192,
        193
200733007 . . . . S5.05[6][b] n.328
200734010 . . . . . S4.13[2] n.6; S18.05[2][e][iv]
        n.113
200735006 . . . . S16.02[9][a] n.574
200736002 . . . . S18.05[2][e][iv] n.108
200736011 . . . . S16.02[9][a] n.574
200736023 . . . . S18.05[2][e][iv] n.108
200738005 . . . . S18.05[2][e][iv] n.108
200740009 . . . . S4.03[1] n.3
200743001 . . . . S9.04[3][g] n.130
200743031 . . . . S5.08[3][b][i] n.92
200744005 . . . . S10.07[2][d] n.80
200745015 . . . . S18.05[2][b][ii] n.41
200746006 . . . . S16.02[9][a] n.574
200746012 . . . . S19.04[4] n.99
200747002 . . . . S4.14[5][b] n.93
200747011 . . . . S10.01[3][g] n.115.4
200748008 . . . S4.13[3] n.20; S10.01[11] n.236
200751022 . . . . S19.03[3][d][i] n.177
200752016 . . . . S6.05[3][b] n.40; S8.09 n.2
200801009 . . . . S10.08[1] n.7
200802010 . . . . S10.07[2][d] n.80
200802024 . . . . S11.02[1][b] n.25

*[Text references are to paragraphs and notes (9"n.");
references to the supplement are preceded by "S."]*

Priv. Ltr. Rul.

200804013 . . . . S17.04[2][a] n.51
200808018 . . . . S11.02[1][b] n.25
200812022   S4.13[6][d] n.76; S18.05[2][b][ii]
                                                        n.41
200814011 . . . . S19.03[3][d][i] n.177;
                                    S19.03[3][d][iii] n.230.1
200814014 . . . . S4.04[6] n.215
200814016 . . . . S17.04[3][b] n.130.1
200815011 . . . . S16.02[9][a] n.574
200816007 . . . . S16.02[9][a] n.574
200816008 . . . S10.01[5] n.150; S18.05[2][b][ii]
                                                        n.44
200816025 . . . . S19.03[3][d][i] n.177;
                                    S19.03[3][d][iii] n.230.1
200817009 . . . . S18.03[2][c] n.49
200818003 . . . . S11.02[2][e] n.103
200821030 . . . . S5.07[3][d] n.117
200822003 . . . . S4.14[4][a] n.40; S10.01[3][g]
                                                        n.115.4
200822011 . . . . S19.03[3][d][i] n.173;
                                    S19.03[3][d][iii] n.230
200825011 . . . . S4.14[4][a] n.40; S10.01[3][g]
                                                        n.115.30
200825014 . . . . S5.05[2][b] n.68
200825032 . . . . S5.06[8][d][iii] n.383;
              S15.03[7][b][ii] n.269; S17.02[1][c][i]
                                                        n.54
200829015 . . . . S5.05[5][b][i] n.227
200829016 . . . . S5.05[5][b][i] n.227
200832011 . . . . S5.06[8][d][iii] n.384
200832015 . . . . S4.13[3] n.20
200832017 . . . . . S5.05[5][b][i] ns. 218, 254;
              S5.06[8][e] n.413; S11.03[4][d] n.102
200832018 . . . . . S10.07[2] n.15; S10.07[2][c]
              n.66; S10.07[2][d][i] n.88
200832021 . . . . S10.06[2][a] n.21
200834013 . . . . S11.02[1][b] n.25
200835021 . . . . S16.02[9][a] n.574
200835022 . . . . S17.02[1][c][i] n.54
200838022 . . . . S15.02[4] n.64; S15.03[7][c][i]
                                                        n.287
200839025–200839027   . . . S18.05[2][e][iv] ns.
                                    107, 110, 113
200839029 . . . . S19.02[4][c][i] n.204;
                                    S19.02[5][a][ii] n.316
200840018 . . . . S4.04[7][b][i] n.272
200840038 . . . . S19.03[4][a] n.282;
                                    S19.03[4][e][i] n.367
200841027 . . . . S18.05[2][e] n.83;
              S18.05[2][e][iv] ns. 107, 110, 113
200842007 . . . . . S4.08[6][a] n.76; S4.10[4][c]
              n.40; S10.01[2][d] n.32
200842012 . . . . S2.02[3][c][ii] n.82
200842013 . . . . S6.05[2][a][i] n.21
200842018 . . . . S5.07[3][d] n.117
200844010 . . . . S10.08[1][a] n.22
200846001 . . . . S19.03[3][b][i] n.141
200846003 . . . . S5.06[8][d][i] n.307;
                                    S10.07[2][d] n.76
200847014 . . . . S5.05[7][e] n.352; S11.02[1][b]
              n.28; S11.02[2][d] n.102

Priv. Ltr. Rul.

200847015 . . . . . S4.13[4][a] n.32; S4.13[7][a]
                                                        n.83
200848002 . . . . S10.01[3][g] n.115.4
200848003 . . . . S19.03[3][d][i] n.177;
              S19.03[3][d][iii] n.230.1
200848009 . . . . S15.03[6] n.227
200848014 . . . . S8.09 n.2
200851013 . . . . S10.01[3][g] n.115.4
200852029 . . . . S19.04[4] n.99
200901013 . . . . S17.04[3] n.81
200901019 . . . S19.03[3][d][iii] n.230.1
200901023 . . . . S5.05[1][c] n.55
200902008 . . . . . . S18.05[2][e][iv] n.106
200904022 . . . . . . S19.03[3][d][iii] n.230.1
200905002 . . . . S16.02[9][a] n.574
200905015 . . . . S5.05[1][b] n.41
200906017 . . . . S16.02[9][a] n.574
200908002 . . . . S17.02[1][c][i] n.54
200908003 . . . . S18.05[2][b][ii] n.34
200910002 . . . . S4.14[4][a] n.40; S10.01[3][g]
                                                        n.115.30
200910003 . . . . S18.05[2][e][iii] n.103
200910004 . . . . S15.03[7][c][i] n.287
200910019 . . . . S5.07[2][b] n.21
200913002 . . . . S18.05[2][e][iv] n.108
200916002 . . . . S17.02[1][c][i] n.54
200917004 . . . . S10.01[3][c] n.97;
              S18.05[2][e][iv] n.106
200917015 . . . . S18.05[2][e][iv] n.106
200918006 . . . . S10.02[1] n.9
200918014 . . . . S5.06[8][d][ii] n.384
200919002 . . S10.02[6][c] n.180; S19.03[4][a]
                                                        n.282
200919003 . . . . S5.06[8][d][ii] n.353
200919005 . . . . S17.02[1][c][i] n.54
200919008 . . . . S4.10[6] n.70; S18.05[2][e][iv]
                                                        n.113
200919013 . . . . S16.02[9][a] n.574
200920033 . . . . S19.03[3][d][iii] n.230.1
200921007 . . . . S16.02[9][a] n.574
200922013–200922027   . . . . . S18.05[2][e][iv]
                                                        n.113
200923012–200923016   . . . . . S18.05[2][e][iv]
                                                        n.109
200925003 . . . S4.14[6] n.103.25; S10.01[3][g]
                                                        n.115.4
200927013 . . . . S5.05[8][c] n.372
200930028 . . . . S4.03[1] n.3
200932020 . . . . S5.03[2][e] n.91
200935004–200935005   . . . . S19.03[3][d][iii]
                                                        n.230.1
200944002 . . . . S4.08[4][c] n.53.1; S4.08[6][a]
              n.76; S4.10[4][c] n.40
200944003 . . . . S16.02[9][a] n.574
200944004 . . . . S16.02[9][a] n.574
200944009 . . . . S16.02[9][a] n.574
200944017 . . . . S18.05[2][d] n.80
200945003 . . . . S16.02[9][a] n.574
200946001 . . . . S16.02[9][a] n.574
200946002 . . . . S16.02[9][a] n.574
200946027 . . . . S17.02[1][c][i] n.52

[Text references are to paragraphs and notes (9"n.");
references to the supplement are preceded by "S."]

Priv. Ltr. Rul.

200947003 . . . . S16.02[9][a] n.574
200947006 . . . . . S4.14[5][b] n.93; S4.14[9][b]
n.137
200947031 . . . . S16.02[9][a] n.574
200948001 . . . . . S4.14[5][b] n.93; S4.14[9][b]
n.137
200949004 . . . . . S4.14[5][b] n.93; S4.14[9][b]
n.137
200949006 . . . . S16.02[9][a] n.574
200949008 . . . . S16.02[9][a] n.574
200949009 . . . . S5.07[5] n.184
200949021 . . . . S16.02[9][a] n.574
200949022 . . . . S4.03[1] n.3
200953002 . . . . S16.02[9][a] n.574
200953003 . . . . S16.02[9][a] n.574
200953004 . . . . S16.02[9][a] n.574
200953010 . . . . S10.07[2][b] n.61; S10.07[2][c]
n.69
200953017 . . . . S16.02[9][a] n.574
201001003 . . . . S16.02[9][a] n.574
201001004 . . . . S16.02[9][a] n.574
201001007 . . . . S10.07[2][b] n.61; S10.07[2][c]
n.69
201001014 . . . . S4.03[1] n.3
201002008 . . . . S17.02[1][c][i] n.54
201002010 . . . . S16.02[9][a] n.574
201002013 . . . . S4.13[3] n.22
201003003 . . . . S16.02[9][a] n.574
201003015 . . . . S18.05[2][e][iv] n.108
201004006 . . . . S10.07[2][b] n.61; S10.07[2][c]
n.69
201006005 . . . . S4.13[3] n.22; S18.05[2][e][ii]
n.99; S18.05[2][e][iii] n.103
201006008 . . . . S16.02[9][a] n.574
201006009 . . . . S16.02[9][a] n.574
201006012 . . . . S19.03[3][d][iii] n.230.1
201010003 . . . . S16.02[9][a] n.574
201010004 . . . . S16.02[9][a] n.574
201010005 . . . . S16.02[9][a] n.574
201010016 . . . . S16.02[9][a] n.574
201011002 . . . . S18.05[2][e][iv] n.108
201011008 . . . . S18.05[2][e][iv] n.108
201013002 . . . . S17.02[1][b] n.32
201013017 . . . . S18.05[2][e][ii] n.99
201013030 . . . . S18.05[2][e][iv] n.108
201014032 . . . . S16.02[9][a] n.574
201014044 . . . . S19.03[3][d][iii] n.230.1
201015003 . . . . . S2.02[3][c][ii] n.57; S4.04[6]
n.215; S5.08[3][b][i] n.92
201015025 . . . . S18.05[2][e][iv] n.113
201016006 . . . . S4.03[1] n.3
201016033 . . . . S5.05[5][b][i] n.254
201019002 . . . . S4.03[1] n.3
201019006 – 201019007 . . . . . S19.03[3][d][iii]
n.230.1
201019012 . . . . S19.03[3][d][iii] n.230.1
201020001 . . . S4.13[3] n.22; S10.04[4][a] n.33
201020002 . . . . S5.06[8][d][iii] n.383
201021003 – 201021011   S18.05[2][e][ii] n.99
201021012 . . . . S16.02[9][a] n.574
201021048 . . . . S10.01[3] n.78.1

Priv. Ltr. Rul.

201022001 . . . . S5.05[2][b] n.68
201022002 . . . . S5.08[3][b][i] n.92
201022003 . . . . S16.02[9][a] n.574
201022004 . . . . S5.06[8][d][iii] n.384;
S17.02[1][c][i] n.42
201023001 – 201023006   S18.05[2][e][ii] n.99
201023007 . . . . S17.02[1][c][i] n.54
201023027 . . . . S18.05[2][e][i] n.96
201023050 . . . . S18.05[2][e] n.84;
S18.05[2][e][iv] n.114
201024006 . . . . S16.02[9][a] n.574
201024008 . . . . S10.08[1][a] n.16
201024009 . . . . S16.02[9][a] n.574
201024012 . . . . S19.03[3][d][iii] n.230.1
201024014 . . . . S18.05[2][e][iv] n.109
201024015 . . . . S18.05[2][e][iv] n.109
201024016 . . . . S18.05[2][e][iv] n.109
201024017 – 201024024 . . . . . S18.05[2][e][iv]
n.109
201024026 . . . . S18.05[2][e][iv] n.108
201024035 . . . . S5.06[8][d][iii] n.384
201024043 . . . . S18.05[2][e][iv] n.109
201024044 . . . . S18.05[2][e][iv] n.109
201025019 . . . . S16.02[9][a] n.574
201025021 . . . . S11.03[4][c] n.56
201025026 . . . . S18.05[2][e][iv] n.109
201025030 . . . . S18.05[2][e][iv] n.111
201025036 . . . . S16.02[9][a] n.574
201026014 . . . . S18.05[2][e][iii] n.103
201026018 . . . . S18.05[2][e][iv] n.108
201026019 . . . . S16.02[9][a] n.574
201026020 . . . . S16.02[9][a] n.574
201026021 . . . . S16.02[9][a] n.574
201026024 . . . . S18.05[2][e][iii] n.103
201026027 . . . . S18.05[2][e][iii] n.103
201027005 . . . . S16.02[9][a] n.574
201027026 . . . . S18.05[2][d] n.80
201027027 . . . . S18.05[2][d] n.80
201027034 . . . . S16.02[9][b] n.584
201029011 . . . . S4.13[8][b] n.122;
S18.05[2][b][ii] n.43
201032002 . . . . S10.07[2][c] n.66; S10.07[2][d]
n.80
201032010 . . . . S10.07[2][c] n.66; S10.07[2][d]
n.80
201032021 . . . . . S9.02[1][a] n.6; S18.03[2][b]
n.42
201032022 . . . . S5.07[5] n.184
201032024 . . . . S16.02[9][a] n.574
201032026 . . . . S18.05[2][e][iv] n.108
201033023 . . . . S4.03[1] n.3
201034008 . . . . S16.02[9][a] n.574
201034009 . . . . S16.02[9][a] n.574
201034013 . . . . S16.02[9][a] n.574
201035001 . . . . S16.02[9][a] n.574
201035008 . . . . S16.02[9][a] n.574
201036010 . . . . S16.02[9][a] n.574
201036011 . . . . S16.02[9][a] n.574
201036013 . . . . S5.06[8][d][iii] n.384
201037002 . . . . S16.02[9][a] n.574
201038004 . . . . S4.13[7][f] n.109

*[Text references are to paragraphs and notes (9"n.");
references to the supplement are preceded by "S."]*

Priv. Ltr. Rul.

201039001 . . . . S19.03[3][d][iii] n.230.1
201039003   S4.13[4][a] n.37; S18.05[2][e][iv]
                                            n.108
201039004 . . . . S16.02[9][a] n.574
201039008–201039009 . . . . . S18.05[2][e][iv]
                                            n.113
201042004 . . . . . S18.05[2][e][iv] ns. 109, 113
201042005 . . . . S16.02[9][a] n.574
201046004 . . . . S5.06[3][a] n.31
201049008 . . . . . S18.05[2][e][iv] ns. 108, 111
201049012 . . . . S16.02[9][a] n.574
201049016 . . . . S18.05[2][e][iii] n.100
201050005 . . . . S18.05[2][e][iv] n.109
201050006 . . . . S18.05[2][e][iv] n.109
201050008 . . . . S18.05[2][e][iv] n.109
201051002 . . . . S18.05[2][e][ii] n.99
201051003 . . . . S18.05[2][e][ii] n.99
201051004 . . . . S18.05[2][e][ii] n.99
201051023 . . . . S18.05[2][e][ii] n.99
201052002 . . . . S18.05[2][e][ii] n.99
201101001–201101009   S18.05[2][e][ii] n.99
201102004–201102024   S18.05[2][e][ii] n.99
201102051–201102052   S18.05[2][e][ii] n.99
201102053 . . . . S16.02[9][a] n.574
201103003 . . . . S4.03[1] n.3
201103004 . . . . S5.07[3][d] n.117
201103016 . . . . S16.02[9][a] n.574
201103023 . . . . S16.02[9][a] n.574
201103024 . . . . S16.02[9][a] n.574
201103039 . . . . S16.02[9][a] n.574
201104001 . . . . S18.05[2][e][ii] n.99
201104003 . . . . . S18.05[2][e][iv] ns. 108, 111
201104012 . . . . S16.02[9][a] n.574
201104022 . . . . S16.02[9][a] n.574
201108002 . . . . S16.02[9][a] n.574
201108005 . . . . S16.02[9][a] n.574
201108010 . . . . S16.02[9][a] n.574
201109004 . . . . S18.05[2][e][iv] n.108
201109005 . . . . S16.02[9][a] n.574
201109009 . . . . S16.02[9][a] n.574
201109012 . . . . S11.03[4][c] n.56
201109016 . . . . S17.02[1][c][i] n.54
201110004 . . . . S16.02[9][a] n.574
201110005 . . . . S16.02[9][a] n.574
201112001 . . . . S5.06[8][d][iii] n.384
201115003 . . . . S5.05[8][c] n.372
201115005 . . . . S15.03[4][d] n.166;
                                   S15.03[4][e][i] n.173
201116003 . . . . S17.04[2][a] n.51secref
             n='201116004'>S17.02[1][c][i] n.54
201116006 . . . . S4.08[7] n.114; S10.06[2] n.14;
                                   S19.03[2][a][ii] n.59
201116008 . . . . S17.04[2][a] n.51
201117005 . . . S5.06[8][d][ii] n.316; S5.06[8][e]
                                            n.413
201118003 . . . . S17.04[2][a] n.51
201118006 . . . . S16.02[9][a] n.574
201118007 . . . . . S8.07[4] n.34; S10.08[1] n.7;
                                   S10.08[1][a] n.13
201118013 . . . . S4.03[1] n.2
201118014 . . . . S19.03[3][d][iii] n.230.1

Priv. Ltr. Rul.

201119003 . . . . S10.08[2] n.31
201119004 . . . . . S8.07[4] n.34; S10.08[1] n.7;
                                   S10.08[1][a] n.13
201121002 . . . . S18.05[2][e][ii] n.99
201121003 . . . . S5.06[8][d][iii] n.383
201121007–201121009 . . . . . S18.05[2][e][iii]
                                            n.103
201121011 . . . . S18.05[2][e][iii] n.103
201122007 . . . . S18.05[2][e][iv] n.110
201122009 . . . . S4.03[1] n.3
201123007 . . . . S16.02[9][a] n.574
201123014 . . . . S18.05[2][e][ii] n.99
201124003 . . . . S16.02[9][a] n.574
201124006 . . . . S16.02[9][a] n.574
201125007 . . . . S5.05[8][c] n.372
201125009 . . . . . S10.07[2] n.21; S10.07[2][c]
                                            n.66
201125016 . . . . S16.02[9][a] n.574
201128011 . . . . S18.05[2][e][iv] n.112
201128016 . . . . S16.02[9][a] n.574
201129016 . . . . S4.04[7][b][i] n.277;
                                   S4.04[7][b][ii] n.285
201129018–201129020   S4.04[7][b][i] n.277;
                                   S4.04[7][b][ii] n.285
201129033 . . . . S5.05[4][a] n.128
201131006 . . . . . . S19.03[3][d][iii] n.230.1
201131011 . . . S5.06[8][d][iii] n.384; S10.08[1]
                       n.3; S17.02[1][c][i] n.42;
                                   S18.05[2][e][iii] n.103
201131012–201131013 . . . S16.02[9][a] n.574
201131014 . . . . S18.05[2][e][iv] n.108
201132017 . . . . S4.13[3] n.22
201133005 . . . . S16.02[9][a] n.574
201133007 . . . . S18.05[2][e][iv] n.108
201134017 . . . . S16.02[5][a] n.301;
                                   S18.05[2][e][i] n.96
201135024 . . . . S16.02[9][a] n.574
201136017 . . . . S18.05[2][b][ii] n.43
201137001 . . . . S16.02[9][a] n.574
201137009 . . . . S16.02[9][a] n.574

ACTIONS ON DECISION

AOD

1987-003 . . . . S5.05[6][a][ii] n.326
2000-04 . . . . S5.03[4][c][i] n.210
2005-01 . . . . S4.02[2][a] n.31
2008-01 . . . . . S4.03[2] n.16; S4.03[3][a] n.40;
                                   S4.03[3][c] n.54.1

ANNOUNCEMENTS

Ann.

83-43 . . . . . . 4.04[3][b][iii] n.53; 4.04[7][b][ii]
                                            n.282
90-54 . . . . 18.02[4][a] n.51
2003-18 . . . . S8.01[2][a] n.41

*[Text references are to paragraphs and notes (9"n.");
references to the supplement are preceded by "S."]*

Ann.

2009-57 . . . . . . S6.07[1][b] n.24; S9.02[1][b][i]
n.10.27

CHIEF COUNSEL ADVICE

CCA

200627023 . . . . S2.02[3][c][iii] n.116
200628042 . . . . S2.02[3][b][ii] n.41;
S2.02[3][c][ii] n.57; S2.02[3][c][vi] n.137
200645027 . . . . S2.02[3][c][iii] n.116
200747019 . . . . S2.02[3][c][iii] n.116
200803016 . . . . S2.02[3][c][iii] n.116
200830001 . . . . S8.02 n.13
200836027   S2.02[3][b][i] n.39; S5.03[3][c][i]
n.119; S5.03[6][a] n.270
200845023 . . . . S2.02[3][c][ii] n.82
200848004 . . . . S2.02[3][c][ii] ns. 55, 57
200909044 . . . . S2.02[3][c][iii] n.116
200915037 . . . . S2.02[3][c][vii] n.156
200916022 . . . . S9.04[10][a] n.219
200928037 . . . . S2.02[3][c][ii] n.82
200941016 . . . . S4.02[4][a] n.146;
S10.02[2][c][iv] n.114
201003013 . . . . S6.04[1] n.1
201020009 . . . S4.07[3][a] n.76; S6.04[2] n.12.1
201024059 . . . S9.04[10][a] n.220; S19.02[5][d]
n.491; S19.03[4][d] n.354
201116018 . . . . S9.04[9] n.206
201129037 . . . . S8.04 n.4

FIELD ATTORNEY ADVICE

FAA

20070801F . . . . S2.02[3][c][iii] n.116

FIELD SERVICE ADVICE

FSA

199919009 . . . . 19.05[3][b] n.53
199920016 . . . . 10.08[2] n.31
199921004 . . . . 5.06[5][b][ii] n.116
199924019 . . . . 4.04[5][b] n.206
199930026 . . . . 4.13[3] n.18
199950014 . . . . 10.01[2][b][ii] n.24;
10.02[2][c][v] n.117
200018020 . . . . 5.06[8][d][ii] n.353
200036012 . . . 4.08[8] n.168; S4.08[8] n.168.5;
4.11 n.3; 4.11[3][a] n.14; 4.11[3][d]
n.34; 19.03[3][b][i] n.120
200051044 . . . . 3.08 n.4
200119013 . . . . 4.16 n.22

FSA

200122011 . . . . 10.01[3][e] n.106; S10.01[3][e]
n.107.1
200143004 . . . 19.04[2] ns. 23, 26; 19.05[3][b]
n.54
200217022 . . . . S5.03[1][b] n.18

GENERAL COUNSEL'S MEMORANDA

GCM

4805 . . . . 5.05[1][b] n.28
16460 . . . . 10.01[3][h] n.123

INCOME TAX UNIT RULINGS

IT

19 . . . 4.15[1][a] n.24; 5.03[5][e] ns. 139, 141;
10.06[1] n.6; 10.06[2] n.18
23 . . . . 5.06[8][b][iv] n.259

IRS LEGAL MEMORANDA

ILM

200141013 . . . . 2.02[3][c][vi] n.151
200141015 . . . . 2.02[3][c][ii] n.100
200147021 . . . . 10.03[1] n.16
200149033 . . . . 5.08[3][b][i] n.92; 5.08[5][b][ii]
n.235
200218003 . . . . S3.05[3][b] n.46

IRS NEWS RELEASES

IR

2007-127 . . . S4.13[4][c][ii] n.41; S10.01[8] ns.
192, 193
2008-4 . . . . S4.02[6][b] n.264.5
2011-33 . . . . S8.10[3][b] n.36

NOTICES

Notice

89-24 . . . . 4.02[5] n.244; 4.08[1][a] n.5;
10.02[2][b][iii] n.57; 16.02[6] n.409
89-60 . . . . 4.02[5] n.244; 4.08[1][a] n.5
94-78 . . . . 5.05[5][a][i] n.169
96-34 . . . . 8.01[1][a][iii] ns. 26, 27
97-19 . . . . . 6.07[1] ns. 12, 14, 15; 9.02[1] n.7

[Text references are to paragraphs and notes (9"n.");
references to the supplement are preceded by "S."]

Notice

97-63 . . . . 5.05[3][b][ii] n.115
98-34 . . . . 6.07[1] n.15
99-31 . . . . 5.05[5][b][i] n.228
2000-37 . . . . 5.05[5][a] n.158; 5.05[5][b] n.214;
    1.02[2][b][i] n.56; 11.02[2][b][ii] n.67
2001-50 . . . . . . 16.02[4][a] n.225; 16.02[9][a]
    n.575; S16.02[9][a] n.574
2001-61 . . . . S8.01[2][a] n.41
2001-62 . . . . 10.07[2][b] n.30
2001-68 . . . . S8.01[2][a] n.41
2002-8 . . . . S10.01[3][g] n.115.4
2002-40 . . . . S8.01[2][a] n.41
2003-72 . . . . S19.03[3][b][i] n.133
2006-15 . . . . S5.05[5][a][i] n.187; S5.05[5][b][i]
    n.242
2007-54 . . . . . S2.02[1] n.7; S4.02[6][b] n.264.5
2007-90 . . . . S2.02[3][c][iii] n.116
2008-11 . . . . S4.02[6][b] n.264.5
2008-13 . . . . S4.02[6][b] n.264.5
2008-63 . . . S4.08[5][a] n.56; S4.10[4][b] n.30;
    S4.13[2][b] n.6; S4.13[3] n.20;
    S18.05[2][e][iv] n.113
2009-5 . . . . S4.02[6][b] ns. 264.5, 264.8
2009-18 . . . . . S4.02[5] n.247; S9.04[3][a] n.48;
    S9.04[3][b] n.61; S10.02[2][b][iii] ns. 55,
    60; S16.02[6] ns. 409, 412
2009-84 . . . . S5.03[1][b][iv] n.54
2009-85 . . . . . S6.07[1] n.8; S6.07[1][a] n.9
2010-19 . . . . S8.10[4] n.138
2011-66 . . . . . S8.10[2] n.15; S8.10[3][b] n.36;
    S8.10[3][d][ii] ns. 112, 116; S15.03[3][c]
    n.70
2011-76 . . . . S2.02[1] n.9; S8.10[2] n.15;
    S8.10[3][a] n.32; S8.10[3][d][ii] ns. 112,
    116; S17.02[1][a] n.7; S18.04[1] n.4
2011-82 . . . . S3.02[1][b][ii] n.52

PRELIMINARY
DETERMINATION
LETTERS

Ltr.

3569 . . . . S10.02[2][d][iii] n.130.3

PROGRAM MANAGER'S
TECHNICAL ADVICE

PMTA

2009-046 . . . . S2.02[3][c][iii] n.116

SMALL BUSINESS/
SELF-EMPLOYED
DIVISION OF IRS
MEMORANDA

SBSE

04-0509-009 . . . . S4.02[6][b] n.264.1
04-0809-015 . . . . S4.02[6][b] n.264.17
04-1010-044 . . . . S4.02[6][b] n.264.1
04-0111-002 . . . . S4.02[3][b] n.84
04-0111-008 . . . . S4.02[3][a] n.59
05-0308-022 . . . . S2.02[3][c][iii] n.116
05-0609-010 . . . . S2.02[3][c][iii] n.116

TECHNICAL ADVICE
MEMORANDA

TAM

8022006 . . . . S5.03[6][a] n.277
8137027 . . . . 6.01[3][b] n.32
8512004 . . . . 3.05[3][b] n.46
8546001 . . . . 19.03[1] n.14
8727003 . . . . 9.04[3][f] n.104
8826003 . . . . S5.03[3] n.80
8837004 . . . . S5.03[4][b][i] n.184
9005001 . . . . 4.05[2][a] n.6
9005002 . . . . 5.06[8][d][ii] n.355
9008003 . . . . 5.06[3][g] n.69
9010004 . . . . 4.07[2][b][ii] n.49
9010005 . . . . 4.07[2][b][ii] n.49
9013001 . . . . 4.04[6] n.218
9015001 . . . . 4.07[2][b][ii] n.49
9016002 . . . . 4.07[2][b][ii] n.49
9017002 . . . . 4.07[2][b][ii] n.49
9018002 . . . . 4.05[2][a] n.6
9021002 . . . . 5.06[8][b][iii] n.250
9023004 . . . . 5.06[8][b][iii] n.250
9027004 . . . . 4.04[6] n.226
9033004 . . . . 5.06[8][d][ii] n.334
9038002 . . . . 4.04[6] ns. 224, 235
9040001 . . . . 5.06[8][d][ii] n.334
9040003 . . . . 6.06[2] n.28
9043074 . . . . 4.08[4][b] n.33; 4.08[7] n.114
9045002 . . . . 9.04[3][f] n.104
9049002 . . . . 4.07[2][b][ii] n.49
9050004 . . . . 5.06[5] n.93
9051002 . . . . 5.03[3][c] n.71
9113028 . . . . 4.04[7][b][i] n.277
9122005 . . . . 4.08[4][b] n.34
9127008 . . . . 10.01[5] n.146
9128001 . . . . 6.04[1] n.6
9128009 . . . . 10.03[2] n.23
9131006 . . . . 9.04[3][e] n.87
9133001 . . . . 10.01[3][e] n.106; S10.01[3][e]
    n.107
9135003 . . . . 6.06[2] n.22
9140003 . . . . 4.08[1][b] n.13
9141008 . . . . 9.04[3][f] n.110

*[Text references are to paragraphs and notes (9"n.");
references to the supplement are preceded by "S."]*

TAM	
9145004	. . . . 3.05[3][b] n.46
9145005	. . . . 5.05[1][a] n.7
9207004	S5.03[4][b] n.173; 5.03[5][a] n.101
9212001	. . . . 4.04[3][b][iii] n.53; 4.04[7][b][ii] n.282
9217004	. . . . . 10.01[3] n.77; 10.02[4] n.139
9220007	. . . . 5.06[8][d][ii] n.328
9225002	. . . . 4.04[6] n.235
9226007	. . . . 4.07[2][b][ii] n.49
9228001	. . . . 5.07[2][b] n.21
9228004	. . . . 5.06[3][h] n.82
9228005	. . . . 4.04[6] n.235
9229004	. . . . 5.06[8][d][ii] n.334
9230002	. . . . 4.04[6] n.220
9231003	. . . . 10.01[5] n.150
9232002	. . . . 10.01[3][c] n.96
9237009	. . . . 5.06[8][d][ii] n.325
9240003	. . . . 4.02[3][g] n.129
9244001	. . . . 5.06[8][e] n.413
9245002	. . . . 4.04[6] n.235
9301005	. . . . 5.06[3][h] n.82
9307001	. . . . . . 5.06[8][d][iii] n.383
9309001	. . . . . 10.01[3][e] n.106; S10.01[3][e] n.107
9315005	. . . . 10.01[2] n.13
9321046	. . . . 19.02[2][a][i] n.55
9323002	. . . . 4.14[9][b] n.137
9326002	. . . . 8.04[2] n.16
9326003	. . . . 5.05[8][b] n.363
9327005	. . . . 5.06[8][d][iii] n.375
9327006	. . . . 5.05[8][b] ns. 364, 365
9328004	. . . . 4.04[5][a] n.180
9333002	. . . . 4.04[7][b][i] ns. 270, 274
9333004	. . . . 5.03[3][c] n.71
9346003	. . . . 4.04[6] n.235
9349002	. . . . 4.14[4][d] n.58
9349003	. . . . 4.03[2] n.16
9403002	. . . . 4.02[4][b][ii] n.155
9409018	. . . . 5.06[5][b][i] n.103; 10.01[3][h] n.124
9411010	. . . . 5.06[8][d][iii] n.383
9414019	. . . . 5.06[8][d][iii] n.383
9419006	. . . . 5.05[3][b][i] n.111
9428002	. . . . 4.04[3][c][ii] n.127
9431004	. . . . 4.13[3] n.18
9432001	. . . . 4.02[4][b][ii] n.151
9434004	. . . . 8.04[2] n.16
9436005	. . . . 10.02[2][c][i] n.79
9441003	. . . . 4.04[6] n.220
9443003	. . . . 4.04[3][b][vi] n.74
9446001	. . . . 4.16 n.13
9447004	. . . 19.02[2][b][ii] n.103; 19.02[4][d] n.217; 19.02[4][d][iv] n.263
9449001	. . . 4.02[4][b][ii] n.151; 4.02[4][b][iv] n.168; 10.02[2][c][i] n.78
9502005	. . . . 4.10[6] n.65
9506001	. . . . 19.03[3][b][i] n.138
9506004	. . . . 4.08[7] n.114
9507044	. . . . 6.04[2] n.17
9508002	. . . . 4.04[6] n.220
9509003	. . . . 10.07[2][d] n.78

TAM	
9511002	. . . . 5.06[8][b][iv] n.26
9533001	. . . . 11.03[5] n.110
9534001	. . . . 13.02[4][b][ii] n.285; 16.02[9][b] n.583
9550002	. . . . 19.04[3] n.35
9601002	. . . . 4.10[4][a] n.25
9604001	. . . . S10.01[3][g] ns. 115.29, 115.31, 115.34
9604002	. . . . 5.03[3][c] n.69
9604005	. . . . 19.03[3][b][i] n.139
9610005	. . . . 10.07[2] n.12
9615004	. . . . 4.14[9][b] n.136
9628004	. . . . 9.04[3][f] n.110
9642001	. . . . . 2.01[2] n.46; S2.01[2] n.56
9707001	. . . . 19.03[3][b][i] n.133
9708004	. . . . 4.10[4][a] n.24
9719001	. . . . 10.02[2][c][iv] n.105
9719006	. . 4.02[4][b][iii] n.164; 19.04[2] ns. 21, 22; 19.04[3][b] n.56; 19.04[3][b][i] n.81
9723009	4.02[4][b][iii] n.164; 19.04[2] n.21; 19.04[3][b] n.56; 19.04[3][b][i] n.81; 19.05[3][b] ns. 54, 56
9725002	4.02[4][b][iii] n.164; 19.04[2] n.21; 19.04[3][b] n.56; 19.04[3][b][i] n.81; 19.05[3][b] n.54
9729005	. . . . 4.07[3][a] n.80
9731003	. . . . 4.10[4][a] n.25
9731004	. . . . . 5.05[1][a] n.5; 9.04[3][f] n.110
9735003	. . . . 19.04[2] n.21; 19.04[3][b] n.56; 19.04[3][b][i] n.81; 19.05[3][b] n.54
9736001	. . . . 10.08[1] n.7
9736004	. . . 19.04[2] n.21; 19.04[3][b] n.56; 19.04[3][b][i] n.81; 19.05[1] n.2; 19.05[3][b] n.54
9741001	. . . . 19.03[3][b][i] n.134
9748004	. . . . 6.04[1] n.3
9750002	. . . . 7.03[3] n.88
9751003	. . . . 9.04[3][e] n.88
9815008	. . . . 5.06[3] n.17
9818005	5.06[3][h] n.82; 5.06[8][d][ii] n.311
9822001	. . . . . . 14.04[1] n.2; 14.04[3] n.16
9826002	. . . . 4.15[1][b][ii] ns. 59, 60
9841005	. . 19.04[3][b][i] n.57; 19.04[4] n.105
9842003	. . 10.01[2][b][ii] n.24; 10.02[2][c][v] n.117
9843001	. . . . 4.04[7][b][ii] n.288
9846002	. . . . 4.03[1] n.2; S4.03[1] n.2
199903031	. . . . 5.06[8][d][ii] n.353
199909001	. . . 4.11[4][a] n.40; S4.11[4][a] n.40
199915001	. . . . 8.05[3] n.10; 8.08[2] n.8
199917001	. . . . 4.08[4][c] n.53
199917066	. . . . 3.05[3][b] n.33
199925043	. . . . 6.06[2] n.21
199933002	. . . . 19.02[3][b] n.174
199935003	. . . . 4.07[2][a][ii] n.32
199938005	. . . . 4.08[6][d] n.101
199940005	. . . . 4.04[7][c][ii] n.324
199941004	. . . . 5.05[8][b] n.363
199943003	. . . . 4.02[4][e][i] n.202
199944005	. . . . 4.10[4][a] n.24

[Text references are to paragraphs and notes (9"n.");
references to the supplement are preceded by "S."]

TAM

200010010 . . . . 19.03[3][b][i] n.121
200011005 . . . . 19.03[3][b][i] n.121
200011008 . . . . 4.15[1][b][i] n.37
200014004 . . . . 10.01[2] n.13
200104008 . . . . S5.03[5] n.245; 5.03[6] n.146;
                             5.06[5][b][i] n.104
200128005 . . . . 5.05[2][b] n.68
200131001 . . . . 5.06[5][b][iii] n.134
200132004 . . . . 5.06[3] n.17
200147021 . . . . 17.02[1][c][ii] n.61
200150003 . . . . 17.01[2][a][i] n.17
200201002 . . . . 17.02[1][c][ii] n.64
200244002 . . . . S5.06[8][b][iii] n.248
200245053 . . . . S10.01[3][e] n.107.1
200247001 . . . . S4.02[4][e][iii] n.219
200252032 . . . . S5.05[2][a] n.58
200303010 . . . . S4.02[3][e] n.100.1
200306002 . . . . S5.05[2][b] n.68
200319001 . . . . . S5.05[2][b] n.72; S10.01[3][e]
                        n.105; S19.03[3][b][i] n.134
200337012 . . . . S10.01[3][e] n.107
200339003 . . . . S5.06[8][b][i] n.220
200341002 . . . . S9.04[3][f] n.110; S11.02[2][c]
                                     n.92
200343002 . . . . S4.03[2] n.20
200352003 . . . . S5.08[3][b][iii] n.100
200407018 . . . . . S4.13[7][a] n.78; S4.16 n.11
200410002 . . . . S5.08[2] n.16
200430030 . . . . S5.08[3][b][iii] n.99;
                             S5.08[3][c][i] n.101
200432015 . . . . S4.07[2][b][i] n.40.1
200432016 . . . . S4.07[3][b] n.85
200437032 . . . . S5.05[1][a] n.7
200444021 . . . . S4.02[4][e][iii] n.219;
         S5.03[3][c][ii] n.127; S5.03[4][b][i]
                                     n.179
200505022 . . . . S5.06[8][b][i] n.218;
                         S5.06[8][d][ii] n.315
200513028 . . . . S5.03[3][c][i] n.118
200532049 . . . . . S4.13[2][b] n.14; S5.03[3][a]
                                     n.92
200648028 . . . . S2.02[3][c][vi] n.142;
         S4.02[4][b][ii] n.155; S4.02[4][e][v]
     n.222; S5.05[3][a] n.97; S10.02[4] n.141;
                            S10.02[5][d] n.167
200840008 . . . . . S5.05[2][b] n.72; S5.05[8][b]
                                   n.367
200907025 . . . . S4.13[3] n.19
200911009 . . . . S4.04[3][c][ii] n.127;
     S4.04[3][c][iii] n.144; S4.04[4] n.165
201004022 . . . . S5.05[2][b] n.68
201126030 . . . . S5.06[3][a] n.24

TREASURY DECISIONS

TD

5032 . . . . 4.14[10] n.150
6296 . . . . 19.04[1][b] n.2
7296 . . . . 3.06 n.4
7786 . . . . 4.04[3][b][viii] n.100
8187 . . . . 18.02[4][a] ns. 42, 44, 51
8395 . . 19.02[5][f][ii] n.512; 19.03[3][b][i] ns.
                                   127, 143
8435 . . . . 4.03[1] n.2
8522 . . . . 5.06[8][b][i] ns. 225, 228, 231;
     5.06[8][d][ii] n.317; 5.06[8][d][iii] n.389
8589 . . . . 2.02[3][a] ns. 28, 32
8613 . . . . 5.07[3][c] n.61
8644 . . . 15.02[1] ns. 29, 30; S15.02[1] ns. 23,
                                     24
8686 . . . . 5.07[3][c] n.53
8744 . . . . 10.07[2][b] n.50
8819 . . . . 4.08[1][a] n.5
8845 . . 2.01[1][b][ii] n.28; S2.01[1][b][ii] n.28
8846 . . . . 5.05[3][b][ii] n.115; 5.06[5][b][ii] ns.
                             109, 112, 114
9068 . . . . S5.05[6][a][ii] n.326
9077 . . . . S10.08[1] n.7
9436 . . . . S4.02[6][b] n.264.17
9443 . . . . S9.04[9] n.209
9448 . . . . . S3.05[3][b] n.29; S4.02[5] ns. 244,
     247; S4.08[1][a] n.5; S4.11[4][a] n.40;
     S5.05[3][a] n.95; S5.05[5][a][ii] n.207;
     S5.05[5][b][iii] n.264; S5.05[5][c][ii]
     n.291; S5.05[6][b] n.327; S5.05[7][a]
     n.333; S5.06[7][d] n.197; S5.06[8][d][ii]
     n.348; S9.04[3][a] n.48; S10.02[2][b][iii]
     n.56; S11.02[1][b] n.27; S16.02[6] n.409;
         S19.03[1] n.3; S19.03[3][b] n.112;
                        S19.03[3][d] n.162
9468 . . . . . S5.03[1][b] n.24; S5.03[1][b][iv] ns.
     50, 54; S5.03[3][a] n.97; S5.03[4][c][iii]
                         ns. 234, 238
9540 . . . . . S3.05[3][b] n.29; S4.02[5] ns. 244,
     247; S4.08[1][a] n.5; S5.05[3][a] n.95;
     S5.05[5][a][ii] n.207; S5.05[5][b][iii]
     n.264; S5.05[5][c][ii] n.291; S5.05[6][b]
     n.327; S5.05[7][a] n.333; S5.06[7][d]
     n.197; S5.06[8][d][iii] n.348; S9.04[3][a]
     n.48; S10.02[2][b][iii] n.56; S11.02[1][b]
     n.27; S16.02[6] n.409; S19.03[1] n.3;
     S19.03[3][b] n.112; S19.03[3][d] n.162
9543 . . . . S10.07[2][b] n.30

Cumulative Table of Cases

*[Text references are to paragraphs and notes (9"n.");
references to the supplement are preceded by "S."]*

A

A. Baer Revocable Trust v. US   S4.02[3][f] n.102

Abell, Estate of v. Comm'r . . . . 4.04[3][b][ii] n.47; 4.04[3][b][iv] n.64

Abely, Estate of v. Comm'r . . . . . 5.06[7][b] n.170

Abraham Estate v. Comm'r . . . . S4.08[4][c] n.49

Abrams v. US . . . . 10.02[6] n.170

Abruzzo, Estate of v. US . . . 4.02[6][c] n.270

Ackerman, Estate of v. Comm'r . . . . 4.14[2] n.6

Acord, Estate of v. Comm'r . . . 5.06[3] n.17

Adams v. US . . . . 4.02[3][f] n.116

Adams, Estate of v. Comm'r . . . 5.06[8][b][iii] n.246

Adec v. US . . . . 5.06[5][a] n.95

Adler, Estate of v. Comm'r . . . S4.02[4][b][ii] n.155

Adolphson v. US . . . . 4.10[6] n.65

Adriance v. Higgins . . . . 4.10[4][b] n.33

Affelder v. Comm'r . . . . . . 10.02[6][d] n.184

Afroyim v. Rusk . . . . 6.01[3][a] n.27

Agnello, Estate of v. Comm'r . . . . 5.06[4] n.83

Agnew, Estate of v. Comm'r . . . 5.03[3] n.40; S5.03[3] n.82; 5.03[3][a] n.48; S5.03[3][a] n.88

Ahlstrom, Estate of v. Comm'r . . . 5.06[3][b] n.37

Ahmanson Found. v. US . . . . 4.02[2][a] n.26; 4.16 n.23; 5.05[3][a] n.97; 5.06[3][a] n.30; 5.06[5] n.93

Alan Baer Revocable Trust Dated February 9, 1996 v. US . . . . . . S5.06[3][a] n.24

Albritton, Estate of v. US . . . . . S5.03[4][a] n.149

Aldrich, Estate of v. Comm'r (5th Cir.) . . . . 4.13[3] n.24

Aldrich, Estate of v. Comm'r (TCM) . . . . 4.03[3][a] n.40; 4.05[4] n.39

Alexander v. US . . . . 10.01[3][i] n.127; 10.02[2][b][i] ns. 38, 39

Alexander, Estate of v. Comm'r   4.08[5][c] n.69; S4.08[5][c] n.69; 4.10[10][d] n.104; 5.06[8][b][i] ns. 230, 231, 233; 10.01[10][e] n.230

All v. McCobb . . . . . 4.11[2][a] n.7; 4.11[3][a] n.19; 4.14[2] n.5

Allen, Brown v. . . . . 4.15[1][b][ii] n.57

Allen v. Comm'r 8.02 n.2

Allen, Comm'r v. . . . . 10.01[5][a] n.15

Allen v. Henggeler   4.05[2][a] n.10; 4.06 ns. 2, 3

Allen, Shukert v. . . . . 4.09[3] n.18; 4.09[7] n.54

Allen v. US (2d Cir.) . . . . . . 5.06[7][b] n.189

Allen v. US (ED Mo.) . . . . 5.06[8][b][i] n.230

Allen, US v. . . . . 4.07[2][b][i] ns. 44, 47; 4.08[4][b] n.33; 4.08[8][a] n.177; 4.08[8][b] ns. 180, 181, 184, 185; 4.09[5] n.46; 4.12[9] & n.76; 4.14[9][b] n.141

Allen, Estate of v. Comm'r (TCM 1990) . . . . 5.06[3][a] n.30

Allen, Estate of v. Comm'r (TC 1963) . . . . 4.11[3][d] n.36

Allison, Estate of v. Comm'r . . . . S5.03[3][c][ii] n.129

Alperstein, Estate of v. Comm'r   4.13[7][a] n.80

Alward, Estate of v. Comm'r . . . . 5.05[1][b] n.36

American Dental Co., Helvering v. . . . . 10.01[2][e] n.34

American Light and Traction, Comm'r v. . . . . 19.02[5][a][iii] n.335

American Nat'l Bank v. US . . . . . 5.06[5][a] n.99; 5.06[7][b] n.177

American Nat'l Bank & Trust Co. v. Comm'r . . . . 4.08[7] n.118

American Nat'l Bank & Trust Co. v. US . . . . 5.06[3][b] n.48

American Nurseryman Publ'g Co. v. Comm'r . . . . 4.05[2][b] n.13

[Text references are to paragraphs and notes (9"n.");
references to the supplement are preceded by "S."]

Amick, Estate of v. Comm'r . . . . . 5.05[1][b]
n.36
Amiel, Estate of v. Comm'r . . . . . 5.06[6][b]
n.157
Amlie, Estate of v. Comm'r . . . . . S10.02[4]
n.141; S19.04[3][a] n.54; S19.04[3][c]
n.93; S19.04[6][a] n.116
Anderson v. Comm'r . . . 4.02[4][b][iii] n.159
Anderson, Estate of v. Comm'r (6th Cir.) . . .
. . . . 19.04[6][a][ii] n.123
Anderson, Estate of v. Comm'r (TCM 1973)
. . . . 4.08[7] n.118
Anderson, Estate of v. Comm'r (TC 1947)
. . . . 10.02[4] n.140
Anderson, Untermyer v. 9.01 n.9
Anderson v. US . . . . S4.02[2][b][iv] n.47;
S4.02[4][c][iii] n.176; S4.02[4][d][ii]
n.186
Andrews, Estate of v. Comm'r . . . 4.02[2][a]
n.28; 4.02[2][b] n.38; 4.02[3][f] n.113;
4.02[4][b][ii] n.152; 4.02[4][d][i] n.185;
4.02[4][e][iii] ns. 212, 215; 4.02[4][f]
n.230; 10.02[2][c][iii] n.100
Andrews, Estate of v. US . . . . 4.02[2][a] n.27
Anglim, Rosenblum v. . . . . 6.05[2][a][i] n.14;
6.05[2][a][ii] n.28
Anglim, Wishon v. . . . . 4.02[3][f] n.107
Anthony v. US (5th Cir.) . . . S4.02[5] n.244;
S4.11[4][a] n.40
Anthony v. US (MD La.) . . . . S4.02[5] n.244
Aquilino, Estate of v. Comm'r . . . .
. . . . 5.06[8][d][iv] n.399
Arbury, Estate of . . . . 10.01[2][f] n.45
Archbold v. Comm'r . . . . . 10.01[3][i] n.127
Arents, Estate of, Comm'r v.   4.08[2] n.15;
4.08[9] n.195
Armstrong v. Comm'r . . . . . 4.07[2][d] n.73;
8.04 n.4
Armstrong, Estate of v. Comm'r (7th Cir.)
. . . . 19.04[6][a][ii] n.129
Armstrong, Estate of v. Comm'r (TC) . . . . .
. . . . S4.07[3][a] ns. 83, 98
Armstrong, Jr. Trust v. US . . . . . 10.02[6][d]
n.185
Aronauer v. US . . . 3.03[2] n.21; 5.09[2] n.14
Aronson, Estate of v. Comm'r . . . .
. . . . S5.06[8][d][ii] n.311
Artall, Estate of v. Comm'r . . . . S5.08[2][a]
n.16; S5.08[2][c][ii] n.56
Asenap v. US . . . . 4.05[2][a] n.5
Askegard, US v. . . . . . . S2.02[3][c][iii] n.115
Astleford v. Comm'r . . . . . . S10.02[2][c][ii]
n.83.1; S10.02[2][c][iv] n.104
Atkinson, Estate of v. Comm'r (11th Cir.)
. . . . S5.05[5][a][i] ns. 160, 189;
S5.05[5][b][i] ns. 215, 244
Atkinson, Estate of v. Comm'r (TC) . . . . . .
. . . . 5.05[5][a][i] ns. 160, 189;
5.05[5][b][i] ns. 215, 244
Auker, Estate of v. Comm'r . . . 4.02[4][e][ii]
n.210
Autin v. Comm'r (5th Cir.) . . . 10.01[4] n.140
Autin v. Comm'r (TC) . . . . 9.04[9] n.206

Awrey, Estate of v. Comm'r . . . 4.12[8] n.69
Awtry, Estate of v. Comm'r . . . 5.06[3][d] &
ns. 51, 54, 55
Axtell v. US . . . 5.03[3][c] n.71; S5.03[3][c][i]
n.125
Ayer, Will of v. Comm'r . . . .
. . . . 10.01[3][g] n.116

B

Baccei, Estate of . . . . S2.02[1] n.11
Bachler v. US (9th Cir.) . . . . S18.05[2][b][ii]
n.39
Bachler v. US (ND Cal.) . . . . . 18.05[2][b][ii]
n.38
Baggett, Estate of v. Comm'r . . . . 4.08[4][c]
n.45; 4.08[6][b] n.83
Bahen, Estate of v. US . . . . . . 4.05[8] n.105;
4.11[3][a] n.19; 4.11[3][c] ns. 27, 30, 32
Bahr, Estate of v. Comm'r . . . . 2.02[3][b][i]
n.39; 5.03[3][c] n.71; S5.03[3][c][i]
n.119
Bailey v. Comm'r . . . . S5.03[4][a] n.146;
5.03[5][a] n.99
Bailly v. Comm'r . . . . 5.03[3][c] n.70;
S5.03[3][c][i] n.115
Baird, Estate of v. Comm'r (TCM 2001) . . .
. . . . 4.02[4][e][i] n.200
Baird, Estate of v. Comm'r (TCM 1997) . . .
. . . . . 5.03[3][a] n.53; S5.03[3][a] n.92
Baker, Estate of v. Comm'r . . . . . 5.06[7][a]
n.160
Balazs, Estate of v. Comm'r . . . 4.12[8] n.58
Baldwin v. Comm'r 2.02 n.3
Baldwin, Estate of v. Comm'r . . . . 5.03[3][a]
n.54; S5.03[3][a] n.93
Ballance v. US . . . . 5.03[3][c] n.69;
S5.03[3][c][i] n.110
Ballard v. Comm'r . . . . 10.02[3] n.132
Ballard, Estate of v. Comm'r 3.06 n.1
Ballas, Estate of v. Comm'r . . . . . 4.02[3][b]
n.79
Baltimore Nat'l Bank v. US   19.04[6][a][ii]
n.124; 19.04[6][a][iii] n.133
Banac, Estate of v. Comm'r . . . 6.05[2][a][ii]
n.25
Bankers Trust Co. v. US . . . 5.03[3][a] n.45;
S5.03[3][a] n.101
Bank of New York v. Helvering   5.03[3][a]
n.50; S5.03[3][a] n.90
Bank of NY v. US (3d Cir.) . . . S5.03[4][a][i]
n.154; 5.03[5][e] n.135
Bank of NY v. US (SDNY) . . . . 4.10[8] n.83
Bank of the West, Trustee v. Comm'r . . . . .
. . . . 2.02 n.5
Baptiste v. Comm'r (8th Cir.) 8.04 n.4;
S8.04 n.4
Baptiste v. Comm'r (11th Cir.) 8.04 n.4;
S8.04 n.4
Bardahl Mfg. Corp. v. Comm'r . . . .
. . . . 5.08[2][b][iv] n.34

*[Text references are to paragraphs and notes (9"n.");
references to the supplement are preceded by "S."]*

Barkey, In re . . . . 5.05[1][c] n.53
Barlow, Estate of v. Comm'r . . . . 4.08[6][c]
   n.85; S19.03[3][d][iii] n.230
Barnes v. Comm'r . . . . . . S4.02[3][f] n.108;
   10.02[2][c][iii] n.100; 10.02[2][c][iv]
   n.110
Barnett v. US . . . . S10.01[2][d] n.69
Barr, Estate of v. Comm'r . . . . 4.05[4] n.38;
   4.11[3][a] ns. 17, 20; 4.14[2] n.18
Barrett, Estate of v. Comm'r   4.15[1][b][i]
   n.40; 10.06[1] n.7
Barritt v. Tomlinson . . . . 4.13[4][a] n.37
Barry, Estate of v. Comm'r (9th Cir.) . . . . .
   . . . . 5.05[1][a] n.8
Barry, Estate of v. Comm'r (TCM) . . . .
   . . . . 4.02[3][b] n.73
Bartberger, Estate of v. Comm'r . . . .
   . . . . . 5.03[3][a] n.53; S5.03[3][a] n.92
Bartlett v. US . . . . 4.09[4][a] n.27
Bartman, Estate of v. Comm'r   10.01[3][g]
   n.118; 10.02[5][c] n.163
Bartol v. McGinnes . . . . 4.13[6][a] n.63
Barton, Estate of v. Comm'r . . . 4.07[2][b][ii]
   n.49
Bartram v. US . . . 4.03[2] n.21; 4.03[2][c] n.29
Barudin, Estate of v. Comm'r . . . .
   . . . . 4.02[4][c][iii] n.176; 4.02[4][d][ii]
   n.190
Bary, Estate of v. Comm'r . . . . . 4.03[1] n.8
Bass, Tips v. . . . . 4.11[5] n.48
Bath, Estate of v. Comm'r . . . . . S5.03[4][a]
   n.147; S5.03[4][a][i] n.157; 5.03[5] n.96
Baumberger, Estate of v. Comm'r . . . .
   . . . . 5.05[3][b][i] ns. 110, 111
Baur v. Comm'r . . . . 9.04[11] & n.244
Bayliss v. US . . . . . 4.08[2] n.15; 4.08[9] n.195
Beal, Estate of v. Comm'r   4.11[4][a] n.41;
   4.11[4][b] n.45
Beat v. US (D. Kan. 2011) . . . .
   . . . . S5.03[3][a] n.99
Beat v. US (D. Kan. 2010) . . . . S5.06[3] n.17
Beauregard, Estate of v. Comm'r . . . .
   . . . . 4.14[4][c] n.53
Becker v. St. Louis Union Trust Co. . . . . . .
   . . . . 4.09[3] n.20
Becklenberg, Estate of v. Comm'r . . . 4.08[4]
   n.23; 4.08[8] n.168; S4.08[8] n.168.5;
   4.11[5] n.47; 5.06[8][d][ii] n.336
Beecher v. US . . . . S5.03[4][a][i] n.155;
   5.03[5][e] n.136
Beeler v. Motter . . . . 4.07[3][b] n.87
Bel v. US . . . . 4.07[3][b] n.91; 4.14[9][b] ns.
   138, 146; 5.06[3][a] n.31
Belcher, Estate of v. Comm'r . . . .
   . . . . 4.05[3] n.28
Bell v. Comm'r . . . . 3.03[2] n.19; 5.09[2] n.12
Bell, Estate of v. Comm'r (9th Cir.) . . . .
   . . . . 2.02[3][c][vi] n.151
Bell, Estate of v. Comm'r (TC 1976) . . . . . .
   . . . . 4.10[5] n.64
Bell, Estate of v. Comm'r (TC 1973) . . . . . .
   . . . . 4.11[5] ns. 48, 50
Bennett v. US . . . . 19.03[3][d][i] n.173

Bennett, Estate of v. Comm'r (TC 1993) . . .
   . . . . 10.07[2][d] n.74
Bennett, Estate of v. Comm'r (TCM 1993)
   . . . 4.02[2][a] n.27; 4.02[4][d][ii] n.195;
   4.02[4][e][iii] n.215
Bensel v. Comm'r . . . . 19.04[1][b] n.3;
   19.04[3][a] n.50; 19.04[6][a][ii] n.129
Berg, Estate of v. Comm'r (8th Cir.) . . . . . .
   . . . . 4.02[2][a] n.13
Berg, Estate of v. Comm'r (TCM) . . . .
   . . . . 4.02[4][c][iii] & n.177
Bergan, Estate of v. Comm'r   4.08[4] n.23;
   4.08[8] n.168; S4.08[8] n.168.5; 4.11[5]
   n.47; 5.06[8][d][ii] n.336; 10.01[3][g]
   n.119; 10.02[6] n.172
Berger v. US . . . . 5.06[7][b] n.174
Bergh v. Warner . . . . 10.02[5][a] n.156
Berkman, Estate of v. Comm'r . . . 5.03[2][a]
   n.17; S5.03[2][a] n.57
Berkowitz v. Comm'r . . . . 4.12[8] n.64
Berman v. Patterson . . . . . . 11.03[4][b] n.52
Bernatschke v. US . . . . 4.15[1][a] n.22
Berzon v. Comm'r . . . . . 9.04[3][b] ns. 62, 66;
   9.05[3] n.39; 10.02[2][b][vi] n.71;
   19.04[6][a][ii] n.126; 19.04[6][b] n.137
Bettenhausen, Estate of v. Comm'r   4.04[6]
   n.226
Bettin, Estate of v. Comm'r . . . 4.12[9] n.71;
   10.01[2][h] n.72; 10.01[5][c] n.167
Bevan, US v. S8.04 n.4
Beveridge v. Comm'r . . . . 10.02[6] n.170
Biagioni, Estate of v. Comm'r . . . . 4.02[2][a]
   n.17
Bianchi, Estate of v. Comm'r . . . . . . 4.08[8]
   n.170
Bies, Estate of v. Comm'r . . . . 9.04[1][b] n.34
Bigelow, Estate of v. Comm'r . . . S4.08[4][c]
   n.49
Bintliff v. US . . . 4.14[3] n.24; 4.14[4][a] n.44;
   4.14[7][b] n.110; 4.14[8] n.122
Bischoff, Estate of v. Comm'r . . . . 4.08[7][d]
   ns. 153, 160; 19.04[1][b] n.6; 19.04[3][a]
   ns. 48, 49; 19.04[3][b][ii] n.60
Bishop Trust Co. v. US . . . . . 4.02[3][f] n.105
Black, Estate of . . . . . S4.08[4][c] n.49; S4.16
   n.19; S5.03[3][c][i] n.118
Black v. Comm'r . . . .
   . . . . 4.12[2] n.17; 4.12[9] n.75
Blackburn, Boulis v. S8.04 n.16
Blackburn v. US . . . . 5.03[2][b] n.24;
   S5.03[2][b] n.66
Blackford, Estate of v. Comm'r . . . 5.05[7][a]
   n.337
Blair v. Comm'r . . . . . 4.05[2][a] n.6; 4.13[3]
   n.24
Blasdel v. Comm'r . . . . 9.04[3][e] n.77
Bliss, Estate of v. Comm'r   5.03[3][c] n.70;
   S5.03[3][c][i] n.115
Blodget v. Comm'r . . . . 4.05[7][b] n.80
Bloise, Estate of v. Comm'r . . . . 4.05[2] n.4
Blood v. Comm'r . . . . 4.12[8] n.60
Bloom, Thornhill v. . . . . S8.04[2] n.17

[Text references are to paragraphs and notes (9"n.");
references to the supplement are preceded by "S."]

Blossom, Estate of v. Comm'r . . . . 5.03[3][c]
n.63; S5.03[3][c][ii] n.129
Blount Estate v. Comm'r . . . . . . S4.02[3][f]
n.102; S19.04[3][c] n.91; S19.04[6][a][i]
n.117; S19.04[7] n.143
Blumberg, US v. . . . . 2.02[1] n.14
Boatmen's First Nat'l Bank of Kan. City v.
US . . . 2.01[1][b][i] n.22; S2.01[1][b][i]
n.22
Bob Jones Univ. v. US . . . . . . 5.05[1][b] n.34
Boeshore, Estate of v. Comm'r . . . .
. . . . 5.05[6][a][ii] n.326; S5.05[6][a][ii]
n.326
Boeving v. US . . . . 4.13[7][a] n.80
Boggs v. Boggs . . . . 5.06[8][d][ii] n.338
Boggs, Boggs v. . . . . 5.06[8][d][ii] n.338
Bogley, Estate of v. US . . . 4.05[4] ns. 37, 38;
4.09[2] n.4
Bograd, Estate of v. Comm'r . . . .
. . . . 4.05[3] n.30
Bohnen v. Harrison . . . . . . 4.14[10] & n.153
Bomash v. Comm'r . . . . 4.08[7][c] n.141
Bommer Revocable Trust v. Comm'r . . . . . .
. . . . 4.02[2][c] n.51
Bond, Estate of v. Comm'r . . . 4.02[3][b] n.69
Bongard, Estate of v. Comm'r . . . S4.08[4][c]
n.49
Bonner, Estate of v. Comm'r   2.02[3][c][ii]
n.107; 4.02[4][b][ii] n.158; 4.16 ns. 20,
22; 5.06[5] n.94
Bookwalter v. Lamar . . . . . . 5.06[7][b] n.175
Borax Estate v. Comm'r . . . . . . 5.06[3] n.17
Bordes, Estate of v. Comm'r . . . 6.06[1] n.12
Borgatello, Estate of v. Comm'r . . . .
. . . . 4.02[4][d][ii] n.192
Borne v. US 3.06 n.3
Borner, Estate of v. Comm'r . . . . . 4.07[2][c]
n.66; 4.12[9] n.75; 10.01[3] n.78
Bosca, Estate of v. Comm'r   10.01[2] n.13;
10.01[3] n.73; 10.02[2][c][ii] n.88
Bosch, Estate of, Comm'r v. . . . 4.05[2][b] &
ns. 12, 13, 17; 4.12[2] n.19; 4.13[3]
n.22; 4.13[4][a] n.36; 5.03[1] & ns. 10,
13, 15; S5.03[1] n.11; S5.03[1][a] & ns.
13, 14, 16; 5.06[3] n.17; 5.06[3][b] n.37;
5.06[5][a] & n.101; 5.06[8][b][iii] ns.
252, 254, 255; 10.01[3] n.74; 10.07[2]
n.26
Bothun, Estate of v. Comm'r . . . . 4.08[7][a]
n.127
Boulis v. Blackburn S8.04 n.16
Bowden v. Comm'r . . . . 10.01[3][b] n.91
Bowers, Sanchez v. . . . . 6.04[1] n.11
Bowers, Schuette v. 4.06 n.4
Bowers, Wilson v. . . . . 19.04[6][a][ii] ns. 131,
132
Bowers, Estate of v. Comm'r   4.15[1][b][i]
ns. 39, 40
Bowes v. US . . . 4.15[1][a] n.21; S5.03[4][a][i]
n.158; 5.03[5][e] n.139; 5.05[3][b][i]
n.105
Bowgren, Estate of v. Comm'r . . . . . 4.08[5]
n.55; 4.10[6] n.65

Bowling, Estate of v. Comm'r . . . .
. . . . 5.06[8][d][ii] ns. 353, 355
Boyd, Estate of v. Comm'r   5.06[3][h] n.83;
8.05[3] n.8; 10.07[2] n.11
Boydstun, Estate of v. Comm'r . . . 5.06[7][b]
n.163
Boykin, Estate of v. Comm'r . . . . 19.02[1][b]
n.11
Boyle, US v. . . . . 2.02[1] ns. 14, 15
Braddock v. US . . . . . 9.04[3] n.46; 9.04[3][d]
n.74
Bradford v. Comm'r . . . . . 10.01[3][i] n.126
Bradford, Estate of v. Comm'r . . . .
. . . . S5.05[3][b][i] n.109
Bradham v. US . . . . 5.06[7][b] n.177
Bradley v. Comm'r . . . . 5.03[2][b] n.28;
S5.03[2][b] n.69
Brainard v. Comm'r . . . . 8.03[2] n.21
Brandon, Estate of v. Comm'r . . . 5.06[3][a]
n.30
Brandt, Estate of v. Comm'r (TCM 1949)
. . . . 4.12[8] n.61
Brandt, Estate of v. Comm'r (TCM 1948)
. . . . 8.02 n.4
Branson, Estate of v. Comm'r . . . .
. . . . 4.02[4][e][ii] n.207
Brantingham v. US . . . . 4.13[4][a] n.34
Braum Family Partnership v. Comm'r . . . . .
. . . . 10.01[3][h] n.122
Bray, Estate of v. Comm'r   5.03[3][d] n.78;
S5.03[6][a] n.273
Breakiron v. Gudonis . . . . . S10.07[2][b] n.36
Bremer v. Luff . . . . 4.12[8] n.66
Brewer, Estate of v. Comm'r . . . . 5.03[3][c]
n.64; S5.03[3][c][iii] n.136
Bridgforth v. US . . . . 4.08[4][c] n.44
Briggs, Davie v. 8.02 n.10
Bright, Estate of v. US . . . . . 4.02[2][a] n.21;
4.02[4][b][ii] n.152; 4.02[4][b][iv] n.167;
4.02[4][e][i] n.197
Brinkley, Estate of v. US . . . . 4.08[4][c] n.44
British Columbia v. Gilbertson . . . . . 7.04[3]
n.19
Broadhead Trust v. Comm'r . . . . 4.05[1] n.1;
S5.03[4][c][i] n.203; 5.03[5][a] n.115
Brocato, Estate of v. Comm'r . . . 4.02[4][e][i]
n.203; 4.02[4][e][ii] n.210
Brock, Estate of v. Comm'r . . . . . 5.05[7][a]
n.331
Brockman v. Comm'r . . . 4.04[3][b][ii] n.47;
4.04[3][c][ii] n.132
Brockway, Estate of v. Comm'r . . 4.07[2][c]
n.66
Brodrick v. Gore . . . . . . 19.04[6][a][ii] n.128
Bromley v. McCaughn . . . . 9.01 n.10; 9.02[3]
n.20
Brooke v. US . . . . 4.08[6][c] n.84
Brooks, Burnet v. . . . 6.03[2][a] n.25; 6.04[1]
n.5; 7.01[2] n.28
Brooks v. Willcuts . . . . 4.02[3][f] n.106
Brookshire, Estate of v. Comm'r . . . .
. . . . . 4.02[2][b][ii] n.43; 4.02[4][d][ii]
n.189

[Text references are to paragraphs and notes (9"n.");
references to the supplement are preceded by "S."]

Brown v. Allen . . . . 4.15[1][b][ii] n.57
Brown v. Comm'r . . . . . 5.06[8][d][iv] n.396;
   10.01[5][d] n.174; 10.01[5][e] n.180
Brown v. Routzhan . . . . 4.13[7][d] n.99;
   10.07[1] n.5; 17.04[3] n.76
Brown v. US (9th Cir.) . . . . S4.07[3][a] n.81;
   S5.06[5][b][ii] n.109
Brown v. US (ND Ala.) . . . . 5.06[7][b] n.164
Brown v. US (MD Tenn.) . . . . . 2.02[1] n.16
Brown v. Webster . . . . . 5.06[8][d][iv] n.392
Brown, Estate of v. Comm'r (5th Cir.) . . . . .
   . . . . 4.02[3][b] n.71
Brown, Estate of v. Comm'r (TCM 1997) . . .
   . . . . 4.08[7] n.114
Brown, Estate of v. Comm'r (TCM 1962) . . .
   . . . . 4.02[3][e] n.100
Bruch v. US . . . . 4.04[3][b][ii] n.47;
   4.04[3][c][ii] n.124
Bruning, Estate of v. Comm'r . . . . 5.06[6][b]
   n.157
Bryan, Estate of v. Comm'r 5.04 n.1
Buchanan v. US . . . . 5.05[3][b][i] n.105
Buchholtz, Estate of v. Comm'r . . . .
   . . . . 2.02[3][b][i] n.39; S5.03[3][c][i]
   n.118
Buck v. Comm'r . . . . 9.04[5][b] n.150
Buckley v. Comm'r   4.12[2] n.17; 4.13[2][a]
   n.10; 9.04[9] n.206
Buckwalter v. Comm'r . . . . 4.05[3] n.32
Budd, Estate of v. Comm'r . . . . . . 4.08[6][a]
   n.76; 4.10[4][c] n.38
Buder v. US . . . . 5.05[1][b] n.38
Buder, Estate of (8th Cir.) S4.16 n.11
Buder, Estate of v. Comm'r (TC) . . . .
   . . . . 9.04[1][b] ns. 37, 39
Budlong, Estate of v. Comm'r . . . . . . 3.04[2]
   n.24ll14842
Bull v. US . . . . 4.05[7][b] n.85
Burdick, Estate of v. Comm'r . . . . . 5.05[2][b]
   ns. 72, 73; S5.05[2][b] n.72
Burford v. Comm'r . . . . . . 10.06[2][a] n.21
Burgess, Estate of v. Comm'r (4th Cir.) . . . .
   . . . . 5.05[2][b] n.72; 5.05[7][a] n.330
Burgess, Estate of v. Comm'r (TCM) . . . . . .
   . . . . 5.06[3][a] n.28
Burghardt, Estate of v. Comm'r   7.02[3] &
   ns. 75, 76, 79
Buring, Estate of v. Comm'r . . . 2.02[1] n.15
Burke v. US . . . . 5.05[3][b][ii] n.115;
   5.06[5][b][ii] n.111
Burnet, Commissioner of Internal Revenue
   (Comm'r) . . . . See individual taxpayer
Burnett v. US . . . . 5.06[8][b][iii] n.246
Burns v. Comm'r . . . . 4.07[2][c] n.60
Burns v. US . . . . 3.04[2] n.24
Burris, Estate of v. Comm'r   4.14[8] n.125;
   S4.14[8] n.125
Burrow Trust v. Comm'r . . . 5.03[3][d] n.75;
   S5.03[6][a] n.271
Busch, Estate of v. Comm'r . . . . . 4.02[3][b]
   n.64; 4.02[4][e][i] n.203
Bush, Estate of v. US   S5.03[4][b][ii] n.198;
   5.03[8] n.161; 5.05[3][b][i] n.104

Byram, Estate of v. Comm'r 4.06 n.13
Byrum, US v. . . . . 4.08[4][a] n.25; 4.08[4][b]
   n.29; 4.08[4][c] n.51; 4.08[5][a] n.58;
   4.08[6][a] ns. 74, 76; 4.08[6][d] & ns.
   92–94, 109; 4.08[9] n.197; 4.10[4][c]
   n.34; 4.14[4][f] n.76

C

Cafaro, Estate of v. Comm'r . . . S5.03[1] n.3;
   S5.03[4][c][i] n.204; 5.03[5][b] n.125
Cain v. Comm'r . . . . 4.11[5] n.47
Calcagno, Estate of v. Comm'r   S5.03[2][a]
   n.57
Calder v. Comm'r . . . . 9.04[3][b] n.62
California Trust Co. v. Riddell . . . . . 4.05[6]
   n.72; 4.14[8] n.118; 5.06[8][a] n.205
Callahan, Estate of v. Comm'r . . . 4.08[4][c]
   n.48
Camp v. Comm'r . . . . . . 4.13[4][c][ii] n.46;
   10.01[8] & ns. 193, 194; 10.01[10][e]
   n.231
Campbell, Universal Oil Prods. Co. v. . . . . .
   . . . . 5.05[1][b] n.23
Campbell, Estate of v. Comm'r (TCM 1991)
   . . . . 2.02[1] n.14
Campbell, Estate of v. Comm'r (TC 1972)
   . . . . . 10.02[4] n.141; 10.04[3][a] n.13
Cameron v. United States . . . . S4.05[2][a] n.6
Canfield, Estate of, Comm'r v. . . . 4.08[1][b]
   n.13
Caplan, Estate of v. Comm'r   19.04[6][a][i]
   ns. 117, 119
Cardeza, Estate of v. Comm'r . . . . 4.05[5][b]
   n.57; 5.03[2][a] n.20; 5.03[2][b] n.23
Cardeza, Estate of, Comm'r v.   S5.03[2][a]
   n.58; S5.03[2][b] n.64
Cardeza, Estate of v. US . . . . . 4.09[4][f] n.41
Carli v. Comm'r . . . . 4.05[3] n.23; 4.15[1][a]
   n.19; S5.03[4][a][i] n.163; 5.03[5][e]
   n.140
Carlson v. Patterson . . . . 11.03[4][b] n.52
Carpenter v. Comm'r . . . . 19.04[1][b] n.1
Carpenter v. US . . . . 10.01[4] n.142
Carpenter, Estate of v. Comm'r   5.05[2][b]
   n.68; 5.06[3][a] n.30; 5.06[8][b][iii]
   n.245
Carpousis, Estate of v. Comm'r . . . . . 4.12[8]
   ns. 59, 64
Carr v. Comm'r . . . . 10.02[2][c][ii] n.89
Carrieres v. Comm'r . . . . 5.06[3][b] n.42
Carroll v. US . . . S8.03[1] n.6; S8.03[2] n.14
Carson v. Comm'r . . . . 9.02[2] n.12
Carson, Estate of v. Comm'r (TCM 1976)
   . . . 5.03[3][b] n.58; S5.03[3][b] n.105;
   S5.03[3][c][ii] n.130
Carson, Estate of v. Comm'r (TCM 1974)
   . . . . 4.13[3] n.22
Carter v. US . . . . 5.03[2][a] n.20; S5.03[2][a]
   n.60
Carter, Estate of v. US . . . . . . 3.05[3][b] n.37

[Text references are to paragraphs and notes (9"n.");
references to the supplement are preceded by "S."]

Cartwright v. US . . . . 4.02[2][c] n.50;
 4.02[3][d] & n.94
Cary, Estate of v. Comm'r . . . . 4.02[3][b] ns.
 66, 72
Casey, Estate of v. Comm'r (4th Cir.) . . . . .
 . . . . 4.10[4][a] ns. 24, 25
Casey, Estate of v. Comm'r (TCM 1996) . . .
 . . . . 4.02[4][c][iii] n.184
Casey, Estate of v. Comm'r (TC 1971) . . . . .
 . . . . 4.10[4][a] n.22
Cass v. Tomlinson . . . . . 5.06[8][b][iii] n.250
Cassidy, Estate of v. Comm'r . . . . 5.05[7][a]
 n.330
Catalano v. US . . . . 4.14[8] n.120
Cavenaugh, Estate of v. Comm'r (5th Cir.)
 . . . . 4.14[8] n.125
Cavenaugh, Estate of v. Comm'r (TC) . . . . .
 . . . . 5.06[8][d][ii] n.329
Cavett, Estate of v. Comm'r . . . . . . 10.02[3]
 n.131
Cederloff, Estate of v. US . . . . . S2.02[1] n.14
Central Nat'l Bank, McDougall v. . . . 8.04[3]
 ns. 18, 19
Central Trust of Cincinnati v. Welch . . . . . .
 . . . . . 5.03[4][a] n.91; S5.03[6][c][iii]
 n.302
Cerf v. Comm'r . . . . . . 10.01[8] ns. 199, 201;
 10.01[9] n.207; 12.01[1] n.10
Cervi v. US . . . . 10.01[4] n.139
Cervin, Estate of v. Comm'r . . . . 4.02[4][e][i]
 n.201; 4.14[8] ns. 126, 128
Chagra, Estate of v. Comm'r . . . .
 . . . . 2.02[1] n.15
Chalmers, Estate of v. Comm'r . . . 4.10[4][c]
 n.40; 4.10[4][d] n.44
Chamberlain, Estate of v. Comm'r . . . .
 . . . . . 10.07[2] n.27; 10.07[2][a] n.28
Chambless v. US . . . . 4.12[2] n.21
Champlin v. Comm'r . . . . 8.03[1] n.6
Chancellor, Estate of v. Comm'r . . . .
 . . . . S4.13[4][a] n.37
Chandler v. US . . . . 4.12[2] n.21
Chandler, US v. . . . . 4.12[2] & n.22
Chanin v. US . . . . 9.04[1][b] ns. 27, 28;
 9.04[3][e] n.90; 10.01[2][b][i] ns. 19, 21;
 10.02[6][a] n.173
Chapman, Estate of v. Comm'r (TCM 1989)
 . . . . 4.14[9][b] n.136
Chapman, Estate of v. Comm'r (TC 1959)
 . . . . 3.04[2] n.24
Charania, Estate of S2.02[1] n.16; S6.04[1]
 n.6
Charles v. Hassett . . . . 9.04[3][a] n.52
Chase Manhattan Bank, Comm'r v. . . . .
 . . . . 10.01[5][d] n.172
Chase Nat'l Bank v. Comm'r (8th Cir.) . . . .
 . . . . 4.08[4][b] n.41; 4.15[1][a] n.26;
 4.15[2] n.71
Chase Nat'l Bank v. Comm'r (TCM) . . . . . .
 . . . . 10.02[4] n.140
Chase Nat'l Bank v. US . . . . . 4.14[10] n.154
Chase Nat'l Bank of NY v. Comm'r . . . . . .
 . . . . 6.03[2][b] n.35

Chase Nat'l Bank of NY, Comm'r v. . . . . . .
 . . . . 4.10[4][b] n.33
Chastain v. Comm'r . . . . . 5.05[3][b][i] n.110;
 8.04[1] n.12
Chenoweth, Estate of v. Comm'r . . . .
 . . . . 4.02[2][a] n.26; 4.16 n.23;
 5.05[5][a][ii] n.205; 5.05[5][b][ii] n.262;
 5.05[5][c][i] n.288; 5.06[5] n.93
Cherokee Tobacco . . . . 7.06 ns. 6, 7
Chesterton, Estate of v. US . . . . S5.03[4][c][i]
 n.209; 5.03[5][b] n.120
Chevron USA v. Natural Resources Defense
 Council, Inc. . . . . S5.03[1][b] n.26
Chew Heong v. US 7.06 n.9
Chickering v. Comm'r . . . . . . 4.10[4][b] n.31
Child v. US . . . . 5.05[1][b] n.36
Childress v. US . . . . . . S5.03[4][a][i] n.155;
 5.03[5][e] n.136
Child's Estate v Comm'r . . . . 19.04[6][a][ii]
 n.132; 19.04[6][a][iii] n.134
Chiles v. US . . . . 5.06[5][a] n.95
Chisholm, Estate of v. Comm'r . . . 4.14[7][a]
 n.105
Chown, Estate of v. Comm'r . . . 4.05[6] n.70
Christ, Estate of v. Comm'r 4.08[1][a] n.7;
 4.08[7][c] ns. 144, 151
Christensen, Estate of v. Comm'r . . . .
 . . . . 4.10[4][a] n.25
Christiansen, Estate of . . . . S5.05[2][c] n.81;
 S10.01[3][e] n.107.1; S10.07[2] n.23;
 S10.07[2][d] n.81
Christiernin v. Manning . . . . 4.05[5][b] n.56;
 4.11[4][a] n.39
Christmas, Estate of v. Comm'r 5.06[6][b]
 n.157
Chrysler, Estate of v. Comm'r . . . 4.08[4][b]
 n.32
Church v. US (5th Cir.) . . . 4.02[4][g] n.238;
 S4.08[4][c] n.49
Church v. US (EDNY) . . . . 2.02[3][b][ii] n.45
Church v. US (WD Tex.) . . . . 10.01[2][b][ii]
 n.25; 10.02[2][c][v] n.122; 19.04[2] ns.
 25, 26; 19.04[3][a] n.48
Church, Estate of, Comm'r v. . . . . . . 4.08[9]
 n.197; 4.11[2][b] n.13
Churchhill v. US . . . . 5.05[2][a] n.58
Cidulka, Estate of v. Comm'r . . . . 9.04[1][b]
 n.34; 10.01[2] n.13; 10.01[2][d] n.31
Citizens & S. Nat'l Bank v. US . . . 5.06[3][a]
 n.29
Citizens Bank & Trust Co. v. Comm'r . . . . .
 . . . . 4.02[2][c] n.53
Citizens Bank & Trust Co. of Bloomington,
 Pearcy v. . . . . 8.05[4] n.13
Citizens Fidelity Bank & Trust Co. v. US . . .
 . . . . 19.04[6][a][ii] n.130
Citizens Nat'l Bank of Evansville v. US . . . .
 . . . . 5.06[8][b][i] n.229
Citizens' Nat'l Bank of Waco v. US . . . .
 . . . . 10.02[2][b][i] n.44
City Bank Farmers Trust Co., Helvering v.
 . . . 4.10[6] ns. 66, 68, 71; 10.01[10][e]
 n.232; 11.03[3][b] n.35

*[Text references are to paragraphs and notes (9"n.");
references to the supplement are preceded by "S."]*

City Bank Farmers Trust Co. v. US . . . . . .
. . . . 6.05[2][a][i] n.16
Clack, Estate of v. Comm'r . . . 5.06[8][d][ii]
n.319
Clark v. Comm'r . . . . 9.04[3][a] n.58; 9.05[1]
n.5; 10.03[3][b] n.44
Clauson v. Vaughan . . . . 4.13[10] n.128
Clayton v. Comm'r . . . . 5.06[8][d][ii] n.319
Cleaveland v. US . . . . 10.07[2][d] n.78
Cleavenger, US v. 8.02 n.5
Clifford, Helvering v. . . . . 4.05[5][c] & n.61;
4.09[4] n.24; 4.14[5][a] n.90;
19.03[2][a][iv] n.71
Clinard, Estate of v. Comm'r . . . .
. . . . 4.04[3][b][viii] n.97
Cline, Estate of v. Comm'r . . . . 5.06[8][b][iii]
n.248
Clise, Comm'r v. . . . . 4.11[7] n.63
Cloutier, Estate of v. Comm'r . . . .
. . . . 4.02[4][d][ii] n.196
Coaxum, Estate of v. Comm'r . . . S4.14[4][a]
n.37
Cobb v. Comm'r . . . 4.02[3][b] n.79; 10.02[4]
n.137; 19.04[3][a] ns. 51, 52
Cockrill v. O'Hara . . . . 4.14[4][c] n.54;
4.14[5][a] n.86
Cohan v. Comm'r . . . . 4.12[8] n.59
Cohen v. Comm'r . . . . 10.01[2][f] n.45
Cohn, Estate of v. US . . . . 4.08[9] n.200;
5.03[3][d] n.75; S5.03[6][a] n.271
Cole, Estate of v. Comm'r   4.08[7][d] & ns.
161, 164
Collino, Estate of v. Comm'r . . . . 4.14[4][c]
n.54; 4.14[7][a] n.108
Collins v. Comm'r . . . . 4.02[3][e] n.100
Collins, US v. . . . . 5.03[2][b] ns. 26, 27;
S5.03[2][b] ns. 67, 68
Collins, Estate of v. US (ED Mich.) . . . .
. . . . 4.07[2][b][iii] n.49
Collins, Estate of v. US (WD Okla.) . . . .
. . . . 4.04[6] ns. 233, 237
Colyear, Estate of v. Comm'r . . . . 4.02[2][a]
n.9
Commissioner of Internal Revenue (Comm'r)
. . . . See individual taxpayer
Commonwealth Trust Co. of Pittsburgh v.
Driscoll . . . . . . 3.03[2] n.20; 4.10[4][d]
n.45; 5.09[2] n.13
Condon Nat'l Bank of Coffeyville v. US . . . .
. . . . 4.13[2][b] n.13; 5.06[8][b][iii] ns.
239, 246
Cone, Estate of v. Comm'r . . . . 4.04[3][b][ix]
n.102; 4.05[2][b] n.20
Connally, Green v. . . . . 5.05[1][b] n.34
Connally, McGlotten v. . . . . 5.05[1][b] n.34
Connecticut Bank & Trust Co. v. US . . . . . .
. . . . 4.05[8] ns. 94, 95
Connell, Estate of v. Comm'r . . . . 4.07[3][b]
n.88
Connelly, Estate of v. US . . . 4.14[4][e] n.69
Constantino v. US . . . . . . 2.02[1] ns. 12, 14
Continental Ill. Nat'l Bank & Trust Co. v.
US (11th Cir.) . . . . 4.02[5] n.253

Continental Ill. Nat'l Bank & Trust Co. v.
US (Ct. Cl.) . . . . 5.05[1][b] n.41
Continental Ill. Nat'l Bank & Trust Co. of
Chicago v. US . . . . . . 3.05[3][b] n.33
Cook v. Comm'r . . . . . 19.03[3][b][i] n.134;
S19.03[3][b][i] n.134
Cook v. US 7.06 n.9
Cook, Estate of v. Comm'r (5th Cir.) . . . . . .
. . . . S4.02[5] n.244; S4.11[4][a] n.40
Cook, Estate of v. Comm'r (TCM 2001) . . . .
. . . . . . 4.02[5] n.244; 4.11[4][a] n.40
Cook, Estate of v. Comm'r (TCM 1970) . . . .
. . . . 4.13[2][a] n.10
Cook, Estate of v. Comm'r (TC 1947) . . . . .
. . . . 4.02[3][f] n.108
Cooper, Estate of v. Comm'r   4.08[2] n.20;
4.08[4][b] n.28
Copley's Estate, Comm'r v. . . . . . 10.01[3][i]
n.127
Correll, US v. . . . . S5.03[1][b] n.26
Corwin, Dimock v. . . . . 4.05[4] n.37
Cosby v. Shackelford . . . . 8.04[3] n.19
Costanza, Estate of (6th Cir.) . . . . . S4.05[3]
n.32
Costanza, Estate of (TC) . . . . . . 4.05[3] n.32
Costin v. Cripe . . . 4.09[4][a] n.26; 4.09[4][g]
n.44; 4.09[6] n.49
Cottage Sav. Assoc. v. Comm'r   18.05[2][e]
n.88
Council, Estate of v. Comm'r . . . . 4.13[7][a]
n.78
Courtney v. US . . . . 4.11[3][a] n.17
Courtney, Estate of v. Comm'r . . . .
. . . . . . S5.03[4][c][i] n.209; 5.03[5][b]
n.120
Cowser, Estate of v. Comm'r . . . .
. . . . 4.04[3][b][ix] n.102
Cox v. US (5th Cir.) . . . . 5.06[5][a] n.99;
5.06[7][b] n.177
Cox v. US (WD La.) . . . . . 10.01[5][d] n.171
Cox, Estate of v. US . . . . 2.02[1] n.14
Coyle, Lake Shore Nat'l Bank v. . . . .
. . . . 4.05[2][b] ns. 17, 19
Craft, Estate of v. Comm'r . . . . . . 5.03[3][a]
n.48; S5.03[3][a] n.88
Craig v. Comm'r . . . . 9.04[5][a] n.147
Crail, Estate of v. Comm'r . . . . . S5.03[5] ns.
247, 249; 5.03[6] ns. 148, 152
Crane v. Comm'r . . . . 4.12[8] n.70;
10.02[2][b][i] ns. 40, 42
Cripe, Costin v. . . . 4.09[4][a] n.26; 4.09[4][g]
n.44; 4.09[6] n.49
Critchfield, Estate of v. Comm'r   4.03[3][a]
n.38
Cristofani, Estate of v. Comm'r . . . 9.04[3][f]
& ns. 105, 107, 108, 110, 113;
15.03[4][b][iii] n.119
Crosby v. US (5th Cir.) . . . . 5.06[3][b] n.40;
5.06[7][b] ns. 176, 178
Crosby v. US (ED Mo.) . . . . . . 4.12[2] n.18
Crosley, Estate of v. Comm'r . . . . 4.14[9][a]
n.130

Cross, Estate of v. Comm'r . . . . . . 4.02[3][g] n.121

Crown v. Comm'r . . . . 9.04[8] n.186; 10.01[2][f] ns. 41, 42

Cruikshank, US v. . . . . 8.03[2] n.18

Crummey v. Comm'r . . . 9.04[3][f] & ns. 94– 96, 102, 104, 113, 115, 118–120; S9.04[3][f] n.110; 9.04[4] & ns. 140, 141; S10.01[3][g] ns. 115.31, 115.34; 10.04[4][c] n.54; 13.02[2][e][ii] & ns. 122, 143; 15.03[4][b][iii] & ns. 119, 122, 142; 16.02[2][b][iii] & ns. 72, 73; 16.02[2][b][iv] & n.108; 16.02[2][b][v] & n.111

Culbertson, Comm'r v. . . . . . 10.07[2][b] n.63

Cullison, Estate of v. Comm'r . . . . 10.02[2][b][iii] n.58

Cummins, Estate of v. Comm'r . . . . 10.01[4] n.142

Curry v. US . . . . 4.12[2] n.21

Curry, Estate of v. Comm'r . . . 4.05[4] n.39

Curry, Estate of v. US . . . . . . 4.02[2][a] n.26

Cutter, Estate of v. Comm'r . . . . . 4.08[6][a] n.80

D

Dailey v. Comm'r . . . . . 10.02[2][c][ii] n.84; 10.02[2][c][iii] n.100

Dallas v. Comm'r . . . . . S10.02[2][c][ii] n.84

Dallman, Second Nat'l Bank of Danville v. . . . 4.05[6] ns. 75, 76; 4.13[2][b] n.16; 4.14[3][c] n.32; 5.06[7][c] n.194; 11.03[3][b] n.40

Daly v. US . . . . 4.14[8] n.114

D'Ambrosio, Estate of . . . 4.08[1][a] ns. 7, 8, 10; 4.08[7][c] ns. 139, 143; 19.03[4][c][ii] n.343; 19.03[4][e][i] ns. 367, 369; S19.03[4][e][i] n.367

Damon, Estate of v. Comm'r . . . 3.03[2] ns. 21, 23; 3.06[4] n.28; 5.09[2] ns. 14, 17

Daniels v. Comm'r . . . . . . 9.04[10][b] n.242

Darby, Estate of v. Wiseman . . . . . 5.03[3][d] n.81; S5.03[6][a] n.276

Darlington, Estate of v. Comm'r . . . . S5.03[4][b][ii] n.199; 5.03[8] n.164

Davenport, Estate of . . . . . S4.02[5] n.244; S4.05[4] n.40; S4.11[4][a] n.40; S5.03[2][a] n.57

Davenport, US v. . . . . S9.04[11] n.245

Davenport, Estate of v. Comm'r . . . 10.01[3] n.75; 10.01[4] n.140

Davie v. Briggs 8.02 n.10

Davies v. US . . . . . 5.05[2][b] n.68; 5.06[3][a] n.30

Davis v. Comm'r (BTA) . . . 5.03[4][a] ns. 86, 90; 5.03[5] n.96

Davis v. Comm'r (TC) . . . . . 9.04[5][b] n.162

Davis, Comm'r v. . . . . 5.03[4][a] ns. 86, 90; 5.03[5] n.96; S5.03[5] n.248; 5.03[6] n.148; S5.03[6][c][iii] n.302

Davis v. US (9th Cir.) . . . 4.04[7][b][i] n.274

Davis v. US (D. NH) . . . . . S4.02[5] n.244; S4.11[4][a] n.40

Davis v. US (ND Tex.) . . . . 10.01[4] n.139; 10.02[6][d] n.183

Davis, US v. . . . . 4.15[1][a] ns. 16, 17; 4.15[1][b][ii] n.55; 5.06[6][a] n.145; 10.02[5][d] n.164

Davis, YMCA v. . . . . 4.05[5][c] n.60

Davis, Estate of v. Comm'r (3d Cir.) . . . . 4.15[2] n.68

Davis, Estate of v. Comm'r (5th Cir.) . . . . 10.02[6][d] n.183

Davis, Estate of v. Comm'r (9th Cir.) . . . . . . S5.06[8][b][i] n.218; S5.06[8][d][ii] n.325

Davis, Estate of v. Comm'r (TC 1998) . . . . 4.02[4][b][iv] n.168; 4.02[4][e][iii] ns. 216, 218; 4.02[4][e][iv] n.220; 10.02[2][c][i] n.80; 10.02[2][c][iv] ns. 106, 108

Davis, Estate of v. Comm'r (TC 1986) . . . . 4.04[3][b][viii] n.96

Davis, Estate of v. Comm'r (TC 1972) . . . . S5.03[4][a][i] n.154; 5.03[5][e] n.135

Davis, Estate of v. Comm'r (TC 1968) . . . . 4.10[4][a] n.22

Davis, Estate of v. Comm'r (TCM 1993) . . . . 4.02[4][e][vii] n.227

Davison, Estate of v. US . . . . . 4.05[7][b] n.82

Dawson, Estate of v. Comm'r (3d Cir.) . . . . 4.14[4][c] n.53

Dawson, Estate of v. Comm'r (TC) . . . . 5.06[5][a] n.98

Deal v. Comm'r . . . . 10.01[3][c] n.99

DeCleene v. Comm'r . . . . . . 4.02[6][a] n.264

De Foucaucourt, Estate of v. Comm'r . . . . 5.03[3][b] n.61; S5.03[3][b] n.107

De Goldschmidt-Rothschild v. Comm'r . . . . 6.04[2] n.13; 9.02[1] n.8; S9.02[1][a] n.7

Delaney v. Gardner . . . . 5.05[1][a] n.9

Delaney v. Murchie . . . 6.03[2][a] ns. 22, 23; 6.04[2] ns. 13, 14

Delaney, Parker v. . . . . 4.12[8] n.70

Del Drago, Riggs v. . . . 5.06[5][a] n.98; 8.04 n.9; 8.04[2] n.15; 8.05[4] n.12

Delaune, Estate of v. US . . . 10.07[2][c] n.66; 10.07[2][d] n.82

De Niro v. US . . . . 8.02 ns. 1, 6

Denison, US v. . . . . 3.05[3][a] n.26

Denman, Estate of . . . . S12.03[1] n.4

Deobald Estate v. US . . . S5.03[4][a][ii] n.167; 5.03[5][a] n.97

De Oliveira v. US . . . . 4.13[4][a] n.37; 4.13[7][c] n.91

De Paoli v. Comm'r . . . . 5.06[3][a] n.30; 10.07[2][d] n.79

Deputy, Estate of v. Comm'r . . . S4.02[2][b] n.38; S4.02[4][c][i] n.172

de St. Aubin, Estate of v. Comm'r . . . . 5.06[6][a] n.151

*[Text references are to paragraphs and notes (9"n.");
references to the supplement are preceded by "S."]*

Detroit Bank & Trust Co. v. US (6th Cir.)
. . . . 4.14[9][b] n.138
Detroit Bank & Trust Co. v. US (ED Mich.)
. . . . 5.05[2][c] n.81
Detroit Trust Co. v. US 8.02 n.4
Devlin, Estate of v. Comm'r . . . 4.05[3] n.28
DeVos, Estate of v. Comm'r . . . . . . S5.03[5]
n.256; 5.03[5][b] n.128
Dewitt, Marcus v.   S5.03[3] n.80; 5.03[3][c]
n.63; S5.03[3][c][ii] n.129
Dewitt, Estate of v. Comm'r . . . . . 4.07[2][c]
n.65
Dickinson v. Comm'r . . . . . 10.01[3][e] n.107
Dickinson, Estate of v. Comm'r . . . 4.05[5][b]
n.52
Dickman v. Comm'r   10.01[2][f] & ns. 41–
43; 13.02[3][b][i] n.219
Dickson v. US . . . . 5.06[3][g] n.72; 5.06[7][b]
n.170
Diedrich v. Comm'r . . . . 4.07[3][a] n.82;
10.02[6][d] n.181
Diehl v. US . . . . 4.08[4][c] n.46
Dietz, Estate of v. Comm'r . . . . . . 4.13[7][f]
n.109
Dillingham, Estate of v. Comm'r . . . . 4.05[3]
n.28
Dillingham v. Comm'r . . . . 10.01[3][h] n.122
Di Marco, Estate of v. Comm'r . . . .
. . . 10.01[2][g] n.64; 10.01[5][b] n.164;
10.02[1][b] ns. 16, 19
Dimen, Estate of v. Comm'r . . . . . 4.14[5][a]
n.86; S4.14[6] n.103.22
Dimock v. Corwin . . . . 4.05[4] n.37
DiSanto, Estate of v. Comm'r 4.16 n.23;
5.06[5] n.94
Disbrow, Estate of v. Comm'r . . . S4.02[4][g]
n.241; S4.08[6][c] n.86
Disston, Comm'r v. . . . . 9.04[3][b] n.60;
9.04[3][d] n.72; 9.04[3][e] n.82; 9.05[1]
n.6; 9.05[3] n.39
Diver v. US . . . . 4.02[3][f] n.108
Dixon v. US . . . . 4.09[6] n.50
Dockery v. Comm'r . . . . 4.02[4][f] n.231
Dodge v. US . . . . S10.07[2][b] n.36
Doerr v. US . . . . 10.01[2] n.13
Doherty, Estate of v. Comm'r (10th Cir.) . . .
. . . . 4.04[6] ns. 233, 237
Doherty, Estate of v. Comm'r (TC) . . . .
. . . . 5.06[8][d][ii] n.325
Dom v. US . . . . 19.04[3][b][i] n.80
Donaldson v. Comm'r . . . . . . 3.05[3][b] n.43
Donaldson, Estate of v. Comm'r . . . . 4.05[6]
n.69
Donehoo v. US . . . . 4.02[2][a] n.17
Donnan, Heiner v. . . . . 4.07[4] n.95; 9.01 n.6
Donovan, Estate of v. United States . . . .
. . . . S4.02[5] n.244; S4.11[4][a] n.40
Dooly, Estate of v. Comm'r . . . . . 4.02[3][f]
n.107; 4.02[4][b][iii] n.159
Dorsey v. Comm'r . . . . 4.02[3][g] n.136;
4.05[8] n.94; 10.01[10][a] n.213
Doster, Estate of v. Comm'r . . . 2.02[3][b][ii]
n.44

Dougherty, Estate of v. Comm'r   4.02[3][b]
n.67; 4.02[4][d][ii] n.194
Doughty, Estate of v. US . . . 5.06[7][b] n.174
Douglas, Estate of v. Comm'r . . . . 4.08[4][c]
n.46
Douglass, Estate of, Comm'r v. . . . 4.08[4][b]
n.32
Dowlin, Estate of v. Comm'r . . . . . 4.02[3][b]
n.67; 5.03[3] n.39; S5.03[3] n.81
Downe, Estate of v. Comm'r . . . . . 4.10[4][d]
n.44
Drake, Estate of v. Comm'r . . . . . 4.13[6][d]
n.76
Draper v. Comm'r . . . . . 5.06[8][b][iv] n.260
Draper Estate v. Comm'r . . . . . 4.14[3] n.21
Drazen, Estate of v. Comm'r . . . . 4.12[7][a]
n.37; 4.12[8] n.61
Driscoll, Commonwealth Trust Co. of Pitts-
burgh v. . . . . . 3.03[2] n.20; 4.10[4][d]
n.45; 5.09[2] n.13
Driscoll, Union Trust Co. of Pittsburgh v.
. . . . 4.10[2] n.7
Drybrough v. US . . . . 10.01[2][e] n.33
Drye v. US . . . . 10.07[2][d] n.82
Duberstein, Comm'r v. . . . . . . 10.01[2][f] n.47;
10.01[10][b] n.219; 10.02[3] n.131
DuCharme, Estate of v. Comm'r . . . .
. . . . . . 4.08[5][b] n.62; 4.10[3] n.12;
4.10[4][e] n.48; 4.10[6] n.69
Dudley, Eggleston v. . . . . . . 5.06[7][b] n.171;
8.05[2] n.6
Duffield v. US . . . . 4.05[4] n.39
Duke v. Comm'r . . . . . . 10.02[2][b][iv] n.63
Dulles v. Johnson . . . . 5.03[3][a] n.53;
S5.03[3][a] n.92; 5.05[1][b] n.28
Dumbrill v. US . . . . 4.12[2] n.22
Dunia, Estate of v. Comm'r . . . . S4.02[3][b]
n.70
Dunigan v. US . . . . 10.01[3][g] n.117
Dunn v. US . . . . 5.06[7][b] n.173
Dunn, Estate of v. Comm'r . . . . . . 4.02[2][a]
n.22; 4.02[2][b][iii] n.45; 4.02[2][b][iv]
n.47; 4.02[4][e][iii] n.218;
S4.02[4][e][iii] n.218; 10.02[2][c][iv]
n.108
du Pont v. Comm'r (TCM 1978) . . . 10.01[2]
n.13
du Pont v. Comm'r (TC 1943) . . . . 10.01[6]
n.183
Du Pont v. US . . . .
. . . . . . 9.02[2] n.13; 9.04[1][b] n.33
DuPont, Estate of v. Comm'r (3d Cir.) . . . . .
. . . . . 4.02[3][h] n.142; 4.05[6] n.69;
4.14[1] n.2; 6.05[1] n.2; 8.01[1][a][ii]
n.12
Du Pont, Estate of v. Comm'r (TC) . . . .
. . . . 4.08[6][c] n.86
DuVal's Estate v. Comm'r . . . . S5.03[4][c][i]
n.207; S5.03[5] n.257; 5.03[5][a] n.118;
5.03[5][b] n.124; 5.03[6] n.155;
10.02[2][b][i] n.45
Dwight's Estate, Comm'r v. . . . . . 4.08[4][b]
n.30; 4.08[8] n.168; 10.02[5][b] n.161

[Text references are to paragraphs and notes (9"n.");
references to the supplement are preceded by "S."]

E

Eagan, Estate of v. Comm'r . . . . . 5.03[3][b]
n.59; S5.03[3][b] n.105
Earl, Lucas v. . . . . 10.01[2][g] n.64;
10.01[10][a] n.208
Eaton, Suisman v. . . . . 5.06[6][a] n.145
Eccles v. Comm'r . . . . 5.06[3] n.19
Eckhardt, Estate of v. Comm'r . . . 4.08[7][d]
n.163
Eddy, Estate of v. Comm'r . . . . . 4.03[1] n.3
Edelman, Estate of v. Comm'r . . . . . 4.13[3]
n.19
Edinburg v. US . . . 3.03[2] n.29; 3.06[4] n.33;
5.09[2] n.31
Edmonds, Estate of v. Comm'r . . . . . 4.08[5]
n.55; 4.10[4][g] n.55; 5.06[7][b] ns. 165,
184
Edwards v. Comm'r (7th Cir.) . . . 9.04[3][d]
n.74; 13.02[2][b][i] n.43; 17.02[3][b]
n.125
Edwards v. Comm'r (TC) . . . . . 5.06[8][b][iii]
n.248
Edwards v. Slocum . . . 5.05[3][b][i] ns. 101–
103; 5.08[4][a][ii] n.177
Edwards v. US . . . . 10.01[2][e] n.33
Edwards Estate, In re . . . .
. . . . 5.06[8][d][iv] n.394
Edwards, Estate of v. Comm'r (TCM 2001)
. . . . 4.02[3][b] n.73
Edwards, Estate of v. Comm'r (TCM 1997)
. . . . 4.15[1][b][i] n.40
Eggleston v. Dudley . . . . . . 5.06[7][b] n.171;
8.05[2] n.6
Ehret, Estate of v. Comm'r . . . . 4.12[8] n.64;
S5.03[4][b] n.173; 5.03[5][a] n.101
Eichheim v. US . . . . 2.02[3][c][vi] n.134
Eichstedt v. US . . . 4.10[4][f] n.50; 4.11[3][a]
n.19; 9.04[5][c] n.168
Eisenberg v. Comm'r . . . 4.02[4][e][iii] n.218;
S4.02[4][e][iii] n.219; 10.02[2][c][iv]
n.108
Eisner v. Macomber . . . . 4.03[2][c] n.28;
4.12[7][a] n.41
Eisner, New York Trust Co. v. . . . . . 9.02[3]
n.21
Elkins, Estate of v. US . . . . S5.03[4][a] n.146;
S5.03[4][a][i] n.155; S5.03[4][b] n.174;
5.03[5] n.96; 5.03[5][a] n.100
Ellingson, Estate of v. Comm'r . . . .
. . . . 5.06[8][d][ii] n.325
Elliot, Estate of v. Comm'r . . . 4.12[2] ns. 21,
22
Ellis v. Comm'r . . . . 10.02[5][b] n.161
Ellis, Comm'r v. . . . .
. . . . 5.06[8][b][iii] ns. 245, 249
Ellis v. US . . . . 4.05[5][c] n.66
Ellis First Nat'l Bank of Bradenton v. US
. . . . 5.05[7][a] n.330
Ellis Sarasota Bank & Trust Co. v. US . . . .
. . . . 10.02[4] n.141

Ellman, Estate of v. Comm'r . . . . 4.15[1][a]
n.24
Emery v. US . . . . 4.13[6][d] n.76
Empire Trust Co. v. US . . . . . . 3.03[2] n.28;
5.09[2] n.29
Endicott Trust Co. v. US . . . . 4.12[7][a] ns. 45,
46
Engelman, Estate of v. Comm'r . . . .
. . . . S5.05[1][a] n.7; S5.05[1][b] n.41;
S10.07[2][c] n.71
English v. US (7th Cir.) . . . . 4.03[2][c] n.31;
4.12[7][a] n.37; 4.12[8] n.61
English v. US (ND Fla.) . . . . . . 2.01[2] n.60;
S2.01[2] n.78; 10.03[2] n.32
Ensley, Estate of v. Comm'r . . . 4.12[8] n.64
Erickson, Estate of v. Comm'r . . . S4.08[4][c]
n.49
Erie RR v. Tompkins . . . . 4.05[2][b] & n.14;
S5.03[1][a] n.14; 10.02[5] & n.152
Erwin v. US . . . . 5.06[6][b] n.157
ESB Fin. v. US . . . . S5.05[8][b] n.367
Essenfeld v. Comm'r . . . . 4.11[2][a] n.7
Estes, Estate of, Nickel v. . . . . . 10.07[2] n.26
Evans v. Comm'r . . . . 9.04[3][c] n.69
Evans v. US . . . . 5.06[8][b][iii] n.250
Evanson v. US . . . . 2.01[1][b][i] n.22;
S2.01[1][b][i] n.22
Evers, Estate of v. Comm'r . . . . 5.06[5] n.87
Ewing, Estate of v. Comm'r . . . . . 4.02[3][f]
n.111
Exchange Bank & Trust Co. of Fla. v. US
. . . 4.08[4][b] n.34; 4.08[7][d] ns. 153,
160; 4.10[4][f] n.52

F

Faber v. US (6th Cir.) . . . . . 9.04[5][a] n.147
Faber v. US (Ct. Cl.) . . . . 6.06[1] n.11
Fabian v. US . . . . 4.10[7] n.73
Fagan, Estate of v. Comm'r . . . 5.05[3][b][i]
n.109
Fahs, Merrill v. . . . . . . 4.06 n.16; 4.15[1] n.5;
4.15[1][b][ii] n.56; 10.02[5][d] n.167;
10.06[1] n.4; 10.06[3] n.33
Fairchild v. Comm'r 8.09 n.1
Falk v. Comm'r . . . . 10.03[1] n.12
Fannon v. Comm'r . . . . 19.04[2] n.33
Farid-Es-Sultaneh v. Comm'r . . . . 4.12[7][a]
n.41
Farish v. Comm'r . . . .
. . . . 9.05[1] n.6; 9.05[3] n.39
Farley v. US . . . . 5.06[3][a] n.31
Farnam, Estate of . . . . S5.08[2][a] n.16;
S5.08[2][c][ii] n.56
Farrell, Estate of v. US . . . . . 4.08[5][a] n.58
Fawcett, Estate of v. Comm'r . . . S5.03[5] ns.
245, 247; 5.03[6] ns. 146, 148
Fay v. Helvering . . . . 5.04[2] n.13
Fehrs v. US . . . . 10.02[3] n.132
Feinberg, Estate of v. Comm'r . . . . S5.03[5]
n.256; 5.03[6] n.153

[Text references are to paragraphs and notes (9"n.");
references to the supplement are preceded by "S."]

Fenton, Estate of v. Comm'r . . . S5.03[4][a][i]
    n.153; 5.03[5][e] n.134
Ferguson v. US . . . . S5.03[3][c][ii] n.129
Fernandez v. Wiener . . . . 4.05[5][a] n.47
Ferrara, Estate of v. US . . . . . . 8.04[2] n.16
Fidelity-Philadelphia Trust Co. v. Rothensies
        . . . . 4.08[8] n.166; 4.09[6] n.52
Fidelity-Philadelphia Trust Co. v. Smith . . . .
     . . . . 4.02[3][h] n.139; 4.11[2][a] n.7;
    4.14[2] n.20; 4.14[9][a] n.129
Fiedler, Estate of v. Comm'r . . . 5.06[8][c] ns.
    278–280
Field, US v. . . . . 4.13[10] n.126
Field, Estate of v. Comm'r . . . . 5.06[8][b][iii]
    n.251
Fields, Estate of v. Comm'r . . . . . 5.06[7][b]
    n.164
Fifth Ave. Bank of NY v. Nunan . . . .
    . . . . 4.10[4][d] n.44
Fifth Ave. Bank of NY, Ex'r v. Comm'r . . .
    . . . . 6.01[3][b] n.31
Fillman v. US . . . . 6.04[1] n.3
Findlay v. Comm'r . . . . 4.05[4] n.35
Fine, Estate of v. Comm'r . . . 5.06[5][a] n.98
Finlay v. US . . . . 4.13[4][a] n.37
Fiorito, Estate of v. Comm'r . . . . . 4.02[2][c]
    n.50; 19.04[3][a] n.48; 19.04[6][a][i] ns.
    120–122
First Huntington Nat'l Bank, US v. . . . .
    . . . . 8.03[1] n.6; 8.03[2] n.13
First Interstate Bank of Ariz. v. US . . . .
    . . . . . S5.03[4][c][i] n.207; 5.03[5][a]
    n.118; 5.03[5][b] n.120
First Ky. Trust Co. v. US . . . . . . 4.12[1] n.4;
    4.14[3] n.21
First Nat'l Bank v. Comm'r . . . . . 4.02[2][a]
    n.13
First Nat'l Bank & Trust Co. of Tulsa v. US
    . . . . 3.03[2] n.17; S5.03[4][b][i] n.186;
    5.03[5][a] n.105; 5.09[2] n.10
First Nat'l Bank of Amarillo v. US . . . .
    . . . . . S5.03[4][a] n.152; 5.03[5][b] ns.
    126, 127
First Nat'l Bank of Birmingham v. US . . . . .
    . . . . . 4.14[4][d] n.59; 4.14[5][a] n.81
First Nat'l Bank of Fayetteville, Ark. v. US
    . . . . 5.05[2][b] n.69
First Nat'l Bank of Fort Smith v. US . . . . . .
    . . . . 4.02[3][f] n.110
First Nat'l Bank of Ft. Worth v. US (US) . . .
    . . . . 5.03[2][b] n.32
First Nat'l Bank of Ft. Worth v. US (ND
    Tex.) . . . S5.03[1][a] n.15; 5.03[3] n.40;
    S5.03[3] n.82
First Nat'l Bank of Kenosha v. US . . . .
    . . . . 4.02[3][b] n.79
First Nat'l Bank of Middlesex County v. US
    . . . . 4.13[2][a] n.10
First Nat'l Bank of Omaha v. US (8th Cir.
    1982) . . . 4.13[3] n.19; 5.05[1][b] n.36
First Nat'l Bank of Omaha v. US (8th Cir.
    1974) . . . . 5.05[3][b][i] n.109

First Nat'l Bank of Ore. v. US . . . 4.14[9][b]
    n.138
First Nat'l Bank of Pa. v. US . . . .
    . . . . . S5.03[4][c][i] n.207; 5.03[5][a]
    n.118
First Nat'l Trust & Sav. Bank, US v. . . . . . .
    . . . . 5.06[8][b][iii] n.243
First Trust Co. of St. Paul v. Reynolds . . . . .
    . . . . 5.05[1][a] n.9
First Trust Co. of St. Paul v. US . . . .
    . . . . 5.06[5][a] n.99
First Victoria Nat'l Bank v. US . . . 4.05[2][a]
    n.5
First Va. Bank v. US . . . . 4.13[4][a] n.37
First Wis. Trust Co. v. US . . . . . 10.01[5][c]
    n.169
Fischer v. Comm'r . . . . 9.04[1][b] n.29;
    9.04[3][e] n.92
Fish v. US . . 4.13[7][a] n.80; 4.13[7][e] n.105;
    4.13[7][f] n.112; 10.04[4][c] n.48
Fisher v. Comm'r (9th Cir.) . . . . . 9.04[3][a]
    n.55
Fisher v. Comm'r (TCM) . . . . . 4.04[7][b][ii]
    n.286
Fisher v. US (Fed. Cl.)   5.05[3][b][ii] n.115;
    5.06[5][b][iii] n.111
Fisher v. US (SD Ind.) . . . . S9.04[3][e] n.88;
    S19.04[3][a] n.48
Fish, Estate of v. Comm'r . . . 4.08[7][d] n.161
Fiske, Estate of (BTA) . . . . . . S5.03[6][c][iii]
    n.302
Fiske, Estate of v. Comm'r (TCM) . . . .
    . . . . 4.10[4][c] n.38
Fitzgerald v. US . . . . 10.07[2][b] n.35
Flake, Estate of v. Comm'r . . . . 5.06[8][b][iii]
    ns. 250, 251
Flanagan, Estate of v. US . . . . 5.05[2][b] n.68
Flanders v. US . . . . . 4.02[3][b] n.60; 4.03[2]
    n.16
Flandreau, Estate of v. Comm'r . . . . 4.15[2]
    n.75; S5.03[4][a][i] n.155; 5.03[5][3]
    n.136; 10.01[1] ns. 9, 11
Flanigan, Estate of v. Comm'r . . . 5.05[2][d]
    n.88
Fleming, Estate of v. Comm'r (7th Cir.) . . . .
    . . . . 10.07[2][b] n.35
Fleming, Estate of v. Comm'r (TCM 1997)
    . . . 4.02[2][a] n.35; 4.02[4][c][iii] n.181
Fleming, Estate of v. Comm'r (TCM 1974)
    . . . . 4.03[2] n.21; 4.05[4] n.45
Florida v. Mellon . . . . 3.03[1] n.9
Florida Bank at Lakeland v. US   5.06[3][b]
    ns. 42, 46
Florida Nat'l Bank v. US . . . . 4.08[9] n.200;
    4.10[4][b] ns. 29, 31
Floyd Estate (No. 2) . . . . . . 10.03[3][a] n.43
Flye, Estate of v. Comm'r . . . . . 4.14[2] n.14
    116136
Focardi, Estate of v. Comm'r . . . .
    . . . . S19.03[3][b][i] n.134
Folkerds v. US . . . . 5.06[5][a] n.99
Folks, Estate of v. Comm'r . . . . 4.02[4][e][ii]
    n.210; 4.10[1] n.2

[Text references are to paragraphs and notes (9"n.");
references to the supplement are preceded by "S."]

Fondren v. Comm'r . . . . . . 9.04[3] & n.47;
  9.04[3][a] n.55; 9.04[3][d] n.72
Forbes, Estate of v. Comm'r . . . . 4.02[4][e][i]
  n.200
Ford v. US . . . . 5.06[3][d] n.54
Ford, Estate of v. Comm'r (2d Cir.) . . . . . .
  . . . . . 4.08[6][a] n.76; 4.10[4][c] n.38;
  4.10[5] n.64
Ford, Estate of v. Comm'r (8th Cir.) . . . . . .
  . . . 4.02[2][a] n.36; 4.02[2][b][iii] n.44;
  4.02[4][c][iii] n.179; 4.02[4][d][ii] n.193
Forrest, Jr., Estate of v. Comm'r . . . .
  . . . . 4.05[2][a] n.6
Forrester, Hollis v. . . . . S8.07[1] n.7
Forsee, US v. . . . . 4.13[4][a] n.37
Fortunato, Estate of v. Comm'r . . . . S4.05[2]
  n.2
Foster v. Neilson 7.06 n.6
Foster, Estate of . . . . . . S4.02[4][e][i] n.196;
  S4.02[4][e][vii] n.225; S5.03[4][c][ii]
  n.215
Foster, Estate of v. Comm'r . . . 5.06[8][b][iv]
  n.262
Fox, Estate of v. Comm'r . . . 4.02[2][a] n.12;
  4.05[1] n.1; 4.12[1] n.7
Frane v. Comm'r . . . . 4.11[5] n.53
Frank, Kuney v. . . . . 4.02[4][g] n.236
Frank, Estate of v. Comm'r . . . . . 4.02[3][g]
  n.118; 4.02[4][b][iii] n.163; 4.02[4][f]
  n.230; 4.07[2][b][ii] n.49
Fratini, Estate of v. Comm'r . . . . 4.02[4][e][i]
  n.198; 4.12[7][a] n.37; 4.12[8] n.59
Frazee v. Comm'r . . . . 4.02[4][g] n.236;
  10.01[2][f] n.48
Frazell v. US . . . . 10.01[2][g] n.63
Frazell, US v. . . . . 4.05[4] n.33
Frazier, Estate of v. Comm'r . . . . 4.05[2][a]
  n.6
Freedman v. US . . . . 4.14[8] n.121
Freedman, Estate of v. Comm'r . . . . 4.12[2]
  n.18
Freeman, Estate of v. Comm'r (TCM 1996)
  . . . . 4.02[2][a] ns. 28, 36
Freeman, Estate of v. Comm'r (TC 1976) . . .
  . . . . 4.13[7][a] n.81
Frick, Lewellyn v. . . . . 4.14[10] n.155
Fried, Estate of v. Comm'r . . . . 4.05[3] n.25;
  4.09[2] n.4; 5.06[7][b] n.175
Frieders, Estate of v. Comm'r . . . . 4.02[3][b]
  n.67
Friedman v. US . . . . 5.06[8][b][ii] n.236
Friedman, Estate of v. Comm'r . . . . 10.02[6]
  n.170
Frizzell, Estate of v. Comm'r . . . . 4.07[2][c]
  n.60
Frost, Estate of v. Comm'r . . . 5.06[3][a] n.29
Frothingham v. Comm'r . . . . . . 4.15[2] n.65
Fruehauf, Estate of v. Comm'r . . . 4.14[4][e]
  n.71; 4.14[4][f] n.75
Fry, Estate of v. Comm'r . . . . 4.08[2] n.20
Fuchs, Estate of v. Comm'r . . . . . 4.14[5][b]
  n.94
Fuentes, Estate of . . . . S2.02[1] n.14

Fulmer, Estate of v. Comm'r . . . .
  S5.03[4][a][ii] n.167; 5.03[5][a] n.97
Fung, Estate of v. Comm'r (9th Cir.) . . . . . .
  . . . . . . S5.06[3][a] n.30; S6.06[1] n.9
Fung, Estate of v. Comm'r (TC)   5.06[3][a]
  n.30; 6.06[1] n.9
Furman, Estate of v. Comm'r . . . . 4.02[2][a]
  n.34; 4.02[2][b] n.38; 4.02[4][e][vi]
  n.224; 4.02[4][f] n.231; 10.01[2] n.13
Fusz, Estate of v. Comm'r . . . 4.11[3][a] n.20

G

Gagliardi, Estate of v. Comm'r . . . . . 4.05[3]
  n.28
Gall v. US . . . . 9.04[5][b] n.152
Gallagher, Estate of v. Comm'r . . . .
  . . . S4.02[2][b][i] n.40; S4.02[2][b][ii]
  n.41; S4.02[4][c][i] n.72; S4.02[4][d][ii]
  n.186
Gallenstein v. US . . . 4.12[10] n.85; 5.06[3][d]
  n.52; 5.06[4] n.86
Galloway v. US . . . . S5.05[4][b] ns. 139, 147;
  S5.05[7][b] n.338
Galt v. Comm'r . . . . . . 10.01[3][a] ns. 84, 87;
  10.01[10][a] ns. 209, 211
Gamble, Estate of v. Comm'r   3.03[2] n.17;
  4.05[2][a] n.8; S5.03[4][b][i] n.186;
  5.03[5][a] n.105; 5.09[2] n.10
Gannon, Estate of v. Comm'r . . . .
  . . . . 19.04[6][a][i] n.117
Gardner, Delaney v. . . . . 5.05[1][a] n.9
Gardner, Estate of v. Comm'r . . . . . . 2.02[1]
  n.10; S2.02[1] n.10
Garret's Estate v. Comm'r . . . . . 6.05[1] n.4
Gartland, Estate of v. Comm'r . . . 4.13[6][a]
  n.69
Gavin, Estate of v. US . . . 4.04[7][b][ii] n.285
Gaynor, Estate of v. Comm'r . . . . 4.10[4][a]
  n.25
Geiger, Estate of v. Comm'r . . . 4.04[3][b][ii]
  n.43
Gelb v. Comm'r . . . . 5.06[8][b][i] n.230;
  9.04[3][b] n.65
General Utilities and Operating Co. v.
  Helvering . . . . . 4.02[4][e][iii] & n.214
Georgia Ketteman Trust v. Comm'r . . . . . .
  . . . . 9.04[1][b] n.28; 9.04[3][e] n.90;
  10.01[2][b][i] n.21
German, Estate of v. US . . . . . 4.08[4][c] n.53
Gerry v. Comm'r . . . . 4.07[3][b] n.86
Gerson, Estate of . . . . . . S18.05[2][b][ii] n.39
Gesner v. US . . . . 4.14[4][e] n.71
Gettysburg Nat'l Bank v. US . . . . 4.02[2][a]
  n.28; 4.04[6] n.236
Giacopuzzi, Estate of v. Comm'r . . . . 3.03[2]
  n.19; 4.12[8] n.60; 5.09[2] n.12
Giannini, Comm'r v. . . . . . . 10.01[2][g] n.65
Gibbs, Estate of v. US . . . . . 4.04[7][b][i] ns.
  272, 273

*[Text references are to paragraphs and notes (9"n.");
references to the supplement are preceded by "S."]*

Gilbertson, British Columbia v. . . . . . 7.04[3] n.19
Gilchrist, Estate of v. Comm'r . . . 4.13[7][a] n.80
Gilford, Estate of v. Comm'r . . . . 4.02[2][a] n.27
Gillespie v. US . . . . 4.02[4][e][ii] n.207; 5.03[3][c] n.62; S5.03[3][c][ii] n.128; 5.03[3][d] n.78; S5.03[6][a] n.273
Gillespie, Estate of v. Comm'r (TC 1994) . . . . 10.03[3][b] n.47
Gillespie, Estate of v. Comm'r (TC 1980) . . . . . . 5.05[4][b] n.147; 11.02[2][b] n.52
Gillespie, Estate of v. Comm'r (TC 1947) . . . . . 5.03[2][a] n.19; S5.03[2][a] n.59
Gillum v. Comm'r . . . . 5.03[4][b] n.92; S5.03[6][c][iii] n.309
Gilman v. Comm'r (2d Cir.) . . . . . 4.08[6][d] n.101
Gilman, Estate of v. Comm'r (TC) . . . . 4.08[4][c] n.51
Gilman, Estate of v. Comm'r (TCM) . . . . S5.03[3][c][i] n.118
Gilmore v. Comm'r . . . . . . 9.04[3][e] n.79; 9.04[4] n.140
Gilruth, Estate of v. Comm'r . . . . 3.05[3][b] n.50
Gimbel, Estate of . . . . . S4.02[4][e][iv] n.220
Ginsberg's Estate, In re . . . . . 5.06[3][b] n.41
Giselman, Estate of v. Comm'r . . . 4.08[6][c] n.85
Gist v. US . . . . 4.08[7][c] n.151
Giustina, Estate of v. Comm'r . . . S4.02[3][f] n.106; S4.02[6][a] n.261
Glade, Estate of v. Comm'r . . . . 4.14[4][a] n.44
Glaser v. US . . . . 4.08[8][a] n.177; 4.12[9] ns. 74, 75
Glass, Estate of v. Comm'r . . . . . 4.05[2] n.4
Glen, Estate of v. Comm'r   4.15[1][a] n.25; 4.15[1][a][ii] n.30; 4.15[1][b][i] n.46; 4.15[1][b][ii] n.58
Glenshaw Glass Co., Comm'r v. 10.01 n.1
Gloeckner, Estate of v. Comm'r   4.02[2][a] n.36; 4.02[2][c] n.50; 19.04[3][b][i] n.59; 19.04[7] n.141
Goelet, Estate of v. Comm'r . . . . . . 10.01[7] n.190
Gokey, Estate of v. Comm'r . . . . . 4.08[4][b] n.30
Goldberg, Estate of . . . . S4.12[9] n.73; S5.03[3][a] ns. 94, 96
Goldman, Estate of v. Comm'r . . . 4.10[4][a] n.25
Goldsborough, Estate of v. Comm'r . . . . 4.12[7][a] n.41
Goldstein v. Comm'r . . . . . . 10.01[5] n.147; 10.01[5][a] n.156
Goldstein, Estate of v. Comm'r . . . 5.06[3][b] n.37
Goldstone, Estate of v. Comm'r . . . . . 4.05[6] n.70; 4.08[4] n.21

Goldwater, Estate of v. Comm'r . . . . 5.06[3] n.17
Goodall, Estate of v. Comm'r . . . . 4.02[2][a] n.17; 4.05[7][b] n.80
Goodin, Estate of v. Comm'r . . . . 4.02[3][g] n.121
Gooding Amusement Co. v. Comm'r . . . . 4.02[3][f] n.101; 4.05[7][a] n.77
Goodman v. Comm'r . . . 4.05[6] n.71; 4.14[8] n.117; 10.01[5][b] n.158
Goodman v. Granger . . . . . 4.02[3][g] n.131; 4.05[4] n.37; 4.05[5][b] n.55; 4.05[8] ns. 95, 106; 4.14[2] ns. 17, 18, 20; 4.14[3][c] n.31
Goodnow v. US . . . . 4.14[9][b] n.146
Goodwin v. McGowan . . . . . 10.01[3][b] n.89
Goodwyn, Estate of . . . . 4.08[5][a] n.58
Gordon, Estate of v. Comm'r . . . . 5.06[3] n.17
Gore, Brodrick v. . . . . . 19.04[6][a][ii] n.128
Gore, Estate of v. Comm'r   S4.05[2][a] n.6; S4.08[4][c] n.49
Goree, Estate of v. Comm'r . . . 10.07[2] n.26
Gorman v. US . . . . 10.02[2][b][ii] n.49
Gould, Estate of v. Comm'r   10.02[2][b][iv] n.63
Goulder v. US . . . . 10.01[3][d] n.101
Gowetz v. Comm'r . . . . . S5.03[4][c][i] n.209; 5.03[5][b] n.120
Grace, Estate of, US v. . . . . . . 4.08[7][d] & ns. 154, 157–160; 9.04[1][b] n.35; 10.02[6][c] n.179; 12.01[1] n.4; 19.02[2][a][iii] n.72
Gradow, Estate of v. US . . . . . 4.08[1][a] n.7; 4.08[7][c] & ns. 140, 142, 144; 19.03[4][e][i] ns. 367, 369; S19.03[4][e][i] n.367
Graegin, Estate of v. Comm'r . . . . 5.03[3][c] ns. 68, 70; S5.03[3][c][i] ns. 116, 118; S5.03[4][a][i] n.163
Gramm, Estate of v. Comm'r . . . . . 10.01[9] n.205
Granger, Goodman v. . . . . 4.02[3][g] n.131; 4.05[4] n.37; 4.05[5][b] n.55; 4.05[8] ns. 95, 106; 4.14[2] ns. 17, 18, 20; 4.14[3][c] n.31
Grant, Estate of v. Comm'r . . . 5.03[3] n.39; S5.03[3] n.81; 5.03[3][c] n.63; S5.03[3][c][ii] n.130
Gray v. Comm'r . . . . . . 4.02[4][d][ii] n.192
Gray, Piatt v. . . . . . . 5.06[8][b][iii] n.251
Gray v. US (3d Cir.) . . . 4.11[3][a] ns. 19, 21
Gray v. US (9th Cir.) . . . . . 4.15[1][b][i] n.40; S5.03[3][a][i] n.158; 5.03[5][b] n.128
Gray, Estate of v. Comm'r (TCM 1997) . . . . 4.02[4][e][iii] n.217; S5.03[4][a] n.149; 5.03[5][a] n.113
Gray, Estate of v. Comm'r (TC 1943) . . . . 5.05[1][b] n.37
Green v. Connally . . . . 5.05[1][b] n.34
Greenburg v. Comm'r . . . S5.03[4][b] n.172; 5.03[5][a] n.99

[Text references are to paragraphs and notes (9"n.");
references to the supplement are preceded by "S."]

Greene, Comm'r v. . . . . . . 10.01[2][h] n.69;
10.02[5] & ns. 145–147, 151
Greene v. US (7th Cir. 1973) . . . . . 5.06[5][a]
n.101
Greene v. US (7th Cir. 1956) . . . . 4.08[8]
n.170; 4.11[5] n.47; 4.15[2] n.74
Green, Estate of v. Comm'r (TC 1975) . . . . .
. . . . 4.07[3][b] n.90
Green, Estate of v. Comm'r (TCM 2003) . . .
. . . . . S8.04[2] n.15.1; S12.03[1] n.4
Green, Estate of v. Comm'r (TCM 1945) . . .
. . . . 4.07[3][b] n.86
Green, Estate of v. US (6th Cir. 1995) . . . . .
. . . . 4.08[7][d] n.153
Green, Estate of v. US (6th Cir. 1971)
. . . . 5.06[7][b] n.170
Greer v. US . . . . 5.06[3][d] n.60
Gregory v. Helvering . . . . 4.02[4][g] n.235
Gregory, Estate of v. Comm'r . . . . 4.08[1][a]
n.7; 4.08[7][c] n.141; 4.15[2] n.77
Gribauskas, Estate of v. Comm'r (2d Cir.)
. . . . S4.02[5] ns. 244, 250; S4.11[4][a]
n.40
Gribauskas, Estate of v. Comm'r (TC) . . . . .
4.02[5] ns. 244, 250; 4.11[4][a] n.40
Grier v. US . . . . . 6.05[2][a][ii] n.27; 10.02[4]
n.138
Grimes, Estate of v. Comm'r . . . . . . 4.04[6]
n.237; 5.06[8][d][iv] n.393
Grinnel, Helvering v. . . . . 4.13[10] n.130
Grissom v. Sternberger . . . . 4.07[3][b] n.88
Groetzinger, Comm'r v. . . . 5.08[2][b][i] n.23
Grootematt, Estate of v. Comm'r . . . .
. . . . 4.02[4][e][ii] n.209
Gross v. Comm'r (TC 1946) . . . 9.04[1][b][ii]
n.29; 9.04[3][e] n.92
Gross v. Comm'r (TCM 2008) . . . .
. . . . S10.01[2][b][ii] n.25.1;
S10.02[2][c][v] n.121
Grossinger, Estate of v. Comm'r . . . .
. . . . 9.04[3][d] n.74
Grynberg v. Comm'r . . . . . . 10.01[5] n.153
Gudonis, Breakiron v. . . . . S10.07[2][b] n.36
Guggenheim, Burnet v. . . . . 10.01[3][i] n.130;
10.01[5] n.144; 10.01[6] & n.182;
10.01[10][e] n.227; 10.02[1][a] n.6;
10.07[2][b] n.37
Guggenheim v. Rasquin . . . . . . 6.05[1] n.5;
10.01[3][g] n.113; 10.02[2][b][ii] & ns.
46–48; 10.02[2][b][iv] n.63
Guida, Estate of v. Comm'r . . . 8.02 ns. 1, 4
Guiney v. US . . . . . 5.06[8][b][iii] n.248
Gulig v. Comm'r . . . . S4.02[2][a] n.34;
S4.02[4][g] ns. 237, 238; S10.02[2][c][v]
n.120; S19.04[2] ns. 25, 26
Gump v. Comm'r . . . . 4.02[3][g] n.124
Gunland, Estate of v. Comm'r . . . . . 4.04[6]
n.223
Gutchess, Estate of v. Comm'r . . . 4.08[4][c]
ns. 44, 53
Guyn v. US . . . . 4.08[4][c] n.45
Gwinn v. Comm'r . . . . 4.12[11] n.98

Gwinn, Estate of v. Comm'r . . . 5.06[5][b][i]
ns. 105, 108; 10.02[2][b][i] ns. 34, 37

H

Hackl v. Comm'r . . . . S9.04[3][e] n.88
Hagar, Estate of, Comm'r v. . . . . 4.10[1] n.2;
4.10[4][c] ns. 35, 41, 43
Hagerman, Estate of v. US . . . 4.02[2][a] n.36
Haggart's Estate v. Comm'r . . . . . 5.03[3][b]
n.61; S5.03[3][b] n.107
Haggett, Estate of v. Comm'r . . . . 4.08[7][b]
n.128
Hagmann, Estate of v. Comm'r . . . 5.03[5][b]
n.120
Hahn v. Comm'r . . . . 4.12[10] n.85;
Hale v. Moore . . . . S5.05[3][b][i] n.109
Hall v. US . . . . 4.09[4][e] ns. 36, 37
Hall, Estate of v. Comm'r (6th Cir.)
. . . . 5.05[8][b] n.367
Hall, Estate of v. Comm'r (TCM 1989) . . . .
. . . . 4.02[3][f] n.111
Hall, Estate of v. Comm'r (TCM 1983) . . . .
. . . . 4.02[3][c] n.85
Hall, Estate of v. Comm'r (TC 1946) . . . . . .
. . . . 4.10[4][d] n.44
Hall, Estate of v. US . . . . 5.06[6][b] n.157
Hallock, Helvering v. . . . . 4.09[3] ns. 20, 23;
4.09[7] n.56
Halpern, Estate of v. Comm'r . . . 4.10[2] n.9;
4.13[2][a] n.8
Halsted v. Comm'r . . . . . . 10.01[3][g] n.113;
11.03[4][b] n.54
Hambleton v. Comm'r . . . . . 10.01[5] n.153;
10.01[5][e] n.180
Hamelsky, Estate of v. Comm'r . . . 5.06[6][a]
n.150
Hamilton v. US . . . . 9.04[3][e] n.80
Hamilton, Estate of v. Comm'r . . . 4.05[5][b]
n.50
Hamilton Nat'l Bank v. US . . . . . . 5.06[7][b]
n.170
Hamlin, Estate of v. Comm'r . . . . 4.02[3][g]
ns. 117, 119, 122
Hammerstein v. Kelley . . . . . . 5.05[1][b] n.28
Hammon, Estate of v. Comm'r . . . 4.02[3][g]
n.125; 5.03[3][c] n.66; S5.03[3][c][iii]
n.137
Hammond, Estate of v. Comm'r . . . .
. . . . 19.04[6][a][i] n.119
Hampton & Co. v. US . . . . 4.10[5] n.63
Hanauer, Estate of v. Comm'r . . . 4.08[7][d]
n.161
Hance, Estate of v. Comm'r . . . . . 4.03[3][b]
n.50; 4.03[4][b] & n.62
Hanch, Estate of v. Comm'r . . . . . 4.05[5][b]
n.53
Haneke v. US . . . . 4.07[3][b] n.90
Hankins, Estate of v. Comm'r . . . 4.04[1] n.5
Hansen v. Vinal . . . . 5.06[8][a] n.205
Harbison v. US . . . . 5.05[8][d] n.382

*[Text references are to paragraphs and notes (9"n.");
references to the supplement are preceded by "S."]*

Harden, US v. . . . . 7.04[3] n.19
Hardenbergh v. Comm'r . . . 4.13[7][d] n.99;
 10.07[1] n.5; 17.04[3] n.76
Harden, Estate of v. Comm'r   4.12[8] n.60;
 S5.03[4][a][i] n.154; 5.03[5][e] n.135;
 5.04[3] n.18
Harkavy's Estate, In re . . . . . . 3.03[2] n.26;
 3.06[4] n.31; 5.09[2] n.23
Harmel, Burnet v. . . . 5.03[1] n.11; 5.03[2][b]
 n.30; 5.06[8][d][iv] n.398
Harmon, Estate of v. Comm'r . . . . 5.06[7][b]
 n.173
Harper, Estate of v. Comm'r (TCM 2002)
 . . . . S4.08[4][c] n.49
Harper, Estate of v. Comm'r (TCM 2000)
 . . . . 4.02[4][g] n.238; 19.05[3][b] n.59
Harper, Estate of v. Comm'r (TC 1989) . . . .
 . . . . 5.06[8][d][i] n.310
Harper, Estate of v. Comm'r (TC 1948) . . . .
 . . . . 4.02[3][g] ns. 128, 129
Harris v. Comm'r (US) . . . 4.15[1][b][i] n.38;
 4.15[1][b][ii] & ns. 49, 51, 58;
 10.01[3][i] n.127; 10.02[4] n.135;
 10.06[1] n.7; 10.06[3] n.32
Harris v. Comm'r (5th Cir.) . . . . . 9.04[5][b]
 n.162
Harris v. US . . . . 4.05[8] ns. 105, 107
Harrison, Bohnen v. . . . . . . 4.14[10] & n.153
Harrison v. Comm'r (TCM 1958) . . . .
 . . . . 4.02[3][f] n.107
Harrison v. Comm'r (TC 1952) . . . .
 . . . . 10.02[6][d] ns. 183, 187
Harrison, Estate of v. Comm'r (TC 2000) . . .
 . . . . 3.05[3][b] n.37
Harrison, Estate of v. Comm'r (TCM 1987)
 5.03[3][c] n.70; S5.03[3][c][i] n.115;
 19.02[1][b] n.11; 19.05[1] & ns. 5, 6;
 19.05[2][d] n.46
Harris Trust & Sav. Bank, US v. . . . .
 . . . . 4.05[5][b] n.55
Harter v. Comm'r . . . . 5.06[3][b] n.39
Hartford-Conn. Trust Co. v. US . . . . 6.06[1]
 ns. 13, 15
Hartshorne v. Comm'r . . . . 4.15[1][b][i] n.42
Hartzell, Estate of v. Comm'r . . . . . . 4.13[9]
 n.124
Harvey v. US . . . . . 4.12[7][a] ns. 41, 44, 46
Harwood v. Comm'r . . . . . 4.02[4][g] n.236;
 10.01[3][e] n.106; 10.02[2][b][vi] n.71
Haskell, Estate of v. Comm'r . . . . 5.06[5][a]
 n.99
Hassett, Charles v. . . . . 9.04[3][a] n.52
Hassett, Liebmann v. . . . . 4.14[8] n.126;
 4.14[9][b] ns. 143, 144; 6.05[1] n.6
Hassett, Stuart v. . . . . 4.12[7][a] n.33
Hassett v. Welch . . . . . 4.08[9] ns. 196, 198
Haupfuhrer, Estate of v. Comm'r . . . .
 . . . . 4.02[3][e] n.100
Hawaiian Trust Co. v. US . . . 5.06[7][b] n.180
Hays v. Heiner . . . . 4.02[2][a] n.11
Hazard v. Comm'r . . . . . . 6.05[2][a][ii] n.27;
 10.02[4] n.138

Hazelton, Estate of v. Comm'r   10.01[3][a]
 n.85
Headrick, Estate of v. Comm'r . . . 4.14[9][b]
 ns. 136–138
Heasty v. US . . . . 4.08[7] n.118; 4.08[8][a] ns.
 175, 177, 179; 4.12[9] ns. 75, 78
Heath v. US . . . . 4.05[7][b] n.80
Heckerman v. US . . . . S10.01[2][b][ii] n.25.1
Hecksher, Estate of v. Comm'r . . . 5.03[3][a]
 n.53; S5.03[3][a] n.92; S5.03[6][c][iii]
 n.305
Heffley, Estate of v. Comm'r   4.04[3][b][ii]
 n.47; 4.04[3][c][ii] n.132
Hefner v. US . . . . 5.03[3] n.38; S5.03[3] n.80
Heidrich v. Comm'r . . . . 9.04[5][a] n.147
Heidt, Estate of v. Comm'r . . . . 4.12[8] n.58
Heim v. Comm'r . . . . 10.01[3][a] n.86
Heim, Estate of v. Comm'r . . . . . . 5.06[7][b]
 n.173
Heiner v. Donnan . . . . 4.07[4] n.95; 9.01 n.6
Heiner, Hays v. . . . . 4.02[2][a] n.11
Heiner, May v. . . . . 4.08[9] & n.190; 4.09[3]
 n.20; 4.09[7] n.56; 4.11[2][b] n.8
Heinold, Estate of v. Comm'r . . . . 5.06[3][f]
 n.65
Helis, Succession of v. US (Fed Cl. 2003) . . .
 . . . . S5.03[3][c][i] ns. 114, 124
Helis, Succession of v. US (Fed. Cl. 2002) . . .
 . . . . S5.03[3] n.82
Helmholtz, Helvering v. . . . . 4.08[5][b] n.63;
 4.10[6] n.70; 4.10[10][d] n.101
Helvering, Commissioner of Internal Revenue
 (Comm'r) . . . . See individual taxpayer
Hemme, US v. . . . . 3.02 n.13; S3.02[1][a] n.18
Hemphill, Estate of v. Washington
 . . . . S3.03[1] n.16
Hempt Bros. v. US . . . . 4.05[4] n.33;
 10.01[2][g] n.63
Henderson v. Rogan . . . . 4.13[6][a] n.72
Henderson v. US 4.06 n.4
Hendrickson, Estate of v. Comm'r . . . .
 4.02[2][b] n.38; 4.02[4][b][iv] n.166;
 4.02[4][d][ii] n.193; S5.03[5] n.257;
 5.03[6] n.154; 10.01[2] n.13
Hendrix, Estate of v. Comm'r   S10.01[3][e]
 n.107.1
Henggeler, Allen v. . . . . 4.05[2][a] n.10; 4.06
 ns. 2, 3
Henricksen, Scott v. . . . . 4.02[2][a] n.9
Henry, Estate of v. Comm'r . . . . . 4.05[5][b]
 n.57
Henslee, May v. . . . . 5.04[2] n.11
Henslee, National Bank of Commerce in
 Memphis v. . . . 4.08[2] n.20; 4.08[4][b]
 n.34
Heringer v. Comm'r   9.04[1][b] ns. 23, 24,
 28; 9.04[3][e] n.90; 10.01[2][b][i] ns. 17,
 18, 21
Herr v. Comm'r . . . . 4.09[3] n.12; 9.04[3][a]
 n.56; 9.04[5][b] ns. 155, 157, 158;
 10.07[2][c] n.67; 16.02[7][b][i] n.450

[Text references are to paragraphs and notes (9"n.");
references to the supplement are preceded by "S."]

Herrmann, Estate of v. Comm'r   4.15[1][a]
    n.16; S5.03[4][a][i] n.163; 5.03[5][e]
    n.140
Hertsche v. US . . . . 4.03[3][a] n.39
Herzberg v. Comm'r . . . . . . 9.04[5][b] n.159
Hess v. Comm'r . . . . . . S10.02[2][c][iii] n.85
Hessenbruch v. Comm'r . . . . . 9.04[3][d] n.74
Hester, Estate of . . . . S4.05[2] n.3
Heyen v. US . . . . 9.04[1][b] n.34; 10.01[2][d]
    n.31
Hibernia Bank v. US . . . . 5.03[3] n.38;
    S5.03[3] n.80; 5.03[3][c] n.68;
    S5.03[3][c][i] n.110
Hicks, Estate of . . . . S5.03[1][b][ii] n.41
Higgins, Adriance v. . . . . 4.10[4][b] n.33
Higgins v. Comm'r . . . . 5.06[8][d][iii] n.386
Higgins, Maass v. . . . . 4.03[2] n.21; 4.03[2][c]
    n.29
Higgins, Marks v. . . . . . 4.08[2] n.17; 4.08[8]
    n.169; 4.11[3][c] n.29
Higgs, Estate of v. Comm'r . . . . 4.11[7] n.67
Hight v. Comm'r . . . . . . 4.04[7][b][ii] n.286
Hilborn v. Comm'r . . . . . . 5.05[7][c] n.347;
    19.04[2] n.33
Hill v. Comm'r . . . 10.02[5] n.150; 10.02[5][a]
    ns. 155, 156
Hill, Estate of v. Comm'r (2d Cir. 1956) . . .
    . . . . 4.09[2] n.4
Hill, Estate of v. Comm'r (2d Cir. 1952) . . .
    . . . . 4.05[5][b] n.57
Hill, Estate of v. Comm'r (5th Cir.) . . . . . .
    . . . . 4.05[2][b] n.13
Hillebrandt, Estate of v. Comm'r . . . .
    . . . . 4.02[3][b] n.80
Hinds, Estate of v. Comm'r . . 4.05[3] n.23
Hinz, Estate of v. Comm'r . . . . 2.02[1] n.14;
    4.02[2][a] n.36
Hinze v. US . . . . 4.05[8] n.105
Hipp v. US . . . . 5.03[3][c] n.71; S5.03[3][c][i]
    n.118
Hite, Estate of v. Comm'r . . . . 4.07[3][b] n.89
Hoagmann, Estate of v. Comm'r . . . .
    . . . . S5.03[4][c][i] n.210
Hockman v. US . . . . 9.04[3][c] n.70
Hodge, Estate of v. Comm'r . . . 4.02[3][g] ns.
    117, 130
Hoey, Lyeth v. . . . . 3.05[1][a] & ns. 7, 9;
    4.05[2][a] n.10; 5.03[1] ns. 7, 8;
    S5.03[1] ns. 8, 9; 5.06[3][a] n.32;
    5.06[8][d][iv] n.398; 10.02[5] n.149
Hoffman v. Comm'r . . . . . 19.04[6][a][i] n.117
Hoffman v. McGinnes . . . .
    . . . . 5.06[8][b][iii] n.249
Hoffman, Estate of v. Comm'r (TCM 2001)
    . . . . 4.02[3][g] n.121
Hoffman, Estate of v. Comm'r (TC 1982) . . .
    . . . . 4.08[7][a] n.123
Hofheimer, Estate of v. Comm'r   4.10[4][g]
    n.54; 4.10[8] n.83
Hogan, Estate of v. Comm'r . . . 4.02[3][f] ns.
    106, 108

Hohensee, Estate of v. Comm'r . . . .
    . . . . 5.05[3][b][ii] n.113; 5.06[5][b][iii]
    n.134
Hohenstein v. Comm'r . . . 4.04[7][b][ii] n.286
Holbrook v. US . . . . 3.05[3][b] n.39
Holderness v. Comm'r . . . . . . 4.10[4][b] n.33
Holl, Estate of v. Comm'r (10th Cir. 1995)
    . . . . 4.03[2][d] n.35
Holl, Estate of v. Comm'r (10th Cir. 1992)
    . . . . 4.03[2][d] n.35
Holland, Estate of v. Comm'r (TCM 1997)
    . . . S5.03[4][a] n.149; 5.03[5][a] n.113;
    9.04[3][f] n.111
Holland, Estate of v. Comm'r (TC 1975) . . .
    . . . . 5.06[8][b][iii] n.251
Hollingshead, Estate of v. Comm'r . . . .
    . . . . 5.06[8][b][i] n.230
Hollingsworth v. Comm'r . . . . . 10.01[2][b][i]
    n.19; 10.02[6][a] n.173
Hollis v. Forrester . . . . S8.07[1] n.7
Holman v. Comm'r (8th Cir.) . . . S4.02[4][g]
    n.238; S10.01[2][b][iii] n.25.1; S19.04[2]
    n.26; S19.04[3][a] n.48; S19.04[3][b][i]
    n.80
Holman v. Comm'r (TC) . . . S10.01[2][b][ii]
    n.25.1
Holmes v. Comm'r. . . . . 4.02[3][f] n.104
Holmes, Estate of v. Comm'r   4.04[3][b][i]
    n.37; 4.04[3][b][iii] n.57; 4.05[2] n.4
Holmes, Estate of, Comm'r v. . . . . 4.08[6][b]
    n.82; 4.10[2] n.6; 4.10[3] n.17;
    4.10[4][e] n.47
Holrick v. Kuhl . . . . 4.02[3][f] n.104
Holtz, Estate of v. Comm'r . . . 10.01[9] n.205
Honickman, Estate of v. Comm'r . . . .
    . . . S5.03[4][b] n.173; 5.03[5][a] n.100
Honigman, Estate of v. Comm'r   4.08[4][c]
    n.45
Hoover v. Comm'r. . . . . 5.03[3][c] n.70;
    S5.03[3][c][i] n.115
Hoover, Estate of v. Comm'r . . . . . . 4.04[5]
    n.171; S4.04[5] n.171
Horne, Estate of v. Comm'r (TC 1988) . . . .
    . . . . 5.06[5][b][iii] n.135
Horne, Estate of v. Comm'r (TC 1975) . . . .
    . . . . 4.14[5][a] n.88
Horner v. US . . . . 4.08[8][a] n.173
Horner, Estate of v. Comm'r . . . .
    . . . . 4.12[3] n.25
Hornor, Estate of v. Comm'r . . . . 4.12[7][a]
    n.33
Horst, Helvering v. . . . . . 10.01[10][a] n.209
Horton v. US . . . 3.03[2] n.17; 4.05[2][a] n.8;
    5.09[2] n.10
Horton, Estate of v. Comm'r . . . . 5.06[7][b]
    n.174
Horvath, Estate of v. Comm'r . . . . 5.03[5][a]
    n.100; S5.03[4][b] n.174
Houston, Estate of v. Comm'r . . . .
    . . . . 4.05[8] n.93
Howard v. US . . . . 3.03[2] n.22; 3.06[4] n.26;
    4.10[4][a] n.22; 5.09[2] n.15

*[Text references are to paragraphs and notes (9"n.");
references to the supplement are preceded by "S."]*

Howard, Estate of v. Comm'r (9th Cir.) . . . .
. . . . 5.06[8][d][ii] n.321
Howard, Estate of v. Comm'r (TC 1988) . . .
. . . 3.05[3][b] n.46; 5.06[8][d][ii] n.321
Howard, Estate of v. Comm'r (TC 1947) . . .
. . . . 4.12[7][a] n.37
Howell, Estate of v. Comm'r . . . 4.11[7] n.64
Howze v. Comm'r . . . . 9.04[3] n.45
Hubbard, Estate of v. Comm'r . . . . . 4.08[9]
n.195
Huber v. Comm'r . . . . S4.02[3][f] n.110
Hubert, Estate of v. Comm'r (US) . . . .
. . . 5.05[3][b][ii] n.115; 5.06[3][a] n.31;
5.06[5][b][ii] & ns. 111, 113, 114;
5.08[4][a][iii] n.185
Hubert, Estate of v. Comm'r (TCM) . . . . . .
. . . . 5.05[1][a] n.7
Hudgins, Estate of v. Comm'r . . . . . . 4.04[6]
n.237
Hudnick, Estate of v. US . . . . . 4.14[8] n.120
Hudson v. US . . . . 4.12[8] n.60
Hughan, Estate of v. Comm'r . . . .
. . . . 4.04[5][a][iii] ns. 194, 195;
4.04[5][b] n.209
Hughes, Estate of v. Comm'r . . . .
. . . . S5.03[4][a][i] n.154
Hull, Estate of v. Comm'r . . . 4.03[3][b] n.50
Humphrey, Estate of v. Comm'r   4.07[2][c]
n.58
Hundemer v. US . . . . 4.05[5][a] n.47
Hundley, Estate of v. Comm'r . . . 10.06[2][c]
n.30
Hunter v. US (8th Cir.) . . . . . 4.14[4][e] n.71
Hunter v. US (WD Pa.) . . . . . 4.13[4][a] n.37
Huntington, Estate of v. Comm'r . . . .
. . . . . S5.03[4][a][i] n.154; 5.03[5][e]
n.135
Huntsman, Estate of v. Comm'r . . . S4.14[6]
n.103.20
Hurd v. Comm'r . . . . 4.10[5] n.62
Hurford, Estate of . . . . S4.08[4][c] n.49
Hutchings, Helvering v. . . . . 9.04[1][b] ns. 17,
18, 25, 38; 10.01[2][a] n.15;
17.01[2][c][i] n.56
Hutson, Estate of v. Comm'r 8.05 n.2
Hyde, Estate of v. Comm'r . . . 4.13[4][a] n.37

I

Iacono, Estate of v. Comm'r . . . . . 4.02[2][a]
n.10
Illinois Nat'l Bank of Springfield v. US . . . .
. . . . 9.04[5][a] n.147
Independent Bank of Waukesha v. US . . . . .
. . . . 4.13[4][a] n.37
Industrial Trust Co. v. Comm'r   4.08[5][c]
ns. 64, 71, 73; 4.10[9][a] ns. 97, 98
Infante, Estate of v. Comm'r . . . . 4.14[4][d]
n.60; 4.14[5][b] n.94
Ingalls v. Comm'r . . . . 2.01[2] n.60; S2.01[2]
n.78; 10.03[2] n.32

Ingleheart v. Comm'r . . . . . . 5.03[2][b] n.23;
S5.03[2][b] n.64
Inman, Estate of v. Comm'r . . . 4.10[9] n.96
Iowa-Des Moines Nat'l Bank v. US . . . .
. . . . 5.06[7][b] n.170
Ithaca Trust Co. v. US . . . . 4.02[3][g] n.136;
S5.03[1][b] n.18; 5.03[5][b] ns. 122,
124; 5.05[2][c] & n.80; 5.05[8][d] n.382
Irvine, US v. . . . . 10.07[1] n.4
Irving Trust Co. . . . . 8.03[1] n.12
Irving Trust Co., Comm'r v. . . . . . 4.08[4][c]
n.53
Irving Trust Co. v. US . . . . . . 5.05[2][e] n.94
Iversen, Estate of v. Comm'r . . . . 4.15[1][a]
n.24

J

Jackman v. Comm'r . . . . 10.02[2][b][i] n.31
Jackson v. US (US) . . . 5.06[1] n.5; 5.06[3][g]
n.70; 5.06[6][a] n.153; 5.06[7][a] n.162;
5.06[7][b] & ns. 168, 169, 182;
5.06[8][d][ii] n.318; 5.06[8][d][iv] n.395
Jackson v. US (ND Tex.) . . . . 4.05[5][a] n.47
Jackson Estate v. US . . . . . . S5.03[2][b] n.68
Jacobs v. Comm'r (8th Cir.) . . . S5.03[1][b]
n.18; S5.03[4][c][i] n.209; 5.03[5][b]
n.124
Jacobs v. Comm'r (BTA) . . . 5.03[5][b] n.124
Jacobs v. Lucas . . . . S5.03[1][b] n.18
Jacobs v. US . . . . 5.03[3][a] n.53; S5.03[3][a]
n.92
Jacobs, US v. . . . . 4.12[11] & n.100
Jacobson, Comm'r v. . . . . 10.01[2][e] n.34
Jacobson v. US . . . . 9.04[3][c] n.67
Jacoby, Estate of v. Comm'r . . . . . 4.10[4][f]
n.50
Jalkut v. Comm'r . . . . 4.07[2][b][ii] n.49
James v. Comm'r . . . . . 19.04[6][a][iii] n.126
Jameson, Estate of v. Comm'r (5th Cir.) . . .
. . . 4.02[4][e][iii] n.218; 10.02[2][c][iv]
n.108
Jameson, Estate of v. Comm'r (TCM) . . . . .
4.02[2][b][iii] n.44; 4.02[4][a] n.146;
4.02[4][d][ii] n.193; 9.02[3] n.20
Jamison, Priedeman v. . . . . 8.05[3] n.10
Janda v. Comm'r . . . . . 10.02[2][c][ii] n.85;
10.02[2][c][iii] ns. 92, 96, 100
Jann, Estate of v. Comm'r . . . . 4.02[2][b][ii]
n.41
Jardell, Estate of v. Comm'r . . . . . 9.04[3][d]
n.73; 10.01[3][a] n.85
Jarecki, McLain v. . . . 4.08[7][d] ns. 156, 158
Jelke, Estate of v. Comm'r . . . S4.02[4][e][iii]
n.218
Jenkins v. US . . . 4.13[2] n.4; 4.13[7][a] n.82
Jenner, Estate of v. Comm'r . . . . 5.03[5] n.38;
S5.03[3] n.79; 5.03[3][c] ns. 62, 68;
S5.03[3][c] n.109; S5.03[3][c][ii] n.128;
5.03[3][d] n.78; S5.03[6][a] n.273
Jennings v. Comm'r . . . . 4.02[5] n.253

[Text references are to paragraphs and notes (9"n.");
references to the supplement are preceded by "S."]

Jennings v. Smith .... 4.10[5] & ns. 60, 61;
 4.10[8] n.79; 4.13[4][a] n.27
Jennings, Estate of v. Comm'r (TCM 1976)
 .... 4.02[3][b] n.68
Jennings, Estate of v. Comm'r (TC 1948) ...
 .... 4.05[5][b] n.50; 4.14[9][b] n.134
Jensen, Estate of v. Comm'r ....
 .... S4.02[4][e][iii] n.218;
 S10.02[2][c][iv] n.108
Jephson, Estate of v. Comm'r ....
 ..... 4.02[2][b][iii] n.45; 4.02[4][d][ii]
 n.196
Jernigan, McAleer v. .... 8.05[4] n.13
Jeschke v. US .... 5.06[5][a] n.98; 5.06[7][b]
 n.164
Jewett v. Comm'r .... 10.07[1] n.4
John Does, In re Tax Liabilities of.......
 .... S9.04[9] n.197
Johnson, Dulles v. .... 5.03[3][a] n.53;
 S5.03[3][a] n.92; 5.05[1][b] n.28
Johnson v. Comm'r ...... 10.02[6][d] n.181;
 19.03[3][d][i] n.176
Johnson v. US .... 5.03[5][a] n.104;
 S5.03[4][b][i] n.183
Johnson, Estate of v. Comm'r (5th Cir.) ....
 .... 4.05[3] n.23
Johnson, Estate of v. Comm'r (TCM) .....
 .... 5.06[8][b][iii] n.251
Johnson, Estate of v. US ..... 5.05[2][b] n.72
Johnston v. Comm'r .... 9.04[3][e] n.83
Johnston v.US .... 4.03[2][d] n.35
Johnstone, Estate of .... 6.06[1] n.9
Johnstone, Estate of v. Comm'r ....
 ..... 6.05[2][a][ii] n.27; 6.06[1] n.10
Jones v. Comm'r (4th Cir.) ..... 10.03[3][a]
 n.40
Jones v. Comm'r (TCM) .... 4.02[3][b] n.70
Jones v. US .... 5.03[5][a] n.100; S5.03[4][b]
 n.173
Jones, Estate of v. Comm'r (TC 2001) .....
 ...... 4.02[4][e][iii] n.216; 4.02[4][g]
 n.238; 4.08[4][c] n.49; 10.01[2][b][ii]
 n.25; 10.02[2][c][iii] n.97; 10.02[2][c][iv]
 n.109; 10.02[2][c][v] n.121; 19.05[3][b]
 ns. 53, 59
Jones, Estate of v. Comm'r (TC 1971) .....
 .... 4.13[4][a] n.37
Jones, Jr., Estate of v. Comm'r ... 4.09[4][e]
 n.35
Jordahl, Estate of v. Comm'r ... S4.08[6][a]
 n.76; S4.10[4][c] n.40; 4.10[4][d] n.44;
 4.14[4][f] & n.74
Jorgensen, Estate of .... S4.08[4][c] n.49
Jorgensen v. US .... 10.04[3][d] n.24
Joslyn v. Comm'r .... 5.03[3][c]
 n.62; S5.03[3][c][ii] n.128; 5.03[3][d]
 n.78; S5.03[6][a] n.273
Jung, Estate of v. Comm'r   4.02[2][a] n.28;
 4.02[4][d][ii] & n.187

K

Kaffie, Estate of v. Comm'r ..... 4.05[7][b]
 n.80
Kahn v. US .... 4.14[6] n.103
Kahn, Estate of v. Comm'r ... S4.02[4][e][iii]
 n.129
Kahn's Estate, Comm'r v. .... 4.11[5] n.48
Kalahasthi, Estate of ...... S8.01[1][b] n.32
Kammerdiner, Rogan v. ...... 4.12[8] n.64
Kane v. US ...... 2.01[3] n.67; 9.02[3] n.20;
 18.05[2][b] n.10
Kaplun v. US .... 5.05[1][b] n.41
Karagheusian, Estate of v. Comm'r ....
 ...... 4.14[4][b] n.50; 4.14[4][e] n.71
Karlson v. Comm'r .... 4.05[5][b] n.50
Kasishke v. US .... 4.08[2] n.17
Kaspar v. Kellar ..... 5.06[7][b] ns. 173, 174;
 5.06[8][a] n.205
Kass v. Comm'r .... 10.03[1] n.14
Katz, Estate of .... S5.06[3][h] n.81
Katz v. US .... 4.08[8] n.171
Katz, Look & Moison, PC v. Shirley .....
 .... S8.07[1] n.7
Kaufman v. US .... 10.01[5][d] n.172
Kaufman, Estate of v. Comm'r ... 4.02[2][a]
 ns. 35, 37
Kearns v. US .... 4.14[4][c] ns. 54, 55
Keating v. Mayer.... 4.13[6] n.60; 4.13[6][a]
 & ns. 63, 64; 4.13[6][c]; 4.13[10] n.129;
 10.04[3][d] n.22
Keeter v. US ..... 4.05[6] n.76; 4.05[8] n.95;
 4.13[2][b] ns. 12, 15; 4.13[6] n.60;
 4.14[3][c] n.32; 5.06[7][c] n.194;
 5.06[8][c] n.288; 11.03[3][b] n.40;
 13.03[4][a] n.82
Keeton, Estate of ..... S5.08[3][c][iii] n.126
Keinath v. Comm'r .... 10.07[1] n.4
Keitel, Estate of v. Comm'r ..... 4.02[3][b]
 n.80; 4.14[4][a] n.35
Kellar, Kaspar v..... 5.06[7][b] ns. 173, 174;
 5.06[8][a] n.205
Keller, Estate of (SD Tex.) .... S5.03[3][c][i]
 n.118; S5.03[6][c][ii] n.295
Keller v. US .... S4.08[4][c] n.49
Keller, Estate of v. Comm'r (US)...... 4.11
 [2][a] n.8
Keller, Estate of v. Comm'r (TCM 1980) ...
 .... 4.02[3][b] n.79
Keller, Estate of v. Comm'r (TCM 1965) ...
 .... 4.15[1][b][ii] n.53
Kelley, Hammerstein v. ..... 5.05[1][b] n.28
Kelley, Estate of v. Comm'r (TC) ....
 .... 10.01[2][e] n.34; 10.01[3][b] n.88
Kelley, Estate of v. Comm'r (TCM) ....
 S4.02[2][b][iii] n.44; S10.02[2][c][ii]
 n.85
Kelley, Estate of v. Comm'r (BTA) ....
 .... 4.12[7][a] n.32
Kellmann v. US .... 5.06[8][d][iv] n.399
Kelly, Estate of v. Comm'r (TC 1974) .....
 .... 4.02[4][g] n.236

[Text references are to paragraphs and notes (9"n.");
references to the supplement are preceded by "S."]

Kelly, Estate of v. Comm'r (TC 1958) . . . . .
. . . . 10.01[5] n.144
Kelm, Struthers v. . . . 4.08[5][c] & ns. 66, 73
Kenan v. Comm'r   4.04[5] n.173; 5.06[6][a]
n.145; 17.04[1][b] n.17
Kendall, Estate of v. Comm'r . . . . 5.06[6][b]
n.157
Kendrick v. Comm'r . . . . 4.13[10] n.128
Kennedy, Estate of v. US . . . 5.06[7][b] n.177
Kerdolff, Estate of v. Comm'r . . . . 4.08[4][c]
n.45
Kern v. US   4.05[5][a] n.47; 4.14[8] ns. 120,
122
Kerr v. Comm'r . . . . 4.02[4][g] ns. 237, 238;
19.05[3][a] n.49; 19.05[3][b] ns. 53, 56,
59
Kess v. US . . . . 4.14[2] n.19
Ketteman, Georgia, Trust v. Comm'r . . . . . .
. . . . 9.04[1][b] n.28; 9.04[3][e] n.90;
10.01[2][b][i] n.21
Khadad, Estate of, In re . . . . 5.06[6][b] n.157
Khan, Estate of v. Comm'r . . . 6.01[3][b] n.31
Kidd v. Patterson . . . . 11.03[4][b] n.53
Kidd v. US . . . . 5.06[7][b] n.175
Kieckhefer v. Comm'r . . . . . 9.04[3][e] n.77;
9.04[4] n.140
Kihchel v. US . . . . 4.05[7][b] n.80
Killion v. Comm'r . . . . . 4.04[6] ns. 233, 237
Kimbell v. US   S4.08[4][c] n.49; S4.08[5][c]
ns. 64, 69
Kime, Estate of, US v. . . . . 8.03[1] n.4
Kincaid v. US . . . . 10.01[2][b][i] n.19;
10.02[6][a] n.173
Kincade, Estate of v. Comm'r . . . .
. . . . 4.12[2] n.17
King v. Comm'r . . . . 9.04[3][e] n.80
King v. US . . . . . 10.01[3][e] n.107; 10.02[4]
n.141
King v. Wiseman . . . . 5.06[3][g] n.72
King, Estate of v. Comm'r (TC 1962) . . . . .
. . . . 4.08[6][a] n.76; 4.10[4][c] n.40;
4.10[4][d] n.44
King, Estate of v. Comm'r (TC 1953) . . . . . .
. . . . 4.05[4] n.36
King, In re v. United Jewish Appeal . . . 8.06
ns. 2, 8
King, Will of, In re . . . . 8.05[4] n.16
Kisling, Estate of v. Comm'r . . . 4.07[2][b][ii]
n.52; 4.10[8] n.91
Kjorvestad, Estate of v. Comm'r . . . .
. . . . 4.05[7][b] n.80
Klafter, Estate of v. Comm'r . . . .
. . . . 4.10[5] n.64
Klauber, Estate of v. Comm'r . . . . 4.09[4][a]
n.26; 4.09[6] n.48
Klauss, Estate of v. Comm'r . . . . 4.02[2][b]
n.38
Klein v. US . . . . 4.09[3] n.19
Klein, Estate of v. Comm'r . . . . . . 5.06[6][b]
n.157
Kleinman v. Comm'r . . . S18.05[2][b][ii] n.39
Klosterman, Estate of v. Comm'r . . . .
. . . . 4.04[5][a][i] n.183

Knight v. Comm'r . . . . 4.02[4][f] n.231;
4.02[4][g] ns. 237, 238, 240;
10.02[2][c][iii] n.94; 10.02[2][c][iv] ns.
111, 114; 19.05[3][b] ns. 53, 59
Knipp, Estate of v. Comm'r . . . . . 4.14[5][b]
n.93
Knoell v. US . . . . 4.02[3][b] n.77
Knowlton v. Moore . . . . 12.01[1] n.1
Koch v. Comm'r . . . . . . 19.04[6][a][ii] n.124
Kohler v. Comm'r . . . . S4.02[6][c] n.265;
S4.03[2] n.16; S4.03[3][a] n.40;
S4.03[3][c] n.54.1
Kohlsaat, Estate of v. Comm'r . . . 9.04[3][f]
& ns. 109, 111
Kokernot, Estate of v. Comm'r . . . . . 4.04[6]
n.218
Kolb, Estate of v. Comm'r . . . . 10.01[5][b]
n.166
Kolczynski, Estate of v. Comm'r . . . .
. . . . S4.02[3][b] n.61
Kolker, Estate of v. Comm'r . . . . . 9.04[3][d]
n.74
Konner v. Comm'r . . . . 9.04[5][b] n.159
Korby, Estate of v. Comm'r . . . . S4.08[4][c]
n.49
Kosman v. Comm'r . . . . 4.02[4][c][iii] n.175;
10.02[2][c][ii] n.86
Kosow, Estate of v. Comm'r . . . 4.15[1][b][i]
n.37; S5.03[4][a][i] n.161; 5.03[5][e]
n.141
Koss, Estate of v. Comm'r . . . S5.03[3][c][ii]
n.132
Koussevitsky, Estate of v. Comm'r   4.12[4]
n.30; 4.12[9] n.80
Krabbenhoft v. Comm'r . . . . . 10.02[3] n.132
Kraft v. Comm'r . . . . 10.01[4] n.139
Krakoff v. US . . . . 4.05[2][b] n.17
Kramer v. US . . . 4.05[8] n.105; 4.11[3][a] ns.
20, 21
Kraemer, Wilson v. . . . . 10.04[3][d] n.21
Krapf v. US . . . . S10.02[1] n.5.1
Krause v. Comm'r . . . . 10.02[6][d] n.183
Krischer, Estate of v. Comm'r . . . . 4.14[4][a]
n.39
Kroger, Estate of v. Comm'r . . . . 4.07[2][c]
n.65
Krohn v. US . . . . 5.05[1][b] n.28
Kroloff v. US . . . . 4.14[8] n.120
Kuhl, Holrick v. . . . . 4.02[3][f] n.104
Kuhl, Van Dyke v. . . . . . 4.02[3][b] ns. 74, 76
Kulhanek, US v. . . . . . S2.02[3][c][iii] n.115
Kuney v. Frank . . . . 4.02[4][g] n.236
Kunkel, Estate of v. US . . . .
. . . . 5.05[3][b][i] n.110
Kurihara, Estate of v. Comm'r . . . .
. . . . 4.07[2][a][ii] n.29
Kurz, Estate of v. Comm'r . . . 4.13[7][a] n.84
Kyle, Estate of v. Comm'r . . . . S5.03[4][c][i]
n.204; 5.03[5][a] n.116; 5.06[8][d][ii]
n.334
Kynett v. US . . . . 4.13[6][d] n.76

L

Labombarde, Estate of v. Comm'r . . . .
. . . . . S5.03[4][a][i] n.155; 5.03[5][e]
n.136
Laird v. Comm'r . . . . 4.02[3][f] n.107
Lake Shore Nat'l Bank v. Coyle   4.05[2][b]
ns. 17, 19
Lakewood Plantation, Inc. v. US   4.05[2][b]
n.17
Lamar, Bookwalter v. . . . . 5.06[7][b] n.175
La Meres, Estate of v. Comm'r . . . 5.05[2][b]
n.72; S5.05[2][b] n.72
Lamson, Estate of v. US . . . . . 5.05[1][a] n.8
Land v. US . . . . 4.03[3][a] n.39
Land, US v. . . . . 4.02[2][a] n.23
Landers, Estate of v. Comm'r . . . . . S2.02[1]
n.14
Landorf v. US . . . . . . 4.14[6] ns. 98, 99, 103
Lang v. US . . . . 4.05[8] n.95
Lang, Estate of v. Comm'r (9th Cir. 1980)
. . . . 3.03[2] n.17; S5.03[4][b][i] n.186;
5.03[5][a] n.105; 5.09[2] n.10; 10.01[4]
n.143
Lang, Estate of v. Comm'r (9th Cir. 1938)
. . . . 5.03[2][b] n.26; S5.03[2][b] n.67
Lange v. US . . . . 10.01[5] n.150
Langer, Estate of v. Comm'r . . . S4.02[3][b]
n.70
Langfitt v. US . . . . 5.05[1][b] n.37
Lanigan, Estate of v. Comm'r . . . . 4.13[4][a]
n.36
Lansburgh v. Comm'r . . . . . 4.02[3][g] n.118
Lappo v. Comm'r . . . . . S10.02[2][c][ii] n.85
Larsh, Estate of v. Comm'r . . . . . 4.14[9][a]
n.130
La Sala, Estate of v. Comm'r . . . . 3.05[3][a]
n.27; 3.05[3][b] n.46
Lasarzig, Estate of v. Comm'r . . . . 5.03[3][c]
n.71; S5.03[3][c][i] n.118
Lasater v. US . . . . 9.04[9] n.206
Lassiter, Estate of v. Comm'r . . . . 5.06[6][b]
n.157; 5.06[8][d][ii] n.325; 10.07[2] n.13
Latta v. Comm'r . . . . 4.13[4][c][ii] n.43;
10.01[5] n.146; 10.01[8] n.198
Latty v. Comm'r . . . . . . S5.03[4][a][i] n.154;
5.03[5][e] n.135
Lauder, Estate of v. Comm'r (TCM 1994)
. . . . . 4.02[2][a] n.35; 4.02[3][f] n.104;
4.02[3][f] n.106; 4.02[4][d][ii] & n.188;
5.06[3] n.23
Lauder, Estate of v. Comm'r (TCM 1992)
. . . . . . 4.02[2][a] n.8; 4.02[2][c] n.52;
19.04[1][b] n.1; 19.04[3][b][i] & ns. 73–
79, 84, 85; 19.04[3][b][iii] ns. 89, 90
Laurin v. Comm'r . . . . . . 5.06[8][b][v] n.273
Law v. US . . . S5.03[4][c][i] n.203; 5.03[5][a]
n.115
Lavelle v. Comm'r . . . . 4.07[3][b] n.88
Lazar v. Comm'r . . . . S5.03[4][a] n.150;
5.03[5][b] n.128

Lazarus v. Comm'r . . . . 4.11[5] n.47;
10.01[3][b] n.88
LDL Research & Dev. II, Ltd. v. Comm'r
. . . . 5.08[2][b][i] n.23
Leach, Estate of v. Comm'r . . . 5.05[3][b][i]
n.110
League of Women Voters v. US . . . 5.05[1][b]
n.27
Le Caer, Estate of v. Comm'r . . . S3.05[2] ns.
22, 22.1; S5.06[8][d][iii] n.388
Leder v. Comm'r . . . . 4.14[9][b] ns. 136–138,
146
Lee v. Comm'r . . . . 5.06[3] n.17
Lee v. US . . . . 4.08[4][c] n.42
Lee, Estate of v. Comm'r (TC 1978) . . . . . .
. . . . 4.02[4][b][ii] n.152; 4.02[4][e][i]
n.197
Lee, Estate of v. Comm'r (TC 1960) . . . . . .
. . . . 4.08[4][b] n.30
Lee, Estate of v. Comm'r (TC 1948) . . . . . .
. . . . 5.03[2][b] n.27; S5.03[2][b] n.68
Lee, Estate of v. Comm'r (TCM 2009) . . . . .
. . . . S2.02[1] n.16; S4.02[6][a] n.264
Lee, Estate of (TCM 2007) . . . . S5.06[3] n.17
Leeds, Estate of v. Comm'r . . . .
. . . . 5.06[5][a] n.99
Leewitz v. US . . . . 5.04[2] ns. 9–11
Le Fever v. Comm'r . . . . 4.04[7] n.254
Le Gierse, Estate of, Helvering v. . . . .
. . . . 4.02[3][h] n.139; 4.11 [2][a] n.7;
4.14[2] n.19; 4.14[10] & n.151
Lehman v. US . . . . 4.13[4][a] n.37
Lehman, Estate of v. Comm'r . . . . 4.08[7][a]
n.122; 4.08[7][d] ns. 153–155, 161;
4.10[1] n.3; 4.10[8] n.83; 5.03[3][c]
n.64; S5.03[3][c][iii] n.135; 12.01[1] n.4
Lehmann, Estate of v. Comm'r . . . 4.02[2][a]
n.20; 4.02[4][g] n.239
Leichter, Estate of v. Comm'r . . . S4.02[2][a]
n.28
Leigh v. Comm'r 2.02 n.5
Lenheim Estate of, ... 10.02[4] n.141
Lennon, Estate of v. Comm'r   2.02[1] n.15;
4.02[2][a] n.17
Leoni, Estate of v. Comm'r . . . . 4.11[7] n.65
Leopold v. US   4.05[3] n.32; 4.08[6][a] n.77;
4.08[8][a] n.173; 4.10[5] n.64;
4.15[1][b][i] n.41; S5.03[4][a][i] n.161;
5.03[5][e] n.135
Lepoutre, Estate of v. Comm'r . . . 4.05[5][a]
n.47
Lester, Estate of v. Comm'r . . . 5.03[5][b] ns.
119, 124
Letts, Estate of v. Comm'r 4.16 n.11
Levin v. Comm'r (4th Cir.) . . . . 2.01[1][b][i]
n.22; S2.01[1][b][i] n.22
Levin v. Comm'r (5th Cir.) . . . . . . 5.03[5][e]
n.136
Levin, Estate of v. Comm'r (TC 1988) . . . . .
. . . . 4.10[1] n.2; 4.10[4][g] n.53
Levin, Estate of v. Comm'r (TCM 1995) . . .
. . . . S5.03[4][a][i] n.165

[Text references are to paragraphs and notes (9"n.");
references to the supplement are preceded by "S."]

Levin, Estate of v. Comm'r (TCM 1951) . . .
. . . . 5.03[5][e] n.145
Levine v. Comm'r . . . . 4.05[2] n.4
Levine, Estate of v. Comm'r . . . . . 9.04[5][b]
n.161
Levitt, Estate of v. Comm'r . . . . . 5.06[6][b]
n.157
Levy v. US . . . . S4.02[3][b] n.79
Levy, Estate of v. Comm'r (TC 1978) . . . . .
. . . . 4.14[5][a] n.87; S4.14[6] n.103.22
Levy, Estate of v. Comm'r (TCM 1983) . . . .
. . . . 4.08[7][d] n.163
Lewellyn v. Frick . . . . 4.14[10] n.155
Lewis, Estate of v. Comm'r
. . . . 5.06[5][a] n.99
Liberty Nat'l Bank & Trust Co. v. US . . . . .
. . . . 5.06[6][b] n.157
Lidbury, Estate of v. Comm'r . . . 10.01[5][e]
n.180
Liebmann v. Hassett . . . . 4.14[8] n.126;
4.14[9][b] ns. 143, 144; 6.05[1] n.6
Lincoln v. US . . . . 4.11[5] n.48
Lincoln, Estate of v. Comm'r . . . . 4.02[3][g]
n.127; 4.05[7][b] n.83
Lincoln Rochester Trust Co. v. US . . . .
. . . . 5.06[8][b][iii] n.246
Linderme, Estate of v. Comm'r . . . 4.08[4][c]
n.45
Lindsey v. Comm'r . . . . 7.06 ns. 9, 17
Lineweaver, Estate of v. Comm'r . . . 5.03[5]
n.96
Lingo v. Comm'r . . . . 10.02[6][d] n.183
Linton v. US . . . . S10.01[2][b][ii] n.25.1
Lion, Estate of v. Comm'r . . . 3.05[3][b] n.37
Litchfield, Estate of . . . S4.02[4][c][iii] n.176;
S4.02[4][d][ii] n.186; S4.02[4][e][iii]
n.218
Litman v. US . . . . S4.02[4][e][iv] n.220
Littick, Estate of v. Comm'r . . . . 19.04[1][b]
n.3; 19.04[3] n.43; 19.04[6][a][ii] ns.
123, 128
Little, Estate of v. Comm'r . . . 4.13[4][a] n.37
Lloyd, Estate of v. US . . . . . 3.05[3][b] n.39
Lloyd, Estate of v. Comm'r . . . 4.02[3][b] ns.
60, 61
Lober v. US . . . . 4.08[5][c] & ns. 67, 70;
4.10[2] n.6; 4.10[3] n.17; 4.10[4][b]
n.32; 4.10[4][e] n.47; 4.10[9][b] n.100;
10.01[7] n.189; 10.01[10][e] n.230
Lockard v. Comm'r . . . . 9.05[4] n.51;
10.01[3][d] n.103
Lockie, Estate of v. Comm'r . . . . 6.04[1] n.8
Loewenstein, Estate of v. Comm'r . . . .
. . . . 4.02[3][b] n.80
Logan, Burnet v. . . . . 4.02[3][g] n.136; 4.05[8]
n.94; 5.03[5][b] n.119; 10.01[10][a]
n.211; 10.02[1][b] ns. 13–15
Lohman, Estate of v. Comm'r 3.02 n.29;
S3.02[3] n.65
Lomb v. Sugden . . . . . . 19.04[6][a][ii] n.124
Lombard, Estate of v. Comm'r . . . 4.13[6][d]
n.76

Longue Vue Found. v. Comm'r . . . 5.05[2][a]
n.58
Looney v. US . . . . 4.11[3][a] n.19
Lopes, Estate of v. Comm'r . . . 4.02[4][b][ii]
n.158; 4.16 n.20; 5.06[5] n.94
Loree, Estate of . . . . S4.03[1] n.3
Loughridge's Estate v. Comm'r . . . . . 4.10[8]
n.80; 4.13[7][a] n.85; 10.01[5][b] n.165
Louisville Trust Co. v. Walter . . . 8.04[3] ns.
18, 19
Love, Estate of v. Comm'r . . . . 5.03[3] n.38;
S5.03[3] n.80
Low, Estate of v. Comm'r . . . .
. . . . 4.02[3][g] n.123
Lowenstein, Estate of v. Comm'r . . . .
. . . . 4.02[2][a] n.10
Lucas, Commissioner of Internal Revenue
(Comm'r) . . . . See individual taxpayer
Lucas, Jacobs v. . . . . S5.03[1][b] n.18
Lucas, Estate of v. US . . . . . . 4.04[6] n.237
Luce v. US . . . S5.03[4][a][i] n.154; 5.03[5][e]
n.135
Ludwick v. Comm'r . . . . . . S10.02[2][c] n.75;
S19.03[3][d][iv] n.257
Lueder's Estate, In re . . . 4.08[7][d] ns. 153,
156, 158
Luff, Bremer v. . . . . 4.12[8] n.66
Lumpkin, Estate of v. Comm'r . . . 4.14[4][e]
n.69; 4.14[6] n.99
Lurie v. Comm'r . . . . S5.06[5][a] n.95;
S5.06[5][b][ii] n.109
Lute II, Estate of v. US . . . . 10.07[2][c] n.66
Lutich v. US . . . . 4.14[8] n.121
Luton, Estate of v. Comm'r . . . 4.02[4][d][ii]
n.191; 4.02[4][e][iii] ns. 212, 217;
4.03[1] n.7
Lyeth v. Hoey . . . . 3.05[1][a] & ns. 7, 9;
4.05[2][a] n.10; 5.03[1] ns. 7, 8;
S5.03[1] ns. 8, 9; 5.06[3][a] n.32;
5.06[8][d][iv] n.398; 10.02[5] n.149
Lykes v. US . . . . 5.03[3][a] ns. 46, 47
Lyman v. Comm'r . . . . 5.04[2] ns. 7, 8
Lyons, Estate of v. Comm'r (TCM 1976) . . .
. . . . 4.12[7][a] n.31; 4.12[8] n.64
Lyons, Estate of v. Comm'r (TC 1945) . . . . .
. . . . 6.01[3] n.20; 6.01[3][a] n.28

M

Maass v. Higgins . . . . 4.03[2] n.21; 4.03[2][c]
n.29
MacKay, Estate of v. Comm'r   5.05[3][b][i]
n.109
Mackie v. Comm'r . . . . 5.06[7][b] n.184
Macomber, Eisner v. . . . . . . 4.03[2][c] n.28;
4.12[7][a] n.41
Madden v. Comm'r . . . . 4.12[8] n.60
Maddox, Estate of v. Comm'r . . . . . . 4.04[5]
n.171
Madsen, Estate of v. Comm'r . . . . . . 4.14[8]
n.120

[Text references are to paragraphs and notes (9"n.");
references to the supplement are preceded by "S."]

Maehling v. US . . . . 5.03[3][c] n.69;
  S5.03[3][c][i] n.120
Maggos, Estate of v. Comm'r . . . . . 10.01[2]
  n.13; 10.02[4] n.141
Magnin, Estate of v. Comm'r (9th Cir.) . . . .
  . . . 4.08[1][a] n.10; 4.08[7][c] ns. 139,
  143; 4.15[2] n.67; 19.03[4][e][i] n.367;
  S19.03[4][e][i] n.367
Magnin, Estate of v. Comm'r (TCM) . . . . . .
  . . . . 4.08[1][a] n.10
Magruder, Mulliken v. . . . 4.02[3][g] ns. 126,
  135, 136
Mahoney v. US . . . . 4.08[7][a] n.121
Malkin, Estate of v. Comm'r . . . S4.08[4][c]
  n.49
Malloch v. Westover . . . . . . 4.02[3][g] n.134
Malone v. US (5th Cir.) . . . . . . 19.03[3][d][i]
  n.176
Malone v. US (SD Tex.) . . . . . . 5.03[3] n.39;
  S5.03[3] n.81
Maltaman v. Comm'r . . . . 2.02[1] n.14
Mandel v. Sturr . . . . 4.05[7][b] n.82
Mandelbaum v. Comm'r   4.02[2][a] ns. 22,
  36; 4.02[3][f] n.114; 4.02[4][d][ii] n.186;
  10.02[2][c][iii] & ns. 93, 95
Mandels, Estate of v. Comm'r . . . . . 10.01[5]
  n.150
Mangels v. US . . . . 4.04[3][c][ii] n.132
Manning, Christiernin v. . . . 4.05[5][b] n.56;
  4.11[4][a] n.39
Manning, Philbrick v. . . . . . 4.02[3][g] n.132
Manscill, Estate of v. Comm'r . . . .
  . . . . 5.06[8][d][ii] n.353
Manufacturers Hanover Trust Co. v. US . . .
  . . . . 10.02[2][b][iii] n.55
Manufacturers Nat'l Bank of Detroit, US v.
  . . . . 4.14[4] n.34; 4.14[10] n.156
Mapes, Estate of v. Comm'r . . . . 4.03[1] n.2;
  S4.03[1] n.2; 4.04[1] n.4; 4.04[3][b][vi]
  n.80
Mappes, US v. . . . . 5.06[7][b] n.175
Marcus v. Dewitt . . . S5.03[3] n.80; 5.03[3][c]
  n.63; S5.03[3][c][ii] n.129
Maresi, Comm'r v. . . . . 5.03[5][b] n.119
Margrave, Estate of v. Comm'r . . . 4.14[4][a]
  n.35
Mariano, Estate of v. Comm'r . . . S5.03[3][a]
  n.96
Marine, Estate of v. Comm'r . . . . 5.05[1][a]
  n.6
Marks v. Higgins . . . . . . 4.08[2] n.17; 4.08[8]
  n.169; 4.11[3][c] n.29
Marks, Estate of v. Comm'r . . . . . 3.05[3][b]
  n.37; 4.14[3][b] n.28
Markwell, Estate of v. Comm'r . . . .
  . . . . . . S5.03[4][a][i] n.157; 5.03[5][e]
  n.138
Marmaduke, Estate of v. Comm'r . . . .
  . . . . 4.02[4][d][ii] n.186
Marshall v. Comm'r . . . 5.05[1][b] ns. 27, 38
Marshall v. US (5th Cir.) . . . .
  . . . . S5.03[4][a] n.149
Marshall v. US (D. Md.) . . . . . 4.10[4][b] n.33

Marshall, Estate of v. Comm'r . . . 4.08[7][a]
  n.125; 4.15[2] n.68
Marshall, Estate of, Comm'r v. . . . 4.09[4][a]
  n.28
Marshall Naify Revocable Trust v. US . . . . .
  . . . S5.03[1][b][iii] n.48; S5.03[4][b][i]
  n.187; S5.03[4][c][i] ns. 203, 210;
  S5.03[4][c][ii] n.215
Martin v. Comm'r . . . . . . 4.04[7][b][ii] n.286
Martin v. US (7th Cir.) . . . . 5.06[5][a] n.101
Martin v. US (Ct. Cl.) . . . . . . 4.05[5][b] n.52
Martinez v. Comm'r . . . . 9.04[3][c] n.67
Maryland Nat'l Bank v. US . . . 9.04[3][b] ns.
  62, 66
Masterson v. Comm'r . . . . 10.01[5][e] n.179
Mather v. McLaughlin . . . . . . 4.07[3][b] n.87
Matheson v. Comm'r . . . . 5.04[2] n.14
Matheson, US v. . . . . 9.02[1] n.5
Mathews v. Comm'r . . . . . . 4.08[6][c] n.84
Mathey v. US . . . . 4.10[4][g] n.55
Matthews v. US . . . . . . 19.04[6][a][ii] n.124
Matthews, Estate of v. Comm'r . . . . . . 4.09[5]
  n.45; 4.14[7][b] n.110; 19.04[6][a][i] ns.
  117, 119
Mauck v. US . . . . 4.07[2][b][i] n.42
Maxcy, Estate of v. Comm'r . . . . 4.02[3][f]
  n.106; 4.05[3] n.27; 5.06[3][f] n.65
Maxwell, Estate of v. Comm'r . . . . 4.08[6][c]
  n.90; 4.15[2] n.75
Maxwell Trust v. Comm'r . . . 4.05[8] ns. 93,
  94, 96
May v. Comm'r . . . 5.06[8][b][iii] ns. 246, 248
May v. Heiner . . . . . 4.08[9] & n.190; 4.09[3]
  n.20; 4.09[7] n.56; 4.11[2][b] n.13
May v. Henslee . . . . 5.04[2] n.11
May, Estate of v. Comm'r (TCM 1978) . . . .
  . . . . 4.12[2] n.17; 4.12[9] n.75
May, Estate of v. Comm'r (TC 1947) . . . . . .
  . . . . . . 5.03[5][a] n.117; S5.03[4][c][i]
  n.206
Mayer, Keating v. . . . 4.13[6] n.60; 4.13[6][a]
  & ns. 63, 64; 4.13[6][c]; 4.13[10] n.129;
  10.04[3][d] n.22
Mayer v. Reinecke . . . . 4.06 ns. 2, 3
Maytag v. US . . . . 4.13[2] n.5
McAleer v. Jernigan . . . . 8.05[4] n.13
McAlpine v. Comm'r . . . . 4.04[6] n.236
McCabe, Estate of v. US . . . 4.08[4][c] ns. 42,
  53; 5.06[8][b][v] n.269
McCann, Comm'r v. . . . 10.02[2][b][vi] n.71;
  19.04[6][b] n.137
McCants, Estate of . . . . . 5.06[8][d][iii] n.386
McCarthy v. US . . . . 4.05[3] n.28
McCaughn, Bromley v. . . . . 9.01 n.10; 9.02[3]
  n.20
McClatchy, Estate of v. Comm'r . . . .
  . . . 4.02[2][a] ns. 24, 26; 4.02[4][e][iv]
  n.220
McClennen v. Comm'r . . . . . . 4.05[7][b] n.82
McCobb, All v. . . . . 4.11[2][a] n.7; 4.11[3][a]
  n.19; 4.14[2] n.5
McCombs v. US . . . . . . 5.06[8][b][iv] n.264

[Text references are to paragraphs and notes (9"n.");
references to the supplement are preceded by "S."]

McCord v. Comm'r (TC) . . . . . . 10.01[3][e]
   n.107.1; S10.02[1] n.5.1; S10.02[2][c][ii]
   n.85; S10.02[2][c][iii] n.93.1;
   S10.02[6][d] n.187; S11.02[2][a] n.47.1
McCord, Succession of v. Comm'r (5th Cir.)
   . . . . S5.03[4][c][i] n.210; S10.01[3][e]
   n.106; S10.02[1] n.5.1; S10.02[2][c][ii]
   n.85; S10.02[2][c][iii] n.93.1;
   S10.02[6][d] n.187; S11.02[2][a] n.47.1
McCormick v. Burnet . . . . 4.08[9] n.191
McCoy v. Shultz . . . . 5.05[1][b] n.34
McCoy, Estate of v. Comm'r (TCM 2009)
   . . . . S5.06[5][a] n.99
McCoy, Estate of v. Comm'r (TCM 1961)
   . . . 4.14[4][a] n.43; 4.15[1][b][ii] n.53;
   5.03[3][a] n.54; S5.03[3][a] n.93
McCuen, Turner v. . . . .
   . . . . 6.05[2][a][ii] ns. 24, 25
McCune, Estate of v. Comm'r . . . . 5.06[7][b]
   n.163
McDonald v. Comm'r . . . . . . 4.04[6] n.237
McDonald's Restaurants of Ill., Inc. v.
   Comm'r . . . . 19.03[4][a] n.276
McDonald Trust v. Comm'r . . . . . 4.15[1][a]
   n.26; 4.15[2] & n.71
McDougall v. Central Nat'l Bank . . . 8.04[3]
   ns. 18, 19
McDowell, Estate of v. Comm'r . . . 5.03[5][b]
   n.125
McElroy, Estate of v. Comm'r . . . . 2.02[1]
   n.18
McFarland v. US . . . . . 3.03[1] n.4; 5.03[5][a]
   n.102; S5.03[4][b][i] n.180; 5.09[1] n.6
McGauley, Estate of, In re . . . 3.05[1][a] n.8;
   3.05[3][b] n.43
McGehee, Estate of v. Comm'r . . . 4.03[2][c]
   ns. 31, 32; 5.06[8][b][iii] n.247
McGhee, Estate of v. Comm'r . . . . 4.07[2][c]
   n.62
McGinnes, Bartol v. . . . . 4.13[6][a] n.63
McGinnes, Hoffman v. . . . .
   . . . . 5.06[8][b][iii] n.249
McGinnes, Silverman v. . . . . . . 4.12[2] n.21
McGinnes, Watson v.   S5.03[4][b][ii] n.199;
   5.03[8] n.164
McGlotten v. Connally . . . . . 5.05[1][b] n.34
McGowan, Goodwin v. . . . . . 10.01[3][b] n.89
McGowan, Williams v. . . . . . 4.05[7][a] n.78
McGuire v. Comm'r . . . . 4.02[2][a] n.8
McHugh v. US . . . . 10.01[3][d] n.103
McKee, Estate of v. Comm'r (TCM 1996)
   . . 5.03[3][c] n.71; S5.03[3][c][i] n.118
McKee, Estate of v. Comm'r (TCM 1978)
   . . . . 4.14[8] n.120
McKeon, Estate of v. Comm'r . . . . 4.08[4][b]
   n.41; 10.02[5][b] n.160; 10.06[2][b] n.24
McKitterick, Estate of v. Comm'r . . . 4.05[4]
   n.36
McLaughlin, Mather v. . . . . . . 4.07[3][b] n.87
McLain v. Jarecki . . . 4.08[7][d] ns. 156, 158
McLean v. US (6th Cir.) . . . . 5.06[3][d] & ns.
   54, 56
McLean v. US (ND Cal.) . . . 10.03[3][b] n.44

McLendon v. Comm'r (TCM) . . . . . . 4.02[5]
   n.253
McLendon, Estate of v. Comm'r (5th Cir.)
   . . . S4.02[5] n.253; S10.01[3][e] n.107
McLoughlin, Van Beuren v. . . . . 4.10[2] n.8;
   4.10[7] n.72
McManus v. Comm'r . . . . 9.04[3][e] n.80
McMillan v. Comm'r . . . 5.06[8][b][iii] n.250
McMorris, Estate of v. Comm'r   5.03[5][a]
   n.115; 5.03[5][b] n.125; S5.03[4][c][i]
   ns. 203, 210
McMullen, Estate of v. Comm'r . . . .
   . . . . 4.02[4][e][i] n.205
McMurtry v. Comm'r . . . . 4.15[1][a] n.17;
   4.15[1][b][i] n.40; 9.05[1] n.3; 10.06[1]
   n.7
McNary, Estate of v. Comm'r . . . .
   . . . . 4.05[4] n.45
McNeely v. US . . . . 4.07[2][b][ii] n.49
McNichol, Estate of v. Comm'r . . . 4.08[4][c]
   n.52
McTighe, Estate of v. Comm'r . . . 4.08[4][b]
   n.36
Mearkle, Estate of v. Comm'r . . . .
   . . . . 4.11[7] n.63
Mellinger, Estate of v. Comm'r . . . .
   4.02[4][b][ii] n.158; 4.16 ns. 20–22;
   5.06[5] n.94
Mellon, Florida v. . . . . 3.03[1] n.9
Mellon Bank NA v. US . . . . . 5.05[1][b] n.36
Melman, US v. 8.04 n.5
Meltzer, Estate of v. Comm'r . . . .
   . . . . 4.05[6] n.70
Melville, Estate of v. Comm'r . . . .
   . . . . 2.02[1] n.14
Mercantile-Commerce Bank & Trust Co.,
   Helvering v. . . . . 4.08[4][b] n.30
Mercantile-Safe Dep. & Trust Co. v. US . . . .
   . . . . 9.04[3][a] n.55
Merchants Nat'l Bank v. US (1st Cir.) . . . . .
   . . . . 5.05[2][c] n.83
Merchants Nat'l Bank v. US (7th Cir.) . . . . .
   . . . . 5.06[5][a] n.101
Merchants Nat'l Bank v. US (ND Iowa) . . . .
   . . . . 5.06[8][b][i] n.218
Merchant's Nat'l Bank, US v. . . . . 4.13[6][a]
   n.63
Merchant's Nat'l Bank of Mobile, US v. . . . .
   . . . . 4.08[1][b] n.13
Merchants Nat'l Bank of Topeka v. US . . . .
   . . . . 3.05[3][b] n.33
Mergott, Estate of v. US . . . . 5.06[3][a] n.30;
   5.06[3][b] n.38
Meriano, Estate of v. Comm'r . . . . 5.03[3][a]
   n.41; 5.04[3] n.15
Merriam, US v.   5.03[3][a] n.50; S5.03[3][a]
   n.90
Merrill v. Fahs . . . . . . 4.06 n.16; 4.15[1] n.5;
   4.15[1][b][ii] n.56; 10.02[5][d] n.167;
   10.06[1] n.4; 10.06[3] n.33
Merwin, Estate of v. Comm'r . . . 4.04[6] ns.
   233, 237

Messing v. Comm'r . . . . 4.02[2][a] n.8;
 4.02[3][f] n.113
Metcalf, Estate of v. Comm'r . . . . 5.03[5][b]
 n.124
Metzger, Estate of v. Comm'r . . . . . . 4.05[3]
 n.28; 10.01[3][h] n.122
Meyer v. US . . . . 5.06[8][c] & n.292
Meyer, Estate of v. Comm'r (2d Cir. 1985)
 . . . . . 3.05[4][a] n.58; 3.05[4][b] n.59
Meyer, Estate of v. Comm'r (2d Cir. 1940)
 . . . . 4.15[1][a] n.23
Meyer, Estate of v. Comm'r (TC) . . . 4.14[8]
 n.120
Michigan Trust Co. v. Comm'r . . . .
 . . . . 19.04[6][a][ii] n.124
Miglio v. US . . . . S3.05[4][a] n.52.1
Miglionico v. US . . . . 4.05[2] n.4
Miller, Estate of . . . . S4.08[4][c] n.49; S4.16
 n.12
Miller v. Comm'r (9th Cir.) . . . 10.01[1] n.9;
 10.01[4] n.143
Miller v. Comm'r (TC) . . . . 5.04[3] n.18
Miller v. US (3d Cir.) . . . . . 4.13[4][c][iii] n.42
Miller v. US (CD Ill.) . . . . . . 4.04[3][c] n.104
Miller v. US (ED Pa.) . . . . . 4.08[8][a] n.177;
 4.10[4][g] n.55; 4.12[9] n.79
Miller, Estate of v. Comm'r . . . . . 4.05[5][b]
 n.53; 4.08[7][a] n.124
Miller, Estate of v. US . . . 5.06[8][d][ii] n.331
Millikin, Estate of v. Comm'r . . . . . . 5.03[3]
 n.38; S5.03[3] n.80
Mills, Comm'r v. . . . . 10.02[6][b] n.174
Mill's Will, In re . . . . 8.04[2] n.17
Mimnaugh v. US . . . . 4.05[6] n.67; 4.14[3][c]
 n.30; 4.14[10] n.148
Minot, Estate of v. Comm'r . . . 4.13[6] n.61;
 4.13[6][a] n.65
Minotto, Estate of v. Comm'r . . . .
 . . . . 4.05[6] n.73
Minskoff v. US . . . . 4.05[7][b] n.85
Minter v. US . . . . 4.04[3][b][v] n.68;
 4.04[7][b][ii] n.286
Mirowski, Estate of v. Comm'r   S4.08[4][c]
 n.49
Mitchell, Estate of v. Comm'r (6th Cir.) . . . .
 . . . . 4.13[6][c] n.74
Mitchell, Estate of v. Comm'r (9th Cir.) . . . .
 4.02[2][a] ns. 13, 31, 37; S4.02[2][a]
 n.31; 4.02[3][b] n.69; 4.02[4][e][vi]
 n.224; 4.02[4][e][vii] n.225; 4.02[4][f]
 n.231
Mitchell, Estate of v. Comm'r (TCM 2011)
 . . . . S4.02[3][a] n.59; S4.02[3][b] n.73
Mitchell, Estate of v. Comm'r (TCM 1981)
 . . . . 4.05[5][b] n.52
Mitchell, Estate of v. Comm'r (TC 1970) . . .
 . . . . 4.08[4][b] n.32
Mitchell, Estate of v. Comm'r (TCM 1968)
 . . . . 4.02[3][b] n.60
Mittelman, Estate of v. Comm'r . . . .
 . . . . 5.06[8][b][i] n.218
Mladinich, Estate of v. Comm'r   4.05[5][a]
 n.46

Moir v. US . . . . 5.03[3][a] n.44; S5.03[3][a]
 n.100
Molter v. US . . . . 4.05[8] n.105
Monroe v. US . . . . 10.04[3][e] n.27
Monroe, Estate of v. Comm'r . . . 10.07[2][c]
 n.73; S12.03[1] n.4
Montgomery, Estate of v. Comm'r 4.11
 [2][a] n.8; 4.11[3][c] n.25; 4.14[2] ns.
 16, 19, 20
Mooneyham v. Comm'r . . . .
 . . . . 10.02[2][c][ii] n.89
Moor, Estate of v. Comm'r . . . . . . 5.05[4][a]
 n.128
Moore v. Comm'r (2d Cir.) . . . . 10.02[6][d]
 n.185
Moore v. Comm'r (TCM) . . . 4.02[3][f] n.115;
 4.02[4][c][ii] n.174
Moore, Hale v. . . . . S5.05[3][b][i] n.109
Moore, Knowlton v. . . . . 12.01[1] n.1
Moore v. US (WD Ky.) . . . . 5.06[7][b] n.179
Moore v. US (ND Ohio) . . . . 5.06[8][c] n.286
Moore, Estate of v. Comm'r . . . . S5.03[4][a]
 n.150; 5.03[5][b] n.128
Moreno, Estate of v. Comm'r . . . . 4.08[7][d]
 n.161
Morgan v. Comm'r . . . 4.05[2][a] n.5; 4.13[3]
 n.24; 4.13[4][a] n.35
Morgens, Estate of v. Comm'r . . . S10.08[3]
 n.49
Morris v. Comm'r . . . . 4.02[3][b] n.70
Morrissey v. Comm'r . . . . . . 4.02[2][a] n.28
Morse, Estate of v. Comm'r . . . S5.03[4][a][i]
 n.163; 5.03[5][e] n.140
Morsman v. Burnet . . . . 4.08[9] n.191
Morton v. Comm'r . . . . 4.02[2][a] n.29
Morton, Taylor v. . . . . 7.06 ns. 6, 8
Morton, Estate of v. Comm'r   4.05[6] n.73;
 4.08[7][b] n.128
Morton, Estate of v. US . . . . . 4.14[4][c] n.53
Motter, Beeler v. . . . . 4.07[3][b] n.87
Mosher v. US . . . . 5.05[3][b][i] n.109
Moss, Estate of v. Comm'r (TCM 1982) . . . .
 . . . . 5.06[3][a] n.31
Moss, Estate of v. Comm'r (TC 1980) . . . . .
 . . . . 4.05[3] n.32; 4.11[5] n.53
Mudry v. US . . . . 7.02[3] & ns. 77, 79
Mueller v. US . . . . 9.04[5][a] n.147
Mueller, Estate of v. Comm'r . . . . 4.02[2][a]
 ns. 27, 33, 35; 4.02[4][e][vii] n.226
Mulliken v. Magruder . . . 4.02[3][g] ns. 126,
 135, 136
Murchie, Delaney v. . . . 6.03[2][a] ns. 22, 23;
 6.04[2] ns. 13, 14
Murphey, Estate of v. Comm'r . . . 4.13[8][b]
 n.122; 4.13[10] n.127
Murphy, Estate of . . . . S4.02[3][a] n.59;
 S4.08[4][c] n.49; S5.03[3][c][i] n.118
Murphy, Estate of v. Comm'r   4.02[4][b][i]
 n.150; 4.02[4][b][iii] n.163; 4.02[4][g]
 n.237; 19.04[2] n.26
Murrah v. Wiseman . . . . 4.05[5][a] n.47
Murray v. US . . . . 5.06[5][b][iii] n.134
Muserlian v. Comm'r . . . . 10.01[1] n.11

*[Text references are to paragraphs and notes (9"n.");
references to the supplement are preceded by "S."]*

Musgrove, Estate of v. Comm'r . . . . . 4.05[3]
n.32; 4.07[2][b][i] n.40; 4.10[4] n.18;
4.15[2] n.75

N

Natchez v. US . . . . . . 4.15[1][b][i] ns. 40, 46
Nathan, Estate of, Comm'r v.   4.08[2] n.17;
4.09[6] n.50
National Bank of Commerce in Memphis v.
Henslee . . . .
. . . . . . 4.08[2] n.20; 4.08[4][b] n.34
National City Bank of Cleveland v. US . . . .
. . . . 4.08[7][a] n.123; 4.14[9][a] n.131
National Metropolitan Bank of Wash. v. US
. . . . 4.14[4][c] n.53
National Sav. Trust Co. v. US . . . . 5.05[1][b]
n.41
National Taxpayers Union v. US . . . . 2.01[3]
n.67
National Westminster Bank, PLC v. US . . . .
. . . . 7.06 n.10
Nationsbank of Tex., NA v. US . . . . . 2.01[3]
n.67
Natural Resources Defense Council, Inc.,
Chevron USA v. . . . . . S5.03[1][b] n.26
Naumoff v. Comm'r . . . . 9.04[4] n.142
Neal v. US . . . . 10.01[5] ns. 150, 153
Neal, Estate of v. Comm'r . . . 4.10[4][d] n.44
Necastro, Estate of v. Comm'r . . . 4.02[2][a]
ns. 27, 37; 4.02[3][b] n.71; 4.02[4][e][v]
ns. 222, 223
Neff v. Comm'r . . . . 4.10[4][a] n.24
Negron v. US . . . S4.02[5] n.244; S4.11[4][a]
n.40
Neisen, Estate of v. Comm'r . . . . . 5.06[6][b]
n.157
Neilson, Foster v. 7.06 n.6
Nelson v. Comm'r . . . . 5.06[7][b] n.187
Nelson, Estate of v. Comm'r (TCM 1983) . . .
. . . . 5.06[8][b][iii] n.245
Nelson, Estate of v. Comm'r (TCM 1980) . . .
. . . . 4.02[2][a] n.10
Nelson, Estate of, Comm'r v.   4.15[1][a][ii]
n.31; 4.15[2] n.73
Nemerov, Estate of v. Comm'r . . . . . 4.05[4]
n.39
Nettleton, Estate of v. Comm'r . . . . . 4.10[5]
n.64
Nettz v. Phillips . . . . 5.06[8][d][iv] n.400
Neumann, Estate of v. Comm'r   18.03[2][a]
n.27
Nevius, Comm'r v. . . . . 6.04[2] n.18
Newberry, Estate of . . . . 4.08[7][d] n.153
Newberry, Estate of v. Comm'r . . . 4.08[7][d]
ns. 156, 161
New England Acceptance Corp. v. US . . . . .
. . . . 9.04[11] n.248

New England Merchant's Nat'l Bank of Bos-
ton v. US . . . . 4.10[6] n.67
Newgass Estate v. Comm'r . . . . . . 5.06[7][b]
n.184
Newhouse, Estate of v. Comm'r . . . 4.02[2][a]
n.34; 4.02[3][f] n.105; 4.02[4][a] n.144;
4.02[4][d][ii] n.193; 10.02[2][c][iii] n.100
Newman, Estate of v. Comm'r . . . . . 4.05[3]
n.28; 10.01[3][h] n.122
Newton, Estate of v. Comm'r
. . . . 2.02[1] n.14
New York Trust Co. v. Comm'r . . . 8.02 ns.
6, 12
New York Trust Co. v. Eisner . . . . . . 9.02[3]
n.21
Nicholson, Estate of v. Comm'r . . . .
. . . . . 5.06[8][b][i] n.218; 5.06[8][d][ii]
n.325
Nickel v. Estate of Estes . . . . . . 10.07[2] n.26
Nicol, Estate of v. Comm'r . . . . 4.08[2] n.20
Nielsen v. US . . . . 5.06[7][b] n.175
Nienhuys, Estate of v. Comm'r . . . 6.01[3][b]
n.30; 6.06[1] n.11
Nilson, Estate of v. Comm'r . . . . . 4.05[2][b]
n.18; S5.03[4][c][i] n.202; 5.03[5][a]
n.114
Nix, Estate of . . . . S5.06[3][h] n.81
Noble, Estate of v. Comm'r . . . . S4.02[2][a]
n.28; S4.02[3][f] n.110
Noel, Estate of, Comm'r v. . . . . . 4.14[2] ns. 6,
7; 4.14[4][a] n.42; 4.14[4][c] n.54
Noland, Estate of v. Comm'r . . . . . 4.05[5][c]
n.65; 4.13[7][f] n.107; 10.02[4] n.141
Norair v. Comm'r . . . . 2.01[2] n.60; S2.01[2]
n.78; 10.03[2] n.32
Nordstrom v. US . . . . 10.03[3][a] n.38
Norstar Bank of Upstate NY v. US   7.03[8]
n.245; 7.06 n.14
Northeastern Pa. Nat'l Bank & Trust Co. v.
US (US) . . . . . 5.06[8][b][i] & ns. 226,
226, 229, 231, 233
Northeastern Pa. Nat'l Bank & Trust Co. v.
US (MD Pa.) . . . . 5.06[5][a] n.99
Northern Trust Co., Burnet v. . . . . . . 4.08[9]
n.191
Northern Trust Co. v. Comm'r . . . 4.02[3][f]
n.108
Northern Trust Co., Reinecke v.   4.08[6][a]
ns. 75, 76; 4.08[9] n.192; 4.09[3] n.20;
4.09[7] n.56; 4.10[4][a] n.19
Northern Trust Co. v. US . . . . . 5.05[2][b] ns.
68, 74
Novotny, Estate of v. Comm'r . . . .
. . . . 5.06[8][d][ii] n.325
Nowell, Estate of v. Comm'r . . . . . 4.02[2][a]
n.26; 4.02[4][b][ii] n.158; 4.16 n.20;
5.06[5] n.94
Nunan, Commissioner of Internal Revenue
(Comm'r) . . . . *See* individual taxpayer

*[Text references are to paragraphs and notes (9"n.");
references to the supplement are preceded by "S."]*

O

Occidental Life Ins. Co. of Cal. v. Comm'r
. . . . 2.02 n.5
Oetting v. US . . . . 5.05[2][b] n.70
Ogarrio, Estate of v. Comm'r . . . 6.05[2][a][i]
n.15
Old Colony Trust Co. v. Comm'r . . . .
. . . 4.08[4][b] n.31; 10.02[2][b][i] n.40;
13.02[2][b][i] n.46; 14.02[4] & ns. 23,
32
Old Colony Trust Co. v. US (1st Cir. 1971)
. . . . 5.05[1][b] ns. 35, 41
Old Colony Trust Co. v. US (1st Cir. 1970)
. . . . 4.08[5][b] n.63; 4.08[6][a] ns. 76,
79; 4.10[4][c] ns. 34, 38; 4.10[4][d] n.44
Old Kent Bank & Trust Co. v. US . . . .
. . . . 3.05[3][b] n.37; 4.05[6] n.70
Old Va. Brick Co. v. Comm'r . . . . . 17.02[2]
n.80
O'Daniel, Estate of v. US . . . 4.14[4][a] n.35;
5.03[3][c] n.71; S5.03[3][c][i] n.125
O'Hara, Cockrill v. . . . . 4.14[4][c] n.54;
4.14[5][a] n.86
O'Keeffe, Estate of v. Comm'r . . . 4.02[3][a]
n.59; 4.02[4][e][ii] n.210
Okerlund v. Comm'r (Fed. Cir. 2004) . . . . .
. . . . S10.02[1] n.5.1
Okerlund v. US (Fed. Cl. 2002) . . . .
. . . . S4.02[4][e][vi] n.224
Olivo, Estate of . . . . S5.03[4][a] n.149
O'Malley, US v. (11th Cir.) . . . . 4.07[2][c] ns.
60, 61; 4.08[4][c] n.51; 4.08[5][c] &
n.65; 4.08[7] n.119; 4.08[8][a] ns. 173,
177; 4.08[9] n.201; 4.10[10][d] n.101;
4.10[10][f] n.112; 4.12[9] n.76;
4.13[2][a] n.9; 10.01[6] n.183;
13.02[4][b][ii] n.277
O'Nan, Estate of v. Comm'r . . . 4.15[1][b][ii]
n.53
O'Neal v. Comm'r . . . . 9.04[11] ns. 246, 247;
9.05[2][a] n.16
O'Neal, Estate of v. US (11th Cir.) . . . .
5.03[3][a] ns. 41, 55; S5.03[3][a] ns.
94, 96; S5.03[4][b][i] n.184;
S5.03[4][c][i] n.210; 5.03[5][a] n.104;
5.03[5][b] n.125
O'Neal, Estate of v. US (ND Ala.) . . . .
. . . . S4.07[3][a] n.78
Opal, Estate of v. Comm'r . . . . 5.06[8][d][iv]
ns. 396, 404
Orcutt, Estate of v. Comm'r . . . . . 5.03[2][b]
n.26; S5.03[2][b] n.67
O'Reilly v. Comm'r (8th Cir.) . . . . . . 4.02[5]
n.253
O'Reilly v. Comm'r (TC) . . . . 9.04[3][b] n.62
Orphanos, Estate of v. Comm'r . . . 5.05[1][a]
n.9; 5.05[1][b] n.41
Otte, Estate of v. Comm'r   4.12[7][a] n.46;
4.12[8] ns. 64, 68
Outwin v. Comm'r . . . . 4.10[4][a] n.23;
10.01[5] n.153

Owen, Estate of v. Comm'r . . . . 3.03[1] n.2;
5.09[1] n.4

P

Palumbo, Estate of v. Comm'r   S5.05[2][b]
n.68
Panama Ref. Co. v. Ryan . . . . . 4.10[5] n.63
Pangas, Estate of v. Comm'r . . . . . 5.06[5][a]
n.101
Paolozzi v. Comm'r . . . . 4.10[4][a] n.23;
10.01[5] n.153; 10.01[9] n.205
Papson, Estate of v. Comm'r . . . . 5.03[3][c]
n.63; S5.03[3][c][iii] n.134
Paquette, Estate of v. Comm'r . . . 6.01[3][b]
n.31
Parsee v. US . . . . 5.06[8][d][ii] n.355
Pardee, Estate of v. Comm'r . . . 4.08[4][b] ns.
36, 38, 39; 4.10[4][c] ns. 36, 38; 4.10[5]
n.64; S5.03[4][b][i] n.189; 5.03[5][a]
n.106
Paris v. US . . . . 5.05[1][a] n.9
Park, Estate of v. Comm'r . . . 5.03[3] n.38;
S5.03[3] n.80
Parker v. Delaney . . . . 4.12[8] n.70
Parker v. US (ED Ark. 1991) . . . . . . 4.04[6]
n.237
Parker v. US (ED Ark. 1990) . . . . . . 4.04[6]
n.233
Parker v. US (ND Ga.) . . . . . 4.08[7][c] n.144
Parker, US v. . . . . 19.04[4] n.100
Parker, Estate of v. Comm'r . . . . . 5.06[3][b]
n.38
Parson v. US . . . 4.05[5][a] n.47; 4.14[8] n.122
Pascal, Estate of v. Comm'r . . . . . 4.02[2][a]
n.17
Past, US v. . . . 4.08[1][a] n.7; 4.15[1][b][ii] &
ns. 54, 55
Pastor v. US . . . . 5.06[3][a] n.31
Patrick v. Patrick . . . . S8.04[2] n.13
Patten v. US . . . . 4.12[10] n.85
Patterson, Berman v. . . . . 11.03[4][b] n.52
Patterson, Carlson v. . . . . . . 11.03[4][b] n.52
Patterson, Kidd v. . . . . 11.03[4][b] n.53
Patterson v. US . . . . 5.06[5][a] n.99;
5.06[8][d][ii] n.319
Patterson, Estate of . . . . 4.05[3] n.31
Pattison, Estate of v. Comm'r . . . . 4.02[2][a]
n.27; 4.02[3][b] n.70
Paul, Estate of v. Comm'r . . . 10.04[3][d] ns.
24, 25
Paxton, Estate of v. Comm'r . . . 2.02[1] n.15;
4.08[4][c] n.53; 4.10[4][a] n.23
Payne v. US (US) . . . . 4.03[2][d] n.35
Payne v. US (MD Fla.) . . . . 5.03[3] n.38;
S5.03[3] n.80
Peabody, Estate of v. Comm'r . . . .
. . . . 4.12[4] n.30
Peacock v. US . . . . 5.06[8][d][ii] n.334
**Pearcy v. Citizens Bank & Trust Co. of
Bloomington** . . . . 8.05[4] n.13

[Text references are to paragraphs and notes (9"n.");
references to the supplement are preceded by "S."]

Peckham, Estate of v. Comm'r . . . 5.03[3][b] n.59; S5.03[3][b] n.105

Peirce v. US . . . . 5.03[3][a] n.53; S5.03[3][a] n.92; 5.06[3][a] n.31

Pelzer, US v. . . . . . 9.04[3][a] n.50; 9.04[3][d] n.71; 10.02[5] & n.148

Penner, Estate of v. Comm'r . . . . . 4.13[4][a] n.37

Penney, Estate of v. Comm'r . . . . 5.06[5][a] n.99

Pennsylvania Bank & Trust Co. v. US . . . . 4.13[7][a] n.80; 5.03[5][b] n.128

Peoples-Pittsburgh Trust Co. v. US . . . . 4.03[2][b] n.26

Peracchio v. Comm'r . . . S10.02[2][c][iii] n.85

Perkins v. Comm'r . . . . 9.04[3][e] n.85; S10.01[5][d] n.169.1

Perrin, Estate of v. Comm'r . . . 4.10[5] n.64

Perry, Estate of v. Comm'r . . . . . 4.14[9][b] n.136

Peters, Estate of v. Comm'r (4th Cir.) . . . . 4.08[8] n.171; 4.12[7][b] & ns. 54– 56

Peters, Estate of v. Comm'r (TCM) . . . . 4.08[6][a] n.76; 4.10[4][c] n.38

Peterson v. Comm'r . . . . 8.03[2] n.13

Peterson Marital Trust v. Comm'r . . . . 18.05[2][b][ii] ns. 36, 38, 39; S18.05[2][b][ii] n.39

Petter, Estate of v. Comm'r . . . . S5.05[4][a] n.128; S10.01[3][e] n.107.1

Pettus v. Comm'r . . . . 9.04[5][a] n.147

Philbrick v. Manning . . . . . . 4.02[3][g] n.132

Phillips, Nettz v. . . . . . . 5.06[8][d][iv] n.400

Phillips, Poage v. . . . . . . 5.06[8][d][iv] n.399

Phillips, Estate of v. Comm'r . . . . 5.06[5][a] n.98

Phinney, Estate of, Stockdick v. 5.06[8][b][iii] n.250

Piatt v. Gray . . . . 5.06[8][b][iii] n.251

Picciano v. US . . . . 4.13[4][c][ii] n.42

Pickard, Estate of v. Comm'r . . . . 5.05[2][e] n.90

Pierre v. Comm'r (TC 2009) . . . . S4.05[7][c] n.88; S10.02[2][c] n.74.1

Pierre v. Comm'r (TCM 2010) (Pierre II) S10.02[2][c] n.74.1; S10.02[3] n.132

Piggott, Estate of v. Comm'r . . . . . 4.14[4][c] n.54

Pillsbury, Estate of v. Comm'r . . . . 4.02[4][e][i] ns. 204, 205; 4.02[4][e][v] n.223

Pinchot v. Comm'r . . . . . 6.05[2][a][ii] n.27; 6.06[1] n.10

Pinkerton, Estate of v. Comm'r . . . 5.03[2][b] ns. 26, 27; S5.03[2][b] ns. 67, 68

Pipe, Estate of v. Comm'r   5.06[8][b][iii] & n.243; 5.06[8][d][iv] n.395

Piper, Estate of v. Comm'r . . . . 4.02[4][e][iii] n.212

Pirrie v. US . . . . 5.06[7][b] n.175

Pitner v. US . . . . 5.03[3] n.38; S5.03[3] n.80; 5.03[3][a] n.56; S5.03[3][a] ns. 95, 96; 5.03[3][c] n.63

Pitt v. US . . . . 4.13[3] n.22

Pittard, Estate of v. Comm'r . . . . . . 2.02 n.5; 5.03[5][b] n.124

Pittman v. US . . . . 4.08[8] n.170

Pittsburgh Nat'l Bank v. US . . . . . 4.13[2][b] n.15; 4.13[4][c][ii] n.43

Pittsfield Nat'l Bank v. US . . 4.13[4][a] n.37

Planters Nat'l Bank & Trust Co. v. US . . . . 5.06[7][b] n.174

Pliske, Estate of . . . . 4.04[3][b][viii] n.96

Poage v. Phillips . . . . . . 5.06[8][d][iv] n.399

Poiner v. Comm'r 8.04 n.4

Polack v. Comm'r . . . . S10.02[1] n.5.1

Poley Estate v. Comm'r . . . . 4.02[3][f] n.108

Pollock, Estate of v. Comm'r . . . . 3.05[3][b] n.39

Polster v. Comm'r . . . . 5.05[2][a] n.58

Poor, White v. . . . 4.10[2] n.8; 4.10[4][a] n.21; 4.10[7] & n.72; 4.14[4][e] n.68

Pope v. US . . . . 4.15[1][b][ii] n.55

Porter v. Comm'r (US) . . . . 4.10[4][b] ns. 29, 31

Porter v. Comm'r (1st Cir.) . . . . . 4.07[3][b] n.91

Porter v. Comm'r (TC) . . . . 4.05[2][b] n.16; 5.03[3][a] n.56; S5.03[3][a] n.95

Porter, Estate of v. Comm'r   4.05[8] n.108; 4.14[2] n.18

Posen, Estate of v. Comm'r . . . 5.03[3] n.38; S5.03[3] n.80; 5.03[3][c] n.63; S5.03[3][c][ii] n.130

Posner, Estate of v. Comm'r . . . . S4.13[7][a] n.78; S5.06[8][b][iii] n.239

Powell, US v. . . . 4.10[4][d] n.44; 4.10[5] n.64

Powell, Estate of v. US . . . . . . 10.02[3] n.131

Powers v. US . . . . 4.13[3] n.22

Preisser, Estate of . . . . . . 5.06[5][b][i] n.104

Prejean v. Comm'r . . . . 9.04[3][c] n.67

Prell, Estate of v. Comm'r   4.03[3][a] n.39; S5.03[3][a] n.96

Price v. Comm'r . . . . S9.04[3][e] n.88

Price v. US (US) . . . . 8.03[1] n.5

Price v. US (5th Cir.) . . . . 4.05[2][a] n.11

Prichard v. US (5th Cir.) . . . . 4.14[4][a] n.44; 4.14[4][e] n.69; 4.14[7][b] n.111

Prichard v. US (ND Tex.) . . . . 4.14[4][a] n.44

Pridmore, Estate of v. Comm'r . . . 4.02[2][a] n.12

Priedeman v. Jamison . . . . 8.05[3] n.10

Pritchard, Estate of v. Comm'r . . . 4.02[3][h] n.142; 4.14[9][b] n.134

Procter, Comm'r v. . . . . . 5.06[5][b][i] n.105; 10.01[3][e] ns. 104, 105; S10.01[3][e] ns.105, 106; 10.02[2][b][i] n.35

Proctor, Estate of v. Comm'r . . . . 4.02[3][b] n.73; 5.05[2][a] n.58

Proesel, Estate of v. US . . . . . . S5.03[4][b][i] n.185; 5.03[5][a] n.104

[Text references are to paragraphs and notes (9"n.");
references to the supplement are preceded by "S."]

Propstra v. US . . . . . . 4.02[4][b][ii] n.152;
   4.02[4][e][i] n.197; S5.03[4][c][i] n.210;
   5.03[5][b] n.125
Proske v. US . . . . S2.02[1] n.10
Prouty, Comm'r v. . . . . 10.01[8] n.196
Provident Nat'l Bank v. US . . . . . 5.06[7][c]
   n.193
Prox, Estate of v. Comm'r . . . . 5.06[8][b][iii]
   n.251; 5.06[8][b][iv] n.257
Prudowsky, Estate of v. Comm'r . . . .
   . . . . 4.10[4][f] n.50; 9.04[5][c] n.168
Pruitt, Estate of v. Comm'r . . . .
   . . . . 4.10[4][a] n.24
Prussner v. US . . . . 4.04[6] ns. 233, 237
Publicker v. Comm'r . . . 10.02[2][b][iv] n.64
Puchner v. US . . . . 4.15[1][a][ii] n.33
Pullian, Estate of v. Comm'r . . . 4.04[6] n.226
Pyle v. US . . . . 10.01[5][e] n.180
Pyle, Estate of v. Comm'r . . . 4.14[9][a] n.131

Q

Quarty v. US . . . . 2.01[3] n.67; 9.02[3] n.20;
   18.05[2][b] n.10
Quatman v. Comm'r . . . . . . 9.04[3][e] n.81
Quinn, Estate of v. US . . . . . . 4.05[2][a] n.6

R

Raab, Estate of v. Comm'r . . . 4.07[3][b] n.86
Rabe, Estate of v. Comm'r . . . . 5.03[3] n.39;
   S5.03[3] n.81
Rabenhorst v. Comm'r . . . . 4.02[2][a] ns. 35,
   37
Racca, Estate of v. Comm'r . . . 5.06[3] n.17
Radel, Estate of v. Comm'r . . . . . 5.06[7][b]
   n.170
Raisler, Estate of v. Comm'r . . . 5.06[8][b][iii]
   n.250
Rakow v. Comm'r . . . . . 4.02[4][c][iii] n.175;
   10.02[2][c][ii] n.82
Ramsey, Estate of v. US . . . . . . 8.04[2] n.17
Rapelje, Estate of v. Comm'r . . . . 4.08[4][c]
   n.45
Rapp, Estate of v. Comm'r . . . . 5.06[8][d][ii]
   n.311
Rasquin, Guggenheim v. . . . . 6.05[1] n.5;
   10.01[3][g] n.113; 10.02[2][b][ii] & ns.
   46–48; 10.02[2][b][iv] n.63
Ratcliffe, Estate of v. Comm'r . . . . 4.02[3][b]
   n.63
Ray v. Comm'r . . . . 5.06[7][b] n.189
Reardon v. US . . . . 4.03[3][a] n.39
Rector, Estate of . . . . S4.02[6][a] n.261;
   S4.08[4][c] n.49
Reed v. Comm'r . . . . 4.05[2] n.3
Reed v. US (7th Cir.) . . . . 3.05[3][b] n.43
Reed v. US (ED Mo.) . . . . 5.06[5][a] n.99
Reed, Estate of . . . . 5.06[5][a] n.98

Reed Estate v. US . . . . . . 4.10[7] ns. 74, 78;
   4.14[4][e] n.68
Regester v. Comm'r . . . . . . 10.04[3][e] n.30;
   13.02[2][e][iii] n.167
Reichart, Estate of v. Comm'r . . . . 4.02[4][g]
   n.241; 4.08[4][c] ns. 48, 49
Reilly v. US . . . . 9.05[2][a] n.14
Reilly, Estate of v. Comm'r (3d Cir.) . . . . . .
   . . . . 5.06[8][c] ns. 290, 291
Reilly, Estate of v. Comm'r (TC) . . . . 5.03[3]
   n.38; S5.03[3] n.80; 5.03[3][a] n.53;
   S5.03[3][a] n.92
Reinecke, Mayer v. . . . . 4.06 ns. 2, 3
Reinecke v. Northern Trust Co. . . . 4.08[6][a]
   ns. 75, 76; 4.08[9] n.192; 4.09[3] n.20;
   4.09[7] n.56; 4.10[4][a] n.19
Reno v. Comm'r . . . . 5.06[5][a] n.99
Rensenhouse, Estate of v. Comm'r . . . .
   . . . . 5.06[3][g] n.74
Reynolds, First Trust Co. of St. Paul v. . . . .
   . . . . 5.05[1][a] n.9
Reynolds, Estate of v. Comm'r   19.04[1][b]
   n.6; 19.04[3][a] n.48; 19.04[3][b][ii] ns.
   89, 90; 19.04[6][a][ii] ns. 126, 127
Rhode Island Hosp. Trust Co. v. US . . . . . .
   . . . . 5.05[1][b] n.28
Rhode Island Hosp. Trust Co., US v. . . . . . .
   . . . . 4.14[4][c] ns. 54, 56
Ribblesdale, Estate of v. Comm'r . . . .
   . . . . S5.03[4][a] n.146; S5.03[4][a][i]
   n.155; 5.03[5][e] n.136
Riccio v. US 3.06 n.3
Richardson v. Comm'r . . . . . . 10.01[4] n.139
Richardson v. Helvering . . . . . . 4.12[8] n.64
Richman, Estate of v. Comm'r . . . 5.06[3][d]
   n.51
Riddell, California Trust Co. v. . . . . . 4.05[6]
   n.72; 4.14[8] n.118; 5.06[8][a] n.205
Ridenour, Estate of v. Comm'r . . . 4.10[4][a]
   n.24
Ridgeway, Estate of, Comm'r v.   4.08[1][b]
   n.13
Riegelman, Estate of v. Comm'r   4.05[7][b]
   n.82
Riese, Estate of v. Comm'r . . . . . S4.08[4][c]
   n.45; S5.03[3][c] n.109; S5.03[4][a]
   n.146; S19.03[3][d][i] n.177
Rifkind v. US . . . . 4.07[2][a] n.19; 4.08[5][a]
   n.56; 5.05[2][e] n.91
Riggs v. Del Drago . . . . . 5.06[5][a] n.98; 8.04
   n.9; 8.04[2] n.15; 8.05[4] n.12
Righter, US v. . . . . 4.15[1][a][ii] n.31; 4.15[2]
   n.76
Riker v. Comm'r . . . . 5.05[1][b] n.31
Rinaldi, Estate of v. US . . . . 5.04[1] n.4;
   5.06[8][d][ii] n.353
Ripley v. Comm'r . . . . 9.04[11] n.247
Risher v. US . . . . 5.06[3][a] n.24
Riter v. Comm'r . . . . 9.04[3][c] n.67
Ritter v. US . . . . 4.10[4][c] ns. 35, 41;
   5.06[3][a] n.24
Rivera, Estate of v. Comm'r 8.09 n.3
Robertson v. Comm'r . . . . 10.03[1] ns. 11, 13

*[Text references are to paragraphs and notes (9"n.");
references to the supplement are preceded by "S."]*

Robertson v. US (5th Cir.) . . . . 5.06[8][b][iii] n.240

Robertson v. US (8th Cir.) . . . . 5.06[8][d][ii] n.319

Robertson v. US (ND Tex.) . . . S14.02[2] n.6; S14.02[3] n.19

Robinette v. Helvering . . . . . . 4.05[8] n.94; 4.09[4][f] n.41; 10.01[3][c] n.95; 10.01[3][d] n.103; 10.01[5][b] n.166; 10.01[8] ns. 195, 199; 10.01[9] n.205; 19.03[1] n.2

Robinson, Estate of (TCM 2010) . . . . S4.02[6][a] n.264

Robinson v. Comm'r (5th Cir.) . . . . 10.01[6] n.186

Robinson v. Comm'r (TC) . . . . . 10.02[6][b] n.178

Robinson v. US (9th Cir. 1980) . . . 4.09[4][e] n.35

Robinson v. US (9th Cir. 1975) . . . 5.06[5][a] n.99

Robinson v. US (SD Ga.) . . . . . 5.06[8][d][iii] n.386

Robinson, Estate of v. Comm'r (TC 1993) . . . . . 4.13[7][c] n.90; 9.04[1][b] n.16

Robinson, Estate of v. Comm'r (TC 1975) . . . . S5.03[5] n.256; 5.03[5][b] n.128

Rockwell v. Comm'r . . . . . . 4.14[4][a] n.45

Rocovich v. US . . . . 2.02[3][c][ii] n.55

Roderick v. Comm'r . . . . . . 9.04[3][d] n.72; 9.04[5][b] n.162

Rodgers, Estate of v. Comm'r . . . . 4.02[4][e][ii] n.210

Rodiek, Frederick, Ancillary Ex'r v. Comm'r . . . . 6.01[3][b] n.33

Roels v. US . . . . 5.06[8][e] n.409

Roemer, Estate of v. Comm'r . . . . 4.08[4][c] n.46

Rogan, Henderson v. . . . . 4.13[6][a] n.72

Rogan v. Kammerdiner . . . . . . 4.12[8] n.64

Rogan, Taylor v. . . . . 4.02[2][a] n.9

Roger's Estate v. Helvering . . . 10.02[5] n.149

Rogers, Estate of v. Comm'r (US) . . . 4.13[10] n.130

Rogers, Estate of v. Comm'r (TCM) . . . . 4.04[5][a][iii] n.198

Rollman v. US . . . . 9.04[5][b] n.157

Roney, Estate of v. Comm'r . . . 5.06[5][b][ii] n.109

Rosano v. US . . . . 4.05[3] n.28

Rose v. US . . . . 4.14[4][e] n.72

Rose, Estate of v. Comm'r . . . . 4.05[2] n.3

Rosen v. Comm'r . . . . 9.04[3][b] ns. 62, 65; 9.04[3][e] n.79

Rosen, Estate of v. Comm'r . . . . S4.08[4][c] n.49

Rosenberg v. Comm'r . . . . . . 5.04[2] n.13

Rosenblatt, Estate of v. Comm'r (10th Cir.) . . . . 4.13[7][a] n.80

Rosenblatt, Estate of v. Comm'r (TCM) . . . . 4.05[2] n.4

Rosenblum v. Anglim . . . . . 6.05[2][a][i] n.14; 6.05[2][a][ii] n.28

Rosenfield v. US . . . . 4.03[1] n.6

Rosenthal v. Comm'r . . . . . 10.01[3][i] n.127; 10.02[1][b] n.12; 10.02[6] n.170; 10.06[1] n.6

Roski, Estate of . . . . . . S2.02[3][c][iii] n.116

Rosser, Comm'r v. . . . . 4.05[5][b] n.54

Rosskam v. US . . . . 4.02[3][g] n.136

Ross v. Comm'r . . . . 9.04[5][b] n.151

Ross v. US . . . . 9.04[5][a] n.147

Roth v. US . . . . 19.04[1][b] n.5

Rothensies, Fidelity-Philadelphia Trust Co. v. . . . . 4.08[8] n.166; 4.09[6] n.52

Round v. Comm'r . . . . 4.10[8] n.79

Routzhan, Brown v. . . . . 4.13[7][d] n.99; 10.07[1] n.5; 17.04[3] n.76

Rowan Cos. v. US 18.03 n.1

Roy, Estate of v. Comm'r . . . . 4.09[4][e] n.35

Rudolph v. US . . . 19.04[1][b] n.1; 19.04[3] ns. 43, 44; 19.04[3][b][i] n.80

Rupert v. United States . . . . . . S5.03[3][c][i] n.118

Rusk, Afroyim v. . . . . 6.01[3][a] n.27

Russell v. US . . . . 5.03[5][b] n.124

Russell, US v. . . . . . 8.02 n.15; S8.03[1] n.10

Ruxton, Estate of v. Comm'r . . . . 4.08[7][d] ns. 158, 165

Ryan, Panama Ref. Co. v. . . . . . 4.10[5] n.63

S

Sachs, Estate of v. Comm'r . . . . . . 4.07[3][a] n.83; S5.03[4][b][i] n.183; S5.03[4][c][i] n.209; 10.02[6][d] n.183; 10.08[3] n.49; S10.08[3] n.49

Safe Deposit & Trust Co., Helvering v. . . . . 4.05[5][c] n.66; 4.13[5] n.54; 4.13[10] n.126; 12.01[1] n.12

Safe Dep. & Trust Co., Tait v. . . . . 4.06 ns. 6, 7

Safe Deposit & Trust Co. of Baltimore, Weinberg v. . . . . 8.05[4] n.13

Sage, Estate of v. Comm'r . . . 5.05[2][e] n.94

Saia, Estate of v. Comm'r . . . . . 4.14[8] n.120

Saigh v. Comm'r S8.04 n.4

St. Joseph Bank & Trust Co. v. US . . . . 10.06[2][b] n.24

St. Louis County Bank v. US . . . 19.04[1][b] & ns. 1, 5, 7; 19.04[2] n.17; 19.04[3] ns. 43, 44; 19.04[3][a] n.48; 19.04[3][b][i] & ns. 63–72, 81–83, 87; 19.04[6][a][iii] n.133

St. Louis Union Trust Co., Becker v. . . . . 4.09[3] n.20

St. Louis Union Trust Co., Helvering v. . . . . 4.09[3] n.20

St. Louis Union Trust Co. v. US . . 5.05[1][b] n.28

St. Louis Union Trust Co., Ex'r v. Comm'r . . . . 6.01[3][a] n.28

Saleh, US v. 8.02 n.5

Salsbury, Estate of v. Comm'r . . . .
. . . . 4.02[4][b][iii] n.159
Salt, Estate of v. Comm'r . . . 19.04[1][b] n.3;
19.04[6][a][ii] n.123
Saltzman v. Comm'r . . . . 10.01[3] n.76
Salyer v. US . . . . 4.14[9][b] n.136
Samuel v. Comm'r . . . . 4.11[5] n.47
Sanchez v. Bowers . . . . 6.04[1] n.11
Sanford's Estate v. Comm'r 3.04 n.5;
4.08[7][c] n.134; 4.10[8] n.83;
4.15[1][b][ii] n.56; 10.01[3][h] n.121;
10.01[6] & ns. 181, 183; 10.01[9];
10.01[10][b] n.216; 10.01[10][c] n.221;
10.01[10][e] n.227; 10.02[6][b] n.178;
10.04[3][a] n.12; 10.07[2][b] n.40;
10.08[1][b] n.26; 11.02[2][b][ii] n.81
Sansone, Estate of v. US . . . . . . 5.06[8][d][ii]
n.351
Sather v. Comm'r . . . . 9.04[1][b] n.36
Satz, Estate of v. Comm'r . . . 4.15[1][b][i] ns.
40, 46
Saunders, Estate of v. Comm'r . . . .
. . . . S5.03[4][c][ii] n.215
Sawade, Estate of v. Comm'r . . . . 4.03[3][a]
n.39; 4.07[3][b] n.88
Sawyer, Estate of v. Comm'r . . . . 5.06[5][a]
n.101
Scanlan, Estate of v. Comm'r . . . . 4.02[2][a]
ns. 28, 33
Scanlon v. Comm'r . . . . . 10.01[2][b][i] n.16;
10.02[6][a] n.173
Schauerhamer v. Comm'r . . . . 4.02[4][g]
n.241; 4.08[4][c] ns. 48, 49
Schecter Poultry Corp. v. US . . . .
. . . . 4.10[5] n.63
Schelberg, Estate of v. Comm'r . . . 4.11[3][a]
n.19
Scher v. US . . . . 4.02[3][g] n.127
Schildkraut, Estate of v. Comm'r . . . .
. . . . 5.06[8][b][i] n.229
Schlesinger v. Wisconsin 9.01 n.7
Schlosser, Estate of v. Comm'r . . . 4.03[2][c]
& n.27; 4.07[2][c] n.62
Schmidt v. US . . . . 4.05[2][b] n.17
Schneider, M. v. US . . . . S4.05[2][a] n.6
Schoenheit v. Lucas . . . . 4.15[2] n.67
Scholl, Estate of v. Comm'r . . . . 4.15[1][a][ii]
n.31; S5.03[4][a][i] n.153; 5.03[5][e]
n.134
Schott v. Comm'r (9th Cir.) . . . .
. . . . S19.03[3][b][i] n.134
Schott v. Comm'r (TCM) . . . . . 19.03[3][b][i]
n.134
Schroeder v. US . . . . 5.06[3][a] n.29
Schuette v. Bowers 4.06 n.4
Schuhmacher v. Comm'r . . . . . 9.04[3] n.45
Schuler, Estate of v. Comm'r . . . 9.04[1][b]
n.35
Schultz, Tax Analysts & Advocates v. . . . . .
. . . . 9.02[2] n.13
Schultz v. US . . . . 9.04[1][b] ns. 16, 36

Schuneman v. US . . . . 3.03[2] n.19;
4.04[3][b][ii] n.46; 4.04[7][b][ii] n.285;
5.09[2] n.12
Schusterman v. US . . . . 10.02[3] n.132
Schutt, Estate of v. Comm'r . . . . S4.08[4][c]
n.49
Schwager v. Comm'r . . . . 4.14[4][a] n.37
Schwan, Estate of v. Comm'r . . . . 5.05[3][a]
n.97
Schwartz v. Comm'r . . . 2.02 n.5; 8.03[1] n.4
Schwartz, Estate of v. Comm'r 3.06 n.3
Scott v. Comm'r . . . . 4.14[8] n.126
Scott v. Henricksen . . . . 4.02[2][a] n.9
Scull, Estate of v. Comm'r . . . 4.02[3][a] n.59
Sears, United States Trust Co. of NY v. . . . .
. . . . 8.05[1] n.5; 8.05[3] n.9; 8.06 n.5;
8.08[2] n.12
Second Nat'l Bank v. US (US) . . . .
. . . . 5.06[3] n.17
Second Nat'l Bank v. US (7th Cir.) . . . .
. . . . 5.06[8][c] n.288
Second Nat'l Bank of Danville v. Dallman
. . . 4.05[6] ns. 75, 76; 4.13[2][b] n.16;
4.14[3][c] n.32; 5.06[7][c] n.194;
11.03[3][b] n.40
Second Nat'l Bank of New Haven v. US (US)
. . . . . . 5.03[2][b] n.31; 8.04[2] n.17
Second Nat'l Bank of New Haven v. US (2d
Cir.) . . . . 3.03[1] n.2; 5.09[1] n.4
Selecman, Estate of v. Comm'r . . . . . 4.12[8]
n.59
Self v. US . . . 10.04[3][e] n.28; 13.02[2][e][iii]
n.167
Seltzer v. Comm'r . . . . 19.04[1][b] n.1
Senda v. Comm'r . . . . S10.01[2][b][ii] n.25.1
Senft v. US . . . . 5.05[2][e] n.90
Sensenbrenner v. Comm'r . . . 9.04[3][a] n.55
Sexton v. US . . . . 4.08[7][a] n.124
Shackelford, Cosby v. . . . . 8.04[3] n.19
Shackleford, Estate of v. US 4.02[5] n.244;
S4.02[5] n.244; 4.11[4][a] n.40;
S4.11[4][a] n.40
Shaeffer, Estate of v. Comm'r . . . . 4.13[2][a]
n.10
Shafer, Estate of v. Comm'r . . . . . 4.08[7][a]
n.121
Shannon, Estate of v. Comm'r . . . . . 8.04[2]
n.17
Shapiro, Estate of v. Comm'r . . . . 5.03[3][c]
n.72
Shapiro, Estate of v. US . . . . . . S5.03[4][a][i]
n.154
Sharp v. Comm'r . . . . 4.05[2] n.4
Sharp, Estate of v. Comm'r . . . 4.02[3][b] ns.
67, 81; 4.02[3][g] n.120; 4.02[4][e][vii]
n.227
Sharpe, Estate of v. Comm'r . . . . . 5.03[3][b]
n.58; S5.03[3][b] n.104
Sharp, Estate of v. US . . . . 4.02[2][a] ns. 25,
29, 32
Shaughnessy, Singer v. . . . . 4.02[2][a] n.10
Shaughnessy, Smith v. . . . . 3.04 ns. 5, 9;
4.02[3][g] n.136; 4.05[8] n.94; 4.09[3]

[Text references are to paragraphs and notes (9"n.");
references to the supplement are preceded by "S."]

n.9; 9.05[1] n.6; 10.01[3][b] n.90;
10.01[3][d] n.102; 10.01[3][h] n.121;
10.01[6] ns. 181, 184; 10.01[3][i] n.129;
10.02[1][b] n.12; 12.01[1] n.7; 19.03[1]
n.1
Shaw v. Comm'r . . . . 4.04[7][b][iii] n.286
Sheaffer's Estate v. Comm'r . . . . 10.02[6][d]
n.183
Shedd's Estate v. Comm'r . . . 3.05[3][b] n.45
Shedd, Estate of v. Comm'r . . . 5.06[8][b][i]
n.210
Shelfer, Estate of v. Comm'r (11th Cir.) . . . .
. . . . 5.06[8][d][ii] n.321
Shelfer, Estate of v. Comm'r (TC) . . . .
. . . . 5.06[8][d][ii] n.321
Shepherd v. Comm'r (11th Cir.) . . . .
. . . . S10.01[2][b][ii] n.25.1;
10.02[2][c][iv] n.102; S10.02[2][c][v]
n.118
Shepherd v. Comm'r (TC) . . . 10.02[2][c][v]
& n.118
Sheppard, Estate of . . . . S8.08[2] n.7
Sherman v. US . . . . 4.15[1][a] n.24
Sherman, Jr. v. US . . . . 4.08[4][b] n.40;
4.15[1][a] n.24
Sherrill v. US . . . . S4.11[6] n.60
Sherrod, Estate of . . . . . . 4.04[3][b][iv] n.64;
4.04[3][b][vi] n.74; 4.04[3][c][ii] n.132
Shirley, Katz, Look & Moison, PC v. . . . . . .
. . . . S8.07[1] n.7
Shively, Estate of, Comm'r v. . . . . 4.02[3][g]
n.136; S5.03[4][c][i] n.209; 5.03[5][b]
n.120
Shlensky, Estate of v. Comm'r   5.04[3] ns.
15, 18
Sholes, Estate of v. Comm'r . . . . . 4.05[2][b]
n.16
Short, Estate of v. Comm'r . . . 5.06[5][a] n.99
Shriners' Hosp. for Crippled Children v. US
(Fed. Cir.) . . . . 5.05[8][d] n.382
Shriners' Hosp. for Crippled Children v. US
(Ct. Cl.) . . . . 5.05[2][c] n.83
Shuhmacher v. Comm'r . . . . . . 9.05[3] n.37
Shukert v. Allen
. . . . 4.09[3] n.18; 4.09[7] n.54
Shultz, McCoy v. . . . . 5.05[1][b] n.34
Shurtz, Estate of v. Comm'r . . . . S4.08[4][c]
n.49
Siegel, Comm'r v. . . . . 4.08[7][c] n.134;
10.01[5][d] ns. 174, 176; 10.02[6][b]
n.178
Siegel, Estate of v. Comm'r (TC 1980) . . . . .
. . . . 4.11 n.3
Siegel, Estate of v. Comm'r (TC 1977) . . . . .
. . . . 5.06[8][d][iv] n.404
Sikler, Estate of v. Comm'r . . . .
. . . . 5.06[3][a] n.29
Silberman v. US . . . . 4.11[3][a] n.2
Silver, Estate of v. Comm'r . . S6.06[2] n.28
Silverman v. McGinnes . . . . . . 4.12[2] n.21
Silvey v. US . . . . 5.06[7][b] n.175
Simmons, US v. . . . . 4.02[3][e] n.100

Simon, Tax Analysts & Advocates v. . . . . . .
. . . . 9.02[2] n.13
Simons v. US . . . . 4.13[6][d] n.76
Simplot, Estate of v. Comm'r . . . . 4.02[2][a]
n.22; 4.02[4][b][iii] & ns. 161, 162;
4.02[4][b][iv] ns. 169, 170
Simpson v. US (8th Cir.)   18.05[2][b][ii] ns.
36, 38, 39; S18.05[2][b][ii] n.39
Simpson v. US (DNM) . . . . 5.06[5] n.90
Singer v. Shaughnessy . . . . 4.02[2][a] n.10
Sirmans, Estate of v. Comm'r . . . . 4.02[3][b]
n.84
Sivyer, Estate of v. Comm'r 8.02 n.4
Skifter, Estate of v. Comm'r . . . . 4.08[6][d]
n.104; 4.10[7] n.74; 4.14[4][e] & ns. 67,
68; 4.14[9][a] n.132
Skinner, Estate of v. US . . . . . 4.08[4][c] n.52
Skouras v. Comm'r . . . . 9.04[3][e] n.75
Slater, Estate of v. Comm'r . . . 4.04[3][b][i]
n.37
Sloane, Estate of v. Comm'r . . . . . 4.03[2][a]
n.23
Slocum, Edwards v. . . . 5.05[3][b][i] ns. 101–
103; 5.08[4][a][ii] n.177
Slocum v. US . . . .
. . . . 19.04[1][b] n.6; 19.04[3] n.43
Slutsky, Estate of v. Comm'r . . . . . 10.02[4]
n.141
Small v. Comm'r . . . . 10.02[4] n.141
Small, Estate of v. Comm'r . . . . . 4.13[2] n.6
Smallwood v. Comm'r 8.09 n.1
Smead, Estate of v. Comm'r . . . 4.14[6] n.102
Smith v. Comm'r (TCM 1999) . . . 4.02[2][a]
n.34
Smith v. Comm'r (BTA 1931) . . . .
. . . . 8.03[1] n.10
Smith, Fidelity-Philadelphia Trust Co. v. . . . .
. . . . . 4.02[3][h] n.139; 4.11[2][a] n.7;
4.14[2] n.20; 4.14[9][a] n.129
Smith, Jennings v. . . . . 4.10[5] & ns. 60, 61;
4.10[8] n.79; 4.13[4][a] n.2
Smith v. Shaughnessy . . . . 3.04 ns. 5, 9;
4.02[3][g] n.136; 4.05[8] n.94; 4.09[3]
n.9; 9.05[1] n.6; 10.01[3][b] n.90;
10.01[3][d] n.102; 10.01[3][h] n.121;
10.01[3][i] n.129; 10.01[6] ns. 181, 184;
10.02[1][b] n.12; 12.01[1] n.7; 19.03[1]
n.1
Smith v. Thompson . . . 5.06[8][d][iv] ns. 392,
394
Smith v. US (D Conn.) . . . . 4.13[3] n.19
Smith v. US (SD Miss.) . . . . 4.02[3][g] n.121
Smith v. US (WD Mo.) . . . . . . 5.05[1][b] n.36
Smith, Estate of v. Comm'r (2d Cir.) . . . . . .
. . . . . 4.02[2][a] n.18; 4.02[3][a] n.59;
S5.03[3] n.80; 5.03[3] n.38; 5.03[3][c]
n.63; S5.03[3][c][ii] n.131
Smith, Estate of v. Comm'r (5th Cir.) . . . . .
. . . . S5.03[4][c][i] ns. 205, 210;
5.03[5][a] n.116; 5.03[5][b] n.125
Smith, Estate of v. Comm'r (7th Cir.) . . . . .
. . . . 5.06[8][b][v] n.273

*[Text references are to paragraphs and notes (9"n.");
references to the supplement are preceded by "S."]*

Smith, Estate of v. Comm'r (TC 1999) . . . .
. . . . . 4.02[2][b][iv] n.47; 4.02[3][f] ns.
108, 111
Smith, Estate of v. Comm'r (TC 1990) . . . . .
. . . . . 2.01[1][b][i] n.22; S2.01[1][b][i]
n.22
Smith, Estate of v. Comm'r (TC 1979) . . . . .
. . . . 4.14[4][a] n.41
Smith, Estate of v. Comm'r (TC 1975) . . . . .
. . . . 4.03[3][a] n.40
Smith, Estate of v. Comm'r (TC 1974) . . . . .
. . . . 5.06[8][b][v] n.268
Smith, Estate of v. Comm'r (TC 1972) . . . . .
4.02[3][g] n.136; 4.02[4][e][ii] n.210
Smith, Estate of v. Comm'r (TC 1954) . . . . .
. . . . 11.03[4][b] n.54
Smith, Estate of v. Comm'r (TC 1950) . . . . .
. . . . 4.02[3][f] n.104
Smith, Estate of v. Comm'r (TCM) . . . . . .
. . . . 5.06[8][b][i] n.220; 5.06[8][b][iii]
ns. 240, 251
Smith, Estate of v. US (5th Cir.) . . . .
. . . . S4.02[4][e][iii] n.219
Smith III, Sidney . . . . S19.04[2] n.19;
S19.04[6][a][i] n.117
Smoot, Estate of v. Comm'r . . . .
. . . 4.04[3][b][viii] n.97; 4.04[6] n.224
Sniveley v. Comm'r 8.02 n.5
Snyder v. US (WD Ky.) . . . . 4.13[2] n.4;
4.13[7][a] n.82; 5.06[8][d][iv] n.401
Snyder v. US (D. Md.) . . . . . . 5.03[3][c] n.70;
S5.03[3][c][i] n.116
Snyder v. Comm'r (TC 1989) . . . . . 10.01[2]
n.13
Snyder v. Comm'r (TC 1976) . . . 10.01[2][d]
n.31
Snyder, Estate of v. Comm'r . . . . . 5.06[7][b]
n.170
Snyder, Estate of v. US . . . . . . 5.03[4] n.84;
S5.03[6][c][ii] ns. 296, 298, 299; 5.03[7]
n.157
Soberdash, Estate of v. Comm'r . . . 4.16 ns.
11, 13
Sochalski, Estate of v. Comm'r . . . 4.02[3][b]
n.65; S5.03[4][a][i] n.165; 5.03[5][e]
n.145
Soliman, Comm'r v. . . . . 19.03[3][d][i] n.181
Sorenson, Estate of v. Comm'r . . . 5.05[2][d]
n.88
Sowder v. United States . . . S5.06[7][b] n.174
Sowell v. Comm'r . . . . 4.13[4][a] n.37
Spalding, Estate of v. Comm'r . . . . . 5.06[3]
n.17
Sparling, Estate of v. Comm'r . . . . 3.05[1][c]
ns. 18, 19; 3.05[3][b] n.44; 4.08[7][c]
n.141
Spencer, Estate of v. Comm'r . . . .
. . . . 5.06[8][d][ii] n.319
Spicer, US v. . . . . 5.06[8][d][iv] n.400
Spiegel, Estate of v. Comm'r . . . . 4.09[3] ns.
18, 20; 4.09[4][c] n.33; 4.09[4][f] n.38;
4.09[7] ns. 55, 57

Spillar, Estate of v. Comm'r . . . 3.03[2] n.26;
3.06[4] n.31; 5.09[2] n.23
Spitzer v. Comm'r . . . . . 10.02[2][b][vi] n.71;
19.04[6][b] ns. 137, 138
Spohn, Estate of . . . . . 5.06[8][d][iii] n.386
Springer, Estate of v. Comm'r . . . 4.02[3][g]
n.132
Spruance v. Comm'r . . . . 4.15[1][b][ii] n.50;
10.06[1] n.7; 10.06[2][a] n.22;
10.06[2][b] n.24
Spruill, Estate of v. Comm'r . . . 4.02[2][a] ns.
27, 29; 4.02[3][b] ns. 64, 80; 4.05[2]
n.4; 4.08[4][c] n.46
Stack v. US . . . . . 5.03[3][d] n.76; S5.03[6][a]
n.277
Stapf, US v. . . . . 4.08[7][c] n.138;
S5.03[4][a][ii] ns. 167, 168; 5.03[5][a]
ns. 97, 98; 5.06[5][b][iii] & ns. 131,
132; 5.06[10] & n.455
Stark v. US . . . 9.04[3][b] n.62; 9.04[3][e] n.79
Starkey v. US . . . . 5.05[1][b] n.37
Starrett v. Comm'r . . . 5.06[8][b][iv] ns. 263,
264, 266
State St. Bank & Trust v. US . . . . 5.05[1][a]
n.11
State St. Trust Co. v. US . . . 4.08[6][a] n.76;
4.10[4][c] n.34
Steffke, Estate of v. Comm'r . . . 5.06[3] n.17
Stephens v. US . . . 5.06[3][b] n.48; 5.06[7][b]
n.183
Stephenson v. US . . . . 4.08[4][c] n.44
Stern v. US . . . . . 9.02[2] n.12; 10.02[4] n.135
Sternberger, Grissom v. . . . . . . 4.07[3][b] n.88
Sternberger, Estate of v. Comm'r . . . 5.03[3]
n.38; S5.03[3] n.80
Stewart, Estate of (2d Cir.) . . . S4.08[4][c] ns.
42, 46; S4.08[8] n.167
Stewart v. US . . . . 4.13[6][a] n.63
Stewart, US v. . . . . 4.05[6] n.72; 4.14[8] n.118
Stewart, Estate of v. Comm'r (TCM) . . . . . .
. . . . . S5.03[4][a] n.149; S5.03[4][a][i]
n.155; S5.03[4][b][i] n.191
Stick, Estate of v. Comm'r
Stick, Estate of v. Comm'r . . . . S5.03[3][c][i]
n.118
Stifel v. Comm'r . . . . 9.04[4] n.140
Stimson, Estate of . . . . 4.05[2] n.4
Stinson Estate v. US . . . . 9.04[1][b] n.28;
9.04[3][e] n.90; 10.01[2][b][i] n.21
Stockdick, Estate of v. Phinney . . . .
. . . . 5.06[8][b][iii] n.250
Stoddard, Estate of v. Comm'r . . . 4.02[3][f]
n.111
Stone v. US . . . . S4.02[4][e][i] n.197
Stone, Estate of v. Comm'r . . . . . S4.08[4][c]
n.49
Stoutz v. US . . . . 4.03[3][a] n.39
Stovall v. Comm'r . . . . . 4.04[7][b][ii] n.286;
4.04[7][g] n.356
Strangi v. Comm'r (5th Cir. 2005) . . . .
. . . S4.02[4][g] n.241; S4.08[4][c] n.49;
S4.08[5][c] n.64; S10.02[2][c][v] n.120

*[Text references are to paragraphs and notes (9"n.");
references to the supplement are preceded by "S."]*

Strangi v. Comm'r (5th Cir. 2002) . . . .
. . . . S10.02[2][c][v] n.120
Strangi, Estate of v. Comm'r (TC 2000) . . . .
. . . 4.02[2][a] n.34; 4.02[4][g] ns. 237,
238, 241; 10.01[2][b][ii] ns. 24, 25;
10.02[2][c][v] & n.118; 19.04[2] ns. 25,
26
Strangi v. Comm'r (TCM 2003) . . . .
. . . . S4.08[4][c] n.49; S4.08[5][c] n.64;
S10.02[2][c][v] n.120
Strauss, Estate of v. Comm'r . . . . 4.13[4][a]
n.37
Streck v. Comm'r . . . . 10.01[6] n.186
Street, Estate of v. Comm'r (5th Cir.) . . . . .
. . . . 4.14[8] n.115
Street, Estate of v. Comm'r (6th Cir.) . . . . .
. . . . 5.05[3][b][ii] n.115; 5.06[5][b][ii]
n.111
Street, Estate of v. Comm'r (TCM 1994) . . .
. . . 5.03[3][c] n.71; S5.03[3][c][i] n.110
Street, Estate of v. Comm'r (TC 1955) . . . . .
. . . . 5.06[7][b] n.173
Streeter, Estate of v. Comm'r . . . . 5.03[3][c]
n.63
Strickland, Estate of v. Comm'r . . . . 4.04[6]
n.237
Strock, Estate of v. US . . . . . . 5.05[2][b] n.68
Struthers v. Kelm . . . 4.08[5][c] & ns. 66, 73
Stuart v. Hassett . . . . 4.12[7][a] n.33
Stubblefield, Estate of v. Comm'r . . . .
. . . . 4.08[6][c] n.85
Stubbs v. US . . . . 5.06[7][b] n.164
Stuit v. Comm'r . . . . 4.10[4][f] n.50; 4.10[5]
n.64
Sturgis, Estate of v. Comm'r . . . S5.03[3][c][i]
n.118
Sturr, Mandel v. . . . . 4.05[7][b] n.82
Sugden, Lomb v. . . . . . . 19.04[6][a][ii] n.124
Suisman v. Eaton . . . . 5.06[6][a] n.145
Sulavich, Estate of v. Comm'r . . . 10.01[5][c]
n.167
Sullivan, Estate of v. Comm'r (9th Cir.) . . . .
. . . . 4.07[2][c] n.66; 4.08[8][a] n.178;
4.14[9][b] n.141
Sullivan, Estate of v. Comm'r (TCM) . . . . .
. . . . 4.08[4][b] n.38
Sunnen, Comm'r v. . . . . 9.05[1] n.6
Sutton v. Comm'r . . . . 4.15[1][a] n.16;
S5.03[4][a][i] n.163; 5.03[5][e] n.140
Suzuki, Estate of v. Comm'r . . . . . 5.06[3][a]
n.30
Swain v. US (7th Cir. 2000) . . . 4.10[6] n.65
Swain v. US (7th Cir. 1998) . . . 4.10[6] n.65
Swallen, Estate of v. Comm'r . . . . 5.06[5][a]
n.101
Swan, Estate of v. Comm'r . . . . . . 4.02[2][a]
n.19; 6.04[2] n.18
Swanson, Estate of v. US . . . . 4.10[4][a] n.25
Swartz v. US . . . . 4.12[7][a] n.40
Swayne, Estate of v. Comm'r . . . .
. . . . S5.03[3][c][ii] n.130
Swenson, Estate of v. Comm'r . . . . 5.06[3][h]
n.76

Swetland v. Comm'r . . . . . . 9.04[3][b] n.62
Swezey, Estate of v. Comm'r . . . .
. . . . 4.05[4] n.43
Swietlik, Estate of v. US . . . . 5.03[3][a] n.44;
S5.03[3][a] n.100
Symington v. Comm'r . . . . . . 19.04[2] n.33

T

Taft v. Comm'r . . . . S5.03[4][a][i] n.166;
5.03[5][e] n.145
Tait v. Safe Dep. & Trust Co. . . . . 4.06 ns. 6,
7
Talbott, Estate of, Comm'r v. . . . . 4.08[1][b]
n.13
Talcott v. US . . . . 5.06[10] n.449
Talge v. US . . . 10.01[1] n.10; 10.01[3][a] n.80;
10.01[5] n.146; 10.01[10][a] n.214
Talman v. US . . . . 5.06[8][d][ii] n.321
Tamulis, Estate of . . . .
. . . . S5.05[8][b] ns. 363, 367
Tarafa y Armas, Jose M., Estate of v.
Comm'r . . . . 6.05[2][a][ii] n.24
Tarver, Estate of v. Comm'r . . . . . 4.09[4][a]
n.25; 8.03[2] n.22
Tate & Lyle, Inc. v. Comm'r 7.06 n.17
Tatum, Estate of . . . . . S10.07[2][d] ns. 76, 82
Tax Analysts & Advocates v. Schultz . . . . . .
. . . . 9.02[2] n.13
Tax Analysts & Advocates v. Simon . . . . . .
. . . . 9.02[2] n.13
Taylor, Helvering v. . . . . 4.02[2][a] n.30
Taylor v. Morton, ... 7.06 ns. 6, 8
Taylor v. Rogan . . . . 4.02[2][a] n.9
Taylor, Estate of v. Comm'r . . . S5.03[4][c][i]
n.209; 5.03[5][b] n.120
Tebb, Estate of v. Comm'r . . . 5.06[3][a] n.29
Tehan, Estate of v. Comm'r . . . . S4.08[4][c]
n.45
Temple v. US . . . . S10.02[2][c][ii] n.86;
S10.02[2][c][iii] n.100; S10.02[2][c][iv]
n.109
Tenenbaum, Estate of v. Comm'r . . . .
. . . . 5.06[5][b][i] n.104
Tennant, Estate of v. Comm'r . . . .
. . . . 4.12[2] n.18
Terhune, Welch v. . . . . 4.10[2] n.7
Terre Haute First Nat'l Bank v. US . . . .
. . . . 5.05[2][b] ns. 68, 75, 76
Terriberry v. US . . . . 4.14[4][e] n.72; 4.14[9][a]
n.132
Texas Commerce Bank v. US . . . .
. . . . 4.13[3] n.17
Thacher, Estate of v. Comm'r . . . . 4.09[3] &
ns. 21–23
Thayn v. US . . . . 5.06[5][a] n.101
Thebaut, Comm'r v. . . . . 9.04[5][b] ns. 156,
157
Theis, Estate of v. Comm'r . . . . S5.03[5] n.257;
5.03[6] n.154

[Text references are to paragraphs and notes (9"n.");
references to the supplement are preceded by "S."]

Theophilos v. Comm'r . . . . 4.02[4][c][iii] ns. 182, 183

Third Nat'l Bank & Trust Co. v. White . . . . 4.12[4] n.29; 4.12[9] n.72

Thomas, White v. . . . . 5.06[3][a] n.34

Thompson v. Comm'r . . . . . 9.04[1][b] n.26; 10.01[2][b][i] n.16

Thompson, Smith v. . . . 5.06[8][d][iv] ns. 392, 394

Thompson, Estate of v. Comm'r (2d Cir. 2010) . . . . S4.02[6][a] n.263

Thompson, Estate of v. Comm'r (2d Cir. 2007) . . . S4.02[3][f] n.113; S4.02[6][a] n.263; S4.02[7][b] ns. 265–267

Thompson, Estate of v. Comm'r (2d Cir. 1974) 4.08[7] n.119; 4.08[9] ns. 200, 201

Thompson, Estate of v. Comm'r (4th Cir.) . . . . 4.04[3][b][viii] ns. 98, 99

Thompson, Estate of v. Comm'r (7th Cir.) . . . S5.03[4][b] n.174; 5.03[5][a] n.101

Thompson, Estate of v. Comm'r (TCM 2002) . . . . S4.08[4][c] n.49

Thompson, Estate of v. Comm'r (TCM 1998) . . . . 4.04[5][a][i] n.182

Thorp, Estate of v. Comm'r . . . . . 4.08[5][b] n.62

Thornhill v. Bloom . . . . S8.04[2] n.17

Thorrez v. Comm'r . . . . 10.03[3][b] n.44

Tilton v. Comm'r . . . . 9.04[11] n.245

Tilyou, Estate of v. Comm'r . . . . . 5.06[7][b] n.174

Timken, Estate of v. US . . . . S18.05[2][b][ii] n.39

Tingley, Estate of v. Comm'r . . . . 5.06[8][b][iv] n.267

Tips v. Bass . . . . 4.11[5] n.48

Titus, Estate of v. Comm'r . . . . . . 4.02[3][f] n.105

Todd v. Comm'r . . . . 10.01[4] n.139

Todd v. US . . . . 6.05[2][a][i] n.17

Todd, Estate of v. Comm'r 5.03[3][c] n.71; S5.03[3][c][i] n.118; 5.06[8][b][i] n.218

Tomerlin, Estate of v. Comm'r . . . . S4.14[6] n.103.16

Tomlinson, Barritt v. . . . . 4.13[4][a] n.37

Tomlinson, Cass v. . . . . . 5.06[8][b][iii] n.250

Tompkins, Erie RR v. . . . 4.05[2][b] & n.14; S5.03[1][a] n.14; 10.02[5] & n.152

Tompkins, Estate of v. Comm'r (TC 1977) . . . . 5.06[7][b] n.184

Tompkins, Estate of v. Comm'r (TC 1949) . . . . 4.02[2][a] n.17

Tooker v. Vreeland . . . . 5.06[8][d][iv] n.392

Touche v. Comm'r . . . . 10.01[5] n.153

Toulmin, Estate of v. US . . . . 5.05[2][e] n.94

Towle, Estate of v. Comm'r . . . 4.13[4][c][ii] n.41

Townsend v. US . . . . 4.10[4][a] n.25

Traders Nat'l Bank v. US . . . 5.06[7][b] n.180

Treganowan, Comm'r v. . . . . . . 4.14[2] n.13; 4.14[4][a] n.41; 4.14[6] n.100

Trenchard, Estate of v. Comm'r 4.02[3][b] n.61; 4.02[4][b][iii] n.159; 4.02[4][d][ii] n.193

Trompeter, Estate of v. Comm'r . . . S4.05[3] n.25

Trotter, Estate of v. Comm'r . . . . 4.08[4][c] n.45

True v. US . . . . 4.02[3][f] n.106

True, Estate of v. Comm'r (10th Cir.) . . . . S4.02[2][c] n.48; S4.02[4][b][iv] n.169; S19.04[3] n.44; S19.04[3][b][i] n.62; S19.04[3][b][ii] n.90; S19.04[3][c] n.97; S19.04[6][a][ii] n.128

True, Estate of v. Comm'r (TCM) . . . . 4.02[2][c] n.48; 4.02[4][b][iv] ns. 169, 170; 19.04[3] n.44; 19.04[3][b][i] n.62; 19.04[3][b][ii] n.90; 19.04[3][c] n.97

Trueman, Estate of v. US . . . . . 4.04[3][b][iv] n.64

Trunk, Estate of v. Comm'r . . . 5.05[3][b][i] n.109

Tubbs v. US . . . . 4.08[4][c] n.42

Tuck, Estate of . . . . S5.03[2][a] n.57

Tuck v. US 4.03[2][c] ns. 31, 32; 4.12[7][a] n.37; 4.12[8] n.61

Tufts, Comm'r v. . . . . 10.02[2][b][i] n.42

Tull, Estate of v. US . . . . . . 4.08[7][a] n.124

Tully, Estate of v. US . . . . 4.05[4] n.37; 4.08[5][c] n.64; 4.10[4] n.18

Tuohy, Estate of v. Comm'r . . . 4.05[6] n.73; 4.08[7][b] n.128

Turner v. Comm'r (3d Cir.) . . . . S4.08[4][c] n.49

Turner v. Comm'r (6th Cir.) . . . 10.02[6][d] n.181

Turner v. Comm'r (TC) . . . . . S4.02[7][b][ii] n.294

Turner v. McCuen . . . 6.05[2][a][ii] ns. 24, 25

Turner v. US . . . . S5.03[3][c][i] n.110

Turner, Estate of v. Comm'r (3d Cir.) . . . . S4.08[4][c] n.49

Turner, Estate of v. Comm'r (TCM) . . . . S4.08[4][c] n.49; S4.08[5][c] n.64; S9.04[3][f] ns. 96, 101

Twogood, Estate of v. Comm'r 4.11[7] ns. 64, 66, 67

Tyler v. US (US) . . . . 4.12[11] & n.99

Tyler v. US (10th Cir.) . . . . 5.06[8][b][iii] n.248

U

Uhl, Estate of v. Comm'r . . . 4.08[4][b] n.29; 4.08[4][c] n.53

Uihlein's Will, In re . . . . . . 5.06[3][h] n.79

Underwood v. US . . . . 4.05[2][b] n.17

Union Guardian Trust Co. . . . . . . 8.03[1] n.9

Union Planters Nat'l Bank v. US . . . . 4.08[4][c] n.44

*[Text references are to paragraphs and notes (9"n.");
references to the supplement are preceded by "S."]*

Union Trust Co. of Pittsburgh v. Driscoll . . .
. . . . 4.10[2] n.7
United Jewish Appeal, In re King v. . . . 8.06
ns. 2, 8
United States (US) . . . *See* specific party name
United States Trust Co., Helvering v. . . . . . .
. . . 10.02[5][b] n.160; 10.06[2][b] n.24
United States Trust Co. of NY v. Sears . . . .
. . . . 8.05[1] n.5; 8.05[3] n.9; 8.06 n.5;
8.08[2] n.12
Universal Oil Prods. Co. v. Campbell . . . . . .
. . . . 5.05[1][b] n.23
Untermyer v. Anderson 9.01 n.9
Upchurch v. Comm'r S8.04 n.4
Upjohn v. US . . . . 9.04[5][a] n.147
Urge, Estate of v. Comm'r . . . . . . 5.06[7][b]
n.164
US Bank, NA v. US . . . . 2.01[3] n.67; 9.02[3]
n.20

V

Vaccaro v. US . . . . . 4.10[4][a] n.22; 10.01[5]
n.152
Vak, Estate of v. Comm'r . . . 4.08[5][a] n.60;
10.01[5] n.146
Valentine, Estate of v. Comm'r . . . 4.09[4][a]
n.26; 4.09[6] n.48
Van, Estate of v. Comm'r . . . . . . S4.02[6][c]
n.265; S4.08[4][c] n.45
Van Beuren v. McLoughlin . . . . . 4.10[2] n.8;
4.10[7] n.72
Van Den Weymelenberg v. US . . . 9.04[3][e]
n.81; 9.04[5][b] n.162
Vander Weele, Comm'r v. . . . 10.01[9] n.205
Van Dever, Estate of v. Comm'r . . . . 4.05[3]
n.27
Van Dyke v. Kuhl . . . . . 4.02[3][b] ns. 74, 76
Vanek, Estate of v. US . . . . 4.05[8] n.95
Van Horne, Estate of v. Comm'r . . . .
. . . S5.03[4][c][i] n.210; 5.03[5][b] ns.
121, 125
Van Tine, Estate of . . . . 4.12[8] n.59
Van Zandt v. Comm'r . . . . . . 4.08[6][c] n.84
Vardell, Estate of v. Comm'r . . . . 4.08[7][c]
n.141; 4.15[2] n.76
Vatter, Estate of v. Comm'r . . . . . 5.03[3][c]
n.63
Vaughan, Clauson v. . . . . 4.13[10] n.128
Vease, Estate of, Comm'r v. . . . . 4.08[7][a] &
n.123
Vermilyea, Estate of v. Comm'r . . . .
. . . . 5.06[8][d][iv] n.400
Vinal, Hansen v. . . . . 5.06[8][a] n.205
Vinikoor v. Comm'r . . . 10.01[1] n.9; 10.01[4]
n.143
Vinson, Estate of v. Comm'r . . . 4.02[3][b] ns.
67, 78
Virginian Hotel Corp. v. Helvering . . . .
. . . . . 5.03[2][b] n.21; S5.03[2][b] n.61
Vissering v. Comm'r . . . . 4.13[4][a] n.37

Vreeland, Tooker v. . . . . 5.06[8][d][iv] n.392

W

Wachovia Bank & Trust Co. v. US . . . .
. . . . 5.06[5][b][i] n.106
Wadewitz, Estate of v. Comm'r . . . . . 4.05[8]
n.105; 4.11[3][b] n.23; 4.11[3][c] ns. 27,
30, 31
Waechter, US v. . . . . 4.05[6] n.72
Wahlfield v. US . . . . 4.13[4][a] n.37
Waite, US v. . . . . 4.06 ns. 2, 3
Waldrop v. US . . . . 5.05[3][b][i] n.105
Waldrup v. US . . . . 5.06[7][b] n.181
Waldstein, Estate of v. Comm'r . . . .
. . . . 6.05[2][a][i] n.16
Walker, Estate of v. Comm'r . . . . 4.02[3][g]
n.133
Wall v. Comm'r . . . . . . 10.02[2][c][ii] n.84;
10.02[2][c][iii] n.98
Wall, Estate of v. Comm'r (TC 1994) . . . . . .
. . . . 4.08[5][a] n.60
Wall, Estate of v. Comm'r (TC 1993) . . . . . .
. . . 4.08[5][a] n.60; 18.05[2][b][i] n.17
Walsh, Estate of v. Comm'r . . . 5.06[8][b][iv]
n.262
Walshire v. US . . . . S10.07[2] n.23
Walston, Comm'r v. . . . . 10.04[3][e] n.28
Walter, Louisville Trust Co. v. . . . . 8.04[3] ns.
18, 19
Walter v. US . . . 4.10[3] n.12; 4.10[4][e] n.48;
4.10[9] n.96
Walton v. Comm'r . . . . 13.03[3][b] n.69;
19.03[3][b][i] ns. 133, 134;
S19.03[3][b][i] ns. 133, 134
Wang v. Comm'r . . . . 10.03[1] n.14;
11.03[3][a] n.28
Want v. Comm'r . . . . 8.03[1] n.6
Ward v. Comm'r . . . . 10.01[3][e] n.106;
S10.01[3][e] n.106; 10.02[2][c][ii] n.89
Warda v. Comm'r . . . . 10.01[4] n.141
Ware, Estate of v. Comm'r . . . . . . 4.08[4][b]
n.33; 4.08[5] n.55
Warner, Bergh v. . . . . 10.02[5][a] n.156
Warner, Comm'r v. . . . . 10.01[6] n.185;
10.01[8] n.200
Warner, Estate of v. US . . . . . S5.06[8][d][iii]
n.328
Warren, Estate of v. Comm'r . . . . 5.05[2][b]
ns. 68, 75; 5.05[3][b][ii] n.115
Washington, Estate of Hemphill v. . . . .
. . . . S3.03[1] n.16
Waters, Estate of v. Comm'r . . . . 4.15[1][a]
n.18; 4.15[1][a][ii] n.30; S5.03[4][a][i]
n.158; 5.03[5][e] n.139
Watson v. Comm'r (US) . . . . . . 4.04[3][b][vi]
n.81
Watson v. Comm'r (TCM) . . . 4.14[4][c] n.53
Watson v. McGinnes S5.03[4][b][ii] n.199;
5.03[8] n.164

[Text references are to paragraphs and notes (9"n.");
references to the supplement are preceded by "S."]

Watson, Estate of v. Comm'r   4.05[4] n.42;
5.06[7][b] n.170
Watson, Estate of, Comm'r v.   4.15[1][b][i]
n.40
Watts, Estate of v. Comm'r . . . 19.05[1] n.9;
19.05[3][b] n.56
Webb, Estate of v. Comm'r . . . . . 4.02[3][f]
n.111
Webster, Brown v. . . . . . 5.06[8][d][iv] n.392
Webster v. Comm'r . . . . 4.14[3][a] n.27
Webster, Estate of v. Comm'r . . . . . . 4.10[8]
n.79; 5.03[3][c] n.71; S5.03[3][c][i] ns.
118, 121
Wegman, Estate of v. Comm'r . . . 5.06[3][a]
n.30
Weil, Estate of v. Comm'r   4.05[7][b] n.81;
19.04[1][b] n.3
Weinberg v. Safe Deposit & Trust Co. of
Baltimore . . . . 8.05[4] n.13
Weinberg, Estate of v. Comm'r . . . .
. . . 4.02[2][b][iv] ns. 46, 47; 4.02[4][g]
n.234
Weisburn, US v. . . . . 8.03[1] n.10
Welch, Central Trust of Cincinnati v. . . . . .
. . . . . 5.03[4][a] n.91; S5.03[6][c][iii]
n.302
Welch, Hassett v. . . . . . . 4.08[9] ns. 196, 198
Welch v. Helvering . . . . S5.03[3][c][i] n.110
Welch v. Terhune . . . . 4.10[2] n.7
Welch v. US . . . . S2.02[1] n.14
Weller v. Comm'r . . . . 9.04[5][b] n.159
Welliver, Estate of v. Comm'r . . . . 4.03[3][b]
ns. 48, 52; 4.11[4][a] n.38
Wells, Estate of v. Comm'r . . . . . . 4.08[4][c]
n.53; 10.01[9] n.204
Wells, Estate of v. US . . 5.06[8][d][ii] n.325
Wells Fargo Bank v. US (9th Cir.) . . . .
. . . . 5.05[8][b] n.363
Wells Fargo Bank v. US (10th Cir.) . . . .
. . . . S11.03[4][c] n.58
Wells Fargo Bank v. US (ND Cal.) . . . .
. . . . 5.05[2][c] n.83
Wells Fargo Bank, US v. (US) . . . .
. . . . 4.05[3] n.30
Wells Fargo Bank, US v. (9th Cir.) . . . .
. . . . 5.03[3][a] n.44; S5.03[3][a] n.100
Wemyss, Comm'r v. . . . . . 4.15[2] ns. 64, 65;
S5.03[4][a][i] n.159; 5.03[5][e] n.143;
10.02[3] n.131; 10.02[4] n.133;
10.02[5][c] n.163; 10.04[4][c] n.53
Werbe's Estate v. US . . . . . . 5.06[7][b] n.175
Westover, Malloch v. . . . . . . 4.02[3][g] n.134
Whalen v. US . . . . 4.04[3][b][ix] n.103
Wheeler v. US . . . . 4.02[4][c][iii] n.180;
4.08[1][a] ns. 9, 10; 4.08[7][c] ns. 139,
143; 19.03[4][e][i] n.367; S19.03[4][e][i]
n.367
Whelan v. US . . . . 4.13[4][a] n.33
Wheless, Estate of v. Comm'r . . . . 5.03[3][c]
n.68; S5.03[3][c][i] n.110
Whipple, Estate of v. US . . . . . 8.04[3] n.20
White v. Comm'r . . . . 5.04[2] n.14

White v. Poor . . . 4.10[2] n.8; 4.10[4][a] n.21;
4.10[7] & n.72; 4.14[4][e] n.68
White, Third Nat'l Bank & Trust Co. v. . . . .
. . . . 4.12[4] n.29; 4.12[9] n.72
White v. Thomas . . . . 5.06[3][a] n.34
White v. US . . . . 4.13[6][a] n.66
White, US v. . . . . . . 5.03[1] n.8; S5.03[1] n.9;
S5.03[3] n.80
Whitt, Estate of v. Comm'r . . . . . 4.02[3][b]
n.70; 4.08[4][c] n.42; 5.03[3][a] n.56;
S5.03[3][a] n.94; 10.01[4] n.141
Wiedemann v. Comm'r . . . 4.15[1][b][i] n.42
Wien, Estate of v. Comm'r . . . . 4.05[6] n.70
Wiener, Fernandez v. . . . . 4.05[5][a] n.47
Wier, Estate of v. Comm'r . . . . 4.08[6][a] n.77
Wildenthal, Estate of v. Comm'r . . . . 4.14[8]
n.116; S5.03[4][c][i] n.208; S5.03[5]
n.250; 5.03[5][b] n.124; 5.03[6] n.149
Wilder v. Comm'r . . . . 5.03[5][b] n.125
Wilder, Estate of, Comm'r v. . . . .
. . . . 4.11[7] n.63
Wilkes v. US . . . . 5.08[4][a] n.172
Willcuts, Brooks v. . . . . 4.02[3][f] n.106
Williams v. McGowan . . . . . 4.05[7][a] n.78
Williams v. US (WD Tex.) . . . .
. . . . 5.03[5][b] n.128
Williams v. US (Ct. Cl.) . . . . 4.05[5][b] n.52;
9.04[5][a] n.147
Williams, Estate of v. Comm'r (TC 1994) . . .
. . . . 5.06[5][b][i] n.104
Williams, Estate of v. Comm'r (TC 1974) . . .
. . . . 4.05[5][b] n.52
Williams, Estate of v. Comm'r (TCM 2009)
. . . . S5.05[2][b] n.68
Williams, Estate of v. Comm'r (TCM 1998)
. . . . 4.02[4][a] n.147; 4.02[4][e][i] ns.
199, 200
Williamson v. Comm'r . . . 4.04[7][b][i] n.270;
4.04[7][b][ii] n.286
Willis, Estate of v. Comm'r . . . . . 4.14[7][a]
n.107
Wilmington Trust Co. v. US . . . . . 4.05[5][a]
n.47
Wilmot, Estate of v. Comm'r . . . . . . 4.14[8]
n.124
Wilson v. Comm'r . . . 4.05[4] n.43; 4.07[3][b]
n.90; 4.08[1][b] n.13
Wilson v. Bowers . . . . . 19.04[6][a][ii] ns. 131,
132
Wilson v. Comm'r . . . . 4.12[2] n.17
Wilson v. Kraemer . . . . 10.04[3][d] n.21
Wilson v. US . . . . S5.03[6][c][ii] n.296
Wilson, Estate of . . . . 4.02[3][b] n.68
Wilson, Estate of v. Comm'r (3d Cir.) . . . . .
. . . . . . 4.10[4][d] n.44; 4.10[5] n.62
Wilson, Estate of v. Comm'r (TCM 1998)
. . . . . . S5.03[4][a][i] n.153; 5.03[5][e]
n.134
Wilson, Estate of v. Comm'r (TCM 1992)
. . . . 5.06[8][b][iv] n.260
Wilson, Estate of v. Comm'r (TC 1943) . . . .
. . . . 8.02 n.11

Wineman, Estate of v. Comm'r . . . . . 4.04[6]
    n.239; 4.08[4][c] n.48
Winer v. US . . . . 3.06[4] n.26
Winkle v. US (SD Ohio) . . . . . . 5.06[8][b][iv]
    n.262
Winkle v. US (WD Pa.) . . . . . 4.05[7][b] n.82
Winkler, Estate of v. Comm'r (TCM 1997)
    . . . . 10.01[3] n.77
Winkler, Estate of v. Comm'r (TCM 1989)
    . . . . 4.02[4][b][iv] n.166
Wisconsin, Schlesinger v. 9.01 n.7
Wisely v. US . . . . 5.06[8][b][i] n.218
Wiseman, Estate of Darby v. . . . . . 5.03[3][d]
    n.81; S5.03[6][a] n.276
Wiseman, King v. . . . . 5.06[3][g] n.72
Wiseman, Murrah v. . . . . 4.05[5][a] n.47
Wishon v. Anglim . . . . 4.02[3][f] n.107
Witkowski v. US . . . . 4.13[4][c][ii] n.43
Wolder v. Comm'r . . . . 5.03[3][a] n.50;
    S5.03[3][a] n.90; S5.03[4][a] n.152;
    5.03[5][b] ns. 126, 127
Wolfe, Estate of v. Comm'r . . . . . 4.02[3][b]
    n.77
Woll, Estate of v. Comm'r . . . 5.03[3][a] n.46
Woll, Estate of v. US . . . . 5.06[5][a] n.99
Wondsel v. Comm'r . . . . 5.06[3] n.17
Wood, Estate of v. Comm'r . . . .
    . . . . 3.05[3][c] n.51
Wooley v. US . . . 9.04[3] n.46; 9.04[3][e] n.93
Woody, Estate of v. Comm'r . . . S5.03[4][a][i]
    n.159; 5.03[5][e] n.143
Wooster, Estate of v. Comm'r . . . . 4.13[6][a]
    n.68
Worcester County Trust Co. v. Comm'r . . . .
    . . . . 19.04[6][a][ii] ns. 124, 126
Worthen v. US . . . . . 4.02[2][a] n.10; 4.05[4]
    n.38
Wragg, Comm'r v. . . . . . S5.03[4][a][i] n.159;
    S5.03[4][c][i] n.207; S5.03[5] n.258;

5.03[5][a] n.118; 5.03[5][e] n.143;
    5.03[6] n.155
Wright, Estate of v. Comm'r . . . . 4.02[2][a]
    n.35; 4.02[4][b][iii] n.160; 4.02[4][e][ii]
    ns. 207, 208; 4.02[4][e][iii] n.212
Wurts, Estate of v. Comm'r . . . . . 4.10[4][c]
    n.38
Wycoff, Estate of v. Comm'r . . . 5.06[5][a]
    n.95
Wyly, Estate of v. Comm'r . . . . . . 4.08[4][b]
    n.29; 4.08[4][c] n.51
Wynekoop, Estate of v. Comm'r   5.06[8][c]
    ns. 285, 286

Y

Yawkey, Estate of v. Comm'r . . . . . . 4.08[2]
    n.20; 4.10[8] n.79
YMCA v. Davis . . . . 4.05[5][c] n.60
Young v. US . . . . S5.03[4][a][i] n.154;
    5.03[5][e] n.135
Young, Estate of v. Comm'r . . . . 4.02[4][e][i]
    n.198

Z

Zabel v. US . . . . . 5.05[4][b] n.137; 5.05[8][b]
    n.367
Zacks, US v. . . . . 4.04[7][b][ii] n.288
Zaiger, Estate of v. Comm'r . . . . . 4.07[3][b]
    n.90
Zanuck v. Comm'r . . . . 4.02[3][f] n.105
Zimmerman v. Comm'r . . . . 5.08[4][a] n.172
Zlotowski, Estate of . . . . S2.02[1] n.14

Cumulative Index

[References are to paragraphs; references to the supplement are preceded by "S".]

A

Acceptance of property interest, disclaimers following . . . . 10.07[2][c]

Actuarial principles, valuation of reversionary interests . . . . 4.09[4][d]

Actuarial valuation, gift tax . . . . . 10.02[2][f]

Additions to property, joint interests
. . . . 4.12[7][b]

Administration expenses
. charitable deductions . . . . . . 5.05[3][c][ii]
. deductions from estate tax . . . . . . 1.02[3][b]

Agreements

   See also Buy-sell agreements
. annuities . . . . 4.11[3][a]
. property settlements not in divorce decree, written agreement requirement . . 10.06[2]
. special-use valuation, real property . . 4.04[6], S4.04[6]
. value determined by, for gross estate inclusion . . . . 4.02[3][g]

Aircraft, treatment under tax conventions
. . . . 7.03[1][b]

Aliens

   See Noncitizen spouses; Nonresident aliens; Resident aliens

Allocations
. estate freezes, between transferred interests and remaining subordinate equity interests
. . . . 19.02[4][d][iii]
. GST exemption

   See Generation-skipping transfer (GST) exemption--allocation of

Alternate valuation date, gross estate inclusion 4.03
. actual estate vs. artificial estate . . . . 4.03[2]
. bond interest . . . . 4.03[2][a]

Alternate valuation date, gross estate inclusion — Cont'd
. cattle . . . . 4.03[2][d]
. changes not due to market conditions
. . . . S4.03[3][c]
. charitable deduction, effect on . . . 4.03[4][b]
. date-of-death rule for valuation . . . . . 4.03[1], 4.14[9][b]
. deductions, effect on . . . . 4.03[4]
. . general impact . . . . 4.03[4][a]
. disposition of property 4.03[3][a], S4.03[3][a]
. dividends, stock . . . . 4.03[2][c]
. election of . . . . 4.03[1], S4.03[1]
. . deductions, effect on . . . . 4.03[4]
. . extension of time for . . . . S4.03[1]
. exceptions to usual alternate date . . . 4.03[3]
. generally . . . . 4.03[1], S4.03[1]
. history . . . . 4.03[1]
. identification of gross estate . . . . . . 4.03[2]
. insurance policy on life of another 4.03[2][d]
. marital deduction, effect on . . . . . 4.03[4][b]
. miscellaneous property . . . . 4.03[2][d]
. oil and gas interests . . . . 4.03[2][d]
. rent . . . . 4.03[2][a]
. Section 2032 provisions . . . . 4.03[1]
. stock, corporate . . . . 4.03[2][b]
. time lapse, effect on value . . . . . . 4.03[3][b]

Annual gift tax exclusion . . 9.04[1], S9.04[1]
. amount of gift, effect on . . . . . . 3.04[1][b]
. charitable organizations, gifts to . . 9.04[1][b]
. corporate gifts . . . . 9.04[1][b]
. credit against estate tax, gift tax as 3.04[2][b]
. Crummey powers with regard to future interests, effect . . . . 9.04[3][f]
. educational expenses . . . . . 1.03[3], 9.04[6], S9.04[6]

Annual gift tax exclusion—Cont'd
. enjoyment of gift
. . brief postponement of, effect . . . 9.04[3][d]
. . right to, effect . . . . 9.04[3][e]
. future interests disqualified for . . . . . 9.04[2]
. generally . . 1.03[3], 9.04[1], S9.04[1], 11.01
. grantor retained income trusts . . 19.03[2][c]
. identification of donees . . . . 9.04[1][b]
. joint donees . . . . 9.04[1][b]
. medical expenses . . . . 1.03[3], 9.04[6]
. other entities, gifts to . . . . 9.04[1][b],
                                              S9.04[1][b][ii]
. prior years . . . . 9.05[3]
. purpose of . . . . 9.04[1][a]
. Qualified State Tuition Programs . . S9.04[6]
. straw man, use of . . . . 9.04[1][b]
. tenancy by the entirety, gifts to . . 9.04[1][b]
. trust, gifts in . . . . 9.04[1][b], 9.04[3][a]
. tuition payments . . 1.03[3], 9.04[6], S9.04[6]
Annuities 4.11
. agreement or contract, requirement 4.11[3][a]
. amount to be included . . . . 4.11[4]
. beneficiary's interest, nature of . . . 4.11[3][d]
. contracts
. . pre-1931 contracts . . . . 4.11[2][b]
. . requirement of contract . . . . 4.11[3][a]
. death benefit arrangements as . . . . . . 4.14[2]
. decedent's interest, nature of . . . . 4.11[3][c]
. estate tax . . . . 1.02[2][b][vi], 4.11[7]
. exempt annuities . . . . 4.11[6]
. generally . . . . 1.02[2][b][vi]
. general rule . . . . 4.11[1]
. gifts of . . . . 10.01[3][g]
. gross estate . . . . 1.02[2][b][vi], 4.05[8], 4.11
. . exceptions . . . . 4.11[2]
. joint-and-survivor . . . . 1.02[2][b][vi], 4.11[7],
                                              11.03[4][c][ii]
. legislative history . . . . 4.11[7]
. life insurance policies . . . . 4.11[2][a]
. nature of interest
. . beneficiary's interest . . . . 4.11[3][d]
. . decedent's interest . . . . 4.11[3][c]
. percentage restriction . . . . 4.11[4][b]
. period for which interest retained . 4.11[3][b]
. pre-1931 contracts . . . . 4.11[2][b]
. private annuities . . . . 4.11[5]
. qualifications . . . . 4.11[3]
. qualified domestic trusts, annuity passing to
   . . . . 5.07[2][c]
. Section 2039 rules 4.11
. . background of Section 2039 . . . . . 4.11[7]
. self-and-survivor 1.02[2][b][vi], 4.11, 4.11[7]

Annuities—Cont'd
. single-life annuity 4.11
. tax conventions, situs rules . . . . . 7.02[2][c]
. types 4.11
. valuation . . . . 4.11[4][a]
Apportionment
. state statutes . . . . 1.02[6]
Armed forces
. combat zone
. . death in, estate tax provisions . . 8.01[2][c]
. . gift tax returns . . . . 9.04[9]
. estate tax provisions 8.01
. . active service requirement . . . . . 8.01[2][a]
. . astronauts . . . . S8.01[1][c]
. . combat zone, death in . . . . 8.01[2][c]
. . generally 8.01
. . member of armed forces, requirement
   . . . . 8.01[2][b]
. . prerequisites for relief . . . . 8.01[2]
. . relief provision, effect of . . . . 8.01[1]
. . service-connected death . . . . . . 8.01[2][d]
. . tax liability . . . . 8.01[1]
. gift tax returns . . . . 9.04[9]
Art works
. charitable deductions . . . . 5.05[8][b]
. gift tax and loans of . . . . 9.04[8]
. gross estate inclusion . . . . 4.02[3][a]
. loans of . . . . 9.04[8]
. nonresident aliens . . . . 6.05[5]
. split interests . . . . 5.05[8][b]
. theft losses . . . . 5.04[3]
. valuation . . . . 4.02[3][a]
Assessment of additional gift tax, limitations
   . . . . 9.04[10], S9.04[10]
Assignment
. generation-skipping transfer tax, assignment
   of generation . . . . 1.04[2], 17.01
. gift tax, assignment of income . . 10.01[10][a]
. group term life insurance, assignment of policy . . . . 4.14[6]
Associations as charitable organizations
   . . . . 5.05[2], 11.01[1]
Astronauts
. armed forces, estate tax provisions
   . . . . S8.01[1][c]
Attorney fees, estate taxation . . . S5.03[3][a]
Attribution rules, estate freezes . 19.02[2][d]
. corporate attribution . . . . 19.02[2][d][i]
. estate attribution . . . . 19.02[2][d][iii]
. generally . . . . . . 19.02[2][a][i], 19.02[2][d]
. indirect transfers . . . . 19.02[2][a][i]
. multiple attribution . . . . 19.02[2][d][iv]

Attribution rules, estate freezes — Cont'd
. partnership attribution . . . . . . 19.02[2][d][ii]
. special valuation rules under Section 2701
  . . . . 19.02[2][d]
. trust attribution . . . . 19.02[2][d][iii]
Austrian convention . . . . 7.03[5]

B

Banks and banking
. checks, gifts of . . . . 10.01[3][h]
. cooperatives (EWOCs) . . . . 5.08[1]
. deposits
. . nonresident aliens   6.04[1], 6.04[3], 6.05[2],
                         6.05[3], 7.02[2][c]
. . tax conventions, situs rules . . . . 7.02[2][c]
. foreign branches of U.S. banks
. . nonresident aliens' deposits in . . . . 6.05[3],
                                        7.02[2][c]
. . tax conventions, situs rules . . . . 7.02[2][c]
. gross estate inclusion of decedent's bank accounts . . . . 4.05[3]
. joint accounts . . . . 1.02[2][b][vii]
. . disclaimers . . . . 10.07[2][b]
. . gross estate . . . . 4.05[3], 4.12[2]
. . revocable transfers . . . . 10.01[5][c]
. nonresident aliens, bank deposits of . 6.04[3],
                                        6.05[2]
. . banking business . . . . 6.05[2][b]
. . contingent interest . . . . 6.05[2][a]
. . domestic institutions . . . . 6.05[2]
. . effectively connected income . 6.05[2][c][ii]
. . foreign branches of U.S. banks . . . 6.05[3]
. . non-U.S.-source income . . . . . . 6.05[2][c]
. . qualifying deposits . . . . 6.05[2][a]
. . tax conventions, situs rules . . . . 7.02[2][c]
. . trade or business, non-U.S.-source income
  . . . . 6.05[2][c][i]
. . use of U.S. banks and trust companies
  . . . . 6.04[1]

Basis
. conservation easement, basis of excluded land
  subject to . . . . S4.02[4][f][iii]
. family-owned business deduction, basis of
  business interest qualifying for
  . . . . S5.08A[6][c][i]
. generation-skipping transfer tax, basis adjustment . . . . 17.04[1]
. . generally . . . . 17.04[1][a]
. . general rule . . . . 17.04[1][b]
. . testamentary direct skips . . . . . 17.04[1][c]
. limited liability companies, step-up in basis
  for assets of . . . . 4.05[7][c]
. special-use valuation of real property, basis
  adjustment for additional tax . . . 4.04[14]

Below-market interest rate loans
. demand loans . . . . 10.01[2][f]
. as indirect gifts . . . . 10.01[2][f]
. term loans . . . . 10.01[2][f]
. types . . . . 10.01[2][f]
Beneficiaries
. annuities, nature of beneficiary's interest
  . . . . 4.11[3][d]
. change of gift beneficiaries, power to make
  . . . . 10.01[6]
. decedent, beneficial interest of
. . gross estate inclusion . . . . 4.05[2]
. . transfers with retained life estate . . 4.08[4]
. generation-skipping transfer tax, classes of
  beneficiaries . . . . 17.01[2]
. . ancestral chain . . . . 17.01[2][a][i],
                                    S17.01[2][a][i]
. . corporations, partnerships, and estates as
  beneficiaries . . . . 17.01[2][c][i]
. . nonindividual beneficiaries . . . 17.01[2][c]
. . nontrust entities . . . . 17.01[2][c][i]
. . overlapping related beneficiaries
  . . . . 17.01[2][a][ii]
. . related beneficiaries . . . . 17.01[2][a]
. . trust entities . . . . 17.01[2][c][ii]
. . unrelated beneficiaries . . . . . 17.01[2][b]
. gifts to, power to change beneficiaries
  . . . . 10.01[6]
. life insurance proceeds . . . . 4.14[4]
. . amount of contribution to tax burden,
  formula for . . . . 8.05[1]
. . contrary will provision regarding estate tax
  liability . . . . 8.05[3]
. . estate tax liability of 8.05
. . marital deduction and estate tax liability,
  special rule . . . . 8.05[2]
. . state law, effect on estate tax liability of
  beneficiary . . . . 8.05[4]
Bequests
. charitable
. . disclaimers . . . . 5.05[3][d]
. . mixed private and charitable . . . . . 5.05[7]
. . nonresident aliens . . . . 6.06[2]
. . outright bequests, charitable deductions
  . . . . 5.05[3][a]
. . partial interests . . . . 5.05[8]
. . temporary interests bequeathed to charity
  . . . . 5.05[9]
. mixed private and charitable . . . . . . 5.05[7]
. patent bequeathed to surviving spouse
  . . . . 5.06[7][c]
. pecuniary bequest to surviving spouse, marital
  deduction . . . . 5.06[6][a]

Bequests —Cont'd
. to surviving spouse, deductions 5.06
   See also Marital deduction
Bona fide sales within three years of death
. . . . S4.07[2][c][i]
Bonds
. flower bonds, valuation . . . . 4.02[3][e]
. gross estate inclusion, valuation . . 4.02[3][e],
                                4.05[3]
. . interest
. . . alternative valuation date . . . . 4.03[2][a]
. . nonresident aliens . . . . 6.05[6]
. interest, valuation for gross estate inclusion
. . alternative valuation date . . . . . 4.03[2][a]
. jointly owned . . . . 4.12[2]
. nonresident aliens . . . . 6.05[6]
. Series E bonds, valuation . . . . . . 4.02[3][e]
. tax conventions, situs rules . . . . . 7.02[2][c]
Bonuses due decedent at death, gross estate
inclusion . . . . 4.05[4]
Burden of proof, joint interests . . . . 4.12[8],
                              S4.12[8]
Business interests
. gross estate inclusion . . . . 4.02[3][f], 4.05[7]
. tax convention, situs rules . . . . . . 7.02[2][c],
                          7.03[1][b]
. . permanent establishment, defined 7.03[1][b]
. valuation . . . . 4.02[3][f]
Buy-sell agreements
. background . . . . 19.04[1][b]
. bona fide business arrangement . 19.04[3][a]
. deemed satisfaction of special valuation rules
. . . . 19.04[4]
. effective dates . . . . 19.04[7]
. estate freezes, special valuation rules . . 19.04
. estate tax valuation . . . . 19.04[6][a]
. . lifetime dispositions, restrictions on
. . . . 19.04[6][a][i]
. . method prescribed by agreement
. . . . 19.04[6][a][iii]
. . obligation of estate to sell . . 19.04[6][a][ii]
. exception from Section 2703, establishing
   valuation . . . . 19.04[6]
. full and adequate consideration, disallowed
   device to transfer property to family for
   less than . . . . 19.04[3][b]
. . full and adequate consideration
. . . . 19.04[3][b][ii]
. . not family device . . . . 19.04[3][b][i]
. generally . . . . 19.04[1][a], 19.04[2]
. generation-skipping transfer tax valuation
. . . . 19.04[6][c]
. gift tax valuation . . . . 19.04[6][b]
. gross estate valuation . . . . 4.02[3][g]

Buy-sell agreements —Cont'd
. life insurance proceeds . . . . 4.14[4][d]
. multiple rights and restrictions . . . . 19.04[5]
. requirements . . . . 19.04[3]
. similar arrangement test . . . . . . 19.04[3][c]
. substantial modification . . . . 19.04[7]
. valuation rules, special 19.04

                       C

Call rights . . . . 19.02[2][b][ii]
Canadian convention . . . . 7.03[8]
Capital transfers in estate freezes
. capital structure transactions . . 19.02[2][a][i]
. contributions to capital . . . . . . 19.02[2][a][i],
                        19.02[4][e]
Casualty losses . . . . 5.04[2]
. deductions . . . . 5.04[2]
. definition of casualty . . . . 5.04[2]
. ejusdem generiso canon of construction (Lord
   Tenderden's rule) . . . . 5.04[2]
. income tax, relation to . . . . 5.04[4]
. securities, loss in value of . . . . 5.04[2]
Cattle, gross estate inclusion, alternate valua-
tion date . . . . 4.03[2][d]
Chapter 13 tax
   See Generation-skipping transfer tax--Chapter
   13 tax
Chapter 14 rules 19.01–19.05
   See also Estate freezes; Special valuation
   rules to combat estate freeze abuses
   (Chapter 14 rules)
. buy-sell agreements 19.04
. definitions . . . . 19.01[2]
. estate freeze abuses . . . . 19.01[1]
. . classic estate freezes 19.02
. . valuation rules to combat . . . 19.01–19.05
. estate maintenance approach of . . . 19.01[3]
. exceptions within . . . . 19.01[4]
. generally . . . . 10.01, 19.01[1]
. lapsing rights and restrictions 19.05
. trusts, transfers of interests in 19.03
. valuation methodology under . . . . . 19.01[3]
. valuation rules to combat estate freeze abuses
. . . . 19.01–19.05
Charitable bequests
   See Bequests
Charitable deductions 5.05
. abuses by exempt organizations . . . . 5.05[4],
                        5.05[5]
. administration expenses . . . . . . 5.05[3][c][ii]
. art works . . . . 5.05[8][b]

Charitable deductions — Cont'd

. associations qualifying as charitable . 5.05[2], 11.01[1]

. charitable lead trusts . . . . 5.05[9]

. . curative amendments . . . . 5.05[10][a]

. charitable organizations, transfers to . 5.05[2], S5.05[2], 11.01[1]

. charitable remainder annuity trust . 5.05[8][c], S5.05[8][c]

. . curative amendments permitted 5.05[10][a]

. charitable remainder unitrust . . . . 5.05[8][d], S5.05[8][d]

. . curative amendments permitted 5.05[10][a]

. charity, defined . . . . 5.05[2]

. classes of recipients . . . . 5.05[1]

. conservation contributions . . . . . . 5.05[8][b]

. corporations qualifying as charitable . 5.05[2], 11.01[1]

. credit against estate tax . 3.04[2][b], 3.05[4][a]

. curative amendments permitted . . . . 5.05[10]

. . generally . . . . 5.05[10][a]

. . qualified reformation . . . . . . 5.05[10][c]

. . reformable and qualified interests . . . . 5.05[10][b] – 5.05[10][d]

. . split interests . . . . 5.05[10][a]

. date-of-death rule, valuation . . . . . 5.05[3][b]

. death taxes . . . . 5.05[3][c][i]

. disclaimers . . . . 5.05[3][d]

. double deductions . . . . 5.05[3][c][ii]

. easements in real property, irrevocable transfers of . . . . 11.02[4]

. educational organizations . . . 5.05[2], 11.01[1]

. ESOPs, transfers to . . . . S5.05[2]

. estate tax . . . . 1.02[3][c]

. expenses of estate . . . . 5.05[3][c]

. . administration expenses . . . . 5.05[3][c][ii]

. . death taxes . . . . 5.05[3][c][i]

. . Section 2053 rules . . . . 5.05[e][c][ii]

. farms, remainders in . . . . 5.05[8][a]

. fraternal organizations . . . . . 5.05[2], 11.01[1]

. generally 5.05

. generation-skipping transfer tax, inclusion ratio . . . . 16.02[3][b][ii]

. gift tax . . . . 1.03[5][a], 11.02, S11.02

. . charitable organizations, gifts to . 9.04[1][b]

. . credit against estate tax, gift tax as . . . . 3.04[2][b]

. . returns S11.02

. gross estate, alternate valuation date . . . . 4.03[4][b]

. lifetime transfers . . . . 5.05[6]

. literary organizations . . . . . 5.05[2], 11.01[1]

. mixed private and charitable gifts and bequests . . . . 5.05[7]

Charitable deductions — Cont'd

. *mixed private — Cont'd*

. . future interests . . . . 11.02[2]

. . present interests . . . . 11.02[3]

. nonresident aliens . . . . 6.06[2]

. organizations qualified . . . . 5.05[2], 11.01[1]

. outright bequests . . . . 5.05[3][a]

. political entities, transfers to 5.05[2], 11.01[1]

. pooled income funds . . . . 5.05[8][e]

. power of decedent, property under 5.05[3][e]

. prior transfers, estate tax credit for tax on . . . . 3.05[4][a]

. private foundations, restrictions on . . 5.05[5]

. qualifications . . . . 5.05[1], 5.05[4]

. qualified recipients . . . . . . 5.05[1], 11.02[1]

. qualified reformation . . . . 5.05[10][c]

. reformable and qualified interests . . . . 5.05[10][b] – 5.05[10][d]

. religious organizations, transfers to . . 5.05[2], 11.01[1]

. remainders . . . . . . 5.05[8], 19.03[3][a][iii]

. residences, remainders in . . . . . . 5.05[8][a]

. routine deductions . . . . 5.05[3]

. . disclaimers . . . . 5.05[3][d]

. . expenses of estate . . . . 5.05[3][c]

. . outright bequests . . . . 5.05[3][a]

. . power of decedent, property under . . . . 5.05[3][e]

. . valuation . . . . 5.05[3][b]

. scientific organizations . . . . 5.05[2], 11.01[1]

. Section 2053 items . . . . 5.05[3][c][ii]

. Section 2055(a) organizations . . . . . . 5.05[2], S5.05[2]

. split interests . . . . 5.05[8]

. . art works . . . . 5.05[8][b]

. . charitable remainder annuity trust . . . . 5.05[8][c], S5.05[8][c]

. . charitable remainder unitrust . . . 5.05[8][d], S5.05[8][d]

. . conservation contributions . . . . . 5.05[8][b]

. . curative amendments permitted 5.05[10][a]

. . exceptions to rules . . . 5.05[8][a], 5.05[8][b]

. . farms, remainders in . . . . 5.05[8][a]

. . generally . . . . 5.05[8]

. . pooled income funds . . . . 5.05[8][e]

. . residential property, remainders in . . . . 5.05[8][a]

. . undivided portion of property, exceptions to . . . . 5.05[7][b], S5.05[7][b]

. tainted organizations . 5.05[1][c], S5.05[1][c], 5.05[5]

. taxable estate 5.05

. tax conventions . . . . 7.03[1][c]

. tax preferences . . . . 5.05[1]

Charitable deductions—Cont'd
. temporary interests bequeathed to charity
  . . . . 5.05[9]
. trusts . . . . 5.05[2]
. valuation . . . . . . 5.05[3][b], 19.03[3][a][iii]
. veterans' organizations . . . . 5.05[2], 11.01[1]
Charitable lead annuity trusts, GST tax inclusion ratio . . . . . . 16.02[4][f], 16.02[6]
Charitable lead trusts
. charitable deductions   5.05[9], 19.03[3][a][iii]
. curative amendments permitted . . 5.05[10][a]
. defined . . . . 5.05[9]
Charitable organizations
. abuses by, qualifications addressing . . 5.05[4],
  5.05[5]
. defined . . . . 5.05[2], 11.01[1]
. gifts to . . . . 9.04[1][b], 11.01[1]
. qualification as . . . . 5.05[2], 11.01[1]
. tainted . . . . 5.05[5]
. transfers to, deductibility . . . . 5.05, 11.01[1]
  See also Charitable deductions
. types . . . . 5.05[2], S5.05[2], 11.01[1]
Charitable remainder annuity trusts
. curative amendments permitted . . 5.05[10][a]
. defined . . . . 5.05[8][c]
. generation-skipping transfer tax . 17.02[3][c]
. split interest, charitable deduction . 5.05[8][c],
  S5.05[8][c]
. valuation rules under Section 2702, exceptions . . . . S19.03[3][c]
Charitable remainder trusts
  *See also Charitable remainder annuity trusts;
  Charitable remainder unitrusts*
. marital deduction, terminable interest rule and
  . . . . 5.06[8][e], S5.06[8][e]
. . gift tax deduction, exception to rule
  . . . . 11.03[4][d]
Charitable remainder unitrusts
. curative amendments permitted . . 5.05[10][a]
. defined . . . . 5.05[8][d]
. generation-skipping transfer tax . 17.02[3][c]
. split interest, charitable deduction . 5.05[8][d],
  S5.05[8][d]
. valuation rules under Section 2702, exceptions . . . . S19.03[3][c]
. value of remainder interest . . . . . 5.05[8][d]
Checks, gifts of . . . . 10.01[3][h]
Children
  See Minors
Citizenship
  See also Noncitizen spouses; Residence
. citizen vs. noncitizen . . . . 6.01[2]

Citizenship —Cont'd
. defined . . . . 6.01[2][a]
. domicile determined with threshold (citizenship) test . . . . 7.03[1][a]
. estate tax liability 8.09
. expatriation . . . . 6.01[2][a]
. loss of . . . . 6.01[2][a]
. possessions of U.S 8.09
. qualification as citizen . . . . 4.04[3][a]
. qualified domestic trusts, exceptions if surviving spouse becomes U.S. citizen . . 5.07[5]
. special-use valuation, residence as qualification for . . . . 4.04[3][a]
Claims
  See also Claims against estate
. creditors' claims, estate tax deductions for
  . . . . 1.02[3][a]
. taxes claimed as credits against estate tax, recovery of 3.08
. tort claims
. . tax convention, situs rules . . . . . 7.02[2][c]
Claims against estate . . . . S5.03[4]
. contingency of claim . . . . S5.03[4][c]
. . actual payment . . . . S5.03[4][c][iii]
. . generally . . . . S5.03[4][c][i]
. . types of contingencies . . . . S5.03[4][c][ii]
. existing at time of death . . . . . . S5.03[4][b]
. . foreign death taxes, limited deductibility
  of--Section 2053(d) . . . S5.03[4][b][ii]
. . taxes as claims . . . . S5.03[4][b][i]
. nonresident aliens . . . . 6.06[1]
. personal obligations of decedent . S5.03[4][a]
. . community property issues . S5.03[4][a][iii]
. . consideration requirement . . S5.03[4][a][ii]
. . related parties, claims by . . . S5.03[4][a][i]
. . Section 2044 claims . . . . . . S5.03[4][a][iv]
Close corporation interests
. discounts and premiums, valuation
. . estate tax . . . . 4.02[3][f]
. . gift tax . . . . 10.02[2][c]
. gross estate inclusion . . . . 4.02[3][f]
. valuation . . . . 4.02[3][f]
Closed and open-end funds
. gross estate inclusion . . . . 4.02[3][d]
. valuation . . . . 4.02[3][d]
Closely held business interests
. continuation of closely held business activities after death, facilitation through special-use valuation . . . . 4.04[1]
  See also Special-use valuation, real property
Collection of tax
. estate tax, reimbursement out of estate . . 8.04

Collection of tax — Cont'd
. qualified domestic trusts, regulatory require-
    ment to ensure collection of deferred tax
    . . . . 5.07[3][c]
. tax conventions . . . . 7.04[3]

Combat zone, member of armed forces in
. death of, estate tax provisions . . . 8.01[2][c]
. gift tax returns . . . . 9.04[9]

Common law
. reimbursement out of estate for estate tax due
    . . . . 8.04[3]
. spouse's economic status in common-law
    states 4.06
. wrongful death acts . . . . 4.05[8]

Community property
. dower or curtesy interests 4.06
. economic status of spouse in community
    property states 4.06
. gifts . . . . 10.01[3][f], 10.01[5][d]
. . valuation . . . . 10.02[6][b]
. legislative background . . . . 5.06[10]
. life estate, election to treat as QTIP
    . . . . S5.06[8][d][ii]
. life insurance
. . policy on life of another, community prop-
    erty interest in proceeds . . . . . . 4.05[6]
. . policy purchased with community property
    funds . . . . 4.14[8]
. marital rights in transfers for insufficient con-
    sideration . . . . 4.15[1][b]
. revocable transfers . 10.01[5][d], S10.01[5][d]
. special-use valuation, estates involving com-
    munity property . . . . 4.04[3][d]
. split gifts and . . . . 10.03[1]

**Compact of Free Association with Microne-
sia and Marshall Islands (Freely Associ-
ated States)** . . . . 7.03[9]

Compact of Free Association with Palau
    . . . . 7.03[10]

Compensation
. for death of decedent . . . . 4.05[8]
. gross estate inclusion
. . compensation due . . . . 4.05[4]
. . compensation for death . . . . 4.05[8]
. . salary due decedent at death . . . . . 4.05[4]
. workers' compensation, gross estate exclusion
    . . . . 4.05[8]

**Competent authority assistance, U.S. estate
and gift tax convention** . . . . 7.04[1]

Computation of tax
. estate tax . . . . 1.02[4]
. . qualified domestic trusts . . . . . . 5.07[4][c]
. generation-skipping transfer tax . . . . 1.04[4]
. gift tax . . . . 1.03[6]

Conditional transfers, gift tax . . . 10.01[3][e],
                            10.01[10][d]

**Conservation contributions, charitable de-
ductions** . . . . 5.05[8][b]

**Conservation easement, gross estate exclu-
sion of value of land subject to** . . S4.02[7]
. amount of exclusion . . . . S4.02[4][d]
. . applicable percentage . . . . . S4.02[7][d][iii]
. . limitation . . . . S4.02[4][d][iv]
. . Section 2055 deduction, reduction for
    . . . . S4.02[4][d][ii]
. . value of land . . . . S4.02[4][d][i]
. applicable land . . . . S4.02[4][b][i]
. capital gains discount . . . . . . S4.02[4][e][iii]
. corporation, land held in . . . . . S4.02[4][e][i]
. debt-financed property . . . . . . S4.02[4][d][i]
. effective date . . . . S4.02[4][g]
. election . . . . S4.02[4][c]
. entity, land held in . . . . S4.02[4][e][i]
. generally . . . . S4.02[4][a]
. generation-skipping transfer tax
    . . . . S4.02[4][f][iii]
. income tax basis . . . . S4.02[4][f][iii]
. interrelationship of Section 2031(c) with other
    tax provisions and taxes . . . . . S4.02[4][f]
. . generally . . . . S4.02[4][f][i]
. . other estate tax provisions . . . S4.02[4][f][ii]
. . other taxes . . . . S4.02[4][f][iii]
. land subject to qualified conservation ease-
    ment . . . . S4.02[4][b]
. location requirements . . . . S4.02[4][b][i]
. National Wilderness Preservation System
    . . . . S4.02[7][b][i]
. ownership of land . . . . S4.02[7][b][i]
. . member of family, defined for ownership
    purposes . . . . S4.02[4][b][i]
. partnership, land held in . . . . . S4.02[4][e][i]
. qualified conservation easement
. . defined . . . . S4.02[4][b][ii]
. . qualified grantors . . . . S4.02[4][b][ii]
. . requirement for exclusion . . . . S4.02[4][a]
. . timing . . . . S4.02[4][b][ii]
. retained development rights
. . defined . . . . S4.02[4][d][i]
. . taxation of . . . . S4.02[4][e][ii]
. Section 2031(c), special rules applicable to
    . . . . S4.02[4][e]
. . Section 303 stock . . . . S4.02[4][f][iii]
. . Section 2032A, relationship to
    . . . . S4.02[4][f][ii]
. . Section 2056, relationship to . S4.02[4][f][ii]
. . Section 2057, relationship to . S4.02[4][f][ii]
. . Section 6166, relationship to . S4.02[4][f][ii]
. . securities law discount . . . . . S4.02[4][e][iv]

**Conservation easement, gross estate exclu-
sion of value of land subject to—Cont'd**
. trust, land held in . . . . S4.02[4][e][i]
. Urban National Forest . . . . . S4.02[4][b][i]

Consideration
. buy-sell agreements, required transfer for full
   and adequate consideration . . 19.04[3][b]
. estate tax, and consideration received
   . . . . 1.03[2][b]
. full and adequate consideration 19.04[3][b][ii]
. generation-skipping transfer tax, reduction for
   consideration . . . . 14.05[3]
. gift tax, and consideration received
   . . . . 1.03[2][b], 10.02[3]
. . money's worth, receipts of . . . . . 10.02[6]
. insufficient consideration, transfers for . . 4.15

   *See also Transfers for insufficient consid-
   eration*
. marital rights in transfers for insufficient consideration . . . . 4.15[1]
. money's worth, gift tax valuation of receipts
   of . . . . 10.02[6]
. partial consideration, transfers for . . . 4.15[2]
. transfers within three years of death
   . . . . S4.07[2][c][i]

Contingent interest
. defined . . . . 6.05[2][a]
. nonresident aliens
. . bank deposits . . . . 6.05[2][a]
. . portfolio debt . . . . 6.05[4]

Contracts
. annuities
. . contract requirement . . . . 4.11[3][a]
. . pre-1931 contracts . . . . 4.11[2][b]
. gifts by . . . . 10.01[4]
. life insurance . . . . 4.14[2]

Contributions
. conservation contributions, charitable deductions . . . . 5.05[8][b]
. estate freezes, contributions to capital
   . . . . 19.02[2][a][i], 19.02[4][e]
. joint interests, contribution by survivor to
   . . . . 4.12[5]
. to political organizations, gift tax . . . 9.02[2]

Control of property, gift tax . . . . 1.03[2][a]

Control premiums for minority interests
. estate tax . . . . 4.02[3][f]
. gift tax . . . . 10.02[2][c]

Conversion rights . . . . 19.02[2][b][ii]
. non-lapsing . . . . 19.02[2][b][ii]

Cooperatives
   *See Eligible worker owned cooperatives
   (EWOCs)*

Copyrights, tax convention situs rules
   . . . . 7.02[2][c]

Corporations
. as charitable organizations . . 5.05[2], 11.01[1]
. close corporation interests, gross estate inclusion . . . . 4.02[3][f]
. conservation easement, corporate-held land
   subject to . . . . S4.02[4][e][i]
. control of, defined . . . . 19.05[2][b][iv]
. domestic, defined . . . . 6.04[1]
. estate freezes, valuation rules to combat
   abuses
. . corporate attribution . . . . . . 19.02[2][d][i]
. . corporate interest requirement
   . . . . 19.02[2][a][ii]
. family-owned, deduction for S5.08A

   See also Family-owned business deduction
. as generation-skipping transfer beneficiaries
   . . . . 17.01[2][c][i]
. gifts by . . . . 9.04[1][b], 10.01[2][c]
. gifts to . . . . 10.01[2][b]
. . money's worth received by, valuation
   . . . . 10.02[6][a]
. interests in, held by decedent, gross estate
   . . . . 4.05[7][a]
. lapsed voting or liquidation rights

   See Lapsed voting or liquidation rights
. shareholders in
. . generation-skipping transfer tax, Shareholders as skip persons . . . . . 13.03[4][b]
. . life insurance proceeds . . . . . . 4.14[5][a]
. stock, corporate

   See Stock

**Credit for state taxes, generation-skipping
transfer tax** . . . . 1.04[4][c], 12.04

Creditors' claims, estate tax deductions for
   . . . . 1.02[3][a]

Credits against estate tax 3.01–3.08

   See also Unified credit
. annual gift tax exclusion . . . . 3.04[2][b]
. charitable deductions . . 3.04[2][b], 3.05[4][a]
. death taxes on remainders 3.07
. deductions compared to credits 3.01
. foreign death taxes, credit for 1.02[5][e], 3.06
. . adjustments, federal estate tax . . 3.06[3][a]
. . computation of credit . . . . 3.06[1]
. . federal estate tax formula . . . . 3.06[3]
. . foreign death tax formula . . . . 3.06[2]
. . gross estate . . . . 3.06[3][c]
. . payment of tax . . . . 3.06[4]
. . value of property . . . . 3.06[3][b]
. generally . . . . 1.02[5], 3.01
. gift tax, credit for . . . . 1.02[5][c], 3.04

Credits against estate tax—Cont'd
. gift tax, credit for—Cont'd
. . amount of gift, computation and   3.04[1][b]
. . annual gift tax exclusion . . . . . .   3.04[2][b]
. . charitable deduction . . . .   3.04[2][b]
. . computation of potential credit . . . .   3.04[1]
. . decedent's gross estate, effect of   3.04[2][c]
. . federal estate tax, limitation on credit and
        . . . .   3.04[2][a]
. . limitation on credit   . . .   3.04[2], 3.04[2][d]
. . marital deduction . . . .   3.04[2][b]
. . nonresident aliens . . . .   6.02[2]
. . split gifts . . . .   3.04[2][b]
. . total gift tax, computation and . .   3.04[1][a]
. . total taxable gifts, computation and
        . . . .   3.04[1][c]
. . value of gift, effect of . . . .   3.04[2][b]
. limitations on credit
. . gift tax . . . .   3.04[2]
. . prior transfers, credit for tax on . . .   3.05[4]
. marital deduction . . . .   3.04[2][b]
. nonresident aliens 6.02
. . gift tax . . . .   6.02[2]
. . prior transfers, tax on . . . .   6.02[3]
. . state death taxes . . . . . .   6.02[1], S6.02[1]
. . unified credit . . . .   6.02[4]
. prior transfers, credit for tax on 3.05
. . additional tax imposed under Section
        2032A, treatment of . . . .   3.05[5]
. . adjustments . . . .   3.05[3]
. . charitable deduction . . . .   3.05[4][a]
. . computation of credit . . . .   3.05[2]
. . death before that of transferor . .   3.05[1][d]
. . decedent's estate, tax caused in .   3.05[4][a]
. . decedent, transfer to . . . .   3.05[1][a]
. . general rule . . . .   3.05[1]
. . limitations on credit . . . .   3.05[4]
. . multiple transferors, property from
        . . . .   3.05[4][b]
. . nonresident aliens . . . .   6.02[3]
. . percentage limitation . . . .   3.05[4][b]
. . property, defined . . . .   3.05[1][b]
. . taxable estate of transferor, adjustment
        . . . .   3.05[3][c]
. . transfer defined . . . .   3.05[1][c]
. . transferor's estate tax, adjustment   3.05[3][a]
. . value of property transferred, adjustment
        . . . .   3.05[3][b]
. property transfers to decedent from another
        decedent, estate tax paid on . . .   1.02[5][d]
. recovery of taxes claimed as credit 3.08

Credits against estate tax—Cont'd
. remainders, death taxes on 3.07
. state death taxes, credit for .   1.02[5][b], 3.03
. . "actually paid" requirement . . . . . .   3.03[1]
. . background of Section 2011 . . . . .   3.03[4]
. . deduction allowed . . . .   3.03[3]
. . limitation on amount of . .   3.03[2], 3.03[3]
. . seasonable payment . . . .   3.03[1]
. tax conventions, credits under .   7.02, 7.02[4]
. . OECD and U.S. model conventions
        . . . .   7.03[1][c]
. . primary credit . . . .   7.02, 7.02[4][a]
. . refunds . . . .   7.04[2]
. . secondary credit . . . . . .   7.02, 7.02[4][b]
Crops, growing
. gross estate inclusion, valuation
. . special-use valuation . . . .   4.04[3][c]
Crossed trusts
    See Reciprocal trusts
Crummey powers
. adverse tax effects, risk of . . . . . .   9.04[3][f]
. powers of appointment and . . . . .   9.04[3][f]
. problems, potential . . . .   9.04[3][f]
. taxable gifts, future interests . . . .   9.04[3][f]
Crummey trusts
. gross estate inclusion, risks . . . . .   4.05[7][c]
. limited liability companies compared
        . . . .   4.05[7][c]
Curtesy interests
. community property and common-law rules
        . . . .   4.05[8]
. defined . . . .   4.05[8]
. estate tax . . . .   4.05[8], 4.15[1]
. gift tax . . . .   10.02[5][d], 10.06[1]
. . valuation . . . .   10.02[5][d]
. gross estate inclusion . . . . .   4.05[8], 4.15[1]
. marital deduction, interests passing to surviv-
        ing spouse . . . .   5.06[3][b]

D

Danish convention . . . .   7.03[6]
Date-of-death rule . . . .   1.02[2][b][ii], 4.03[1],
        S4.03[1], 4.14[9][b], 5.05[3][b]
Death of individual
. armed services, estate tax provisions . . .   8.01
. . combat zone, death in . . . .   8.01[2][c]
. . service-connected death . . . . . .   8.01[2][d]
. compensation for, gross estate inclusion
        . . . .   4.05[8]

Death of individual —Cont'd

. continued use of certain real property after death, facilitation through special-use valuation . . . . 4.04[1], S4.04[1]

   See also Special-use valuation, real property

. date-of-death rule for valuation . 1.02[2][b][ii], 4.03[1], S4.03[1], 4.14[9][b]
. generation-skipping transfer tax
. . taxable terminations at death . . 14.05[2][b]
. . transfers at death, deferral of payment . . . . 18.01[2][a], S18.01[2][a]
. gross estate valuation, date of decedent's death as time for 4.01
. physical condition of decedent before, effect on transfers effective at death . 4.09[4][e]
. prior transfers, credit for tax on, death before that of transferor . . . . 3.05[1][d]
. property owned at . . . . 1.02[2][a]
. simultaneous death, life insurance proceeds . . . . 4.14[3][b]
. transfers near . . . . 1.02[2][b][i], S4.07
. transfers taking effect at 4.09
. wrongful death acts . . . . 4.05[8]

Death taxes

   See also Estate tax; Foreign death taxes; State death taxes

. charitable deductions for estate expenses . . . . 5.05[3][c][i]
. international system of death taxation 7.01[2]
. . death taxes involved . . . . 7.01[2][b]
. on remainders, credit against estate tax . 3.07
. tax conventions . . . . 7.01[2]

Debt

   See Indebtedness

Debt instruments

   See Bonds; Notes; Securities

Decedent

   See also Death of individual; Transfers within three years of death

. beneficial interests of, gross estate . . 4.05[2]
. . state decrees . . . . 4.05[2][b]
. . state law . . . . 4.05[2][a]
. beneficial interests of, transfers with retained life estate . . . . 4.08[4]
. . enjoyment "retained" 4.08[4][c], S4.08[4][c]
. . possession or enjoyment . . . . . . 4.08[4][a], 4.08[4][c], S4.08[4][c]
. . right to income . . . . 4.08[4][b]
. business interests of, gross estate . . . 4.05[7]
. . corporations . . . . 4.05[7][a]
. . limited liability companies . . . . 4.05[7][c], S4.05[7][c]

Decedent —Cont'd
. *business interests of, gross estate—Cont'd*
. . partnerships . . . . 4.05[7][b]
. . proprietorships . . . . 4.05[7][a]
. charitable deductions, property over which decedent had power . . . . 5.05[3][e]
. estate tax liability of recipient of property over which decedent had power 8.06
. gross estate inclusion of property in which decedent had interest 4.05

   See also Gross estate

. . bank accounts . . . . 4.05[3]
. . beneficial interest . . . . 4.05[2]
. . bonuses . . . . 4.05[4]
. . business interests . . . . 4.05[7]
. . compensation due at death . . . . . . 4.05[4]
. . compensation for death . . . . 4.05[8]
. . corporations . . . . 4.05[7][a]
. . dividends . . . . 4.05[4]
. . generally . . . . 4.05[1]
. income items . . . . 4.05[4]
. . insurance proceeds . . . . 4.05[6]
. . intangible property interests . . . . . . 4.05[3]
. . limited liability companies . . . . 4.05[7][c], S4.05[7][c]
. . partial interests in property . . . . . . 4.05[5]
. . partnerships . . . . 4.05[7][b]
. . proprietorships . . . . 4.05[7][a]
. . rent accrued at death . . . . 4.05[4]
. . routine inclusions . . . . 4.05[3]
. . stocks, bonds, and notes . . . . 4.05[3]
. . tangible personal property . . . . . . 4.05[3]
. gross estate of

   See Gross estate

. marital deduction, property over which decedent had power . . . . 5.05[3][e]
. partial interests in property, gross estate and . . . . 4.05[5]
. . cautions . . . . 4.05[5][c]
. . shared interests . . . . 4.05[5][a]
. . successive interests . . . . 4.05[5][b]
. power in decedent, revocable transfers 4.10[4]

   See also Revocable transfers

. power over property
. . charitable deductions . . . . 5.05[3][e]
. . estate tax liability of recipient of property 8.06
. . marital deduction . . . . 5.05[3][e]
. prior transfers to, estate tax credit for tax on . . . . 3.05[1][a]
. property transfers to decedent from another decedent, credit for estate tax paid on . . . . 1.02[5][d]

Decedent —Cont'd

. recovery, right of, decedent-retained interest
. . . . 8.08

. . effective dates . . . . 8.08[4]

. . estate tax recovery . . . . 8.08[2]

. . generally . . . . 8.08[1]

. . gift tax recovery . . . . 8.08[3]

. special-use valuation, property acquired from
    decedent . . . . 4.04[3][b][viii]

. taxable estate of

    See Taxable estate

. transfers with retained life estate

. . beneficial interests in decedent . . . . 4.08[4]

. . election, transfers by . 4.08[7][b], 4.08[7][c]

. . indirect transfers by decedent . . 4.08[7][a]

. . reciprocal trusts . . . . 4.08[7][d]

. . transfers by decedent . . . . 4.08[7]

. . widow's election . . . . 4.08[7][c]

Deductible gifts . . . . 11.01 – 11.04

    See also Deductions; Gifts; Gift tax

. charitable gifts . . . 1.03[5][a], 11.02, S11.02

. . easements in real property, irrevocable
        transfers of . . . . 11.02[4]

. . extent of deduction . . . . 11.04[1]

. . mixed private and charitable gifts . 11.02[2],
                                            11.02[3]

. . qualified recipients . . . . 11.02[1]

. easements in real property, irrevocable trans-
        fers of . . . . 11.02[4]

. extent of deductions 11.04

. . charitable deduction . . . . 11.04[1]

. . marital deduction . . . . 11.04[2]

. generally 11.01

. irrevocable transfers of easements in real
        property . . . . 11.02[4]

. mixed private and charitable gifts

. . future interests . . . . 11.02[2]

. . present interests . . . . 11.02[3]

. noncitizen donee spouses . . . . 11.03[5]

. prior years . . . . 9.05[4]

. to spouse 11.03

. . caveat on powers . . . . 11.03[3][a]

. . charitable remainder trusts . . . . 11.03[4][d]

. . donor retains interest . . . . 11.03[3][a]

. . exceptions to terminable interest rule
        . . . . 11.03[4]

. . generally . . . . 11.03[1]

. . joint-and-survivor annuities . 11.03[4][c][ii]

. . joint interests . . . . 11.03[4][a]

. . life interests with powers . . . . 11.03[4][b]

. . noncitizen spouses . . . . 11.03[5]

. . qualified terminable interest property
        . . . . 11.03[4][c]

Deductible gifts—Cont'd
. *to spouse—Cont'd*

. . requirements . . . . 11.03[2]

. . Section 2523(b)(1) transfers . . . 11.03[3][a]

. . Section 2523(b)(2) transfers . . . 11.03[3][b]

. . "tainted" asset rule . . . . 11.03[3][c]

. . terminable interest rule . . 11.03[3], 11.03[4]

. . third party acquires interest . . . 11.03[3][a]

Deductions

    *See also Charitable deductions; Deductible
        gifts; Marital deduction*

. administration expenses . . . . S5.03[3]

. alternate valuation date for gross estate inclu-
        sion, effect of . . . . 4.03[4]

. . charitable and marital deductions 4.03[4][b]

. . general impact . . . . 4.03[4][a]

. attorney fees . . . . S5.03[3][a]

. casualty losses . . . . 5.04[2]

. claims against estate . . . . S5.03[4]

. . contingency of claim . . . . S5.03[4][c]

. . . actual payment . . . . S5.03[4][c][iii]

. . . generally . . . . S5.03[4][c][i]

. . . types of contingencies . . . S5.03[4][c][ii]

. . existing at time of death . . . . . S5.03[4][b]

. . . foreign death taxes, limited deductibility
        of--Section 2053(d) . . . S5.03[4][b][ii]

. . . taxes as claims . . . . S5.03[4][b][i]

. . personal obligations of decedent S5.03[4][a]

. . . community property issues S5.03[4][a][iii]

. . . consideration requirement . S5.03[4][a][ii]

. . . related parties, claims by . . S5.03[4][a][i]

. . . Section 2044 claims . . . . S5.03[4][a][iv]

. creditors' claims . . . . 1.02[3][a]

. credits compared 3.01

. double deductions

. . charitable deductions . . . . . . S5.05[3][c][ii]

. eligible worker owned cooperatives (EWOCs)
        . . . . 5.08

. employee stock ownership plans (ESOPs)
        . . . . 5.08

. estate tax . . . . 1.02[3], 5.01 – 5.08

. . creditors' claims . . . . 1.02[3][a]

. . expenses, deductions for . . . . . . 1.02[3][b]

. . losses, deductions for . . . . 1.02[3][b]

. executor commissions . . . . S5.03[3][a]

. family-owned business deduction . . . S5.08A

    See also Family-owned business deduction

. funeral expenses . . . . 1.02[3][b]

. interest expenses . . . . S5.03[3][c][i]

. losses . . . . 1.02[3][b], 5.04

. miscellaneous administration expenses
        . . . . S5.03[3][c]

. mortgages . . . . S5.03[5]

Deductions — Cont'd

. nonresident aliens

. . charitable bequests . . . . 6.06[2]

. . expenses, claims, and losses . . . . . 6.06[1]

. . generally . . . . 6.06[1]

. . marital deduction . . . . 6.06[3]

. . prerequisite to deductions . . . . 6.06[4]

. other deductible administration expenses
. . . . S5.03[3][c][iii]

. prior years, gift tax deductions for . . 9.05[4]

. rules and limitations related to Section 2053
deductions . . . . S5.03[6]

. . property not subject to claims, special rules
for

. . . administration expenses: Section 2053(b)
. . . . S5.03[6][c][iii]

. . . generally . . S5.03[6][c][i], S5.03[6][c][ii]

. . . value of property subject to claims, limitation based on––Section 2053(c)(2)
. . . . S5.03[6][c][iv]

. . Section 213(c)(2) election . . . . S5.03[6][b]

. . Section 642(g) election . . . . . . S5.03[6][a]

. selling expenses . . . . S5.03[3][c][ii]

. state death tax deduction, effect on death tax
credit . . . . 3.03[3]

. taxable estate, Subtraction of deductions in
determination of 5.01, 5.02

. tax conventions . . . . 7.02[3]

. . OECD and U.S. model conventions
. . . . 7.03[1][c]

. taxes 5.01

. theft losses . . . . 5.04[3]

Deferred estate tax

. generally . . . . 2.02[3]

. interest on deferred payment . . . . 2.02[3][c],
S2.02[3][c]

. maximum amount of deferral . . . . 2.02[3][c]

. qualified domestic trusts, regulatory requirements to ensure collection of deferred tax
. . . . 5.07[3][c]

Demand loans . . . . 10.01[2][f]

Dependents, support of

. right to support . . . . 4.15[1][d]

. valuation of family obligations, gift tax
. . . . 10.02[5]

**Depression of 1930s, gross estate alternate
valuation date and** . . . . 4.03[1]

Direct skips

See Generation-skipping transfer tax

Disability

. defined . . . . 4.04[3][c][ii]

. special-use valuation qualification and
. . . . 4.04[3][c][ii]

Disasters

. casualty losses . . . . 5.04[2]

. terminable interest rule and marital deduction,
effect of common disasters . . . 5.06[8][a]

Discharge of indebtedness, as indirect gift
. . . . 10.01[2][e]

Disclaimers

. acceptance, disclaimer may not follow
. . . . 10.07[2][c]

. charitable bequests . . . . 5.05[3][d]

. charitable deductions . . . . 5.05[3][d]

. date-of-creation rules . . . . 10.07[2][b]

. defined . . . . 10.07[2]

. effective date . . . . 10.07[3]

. estate tax . . . . . . 4.13[7][d], 4.18, 10.07[1]

. generally . . . . 10.07[1]

. generation-skipping transfer tax . . . 10.07[1],
17.04[3], S17.04[3]

. gift tax . . . . . . 1.03[2][f], 4.13[7][d], 10.07

. . acceptance, disclaimer may not follow
. . . . 10.07[2][c]

. . definition of qualified disclaimer . 10.07[2]

. . effective date . . . . 10.07[3]

. . generally . . . . 10.07[1]

. . persons to whom interest must pass
. . . . 10.07[2][d]

. . timeliness requirement . . . . . . 10.07[2][b],
S10.07[2][b]

. . uniform treatment under gift tax, estate tax,
and generation-skipping transfer taxes
. . . . 10.07[1]

. . writing requirement . . . . 10.07[2][a]

. gross estate 4.18

. irrevocability of . . . . 10.07[2]

. joint bank accounts . . . . 10.07[2][b]

. joint tenancies . . . . 10.07[2][b], S10.07[2][b]

. local law, disclaimers ineffective under
. . . . 10.07[2][d][ii]

. marital deduction, interests passing to surviving spouse . . . . 5.06[3][h]

. persons to whom interest must pass
. . . . 10.07[2][d]

. powers of appointment

. . estate tax . . . . 4.13[7][d]

. . gift tax . . . . 10.04[4][b], 10.07[2][b]

. qualified disclaimer, defined . . . . . 10.07[2]

. qualified terminable interest property
. . . . 10.07[2][b]

. surviving spouse, disclaimer by 10.07[2][d][i]

. tenancies by the entirety . . . . . . 10.07[2][b],
S10.07[2][b]

. timeliness requirement . . . . 10.07[2][b]

. uniform treatment under estate, gift, and generation-skipping transfer taxes . . 10.07[1]

. writing requirement . . . . 10.07[2][a]

Discounts and premiums for minority interests
. estate tax . . . . 4.02[3][f]
. gift tax . . . . 10.02[2][c]
Distribution rights
. defined . . . . 19.02[2][b][ii], 19.02[4][c]
. estate freezes . . . 19.02[2][b][ii], 19.02[4][c]
. qualified payment rights . . . . . 19.02[4][c][i]
. . extraordinary payment rights, combined
         with . . . . 19.02[4][c][ii]
Distributions

  See also Generation-skipping transfers
. ESOPs . . . . 5.08[1]
. estate freezes, distribution rights
         . . . . 19.02[2][b][ii], 19.02[4][c]
. . qualified payment rights . . . . 19.02[4][c][i]
. . . combined with extraordinary payment
         rights . . . . 19.02[4][c][ii]
Dividends
. gross estate inclusion . . . . 4.05[4]
. . alternate valuation date . . . . 4.03[2][c]
Divorce

  *See also Property settlements not in divorce
  decree*
. gift tax
. . divorce transfers . . . . 1.03[2][e]
. . family obligations, valuation of   10.02[5][c]
. . settlements not in divorce decree . . . 10.06
. marital rights in transfers for insufficient con-
         sideration . . . . 4.15[1][e]
Domicile, defined . . . . 6.01[2][b], 7.01[2][b],
                                              7.03[1][a]
. hierarchy-of-criteria test . . . . 7.03[1][a]
. threshold (citizenship) test . . . . . . 7.03[1][a]
Donees, gift tax
. identification of donees, annual exclusion
         . . . . 9.04[1][b]
. . charitable organizations, gifts to . 9.04[1][b]
. . corporate gifts . . . . 9.04[1][b]
. . gifts in trust . . . . 9.04[1][b]
. . other entities, gifts to . . . . 9.04[1][b]
. . straw man, use of . . . . 9.04[1][b]
. joint donees . . . . 9.04[1][b]
. liability of . . . . 9.04[11]
. minor donees . . . . 9.04[4]
. . first donee requirement . . . . 9.04[5][a]
. . requirements . . . . 9.04[5]
. . second donee requirement . . . . . 9.04[5][b]
. . state statutes simplifying gifts . . 9.04[5][c]
. noncitizen spouses . . . . 11.03[5]
. payment of tax by, valuation . . . 10.02[6][d]
Donors
. gift tax liability . . . . 9.02[3]

Donors —Cont'd
. nonresident aliens . . . . 10.01[11]
. nonresident noncitizens . . . . S10.01[11]
. revocable transfers, termination of donor's
         control . . . . 10.01[5][b]
Double taxation
. special valuation rules, double taxation regu-
         lation . . . . 19.03[4][c]
. . estate tax . . . . 19.03[4][c][ii]
. . gift tax . . . . 19.03[4][c][i]
. tax conventions, avoidance through 7.02,
                                                      7.02[1]
Dower interests
. community property and common-law rules
         . . . . 4.05[8]
. defined . . . . 4.05[8]
. estate tax . . . . 4.05[8], 4.15[1]
. gift tax . . . . 10.02[5][d], 10.06[1]
. . valuation . . . . 10.02[5][d]
. gross estate inclusion . . . . . 4.05[8], 4.15[1]
. marital deduction, interests passing to surviv-
         ing spouse . . . . 5.06[3][b]

E

Easements
. conservation easement, gross estate exclusion
         of value of land subject to . . . . . S4.02[4]
. in real property, irrevocable transfers of
         . . . . 11.02[4]
**Economic Growth and Tax Relief Reconcilia-
tion Act of 2001**
. estate tax
. . "sunset provisions" . . . . S1.05[4]
. . termination after December 31, 2001   S1.05
. generation-skipping transfer tax
. . termination S1.05
Economic Recovery Tax Act (ERTA)
. marital deduction . 4.15[1], 5.06[1], 5.06[10],
                                                      7.03[6]
. partial consideration, transfers for . 4.15[2][a]
. transfers within three years of death   S4.07[1]
Educational expenses
. annual gift tax exclusion . . 9.04[6], S9.04[6]
. generation-skipping transfer tax exclusion
         . . . . . 1.04[3][d], 13.01[2][a], S13.01[2][a]
. gift tax exclusion . . 1.03[3], 9.04[6], S9.04[6]
. Qualified State Tuition Programs . . S9.04[6],
                                                      S13.01[2][a]
**Educational organizations, charitable trans-
fers to** . . . . 5.05[2], 11.01[1]
Education IRAs . . . . S13.01[2][a]
. gift tax . . . . S9.04[6], S10.01[3][c]

Effectively connected income, nonresident aliens' bank deposits . . . . . 6.05[2][c][ii]

Ejusdem generiso canon of construction (Lord Tenderden's rule) . . . . 5.04[2]

Eligible worker owned cooperatives (EWOCs) 5.08
. deductions 5.08
. defined . . . . 5.08[1]
. ESOPs compared . . . . 5.08[1]
. generally . . . . 5.08[1]
. qualified employer securities, sale to plan of
. . . . 5.08[2]
. . definition of qualified employer securities
. . . . 5.08[2], S5.08[2][a]
. . effective dates . . . . 5.08[6]
. . employer, defined . . . . 5.08[2]
. . excise tax limitations . . . . 5.08[4]
. . generally . . . . 5.08[1]
. . miscellaneous proceeds limitations
. . . . 5.08[3][c]
. . net sale amount limitation . . . . . 5.08[3][a]
. . procedural requirements . . . . 5.08[5]
. . proceeds limitations . . . . 5.08[3]
. . Section 4978A tax . . . . 5.08[4][a]
. . Section 4979A tax . . . . 5.08[4][b]
. . taxable events . . . . 5.08[4][a]
. . transferred assets limitation . . . . 5.08[3][b]
. repeal, restrictions due to 5.08
. Section 2057 rules . . . . 5.08[1]
. . limitations . . . . 5.08[1]
. . repeal restrictions 5.08
. taxable estate 5.08
. tax incentive for formation of . . . . . 5.08[1]
. types . . . . 5.08[1]

Employee plan benefits passing to qualified domestic trust . . . . 5.07[2][c]

Employee stock ownership plans (ESOPs)
. . . . 5.08
. charitable transfers to . . S5.05[2], S5.06[8][e]
. deductions 5.08
. defined . . . . 5.08[1]
. distributions . . . . 5.08[1]
. EWOCs compared . . . . 5.08[1]
. generally . . . . 5.08[1]
. qualified employer securities, sale to plan of
. . . . 5.08[2]
. . definition of qualified employer securities
. . . . 5.08[2], S5.08[2][a]
. . effective dates . . . . 5.08[6]
. . employer, defined . . . . 5.08[2]
. . excise tax limitations . . . . 5.08[4]
. . generally . . . . 5.08[1]
. . miscellaneous proceeds limitations
. . . . 5.08[3][c]

Employee stock ownership plans (ESOPs)— Cont'd
. qualified employer securities, sale to plan of—Cont'd
. . net sale amount limitation . . . . . 5.08[3][a]
. . procedural requirements . . . . 5.08[5]
. . proceeds limitations . . . . 5.08[3]
. . Section 4978A tax . . . . 5.08[4][a]
. . Section 4979A tax . . . . 5.08[4][b]
. . taxable events . . . . 5.08[4][a]
. . transferred assets limitation . . . . 5.08[3][b]
. repeal, restrictions due to 5.08
. retiring or near-retirement employees . 5.08[1]
. Section 2057 rules . . . . 5.08[1]
. . limitations . . . . 5.08[1]
. . repeal restrictions 5.08
. taxable estate 5.08
. tax incentive for formation of . . . . . 5.08[1]

Encumbered property
. gifts, valuation . . . . 10.02[2][a]
. marital deduction, valuation of encumbrances
. . on surviving spouse's interest . 5.06[5][b]

Enjoyment
. change in, revocable transfers . . . . . 4.10[3]
. defined . . . . 4.08[6][b]
. postponement of enjoyment of gift, brief
. . . . 9.04[3][d]
. right to enjoyment of gift . . . . . 9.04[3][e]
. transfers with retention of
. . beneficial interests in decedent . . 4.08[4][a],
. . . . 4.08[4][c], S4.08[4][c]
. . commercial transactions . . . . . . 4.08[6][b]
. . generally . . . . 1.02[2][b][iii]

ERTA

See Economic Recovery Tax Act (ERTA)

ESOPs

See Employee stock ownership plans (ESOPs)

Estate freezes 19.01–19.05

See also Special valuation rules to combat estate freeze abuses (Chapter 14 rules)
. abuses of . . . . 19.01[1]
. . efforts to curb . . . . 19.01[1], 19.02[1]
. . valuation rules addressing . . . 19.01–19.05
. adjustments to value of transferred interests
. . . . 19.02[4][d][iv]
. applicable retained interest, defined
. . . . 19.02[2][b][ii]
. attribution rules . . . . 19.02[2][d]
. . corporate attribution . . . . 19.02[2][d][i]
. . estate attribution . . . . 19.02[2][d][iii]
. . multiple attribution . . . . . . 19.02[2][d][iv]
. . partnership attribution . . . . . 19.02[2][d][ii]

Estate freezes—Cont'd
. *attribution rules—Cont'd*
. . trust attribution . . . . 19.02[2][d][iii]
. bifurcation of entity into two interests
. . . . 19.02[1][a]
. buy-sell agreements, valuation rules . . 19.04

    See also Buy-sell agreements
. call rights . . . . 19.02[2][b][ii]
. capital structure transactions . . 19.02[2][a][i]
. Chapter 14 rules
. . combating estate freeze abuses, generally
. . . . 19.01[1]
. . definitions . . . . 19.01[2]
. . exceptions within . . . . 19.01[4]
. . generally . . . . 19.01[1]
. . requirements for applicability . . . . 19.02[2]
. . valuation methodology under . . . . 19.01[3]
. . valuation rules under, addressing freeze
. . . . . abuses 19.01–19.05
. classic freezes 19.02
. contributions to capital . . . . . . 19.02[2][a][i],
. . . . 19.02[4][e]
. conversion rights . . . . 19.02[2][b][ii]
. . non-lapsing . . . . 19.02[2][b][ii]
. corporations
. . corporate attribution . . . . 19.02[2][d][i]
. . interest in corporation . . . . 19.02[2][a][ii]
. definitions . . . . 19.01[2], 19.02[1][a]
. distribution rights . 19.02[2][b][ii], 19.02[4][c]
. . qualified payment rights . . . . 19.02[4][c][i]
. . . combined with extraordinary payment
. . . . . rights . . . . 19.02[4][c][ii]
. double taxation regulation . . . . . 19.03[4][c]
. estate attribution . . . . 19.02[2][d][iii]
. estate tax
. . relationship to . . . 19.02[5][f], 19.03[4][e][i]
. . relief from . . . . 19.02[5][c][iv]
. extraordinary payment rights . 19.02[2][b][ii],
. . . . 19.02[4][b]
. . qualified payment rights combined with
. . . . 19.02[4][c][ii]
. family-held interests
. . subordinate equity interests . 19.02[4][d][iii]
. . valuation . . . . 19.02[4][d][i]
. frozen interest . . . . 19.02[1][a]
. . minimal valuation of retained interest
. . . . 19.02[1][c]
. generally . . . . 19.01[1], 19.02[1]
. generation-skipping transfer tax, relationship
. . . . to . . . . 19.02[5][f], 19.03[4][e][iii]
. gift tax
. . relationship of Section 2701 to other provi-
. . . . sions of . . . . 19.02[5][e]
. . relief from . . . . 19.02[5][c][iii]

Estate freezes—Cont'd
. grantor retained income trusts . . . . 19.03[1],
. . . . 19.03[2]

    *See also Grantor retained income trusts
    (GRITs)*
. growth interest . . . . 19.02[1][a]
. guaranteed payment rights . . . 19.02[2][b][ii]
. historical background . . . . 19.01[1]
. income tax, relationship to . . . . . 19.02[5][f],
. . . . 19.03[4][e][ii]
. indirect transfers under attribution rules
. . . . 19.02[2][a][i]
. joint purchases . . . . . . 19.03[1], 19.03[4][a]
. junior equity interest, minimum valuation of
. . . . 19.02[4][f]
. lapsing rights and restrictions, valuation rules
. . . . for certain 19.05
. liquidation
. . extraordinary payment (liquidation) rights
. . . . 19.02[2][b][ii]
. . lapsed liquidation rights . . . . 19.05[2]
. . liquidation rights . . 19.02[2][b][ii], 19.05[2]
. . restrictions on . . . . 19.05[3]
. mandatory payment rights . . . 19.02[2][b][ii]
. minimal valuation of retained frozen interest
. . . . 19.02[1][c]
. multiple attribution . . . . 19.02[2][d][iv]
. nature of . . . . 19.02[1][a]
. options 19.04

    See also Options
. partnerships
. . interest in partnership . . . . . 19.02[2][a][ii]
. . partnership attribution . . . . . 19.02[2][d][ii]
. preferred stock frozen . . . . 19.02[1][a]
. prior attacks on . . . . 19.02[1][b]
. put rights . . . . 19.02[2][b][ii]
. qualified payment interest . . . . . 19.02[5][a]
. . amount of transfer . . . . 19.02[5][a][iv]
. . generally . . . . 19.02[5][a][i]
. . qualified payment elections . 19.02[5][a][ii]
. . taxable events . . . . 19.02[5][a][iii]
. recapitalization, tax-free, freeze as result of
. . . . 19.02[1][a], 19.02[2][a][i]
. redemptions . . . . 19.02[2][a][i]
. relief rule . . . . 19.02[5][c]
. . amount of reduction . . . . . . 19.02[5][c][ii]
. . duplicated amount . . . . 19.02[5][c][ii]
. . estate tax relief . . . . 19.02[5][c][iv]
. . generally . . . . 19.02[5][c][i]
. . gift tax relief . . . . 19.02[5][c][iii]
. . split gifts, special rules for . . 19.02[5][c][v]
. . subsequent taxation, relief from
. . . . 19.02[5][c][i]

Estate freezes—Cont'd

. requirements . . . . 19.02[2]

. rights and restrictions disregarded 19.04

. . background . . . . 19.04[1][b]

. . enactment of Section 2703 . . . 19.04[1][c]

. . generally . . . . 19.04[1]

. . general principles . . . . 19.04[1][a]

. senior equity interests, reduction for value of
. . . . 19.02[4][d][ii]

. separate interest rule . . . . 19.02[5][b]

. subordinate equity interests

. . allocations between transferred interests and
. . . . 19.02[4][d][iii]

. . family-held . . . . 19.02[4][d][iii]

. . reduction for value . . . . . . 19.02[4][d][ii]

. tangible property, transfers of certain
. . . . 19.03[4][b]

. transferred interests

. . adjustments to value of . . . . 19.02[4][d][iv]

. . allocations between subordinate equity interests and . . . . 19.02[4][d][iii]

. transfer rules . . . . 19.02[2][a]

. . applicable retained interest held by applicable family member, requirement
. . . . 19.02[2][b], 19.03[2][a][iii]

. . limitation on . . . . 1.02[2][a][i]

. trusts

. . transfers of interests in, valuation rules
. . . . 19.03

. . trust attribution . . . . 19.02[2][d][iii]

. zero valuation rule . . . . . 19.03[1], 19.03[2]

. . exceptions to . . . . 19.03[3]

Estates

See also Estate freezes; Estate tax

. as generation-skipping transfer beneficiaries
. . . . 17.01[2][c][i]

. as skip persons . . . . 13.03[4][a]

Estate tax 1.02, 2.02

*See also Credits against estate tax; Estate
freezes; Gross estate; State death taxes;
Taxable estate; Unified credit*

. annuities . . . . 1.02[2][b][vi], 4.11[7]

. armed forces 8.01

. . active service requirement . . . . . 8.01[2][a]

. . astronauts . . . . S8.01[1][c]

. . combat zone, death in . . . . 8.01[2][c]

. . generally 8.01

. . member of armed forces, requirement
. . . . 8.01[2][b]

. . prerequisites for relief . . . . 8.01[2]

. . relief provision, effect of . . . . . . 8.01[1]

. . service-connected death . . . . . . 8.01[2][d]

. buy-sell agreements, valuation . . 19.04[6][a]

Estate tax—Cont'd

. carryover basis regime following estate tax
elimination . . . . S1.05[3]

. charitable deductions . . . . 1.02[3][c]

. citizenship and liability for 8.09

. collection of tax, reimbursement out of estate
as 8.04

. common law, reimbursement out of estate
. . . . 8.04[3]

. computation . . . . 1.02[4]

. . gross estate, effect of 4.01

. conservation easement under Section 2031(c),
interrelationship with other estate tax provisions . . . . S4.02[4][f][ii]

. consideration received . . . . 1.03[2][b]

. control premiums . . . . 4.02[3][f]

. creditors' claims, deductions for . . 1.02[3][a]

. curtesy interests . . . . 4.05[8], 4.15[1]

. decedent-retained interest, right of recovery
. . . . 8.08

. deductions . . . . 1.02[3], 5.01–5.08

. deferred

. . generally . . . . 2.02[3]

. . interest on . . . . 2.02[3][c], S2.02[3][c]

. . maximum amount of deferral . . . 2.02[3][c]

. disclaimers . . . . . . 4.13[7][d], 4.18, 10.07[1]

. discounts for minority interests . . . 4.02[3][f]

. double taxation regulation . . . 19.03[4][c][ii]

. dower interests . . . . 4.05[8], 4.15[1]

. elimination of, Act Section 501 and IRC Section 2210 . . . . S1.05[1]

. estate freezes

. . estate tax relief . . . . 19.02[5][c][iv]

. . relationship to estate tax . . . . . 19.02[5][f],
19.03[4][e][i]

. excise tax nature of . . . . 1.03[1]

. executor

See also Executor

. . defined 8.02

. . personal liability, discharge from 8.03

. expenses, deductions for . . . . 1.02[3][b]

. extension of time for payment . . . . . 2.02[3]

. . election for . . . . 2.02[3][c]

. . interest . . . . 2.02[3][c], S2.02[3][c]

. . maximum amount of deferral . . . 2.02[3][c]

. . penalty for late payment . . . . . . 2.02[3][c]

. . period of extension . . . . 2.02[3][c]

. . qualification for . . . . 2.02[3][c]

. . reasonable cause extensions . . . . 2.02[3][b]

. . Section 6159 rules . . . . 2.02[3][a]

. . Section 6161 rules . . . . 2.02[3][b]

. . Section 6166 rules . . 2.02[3][c], S2.02[3][c]

. . short extensions . . . . 2.02[3][b]

Estate tax—Cont'd
. family-owned business deduction
. . estate qualifications . . . . S5.08A[3]
. . estate tax savings, recapture of
     . . . . S5.08A[5][c][ii]
. . interest on estate tax, recapture of
     . . . . S5.08A[5][c][iii]
. generally . . . . 1.01, 1.02[1]
. generation-skipping transfer tax
. . comparison of . . . . 1.04[1]
. . inclusion period . . . . 16.02[7]
. gift tax and . 1.03[1], 1.03[2][a], 1.04[1], 9.01
. . federal estate tax as limitation on gift tax
     credit . . . . 3.04[2][a]
. . gift tax as credit against estate tax
     . . . . 1.02[5][c], 3.04
. . integration of estate and gift tax 3.04
. . marital rights . . . . . 4.15[1][f], 10.02[5][d]
. . relationship . . . . 10.01[10]
. gross estate tax . . . . 1.02[5]
. history . . . . 1.02[1]
. insufficient consideration, transfers for . . 4.15,
     4.15[1], 4.15[1][f], 4.15[2]
. interest on deferred payment . . . . 2.02[3][c],
     S2.02[3][c]
. . penalty for late payment . . . . . . 2.02[3][c]
. international system of death taxation
     . . . . 7.01[2][a]
. interspousal transfers, exclusion 4.16
. joint interests . . . 4.12[6], 4.12[10], 4.12[11]
. lapsed voting or liquidation rights 19.05[2][a]
. life insurance beneficiaries, liability of . . 8.05
. . amount of, formula for . . . . 8.05[1]
. . contrary will provision . . . . 8.05[3]
. . marital deduction, special rule . . . . 8.05[2]
. . state law, effect . . . . 8.05[4]
. life insurance proceeds
. . beneficiaries, liability of 8.05
. . gross estate . . 1.02[2][b][ix], 4.05[6], 4.14
. limited liability companies, advantages of
     . . . . 4.05[7][c], S4.05[7][c]
. liquidation restrictions . . . . 19.05[3][a]
. losses, deductions for . . . . 1.02[3][b]
. marital deduction . . . . 1.02[3][d]
. . credit against estate tax, gift tax as
     . . . . 3.04[2][b]
. . life insurance beneficiaries, estate tax liabil-
     ity of . . . . 8.05[2]
. . right of recovery 8.07
. marital rights in transfers for insufficient con-
     sideration . . . . 4.15[1], 4.15[1][f]
. minority interests, discounts in valuation of
     . . . . 4.02[3][f]
. nonresident aliens . . . . . . 6.01[1], S6.01[1]

Estate tax—Cont'd
. *nonresident aliens—Cont'd*
. . credits against 6.02
. . pre-1967 estate tax provisions 6.08
. . tax rates . . . . S6.01[1]
. options . . . . 19.04[6][a]
. overpayment of, effect . . . . 2.02[3][c]
. partial consideration, transfers for . . . 4.15[2]
. payment of . . . . 1.02[6], 2.02[2]
. . executor, liability of 2.02
. . extension of time for . . . . 2.02[3]
. . liability for 2.02
. . overpayment, effect . . . . 2.02[3][c]
. powers of appointment
. . disclaimers . . . . 4.13[7][d]
. . estate tax liability of recipient of property
     over which decedent had power . . 8.06
. . generally . . . . 1.02[2][b][viii]
. prior interests 4.17
. private annuities . . . . 4.11[5]
. qualified domestic trusts . . . . 5.07[4]
. . computation of tax . . . . 5.07[4][b]
. . events triggering tax . . . . 5.07[4][a]
. . liability for tax . . . . 5.07[4][c]
. . payment of tax . . . . 5.07[4][c]
. rate of tax . . . . 1.02[1]
. . generally . . . . 1.02[1]
. . graduated rate table . . . . 1.02[1]
. recovery, right of
. . decedent-retained interest 8.08
. . marital deduction 8.07
. reimbursement out of estate 8.04
. . state common law . . . . 8.04[3]
. . state statutes . . . . 8.04[2]
. . will provisions . . . . 8.04[1]
. residence and liability for 8.09
. returns . . . . 2.02[1]
. . executor, timely filing by . . . . 2.02[1]
. . reasonable cause test . . . . 2.02[1]
. . will filed with . . . . 2.02[1]
. rights and restrictions on property, valuation
     . . . . 19.04[6][a]
. state common law, reimbursement out of es-
     tate . . . . 8.04[3]
. state statutes, reimbursement out of estate
     . . . . 8.04[2]
. "sunset provisions" . . . . S1.05[4]
. tax planning . . . . 5.06[6][b]
. tax treaties, effect
     See Tax conventions
. termination after December 31, 2001 . . S1.05
. transfers subject to . . . . 1.03[2]

Estate tax—Cont'd
. *transfers subject to—Cont'd*
. . within three years of death . . 1.02[2][b][i], S4.07[2][c]
. will provisions, reimbursement out of estate . . . . 8.04[1]

Estate trusts, marital deduction . . 5.06[7][b]

EWOCs

See Eligible worker owned cooperatives (EWOCs)

Excise taxes
. ESOPs and EWOCs, excise tax limitations in sale of qualified employer securities to . . . . 5.08[4]
. estate tax . . . . 1.03[1]
. gift tax . . . . 1.03[1]
. . valuation of gifts . . . . 10.02[2][g]

Executor
. defined . . . . 1.02[6], 4.14[3][a], 8.02
. discharge from personal liability 8.03
. . debts due the United States . . . . . . 8.03[1]
. . procedure to gain release . . . . 8.03[2]
. embezzlement of estate assets by, theft losses . . . . 5.04[3]
. liability of, personal
. . discharge from 8.03
. . estate tax payment . . . . 2.02, 2.02[1]
. terminable interest rule, executor-purchaser provision . . . . 5.06[7][d]

Executor commissions, estate taxation
. . . . S5.03[3][a]

Exemptions

See also Generation-skipping transfer (GST) exemption
. annuities, exemption from gross estate . . . . 4.11[6]
. prior years, gift tax exemptions for . . 9.05[4]
. tax conventions . . . . 7.03[1][c]

Expatriation
. determination of citizenship . . . . . 6.01[2][a]
. tax avoidance and 6.07, S6.07
. . Section 2107 . . . . S6.07[2]
. . . credit . . . . S6.07[2][c]
. . . requirements . . . . S6.07[2][a]
. . . special situs rule . . . . S6.07[2][b]
. . Section 2801 . . . . S6.07[1]
. . . requirements . . . . S6.07[1][a]
. . . tax imposed . . . . S6.07[1][b]

Expenses

See also Administration expenses; Educational expenses; Funeral expenses
. charitable deductions for estate expenses . . . . 5.05[3][c]

Expenses —Cont'd
. *charitable deductions for estate expenses—Cont'd*
. . administrative expenses . . . . 5.05[3][c][ii]
. . death taxes . . . . 5.05[3][c][i]
. . Section 2053 items . . . . 5.05[3][c][ii]
. deductions . . . . 1.02[3][b]
. medical

See Medical expenses
. nonresident aliens . . . . 6.06[1]
. tuition

See Tuition payments

Extraordinary payment rights
. defined . . . . 19.02[2][b][ii], 19.02[4][b]
. estate freezes, special valuation rules . . . . 19.02[2][b][ii], 19.02[4][b]
. qualified payment rights combined with . . . . 19.02[4][c][ii]

F

Fair market value
. defined . . . . 4.02[2], 4.04[1]
. gross estate . . . . 4.02[2]
. interest in property, measurement of gift of . . . . 19.03[1]

Family members
. conservation easement, gross estate exclusion for family-owned land subject to . . . . S4.02[4][b][i]
. defined . . . . 19.05[2][b][iii]
. estate freezes, special valuation rules to combat abuses of
. . applicable family member . . 19.02[2][b][i], 19.02[5][a][iii], 19.03[2][a][iii]
. . grantor retained income trusts . . . . 19.03[2][a][ii]
. . member of family, required transfer or benefit of . . . . 19.02[2][a][iii]
. family-owned business deduction . . . S5.08A
. gross estate exclusion for family-owned property
. . conservation easement, land subject to . . . . S4.02[4][b][i]
. joint purchases by . . . . 19.03[4][a]
. lapsed voting or liquidation rights . . . . 19.05[2][b][iii]
. special-use valuation qualification . . . . 4.04[3][b][vii]

Family obligations, gift tax valuation
. . . . 10.02[5]
. divorce . . . . 10.02[5][c]
. dower and curtesy rights . . . . . . 10.02[5][d]
. extent and value of obligation . . 10.02[5][a]
. marital rights, elective share . . . 10.02[5][d]

Family obligations, gift tax valuation—Cont'd
. trust, creation of . . . . 10.02[5][b]
Family-owned business deduction . . . S5.08A
. amount of deduction . . . . S5.08A[4]
. assets excluded from value . S5.08A[2][b][iv]
. corporate or partnership entities, requirements with respect to . . . . S5.08A[2][c]
. . general requirements . . . . S5.08A[2][b]
. . non-publicly traded equity and debt . . . . S5.08A[2][c][i]
. . ownership requirements . . S5.08A[2][c][ii]
. definition of qualified family-owned business interest . . . . S5.08A[2]
. effective date . . . . S5.08A[7]
. estate qualifications . . . . S5.08A[3]
. . adjusted gross estate . . . . S5.08A[3][c][v]
. . adjusted value of qualified family-owned business . . . . S5.08A[3][c][iii]
. . agreement . S5.08A[3][b], S5.08A[3][b][ii]
. . citizens or residents only . . . S5.08A[3][a]
. . election . . . . S5.08A[3][b], S5.08A[3][b][i]
. . 50 percent test . . . . S5.08A[3][c], S5.08A[3][c][i]
. . includible qualified family-owned business interests . . . . S5.08A[3][c][ii]
. . . gifts of . . . . S5.08A[3][c][iv]
. . material participation requirement . . . . S5.08A[3][e]
. . ownership requirement . . . . . S5.08A[3][d]
. . qualified heir requirement . S5.08A[3][c][ii], S5.08A[3][f]
. generally . . . . S5.08A[1]
. GST tax, interrelationship of exclusion with . . . . S5.08A[6][c][ii]
. income tax basis . . . . S5.08A[6][c][i]
. interrelationship of Section 2057 deduction to other estate tax Sections and other taxes . . . . S5.08A[6]
. . generally . . . . S5.08A[6][a]
. . other estate tax provisions . . . S5.08A[6][b]
. . Section 2031(c), interrelationship with . . . . S5.08A[6][b][i]
. . Section 2032A, interrelationship with . . . . S5.08A[6][b][ii]
. . Section 2056, interrelationship with . . . . S5.08A[6][b][iii]
. . Section 6166, interrelationship with . . . . S5.08A[6][b][iv]
. limitations . . . . S5.08A[2][b]
. marital deduction, interrelationship with . . . . S5.08A[6][b][iii]
. noncitizens, interest passing to . . . . S5.08A[2][b][v]
. personal holding company income, ceiling on . . . . S5.08A[2][b][iii]

Family-owned business deduction—Cont'd
. qualified family-owned business interest . . . . S5.08A[2][a]
. recapture rules . . . . S5.08A[5]
. . adjusted tax difference . . . S5.08A[5][c][ii]
. . amount of recapture tax . . . S5.08A[5][c][i]
. . applicable percentage . . . . S5.08A[5][c][ii]
. . citizenship, loss of . . . . . S5.08A[5][b][iii]
. . dispositions . . . . S5.08A[5][b][ii]
. . due date for tax . . . . S5.08A[5][e]
. . estate tax savings . . . . . . S5.08A[5][c][ii]
. . failure to meet material participation requirements . . . . S5.08A[5][b][i]
. . foreign principal place of business . . . . S5.08A[5][b][iv]
. . generally . . . . S5.08A[5][a]
. . interest . . . . S5.08A[5][c][iii]
. . liability for tax . . . . S5.08A[5][f]
. . measuring recapture tax . . . . S5.08A[5][c]
. . only one additional tax . . . . . S5.08A[5][d]
. . recapture events . . . . S5.08A[5][b]
. . statute of limitations . . . . . . S5.08A[5][g]
. requirements . . . . S5.08A[2][b], S5.08A[2][c]
. Section 303 stock . . . . S5.08A[6][c][i]
. Section 2031(c), interrelationship of Section 2057 deduction with . . . . . S5.08A[6][b][i]
. Section 2032A, interrelationship of Section 2057 deduction with . . . . S5.08A[6][b][ii]
. Section 2056, interrelationship of Section 2057 deduction with . . . . S5.08A[6][b][iii]
. Section 6166, interrelationship of Section 2057 deduction with . . . . S5.08A[6][b][iv]
. trade or business requirement . S5.08A[2][b][i]
. United States as principal place of business requirement . . . . S5.08A[2][b][ii]
Farms and farming
. absence from farm, special-use valuation qualification . . . . 4.04[3][c][ii]
. cattle, alternate valuation date for gross estate inclusion . . . . 4.03[2][d]
. charitable bequests of remainders in . . . . 5.05[8][a]
. comparability of land, valuation and . . . . 4.04[5][a][iii]
. continued use of farm for farming after death, facilitation through special-use valuation . . . . 4.04[1]
. defined . . . . 4.04[3][b][iii]
. eligible worker owned cooperatives (EWOCs) . . . . 5.08[1]
. farming purposes, defined . . . . 4.04[3][b][iii]
. formula farm valuation method . . . 4.04[5][a]
. . comparable land . . . . 4.04[5][a][iii]
. . divisor . . . . 4.04[5][a][v]
. . gross cash rental . . . . 4.04[5][a][i]

Farms and farming —Cont'd
. *formula farm valuation method—Cont'd*
. . interest rate and . . . . 4.04[5][a][v]
. . net share rental . . . . 4.04[5][a][ii]
. . real estate taxes . . . . 4.04[5][a][iv]
. . speculative inflation of farm real estate val-
    ues, elimination of . . . . 4.04[5][b]
. growing crops, valuation for gross estate in-
    clusion purposes
. . special-use valuation . . . . 4.04[3][c]
. multiple-factor method of valuation 4.04[5][c]
. production of agricultural/horticultural com-
    modities, special-use valuation
    . . . . 4.04[3][c][ii]
. remainders in, charitable bequests of
    . . . . 5.05[8][a]
. special-use valuation, gross-estate inclusion
    . . . . 4.04

    See also Special-use valuation, real prop-
    erty
. types of farms . . . . 4.04[3][b][iii]
. valuation methods . . . . 4.04[5]

**Federal Coal Mine Health and Safety Act of
1969**
. gross estate exclusion of payments under
    . . . . 4.05[8]

Federal Housing Act of 1937
. public housing bonds, gross estate and
    . . . . 4.05[3]

Federal Railroad Retirement Act
. gross estate exclusion of payments under
    . . . . 4.05[8]

Federal redeemable bonds
. valuation . . . . 4.02[3][e]

**Federal statutory law, conflicts between tax
conventions and** 7.06

Fiduciary liability, gift tax . . . . 9.04[11]

Fires, casualty losses . . . . 5.04[2]

Five and five rule
. powers of appointment . . . . 4.13[7][f]

Flower bonds
. valuation . . . . 4.02[3][e]

**Foreign branches of U.S. banks, deposits by
nonresident aliens** . . . . 6.05[3]

Foreign corporate stock of nonresident aliens
    . . . . 6.04[1]

Foreign death taxes
. credit against estate tax . . . . 1.02[5][e], 3.06
. . adjustments, federal estate tax . . 3.06[3][a]
. . computation of credit . . . . 3.06[1]
. . federal estate tax formula . . . . . . 3.06[3]
. . foreign death tax formula . . . . . . 3.06[2]
. . gross estate . . . . 3.06[3][c]

Foreign death taxes —Cont'd
. *credit against estate tax—Cont'd*
. . payment of tax . . . . 3.06[4]
. . remainders, tax on 3.07
. . value of property . . . . 3.06[3][b]
. tax conventions 3.06

Foreign Investors Tax Act of 1966
. expatriation 6.07
. . Section 2107 . . . . S6.07[2]
. . . credit . . . . S6.07[2][c]
. . . requirements . . . . S6.07[2][a]
. . . special situs rule . . . . S6.07[2][b]
. . Section 2801 . . . . 6.07[1]
. . . requirements . . . . 6.07[1][a]
. . . tax imposed . . . . 6.07[1][b]
. foreign death taxes 3.06
. nonresident aliens, taxation of 7.02
. . bank accounts . . 6.04[3], 6.05[2], 6.05[2][b]
. tax conventions and . 7.02, 7.02[2][c], 7.03[2]

Fraternal organizations
. charitable deductions . . . . . 5.05[2], 11.01[1]
. death benefits paid by fraternal beneficial so-
    cieties . . . . 4.14[2]

**Freely Associated States, Compact of Free
Association with** . . . . 7.03[9]

Freezing of estate
    See Estate freezes

French convention . . . . 7.03[3]

Funeral expenses
. deductions from estate tax . . . . . . 1.02[3][b]

Funeral expenses, estate taxation
. "allowable" test . . . . S5.03[2][b]
. generally . . . . S5.03[2][a]

Future interests
. defined . . . . 9.04[3]
. gift tax . . . . 9.04[2], 9.04[3]
. . Crummey powers . . . . 9.04[3][f]
. . definition of future interests . . . . . 9.04[3]
. . disqualification for exclusion . . . . . 9.04[2]
. . enforceable future rights, gifts of
    . . . . 10.01[3][i]
. . minors, gifts to . . . . 9.04[4]
. . mixed private and charitable gifts . 11.02[2]
. . non-income-producing property . 9.04[3][b]
. . postponement of enjoyment of gift, brief
    . . . . 9.04[3][d]
. . present interests, powers affecting
    . . . . 9.04[3][c]
. . right to enjoyment of gift . . . . . 9.04[3][e]
. . separate interests tested . . . . . . 9.04[3][a]

G

Generation-skipping transfer (GST) exemption
. allocation of
. . deferral of effect on inclusion ratio 16.02[7]
. . direct skips . . . . 16.02[7]
. . generally 15.01
. . inclusion ratio . . . . 16.02[4][a], 16.02[5][b],
16.02[7]
. direct skips, allocation to
. . deferral of effect, inclusion ratio and
. . . . 16.02[7]
. . inclusion ratio . . . . 16.02[7]
. generally 15.01
. inclusion ratio, relationship with . . . 16.02[1]
. $1 million, exemption amount 15.01

Generation-skipping transfers . 13.01 – 13.03

See also Generation-skipping transfer (GST)
exemption; Generation-skipping transfer
tax
. Act Section 501 and Code Section 2664, applicability . . . . S1.05[2]
. defined 13.01
. direct skips . . . . 1.04[3][a]
. . computation of taxable amount . . 14.04[1]
. . defined . . . . 1.04[3][a]
. . generally . . . . 1.03[2][d], 1.04[3][a], 12.02
. . gift tax on . . . . 1.03[2][d]
. . gross estate of transferor, property included
in . . . . 14.05[2][a]
. . inclusion ratio . . . . . . 16.02[2], 16.02[7],
16.02[8][a]
. . inter vivos transfers . 1.03[2][d], 1.04[3][a],
12.02
. . payment of tax . . . . 1.04[5]
. . reductions . . . . 14.04[3]
. . returns . . . . 18.02[2][b]
. . taxable amount . 1.04[4][a][i], 12.02, 14.04,
14.05[1]
. . tax exclusive transfers 12.02
. . tax inclusive transfers 12.02
. . tax liability . . . . 12.03[1]
. . testamentary . 12.02, 17.04[1][c], 18.03[1][a]
. . valuation of property received by transferee
. . . . 14.04[2]
. excluded transfers . . . . . 1.04[3][d], 13.01[2]
. . educational expenses, transfers for
. . . 1.04[3][d], 13.01[2][a], S13.01[2][a]
. . medical expenses, transfers for . . 1.04[3][d],
13.01[2][a]
. . previously taxed transfers . . . . 13.01[2][b]
. generally . . . . 13.01[1]
. reductions
. . direct skips . . . . 14.04[3]

Generation-skipping transfers—Cont'd
. *reductions —Cont'd*
. . taxable distributions . . . . 14.02[3]
. . taxable terminations . . . . 14.03[3]
. "sunset provisions" . . . . S1.05[4]
. taxable distributions . . . . 1.04[3][c]
. . computation of taxable amount . . 14.02[1]
. . defined . . . . 1.04[3][c]
. . generally . . . . . . 1.04[3], 1.04[3][c], 12.02
. . inclusion ratio . . . . . . 16.02[3], 16.02[8][b]
. . payment of tax . . . . 1.04[5], 14.02[4]
. . reductions . . . . 14.02[3]
. . returns . . . . 18.02[2][a]
. . taxable amount 1.04[4][a][iii], 12.02, 14.02,
14.05[1]
. . tax inclusive transfers 12.02
. . tax-payment taxable distributions . 14.02[4]
. . valuation of property received by transferee
. . . . 14.02[2]
. taxable terminations . . . . 1.04[3][b]
. . computation of taxable amount . . 14.03[1]
. . death, valuation of terminations on
. . . . 14.05[2][b]
. . defined . . . . 1.04[3][b]
. . generally . 1.04[3], 1.04[3][b], 1.04[4][a][ii],
12.02
. . inclusion ratio . . . . . . 16.02[3], 16.02[8][b]
. . payment of tax . . . . 1.04[5]
. . reductions . . . . 14.03[3]
. . returns . . . . 18.02[2][a]
. . taxable amount . 1.04[4][a][ii], 12.02, 14.03,
14.05[1]
. . tax inclusive transfers 12.02
. . valuation of property involved in . 14.03[2]
. testamentary transfers
. . basis adjustment . . . . 17.04[1][c]
. . direct skips . . 12.02, 17.04[1][c], 18.03[1][a]
. . inclusion ratio . . . . 16.02[4][d]
. . recapture tax . . . . . 18.03[1][a], 18.03[1][b]
. types . . . . 1.04[3]

Generation-skipping transfer tax 1.04, 18.01 –
18.05

See also Generation-skipping transfer (GST)
exemption; Generation-skipping transfers
. administration 18.01
. . deferral of payment . . . . 18.01[2]
. . generally . . . . 18.01[1]
. . transfers at death, deferral of payment
. . . . 18.01[2][a], S18.01[2][a]
. . transfers other than at death, deferral of
payment . . . . 18.01[2][b]
. amount taxable . . . 1.04[4][a], 12.02, S12.02,
14.01 – 14.05
. applicable rate . . . . 1.04[4][b]

Generation-skipping transfer tax — Cont'd

. assignment of generation . . . . 1.04[2], 17.01
. assignment of trust interests . . . . 17.02[3][e]
. . beneficiary assignor, consequences to
. . . . 17.02[3][e][i]
. . trust, consequences to . . . . . 17.02[3][e][iii]
. basis adjustment . . . . 17.04[1]
. . generally . . . . 17.04[1][a]
. . general rule . . . . 17.04[1][b]
. . testamentary direct skips . . . . . 17.04[1][c]
. beneficiaries, classes of . . . . 17.01[2]
. . ancestral chain . . . . 17.01[2][a][i],
. . . . S17.01[2][a][i]
. . assignment of trust interests, consequences
. . . . to beneficiary . . . . 17.02[3][e][i]
. . corporations, partnerships, and estates as
. . . . beneficiaries . . . . 17.01[2][c][i]
. . nonindividual beneficiaries . . . 17.01[2][c]
. . nontrust entities . . . . 17.01[2][c][i]
. . overlapping related beneficiaries
. . . . 17.01[2][a][ii]
. . related beneficiaries . . . . 17.01[2][a]
. . trust entities . . . . 17.01[2][c][ii]
. . unrelated beneficiaries . . . . . . 17.01[2][b]
. buy-sell agreements, valuation . . 19.04[6][c]
. Chapter 13 tax
. . nonresident aliens, trusts partially subject to
. . . . Chapter 13 . . . . 18.03[2][c]
. . repeal of 1976 version 18.05
. charitable remainders, special rule 17.02[3][c]
. charitable remainder trusts . . . . . 17.02[3][c]
. classes of beneficiaries . . . . 17.01[2]
. computation . . . . 1.04[4], 14.01
. conservation easement . . . . . S4.02[4][f][iii]
. consideration, reduction for . . . . . . 14.05[3]
. corporations as beneficiaries . . 17.01[2][c][i]
. credit for state taxes . . . . . . 1.04[4][c], 12.04
. deferral of payment . . . . 18.01[2]
. . transfers at death . 18.01[2][a], S18.01[2][a]
. . transfers other than at death . . 18.01[2][b]
. definitions 17.01, 17.02
. direct skips . . . . 1.04[3][a]

See also Generation-skipping trans-
fers--direct skips

. disclaimers . . . 10.07[1], 17.04[3], S17.04[3]
. double imposition, avoidance . . . 13.01[2][b]
. . general rule . . . . 13.01[2][b][i]
. . limitation . . . . 13.01[2][b][ii]
. . scope of exclusion . . . . 13.01[2][b][iii]
. educational expenses, exclusion . . 1.04[3][d],
. . . . 13.01[2][a], S13.01[2][a]
. estate freezes, relationship to . . . 19.02[5][f],
. . . . 19.03[4][e][iii]

Generation-skipping transfer tax — Cont'd

. estates
. . as beneficiaries . . . . 17.01[2][c][i]
. . as skip persons . . . . 13.03[4][a]
. estate tax, comparison . . . . 1.04[1]
. estate tax inclusion period (ETIP) . . 16.02[7]
. . death, termination at . . . . . 16.02[7][e][ii]
. . inclusion ratio . . . . 16.02[7]
. . lifetime termination of . . . . 16.02[7][e][iii]
. . nonresident aliens . . . . 18.03[2][d]
. . termination of . . . . 16.02[7][c]
. family-owned business deduction, interrela-
. . . . tionship of GST tax with   S5.08A[6][c][ii]
. generally . . . . 1.03[2][d], 1.04[1]
. generation
. . assignment of . . . . 1.04[2], 17.01
. . defined . . . . 17.01[1]
. . multiple skips, generation level of transfer-
. . . . ors of . . . . 17.03[1]
. gift tax and . . . . 1.04[1], 10.05, S10.05
. history . . . . 1.04[1]
. imposition of
. . double imposition, avoidance . . 13.01[2][b]
. inclusion ratio . . . . 1.04[4][b][ii], 16.02
. . allocation of GST exemption . . 16.02[4][a],
. . . . 16.02[5][b], 16.02[5][b][i],
. . . . 16.02[5][b][iii], 16.02[7]
. . applicable fraction . . . . 1.04[4][b][ii],
. . . . 16.02[2][c][i], 16.02[3][b],
. . . . . 16.02[4][d][i], 16.02[5], 16.02[7][e]
. . calculation of . 16.02[1], 16.02[2], 16.02[3]
. . charitable deduction reduction
. . . . 16.02[3][b][ii]
. . charitable lead annuity trusts . . 16.02[4][f],
. . . . 16.02[6]
. . consolidation of separate trusts   16.02[5][c]
. . deferral of effect of GST exemption alloca-
. . . . tion and of direct skips on certain inter
. . . . vivos transfers . . . . 16.02[7]
. . defined . . . . 1.04[4][b][ii], 16.02[1]
. . denominator, applicable fraction
. . . . 16.02[3][b][ii]
. . direct skips . 16.02[2], 16.02[7], 16.02[8][a]
. . estate tax inclusion period . . . . . 16.02[7]
. . finality of . . . . 16.02[8]
. . generally . . . . 1.04[4][b][ii], 16.02[1]
. . gross estate, inter vivos transfers includible
. . . . in . . . . 16.02[4][b], 16.02[7][a],
. . . . 16.02[7][b][i], 16.02[7][b][ii],
. . . . 16.02[7][c][i]
. . GST exemption relationship with . 16.02[1]
. . illustrations of deferral rules . . 16.02[7][d]
. . inter vivos transfers . . . . 16.02[4][b],
. . . . 16.02[4][c], 16.02[7]

Generation-skipping transfer tax—Cont'd
. *inclusion ratio—Cont'd*
. . lifetime termination of estate tax inclusion
     period . . . . 16.02[7][e][iii]
. . marital deduction transfers . 16.02[7][b][ii]
. . multiple skips, effect of . . . . 17.03[2]
. . nontaxable gifts . . . . 16.02[2][b]
. . numerator, applicable fraction 16.02[3][b][i]
. . ongoing inclusion ratio, taxable terminations
     and distributions . . . . . . 16.02[3][b][iii]
. . ongoing nontaxable gift transfers to trust,
     direct transfers . . . . 16.02[2][b][v]
. . other-than-nontaxable gifts, direct skips
     . . . . 16.02[2][c]
. . pecuniary amounts . . . . 16.02[4][d][ii],
     16.02[4][d][iii]
. . post-March 31, 1988 transfers to trust, di-
     rect skips . . . . 16.02[2][b][iii]
. . pre-April 1, 1988 nontaxable gift transfers
     to trust, direct transfers . 16.02[2][b][iv]
. . qualified terminable interest property
     . . . . 16.02[4][e]
. . redetermination of applicable fraction
     . . . . 16.02[5]
. . residual transfer after pecuniary payment
     . . . . 16.02[4][d][iii]
. . split gifts . . . 16.02[7][b][ii], 16.02[7][c][ii]
. . subsequent transfers, continuation of inclu-
     sion ratio for 16.02[2][c][ii], 16.02[5][a]
. . taxable terminations and taxable distribu-
     tions . . . . 16.02[3], 16.02[8][b]
. . . calculation for . . . . 16.02[3][a]
. . tax imposed on GST transfer . . 16.02[5][d]
. . tax reduction . . . . 16.02[3][b][ii]
. . termination of estate tax inclusion period
     . . . . 16.02[7][c]
. . . at death . . . . 16.02[7][e][ii]
. . testamentary transfers . . . . 16.02[4][d]
. . timely gift tax return . . . . 16.02[4][a]
. . transferor's spouse . . . . 16.02[7][b][ii],
     16.02[7][c][iii]
. . transfers in trust, additional . 16.02[5][b][ii],
     16.02[5][b][iii]
. . transfers not in trust, direct skips
     . . . . 16.02[2][b][ii]
. . trust severance . . . . S16.02[5][e]
. . valuation rules . . . . 16.02[4]
. . zero inclusion ratio 16.02[2][a], 16.02[2][b]
. information returns . . . . 18.02[6]
. interests in property . . . . 17.02[3]
. . avoidance of GST . . . . 17.02[3][d]
. . charitable remainders, special rule
     . . . . 17.02[3][c]
. . defined . . . . 17.02[3][a]
. . generally . . . . 17.02[3][a]

Generation-skipping transfer tax—Cont'd
. *interests in property—Cont'd*
. . permissible noncharitable current recipient
     of trust income or corpus . . 17.02[3][b]
. . postponement of GST . . . . . . 17.02[3][d]
. . present right to . . . . 17.02[3][b]
. . trusts, assignment of interests . 17.02[3][e]
. inter vivos transfers
. . direct skips . . . 1.03[2][d], 1.04[3][a], 12.02
. . gift tax and, transfers subject to both taxes
     . . . . 10.05, S10.05
. . gross estate . . . 16.02[7][a], 16.02[7][b][i],
     16.02[7][b][ii], 16.02[7][c][i]
. . GST exemption allocated to inter vivos
     transfers other than direct skips
     . . . . 16.02[4][c]
. . inclusion ratio . . . . 16.02[4][b], 16.02[4][c],
     16.02[7]
. introduction . . . . S17.02[1][a]
. lapsed voting or liquidation rights 19.05[2][a]
. liability for . . . . 1.04[5], 12.03
. . general rules . . . . 12.03[1]
. . trustee's liability, limitation of . . . 12.03[3],
     17.04[4]
. . trust equivalent arrangements . . . . 12.03[2]
. liquidation restrictions . . . . 19.05[3][a]
. medical expenses, exclusion . . . . . 1.04[3][d],
     13.01[2][a]
. multiple skips 17.03
. . generation level of transferors of . 17.03[1]
. . inclusion ratio, effect on . . . . 17.03[2]
. . pour-over trusts . . . . 17.03[2][b]
. . taxable terminations, multiple, with same
     trust transferor . . . . 17.03[2][a]
. multiple transferors . . . . 17.02[1][d]
. nonindividual beneficiaries . . . . . 17.01[2][c]
. . nontrust entities . . . . 17.01[2][c][i]
. . trust entities . . . . 17.01[2][c][ii]
. nonresident alien transferors . . . . . . 18.03[2]
. . ETIP rules . . . . 18.03[2][d]
. . generally . . . . 18.03[2][a]
. . property within United States, transfer of
     . . . . 18.03[2][b]
. . trusts partially subject to Chapter 13
     . . . . 18.03[2][c]
. non-skip persons . . . . 13.03[5]
. . defined . . . . 13.03[1], 13.03[5]
. . generally . . . . 13.03[1]
. nontrust entities as skip persons . . . 13.03[4]
. options . . . . 19.04[6][c]
. partnerships beneficiaries . . . . . 17.01[2][c][i]
. payment of tax . . . . 1.04[5]
. . deferral of payment . . . . 18.01[2]
. . taxable distributions, tax-payment . 14.02[4]

Generation-skipping transfer tax—Cont'd
. *payment of tax—Cont'd*
. . transfers at death, deferral of payment
. . . . 18.01[2][a], S18.01[2][a]
. . transfers other than at death, deferral of
payment . . . . 18.01[2][b]
. pooled income funds . . . . 17.02[3][c]
. pour-over trusts . . . . 17.03[2][b]
. predeceased parent provision . S17.01[2][a][i]
. qualified terminable interest property
. . inclusion ratio . . . . 16.02[4][e]
. . transferors . . . . 17.02[1][c][i]
. rate of tax . . . . 1.04[4][b]
. . applicable rate . . . . 1.04[4][b]
. . inclusion ratio . . . . 1.04[4][b][ii]
. . maximum federal estate tax rate
. . . . 1.04[4][b][i]
. recapture tax
. . regulations . . . . 18.03[1]
. . testamentary direct skips . . . . . 18.03[1][a]
. . testamentary transfers other than direct
skips . . . . 18.03[1][b]
. reductions
. . for consideration . . . . 14.05[3]
. regulations 18.03
. . nonresident alien transferor . . . . . 18.03[2]
. . recapture tax . . . . 18.03[1]
. . trust equivalent arrangements . . . . 18.03[3]
. related beneficiaries . . . . 17.01[2][a]
. . ancestral chain . . . . 17.01[2][a][i],
S17.01[2][a][i]
. . overlapping . . . . 17.01[2][a][ii]
. returns 18.02
. . direct skips . . . . 18.02[2][b]
. . extensions of time to file . . . . 18.02[4][b]
. . generally . . . . 1.04[5], 18.02[1]
. . information returns . . . . 18.02[6]
. . parties who must file . . . . 18.02[3]
. . place for filing . . . . 18.02[5]
. . requirement of return . . . . 18.02[2]
. . taxable distributions and taxable terminations . . . . 18.02[2][a]
. . time for filing . . . . 18.02[4]
. . timely filing . . . . 18.02[4][a]
. skip persons 13.03
. . defined . . . . 1.04[2], 13.03[1]
. . estates . . . . 13.03[4][a]
. . generally . . . . 1.04[2], 13.03[1]
. . individuals as . . . . 13.03[2]
. . nontrust entities . . . . 13.03[4]
. . shareholders as . . . . 13.03[4][b]
. . trusts as . . . . 13.03[1], 13.03[3]
. special rules 17.04

Generation-skipping transfer tax—Cont'd
. split gifts
. . inclusion ratio . . . . 16.02[7][b][ii],
16.02[7][c][ii]
. . transferors . . . . 17.02[1][c][ii], 17.02[1][d]
. taxable amount . . . 1.04[4][a], 12.02, S12.02,
14.01–14.05
. . direct skips . . . . 14.04, 14.05[1]
. . generally 14.01
. . taxable distributions . . . . . . 14.02, 14.05[1]
. . taxable terminations . . . . . . 14.03, 14.05[1]
. . valuation 14.05
. taxable distributions . . . . 1.04[3][c]

*See also Generation-skipping trans-
fers--taxable distributions*

. taxable terminations . . . . 1.04[3][b]

*See also Generation-skipping trans-
fers--taxable terminations*

. tax conventions 7.05
. terminology . . . . 1.04[2]
. transferors . . . . 17.02[1]
. . defined . . . . 1.04[2]
. . generally . . . . 1.04[2]
. . general rules . . . . 17.02[1][b]
. . gift-splitting by spouses . . . 17.02[1][c][ii],
17.02[1][d]
. . multiple . . . . 17.02[1][d]
. . multiple skips . . . . 17.03[1]
. . multiple taxable terminations with same
trust transferor . . . . 17.03[2][a]
. . nonresident aliens . . . . 18.03[2]
. . qualified terminable interest property
. . . . 17.02[1][c][i]
. . special rules . . . . 17.02[1][c]
. trustees
. . defined . . . . 17.02[2]
. . liability of, limitation . . . 12.03[3], 17.04[4]
. trusts and
. . assignment of interests in . . . . 17.02[3][e]
. . beneficiaries, trusts as . . . . 17.01[2][c][ii]
. . charitable lead annuity trusts . . 16.02[4][f],
16.02[6]
. . consolidation of separate trusts, inclusion
ratio . . . . 16.02[5][c]
. . definition of trust . . . . 17.02[2]
. . division of single trust . . . . . 17.04[2][b]
. . equivalent arrangements . . . . 12.03[2],
13.03[3][c], 18.03[3]
. . inclusion ratio . . . . 16.02[4][f], 16.02[5][b],
16.02[5][b][iii], 16.02[5][c], 16.02[6]
. . interests held in . . . . 17.02[3]
. . multiple taxable terminations with same
trust transferor . . . . 17.03[2][a]

Generation-skipping transfer tax—Cont'd
. *trusts—Cont'd*
. . multiple trusts, single trust treated as
. . . . 17.04[2][a]
. . nonresident alien transferors, trusts partially
. . . . subject to Chapter 13 . . . . 18.03[2][c]
. . permissible noncharitable current recipient
. . . . of trust income or corpus . . 17.02[3][b]
. . pour-over trusts . . . . 17.03[2][b]
. . single trust treated as multiple trusts
. . . . 17.04[2][a]
. . skip persons, trusts as . . . . 13.03[3]
. . . all trust interests held by skip persons
. . . . 13.03[3][a]
. . . distributions to skip persons . 13.03[3][b]
. . . generally . . . . 13.03[1]
. . . trust equivalent arrangements . . 12.03[2],
. . . . 13.03[3][c]
. tuition expenses, exclusion . . . . . 1.04[3][d],
. . . . 13.01[2][a], S13.01[2][a]
. unrelated beneficiaries . . . . 17.01[2][b]
. valuation of inclusion ratio . . . . . . 16.02[4]
. valuation of taxable amount 14.05
. . direct skips . . . . 14.04[2], 14.05[2][a]
. . fair market valuation on date of transfer,
. . . . exceptions to . . . . 14.05[2]
. . general rule . . . . 14.05[1]
. . reduction for consideration . . . . . 14.05[3]
. . taxable distributions . . . . 14.02[2]
. . taxable terminations . . 14.03[2], 14.05[2][b]
Generation-skipping transfer tax in 2010,
2013 and thereafter S18.04
. in the year 2013 and thereafter . . . S18.04[2]
German convention . . . . . . 7.03[4], S7.03[4]
Gifts

See also *Deductible gifts; Gift tax; Split gifts*
. adjusted taxable gifts
. . defined . . . . 6.01[1]
. . nonresident aliens . . . . . 6.01[1], S6.01[1]
. alteration of time or manner of gift, power of
. . . . 10.01[7]
. amount of gift . . . . 3.04[1][b]
. annuities . . . . 10.01[3][g]
. below-market interest rate loans, as indirect
. . . . gifts . . . . 10.01[2][f]
. beneficiaries of, power to change . . 10.01[6]
. charitable organizations, gifts to . . 9.04[1][b],
. . . . 11.01[1]
. checks . . . . 10.01[3][h]
. community property . 10.01[3][f], 10.01[5][d]
. . valuation . . . . 10.02[6][b]
. completion of gift
. . determination . . . . 10.01[4]
. . valuation on . . . . 10.02[1][a]

Gifts —Cont'd
. conditional transfers 10.01[3][e], 10.01[10][d]
. contract, gifts by . . . . 10.01[4]
. corporations
. . gifts by . . . . 9.04[1][b], 10.01[2][c]
. . money's worth received by, valuation
. . . . 10.02[6][a]
. . transfers to . . . . 10.01[2][b]
. defined . . . . 1.03[2][b], 9.04
. determination of gift . . . . 10.01[4]
. direct gifts . . . . 10.01[1]
. discharge of indebtedness . . . . . 10.01[2][e]
. enjoyment of
. . postponement, brief . . . . 9.04[3][d]
. . right to . . . . 9.04[3][e]
. family obligations, valuation . . . . . 10.02[5]
. . divorce . . . . 10.02[5][c]
. . dower and curtesy rights . . . . . 10.02[5][d]
. . extent and value of . . . . 10.02[5][a]
. . marital rights, elective share . . 10.02[5][d]
. . money's worth, receipts of . . . . . 10.02[6]
. . trust, creation of . . . . 10.02[5][b]
. future rights, enforceable . . . . . . 10.01[3][i]
. generally 1.01
. gratuitous services . . . . 10.01[2][g]
. gross gifts 9.02
. husband or wife, gifts to third party by 10.03
. incompetent persons, indirect gifts by
. . . . 10.01[2][h]
. indirect gifts . . . . 10.01[2]
. . below-market interest rate loans . 10.01[2][f]
. . corporations, gifts by . . . . 10.01[2][c]
. . discharge of indebtedness . . . . 10.01[2][e]
. . gratuitous services . . . . 10.01[2][g]
. . incompetent persons, gifts by . . 10.01[2][h]
. . marital deduction property, right of recovery
. . . . 8.07[5]
. . nature of transfer . . . . 10.01[2][d]
. . private corporations, transfers to 10.01[2][b]
. . trust, transfers in . . . . 10.01[2][a]
. insurance . . . . 10.01[3][g], 10.02[2][e]
. . split dollar life insurance . . . S10.01[3][g]
. intention to make . . . . 10.01[4]
. joint accounts . . . . 10.01[5][c]
. joint and mutual wills . . . . 10.01[5][e]
. joint donees . . . . 9.04[1][b]
. joint interests . . . . 4.12[6], 10.01[3][f]
. life insurance policies . . . . 10.01[3][g]
. limited liability companies compared to gift
. . . . giving . . . . 4.05[7][c]
. loans, gift . . . . 10.01[2][f]
. minors, gifts to . . . . 9.04[4]

Gifts —Cont'd
. *minors, gifts to—Cont'd*
. . donee requirements, special statutory rule
. . . . 9.04[5]
. . gift tax credit for gifts to . . . . . 3.04[1][b]
. . revocable transfers . . . . 4.10[4][f]
. mixed private and charitable gifts
. . future interests . . . . 11.02[2]
. . present interests . . . . 11.02[3]
. near death . . . . 1.02[2][b][i], S4.07

　　*See also Transfers within three years of
　　death*
. nonresident aliens . . . . . . 6.02[2], 10.01[11]
. notes . . . . 10.01[3][h]
. other entities, gifts to . . . . 9.04[1][b]
. powers of appointment 10.04
. property interests . . . . 10.01[3]
. . annuities . . . . 10.01[3][g]
. . checks . . . . 10.01[3][h]
. . classes of property . . . . 10.01[3][a]
. . community property . . . . 10.01[3][f]
. . conditional transfers, not subject to tax
. . . . 10.01[3][e]
. . discounts and premiums . . . . . 10.02[2][c]
. . future rights, enforceable . . . . . 10.01[3][i]
. . identification of . . . . 10.01[3]
. . insurance . . . . 10.01[3][g]
. . joint interests . . . . 10.01[3][f]
. . life insurance policies . . . . 10.01[3][g]
. . notes . . . . 10.01[3][h]
. . remainders . . . . 10.01[3][b]
. . reversionary interests . . . . 10.01[3][d]
. . types of . . . . 10.01[3][a]
. . uncertain interests 10.01[3][c], S10.01[3][c]
. reciprocal trusts . . . . 10.02[6][c]
. remainders . . . . 9.04[3], 10.01[3][b]
. reversionary interests . . . . 10.01[3][d]
. revocable transfers . . . . 10.01[5]
. . community property . . . . 10.01[5][d],
. . . . S10.01[5][d]
. . joint accounts . . . . 10.01[5][c]
. . joint and mutual wills . . . . . . 10.01[5][e]
. . minor's right to revoke . . . . . . 10.01[5][a]
. . termination of donor's control . 10.01[5][b]
. split dollar life insurance . . . . . S10.01[3][g]
. split gifts 10.03
. . consent, signifying . . . . 10.03[3]
. . election, effect of . . . . 10.03[2]
. . generally . . . . 10.03[1]
. . manner of signifying consent . . 10.03[3][a]
. . rate of tax . . . . 10.03[2]
. . return requirement, effect of election on
. . . . 10.03[4]

Gifts —Cont'd
. *split gifts—Cont'd*
. . revocation of consent . . . . . . 10.03[3][c]
. . time of consent . . . . 10.03[3][b]
. straw man, use of . . . . 9.04[1][b]
. taxable . . . . 1.03[3], 1.03[5], 9.04, 11.01
. . adjusted taxable gifts . . . 6.01[1], S6.01[1]
. . preceding calendar periods, taxable gifts for
. . . . 9.05
. tax-free . . . . 1.03[3]
. tenancy by the entirety, gifts to . . 9.04[1][b]
. third parties, gifts by husband or wife to
. . . . 10.03
. timing problem . . . . 10.01[4]
. total taxable gifts . . . . 3.04[1][c]
. trust
. . gifts in . . . . 9.04[1][b], 9.04[3][a]
. . transfer in (indirect gifts) . . . . 10.01[2][a]
. uncertain interests . 10.01[3][c], S10.01[3][c]
. valuation 10.02
. . actuarial valuation . . . . 10.02[2][f]
. . community property . . . . 10.02[6][b]
. . completion of gift . . . . 10.02[1][a]
. . consideration received for transfer 10.02[3]
. . corporate recipients . . . . 10.02[6][a]
. . credit for gift tax, value of gift and
. . . . 3.04[2][b]
. . discounts and premiums, interests in prop-
. . . erty . . . . 10.02[2][c]
. . donee payment of tax . . . . 10.02[6][d]
. . encumbered property . . . . . . 10.02[2][a]
. . excise tax and other charges . . 10.02[2][g]
. . family obligations . . . . 10.02[5]
. . generally 10.02
. . insurance contracts . . . . 10.02[2][e]
. . methods of . . . . 10.02[2], S10.02[2]
. . money's worth, receipts of . . . . 10.02[6]
. . mutual fund shares . . . . 10.02[2][d]
. . open transactions . . . . 10.02[1][b]
. . ordinary course of business, transfers in
. . . . 10.02[4]
. . reciprocal trusts . . . . 10.02[6][c]
. . restrictions on use or disposition
. . . . 10.02[2][b]
. . rules for . . . . 1.03[2][a]
. . statement of valuation, furnishing on request
. . . . 10.02[7]
. . statutes applicable to
. . . Section 7477 revised . . . S10.02[2][d][iii]
. . time of . . . . 10.02[1]

Gift tax 1.03, 10.01–10.08

See also Annual gift tax exclusion; Deductible gifts; Gifts

. amnesty rule . . . . 4.15[1][e]
. annuities, gifts of . . . . 10.01[3][g]
. art works, loans of . . . . 9.04[8]
. assessment of additional tax, limitations
. . . . 9.04[10], S9.04[10]
. assignment of income . . . . 10.01[10][a]
. background 9.01
. below-market interest rate loans, as indirect
. . gifts . . . . 10.01[2][f]
. buy-sell agreements, valuation . . 19.04[6][b]
. Chapter 14 rules 10.01
. charitable deduction 1.03[5][a], 11.02, S11.02
. charitable organizations, gifts to . . 9.04[1][b]
. checks, gifts of . . . . 10.01[3][h]
. community property, transfers of   10.01[3][f],
. . . . 10.01[5][d]
. . valuation . . . . 10.02[6][b]
. completion of gift
. . determination . . . . 10.01[4]
. . valuation on . . . . 10.02[1][a]
. computation . . . . 1.03[6]
. conditional transfers 10.01[3][e], 10.01[10][d]
. consideration received for transfer . 1.03[2][b],
. . . . 10.02[3]
. control premiums . . . . 10.02[2][c]
. corporations
. . gifts by . . . . 9.04[1][b], 10.01[2][c]
. . money's worth received by, valuation
. . . . 10.02[6][a]
. . transfers to . . . . 10.01[2][b]
. as credit against estate tax . . 1.02[5][c], 3.04
. . amount of gift, computation and   3.04[1][b]
. . annual gift tax exclusion . . . . . . 3.04[2][b]
. . charitable deduction . . . . 3.04[2][b]
. . computation of potential credit . . . . 3.04[1]
. . decedent's gross estate, effect of   3.04[2][c]
. . federal estate tax, limitation on credit and
. . . . 3.04[2][a]
. . limitation on credit . . . 3.04[2], 3.04[2][d]
. . marital deduction . . . . 3.04[2][b]
. . nonresident aliens . . . . 6.02[2]
. . split gifts . . . . 3.04[2][b]
. . total gift tax, computation and . . 3.04[1][a]
. . total taxable gifts, computation and
. . . . 3.04[1][c]
. . value of gift, effect of . . . . 3.04[2][b]
. curtesy interests . . . . . . 10.02[5][d], 10.06[1]
. direct gifts . . . . 10.01[1]
. discharge of indebtedness . . . . . 10.01[2][e]
. disclaimers . . . . 1.03[2][f], 4.13[7][d], 10.07,
. . . . S10.07[2][b]

Gift tax—Cont'd
. discounts for minority interests . . 10.02[2][c]
. divorce
. . property settlements not in divorce decree
. . . . 10.06
. . transfers in . . . . 1.03[2][e]
. dominion and control . . . . 1.03[2][a]
. donees
. . identification of, annual exclusion
. . . . 9.04[1][b]
. . joint . . . . 9.04[1][b]
. . liability of . . . . 9.04[11]
. . minor donees . . . . 9.04[4], 9.04[5]
. . noncitizen spouses . . . . 11.03[5]
. . payment of tax by, valuation . . 10.02[6][d]
. donors
. . liability of . . . . 9.02[3]
. . nonresident aliens . . . . 10.01[11]
. . nonresident noncitizens . . . . S10.01[11]
. . revocable transfers, termination of donor's
. . . control . . . . 10.01[5][b]
. double taxation regulation . . . . 19.03[4][c][i]
. dower interests . . . . . . 10.02[5][d], 10.06[1]
. educational expenses . . . . . 1.03[3], 9.04[6],
. . . . S9.04[6]
. education IRAs . . . . . S9.04[6], S10.01[3][c]
. enforceable future rights, gifts of . 10.01[3][i]
. estate freezes
. . gift tax relief . . . . 19.02[5][c][iii]
. . relationship to other gift tax provisions
. . . . 19.02[5][e], 19.03[2][c]
. estate tax and . . 1.03[1], 1.03[2][a], 1.04[1],
. . . . 9.01
. . federal estate tax as limitation on gift tax
. . . credit . . . . 3.04[2][a]
. . gift tax as credit against estate tax
. . . . 1.02[5][c], 3.04
. . integration of gift tax and estate tax . . 3.04
. . marital rights . . . . . 4.15[1][f], 10.02[5][d]
. . relationship . . . . 10.01[10]
. excise tax nature of . . . . 1.03[1]
. exclusions . . . . . 1.03[3], 9.04[1], S9.04[1]
. . future interests disqualified for exclusion
. . . . 9.04[2]
. . prior years . . . . 9.05[3]
. exemptions for prior years . . . . 9.05[4]
. family obligations, valuation . . . . . 10.02[5]
. fiduciary liability . . . . 9.04[11]
. future interests . . . . 9.04[2], 9.04[3]
. . Crummey powers . . . . 9.04[3][f]
. . defined . . . . 9.04[3]
. . disqualification for exclusion . . . . . 9.04[2]
. . enforceable future rights . . . . . . 10.01[3][i]
. . minors, gifts to . . . . 9.04[4]

Gift tax—Cont'd
. *future interests—Cont'd*
. . non-income-producing property . 9.04[3][b]
. . postponement of enjoyment of gift, brief
　. . . . . 9.04[3][d]
. . present interests, powers affecting
　. . . . . 9.04[3][c]
. . right to enjoyment of gift . . . . . 9.04[3][e]
. . separate interests tested . . . . . . 9.04[3][a]
. generally . . . . 1.01, 1.03[1], 9.01
. generation-skipping transfer tax and . 1.04[1],
　　　　　　　　　　　　　10.05, S10.05
. gift-splitting . . . . 1.03[4]
. gratuitous services . . . . 10.01[2][g]
. gross gifts 9.02
. history . . . . 1.03[1]
. husband or wife, gifts to third party by 10.03
. imposition of 9.02
. . gift taxation of some expatriates S9.02[1][b]
. . . Section 2501(a)(3) . . . . . . S9.02[1][b][ii]
. . . Section 2801 . . . . S9.02[1][b][i]
. . nonresident aliens, transfers of intangibles
　　by . . . . 9.02[1]
. . nonresident noncitizens . . . . S9.02[1]
. . . general rules for . . . . S9.02[1][a]
. . . rule treating nonresident noncitizens as re-
　　　sidents or citizens . . . . . . S9.02[1][c]
. . periodic imposition . . . . 9.02[3]
. . political organizations, transfers to . 9.02[2]
. income tax and . . . . 9.01, 10.01[10]
. incompetent persons, indirect gifts by
　. . . . . 10.01[2][h]
. indirect gifts . . . . 10.01[2]
. . nature of transfer . . . . 10.01[2][d]
. insurance, gifts of . . 10.01[3][g], 10.02[2][e]
. . split dollar life insurance . . . S10.01[3][g]
. intangibles, transfers by nonresident aliens
　. . . . . 9.02[1]
. interspousal transfers, exclusion 4.16
. inter vivos direct skip . . . . 1.03[2][d]
. joint and mutual wills . . . . 10.01[5][e]
. joint donees . . . . 9.04[1][b]
. joint interests, gifts creating . . . . . . 4.12[6],
　　　　　　　　　　　　　10.01[3][f]
. lapsed voting or liquidation rights 19.05[2][a]
. legislative background 9.01
. liability, determination of
. . donee liability . . . . 9.04[11]
. . donor liability . . . . 9.02[3]
. . fiduciary liability . . . . 9.04[11]
. . generally 9.01
. . imposition of tax 9.02
. . preceding calendar periods, taxable gifts for
　. . . . . 9.05

Gift tax—Cont'd
. *liability, determination of —Cont'd*
. . taxable gifts 9.04, 9.05
. life estates
. . dispositions of certain 10.08
. . election to treat as QTIP . . . . . . 1.03[2][g]
. life insurance policies, gifts of . . 10.01[3][g]
. life interests retained, transfers with
　. . . . . 10.01[10][c]
. limitations on assessment 9.04[10], S9.04[10]
. liquidation restrictions . . . . 19.05[3][a]
. loans of qualified art works . . . . . . 9.04[8]
. marital deduction . . . . 1.03[5][b]
. marital rights in transfers for insufficient con-
　　sideration . . . . 4.15[1][f]
. medical expenses . . . . 1.03[3], 9.04[6]
. minority interests, discounts in valuation of
　. . . . . 10.02[2][c]
. minors, gifts to . . . . 9.04[4]
. . donee requirements, special statutory rule
　. . . . . 9.04[5]
. . first donee requirement . . . . 9.04[5][a]
. . gift tax credit . . . . 3.04[1][b]
. . revocable transfers . . . . 4.10[4][f]
. . second donee requirement . . . . . 9.04[5][b]
. . state statutes simplifying gifts . . 9.04[5][c]
. near-death transfers . . . . S4.07[1], S4.07[3],
　　　　　　　　　　　　　10.01[10][b]
. nonresident aliens . . . . . . S6.01[1], 6.02[2],
　　　　　　　　　　　　　10.01[11]
. . intangibles, transfers of . . . . 9.02[1]
. . nonresident noncitizens . . . . S10.01[11]
. . Section 2511(b) rules for situs of intangible
　　property owned by . . . . S10.01[11]
. notes, gifts of . . . . 10.01[3][h]
. open transaction doctrine . . . . . . 10.02[1][b]
. options, valuation . . . . 19.04[6][b]
. other entities, gifts to . . . . 9.04[1][b]
. payment of . . . . 1.03[8]
. periodic imposition of . . . . 9.02[3]
. political organizations, transfers to . . 9.02[2]
. powers of appointment 10.04

　See also Powers of appointment
. . general power . . . . 1.03[2][c]
. . present interests, powers affecting
　. . . . . 9.04[3][c]
. preceding calendar periods, taxable gifts for
　. . . . . 9.05
. prior years 9.05
. . deductions for . . . . 9.05[4]
. . exclusions for . . . . 9.05[3]
. . exemptions for . . . . 9.05[4]
. . generally 9.05
. . transfers included for . . . . 9.05[1]

Gift tax—Cont'd
. *prior years—Cont'd*
. . valuation for . . . . 9.05[2], S9.05[2]
. private annuities . . . . 4.11[5]
. property interests, gifts of . . . . 10.01[3]
. property settlements not in divorce decree
  . . . . 10.06
. . child support, amount for . . . . 10.06[2][b]
. . comparative estate tax treatment . . 10.06[3]
. . generally . . . . 10.06[1]
. . income tax aspects . . . . 10.06[4]
. . statutory requirements . . . . 10.06[2]
. . three-year rule . . . . 10.06[2][c]
. . type of transfer, requirement . . 10.06[2][a]
. . written agreement requirement . . . 10.06[2]
. Qualified State Tuition Programs . . S9.04[6],
                                        S10.01[3][c]
. qualified terminable interest property
  . . . . 1.03[2][g], 10.08
. rate of tax
. . generally . . . . 1.03[1]
. . graduated rate table . . . . 1.03[1]
. reciprocal trusts . . . . 10.02[6][c]
. recovery, right of
. . decedent-retained interest . . . . . . 8.08[3]
. . marital deduction property . 8.07[3]–8.07[5]
. remainders, gifts of . . . . 9.04[3], 10.01[3][b]
. returns . . . . 9.02[3], 9.04[9], S9.04[9]
. . charitable gifts S11.02
. . fraudulent . . . . 9.04[10]
. reversionary interests, gifts of . . 10.01[3][d]
. revocable transfers . . . . 10.01[5]
. rights and restrictions on property, valuation
  . . . . 19.04[6][b]
. scope of 10.01
. split gifts 10.03
. . consent, signifying . . . . 10.03[3]
. . election, effect of . . . . 10.03[2]
. . generally . . . . 10.03[1]
. . manner of signifying consent . . 10.03[3][a]
. . rate of tax . . . . 10.03[2]
. . return requirement, effect of election on
  . . . . 10.03[4]
. . revocation of consent . . . . 10.03[3][c]
. . time of consent . . . . 10.03[3][b]
. straw man, use of . . . . 9.04[1][b]
. survivorship benefits, waiver of . . 9.04[7]
. taxable gifts . . . 1.03[3], 1.03[5], 9.04, 11.01
. . adjusted taxable gifts . . . . 6.01[1]
. . annual exclusion . . . . 9.04[1]
. . determination of 9.04
. . limitations on assessment . . . . . . 9.04[10],
                                        S9.04[10]

Gift tax—Cont'd
. *taxable gifts—Cont'd*
. . preceding calendar periods, taxable gifts for
  . . . . 9.05
. . specific gifts . . . . 9.04[2]–9.04[8]
. tax conventions 7.05
. tenancy by the entirety, gifts to . . 9.04[1][b]
. third persons
. . donor's power exercisable only with
  . . . . 10.01[8]
. . husband or wife, gifts to third party by
  . . . . 10.03
. . powers held only by . . . . 10.01[9]
. . split gifts 10.03
. timing problem . . . . 10.01[4]
. total gift tax . . . . 3.04[1][a]
. transferor, powers held by . . . . 10.01[10][e],
                                      S10.01[10][e]
. transfers subject to 10.01–10.08
. . alteration of time or manner of gift, power
    of . . . . 10.01[7]
. . beneficiary change, power to make 10.01[6]
. . completion of transfer . . . . 10.01[4]
. . conditional transfers . . . . 10.01[3][e],
                                      10.01[10][d]
. . direct gifts . . . . 10.01[1]
. . disclaimers 10.07
. . estate tax, relationship of gift tax to
  . . . . 10.01[10]
. . generally 10.01
. . generation-skipping transfers tax, treatment
    of 10.05, S10.05
. . husband or wife, gifts to third party by
  . . . . 10.03
. . income tax, relationship of gift tax to
  . . . . 10.01[10]
. . indirect gifts . . . . 10.01[2]
. . life estates, dispositions of certain . . 10.08
. . life interests retained, transfers with
  . . . . 10.01[10][c]
. . nonresident aliens . . . . 10.01[11]
. . powers of appointment 10.04
. . prior years . . . . 9.05[1]
. . property interests . . . . 10.01[3]
. . property settlements not in divorce decree
  . . . . 10.06
. . revocable transfers . . . . 10.01[5]
. . split gifts 10.03
. . third persons
. . . donor's power exercisable only with
  . . . . 10.01[8]
. . . powers held only by . . . . 10.01[9]
. . within three years of death . . . . . S4.07[1],
                                  S4.07[3], 10.01[10][b]

Gift tax—Cont'd
. transfers subject to—Cont'd
. . transferor, powers held by . . . 10.01[10][e],
S10.01[10][e]
. . valuation of gifts 10.02
. trust
. . gifts in . . . . 9.04[1][b], 9.04[3][a]
. . transfers in (indirect gifts) . . . . 10.01[2][a]
. tuition payments . . 1.03[3], 9.04[6], S9.04[6]
. uncertain interests, gifts of . . . . . 10.01[3][c],
S10.01[3][c]
. valuation . . . . 10.02, 10.02[4]
. . actuarial valuation . . . . 10.02[2][f]
. . community property . . . . 10.02[6][b]
. . completion of gift . . . . 10.02[1][a]
. . consideration received for transfer   10.02[3]
. . corporate recipients . . . . 10.02[6][a]
. . discounts and premiums, interests in property . . . . 10.02[2][c]
. . donee payment of tax . . . . . . 10.02[6][d]
. . encumbered property . . . . 10.02[2][a]
. . excise tax and other charges . . 10.02[2][g]
. . family obligations . . . . 10.02[5]
. . generally . . . . 1.03[2][a], 10.02
. . insurance contracts . . . . 10.02[2][e]
. . methods of . . . . 10.02[2]
. . money's worth, receipts of . . . . . 10.02[6]
. . mutual fund shares . . . . 10.02[2][d]
. . open transactions . . . . 10.02[1][b]
. . ordinary course of business, transfers in
. . . . 10.02[4]
. . prior years . . . . 9.05[2], S9.05[2]
. . reciprocal trusts . . . . 10.02[6][c]
. . restrictions on use or disposition
. . . . 10.02[2][b]
. . statement of valuation, furnishing on request
. . . . 10.02[7]
. . time of . . . . 10.02[1]
. waiver of survivorship benefits . . . . . 9.04[7]
**Government bonds, notes, and bills, tax con-
vention situs rules** . . . . 7.02[2][c]
Grandchildren
*See Generation-skipping transfers; Genera-
tion-skipping transfer tax*
Grantor retained income trusts (GRITs)
. . . . 19.03[2]
. annual gift tax exclusion . . . . . . 19.03[2][c]
. defined . . . . 19.03[1]
. as estate freezing techniques . . . . . 19.03[1]
. family members
. . applicable family members . 19.03[2][a][iii]
. . defined . . . . 19.03[2][a][ii]
. . required retained interest by   19.03[2][a][ii]

**Grantor retained income trusts (GRITs)—
Cont'd**
. generally . . . . 19.03[1]
. general rule . . . . 19.03[2]
. gift tax provisions, relationship to other
. . . . 19.03[2][c]
. interest rates, effect . . . . 19.03[1]
. intra-family GRITs . . . . 19.03[1]
. portion of interest in trust, transfer of
. . . . 19.03[2][b]
. requirements . . . . 19.03[2][a]
. retained interest requirement . 19.03[2][a][iv]
. special valuation rules to combat estate freeze
abuses of . . . . 19.03[1], 19.03[2]
. split gifts . . . . 19.03[2][c]
. transfer in trust requirement . . . 19.03[2][a][i]
. unified credit . . . . 19.03[1]
. zero valuation rule . . . . . 19.03[1], 19.03[2]
Gratuitous services, as indirect gifts
. . . . 10.01[2][g]
Gratuitous transfers of wealth, overview
. . . . 1.01, S1.06
Grievance procedures, tax conventions
. . . . 7.04[4]
GRITs
See Grantor retained income trusts (GRITs)
Gross estate 4.01–4.18
*See also Alternate valuation date, gross es-
tate inclusion*
. actual estate and artificial estate comprising
. . . . 4.03[2]
. annuities . . . . . 1.02[2][b][vi], 4.05[8], 4.11
See also Annuities
. . amount to be included . . . . 4.11[4]
. . background of Section 2039 . . . . . 4.11[7]
. . exceptions . . . . 4.11[2]
. . exempt annuities . . . . 4.11[6]
. . general rule . . . . 4.11[1]
. . life insurance policies . . . . 4.11[2][a]
. . pre-1931 contracts . . . . 4.11[2][b]
. . private annuities . . . . 4.11[5]
. . qualifications . . . . 4.11[3]
. . Section 2039 rules 4.11
. artificial aspects of . . . . 1.02[2][b]
. background of Section 2041 . . . . . 4.13[10]
. bank accounts, joint . . . . . . 4.05[3], 4.12[2]
. beneficial interest of decedent . . . . . 4.05[2]
. . state decrees . . . . 4.05[2][b]
. . state law . . . . 4.05[2][a]
. conservation easement, exclusion of value of
land subject to . . . . S4.02[4]
. . amount of exclusion . . . . S4.02[4][d]
. . effective date . . . . S4.02[4][g]

Gross estate—Cont'd
. *conservation easement, exclusion of value of land subject to—Cont'd*
. . election . . . . S4.02[4][c]
. . generally . . . . S4.02[4][a]
. . interrelationship of Section 2031(c) with other estate tax provisions and other taxes . . . . S4.02[4][f]
. . land subject to qualified conservation easement . . . . S4.02[4][b]
. . Section 2031(c), special rules applicable to . . . . S4.02[4][e]
. curtesy interest . . . . 4.05[8], 4.15[1]
. death, transfers taking effect at 4.09
. decedent, property in which interest held by 4.05
. . bank accounts . . . . 4.05[3]
. . beneficial interest . . . . 4.05[2]
. . business interests . . . . 4.05[7]
. . cautions concerning partial interests . . . . 4.05[5][c]
. . compensation for death . . . . 4.05[8]
. . corporations . . . . 4.05[7][a]
. . dividends . . . . 4.05[4]
. . generally . . . . 4.05[1]
. . income items . . . . 4.05[4]
. . insurance proceeds . . . . 4.05[6]
. . intangible property interests . . . . . . 4.05[3]
. . limited liability companies . . . . 4.05[7][c], S4.05[7][c]
. . partial interests in property . . . . . . 4.05[5]
. . partnerships . . . . 4.05[7][b]
. . proprietorships . . . . 4.05[7][a]
. . routine inclusions . . . . 4.05[3]
. . shared interests in property . . . . 4.05[5][a]
. . stocks, bonds, and notes . . . . 4.05[3]
. . successive interests . . . . 4.05[5][b]
. . tangible personal property . . . . . . 4.05[3]
. defined 4.02
. . nonresident aliens 6.03
. determination of 4.01
. disclaimers 4.18
. dividends . . . . 4.05[4]
. dower interest . . . . 4.05[8], 4.15[1]
. enjoyment retained, transfers with . . . . 1.02[2][b][iii]
. estate tax computation, effect on 4.01
. fair market value . . . . 4.02[2]
. family-owned business deduction . . . S5.08A
. . adjusted gross estate, 50 percent test and . . . . S5.08A[3][c][v]
. . 50 percent test . . . . S5.08A[3][c]
. . generally . . . . S5.08A[1]

Gross estate—Cont'd
. *family—Cont'd*
. . includible qualified family-owned business interests . . . . S5.08A[3][c][ii]
. foreign death taxes, credit against estate tax . . . . 3.06[3][c]
. generally . . . . 1.02[2], 4.01
. generation-skipping transfer tax
. . direct skip property included in transferor's gross estate . . . . 14.05[2][a]
. . inclusion ratio, inter vivos transfers includible . . . . 16.02[4][b], 16.02[7][a], 16.02[7][b][i], 16.02[7][b][ii], 16.02[7][c][i]
. gift tax credit against estate tax, effect of decedent's gross estate on . . . . . 3.04[2][c]
. identification of . . . . 4.03[2]
. included interests, valuation of . . . . . 4.02[1]
. insufficient consideration, transfers for . . 4.15
. joint interests 4.12
. . additions to property . . . . 4.12[7][b]
. . amount to be included . . . . 4.12[4]
. . burden of proof . . . . 4.12[8], S4.12[8]
. . co-owners, property paid for by . . . 4.12[7]
. . exception to general rule . . . . 4.12[10]
. . forms of ownership covered . . . . . 4.12[2]
. . generally . . . . 4.12[1]
. . gift, property acquired by . . . . 4.12[6]
. . improvements to property . . . . . 4.12[7][b]
. . misconceptions concerning . . . . . . 4.12[3]
. . survivor's contribution . . . . 4.12[5]
. . termination prior to death . . . . 4.12[9]
. . tracing requirement . . . . 4.12[7][a]
. jointly held property . . . . . . 1.02[2][b][vii]
. joint tenancies . . . 4.12[2], 4.12[10], 4.12[11]
. life insurance policies on life of another . . . . 4.02[3][i], 4.03[2][d], 4.05[6]
. life insurance proceeds . . . . . 1.02[2][b][ix], 4.05[6], 4.14
. . amounts receivable
. . . by or for estate . . . . 4.14[3]
. . . by other beneficiaries . . . . 4.14[4]
. . amount to be included . . . . 4.14[7]
. . background of Section 2042 . . . . 4.14[10]
. . buy-sell agreements . . . . 4.14[4][d]
. . community property funds, policy purchased with . . . . 4.14[8]
. . constitutional challenges . . . . . . 4.14[10]
. . economic benefit . . . . 4.14[4][f]
. . executor, defined . . . . 4.14[3][a]
. . full amount, inclusion of . . . . . . 4.14[7][a]
. . generally . . . . 4.14[1]
. . group term insurance, assignment of 4.14[6]
. . incidents incidentally held . . . . . . 4.14[5]

Gross estate—Cont'd
. *life insurance proceeds—Cont'd*
. . "incidents" in context . . . . 4.14[4][e]
. . incidents of ownership . . . . 4.14[4][a]
. . incomplete near-death transfers . 4.14[9][b]
. . insurance, defined . . . . 4.14[2]
. . legislative background . . . . 4.14[10]
. . near-death transfers . . . . 4.14[9][b]
. . partnership's insurance on partner
     . . . . 4.14[5][b]
. . portion of proceeds, gross estate inclusion
     . . . . 4.14[7][b]
. . premiums payable after transfer . 4.14[9][b]
. . relation of Section 2042 to other Sections
     defining gross estate . . . . 4.14[9]
. . remainder interest . . . . 4.14[4][b]
. . reversionary interest . . . . 4.14[4][b]
. . Section 2042 rules . . . . . . 4.14[1], 4.14[9],
                                      4.14[10]
. . shareholder in corporation . . . . S4.14[5][a]
. . simultaneous death . . . . 4.14[3][b]
. . terms of policy, effect . . . . 4.14[4][c]
. . transfers . . . . 4.14[9][a], 4.14[9][b]
. . transmittal of wealth . . . . 4.14[3][c]
. marital deduction . . . 4.03[4][b], 4.16, 5.06[4]
. near death transfers . . . . 1.02[2][b][i], S4.07
. nonresident aliens 6.03
. . definition of gross estate 6.03
. . generally 6.06
. . general principles . . . . 6.03[1]
. . intangibles . . . . 6.03[2][b], 6.04[3]
. . limitations . . . . 6.03[2]
. . real property . . . . 6.03[2][a]
. . tangible personal property . . . . . 6.03[2][a]
. powers of appointment 4.13
. . amount to be included in gross estate
     . . . . 4.13[9]
. . another person, powers with . . . 4.13[4][c]
. . background of Section 2041 . . . . 4.13[10]
. . complete release of pre-1942 power
     . . . . 4.13[6][c]
. . defined . . . . 4.13[2]
. . . general power . . . . S4.13[3]
. . denunciation . . . . 4.13[7][d]
. . disclaimer . . . . 4.13[7][d]
. . exceptions to general definition . . . 4.13[4]
. . exercise of . . . . 4.13[7][b]
. . . pre-1942 power . . . . 4.13[6][a]
. . existence of . . . . 4.13[2]
. . failure to exercise 1942 power . . 4.13[6][b]
. . five and five rule . . . . 4.13[7][f]
. . generally . . . . 4.13[1]

Gross estate—Cont'd
. *powers of appointment—Cont'd*
. . general powers . . 1.02[2][b][viii], 4.13[3]–
                                      4.13[7]
. . judicious use of . . . . 4.13[4][d]
. . lapse of power . . . . 4.13[7][e]
. . legislative background . . . . 4.13[10]
. . limitation of power by standard . 4.13[4][a]
. . nongeneral power . . . . 4.13[8]
. . overlapping of interests . . . . . . 4.13[2][b]
. . partial release of pre-1942 power 4.13[6][d]
. . possession of . . . . 4.13[7][a]
. . post-1942 powers . . . . . 4.13[4][c], 4.13[7]
. . pre-1942 powers . . . . . 4.13[4][b], 4.13[6]
. . relationship of Section 2041 to other Sec-
     tions . . . . 4.13[2][a]
. . release of . 4.13[6][c], 4.13[6][d], 4.13[7][c]
. . Section 2041
. . . powers within . . . . 4.13[2]
. . . rules . . . . 4.13[1], 4.13[10]
. . special powers . . . . 4.13[8]
. . treatment of general powers . . . . . 4.13[5]
. prior interests 4.17
. property owned at death . . . . 1.02[2][a]
. qualified terminable interest property
     . . . . 1.02[2][b][x]
. rent . . . . 4.03[2][a], 4.05[4]
. retained life estate, transfers with 4.08
. revocable transfers . . . . . 1.02[2][b][v], 4.10
     See also Revocable transfers
. . amount to be included . . . . 4.10[9]
. . change in enjoyment, effect . . . . . . 4.10[3]
. . excluded transfers . . . . 4.10[2]
. . existence of power, time requirement
     . . . . 4.10[8], S4.10[8]
. . generally . . . . 4.10[1]
. . lifetime transfer rules under Code Sections
     . . . . 4.10[10]
. . power exercisable only with another 4.10[6]
. . power in decedent . . . . . . 4.10[4]–4.10[7]
. . restriction of power . . . . 4.10[5]
. . source of power . . . . 4.10[7]
. Social Security benefits exclusion . . . 4.05[8]
. special-use valuation, real property
     . . . . 1.02[2][b][iv], 4.04
     See also Special-use valuation, real prop-
     erty
. tenancies by the entirety . . . 4.12[2], 4.12[10]
. transfers for insufficient consideration . . 4.15
     See also Transfers for insufficient consid-
     eration
. . marital rights, negative rule . . . . . . 4.15[1]

Gross estate—Cont'd
. *transfers for insufficient consideration— Cont'd*
. . partial consideration, affirmative rule .... 4.15[2]
. transfers taking effect at death 4.09
 See also Transfers effective at death
. . amount to be included .... 4.09[6]
. . background of Section 2037 covering .... 4.09[7]
. . excluded transfers .... 4.09[2]
. . generally .... 4.09[1]
. . reversionary interest, retention of . . 4.09[4]
. . survivorship requirement .... 4.09[3]
. . termination of reversion, pre-death . 4.09[5]
. transfers within three years of death .... 1.02[2][b][i], S4.07
. . generally .... S4.07[1]
. . gross estate inclusion under Section 2035(a) .... S4.07[2]
. . gross-up of gift tax under Section 2035(b) .... S4.07[3]
. . pre-1982 Section 2035 and its background .... S4.07[4]
. transfers with retained life estate 4.08
 See also Transfers with retained life estate
. . amount to be included .... 4.08[8]
. . background of Section 2036 covering .... 4.08[9]
. . beneficial interests in decedent .... 4.08[4]
. . control over others' interests ..... 4.08[5]
. . decedent, transfers by .... 4.08[7]
. . excluded transfers .... 4.08[1]
. . indirect interests or controls ..... 4.08[6]
. . nature of interest retained ...... 4.08[3]
. . period for which interest retained . . 4.08[2]
. valuation .... 4.02[3]
. . agreements, determination by . . . 4.02[3][g]
. . alternative valuation date 4.03
. . art works .... 4.02[3][a]
. . basic approaches to .... 4.02[3]
. . bonds .... 4.02[3][e]
. . business interests .... 4.02[3][f]
. . buy-sell agreements .... 4.02[3][g]
. . close corporation interests ..... 4.02[3][f]
. . closed-end funds .... 4.02[3][d]
. . conservation easement, exclusion of value of land subject to .... S4.02[4]
. . crops, growing .... 4.04[3][c]
. . date of decedent's death as time for . . 4.01
. . fair market value .... 4.02[2]
. . generally .... 1.02[2][b][ii]
. . included interests .... 4.02[1]

Gross estate—Cont'd
. *valuation—Cont'd*
. . notes .... 4.02[3][h]
. . open-end funds .... 4.02[3][d]
. . optional methods 4.04
. . partial property interests ...... 4.02[3][i]
. . real property .... 4.02[3][b], 4.04
. . securities .... 4.02[3][c]
. . special-use valuation, real property . . . 4.04
. . statutes related to .... 4.02[6]
. . . Section 7491 .... S4.02[6][c]
. . . understatement of taxpayer liability by return preparer: Section 6694 S4.02[6][b]
. . . understatement penalty and reasonable cause: Sections 6662 and 6664 .... S4.02[6][a]
. . tangible personal property ..... 4.02[3][a]
. . temporal property interests ..... 4.02[3][i]
. . terminally ill person, valued interest measured by life of .... 4.02[3][i]
. workers' compensation exclusion ... 4.05[8]
Gross-up of gift tax, transfers within three years of death .... S4.07[3]
Group term insurance, assignment of 4.14[6]
GST
 See Generation-skipping transfers; Generation-skipping transfer tax
Guaranteed payment rights
. defined .... 19.02[2][b][ii]
. estate freezes, special valuation rules .... 19.02[2][b][ii]

H

Heirs, qualified, special-use valuation .... 4.04[3][b][ix]
Husbands and wives
 See Divorce; Marital deduction; Marital rights; Property settlements not in divorce decree; Split gifts; Spouses

I

Illness
. physical condition of decedent before death, effect on transfers effective at death .... 4.09[4][e]
. terminally ill persons, defined, gross estate valuation .... 4.02[3][i]
Immigration and Naturalization Act
. citizenship, determination of .... 4.04[3][a], 6.01[2][a]
Improvements of property, joint interests .... 4.12[7][b]

Inclusion ratio, GST tax

　See Generation-skipping transfer
　　tax--inclusion ratio

Income in respect of decedent

. salary due decedent at death, gross estate in-
　clusion . . . . 4.05[4]

Income tax

. casualty losses, relation to . . . . 5.04[4]
. estate freezes, relationship to . . . 19.02[5][f],
　　　　　　　　　　　　　　　　　19.03[4][e][ii]
. family-owned business deduction, income tax
　basis . . . . S5.08A[6][c][i]
. gift tax and 9.01
. . property settlements . . . . 10.06[4]
. . relationship . . . . 10.01[10]
. losses, relation to . . . . 5.04[4]
. private annuities . . . . 4.11[5]
. property settlements not in divorce decree, in-
　come tax aspects . . . . 10.06[4]

Incompetent persons, indirect gifts by
　. . . . . 10.01[2][h]

Incomplete transfers

. exception to Section 2702 special valuation
　rules . . . . 19.03[3][a]
. undivided proportionate share, proportionate
　share rule . . . . 19.03[3][a]
. valuation . . . . 19.03[3][a]
. zero valuation rule, application of 19.03[3][a]

Indebtedness

. discharge of, as indirect gift . . . 10.01[2][e]
. gross estate inclusion of personal debt, valua-
　tion . . . . 4.02[3][h]
. judgment debts, tax convention situs rules
　. . . . . 7.02[2][c]
. nonresident aliens . . . . 6.04[3]
. . portfolio interest . . . . . . 6.05[4], S6.05[4]
. portfolio interest . . . . 6.05[4], S6.05[4]
. tax conventions, situs rules . . . . . 7.02[2][c]
. United States, debts due to, executor's dis-
　charge from personal liability for . 8.03[1]

Information exchange under tax conventions
　. . . . . 7.04[3]

Information returns

　See also Returns
. generation-skipping transfer tax . . . 18.02[6]

Inheritance

. interests passing to surviving spouse by, mari-
　tal deduction . . . . 5.06[3][a]
. international system of death taxation, inheri-
　tance taxes . . . . 7.01[2][a]

Installment sales notes

. gross estate inclusion of, valuation 4.02[3][h]

Insufficient consideration, transfers for . 4.15

　See also Transfers for insufficient considera-
　　tion

Insurance

　See also Life insurance; Life insurance poli-
　　cies; Life insurance proceeds
. cooperatives (EWOCs) . . . . 5.08[1]
. defined . . . . 4.14[2]
. gifts of . . . . 10.01[3][g]
. . split dollar life insurance . . . S10.01[3][g]
. . valuation . . . . 10.02[2][e]
. qualified personal residence trusts, insurance
　proceeds . . . . 19.03[3][d][iii]

Intangible property

. gift tax on transfers by nonresident aliens
　. . . . . 9.02[1]
. gross estate inclusion
. . decedent, property interest held by . 4.05[3]
. . nonresident aliens . . . . 6.03[2][b], 6.04[3]
. nonresident aliens 6.03[2][b], 6.04[3], 9.02[1]
. special-use valuation . . . . 4.04[3][b][vi]
. tax conventions, situs rules . . . . . 7.02[2][c]

Interest

. bonds, gross estate inclusion of interest ac-
　crued on
. . alternative valuation date . . . . . 4.03[2][a]
. on deferred estate tax payment . . . 2.02[3][c],
　　　　　　　　　　　　　　　　　S2.02[3][c]
. family-owned business deduction, recapture of
　interest on estate tax . . . S5.08A[5][c][iii]
. formula farm special-use valuation method,
　effect of interest rate on . . . 4.04[5][a][v]
. grantor retained income trusts, effect of inter-
　est rates . . . . 19.03[1]
. interest-free loans . . . . 10.01[2][f]
. nonresident aliens
. . bank deposits . . . . 6.05[2][a]
. . contingent interest . . . . . 6.05[2][a], 6.05[4]
. . portfolio interest . . . . . . 6.05[4], S6.05[4]
. portfolio interest . . . . 6.05[4], S6.05[4]

Interest Equalization Tax Extension Act of 1971

. nonresident aliens' debt obligations and bank
　accounts . . . . 6.04[3]

Internal Revenue Act of 1962

. tax conventions 7.06

Internal Revenue Code, tax conventions and
　. . . . . 7.06

International system of death taxation
　. . . . . 7.01[2]

　See also Tax conventions
. death taxes . . . . 7.01[2][b]
. domicile, defined . . . . 7.01[2][b]

International system of death taxation—Cont'd
. estate tax . . . . 7.01[2][a]
. historical background 7.02
. inheritance tax . . . . 7.01[2][a]
Inter vivos transfers
. direct skips
. . generally . . . . 1.04[3][a], 12.02
. . gift tax on . . . . 1.03[2][d]
. generation-skipping transfer tax
. . gift tax and, transfers subject to both taxes
. . . . 10.05, S10.05
. . gross estate . . . 16.02[7][a], 16.02[7][b][i],
     16.02[7][b][ii], 16.02[7][c][i]
. . GST exemption allocated to inter vivos
     transfers other than direct skips
     . . . . 16.02[4][c]
. . inclusion ratio . . . . 16.02[4][b], 16.02[4][c],
     16.02[7]
. gift tax and generation-skipping transfer tax,
     transfers subject to both . . . 10.05, S10.05
. marital deduction . . . . 5.06[3][c]
. reciprocal trusts . . . . . 4.08[7][d], 10.02[6][c]
. revocable transfers 4.10
. within three years of death S4.07
Investment
. revocable transfers, investment powers of de-
     cedent . . . . 4.10[4][d]
**Involuntary conversions, special-use valua-
tion of real property** . . . . 4.04[3][c][i]
Irrevocable actions
. disclaimers . . . . 10.07[2]
. easements in real property, irrevocable trans-
     fers of . . . . 11.02[4]
. qualified domestic trust (QDOT) election
     . . . . 5.07[3][d]
. special-use valuation of real property, election
     of . . . . 4.04[6]

J

Joint-and-survivor annuities . . 1.02[2][b][vi],
     4.11[7], 11.03[4][c][ii]
Joint bank accounts . . . . 1.02[2][b][vii]
. disclaimers . . . . 10.07[2][b]
. gross estate . . . . 4.05[3], 4.12[2]
. revocable transfers . . . . 10.01[5][c]
Joint donees, annual gift tax exclusion
     . . . . 9.04[1][b]
Joint interests 4.12
. additions to property . . . . 4.12[7][b]
. alien spouses . . . . 4.12[10]
. amount to be included . . . . 4.12[4]
. bank accounts, joint . . . . 4.12[2]

Joint interests—Cont'd
. bonds . . . . 4.12[2]
. burden of proof . . . . 4.12[8], S4.12[8]
. co-owners, property paid for by . . . . 4.12[7]
. creation by gift . . . . 10.01[3][f]
. disclaimers . . . . . . 10.07[2][b], S10.07[2][b]
. estate tax . . . . . . 4.12[6], 4.12[10], 4.12[11]
. exception to general rule . . . . 4.12[10]
. forms of ownership covered . . . . . . 4.12[2]
. generally . . . . 1.02[2][b][vii], 4.12[1]
. gift, property acquired by 4.12[6], 10.01[3][f]
. . deductible gifts to spouse . . . . 11.03[4][a]
. gross estate 4.12
. improvements to property . . . . . . 4.12[7][b]
. joint tenancies . . . 4.12[2], 4.12[10], 4.12[11]
. legislative background . . . . 4.12[11]
. marital deduction, interests passing to surviv-
     ing spouse . . . . 5.06[3][d], 5.06[8][d][iv]
. misconceptions concerning . . . . 4.12[3]
. qualified domestic trust, transfer of interest to
     . . . . 4.12[10], 5.07[1], 5.07[2][b]
. Section 2040 rules . . . . 4.12[1]
. survivor's contribution . . . . 4.12[5]
. survivorship rights . . . . 4.12[1]
. tenancies by the entirety . . . 4.12[2], 4.12[10]
. termination prior to death . . . . 4.12[9]
. tracing requirement . . . . 4.12[7][a]
. U.S. savings bonds . . . . 4.12[2]
. wills, joint and mutual . . . . 5.06[3][d],
     5.06[8][d][iv], 10.01[5][e]
Jointly held property, generally
     . . . . 1.02[2][b][vii]
     See also Joint interests
Joint purchases . . . . 19.03[1], 19.03[4][a]
Joint tenancies
. disclaimers . . . . . . 10.07[2][b], S10.07[2][b]
. gross estate . . . . . 4.12[2], 4.12[10], 4.12[11]
. state law . . . . 4.12[2]
Judgment debts, tax convention situs rules
     . . . . 7.02[2][c]
Judicial doctrine of reciprocal trusts
     . . . . 4.08[7][d]

L

Lapsed voting or liquidation rights . . . 19.05
. control, defined . . . . 19.05[2][b][iv]
. definitions . . . . 19.05[2][b]
. effective date . . . . 19.05[4]
. estate tax . . . . 19.05[2][a]
. exceptions for certain lapses . . . 19.05[2][c]
. generally . . . . 19.05[1]
. general rule . . . . 19.05[2][a]

Lapsed voting or liquidation rights — Cont'd

. generation-skipping transfer tax . 19.05[2][a]
. gift tax . . . . 19.05[2][a]
. lapses, defined . . . . 19.05[2][b][ii]
. members of family, defined . . 19.05[2][b][iii]
. restrictions on liquidation . . . . 19.05[3]
. Section 2704 valuation rules 19.05
. valuation rules for estate freezes 19.05
. voting and liquidation rights, defined
. . . . 19.05[2][b][i]

Liability for tax

See Tax liability

Life estate retained, transfers with

See Transfers with retained life estate

Life insurance

See also Life insurance policies; Life insurance proceeds

. death benefit arrangements as . . . . . . 4.14[2]
. defined . . . . 4.14[2]
. fraternal beneficial societies, death benefits
. . . paid as insurance . . . . 4.14[2]
. group term insurance, assignment of . 4.14[6]
. split dollar insurance . . . . S4.14[6]

Life insurance policies

. annuities, gross estate . . . . 4.11[2][a]
. endowment policies . . . . 4.14[2]
. gifts of . . . . 10.01[3][g], 10.02[2][e]
. . split dollar life insurance . . . S10.01[3][g]
. gross estate inclusion of insurance policy on
. . . life of another, valuation . . . . . 4.02[3][i],
. . . . 4.05[6]
. . alternate valuation date . . . . 4.03[2][d]
. . community property interest . . . . . 4.05[6]
. group term life insurance, assignment of pol-
. . . icy . . . . 4.14[6]
. split dollar insurance . . . . S4.14[6]
. terms of policy, effect on proceeds 4.14[4][c]

Life insurance proceeds 4.14

. amounts receivable
. . by or for estate . . . . 4.14[3]
. . by other beneficiaries . . . . 4.14[4]
. amount to be included . . . . 4.14[7]
. beneficiaries of, estate tax liability of . . 8.05
. . amount of liability, formula for . . . 8.05[1]
. . contrary will provision . . . . 8.05[3]
. . marital deduction, special rule . . . . 8.05[2]
. . state law, effect . . . . 8.05[4]
. buy-sell agreements . . . . 4.14[4][d]
. community property funds, policy purchased
. . . with . . . . 4.14[8]
. constitutional challenges . . . . 4.14[10]
. economic benefit . . . . 4.14[4][f]

Life insurance proceeds — Cont'd

. estate tax . . . . . 1.02[2][b][ix], 4.05[6], 4.14
. executor, defined . . . . 4.14[3][a]
. full amount, inclusion of . . . . . . 4.14[7][a]
. generally . . . . 1.02[2][b][ix], 4.14[1]
. gross estate . . . . 1.02[2][b][ix], 4.05[6], 4.14
. . relation of Section 2042 to other Sections
. . . defining gross estate . . . . 4.14[9]
. . Section 2042 rules covering . . . . . 4.14[1]
. group term insurance, assignment of . 4.14[6]
. incidents incidentally held . . . . 4.14[5]
. "incidents" in context . . . . 4.14[4][e]
. incidents of ownership . . . . 4.14[4][a]
. incomplete near-death transfers . . . 4.14[9][b]
. insurance, defined . . . . 4.14[2]
. legislative background . . . . 4.14[10]
. life of another, policy on
. . gross estate inclusion . . . . 4.05[6]
. . marital deduction . . . . 5.06[3][f], 5.06[8][c]
. marital deduction
. . insurance with powers . . . . 5.06[8][c]
. . interests passing to surviving spouse
. . . . 5.06[3][f]
. near-death transfers . . . . 4.14[9][b]
. . premiums payable after . . . . . . 4.14[9][b]
. nonresident aliens . . . . 6.05[1]
. partnership's insurance on partner . 4.14[5][b]
. portion of proceeds, gross estate inclusion
. . . . 4.14[7][b]
. powers of appointment . . . . 4.14[9][a]
. premiums payable after transfer . . 4.14[9][b]
. remainder interest . . . . 4.14[4][b]
. reversionary interest . . . . 4.14[4][b]
. Section 2042 rules . . . . 4.14[1]
. . background of Section . . . . 4.14[10]
. . relation of Section 2042 to other Sections
. . . defining gross estate . . . . 4.14[9]
. shareholder in corporation . . . . . 4.14[5][a]
. simultaneous death . . . . 4.14[3][b]
. tax conventions, situs rules . . . . . 7.02[2][c]
. terms of policy, effect . . . . 4.14[4][c]
. transfers . . . . 4.14[9][a], 4.14[9][b]
. transmittal of wealth . . . . 4.14[3][c]

Life insurance trusts

. gross estate inclusion . . . . 4.05[7][c]
. limited liability companies compared
. . . . 4.05[7][c]

Life interests

. with powers, marital deduction and termina-
. . . ble interest rule . . . . 5.06[8][b]
. . annual or more frequent payments to sur-
. . . viving spouse . . . . 5.06[8][b][ii]

Life interests —Cont'd
. with powers, marital deduction—Cont'd
. . entitlements of surviving spouse
    . . . . 5.06[8][b][i], S5.06[8][b][i]
. . exercise of power . . . . 5.06[8][b][iv]
. . powers of surviving spouse . 5.06[8][b][iii]–
    5.06[8][b][v]
. . scope of powers . . . . 5.06[8][b][iii]
. . sole power in surviving spouse, requirement
    . . . . 5.06[8][b][v]
. transfers with interest retained . . 10.01[10][c]
Lifetime transfers
    See also Inter vivos transfers
. charitable deductions . . . . 5.05[6]
. nonresident aliens, property subject to lifetime
    transfer . . . . 6.04[2]
. revocable transfers 4.10
**Like-kind exchanges, special-use valuation of
    real property** . . . . 4.04[3][c][i]
Limited liability companies
. advantages . . . . 4.05[7][c]
. basis of assets, step-up in . . . . . . 4.05[7][c]
. Crummey trusts compared . . . . . . 4.05[7][c]
. defined . . . . 4.05[7][c]
. estate tax benefits . . . . 4.05[7][c]
. gift giving compared . . . . 4.05[7][c]
. interests in, held by decedent, gross estate
    . . . . 4.05[7][c], S4.05[7][c]
. life insurance trusts compared . . . 4.05[7][c]
. limited partnerships compared . . . 4.05[7][c]
. partnership treatment of . . . . 4.05[7][c]
. S corporations compared . . . . 4.05[7][c]
. voting control . . . . 4.05[7][c]
Liquidation rights
. defined . . . . 19.05[2][b][i]
. as extraordinary payment rights
    . . . . 19.02[2][b][ii]
. lapsed . . . . 19.05[2]
    *See also Lapsed voting or liquidation
    rights*
**Liquidation, special valuation rules for estate
    freezes**
    See also Liquidation rights
. effective date . . . . 19.05[4]
. estate tax . . . . 19.05[3][a]
. generation-skipping transfer tax . 19.05[3][a]
. gift tax . . . . 19.05[3][a]
. liquidation participation rights 19.02[2][b][ii]
. restrictions on . . . . 19.05[3]
. . applicable restrictions . . . . . . 19.05[3][b]
. . general rule . . . . 19.05[3][a]
**Literary organizations, charitable transfers
    to** . . . . 5.05[2], 11.01[1]

Load funds
. valuation . . . . 4.02[3][d]
Loans
. art works, gift tax and loans of . . . . 9.04[8]
. below-market interest rate loans, as indirect
    gifts . . . . 10.01[2][f]
. . demand loans . . . . 10.01[2][f]
. . term loans . . . . 10.01[2][f]
Local law
    See State and local law
Lord Campbell's Act
. wrongful death . . . . 4.05[8]
**Lord Tenderden's rule (ejusdem generiso ca-
    non of construction)** . . . . 5.04[2]
Losses
. amount of, determination . . . . 5.04[1]
. casualty losses . . . . 5.04[2]
. deductions . . . . 1.02[3][b], 5.04
. estate tax . . . . 1.02[3][b]
. income tax, relation to . . . . 5.04[4]
. nonresident aliens . . . . 6.06[1]
. taxable estate 5.04
. theft losses . . . . 5.04[3]

M

Mandatory payment rights
. defined . . . . 19.02[2][b][ii]
. estate freezes, special valuation rules
    . . . . 19.02[2][b][ii]
Marital deduction 5.06
. background . . . . 5.06[1], 5.06[10]
. credit against estate tax, gift tax as 3.04[2][b]
. curtesy, interests passing to surviving spouse
    by . . . . 5.06[3][b]
. description, general . . . . 5.06[2]
. disclaimers . . . . 5.06[3][h]
. dower, interests passing to surviving spouse
    by . . . . 5.06[3][b]
. encumbrances on surviving spouse's interest,
    valuation . . . . 5.06[5][b]
. estate tax . . . . 1.02[3][d]
. . credit against estate tax, gift tax as
    . . . . 3.04[2][b]
. . life insurance beneficiaries, liability of
    . . . . 8.05[2]
. . right of recovery 8.07
. estate trusts . . . . 5.06[7][b]
. extent of deduction . . . . 11.04[2]
. family-owned business deduction, interrela-
    tionship with . . . . S5.08A[6][b][iii]
. formula clauses . . . . 5.06[6]
. . generally . . . . 5.06[6]

Marital deduction—Cont'd
. formula clauses—Cont'd
. . outdated . . . . 5.06[6][b]
. . pecuniary bequest to surviving spouse, spe-
        cial problem . . . . 5.06[6][a]
. . transitional rule . . . . 5.06[6][b]
. . unlimited marital deduction . . . . 5.06[6][b]
. generally . . . . 5.06[1], 5.06[2]
. generation-skipping transfer tax, inclusion ra-
        tio . . . . 16.02[7][b][ii]
. gift tax . . . . 1.03[5][b], 11.03
. . credit against estate tax, gift tax as
        . . . . 3.04[2][b]
. . exceptions to terminable interest rule
        . . . . 11.03[4]
. . extent of marital deduction . . . . . 11.04[2]
. . generally . . . . 11.03[1]
. . gift tax counterpart of marital deduction
        . . . . 11.03[1]
. . noncitizen donee spouses . . . . . . 11.03[5]
. . requirements . . . . 11.03[2]
. . terminable interest rule . . 11.03[3], 11.03[4]
. gross estate
. . alternate valuation date . . . . 4.03[4][b]
. . previously allowed deduction 4.16
. . requirement . . . . 5.06[4]
. inheritance, interests passing to surviving
        spouse by . . . . 5.06[3][a]
. interests passing to surviving spouse . 5.06[3]
. . concept of passing . . . . 5.06[2]
. . curtesy . . . . 5.06[3][b]
. . deductible interest, requirement of . 5.06[2]
. . defined . . . . 5.06[3][g]
. . disclaimers . . . . 5.06[3][h]
. . dower . . . . 5.06[3][b]
. . encumbrances on surviving spouse's interest
        . . . . 5.06[5][b]
. . inheritance . . . . 5.06[3][a]
. . jointly held property . . . . 5.06[3][d]
. . life insurance proceeds . . . . 5.06[3][f]
. . power of decedent, property subject to
        . . . . 5.06[3][e]
. . problems with passing of interests
        . . . . 5.06[3][g]
. . support payments . . . . 5.06[3][g]
. . taxes on surviving spouse's interest
        . . . . 5.06[5][a]
. . transfers within requirements . . . 5.06[3][c]
. . valuation of . . . . 5.06[5]
. . will . . . . 5.06[3][a]
. inter vivos transfers . . . . 5.06[3][c]
. jointly held property 5.06[3][d], 5.06[8][d][iv]
. legislative background . . . . 5.06[1], 5.06[10]

Marital deduction—Cont'd
. life estate, election to treat as QTIP
        . . . . 5.06[8][d]
. . election . . . . 5.06[8][d][iii]
. . generally . . . . 5.06[8][d]
. . income interest . . . . 5.06[8][d][ii],
                                        S5.06[8][d][ii]
. . interrelationship of terminable interest ex-
        ceptions . . . . 5.06[8][f]
. . joint and mutual wills . . . . . 5.06[8][d][iv]
. . passing requirement . . . . 5.06[8][d][i]
. . powers over property during surviving
        spouse's life . . . . 5.06[8][d][ii],
                                        S5.06[8][d][ii]
. . qualifying income interest requirement
        . . . . 5.06[8][d][ii], S5.06[8][d][ii]
. life insurance proceeds . . . . 5.06[3][f]
. . liability of beneficiaries for estate tax
        . . . . 8.05[2]
. mandatory nature of . . . . 5.06[1]
. marital rights in transfers for insufficient con-
        sideration, relation to . . . . 4.15[1]
. noncitizen surviving spouse . 5.06[1], 5.06[9],
                                        11.03[5]
. nonresident aliens . . . . 6.06[3]
. power of decedent, property subject to
        . . . . 5.06[3][e]
. property for which deduction previously al-
        lowed 4.16
. qualified domestic trusts . . . 5.06[1], 5.07[1],
                                        5.07[3][e], 6.06[3]

        *See also Qualified domestic trusts
        (QDOTs)*
. qualifying terminable interests . . . . . 5.06[8]
. recovery, right of, certain marital deduction
        property 8.07
. . estate tax recovery . . . . 8.07[2]
. . generally . . . . 8.07[1]
. . gift tax recovery . . . . 8.07[3]
. . indirect gifts, possibility of . . . . . . 8.07[5]
. . tax liability . . . . 8.07[4]
. tax conventions . . . . 7.03[1][c]
. taxes on surviving spouse's interest, valuation
        . . . . 5.06[5][a]
. terminable interest rule . . . . 5.06[7]
. . charitable remainder trusts, special rules
        . . . . 5.06[8][e], S5.06[8][e]
. . common disasters . . . . 5.06[8][a]
. . estate tax . . . . 1.02[3][d], 5.06[7]
. . exceptions to . . . . . . 5.06[8][f], 11.03[4]
. . executor-purchaser provision . . . 5.06[7][d]
. . generally . . . . 5.06[7], 5.06[7][c]
. . general rule . . . . 5.06[7][a]
. . gift tax . . . . 1.03[5][b], 11.03[3], 11.03[4]

Marital deduction — Cont'd
. *terminable interest rule — Cont'd*
. . identification of terminable interests
.... 5.06[7][b]
. . insurance with powers .... 5.06[8][c]
. . life estate for surviving spouse, election
with respect to .... 5.06[8][d]
. . life interests with powers ..... 5.06[8][b]
. . patents................. 5.06[7][c]
. . purpose .... 5.06[7][a]
. . qualifying terminable interests .... 5.06[8]
. . tainted asset rule .... 5.06[7][e]
. transitional rule .... 5.06[6][b]
. trusts
. . estate trusts .... 5.06[7][b]
. . unlimited marital deduction .... 5.06[6][b]
. unlimited marital deduction ..... 5.06[6][b]
. valuation
. . alternate valuation date .... 4.03[4][b]
. . encumbrances on surviving spouse's interest
.... 5.06[5][b]
. . of interests passing .... 5.06[5]
. . taxes on surviving spouse's interest
.... 5.06[5][a]
. will, interests passing to surviving spouse by
.... 5.06[3][a]

Marital rights
. estate tax and gift tax, interrelationship
.... 4.15[1][f], 10.02[5][d]
. gift tax
. . interrelationship with estate tax . 4.15[1][f],
10.02[5][d]
. . property settlements not in divorce decree
.... 10.06
. . valuation of elective share of marital rights
.... 10.02[5][d]
. transfers for insufficient consideration 4.15[1]
. . community property, interest in . 4.15[1][b]
. . disqualified marital rights ..... 4.15[1][a]
. . divorce, effect .... 4.15[1][e]
. . dower or curtesy interests, relinquishment of
.... 4.15[1]
. . estate tax .... 4.15[1], 4.15[1][f]
. . generally .... 4.15[1]
. . gift tax amnesty rule .... 4.15[1][e]
. . gift tax/estate tax anomaly .... 4.15[1][f]
. . gross estate .... 4.15[1]
. . intestate succession, state statute on
.... 4.15[1][c]
. . marital deduction, relation to ..... 4.15[1]
. . support, right to .... 4.15[1][d]

**Market quotations availability, valuation of
discretionary rights** .... 19.02[3][a]

Married couples
*See Divorce; Marital Deduction; Marital
rights; Property settlements not in divorce
decree; Spouses*

**Marshall Islands, Compact of Free Associa-
tion with** .... 7.03[9]

Medical expenses
. generation-skipping transfer tax exclusion
.... 1.04[3][d], 13.01[2][a]
. gift tax exclusion . . 1.03[3], 9.04[6], S9.04[6]
. local law, effect............ 9.04[6]

**Micronesia, Compact of Free Association
with** .... 7.03[9]

Minority interests, discounts and premiums
. estate tax .... 4.02[3][f]
. gift tax .... 10.02[2][c]

Minors
. as donees, requirements .... 9.04[5]
. . first requirement .... 9.04[5][a]
. . second requirement .... 9.04[5][b]
. . state statutes simplifying gifts . . 9.04[5][c]
. gifts to.................... 9.04[4]
. . checks, gifts of .... 10.01[3][h]
. . donee requirements, special statutory rule
.... 9.04[5]
. . as future interests .... 9.04[4]
. . gift tax credit for........... 3.04[1][b]
. . revocable transfers.......... 4.10[4][f]
. . . minor's right to revoke .... 10.01[5][a]
. support
. . property settlements outside divorce decree,
amount for child support . . 10.06[2][b]

Model tax conventions
*See Organization for Economic Cooperation
and Development (OECD) convention;
United States--model U.S. tax conventions*

**Mortality tables, valuation of reversionary
interests** .... 4.09[4][d]

Mortgages .... S5.03[5]
. gross estate inclusion of mortgage obligations,
valuation .... 4.02[3][h]

**Mutual fund shares, valuation for gift tax
purposes**................ 10.02[2][d]

N

National Wilderness Preservation System
.... S4.02[4][b][i]

Near-death transfers .... 1.02[2][b][i], S4.07,
4.14[9][b], 10.01[10][b]

*See also Transfers within three years of
death*

Netherlands convention .... 7.03[2]

No-load funds
. valuation . . . . 4.02[3][d]

Noncitizens

  See also Noncitizen spouses
. expatriation to avoid tax 6.07, S6.07
. . Section 2107 . . . . 6.07[2]
. . . credit . . . . 6.07[2][c]
. . . requirements . . . . 6.07[2][a]
. . . special situs rule . . . . 6.07[2][b]
. . Section 2801 . . . . 6.07[1]
. . . requirements . . . . 6.07[1][a]
. . . tax imposed . . . . 6.07[1][b]
. nonresident noncitizens

    See Nonresident aliens

Noncitizen spouses
. as donees, gift tax . . . . 11.03[5]
. gifts to, nondeductibility . . . . 11.03[5]
. joint interests . . . . 4.12[10]
. marital deduction, surviving spouse . . 5.06[1],
                           5.06[9]
. qualified domestic trusts . . 4.12[10], 5.06[1],
                            5.07

    See also Qualified domestic trusts
    (QDOTs)
. . exceptions if surviving spouse becomes
    U.S. citizen . . . . 5.07[5]

Nondiscrimination provisions, tax conven-
tions . . . . 7.04[6]

Non-lapsing conversion rights
. defined . . . . 19.02[2][b][ii]
. estate freezes, special valuation rules
  . . . . 19.02[2][b][ii]

Nonresident aliens 6.01–6.08
. adjusted taxable gifts . . . . 6.01[1], S6.01[1]
. art works . . . . 6.05[5]
. bank deposits . . . . 6.04[3], 6.05[2]
. . banking business . . . . 6.05[2][b]
. . contingent interest . . . . 6.05[2][a]
. . domestic institutions . . . . 6.05[2]
. . effectively connected income . 6.05[2][c][ii]
. . foreign branches of U.S. banks . . . 6.05[3]
. . non-U.S.-source income . . . . . . 6.05[2][c]
. . qualifying deposits . . . . 6.05[2][a]
. . trade or business, non-U.S.-source income
  . . . . 6.05[2][c][i]
. bonds . . . . 6.05[6]
. charitable bequests . . . . 6.06[2]
. citizenship, defined . . . . 6.01[2][a]
. claims . . . . 6.06[1]
. credits against estate tax 6.02
. . gift tax . . . . 6.02[2]
. . prior transfers, tax on . . . . 6.02[3]

Nonresident aliens—Cont'd
. *credits against estate tax—Cont'd*
. . state death taxes . . . . . 6.02[1], S6.02[1]
. . unified credit . . . . 6.02[4]
. debt obligations . . . . 6.04[3]
. . portfolio interest . . . . . 6.05[4], S6.05[4]
. deductions
. . charitable . . . . 6.06[2]
. . expenses, claims, and losses . . . . . 6.06[1]
. . generally . . . . 6.06[1]
. . marital deduction . . . . 6.06[3]
. . prerequisite to . . . . 6.06[4]
. estate tax . . . . 6.01[1], S6.01[1]
. . citizenship and residence, tax liability and
  . . . . 8.09
. . credits against 6.02
. . pre-1967 estate tax provisions 6.08
. . tax rates . . . . S6.01[1]
. expatriation to avoid tax 6.07, S6.07
. . Section 2107 . . . . S6.07[2]
. . . credit . . . . S6.07[2][c]
. . . requirements . . . . S6.07[2][a]
. . Section 2801 . . . . S6.07[1]
. . . requirements . . . . S6.07[1][a]
. . . tax imposed . . . . S6.07[1][b]
. expenses . . . . 6.06[1]
. foreign corporate stock . . . . 6.04[1]
. generation-skipping transfer tax, nonresident
  alien transferor . . . . 18.03[2]
. . ETIP rules . . . . 18.03[2][d]
. . generally . . . . 18.03[2][a]
. . property within United States, transfer of
  . . . . 18.03[2][b]
. . trusts partially subject to Chapter 13
  . . . . 18.03[2][c]
. gift tax . . . . 6.02[2], 10.01[11]
. gross estate 6.03
. . defined 6.03
. . generally 6.06
. . general principles . . . . 6.03[1]
. . intangibles . . . . 6.03[2][b], 6.04[3]
. . limitations . . . . 6.03[2]
. . real property . . . . 6.03[2][a]
. . tangible personal property . . . . . 6.03[2][a]
. . valuation . . . . 6.03[1]
. intangible property
. . gift tax . . . . 9.02[1]
. . gross estate . . . . 6.03[2][b], 6.04[3]
. life insurance proceeds . . . . 6.05[1]
. lifetime transfers, property subject to . 6.04[2]
. limitations on gross estate inclusion . 6.03[2]
. losses . . . . 6.06[1]
. marital deduction . . . . 6.06[3]

Nonresident aliens — Cont'd

. portfolio interest . . . . 6.05[4], S6.05[4]

. pre-1967 estate tax provisions 6.08

. prerequisite to deductions . . . . 6.06[4]

. prior transfers, credit for tax on . . . . 6.02[3]

. property within United States 6.04

. . generation-skipping transfer tax, nonresident alien transferor . . . . 18.03[2][b]

. . situs rules, summary . . . . 6.05[7]

. property without United States 6.05

. . situs rules, summary . . . . 6.05[7]

. qualified domestic trusts . . . . 6.06[3]

    See also Qualified domestic trusts (QDOTs)

. real property, gross estate . . . . . . 6.03[2][a]

. residence, defined . . . . 6.01[2][b]

. resident vs. nonresident . . . . 6.01[2]

. situs of property

. . generally 6.04

. . property within United States   6.04, 6.05[7]

. . property without United States 6.05, 6.05[7]

. . summary of situs rules . . . . 6.05[7]

. spouses

    See Noncitizen spouses

. state death taxes . . . . . . 6.02[1], S6.02[1]

. stock, corporate . . . . 6.04[1]

. stock in regulated investment company (RIC) . . . . S6.05[5]

. tangible personal property, gross estate . . . . 6.03[2][a]

. taxable estate 6.06

. . expenses, claims, and losses . . . . . 6.06[1]

. tax imposed 6.01

. . citizen or noncitizen . . . . 6.01[2]

. . credits against 6.02

. . generally . . . . 6.01[1], S6.01[1]

. . property within vs. property without United States 6.04

. unified credit . . . . 6.02[4]

. United States, defined . . . . 6.03[2]

. valuation of gross estate . . . . 6.03[1]

Non-U.S.-source income, nonresident aliens' bank deposits . . . . 6.05[2][c]

. effectively connected income . . 6.05[2][c][ii]

. trade or business, engagement in 6.05[2][c][i]

Notes

. gifts of . . . . 10.01[3][h]

. gross estate inclusion, valuation . . 4.02[3][h], 4.05[3]

. installment sales notes, valuation . 4.02[3][h]

. tax conventions, situs rules . . . . . 7.02[2][c]

O

OBRA

    See Omnibus Budget Reconciliation Act (OBRA) of 1989

OECD

    See Organization for Economic Cooperation and Development (OECD) convention

Oil and gas interests

. gross estate inclusion, valuation for

. . alternate valuation date . . . . 4.03[2][d]

Omnibus Budget Reconciliation Act (OBRA) of 1989

. ESOPs and EWOCs, repeal restrictions on 5.08

$1 million GST exemption

    See Generation-skipping transfer (GST) exemption

Open and closed-end funds

. gross estate inclusion . . . . 4.02[3][d]

. valuation . . . . 4.02[3][d]

Open transaction doctrine, gift tax . . . . 10.02[1][b]

Options 19.04

. background . . . . 19.04[1][b]

. bona fide business arrangement . 19.04[3][a]

. deemed satisfaction of special valuation rules . . . . 19.04[4]

. effective dates . . . . 19.04[7]

. estate freezes, special valuation rules . . 19.04

. estate tax valuation . . . . 19.04[6][a]

. . lifetime dispositions, restrictions on . . . . 19.04[6][a][i]

. . method prescribed by agreement . . . . 19.04[6][a][iii]

. . obligation of estate to sell . . 19.04[6][a][ii]

. exception from Section 2703, establishing valuation . . . . 19.04[6]

. full and adequate consideration, disallowed device to transfer property to family for less than . . . . 19.04[3][b]

. . not family device . . . . 19.04[3][b][i]

. generally . . . . 19.04[1][a], 19.04[2]

. generation-skipping transfer tax valuation . . . . 19.04[6][c]

. gift tax valuation . . . . 19.04[6][b]

. multiple rights and restrictions . . . . 19.04[5]

. requirements . . . . 19.04[3]

. similar arrangement test . . . . . . 19.04[3][c]

. substantial modification . . . . 19.04[7]

. valuation rules, special 19.04

Ordinary course of business, transfers in . . . . 10.02[4]

Organization for Economic Cooperation and Development (OECD) convention . 7.03[1]
. changes in tax laws, advisement of 7.06
. charitable deductions . . . . 7.03[1][c]
. credits . . . . 7.03[1][c]
. deductions . . . . 7.03[1][c]
. exemptions . . . . 7.03[1][c]
. fiscal domicile . . . . 7.03[1][a]
. marital deduction . . . . 7.03[1][c]
. situs rules . . . . 7.03[1][b]

Overpayment of estate tax, effect . 2.02[3][c]

Ownership of property
. conservation easement, family-owned property subject to, gross estate exclusion
. . . . S4.02[4][b][i]
. family-owned business deduction . . . S5.08A
. joint interests
. . co-owners, property paid for by . . . 4.12[7]
. . forms of ownership of . . . . 4.12[2]
. life insurance proceeds, incidents of owner-ship . . . . 4.14[4][a]
. . incidents incidentally held . . . . . . 4.14[5]
. . "incidents" in context . . . . 4.14[4][e]
. special-use valuation of real property
. . indirect ownership and use, 50 percent test
. . . . 4.04[3][b][v]
. . ownership and use requirements, 25 percent test . . . . 4.04[3][c][i]

P

Palau, Compact of Free Association with
. . . . 7.03[10]

Partial consideration, transfers for . . 4.15[2]
. estate tax . . . . 4.15[2]
. Past rule . . . . 4.15[2][b]
. reduction for partial consideration . 4.15[2][a]

Partial property interests
See also Split gifts
. charitable bequests of . . . . 5.05[8]
. gross estate inclusion . . . . 4.02[3][i]
. qualified terminable interest property, disposition of portion of . . . . 10.08[1][a]
. valuation . . . . 4.02[3][i]

Partnerships
. conservation easement, partnership-held land subject to . . . . S4.02[4][e][i]
. control of, defined . . . . 19.05[2][b][iv]
. estate freezes, valuation rules to combat abuses
. . partnership attribution . . . . . 19.02[2][d][ii]
. . partnership interest requirement
. . . . 19.02[2][a][ii]

Partnerships —Cont'd
. family-owned business deduction . S5.08A[1], S5.08A[2][b], S5.08A[2][c]
See also Family-owned business deduction
. as generation-skipping transfer beneficiaries
. . . . 17.01[2][c][i]
. interests in, held by decedent, gross estate
. . . . 4.05[7][b]
. lapsed voting or liquidation rights
See Lapsed voting or liquidation rights
. life insurance proceeds, partnership's insurance on partner . . . . 4.14[5][b]
. limited liability companies
. . limited partnerships compared . . 4.05[7][c]
. . partnership treatment of . . . . . . 4.05[7][c]

Patents
. marital deduction, terminable interest rule
. . . . 5.06[7][c]
. tax convention, situs rules . . . . . . 7.02[2][c]

Payment of tax
. estate tax . . . . 1.02[6], 2.02[2]
. . deferred . . . . 2.02[3], 5.07[3][c]
. . extension of time for payment . . . . 2.02[3]
. . foreign death taxes, credit for . . . . 3.06[4]
. . liability for payment 2.02
. . overpayment, effect . . . . 2.02[3][c]
. . qualified domestic trusts . . . . . . 5.07[4][c]
. extension of time for payment, section 6159 rules . . . . 2.02[3][a]
. generation-skipping transfer tax . . . . 1.04[5]
. . deferral of payment . . . . 18.01[2]
. . taxable distributions, tax-payment . 14.02[4]
. . transfers at death, deferral of payment
. . . . 18.01[2][a], S18.01[2][a]
. . transfers other than at death, deferral of payment . . . . 18.01[2][b]
. gift tax . . . . 1.03[8]
. . donee payment of, valuation . . 10.02[6][d]

Pensions, tax convention situs rules
. . . . 7.02[2][c]

Personal holding company income
. defined . . . . S5.08A[2][b][iii]
. family-owned business deduction, income ceiling for . . . . S5.08A[2][b][iii]

Personal property
See Tangible personal property

Personal residence trusts
. defined . . . . 19.03[3][d]
. exception to Section 2702 special valuation rules . . . . 19.03[3][d]
. personal residence, defined . . . 19.03[3][d][i]
. qualified personal residence trust
. . . . 19.03[3][d][iii]

Personal residence trusts —Cont'd
. *qualified personal residence trust*—*Cont'd*
. . cash and other assets . . . . . 19.03[3][d][iii]
. . cessation of trust . . . . 19.03[3][d][iii]
. . insurance proceeds . . . . 19.03[3][d][iii]
. . sale proceeds . . . . 19.03[3][d][iii]
. . transfer of real property in trust to another
        trust . . . . S19.03[3][d][iii]
. regular personal residence trust 19.03[3][d][ii]
. . generally . . . . 19.03[3][d][ii]
. . qualified proceeds . . . . 19.03[3][d][ii]
. . trust imputation . . . . 19.03[3][d][ii]
. requirements . . . . 19.03[3][d][i]
. two personal residence trusts limitation
        . . . . 19.03[3][d][iv]
. two types . . . . 19.03[3][d]
. use of residence . . . . 19.03[3][d][i]
. valuation . . . . 19.03[3][d]

Political entities, charitable transfers to
        . . . . 5.05[2], 11.01[1]

**Political organizations, gift tax on transfers
to** . . . . 9.02[2]

Pooled income funds
. generation-skipping transfer tax . 17.02[3][c]
. split interest, charitable deduction . 5.05[8][e],
        19.03[3][a][iii]

Possessions of U.S.
. estate tax liability, citizenship and residence
        . . . . 8.09
. tax conventions and . . . . 7.04[5]

Pour-over trusts . . . . 17.03[2][b]

Powers of appointment 4.13, 10.04
. amount to be included in gross estate 4.13[9]
. another person, powers with . . . . 4.13[4][c]
. charitable deductions, property over which
        decedent had power . . . . 5.05[3][e]
. complete release of pre-1942 power
        . . . . 4.13[6][c]
. Crummey powers and . . . . 9.04[3][f]
. decedent's power over property
. . charitable deductions . . . . 5.05[3][e]
. . estate tax liability of recipient of property
        . . . . 8.06
. . marital deduction . . . . 5.05[3][e]
. defined . . . . 4.13[2], 10.04[2][a]
. disclaimers
. . estate tax . . . . 4.13[7][d]
. . gift tax . . . . 10.04[4][b], 10.07[2][b]
. estate tax 4.13
. . definition of general power . . . . . . 4.13[3]
. . disclaimers . . . . 4.13[7][d]
. . exercise of power . . . . 4.13[6][a]
. . generally . . . . 1.02[2][b][viii]

Powers of appointment—Cont'd
. *estate tax*—*Cont'd*
. . general power . . . . 4.13[3]–4.13[7]
. . liability of recipient of property over which
        decedent had power 8.06
. . nongeneral power . . . . 4.13[8]
. . post-1942 powers . . . . . 4.13[4][c], 4.13[7]
. . pre-1942 powers . . . . 4.13[4][b], 4.13[6]
. . release of power . . . 4.13[6][c], 4.13[6][d],
        4.13[7][c]
. exceptions to general definition of . . 4.13[4]
. exercise of power
. . estate tax . 4.13[6][a], 4.13[6][b], 4.13[7][b]
. . failure to exercise . . . . 4.13[6][b]
. . gift tax 10.04[3][c], 10.04[3][d], 10.04[3][f],
        10.04[4][a]
. . indirect exercise of power . . . . . 10.04[3][f]
. . ineffective exercise . . . . 10.04[3][d]
. . partial exercise . . . . 10.04[3][c]
. . post-1942 powers . 4.13[7][b], 10.04[4][a]
. . pre-1942 powers . . . 4.13[6][a], 4.13[6][b],
        10.04[3][a], 10.04[3][c], 10.04[3][f]
. existence of . . . . 4.13[2]
. failure to exercise pre-1942 power 4.13[6][b]
. five and five rule . . . . 4.13[7][f]
. generally . . . . 1.02[2][b][viii], 4.13[1]
. general power . . . . 4.13[3]–4.13[7]
. . defined . . . . . 4.13[2], 4.13[3], 10.04[2][a]
. . estate tax . . . . 4.13[3]–4.13[7]
. . exceptions to . . . . 4.13[4], 10.04[2][b]
. . generally . . . . 1.02[2][b][viii]
. . gift tax . . . . 1.03[2][c], 10.04[2]
. . treatment of . . . . 4.13[5]
. gift tax 10.04
. . alteration of time or manner of gift, power
        of . . . . 10.01[7]
. . change of gift beneficiaries, power to make
        . . . . 10.01[6]
. . definition of general power . . . 10.04[2][a]
. . disclaimers under . . . . 4.13[7][d]
. . exceptions to general power . . 10.04[2][b]
. . exercise of power . 10.04[3][a], 10.04[3][c],
        10.04[3][d], 10.04[3][f], 10.04[4][a]
. . generally . . . . 10.04[1]
. . general power . . . . . . 1.03[2][c], 10.04[2]
. . indirect exercise of power . . . . . 10.04[3][f]
. . ineffective exercise of power . . 10.04[3][d]
. . interest accompanying power . . 10.04[3][e]
. . lapse of power . . . . 10.04[4][c]
. . life interests with powers, deductible gifts
        to spouse of . . . . 11.03[4][b]
. . nongeneral power, special rule . . . 10.04[5]
. . partial exercise of power . . . . . 10.04[3][c]

Powers of appointment—Cont'd
. *gift tax—Cont'd*
.. post-1942 powers . . . . 10.04[4]
.. pre-1942 powers . . . . 10.04[3]
.. present interests, powers affecting
. . . . 9.04[3][c]
.. release of power . . . . 10.04[3][b]
.. rule for general power . . . . . . 10.04[2][a]
.. terminable interest rule, caveat on powers
. . . . 11.03[3][a]
.. third persons
... donor's power exercisable only with
. . . . 10.01[8]
... powers held only by . . . . 10.01[9]
.. transferor, powers held by . . . 10.01[10][e],
S10.01[10][e]
. gross estate 4.13
. insurance with powers, marital deduction
. . . . 5.06[8][c]
. judicious use of . . . . 4.13[4][d]
. lapse of power
.. estate tax . . . . 4.13[7][e]
.. gift tax . . . . 10.04[4][c]
.. post-1942 powers . . 4.13[7][e], 10.04[4][c]
. legislative background . . . . 4.13[10]
. life insurance proceeds . . . . 4.14[9][a]
. life interests with powers, marital deduction
and terminable interest rule . . . 5.06[8][b]
.. annual or more frequent payments to surviving spouse . . . . 5.06[8][b][ii]
.. entitlements of surviving spouse
. . . . 5.06[8][b][i], S5.06[8][b][i]
.. exercise of power . . . . 5.06[8][b][iv]
.. powers of surviving spouse . 5.06[8][b][iii]–
5.06[8][b][v]
.. scope of powers . . . . 5.06[8][b][iii]
.. sole power in surviving spouse, requirement
. . . . 5.06[8][b][v]
. limitation of power by standard . . 4.13[4][a]
. marital deduction
.. insurance with powers . . . . 5.06[8][c]
.. life estate treated as QTIP, powers over
property during surviving spouse's life
. . . . 5.06[8][d][ii], S5.06[8][d][ii]
.. property over which decedent had power
. . . . 5.06[3][e], 5.06[8][b]
. nongeneral power
.. estate tax . . . . 4.13[8]
.. gift tax . . . . 10.04[5]
. overlapping of interests . . . . 4.13[2][b]
. partial release of pre-1942 power . 4.13[6][d]
. possession of power . . . . 4.13[7][a]
. post-1942 powers . . . . . . 4.13[4][c], 4.13[7],
10.04[4]
.. with another person . . . . 4.13[4][c]

Powers of appointment—Cont'd
. *post—Cont'd*
.. disclaimer or renunciation . . . . . 4.13[7][d],
10.04[4][b]
.. estate tax . . . . 4.13[4][c], 4.13[7]
.. exercise of . . . . . . 4.13[7][b], 10.04[4][a]
.. five and five rule . . . . 4.13[7][f]
.. gift tax . . . . 10.04[4]
.. lapse of power . . . . 4.13[7][e], 10.04[4][c]
.. possession of . . . . 4.13[7][a]
.. release of . . . . 4.13[7][c], 10.04[4][c]
.. treatment of . . . . 4.13[7], 10.04[4]
. pre-1942 powers 4.13[4][b], 4.13[6], 10.04[3]
.. complete release of . . . . 4.13[6][c]
.. estate tax . . . . 4.13[4][b], 4.13[6]
.. exercise of . . . . . . 4.13[6][a], 10.04[3][a]
.. failure to exercise . . . . 4.13[6][b]
.. gift tax . . . . 10.04[3]
.. partial release of . . . . 4.13[6][d]
.. treatment of . . . . 4.13[6], 10.04[3]
. release of power
.. complete release . . . . 4.13[6][c]
.. estate tax . 4.13[6][c], 4.13[6][d], 4.13[7][c]
.. gift tax . . . . 10.04[3][b]
.. partial release . . . . 4.13[6][d]
.. post-1942 powers . 4.13[7][c], 10.04[4][b],
10.04[4][c]
.. pre-1942 powers . . . . 4.13[6][c], 4.13[6][d]
. renunciation . . . . 4.13[7][d]
. Section 2041
.. background of Section . . . . 4.13[10]
.. powers within . . . . 4.13[2]
.. relationship to other Sections . . . 4.13[2][a]
.. rules . . . . 4.13[1]
. special powers . . . . 4.13[8]
. surviving spouse . . . . 5.06[8][b]
. terminable interest rule
.. caveat on powers . . . . 11.03[3][a]
.. life interests with powers, exception to rule
. . . . 11.03[4][b]
Powers of Appointment Act of 1951 4.13[10]
**Prior interests, gross estate inclusion/exclu-
sion** 4.17
Prior transfers, estate tax credit for tax on
. . . . 3.05
. additional tax imposed under Section 2032A,
treatment of . . . . 3.05[5]
. adjustments . . . . 3.05[3]
. charitable deduction . . . . 3.05[4][a]
. computation of credit . . . . 3.05[2]
. death before that of transferor . . . 3.05[1][d]
. decedent's estate, tax caused in . . 3.05[4][a]
. decedent, transfer to . . . . 3.05[1][a]

Prior transfers, estate tax credit for tax on—Cont'd
. general rule . . . . 3.05[1]
. limitations on credit . . . . 3.05[4]
. multiple transferors, property from   3.05[4][b]
. nonresident aliens . . . . 6.02[3]
. percentage limitation . . . . 3.05[4][b]
. property, defined . . . . 3.05[1][b]
. taxable estate of transferor, adjustment
      . . . . 3.05[3][c]
. transfer defined . . . . 3.05[1][c]
. transferor's estate tax, adjustment . 3.05[3][a]
. value of property transferred, adjustment
      . . . . 3.05[3][b]

Private annuities
. estate tax . . . . 4.11[5]
. gift tax . . . . 4.11[5]
. gross estate . . . . 4.11[5]
. income tax . . . . 4.11[5]

Private foundations, restrictions on charitable deductions . . . . 5.05[5]

Property

    See also Intangible property; Real property; Tangible personal property
. additions to, joint interests . . . . . . 4.12[7][b]
. death, property owned at . . . . 1.02[2][a]
. defined . . . . 10.01[3][a]
. dispositions of
. . alternate valuation date, gross estate
      . . . . 4.03[3][a], S4.03[3][a]
. . recapture, special-use valuation of real property . . . . 4.04[8][a], S4.04[8][a]
. . terminable interest property 10.08
. encumbered
. . gifts of, valuation . . . . 10.02[2][a]
. . marital deduction, valuation for . 5.06[5][b]
. everyday classes of . . . . 10.01[3][a]
. foreign death taxes, effect of property value on estate tax credit . . . . 3.06[3][b]
. future interests in
    See Future interests
. gift tax
. . classes of property . . . . 10.01[3][a]
. . property interests subject to . . . . . 10.01[3]
. . property settlements subject to 10.06
. gross estate inclusion of property interests, valuation rules
. . beneficial interests of decedent . . . 4.05[2]
. . nonresident aliens . . . . 6.03[2][a]
. . partial and temporal property interests
      . . . . 4.02[3][i]
. . . decedent, partial interests of . . . . 4.05[5]
. . real property . . . . 4.02[3][b]

Property —Cont'd
. gross estate inclusion of property interests, valuation rules —Cont'd
. . tangible personal property . . . . . 4.02[3][a]
. improvements of . . . . 4.12[7][b]
. jointly held . . . . 1.02[2][b][vii]
    See also Joint interests
. nonresident aliens
. . intangible property . . . . 6.03[2][b], 6.04[3]
. . lifetime transfers, property subject to
      . . . . 6.04[2]
. . property within United States 6.04
. . property without United States 6.05
. . real property . . . . 6.03[2][a]
. . tangible personal property . . . . . 6.03[2][a]
. partial interests of decedent in, gross estate and . . . . 4.05[5]
. . cautions . . . . 4.05[5][c]
. . shared interests . . . . 4.05[5][a]
. . successive interests . . . . 4.05[5][b]
. partial property interests, valuation for gross estate inclusion . . . . 4.02[3][i]
. prior transfers of, estate tax credit for tax on
      . . . . 3.05[1][b]
. . multiple transferors, property from
      . . . . 3.05[4][b]
. residential property, charitable bequests of remainders in . . . . 5.05[8][a]
. tax convention situs rules, property rights
      . . . . 7.02[2][c], 7.03[1][b]
. temporal property interests, valuation for gross estate inclusion . . . . 4.02[3][i]

Property not subject to claims, special rules for
. administration expenses: Section 2053(b)
      . . . . S5.03[6][c][iii]
. definitions . . . . S5.03[6][c][ii]
. generally . . . . S5.03[6][c][i]
. value of property subject to claims, limitation based on--Section 2053(c)(2)
      . . . . S5.03[6][c][iv]

Property settlements not in divorce decree
      . . . . 10.06
. child support, amount for . . . . . . 10.06[2][b]
. comparative estate tax/gift tax treatment
      . . . . 10.06[3]
. generally . . . . 10.06[1]
. gift tax on 10.06
. income tax aspects . . . . 10.06[4]
. statutory requirements . . . . 10.06[2]
. three-year rule . . . . 10.06[2][c]
. type of transfer, requirement . . . 10.06[2][a]
. written agreement requirement . . . . 10.06[2]

Proportionate transfers, valuation 19.02[3][c]

Proprietorships, decedent-held interests in, gross estate . . . . 4.05[7][a]

Public Safety Officers' Benefit Act

. gross estate exclusion of payments under
. . . . 4.05[8]

Public uses, transfers for

See Charitable deductions

Put rights . . . . 19.02[2][b][ii]

Q

QDOTs

See Qualified domestic trusts (QDOTs)

QTIP

See Qualified terminable interest property (QTIP)

Qualified domestic trusts (QDOTs) 5.07

. annuity or other arrangement passing to
. . . . 5.07[2][c]

. collection of deferred tax, regulatory requirements to ensure . . . . 5.07[3][c]

. . applicable rules . . . . 5.07[3][c][iii], S5.07[3][c][iii]

. . assets not exceeding $2 million in value
. . . . 5.07[3][c][i], 5.07[3][c][ii], S5.07[3][c][ii]

. defined . . . . 5.07[1], 6.06[3]

. election

. . irrevocability of . . . . 5.07[3][d]

. . requirement of QDOT election . . 5.07[3][d]

. employee plan benefits passing to . 5.07[2][c]

. estate taxation of QDOT property . . . 5.07[4]

. . computation of tax . . . . 5.07[4][b]

. . events triggering . . . . 5.07[4][a]

. . liability for tax . . . . 5.07[4][c]

. . payment of tax . . . . 5.07[4][c]

. exceptions if surviving spouse becomes U.S. citizen . . . . 5.07[5]

. generally . . . . 5.07[1]

. joint interest transferred to . 4.12[10], 5.07[1], 5.07[2][b]

. marital deduction 5.06[1], 5.07[1], 5.07[3][e], 6.06[3]

. noncitizen spouse . . 4.12[10], 5.06[1], 5.07[1]

. . exceptions if surviving spouse becomes U.S. citizen . . . . 5.07[5]

. . transfer by surviving spouse to QDOT
. . . . 5.07[2][b]

. nonresident aliens . . . . 6.06[3]

. passing requirement . . . . 5.07[2]

. . annuity or other arrangement satisfying
. . . . 5.07[2][c]

. . direct passing of property . . . . 5.07[2]

. . reformation into QDOT . . . . . . 5.07[2][a]

Qualified domestic trusts (QDOTs)—Cont'd

. *passing requirement—Cont'd*

. . transfer by surviving spouse to QDOT
. . . . 5.07[2][b]

. qualification as . . . . 5.07[3]

. reformation into QDOT . . . . 5.07[2][a]

. requirements . . . . 5.07[3]

. . collection of deferred tax, regulatory requirements to ensure . . . . . 5.07[3][c]

. . marital deduction qualification . . 5.07[3][e]

. . passing requirement . . . . 5.07[2]

. . QDOT election . . . . 5.07[3][d]

. . U.S. trustee . . . . . 5.07[3][a], S5.07[3][a], 5.07[3][b]

. U.S. trustee

. . requirement of . . . . 5.07[3][a], S5.07[3][a]

. . right of trustee to withhold tax . 5.07[3][b]

. valuation of QDOT property . . . . . 5.06[1]

Qualified interests, valuation

. exception to Section 2702 special valuation rules . . . . . . 19.03[3][b], S19.03[3][b][i]

. generally . . . . 19.03[3][b]

. qualified income interests . . . 19.03[3][b][i], S19.03[3][b][ii]

. qualified remainder interests . 19.03[3][b][ii]

. zero valuation rule, application of 19.03[3][a]

Qualified State Tuition Programs . . S9.04[6], S10.01[3][c], S13.01[2][a]

Qualified terminable interest property (QTIP) 10.08

See also Terminable interest rule

. disclaimers . . . . 10.07[2][b]

. disposition of 10.08

. . definition of disposition 10.08[2], S10.08[2]

. . effective dates . . . . 10.08[4]

. . general rule . . . . 10.08[1]

. . gift tax liability . . . . 10.08[3]

. . portion of transferee spouse's qualifying income interest . . . . 10.08[1][a]

. . Section 2519 transfer . . . . 10.08[1][b]

. generally . . . . 1.02[2][b][x], 5.06[8][d]

. generation-skipping transfer tax

. . inclusion ratio . . . . 16.02[4][e]

. . transferors . . . . 17.02[1][c][i]

. gift tax . . . . 1.03[2][g], 10.08

. . deductible gifts to spouse . . . . 11.03[4][c]

. . liability for . . . . 10.08[3]

. . QTIP consequences . . . . 11.03[4][c][i]

. life estate, election to treat as QTIP
. . . . 5.06[8][d], 10.08

. . election . . . . 5.06[8][d][iii]

. . generally . . . . 5.06[8][d]

. . income interest . . . . 5.06[8][d][ii], S5.06[8][d][ii]

Qualified terminable interest property (QTIP)—Cont'd
. *life estate, election to treat as QTIP—Cont'd*
. . interrelationship of terminable interest exceptions . . . . 5.06[8][f]
. . joint and mutual wills . . . . . 5.06[8][d][iv]
. . passing requirement . . . . 5.06[8][d][i]
. . powers over property during surviving spouse's life . . . . 5.06[8][d][ii], S5.06[8][d][ii]
. . qualifying income interest requirement . . . . 5.06[8][d][ii], S5.06[8][d][ii]
. marital deduction, recovery right, estate tax . . . . 8.07[2]

R

Rate of tax
See Tax rates

Real property
. charitable bequests of remainders in residential property . . . . 5.05[8][a]
. conservation contributions, charitable deductions . . . . 5.05[8][b]
. easements in real property
. . gross estate exclusion of land subject to qualified conservation easement . . . . S4.02[4]
. . irrevocable transfers of . . . . 11.02[4]
. gross estate inclusion . . . . . 4.02[3][b], 4.04
. . nonresident aliens . . . . 6.03[2][a]
. nonresident aliens . . . . 6.03[2][a]
. tax conventions, situs rules . . . . . 7.02[2][a], 7.03[1][b]
. valuation . . . . 4.02[3][b], 4.04
See also Special-use valuation, real property

Recapitalization, tax-free, estate freeze as result of . . . . 19.02[1][a], 19.02[2][a][i]

Recapture tax
. family-owned business deduction, recapture rules . . . . S5.08A[5]
. . due date for tax . . . . S5.08A[5][e]
. . generally . . . . S5.08A[5][a]
. . liability for tax . . . . S5.08A[5][f]
. . measuring recapture tax . . . . S5.08A[5][c]
. . only one additional tax . . . . . S5.08A[5][d]
. . recapture events . . . . S5.08A[5][b]
. . statute of limitations . . . . . . S5.08A[5][g]
. generation-skipping transfer tax . . . 18.03[1]
. . regulations . . . . 18.03[1]
. . testamentary direct skips . . . . . 18.03[1][a]
. . testamentary transfers other than direct skips . . . . 18.03[1][b]
. . trust severance . . . . S16.02[5][e]

Recapture tax —Cont'd
. special-use valuation of real property . . . . 4.04[7]–4.04[9]
. . adjusted tax difference . . . . 4.04[9][b]
. . cessation of qualified use . . . . . 4.04[8][b], S4.04[8][b]
. . dispositions of property . . . . . . 4.04[8][a], S4.04[8][a]
. . generally . . . . 4.04[7]
. . measurement of recapture tax, generally . . . . 4.04[9][a]
. . portions of an interest . . . . 4.04[9][c]
. . recapture events . . . . 4.04[8]
. . recapture tax, measurement of . . . . 4.04[9]
. . successive interests . . . . 4.04[9][d]
. . ten-year period . . . . 4.04[7]
. . timber dispositions . . . . 4.04[9][e]

Reciprocal trusts
. defined . . . . 4.08[7][d]
. doctrine of . . . . 4.08[7][d]
. gift tax valuation . . . . 10.02[6][c]
. inter vivos creation of . 4.08[7][d], 10.02[6][c]
. transfers with retained life estate . 4.08[7][d]
. unequal trusts as . . . . 4.08[7][d]

Recovery, right of
. decedent-retained interest 8.08
. . effective dates . . . . 8.08[4]
. . estate tax recovery . . . . 8.08[2]
. . generally . . . . 8.08[1]
. . gift tax recovery . . . . 8.08[3]
. estate tax recovery
. . credits against estate tax, recovery of taxes claimed as 3.08
. . decedent-retained interest . . . . 8.08[2]
. . marital deduction property . . . . . . 8.07[2]
. gift tax recovery
. . decedent-retained interest . . . . 8.08[3]
. . marital deduction property . . . . . . 8.07[3]
. marital deduction property 8.07
. . estate tax recovery . . . . 8.07[2]
. . generally . . . . 8.07[1]
. . gift tax recovery . . . . 8.07[3]
. . indirect gifts, possibility of . . . . . . 8.07[5]
. . tax liability . . . . 8.07[4]
. wrongful death recovery . . . . 4.05[8]

Redemptions, estate freezes . . . 19.02[2][a][i]

Refunds of credits provided by tax conventions . . . . 7.04[2]

Regulated investment company (RIC)
. stock in . . . . S6.05[5]

Reimbursement out of estate for estate tax due 8.04
. state common law . . . . 8.04[3]

Reimbursement out of estate for estate tax due — Cont'd
. state statutes . . . . 8.04[2]
. will provisions . . . . 8.04[1]

Religious organizations
. charitable transfers to . . . . . 5.05[2], 11.01[1]

   See also Charitable deductions

Remainders
. charitable remainders . . . . 5.05[8]
. contingent . . . . 9.04[3]
. death taxes on, credit against estate tax for
  . . . . 3.07
. farms, charitable bequests of remainders in
  . . . . 5.05[8][a]
. gifts of . . . . 9.04[3], 10.01[3][b]
. life insurance proceeds . . . . 4.14[4][b]
. qualified remainder interests . 19.03[3][a][ii]
. residences, charitable bequests of remainders
  in . . . . 5.05[8][a]

Rent
. gross estate inclusion
. . alternative valuation date . . . . . 4.03[2][a]
. . rent accrued at death . . . . 4.05[4]
. transfers with retained life estate, rent paid by
  transferor . . . . 4.08[6][c]

Residence
. classification as resident . . . . 4.04[3][a]
. defined . . . . 6.01[2][b]
. domicile, defined . . . . 6.01[2][b], 7.01[2][b],
  7.03[1][a]
. . hierarchy-of-criteria test . . . . . . 7.03[1][a]
. . threshold (citizenship) test . . . . . 7.03[1][a]
. estate tax liability 8.09
. possessions of U.S 8.09
. resident, defined . . . . 6.01[2][b]
. resident vs. nonresident . . . . 6.01[2]
. special-use valuation, residence as qualification for . . . . 4.04[3][a]
. tax conventions 7.02

Resident aliens

  See also Nonresident aliens
. expatriation to avoid tax S6.07
. . Section 2107 . . . . S6.07[2]
. . . credit . . . . S6.07[2][c]
. . . requirements . . . . S6.07[2][a]
. . . special situs rule . . . . S6.07[2][b]
. . Section 2801 . . . . S6.07[1]
. . . requirements . . . . S6.07[1][a]
. . . tax imposed . . . . S6.07[1][b]

Residential property, charitable bequests of remainders in . . . . 5.05[8][a]

Retained interests, valuation
. estate freezing
. . special valuation rules to combat abuses of

   See Estate freezes; Special valuation
   rules to combat estate freeze abuses
   (Chapter 14 rules)
. grantor retained income trusts, retained interest requirement . . . . 19.03[2][a][iv]
. incomplete transfers . . . . 19.03[3][a]
. interests of same class . . . . . . 19.02[3][b]
. interests proportionate to class . . 19.02[3][b]
. market quotations availability . . . 19.02[3][a]
. personal residence trusts . . . . . . 19.03[3][d]
. proportionate transfers . . . . 19.02[3][c]
. qualified interests . 19.03[3][b], S19.03[3][b][i]

Retained life estate, transfers with

  See Transfers with retained life estate

Retirement
. employee stock ownership plans (ESOPs)
  . . . . 5.08[1]
. pensions, tax convention situs rules 7.02[2][c]

Returns
. armed forces in combat zone . . . . . . 9.04[9]
. estate tax . . . . 2.02[1]
. . executor, timely filing by . . . . 2.02[1]
. . reasonable cause test . . . . 2.02[1]
. . will filed with return . . . . 2.02[1]
. generation-skipping transfer tax 18.02
. . direct skips . . . . 18.02[2][b]
. . extensions of time to file . . . . 18.02[4][b]
. . generally . . . . 1.04[5], 18.02[1]
. . information returns . . . . 18.02[6]
. . parties who must file . . . . 18.02[3]
. . place for filing . . . . 18.02[5]
. . requirement of return . . . . 18.02[2]
. . taxable distributions and taxable terminations . . . . 18.02[2][a]
. . time for filing . . . . 18.02[4]
. . timely filing . . . . 18.02[4][a]
. gift tax . . 9.02[3], 9.04[9], S9.04[9], S11.02
. . armed forces in combat zone . . . . . 9.04[9]
. . fraudulent . . . . 9.04[10]
. . split gifts . . . . 9.04[9], 10.03[4]
. . timely return, GST inclusion ratio valuation
  . . . . 16.02[4][a]

Revenue Act of 1948
. community property . . . . 5.06[10]
. marital deduction . . . . 5.06[10]

Revenue Act of 1950
. marital deduction . . . . 5.06[3][g]

Revenue Act of 1986
. generation-skipping transfer tax . 17.02[1][d]

Revenue Act of 1987
. eligible worker owned cooperatives (EWOCs)
. . . . 5.08[6]
. employee stock ownership plans (ESOPs)
. . . . 5.08[6]

Revenue Reconciliation Act of 1993
. portfolio interest . . . . 6.05[4]

Reversionary interests
. actuarial principles, valuation using 4.09[4][d]
. defined . . . . 4.09[4][a], 4.14[4][b]
. 5 percent test
. . application of . . . . 4.09[4][f]
. . base for . . . . 4.09[4][g]
. gifts of . . . . 10.01[3][d]
. gross estate . . . . 4.09[4], 4.14[4][b]
. life insurance proceeds . . . . 4.14[4][b]
. method of retaining interest . . . . . 4.09[4][b]
. mortality tables, valuation using . . 4.09[4][d]
. negligible interests . . . . 4.09[4][c]
. physical condition of decedent before death,
. . . effect . . . . 4.09[4][e]
. retention of . . . . 4.09[4]
. valuation of interests . . . . 4.09[4][d]

Revocable transfers 4.10
. administrative powers of decedent . 4.10[4][c]
. alteration or amendment powers of decedent
. . . . 4.10[4][b]
. amount to be included . . . . 4.10[9]
. . change, interests subject to . . . . 4.10[9][a]
. . comparison of Sections 2036 and 2038
. . . . 4.10[9][b]
. change in enjoyment . . . . 4.10[3]
. community property 10.01[5][d], S10.01[5][d]
. consent of another party, power exercisable
. . . only with . . . . 4.10[6]
. defined . . . . 4.10[1]
. excluded transfers . . . . 4.10[2]
. generally . . . . 1.02[2][b][v], 4.10[1]
. gifts, disqualification as . . . . 10.01[5]
. investment powers of decedent . . . 4.10[4][d]
. joint accounts . . . . 10.01[5][c]
. joint and mutual wills . . . . 10.01[5][e]
. lifetime transfer rules under Code Sections
. . . . 4.10[10]
. . applicability of . . . . 4.10[10][f]
. . interest taxed, identification of . . 4.10[10][f]
. . overlapping Sections . . . . 4.10[10][a],
. . . . 4.10[10][b]
. . Section 2035 rules . . . . 4.10[1], 4.10[10][e]
. . Section 2036 rules . . . . 4.10[1], 4.10[9][b],
. . . . 4.10[10][a], 4.10[10][c]
. . Section 2037 rules . . . 4.10[1], 4.10[10][a],
. . . . 4.10[10][b]

Revocable transfers—Cont'd
. *lifetime transfer rules under Code Sections—*
. . *Cont'd*
. . Section 2038 rules . . . . 4.10[1], 4.10[9][b],
. . . . 4.10[10][a], 4.10[10][d]
. minors, gifts to . . . . 4.10[4][f]
. . revocation, minor's right of . . . 10.01[5][a]
. power in decedent . . . . 4.10[4]–4.10[8]
. . administrative powers . . . . 4.10[4][c]
. . alteration or amendment, power of
. . . . 4.10[4][b]
. . consent of another party, power exercisable
. . . only with . . . . 4.10[6]
. . existence of power, time requirement
. . . . 4.10[8], S4.10[8]
. . generally . . . . 4.10[4]
. . investment, powers of . . . . 4.10[4][d]
. . minors, gifts to . . . . 4.10[4][f]
. . restriction by standards . . . . 4.10[5]
. . revocation, power of 4.10[4][a], S4.10[4][a]
. . Section 2035(e) . . . . S4.10[8]
. . source of . . . . 4.10[7]
. . termination, power of . . . . 4.10[4][e]
. . "whatever" capacity, power in . . 4.10[4][g]
. revocation power of decedent . . . . 4.10[4][a],
. . . . S4.10[4][a]
. termination of donor's control . . 10.01[5][b]
. termination power of decedent . . . 4.10[4][e]

Revocable trusts
. transfers within three years of death
. . . . S4.07[2][c][ii]

Rights and restrictions on property . . 19.04
. background . . . . 19.04[1][b]
. bona fide business arrangement . 19.04[3][a]
. deemed satisfaction of special valuation rules
. . . . 19.04[4]
. disregard of 19.04
. effective dates . . . . 19.04[7]
. estate freezes, special valuation rules . . 19.04
. estate tax valuation . . . . 19.04[6][a]
. . lifetime dispositions, restrictions on
. . . . 19.04[6][a][i]
. . method prescribed by agreement
. . . . 19.04[6][a][iii]
. . obligation of estate to sell . . 19.04[6][a][ii]
. exception from Section 2703, establishing
. . . valuation . . . . 19.04[6]
. full and adequate consideration, disallowed
. . . device to transfer property to family for
. . . less than . . . . 19.04[3][b]
. . full and adequate consideration
. . . . 19.04[3][b][ii]
. . not family device . . . . 19.04[3][b][i]
. generally . . . . 19.04[1][a], 19.04[2]

Rights and restrictions on property — Cont'd
. generation-skipping transfer tax valuation
.... 19.04[6][c]
. gift tax valuation .... 19.04[6][b]
. multiple rights and restrictions .... 19.04[5]
. requirements .... 19.04[3]
. similar arrangement test ...... 19.04[3][c]
. substantial modification .... 19.04[7]
. valuation rules, special 19.04

S

Salary due decedent at death, gross estate inclusion .... 4.05[4]

Sales
. bona fide sales within three years of death
.... S4.07[2][c][i]
. ESOPs and EWOCs, sale of qualified employer securities to 5.08
. installment sales notes, gross estate inclusion
.... 4.02[3][h]
. qualified personal residence trusts, sale proceeds .... 19.03[3][d][iii]
. restrictions on sale of certain property, special valuation rules 19.04

Scientific organizations, charitable transfers to .... 5.05[2], 11.01[1]

S corporations compared to limited liability companies .... 4.05[7][c]

Section 213(c)(2) election ...... S5.03[6][b]

Section 303 stock
. conservation easement, Section 2031(c) interrelationship with Section 303
.... S4.02[4][f][iii]
. family-owned business deduction
.... S5.08A[6][c][i]

Section 642(g) election .... S5.03[6][a]

Section 2001: Imposition and rate of tax
.... S2.01
. computation of tentative tax ..... S2.01[1]
.. adjusted taxable gifts ...... S2.01[1][b]
... gifts made after August 5, 1997
.... S2.01[1][b][ii]
... gifts made through August 5, 1997
.... S2.01[1][b][i]
.. taxable estate .... S2.01[1][a]
.. tax rates .... S2.01[1][c]
. planning .... S2.01[3]
. reductions in tentative tax .... S2.01[2]

Section 2010: Unified credit against estate tax S3.02
. amount of credit .... S3.02[1]
.. basic exclusion amount ...... S3.02[1][a]
.. deceased spousal unused exclusion amount
.... S3.02[1][b]

Section 2010: Unified credit against estate tax — Cont'd
. amount of credit — Cont'd
.. deceased spousal unused exclusion amount — Cont'd
... amount of unused exclusion S3.02[1][b][i]
... election .... S3.02[1][b][ii]
. estate tax return filing requirements . S3.02[3]
. Section 2505 credit, relationship to . S3.02[2]

Section 2107
. expatriation to avoid tax S6.07
.. credit .... S6.07[3]
.. requirements of Section .... S6.07[1]
.. special situs rule .... S6.07[2]

Section 2210 estate tax for year 2010 . S8.10
. election .... S8.10[2]
. generally .... S8.10[1]
. income tax consequences .... S8.10[3]
.. carry-over basis, adjustments to S8.10[3][b]
... allocation of basis adjustments
.... S8.10[3][b][v]
... increase in basis regardless of recipient
.... S8.10[3][b][i]
... ineligible property ...... S8.10[3][b][iv]
... ownership .... S8.10[3][b][iii]
... surviving spouses, increase in basis for
.... S8.10[3][b][ii]
.. gain, special rules for treatment of
.... S8.10[3][c]
... character .... S8.10[3][c][i]
... foreign transfers .... S8.10[3][c][v]
... liability in excess of basis S8.10[3][c][iii]
... pecuniary bequests ..... S8.10[3][c][ii]
... sale of residence ...... S8.10[3][c][iv]
.. generally .... S8.10[3][a]
.. reporting requirements ..... S8.10[3][d]
... death, transfers at ..... S8.10[3][d][ii]
... failure to file required information, penalties for .... S8.10[3][d][iii]
... lifetime gifts .... S8.10[3][d][i]

Section 2502: Rate of tax S9.03
. computation method .... S9.03[3]
. liability for gift tax .... S9.03[4]
. periodic accounting for gifts ..... S9.03[1]
. rates .... S9.03[2]

Section 2505: Unified credit against gift tax
.... S9.06
. amount of credit .... S9.06[1]
. Section 2010 credit, relationship to . S9.06[2]

Section 2631: GST exemption S15.02
. exemption
.. duration of .... S15.02[4]
.. use of .... S15.02[2]

Section 2631: GST exemption—Cont'd
. individual allocation . . . . S15.02[1]
. transferor requirement . . . . S15.02[3]
Section 2641: Applicable rate S16.01
Securities
. casualty losses . . . . 5.04[2]
. ESOPs and EWOCs, sale of qualified employer securities to . . . . 5.08[2]
. . definition of qualified employer securities
. . . . 5.08[2], S5.08[2][a]
. . effective dates . . . . 5.08[6]
. . excise tax limitations . . . . 5.08[4]
. . generally . . . . 5.08[1]
. . procedural requirements . . . . 5.08[5]
. . proceeds limitations . . . . 5.08[3]
. gross estate inclusion . . . . 4.02[3][c]
. valuation . . . . 4.02[3][c]
Self-and-survivor annuities . . . 1.02[2][b][vi],
4.11, 4.11[7]
Series E bonds
. valuation . . . . 4.02[3][e]
Services, gratuitous, as indirect gifts
. . . . 10.01[2][g]
Settlor trustee, transfers with retained life
estate . . . . 4.08[6][a]
Shareholders in corporations
. generation-skipping transfer tax, shareholders
as skip persons . . . . 13.03[4][b]
. life insurance proceeds . . . . 4.14[5][a]
Ships
. casualty losses due to shipwrecks . . . 5.04[2]
. tax conventions, treatment under . . 7.03[1][b]
Simultaneous death, life insurance proceeds
. . . . 4.14[3][b]
Single-life annuity 4.11
Skip persons
See Generation-skipping transfer tax--skip
persons
Social Security benefits
. gross estate exclusion . . . . 4.05[8]
Special-use valuation, real property . . . 4.04
. absence from business, material participation
and . . . . 4.04[3][c][ii]
. acquisition from decedent . . . 4.04[3][b][viii]
. active business . . . . 4.04[3][b][iv]
. active management . . . . 4.04[3][c][iii]
. additional tax . . . . 4.04[9]–4.04[14]
. . basis adjustment for . . . . 4.04[14]
. . due date for . . . . 4.04[11]
. . imposition of . . . . 4.04[10]
. . liability for . . . . 4.04[12]
. . only one additional tax allowed . . 4.04[10]

Special-use valuation, real property—Cont'd
. *additional tax—Cont'd*
. . recapture tax . . . . 4.04[9]
. . statute of limitations . . . . 4.04[13]
. adjusted value
. . 50 percent test . . . . 4.04[3][b][i]
. . 25 percent test . . . . 4.04[3][c]
. agreement . . . . 4.04[6], S4.04[6]
. community property, estates involving
. . . . 4.04[3][d]
. continued use of property, facilitation of
. . . . 4.04[1]
. disability, material participation and
. . . . 4.04[3][c][ii]
. election of . . . . . . 4.04[1], 4.04[6], S4.04[6]
. . effect of . . . . 4.04[6]
. . irrevocability of . . . . 4.04[6]
. family members . . . . 4.04[3][b][vii]
. 50 percent test . . . . 4.04[3][b]
. formula farm valuation method . . . 4.04[5][a]
. . comparable land . . . . 4.04[5][a][iii]
. . divisor . . . . 4.04[5][a][v]
. . gross cash rental . . . . 4.04[5][a][i]
. . interest rate and . . . . 4.04[5][a][v]
. . net share rental . . . . 4.04[5][a][iii]
. . real estate taxes . . . . 4.04[5][a][iv]
. generally . . . . 4.04[1]
. growing crops . . . . 4.04[3][c]
. indirect ownership and use . . . 4.04[3][b][v]
. intangible personal property . . . 4.04[3][b][vi]
. involuntary conversions . . . . . . 4.04[3][c][i]
. like-kind exchanges . . . . 4.04[3][c][i]
. material participation . . . . . . 4.04[3][c][ii]
. methods of valuation . . . . 4.04[5]
. . formula farm valuation . . . . . . 4.04[5][a]
. . multiple-factor valuation . . . . . 4.04[5][c]
. . objectives of formula valuation . 4.04[5][b]
. multiple-factor valuation . . . . . . 4.04[5][c]
. nature of use of property . . . . 4.04[3][b][vi]
. objectives of formula valuation . . . 4.04[5][b]
. ownership and use requirements . 4.04[3][c][i]
. percent test . . . . 4.04[3][c][ii]
. production of agricultural/horticultural com-
modities 25
. qualification . . . . 4.04[2]–4.04[4]
. . active business requirement . . 4.04[3][b][iv]
. . citizens or residents only . . . . . 4.04[3][a]
. . community property, estates involving
. . . . 4.04[3][d]
. . estate qualification . . . . 4.04[3]
. . farm and farming . . . . 4.04[3][b][iii]
. . 50 percent test . . . . 4.04[3][b]
. . generally . . . . 4.04[2]

Special-use valuation, real property—Cont'd
. *qualification—Cont'd*
. . qualified use . . . . 4.04[3][b][ii]
. . real property qualification . 4.04[1], 4.04[4]
. . 25 percent test . . . . 4.04[3][c]
. qualified heirs . . . . 4.04[3][b][ix]
. qualified use . . . . 4.04[3][b][ii]
. real property qualification . . 4.04[1], 4.04[4]
. recapture . . . . 4.04[7]–4.04[9]
. . adjusted tax difference, recapture tax and
. . . . 4.04[9][b]
. . cessation of qualified use . . . . . 4.04[8][b],
                                        S4.04[8][b]
. . dispositions of property . . . . . . 4.04[8][a],
                                        S4.04[8][a]
. . generally . . . . 4.04[7]
. . portions of an interest . . . . 4.04[9][c]
. . recapture events . . . . 4.04[8]
. . recapture tax, measurement of . . . . 4.04[9],
                                        4.04[9][a]
. . successive interests . . . . 4.04[9][d]
. . ten-year period . . . . 4.04[7]
. . timber dispositions . . . . 4.04[9][e]
. substantial compliance test . . . . 4.04[6]
. tangible personal property . . . . 4.04[3][b][vi]
. trade or business use . . . . 4.04[3][b][iv]
. 25 percent test . . . . 4.04[3][c]
. woodland, qualified . . . . 4.04[3][c]
. written agreement . . . . 4.04[6]
Special valuation rules to combat estate
freeze abuses (Chapter 14 rules) . . 19.01–
                                        19.05

    See also Estate freezes
. applicable retained interest held by applicable
    family member, requirement . 19.02[2][b],
                19.03[2][a][iii], 19.03[2][a][iv]
. . applicable family member, defined
. . . . 19.02[2][b][i]
. . applicable retained interest, defined
. . . . 19.02[2][b]
. attribution rules . . . . 19.02[2][d]
. . corporate attribution . . . . . . 19.02[2][d][i]
. . estate attribution . . . . 19.02[2][d][iii]
. . indirect transfers under . . . . . 19.02[2][a][i]
. . multiple attribution . . . . . . 19.02[2][d][iv]
. . partnership attribution . . . . . 19.02[2][d][ii]
. . trust attribution . . . . 19.02[2][d][iii]
. buy-sell agreements 19.04

    See also Buy-sell agreements
. call rights . . . . 19.02[2][b][ii]
. capital structure transactions . . 19.02[2][a][i]
. charitable deductions, exception
. . . . 19.03[3][a][iii]

Special valuation rules to combat estate
freeze abuses (Chapter 14 rules)—Cont'd
. charitable lead trusts, exception
. . . . 19.03[3][a][iii]
. contributions to capital . . . . . 19.02[2][a][i],
                                        19.02[4][e]
. conversion rights . . . . 19.02[2][b][ii]
. . non-lapsing . . . . 19.02[2][b][ii]
. distribution rights . 19.02[2][b][ii], 19.02[4][c]
. . qualified payment rights . . . . 19.02[4][c][i]
. . . combined with extraordinary payment
        rights . . . . 19.02[4][c][ii]
. double taxation regulation . . . . . 19.03[4][c]
. . estate tax . . . . 19.03[4][c][ii]
. . gift tax . . . . 19.03[4][c][i]
. estate freeze abuses 19.01
. . Chapter 14 valuation methodology 19.01[3]
. . definitions . . . . 19.01[2]
. . generally . . . . 19.01[1]
. . rules to combat 19.01–19.05
. estate maintenance approach in . . . . 19.01[3]
. exceptions to . . . 19.01[4], 19.02[3], 19.03[3],
                                        S19.03[3]
. . interests of same class and interests propor-
        tionate to class . . . . 19.02[3][b]
. . market quotations available . . . 19.02[3][a]
. . proportionate transfers . . . . . . 19.02[3][c]
. extraordinary payment rights . 19.02[2][b][ii],
                                        19.02[4][b]
. . qualified payment rights combined with
. . . . 19.02[4][c][ii]
. generally 19.02
. grantor retained income trusts . . . . 19.03[1],
                                        19.03[2]

    See also Grantor retained income trusts
    (GRITs)
. guaranteed payment rights . . . 19.02[2][b][ii]
. incomplete transfers, exception . . 19.03[3][a]
. indirect transfers under attribution rules
. . . . 19.02[2][a][i]
. interest transferred requirement . . 19.02[2][a]
. . corporate or partnership interest
. . . . 19.02[2][a][ii]
. . member of family, required transfer or ben-
        efit of . . . . 19.02[2][a][i]
. . transfer defined . . . . 19.02[2][a][i]
. joint purchase rule . . . . 19.03[1], 19.03[4][a]
. junior equity interest, minimum valuation of
. . . . 19.02[4][f]
. lapsing rights and restrictions, treatment of
    certain 19.05
. liquidation
. . lapsed liquidation rights . . . . 19.05[2]
. . liquidation rights . . 19.02[2][b][ii], 19.05[2]
. . restrictions on . . . . 19.05[3]

Special valuation rules to combat estate freeze abuses (Chapter 14 rules) — Cont'd

. mandatory payment rights . . . 19.02[2][b][ii]

. options 19.04

    See also Options

. other regulatory exceptions . . . . 19.03[3][c], S19.03[3][c]

. personal residence trusts, exception

    . . . . 19.03[3][d]

. pooled income funds, exception

    . . . . 19.03[3][a][iii]

. put rights . . . . 19.02[2][b][ii]

. qualified interests, exception . . . 19.03[3][b], S19.03[3][b][i]

. qualified payment interest . . . . . 19.02[5][a]

. . amount of transfer . . . . 19.02[5][a][iv]

. . applicable family member, transfer to

    . . . . 19.02[5][a][iii]

. . ceiling rule . . . . 19.02[5][a][iv]

. . computation . . . . 19.02[5][a][iv]

. . death of transferor . . . . . . 19.02[5][a][iii]

. . elective transfer . . . . 19.02[5][a][iii], 19.02[5][a][iv]

. . generally . . . . 19.02[5][a][i]

. . inter vivos transfer of applicable retained interest providing . . . . . 19.02[5][a][iii]

. . qualified payment elections . 19.02[5][a][ii]

. . spouse, transfer to . . . . 19.02[5][a][iii]

. . taxable events . . . . 19.02[5][a][iii]

. relief rule . . . . 19.02[5][c]

. . amount of reduction . . . . . . 19.02[5][c][ii]

. . duplicated amount . . . . 19.02[5][c][ii]

. . estate tax relief . . . . 19.02[5][c][iv]

. . generally . . . . 19.02[5][c][i]

. . gift tax relief . . . . 19.02[5][c][iii]

. . split gifts, special rules for . . 19.02[5][c][v]

. . subsequent taxation, relief from

    . . . . 19.02[5][c][i]

. requirements for applicability . . . . . 19.02[2]

. . examples . . . . 19.02[2][c]

. rights and restrictions disregarded 19.04

    See also Rights and restrictions on property

. Section 2701 rules 19.02

. . effective dates . . . . 19.02[5][g]

. . estate tax, relationship to . . . . . 19.02[5][f]

. . examples . . . . 19.02[2][c]

. . exceptions . . . . 19.02[3]

. . generally . . . . 19.02[1], 19.02[1][c]

. . generation-skipping transfer tax, relationship to . . . . 19.02[5][f]

. . income tax, relationship to . . . . 19.02[5][f]

. . other gift tax provisions, relationship to

    . . . . 19.02[5][e]

Special valuation rules to combat estate freeze abuses (Chapter 14 rules) — Cont'd

. *Section 2701 rules* — Cont'd

. . other taxes, relationship of Section 2701 transfers to . . . . 19.02[5][f]

. . requirements of . . . . 19.02[2]

. . special rules . . . . 19.02[5]

. . statute of limitations, open . . . 19.02[5][d]

. . valuation rules . . . . 19.02[4]

. Section 2702 rules 19.03

. . double taxation regulation . . . . 19.03[4][c]

. . effective dates . . . . 19.03[4][f]

. . estate tax, relationship to . . . 19.03[4][e][i]

. . exceptions . . . . 19.03[3]

. . generally . . . . 19.03[1]

. . general rules . . . . 19.03[2]

. . generation-skipping transfer tax, relationship to . . . . 19.03[4][e][iii]

. . grantor retained income trusts (GRITs)

    . . . . 19.03[1], 19.03[2]

. . income tax, relationship to . 19.03[4][e][ii]

. . joint purchases . . . . 19.03[4][a]

. . other gift tax provisions, relationship to

    . . . . 19.03[2][c]

. . relationship to other taxes . . . . 19.03[4][e]

. . special rules . . . . 19.03[4]

. . statute of limitations, open . . . 19.03[4][d]

. . tangible property, transfers of certain

    . . . . 19.03[4][b]

. Section 2703 rules 19.04

. . deemed satisfaction . . . . 19.04[4]

. . effective dates . . . . 19.04[7]

. . enactment of Section 2703 . . . 19.04[1][c]

. . exception of right or restriction . . 19.04[6]

. . generally . . . . 19.04[1]

. . general rule . . . . 19.04[2]

. . multiple rights and restrictions . . . 19.04[5]

. . requirements . . . . 19.04[3]

. . substantial modification . . . . 19.04[7]

. Section 2704 rules 19.05

. . effective date . . . . 19.05[4]

. . generally . . . . 19.05[1]

. . lapsed voting or liquidation rights 19.05[2]

. . restrictions on liquidation . . . . . . 19.05[3]

. separate interest rule . . . . 19.02[5][b]

. statute of limitations, open . . . . . 19.02[5][d], 19.03[4][d]

. subtraction method of valuation . 19.02[4][d]

. . adjustments to value of transferred interests

    . . . . 19.02[4][d][iv]

. . allocation between transferred interests and family-held subordinate equity interests

    . . . . 19.02[4][d]

. . examples . . . . 19.02[4][d][v]

Special valuation rules to combat estate freeze abuses (Chapter 14 rules) — Cont'd

. *subtraction method of valuation* — *Cont'd*

. . family-held interests, valuation of
. . . . 19.02[4][d][i]

. . reduction for value of senior equity and subordinate equity interests
. . . . 19.02[4][d][ii]

. tangible property, transfers of certain
. . . . 19.03[4][b]

. transfer requirement . . . . 19.02[2][a][i]

. . limitation on transfer rules . . 19.02[2][a][i]

. trusts, transfers of interests in 19.03

. zero valuation rule . . 19.03[2][a], 19.03[2][b]

. . exceptions to . . . . 19.03[3]

Split dollar life insurance . . . . S4.14[6], S10.01[3][g]

Split gifts 10.03

. charitable bequests of split interests . . 5.05[8]

. community property and . . . . 10.03[1]

. consent . . . . 10.03[3]

. . manner of signifying . . . . 10.03[3][a]

. . revocation of . . . . 10.03[3][c]

. . signifying of . . . . 10.03[3]

. . time of . . . . 10.03[3][b]

. election, effect of . . . . 10.03[2]

. . return requirement, effect on . . . . 10.03[4]

. estate freezes, relief rule . . . . . 19.02[5][c][v]

. generally . . . . 1.03[4], 10.03[1]

. generation-skipping transfer tax

. . inclusion ratio . . . . 16.02[7][b][ii], 16.02[7][c][ii]

. . transferors . . . . 17.02[1][c][ii], 17.02[1][d]

. gift tax . . . . 1.03[4], 10.03

. . credit against estate tax, gift tax as
. . . . 3.04[2][b]

. . rate of tax . . . . 10.03[2]

. . returns . . . . 9.04[9], 10.03[4]

. grantor retained income trusts (GRITs)
. . . . 19.03[2][c]

. legislative background . . . . 10.03[1]

. requirements . . . . 10.03[1]

. returns, gift tax . . . . 9.04[9], 10.03[4]

Spouses

See also Divorce; Marital deduction; Marital rights; Noncitizen spouses; Property settlements not in divorce decree; Survivorship

. common-law states, economic status in . 4.06

. community property states, economic status in
. . . . 4.06

. disclaimers by surviving spouses
. . . . 10.07[2][d][i]

. dower or curtesy interests

. . gift tax valuation . . . . 10.02[5][d]

Spouses — Cont'd

. *dower or curtesy interests* — *Cont'd*

. . gross estate . . . . 4.06, 4.15[1]

. . relinquishment of . . . . 4.15[1]

. entitlements of surviving spouse 5.06[8][b][i], S5.06[8][b][i]

. gifts to, deductions . . . . 5.06[3], 11.03

. interspousal transfers, estate and gift tax exclusion 4.16

. joint-and-survivor annuities . . 1.02[2][b][vi], 4.11[7], 11.03[4][c][ii]

. noncitizen spouse, joint interests . . . 4.12[10]

. powers of appointment of surviving spouse
. . . . 5.06[8][b]

. status of surviving spouse, determination
. . . . 5.06[3]

. support

. . marital deduction and . . . . 5.06[3][g]

. . right to . . . . 4.15[1][d]

. . valuation of family obligations, gift tax
. . . . 10.02[5]

. tenancies by the entirety . . . . 4.12[2]

State and local law

. apportionment statutes . . . . 1.02[6]

. beneficial interest of decedent, gross estate and . . . . 4.05[2][a]

. . generally . . . . 4.05[2]

. . state decrees . . . . 4.05[2][b]

. disclaimers ineffective under local law
. . . . 10.07[2][d][ii]

. estate tax liability

. . life insurance proceeds, beneficiaries of
. . . . 8.05[4]

. . reimbursement out of estate for estate tax due . . . . 8.04[2]

. intestate succession, marital rights in transfers for insufficient consideration . . 4.15[1][c]

. joint tenancies . . . . 4.12[2]

. medical expenses . . . . 9.04[6]

. minor donees, state statutes simplifying gifts
. . . . 9.04[5][c]

. reimbursement out of estate for estate tax due
. . . . 8.04[2]

. . state common law . . . . 8.04[3]

. tuition payments . . . . 9.04[6]

State and local taxes

See also State death taxes

. real estate taxes, effect on special-use valuation . . . . 4.04[5][a][iv]

State death taxes

. credit for 3.03

. . "actually paid" requirement . . . . . 3.03[1]

. . background of Section 2011 . . . . . 3.03[4]

. . deduction allowed . . . . 3.03[3]

State death taxes —Cont'd
. *credit for—Cont'd*
. . generally . . . . 1.02[5][b]
. . generation-skipping transfer tax . 1.04[4][c],
　　　　　　　　　　　　　　　　　　　12.04
. . limitation on amount of . . 3.03[2], 3.03[3]
. . nonresident aliens . . . . . 6.02[1], S6.02[1]
. . remainders, tax on 3.07
. . seasonable payment . . . . 3.03[1]
. nonresident aliens . . . . . . 6.02[1], S6.02[1]

Statute of limitations
. estate freezes, open statute of limitations
　　. . . . . 19.02[5][d], 19.03[4][d]
. special-use valuation of real property, limita-
　　tion on additional tax . . . . 4.04[13]

Statutory relief provision
. election relief . . . . S16.02[9][a]

Stock

See also Bonds; Notes; Securities
. control of . . . . 19.05[2][b][iv]
. dividends, alternate valuation date . 4.03[2][c]
. foreign corporate stock of nonresident aliens
　　. . . . . 6.04[1]
. frozen preferred stock in estate freezes
　　. 19.02[1][a]
. gross estate inclusion, valuation . . . . 4.05[3]
. . alternate valuation date . . . . 4.03[2][b]
. . dividends, alternate valuation date
　　. 4.03[2][c]
. . generally . . . . 4.02[3][c]
. . nonresident aliens . . . . 6.04[1]
. nonresident aliens . . . . 6.04[1]
. redemptions, estate freezes . . . 19.02[2][a][i]
. tax conventions, situs rules . . . . . 7.02[2][c]
. transfers with retained life estate . 4.08[6][d]
. voting rights retained
. . limited liability companies . . . . 4.05[7][c]
. . transfers with retained life estate 4.08[6][d]

**Stock market crash of 1929, gross estate al-
ternate valuation date and** . . . . . . 4.03[1]

Storms, casualty losses . . . . 5.04[2]

Straw man, gifts with use of . . . . 9.04[1][b]

"Sunset provisions" S8.11
. estate tax . . . . S1.05[4], S8.11[1]
. generation-skipping transfer tax . . . S1.05[4],
　　　　　　　　　　　　　　　　　　S8.11[3]
. gift tax . . . . S8.11[2]

Support
. children
. . property settlements outside divorce decree,
　　amount for child support . . 10.06[2][b]
. marital deduction and . . . . 5.06[3][g]

Support —Cont'd
. property settlements outside divorce decree,
　　amount for child support . . . . 10.06[2][b]
. right to . . . . 4.15[1][d]
. valuation of family obligations, gift tax
　　. . . . . 10.02[5]
. . divorce . . . . 10.02[5][c]
. . dower and curtesy rights . . . . . 10.02[5][d]
. . extent and value of obligation . 10.02[5][a]
. . marital rights, elective share . . 10.02[5][d]
. . trust, creation of . . . . 10.02[5][b]

Survivorship
. contribution by survivor to joint interests
　　. . . . . 4.12[5]
. joint-and-survivor annuities . . 1.02[2][b][vi],
　　　　　　　　　　　　4.11[7], 11.03[4][c][ii]
. joint bank accounts . . . . 4.12[2]
. joint interests . 4.12, 5.06[3][d], 5.06[8][d][iv]
. joint tenancies . . . . 4.12[2]
. self-and-survivor annuities . . . 1.02[2][b][vi],
　　　　　　　　　　　　　4.11, 4.11[7]
. spouse

　See also Marital deduction; Marital rights
. . disclaimers by surviving spouses
　　. . . . . 10.07[2][d][i]
. . life interests with powers, marital deduction
　　for surviving spouse and terminable in-
　　terest rule . . . . 5.06[8][b]
. tenancies by the entirety . . . . 4.12[2]
. transfers conditioned upon survival
　　. . . . . 1.02[2][b][iv]
. transfers effective at death, survivorship re-
　　quirement . . . . 4.09[3]
. waiver of survivorship benefits . . . . . 9.04[7]

Swedish convention . . . . 7.03[7]

T

Tainted assets, terminable interest rule
. . . . 5.06[7][e]

Tainted organizations, charitable deductions
. . . . 5.05[5]

Tangible personal property
. creative, loans of, gift tax and . . . . . 9.04[8]
. gross estate inclusion . . . . 4.02[3][a]
. . decedent, property in which interest held by
　　. 4.05[3]
. . nonresident aliens . . . . 6.03[2][a]
. nonresident aliens . . . . 6.03[2][a]
. tax conventions, situs rules . . . . . 7.02[2][b]
. valuation . . . . 4.02[3][a]
. . special-use valuation . . . . . . 4.04[3][b][vi]
. . special valuation rules . . . . . . 19.03[4][b]

Taxable distributions

See Generation-skipping transfers--taxable distributions

Taxable estate 5.01–5.08
. administration expenses
. . charitable deductions . . . . . . 5.05[3][c][ii]
. casualty losses . . . . 5.04[2]
. charitable deductions 5.05
. . abuses by exempt organizations . . . 5.05[4], 5.05[5]
. . administration expenses . . . . 5.05[3][c][ii]
. . art works . . . . 5.05[8][b]
. . charitable lead trusts . . . . 5.05[9]
. . charitable organizations . 5.05[2], S5.05[2], 11.01[1]
. . charitable remainder annuity trust
. . . . 5.05[8][c], S5.05[8][c]
. . charitable remainder unitrust . . . 5.05[8][d], S5.05[8][d]
. . classes of recipients . . . . 5.05[1]
. . conservation contributions . . . . . 5.05[8][b]
. . curative amendments permitted . . 5.05[10]
. . death taxes . . . . 5.05[3][c][i]
. . disclaimers . . . . 5.05[3][d]
. . educational organizations . 5.05[2], 11.01[1]
. . expenses of estate . . . . 5.05[3][c]
. . generally 5.05
. . lifetime transfers . . . . 5.05[6]
. . literary organizations . . . . 5.05[2], 11.01[1]
. . mixed private and charitable bequests
. . . . 5.05[7]
. . organizations qualified . . . . 5.05[2]
. . outright bequests . . . . 5.05[3][a]
. . political entities . . . . 5.05[2], 11.01[1]
. . pooled income funds . . . . 5.05[8][e]
. . power of decedent, property under
. . . . 5.05[3][e]
. . private foundations, restrictions on . 5.05[5]
. . qualifications . . . . 5.05[1], 5.05[4]
. . qualified recipients . . . . 5.05[1]
. . qualified reformation . . . . 5.05[10][c]
. . reformable and qualified interests
. . . . 5.05[10][b]–5.05[10][d]
. . religious organizations . . . 5.05[2], 11.01[1]
. . remainders in residences and farms
. . . . 5.05[8][a]
. . routine deductions . . . . 5.05[3]
. . scientific organizations . . . 5.05[2], 11.01[1]
. . Section 2055(a) organizations . . . . 5.05[2], S5.05[2]
. . split interests . . . . . . 5.05[8], S5.05[8][c], S5.05[8][d]
. . tainted organizations 5.05[1][c], S5.05[1][c], 5.05[5]

Taxable estate—Cont'd
. *charitable deductions—Cont'd*
. . temporary interests bequeathed to charity
. . . . 5.05[9]
. . valuation . . . . 5.05[3][b]
. deductions 5.01, 5.02
. defined 5.02
. determination of . . . . 1.02[1], 5.01
. eligible worker owned cooperatives 5.08

. . *See also Eligible worker owned cooperatives (EWOCs)*

. employee stock ownership plans 5.08

. . *See also Employee stock ownership plans (ESOPs)*

. generally . . . . 1.02[1], 5.01
. interests passing to surviving spouse . 5.06[3], 5.06[5]
. losses 5.04
. . amount of, determination . . . . 5.04[1]
. . casualty losses . . . . 5.04[2]
. . deductions 5.04
. . income tax, relation to . . . . 5.04[4]
. . theft losses . . . . 5.04[3]
. marital deduction 5.06
. . background . . . . 5.06[1], 5.06[10]
. . description, general . . . . 5.06[2]
. . formula clauses . . . . 5.06[6]
. . generally . . . . 5.06[1], 5.06[2]
. . gross estate requirement . . . . 5.06[4]
. . interests passing to surviving spouse
. . . . 5.06[3], 5.06[5]
. . legislative background . . . 5.06[1], 5.06[10]
. . noncitizen surviving spouse 5.06[1], 5.06[9]
. . qualified domestic trusts . . . . 5.06[1], 5.07
. . qualifying terminable interests . . . 5.06[8]
. . terminable interest rule . . . 5.06[7], 5.06[8]
. . valuation of interests passing . . . . . 5.06[5]
. nonresident aliens 6.06
. . expenses, claims, and losses . . . . . 6.06[1]
. prior transfers, estate tax credit for tax on, adjustment for taxable estate of transferor
. . . . 3.05[3][c]
. property owned at death . . . . 1.02[2][a]
. public uses, transfers for 5.05
. qualified domestic trusts 5.07
. . computation of tax . . . . 5.07[4][b]
. . estate tax triggered . . . . 5.07[4][a]
. . exceptions . . . . 5.07[5]
. . generally . . . . 5.07[1]
. . liability for tax . . . . 5.07[4][c]
. . passing requirement . . . . 5.07[2]
. . payment of tax . . . . 5.07[4][c]
. . reformation into . . . . 5.07[2][a]

Taxable estate — Cont'd
. *qualified domestic trusts — Cont'd*
. . requirements . . . . 5.07[2], 5.07[3]
. . taxation of QDOT property . . . . . . 5.07[4]
. religious uses, transfers for 5.05
. Section 2053
. . administration expenses . . . . S5.03[3]
. . . attorney fees . . . . S5.03[3][a]
. . . executor commissions . . . . . S5.03[3][a]
. . . interest expenses . . . . S5.03[3][c][i]
. . . miscellaneous expenses . . . . S5.03[3][c]
. . . other deductible administration expenses
. . . . S5.03[3][c][iii]
. . . selling expenses . . . . S5.03[3][c][ii]
. . . trustee, commissions paid to . S5.03[3][b]
. . amount and payment requirement
. . . . S5.03[1][b]
. . . liability, bona fide . . . . . . S5.03[1][b][ii]
. . . liability, methods of establishing
. . . . S5.03[1][b][i]
. . . liability, payment of . . . . S5.03[1][b][iii]
. . . timing of post-death events
. . . . S5.03[1][b][iv]
. . claims against estate . . . . S5.03[4]
. . . community property issues S5.03[4][a][iii]
. . . consideration requirement . S5.03[4][a][ii]
. . . contingency of claim . . . . . . S5.03[4][c],
. . . . S5.03[4][c][i], S5.03[4][c][ii],
. . . . S5.03[4][c][iii]
. . . existing at time of death . . . . S5.03[4][b]
. . . foreign death taxes, limited deductibility
. . . of--Section 2053(d) . . . S5.03[4][b][ii]
. . . personal obligations of decedent
. . . . S5.03[4][a]
. . . related parties, claims by . . S5.03[4][a][i]
. . . Section 2044 claims . . . . S5.03[4][a][iv]
. . . taxes as claims . . . . S5.03[4][b][i]
. . deductions, four categories of . . . S5.03[1]
. . funeral expenses
. . . "allowable" test . . . . S5.03[2][b]
. . . generally . . . . S5.03[2][a]
. . generally . . . . S5.03[1]
. . mortages . . . . S5.03[5]
. . rules and limitations related to . . . S5.03[6]
. . . administration expenses for property not
. . . subject to claims: Section 2053(b)
. . . . S5.03[6][c][iii]
. . . property not subject to claims, special
. . . rules for . S5.03[6][c][i], S5.03[6][c][ii]
. . . Section 213(c)(2) election . . . S5.03[6][b]
. . . Section 642(g) election . . . . S5.03[6][a]
. . . value of property subject to claims, limita-
. . . tion based on--Section 2053(c)(2)
. . . . S5.03[6][c][iv]
. . state law allowance requirement S5.03[1][a]

Taxable estate — Cont'd
. . taxes 5.01
. . deductions 5.01
. theft losses . . . . 5.04[3]
. transfers for public, charitable, and religious
. uses 5.05

Taxable gifts
. *See Gift tax--taxable gifts*

Taxable terminations
. *See Generation-skipping transfers--taxable*
. *terminations*

Tax avoidance, expatriation for purpose of
. . . . 6.07, S6.07
. Section 2107 . . . . S6.07[2]
. . credit . . . . S6.07[2][c]
. . requirements . . . . S6.07[2][a]
. . special situs rule . . . . S6.07[2][b]
. Section 2801 . . . . S6.07[1]
. . requirements . . . . S6.07[1][a]
. . tax imposed . . . . S6.07[1][b]

Tax conventions 7.01–7.06
. aircraft, treatment of . . . . 7.03[1][b]
. annuities . . . . 7.02[2][c]
. Austrian convention . . . . . . 7.03[4], 7.03[5]
. bank deposits . . . . 7.02[2][c]
. bonds . . . . 7.02[2][c]
. business interests . . . . . 7.02[2][c], 7.03[1][b]
. . permanent establishment, defined 7.03[1][b]
. Canadian convention . . . . 7.03[8]
. charitable deductions . . . . 7.03[1][c]
. collection of taxes . . . . 7.04[3]
. Compact of Free Association with Micronesia
. and Marshall Islands (Freely Associated
. States) . . . . 7.03[9]
. Compact of Free Association with Palau
. . . . 7.03[10]
. competent authority assistance . . . . . 7.04[1]
. conflicts between treaties and U.S. statutory
. law 7.06
. copyright . . . . 7.02[2][c]
. corporate stock and bonds . . . . . . 7.02[2][c]
. credits under . . . . 7.02, 7.02[4]
. . OECD and U.S. model conventions
. . . . 7.03[1][c]
. . primary credit . . . . 7.02, 7.02[4][a]
. . refunds . . . . 7.04[2]
. . secondary credit . . . . 7.02, 7.02[4][b]
. Danish convention . . . . 7.03[6]
. death taxation, international system of 7.01[2]
. . death taxes involved . . . . 7.01[2][b]
. . domicile, defined . . . . 7.01[2][b]
. . estate tax . . . . 7.01[2][a]
. historical background 7.02

Tax conventions—Cont'd
. *death taxation, international system of—*
    Cont'd
. . inheritance tax . . . . 7.01[2][a]
. debt . . . . 7.02[2][c]
. deductions . . . . 7.02[3]
. . OECD and U.S. model conventions
    . . . . 7.03[1][c]
. domicile, determination . . . . 7.03[1][a]
. . hierarchy-of-criteria test . . . . . . 7.03[1][a]
. . threshold (citizenship) test . . . . . 7.03[1][a]
. double taxation, avoidance . . . . 7.02, 7.02[1]
. exemptions . . . . 7.03[1][c]
. fiscal domicile, determination . . . . 7.03[1][a]
. foreign death tax credit 3.06
. Freely Associated States, Compact of Free
    Association with . . . . 7.03[9]
. French convention . . . . 7.03[3]
. generally 7.01
. generation-skipping transfer tax conventions
    . . . . 7.05
. German convention . . . . . 7.03[4], S7.03[4]
. gift tax conventions 7.05
. government bonds, notes, and bills 7.02[2][c]
. grievance procedures . . . . 7.04[4]
. historical background 7.02
. indebtedness . . . . 7.02[2][c]
. information exchange . . . . 7.04[3]
. intangible personal property . . . . . 7.02[2][c]
. Internal Revenue Code 7.06
. judgment debts . . . . 7.02[2][c]
. life insurance . . . . 7.02[2][c]
. marital deduction . . . . 7.03[1][c]
. Marshall Islands, Compact of Free Associa-
    tion with . . . . 7.03[9]
. Micronesia, Compact of Free Association
    with . . . . 7.03[9]
. modern treaties 7.03
. Netherlands convention . . . . 7.03[2]
. nondiscrimination provisions . . . . . . 7.04[6]
. notes . . . . 7.02[2][c]
. older treaties, interpretation of 7.02
. Organization for Economic Cooperation and
    Development (OECD) convention . 7.03[1]
. . changes in tax laws, advisement of . . . 7.06
. . charitable deductions . . . . 7.03[1][c]
. . credits . . . . 7.03[1][c]
. . deductions . . . . 7.03[1][c]
. . exemptions . . . . 7.03[1][c]
. . fiscal domicile . . . . 7.03[1][a]
. . marital deduction . . . . 7.03[1][c]
. . situs rules . . . . 7.03[1][b]
. patents . . . . 7.02[2][c]

Tax conventions—Cont'd
. pensions . . . . 7.02[2][c]
. possessions of U.S. and other countries
    . . . . 7.04[5]
. procedural provisions 7.04
. property rights . . . . 7.02[2][c]
. . defined . . . . 7.03[1][b]
. purpose of . . . . 7.01[1]
. real property . . . . 7.02[2][a], 7.03[1][b]
. refunds or credits . . . . 7.04[2]
. ships, treatment of . . . . 7.03[1][b]
. situs rules
. . determination of situs . . . . 7.02[1]
. . generally . . . . 7.02[1]
. . OECD convention . . . . 7.03[1][b]
. . specific rules . . . . 7.02[2]
. . taxation based on situs . . . . 7.02[3]
. . U.S. model conventions . . . . . . 7.03[1][b]
. stock . . . . 7.02[2][c]
. Swedish convention . . . . 7.03[7]
. tangible personal property, situs rules
    . . . . 7.02[2][b]
. termination . . . . 7.04[7]
. territorial extensions . . . . 7.04[5]
. tort claims . . . . 7.02[2][c]
. typical convention 7.01
. unified credit . . . . 7.02[3]
. United Kingdom convention . . . . 7.03[3]
. U.S. model conventions . . . . 7.03[1]
. . changes in tax laws, advisement of . . . 7.06
. . charitable deductions . . . . 7.03[1][c]
. . credits . . . . 7.03[1][c]
. . deductions . . . . 7.03[1][c]
. . exemptions . . . . 7.03[1][c]
. . fiscal domicile . . . . 7.03[1][a]
. . marital deduction . . . . 7.03[1][c]
. . nondiscrimination provision . . . . . . 7.04[6]
. . situs rules . . . . 7.03[1][b]
. U.S. statutory law, conflicts between treaties
    and 7.06

Taxes
  See also Estate tax; Generation-skipping
    transfer tax; Gift tax; State death taxes;
    Tax conventions; Tax liability; Tax rates
. deductions for 5.01
. interests passing to surviving spouse, marital
    deduction, valuation of taxes on 5.06[5][a]
. taxable estate, determination of 5.01

Tax liability
. estate tax 2.02, 5.01
. . armed forces, members of . . . . 8.01[1]
. . . astronauts . . . . S8.01[1][c]
. . citizenship 8.09

Tax liability —Cont'd
. *estate tax—Cont'd*
. . life insurance proceeds, liability of benefi-
    ciaries 8.05
. . marital deduction property, right of recovery
    . . . . 8.07[4]
. . power over property, liability of recipient of
    property over which decedent had . 8.06
. . qualified domestic trusts . . . . . . 5.07[4][c]
. . residence 8.09
. of executor
. . debts due the United States, discharge of li-
    ability for . . . . 8.03[1]
. . discharge from 8.03
. . estate tax payment . . . . 2.02, 2.02[1]
. . procedure to gain release from liability
    . . . . 8.03[2]
. generation-skipping transfer tax . . . . 1.04[5],
                                             12.03
. . general rules . . . . 12.03[1]
. . trustee's liability, limitation of . . . 12.03[3],
                                             17.04[4]
. . trust equivalent arrangements . . . . 12.03[2]
. gift tax
. . determination of liability 9.01
. . donee liability . . . . 9.04[11]
. . donor liability . . . . 9.02[3]
. . fiduciary liability . . . . 9.04[11]
. . imposition of tax 9.02
. . marital deduction property, right of recovery
    . . . . 8.07[4], S8.07[4]
. . preceding calendar periods, taxable gifts for
    . . . . 9.05
. . qualified terminable interest property
    . . . . 10.08[3]
. . taxable gifts 9.04, 9.05

Taxpayer Relief Act of 1997
. charitable transfers . . . . S5.06[8][d][ii],
                                        S5.06[8][e]
. community property interest of surviving
    spouse . . . . S5.06[8][d][ii]
. education IRAs . . . . S13.01[2][a]
. gift tax returns . . . . S9.04[9]
. Qualified State Tuition Programs S13.01[2][a]
. special-use valuation of real property, election
    and agreement . . . . S4.04[6]
. taxable gifts
. . limitations on assessment . . . . . S9.04[10]
. . returns . . . . S9.04[9]
. . valuation . . . . S10.02[2]
. transfers within three years of death S4.07[1]

Tax planning
. estate freeze abuses, Chapter 14 valuation
    rules combating 19.01
. estate tax . . . . 5.06[6][b]

Tax planning —Cont'd
. marital deduction . . . . 5.06[6][b]
Tax preferences, charitable . . . . 5.05[1]
Tax rates
. estate tax . . . . 1.02[1]
. . generally . . . . 1.02[1]
. . graduated rate table . . . . 1.02[1]
. generation-skipping transfer tax . . 1.04[4][b]
. . applicable rate . . . . 1.04[4][b]
. . inclusion ratio . . . . 1.04[4][b][ii]
. . maximum federal estate tax rate
    . . . . 1.04[4][b][i]
. gift tax
. . generally . . . . 1.03[1]
. . graduated rate table . . . . 1.03[1]
. . split gifts . . . . 10.03[2]
Tax Reduction Act of 1986
. tax conventions 7.06
Tax Reform Act of 1969
. nonresident aliens' debt obligations and bank
    accounts . . . . 6.04[3]
Tax Reform Act of 1976
. integration of gift tax and estate tax . . . 3.04
. marital deduction . . . . 5.06[1], 5.06[10]
. nonresident aliens . . . . 7.03[3]
. . debt obligations and bank accounts . 6.04[3]
. tax conventions and . . . 7.02[3], 7.03[3], 7.06
. transfers within three years of death   S4.07[1]
Tax Reform Act of 1984
. exempt annuities . . . . 4.11[6]
. portfolio interest . . . . 6.05[4]
. public housing bonds, gross estate inclusion
    . . . . 4.05[3]
Tax Reform Act of 1986
. eligible worker owned cooperatives (EWOCs)
    . . . . 5.08[4][b]
. employee stock ownership plans (ESOPs)
    . . . . 5.08[4][b]
Tax return preparers
. penalties imposed by Section 6694
. . understatement of liability . . . . S4.02[6][b]
Tax returns
  See Returns
Tax treaties
  See Tax conventions
**Technical and Miscellaneous Revenue Act of
  1988 (TAMRA)**
. marital deduction . . . . 7.03[8]
Technical Changes Act of 1949
. annuities . . . . 4.11[7]

Temporal property interests
. gross estate inclusion . . . . 4.02[3][i]
. valuation . . . . 4.02[3][i]
**Temporary interests bequeathed to charity
(charitable lead trusts)** . . . . 5.05[9]
Tenancies by the entirety
. disclaimers . . . . . 10.07[2][b], S10.07[2][b]
. gift tax on gifts to, annual exclusion
. . . . 9.04[1][b]
. gross estate . . . . 4.12[2], 4.12[10]
Terminable interest rule

*See also Qualified terminable interest prop-
erty (QTIP)*
. charitable remainder trusts, special rules
. . gift tax deduction, exception to terminable
interest rule . . . . 11.03[4][d]
. . marital deduction . . . 5.06[8][e], S5.06[8][e]
. gift tax deductions . . . . 11.03[3]
. . caveat on powers . . . . 11.03[3][a]
. . charitable remainder trusts . . . . 11.03[4][d]
. . donor retains interest . . . . . . 11.03[3][a]
. . exceptions to terminable interest rule
. . . . 11.03[4]
. . generally . . . . 11.03[3]
. . joint-and-survivor annuities . 11.03[4][c][ii]
. . joint interests, exception to rule   11.03[4][a]
. . life interests with powers, exception to rule
. . . . 11.03[4][b]
. . Section 2523(b)(1) transfers . . . 11.03[3][a]
. . Section 2523(b)(2) transfers . . . 11.03[3][b]
. . "tainted" asset rule . . . . 11.03[3][c]
. . third party acquires interest . . . 11.03[3][a]
. marital deduction . . . . 5.06[7]
. . charitable remainder trusts, special rules
. . . . 5.06[8][e], S5.06[8][e]
. . common disasters . . . . 5.06[8][a]
. . executor-purchaser provision . . . 5.06[7][d]
. . generally . . . . 5.06[7], 5.06[7][c]
. . general rule . . . . 5.06[7][a]
. . identification of terminable interests
. . . . 5.06[7][b]
. . insurance with powers . . . . . . 5.06[8][c]
. . life estate for surviving spouse, election
with respect to . . . . 5.06[8][d]
. . life interests with powers . . . . . 5.06[8][b]
. . patents . . . . 5.06[7][c]
. . purpose . . . . 5.06[7][a]
. . qualifying terminable interests . . . . 5.06[8]
. . tainted asset rule . . . 5.06[7][e], 11.03[3][c]
Terminally ill persons
. defined, for gross estate valuation purposes
. . . . 4.02[3][i]

Terminally ill persons — Cont'd
. physical condition of decedent before death,
effect on transfers effective at death
. . . . 4.09[4][e]
Terminations

*See also Generation-skipping trans-
fers--taxable terminations*
. joint interests, termination prior to death
. . . . 4.12[9]
. revocable transfers, termination power of decedent . . . . 4.10[4][e]
. tax conventions . . . . 7.04[7]
. transfers effective at death, pre-death termination of reversion . . . . 4.09[5]
Term loans . . . . 10.01[2][f]
Territorial extensions under tax conventions
. . . . 7.04[5]
Theft losses . . . . 5.04[3]
. art works . . . . 5.04[3]
. deductions . . . . 5.04[3]
. defined . . . . 5.04[3]
. embezzlement of estate assets by executor
. . . . 5.04[3]
Third parties
. gift tax
. . donor's power exercisable only with third
person . . . . 10.01[8]
. . husband or wife, gifts to third party by
. . . . 10.03
. . powers held only by third person . 10.01[9]
. . split gifts 10.03
. . terminable interest rule, third party acquires
interest . . . . 11.03[3][a]
Three-year rule
. property settlements not in divorce decree
. . . . 10.06[2][c]
Threshold (citizenship) test
. domicile, defined . . . . 7.03[1][a]
**Timber dispositions, recapture, special-use
valuation** . . . . 4.04[9][e]
Tort claims
. tax convention, situs rules . . . . . . 7.02[2][c]
Trade or business
. nonresident aliens' bank deposits, engagement
in trade or business, non-U.S.-source income . . . . 6.05[2][c][i]
. special-use valuation of real property 50 percent test, trade or business use
. . . . 4.04[3][b][iv]
Transfers conditioned upon survival
. . . . 1.02[2][b][iv]
Transfers effective at death 4.09
. amount to be included . . . . 4.09[6]
. background of Section 2037 covering 4.09[7]

Transfers effective at death — Cont'd
. excluded transfers . . . . 4.09[2]
. generally . . . . 4.09[1]
. reversionary interest, retention of . . . 4.09[4]
. . actuarial principles . . . . 4.09[4][d]
. . definition of reversionary interest 4.09[4][a]
. . 5 percent test . . . . . . 4.09[4][f], 4.09[4][g]
. . method of retaining interest . . . . 4.09[4][b]
. . mortality tables . . . . 4.09[4][d]
. . negligible interests . . . . 4.09[4][c]
. . physical condition of decedent before death,
     effect . . . . 4.09[4][e]
. Section 2037 rules . . . . 4.09[1]
. . background of Section . . . . 4.09[7]
. survivorship requirement . . . . 4.09[3]
. termination of reversion, pre-death . . 4.09[5]
Transfers for insufficient consideration . 4.15
. estate tax 4.15
. gross estate 4.15
. marital rights, negative rule . . . . 4.15[1]
. . community property, interest in . 4.15[1][b]
. . disqualified marital rights . . . . . 4.15[1][a]
. . divorce, effect . . . . 4.15[1][e]
. . dower or curtesy interests, relinquishment of
     . . . . 4.15[1]
. . estate tax . . . . 4.15[1], 4.15[1][f]
. . generally . . . . 4.15[1]
. . gift tax amnesty rule . . . . 4.15[1][e]
. . gift tax/estate tax anomaly . . . . 4.15[1][f]
. . gross estate . . . . 4.15[1]
. . intestate succession, state statute on
     . . . . 4.15[1][c]
. . marital deduction, relation to . . . . . 4.15[1]
. . support, right to . . . . 4.15[1][d]
. partial consideration, affirmative rule . 4.15[2]
. . estate tax . . . . 4.15[2]
. . Past rule . . . . 4.15[2][b]
. . reduction for partial consideration
     . . . . 4.15[2][a]
Transfers for public, charitable, and relig-
ious uses
    See Charitable deductions
Transfers, revocable
    See Revocable transfers
Transfers subject to gift tax
    See Gift tax--transfers subject to
Transfers with enjoyment retained
    . . . . 1.02[2][b][iii]
Transfers within three years of death . S4.07
. generally . . . . S4.07[1]
. adjustments to gross estate S4.07
. background . . . . S4.07[4]

Transfers within three years of death —
   Cont'd
. estate tax . . . . 1.02[2][b][i], S4.07[4]
. generally . . . . 1.02[2][b][i]
. gift tax . . . . S4.07[1], 10.01[10][b]
. . gross-up under Section 2035(b) . . S4.07[3]
. gross estate inclusion under Section 2035(a)
    . . . . S4.07[2]
. . amount to be included . . . . . . S4.07[2][d]
. . bona fide sales . . . . S4.07[2][c][i]
. . exceptions to 2035(a) inclusion S4.07[2][c]
. . revocable trusts, transfers from
    . . . . S4.07[2][c][ii]
. . Section 2035(a) inclusion . . . . . . S4.07[2]
. . Section 2035(a)(1) transfers . . . S4.07[2][a]
. . Section 2035(a)(2) transfers . . . S4.07[2][b]
. . Section 2035(d) transfers . . . S4.07[2][c][i]
. . Section 2035(e) transfers . . S4.07[2][c][ii]
. . special applications . . . . S4.07[2][e]
. gross-up of gift tax under Section 2035(b)
    . . . . S4.07[3][a]
. . determination of transfer . . . . . S4.07[3][b]
. legislative history . . . . S4.07[1], S4.07[4]
. life insurance proceeds . . . . 4.14[9][b]
. pre-1982 Section 2035 and background
    . . . . S4.07[4]
Transfers with retained life estate 4.08
. accumulated income, amount to be included
    . . . . 4.08[8][a]
. amount to be included . . . 4.08[8], S4.08[8]
. background of Section 2036 covering 4.08[9]
. beneficial interests in decedent . . . . . 4.08[4]
. . enjoyment "retained" 4.08[4][c], S4.08[4][c]
. . family limited partnership securities
    . . . . S4.08[4][c]
. . possession or enjoyment . . . . . . 4.08[4][a],
                  4.08[4][c], S4.08[4][c]
. . right to income . . . . 4.08[4][b]
. control over others' interests . . . . . . 4.08[5]
. . designation of party who benefits, right of
    . . . . 4.08[5][c]
. . illusory control . . . . 4.08[5][b]
. . indirect retention of right to designate
    . . . . 4.08[5][a]
. death bed relinquishment of life interests
    . . . . 4.08[8][b]
. decedent, transfers by . . . . 4.08[7]
. . election, transfers by . 4.08[7][b], 4.08[7][c]
. . indirect transfers . . . . 4.08[7][a]
. . reciprocal trusts . . . . 4.08[7][d]
. . widow's election . . . . 4.08[7][c]
. enjoyment
. . beneficial interests in decedent . . 4.08[4][a],
                  4.08[4][c], S4.08[4][c]

Transfers with retained life estate — Cont'd
. *enjoyment* — *Cont'd*
. . commercial transactions . . . . . . 4.08[6][b]
. excluded transfers . . . . 4.08[1]
. generally 4.08
. indirect interests or controls . . . . . . 4.08[6]
. . commercial transactions, enjoyment retained
　　in . . . . 4.08[6][b]
. . legislative possibilities . . . . 4.08[6][e]
. . rent paid by transferor . . . . 4.08[6][c]
. . settlor trustee . . . . 4.08[6][a]
. . stock transfers . . . . 4.08[6][d]
. indirect transfers by decedent . . . . 4.08[7][a]
. legislative history . . . . 4.08[9]
. lifetime relinquishment of prescribed interests
　　. . . . . 4.08[8][b]
. nature of interest retained . . . . 4.08[3]
. period for which interest retained . . . 4.08[2]
. rules under Section 2036
. . background of Section . . . . 4.08[9]
. stock transfers . . . . 4.08[6][d]
. voting rights . . . . 4.08[6][d]

Treaties

　See Tax conventions

**Trees, planting, cultivating, care, or cutting
of**
. qualified woodland . . . . 4.04[3][c]
. special-use valuation . . . . 4.04[3][b][iii],
　　　　　　　　　　　　　　　　4.04[3][c]

Trustees
. commissions paid to . . . . S5.03[3][b]
. generation-skipping transfer tax
. . definition of trustee . . . . 17.02[2]
. . liability, limitation on . . . 12.03[3], 17.04[4]
. qualified domestic trust requirement of U.S.
　　trustee . . . . 5.07[3][a], S5.07[3][a]
. . right of U.S. trustee to withhold tax
　　. . . . . 5.07[3][b]
. transfers with retained life estate, settlor trus-
　　tee . . . . 4.08[6][a]

Trusts

　*See also Grantor retained income trusts
　　(GRITs); Personal residence trusts; Quali-
　　fied domestic trusts (QDOTs)*
. charitable deductions . . . . 5.05[2]
. charitable lead trusts, charitable deduction
　　. . . . . 5.05[9]
. charitable remainder annuity trusts, charitable
　　deduction . . . . . . 5.05[8][c], S5.05[8][c]
. charitable remainder trusts, marital deduction
　　. . . . . 5.06[8][e], S5.06[8][e]
. . gift tax deduction, exception to rule
　　. . . . . 11.03[4][d]

Trusts — Cont'd
. charitable remainder unitrusts, charitable de-
　　duction . . . . 5.05[8][d], S5.05[8][d]
. conservation easement, trust-held land subject
　　to . . . . S4.02[4][e][i]
. Crummey trusts
. . gross estate inclusion . . . . 4.05[7][c]
. . limited liability companies compared
　　. . . . . 4.05[7][c]
. defined . . . . 13.03[3]
. estate freezes
. . grantor retained income trusts (GRITs)
　　. . . . . 19.03
. . transfers of interests in trusts, valuation
　　rules 19.03
. . trust attribution . . . . 19.02[2][d][iii]
. generation-skipping transfer tax
. . assignment of trust interest . . . 17.02[3][e]
. . beneficiaries, trusts as . . . . 17.01[2][c][ii]
. . charitable lead annuity trusts . . . . 16.02[6]
. . consolidation of separate trusts, inclusion
　　ratio . . . . 16.02[5][c]
. . definition of trust . . . . 17.02[2]
. . division of single trust . . . . 17.04[2][b]
. . inclusion ratio . . . . 16.02[4][f], 16.02[5][b],
　　　16.02[5][b][iii], 16.02[5][c], 16.02[6]
. . interests held in . . . . 17.02[3]
. . multiple taxable terminations with same
　　trust transferor . . . . 17.03[2][a]
. . multiple trusts, single trust treated as
　　. . . . . 17.04[2][a]
. . nonresident alien transferors, trusts partially
　　subject to Chapter 13 . . . . 18.03[2][c]
. . permissible noncharitable current recipient
　　of trust income or corpus . . 17.02[3][b]
. . pour-over trusts . . . . 17.03[2][b]
. . single trust treated as multiple trusts
　　. . . . . 17.04[2][a]
. . skip persons, trusts as . . 13.03[1], 13.03[3]
. . trust equivalent arrangements . . . . 12.03[2],
　　　　　　　　　　13.03[3][c], 18.03[3]
. gifts in trust . . . . 9.04[1][b], 9.04[3][a]
. life insurance trusts
. . gross estate inclusion . . . . 4.05[7][c]
. . limited liability companies compared
　　. . . . . 4.05[7][c]
. marital deduction
. . estate trusts . . . . 5.06[7][b]
. . unlimited . . . . 5.06[6][b]
. pour-over trusts . . . . 17.03[2][b]
. reciprocal trusts . . . . . 4.08[7][d], 10.02[6][c]
. separate interests in, gift tax . . . . 9.04[3][a]
. single trust, GST tax
. . division of single trust . . . . . . 17.04[2][b]
. . multiple trusts, treatment as . . . 17.04[2][a]

Trusts — Cont'd

. support obligations, creation of trust to discharge . . . . 10.02[5][b]
. transfers within three years of death, revocable trusts . . . . S4.07[2][c][ii]

Tuition payments

. annual gift tax exclusion . . . 1.03[3], 9.04[6], S9.04[6]
. education IRAs . . . . . S9.04[6], S10.01[3][c], S13.01[2][a]
. generation-skipping transfer tax exclusion . . . . . 1.04[3][d], 13.01[2][a], S13.01[2][a]
. gift tax exclusion . . 1.03[3], 9.04[6], S9.04[6]
. local law, effect . . . . 9.04[6]
. Qualified State Tuition Programs . . S9.04[6], S10.01[3][c], S13.01[2][a]

U

Uncertain interests, gifts of . . . . 10.01[3][c], S10.01[3][c]

Unified credit

. estate tax . . . . 1.02[5][a]
. generally . . . . 1.02[5][a], 1.03[7]
. gift tax . . . . 1.03[7]
. grantor retained income trusts . . . . 19.03[1]
. nonresident aliens . . . . 6.02[4]
. tax conventions . . . . 7.02[3]

Uniform Gift to Minors Act

. gift tax credit . . . . 3.04[1][b]

Uniform Simultaneous Death Act

. life insurance proceeds, gross estate inclusion . . . . 4.05[6]

United Kingdom convention . . . . 7.03[3]

United States

. debts due to, executor's discharge from personal liability for . . . . 8.03[1]
. defined . . . . 6.03[2]
. model U.S. tax conventions . . . . 7.03[1]
. . changes in tax laws, advisement of . . . 7.06
. . charitable deductions . . . . 7.03[1][c]
. . credits . . . . 7.03[1][c]
. . deductions . . . . 7.03[1][c]
. . exemptions . . . . 7.03[1][c]
. . fiscal domicile . . . . 7.03[1][a]
. . marital deduction . . . . 7.03[1][c]
. . nondiscrimination provisions . . . . . 7.04[6]
. . situs rules . . . . 7.03[1][b]
. possessions of U.S.
. . estate tax liability, citizenship and residence 8.09
. . tax conventions and . . . . 7.04[5]
. tax conventions with 7.01–7.06

United States — Cont'd
. *tax conventions with — Cont'd*
. . competent authority assistance under U.S. convention . . . . 7.03[1]
. . conflicts between treaties and U.S. statutory law 7.06
. . possessions of U.S. and . . . . 7.04[5]

Urban National Forest . . . . S4.02[4][b][i]

U.S. citizenship

See Citizenship

U.S. residence

See Residence

U.S. savings bonds

. jointly owned . . . . 4.12[2]
. valuation . . . . 4.02[3][e]

V

Valuation

See also Alternate valuation date, gross estate inclusion; Special-use valuation, real property; Special valuation rules to combat estate freeze abuses (Chapter 14 rules)

. actuarial valuation, gift tax . . . . . 10.02[2][f]
. annuities . . . . 4.11[4][a]
. charitable deductions . . . . 5.05[3][b], 19.03[3][a][iii]
. charitable remainder unitrust, value of remainder interest . . . . 5.05[8][d]
. date-of-death rule . . . . 1.02[2][b][ii], 4.03[1], S4.03[1], 4.14[9][b], 5.05[3][b]
. encumbered property . 5.06[5][b], 10.02[2][a]
. encumbrances on surviving spouse's interest . . . . 5.06[5][b]
. estate freezes, special valuation rules to combat abuses of 19.01–19.05
. generation-skipping transfer tax
. . direct skips . . . . 14.04[2], 14.05[2][a]
. . fair market valuation on date of transfer, exceptions to . . . . 14.05[2]
. . general rule . . . . 14.05[1]
. . inclusion ratio . . . . 16.02[4]
. . reduction for consideration . . . . . 14.05[3]
. . taxable amount 14.05
. . taxable distributions . . . . 14.02[2]
. . taxable terminations . . 14.03[2], 14.05[2][b]
. gift tax 10.02
. . actuarial valuation . . . . 10.02[2][f]
. . community property . . . . 10.02[6][b]
. . completion of gift . . . . 10.02[1][a]
. . consideration received for transfer 10.02[3]
. . corporate recipients . . . . 10.02[6][a]
. . credit for gift tax, value of gift and . . . . 3.04[2][b]

Valuation —Cont'd
. gift tax—Cont'd

. . discounts and premiums, interests in prop-
　　erty . . . . 10.02[2][c]
. . donee payment of tax . . . . . . 10.02[6][d]
. . encumbered property . . . . 10.02[2][a]
. . excise tax and other charges . . 10.02[2][g]
. . family obligations . . . . 10.02[5]
. . generally . . . . 1.03[2][a], 10.02
. . insurance contracts . . . . 10.02[2][e]
. . methods of valuation . . 10.02[2], S10.02[2]
. . mutual fund shares . . . . 10.02[2][d]
. . open transactions . . . . 10.02[1][b]
. . ordinary course of business, transfers in
　　. . . . . 10.02[4]
. . prior years . . . . 9.05[2], S9.05[2]
. . reciprocal trusts . . . . 10.02[6][c]
. . restrictions on use or disposition
　　. . . . . 10.02[2][b]
. . rules, generally . . . . 1.03[2][a]
. . statement of valuation, furnishing on request
　　. . . . . 10.02
. . statutes applicable to
. . . Section 7477 revised . . . S10.02[2][d][iii]
. . time of valuation . . . . 10.02[1]
. gross estate . . . . 4.02[3]
. . agreements, value determined by 4.02[3][g]
. . alternative valuation date 4.03
. . art works . . . . 4.02[3][a]
. . basic valuation approaches . . . . . . 4.02[3]
. . bonds . . . . 4.02[3][e]
. . business interests . . . . . . 4.02[3][f], 4.05[7]
. . buy-sell agreements . . . . 4.02[3][g]
. . close corporation interests . . . . . 4.02[3][f]
. . closed-end funds . . . . 4.02[3][d]
. . crops, growing . . . . 4.04[3][c]
. . date of decedent's death as time for . . 4.01
. . fair market value . . . . 4.02[2]
. . generally . . . . 1.02[2][b][ii]
. . included interests . . . . 4.02[1]
. . nonresident aliens . . . . 6.03[1]
. . notes . . . . 4.02[3][h]
. . open-end funds . . . . 4.02[3][d]
. . optional methods 4.04
. . partial property interests . . . . 4.02[3][i]
. . real property . . . . 4.02[3][b], 4.04
. . securities . . . . 4.02[3][c]
. . tangible personal property . . . . . 4.02[3][a]
. . temporal property interests . . . . . 4.02[3][i]
. . terminally ill person, valued interest mea-
　　sured by life of . . . . 4.02[3][i]
. lapsed voting or liquidation rights 19.05
. marital deduction

Valuation —Cont'd
. marital deduction —Cont'd

. . alternate valuation date . . . . 4.03[4][b]
. . interests passing, valuation of . . . . 5.06[5]
. market quotations availability, valuation of
　　discretionary rights . . . . 19.02[3][a]
. nonresident aliens, gross estate of . . . 6.03[1]
. personal residence trusts . . . . . . 19.03[3][d]
. proportionate transfers . . . . 19.02[3][c]
. QDOT property . . . . 5.06[1]
. retained interests
. . estate freezing, exceptions to . . . . 19.02[3]
. . incomplete transfers . . . . 19.03[3][a]
. . interests of same class . . . . . . 19.02[3][b]
. . interests proportionate to class . 19.02[3][b]
. . market quotations availability . 19.02[3][a]
. . proportionate transfers . . . . . . 19.02[3][c]
. . qualified interests . . . . 19.03[3][b],
　　　　　　　　　　　　　　　　S19.03[3][b][i]
. reversionary interests, valuation using mortal-
　　ity tables and actuarial principles
　　. . . . . 4.09[4][d]
. stock, generally . . . . 4.02[3][c]
. taxes on surviving spouse's interest 5.06[5][a]
**Veterans' organizations, charitable deduc-
tions** . . . . 5.05[2], 11.01[1]
Voting rights

　　See also Lapsed voting or liquidation rights
. defined . . . . 19.05[2][b][i]
. retained
. . limited liability companies . . . . 4.05[7][c]
. . transfers with retained life estate 4.08[6][d]

W

Waiver of survivorship benefits . . . . 9.04[7]
Wills
. estate tax liability
. . life insurance beneficiaries, contrary will
　　provision regarding . . . . 8.05[3]
. . reimbursement out of estate for estate tax
　　due, will provisions for . . . . . . 8.04[1]
. estate tax return, will filed with . . . . 2.02[1]
. joint and mutual . . 5.06[3][d], 5.06[8][d][iv],
　　　　　　　　　　　　　　　　　10.01[5][e]
. marital deduction
. . interests passing to surviving spouse
　　. . . . . 5.06[3][a]
. . joint and mutual wills . . . . . . 5.06[3][d],
　　　　　　　　　　　　　　　　5.06[8][d][iv]
. . unlimited deduction . . . . 5.06[6][b]
. reimbursement out of estate for estate tax
　　due, will provisions for . . . . 8.04[1]

Withholding
. qualified domestic trust, right of U.S. trustee
    to withhold tax . . . . 5.07[3][b]
Within three years of death, transfers made

See Transfers within three years of death
Woodland, qualified for special-use valuation
. . . . 4.04[3][c]
Worker owned cooperatives

*See Eligible worker owned cooperatives
(EWOCs)*

Workers' compensation
. gross estate exclusion . . . . 4.05[8]
Wrongful death acts . . . . 4.05[8]

Z

Zero valuation rule . . . . . . 19.03[1], 19.03[2]

*See also Grantor retained income trusts
(GRITs)*
. exceptions to . . . . 19.03[3]